CORPORATE FINANCE

DEBT, EQUITY, AND DERIVATIVE MARKETS AND THEIR INTERMEDIARIES

Third Edition

■ ■ ■

By

Jerry W. Markham

Professor of Law, College of Law, Florida International University, Miami

José M. Gabilondo

*Associate Dean for Academic Affairs, Associate Professor of Law
College of Law, Florida International University, Miami*

Thomas Lee Hazen

*Professor of Law, Cary C. Boshamer Distinguished Professor of Law,
University of North Carolina*

AMERICAN CASEBOOK SERIES®

WEST®

A Thomson Reuters business

Mat #41032880

Thomson Reuters created this publication to provide you with accurate and authoritative information concerning the subject matter covered. However, this publication was not necessarily prepared by persons licensed to practice law in a particular jurisdiction. Thomson Reuters does not render legal or other professional advice, and this publication is not a substitute for the advice of an attorney. If you require legal or other expert advice, you should seek the services of a competent attorney or other professional.

American Casebook Series is a trademark registered in the U.S. Patent and Trademark Office.

© West, a Thomson business, 2004, 2008
© 2011 Thomson Reuters
    610 Opperman Drive
    St. Paul, MN 55123
    1–800–313–9378
Printed in the United States of America

ISBN: 978–0–314–26510–4

For Oscar, Lola, and Sophie

JWM

For Nico, James, and Michael

JMG

For Lisa, Elliott, and George

TLH

Preface to the Third Edition

This book introduces students to the major instruments issued by corporations to fund their activities and to manage risk–debt, equity, and derivatives–and explains both their financial and legal nature. After two introductory chapters on financial history, market structure, accounting standards, and the professional expectations that apply to corporate lawyers, the book moves down the balance sheet–starting with the short term debt instruments of the money market, followed by medium-and long-term debt instruments, introducing junior equity through preferred stock, and, then, examining the major legal issues of common stock. In these chapters, we start with the financial structure of the instruments and then examine their legal and regulatory aspects, which are best appreciated after understanding the instruments themselves.

Moving beyond the primary market of issuance, the book also puts these instruments in the context of the trading markets where financial intermediaries deal and invest. In addition to explaining the state and federal law framework for these instruments, the book focuses on cases that contain good lessons for the practitioner. To economize on coverage, we have eliminated the chapters on retirement plans and insurance from previous editions. Since the Second Edition, the Dodd–Frank Act has changed the regulatory framework for the debt markets. Hence, this edition incorporates the implications of the Dodd–Frank Act throughout the text. To help students track their progress, a set of chapter objectives has been added at the beginning of each chapter.

The authors would like to thank Timothy McFarland and Rigers Gjyshi, students at the College of Law, Florida International University, for their fine work in compiling the statutory and other materials contained in the supplement that accompanies this casebook.

Jerry W. Markham
José M. Gabilondo
Thomas Lee Hazen

December 2010

ACKNOWLEDGMENTS

We are indebted to the following authors and publishers for their generosity in giving us permission to reprint excerpts from copyrighted materials:

William T. Allen, "Contracts and Communities in Corporation Law," 50 Washington & Lee Law Review 1395 (1993). Reprinted with permission.

Bank of America Web Site Material provided as a courtesy of Bank of America.

Michael S. Bennett & Michael J. Marin, "The Casablanca Paradigm: Regulatory Risk in the Asian Financial Derivatives Markets," 5 Stan. J. L. Bus. & Fin. 1, 7 (1999). Reprinted with permission.

Carl S. Bjerre, "International Project Finance Transactions: Selected Issues Under Revised Article 9," 73 Am. Bankr. L.J. 261B266 (1999). Reprinted with the permission of the copyright owner, the National Conference of Bankruptcy Judges.

Committee on Bankruptcy and Corporate Reorganization of the Association of the Bar of the City of New York, "Structured Financing Techniques," 50 Bus. Law. 527 (1995). Reprinted by permission.

"Federal Regulation of Securities: Regulatory Developments," 48 Bus. Law. 997 (1993). Reprinted by permission.

CBOE Web Site Material provided as a courtesy by Chicago Board Options Exchange, Incorporated.

Nicole Chu, "Bowie Bonds: A Key to Unlocking the Wealth of Intellectual Property," 21 Hastings Comm. & Ent. L. J. 469 (1999). Reprinted with permission.

Todd H. Eveson, "Financial and Bank Holding Company Issuance of Trust Preferred Securities," 6 N.C. Banking Institute 315B317 (2002). Reprinted with permission.

Thomas R. Fileti & Carl R. Steen, "Synthetic Lease Financing For the Acquisition and Construction of Power Generation Facilities in a Changing U.S. Energy Environment," 24 Fordham Int'l L. J. 1083 (2001). Reprinted with permission of the authors.

Ann Judith Gellis, "Municipal Securities Market: Same Problem No Solution," 21 Delaware Journal of Corporation Law 427 (1996). Reprinted with permission.

Thomas S. Harman, "Emerging Alternatives to Mutual Funds: Unit Investment Trusts and Other Fixed Portfolio Investment Vehicles," 1987 Duke L. J. 1045. Reprinted with permission.

Timothy J. Harris, "Modeling the Conversion Decisions of Preferred Stock," 58 Bus. Law. 587 (2003). Reprinted by permission.

Excerpts from <www.isda.org> are reprinted with the permission of the International Swaps and Derivatives Association, Inc.

Jonathan R. Macey, "Wall Street Versus Main Street: How Ignorance, Hyperbole, and Fear Lead to Regulation," 65 U. Chi. L. Rev. 1487, 1497B 1498 (1998). Reprinted with permission.

Paul S. Maco, "Building a Strong Subnational Debt Market: A Regulator's Perspective," 2 Rich. J. Global L. & Bus. 1, 12 (2001). Reprinted with permission.

Jack H. McCall, "A Primer on Real Estate Trusts: The Legal Basics of REITS," 2 Transactions 1 (2001). Reprinted with permission.

Norman Menachem Feder, "Deconstructing OverBTheBCounter Derivatives," 2002 Columbia Business Law Review 677. Reprinted with permission.

Donna M. Nagy, Is the PCAOB a "Heavily–Controlled Component" of the SEC? An Essential Question in the Constitutional Controversy, 71 U. Pitt. L. Rev. 361. Reprinted with permission.

Frank Partnoy, F.I.A.S.C.O., Blood in the Water on Wall Street, 55B56 (1997). Used by permission of W.W. Norton & Company, Inc. and by permission of the author.

Frank Partnoy, "The Siskel and Ebert of Financial Markets? Two Thumbs Down for the Credit Rating Agencies," 77 Wash. U. L. Q. 619, 648, n. 139 (1999). Reprinted with permission.

Edward L. Pittman, "Economic and Regulatory Developments Affecting Mortgage Related Securities," 64 Notre Dame L. Rev. 497 (1989). Reprinted with permission.

Robert A. Robertson & Bradley W. Paulson, "Regulation of Financial Derivatives: A Methodology for Mutual Fund Derivative Instruments," 1 Stanford Journal of Law, Business & Finance 237 (1995). Reprinted with permission.

Lee A. Sheppard, "News Analysis: Equipment Leasing Shelters for Corporate Customers," 66 Tax Notes 1591 (1995). Reprinted with permission.

Norman P. Stein, "An Alphabet Soup Agenda for Reform of the Internal Code and ERISA Provision Applicable to Qualified Deferred Compensation Plans," originally appearing in Vol. 56, No. 1 of the SMU Law Review. Reprinted with permission from the SMU Law Review and the Southern Methodist University Dedman School of Law.

"The Commercial Paper Market and the Securities Acts," 39 University of Chicago Law Review 362, 363B64 (1972). Reprinted with permission.

Arthur E. Wilmarth, Jr., "The Transformation of the U.S. Financial Services Industry 1975B2000: Competition, Consolidation, and Increased Risk," 2002 U. Ill. L. Rev. 215, 235B236. Reprinted with permission.

Charles E. Wren III, "Sparing Cain: Executive Clemency in Capital Cases: The Stapled REIT on Ice: Congress' 1988 Freeze of the Grandfather Exception for Stapled REITs," 28 Capital University Law Review 717 (2000). Reprinted with permission.

Edward A. Zelinsky, "The Cash Balance Controversy," 19 Va. Tax. Rev. 683 (2000). Reprinted with permission.

Summary of Contents

TABLE OF CONTENTS

TABLE OF CASES

The principal cases are in bold type. Cases cited or discussed in the text
are in roman type. References are to pages. Cases cited in principal
cases and within other quoted materials are not included.

CORPORATE FINANCE

DEBT, EQUITY, AND DERIVATIVE MARKETS AND THEIR INTERMEDIARIES

Third Edition

CHAPTER ONE

CORPORATE FINANCE—AN OVERVIEW

■ ■ ■

Chapter objectives

- To understand the recent history of corporate finance.
- To learn the institutional landscape of corporate finance.
- To appreciate the market structure for the issuance and trading of financial products.
- To understand a lawyer's role in advising clients on corporate finance matters.

SECTION 1. INTRODUCTION

A corporate lawyer needs to be familiar with several areas of finance in order to advise clients. Although they need not be accountants or investment bankers themselves, corporate lawyers must also be able to break down complex transactions into their basic elements for analysis and application of sometimes complex regulatory requirements. A corporate lawyer must further be able to understand the risks, as well as potential rewards, of financial transactions. That knowledge is necessary in order to make required disclosures and to advise clients on risks being incurred. This may require an understanding of how particular financial instruments will perform under changed market or economic conditions. This casebook examines a broad range of financial instruments that will expose you to those considerations.

Traditionally, the focus in corporation finance has been on dividend restrictions, valuation of enterprises and some other classic matters such as bond financings. Today, corporate finance extends into many other areas. Structured finance, derivatives, cash management programs and financing arrangements such as repos, money market funds and securitizations are basics for lawyers dealing with corporate finance. On the principle that one must crawl before walking, this book will first address the more traditional areas of corporate finance that lawyers must still be familiar with, including such things as loans, classic corporate bonds, dividend restrictions and stock subscriptions. The materials will then

1

proceed to some of the more modern and complex instruments now used in corporate finance.

SECTION 2. CORPORATE FINANCE— SOME HISTORY[1]

Commercial corporations did not become prevalent in America until after the Revolution freed business development from the restrictions imposed by the English government on corporate charters. The Bank of North America was formed at the end of the Revolution by Robert Morris, the Superintendent of Finance for the Continental Congress, in order to shore up the country's faltering finances. Its ownership was divided among the government and a number of wealthy merchants who subscribed to purchase its stock. After the Revolution, the bank obtained new stock subscriptions to increase its capital and the value of its stock rose. The bank paid its shareholders dividends of 10 percent. Soon other banks, including the Bank of New York, were in competition with the Bank of North America and were selling their own stock. At the urging of the Secretary of the Treasurer, Alexander Hamilton, Congress created a Bank of the United States. Part of its capital stock was sold to the public. It was a "hot" issue and was heavily oversubscribed. More banks followed and their stocks became the subject of trade and speculation.

Other commercial corporations followed. Canal and turnpike companies were all demanding great amounts of capital. Their shares were popular. The stock of the Philadelphia and Lancaster Turnpike Company were so heavily over subscribed that the shares had to be allocated by lottery. Speculation nearly doubled share prices between 1789 and 1791. A market panic then occurred when one speculator, William Duer, the former Assistant Secretary of the Treasury, defaulted on loans and commitments he had obtained in his speculations. This resulted in our first stock market panic.

The first stock exchange was formed in Philadelphia in 1790. That city was also the home of the country's two largest banks, the Bank of North America and the first Bank of the United States. An auction market for securities was managed by John Sutton and Benjamin Jay in New York. It was conducted at 22 Wall Street. Dissatisfaction with that process led to a meeting of brokers at Corre's Hotel on March 21, 1792, which formed the foundation for the institution that ultimately became the New York Stock Exchange. The brokers attending the meeting wanted to exclude auctioneers from the stock business, and they reached an agreement that was signed by twenty-four stock brokers under a buttonwood tree on May 17, 1792. That agreement stated that:

---

1. The following history is based on 23 Jerry W. Markham & Thomas Lee Hazen, Broker–Dealer Operations Under Securities and Commodities Laws (2d ed. 2002) and Jerry W. Markham, Accountants Make Miserable Policemen—Rethinking the Federal Securities Laws, 28 North Carolina Journal of International Law and Commercial Regulation 725 (2003).

We the Subscribers, Brokers for the Purchase and Sale of Public Stock, do hereby solemnly promise and pledge ourselves to each other that we will not buy or sell, from this day for any person whatsoever any kind of public stock at a less rate than one-quarter per cent commission on the specie value, and that we will give preference to each other in our negotiations.

By 1817, eight brokerage firms and nineteen individuals were engaged in the brokerage business in New York. In that year, the New York Stock and Exchange Board was formed. It was renamed the New York Stock Exchange at the close of the Civil War. Composed originally of seven brokerage firms and thirteen individual brokers, the exchange operated at 40 Wall Street, and approximately thirty stocks were traded.

The New York Stock and Exchange Board grew rapidly in the next few decades, paralleling the increased need for borrowing by the states as a result of the growth of canal building. One successful flotation was for the Erie Canal that was completed in 1825.

In 1829, a locomotive pulled a train for the first time in the United States. A year later, the first railroad company stock was listed on the New York Stock and Exchange Board—the Mohawk and Hudson Railroad. Trading in railroad stocks grew quickly. By 1837, exchange listings included some eight railroads, two canal companies and twelve banks.

Trading in stocks were also conducted in curb market on the streets of New York before the Civil War. This grew into a colorful spectacle as traders in the streets signaled prices and transactions to clerks hanging from office windows. Trading would swell to levels that required streets to be cordoned off in order to accommodate the trading crowds. The phenomena of market crashes and recessions was an unwelcome part of these markets. Panics in 1837 and 1857 resulted in job losses and firm failures across the country. These events were often triggered by the failure of financiers or large firms. The panic of 1837 was touched off by the failure of some large cotton dealers. A severe recession followed. The failure of the Ohio Life insurance and Trust Company and the sinking of the *SS Central America* that was carrying a large shipment of gold (which was not recovered until the end of the twentieth century) touched off the panic of 1857.

The call market for money was developing as a source of funds for the speculative trading of stocks. These were loans made by banks and others to brokers for their trading. The loans were on call, which meant that the banks could demand repayment at any time. The loaned funds could be pyramided into large holdings by margin trading, i.e., stock could be purchased with only a small payment, the rest being borrowed on margin in the call market. The loan value of the stocks on margin had to be maintained through margin calls. For example, a stock priced at $10 and purchased on a margin of 10 percent required the broker to put up only $1 in his own funds, with the rest borrowed. If, however, the stock dropped value to say $9, the broker would have to put up another $1 to maintain the margin loan.

Margin had its dangers. For example, country banks would recall their funds held with their New York correspondent banks in the fall. This required the New York banks to call their margin loans, which required the brokers to sell their stocks in order to repay their margin loans. Those sales would result in a drop in stock market prices, which would in turn cause more sales and even lower prices as brokers sold more stock to meet margin calls.

Much of the capital in the market was coming from abroad in the early stages of market development in the United States. This would change after the Civil War. That war would have even greater effects on the American markets. Trading in the stock markets increased, giving rise to several new exchanges. The commodity markets also were developed during that era. See Chapter 11. A national currency was created during the Civil War—the Greenback. National banks were another development arising from the war.

Speculation was often frantic in New York during the Civil War. Gold was a favorite subject of trading. Its price rose and fell with Union victories and defeats in the field. The telegraph was a boon to markets as information began to move rapidly, a development akin to the introduction of the Internet during more recent years.

After the Civil War, "Robber Barons" such as Jay Gould, Jim Fisk and Daniel Drew, became legends as they plundered railroads and manipulated markets. Fisk and Gould's attempted corner of the gold market is still a legend in the financial history of the United States. The failure of Jay Cooke's firm in 1873 (he had been a leading financier and salesman of Union bonds during the Civil War) touched off another devastating panic.

The foundation for American financial leadership was laid by the capital raising efforts and speculations of the Robber Barons of the nineteenth century and the growth of the more professional investment bankers such as J.P. Morgan & Co. and E.H. Harriman. At the beginning of the twentieth century, the investment bankers were consolidating whole industries, making them more efficient and competitive on the world stage. They created a national economy and provided vast amounts of new finance for what were then fledgling hi-tech industries such as automobiles, electricity, telephones, radios and motion pictures. At the time of the outbreak of World War I, these financiers controlled vast amalgamations of capital and could raise enormous sums for investment through sophisticated underwriting methods. That skill proved handy when the European nations turned to America to fund their armies. America responded by providing a significant portion of the capital used to wage that conflict, while at the same time allowing America to field its own forces. The United States was the financial as well as political center of the world at the conclusion of that war.

Regulation of securities trading and sales was largely a matter of state law before the advent of the SEC. That regulation was limited. Kansas enacted the first "blue sky" law in 1911. It required companies selling securities in Kansas to register with the bank commissioner and disclose information about their operations. Stockbrokers were required to be registered. This legislation became a model for other states. Over twenty states adopted some form of blue sky law shortly after the enactment of the Kansas legislation. The Martin Act that was adopted in New York in 1921 sought to curb securities fraud scandals that were occurring after World War I. That act authorized the New York attorney general to investigate and seek injunctions against fraudulent securities practices or manipulative activities. The Martin Act was a broad based anti-fraud measure, rather than a disclosure device. It would become a popular means for New York to establish near predominance over securities regulation early in that century.

Important to the effort to impose federal regulation was the congressional investigation that followed the Panic of 1907 and which sought to determine if there was a money trust that was controlling American business. That inquiry was the result of the muckraking journalists and "progressive" legislators such as Charles Lindbergh, a congressman from Minnesota and the father of the famous flier. Lindbergh's claims led to a congressional investigation conducted by the House Committee on Banking, chaired by Arsene Pujo of Louisiana. The Committee did indeed find that J.P. Morgan & Co., the First National Bank and the National City Bank and a few others controlled vast railroad and other enterprises through interlocking directorships. The Pujo Committee also discovered numerous abuses in the securities markets, including insider trading.

Despite these revelations, Congress did not choose to regulate the securities markets. Instead, it passed the Clayton Antitrust Act and created the Federal Trade Commission in order to stop non-competitive practices and abuses of inter-locking directorships. Banking regulation was also enhanced in 1913 with the creation of the Federal Reserve System. That institution was formed in the aftermath of the Panic of 1907 at the behest of a group of bankers and was intended to assure that there was adequate liquidity in the money markets during times of stress.

The next serious effort to regulate securities trading arose during World War I. The Liberty Loan Committee in New York that was administered by the Federal Reserve Board, established a subcommittee on money rates (the "Money Committee") that sought to regulate the call money market to assure adequate liquidity so as to avert market panics. The Treasury Department and the Federal Reserve also formed a Capital Issues Committee ("CIC") that at first operated on a voluntary basis but was later given congressional authority to require submission of security issues for review and approval. The CIC reviewed securities offering in excess of $100,000 to assure they were compatible with the war effort. This was basically a way to bar speculative enterprises from tapping the capital markets. Unless approved as meeting that standard, securities offerings could not go forward. Before concluding its operations, the CIC submitted a report to Congress recommending the continuance of its operations after the war. The committee reported that market operators were fleecing unsophisticated individuals through schemes in which valuable Liberty bonds were exchanged for worthless securities. The CIC concluded that state blue sky laws were inadequate to deal with such problems. Congress failed to respond to the CIC's concerns.

The CIC had administered a substantive review process for approving the use of funds being raised by underwritings, but the legislation it sought was disclosure based. President Woodrow Wilson asked congress for the legislation sought by the CIC in order to "stop speculation and to prevent the fraudulent methods of promotion by which our people are annually fleeced on many millions of hard earned money." This legislation was not adopted, but the Federal Reserve Board, at the urging of the Secretary of Commerce, did publish a pamphlet in 1917 entitled "Approved Methods for the Preparation of Balance Sheets."

The Stock Market Crash and the New Deal

The causes of the Stock Market Crash of 1929 are still debated. Variously blamed are excessive speculation through margin accounts and abusive market practices such as the organized pools that were operating in over one hundred New York Stock Exchange stocks. Margin trading was claimed to have induced excessive speculation and soaked up credit needed for industrial use. More recent focus has centered on the blunders of the Federal Reserve System (the "Fed"). The Fed first eased credit in order to support England's effort to return to the gold standard, thereby boosting the market. The Fed then reversed course and sought to curb the market through ill-conceived interest rate increases. * * *

The congressional investigations that followed the stock market crash of 1929 resulted in the enactment of the federal securities laws. Those statutes sought to assure investors of "complete and truthful information from which he may intelligently appraise the value of a security, and to safeguard against the negligent and fraudulent practices perpetrated upon him in the past by incompetent and unscrupulous bankers, underwriters, dealers, and issuers."

The federal securities laws did not end the Great Depression. Controversy exists over what caused and prolonged the Great Depression. Some claimed that the market crash caused the depression, *post hoc ergo propter hoc*. Indeed, recessions and depressions often followed a market crash. The depression that began in 1893 was particularly prolonged and deep. But that claim does no more than suggest that the market anticipates the decline. The current view seems to be that the stock market crash of 1929 "was probably an event of relatively minor significance" in causing the Great Depression. Others suggest that the tariff wars raging around the world as the depression worsened prolonged and deepened its effects by almost stopping international trade. More blundering by the Federal Reserve pushed the country back into depression when a recovery appeared imminent in 1937. As the *Economist* noted, the depression "was caused by wrong-headed monetary and fiscal policy, combined with the Smoot–Hawley tariffs, and not by happenings on Wall Street."

In fact, the enactment of the Glass–Steagall Act assured that the investment bankers would be too weak to lead a recovery. They were cut off from the financial strength provided theretofore by commercial banks. The enactment of the federal securities laws also added further burdens, and the investment bankers turned to private placements with large institutions, which were not covered by the registration requirements. In many instances, this involved insurance companies that wanted only fixed income instruments. That dependency on debt resulted in a distortion of corporate balance sheets as they increased debt and reduced equity positions. The private placement market was also unavailable to small and medium size entrepreneurs.

The Great Depression ended only when war broke out in Europe. The stock markets still languished until after the end of World War II, when the consumer economy began to boom. It was not until November 17, 1954, however, that the market returned to its 1929 high under a more business friendly Eisenhower administration. At that point, institutional investors were firmly entrenching themselves in the market. Their strength grew. By 1990, the institutional investor would dominate the capital markets. Individual investors were net sellers of stock at the rate of about 3.5 million shares per day. This result should not surprise as many small investors found themselves being fleeced by penny stock promotions after the war, speculative forays into technology stocks, which presaged the Internet boom of the 1990's, and an underworld of felons were concocting various schemes to loot publicly traded companies.

Amendments were made in 1964 to strengthen financial reporting by public companies. The Williams Act regulated tender offers in 1968 but failed to halt the merger mania of the 1980's and 1990s. The SEC also became a more aggressive agency in the 1960s. Despite this new aggression on the part of the SEC, scandals continued. There was the implosion of Investors Overseas Services ("IOS"), a giant off-shore mutual fund that had been structured to avoid regulation in the United States. IOS was managed by a very colorful character, Bernie Cornfeld, whose loose administration led to sales to United States investors, as well as fraud and dubious investments. That activity gave rise to regulatory action by the SEC, and IOS was crippled. IOS was then sold to Robert Vesco, who then looted the company of hundreds of millions of dollars. Vesco fled to the Caribbean. He was subsequently jailed in Cuba for ten years but remained a fugitive from United States justice. Other scandals included the stock sales of Four Seasons Nursing Centers and the National Student Marketing Corporation and the pyramid sales scheme of Glenn W. Turner, all of which were disasters for public investors.

During what was known as the "go-go" years of the 1960s, the securities industry nearly imploded because it was not equipped to handle the stock volumes. The resulting "paperwork crisis" led to account insurance with the creation of the enactment of the Securities Investor Protection Act or 1970 and its creation of the Securities Investor Protection Corporation (SIPC). The SIPC provides insurance for customers with securities at a failed broker-dealer. This created a new moral hazard since customers were relieved of the obligation to monitor the financial health of their broker-dealer. Account insurance also led to more regulation in the form of an incredibly complex set of regulations governing the net capital of broker-dealers and their treatment of customer funds, all in the name of safeguarding the SIPC insurance fund. These regulatory "improvements" did nothing for the market, which was cut nearly in half during the recession that occurred in 1973–74.

Legislation enacted in 1975 regulated clearing and settlement activities, imposed more stringent regulation over broker-dealer operations and sought to create a National Market System (NMS). The SEC also devised a "central market" system concept as a result of a study it directed of institutional traders. This scheme posited that investors would be better served by a centralized trading system that would assure that every investor received the "best" execution price available for orders. The SEC never was able to articulate exactly how this concept would work in practice, but it was able to convince Congress that this should be a national goal. Although congress mandated a central market system in 1975, nothing much happened except for some consolidated reporting and a link among exchange specialists. The SEC did seek to put some teeth in NMS through a "trade through" rule in 2006, which required orders to be executed at the best available prices in all markets.

A series of scandals involving "questionable payments" to foreign government officials also arose in the 1970s. Those payments were funded from off-the-books slush funds of public companies. A long list of public companies made those bribes, but Lockheed was the leader, handing out $30 million to government officials in Japan, Germany, Netherlands, Italy, and numerous other countries. Disclosure of those bribes led to the collapse of several governments. That scandal resulted in the passage of the Foreign Corrupt Practices Act in 1977. That legislation prohibited such payments, more importantly it required public companies to maintain accurate books and records, a requirement that proved to be a myth in the scandals surfacing as this century began.

Scandals involving "bond daddies" in various southern cities and a funding crisis in New York City led to more regulation in the 1970s. A Municipal Securities Rulemaking Board was created by the 1975 amendments to the federal securities laws as a means to bring full disclosure to municipal securities. Unregistered dealers continued their sale of United States government securities utilizing a transaction called "repos." A default of a stunning proportions occurred 1982 when the Washington Public Power Supply System ("WPPS") defaulted on $2.25 billion in bonds it had issued to build nuclear power plants. A new layer of regulation was added with the enactment of the Government Securities

Act of 1986. Another massive default occurred in 1994, however, when Orange County, California announced large losses from speculative trading by its Treasurer. It was the largest municipal bankruptcy in history. Losses amounted to almost $1,000 for every man, woman and child in the county. More problems followed with "pay-to-play" underwriting abuses in which political contributions were made in order to obtain underwriting business and "yield burning" that was used to avoid IRS restrictions on refunding yields.

The savings and loan debacle of the 1980s witnessed the failure of hundreds of those institutions. Many of those S & Ls had been taken over by criminals after regulatory controls nearly bankrupted those institutions. Regulatory changes opened the door fraudulent schemes in which federal deposit insurance was used to obtain monies that could be spent on speculative operations, yachts, jets, mansions, expensive art works and other executive necessities. Most of the larger failed S & Ls were public companies.

Banking failures like the Bank of Credit and Commerce International ("BCCI") were another concern. That bank was found to be a giant criminal enterprise that bank regulators had permitted to operate globally. Accountants also failed to unravel the accounting shell game utilized by the Penn Square Bank in Oklahoma to sell $2.5 billion in loan participations to other banks. The failure of that shopping center bank caused a national crisis. One victim, the giant Continental Bank in Chicago had to be nationalized by the government.

Insider trading scandals of the 1980s involving the likes of Ivan Boesky, was another matter of concern. Sanctions were later strengthened after a series of scandals, but insider trading continued. Investors also poured $10 billion into penny stocks in the 1980s. Hundreds of thousands of those investors were thoroughly swindled by their brokers that included the likes of Blinder Robinson and First Jersey Securities. Additional legislation was enacted to deal with those penny stock frauds, but they would be succeeded by the "microcap" and "pump and dump" schemes of the 1990s.

The stock market crash of 1987 set a new record for the most severe one-week decline in stock market history, exceeding that of the 1929 crash. The SEC blamed that event on the speculative excesses of commodity futures traders operating on low margins in stock index futures contracts. The commodity futures markets, however, according to the SEC's own reports had become "synthetic" stock markets and were being used to price stocks. In other words, the commodity markets were viewed to be more efficient than the stock markets.

Market Run Up

The market run up at the end of the twentieth century had many eerie similarities to that of 1929. Even the Federal Reserve Board's blundering efforts to squelch the market at the end of the century, by ratcheting up interest rates, smacked of past errors forgotten. The market rise in the 1920s was a reflection of a revolution in communications and transportation. The radio, motion pictures and automobiles spurred the economy to new heights during that era. In the 1990s, the computer and the Internet changed society in ways that are too numerous to even catalogue. The stock market mania in the 1920s that was induced by the advances of that period caused problems with speculators who were overextended and trading on margin. That problem would be mimicked by customers at speculative "day trading" shops in the 1990s. At one point there were 400,000 day-traders, a large number, but one that was outmatched by the margin accounts of the 1920s.

The initial public offerings ("IPOs") of the dot.com companies at the end of the last century were reflective of the speculative excesses of the 1920s. These highly speculative Internet operations became "hot issues," which quickly traded in multiples of their offering price. Many of those enterprises just as quickly crashed. For example, the price of Scient rose from $10 to $133 before falling to $1.81. Priceline.com stock fell from $162 to $1.12. Yahoo stock dropped 92 percent. Stock values at Cisco Systems were reduced by $148 billion. Other big losers were EMC Networks, Oracle, Nortel Networks, Merck and General Electric. Nasdaq stocks lost seventy percent of their value, and hundreds of companies were dropped from trading in that market following the collapse of market prices in 2000. Estimates have ranged as high as $8.5 trillion as to the market value lost on the Nasdaq during the market reverse that began in 2000.

Some comparable figures are available from 1929. Stocks listed on the NYSE dropped in value from $90 billion to $16 billion, a drop of over 80 percent. The investment trusts of that era were closed end funds that owned many speculative securities. The fall in their share prices would have done a dot.com company proud. For example, the Goldman Sachs Trading Corporation saw its share prices fall from $326 to $1.75. The Blue Ridge Corp. stock price went from $100 to $3, and the American Founders Corp. shares dropped from $30 to 38 cents.

Scandals

The stock analyst scandals that followed the market collapse in this century had overtones of abuses from the 1920s. Harry Blodget, an analyst at Merrill Lynch, described one stock he had publicly praised as a "piece of junk" in an internal email. An investigation of Blodget by Eliot Spitzer, New York attorney general, caused Merrill Lynch to have to pay $100 million in fines and also exposed conflicts of interest in Merrill Lynch's research department. Internal emails had shown that firm analysts were privately disparaging company stocks, calling some "crap" while publicly recommending those shares. Mary Meeker, an analyst at Morgan Stanley, was given the title of "queen of the net" for hyping IPO internet stock offerings that her firm was underwriting. The State of Massachusetts claimed that analysts employed at Credit Suisse First Boston were touting stocks that they were privately disparaging in order to obtain investment banking business. Jack Grubman, an analyst at Salomon Smith Barney, was alleged to have pumped telecommunications stocks so that his firm could obtain their underwriting business. Even more juicy was the charge that Grubman had been induced to upgrade his rating on AT & T by Sandy Weill, the head of Citigroup in order to please that client. Such abuses led to a $1.4 billion settlement with regulators by several investment banking firms.

SECTION 3.   ENRON: FINANCIAL MORAL PANIC

A seismic shift in the world of corporate finance arrived when the Enron Corp. declared bankruptcy in October 2001. The company's failure occurred after it was forced to restate its accounts because of improper practices by some of its executives. More scandals soon followed.

The SEC was observing a number of accounting problems as the market bubble grew at the end of the 1990s. Accounting restatements were rare before 1995 but their use grew rapidly. Between 1998 and 2002, there were over 650 accounting restatements by public corporations. Accounting failures were said to have cost investors $88 billion between 1993 and 2000. The market collapse that began in 2000 exposed even more disturbing flaws in the financial system. At the center of this debacle were failures in accounting. Enron and its auditor, Arthur Anderson, came under scrutiny for failing to disclose the off-sheet accounting practices of Enron that allowed the company to keep large liabilities off its balance sheet, sometimes using special purpose vehicles in which management had invested. Enron announced a $1.01 billion charge resulting from limited partnerships, including one operated by the firm's chief financial officer. This resulted in a $618 million third quarter loss for the company in 2001.

Enron did not survive the resulting firestorm, and it became the largest bankruptcy in American history, although that record was soon bested. At the time of its bankruptcy, Enron was the seventh largest company in the United States. One newspaper claimed, however, that if Enron had properly accounted for its operations the firm would have ranked only 287 in the list of the country's largest companies. Arthur Anderson was also destroyed in the Enron scandal, after being convicted of obstruction of justice in connection with its handling of Enron documents. That conviction was later set aside by the Supreme Court, but that decision came too late to save the firm.

JERRY MARKHAM
ACCOUNTANTS MAKE MISERABLE POLICEMEN: RETHINKING THE FEDERAL SECURITIES LAWS
28 N.C.J. Int'l L. & Com. Reg. 725, 777 (2003)

The political outcry over Enron and other accounting problems undermined confidence in the SEC's full disclosure system and accounting in general. To restore confidence, the SEC required chief executive officers and chief financial officers of the largest publicly traded companies to swear that their financial statements were accurate. A total of sixteen of about 950 responding companies were unable to certify to the accuracy and completeness of their companies' reports. * *

Accounting scandals were endemic elsewhere. Xerox confessed that it had accelerated revenue improperly from 1997 through 2001 in an amount that could exceed $6 billion. Bristol–Myers Squibb, the pharmaceutical company, announced in October of 2002 that it was restating over $2 billion in inflated sales figures. The Rite Aid Corporation's restatement was for $1.6 billion in various years in the late 1990s. Former executives at Rite Aid were indicted for fraudulently inflating profits of the company. Its chief executive officer was facing charges of accounting fraud, false statements to the government and obstruction of justice by tampering with a witness.

The president of Critical Path Inc. pleaded guilty to charges that he falsified company revenues for 2000. The company's stock value subsequently dropped from $3.8 billion to $192 million. At the same time, Take–Two announced that it was the subject of an SEC investigation for certain of its accounting practices. Cendant Corp. inflated $500 million in earnings on its records, embarrassing its auditor—Ernst & Young. PNC Financial was required to restate its earnings twice for 2001. The total restatement reduced earnings by $377 million, a reduction of about one third of the previously reported earnings.

Vivendi wrote down over $12 billion of corporate goodwill, but that paled in comparison to the $54.2 billion written off by AOL Time Warner. Cisco Systems, Inc. took a $2.8 billion write down on inventory. An executive at Tyco, who had been indicted for not paying state sales taxes on expensive paintings, was also found to have looted as much as $175 million from the corporation. He used the funds for such things as a $6,000 shower curtain and a $2.1 million birthday party for his wife on the island of Sardinia where singer Jimmy Buffett was imported for her entertainment. Tyco, thereafter, announced a $6 billion charge against earnings that was said to be the result of "a pattern of aggressive accounting" designed to inflate earnings. Other executives had been similarly greedy. A survey by the *Financial Times* concluded that in the three years prior to August 2002 the top executives and directors involved in major business collapses in the United States were paid about $3.3 billion. At the same time these enormous sums were being paid out, those companies laid off some 100,000 workers, and hundreds of billions of dollars in shareholder value were lost.

The telecoms were at center of an ocean of red ink and accounting fraud. AT & T took a $1 billion restructuring charge in the last quarter of 2001 and cut 10,000 jobs. Global Crossing, a fiber optic telecom carrier whose valuation had reached $50 billion, filed for bankruptcy. It became the fourth largest bankruptcy in United States history. Nortel Networks, a telecommunications firm, saw its chief financial officer resign as a result of some improper personal investments. Nortel's stock price had dropped almost ninety percent in the prior two years. That was a loss of $140 billion in market value. WorldCom and Qwest Communications International had write-offs of $60 billion in goodwill as a result in the change in accounting rules for merger-acquired goodwill. Qwest Communications was defending itself in the press against claims that it had improperly accounted for certain equipment sales to KMC Telecom Holdings, Inc.

Thereafter, WorldCom announced that it had engaged in a staggering $9 billion in fraudulent accounting entries. That fraud was designed to boost its stock performance. The company was delisted from Nasdaq. WorldCom filed for Chapter 11 bankruptcy on July 21, 2002. This gave WorldCom the dubious title of the largest bankruptcy in history, shoving aside Enron for that honor. On October 1, 2002, Elliot Spitzer, the New York attorney general, brought charges against five individuals including former WorldCom CEO Bernard Ebbers, claiming that they had improperly profited by more than $1.5 billion from shares given to them in IPOs as an inducement for them to direct their company's business to investment banking firms such as Salomon Smith Barney. This practice was similar to the use of "preferred" accounts used by J.P. Morgan and others back in the 1920s and for which were roundly criticized. In a return of pre-SEC regulation, Spitzer used the Martin Act to investigate and prosecute those executives.

Adelphia, the cable company, announced that it had overstated revenue and cash flow by some $500 million over a two year period. Adelphia was also a co-borrower of $3.1 billion in loans to a partnership owned by its founders, the Rigas family. The family used $1.4 billion of that loan to buy company stock. Adelphia filed for bankruptcy on June 25, 2002. It was then the nation's sixth largest cable company. The founder of Adelphia along with his son, was convicted of looting the company. Two senior executives at the Sprint Corp. were forced to resign after it was revealed to their board of directors that they had used a dubious tax shelter to avoid paying taxes on over $100 million of income from stock options they had been awarded as bonuses.

Firms outside the telecom industry were also suffering. Conseco became the third largest bankruptcy in history in 2002. Polaroid filed for bankruptcy in September of 2001. Kmart filed for Chapter 11 bankruptcy on January 22, 2002. This was the largest retail bankruptcy in history. Kmart had almost $40 billion in annual sales before filing for bankruptcy. As concern arose about Kmart's continued viability, its share prices dropped dramatically, by seventy percent in a single week. There was also bad news for investors interested in the airlines industry. US Airways declared bankruptcy, and American Airlines announced that it was laying off 7,000 workers. United Airlines filed for bankruptcy in December of 2002. This was the largest bankruptcy of an airline in history.

Losses were also mounting as further management failures were exposed by the downturn in the economy. In 2001, there were 257 bankruptcies of publicly owned companies. This was a record high. * * *

Financial reform may have been in order after these scandals, but the resulting legislation—the Sarbanes–Oxley Act of 2002—displayed the hallmarks of legislative overreaction.

JOSÉ GABILONDO
FINANCIAL MORAL PANIC! SARBANES–OXLEY, FINANCIER FOLK DEVILS, AND OFF–BALANCE–SHEET ARRANGEMENTS

36 Seton Hall L. Rev. 781 (2006)

... Moral panic theory claims that the media, moral entrepreneurs, government authorities, and special interest groups (including values communities) often react to a perceived threat to a fundamental social interest by invoking a deviant to blame for the perceived threat....

Financial moral panic is the expression in the explicitly economic sphere of the more general form of moral panic. The public discourse about [Enron and related scandals] was framed in the familiar terms of a moral panic. In this panic narrative, rogue managers and auditors threatened public confidence in a vital public good—the capital market—risking the solvency of every investor's financial future. A national auto de fe against financial heresy, the congressional hearings leading up to the Act opened on this tone. Consistent with popular accounts of accounting scandals, the legislative history of the Sarbanes–Oxley Act similarly reflects the reception of the blame narrative. Some witnesses did testify to the technical nature of the accounting problems which underlay Enron, but these voices were outnumbered by the gnashing of teeth over lapses in professional ethics. Imputing a simple intent to Congress's 535 independent members often seems farfetched, but not so with respect to the sentiment that the corporate officials and auditors in question had behaved wantonly. Though stopping short of phrenology, the floor debate from the Act contains numerous aspersions about chief executive officers, chief financial officers, and accountants—the folk devils of this financial moral panic. (Lawyers played a key role in the media construction of this moral panic, confirming their complicity in feeding a moral panic which they were also in a position to critically evaluate.)

... In a general moral panic, though, economic anxiety is displaced away from the market and onto social issues. [I]n a financial moral panic the economic anxiety stays in the economic sphere but plays out in a new form. Put another way, the logic of the financial moral panic must explain the losses caused by the scandals without undermining the basic optimism in capital markets overall. Since indifferent markets could not be blamed for these investment and employment losses, bad people would have to be. A parody of Calvinist predestination, causation in this instance explained financial losses in terms of personal morality, not market movements, as reflected in the moral critiques of accounting scandals issued at the time.

... Against this background of ambient economic insecurity, the narrative about rogue officers who robbed workers of their life savings is poignant but no less misleading for being so. An explanation of these financial losses in terms of individual misconduct misses the point. After all, it was the same accounting and business practices here repudiated that had created much of the wealth and many of the jobs whose evaporation had triggered the financial moral panic in the first place. In fact, Enron, in particular, had become a poster firm for "best practices" in financial engineering, associated with the production of financial wealth. This poignant narrative about investor and worker losses also reflects a common misconception about the nature of unrealized appreciation in financial assets. Again, most of what Enron employees lost was unrealized value, which, for example, the federal income tax laws do not tax as income. Evoking tulip bulbs, Enron reminded us of the ephemeral nature of unrealized gain, striking a chord since such gain makes up much of our wealth. Would a retirement based on unrealized appreciation in corporate equities be rosy? Maybe not, given the nature of market risk. John Kenneth Galbraith argues that during a price bubble, a collective psychology built on denial of financial realities sets in with investors. The psychology leads to financial speculation and concomitant disaster. Financial moral panic is a defense mechanism of this mind set. More specifically, my point is that panics of this type deny the unavoidable underlying volatility of financial assets, of which capital market investment is simply the most popular example ...

In the absence of any meaningful opposition to the blame narrative, Congress acted accordingly. Since the evil calling for Congress's attention was framed as mischief by officials and auditors, the [Sarbanes–Oxley] Act ended up with a punitive rather than technical focus. The traditional focus of federal securities law is disclosure. However, only three of Sarbanes–Oxley's sixty-six substantive provisions address disclosure. Instead, criminalizing corporate and managerial activity is the overriding purpose of the Act; three titles are dedicated to fraud and criminal penalties. Targeting folk devils, the Act increased the liability of the chief financial officer (CFO) by requiring the CFO to attest to the accuracy of periodic reports under pain of criminal prosecution. Moreover, by setting up the Public Company Accounting Oversight Board, the Act puts auditors squarely in the sights of the SEC, now empowered to increase its criminal referrals and disciplinary action over a profession that had previously been largely self-regulated. Again, this emphasis on individual criminality reflects the influence of moral panic in the legislative process. Consistent with the national mood, financiers convicted in related prosecutions have received heavy sentences, in particular the contumaciously intransigent ones who refused to plea bargain. Other prosecutions and civil actions brought against corporate officials have also tried to expand the concept of financial loss beyond the previous legal definition. Constructing the problem in question in terms of corporate rogues has also dovetailed with the SEC's self-concept as an enforcement agency, rather than as a knowledge center about capital market structure.

Granted, public floggings do deter misconduct, but they are not likely to solve the technical problems about financial reporting.

SECTION 4. THE ROLE OF THE CORPORATE LAWYER

The highly publicized failure of Enron Corp. led to much criticism of the role played by lawyers in corporate fraud. The Enron and other scandals suggested to many that lawyers were neglecting their professional obligations.

THOMAS LEE HAZEN
ADMINISTRATIVE LAW CONTROLS ON ATTORNEY PRACTICE—A LOOK AT THE SECURITIES AND EXCHANGE COMMISSION'S LAWYER CONDUCT RULES

55 Administrative Law Review 323 (2003).

When representing clients of regulated industries, lawyers play various roles in dealing with the applicable administrative agencies. Administrative agencies frequently function as tribunals and as such may implement rules regulating the practice of law before the agency. Since 1935 the Securities and Exchange Commission has regulated the conduct of lawyers who practice before it. The SEC adopted the predecessor to its current Rule 102(e) of its Rules of Practice "in order to protect the integrity of its processes from incompetent, unethical or dishonest professionals, including attorneys." The SEC has explained that the rule is premised not only on its "inherent authority" but also on its statutory authority to adopt rules "as may be necessary or appropriate to implement the [securities laws]."

Rule 102(e) and its predecessors have had a controversial history. In 2002, in response to the corporate governance crisis unearthed by high profile investigations such as the one involving Enron Corporation, Congress enacted numerous amendments to the federal securities laws under the aegis of the Sarbanes–Oxley Act of 2002. Section 307 of that Act directed the SEC to adopt rules defining proper client representation in SEC matters. * * *

Lawyers, like anyone else, can violate the securities laws. The SEC has a wide range of enforcement tools that may be used against persons who violate the securities laws. Each of the securities acts gives the SEC the authority to seek either temporary or permanent injunctive relief in the courts "whenever it shall appear to the Commission that any person is engaged or about to engage in any acts or practices which constitute or will constitute a violation." Courts will not invoke their injunctive power without "positive proof of a reasonable likelihood that past wrongdoing will occur" and proof that there is "something more than the mere possibility which keeps the case alive." Accordingly, even where the SEC can establish that a violation has occurred, failure to prove a reasonable likelihood of future violations is likely to mean that no injunction will be granted. SEC injunctive relief frequently is accompanied by ancillary relief such as disgorgement of ill-gotten gains and in appropriate cases, the imposition of a civil penalty. The SEC has broad adjudicatory authority under which it may bring administrative proceedings and may impose a wide variety of sanctions, including the imposition of civil penalties. In addition the SEC has cease and desist power. In extreme cases lawyers who violate the securities laws will be subject to criminal prosecution.

Lawyers who assist clients' securities law violations have been pursued as aiders and abettors. A 1994 Supreme Court decision held that private parties may not seek damages against persons who aid and abet securities law violations. In 1995, Congress made it clear, however, that the SEC may bring enforcement actions and administrative proceedings against aiders and abettors. Mere lawyering for a client who violates the securities laws does not constitute aiding and abetting but active involvement in furthering the violations will put the lawyer at risk of exposure to aiding and abetting liability.

The SEC's authority is not limited to pursuing lawyers as aiders and abettors or primary violators of the securities laws. Section 15(c)(4) of the Securities Exchange Act of 1934 gives the SEC extremely broad authority to institute administrative proceedings and impose sanctions against anyone who is a "cause" of a securities law violation. As enacted, section 15(c)(4) gave the SEC the authority to pursue persons whose conduct was sufficiently egregious to constitute a violation of the Act. However, as part of the Insider Trading Sanctions Act of 1984, Congress significantly expanded the SEC's administrative powers with regard to an individual or entity who was a "cause" of a failure to comply with the Act's reporting requirements. Under section 15(c)(4), after notice and opportunity for a hearing, the SEC may issue an order calling for compliance or steps towards compliance with any SEC Rule or Regulation. The SEC's authority under section 15(c)(4) includes the power to issue administrative sanctions against officers, directors and employees of such issuer, or anyone else responsible for, or who could have prevented, the violation. Lawyers could be included into this latter category. The broad terms of section 15(c)(4) do not place any limits on the types of orders that the Commission may issue. Thus, for example, the SEC could rely on section 15(c)(4) to issue an order barring an individual from being associated with a 1934 Act reporting company.

The SEC invoked its authority under section 15(c)(4) in *In re Kern* [50 S.E.C. 596 (1991)] to pursue an attorney's involvement in SEC filing violations. In that case, the administrative law judge (ALJ) indicated that an attorney whose negligence resulted in the filing of a false document might be found to have been a cause of a violation of the Act. The ALJ held, however, that he was without power to issue any bar order because at the time of the decision, the respondent was no longer associated with the company in question. The full Commission has affirmed the ALJ's decision solely on the grounds that it was beyond the ALJ's authority once the respondent was no longer in a position to control the company's future compliance. The *Kern* proceeding demonstrated the SEC's imaginative use of its administrative authority to pursue an attorney whose conduct was not sufficient in itself to constitute a violation of the Act.

The most direct route for the SEC to pursue attorneys practicing before the Commission is through its rules of Practice. In particular, SEC Rule of Practice 102, specifically addresses practice before the Commission. * * *

Under the terms of Rule 102(e), the SEC may limit or deny an attorney's or other professional's practice before the Commission if the Commission finds that the person lacks the qualifications necessary to represent others, lacks sufficient character or integrity, has engaged in improper professional conduct, or has willfully violated or aided and abetted any violation of the federal securities laws or the rules and regulations thereunder. * * *

On March 7, 2002, a group of law professors sent a letter to SEC Chairman Harvey Pitt urging the SEC to amend its rules of practice to better define what constitutes proper representation of public companies. In particular, the letter asked that the Commission adopt a rule to conform to Rule 1.13 of the American Bar Association's Model Rules of Professional Conduct. In relevant part, Rule 1.13 requires that when an attorney who is representing a corporation is made aware of serious wrongdoing, the attorney must take steps to correct the problem. Those steps include what is sometimes referred to as "climbing the corporate ladder"—reporting the violation to someone within the corporation in a position of authority to take corrective action. The Model Rule requires the attorney to continue to climb the ladder, even to the Board of Directors until the attorney is satisfied that the matter will be attended to properly. The letter to Chairman Pitt asked that the SEC adopt a rule indicating that a lawyer who does not take this action can be suspended from practice before the SEC. On March 28, David Becker, the SEC's General Counsel responded on Chairman Pitt's behalf that since 1981 the SEC "has not brought Rule 102(e) proceedings against on allegations of professional conduct, or otherwise used the Rule to establish professional responsibilities of lawyers." Mr. Becker's letter further stated that "[t]here is a strong view among the bar that these matters are more appropriately addressed by state bar rules ..." Later in the spring of 2002, Senator John Edwards' office submitted a proposed provision that was made part of the Sarbanes–Oxley Act as section 307 of that Act. Section 307 of the Sarbanes–Oxley Act provides:

> Not later than 180 days after the date of enactment of this Act, the Commission shall issue rules, in the public interest and for the protection of investors, setting forth minimum standards of professional conduct for attorneys appearing and practicing before the Commission in any way in the representation of issuers, including a rule—
>
>> (1) requiring an attorney to report evidence of a material violation of securities law or breach of fiduciary duty or similar violation by the company or any agent thereof, to the chief legal counsel or the chief executive officer of the company (or the equivalent thereof); and
>>
>> (2) if the counsel or officer does not appropriately respond to the evidence (adopting, as necessary, appropriate remedial measures or sanctions with respect to the violation), requiring the attorney to report the evidence to the audit committee of the board of directors of the issuer or to another committee of the board of directors comprised solely of directors not employed directly or indirectly by the issuer, or to the board of directors.

The Act thus requires the SEC to impose the obligations to report the wrongdoing within the corporation. The Act does not require the attorney to blow the whistle outside of the corporate entity. However, in the late 1970s the SEC took the position that reporting violations to the SEC might be required at some point. This was a controversial position that was opposed by the American Bar Association because of its perceived conflict with the attorney's obligation of confidentiality and was never implemented.

Section 307 of Sarbanes–Oxley mandates only a climbing the ladder requirement within the corporate entity and thus does not implicate the attorney client privilege. However, in its proposed rules, the SEC went even further in calling for a noisy withdrawal from representation and notification of the SEC if the attorney is not satisfied that the course taken by the client would correct the wrongful conduct. The SEC recognized that this proposal went beyond the mandate of the statute and in light of the anticipated controversy, specifically solicited comments on this expansion. As expected, the noisy withdrawal requirement met with opposition from large portions of the securities bar. Not surprisingly, the majority of comments to the SEC opposed the noisy withdrawal proposal.
* * *

On January 23, 2003, the SEC announced that it was adopting a modified version of the proposed rules. In the first instance, the Commission deferred for further consideration the most controversial aspect of the rule proposal—the noisy withdrawal requirement. It has been suggested that the SEC is likely at some point to implement a noisy withdrawal requirement in some form. In doing so, the SEC solicited additional comments on the noisy withdrawal requirement. The new rules as adopted contain the up the ladder requirement mandated by section 307 of Sarbanes–Oxley but at the same time the rules diluted the threshold for triggering the internal reporting requirement. In particular, while the original rules spoke in terms of requiring the lawyer to begin climbing the ladder, if the attorney "reasonably believes" that a material violation might have occurred. In place of this "reasonably believes" trigger, the SEC substituted a threshold formulated as a double negative: the internal reporting requirement is triggered by "credible evidence based upon which it would be *unreasonable*, under the circumstances, for a prudent and competent attorney *not to conclude* that a material violation has occurred, is ongoing, or is about to occur." This is a difficult standard to prove in an enforcement action. A more troubling problem with this high threshold of proof is that it may actually operate to discourage communication to information to attorneys so as to create deniability. In other words, as one commentator has suggested, under the rules as adopted ignorance may be bliss. * * *

The "up the ladder" reporting operates as follows. Under Rule 205.3(b) an attorney who is practicing before the SEC in representation of a public company who becomes aware of a material violation must "report such evidence to the issuer's chief legal officer (or the equivalent thereof) or to both the issuer's chief legal officer and its chief executive officer (or the equivalents thereof) forthwith." Since the reporting is within the corporation, the attorney-client privilege is in no way diminished, although the proposed rules would have also required documentation of the report.

The first step of the ladder thus is the report to the company's chief legal officer or equivalent officer. The chief legal officer (or equivalent) must then investigate the situation (or turn the matter over to a Qualified Legal Compliance Committee (QLCC) within the corporation). If the chief legal officer (CLO) concludes that a material violation "has occurred, is ongoing, or is about to occur, he or she shall take all reasonable steps to cause the issuer to adopt an appropriate response, and shall advise the reporting attorney thereof."

If the attorney making the original report is satisfied that the CLO has taken appropriate action, then nothing further needs to be done by the reporting attorney. If however, the reporting attorney is not satisfied that appropriate action has been taken, the reporting attorney must climb the next rung of the corporate ladder. Specifically:

(3) Unless an attorney who has made a report under paragraph (b)(1) of this section reasonably believes that the chief legal officer or the chief executive officer of the issuer (or the equivalent thereof) has provided an appropriate response within a reasonable time, the attorney shall report the evidence of a material violation to:

(i) The audit committee of the issuer's board of directors;

(ii) Another committee of the issuer's board of directors consisting solely of directors who are not employed, directly or indirectly, by the issuer and are not, in the case of a registered investment company, "interested persons" as defined in section 2(a)(19) of the Investment Company Act of 1940 (15 U.S.C. 80a–2(a)(19)) (if the issuer's board of directors has no audit committee); or

(iii) The issuer's board of directors (if the issuer's board of directors has no committee consisting solely of directors who are not employed, directly or indirectly, by the issuer and are not, in the case of a registered investment company, "interested persons" as defined in section 2(a)(19) of the Investment Company Act of 1940 (15 U.S.C. 80a–2(a)(19))).

In the process of making the necessary investigations, the corporation is likely to use additional attorneys. The rules expressly provide that attorneys retained to investigate reports of a material violation are practicing before the SEC and this become subject to the up the ladder reporting requirements. However, an attorney retained by the company's CLO or QLCC to investigate the situation does not have an up the ladder reporting obligation so long as he or she makes a report to the CLO or QLCC (as the case may be). * * *

Notes

1. The role of a corporate lawyer is often a leading one in negotiating financial transactions. The corporate lawyer will also be "signing off" on a deal, i.e., assuring the participants that the deal is legal. Rarely, however, will a complex transaction be completely without legal doubt. If it were otherwise there would be little need for lawyers. Indeed, if certainty is required, few complex financial transactions would be completed. Lawyers (and clients) must make judgments as to whether the legal risks justify going forward. Assessing those risks requires good judgment. A too timid lawyer is not useful to society, a reckless one is even more of a menace. How will you draw the line in giving advice to your clients?

2. How will you decide whether to report an executive you are working for who you think may be violating the law by refusing to disclose some fact that may be material? What if the issue is a close one? Do you think an executive will hire you in the future if you report her to the board of directors? Remember if you cannot afford to lose the business, you cannot afford to do it.

SECTION 5. INSTITUTIONS

Corporate lawyers need to be familiar with a number of institutions that play key roles in corporate finance. These include broker-dealers, investment bankers and institutional investors such as mutual funds. Subsequent chapters will focus on the role of these institutions. Banks and thrifts are other institutions playing a key role in corporate finance. The regulation of banks and thrifts is the subject of a separate course in many law schools, but some understanding of their growth and development is necessary for this course.

Banks and Thrifts—Some History and Background[2]

Banking in America and its regulation has a long and tangled history. Robert Morris, the Superintendent of Finance for the Continental Congress, laid the groundwork for the existing structure during the Revolution. Assisting Morris in that effort was Alexander Hamilton who, as a reader of Adam Smith's *The Wealth of Nations* that was published in 1776, became an advocate of a central bank that would guide and help build America into a world power. Hamilton proposed such an institution in a letter to Robert Morris that was written while the Continental Army was in winter quarters. Morris set that plan in motion through the "Bank of North America," which began operations in 1782 and aided the Continental army during some of its darker hours. Hamilton used the Bank of England as the model for the creation of this bank. Hamilton wanted the Bank of the United States ("BUS") to be a private bank. Congress approved Hamilton's recommendations and authorized the creation of this national bank in 1791.

The BUS was not the only bank in America. A number of banks were created in the years following the Revolution. Between 1782 and 1837, over 700 banks sprang up in the United States. Since there was no national currency, the notes issued by the banks began circulating as a substitute. It was sometimes an unstable currency. As John Adams noted in 1799, "the fluctuations of our circulating medium have committed greater depredations upon the property of honest men than all the French piracies."

The states began to take some rudimentary efforts to regulate banking. Massachusetts and New Hampshire prohibited unincorporated banks in 1799. New York imposed a similar measure in 1804. These prohibitions were based on the English Bubble Act of 1720, which had sought to curb speculative enterprises by requiring businesses to obtain a government approved charter before stock could be sold to the public or notes issued.

Despite the competition, the BUS continued as the premier bank. It had branches in Boston, New York, Washington, Norfolk, Charleston, Savannah and New Orleans. Ironically, the success of the BUS spelled its doom. It was a threat to the state banks that were appearing in ever increasing numbers, and Congress refused to renew its charter in 1811. The expiration of the bank's Congressional charter created a vacuum that was soon filled by the state banks. Over 120 new state banks were

---

2. The following material is excerpted from Jerry W. Markham, Banking Regulation: Its History and Future, 4 N.C. Banking Inst. 221 (2000).

chartered between 1811 and 1815. Difficulties encountered during the War of 1812, however, resulted in the creation of a new Bank of the United States. The states did not react favorably toward this institution. Fourteen states passed laws that tried to prevent the second BUS from collecting its debts. Six states tried to tax the branches of the second BUS in their borders. In *McCulloch v. Maryland*, 17 U.S. 316, 4 L.Ed. 579 (1819), however, the Supreme Court held that a Maryland tax directed against BUS violated the Constitution. That ruling freed BUS from restrictive state regulations.

The BUS became the center of a political battle that has reverberated through the centuries. Andrew Jackson viewed the bank to be a "monster." Henry Clay, his political rival, wanted to make the BUS's charter a political issue to further Clay's own Presidential ambitions. Clay and his supporters, who included Daniel Webster, had control of both the House and the Senate. They rechartered the Second Bank in 1832. Jackson responded by vetoing that legislation. His veto was upheld, and he ordered the government's deposits to be removed from the BUS to state banks that were politically aligned with Jackson. They were derisively referred to by Jackson's opponents as the "pet" banks. At Clay's urging, Jackson was censured by the Senate for his removal order, but Clay suffered a severe defeat when the Senate voted to expunge that censure from Senate records in 1837.

The struggle over the BUS set back the effort to create a central banking authority until the next century, and its demise led to a "bank mania." The number of state banks more than doubled between 1829 and 1837. New York furthered their growth by allowing banks to be incorporated without requiring a special charter from the legislature. Several other states followed this "free banking" approach to chartering. More affirmative regulation was also being adopted. New York set up a bank supervisory authority in 1829, and a more formal banking commission was created in New York to oversee banks after the Panic of 1837. Reserve requirements were imposed. The first insurance for bank depositors appears to have been developed by the New York safety fund law that was passed in 1829. It was not successful.

By the time of the Civil War, America's principal currency was the bank notes that were being issued by the state banks, which fluctuated in value according to their quality. Thousands of bank notes were then in circulation, many of which were counterfeit. The Union government created the "greenback" and made it legal tender as a way to fund its expenditures during the Civil War. This became our national currency, and the creation of the national banks was closely tied to its success. The federal government's elimination of state bank notes as a currency was accomplished through a two-step process. The first step was to create a national banking system. The second step was to tax the state bank notes out of existence. The first of these measures was taken with the passage of the National Banking Act that became law on February 25, 1863. It authorized the creation of "national" banks that would be regulated by the federal government. The Office of the Comptroller of the Currency was directed to administer this legislation. This resulted in a "dual" system of banking regulation between the states and the federal government.

The bank clearing houses were a key part of the banking system after the Civil War. They served in the place of a central bank. Clearinghouse certificates were used as a means of relieving temporary stringencies in the money supply. The value of the clearinghouse certificates proved themselves during the panics in 1873, 1884, 1890 and 1893.

The trust companies became popular at the turn of the century as a mechanism for avoiding the functional regulation that was being imposed on commercial banks. The Knickerbocker Trust Company was the third largest trust company in New York with deposits in excess of $60 million when it failed on October 22, 1907. The Knickerbocker's failure touched off a panic that was one of the worst in the history of the United States. The federal government appeared to be helpless in dealing with the crisis. Instead, a single individual emerged as the country's savior. He was an unlikely, unappreciated, but well paid hero. That individual, J.P. Morgan, acted as a "one-man Federal Reserve Bank" in stopping the panic. Even so, the country was left stunned by the suddenness and force of that economic catastrophe.

Congress created a Monetary Commission to examine the causes of the Panic of 1907 and to propose measures to prevent such an occurrence in the future. The Commission was chaired by Senator Nelson Aldrich. He conducted an extensive investigation that lasted almost four years. Senator Nelson Aldrich introduced legislation in 1912 that proposed the creation of such a central banking authority in the United States. Following much debate and various compromises, the Federal Reserve Act of 1913 was enacted. It created a further division in bank regulation. In addition to state regulation, federal bank regulatory authority was being split between the Treasury Department and the Federal Reserve System (the "Fed"). The Comptroller of the Currency at the Treasury retained responsibility for examining and regulating the national banks, while the Fed managed monetary issues.

Another regulatory issue affecting banking was restrictions on branch banking. Branch banking was an established practice in the United States almost from the country's inception, but branch banking by national banks was restricted under the National Banking Act. By 1895, branching was permitted in twenty states, but most branch banks were intra-city branches, and eight of those states later prohibited branching. By 1896, thirteen states prohibited branch banking and many other states considered the practice to be illegal. This resulted in "unit" banking in the United States, i.e., single bank units. These individual banks established correspondent banking arrangements with other banks in order to conduct interstate or even inter-city banking transactions. The correspondents borrowed from each other and referred business outside their geographical area. Most country banks were strongly dependent on their correspondent banking relationships in New York, which was the nation's money center by the time of the Civil War. Nevertheless, correspondent banking frustrated efforts by the city banks and their clearinghouses to stabilize liquidity during times of panic because the country banks would withdraw their deposits according to crop cycles and in times of trouble.

The McFadden Act that was adopted in 1926 sought to allow national banks to establish branches under conditions similar to those permitted by state banks. The McFadden Act provided for the creation of new branches by national banks in states that permitted banks to have branches and in cities with a population of more than 25,000. Actually, "the ultimate effect of the McFadden Act was to allow state legislators and regulators to prevent out-of-state banks from opening branches within their borders." This assured that small communities would only be served by their local banks. They would be spared the competition and services of the larger and better capitalized big city banks. More significantly, restrictions on branch banking resulted in a large number of very weak banks that would be unable to cope with a serious economic downturn.

Bank failures reached epidemic proportions after the stock market crash of 1929. In December of 1930, the Bank of United States failed. It was the largest bank failure in history at that time, but there were many joining it. By 1932, one in four banks in the United States had failed. Franklin Roosevelt was sworn in as President during the bank panic that struck America. He declared a national bank holiday on March 6, 1933, and new legislation, including the Glass–Steagall Act, was enacted to strengthen the banking system. Federal insurance was created to protect customer bank deposits and to maintain faith in the banks in order to prevent depositor runs. This insurance was to be administered by the Federal Deposit Insurance Corporation ("FDIC").

The Glass–Steagall Act sought the "complete divorcement" of commercial and investment banking. There is still uncertainty as to why Congress mandated such an approach. Presumably, it was due to the failure of the Bank of United States and its securities affiliate—the City Financial Corporation. The affiliate, however, was not shown to have caused the bank's failure.

The Fed only slowly grasped the reigns of control over monetary policy. That agency was accused of pushing the country back into recession in 1937 by its restrictive policies. The Fed was also forced to bow to the Treasury Department on issues of monetary policy during World War II. In order to reduce government costs caused by that conflict, the Treasury Department decreed that interest rates would be kept at artificially low levels. The Fed agreed to that policy until post-war inflation became more of a threat than high government borrowing costs. Friction between the Fed and the Treasury on this issue increased until the adoption of the so-called "Treasury–Federal Reserve Accord" that was entered into by the Fed and the Treasury in March of 1951. The agreement strengthened the role of the Fed in managing federal monetary policy.

The Fed's Regulation Q restricted interest rates paid on time deposits by national banks. Because of Regulation Q, banking was not viewed to be a very complicated business in the 1950s. It was claimed that bankers operated on a "3–6–3" rule. This meant that the bankers borrowed money at the Regulation Q interest rate of three percent and loaned the money at six percent. The bankers were then free to play golf by three o'clock, since there was nothing else to do. Advertising premiums were offered in the 1950s for new business. This allowed banks to avoid Regulation Q ceilings. Toasters and other giveaways were used to attract depositors to these programs.

The 1960s marked the beginning of an era in which financial service firms sought to expand and diversify their businesses across regulatory boundaries. James J. Saxon, who was appointed by President Kennedy to the position of Comptroller of the Currency, sought to open the door to such diversification to the banks. Saxon and his successors took an expansive view of the banking laws in allowing the banks to broaden their business base. Saxon's rulings upset a delicate balance between the banking and other financial service industries. He started an effort that continued until the financial crisis that began in 2007 to remove restrictions on banks that prevent them from aggressively expanding their business activities. The rulings of the Comptroller were challenged in court by competitors and were sometimes stricken down, but the effort to ease restrictions on bank activities continued.

The banks began looking for other loopholes to expand their business and avoid banking regulations. The Bank Holding Company Act of 1956 restricted the ability of bank holding companies to enter into other lines of business or to purchase other banks. Such activities required Fed approval, but the Bank Holding Company Act of 1956 did not apply to one-bank holding companies. The number of one-bank holding companies grew rapidly as this loophole was exploited. These entities held about one third of total bank deposits. This concerned Congress, and it acted to close the one bank holding company exception through the Bank Holding Company Act Amendments of 1970.

As inflation increased, the Fed's interest rate ceilings began to interfere with the ability of the banks to attract deposits. Credit "crunches" were occurring in which loan demand was out stripping the amount of funds banks had available to lend. The banks were seemingly helpless in dealing with these crunches. They could not attract sufficient deposits to meet loan demand at Regulation Q rates. This gave rise to a growing concern with "disintermediation" in which funds were being drawn from deposit institutions such as banks and savings and loan associations ("S & Ls") and invested in other investments such as securities. One source of competition for funds was the money market funds. In June of 1976, money market funds held less than $3 billion. By December of 1982, over

$230 billion was held in money market funds at broker-dealers. Those money market funds became substitutes for bank accounts and allowed consumers to earn market rates on their liquid funds.

The banks turned to NOW accounts, negotiable CDs, Eurodollars, Eurobonds and other sources for funds. They also looked elsewhere for profits. Foreign exchange operations grew, although not always without loss, as demonstrated by the failure of the Franklin National Bank and the Bankhaus Herstatt. The latter's failure nearly caused a breakdown in the American CHIPS (interbank) payment system. Competition was causing the banks to make questionable loans. In 1975, non-performing loans at Chase Manhattan Bank were over $1.8 billion. That amount increased by another $400 million in 1976. Earlier, in 1974, the Secretary of the Treasury, George Schultz, announced that controls established ten years before on credit extensions by banks outside of the United States were being abolished. Thereafter, international lending grew faster than domestic lending for many banks. This business included large Latin American investments that would cause enormous losses. Years later, the largest banks in the United States were setting aside billions of dollars as loss reserves for loans to Latin America.

Deposits were becoming a smaller factor in banking. As banking expanded, and regulatory limits on interest payments squeezed out deposits, "borrowed money, rather than demand deposits were used to provide the fuel for bank growth." Restrictions on the ability of banks to expand their business base and Regulation Q restrictions on their ability to compete for funds was crippling the banking sector. American banks had dominated world finance beginning as early as World War I. By the middle of the 1970s, however, only four of the top twenty banks in the world were American. That number was reduced to three in 1979.

Over forty banks failed each year in the United States during the middle of the 1980s. The number of "problem" depository institutions on the FDIC watch list rose substantially. In 1984, the FDIC had a list of over 500 problem banks. That number soon increased to 800. By 1986, over 1,000 institutions were on the FDIC watch list.

The thrifts were another group in the banking sector that were being hurt by artificial regulatory restraints on their business and disintermediation. Congress lifted the interest rate ceilings on the amount of interest these institutions could pay for deposits as interest rates rose. When the interest rate ceilings were raised, the thrifts were, nonetheless, left with a problem. The loans on their books were still paying interest rates lower than what they had to pay for deposits at market rates. In 1981, after enactment of the Depository Institutions Deregulation and Monetary Control Act of 1980, the thrifts were paying an average of eleven percent for their funds, while their mortgage portfolios were yielding only ten percent. The thrifts lost a total of $8.9 billion in 1981 and 1982. Eighty-one thrifts failed in 1981 and over 250 failed in the following year. By

1984, over thirty percent of all FSLIC insured institutions were operating at a loss.

Congress and the states tried to assist the thrifts by lifting restrictions on their investments. This laid the groundwork for arguably the worst financial disaster in history. The S & Ls in particular went on a binge in investing in shopping centers, malls, buildings and other projects, particularly in the southwest, after investment restrictions were eased. The "go-go" thrifts of this era invested in a number of speculative enterprises that included oil and gas operations and such things as windmill farms. S & Ls became a favorite dumping ground for junk bonds, many of which were purchased from Drexel Burnham Lambert and Michael Milken. The S & Ls owned about seven percent of outstanding junk bonds at one point. Those holdings were concentrated into a few large S & Ls. Total thrift liabilities grew from $674 billion to $1.1 trillion dollars.

When real estate values collapsed at the end of the 1980s, all of the problems that had been building in the S & Ls were exposed and hundreds of S & Ls failed. A majority of the distressed thrift associations were in California and Texas. In 1987, the S & L industry lost some $7 billion. In 1988, over 700 banks and over 1,000 S & Ls were being closed down. Costs to taxpayers from the failed S & Ls were predicted to range from $500 billion to $1 trillion. One congressional subcommittee called the S & L crisis "the greatest financial fiasco the United States has ever seen." Regulators estimated that forty percent of the thrift failures were due to fraud or insider abuse. By 1992, some 1,000 individuals had been charged with crimes in connection with S & L activities.

The Financial Institutions Reform, Recovery and Enforcement Act of 1989 ("FIRREA") set aside federal funds to protect the customers of S & Ls that had failed. This legislation reorganized the regulation and insurance system for S & Ls. FSLIC was replaced by the Savings Association Insurance Fund, and the FDIC was put in charge of administrating that fund. The legislation appropriated an initial allocation of $50 billion to close down insolvent thrifts and pay off depositors. The legislation also abolished the Federal Home Loan Bank Board and replaced it with the newly formed Office of Thrift Supervision, which was a bureau of the Treasury Department until it was abolished in 2010.

The Resolution Trust Corporation ("RTC") was established in 1989 to take over failed S & Ls, pay off their depositors and then sell their assets. The RTC quickly became one of the largest managers of financial and real estate properties in the United States. The final cost to American taxpayers for the S & L crisis proved to be much less than originally estimated, but still totaled at least $90 billion. This entire debacle was strong evidence that the regulatory structure in the United States was not constructed on the basis of scientific principles. A prime culprit appeared to be the artificial regulatory restrictions on S & Ls that led them to try to play catch-up through speculative investments. The fact that they were dealing with insured funds relieved the depositors of any responsibility for monitoring the S & Ls investments. It was free money, and the unscrupulous were quick to take advantage.

In the early 1990s, the only states that allowed interstate branches were Alaska, Nevada, New York, North Carolina, Oregon and Rhode Island. By the middle of the 1990s, every state was permitting multi-office banking. Yet, "no commercial banking organization was even close to establishing a truly nationwide franchise." That situation would quickly change. Interstate banking on a regional basis had begun in the 1980s, and the Riegle–Neal Interstate Banking and Branching Efficiency Act of 1994 finally opened the door widely to interstate banking. That legislation allowed bank holding companies to acquire banks in any state, and after July 1, 1997, merge multiple banks together, retaining the interstate as branches of the main bank.

Banks also began to introduce ATMs (automated teller machines) as a way of expanding their reach. When the Comptroller of the Currency ruled that those machines were not branches, ATMs spread across America. By 1996, there were some 120,000 ATMs in the United States that were dispensing $9 billion in cash a year. Grocery stores even became a favorite location for banking centers.

The 1980s witnessed a change from "relationship" banking to "transactional" banking. Previously, banks had depended on established relationships with customers as the basis for their lending business. The banks were constantly trying to expand their relationships by acquiring new customers. That approach was being abandoned. Instead, banks began selling by product line to customers with whom they did not always have a relationship. Banks had several products to offer, including cash management services and computerized programs that allowed corporations to readily access their cash positions and bank accounts, as well as to transfer balances and funds.

The securitization of assets transformed banks from deposit takers and loan makers into conduits for loans as underwriters and distributors. Mezzanine finance became an important market for banks. This is debt located between senior debt and common equity in corporate capital structures. Banks were engaging in loan participations in which loans were originated and sold off to a group of banks to spread the risk. Syndicated lending reached a value of $1 trillion in 1997. Banks continued to account for a significant portion of the underwriting of state and municipal bonds. Home equity lines became popular in the 1980s. Driven by floating exchange rates, foreign exchange trading in the inter-bank currency market was totaling about $60 billion a day in New York in 1986. That figure would increase to over $100 billion in 1989. Worldwide, average daily foreign exchange trading at that time was $1 trillion. The banks appeared to be less and less like banks and more and more like financial services firms.

The banks increased their role in providing financial services. This included "selling stocks and bonds, providing advice on mergers and acquisitions, concocting new fangled financial products and trading." Banks were offering instruments that had elements of securities and commodity futures and options. One such product was indexed certificates of deposit. These included the bulls/bears CDs that were issued by Chase Manhattan Bank. The return on this certificate was based on fluctuations in the Standard & Poor's 500 stock market index. The College Savings Bank of Princeton, New Jersey offered tuition-linked certificates of deposit. The depositor's return from these CDs was based on an increase in an index of tuition, room and board for 500 colleges and universities. Franklin Savings and Loan Association in Kansas began offering certificates of deposit that provided a rate of return of three percentage points above the rate of inflation. Banks were becoming more involved in commodity futures markets activities.

The banks were intruding into the securities business. The securities industry was able to slow this process by court challenges. Nevertheless, the reintegration of the banks back into the securities business was inexorable, especially since it appeared that their very survival was dependent on it. The bank regulators recognized this fact and continued to open the door wider for the banks to expand their securities activities.

The banks then began to exploit the provisions of section 20 of the Glass–Steagall Act, which prohibited bank securities affiliates from being "principally engaged" in the investment banking aspects of non-exempt securities transactions. The District of Columbia Circuit Court of Appeals held that the Fed could properly allow bank affiliates to engage in up to five percent of ineligible securities activities without running afoul of the Glass–Steagall prohibition that bank affiliates not be "principally engaged" in such activity.

The Comptroller of the Currency authorized the Security Pacific National Bank to create a subsidiary called Discount Brokerage Service in August of 1982. Thereafter, more than 200 banks created joint ventures with discount brokers. The Fed also concluded that discount brokerage services were closely related to bank activities and, therefore, permissible under the Bank Holding Company Act. In 1983, the Fed approved the acquisition by BankAmerica Corporation of Charles Schwab, the nation's largest discount broker. That action was upheld by the Supreme Court.

A new form of bank was emerging in the early 1990s. These were super-regional banks. They included Banc One Corporation, First Chicago/NBD Corporation, Fleet Financial, Norwest Corporation, CoreStates, First Union, Wachovia Corporation, Wells Fargo and NationsBank. These enterprises became even more aggressive in seeking to expand their business base because they could no longer depend on the deposit business as their prime basis for generating revenues. This was underscored by the fact that, by 1993, commercial bank deposits were exceeded in amount by the funds held by mutual funds. The banks responded to that threat by creating their own mutual funds, and continued their efforts of aggressively pursuing other securities related business. In 1993, a third of all mutual funds were being sold through banks.

As the century aged, the banks continued to drop their traditional lending business and increase their role in financial services such as selling insurance and securities, engaging in repos, providing advice on mergers and creating and selling derivative instruments such as swaps. By the middle of the 1990s, many of the larger banks were receiving from one-third to over fifty percent of their revenues from non-interest income. By 1994, banks were involved in selling United States Treasury securities, lease and other asset backed securities, municipal securities, corporate bonds, corporate equities, financial and precious metal futures, as well as bullion. They were acting in private placements as agents, were sponsoring closed end investment funds and were offering deposit accounts with returns that were tied to stock market performance. Other bank activities included Eurodollar dealings, mergers and acquisitions, trust investments, automatic investment services, dividend investment services, custodial services, financial advising, discount brokerage activities, securities swaps and research services.

The Fed announced in December of 1996 that it was increasing from ten to twenty-five percent the amount of total revenues that a non-bank subsidiary of a bank holding company could derive from underwriting and dealing in securities. This allowed banks to expand their securities activities in their Section 20 affiliates under the Glass–Steagall Act. It was thought that these changes would allow "one stop financial shopping at banks and bank holding companies." This change enabled Bankers Trust to acquire Alexander Brown in 1997 through a share swap transaction valued at $1.7 billion. U.S. Bancorp announced the acquisition of Piper Jaffrey Co. in December of 1997. Piper Jaffrey was then the eleventh largest securities firm in the United States.

These changes were dramatically altering the business of banking. The erosion of the barriers between investment banking and commercial banking led one paper to conclude that J.P. Morgan was looking increasingly more like an investment bank. The new role being played by banks was illustrated by a two page advertisement in the Wall Street Journal in February of 1998 that announced NationsBank's results for the prior year. In that year, the bank handled initial public offerings worth $4.5 billion; high-yield ("junk bond") transactions worth $16.7 billion; mergers and acquisitions worth $14.5 billion; "follow-ons" worth $11.8 billion; syndicated floating rate debt of $442 billion; convertible securities underwritten in the amount of $3.7 billion; private placements worth $940 million; real estate finance valued at $30.2 billion; high-grade securities underwritings of $30.6 billion; asset-backed securities underwritings at $22.5 billion and project finance of $5.7 billion.

In April of 1998, Citicorp announced a planned merger with Travelers Group, Inc. which owned Salomon Brothers and Smith Barney, two traditional investment banking firms. The value of this merger was set at $83 billion. Before its merger with Travelers Group, Citicorp had relationships with one in five households in the United States. The combined entity had more than 100 million customers world wide, and it offered a wide range of products that varied from corporate finance to consumer banking and securities. The Citigroup amalgamation was matched by the merger of BankAmerica and NationsBank.

Agreement was finally reached in October of 1999 on the passage of legislation to repeal the Glass–Steagall Act. The legislation, the Gramm–Leach–Bliley Act, authorized the creation of financial holding companies that could engage in a broad array of financial services including commercial and investment banking, securities and insurance. Restrictions were eased on the grand-fathered non-bank banks, and operating subsidiaries of national banks were given similarly expanded powers. Unfortunately, the legislation continued efforts by Congress to control the delivery of financial services. Even the new financial holding companies were restricted in their ability to engage in non-financial services. The statute also imposed restrictions on commercial firms that were seeking to enter the banking business by buying or chartering thrifts, by eliminating the unitary thrift holding company loophole that permitted companies owning only a single thrift to engage in any other business without limitation under the Savings and Loan Holding Company Act. This was directed at stopping Wal–Mart from buying or chartering a thrift or from operating Wal–Mart brand banking operations in its stores.

Banking continued to evolve. Cash was becoming an anachronism. Coin and paper money accounted for only eight percent of the worldwide supply of American dollars as the century closed. Checks were still popular, but electronic money was replacing such traditional currency in many transactions. The amount of funds being transferred electronically by wire transfers each day was estimated to be in the trillions of dollars. By 1993, electronic transfers totaled $400 trillion in the United States. Credit cards were another form of electronic payment that was increasing in popularity. The credit card was becoming a substantial substitute for cash in retail transactions. In October of 1998, Americans owned an average of three credit cards and used them for about twenty-five percent of their spending. Visa and MasterCard were responsible for seventy-five percent of all credit card purchases in the United States. Their cards were accepted by more than 3.4 million stores. Almost 600 million Visa cards were outstanding by 1997, and they were being accepted at more than fourteen million locations. Those cards were used to purchase over $1 trillion dollars in goods and services. The credit card lending activities of United States banks were their most profitable business.

Debit cards were gaining popularity in the United States. These cards acted essentially as electronic checks in that the funds were withdrawn from the customer's account upon use of the card. By the year 2005 debit card payments accounted for forty-eight percent of total credit card transactions, as compared to twenty-one percent in 1997. Experiments with "stored value cards" were being carried out as a substitute for money. These "smart" cards were a variation of the traveler's check. They operated through a micro chip embedded in the card. Smart cards could be recharged at cash machines or payment could be made from an account or in cash to load the card up for use for purchases. Super smart cards were being developed that allowed holders to check their bank balance, make securities transactions and perform other functions. Smart cards sought to act as substitutes for money and were sometimes referred to as "e-purses." More than seventy million smart cards were distributed in 1996. At that time, their use was doubling annually. By the end of 1998, however, it seemed that the banks were going to have to reconsider smart cards because consumers were not expressing a great deal of enthusiasm for this payment medium.

An effort was underway to develop an electronic check that could be written through the Internet on a computer screen using a digital signature. A Cybercash system allowed a consumer to transfer funds through the Internet when purchasing goods. DigiCash was developed in 1997 as a means to provide electronic cash for making payments to an Internet merchant. Another system called NetCash transmitted cash through the Internet using an encryption scheme. PayPal also allowed secure payment to be made through the internet.

Banks had begun examining the concept of home banking as early as 1970. Initially, this was carried out through touch tone telephones and proprietary software that allowed customers to access account balances and transfer funds. Web-based banking allowed greater access. Customers could transfer funds, obtain checking account balances, pay bills, write checks, and transfer funds between accounts and obtain current interest rates. Internet banks were being established. These "virtual" banks operated only online. They allowed their customers to open accounts and to perform most of their banking activities through the Internet.

The Subprime Crisis[3]

The new century began with the bursting of a stock market bubble in Internet and Telecom stocks after a period of sharp interest rate increases by the Federal Reserve Board that threw the economy into a near recession. That crash was followed by a series of financial accounting scandals at the Enron Corp., WorldCom Inc. and others. Congress responded to those scandals with the Sarbanes–Oxley Act Corporate Reform Act of 2002 that imposed costly corporate governance and accounting reforms on public companies. In order to right the economy, the Fed drastically cut interest rates starting in 2001. The fed funds rate was 6.50 percent in 2000 but had been reduced to one percent by June 2003. This triggered a residential real estate bubble.

---

3. For a more complete description of the subprime crisis see Jerry W. Markham, *A Financial History of the United States*: The Subprime Crisis (2006–2009) (2011).

As housing prices soared, the practice of "flipping" houses and condos for a quick profit became a popular American pastime. The real estate bubble was fueled by liberal credit extensions at quite low "teaser" interest rates to "subprime" borrowers. These subprime borrowers had credit problems that disqualified them from obtaining a conventional mortgage.

Fueling this subprime lending boom were mortgage brokers promoting "no-doc" or "low doc" loans that did not require the normal documentation of the borrower's creditworthiness. Credit quality was of no concern to the mortgage brokers and lenders making those loans because the loans were immediately resold by securitizing them in a pool, which was then sold to investors as a collateralized debt obligation (CDO). The CDOs often had complex payment streams, and they were frequently insured against default by "monoline" insurance companies with little capital, or hedged by a new financial instrument in the form of credit default swaps. Those protections allowed the "super senior" tranches in subprime securitizations to obtain a triple-A credit ratings from the leading rating agencies, making them highly marketable in the U.S. and Europe. However, there was a major hidden flaw in the ratings process. The rating agencies used risk models for awarding the triple-A rating that did not take into account the possibility of a major downturn in the real estate market.

Subprime mortgages were sometimes pooled to fund off-balance sheet commercial paper borrowings called "structured investment vehicles" (SIVs) or "asset-backed commercial paper" (ABCP), as they were sometimes called. Banks, such as Citigroup, used short-term commercial paper borrowings to purchase mortgages held in their SIVs. Those commercial paper borrowings funded the mortgages and provided a profit through the spread between the higher rates paid by mortgages and the lower rates then existing in the commercial paper market. There was a flaw in these carry trade programs. In the event that commercial paper borrowers refused to roll over their loans, the SIV would have to liquidate their mortgages. That roll over might not be possible in a credit crunch or major market downturn. Another danger was that short-term rates could rise faster than long-term rates, erasing the spread, or even inverting the payment stream.

In order to crush the real estate bubble that was feeding on low rates, Fed Chairman Alan Greenspan began a series of seventeen consecutive interest rate increases beginning on June 30, 2004. Ben Bernanke, who replaced Alan Greenspan as the Chairman of the Federal Reserve Board on February 1, 2006, made still more interest rate increases. The effects of those actions were already manifesting themselves as Bernanke assumed office. The housing market experienced the largest decline in new home sales in nine years in the month after Bernanke became the Fed Chairman. This did not deter the Fed. The Fed announced its seventeenth consecutive increase on June 29, 2006, increasing short-term rates to 5.25 percent. The effect of this onslaught on the real estate market turned into a financial crisis in 2007. Home sales and new residential construction slowed dramatically, and the market became glutted with unsold homes.

Construction firms, such as Toll Brothers, cut back their building programs, and the housing construction industry experienced its worst slump in forty years. Speculators who had been gaining unprecedented profits by buying and quickly reselling properties, often after only a cosmetic touch up, found that they could no longer flip their properties for a quick profit, and they were left holding highly depreciated properties. "Short" sales, in which foreclosed homes were sold for less than their outstanding mortgage, became common as speculators defaulted, and as homeowners could no longer meet their payments due to the rising interest rates. Subprime homeowners, in many instances, simply walked away from their homes and mortgages when the value of their home dropped below the amount of the mortgage, a condition known as being "underwater."

The growing crisis in the real estate market caused the banks to tighten credit requirements and to cut back on credit, creating a credit crunch in the summer of 2007. Foreclosures continued to mount and subprime defaults skyrocketed. This caused a crisis in the financial markets when the banks were unable to rollover their commercial paper. As the crisis deepened, some SIVs tried to sell their mortgage collateral, but they could only do so at steep discounts. Concerned with losses from SIVs and CDOs, the banks cut back further on lending, worsening the credit crunch that was causing funding problems throughout the economy.

Subprime problems spread abroad. European investors had become deeply involved in the subprime market, and some financial institutions there faced massive losses. Customers began a run on Northern Rock PLC in England in September 2007, after they became concerned with its mortgage exposure. That was the first bank run in England in over 100 years. Depositors withdrew $2 billion before the run was stopped by a $28 billion cash infusion from the Bank of England. The English government later nationalized Northern Rock, as well as the Royal Bank of Scotland. The Bank of England and the European Central Bank also worked in tandem with the Federal Reserve Board to make unlimited funds available to their banks for borrowing in order to ease the credit crunch.

Citigroup and Merrill Lynch announced billions of dollars in losses from subprime loans as 2007 ended, causing the removal of their CEOs and the injection of billions of dollars obtained from sovereign wealth funds to shore up their capital. Other financial institutions also announced billions of dollars of losses from subprime loans, including Morgan Stanley. Congress enacted a $160 billion economic stimulus package. The action had little effect, and the Fed was forced to arrange a dramatic takeover of Bear Stearns, one of the nation's largest brokerage firms, by the JPMorgan Chase bank in March 2008. Bear Stearns was brought down by a liquidity crisis that arose after traders refused to roll over Bear Stearns' positions in the money market. Assets of clients were pulled from the firm in large amounts, and counterparties were refusing to trade with Bear Stearns because of concerns that it would fail, which it did. In order to close the deal, the Fed agreed to guarantee some $30 billion of Bear Stearns assets. The Fed also threw open its lending window to the investment banks, as well as to the commercial banks, and was accepting mortgage backed securities, the very instruments that led to the crisis, as good collateral.

Some other giants on Wall Street were forced to merge as a result of massive losses from subprime mortgage exposure. Merrill Lynch was taken over by Bank of America. Wachovia Bank was folded into Wells Fargo. JPMorgan Chase took over Washington Mutual, the largest savings and loan association in the country. Still, the situation worsened, becoming a full-scale panic, after another giant brokerage firm, Lehman Brothers, failed in September 2008. A money market fund then "broke-the-buck" and touched off an investor run on money market funds in which over $500 billion was withdrawn before the government stepped in to guarantee the funds. The American International Group Inc., a giant global insurance firm, had to be rescued by the federal government at a cost of over $180 billion.

An unprecedented $700 billion bailout package passed by Congress, called the Troubled Assets Relief Program ("TARP"), failed to halt the ensuing stock market panic. The Treasury Department used TARP funds to inject capital into the largest financial institutions, including $25 billion into Citigroup, but then paused. That pause further destabilized an already historically volatile market. Citicorp's stock dropped sixty percent in a single week, and its existence was threatened until the government stepped in to guarantee some $250 billion of its mortgage holdings and to inject another $20 billion in capital into the bank. General Motors and Chrysler were given funds for a bailout, and they were later partially nationalized.

The Federal Reserve Board introduced various new lending programs in order to restart the credit markets. The newly elected president, Barack Obama, also stepped into the crisis with an $838 billion stimulus package, but the subprime crisis bottomed out in March 2009 before that stimulus could have any effect. Congress and the still new administration began considering a near complete revamping of the existing financial regulatory structure. Consideration was also being given to regulating executive compensation and to limiting business risk-taking, two uncharted areas for government intervention. That reform emerged in the form of the 2,300 page Dodd–Frank Wall Street Reform and Consumer Protection Act of 2010 that affected nearly every area of finance.

Institutional Investors[4]

One of the most striking developments in financial markets during the latter half of this century has been the growing dominance of the

---

4. This discussion is excerpted from Jerry W. Markham, Protecting the Institutional Investor—Jungle Predator or Shorn Lamb, 12 Yale J. on Reg. 345 (1995).

institutional investor. The expanding role of large, institutional investors has been accompanied by demands for lessened regulation of these entities, because institutions are said to have the sophistication to protect themselves from fraud and overreaching. Regulators have been receptive to such demands. Consequently, many institutional traders have been freed of the regulatory shackles imposed in markets where the proverbial widows and orphans invest. The result amounts to a virtual two-track regulatory system: one set of rules governs trading by sophisticated institutions, and another more restrictive set of rules governs trading by unsophisticated "retail" customers.

The mix of participants in financial markets has changed dramatically in the latter half of the twentieth century. One of the "most profound developments" in the markets has been the shift in stock ownership from individuals to institutions. In the 1950s, individual investors held ninety percent of American equities. Now, just forty years later, institutions control more than half of all stock. This "institutionalization" of the financial markets has steadily increased over the decades. In 1958, institutions held twenty-six percent of outstanding stock. That figure grew to almost forty percent by 1970. Block sales by institutions accounted for about fifteen percent of trading volume on the New York Stock Exchange in 1970. By 1986, their share of trading volume had grown to fifty percent. In 1990, institutions held thirty-nine percent of all over-the-counter stocks and eighty-seven percent of privately placed securities.

Naturally, the drop in individual ownership was equally dramatic. Between 1980 and 1990, individual investors' share of all outstanding stock dropped by one fourth. Direct stock ownership by individuals dropped from approximately eighty-four percent of outstanding holdings in 1965 to about fifty-three percent in 1991. By 1989, individuals were net sellers of stock at the rate of about 3.5 million shares per day.

The shift in ownership patterns is reflected by the growth of financial colossuses. In 1994, pension funds held securities valued in excess of $2 trillion, insurance company holdings exceeded $1 trillion, and mutual fund securities holdings were valued at over $800 billion. Mutual funds' holdings increased even more dramatically in the early 1990s as interest rates dropped sharply. Their assets expanded to over $1.8 trillion by August of 1993. This helped push the Dow Jones Industrial Average to previously undreamed-of levels.

Surveys of the futures exchanges also indicate significant change in the nature of those markets. The futures markets were largely devoted to agricultural commodities before the 1980s. At that time, the so-called "financial" futures began to intrude into these markets. Financial futures now account for about eighty-three percent of the trading volume on the Chicago Board of Trade, up from some forty percent in 1983, and ninety-seven percent of the trading volume on the Chicago Mercantile Exchange.

Many factors have contributed to the growth of institutional investing in the securities and futures markets. The growth of private and governmental pension funds has played a significant role. Another contributing factor has been the demand for diversification and expertise in trading as the markets have grown more complex. Those factors led to the growth of mutual funds, as did the almost continual rise in stock prices since World War II. The increased complexity of the markets and the willingness of institutions to engage in more speculative activities have also led to the development of hedge funds that seek to take advantage of leveraged opportunities.

Other legal factors have also spurred the rise of the institutional investor. The "prudent man rule" for trustees has been modified to allow increased participation in equity markets. The Department of Labor's decision to ease the restrictions on pension fund investments under ERISA also allowed greater flexibility in investment decisions. These legal changes freed institutions from investing in only a limited list of investment devices, setting the stage for expansion in investment portfolios by the growing number of pension funds, insurance companies, mutual funds, and other institutions.

Theoretical developments also contributed: the advent of modern portfolio theory led investors to seek increasingly diversified investment portfolios. Under this theory, an investment portfolio is to be judged by its overall performance. This has led to the increasing use of "passive" institutional investment strategies that track market moves through diversified portfolios. Modern portfolio theory also induced experimentation in the world of leveraged investments, including futures and options. Futures markets have been particularly attractive because they offer broadly indexed contracts at relatively low transaction costs. Institutions soon found indexed instruments to be to their liking, and now dominate those markets. The increased participation of institutions in the futures and options markets has spurred the development of even more complex instruments to accommodate their needs and desires. The steadily growing over-the-counter derivatives market is largely an institutional market.

The growing dominance of the institutional investor, and of markets in derivatives tailored to its needs, soon led to demand for reduced regulation. The institutions wanted greater freedom in their investment decisions, and they wanted to be free of restrictive regulations that had been adopted to protect unsophisticated investors such as those who had been so badly damaged by the Stock Market Crash of 1929. The institutions particularly chafed at being shackled with the restrictive regulations of the Securities and Exchange Commission (SEC), nearly all of which had been adopted to protect the small investor. Clearly, it was argued, the institutions were too sophisticated to be regulated like the typical retail customer of a broker-dealer.

Regulators have responded favorably to requests for the removal of restrictive regulations on institutions. The SEC has been particularly supportive of the development of a two track regulatory system—one for institutional investors and one for unsophisticated investors. For example, it has allowed the development of the so-called private placement of securities to institutional investors and wealthy individuals, without requiring compliance with many of the cumbersome registration requirements imposed on public offerings. The SEC's Regulation D exempts issuers from many of the registration requirements of the federal securities laws when they place their securities with "accredited" investors. Accredited investors are defined to include banks, savings and loans, pension funds, and tax exempt organizations and trusts with assets in excess of $5 million. Accredited investors may also include natural persons whose net worth exceeds $1 million or who have had income in excess of $200,000 in each of the two preceding years. When accredited investors are the only participants in a securities issue, the amount of disclosure required is greatly reduced. In fact, there are no specific disclosures required. The private placement market has grown rapidly and is a popular investment medium for institutions. In 1993 alone, almost $220 billion in debt and equity was raised through private placements.

The SEC's efforts have resulted in the development of an institutional market in the securities industry in which the participants are viewed as having the resources and sophistication to protect themselves when assessing the risks of their investments. Many institutions have the bargaining power to demand instruments tailored to their particular needs and to receive customized investment opportunities. A public shareholder has no such power and often lacks the ability to assess the risks of the investment without the analysis and advice of a broker-dealer or investment adviser.

Institutions are accorded special treatment in the futures markets. Congress passed legislation in 2000 (the Commodity Futures Modernization Act of 2000) that exempted institutional traders from most regulation, except where they participate in a market that also includes retail traders. Institutions engaging in interbank currency and certain other financial transactions are also exempted from most regulation, other than general oversight by bank regulators.

Several assumptions underlie regulators' decisions to exempt institutions from regulatory requirements. One basic assumption is that regulation, in terms of its sheer cost in any particular transaction as well as its more general effects on market competition and efficiency, is expensive and therefore needs to be fully justified. The SEC requirements that mandate filings of a prospectus and detailed disclosures are expensive to comply with and result in delays in awaiting review by the SEC staff. These expenses and delays should be eliminated if the investor does not need the protection that the disclosure regime is intended to provide.

The SEC assumes that commercial institutions and wealthy and sophisticated investors can determine for themselves what information is needed before making an investment decision. Institutions probably have the bargaining power to demand the information they need from issuers or underwriters. The same is not true of small retail customers. These small investors arguably need the protection of the SEC's prospectus requirements, which seeks to guarantee small investors from fraud thorough disclosure.

Another perceived difference between institutions and retail customers is that institutions are already better protected by diversification. If a particular investment fails, the overall damage to the diversified investor should not be fatal. Most retail customers do not have sufficient assets to diversify their holdings in such a manner, except through their investments in such institutions as mutual funds. Of course, institutions do make mistakes. A series of losses by large corporations in derivatives in the early 1990s raised concern that even sophisticated institutions might need some regulatory protections. Only limited relief was given. The Enron Corp. scandals also resulted in claims that institutions were using unregulated markets to manipulate energy prices. Until the subprime crisis, there was a general reluctance to broadly regulate institutional transactions that do not involve retail customers.

Functional Regulation

Most countries around the world have adopted a single regulator model for financial services. The United States does not follow that approach. Instead, it uses a model called "functional" regulation.

JERRY W. MARKHAM
MERGING THE SEC AND CFTC—
A CLASH OF CULTURES

78 U. Cin. L. Rev. 537 (2009)

Functional Regulation

The United Sates operates under a "functional" regulatory system. Under this system, different regulators are appointed to regulate particular financial services, even if those services are offered by the same firm. This has resulted in much overlap and regulatory conflict, and created a system that failed to anticipate the subprime crisis that arose between 2007 and 2009. That the functional regulatory system failed should not be a surprise. It is a haphazard system of regulation that is not the result of a design or reasoned blueprint.[5] Rather, it is a set of accumulated responses

---

5. The Treasury study was the first effort to undertake a comprehensive review of financial services regulation in the United States since the 1984 report by the Task Group on Regulation of Financial Services that was headed by then Vice President George H.W. Bush. Its members included Donald T. Regan, Treasury Secretary and former Merrill Lynch CEO, the chairman of the Federal Reserve Board, representatives from the Attorney General's office, the Office of Management and Budget, and the heads of several agencies responsible for regulating financial services. The Bush task force concluded that financial services in the United States were the "central nervous system of the economy" and that this industry was suffering from too much regulation. The Bush task force recommended reducing federal bank regulators from three to two, creating a new Federal Banking Agency in the Treasury Department and reducing financial services regulators. U.S. TASK GROUP ON REGULATION OF FINANCIAL SERVICESSERVS. BLUEPRINT FOR REFORM: THE REPORT OF THE TASK GROUP ON REGULATION OF FINANCIAL SERVICES 8 (1984). Chicago: Commerce Clearing House, 1984. Those recommendations were not implemented. Instead, in 1999, Congress embraced "functional" regulation in the Gramm–Leach–Bliley Act in 1999 (Pub. L. No. 106–102, 113 Stat.1338), which repealed the provisions of the Glass–Steagall Act (Pub. L.

to a long history of financial crises, scandals, happenstance, personalities, and compromises among a broad and competing array of industry and governmental bodies.[6]

Under functional regulation, financial service firms are regulated by fifty state insurance commissioners acting collectively through the National Association of Insurance Commissioners (NAIC), fifty state securities commissioners (plus the District of Columbia) acting collectively through the North American Securities Administrators Association (NASAA), fifty state attorneys general who operate in wolf packs when attacking financial service firms, and fifty state bank regulators. Union pension funds support that cast by acting as "private attorneys general" in bringing class action lawsuits whenever a company announces bad news.

At the federal level, functional regulators include the Federal Reserve Board (Fed), the Office of the Comptroller of the Currency in the Treasury Department (OCC), the Federal Deposit Insurance Corporation (FDIC), the Office of Thrift Supervision (OTS), the Treasury Department's anti-money laundering group (FinCEN), and the Office of Foreign Asset Control (OFAC), which is also in the Treasury Department and handles financial embargoes imposed on troublesome countries. The Justice Department, together with the FBI and Postal Inspectors, has also become a financial services regulator by criminalizing bad corporate decision making. In addition, the SEC, CFTC, Federal Trade Commission (FTC), Occupational Safety & Health Agency (OSHA) (for SOX whistleblower claims), and self-regulatory bodies such as the Financial Industry Regulatory Authority (FINRA) and National Futures Association (NFA) regulate various aspects of the financial services industry.

Treasury Report

In 2006, Treasury Secretary Henry Paulson warned that the country was "creating a thicket of regulation that impedes competitiveness."[7] The Treasury Department sought public comment on regulatory efficiency issues in its study on the flaws in functional regulation. Of particular interest was the Department's request for comment on whether the "increasing convergence of products across the traditional 'functional' regulatory lines of banking, insurance, securities, and futures" justifies changes in the regulatory system to ensure that regulatory boundary lines

---

No. 73–66, ch. 89, 48 Stat. 162 (1933)). *See* LISSA L. BROOME & JERRY W. MARKHAM, REGULATION OF BANKING FINANCIAL SERVICE ACTIVITIES, CASES AND MATERIALS 239–240 (3d edition 2008) (discussing functional regulation).

Still another study, this one entitled *Financial Institutions and the Nation's Economy* (FINE), was undertaken by the House Committee on Banking Currency and Housing in 1975. FINE recommended that all depository institutions be regulated by a single regulator, a recommendation ahead of its time. *See generally Financial Institutions and the Nation's Economy (FINE) "Discussion Principles": Hearings Before the H. Subcomm. on Fin. Insts. Supervision, Regulation & Ins. of the Comm. on Banking, Currency & Hous.,* 94th Cong. (1975).

6. *In re Methyl Tertiary Butyl Ether ("MTBE") Products Prods. Liability Litigation*, 559 F. Supp. 2d 424, 436, n. 75 (S.D.N.Y. 2008) (quoting the author).

7. Deborah Solomon, *"Treasury's Paulson Warns of the Costs of Rules Overlap,"* WALL ST. J., Nov. 21, 2006, at A2.

do not unnecessarily inhibit competition.[8] The Department received more than 350 letters in response, indicating the financial community's interest.[9] The Treasury Department published its report in March 2008 (Treasury Blueprint).[10]

The study that led to the Treasury Blueprint was commenced at a time when inefficient regulation was thought to be impairing financial services. Even while the Treasury study was ongoing, however, a sea change was occurring as the subprime crisis arose and intensified. The *Wall Street Journal* declared in a front-page article on March 24, 2008, that a new era of increased regulation could be expected due to problems in the subprime market.[11] The Treasury Blueprint, which recommended a broad restructuring of the chaotic financial services regulatory structure, was published a few days after the *Wall Street Journal* article.[12] It sought more centralized and rational regulation because of concern that functional regulation was ineffective and was undermining America's traditional competitive advantage in financial services.[13] The Treasury Blueprint prophetically found that functional regulation:

> exhibit[ed] several inadequacies, the most significant being the fact that no single regulator possesses all of the information and authority necessary to monitor systemic risk, or the potential that events associated with financial institutions may trigger broad dislocation or a series of defaults that affect the financial system so significantly that the real economy is adversely affected.[14]

The Blueprint contrasted the functional regulatory approach in America with regulatory mechanisms abroad. England, Germany, Japan, and dozens of other countries use a single consolidated regulator, along with a central bank, to regulate; those countries eschew the "rules-based" approach used by most of the most regulators in the United States.[15] Rather, foreign regulators use a "principles-based" approach that sets broad

---

8. Request for Comments, Review by the Treasury Department of the Regulatory Structure Associated With Financial Institutions, 72 Fed. Reg. 58,939, 58,940 (October 17, 2007).

9. U.S. Treasury Assistant Secretary for Financial Institutions David G. Nason, U.S. Treasury Assistant Sec'y for Fin. Insts., Remarks Before the City of London Corporation: Redesigning U.S. Financial Regulation for a Global Marketplace (December Dec. 11, 2007), *available at* http://www.treas.gov/press/releases/hp726.htm.

10. *See* DEPARTMENT OF THE TREASURY, BLUEPRINT FOR A MODERNIZED FINANCIAL REGULATORY STRUCTURE (March 2008).

11. Elizabeth Williamson, *Political Pendulum Swings Toward Stricter Regulation—Safety Scares, Crisis In Housing Rupture A Long Consensus*, WALL ST. J. March. 24, 2008, at A1.

12. TREASURY BLUEPRINT, *supra* n. 10.

13. The Blueprint noted:

Due to its sheer dominance in the global capital markets, the U.S. financial services industry for decades has been able to manage the inefficiencies in its regulatory structure and still maintain its leadership position. Now, however, maturing foreign financial markets and their ability to provide alternate sources of capital and financial innovation in a more efficient and modern regulatory system are pressuring the U.S. financial services industry and its regulatory structure.

TREASURY BLUEPRINT, *supra* n. 10 at p. 2.

14. TREASURY BLUEPRINT, *supra* n. 10 at p. 4.

15. TREASURY BLUEPRINT, *supra* n. 10 at p. 141.

regulatory goals and permits the industry to decide how to meet those goals. A principles-based approach reduces the need for volumes of regulations that seek to control every aspect of financial services operations— which is the approach taken by the SEC. The SEC has an institutional culture that seeks to dictate every aspect of corporate behavior. In contrast, the CFTC administers a principles-based regulatory structure put in place by the Commodity Futures Modernization Act of 2000.[16]

* * *

Twin Peaks

In seeking to abandon functional regulation, the Treasury Blueprint did not advocate a single regulator system for the United States. The Blueprint rejected a single regulator model for many reasons:

> While the consolidated regulator approach can deliver a number of benefits, several potential problems also arise. First, housing all regulatory functions related to financial and consumer regulation in one entity may lead to varying degrees of focus on these key functions. Limited synergies in terms of regulation associated with financial and consumer protection may lead the regulator to focus more on one over the other. There may also be difficulties in allocating resources to these functions. Second, a consolidated regulatory approach to financial oversight might also lead to less market discipline as the same regulator would regulate all financial institutions, whether or not they have explicit government guarantees. This would seem to be particularly important in the United States where a number of financial institutions have access to explicit government guarantees of varying degrees. Third, since regulatory reform must consider the role of the central bank, the consolidated regulatory approach must maintain some degree of close coordination with the central bank if the central bank is going to be ultimately responsible for some aspect of market stability. The United Kingdom's recent experience with Northern Rock highlights the importance of this function in the consolidated regulator approach. Finally, the scale of operations necessary to establish a single consolidated regulator in the United States could make the model more difficult to implement in comparison to other jurisdictions.[17]

Instead of a single regulator, the Blueprint recommended that the United States adopt the "twin peaks" approach used in Australia and the Netherlands.[18] This concept is attributed to Michael Taylor, a former official at the Bank of England who wrote a 1995 article entitled *'Twin Peaks': A Regulatory Structure for the New Century*.[19] The Twin Peaks approach is objectives-based and focuses on specific regulatory goals.

---

16. Commodity Futures Modernization Act of 2000, Pub. L. No. 106–554, 114 Stat. 2763.

17. TREASURY BLUEPRINT, *supra* n. 10 at p. 141.

18. TREASURY BLUEPRINT, *supra* n. 10 at p. 139.

19. Jill Treanor, *Regulators Back Taylor's Twin Peaks Theory*, INDEPENDENT (London), Oct. 29, 1996, http://www.independent.co.uk/news/business/regulators-back-taylors-twinpeaks-theory-1360780.html.

Twin Peaks envisions a central bank that focuses on prudential supervision, and a single business practices regulator that focuses on business conduct and consumer protection. From this the Treasury Blueprint created a "Three Peaks" approach that would have three separate bodies implementing three specific regulatory goals: (1) market stability regulation, (2) prudential financial regulation, and (3) business conduct regulation. This objectives-based approach would require consolidating and reshuffling the existing functional regulators in the United States into essentially three principal regulators. The market stability regulator would be the Federal Reserve Board. A new agency would be created for prudential financial regulation that would regulate financial institutions with a government guarantee, such as banks insured by the FDIC and broker-dealers insured by the Securities Investor Protection Corporation (SIPC). A new agency would also have to be created for the business conduct regulator, which would create and apply principles-based regulation.[20]

The Treasury Department Blueprint was a non-starter because of the then ongoing subprime crisis. Elizabeth Williamson, Political Pendulum Swings Toward Stricter Regulation—Safety Scares, Crisis In Housing Rupture A Long Consensus, Wall St. J. March 24, 2008, at A1. The Obama administration replaced the Blueprint with its own regulatory reform proposals that sought more, not less, regulation. Department of the Treasury, Financial Regulatory Reform, A New Foundation: Rebuilding Financial Supervision and Regulation (2009). That proposal resulted in enactment of the Dodd–Frank Wall Street Reform and Consumer Protection Act of 2010. That legislation only furthered functional regulation by creating still more regulatory layers, including a new Financial Stability Oversight Council, a Bureau of Consumer Financial Protection Bureau, a Federal Insurance Office, and an Office of Financial Research, while eliminating only one agency, the Office of Thrift Administration.

SECTION 6. FINANCE AND ECONOMICS

Finance is closely rated to, but distinguishable from, economics. Corporate finance is concerned with *how* corporations use financial tools to fund their business. Economics is a study of *why* corporations behave as they do in their financial operations. This course will not address law and economics. That is itself a separate course as the following excerpt suggests.

WILLIAM T. ALLEN
CONTRACTS AND COMMUNITIES IN
CORPORATION LAW

50 Washington & Lee Law Review 1395 (1993)

Until rather recently the liberal-utilitarian explanation and prescription for the social order of our economy did not focus upon what happened

---

20. TREASURY BLUEPRINT, *supra* n. 10 at p. 144.

(or what should happen) within corporations. The "market" focus of the perspective implied that the internal operation of corporate actors was no more interesting than the internal operation of human actors. In a long ignored but now famous 1937 article, Ronald Coase for the first time offered a theory that looked inside the firm. Coase asked why some transactions are accomplished within firms while others are accomplished in markets. This question and Coase's efficiency-based answer to it were finally taken up by economists in the 1970s, most notably by Armen Alchian and Harold Demsetz, Oliver Williamson, Michael Jensen and William Meckling and others. This work re-energized the field of institutional economics. This scholarship employed two related perspectives—transaction cost economics and agency cost economics—to generate both a conceptual account of why firms exist and why they are structured as they are, and a prescriptive account of how they should function. When applied by legal scholars to the institutional detail of corporation law, the agency cost perspective supplied for the first time a unified theory of corporation law. This work was carried on by a number of brilliant legal scholars. Perhaps most prominent in that effort have been Judge Frank Easterbrook and Professor Daniel Fischel, the authors of The Economic Structure of Corporate Law.

The work of the law and economics scholars has come, I believe, to dominate the academic study of corporate law, even if some of the field's most respected minds remain among the unconverted. This work has left academic corporate law far more coherent than it had been and constitutes a substantial intellectual accomplishment.

The dominant legal academic view does not describe the corporation as a social institution. Rather, the corporation is seen as the market writ small, a web of ongoing contracts (explicit or implicit) between various real persons. The notion that corporations are "persons" is seen as a weak and unimportant fiction. The corporation is regarded as a minor utilitarian invention designed to reduce the costs necessary to plan, coordinate and accomplish the complex contracts that large-scale ongoing projects would require.

Since the corporate contract governs an ongoing venture, there is much that cannot be specified before the relationship among the real persons involved commences. Thus, a corporation can be seen as a form of relational contract, in which rather large contractual gaps will necessarily exist. The essence of the corporate form may therefore be seen, on this view, as the identification of structures or processes by which (1) persons will be designated to make certain sorts of discretionary judgments, and (2) those so designated will be monitored. Thus, in the dominant view, a corporation may be said most fundamentally to be a contractual governance structure.

Corporate law is seen as a way to provide a standard set of instructions for the operation of such a governance structure. In the corporate charter much of this standard set can be replaced by terms better suited to the perceived needs of the parties involved, if that is efficient and desired, but the cheaper, "off-the-rack" terms set forth in the corporate statute will often serve well enough. United States corporate law is thus chiefly enabling in character, not regulatory.

The transaction costs that corporation law can reduce include costs of negotiation and documentation of the corporate form, but in the dominant academic vision, most importantly they include other so-called agency costs. Agency costs are all the costs incurred by a principal by reason of the utilization of an agent to manage the principal's property. In the nexus of contracts model, the principals are the residual risk bearers—shareholders—and the agents are directors and management. Agency costs include market rate salaries and other irreducible costs, but more importantly they include various forms of sub-optimizing behavior by agents. Certain implicit costs, for example, will arise from a disjunction between the kinds and amounts of investments made by agents and their principals and the returns available to each. In addition, shirking, empire-building or venal diversion of corporate property or prospects all constitute agency costs of the corporate form.

It is, of course, a simplification to speak of a single economics-inspired theory of corporations. There is diversity and richness among the economists, too, running from those most closely associated with a neo-classical position (such as Michael Jensen, Easterbrook and Fischel) to those whose micro-analytic techniques and assumptions move them some distance from the liberal-utilitarian core (such as Williamson). These models, however, all share a view of persons as "undersocialized," self-interested maximizers.

Such is the dominance of the nexus of contracts model of the corporation in the legal academy that this symposium on new directions in corporate law can be understood only in opposition to this paradigm. One of the marks of a truly dominant intellectual paradigm is the difficulty people have in even imagining any alternative view. This is often the case in the legal academy with respect to the nexus of contracts model of the corporation. For many corporation law scholars this view is indisputably correct; its statement is seen as one of fact. Corporations, we are told, do not really exist; when we refer to one—General Motors or RJR Nabisco, for example—we are just using a rhetorical shortcut to refer to the vast network of contracts or implicit contracts that is the "reality."

There is, of course, force in this position. But, as my simplistic analysis suggests, another view of corporations is possible. In opposition to the philosophical nominalism of economics stands the philosophical realism of sociology. To the philosophical realist, to call a corporation a network of contracts is to overlook an essential part of the empirical reality of social interactions within corporations. It implies that the circumstances that any participant in the enterprise may confront at any moment are fully accounted for by reference to one or more earlier negotiated (or implicit) bargains he or she made. This, to realists, is a palpably impoverished way to interpret much of what goes on within corporations. Contract, for example, can provide only a thin and weak account of the experience of long-term stockholders of a large public corporation that has recently started paying grossly excessive compensation to its senior management; or whose management wants to deploy a newly created "poison pill" to foreclose a hostile tender offer. Or consider an instance in which employees work especially diligently in order that a team, department or division can reach a production goal. It very plausibly could be the case that contract would provide only a very partial and inadequate explanation of their behavior.

On the realist view corporations can be, indeed inevitably are, more than contracts. Actual bargains, explicit or implicit, provide an incomplete account of the social order we find in organizations. That social order can exist only because contracts are embedded in a social context that permits trust and expectations of fair dealing.

More than a network of contracts, corporations are seen by realists as collective entities that have identities apart from those of any of the individuals who temporarily fill roles within them. The history of such an institution, the "culture" and values it comes to embody and the institutional goals it formally and informally moves toward affect in every sense (legal, social or economic) the relationships among those who participate in the corporate enterprise. Such an institution to succeed over time must employ learning (about markets, about technology, about organization and about improving human skills). It must create and sustain an evolving capacity to learn to recall, to plan and to coordinate action. Achievement of corporate goals may depend importantly on the trust and loyalty of the human actors involved in circumstances in which monitoring and incentives are difficult and costly to establish and implement.

The provision of pre-defined roles and rules in the ongoing organization and the social-psychological processes of identification that successful organizations promote are seen by some as vital components of economic organizations that simply are not visible to the "network of contracts" vision of the firm. When Judge Easterbrook and Professor Fischel, for example, state that "[e]verything to do with the relation between the firm and the suppliers of labor ... is contractual," they underline the word "[e]verything." Those who tend towards the social model of human behavior see this sort of description of corporations as brittle, partial and flawed.

Some of those who hold a social or realist perspective tend normatively to be concerned with a corrosive effect that interpreting social life as a continuous, self-interested negotiation may have. Thus they do not accept the assertion that corporate management owes a duty to exercise discretion so as to maximize financial returns to stockholders. Rather, they look

Alibaba

for ways in which workers can participate in firm governance and thus gain a greater sense of the meaning of community membership. Perhaps incidentally, it is sometimes urged that steps that will increase worker engagement and responsibility will also increase corporate productivity.

Seeing the business corporation as a social institution can supply justification for a variety of organizational forms that differ from the share value maximization model promoted by the dominant academic conception of the corporation. The social model, in one of its weaker forms, is highly consistent with the managerialist concept of the corporation that has, in fact, dominated the real world of business and politics since the great depression. That view sees senior management as empowered to give fair consideration to workers, communities, and suppliers as well as to suppliers of capital. The statutory law in more than half of the U.S. jurisdictions has arguably come to reflect the managerialist concept of the corporation.

Equally evidently the social model of philosophical realists is consistent with various forms of worker involvement in management, such as may accompany an Employee Stock Ownership Plan (ESOP), and with worker representation, such as is present in the German co-determination structure. At its most extreme, this conception may yield more "radical" forms of corporate organizations, such as the kibbutz or other worker communes.

Many corporation law issues do not, of course, penetrate the dense superstructure of the field to reach the level of philosophical disagreement. Think of the issues in an appraisal proceeding, for example. From the host of technical questions relating to whether a right to an appraisal has been duly exercised, to the financial issues of "fair price," one's view of the meaning of human social life simply doesn't enter into the matter. Or consider the corporation law issues involved in that most common of all legal opinions, that a corporation is validly organized and in good standing, or an opinion that an act has been duly authorized by effective board action. In resolving such questions, formality, not contestable assertions of social meaning, is critical. Similarly, the experienced legal practitioner expects questions concerning the validity of by-laws, the need for a class vote, the rights of preferred stock, the proper way to count the vote at an election, and a host of other technical corporation law questions to be decided as matters of form according to clear pre-existing rules.

It is when the directors' duty of loyalty is properly called into issue that the corporate law may tend to cast off its heavy reliance upon formality to look beneath the surface of things. It is the concept of loyalty, which necessarily is grounded in the moral order of some community, that most evidently introduces into corporation law the dichotomy that I have mentioned: between a positivistic, utilitarian, rules-bound worldview on one hand and a flexible, moralistic one on the other. Fiduciary duty claims are equitable in origin. They tend to be analyzed in a particularistic *ex post* style. Their evaluation entails a moral account or prescription for a dispute that is in its own terms independent of, and sometimes inconsistent with, the positivistic, *ex ante* style of the liberal-utilitarian approach.

Large parts of the fabric of our corporation law have been woven on the loom of equity. In his classic article, Corporate Powers as Powers in Trust, Professor Berle, for example, demonstrated the early origin of the doctrine of stockholder preemptive rights in the equitable powers of chancery. In *Speiser v. Baker* I had the occasion to trace back the equity cases from which evolved the statutory prohibition on a corporation voting its own stock. In fact, in every corporation law case in which the gist of the complaint is a breach of loyalty—in every case involving self-dealing by a controlling shareholder or involving any manipulation of the voting process, for example—compliance with the more or less clear technical rules of corporation law is not the determinative issue. A contestable judgment about fairness—the historic mission of chancery—is.

Thus, fiduciary duties, pre-eminently the duty of loyalty, introduce tension and ambiguity into corporation law. It is when questions of loyalty are at issue that the philosophical differences that I have mentioned begin to appear near the surface, visible to even judges and lawyers in practice. Most especially is this true, as the experience of the 1980s demonstrated, when the question of fiduciary duty arises in connection with a proposed sale of a company. One of the things that was so remarkable about that period in corporation law was the way in which deep philosophical conflict concerning the purpose of corporations and political questions concerning our commitment to the values of the liberal economy were forced to the surface. In that setting, the philosophical divergence between the liberal model and the social model did not appear ethereal or academic but vital.

The law and economics paradigm offers a highly coherent conception of corporation law as a system of rules facilitating wealth maximization through contracts, explicit or implicit. This is, to a substantial extent, an idealized version of the corporation law in action. Like much of neoclassical economics, the law and economics account of corporation law is at bottom not empirical description, but normative prescription. It means to tell us how people would act with respect to formation of legal rules concerning corporations if people acted rationally (as they sometimes, if imperfectly, do). It thus means to create an ideal corporation law to guide those who fill in "contractual gaps" to act rationally when they do so. I suppose that even those who prefer to think about life as a world of complete markets drifting in and out of equilibrium do not believe that in fact people always do act rationally. But that recognition does not, of course, mean that the law should not take rationality as a standard. It is the further step taken by the law and economics theorists, their attempts to forge an equivalence between rationality and profit maximization, that does give rise to warm disagreement.

The idealized law and economics version of corporation law makes a tremendous contribution to our understanding of the nature of the firm, but it is not complete. My own understanding, which is, I confess, incomplete as well, acknowledges the power and utility of much of the law and economics story, but recognizes as well the pressures on rule-creating agencies to view corporate directors as men and women with obligations of loyalty which will be evaluated *ex post* on a fairness standard. Courts have felt and responded to these pressures for over two hundred years. To whom director duties of loyalty are owed can and has sustained earnest debate in legislative chambers, in the press, and in the academy. Thus, either a descriptive account or a normative account of corporation law that I might advance would include a powerful element of wealth maximization, but it would inescapably include as well a political-moral component. Corporation law is a system of rules, principles and roles and a process by which they are defined, redefined in legally significant interactions, and enforced. In that process the law, or legal agents, mediate, pursuant to the processes of law, between the wealth maximizing value and the ex ante analytical style of the liberal model and the fairness value and the *ex post* analytical style of equity. I offer no theory to explain that mediation here.

The "efficient market" hypothesis propounded by the law and economics scholars has received much criticism, despite its adoption by the Supreme Court in *Basic Inc. v. Levinson*, 485 U.S. 224, 108 S.Ct. 978, 99 L.Ed.2d 194 (1988). Eugene Fama, the father of the efficient market hypothesis, was among those conceding its shortcomings. A new school of "behavioral economics" led by Richard Thaler also attacked the efficient market theory stating that: "conventional finance theorists assume that only 'rational' behavior affects equity prices, behavioral finance theorists argue that how people actually behave makes a difference to stock prices. Specifically, behavioral finance is based on the observation (based on cognitive psychology and decision theory) that in some circumstances humans make systematic errors in judgment and that these behavioral biases affect equity prices." Martin Lipton and Paul K. Rowe, Pills, Polls and Professors: A Reply to Professor Gilson, 27 Del. J. Corp. L. 1, 23 (1999).

As has also been noted:

During the last three decades, while law faculties across the nation were succumbing to the brilliant simplicity of the Coase theorem and the analytical force of the law and economics movement, social scientists in other departments were discovering evidence that should have given pause to even the most ardent legal economic positivist. Those scientists—cognitive psychologists, behavioral researchers, probability theorists, and others—were discovering powerful evidence that the rational actor model, upon which the law and economics project depends, is significantly flawed. In place of the rational actor model, those scientists were developing a human decisionmaker model replete with heuristics and biases, unwarranted self-confidence, a notable ineptitude for probability, and a host of other nonrational cognitive features.

Jon D. Hanson & Douglas A. Kysar, Taking Behavioralism Seriously: The Problem of Market Manipulation, 74 N.Y.U.L. Rev. 630, 640 (1999).

All of these theorists may be presuming too much. The market is neither perfect nor irrational. Rather, to paraphrase Winston Churchill, free market discipline may be the worst possible system, except for any other.

CHAPTER TWO

SOME BASIC ACCOUNTING ISSUES

■ ■ ■

Chapter objectives

- To understand the different financial reporting roles played by the balance sheet, the income statement, and the statement of cash flows.

- To appreciate the role of the accountant as a financial auditor and to understand the limits of an accountant's liability when issuing audit opinions.

- To see the relevance of accounting standards to the federal securities laws.

SECTION 1. ACCOUNTING STATEMENTS

This chapter focuses on some basic accounting standards that you should be familiar with in order to understand corporate finance. Do not be alarmed; we have no intention of transforming you into an accountant. Indeed, you may already be familiar with all or most of these concepts from your basic corporate law course.

The Balance Sheet

A useful tool for understanding the finances of a corporation is the balance sheet. An example of a balance sheet is set forth below. The balance sheet identifies the assets of the corporation and sets forth the source of funds for those assets. The balance sheet must balance. This means the amount of the assets on the left side of the balance sheet must equal the liabilities, equity investments and retained earnings (profits) on the right side of the balance sheet.

BALANCE SHEET

Assets		Liabilities	
Current Assets		**Current Liabilities**	
Cash	$250,000	Accounts payable	$100,000
Acct.s receivable	$500,000	Notes payable	$100,000
Inventory (FIFO)	$250,000	Income taxes payable	$20,000
Fixed Assets		**Long Term Liabilities**	
Land	$500,000	5yr notes payable	$780,000
Building	$300,000		
Equip.	$200,000	Total Liabilities	$1,000,000
Total	$2,000,000		
Less Depr.	-100,000		
	$1,900,000		
		Shareholder Equity	
		Preferred Stock	
		2500 @ $100 liquidating	$250,000
		value preference	
		Common Stock	
Intangibles	$100,000	250,000 common stock @ $1	
		par:	
		Stated Capital =	$250,000
		Capital Surplus =	$250,000
		Retained Earnings =	$250,000
		Total Shareholders' Equity	$1,000,000
TOTAL ASSETS =	$2,000,000	TOTAL EQUITY AND LIABILITIES =	$2,000,000

Assets on the balance sheet may be short or long-term. A short-term asset is cash or an asset that is readily convertible into cash. This could include such things as accounts receivable or tax refunds due to the corporation. A long-term asset is one that will not be converted into cash within a year. Long-term assets include such things as real property, buildings and equipment. The corporation's assets need to be valued before their inclusion on the balance sheet. Usually, the value of the asset will be its purchase price, but that valuation is not always easy to arrive at, particularly in the case of inventory. To illustrate: a shoe store's inventory of goods must be valued. Assume that the company has sold some shoes it ordered, but not all of them. A new shipment arrives subsequently, but the prices for the shoes are different. The corporation could possibly count the old shoes still on the shelf, value them individually and then use the new price for the new shoes. Over time, however, the shoes became intermingled. Some of the new shoes were sold, and some of the old ones remain. Rather than trying to sort them out, we can simply use one of several common inventory valuation techniques such as FIFO (first-in-first-out) or LIFO (last-in-first-out). Under FIFO, we simply assume that the first goods purchased were the first ones sold. Under LIFO, we assume that the last shoes purchased were the first ones sold on the theory that the new shoes were put on the front of the shelf and sold first before the older shoes on the back of the shelf. These assumptions may not be completely accurate, but they provide a convenient way to value inventory.

Valuing assets on the balance sheet raises additional issues. For example, assets could be carried on the balance sheet at their purchase price ("book value"), but that may not accurately reflect their current market value. In some instances, accounting principles will require "mark-to-market" accounting for assets, requiring them to be valued at their current market value. Even where assets are not required to be marked-to-the-market, however, their value needs to be adjusted to reflect the decline in their value as they wear out from use. To deal with that concern, these assets are depreciated each year on the balance sheet using any number of depreciation methods that range from the simple (*e.g.*, dividing the cost of the asset by the number of years of its expected life and deducting the resulting amount each year) to the complex (*e.g.*, accelerating depreciation in early years to reduce taxes or deferring depreciation to later years in order to increase earnings). Land is not depreciated.

Still another asset valuation concern is the collection of accounts receivable, which are carried as assets on the balance sheet. Say that the corporation sells some of its goods on credit, allowing purchasers 90 days to pay. Some purchasers will fail to pay and their accounts become uncollectable. The corporation needs to reserve an amount on its balance sheet to reflect its loss experience from such bad accounts. That reserve amount is deducted from its account receivable on the balance sheet to provide a more realistic valuation of the corporation's assets.

More complex valuation issues are raised by intangible assets, such as patents and goodwill. A patent has a limited life and its value is intangible, but may be valued in a reasonable manner on the balance sheet. This means that its value may be amortized over the expected life of the patent so that a huge write-off will not be required when it expires. Another intangible asset is goodwill. This asset will arise where a corporation purchases another business and pays more for that business than its tangible assets will justify. The excess of the price over the value of those tangible assets is treated as goodwill. Why would a corporation pay more for another business than the value of that business's assets? Assume that ABC, LLC is a shoe store. Its only significant asset is an inventory of shoes valued (by LIFO) at $90,000. The only other assets are a cash register, some computers, lamps and other equipment at the store it rents valued at $10,000. XYZ, Inc. has agreed to pay $1 million for ABC's business. Why would XYZ make such an offer? The answer is that ABC sells a lot of shoes, turning its inventory over rapidly and making nice profits. XYZ wants that revenue flow and its profits. The tangible assets acquired from ABC will be carried on XYZ's balance sheet at a value of $100,000. The remainder of the purchase price ($900,000) will be carried as goodwill on XYZ's balance sheet. Under current accounting rules, goodwill must be written off if the acquired business declines in value.

The right side of the balance sheet must also be analyzed. It is divided into liabilities and equity capital. The liabilities section sets forth the funds borrowed by the corporation. Liabilities are divided into long and short-term. Liabilities that must be repaid within a year are short-term, while those with a maturity of more than one year are long-term. Short-term liabilities include bank loans with maturities of less than one year. These could be a revolving credit line used by the corporation for working capital needs or simply a short-term loan such as commercial paper, which is simply a promissory note sold to institutional investors. Long-term debt includes bank loans of longer duration, secured loans that are collateralized by particular assets of the corporation and debentures (general obligation bonds) that are usually unsecured. Debt on the balance sheet may be senior or junior. Senior debt will have priority in bankruptcy over more junior debt. Remember that all debt must be paid in full before stockholders receive anything in bankruptcy.

Below the liabilities on the right side of the balance sheet is equity capital, which may include preferred stock. Where preferred stock has been issued, its liquidation value is listed. This is the preference for the preferred shareholder (over common stockholders) in the event of liquidation or insolvency. Model Business Corporation Act § 6.40(c) restricts a corporation from paying dividends to common shareholders where the dividend would impair the corporation's ability to pay liquidation preferences.

As you can see from the balance sheet, there may be two accounts on the right side of the balance sheet that describe the contribution to the corporation's assets by the common stockholders—a "stated" capital account and a capital "surplus" account. The stated capital account is used to reflect the "par" value of the common stock. This confusing concept is the result of history and not economics. In earlier years, par value was what the stock was sold for and was used to value the stock when sold. Common stock is no longer traded on the basis of par value, but the concept still lingers. Some states prohibit payment of dividends out of stated capital, and some states restrict dividends from capital surplus, which is the amount the corporation received for the stock in excess of its par value. Therefore, distinction must be made between the two. Corporations usually set a low par value for their stock to avoid such restrictions. To add further confusion, the Model Bus. Corp. Act does not require par value for common stock. This is because that statute ties dividend restrictions to solvency tests, rather than to capital accounts. Model Bus. Corp. Act § 6.40(c). Delaware also authorizes no-par stock (Del. § 151) but then provides for the corporation to designate an amount that acts as stated capital or provides a formula for such a computation in the absence of such a determination. Del. § 154. The latter requirement is tied to Delaware's limitations on dividends from a corporation's capital. Del. § 170. For a further description of dividend limitations see Chapter 6. For present purposes, you need only remember that stated capital and surplus, when added together, tell you what the corporation sold its stock for to the original purchaser.

Still another capital account is for retained earnings or earned surplus. This account simply reflects profits of the corporation that have not been paid out in dividends. The retained earnings account may be in deficit if the company has lost money in excess of any retained earnings. Retained earnings are the usual source for dividends.

Much of this book concerns the law of particular items on the balance sheet, both its liability and its asset side. Indeed, you can plot several of the chapters in this book on a balance sheet thus:

By the end of the course, you'll appreciate the laws which apply to the following items on the balance sheet.

OFF-BALANCE SHEET ASSETS	ASSETS	LIABILITIES	OFF-BALANCE SHEET LIABILITIES
Futures and Options (Chapter 11) Swaps (Chapter 12)	Money market assets (Chapter 3)	Money market liabilities (Chapter 3)	Futures and Options (Chapter 11) Swaps (Chapter 12)
	Receivables (Chapter 10)	Short-term notes or bills (Chapter 3)	
		Medium-term notes (Chapter 4)	
		Long-term bonds or debentures (Chapter 4)	
		Subordinated debt (Chapter 4)	
		Hybrid instruments (Chapter 10)	
		EQUITY ACCOUNTS	
		Preferred stock (Chapter 5)	
		Common stock Par value Revaluation surplus Capital surplus Retained earnings (Chapter 6)	
	Total Assets	Liabilities plus equity	

Off–Balance Sheet Arrangements

Accounting standards provide corporate managers with discretion to avoid public reporting of certain assets and liabilities by booking these items 'off-the-balance-sheet,' a practice that the Sarbanes–Oxley Act of 2002 curtailed somewhat by mandating public disclosure of certain off-balance-sheet arrangements.

JOSÉ GABILONDO
FINANCIAL MORAL PANIC! SARBANES–OXLEY, FINANCIER FOLK DEVILS, AND OFF–BALANCE–SHEET ARRANGEMENTS

36 Seton Hall L. Rev. 781, 812 (2006)

. . . The numbers on the balance sheet matter dearly. If they hint at illiquidity or capital shortfalls, the firm may have to pay more for credit, face the white-hot glare of regulators, or trigger adverse contractual rights of demanding counterparties. For example, some credit covenants let a creditor sue if the borrowing firm's (balance sheet) debt to equity ratio drops below a contractually-set point. To mitigate these business risks, the careful manager optimizes the presentation of information on the balance sheet. For example, firms may reclassify debt from short-term to long-term in order to improve their liquidity ratios. Shifting numerical values only in the assets column (left-hand side), only in the liabilities column (right-hand side), or only between the liability and the equity accounts (both on the right-hand side) does not change the overall size of the balance sheet. To modify the size of the visible balance sheet, managers must move off the balance sheet (OBS), using reporting discretion which is customary in accrual accounting. For example, the classification of operating leases is subject to significant discretion. The generalized practice of funding with OBS items leads finance practitioners to distinguish between a firm's "book leverage" and its "financial leverage." Some arrangements are hard to classify as on- or off-balance-sheet.

Managers may seek shelter from balance sheet disclosure both for fiduciary and opportunistic reasons. Conducting a transaction off the balance sheet gives managers more flexibility by reducing the discipline of oversight from creditors or owners who would be able to monitor publicly-reported financial details. Common fiduciary motivations include managing the firm's book leverage, credit rating, or risk profile for the sake of protecting the trading value of the firm's shares. For example, an OBS deal may boost the firm's book income without worsening the firm's book leverage. A firm may deduct the OBS debt interest from some special purpose entities on its federal taxes without having to report the underlying liability on its balance sheet Firms also use OBS partnerships to optimize the tax value of their research and development expenditures. Segregating a business project off-balance-sheet insulates the firm from the risk of loss from the investment. Stealth funding through OBS arrangements may avoid covenants limiting investment in new business opportunities in bank loan documents, bondholder indenture agreements, or a firm's certificate of incorporation. Such deals may, however, violate explicit contractual duties of good faith and fair dealing.

Apart from fiduciary brinksmanship for the sake of shareholders, managers may also use an OBS arrangement for their own opportunistic ends, which may be antithetical to the interests of their principals, i.e. shareholders. When executive compensation is pegged to balance sheet ratios such as return on assets, return on equity, and debt-to-equity, a manager would likely prefer, all else being equal, an OBS deal which increases his compensation by improving one of these ratios.

Undisclosed OBS arrangements bear on conflicts between a firm's competing claimants, including the stockholder-bondholder conflict over the firm's exposure to financial risk OBS cash flow may also increase existing agency costs for shareholders. Management accounting will carefully monitor these arrangements to the extent that they are material to the decisions faced by a firm's managers. Some firm outsiders such as institutional creditors may also bargain for this type of information. Financial databases, an important public source of firm-level information, however, usually lack much information about OBS items. . . .

The Income Statement

Another useful tool for corporate finance is the income statement (or profit and loss statement as it is sometimes called). This statement shows the company's revenues, expenses and income for a stated period of time.

Income Statement

Net Sales	$10,000
Costs of Goods Sold and Operating Expenses	$7,000
Depreciation	$1,000
Selling and Administrative Expenses	$1,000
Operating Income	$1,000
Less Interest on Long Term Notes	$100
Income Before Taxes	$900
Income Taxes	$200
Net Income	$700
Net Income Per Share (1000 shares) =	00.70

The income statement is useful for several reasons. This information allows planning by the corporation (*e.g.*, the officers of the corporation may perceive the need to cut certain expenses or add resources in an effort to increase revenues). Managers and stockholders are also provided a picture of whether, and to what extent, the corporation is profitable. In evaluating a corporation's performance, various financial ratios are helpful and may be used to compare its performance with other corporations. For example "ROE" (return on equity) may be computed by dividing the dollar amount of the corporation's earnings by the dollar amount of equity capital obtained from the balance sheet. "ROA" (return on assets) is determined by dividing income by the dollar figure for assets from the balance sheet. Another useful measure is a corporation's PE ratio. This is the market price of a share of stock divided by the corporation's earnings per share. A high ratio may suggest a belief that the company's prospects for future growth is high, while a lower ratio could suggest that a lot of growth is not expected. Of course, other market factors can also affect this ratio.

A statement of cash flows is similar to the income statement except that depreciation is added back to the income figure along with any other non-cash charges, including amortization. The statement will disclose cash received and paid out from operating activities, payments of interest and taxes. Cash received from investments by the corporation will be disclosed. Those investments may be the result of excess cash flows. The statement of cash flows will further disclose cash received from financing activities. This could include cash received from borrowings or stock sales. Dividend payments will also be disclosed.

Because of accrual accounting, which is discussed below, the income statement may show a sale even though cash has not been received or an expense incurred even though it has not been paid. The statement of cash flows, however, shows only actual cash received or paid out. It allows managers to manage cash flows and determine if there is excess cash that may be used for productive purposes and to determine in the event of a shortfall whether they should borrow additional funds or raise additional capital by selling ("issuing") stock.

Another useful computation for managers is "EBITDA" (earnings before interest, taxes, depreciation and amortization). *See* In re PWS Holding Corp., 228 F.3d 224, 233 (3d Cir.2000) (defining EBITDA). EBITDA tells you what the company is producing from its assets and operations.

JOSÉ GABILONDO
FINANCIAL MORAL PANIC! SARBANES–OXLEY, FINANCIER FOLK DEVILS, AND OFF–BALANCE–SHEET ARRANGEMENTS
36 Seton Hall L. Rev. 781, 812 (2006)

Statement of Cash Flows

"Comprehensively measuring cash flow is a key aspect of effective capital structure. A firm manages its day-to-day liquidity on the basis of financial cash flow. Though valuable, financial cash flow is hard to square with the balance sheet and the income statement, which use different accounting methods to present financial information. Examples like the cash flow games played by Enron illustrate the gap between tracking financial cash flow and reported cash flow. Instead of financial cash flow, the statement of cash flows reflects accounting cash flow, the best publicly available proxy for a firm's financial cash flow. . . . The statement of cash flows nets cash inflows and cash outflows for a time period between two balance sheets. The statement does not reflect accrual losses or gains. Rather, it reflects only accounting cash outflows and inflows. The statement lets a reader compare accrual-based earnings or balance sheet values with accounting cash flow, sourced on- or off-balance-sheet. Any single financial indicator has its limits and this is also true for measures that track cash flow. . .

"The statement of cash flows was the last major financial report to become widely used by firms. Ever reactive on accounting matters, the SEC began to mandate the disclosure of cash flow information by firms for the first time after an agency study recommended the mandatory disclosure of accounting cash flow. During this same period cash flow became a popular way of valuing the firm. In 1985, the Financial Accounting Standards Board (FASB) began to adopt cash flow valuation for selected situations, starting with the treatment of pensions. Only in 1987 did FASB require the disclosure of accounting cash flow in a firm's financial reports. Beginning in that year, firms had to report cash flow classified according to whether it was related to operating, investing, or financing activity. . .

"The statement of cash flows distinguishes between investment, operational, and financing cash flows. However, the statement currently blurs two streams of investment cash flow that would have more informational value if unbundled: (1) that from investment in assets related to a firm's core functions; and (2) that due to investments in other than operational assets. By separating operational investment cash flow from market investment cash flow the classification would let the reader distinguish between investment required by the firm's core activities and that from the firm's activities as a speculative investor in the market. Such a distinction would help an investor to appreciate whether cash flow is attributable to business decisions about operations or to speculative investment decisions."

Accounting Principles and Practices

Before World War I accounting doctrine was based on the precept of "anticipate no profits and provide for all possible losses." *Cf.* Space Controls, Inc. v. Commissioner, 322 F.2d 144, 148 (5th Cir.1963) (citing rule). This principle of conservatism required assets to be carried on the balance sheet at their historical cost rather than their market value. Transactions had to be accounted for on a cash basis. D Herwitz, Materials on Accounting for Lawyers 149–150 (1980). This historical cost or book value approach itself replaced the use of par value to value companies. Jonathan B. Baskin & Paul J. Miranti, Jr., A History of Corporate Finance 183 (1997). Modern accounting, however, shifted its focus to the income statement, which led to "accrual" accounting. Accrual accounting requires a corporation to recognize revenues when earned and liabilities when incurred. This means that income must be recorded when a sale is made (*i.e.*, when the goods are transferred or services rendered) even if cash is not received until later. *See generally In re Clinger & Co.*, Securities Exchange Act Release No. 393390 (S.E.C. 1997) ("The accrual method of accounting requires that revenue be recognized when the earnings process is complete and an exchange has taken place, as opposed to the 'cash' method of accounting, which allows for revenue recognition only when a cash payment is actually received."). As one commentator notes:

> Accounting is not precise or scientific. It is an art, and a highly developed one. To begin with, rather than keeping its books on a cash basis, which might seem ever so simple, GAAP (generally accepted accounting principles) requires industry to use accrual basis accounting. Income is thus recognized when it is earned rather than when cash is received. The essence of the accrual basis is the matching of expenses with revenues, so as to produce a truer picture of a company's profitability. The rub is that accrual-basis accounting affords a great deal of flexibility and judgment in the timing of income and expense recognition. Will American Airlines' new airplanes be serviceable for thirty years or should they be depreciated over just twenty? Should research and development expenses be charged to earnings as they are incurred, or should some portion be capitalized and charged only over time? And so on.

Louis Lowenstein, Financial Transparency and Corporate Governance: You Manage What You Measure, 96 Colum. L. Rev. 1335, 1345–1346 (1996).

　　To illustrate, a computer is sold and delivered to a customer on December 1, 2010 for $2,500. The transaction was on credit, and payment was not actually received until January 3, 2011. Under the accrual method, the sale occurred on December 1, 2010. The theory is that to record the sale on January 3, 2011 would distort the corporation's accounting picture, *i.e.*, shareholders would think that the sale was actually made in 2011 rather than 2010, thereby understating sales in 2010 and overstating in 2011. Under the cash method, the sale would nevertheless have been recorded in 2011. Liabilities are treated similarly under the accrual method. For example, taxes are treated as an expense for the period incurred even if they are not paid until later. In other words, expenses are matched to the period where the sales were made to which those expenses are attributed. This conforms to another accounting assumption, *i.e.*, accounting reports are for a specific time period (in the case of an income statement) or just a "snapshot" on a particular day (as in the case of a balance sheet).

NOTES

1. A basic practice for accountants is the use of so-called "T" accounts that provide for double entries to record accounting events. Assume that a corporation has received a cash payment of $1,000 from one of its accounts receivable. That transaction might be recorded in two T accounts as follows:

Smith Account Receivable		Cash	
Debit	Credit	Debit	Credit
$1,000			$1,000

The account receivable has been debited on the left side with $1,000 and the corporation's cash account has been credited on the right side with the same $1,000, hence the double entry. When a new account receivable owed by Smith is created, the Smith Account Receivable T account is credited with that amount and goods sold or similar T account will be debited. The T account entries are posted to journals and then transferred to a general ledger that records all accounts receivable and cash accounts. The ledgers are used to create trial balances that are posted to the balance sheet.

2. The following warning should be heeded:

"Watch Those Footnotes"

The annual reports of many companies contain this statement: 'The accompanying footnotes are an integral part of the financial statements.' The reason is that the financial reports themselves are kept concise and condensed. Therefore, any explanatory matter that cannot readily be abbreviated is set out in greater detail in footnotes. * * *

Most people do not like to read footnotes because they may be complicated and are almost always hard to read. That's too bad, because footnotes are very informative. Even if they don't reveal that the corporation has been forced into bankruptcy, footnotes can still reveal many fascinating sidelights on the financial story."

Merrill Lynch, How to Read a Financial Report 26 (1990).

3. Keep in mind that "legal" accounting requirements for dividends and other purposes under state corporation laws may vary from GAAP or accounting terminology. See Chapter 6.

Fair Value Accounting

In keeping with the principle of conservatism, some members of the accounting profession have argued that assets should be carried on corporate balance sheets at their historical cost rather than at their present market value. If valued at current market prices, the value of the assets on the balance sheet could fluctuate up or down and add volatility to the balance sheet and raise issues as to whether increases or decreases should affect the income statement. The concept of using market value instead of cost to value assets is variously referred to as "mark-to-market" or "fair value" accounting.

RIGERS GJYSHI[1]
A HISTORY OF MARK–TO–MARKET ACCOUNTING

The Rise of Mark-to-Market Accounting for Financial Instruments

Mark-to-market accounting was first used by futures traders on commodities exchanges in the late nineteenth and twentieth centuries. Fair market value accounting existed in the early twentieth century, when companies were free to choose which accounting method to use for asset valuation purposes. A common practice was the use of 'current values,' or appraised asset values, which in many cases resulted in large asset write-ups that did not accurately reflect their true economic worth.[2] In addition, prior to 1938, banking organizations were required to use mark-to-market accounting on their investment portfolios for regulatory purposes. However, as the U.S. economic recovery was still being battered by the lingering effect of the Great Depression in 1938,[3] the U.S. Treasury and banking regulators decided to abandon the mark-to-market accounting method to supervise banks.[4] The concern was that mark-to-market accounting caused bank loans and investments to be recorded at a much lower value, especially in times of economic contraction, which placed downward pressure on bank liquidity, even though these loans and investments were deemed ultimately sound.[5]

Concerns about the effects of this valuation method, and inherent skepticism about the fairness of mark-to-market accounting caused regulators to abandon it in favor of what was known as 'the doctrine of

---

1.　Research Fellow, Florida International University College of Law at Miami (2010).

2.　*See* Solomon Fabricant, *Revaluations of Fixed Assets, 1925–1934*, National Bureau of Economic Research Bulletin (December 1936).

3.　*See* Milton Friedman and Anna Schwartz, *A Monetary History of the United States* (Princeton University Press 1971).

4.　Report and Recommendations Pursuant to Section 133 of the Emergency Economic Stabilization Act of 2008: Study on Mark–To–Market Accounting 34,[hereinafter SEC Study], citing letter from Federal Reserve Chairman Alan Greenspan to SEC Chairman Richard Breeden (Nov. 1, 1990).

5.　Eds. Note: "What many people do not realize is that mark-to-market accounting existed in the Great Depression and, according to Milton Friedman, was an important reason behind many bank failures. In 1938, Franklin Delano Roosevelt called on a commission to study the problem and the rule was finally suspended." Brian S. Wesbury & Robert Stein, *Mr. President, Suspend Mark–To–Market*, Forbes.com, Jan. 21, 2009, http://www.forbes.com/2009/01/20/accounting-treasury-obama-oped-cx_bw_rs_0121wesburystein.html (last visited Nov. 12, 2009). The Reconstruction Finance Corp. (RFC) also dropped fair value accounting requirements, during the Great Depression. The RFC "deemphasized the liquidity and marketability of bank assets, and evaluated high-grade securities at their potential, not market, value. The RFC gave book or cost value to the highest grade bonds, market value for bonds in default, face value for slow but sound assets, and a reasonable valuation for doubtful assets like real estate." JAMES S. OLSON, SAVING CAPITALISM: THE RECONSTRUCTION FINANCE CORPORATION AND THE NEW DEAL, 1933–1940 79–80 (1988).

ultimate collectability'.[6] Some have even argued that the ultimate decision to suspend mark-to-market accounting was made more out of a desire to ease banking credit than it was out of a concern about sound accounting principles.[7]

After the Great Depression, as often happens after a severe crisis, there was a general movement towards more conservative accounting methods. This movement was spearheaded by Robert E. Healy, who led a six year long congressionally mandated investigation by the FTC on the accounting practices that contributed to the severity of the Great Depression.[8] In his investigation, Healy was shocked by the loose accounting practices and asset write-ups that companies had engaged in before the market crash. In 1934, Healy became one of the five founding members of the SEC, which Congress created with the Securities Exchange Act of 1934, to supervise and regulate the stock market. His investigation on asset write-ups had caused him to be a strong supporter of historical cost accounting and to detest asset writ-ups.

Healy used his position at the SEC to push for the wide spread adoption of historical cost accounting and began an active and remarkably effective campaign for the eradication of other accounting methods, like current value accounting. By the 1940s, Healy and other like-minded commissioners had succeeded in making historical cost the de facto accounting practice for disclosure and reporting purposes. This practice virtually eliminated asset write-ups and influenced a generation of SEC accountants to be staunch supporters of historical cost accounting for nearly half a century.

The SEC's unconditional acceptance of historical cost accounting minimized the use of other accounting practices as valuation methods in income statements and balance sheets.[9] Consequently, mark-to-market accounting was largely silent until it reappeared during the economic decline of the early 1970s. The rigidity of historical cost accounting in asset valuation caused many accounting industry leaders to continuously lobby the SEC to allow for other valuation methods, like price-level depreciation or even value accounting. These calls for accounting reform, although of limited initial success, began to gain momentum.

In December of 1975, the FASB issued FAS 12, which required companies to record their marketable equity securities at lower-of-cost-or-fair-value, in an attempt to create some uniformity in accounting methods used to report these instruments.[10] FAS 12's definition of equity security

---

6. Donald J. Kirk, Commentary: Competitive Disadvantage and Mark–To–Market Accounting, 5 Acct. Horizons, June 98, at 102.

7. *See* Donald G. Simonson & George H. Hempel, *Banking Lessons from the Past: The 1938 Regulatory Agreement Interpreted,* 7 J. Fin. Servs. Res. 249 (1993).

8. Stephen Zeff, *The SEC Rules Historical Cost Accounting: 1934 to the 1970s,* 37 Accounting and Business Research (International Accounting Policy Forum Issue) (2007).

9. Homer Kripke, *The SEC, the Accountants, Some Myths and Some Realities,* 45 N.Y.U. L. Rev. 1151, 1189. (1970)

10. FASB Statement No. 12, *Accounting for Certain Marketable Securities* (December 1975).

encompassed any ownership instrument like common, preferred, and other capital stock, or the right to acquire ownership shares, like warrants, rights, and call options, or the right to dispose of ownership shares, like put options. Moreover, a marketable security was defined to include any equity security as to which a bid and ask price was available on a national securities exchange or over-the-counter market.

In the late 1970s, the SEC further departed from its allegiance to historical cost accounting when it began requiring oil and gas companies to provide current value information in their financial statements. This change was the result of the Energy Policy and Conservation Act of 1975, which directed the SEC to eliminate the diverse accounting practice used by oil and gas companies. In 1977, the FASB issued FAS 19 where it mandated 'successful efforts costing' in an effort to streamline the accounting practice in the oil and gas business.[11]

The fair value accounting movement gained full momentum during the savings and loan crisis in the 1980s, when there was a general agreement that historical cost accounting was one of the main reasons for failed capital measurements that led to the crisis.[12] Policymakers argued that institutions should be required to provide a better picture of their capital through a system of current value accounting.[13] In 1986, as a response to the savings and loan crisis, the FASB began a thorough review accounting standards. The result was two-phase project that intended to move away from the use of historical cost accounting and toward the use of fair value. In March of 1990, the FASB announced the first phase of the project when it issued FAS 105 and FAS 107. FAS 105 indicated new reporting requirements regarding financial instruments and other off-balance-sheet risks.[14]

In 1993, the FASB continued its move towards fair value when it issued FAS 115, which sets forth the accounting and financial reporting requirements for investments in equity securities with determinable fair market value and for all investments in debt securities.[15] In 1998, the FASB renewed its move towards a fair value system when it issued FAS 133, which imposed fair value reporting requirements for derivatives for fiscal years beginning after June 15, 1999.[16] FAS 133 required that the

---

11. FASB Statement No. 19, *Financial Accounting and Reporting by Oil and Gas Producing Companies* (December 1977).

12. *See* James R. Bath, *The Great Savings and Loan Debacle* 64 (The AEI Press 1991); Franklin Allen and Elena Carletti, *Mark-to-Market Accounting and Liquidity Pricing*, 45 Journal of Accounting and Economics 385 (2008).

13. *See* Richard T. Pratt, *Annual Report 1982*, Federal Home Loan Bank Board Journal 15, at 5, (April 1983).

14. *See* FASB Statement No. 105, *Disclosure of Information about Financial Instruments with Off–Balance–Sheet risk and Finical Instruments with Concentrations of Credit Risk* (March 1990).

15. FASB Statement No. 115, *Accounting for Certain Investments in Debt and Equity Securities* (May 1993).

16. FASB Statement No. 133, *Accounting for Derivative Instruments and Hedging Activities* (July 1998). The effective date was later deferred until June 15, 2000, by FASB Statement No. 137, *Accounting for derivative instruments and Hedging Activities—Deferral of the Effective Date of FASB Statement Number 133* (June 199).

balance sheet record some derivatives at their fair value. The financial statement must recognize the changes in the fair value of derivatives when they occur. In addition, FAS 133 discusses three types of hedges, fair value hedge, cash flow hedge and foreign currency hedge, and it provides specifications on their accounting requirements, with fair value hedges generally being recorded at fair value.

In 2002, in response to the Enron collapse and the accounting scandal associated with it, Congress passed the Sarbanes–Oxley Act, which among other things amended Section 13 of the Securities Exchange Act of 1934 to require real time disclosures of material changes in the financial condition of the issuer.[17] This portion of the Sarbanes–Oxley Act was designed to restore public confidence in the stock market by attempting to make the issuers more transparent, thus allowing the market to appropriately value the risks associated with each issuer.[18] Even though there are some critics who have argued that the mark-to-market method was partially responsible to the fraud perpetrated by Enron.[19]

The New Sheriff in Town: Mark–To–Market Defined

One of the main problems of fair value accounting has always been the inherent subjectivity in determining the fair value of an asset and the lack of definite measuring guidelines. Past attempts to define fair value have resulted in inconsistent measurement. In 2000, the FASB tried to resolve these inconsistencies when it attempted to define fair value in Concept Statement 7, which focused on price that an asset or liability could be bought or sold for, in a current transaction between willing parties.[20] Though a good start, Concept Statement 7 had limited success because it lacked the clear guidelines that complex financial institutions require in valuing their assets.

In 2006, the FASB tried to refine the fair value definition when it issued FAS 157. FAS 157 defines fair value as the price that would be received to sell an asset or paid to transfer a liability in an orderly transaction between market participants at the measurement date.[21] Inherent in this fair value definition is a focus on the asset or liability, the price, principal market and market participant.

---

17. Sarbanes–Oxley Act of 2002, PL 107–204 (2002).

18. Evan N. Turgeon, Note, *Boom and Bust for Whom? The Economic Philosophy Behind the 2008 Financial Crisis*, 4 Va. L. & Bus. Rev. 139 (2009).

19. *See* Stewart Hamilton and Alicia Micklethwait, *Greed and Corporate Failure, The Lessons from Recent Disasters* 39, (Palgave 2006), discussing the SEC's decision to allow Enron in 1991, to mark-to-market the value volumetric production payments contracts. This was the first instance that a company was allowed to adopt this method outside the financial sector, and allowed Enron to take upfront almost all of the anticipated profits on such contracts, but it had to recognize the losses if their value was diminished. Enron took advantage of the limited price horizons that trading markets provided and extended its price projections far beyond what the market curves could predict, which allowed it to set its own values. Moreover, Enron used the SEC permission to mark-to-market other types of long-term contracts, like broadband deals.

20. FASB Concepts Statement No. 7, *Using Cash–Flow Information and Present Value in Accounting Measurements* (February 2000).

21. FASB Statement No. 157, *Fair Value Measurement*, paragraph 5, (September 2006).

FAS 157, unlike previous fair value frameworks, focuses on exit price based on an assumption of orderly and active markets. FAS 157 consolidates previous attempts to define fair value and provides the clearest definition and application guidelines for fair value accounting to date. FAS 157, however, does not mandate the use of fair value accounting for financial instruments, it merely dictates the method of valuation when fair value is used. FAS 157 became effective for the fiscal years beginning after November 15, 2007, for financial assets. As to non-financial assets, the effective date was deferred one year in order for the Board to have more time to analyze the effect of implementation problems that may arise from FAS 157.[22]

One of the main criticisms is that the FAS 157 framework is premised on quotes obtained from an orderly market and when the markets are disorderly and erratic, an accurate estimation of fair market value is down right impossible. These criticisms were fueled by the economic crisis of 2008, which resulted in temporarily illiquid and disorderly markets, forcing financial companies to take enormous write-downs on their investments in order to comply with fair value requirements, regardless of the underlying economic strength of those investments.

In September 2008, in order to address these criticisms, the SEC staff and the FASB staff issued a joint press release clarifying FAS 157 fair value measurements in the case of illiquid/inactive markets, specifically encouraging the consideration of intra company unobservable inputs, so called level 3 inputs, and make necessary adjustments to make up for the lack of market data. In addition, in October of 2008, the FASB further clarified the September press release by issuing FASB Staff Position No. 157–3, which explained how to conduct fair value calculations during inactive markets, and specifically permitting the use of Level 3 inputs to value what were believed to be severely undervalued financial instruments.[23]

In that same month, Congress passed the Emergency Economic Stabilization Act, which, among other things, authorized the SEC to suspend the application of the mark-to-market rules under FASB 157 to any issuer if it deemed it in the public interest.[24] The EESA further directed the SEC to conduct a study on the role of mark-to-market accounting in the then current financial crisis, and ordered it to make recommendations as to its future in financial reporting.[25] Pursuant to the EESA mandate, the SEC issued its report on the effect of mark-to-market in December of 2008. In the report, the SEC recommended that although fair value standards should be improved, they are an adequate accounting method and should not be suspended. One of the main recommendations

---

22. FASB Staff Position No. 157–2, *Effective Date of FASB Statement NO. 157* (February 2008).

23. FASB Staff Position 157–3, *Determining the Fair Value of a Financial Asset When the Market for That Asset Is Not Active* (October 2008), superseded by FSP 157–4.

24. Emergency Economic Stabilization Act of 2008 (EESA), 12 U.S.C.A § 5237 (2008).

25. EESA section 133, 12 U.S.C.A. § 5238 (2008).

of the report was the need to develop accounting practices that would allow fair value estimation during times of illiquid or inactive markets. At the heart of the SEC recommendation was the notion that the FAS 157 fair value definition assumed a sale in an orderly and active market, and not in distressed or forced sales, like the ones in the latest economic crisis. The report seemed to suggest that, because FAS 157 guidelines were not meant for such disorderly markets, other valuation methods should be developed to reach a fair value estimation.

On April 9, 2009, the FASB responded to the report by issuing Staff Position No. 157–4, which superseded Staff Position No. 157–3 and gave companies that were using fair value accounting even greater leeway in reporting their depressed securities, especially market-less mortgage-backed securities.[26] Staff Position No. 157–4 provided an eight-factor list to determine whether "there has been a significant decrease in the volume and level of activity for the asset or liability."[27] If the reporting entity concludes that there is such a decrease, it may find it necessary to make significant adjustments to the depressed market price through the valuation techniques described in FAS 157.

Although Staff Position No. 157–4 tried to continue the spirit of 157, i.e. using objective, market-driven criteria to estimate the true value of an asset, there was a widespread perception that the FASB move was more a response to political pressures instead of genuine accounting reform.[28]

As noted in the preceding essay, mark-to-market accounting has caused some problems. The Enron Corp. used mark-to-market accounting to inflate its assets and revenues, causing the company to declare bankruptcy when its accounting abuses were discovered. Among other things, FAS 133 allowed Enron to report large increases in income, but without any corresponding increase in cash. They were paper profits only that were based on doubtful valuation increases. *See* Jerry W. Markham, *A Financial History of Modern U.S. Corporate Scandals: From Enron to Reform*, 58–59 (2005).

Fair value accounting was also a center of controversy during the subprime crisis that occurred between 2007 and 2009. As Peter Wallison, an American Enterprise Institute Fellow, noted in the midst of the subprime crisis:

> As losses mounted in subprime mortgage portfolios in mid–2007, lenders demanded more collateral. If the companies holding the assets did not have additional collateral to supply, they were compelled to

---

26. FASB Staff Position 157–4, *Determining Fair Value When the Volume and Level of Activity for the Asset or Liability Have Significantly Decreased and Identifying Transactions That Are Not Orderly* (April 9, 2009).

27. *Id.* at paragraph 12.

28. Floyd Norris, *Banks Get New Leeway in Valuing their Assets*, N.Y. Times, April 3, 2009, at B1.

sell the assets. These sales depressed the market for mortgage-backed securities (MBS) and also raised questions about the quality of the ratings these securities had previously received. Doubts about the quality of ratings for MBS raised questions about the quality of ratings for other asset-backed securities (ABS). Because of the complexity of many of the instruments out in the market, it also became difficult to determine where the real losses on MBS and ABS actually resided. As a result, trading in MBS and ABS came virtually to a halt and has remained at a standstill for almost a year. Meanwhile, continued withdrawal of financing sources has compelled the holders of ABS to sell them at distressed or liquidation prices, even though the underlying cash flows of these portfolios have not necessarily been seriously diminished. As more and more distress or liquidation sales occurred, asset prices declined further, and these declines created more lender demands for additional collateral, resulting in more distress or liquidation sales and more declines in asset values as measured on a mark-to-market basis. A downward spiral developed and is still operating.[29]

"The difficulty in putting a value on loans, securities, and exotic financial instruments banks were carrying on their books became one of the most debilitating features of the Great Panic" in 2008.[30] Critics of fair value accounting charged that, because liquidity in subprime investments had dried up as the subprime crisis blossomed, the only prices available for "fair value" accounting were fire sale prices from desperate sellers. Those prices in no way reflected the actual value of the more senior mortgage-backed securities being written down as measured by their cash flows and default rates. One accountant complained to the FASB that: "May the souls of those who developed FAS 157 burn in the seventh circle of Dante's Hell."[31] Warren Buffett likened mark-to-market requirements for measuring bank regulatory capital to throwing "gasoline on the fire in terms of financial institutions."[32]

The markets began their recovery after some relief was given from the requirement for fair value accounting.

---

29. Peter J. Wallison, *Fair Value Accounting: A Critique*, FIN. SERVS. OUTLOOK (Am. Enterprise Inst. for Pub. Pol'y, Washington D.C.), July 2008, at 2.

30. DAVID WESSEL, IN FED WE TRUST, 128 (2009).

31. *Accounting Principles*, 40 SEC. REG. & L. REP. (BNA) 1767 (2008).

32. Holman W. Jenkins, Jr., *Buffett's Unmentionable Bank Solution*, WALL ST. J., Mar. 11, 2009, at A13. As one author noted:

> The argument against fair value is a compelling one: volatile markets make securities valuation difficult and undermine investors' confidence, forcing companies to mark down values, leading to greater illiquidity and further markdowns. The more the markdowns impair capital, the greater the loss of investor confidence, and the faster the churn of the self-reinforcing cycle.

Todd Davenport. *Fair Value: Few Fans, But Fewer Alternatives; Despite Widespread Frustration, Changes Don't Seem Likely*, 173 AM. BANKER 1 (Mar. 24, 2008).

SECTION 2. ACCOUNTANT'S LIABILITY UNDER STATE LAWS

BILY v. ARTHUR YOUNG & CO.

3 Cal.4th 370, 11 Cal.Rptr.2d 51, 834 P.2d 745 (1992).

Lucas, Chief Justice.

We granted review to consider whether and to what extent an accountant's duty of care in the preparation of an independent audit of a client's financial statements extends to persons other than the client.

Since Chief Judge Cardozo's seminal opinion in *Ultramares Corp. v. Touche* (1931) 255 N.Y. 170, 174 N.E. 441 (*Ultramares*), the issue before us has been frequently considered and debated by courts and commentators. Different schools of thought have emerged. At the center of the controversy are difficult questions concerning the role of the accounting profession in performing audits, the conceivably limitless scope of an accountant's liability to non-clients who may come to read and rely on audit reports, and the effect of tort liability rules on the availability, cost, and reliability of those reports.

Following a summary of the facts and proceedings in this case, we will analyze these questions by discussing the purpose and effect of audits and audit reports, the approaches taken by courts and commentators, and the basic principles of tort liability announced in our prior cases. We conclude that an auditor owes no general duty of care regarding the conduct of an audit to persons other than the client. An auditor may, however, be held liable for negligent misrepresentations in an audit report to those persons who act in reliance upon those misrepresentations in a transaction which the auditor intended to influence, in accordance with the rule of section 552 of the Restatement Second of Torts, as adopted and discussed below. Finally, an auditor may also be held liable to reasonably foreseeable third persons for intentional fraud in the preparation and dissemination of an audit report.

This litigation emanates from the meteoric rise and equally rapid demise of Osborne Computer Corporation (hereafter the company). Founded in 1980 by entrepreneur Adam Osborne, the company manufactured the first portable personal computer for the mass market. Shipments began in 1981. By fall 1982, sales of the company's sole product, the Osborne I computer, had reached $10 million per month, making the company one of the fastest growing enterprises in the history of American business.

In late 1982, the company began planning for an early 1983 initial public offering of its stock, engaging three investment-banking firms as underwriters. At the suggestion of the underwriters, the offering was postponed for several months, in part because of uncertainties caused by the company's employment of a new chief executive officer and its plans to introduce a new computer to replace the Osborne I. In order to obtain "bridge" financing needed to meet the company's capital requirements until the offering, the company issued warrants to investors in exchange for direct loans or letters of credit to secure bank loans to the company (the warrant transaction). The warrants entitled their holders to purchase blocks of the company's stock at favorable prices that were expected to yield a sizable profit if and when the public offering took place.

Plaintiffs in this case were investors in the company. They include individuals as well as pension and venture capital investment funds. Several plaintiffs purchased warrants from the company as part of the warrant transaction. Others purchased the common stock of the company during early 1983. For example, one plaintiff, Robert Bily, who was also a director of the company, purchased 37,500 shares of stock from company founder Adam Osborne for $1.5 million.

The company retained defendant Arthur Young & Company (hereafter Arthur Young), one of the then-"Big Eight" public accounting firms, to perform audits and issue audit reports on its 1981 and 1982 financial statements. (Arthur Young has since merged with Ernst & Whinney to become Ernst & Young, now one of the "Big Six" accounting firms.).[33] (In its role as auditor, Arthur Young's responsibility was to review the annual financial statements prepared by the company's in-house accounting department, examine the books and records of the company, and issue an audit opinion on the financial statements.)

Arthur Young issued unqualified or "clean" audit opinions on the company's 1981 and 1982 financial statements. Each opinion appeared on Arthur Young's letterhead, was addressed to the company, and stated in essence: (1) Arthur Young had performed an examination of the accompanying financial statements in accordance with the accounting profession's "Generally Accepted Auditing Standards" (GAAS); (2) the statements had been prepared in accordance with "Generally Accepted Accounting Principles" (GAAP); and (3) the statements "present[ed] fairly" the company's financial position. The 1981 financial statement showed a net operating loss of approximately $1 million on sales of $6 million. The 1982 financial statements included a "Consolidated Statement of Operations" which revealed a modest net operating profit of $69,000 on sales of more than $68 million.

Arthur Young's audit opinion on the 1982 financial statements was issued on February 11, 1983. The Arthur Young partner in charge of the audit personally delivered 100 sets of the professionally printed opinion to the company. With one exception, plaintiffs testified that their investments were made in reliance on Arthur Young's unqualified audit opinion on the company's 1982 financial statements.

As the warrant transaction closed on April 8, 1983, the company's financial performance began to falter. Sales declined sharply because of manufacturing problems with the company's new "Executive" model computer. When the Executive appeared on the market, sales of the

---

33. [Authors' note: The number of "big" accounting firms was down to four in 2003—the "Final Four."]

Osborne I naturally decreased, but were not being replaced because Executive units could not be produced fast enough. In June 1983, the IBM personal computer and IBM-compatible software became major factors in the small computer market, further damaging the company's sales. The public offering never materialized. The company filed for bankruptcy on September 13, 1983. Plaintiffs ultimately lost their investments.

Plaintiffs brought separate lawsuits against Arthur Young in the Santa Clara County Superior Court. Plaintiffs J.F. Shea & Co., et al. (the "Shea plaintiffs"), brought one lawsuit; plaintiff Robert Bily brought another. The two actions were consolidated for trial. The focus of plaintiffs' claims was Arthur Young's audit and audit opinion of the company's 1982 financial statements.

Plaintiffs' principal expert witness, William J. Baedecker, reviewed the 1982 audit and offered a critique identifying more than 40 deficiencies in Arthur Young's performance amounting, in Baedecker's view, to gross professional negligence. In his opinion, Arthur Young did not perform its examination in accordance with GAAS. He found the liabilities on the company's financial statements to have been understated by approximately $3 million. As a result, the company's supposed $69,000 operating profit was, in his view, a loss of more than $3 million. He also determined that Arthur Young had discovered material weaknesses in the company's accounting controls, but failed to report its discovery to management.

Although most of Baedecker's criticisms involved matters of oversight or nonfeasance, e.g., failures to detect weaknesses in the company's accounting procedures and systems, he also charged that Arthur Young had actually discovered deviations from GAAP, but failed to disclose them as qualifications or corrections to its audit report. For example, by January 1983, a senior auditor with Arthur Young identified $1.3 million in unrecorded liabilities including failures to account for customer rebates, returns of products, etc. Although the auditor recommended that a letter be sent to the company's board of directors disclosing material weaknesses in the company's internal accounting controls, his superiors at Arthur Young did not adopt the recommendation; no weaknesses were disclosed. Arthur Young rendered its unqualified opinion on the 1982 statements a month later. * * *

The jury exonerated Arthur Young with respect to the allegations of intentional fraud and negligent misrepresentation, but returned a verdict in plaintiffs' favor based on professional negligence. No comparative negligence on plaintiffs' part was found. The jury awarded compensatory damages of approximately $4.3 million, representing approximately 75 percent of each investment made by plaintiffs. The Court of Appeal affirmed the resulting judgment in plaintiffs' favor with respect to all matters relevant to the issue now before us.

Although certified public accountants (CPA's) perform a variety of services for their clients, their primary function, which is the one that most frequently generates lawsuits against them by third persons, is financial auditing. (Hagen, *Certified Public Accountant's Liability for Malpractice: Effect of Compliance with GAAP and GAAS* (1987) 13 J.Contemp. Law 65, 66 [hereafter Hagen]; Siliciano, *Negligent Accounting and the Limits of Instrumental Tort Reform* (1988) 86 Mich.L.Rev.1929, 1931 [hereafter Siliciano].) "An audit is a verification of the financial statements of an entity through an examination of the underlying accounting records and supporting evidence." (Hagen, *supra*, 13 J.Contemp. Law at p. 66.) "In an audit engagement, an accountant reviews financial statements prepared by a client and issues an opinion stating whether such statements fairly represent the financial status of the audited entity." (Siliciano, *supra*, 86 Mich.L.Rev. at p. 1931.)

In a typical audit, a CPA firm may verify the existence of tangible assets, observe business activities, and confirm account balances and mathematical computations. It might also examine sample transactions or records to ascertain the accuracy of the client company's financial and accounting systems. For example, auditors often select transactions recorded in the company's books to determine whether the recorded entries are supported by underlying data (vouching). Or, approaching the problem from the opposite perspective, an auditor might choose particular items of data to trace through the client's accounting and bookkeeping process to determine whether the data have been properly recorded and accounted for (tracing).

For practical reasons of time and cost, an audit rarely, if ever, examines every accounting transaction in the records of a business. The planning and execution of an audit therefore require a high degree of professional skill and judgment. Initially, the CPA firm plans the audit by surveying the client's business operations and accounting systems and making preliminary decisions as to the scope of the audit and what methods and procedures will be used. The firm then evaluates the internal financial control systems of the client and performs compliance tests to determine whether they are functioning properly. Transactions and data are sampled, vouched for, and traced. Throughout the audit process, results are examined and procedures are reevaluated and modified to reflect discoveries made by the auditors. "For example, if the auditor discovers weaknesses in the internal control system of the client, the auditor must plan additional audit procedures which will satisfy himself that the internal control weaknesses have not caused any material misrepresentations in the financial statements." (Hagen, *supra*, 13 J. Contemp. Law at pp. 67–68.)

The end product of an audit is the audit report or opinion. The report is generally expressed in a letter addressed to the client. The body of the report refers to the specific client-prepared financial statements which are attached. In the case of the so-called "unqualified report" (of which Arthur Young's report on the company's 1982 financial statements is an example), two paragraphs are relatively standard.

In a scope paragraph, the CPA firm asserts that it has examined the accompanying financial statements in accordance with GAAS. GAAS are promulgated by the American Institute of Certified Public Accountants (AICPA), a national professional organization of CPA's, whose membership is open to persons holding certified public accountant certificates issued by state boards of accountancy.

The GAAS include 10 broadly phrased sets of standards and general principles that guide the audit function. They are classified as general standards, standards for fieldwork, and standards of reporting. General Standard No. 1 provides: "The examination is to be performed by a person or persons having adequate technical training as ... auditor[s]." General Standard No. 3 provides: "Due professional care is to be exercised in the performance of the examination and the preparation of the report." Standard of Fieldwork No. 2 provides: "A sufficient understanding of the internal control structure is to be obtained to plan the audit and to determine the nature, timing, and extent of tests to be performed."

The generality of these statements is somewhat mitigated by the Statements on Auditing Standards (SAS), which are periodic interpretations of the standards issued by the Auditing Standards Board of the AICPA. (Miller & Bailey, Comprehensive GAAS Guide (1991) pp. 5.03, 5.11, 6.07 [hereafter GAAS Guide].) For example, SAS–55, which relates to internal financial control structure, includes steps to be followed in understanding and testing accounting control systems in relation to information provided in financial statements. (GAAS Guide at p. 7.03 et seq.) The GAAS Guide, a commonly used summary of GAAS, that purports to integrate and comprehensively restate pertinent auditing standards, includes 140 major sections and more than 1,000 pages.

In an opinion paragraph, the audit report generally states the CPA firm's opinion that the audited financial statements, taken as a whole, are in conformity with GAAP and present fairly in all material respects the financial position, results of operations, and changes in financial position of the client in the relevant periods.

The GAAP are an amalgam of statements issued by the AICPA through the successive groups it has established to promulgate accounting principles: the Committee on Accounting Procedure, the Accounting Principles Board, and the Financial Accounting Standards Board. Like GAAS, GAAP include broad statements of accounting principles amounting to aspirational norms as well as more specific guidelines and illustrations. The lack of an official compilation allows for some debate over whether particular announcements are encompassed within GAAP. One standard text purporting to comprehensively restate GAAP includes 90 major sections and more than 500 pages. (M. Miller, GAAP Guide (1991).)

In addition to or in place of the standardized statements in an audit report, the auditing CPA firm may also qualify its opinion, noting exceptions or matters in the financial statements not in conformity with GAAP or significant uncertainties which might affect a fair evaluation of the statements. The report may also contain a disclaimer stating the accountant's inability to express any opinion about the statements or an adverse opinion that the statements do not fairly present the financial position of the client in conformity with GAAP.

Arthur Young correctly observes that audits may be commissioned by clients for different purposes. Nonetheless, audits of financial statements and the resulting audit reports are very frequently (if not almost universally) used by businesses to establish the financial credibility of their enterprises in the perceptions of outside persons, e.g., existing and prospective investors, financial institutions, and others who extend credit to an enterprise or make risk-oriented decisions based on its economic viability. The unqualified audit report of a CPA firm, particularly one of the "Big Six," is often an admission ticket to venture capital markets—a necessary condition precedent to attracting the kind and level of outside funds essential to the client's financial growth and survival. As one commentator summarizes: "In the first instance, this unqualified opinion serves as an assurance to the client that its own perception of its financial health is valid and that its accounting systems are reliable. The audit, however, frequently plays a second major role: it assists the client in convincing third parties that it is safe to extend credit or invest in the client." (Siliciano, *supra*, 86 Mich.L.Rev. at p. 1932.)

The GAAP acknowledge that financial audit reporting is "a principal means of communicating accounting information to those outside an enterprise." (Statement of Financial Accounting Concepts of the Financial Accounting Standards Board of the AICPA No. 1, ¶ 6, p. 7.) As the AICPA recently stated: "The independent audit, through the process of examining evidence underlying the financial statements, adds credibility to management's representations in the statements. In turn, the audit provides investors, bankers, creditors, and others with reasonable assurance that the financial statements are free of material misstatement." (AICPA, Understanding Audits and the Auditor's Report, A Guide for Financial Statement Users (1989) p. 36; see also Bus. & Prof.Code, § 5051, subd. (d) [practice of accountancy includes preparation of reports on audits for purpose of obtaining credit or filing documents with government agencies]; Cal.Code Regs., tit. 16, § 58.3 [accountant may not issue report on unaudited financial statements to client or others without complying with professional standards].)

The AICPA's professional standards refer to the public responsibility of auditors: "A distinguishing mark of a profession is acceptance of its responsibility to the public. The accounting profession's public consists of clients, credit grantors, governments, employers, investors, the business and financial community, and others who rely on the objectivity and integrity of certified public accountants to maintain the orderly functioning of commerce. This reliance imposes a public interest responsibility on certified public accountants." (2 AICPA Professional Standards (CCH 1988) § 53.01.)

The United States Supreme Court had also recognized the public function of the CPA auditor as a reason to deny work product protection to the auditor's work papers. Distinguishing CPA firms from lawyers and other professionals who perform services for clients, the high court stated: "By certifying the public reports that collectively depict a corporation's financial status, the independent auditor assumes a *public* responsibility transcending any employment relationship with the client. The independent public accountant performing this special function owes ultimate allegiance to the corporation's creditors and stockholders, as well as to the investing public. This 'public watchdog' function demands that the accountant maintain total independence from the client at all times and requires complete fidelity to the public trust." (*United States v. Arthur Young & Co.* (1984) 465 U.S. 805, 817–818, 104 S.Ct. 1495, 1503, 79 L.Ed.2d 826.)

The complex nature of the audit function and its economic implications has resulted in different approaches to the question whether CPA auditors should be subjected to liability to third parties who read and rely on audit reports. Although three schools of thought are commonly recognized, there are some variations within each school and recent case law suggests a possible trend toward merger of two of the three approaches.

A substantial number of jurisdictions follow the lead of Chief Judge Cardozo's 1931 opinion for the New York Court of Appeals in *Ultramares, supra,* 174 N.E. 441, by denying recovery to third parties for auditor negligence in the absence of a third party relationship to the auditor that is "akin to privity." In contrast, a handful of jurisdictions, spurred by law review commentary, have recently allowed recovery based on auditor negligence to third parties whose reliance on the audit report was "foreseeable."

Most jurisdictions, supported by the weight of commentary and the modern English common law decisions cited by the parties, have steered a middle course based in varying degrees on Restatement Second of Torts section 552, which generally imposes liability on suppliers of commercial information to third persons who are intended beneficiaries of the information. Finally, the federal securities laws have also dealt with the problem by imposing auditor liability for negligence-related conduct only in connection with misstatements in publicly filed and distributed offering documents. * * *

The New York Court of Appeals restated the law in light of *Ultramares, White v. Guarente,* and other cases in *Credit Alliance v. Arthur Andersen & Co.* (1985) 65 N.Y.2d 536, 493 N.Y.S.2d 435, 483 N.E.2d 110. *Credit Alliance* subsumed two cases with different factual postures: in the first case, plaintiff alleged it loaned funds to the auditor's client in reliance on audited financial statements overstating the client's assets and net worth; in the second, the same scenario occurred, but plaintiff also alleged the auditor knew plaintiff was the client's principal lender and communicated directly and frequently with plaintiff regarding its continuing audit reports. The court dismissed plaintiff's negligence claim in the first case, but sustained the claim in the second.

The New York court promulgated the following rule for determining auditor liability to third parties for negligence: "Before accountants may be held liable in negligence to non-contractual parties who rely to their detriment on inaccurate financial reports, certain prerequisites must be satisfied: (1) the accountant must have been aware that the financial reports were to be used for a particular purpose or purposes; (2) in the furtherance of which a known party or parties was intended to rely; and (3) there must have been some conduct on the part of the accountants linking them to that party or parties, which evinces the accountants' understanding of that party or parties' reliance." (*Credit Alliance v. Arthur Andersen & Co., supra,* 493 N.Y.S.2d at p. 443, 483 N.E.2d at p. 118.) * * *

From the cases cited by the parties, it appears at least nine states purport to follow privity or near privity rules restricting the liability of auditors to parties with whom they have a contractual or similar relationship. In five states, this result has been reached by decisions of their highest courts. In four other states, the rule has been enacted by statute. Federal court decisions have held that the rule represents the law of three additional states whose highest courts have not expressly considered the question. The more recent of the cited cases generally follow the New York rule as reformulated in *Credit Alliance.*

Arguing that accountants should be subject to liability to third persons on the same basis as other tortfeasors, Justice Howard Wiener advocated rejection of the rule of *Ultramares* in a 1983 law review article. (Wiener, *Common Law Liability of the Certified Public Accountant for Negligent Misrepresentation* (1983) 20 San Diego L.Rev. 233 [hereafter Wiener].) In its place, he proposed a rule based on foreseeability of injury to third persons. Criticizing what he called the "anachronistic protection" given to accountants by the traditional rules limiting third person liability, he concluded: "Accountant liability based on foreseeable injury would serve the dual functions of compensation for injury and deterrence of negligent conduct. Moreover, it is a just and rational judicial policy that the same criteria govern the imposition of negligence liability, regardless of the context in which it arises. The accountant, the investor, and the general public will in the long run benefit when the liability of the certified public accountant for negligent misrepresentation is measured by the foreseeability standard." (*Id.* at p. 260.) Under the rule proposed by Justice Wiener, "[f]oreseeability of the risk would be a question of fact for the jury to be disturbed on appeal only where there is insufficient evidence to support the finding." (*Id.* at pp. 256–257.)

Following in part Justice Wiener's approach, the New Jersey Supreme Court upheld a claim for negligent misrepresentation asserted by stock purchasers against an auditor who had rendered an unqualified audit report approving fraudulently prepared financial statements. (*Rosenblum v. Adler* (1983) 93 N.J. 324, 461 A.2d 138.) The court found no reason to distinguish accountants from other suppliers of products or services to the public and no reason to deny to third party users of financial statements recovery for economic loss resulting from negligent misrepresentation. From its review of the purpose and history of the audit function, it concluded: "The auditor's function has expanded from that of a watchdog for management to an independent evaluator of the adequacy and fairness of financial statements issued by management to stockholders, creditors, and others." Noting the apparent ability of accounting firms to obtain insurance against third party claims under the federal securities laws, the court posited the same or similar protection would be available for common law negligent misrepresentation claims.

From a public policy standpoint, the court emphasized the potential deterrent effect of a liability-imposing rule on the conduct and cost of audits: "The imposition of a duty to foreseeable users may cause accounting firms to engage in more thorough reviews. This might entail setting up stricter standards and applying closer supervision, which should tend to reduce the number of instances in which liability would ensue. Much of the additional cost incurred either because of more thorough auditing review or increased insurance premiums would be borne by the business entity and its stockholders or its customers."

Notwithstanding its broad pronouncements about the public role of auditors and the importance of deterring negligence by imposing liability, when the New Jersey court formulated a rule of liability it restricted the auditor's duty to "all those whom that auditor should reasonably foresee as recipients *from the company* of the statements for its proper business purposes, provided that the recipients rely on the statements pursuant to those business purposes." (*Rosenblum v. Adler, supra,* 461 A.2d at p. 153, italics added.) According to the court, its rule would preclude auditor liability to "an institutional investor or portfolio manager who does not obtain audited statements from the company" or to "stockholders who purchased the stock after a negligent audit" unless they could demonstrate "the necessary conditions precedent."

The New Jersey court offered no principled basis for its "conditions precedent" requirement. Institutional investors, portfolio managers, or prospective stock purchasers who may pick up an audit report from a stockbroker, friend, or acquaintance or otherwise acquire it indirectly are no less "foreseeable" users. In view of the lack of any effective limits on access to audit reports once they reach the client, an auditor can foresee its reports coming into the hands of practically anyone. Thus, the court's approach evinces an *Ultramares*-like concern about the prospect of unlimited auditor liability, but offers no reasoned explanation of its decision to establish a limit based solely on the company's distribution, a factor over which the auditor has no control.

Two other state high courts—those of Wisconsin and Mississippi—have endorsed foreseeability rules. * * *

In the nearly 10 years since it was formally proposed, the foreseeability approach has not attracted a substantial following. And at least four state supreme courts have explicitly rejected the foreseeability approach in favor of the Restatement's "intended beneficiary" approach since the New Jersey court's decision in *Rosenblum.*

The foreseeability approach has also encountered substantial criticism from commentators, who have questioned, among other matters, its failure to consider seriously the problem of indeterminate liability and its prediction of a significant deterrent effect that will improve the quality of audit reporting. Other commentators have disagreed. The body of scholarly and practical literature is substantial. * * *

Auditors may also incur liability to third persons under the federal securities laws. Under section 10(b) of the Securities and Exchange Act of 1934 (1934 Act) and rule 10(b)–5 of the Securities Exchange Commission (SEC), accountants may be held liable to actual purchasers or sellers of securities for fraud or gross negligence. (15 U.S.C. § 78j(b); see *Ernst & Ernst v. Hochfelder* (1976) 425 U.S. 185, 96 S.Ct. 1375, 47 L.Ed.2d 668; *Blue Chip Stamps v. Manor Drug Stores* (1975) 421 U.S. 723, 95 S.Ct. 1917, 44 L.Ed.2d 539.)

Accountants may incur liability to third parties without a showing of fraud or gross negligence under section 18 of the 1934 Act, 15 United States Code § 78r, or section 11 of the Securities Act of 1933 (1933 Act), 15 United States Code § 77k. Section 11 of the 1933 Act provides in part: "In case any part of the registration statement . . . contained an untrue statement of a material fact or omitted to state a material fact required to be stated therein or necessary to make the statements therein not misleading, any person acquiring such security (unless it is proved that at the time of such acquisition he knew of such untruth or omission) may, either at law or in equity, in any court of competent jurisdiction sue—. . . (4) every accountant, engineer, or appraiser, or any person whose profession gives authority to a statement made by him, who has with his consent been named as having prepared or certified any part of the registration statement, or as having prepared or certified any report or valuation which is used in connection with the registration statement, with respect to the statement in such registration statement, report, or valuation, which purports to have been prepared or certified by him." (15 U.S.C. § 77k(a)(4).) An accountant or other professional within the scope of section 11 can escape liability for a false or misleading statement by proving due diligence, i.e., that after "reasonable investigation" he or she had "reasonable ground to believe and did believe" that the statement was "true and not misleading." (*Id.,* § 77k(b)(3).)

The liability of accountants and other professionals to third parties under section 11 of the 1933 Act is circumscribed by several factors: (1) the accountant's liability is limited to situations in which he or she prepares or certifies the accuracy of a portion of a registration statement and thus is aware he or she is creating part of a communication *to the public;* (2) liability is limited to third parties who actually purchase securities; (3) damage exposure is limited to the out-of-pocket loss suffered by the purchaser and can be no greater than the amount of the offering. (15 U.S.C. § 77k(a), (e) and (g).) Thus, under section 11: "[T]he plaintiff class, the proof of violation, and the measure of damages are statutorily defined in a manner that enhances the accountant's ability to gauge, *ex ante,* its liability exposure." (Siliciano, *supra,* 86 Mich.L.Rev. at p. 1954, fn. 131, italics in original.)

Section 18 of the 1934 Act imposes liability on accountants for misstatements contained in documents filed with the SEC. Liability is limited to third persons who, in reliance on the accountant's statement, "have purchased or sold a security at a price which was affected by such statement, for damages caused by such reliance." (15 U.S.C. § 78r(a).) The accountant may successfully defend the action by proving that "he acted in good faith and had no knowledge that such statement was false or misleading." (*Ibid.*)

In summary, under the federal securities laws, an auditor's liability to third persons on theories akin to common law negligence is limited to those situations in which the third party suffers a loss in the purchase or sale of a security in reliance on an auditor's misstatement in a public registration statement or other public document filed with the SEC for use in connection with an identified securities registration. In these situations, the auditor is placed on notice of the extent of its potential liability exposure. * * *

An auditor is a watchdog, not a bloodhound. (*In re Kingston Cotton Mill Co.* (1896) 2 Ch. 279, 288.) As a matter of commercial reality, audits are performed in a client-controlled environment. The client typically prepares its own financial statements; it has direct control over and assumes primary responsibility for their contents. (See *In re Interstate Hosiery Mills, Inc.* (1939) 4 S.E.C. 721 ["The fundamental and primary responsibility for the accuracy [of financial statements] rests upon management."]) The client engages the auditor, pays for the audit, and communicates with audit personnel throughout the engagement. Because the auditor cannot in the time available become an expert in the client's business and record-keeping systems, the client necessarily furnishes the information base for the audit.

The client, of course, has interests in the audit that may not be consonant with those of the public. "Management seeks to maximize the stockholders' and creditors' confidence in the company, within the bounds of [GAAP and GAAS]; whereas, the public demands a sober and impartial evaluation of fiscal performance." (*First Nat. Bank of Commerce v. Monco Agency Inc., supra,* 911 F.2d at p. 1058.)

Client control also predominates in the dissemination of the audit report. Once the report reaches the client, the extent of its distribution and the communications that accompany it are within the exclusive province of client management. Thus, regardless of the efforts of the auditor, the client retains effective primary control of the financial reporting process.

Moreover, an audit report is not a simple statement of verifiable fact that, like the weight of the load of beans in *Glanzer v. Shepard, supra,* 233 N.Y. 236, 135 N.E. 275, can be easily checked against uniform standards of indisputable accuracy. Rather, an audit report is a professional opinion based on numerous and complex factors. The report is based on the auditor's interpretation and application of hundreds of professional standards, many of which are broadly phrased and readily subject to different constructions. Although ultimately expressed in shorthand form, the report is the final product of a complex process involving discretion and judgment on the part of the auditor at every stage. Using different initial assumptions and approaches, different sampling techniques, and the wisdom of 20–20 hindsight, few CPA audits would be immune from criticism.

Although the auditor's role in the financial reporting process is secondary and the subject of complex professional judgment, the liability it faces in a negligence suit by a third party is primary and personal and can be massive. The client, its promoters, and its managers have generally left the scene, headed in most cases for government-supervised liquidation or the bankruptcy court. The auditor has now assumed center stage as the remaining solvent defendant and is faced with a claim for all sums of money ever loaned to or invested in the client. Yet the auditor may never have been aware of the existence, let alone the nature or scope, of the third party transaction that resulted in the claim.

The character of the damages claimed from the auditor—economic loss resulting from investment and credit decisions—introduces further uncertainties into the negligence suit against the auditor. An award of damages for pure economic loss suffered by third parties raises the spectre of vast numbers of suits and limitless financial exposure.

Investment and credit decisions are by their nature complex and multifaceted. Although an audit report might play a role in such decisions, reasonable and prudent investors and lenders will dig far deeper in their "due diligence" investigations than the surface level of an auditor's opinion. And, particularly in financially large transactions, the ultimate decision to lend or invest is often based on numerous business factors that have little to do with the audit report. The auditing CPA has no expertise in or control over the products or services of its clients or their markets; it does not choose the client's executives or make its business decisions; yet, when clients fail financially, the CPA auditor is a prime target in litigation claiming investor and creditor economic losses because it is the only available (and solvent) entity that had any direct contact with the client's business affairs.

The facts of this case provide an apt example. Although plaintiffs now profess reliance on Arthur Young's audit report as the sine qua non of their investments, the record reveals a more complicated decision making process. As a group of corporate insiders and venture capitalists who were closely following the Cinderella-like transformation of the company, plaintiffs perceived an opportunity to make a large sum of money in a very short time by investing in a company they believed would (literally within months) become the dominant force in the new personal computer market.

Although hindsight suggests they misjudged a number of major factors (including, at a minimum, the product, the market, the competition, and the company's manufacturing capacity), plaintiffs' litigation-focused attention is now exclusively on the auditor and its report. Plaintiffs would have us believe that, had the Arthur Young report disclosed deficiencies in accounting controls and the $3 million loss (on income of over $68 million), they would have ignored all the other positive factors that triggered their interest (such as the company's rapid growth in sales, its dynamic management, and the intense interest of underwriters in a public offering) and flatly withheld all their funds. Plaintiffs' revisionist view of the company's history, the audit, and their own investments, suggests something less than a "close connection" between Arthur Young's audit report and the loss of their invested funds.

In view of the factors discussed above, judicial endorsement of third party negligence suits against auditors limited only by the concept of forseeability raises the spectre of multibillion-dollar professional liability that is distinctly out of proportion to: (1) the fault of the auditor (which is necessarily secondary and may be based on complex differences of professional opinion); and (2) the connection between the auditor's conduct and the third party's injury (which will often be attenuated by unrelated business factors that underlie investment and credit decisions).

As other courts and commentators have noted, such disproportionate liability cannot fairly be justified on moral, ethical, or economic grounds. As one commentator has summarized: "The most persuasive basis for maintaining the limited duty [of auditors] is a proportionality argument.... It can be argued as a general proposition in these cases that the wrongdoing of an accountant is slight compared with that of the party who has deceived him (his client) as well as the plaintiff. This rationale for nonliability is similar to the proximate cause grounds on which willful intervening misconduct insulates a 'merely negligent' party from liability." (Rabin, *supra,* 37 Stan.L.Rev. at pp. 1536–1537, fn. 74.)

Courts advocating unlimited auditor liability to all foreseeably injured third parties often analogize the auditor's opinion to a consumer product, arguing that the demise of privity as a barrier to recovery for negligence in product manufacture implies its irrelevance in the area of auditor liability as well. (See, e.g., *Rosenblum v. Adler, supra,* 461 A.2d at pp. 145–147.) Plaintiffs advance similar arguments. The analogy lacks persuasive force for two reasons. Initially, as noted above, the maker of a consumer product has complete control over the design and manufacture of its product; in contrast, the auditor merely expresses an opinion about its client's financial statements—the client is primarily responsible for the content of those statements in the form they reach the third party.

Moreover, the general character of the class of third parties is also different. Investors, creditors, and others who read and rely on audit reports and financial statements are not the equivalent of ordinary consumers. Like plaintiffs here, they often possess considerable sophistication in analyzing financial information and are aware from training and experience of the limits of an audit report "product" that is, at bottom, simply a broadly phrased professional opinion based on a necessarily confined examination.

In contrast to the "presumptively powerless consumer" in product liability cases, the third party in an audit negligence case has other options—he or she can "privately order" the risk of inaccurate financial reporting by contractual arrangements with the client. (Siliciano, *supra*, 86 Mich.L.Rev. at pp. 1956–1957.) For example, a third party might expend its own resources to verify the client's financial statements or selected portions of them that were particularly material to its transaction with the client. Or it might commission its own audit or investigation, thus establishing privity between itself and an auditor or investigator to whom it could look for protection. In addition, it might bargain with the client for special security or improved terms in a credit or investment transaction. Finally, the third party could seek to bring itself within the *Glanzer* exception to *Ultramares* by insisting that an audit be conducted on its behalf or establishing direct communications with the auditor with respect to its transaction with the client.

As a matter of economic and social policy, third parties should be encouraged to rely on their own prudence, diligence, and contracting power, as well as other informational tools. This kind of self-reliance promotes sound investment and credit practices and discourages the careless use of monetary resources. If, instead, third parties are simply permitted to recover from the auditor for mistakes in the client's financial statements, the auditor becomes, in effect, an insurer of not only the financial statements, but of bad loans and investments in general.

Courts and commentators advocating auditor negligence liability to third parties also predict that such liability might deter auditor mistakes, promote more careful audits, and result in a more efficient spreading of the risk of inaccurate financial statements. For example, the New Jersey Supreme Court reasoned: "The imposition of a duty to foreseeable users may cause accounting firms to engage in more thorough reviews. This might entail setting up stricter standards and applying closer supervision, which would tend to reduce the number of instances in which liability would ensue. Much of the additional cost incurred because of more thorough auditing review or increased insurance premiums would be borne by the business entity and its stockholders or its customers.... Accountants will also be encouraged to exercise greater care leading to greater diligence in audits." (*Rosenblum v. Adler, supra,* 461 A.2d at p. 152.)

We are not directed to any empirical data supporting these prognostications. From our review of the cases and commentary, we doubt that a significant and desirable improvement in audit care would result from an expanded rule of liability. Indeed, deleterious economic effects appear at least as likely to occur.

In view of the inherent dependence of the auditor on the client and the labor-intensive nature of auditing, we doubt whether audits can be done in ways that would yield significantly greater accuracy without disadvantages. Auditors may rationally respond to increased liability by simply reducing audit services in fledgling industries where the business failure rate is high, reasoning that they will inevitably be singled out and sued when their client goes into bankruptcy regardless of the care or detail of their audits. As a legal economist described the problem: "The deterrent effect of liability rules is the difference between the probability of incurring liability when performance meets the required standard and the probability of incurring liability when performance is below the required standard. Thus, the stronger the probability that liability will be incurred when performance is adequate, the weaker is the deterrent effect of liability rules. Why offer a higher quality product if you will be sued regardless whenever there is a precipitous decline in stock prices?" (Fischel, *The Regulation of Accounting: Some Economic Issues* (1987), 52 Brooklyn L.Rev. 1051, 1055.) Consistent with this reasoning, the economic result of unlimited negligence liability could just as easily be an increase in the cost and decrease in the availability of audits and audit reports with no compensating improvement in overall audit quality.

In light of the relationships between auditor, client, and third party, and the relative sophistication of third parties who lend and invest based on audit reports, it might also be doubted whether auditors are the most efficient absorbers of the losses from inaccuracies in financial information. Investors and creditors can limit the impact of losses by diversifying investments and loan portfolios. They effectively constitute a "broad social base upon which the costs of accounting errors can be spread." (Siliciano, *supra,* 86 Mich.L.Rev. at p. 1973.) In the audit liability context, no reason appears to favor the alleged tortfeasor over the alleged victim as an effective distributor of loss. * * *

For the reasons stated above, we hold that an auditor's liability for general negligence in the conduct of an audit of its client financial statements is confined to the client, i.e., the person who contracts for or engages the audit services. Other persons may not recover on a pure negligence theory.

There is, however, a further narrow class of persons who, although not clients, may reasonably come to receive and rely on an audit report and whose existence constitutes a risk of audit reporting that may fairly be imposed on the auditor. Such persons are specifically intended beneficiaries of the audit report who are known to the auditor and for whose benefit it renders the audit report. While such persons may not recover on a general negligence theory, we hold they may * * * recover on a theory of negligent misrepresentation.

The sole client of Arthur Young in the audit engagements involved in this case was the company. None of the plaintiffs qualify as clients. Under the rule we adopt, they are not entitled to recover on a pure negligence theory. Therefore, the verdict and judgment in their favor based on that theory are reversed. * * *

Having determined that intended beneficiaries of an audit report are entitled to recovery on a theory of negligent misrepresentation, we must consider whether they may also recover on a general negligence theory. We conclude they may not. Non-clients of the auditor are connected with the audit only through receipt of and express reliance on the audit report. Similarly, the gravamen of the cause of action for negligent misrepresentation in this context is actual, justifiable reliance on the representations in that report. Without such reliance, there is no recovery regardless of the manner in which the audit itself was conducted. (See *Garcia v. Superior Court* (1990) 50 Cal.3d 728, 737, 268 Cal.Rptr. 779, 789 P.2d 960 (maj. opn.), 741–744, 268 Cal.Rptr. 779, 789 P.2d 960 (Lucas, C.J., conc.) [both opinions emphasizing importance of justifiable reliance element in cause of action for negligent misrepresentation based on furnishing false information].) * * *

PANELLI, ARABIAN, BAXTER and GEORGE, JJ., concur.

KENNARD, JUSTICE, dissenting. * * *

MOSK, J., concurs.

NOTES

1.   Auditing in all events is not a precise science, as noted in one court's opinion:

> "Inherent in rendering an audit opinion is the recognition that financial statements cannot 'precisely' or 'exactly' present financial position, results of operations and cash flows. Such precision is unattainable...." Consequently, an accountant's opinion that "the financial statements fairly present the financial condition of the Company in accordance with generally accepted accounting principles" is not the same as stating that everything in the financial statement is perfect; rather, it means the financial statements are materially accurate and provide sufficient disclosure to users of the financial statements. "Materiality is 'the magnitude of an omission or misstatement of accounting information that, in the light of surrounding circumstances, makes it probable that the judgment of a reasonable person relying on the information would have been changed or influenced by the omission or misstatement.' " "A concept of

materiality is a practical necessity in both auditing and accounting. Allowing immaterial items to complicate and clutter up the auditing process or financial statements is uneconomical and diverts users' attention from significant matters in the financial statements."

Koch v. Koch Industries, 969 F.Supp. 1460, 1558–59 (D.Kan.1997) (citations omitted).

2. Still another flaw is the fact that accounting provides backward looking information, particularly trailing quarterly earnings. In addition, "[i]t is driven by accounting standards that are a function of habit and history, of often archaic and abstract principle, and of a shortsighted conviction that it is better to obscure rather than illuminate the real source of earnings." Treasury Official Sees Need for Relevant Disclosure, Supports SEC Proposals, Fed. Sec. L. Rep. No. 2054 (2002) (Describing speech of Treasury Undersecretary for Domestic Finance Peter Fisher before the Securities Industry Association). Forward looking reports are also criticized because management has a tendency to exaggerate and because they focus investors on short term results. In response to such criticism, Coca Cola announced that it would no longer make quarterly profit forecasts. Betty Liu & Andrew Hill, Coca–Cola Attacks Wall St Focus on Short–Term Outlook, Financial Times (London), Dec. 14–15, 2002, at 1.

3. More emphasis has been suggested on cash accounting as a way to assure corporate managers do not use accrual accounting to inflate earnings, which analysts now rely on in recommending stocks. Peter J. Wallison, Give Us Disclosure, Not Audits, Wall St. J., June 2, 2003, at A16 ("As Wall Streeters have always noted, 'Earnings are an opinion, but cash is a fact.' ") Another suggestion is that managers should be judged on the rate of return they generate over that which would be earned by an investor in other investments of comparable risk. G. Bennett Stewart III, Why Smart Managers Do Dumb Things, Wall St. J., June 2, 2003, at A16. Do you agree with these approaches? Remember cash based accounting may be manipulated by deferring payment of expenses or receipt of income.

4. At the beginning of the twentieth century, accounting for manufacturing firms was not for external use for investors but rather for management purposes. See Jonathan Barron Baskin & Paul J. Miranti, Jr., A History of Corporate Finance, Cambridge, 183–84 (1997). Should accounting statements be limited to that role? Accountants are not policeman and cannot assure the accuracy of financial statements for investors, so why suggest to investors that they are something more?

SECTION 3. SEC REGULATION

The role of accountants was expanded by the adoption of the federal securities laws, which required publicly owned companies to publish certified accounting statements. Section 12(g) of the Securities Exchange Act of 1934 requires registration with the SEC of any company that has total assets exceeding $1,000,000 (raised to $10,000,000 by SEC rule) and a class of equity securities with at least 500 shareholders of record. 15 U.S.C. § 78l. Section 13 of the Securities Exchange Act (15 U.S.C. § 78m) imposes periodic disclosure and other requirements on companies required to register under Section 12. Those companies must file with the SEC audited annual financial reports, unaudited quarterly reports and reports of material events affecting the company whenever they occur. The SEC makes these reports publicly available.

Among the periodic reports that must be filed by an issuer under Section 13 are annual reports on Commission Form 10–K. See 17 C.F.R. § 240.13a–1 (SEC requirement for annual report). These reports must include financial statements, including a balance sheet, that have been audited in accordance with generally accepted accounting principles ("GAAP") by an independent certified public accountant. Information about the company's business and its officers and directors must also be included. The company is required to disclose legal proceedings against it, and the registrant must make available quantitative and qualitative information about market risks it is incurring. This rather comprehensive statement, *i.e.*, Form 10–K, provides investors with a wealth of information on the company. The Form 10–K must be signed by the corporation's principal executive, financial and accounting officers and by at least a majority of the board of directors. In adopting this requirement, the SEC stated the reason for it was that the "attention of the private sector, including management, directors, accountants, and attorneys, must ... be refocused towards Exchange Act filings if a sufficient degree of discipline is to be instilled in the system to make it work." Sec.Ex.Act Rel. No. 17114 (Sept. 2, 1980).

To assure more current information, the issuer must file a quarterly financial report with the SEC on Form 10–Q. 17 C.F.R. § 240.13a–13. This financial statement need not be audited because such a requirement would delay its filing and thereby impair the usefulness of that information to investors. Another important requirement is that the issuer file a Form 8–K with the SEC promptly after the occurrence of certain material events. 17 C.F.R. § 240.13a–11. This assures that investors are advised promptly of such events; they need not await the filing of the quarterly or annual reports before being advised of such information. Disclosure is required under Form 8–K of such things as a change in control of the registrant, resignations of directors, changes in accountants and bankruptcy.

The disclosure requirements of the federal securities laws led to attempts to impose liability on accountants under those statutes. Accountants were often the target, as the "deep pocket," when public companies failed. The accounting profession fought off those efforts first in their challenges to liability based on negligence in their audits. Ernst & Ernst v. Hochfelder, 425 U.S. 185, 96 S.Ct. 1375, 47 L.Ed.2d 668 (1976). Further protection was received when the Supreme Court rejected private rights of action for aiding and abetting on the part of professionals such as accountants and lawyers. Central Bank v. First Interstate Bank, 511 U.S.

164, 114 S.Ct. 1439, 128 L.Ed.2d 119 (1994). In Touche Ross & Co. v. Redington, 442 U.S. 560, 99 S.Ct. 2479, 61 L.Ed.2d 82 (1979), the Supreme Court held that there was no private right of action against accountants under the books and records provisions of the Securities Exchange Act of 1934. Liability for filing false documents could still be based on Section 18(a) of 1934, 15 U.S.C. § 78r(a), but that provision allows a good faith defense, and Section 11 of the Securities Act of 1933 also somewhat circumscribes accountant liability. 15 U.S.C. § 77k. *See also* Reves v. Ernst & Young, 507 U.S. 170, 113 S.Ct. 1163, 122 L.Ed.2d 525 (1993) (rejecting RICO liability for accounting activities).

The Securities and Exchange Commission ("SEC") deferred for the most part to the accounting profession in developing what are called "generally accepted accounting principles" or "GAAP." 2 *Thomas L. Hazen, Treatise on the Law of Securities Regulation* § 9.6 (4th ed.2002). The Financial Accounting Standards Board ("FASB"), an industry group that worked with the SEC, had taken the lead in developing or changing particular GAAP standards. *See generally* Marshall S. Armstrong, "The Work and Workings of the Financial Accounting Standards Board," 29 Bus. Law. 145 (1974).

Accounting standards change from time-to-time, *albeit* slowly. The SEC did not always defer to the FASB. The SEC imposed particular standards in its filings by rule and issues Accounting Series Releases on matters it deems are not adequately addressed by the accounting profession. Regulation S–X imposed various accounting requirements in public offerings. 17 C.F.R. §§ 210.1 *et seq.* The SEC further assumed the authority to discipline accountants that failed to meet what the SEC deemed are appropriate auditing standards. 17 C.F.R. § 210.102(e).

Another key aspect of the audit process are generally accepted auditing standards ("GAAS"), which GAAS are produced by the Auditing Standards Board of the American Institute of Certified Public Accountants ("AICPA"). The AICPA is a private professional organization of certified public accountants ("CPAs"), i.e., accountants passing rigorous examinations conducted by state boards of accountancy in order to assure proficiency in the profession. CPAs are the accountants qualified to conduct audits and certify that a corporation's books and records are properly prepared.

Section 10A of the Securities Exchange Act of 1934 requires audits to be conducted in accordance with GAAP and GAAS. Independent auditors are also required to conduct their audits in a way that would uncover illegal activities and to report such conduct to management and to the board of directors if management fails to act. The board of directors must then report the violative activity to the SEC or, if it fails to do so, the auditor must inform the SEC. 15 U.S.C. § 78j–1. The SEC has also adopted rules that sought to assure auditor competency and independence from audit clients. 17 C.F.R. § 210.2–01(b). Those independence standards were questioned after the SEC discovered that numerous partners in audit

firms held stock in their audit clients. The SEC found in one large
accounting firm that thirty one of the top forty-three partners held stock *conflict*
in audit clients. A total of 8,000 violations of independence standards were *of interest*
found by partners and employees of the accounting firm. Consulting
operations created by accounting firms were also creating conflicts. In
announcing proposals to strengthen the independence of auditors, the
SEC noted that:

> Independent auditors have an important public trust. Every day,
> millions of people invest their savings in our securities markets in
> reliance on financial statements prepared by public companies and
> audited by independent auditors. These auditors, using Generally
> Accepted Auditing Standards ("GAAS"), examine issuers' financial
> statements and issue opinions about whether the financial state-
> ments, taken as a whole, are fairly presented in conformity with
> Generally Accepted Accounting Principles ("GAAP"). While an audi-
> tor's opinion does not guarantee the accuracy of financial statements,
> it furnishes investors with critical assurance that the financial state-
> ments have been subjected to a rigorous examination by an impartial
> and skilled professional and that investors can therefore rely on them.
> Providing that assurance to the public is the auditor's over-arching
> duty.
>
> Investors must be able to put their faith in issuers' financial state-
> ments. If investors do not believe that the auditor is truly indepen-
> dent from the issuer, they will derive little confidence from the
> auditor's opinion and will be far less likely to invest in the issuer's
> securities. Fostering investor confidence, therefore, requires not only
> that auditors actually be independent of their audit clients, but also
> that reasonable investors perceive them to be independent.
>
> One of our missions is to promote investor confidence in the reliabili-
> ty and integrity of issuers' financial statements. To promote investor
> confidence, we must ensure that our auditor independence require-
> ments remain relevant, effective, and fair in light of significant
> changes in the profession, structural reorganizations of accounting
> firms, and demographic changes in society. Some of the important
> developments in each of these areas since we last amended our
> auditor independence requirements in 1983 include the following:
>
> > — Firms are becoming primarily business advisory service firms
> > as they increase the number, revenues from, and types of non-
> > audit services provided to audit clients,
> >
> > — Firms and their audit clients are entering into an increasing
> > number of business relationships, such as strategic alliances, co-
> > marketing arrangements, and joint ventures,
> >
> > — Firms are divesting significant portions of their consulting
> > practices or restructuring their organizations,

— Firms are offering ownership of parts of their practices to the public, including audit clients,

— Firms are in need of increased capital to finance the growth of consulting practices, new technology, training, and large unfunded pension obligations,

— Firms have merged, resulting in increased firm size, both domestically and internationally,

— Firms have expanded into international networks, affiliating and marketing under a common name,

— Non-CPA financial service firms have acquired accounting firms, and the acquirers previously have not been subject to the profession's independence, auditing, or quality control standards,

— Firms' professional staffs have become more mobile, and geographical location has become less important due to advances in telecommunications and internet services, and

— Audit clients are hiring an increasing number of firm partners, professional staff, and their spouses for high level management positions.

Proposed Rules, Securities Exchange Act Release No. 42994 (July 12, 2000).

The SEC thereafter adopted rules to reflect these changes which, among other things, clarified the circumstances under which an auditor would retain independence in light of investments by auditors or their family members in audit clients, employment relationships between auditors or their family members and audit clients, and the scope of services provided by audit firms to their audit clients. The rules identified certain non-audit services that could impair the auditor's independence. Revision of the Commission's Auditor Independence Requirements, Securities Exchange Act Release No. 43602 (Nov. 21, 2000). Some large accounting firms spun off consulting services. Accenture was one such spin off and IBM purchased the consulting operations of another giant accounting firm. William Bulkeley & Kemba Dunham, "IBM Speeds Move to Consulting With $3.5 Billion Acquisition," Wall St. J., July 31, 2002, at A1.

NOTES

1. If you would like to examine the financial reports of a public company in which you have an interest, they are available online through the SEC's EDGAR filing system at: www.sec.gov/edgar.shtml. Take a minute to review the company's balance sheet. It will be more complex than the one set forth in this chapter, but the structure is the same. Do you understand how the company's assets are valued? Check the footnotes for that information.

2. Do you think the balance sheet provides a better valuation of the company than an income statement? Are both needed to make a valuation?

SECTION 4. APPLICATION OF ACCOUNTING STANDARDS

S.E.C. v. DUNLAP

Fed. Sec. L. Rep. ¶ 91,771 (S.D.Fla.2002).

* * * The facts of the complaint, in brief and as they pertain to Griffith are as follows. Because the motion to dismiss tightly focuses on the allegations of the complaint as it is now constituted, the Court shall quote heavily from that document. This case as a whole concerns the SEC's allegations that "[f]rom the last quarter of 1996 until June of 1998, senior management of Sunbeam Corporation ... orchestrated a fraudulent scheme to create the illusion of a successful restructuring of Sunbeam and facilitate a sale of the Company at an inflated price." Top Sunbeam officials assured investors that as a result of certain restructuring, "Sunbeam would meet very aggressive revenue and earnings targets." These figures were the goal; Lee B. Griffith was enlisted to help attain this goal. Griffith was Vice President for Sales for the Sunbeam Corporation from August of 1996 until April of 1998. After this, Griffith assumed the position of President of the Household Division, a vacancy that came up when Al Dunlap, Sunbeam's relatively new Chief Executive Officer, dismissed Donald Uzzi from that position. Griffith resigned from this position just three months later. Together with other top Sunbeam officials, Griffith participated in a scheme in which "improper accounting and misleading disclosures" duped investors into believing that the projected goals had been or were being met. This false information caused Sunbeam share prices to rise, which was designed to obtain an artificially inflated price for the sale of the company.

The allegations include creation of improper accounting reserves "into which management could and did dip its hand to artificially and improperly inflate income in 1997, further contributing to the picture of a rapid turnaround." In furtherance of the plan to give a booster shot to Sunbeam's 1997 revenue, the defendants, including Griffith, engaged in improper accounting procedures which "caused Sunbeam to recognize revenue from sales that did not meet applicable accounting rules." Some of this revenue gain was accomplished through "channel stuffing," which the complaint describes as "overloading channels of distribution by offering discounts and other inducements in order to sell product now that would otherwise be sold in the future." "Since many customers could not burden their warehouses with seasonal merchandise before the season began, Griffith proposed that the Company combine its discount offers with the option to have Sunbeam hold this merchandise until the normal time for delivery." This directly implicates the sales practices at Sunbeam, of which Griffith was Vice President.* * *[S]ales were poor in April "primarily due to mortgaging April to achieve Q1." * * *

What the complaint then describes can best be termed the "snowball effect" of this fraudulent scheme. In order to effectuate the scheme, and obtain an inflated price for the sale of Sunbeam, the defendants had wrongfully pumped up the revenue and sales figures for 1997. "Among other things, the [ ] Defendants ... engaged in deceptive and improper sales practices. As a result of these practices, more than 50% of Sunbeam's reported second-quarter 1997 income of $40.5 million did not comply with GAAP requirements." Further, by mid-November of 1997, these inflated revenue levels were extremely difficult to sustain. Therefore, "Dunlap, Kersh, Griffith, and Uzzi approved plans specifically intended to pull 1998 sales into 1997. These included plans to pull $52 million in 1998 barbecue-grill sales into 1997 by offering discounts, extended terms and additional local advertising support for retailers willing to purchase grills in December." Additionally, in December of 1997, Griffith assisted in creating a "distributor program," whereby "Sunbeam accelerated recognition of sales revenue by placing merchandise, including merchandise specifically slated for some of its retail customers, with certain distributors in advance of actual retail demand." In order to accomplish this, Sunbeam offered favorable terms and, "consistently, the right to return unsold product."

However, because of the actions undertaken in 1997, the company was faced with "the prospect of poor 1998 results." Therefore, "[i]n early 1998, the Sunbeam Defendants [of which Griffith is one] took increasingly desperate measures to conceal the Company's mounting financial problems ...," including "again engag[ing] in, and recogniz[ing] revenue for, sales that did not meet the applicable accounting rules," accelerating future sales revenue into present recognition periods, eliminating return authorizations "to conceal pending returns of merchandise," and "misrepresent[ing] the Company's performance and future prospects in its financial statements ... and its communications with analysts." Each of the named defendants, top Sunbeam officials during the relevant time period, "knew or recklessly disregarded facts indicating that their activities, together with the activities of other Sunbeam Defendants, would cause Sunbeam's books and records and period filings to be materially false and misleading." "Griffith's primary role was to develop and implement the specific sales programs that were the vehicle for the Company's improper accounting and misleading disclosure."

Additionally, during the first quarter of 1998, Sunbeam was faced with the consequences of its right-of-return sales policy and the "parking arrangements" into which it had entered.[34] Therefore, defendant Kersh, "in the presence of Uzzi and Gluck, ordered the deletion of all return authorizations from the Company's computer system. Griffith learned

34. These "parking arrangements" involved wholesalers holding merchandise over a financial quarter's end, without the wholesaler "accepting any of the risks or rewards of ownership." This was direct violation of GAAP revenue-recognition requirements.

about Kersh's instruction immediately." The deletion of these return authorizations caused these pending returns to be delayed, obviously resulting in an artificial inflation in the net sales figures.

On May 11, 1998, a press conference was held, following the release that same day of Sunbeam's first-quarter 1998 earnings release. That release reflected a loss of 52 [cents] per share. At the press conference, attended by Sunbeam officials Dunlap, Kersh, and Griffith, these three men addressed that shortfall. Dunlap stated without caveat that he "categorically reject[ed] all accusations that [Sunbeam officials] tried to stuff the channel and artificially pump up the fourth quarter." Following Kersh's comments, Griffith addressed the conference attendees, remarking that he and his colleagues "were not overloading the channel. We were pursuing a sound marketing idea. . . ." As a pensive Hamlet might say, "Aye, there's the rub." William Shakespeare, *Hamlet,* act III, sc. I, line 64.
* * *

The statement denying all allegations of channel stuffing and painting the scene as nothing more than a "sound marketing idea," especially in light of Griffith's elevated position in Sunbeam such that investors reasonably rely on his statements concerning the company's sales policies, is sufficient at the motion to dismiss stage to keep Griffith as a defendant in this action. Griffith's argument that the statement was immaterial as a matter of law based on Sunbeam's same-day releases concerning its financial status does not carry the day for him; the flat denial was not made immaterial by these releases where the investing public heard the denial from the mouth of the President of Sunbeam's Household Division.

The SEC's complaint also satisfies the scienter requirement. *See Ernst & Ernst v. Hochfelder,* 425 U.S. 185, 193 n. 12 (describing scienter as "refer[ring] to a mental state embracing intent to deceive, manipulate, or defraud."). The scienter requirement may be met by a showing of severe recklessness, *see Ziemba,* 256 F.3d at 1202 (citing *McDonald,* 863 F.2d at 814), and circumstantial evidence (especially at the motion to dismiss stage) may be probative of a defendant's scienter. *See, e.g., Greebel v. FTP Software, Inc.,* 194 F.3d 185, 194–97 (1st Cir.1999) (PSLRA context); *In re Silicon Graphics Inc. Secs. Litig.,* 183 F.3d 970, 977 (9th Cir.1999) (same). The allegations here, taken as true for the present purposes, include (but are not limited to) that Griffith proposed some of the non-GAAP sales practices,[35] that he drafted an internal memorandum acknowledging the reasons in part for the company's revenue shortfalls, affirmatively participated in accelerating sales revenue recognition, and made a material misstatement concerning the channel stuffing allegations. "Courts have held that allegations of omissions and misrepresentations regarding channel stuffing . . . are actionable." *Harvey M. Jasper Retirement Trust v. IVAX Corp.,* 920 F.Supp. 1260, 1266 (S.D.Fla.1995). Fur-

---

35. Although Griffith is not an accountant, his position at Sunbeam was such that it was at least "severely reckless" for him to propose and participate in such egregious GAAP violations, even if he did not definitively know that such accelerated sales and revenue recognition practices, for example, were problematic.

ther, while the Court clearly recognizes that "[t]he mere publication of inaccurate accounting figures, or a failure to follow GAAP, without more, does not establish scienter," *In re Software Toolworks Inc. Secs. Litig.*, 50 F.3d at 627, the situation here is *not* "without more." "The more serious the error, the less believable are defendants [*sic*] protests that they were completely unaware of [the corporation's] true financial status and the stronger is the inference that defendants [several executive officers] must have known about the discrepancy." *Rehm v. Eagle Fin. Corp.*, 954 F.Supp. 1246, 1256 (N.D.Ill.1997). The Court concludes that the SEC's complaint sufficiently sets forth a strong inference that Griffith acted with the requisite state of mind. * * *

NOTES

1. The Sunbeam Corp. chairman, Al Dunlap, earned the sobriquet "Chainsaw Al" for his cut and slash polices at another corporation, Scott Paper Co. Jerry W. Markham, A Financial History of the United States, From the Age of Derivatives into the New Millennium (1970–2001) 314 (2002). Dunlap was sanctioned by the SEC for his conduct at Sunbeam. He was banned permanently from serving as an officer in a public company and was fined $500,000 by the SEC in September of 2002. Michael Schroeder, Dunlap Settles Fraud Charges with the SEC, Wall St. J., Sep. 5, 2002, at C1.

2. Some less imaginative executives at other companies simply listed expenses as assets and over stated accounts receivable. *See e.g.*, SEC Sanctions FLIR Systems, Sues Former Officers for Inflating Earnings, 34 Sec. Reg. & L. Rep. No. 43, at 1806 (Nov. 4, 2002).

IN THE MATTER OF TRUMP HOTELS & CASINO RESORTS, INC., SECURITIES EXCHANGE ACT RELEASE NO. 45287

(Jan. 16, 2002).

The Securities and Exchange Commission ("Commission") deems it appropriate that cease-and-desist proceedings pursuant to Section 21C of the Securities Exchange Act of 1934 ("Exchange Act") against Respondent Trump Hotels & Casino Resorts, Inc. ("THCR" or "the Company") be, and hereby are, instituted.

In anticipation of the institution of these cease-and-desist proceedings, THCR has submitted an Offer of Settlement ("Offer"), which the Commission has determined to accept. Solely for the purpose of these proceedings and any other proceedings brought by or on behalf of the Commission, or in which the Commission is a party, and without admitting or denying the findings set forth herein, except that THCR admits the jurisdiction of the Commission over it and over the subject matter of these proceedings, THCR, by its Offer of Settlement, consents to the entry of this Order Instituting Cease-and-Desist Proceedings Pursuant to Section 21C of the Securities Exchange Act of 1934, Making Findings, and Issuing Cease-and-Desist Order ("Order").

On the basis of this Order and the Offer, the Commission makes the following findings:

SUMMARY

On October 25, 1999, THCR issued a press release announcing its results for the third quarter of 1999 (the "Earnings Release" or the "Release"). To announce those results, the Release used a net income figure that differed from net income calculated in conformity with generally accepted accounting principles ("GAAP"). Using that non-GAAP figure, the Release touted THCR's purportedly positive operating results for the quarter and stated that the Company had beaten analysts' earnings expectations.

The Earnings Release was materially misleading because it created the false and misleading impression that the Company had exceeded earnings expectations primarily through operational improvements, when in fact it had not. The Release expressly stated that the net income figure excluded a one-time charge. The statement that this one-time charge was excluded implied that no other significant one-time items were included in THCR's stated net income. Contrary to that implication, however, the stated net income included an undisclosed one-time gain of $17.2 million.

The misleading impression created by the reference to the single one-time charge and the undisclosed inclusion of the one-time gain was reinforced by the comparison of the stated earnings-per-share figure with analysts' earnings estimates and by statements in the Release that the Company had been successful in improving its operating performance. In fact, without the one-time gain, the Company's revenues and net income would have decreased from the prior year and the Company would have failed to meet analysts' expectations. The undisclosed one-time gain was thus material, because it represented the difference between positive trends in revenues and earnings and negative trends in revenues and earnings, and the difference between exceeding analysts' expectations and falling short of them.

By knowingly or recklessly issuing a materially misleading press release, THCR violated Section 10(b) of the Exchange Act and Rule 10b–5 thereunder.

SETTLING RESPONDENT

THCR is a publicly-held Delaware corporation. Through various subsidiaries, it owns and operates the Trump Taj Mahal Casino Resort (the "Taj Mahal") located in Atlantic City, New Jersey, as well as other casino resorts. THCR and its subsidiaries file reports, including their financial statements, on a consolidated basis. The Company's common stock is registered with the Commission pursuant to Section 12(b) of the Exchange Act and is traded on the New York Stock Exchange. The Company's executive offices are in New York City, and its business and financial operations are centered in Atlantic City.

The All Star Gain

In September 1999, Taj Mahal Associates ("Taj Associates"), a THCR subsidiary, took over the All Star Cafe located in the Taj Mahal Casino from Planet Hollywood International, Inc. On September 15, 1999, Taj Associates, Planet Hollywood, and the All Star Cafe, Inc. reached an agreement pursuant to which, effective September 24, 1999, the All Star Cafe's lease of space at the Taj Mahal would be terminated and All Star would be relieved of its rental obligations to THCR. In return, Taj Associates would receive the All Star Cafe's leasehold improvements, alterations, and certain personal property. Because the Taj Mahal was going to continue to use the space as a restaurant, the Company's outside auditor advised that Taj Associates should record as operating income the fair market value of the leasehold improvements, alterations and personal property reverting to Taj Associates. Based on this advice and on an independent appraisal, and in conformity with GAAP, Taj Associates (and, on a consolidated basis, THCR) recorded $17.2 million, the estimated fair market value of these assets, as a component of operating income for the third quarter of 1999.

The Earnings Release

On October 25, 1999, THCR issued the Earnings Release, publicly announcing its results for the third quarter of 1999. The Release, and the accompanying financial data, defined net income, or net profit, for the quarter as income before a one-time Trump World's Fair closing charge of $81.4 million. Using this "pro forma" net income,[36] the Release announced that the Company's quarterly earnings exceeded analyst's expectations, stating:

> Net income increased to $14.0 million, or $0.63 per share, before a one-time Trump World's Fair charge, compared to $5.3 million or $0.24 per share in 1998. THCR's earnings per share of $0.63 exceeded First Call estimates of $0.54.

The Release fostered the false and misleading impression that the positive results and improvement from third-quarter 1998 announced by

---

36. Although neither the text of the Release nor the accompanying financial data used the term "pro forma," the net income figure was pro forma in that it differed from net income calculated in conformity with GAAP by excluding the one-time charge. (Accordingly, the net income figure is hereafter referred to as "pro forma net income" and the earnings-per-share figure derived from the pro forma net income is referred to as "pro forma EPS.") The Release also used another pro forma figure, EBITDA, which it defined as earnings before interest, taxes, depreciation, amortization, corporate expenses and the $81.4 million Trump World's Fair closing charge.

the Company were primarily the result of operational improvements. In the Release, THCR's chief executive officer ("CEO") was quoted as saying:

Our focus in 1999 was three-fold: first, to increase our operating margins at each operating entity; second, to decrease our marketing costs; and third, to increase our cash sales from our non-casino operations. We have succeeded in achieving positive results in each of the three categories. The third quarter and nine month results for the company indicate that we have successfully instituted the programs that we focused on during 1999.

The Release failed to disclose, however, that the Company's pro forma net income for the quarter included the one-time gain resulting from the All Star Cafe lease termination. Accordingly, it failed to disclose the impact of that $17.2 million one-time gain upon the Company's $14 million pro forma net income or upon any of the other figures cited in the Release. Not only was there no mention of the one-time gain in the text of the Release, but the financial data included in the Release gave no indication of it, because, as discussed below, all revenue items were reflected in a single line item.

In fact, quarterly pro forma results that excluded the one-time gain as well as the one-time charge would have reflected a decline in revenues and net income and would have failed to meet analysts' expectations. The table below illustrates the impact of the one-time gain on the trends reported in the Earnings Release:

(In thousands)	3rd Q 1998	3rd Q 1999 Per Release	3rd Q 1999 Excluding One–Time Gain
Revenues	$397,387	$403,072	$385,872
Net Income	$5,312	$13,958	$3,048
EPS	$0.24	$0.63	$0.14

The Earnings Release was misleading. The Release used pro forma numbers that implied that all significant one-time items had been excluded, when they had not. The Release compared the pro forma EPS to analysts' expectations for quarterly EPS, which are generally and were in this case calculated on the basis of continuing business operations, thus reinforcing the false implication that all one-time items had been excluded. Moreover, the Release highlighted improvements in the Company's operations, i.e., the Company's increased operating margins, decreased marketing costs, and increased cash sales from non-casino operations.[37] By

---

37. Although the statements about increased operating margins, decreased marketing costs, and increased cash sales from non-casino operations were nominally true, in the context of the Earnings Release they were misleading, because, without the $17.2 million one-time gain, the increases in margins and cash from non-casino operations were negligible. Excluding the one-time gain, THCR's operating margins increased by 0.4% from third-quarter 1998 and its non-gaming

making these representations about THCR's quarterly performance, without disclosing the existence or impact of the one-time gain, the Release created the false and misleading impression that the Company's third-quarter results had improved over the results for third-quarter 1998 and had exceeded analysts' expectations primarily because management had been effective in improving the Company's operating performance.

Preparation of the Earnings Release

Historically, THCR announced its quarterly results in an earnings release that included financial data presented in a format similar to that of a Form 10–Q or Form 10–K financial statement. Among other things, financial data in these earlier earnings releases itemized revenues (on a Company-wide basis and also by property) by "Casino," "Rooms," "Food & Beverage," and "Other." In the third quarter of 1999, however, at the direction of the Company's CEO, and following similar models used by some of THCR's competitors, the Company adopted a less detailed, or "streamlined," format for the financial data contained in its earnings releases. Unlike the more detailed format used in earlier quarters, the new, streamlined format did not break out revenue items, but instead disclosed revenue as a single line item for each casino. Thus, the streamlined format did not break out "other revenue," the line-item classification in which the $17 million one-time All Star Cafe gain would have been reported under the old format.

The Earnings Release was prepared by the Company's corporate treasurer ("Treasurer") and its chief financial officer ("CFO"), under the supervision of the CEO, who approved the contents of the Release and made the decision to issue it. The contract of the CEO expired in June 2000 and was not renewed; he is no longer associated with the Company.

When the Release was issued, THCR knew that the estimated fair market value of the All Star Cafe lease termination would be recorded as part of operating income for third-quarter 1999 and that the estimated fair market value of the transaction was $17.2 million. The Company also knew that the Earnings Release used a pro forma net income figure that expressly excluded the $81.4 million one-time charge but did not disclose the existence or impact of the $17.2 million one-time gain.

Publication of the Earnings Release and the Aftermath

At 10:00 a.m. on October 25, 1999, the day the Earnings Release was issued, THCR held a conference call with analysts. During the call, the CEO told the analysts that increasing non-casino sales at the Taj Mahal had been a priority over the past year, and cited the Taj Mahal's third-quarter revenues as evidence that the emphasis had paid off. The CEO did

---

revenue increased by $1.8 million, or approximately 2.25%. The Company's marketing costs (as represented by promotional allowances) decreased by approximately $549,000, or approximately 1%.

not say that the Taj Mahal's non-casino revenue had increased primarily because of the All Star Cafe transaction.[38]

Immediately after the issuance of the Earnings Release and the conference call, analysts began asking questions about the details of the Company's increase in revenues. Within hours of the conference call, THCR's CFO spoke to several analysts who called with questions about specific aspects of Company's third-quarter results, and he provided them with information about the All Star Cafe gain. Over the next few days, additional analysts raised questions about the quarterly results, and the lack of detail in the Earnings Release. As a result, the Company's CFO and Treasurer attempted to speak to every analyst who had been on the conference call to explain the All Star Cafe transaction. In addition, the Company decided to accelerate the filing of its 10–Q for the quarter, which would contain a description of the one-time gain.

After learning about the one-time gain, certain analysts informed their clients of its impact. One analyst at Bear, Stearns & Co. notified his clients on October 27, 1999 that the increased third-quarter EPS resulted from the inclusion in revenue of the one-time All Star Cafe gain. On October 28th, analysts at Deutsche Banc Alex Brown issued a report on the effect of the one-time gain, which was disseminated to subscribers to Deutsche Banc research over the First Call Research Network. The Deutsche Banc analysts reported that Company management had disclosed that day that roughly $0.47 of the $0.63 third-quarter pro forma EPS the Company had previously reported "were not operating EPS but were actually the result of an accounting gain." The analysts determined that after backing out the one-time $17 million gain, THCR's net revenues would have fallen 2.7%, rather than rising 1.5% as they did when the one-time gain was included. The Deutsche Banc report also explained that, without the one-time gain, the Company experienced negative trends in Company-wide cash flows and margins, as well as in Taj Associates' revenues from operations, rather than the positive trends indicated by the Earnings Release. Adjusting for the impact of the one-time gain, the Deutsche Banc analysts lowered their 1999 EPS estimate from -$1.17, contained in their initial report on THCR's third-quarter results, to -$1.64.

On October 25th, the day the Earnings Release was issued, the price of the Company's stock rose 7.8% (from $4 to $4.3125), on volume approximately five times the previous day's volume. On October 28th, the day of the second Deutsche Banc analysts' report, the stock price fell approximately 6%, on volume approximately four times the previous day's volume.

On November 4, 1999, THCR filed its quarterly report on Form 10–Q. The 10–Q disclosed the existence and amount of the one-time gain in a footnote to the financial statements.

---

38. Without the $17.2 million one-time gain, non-casino sales at the Taj Mahal increased by only $300,000, or less than one percent, from third-quarter 1998 to third-quarter 1999.

THCR Violated Section 10(b) of the Exchange Act and Rule 10b–5 Thereunder

Section 10(b) of the Exchange Act and Rule 10b–5 thereunder make it unlawful, in connection with the purchase or sale of securities, "to make any untrue statement of a material fact or to omit to state a material fact necessary in order to make the statements made, in light of the circumstances under which they were made, not misleading."

To violate Section 10(b) of the Exchange Act and Rule 10b–5 thereunder, a misrepresentation or omission must be material, meaning that a reasonable investor would have considered the misrepresented or omitted fact important when deciding whether to buy, sell or hold the securities in question. *See Basic Inc. v. Levinson*, 485 U.S. 224, 231–32, 108 S.Ct. 978, 983 (1988). To constitute a violation, the material misstatement or omission must be made with scienter. *Aaron v. SEC*, 446 U.S. 680, 701–02, 100 S.Ct. 1945, 1958 (1980). Scienter can be shown by knowledge of the misrepresentation and, in the Second Circuit, by reckless disregard for the truth or falsity of a representation. *Sirota v. Solitron Devices, Inc.*, 673 F.2d 566, 575 (2d Cir.1982), cert. denied, 459 U.S. 838 (1982). Recklessness is defined as "conduct which is highly unreasonable and which represents an extreme departure from the standards of ordinary care . . . to the extent that the danger was either known to the defendant or so obvious that the defendant must have been aware of it." *Rolf v. Blyth, Eastman Dillon & Co.*, 570 F.2d 38, 47 (2d Cir.), cert. denied, 439 U.S. 1039 (1978); *see also SEC v. McNulty*, 137 F.3d 732, 741 (2d Cir.1998) (applying *Rolf* recklessness standard).

Thus, an issuer that knowingly or recklessly makes false or misleading statements in public announcements to investors, including press releases and other public statements, violates Section 10(b) and Rule 10b–5. *See SEC v. Koenig*, 469 F.2d 198 (2d Cir.1972); *SEC v. Great American Industries, Inc.*, 407 F.2d 453 (2d Cir.1967), cert. denied, 395 U.S. 920 (1969). *See also SEC v. Texas Gulf Sulphur Co.*, 401 F.2d 833, 861–63 (2d Cir.1968) (en banc), cert. denied, 394 U.S. 976 (1969). In *Public Statements by Corporate Representatives*, Securities Act Rel. No. 6504 (January 1984), the Commission reminded registrants that Section 10(b) and Rule 10b–5 apply to all public statements by persons speaking on behalf of a public company. The Commission also made clear that public announcements and press releases constitute public statements. *Id.*; *see also In re Carter–Wallace, Inc. Sec. Litig.*, 150 F.3d 153 (2d Cir.1998) (advertisements by issuer can be "in connection with" the purchase or sale of securities); *Sunbeam Corporation*, Exchange Act Rel. No. 44305 (May 15, 2001) (issuer violated Section 10(b) and Rule 10b–5 when it disseminated materially false and misleading press releases).

The omission from the Earnings Release of the information that THCR's pro forma net income included a $17.2 million one-time gain was misleading, for several reasons. Absent disclosure to the contrary, the use of pro forma numbers in an earnings release reasonably implies that any adjustments to GAAP numbers were made on a consistent basis and do not obscure a significant result or a trend reflected in the GAAP numbers. Here, THCR's express exclusion of a one-time charge reasonably implied that no other significant one-time item was included in the pro forma net income figure. This implication was reinforced by the Company's assertions in the Release that its quarterly results had exceeded analysts' EPS expectations, which are generally, and were in this case, a measure of expected operating performance. Moreover, the misleading impression created by the use of the pro forma net income figure without disclosing the inclusion of the one-time gain was reinforced by the statements in the Release about improvements in the Company's operating performance, specifically, improvements in operating margins, marketing costs, and sales from non-casino operations.

In the context of the express exclusion from pro forma net income of the one-time charge, the comparison to analysts' earnings expectations, and the statements about the Company's operational improvements, the omission of information about the one-time gain was material, because the undisclosed one-time gain represented the difference between positive trends in revenues and earnings and negative trends in revenues and earnings, and the difference between exceeding analysts' expectations and falling short of them. Thus, the omission of information about the one-time gain obscured a negative trend and a failure to meet analysts' expectations, and therefore could reasonably have led analysts and investors to draw false conclusions about THCR's quarterly results.

THCR, through the THCR officers involved in the drafting and issuance of the Earnings Release, knew that the estimated fair market value of the All Star Cafe lease termination was recorded as part of operating income for third-quarter 1999 and that the estimated fair market value of the transaction was $17.2 million. THCR knew that the Earnings Release used a pro forma net income figure that expressly excluded the one-time charge but did not disclose the existence or impact of the one-time gain. Accordingly, THCR knew or recklessly disregarded that the Earnings Release was materially misleading. * * *

In view of the foregoing, the Commission deems it appropriate to accept the Offer submitted by THCR and impose the cease-and-desist order specified in the Offer. In determining to accept the Offer, the Commission considered remedial acts promptly undertaken by THCR, and the limited duration of the violations.

Accordingly, IT IS ORDERED, pursuant to Section 21C of the Exchange Act, that THCR cease and desist from committing or causing any violation, and any future violation, of Section 10(b) of the Exchange Act and Rule 10b–5 thereunder.

By the Commission.

NOTES

1. *Pro forma* results may exclude certain events such as a one-time charge in order to allow investors to assess the underlying business unaffected by an extraordinary event. As set forth in the preceding case, the SEC is concerned where one-time bad events are excluded, while good events are included in the *pro forma* results.

2. The Sarbanes–Oxley Act of 2002, Pub. L. No. 107–204, 116 Stat. 745 directed the SEC to adopt rules that require reporting companies to reconcile pro forma results with GAAP. The SEC proposed and later adopted such a requirement. 17 C.F.R. § 244.100 *et seq. See* Michael Schroeder, SEC Orders New Disclosures on Company Earnings, Wall St. J., Jan. 16, 2003, at A2 (discussing adoption and purpose of the rule).

3. Consider the following case brought by the SEC against a company that sought to assure that analysts' projections were exceeded, thereby boosting the company's stock price:

> This matter involves the misstatement of Ashford.com's financial results, which allowed the company to beat analysts' pro forma earnings expectations. In March 2000, Ashford.com and two of its executives improperly deferred $1.5 million in expenses under a contract with Amazon.com, causing Ashford.com to materially understate its marketing expenses. The improper deferral resulted from Ashford.com's settlement of a dispute with Amazon.com using two separate documents (prepared at Ashford.com's request), one of which Ashford.com subsequently failed to disclose to its auditors.

> In September 2000, Ashford.com misstated its pro forma results by changing the classification of expenses on its income statement. For the quarters ended March 31 and June 30, 2000, Ashford.com had properly classified these expenses as marketing expenses. But in September 2000, without disclosing that it had made a change, Ashford.com classified the expenses as "depreciation and amortization," which inflated its pro forma results (which did not take depreciation and amortization into account).

> Additionally, during 2000, Ashford.com misclassified a material portion of the expenses arising under a second contract with Amazon.com. Under this agreement, Ashford.com issued new Ashford.com stock to Amazon.com in exchange for advertising placements and an agreement not to compete. Ashford.com, however, classified 100% of the expenses under this contract as "depreciation and amortization," materially understating its true marketing expenses each quarter and improving its pro forma results.

In the Matter of Ashford.com, Inc. Securities Exchange Act Release No. 46052 (June 10, 2002) (settled by consent).

IN THE MATTER OF DYNEGY INC., SECURITIES EXCHANGE ACT OF 1934 RELEASE NO. 46537

(September 24, 2002).

The Securities and Exchange Commission ("Commission") deems it appropriate to institute cease-and-desist proceedings pursuant to Section 8A of the Securities Act of 1933 (the "Securities Act") and Section 21C of the Securities Exchange Act of 1934 (the "Exchange Act") against Dynegy Inc. ("Dynegy" or "Respondent").

In anticipation of the institution of these proceedings, Dynegy has submitted an Offer of Settlement ("Offer") that the Commission has determined to accept. * * *

On the basis of this Order and Respondent's Offer, the Commission makes the following findings.

Dynegy is an Illinois corporation headquartered in Houston, Texas. Dynegy's shares are registered with the Commission under Section 12(b) of the Exchange Act and trade on the New York Stock Exchange under the symbol DYN. Dynegy produces and delivers energy, including natural gas, electricity, natural gas liquids and coal, to customers in North America, the United Kingdom and Continental Europe. In addition to energy production and delivery, energy trading is a key component of Dynegy's business.

Other Relevant Entitles

ABG Gas Supply LLC ("ABG Supply") is a Delaware limited liability company headquartered in New York, New York. It is a special-purpose entity sponsored by Dynegy. Dynegy has no direct or indirect ownership interest in ABG Supply, nor is Dynegy affiliated with any of ABG Supply's owners.

ABG Holding LLC ("ABG Holding") is a Delaware limited liability company. It is the immediate parent company of ABG Supply. ABG Holding is a special-purpose entity sponsored by a member of the syndicate of lenders involved in Alpha. Dynegy has no ownership interest in ABG Holding.

NGAI Funding LLC ("NGAI Funding") is a Delaware limited liability company headquartered in San Francisco, California. NGAI Funding is a special-purpose entity sponsored by Dynegy. Dynegy has no ownership interest in NGAI Funding.

DMT Supply LP ("DMT Supply") is a Delaware limited partnership and is a wholly-owned subsidiary of Dynegy.

This matter involves Dynegy's materially misleading (i) use of special-purpose entities ("SPEs") and (ii) pre-arranged, "wash" or "round-trip" energy transactions. First, in a series of transactions code-named "Project

Alpha" ("Alpha"), Dynegy used SPEs to report as cash flow from operations what was in actuality nothing more than a loan. Specifically, Dynegy implemented Alpha to enhance cash flow from operations by $300 million in 2001, and to achieve an Alpha-linked $79 million tax benefit. Dynegy failed to disclose the financing transactions underlying Alpha, and failed to otherwise clarify that the $300 million Alpha-related cash flow enhancing Dynegy's 2001 Statement of Cash Flows derived from financing, not operations. These omissions by Dynegy were materially misleading. Moreover, even when Dynegy admitted Alpha's existence following an April 3, 2002 newspaper article, Dynegy's then—now former—Chief Financial Officer ("CFO") claimed falsely that Alpha's primary purpose was to ensure a stable supply of gas, and Dynegy continued to assert that its obtaining a long-term gas supply was a principal purpose of Alpha. It was not until Dynegy filed its Form 8–K that Dynegy acknowledged that Alpha's principal purposes were to minimize the gap between Dynegy's reported net income and reported operating cash flow and to realize an associated tax benefit. Dynegy then announced that it would reverse Alpha's impact by restating its 2001 financial statements.

According to Dynegy, the restatement will include, at least, the following: 1) reclassification of the cash flow associated with Alpha as deriving from financing activities, rather than operations—reducing, as a consequence, Dynegy's cash flow from operations in 2001 by 37%; 2) consolidation in Dynegy's financial statements of a certain SPE with Dynegy; and 3) reduction of Dynegy's 2001 net income by 12%—the amount of the purported $79 million tax benefit. Alpha's impact on Dynegy's financial statements was especially significant because the Statement of Cash Flows has historically been considered immune from cosmetic tampering. * * *

Energy trading is a prominent part of Dynegy's business. Accounting rules require Dynegy and other energy traders to record today the value of contracts for the future delivery of gas, electricity and other commodities. Financial Accounting Standard 133 and EITF 98–10. Under this "mark-to-market" accounting, the total contract values are recorded as assets (or liabilities) on the balance sheet. Likewise, an increase (decrease) in a contract's value is recorded as unrealized gain (loss) and reflected as net income on the income statement, even though it generates no current cash flow.

By 2000, some energy analysts following Dynegy had noticed the widening gap between Dynegy's net income and operating cash flow. Some analysts viewed this widening gap as possible evidence that Dynegy's energy contracts were overvalued, and that Dynegy's liquidity and access to capital were potentially impaired.

In late 2000, Dynegy began exploring means of narrowing the gap between its net income and operating cash flow. After months of high-level discussion, meetings and document exchanges among Dynegy's independent auditor-consultant ("auditor-consultant") and other outside consultants, Alpha emerged as the chosen strategy for accomplishing Dynegy's purpose of narrowing that gap, while at the same time securing for Dynegy an Alpha-linked tax benefit. In its final form, Alpha embodied both a basis-shifting tax structure marketed to Dynegy by its auditor-consultant, and a "pre-paid" natural gas transaction. Internal Dynegy documents make clear that one of Alpha's principal purposes was to address the "disconnect ... between book and cash earnings" and to improve "quality of earnings"—*i.e.*, to create the appearance that Dynegy's operations were generating far more cash than they actually were. In 2001, Dynegy recorded $300 million in operating cash flow from Alpha. The $300 million was 37% of Dynegy's reported cash flow from operations in 2001. In addition, through Alpha, Dynegy recorded a tax savings in 2001 of $79 million, or 12% of its net income.

The lengths to which Dynegy went to reap Alpha's accounting and tax benefits are best conveyed by Alpha's inordinate complexity and its $35.8 million cost. Alpha can be conceptualized as a flow-through matrix involving two SPEs, three interconnected loans, a gas purchase agreement, hedging transactions, and a transfer of basis and intended tax benefit. The first Alpha "loan" was effected through a capital contribution made by an SPE, NGAI Funding, to a limited partnership, DMT Supply—a trading partnership established to conduct natural gas trades with another SPE, ABG Supply. NGAI Funding received in return for its capital contribution a 99%, 9–month term limited partnership interest in DMT Supply; Dynegy held a 1% general partnership and remainder interest in DMT Supply. NGAI Funding borrowed $310 million from a syndicate of lenders and, of that amount, contributed $307 million to DMT Supply's capitalization. By making the $307 million capital contribution to DMT Supply, NGAI Funding created $307 million in initial tax basis.

The second Alpha "loan" was from DMT Supply to Dynegy in the amount of $300 million and payable by Dynegy upon demand of DMT Supply. When NGAI Funding's interest in the partnership expired at the end of the first nine months of the Alpha transaction, its $307 million tax basis migrated to a wholly-owned subsidiary of Dynegy as the sole limited partner with the remainder interest in DMT Supply. Through this tax basis shift, Dynegy planned to save $79 million in taxes and increase its net income by an equal amount in 2001. Under this second loan arrangement, Dynegy is required to repay the "demand" loan to DMT Supply—noting however, that by that time, DMT Supply will be wholly owned by Dynegy.

In the gas purchase portion of Alpha, ABG Supply entered into a five-year trading contract (the "Gas Contract") with DMT Supply, commencing in April 2001. The purchase price of the gas under the Gas Contract was 86% variable and 14% fixed. Under the Gas Contract, DMT Supply bought natural gas from ABG Supply at below-market prices for the first nine months of the Gas Contract—for re-sale by DMT Supply on the open market at a profit. ABG Supply borrowed from various lenders (the third

Alpha loan) to fund the losses it would incur over these first nine months of the Gas Contract.

DMT Supply allocated 99% of the profits generated during the first nine months of the Gas Contract to NGAI Funding and distributed cash of approximately $300 million to NGAI Funding, thereby enabling NGAI Funding to repay a portion of its loan payable to the syndicate of lenders. After this initial nine-month period, NGAI Funding ceased to hold an interest in DMT Supply, and Dynegy became DMT Supply's sole owner. For the remaining 51 months of the Gas Contract, DMT Supply will pay ABG Supply above-market prices for gas, incurring losses. As owner of DMT Supply, Dynegy will incur the losses generated during the latter 51 months of the Gas Contract.

Dynegy's classification of Alpha's $300 million cash flow as operations-based was materially misleading: in essence, the $300 million transaction was a loan to Dynegy, not the result of Dynegy's operations. Moreover, Dynegy's classification of the $300 million as cash flow from operations was inconsistent with generally accepted accounting principles ("GAAP").

Alpha reduced by a significant amount the gap between Dynegy's net income and operational cash flow, thereby concealing from the investing public the true extent of this gap. Furthermore, Dynegy failed to disclose the true financing nature of the $300 million Alpha-related cash flow, which Dynegy could have done by disclosing the complex financing transactions underlying Alpha. Instead of making this disclosure, Dynegy made no reference to the underlying transactions in its second and third quarter 2001 Forms 10–Q or its 2001 Form 10–K, even though Alpha fell outside Dynegy's normal course of business. * * *

The substance of Alpha was a $300 million loan to Dynegy. That loan was funded indirectly through contractually assured profits on the resale of gas at below-market prices in the first nine months of the Gas Contract. Dynegy's promise to repay the loan was embedded in its promise to pay above-market prices for the remaining term of the Gas Contract. Consequently, under Financial Accounting Standard 95 ("FAS 95"), the cash flow associated with Alpha should have been classified as cash flow from financing activities—not operations. Where certain cash receipts and payments may have aspects of different types of cash flow, "the appropriate classification shall depend on the activity that is likely to be the *predominant* source of cash flow for the item." (FAS 95, P 24, emphasis added).

Dynegy's treatment of the Alpha cash flow as operating cash flow did not conform to GAAP for an additional reason: the equity investment in the SPE, ABG Supply, by its owners did not meet the requisite minimal exposure to the "substantive risks and rewards of ownership" during the entire term of the Gas Contract between ABG Supply and DMT Supply. Accounting guidelines state that independent owners of an SPE must make a substantive capital investment in the SPE, and that a prescribed minimum portion of the investment must demonstrate the substantive risks and rewards of ownership, during the entire term of the transaction. This *minimum* is 3% of the total capital invested in the SPE, but the appropriate level for any particular SPE depends on the prevailing facts and circumstances. Investments are not at risk if they are supported by a letter of credit or other form of guaranty on the initial investment or have a guaranteed return. Rather than maintain the requisite 3% risk exposure, the owners of ABG Supply avoided all commodity price risk using hedging transactions entered into by ABG Supply or ABG Holding with a member of the lending syndicate. As a result, ABG Supply should have been consolidated in Dynegy's financial statements, and the $300 million loan to ABG Supply—covering its initial losses under the Gas Contract—should have been reflected by Dynegy, on a consolidated basis, as cash flow from financing.

Dynegy's auditor-consultant instructed Dynegy that improper hedging of the risk to the equity investment in ABG Supply would require consolidation of ABG Supply with Dynegy, requiring Dynegy to classify the Alpha-related cash flow as financing. Dynegy knew, or was reckless in not knowing, that its presentation of its financial statements—without consolidating ABG Supply—was not in conformity with GAAP. * * *

Dynegy also overstated in public disclosures the amount of trading on its electronic trading platform, Dynegydirect. On November 15, 2001, Dynegy entered into two massive round-trip trades of electricity with another energy trading company on Dynegydirect. The round-trip trades, in which Dynegy simultaneously bought and sold power at the same price, terms and volume, resulted in neither profit nor loss to either transacting party. Dynegy conducted the trades on Dynegydirect, which Dynegy was developing with an eye toward its potential for rapid growth.

The two round-trip trades—the largest power trades, by volume, that Dynegy had ever conducted on Dynegydirect—required for their execution that Dynegy override the platform's normal volume limits. The trades involved the simultaneous purchase and sale of 5000 megawatts of on-peak electricity at $34/mwh for calendar year 2002, and the simultaneous purchase and sale of 15,000 megawatts of on-peak electricity at $25.50 for December 2001 (a combined total of over 25 million megawatt hours of electricity).

* * * In a January 23, 2002 press release, Dynegy reported on Dynegydirect, for the fourth quarter of 2001, $13 billion in notional trading value (absolute value of all trading traffic), of which $1.7 billion was attributable to the round-trip trades. Later, in an April 30, 2002 press release, Dynegy reported 89.7 million megawatt hours of electricity traded in the first quarter of 2002, of which approximately five million megawatt hours were the product of round-trip trades. In that same press release, Dynegy improperly reported $236 million in revenue (and $236 million in offsetting costs) from the round-trip trades.[39] Dynegy's disclosures of

---

39. Before, during and after both the January 2002 and April 2002 press releases, Dynegy was conducting an ongoing offering of its common stock, in connection with its employee stock option

results attributable to the round-trip transactions conveyed a false picture of Dynegy's financial status and business activity. * * *

Dynegy violated the antifraud provisions of the Securities Act and the Exchange Act. As demonstrated in this Order's findings, Alpha was an undisclosed, highly complex transaction that incorrectly reported Dynegy's true cash position and dramatically overstated Dynegy's cash flow from operations—in violation of Sections 17(a)(1), 17(a)(2) and 17(a)(3) of the Securities Act and Section 10(b) of the Exchange Act and Rule 10b–5 thereunder. In addition, as a result of inadequate internal controls, Dynegy negligently disclosed to the public material information concerning the results of the round-trip trades, specifically, volumes and revenues, in violation of Sections 17(a)(2) and 17(a)(3) of the Securities Act. As a consequence of Alpha's impact on Dynegy's financial statements, Dynegy's failure to disclose the financing transactions underlying Alpha, and the negligent disclosure of the results of the round-trip trades, Dynegy materially misrepresented its financial performance. There is a substantial likelihood that these false representations and associated omissions would have assumed actual significance in the investment deliberations of a reasonable investor by casting doubt on Dynegy's financial position, credit-worthiness and management team. Dynegy's false accounting treatment and inadequate disclosure of Alpha would have violated the antifraud provisions, even if Alpha had technically conformed to GAAP—which it did not. As the Fourth Circuit pointed out in *Malone v. Microdyne Corp.:*

> The Financial Accounting Standards of GAAP and the antifraud rules promulgated under § 10(b) of the 1934 Act serve similar purposes, and courts have often treated violations of the former as indicative that the latter were also violated. The prohibitions contained in GAAP and in Rule 10b–5, however, are not perfectly coextensive. In some circumstances, courts have found defendants liable for securities fraud under Rule 10b–5 despite having complied with GAAP.

26 F.3d 471, 478 (4th Cir.1994) (citations omitted).

Consistent with *Malone,* a public company cannot wield technical conformity with GAAP as a shield against substantiated charges that the underlying transaction materially misled investors. Because Dynegy failed to disclose Alpha, and the financing nature of the $300 million Alpha-related cash flow Dynegy presented in its 2001 Statement of Cash Flows, Dynegy violated the antifraud provisions—notwithstanding any argument that Alpha's accounting treatment conformed to GAAP. In fact, Alpha's accounting treatment failed to conform to GAAP in two important respects. First, pursuant to FAS 95, the predominant characteristic of the

---

plans, pursuant to a Form S–8 registration statement filed with the Commission. The April 30 press release included text, which contained the round-trip *volume* information, and a financial attachment, which included both the round-trip *volume* information and the round-trip *revenue* information. Dynegy posted the complete press release (text and attachment) on its website where it was readily accessible to the general public. Dynegy also e-mailed the textual portion of the April 30 press release to all of its employees, including participants in Dynegy's stock option plans.

cash flow associated with Alpha was financing, not operations. Alpha was essentially a $300 million loan, disguised as operating cash flow. Second, certain representatives of Dynegy knew that the equity investors did not maintain the requisite 3% minimum investment at risk in the SPE. The improper hedging rendered Dynegy's accounting treatment of Alpha inconsistent with GAAP.

Section 13(a) of the Exchange Act requires issuers such as Dynegy to file periodic reports with the Commission containing such information as the Commission prescribes by rule. Exchange Act Rule 13a–1 requires issuers to file annual reports, and Exchange Act Rule 13a–13 requires issuers to file quarterly reports. Under Exchange Act Rule 12b–20, the reports must contain, in addition to disclosures expressly required by statute and rules, such other information as is necessary to ensure that the statements made are not, under the circumstances, materially misleading. The obligation to file reports includes the requirement that the reports be true and correct. *United States v. Bilzerian*, 926 F.2d 1285, 1298 (2d Cir.), *cert. denied*, 502 U.S. 813 (1991). The reporting provisions are violated if false and misleading reports are filed. *SEC v. Falstaff Brewing Corp.*, 629 F.2d 62, 67 (D.C.Cir.1980). *Scienter* is not an element of a Section 13(a) violation. *SEC v. Savoy Indus., Inc.*, 587 F.2d 1149, 1167 (D.C.Cir.1978).

Dynegy violated these provisions by filing second and third quarter 2001 Forms 10–Q and a 2001 Form 10–K that were false and misleading. Dynegy's false accounting treatment of Alpha, and the absence of any clarifying disclosure of Alpha's true purpose and effect, caused the violations. Dynegy should have treated the cash flow from Alpha as a loan and ABG Supply should have been consolidated in Dynegy's financial statements, which would have had numerous material effects on Dynegy's financial statements. If consolidated, ABG Supply's $300 million borrowing to fund the losses during the first nine months of the Gas Contract would have been reflected as cash flow from financing activities, rather than operations, on Dynegy's Statement of Cash Flow; the liability associated with Alpha would have appeared as debt on Dynegy's Balance Sheet, rather than risk-management liability; and the tax benefit would not have been available to Dynegy, meaning that Dynegy's net income would have been reduced by $79 million on Dynegy's Income Statement.

Section 13(b)(2)(A) of the Exchange Act requires all issuers to make and keep books, records, and accounts that, in reasonable detail, accurately and fairly reflect their transactions and dispositions of their assets. *Scienter* and materiality are not elements of primary violations of this provision. *SEC v. World–Wide Coin Inv., Ltd.*, 567 F.Supp. 724, 749–50 (N.D.Ga.1983). Dynegy, through its treatment of Alpha and the round-trip energy trades, violated Section 13(b)(2)(A) by failing to keep books, records and accounts that accurately and fairly reflected its assets and financial results.

Section 13(b)(2)(B) of the Exchange Act requires issuers to devise and maintain an adequate system of internal accounting controls. *Scienter* and materiality are not elements of a violation of this provision. *World–Wide Coin,* 567 F. Supp. at 749–50. Dynegy violated Section 13(b)(2)(B) by failing to devise and maintain a system of internal controls sufficient to provide reasonable assurances that structured transactions involving special purpose entities are recorded as necessary to permit preparation of financial statements in conformity with GAAP. Dynegy violated Section 13(b)(2)(B) for the additional reason that it failed to ensure against the inclusion of results from round-trip trades in Dynegy's computation and public disclosure of its trading volume and trading revenues. Dynegy's reporting of revenue derived from these transactions was inconsistent with GAAP. (Statement of Financial Accounting Concepts No. 5; *see also* Staff Accounting Bulletin 101).

Exchange Act Rule 13b2–1 (promulgated under Section 13(b)(2) of the Exchange Act) prohibits any person from falsifying or causing to be falsified any accounting books and records of reporting public companies. *Scienter* is not an element of a violation of Rule 13b2–1. *SEC v. McNulty,* 137 F.3d 732 (2d Cir.1998). Dynegy's falsification of its books in connection with Alpha effectively disguised a loan as operating cash flow. Dynegy's failure to maintain adequate controls caused Dynegy to falsify its books in connection with the round-trip trades, effectively inflating Dynegy's trading volume and revenues. Both falsifications were violations of Rule 13b2–1. * * *

In view of the foregoing, the Commission deems it appropriate to impose the sanctions agreed to in the Offer.[40]

Accordingly, IT IS HEREBY ORDERED, pursuant to Section 8A of the Securities Act and Section 21C of the Exchange Act, that Respondent Dynegy cease and desist from committing or causing any violation and any future violation of Section 17(a) of the Securities Act, and Sections 10(b), 13(a) and 13(b)(2) of the Exchange Act and Rules 10b–5, 12b–20, 13a–1, 13a–13 and 13b2–1 thereunder; and IT IS HEREBY FURTHER ORDERED that Dynegy * * * shall restate its financial statements for its fiscal year 2001 in a manner that conforms to Generally Accepted Accounting Principles, which shall include the consolidation of ABG Gas Supply LLP in Dynegy's financial statements.

By the Commission.

NOTES

1. The "inordinate complexity" of the Dynegy arrangements make them difficult to understand. In essence, however, they were designed to cover the

---

40. Dynegy has agreed to pay a $3 million civil penalty in connection with a parallel civil action.

divergence in the company's accounts between accrual accounting system and cash flow analysis. Why was there such a gap? Is there any means that you can suggest to prevent such arrangements? Cash-in income and "cash-out" expenses become meaningless in measuring financial performance if borrowings are included in cash income, but should not debt payments be included in cash out calculations?

2.   Reliant Resources Inc. announced in July of 2002 that it was restating its earning for a three-year period as a result of an artificial inflation of its revenues. That inflation was the result of so-called "round trip" trades in electricity that bought and sold at the same quantity and price in order to increase the firm's trading volumes and increase the perception that the firm was a major energy trader. The trades also increased gross revenues by almost $8 billion. In the Matter of Reliant Resources, Securities Exchange Act Release No. 47828 (S.E.C. May 12, 2003) Although offset by expenses in the same amount, the increased revenues were claimed to give the appearance of actual business growth, a factor viewed favorably by analysts even if not generating profits. Should those analysts be more perceptive?

3.   The SEC's Dynegy opinion refers to the court's decision in *Malone v. Microdyne* Corp., 26 F.3d 471 (4th Cir.1994). There, the court noted:

> Microdyne issued a series of misleading statements throughout the spring and summer before finally correcting the public record in October. The market relied upon the misleading statements and thereby kept Microdyne's stock price artificially inflated, much to the detriment of the stock's purchasers.

> At trial the plaintiffs called to the stand three former Microdyne employees—the vice president of sales, the national sales manager for distribution, and a regional sales manager—to testify regarding the rights of return. They testified that the number of NAS units that management demanded be shipped was not based on what the salespeople thought could be sold, but rather on commitments that Microdyne Chairman and President Cunningham had made to the financial community. Microdyne's Vice President of Sales, who was responsible for selling NAS and NACS to distributors, testified that in order to sell the products, distributors were told, "If they don't sell, then you could return the product," that this return privilege was not "normal," that the normal limited right of return was part of a stock-rotation plan in which the distributor had to give a "corresponding purchase order to buy another product," and that, by contrast, "in the case of the NAS/NACS, we allowed them to return product without any replacement purchase order. They could just return the product."

> The national sales manager testified that Microdyne never tried "to make a distributor pay for NAS/NACS products that he wished to return," and that "full return privileges" were extended in writing to one distributor and verbally to other distributors. The regional sales manager testified that Microdyne's distributors "would take the [NAS/NACS] product down with the understanding that they could return the product at any time they wanted without having to issue an offsetting purchase

order," and that those distributors did in fact return NAS/NACS products.

At trial, the plaintiffs also called Harris Devor, a C.P.A., as an expert in accounting. Prior to testifying, Devor had examined each of the allegedly false or misleading statements and had attended the depositions of Microdyne's accountants. He also had reviewed deposition transcripts, pleadings, and briefs in the case, as well as invoice and return authorizations issued by Microdyne.

Devor testified that, in his expert opinion, Microdyne had failed to comply with Financial Accounting Standard No. 48 (FAS 48) of the Generally Accepted Accounting Principles (GAAP), which Microdyne concedes it was required to follow. FAS 48 establishes six conditions that must be met before a company can recognize revenue when it sells its product but gives the buyer a right to return the product. One of the six conditions is that "[t]he amount of future returns can be reasonably estimated." Statement of Financial Accounting Standards No. 48, ¶ 6 (Fin. Accounting Standards Bd.1981) (footnote omitted). FAS 48 specifies several factors that may impair a company's ability to make a reasonable estimate of the amount of future returns, including the "[a]bsence of historical experience with similar types of sales of similar products." *Id.* ¶ 8. If the company cannot reasonably estimate the amount of future returns at the time of sale, it should not recognize any sales revenue from the transaction until either (1) the return privilege has substantially expired, or (2) the company has become capable of making a reasonable estimate of future returns, whichever occurs first. When sales revenues do become properly recognizable, they must be reduced to reflect actual past returns and estimated future returns, *e.g.*, by establishing a "reserve" for returned merchandise.

Devor testified that, in his expert opinion, Microdyne violated FAS 48 repeatedly, beginning with the issuance of its second-quarter press release on April 23 and continuing up until the issuance of its corrective press release on October 6, 1992. Devor explained that, in the spring of 1992, Microdyne had no experience with NAS or any similar products, and thus it was incapable of reasonably estimating the amount of future returns of NAS. Therefore, in keeping with FAS 48, Microdyne's April and May statements should not have recognized *any* of the $2.9 million in NAS-related, second-quarter revenue for which distributors had a right of return. Including the entire $2.9 million in Microdyne's reported second-quarter revenues made those statements untrue.

Devor testified that Microdyne's July and August statements were also improper because they indicated no "reserve" reflecting Microdyne's best estimate for the total amount of NAS returns (approximately $1.2 million worth, according to the company's internal figures in July). Devor further testified that Microdyne's failure to record the NAS transactions properly left the investing public with the impression that Microdyne's second-quarter income (before taxes) had increased about $600,000 from the same quarter in the prior year, when in fact it had *decreased* about $600,000. Therefore, Devor concluded, the omissions of any reference to the $1.2 million in product returns made Microdyne's statements not only misleading, but misleading in a material way.

4. As noted in the Dynegy case, the Securities and Exchange Act of 1934, 15 U.S.C. § 78m(b)(2)(B) requires that:

> Every issuer which has a class of securities registered pursuant to section 78l of this title and every issuer which is required to file reports pursuant to section 78o(d) of this title shall—* * *

>> (B) devise and maintain a system of internal accounting controls sufficient to provide reasonable assurances that—

>>> (i) transactions are executed in accordance with management's general or specific authorization;

>>> (ii) transactions are recorded as necessary (I) to permit preparation of financial statements in conformity with generally accepted accounting principles or any other criteria applicable to such statements, and (II) to maintain accountability for assets;

>>> (iii) access to assets is permitted only in accordance with management's general or specific authorization; and

>>> (iv) the recorded accountability for assets is compared with the existing assets at reasonable intervals and appropriate action is taken with respect to any differences; * * *

Does this provision provide a basis for an SEC action anytime there is a breakdown in accounting procedures? Are shareholders damaged when this occurs? Who should pay such damages? What is the auditor's responsibility in detecting such breakdowns?

5. The mark-to-market accounting required by Financial Accounting Standard 133 described in the Dynegy case led the Enron Corp. to engage in aggressive accounting ploys to move volatile assets off its books. Enron also used special purpose entities ("SPEs") to reduce debt on its balance sheet, enhancing the company's credit rating and boosting its stock price. Enron's stock traded as high as $90, but after it announced a restatement of its earnings (taking an initial $544 million after tax charge and reducing shareholders' equity by $1.2 billion and later amounts of a similar magnitude) the stock dropped below $1 just before the company declared bankruptcy. Enron's SPEs' were called such things as "Raptors," "Chewco" and "JEDI." They operated as limited partnerships. Accounting rules allowed an entity that was only three percent owned by outside parties to be removed from the books of a company owning 97 percent. Chewco failed to meet this requirement, falling short by about one percent or $3 million. *See generally* Report of Investigation by the Special Investigative Committee of the Board of Directors of Enron Corp. (Feb. 1, 2002) (describing accounting short cuts taken by Enron); Loren Fox, Enron The Rise and Fall (2003) (describing Enron's business and accounting practices).

6. Another financial instrument used by Enron was something called monthly income preferred shares ("MIPS"). These instruments made periodic payments to investors that were treated as interest payments for income tax purposes but were used for accounting purposes as equity in order to reduce

the amount of leverage on the company's balance sheet. In other words, it was both a stock and a loan at the same time. John D. McKinnon & Greg Hitt, Double Play, How Treasury Lost a Battle to Quash a Dubious Security, Wall St. J., Feb. 4, 2002, at A1. Enron also used synthetic leases as substitutes for loans, allowing those obligations to be kept off the balance sheet. Loren Fox, Enron The Rise and Fall, 120 (2003).

7. Another device used were so-called prepaid forward contracts that were later claimed to be simply disguised loans made to Enron by J.P. Morgan–Chase. Several surety firms refused to pay on the defaults on those contracts when they learned that the delivery obligations from Enron were simply circular in nature and did not involve delivery to a bona fide third party. See Chapter 10.

SECTION 5.   SARBANES–OXLEY ACT OF 2002: A FINANCIAL MORAL PANIC

Congress responded to the Enron and other accounting scandals described in Chapter 1 with the Sarbanes–Oxley Act of 2002. This legislation created a new public regulatory organization (the "Public Company Accounting Oversight Board") ("PCAOB" or to some "peekaboo") that took control of auditing standards away from the accounting profession. Accountants certifying the financial standards of public companies are now required to register with the board, and those firms must conform to its standards. Accountants were also prohibited from offering certain consulting services to their audit clients. Pub. L. No. 107–204, 116 Stat. 745 (2002).

To further assure the integrity of the audit process, the Sarbanes–Oxley Act mandates that the corporate audit committees of public companies be composed entirely of outside directors. A question raised by this change is how will it be possible for those persons to understand the audit process of the corporation if they are not working full time for the company? If they do work full time, will that status convert them into insiders?

The FASB continues its role of setting accounting standards (GAAP). See Securities Exchange Act Release No. 47743 (April 25, 2003) (SEC rules that FASB will continue to establish financial accounting standards that will be recognized as GAAP under the federal securities laws).

A particularly contentious issue that arose after the Enron bankruptcy was the accounting treatment for options given to corporate executives. This compensation was diluting the holdings of other shareholders. These option grants were not being expensed, causing much criticism because many companies were paying executives large sums without accounting recognition of this income as an expense to the corporation.

Options as executive compensation had become popular for many reasons. Congress decided that tax penalties should be imposed on salary payments in excess of $1 million. *See* Omnibus Revenue Reconciliation Bill of 1993, H.R. 2264, 103d Cong., 1st Sess. (1993) (prohibiting a corporation from deducting more than $1 million for an executive's salary without, among other things, obtaining shareholder approval, a vote that a highly paid executive would not want to occur). This made options attractive to high roller executives because there was no cap, and options can have tax advantages. Options were also attractive to start up companies and their employees as a way of attracting highly motivated employees who would be well compensated in a market bubble such as that of the 1990s. Some 80 percent of executive compensation was paid in stock options as the new century began. Arthur Levitt, Take On the Street, What Wall Street and Corporate America Don't Want You to Know, What You Can Do to Fight Back 111 (2002).

The use of options also satisfied a demand by corporate critics that executives be made more accountable to shareholders by tying compensation to the share price. In fact, the opposite occurred. Shareholders, at least most small investors, have a long-range investment goal. They buy and hold. A senior executive is seeking to receive as much cash as possible in as short a time as possible for retirement and to gratify a life-style they demand from their business success.[41] These executives have a tremendous incentive to boost their stock on a short-term basis so that they can realize cash from their options. In order to do that, earnings must continually increase earnings, giving rise to imaginative schemes to manage or manipulate earnings in order to pump up stock prices for purposes of their option exercises. Further, as noted, the issuance of options dilutes the holdings of the long-term investors, a matter that a liquidating executive will care little about.

The FASB in the early 1990s proposed to require corporations to treat option grants as an expense on the income statement and as a charge against earnings. This met widespread opposition, not only from overpaid executives, but also employees and participants in the numerous startup companies that were seeking to exploit the Internet. After this became a controversial political football in Congress, the FASB backed off the proposal. The issue was raised anew with the Enron debacle. Although it is not clear how option grants caused that company's demise (they were not a cash drain), Enron executives did receive $1.2 billion in options during the two years preceding its bankruptcy. After, the collapse of Enron, some companies, including General Electric and Coca–Cola, announced that they would expense options in their future financial reports.

---

41. As an example of the incredible size of option payouts, Michael Eisner at Walt Disney Co. exercised option in 2000 worth some $60 million and was holding additional options valued at $266 million. Thomas L. Hazen & Jerry W. Markham, Corporations and Other Business Organizations 315–316 (Unabridged 2003). Larry Ellison, the head of Oracle Corp., made $706 million on his options. Michael Dell of Dell Computer made $233 million, Sanford Weill at Citigroup made $220 million and Thomas Siebel of Siebel Systems made $174 million from option grants. Matt Murray, Options Frenzy: What Went Wrong, Wall St. J., Dec. 17, 2002, at B1.

FASB thereafter decided to expense options. Placing a value on the options, however, remains a contentious issue, some suggesting using the Black–Scholes economic model for options pricing. See chapter 11. Arthur Levitt, Take On the Street, What Wall Street and Corporate America Don't Want You to Know, What You Can Do to Fight Back 108 (2002). For criticism of such an approach see Robert Bartley, The Options–Accounting Sideshow, Wall St. J., July 29, 2002, at A15. In Seinfeld v. Bartz, 322 F.3d 693 (9th Cir.2003), the court dismissed claims that a proxy statement was misleading because it did not disclose the value of options granted to executives under the Black–Scholes model.

A study at the University of Michigan concluded that the requirement that options be expensed had not reduced the number of firms granting options to executives. In fact, option grants were up some 24 percent.

Option problems continued. Executives at a large number of public companies were caught up in scandals involving the backdating of their option grants. Backdating options was a more simple and effective way of increasing compensation. These practices were uncovered by a study by the Center for Financial Research and Analysis. Another study estimated that some 2,000 companies had been engaged in this practice. Apparently, the intense scrutiny of accounting statements was preventing companies from manipulating their earnings to boost stock prices and profits from option grants, so they resorted to back dating. The scandal widened with the discovery that "spring loaded" options were being granted to executives just in advance of the announcement of good news by the company. Another popular practice is called "bullet dodging," which involves granting options right after some unexpected event has driven down stock prices. The *Wall Street Journal* also reported that some ninety public companies made large options grants to their executives just after the terrorist attacks on 9/11. As a result of that attack, stock prices were reduced by the greatest percentage since the outbreak of World War II. However, the market recovered and generated huge profits to those executives. Of course, that might be an object lesson for those who doubt the strength or resilience of the U.S. stock market.

Notes

1. The Dutch East India Company at the beginning of the seventeenth century was required to sell all of its assets and distribute them to shareholders every ten years as a way of assuring management honesty. Jonathan B. Baskin & Paul J. Miranti, Jr., A History of Corporate Finance 97 (1997) (describing this arrangement). Do you think such an approach would assure accurate accounting? Is there a practical alternative, such as having "independent" appraisers periodically value the company?

2. The SEC was directed by Section 404 of the Sarbanes–Oxley Act to adopt rules requiring management to implement internal controls for finan-

cial reporting and to assess the effectiveness of those controls annually. This proved to be an extremely expensive exercise and caused much complaint. The results were also disheartening. Some 200 companies reported flaws in their internal financial controls. Although Sarbanes–Oxley imposed massive costs on public companies, it does not appear to have increased the reliability of audits. "Almost 10% of U.S. public companies announced 1,420 financial restatements in 2006," setting a new record. Robert C. Pozen, "The SEC's Fuzzy Math," Wall St. J., March 23, 2007, at A11.

SECTION 6.   PUBLIC COMPANY ACCOUNTING OVERSIGHT BOARD

The PCAOB's legal structure as a corporation with regulatory powers has raised questions about its authority.

DONNA M. NAGY
IS THE PCAOB A "HEAVILY CONTROLLED COMPONENT" OF THE SEC?: AN ESSENTIAL QUESTION IN THE CONSTITUTIONAL CONTROVERSY

71 U. Pitt. L. Rev. 361 (2010).

The U.S. Supreme Court recently heard oral arguments in Free Enterprise Fund v. Public Company Accounting Oversight Board, described as "the most important separation-of-powers case regarding the President's appointment and removal powers to reach the courts in the last 20 years." Established by Congress as the cornerstone of the Sarbanes–Oxley Act of 2002 ("Sarbanes–Oxley" or the "Act"), the Public Company Accounting Oversight Board (the "PCAOB" or the "Board") was structured as "a strong, independent board to oversee the conduct of the auditors of public companies." Its principal mission was to prevent the type of auditing failures that contributed to the scandals at Enron, WorldCom, and numerous other public companies in the period leading up to the passage of the Act.

The PCAOB's unique design as a private-sector corporation with vast regulatory powers sparked controversy from the start. ... [T]he controversy now centers on whether the PCAOB's structure complies with the Appointments Clause and the doctrine of separation of powers. That structure has been called into question because the five members who head the PCAOB are neither appointed nor removable by the President. Instead, PCAOB members are appointed for fixed, five-year terms by the Securities and Exchange Commission (the "SEC" or "Commission"), an independent regulatory agency that is itself insulated from direct presidential control. Moreover, PCAOB members are removable only by the SEC and only for willful or unjustifiable transgressions.* * *

In establishing the PCAOB "to oversee the audit of public companies," Congress recognized that it was creating a "strange kind of entity."

As Senator Phil Gramm explained: "We want it to be private, but we want it to have governmental powers. We have tried to structure it in ways to try to accommodate this."

There is no dispute that Sarbanes–Oxley, enacted in the wake of the massive accounting and corporate governance scandals at Enron, World-Com, and other public companies, vested the PCAOB with broad governmental powers and responsibilities. These powers and responsibilities encompass substantial enforcement, rulemaking, and adjudicative functions, and include the authority to register accounting firms that audit public companies; enact rules setting standards for auditing, quality control, ethics, and independence; inspect on a yearly basis the nation's largest accounting firms and inspect other firms at least once every three years; investigate accounting firms and their associated persons for possible violations of PCAOB rules or the federal securities laws; and impose discipline for established violations through a range of sanctions including censures, temporary suspensions, permanent bars, and substantial monetary fines. Willful violations of PCAOB rules may be prosecuted by the DOJ as federal crimes. In addition, the Act authorizes the PCAOB to set its own budget, and to fund that budget through the imposition of an "accounting support fee" levied on public companies.* * *

The legislative history of Sarbanes–Oxley reinforces the text's design of a board that is substantively independent, not only from the accounting industry that it regulates, but also from the SEC and elected officials to whom the SEC is answerable. The Senate Report explains that the Act "creates a strong, independent board to oversee the conduct of the auditors of public companies" and emphasizes the Board's "plenary" rulemaking, and its "broad authority to investigate" possible violations of PCAOB rules, the Act, or the federal securities laws. The congressional record is also replete with references to the PCAOB as a "strong, independent ... board with significant authority," and with respect to PCAOB rulemaking, states specifically that "[t]he board would possess plenary authority to establish or adopt auditing, quality control, ethics, and independence standards for the auditing of public companies." The record further reflects at least one Senator's view of the Board as an entity with "massive power, unchecked power, by design."

Senator Phil Gramm's reference to the PCAOB's "massive power, unchecked power" merits more than a mere snippet. Less than three weeks before the passage of the Act, Senator Gramm shared with his colleagues the view that:

> Anybody who thinks this board is just going to slap around a few accountants does not understand this bill. This board is going to have massive power, unchecked power, by design. I would have to say the board that Senator Enzi and I set up in our bill has massive unchecked power as well. I mean, that is the nature of what we are trying to do here. I am not criticizing Senator Sarbanes. I am just reminding people that there are two edges of this sword. We are

setting up a board with massive power that is going to make decisions that affect all accountants and everybody they work for, which directly or indirectly is every breathing person in the country. They are going to have massive unchecked powers.

* * *

The legislative record also facilitates our understanding of why Congress was particularly concerned about the PCAOB's ability to exercise independent judgment in connection with auditor oversight: As the D.C. Circuit recognized and acknowledged, "the level of Presidential control over the Board reflects Congress's intention to insulate the Board from partisan forces." In particular, Congress sought to avert the "extraordinary amount of political pressure" previously directed at the SEC's Commissioners, when the SEC had attempted during the 2000 election year to promulgate stricter requirements for auditor independence. As Senator Paul Sarbanes recounted during a hearing, several witnesses had advised Congress that "if we can structure the board well enough, it might actually have more independence from political influence than the SEC would have." And Senator Debbie Stabenow raised her own concern "about finding a better way to insulate the establishment of accounting standards from politics and pressure, both from the industry, and frankly, from Congress."

Congress's intention to insulate the PCAOB from political influence and partisan forces would be thwarted if the PCAOB could, in the words of the D.C. Circuit, be "micromanag[ed]" by the SEC. Recognizing that the past is prologue, Congress feared that its own members and the President might be tempted to persuade the SEC to adopt positions favored by their powerful constituents and contributors. Congress also may have surmised that the SEC, headed by a Chairman who serves at the pleasure of the President, and composed (at the time) of a majority of members from the President's political party, would be more inclined to favor the President's policy preferences. Accordingly, fueled with bipartisan spirit in the wake of the collapses of Enron and WorldCom, Congress designed the PCAOB to be doubly insulated from political and partisan pressure.

Public company accounting oversight could have been placed in a new unit within the SEC-and that new unit could have been self-funded through fees paid by public companies. But a new unit within the SEC (even a self-funded unit) would have been subject to the SEC's plenary control, and thus the new unit would have more susceptible to indirect control by the President and Congress. Although subject to SEC oversight and enforcement authority, Board members with fixed five-year terms and strict restrictions on removal were far more likely to bring their independent judgment to bear on the critical issues that faced the auditing industry in the wake of the scandals. The PCAOB's independence from the SEC was not an end in itself, but rather a means to the end of depoliticizing the PCAOB.

In its 5–4 ruling, the Supreme Court mandated a small, technical change to the Sarbanes–Oxley Act by giving the Securities and Exchange Commission the power to remove any member of the Accounting Oversight Board 'at will'. Free Enterprise Fund v. PCAOB, ___ U.S. ___, 130 S.Ct. 3138, 177 L.Ed.2d 706, 22 Fla. L. Weekly Fed. S 685 (2010). Otherwise, the Court left the PCAOB intact.

SECTION 7. INTERNATIONAL ACCOUNTING STANDARDS

The SEC, even before Enron, had been concerned with accounting schemes that were designed to enhance a company's revenues and boost its stock price. One such practice, as seen in the Sunbeam case, *supra*, involved the use of so-called "cookie jar reserves" that were being used by companies to manage their earnings. Cookie jar reserves are inflated loss reserves that can be reduced in the future to increase earnings. Arthur Levitt, Take On the Street: What Wall Street and Corporate America Don't Want You to Know, What You Can Do to Fight Back 163 (2002).

The use of hidden reserves to manage earnings was actually an accepted practice in many other countries. The SEC has for years been on a crusade against the acceptance of international accounting standards that allow the use of such secret reserves, which excluded many foreign companies from United States markets, impeding cross-border capital flows. The SEC required foreign firms seeking access to American markets to reconcile their financial statements with GAAP.

More recently, the SEC has been softening its opposition to international standards. The creation of an International Accounting Standards Committee by some 100 accounting firms world wide, and its governing board, the International Accounting Standards Board ("IASB") that the SEC was given a role in selecting, has been trying to lessen the SEC's concerns. The SEC issued a concept release in 2000 that sought comment on the development of a set of broad standards for determining whether an international accounting method met the SEC's goals of full disclosure. International Accounting Standards, Securities Exchange Act Release No. 42430 (Feb. 16, 2000). The subsequent collapse of Enron Corp. and ensuing scandals has thrown that project into an era of uncertainty, but work continues.

Enron also gave rise to debates over whether American generally accepted accounting principles standards are so flawed and rigid that they should be abandoned in favor of international accounting standards that allow more discretion. The Impossible Dream, Economist, Mar. 2, 2002, at

69. International standards are "principle based." That is, those standards set forth general principles and the company and its accountants apply those broad principles to their specific transactions. In contrast, GAAP is a set of specific rules that try to define with particularity how a specific transaction is to be treated. GAAP has been compiled in a 4,500 page three volume set; some rules are said to consume over 700 pages to how to book a single transaction. Walter Wriston, The Solution to Scandal? Simpler Rules, Wall St. J., Aug. 5, 2002, at A10. The SEC has issued a report embracing a more "principled" based approach but does want to retain some rules based requirements—a hybrid approach. Adrian Michaels, SEC in Principled Stand on GAAP: Regulator Finds Rules–Based Approach of US Guidelines Imperfect, Preferring 'Objectives–Based' Approach, Financial Times (London), July 26, 2003, at 8. The SEC was considering a proposal in 2007 that would allow issuers to use either GAAP or International Financial Reporting Standards ("IFRS"). The SEC has also proposed dropping the requirement that foreign issuers reconcile their international standards to GAAP. One critic has argued that moving to principle based accounting will not work because our entire financial and regulatory system is rule based. The discretion in a principles based system may also be turned against participants by regulators and class action plaintiffs who will always use discretion in its most restrictive fashion. Peter J. Wallison, Why the Americans Will Prefer to Rely on Rules, Not Principles, Fin. Times (London), July 6, 2007.

Compounding this picture, the European Union required its companies to use IASB standards by 2005, which will cause difficulties for European firms listing their stock in the United States unless reconciliation is achieved. Institutional investors in America would also like a single standard. Michael Skapinker, Investors Look for Single Accounting Standard, Fin. Times (London), July 8, 2002, at 13.

On August 7, 2007, the SEC published a Concept Release seeking public comment on whether public companies in the United States should be allowed to prepare financial statements in accordance with International Financial Reporting Standards as published by the International Accounting Standards Board. Securities Act Release No. 33–831 (Aug. 7, 2007).

In November 2008, in an almost complete switch from its long held, sometimes almost fanatical, support of GAAPs, the SEC announced that it was proposing the mandatory use of IFRS by 2016. In the meantime, the largest U.S. companies were allowed to adopt such standards voluntarily. However, the subprime crisis upended this program. Mary Schapiro, the new SEC chairman appointed by President Barack Obama when he took office, expressed the view that the adoption of those international standards should be done only cautiously, which appeared to be a signal that she was considering retaining the complex and outmoded GAAP rule formulations.[42] However, a senior SEC staff member later stated that the agency remained committed to moving toward the use of IFRS.

---

42. Mary Schapiro Vows to Be Tough Enforcer, CFO Magazine, Jan. 15, 2009, http://www.cfo.com/article.cfm/12958299/c_12931795

RIGERS GJYSHI[43]
A HISTORY OF MARK–TO–MARKET ACCOUNTING

Like the FASB, the International Accounting Standard Board [hereinafter IASB] has been working on integrating fair value disclosure, especially with financial instruments. For example, in 2008, the IASB issued a discussion paper requesting ideas on how to improve financial instrument reporting.[44] A major part of that paper focused on how to use fair values in reporting financial instruments.

IASB has defined fair value as the amount for which an asset could be exchanged, or a liability settled, between knowledgeable, willing parties in an arm's length transaction.[45] Clearly, this definition assumes a hypothetical transaction that could occur, and which is assumed to occur between two parties who know the real value of the asset and who are trying to value the exchange to their own benefit.[46]

IAS 39 also includes a fair value option for certain financial instruments, much like FAS 133. For example, IAS 39 is similar to FAS 133 in that it requires election of the fair value option at the recognition of the financial asset or liability, and once made that recognition is irrevocable.

There are three main differences between the IAS 39 and FAS 157 definitions, however. First, the IAS 39 looks at the exchange price of an asset or liability, unlike FAS 157, which reaches a value by looking at the exit price, i.e. the value of an asset when it is sold or liability when it is settled. Second, IAS 39 refers to knowledgeable, willing parties in an arm's length transaction, whereas FAS 157 refers to market participants. While market participants could fit into the IAS 39 definition, the reverse is not true, as these transactions may occur in private settings. Third, under the FAS 157 definition, the liability is transferred, i.e. continues to exist, even though a different party is responsible for it, whereas under IAS 39 the liability is considered settled and not assumed.

———

The IASB agreed with FASB, on March 24, 2009, that the two bodies would work together to jointly achieve common accounting standards. That agreement lasted less than two weeks. IASB refused to follow the FASB's interpretative guidance on fair value accounting that was issued on April 2, 2009. Instead, IASB announced that it would be conducting a six-month study of the issue. The Group of Twenty, at their meeting in London on April 2, 2009, also called on the FASB and IASB to further

---

43.   Research Fellow, Florida International University College of Law at Miami (2010),

44.   IASB Discussion Paper, *Reducing Complexity in Reporting Financial Instruments* (March 19, 2008).

45.   IASC Standard No. 39, *Financial Instruments*, paragraph 11.

46.   Portfolio 5403–1st, *supra* note 1, at section II–B.

address fair value accounting issues. They sought more clarity and consistency. The result of all of this debate was confusion and uncertainty, the very thing accounting standards were supposed to prevent.

CHAPTER THREE

INTEREST RATES, THE MONEY MARKET, AND FIRM LIQUIDITY MANAGEMENT

■ ■ ■

Chapter objectives

- To learn basic concepts about corporate borrowing and the yield curve.

- To appreciate the difference between leverage, firm liquidity, market liquidity, and firm solvency.

- To understand the instruments of the money market, including commercial paper and repurchase agreements.

- To appreciate the role of, and changing regulatory climate for, credit rating agencies.

SECTION 1. BORROWING FUNDS— SOME FUNDAMENTALS

This chapter focuses on the role of interest rates in corporate finance and the use of short-term liabilities for working capital needs and as an investment for excess funds generated by corporations. Therefore, we are concerned with how a corporation manages its assets and liabilities maturing over a short period, typically one year. Short-term assets and liabilities are said to be more 'liquid.' A key concern with short-term liabilities is the interest rate to be paid for the use of the funds.

Risk and Interest Rates

Interest rates are usually expressed in terms of a percentage of the loan being made and are measured by a one year term. For example, a loan of $100 for a period of five years at five percent interest would require the borrower to pay $5 in interest in each of the five years and return the principal as well at the end of the fifth year.

The amount or percentage of the interest payment will be determined by a number of factors. A principal consideration is the risk of default.

The interest rate will rise as the level of risk increases. The risk factor in setting the interest rate is measured against a baseline of the rate for U.S. government securities. There is said to be no default risk for investment in U.S. government securities that are backed by the full faith and credit of the United States. As long as the flag is flying, the government will meet its commitments. In reality, there still remains some risk, as where Congress fails to fund the government, but even that risk is small because of the political implications of a default.

Corporate obligations will have more risk and will pay higher rates than comparable obligations of the United States Government. The rate paid will depend on the particular risks associated with each issuing company as well as general economic factors. The creditworthiness of particular corporations are measured by the ratings agencies or, as they are more formally know, Nationally Recognized Statistical Rating Organizations ("NRSOs").

The two leading ratings agencies are Moodys and Standard & Poors. Their ratings have been described as follows:

Moody's	S & P/Others	Meaning
Aaa	AAA	Highest quality
Aa1	AA+	High quality
Aa2	AA	
Aa3	AA-	
A1	A+	Strong payment capacity
A2	A	
A3	A-	
Baa1	BBB+	Adequate payment capacity
Baa2	BBB	
Baa3	BBB-	
Ba1	BB+	Likely to repay; ongoing uncertainty
BA2	BB	
Ba3	BB-	
B1	B+	High risk obligations
B2	B	
B3	B-	
	CCC+	Vulnerable to default, or in default
Caa	CCC	
	CCC-	
Ca	C	In bankruptcy, or default
Moody's has no D rating	D	

A different system is used for rating commercial paper. (*see* section 2 of this chapter). Frank Partnoy, *The* Siskel and Ebert of Financial Markets? Two Thumbs Down for the Credit Rating Agencies, 77 Wash. U. L. Q. 619, 648, n. 139 (1999).

Interest Rates and Inflation

Another component of the amount of the interest rate is inflation. Inflation will devalue the dollars borrowed today and returned at a later date. For example, consider the following: the original $5 from a loan will buy a certain number of hamburgers on the day the funds are borrowed, but will buy a lesser number on the day they are returned (say five years later) if prices have increased as a result of inflation. To compensate for that risk, interest rates will rise or fall as the threat of inflation increases or decreases. The risk of inflation and default on a loan is greater over longer periods, giving rise to the "yield curve." This is a reference to the fact that longer-term loans tend to carry higher interest rates than shorter-term obligations in order to compensate for inflation and increased longer-term risks.

The Federal Reserve Board ("Fed") plays an important role in the setting of interest rates. It seeks to influence monetary policy and to curb inflation by raising rates to curb inflationary tendencies or lowering them to boost the economy. The Fed also uses interest rates to command and control the economy such as, in the words of the Fed chairman, curbing "irrational exuberance" in the stock market. In 1999 and 2000, the Fed increased rates several times in order to stop a rise in the stock market that was taking on the appearance of a bubble. That action did indeed crush the market. It lost over $8 trillion in value and the economy was thrown into a recession. The Fed then desperately cut interest rates to levels not seen in decades. After the Federal Reserve Board cut rates for the thirteenth time since the beginning of 2001, the interest rate on overnight loans between banks was 1 percent on June 25, 2003, the lowest level in forty-five years. Those low rates touched off a boom in the housing market that was crushed by the Fed through seventeen consecutive rate increases—creating a credit crunch and laying the groundwork for the financial crisis that arose between 2007 and 2009.

Current interest rates may be obtained from several sources. The "Fed funds" rate is the short term rate set by the Fed. "Libor", which is the London interbank offered rate, is another popular index for determining rates. It is an index of rates charged by several large banks. The "prime" rate was a popular measure used by large United States banks for many years. It was the rate that large banks charged their most creditworthy customers. The prime rate has lost favor to Libor and other measures.

A loan may be based on a fixed or floating rate. If fixed, the same rate is charged over the life of the loan, say a fixed 5 percent in the example given at the beginning of this section. If floating, the rate will be periodically reset on the basis of any changes in a specified interest rate index such as Libor. For example, if the loan just mentioned was a floating rather than fixed rate obligation, the rate would be changed, say quarterly, to reflect changes in the Libor rate. If the Libor rate had increased at the end of the quarter, the rate would be increased for the next quarter. If at the end of that second quarter rates had gone down, the borrower would then pay that lower rate for the next quarter.

Fixed and floating rate loans have advantages and disadvantages. In the case of the fixed rate loan, the borrower does not have to worry about increased interest payments if market rates increase. The lender, however, will be receiving less on that loan than otherwise available in the market, making the loan less valuable as an investment. A floating rate loan will expose the borrower to higher interest payments if rates increase but lower payments will be made if rates decrease. Conversely, the lender receives more if rates go up, making the investment more valuable, but less if rates decrease.

Once the decision is made to borrow funds, the maturity and form of the debt must be considered. Corporate debt is classified on the balance sheet as long term (with a maturity of more than 10 years), medium term (with a maturity of one year to ten years) and short term (with a maturity of less than one year, but for some purposes, short term debt may be defined as having a maturity of less than nine months). *See generally* In re Bevill, Bresler & Schulman Asset Management Corp., 67 B.R. 557, 567 (D.N.J.1986) (describing debt with differing maturities).

Interest rate obligations may be met by discounts or coupon payments. In the case of a coupon debt instrument, payments of interest will be paid periodically over the life of the instrument, perhaps semi-annually, quarterly or even monthly, as is the case for your home mortgage. Say, you have borrowed $100 for five years with a five percent interest rate to be paid semi-annually. This is a coupon debt that requires you to pay $2.50 each six months for five years. The interest could be paid in advance. In this example, the $2.50 would be paid initially when the loan was paid and every six months thereafter until the last six months of the loan's term. Alternatively, the interest could be paid in arrears, which means that the initial interest payment is made at the end of the first six months and is thereafter, with the final interest be paid on the same day the principal is returned.

A discount obligation does not make a periodic interest payment. Rather, the amount returned on maturity will be increased over the amount of principal loaned. For example, assume you loaned another person $95 The borrower does not agree to pay you periodic interest. Rather, you will be paid $100 at the end of the year, reflecting the return of principal and interest on your funds. Discount obligations may be short or long term. Short-term discount obligations are often referred to as bills, while long term discounts are referred to as zero coupon bonds. (As will be seen in Chapter 4, zero coupon bonds have some tax disadvantages).

A corporation must determine what amount of the funds it needs should be borrowed and what amount should be obtained through sales of stock. Borrowing funds will require payments of interest (which are tax deductible if there are profits) and repayment of the principal. A sale of stock will raise funds, without interest charges, and the funds are contributed permanently, which means that they need not be repaid. However, the number of owners is increased and existing shareholders will have to share future profits and control with the new stockholders, thereby diluting the ownership interest of the existing shareholders. For that reason, borrowing may be preferred, *i.e.*, borrowing provides existing shareholders with "leverage" and avoids dilution.

To understand the concept of leveraging, think about the purchase of a single-family residence. The family buying the home will make a down payment to the bank of, say, 20% ($80,000) in order to borrow the balance on a $400,000 home. The family will then make fixed monthly payments that will reflect annual interest payments of, say, 6% on the balance plus a remaining amount that will repay a portion of the principal each month over the life of the loan. The leverage gained from borrowing will allow this family to live in a $400,000 house even though they only had $80,000 available for such an investment. Leverage has another effect. Assume that the value of this real estate increased to $500,000 in a single year. Assume that the family has a pre-tax profit from the sale of a house of $50,000, after real estate commissions, closing costs and adjustment for interest on the loan. This is a return of 62.5% on the family's investment of $80,000. Now consider what the return on this property would be if the family had paid the entire $400,000 purchase price with cash. The return on their investment of $400,000 with a profit from the sale of the house of $50,000 would only be a relatively paltry 12.5%, rather than the rather robust 62.5 percent obtained by the leverage from a mortgage. Remember, however, that leverage works both ways. If the value of the real estate had gone down, the loss in percentage terms would be far greater for the leveraged purchase than for full payment.

Careful financial officers seek to prevent their corporations from being over-leveraged, while at the same time seeking to use the advantages of at least some leverage. Banks are also careful in extending loans to make sure that a corporate borrower is not over-leveraged. Investors in corporate debt must also be concerned with the effects of leverage. Nevertheless, more than ninety cents of every investment dollar raised in the United States at the end of the last century was through bond sales rather than equity. The effects of leveraging was apparent during the financial crisis in 2007–2009 and Congress acted to limit leveraging by banks.

A popular tool for financing a corporate takeover is through the leveraged buyout, a technique described by one court as follows:

> A leveraged buy-out occurs when a group of investors, usually including members of a company's management team, buy the company under financial arrangements that include little equity and significant new debt. The necessary debt financing typically includes mortgages or high risk/high yield bonds, popularly known as "junk bonds." Additionally, a portion of this debt is generally secured by the company's assets. Some of the acquired company's assets are usually sold

after the transaction is completed in order to reduce the debt incurred in the acquisition.

Metropolitan Life Ins. Co. v. RJR Nabisco, Inc., 716 F.Supp. 1504, 1505, n. 1 (S.D.N.Y.1989).

Cash Management

The time value of money requires corporations to manage their cash carefully. A cash shortage requires borrowing that will incur an expense. Excess cash on hand needs to be reinvested to gain the value of interest. Most large corporations have specialized and complex cash management systems that assure that they will have access to short term loans when cash is short and that excess funds will be invested until needed.

These cash management systems often use "controlled disbursement" accounts. These accounts include "sweep" accounts that allow a company to pull excess cash from all of its accounts and branches. The swept funds are then deposited into a "concentration" account. The concentration account is coupled with a "zero balance" account. In brief, here is how the system works. A financial officer for the corporation will require that excess funds in all of its bank accounts be swept each night into the concentration account. On the following morning, the bank notifies the officer of any pending checks or withdrawals. That amount is sent to the zero balance account from the concentration account, and those items are paid. The remaining funds in the concentration account are then invested by the financial officer in a number of possible ways that will be discussed later in this chapter. The banks are compensated for this service by fees or by "targeted balancing," which means that the corporation agrees to leave a specified amount of funds on hand as a compensating balance for the bank, i.e., the bank can invest those funds for its own account and obtain compensation in that manner.

IN RE MONTGOMERY
983 F.2d 1389 (6th Cir.1993).

DAVID A. NELSON, CIRCUIT JUDGE.

The debtors in this complex bankruptcy case operated a massive check kiting scheme through which they obtained what amounted to unauthorized loans from a number of different banks. On March 21, 1988—a date within the 90–day preference period before the filing of bankruptcy petitions against the debtors—the level of unauthorized loans at one of the banks, defendant Third National Bank in Nashville, reached a high point of more than $2 million. A month later that figure had been reduced to zero, the debtors having paid off the unauthorized loans at Third National with commingled funds generated partly through legitimate business activities and partly through the kiting of checks at other banks.

The trustee in bankruptcy brought an adversary proceeding against Third National to recover the value of the payoff as a voidable preference.

The bankruptcy court decided the case in favor of the trustee. The district court affirmed the bankruptcy court's final order, which included an award of prejudgment interest from the date of demand, and this appeal followed.

The main questions we must answer are whether transfers of property to Third National were properly identified, and, if so, whether the debtors had an interest in such property. Like the district court, we think both questions should be answered in the affirmative. Accordingly, and because we find no abuse of discretion in the award of prejudgment interest, we shall affirm the challenged judgment.

The individual debtor, N. Eddie Montgomery, was the sole owner of Southland Escrow Services, Inc., a real estate closing firm. Involuntary petitions in bankruptcy were filed against Mr. Montgomery and Southland Escrow on June 3, 1988, and the cases were consolidated. We shall refer to the debtors interchangeably, the distinction between them having no practical significance here.

Mr. Montgomery established a banking relationship with defendant Third National in the summer of 1987, when the bank set up an elaborate cash management system for the escrow business. Among the elements of the cash management system were a "Main Funding Account," where receipts from real estate closings were to be concentrated, and a "Zero Balance Account" on which checks were to be written. All funds placed in the Main Funding Account were available to Mr. Montgomery immediately, whether or not they had actually been collected. Positive balances in the Main Funding Account were to be invested automatically so as to earn interest, and funds were to be transferred automatically each day from that account to the Zero Balance Account in amounts sufficient to cover Third National checks presented for payment that day.[1] A computer program called "INTERLINK" gave Mr. Montgomery direct access to detailed credit and debit information on these accounts and others through a computer terminal in his office.

Third National's computer system proved unable to clear the Zero Balance Account in a timely manner, and all checks presented on a given day were therefore recorded initially as "overdrafts." On the day following presentment a bank employee would debit the Main Funding Account in the amount necessary to "zero out" the previous day's negative balance.

The Main Funding Account would be debited in this manner regardless of the sufficiency of the funds it contained. When the balance in the Main Funding Account was insufficient—and this proved to be the norm throughout most of the period during which Mr. Montgomery did business at Third National—an overdraft notice would be generated on the second day after presentment of the checks in question. The overdrafts were paid

---

1. As explained in *First Federal of Michigan v. Barrow*, 878 F.2d 912, 914 n.2 (6th Cir.1989), "zero balance accounts are open accounts without cash balances which are designed to maximize the viability of idle investment capital by affording a system of automatic inter-account fund transfers from a central account to subsidiary accounts on an 'as needed' basis."

initially through a $500,000 line of credit. The line of credit was soon exhausted, and Mr. Montgomery then started paying "analysis charges"—calculated at a rate of 10 1/2 percent per annum—on the negative balances in both accounts. The analysis charges were very large; the charge for January of 1988, for example, came to more than $30,000, which was unprecedented at this bank.

As early as November of 1987 Third National suspected Mr. Montgomery and an associate of kiting checks in an account they maintained at the bank for a real estate syndication business called Southland Properties. The Southland Properties account—which was not part of the cash management system—was promptly closed by the bank.

Officers of Third National Bank were assured by Mr. Montgomery at meetings held in January and February of 1988 that the negative balances in the cash management accounts would be reduced. These promises were not kept, and it is now clear that Mr. Montgomery was using the cash management accounts at Third National and accounts he maintained at Sovran Bank and elsewhere to augment the funds under his control by kiting checks. The bankruptcy court gave the following explanation of the workings of this "colossal" check kiting scheme, as the court characterized it:

> "March 14, 1988, was typical of the operation of the debtors' check kite during the preference period. On March 14, the bank statement for the ZBA account [Zero Balance Account] at Third National Bank showed an overdraft of $2,056,721. Not included in that amount were checks totalling $1,591,799 written on the ZBA account and already presented and posted as an increase in cash in a Montgomery controlled bank account at Sovran Bank. On March 14, the bank statement for this Montgomery controlled account at Sovran Bank showed a balance of $1,705,375. Not included in that amount were checks totalling $1,625,600 written on the Sovran account and already presented and posted as an increase in cash in the Main Funding Account at Third National. The $1,591,799 drawn on the ZBA account at Third and the $1,625,600 drawn on the Montgomery controlled account at Sovran were uncollected funds in use by the debtors on March 14 that do not appear as decreases in the respective drawee bank balances on that day because the items representing these amounts were 'floating' in the collection process between the banks."

Almost every business day during the preference period and before April 18, 1988, there were similar multi-million dollar "interbank" transfers of funds among Montgomery controlled accounts at Third National and other Nashville banks that were not tied to the closing of real estate transactions. The volume of "interbank" checks exceeded by almost four-to-one the banking transactions traceable to legitimate real estate closings. The precision with which Montgomery timed and shifted this float among the banks betrays an unintended use of INTERLINK—to determine how much and where to fuel the kite to keep it floating.

Early in April of 1988 Third National decided, according to an internal bank memorandum, to "delete" the cash management services it had been providing Montgomery/Southland Escrow. Mr. Montgomery was called into the bank to discuss the mechanics of shutting the system down, and on April 18, 1988, Southland stopped using the Zero Balance Account for routine disbursements. Deposits continued to be made in the Main Funding Account until May 3, 1988; it appears that funds commingled in that account were used to clear up the arrearages in all of the Third National accounts. "By the end of the second week in May," the bankruptcy court found, "the balances in all [Third National] accounts were reduced to insignificance."

Bankruptcy proceedings were commenced against Mr. Montgomery and Southland Escrow on June 3, as noted above, and the trustee subsequently made demand on Third National for the return of nearly $2 million in preferential transfers. The bank declined to pay, and the trustee then filed his complaint. The complaint alleged, among other things, that on March 14, 1988, Southland Escrow had a combined negative balance of $1,971,978.75 in all its Third National accounts; that Montgomery and Southland Escrow subsequently made several hundred deposits and withdrawals, with the total deposits exceeding the total withdrawals to such an extent that on May 25, 1988, Southland Escrow had a combined positive balance of $1,179.20 in its Third National accounts; that the aggregate of all the transfers from Southland Escrow to Third National caused the bank to recover all its losses to the prejudice of Southland Escrow's other creditors; that the transfers would enable the bank to recover more than it would otherwise be able to receive as a creditor; and that the aggregate of the transfers constituted a preferential transfer within the meaning of 11 U.S.C. § 547.

The bank's answer to the complaint denied the existence of any preferential transfers and, among other things, pleaded affirmatively that the alleged transfers represented contemporaneous exchanges for new value. The affirmative defenses seem to have received most of the attention of the parties at the trial conducted before the bankruptcy court, but on appeal to the district court the focus of the parties' arguments shifted to the questions whether any "transfers" had actually been identified and whether property interests of the debtor had been transferred. Third National argued before the district court, as it argues here, that there had been no identification of any transfers from the debtors to Third National of property in which the debtors had an interest. A debtor cannot have an interest in a property that would not be available for distribution to creditors in the event of bankruptcy, the bank points out, and it goes on to assert that the shift in the locus of Mr. Montgomery's check kiting activities did not deplete assets that would otherwise have been available to general creditors of Montgomery and his company.

The district court concluded (1) that the bankruptcy court properly identified the existence of a voidable transfer, (2) that property interests of the debtor were transferred to Third National during the preference period, and (3) that the transfers resulted in depletion of the debtors' estate. We agree with each of these conclusions.

McMAHAN & CO. v. PO FOLKS, INC.

206 F.3d 627 (6th Cir.2000).

AVERN COHN, DISTRICT JUDGE sitting by designation

On February 28, 1995, McMahan obtained a default judgment in the United States District Court of Delaware against Po Folks for failure to pay on a promissory note given to McMahan. The judgment, in the amount of $288,763.14 (including interest), was registered in the United States District Court for the Eastern District of Kentucky on April 3, 1995. McMahan thereafter attempted to enforce its judgment through more than twenty garnishment orders issued to the Bank, at which Po Folks maintained accounts. However, McMahan's efforts were largely unsuccessful, with less than $12,000 being remitted to McMahan by the Bank.

McMahan therefore moved for a writ of execution, attachment and/or sequestration against Po Folks' property held by the Bank, as is the standard procedure to challenge a bank's garnishment disclosure in Kentucky. The district court denied McMahan's motion, finding that the Bank did not possess any Po Folks property on the date and the time the garnishment orders were received. On appeal, we reversed the district court's decision and ordered that discovery be conducted. McMahan & Co. v. Po Folks, Inc., 107 F.3d 871, 1997 WL 78497 (6th Cir. Feb. 24, 1997).

On remand, discovery revealed that the reason the Bank did not satisfy the garnishment orders served by McMahan was because of the internal procedures of the Bank, and the structure of Po Folks' accounts. Po Folks had several accounts with the Bank, specifically, a general account and 5 independent, named accounts. The named accounts were "zero balance" accounts, which meant that at the close of business every day, the account funds would be "swept" into the general account, leaving a zero balance. Po Folks paid the Bank a monthly fee to allow Po Folks to significantly overdraw on its general account. When a garnishment order was served, the Bank's policy was to check the balance of the account by computer, which only reflected the account balances as of the close of business the previous day and did not show any deposits or withdrawals made during the day the garnishment orders were served. Thus, since all of Po Folks' accounts were either "zero balance" accounts, or overdrawn as of the close of business the preceding day, whenever a garnishment order was served the Bank would respond that no monies were in Po

Folks' account, even if deposits had been made the day that the garnishment order was served, and particularly that part of the day preceding the exact time the garnishment order was served.* * *

The district court's opinion focused on the fact that the Bank, in following their ordinary garnishment procedures, could not have discovered property belonging to Po Folks, absent "manually processing all items on hand at that particular moment." The district court therefore concluded that since the Bank could not locate Po Folks' property in the "ordinary course of business," it did not possess any of Po Folks' property. Nowhere in the statute does it say that locating garnished property is required only if it can be done in the "ordinary course of business" or without being unduly burdensome.

Moreover, even assuming that such a requirement exists, the record reflects that the Bank had the ability to locate property belonging to Po Folks in the "ordinary course of business." Although the Bank was unable to view a current daily account balance from the computer terminals since the computer always had a one day lag, several Bank employees testified that it was common practice, in a number of situations including garnishments, for the Bank to place a "hold" on an account for up to 14 days. A "hold" prevents any withdrawals or deposits from the account until it is lifted. If the Bank had placed a "hold" on any of Po Folks' accounts for even 24 hours, which the Bank was able to do, the Bank would have been able to process the deposits and debits received prior to the hold in its normal procedure, and ascertained if there was any surplusage the next day. * * *

NOTES

1. Consider the following description of a cash management plan used by one entity:

> The fertilizer industry, reflecting conditions in the agricultural industry that is its only customer, is both highly seasonal and highly volatile. Farmers buy fertilizer primarily in the spring and in the fall, and the amount they buy depends on the vicissitudes of weather, fluctuations in demand for farm products, and other factors difficult to predict. Another source of uncertainty for producers of chemical fertilizers is that the prices of the chemicals that are the principal inputs into such fertilizers also fluctuate a great deal. All this makes cash management a matter of acute concern for an enterprise like CF. It needs more cash in winter and summer, when it is producing for inventory to supply the farmers' needs in the spring and fall, than it does in the spring and fall, when it is selling and being paid for the fertilizer it has produced. It cannot be certain how much cash it must have at any time, because it must have cash to meet sudden increases in the prices of its chemical raw materials and sudden surges in

demand for fertilizer, requiring it to expand production on short notice. In fact it cannot forecast its cash needs accurately more than a month in advance, and therefore it wants to be able to increase or reduce its cash balances on short notice. It could try to go cashless and borrow short term whenever it needed cash to pay its bills, or, as it does, it could place some of its assets in short-term financial instruments that are cash equivalents, such as bank certificates of deposit, U.S. government financial instruments, repurchase agreements, and money-market funds—all of which are available with short maturities. Roughly 75 percent of the cash equivalents used by CF in its cash management program have maturities of 7 days or less, and 92 percent have maturities of less than 30 days. A few have much longer maturities but are the equivalent of short-term cash-equivalent instruments because of conversion features. Apparently the assets in CF's cash-management account are generated by revenues from the sale of the cooperative's products.

CF Industries, Inc. (and Subsidiaries) v. Commissioner of Internal Revenue, 995 F.2d 101, 102–03 (7th Cir.1993). Cash management was driven in part by the fact that banks could not pay interest on demand accounts. However, section 627 of the Dodd–Frank Wall Street Reform and Consumer Protection Act of 2010 allowed interest to be paid on such accounts beginning in 2011.

2. Cash management services are available for consumers. The "Cash Management Account" created by Merrill Lynch, Pierce, Fenner & Smith Inc. and adopted by most other large broker-dealers, links customer securities accounts with a money market fund in which excess cash balances are invested in short term liability instruments that pay the customer interest. When cash is needed, the investment is liquidated and withdrawn by check or debit card. The customer may also borrow money by using securities in his or her securities accounts as collateral. For a description of this program see In re Merrill Lynch, Pierce, Fenner & Smith, Inc., 230 U.S.P.Q. (BNA) 128 (TTAB 1986), rev'd, 828 F.2d 1567 (Fed.Cir.1987).

3. As seen in the In re Montgomery case, cash management practices may become too aggressive. E.F. Hutton & Co., at the time one of the nation's largest broker-dealers, pleaded guilty to a 2,000 count indictment for mail and wire fraud in connection with its cash management program. The firm was actually engaged in an elaborate check-kiting scheme in which it deposited checks drawn on other accounts that had uncleared funds. Those uncleared funds were actually checks deposited by E.F. Hutton. Knowing they would take a few days to clear, E.F. Hutton personnel would obtain immediate funds on the account, thereby acquiring an interest free loan. Merrill Perlman, E.F. Hutton Admits It Defrauded Banks, N.Y. Times, May 5, 1985, 3, at 14. Other broker-dealers were drawing checks on remote accounts for use in paying customer obligations. Say a customer in New York would be paid with a check drawn on a California bank. The broker-dealer would use the use the customer's funds during the additional time it took for the funds to clear. The SEC asked that such "remote disbursement" practices be stopped. III Jerry W. Markham, A Financial History of the United States: From the Age of Derivatives Into the New Millennium (1970–2001) 101 (2002).

4.   Another example of the time value of money is found in the traveler's check. Cash is paid for the check, but it frequently is not used for some period of time. Some travelers even save unused checks for their next trip. During that period, the issuer of the traveler's check has use of those funds. As a measure of the size of that "float," the American Express Company sold $26 billion in travelers checks in 1995. III Jerry W. Markham, A Financial History of the United States: From the Age of Derivatives Into the New Millennium (1970–2001) 285 (2002).

5.   You may have a "smart card," but is it so smart? Someone has the use of the funds that you loaded on that card until you use the card and disburse the funds to a vendor.

6.   If the balance is paid on a credit card each month, the holder is receiving an interest free loan from the time of purchase until the credit card bill is paid. If the balance is carried over, however, the holder will then pay a high price for the use of the bank's funds.

SECTION 2.   THE MONEY MARKET AND OTHER SHORT TERM DEBT

This section considers the instruments of the money market, which comprises short term debt, i.e., debt with a maturity of less than one year (in some cases the definition of short term debt may be limited to debt with a maturity of less than nine months). Because of its short short term, the money market is where corporations manage their short-term liquidity by, on the liability-side of the balance sheet, borrowing cash for short periods or, on the asset-side of the balance sheet, investing excess cash in short-term obligations. Corporations often have cash shortages they must cover by borrowing or by tapping some other funding mechanism, thereby incurring a short-term liability. This activity takes many forms, and funds may be obtained from a number of sources. Conversely, when corporations have excess liquidity that they want to lend out without tying up for very long, they may also lend out this liquidity in the money market, thereby incurring a short-term asset.

Bank Credit

Short-term debt is often used by corporations to meet working capital needs. A corporation may thus need funds to pay bills before revenues are received from sales that are to be used to make such payments. Short-term debt is used to fill that gap. A popular mechanism for meeting short-term working capital needs is a line of credit from a bank. This allows the corporation to borrow cash whenever needed up to a specified amount. This line of credit may be extended as a "revolving line of credit," or more loosely a "revolver." This is a commitment by the bank to lend money to the corporation up to a set limit for a specified period of time, generally one to three years, during which the company may draw from and repay funds as needed. A "non-revolving line of credit" is similar to a revolving line of credit except that the available credit limit is reduced each time a repayment is made. For a description of a revolving credit facility see Venetis v. Global Financial Services, Inc., 174 F.R.D. 238 (D.Mass.1997).

The advantages of a line of credit are that a company may borrow as needed and repay when funds become available. The term of the debt is thus matched to the company's needs. The line of credit also provides a backup facility for unexpected demands, providing the company with liquidity.

A loan such as a line of credit, and other loans, may be secured or unsecured. In the case of a secured loan, specific corporate property is pledged to the bank as security for the loan. This may involve the use of the Uniform Commercial Code and related filings in order to perfect this security interest. If properly secured, the bank will have a prior lien (ahead of all other creditors) in the event of bankruptcy. An unsecured loan merely gives the bank a claim against the corporation's general assets in the event of bankruptcy. The bank will have to share with other creditors in the event of a shortfall.

Another concept to consider is recourse and non-recourse debt. In the simplest example this means, in the case of a recourse loan, that the owners of the corporation must guarantee the debt. This is often required for small corporations and effectively removes the corporate shield of limited liability for such owners, at least for that debt. The bank may make a non-recourse when the corporation has enough capital and earning power to assure the bank that the loan will be repaid.

NOTE

Credit facilities may have some unconventional terms. For example, the Michelin tire company obtained a $1 billion subordinated loan facility from its banks that could be drawn down only if the GDP in its principal markets declined. This would provide working capital during an economic downturn when tire revenues predictably will decline with the drop in GDP. Robert J. Shiller, The New Financial Order, Risk in the 21st Century 142–43 (2003).

Financing of Inventory

There are numerous ways for corporations to obtain funds in advance of cash payment from customers. These methods are often industry specific. For example, in the automobile industry, dealers finance their inventory of automobiles by pledging the proceeds of their sales. This is called "floor plan" financing. *See* Fleet Capital Corp. v. Yamaha Motor Corp., U.S.A., 48 U.C.C. Rep. Serv.2d (Callaghan) 1137 (S.D.N.Y. 2002) ("'floor plan' line of credit is typically employed to purchase and secure specific inventory assets, such as cars). See Black's Law Dictionary, (7th ed. 1999) ('Floor-plan financing' is a loan that is secured by merchandise and paid off as the goods are sold. Usually such a loan is given by a manufacturer to a retailer or other dealer (as a car dealer)."). The danger to the creditor in these transactions is an "out of trust" sale in which the dealer sells a car but keeps the proceeds and does not report the sale to the lender. See Motorcity of Jacksonville v. Southeast Bank, N.A., 83 F.3d 1317, 1322 (11th Cir.1996), vacated and remanded, 519 U.S. 1087, 117 S.Ct. 760, 136 L.Ed.2d 708 (1997) (describing concerns with out of trust sales). Another concern is the perfection of the security interest in the automobiles:

IN RE BLUEGRASS FORD–MERCURY, INC.

942 F.2d 381 (6th Cir.1991).

GUY, JR., CIRCUIT JUDGE:

Defendant, Farmers National Bank of Cynthiana (Farmers), appeals the district court's decision, which affirmed the bankruptcy court's order, setting aside certain liens held on Bluegrass Ford–Mercury's (Bluegrass or debtor) property as preferential and allowing Bluegrass to recover certain payments made during the preference period from the bank.

Farmers argues that it was a perfected, secured creditor and, thus, did not receive any preferential transfers. Additionally, Farmers argues that the plaintiff has failed to prove all of the essential elements of a preferential transfer. Finally, Farmers argues that the exceptions to the rule against preferential transfers, as provided in 11 U.S.C. § 547(c), should apply and therefore Bluegrass is not entitled to avoid the payments made to Farmers. We find defendant's arguments without merit and affirm, essentially on the basis of the bankruptcy and district court opinions, although our rationale differs slightly from both the bankruptcy and district courts.

Farmers entered into a floor plan financing arrangement with Bluegrass Ford, Bluegrass Ford–Mercury's predecessor, in the mid–1970s.

"Floor planning is a form of inventory financing." Ruda, *Floor Planning*, Commercial Finance, Factoring, and Other Asset–Based Lending 1984, 339 PLI/Comm. 135, 135 (1984) (hereinafter Floor Planning). It provides a means of "lending to a dealer against the security of its automobile inventory." *Id.* Generally, "the borrower is a seller or lessor of personal property...." and "the lender may be a bank or finance company." *Id.*

As new vehicles were shipped to Bluegrass Ford, it would forward a draft for payment to the bank. A representative of the dealership would go to the bank upon its receipt of these drafts and execute a 90–day "Precomputed Installment Note, Disclosure & Security Agreement." Once these notes were executed, the bank would pay the drafts directly to the Ford Motor Company. The notes covered one or more cars, depending on the number of drafts. As the vehicles were sold, the principal amount of the note was paid to the bank. Upon the sale of the last vehicle covered under the agreement, or when the 90–day period had expired and the agreement was up for renewal, the interest was paid.

To perfect its security interest in the proceeds from the sales of the automobiles, Farmers filed a Uniform Commercial Code (UCC) financing statement on June 7, 1977. This financing statement covered "all new cars and demonstrators in the inventory of Bluegrass Ford, Inc." Although new floor plan notes were executed, no new financing statements were filed.

In August of 1979, the assets of the dealership were sold by William A. Webber to James A. Morris. These assets included all new cars in Bluegrass Ford's inventory. As part of the same sales contract, Bluegrass Ford conveyed its real property to James A. Morris and his wife, Betty C. Morris.

After the sale, the dealership was transferred to a new corporate entity called Bluegrass Ford–Mercury, Inc., the plaintiff in this action. James Morris executed new notes and security agreements with the bank in order to assume the indebtedness of the old dealership. The floor plan financing arrangement continued as before, until just before Bluegrass Ford–Mercury filed its petition for relief. No new financing statement to perfect Farmers' security interest in Bluegrass Ford–Mercury's inventory was filed as a result of the change in ownership or corporate name of the dealership.

In the spring of 1981, Bluegrass developed financial problems and stopped paying proceeds from sold vehicles to the bank. In total, the amount of income realized by Bluegrass Ford–Mercury from vehicles sold out of trust[2] was $160,220.39.

On April 9, 1981, Bluegrass Ford–Mercury, Inc., owed Farmers $232,084.24 on floor plan vehicles that were subject to installment notes. This includes the proceeds owed for the sales of vehicles out of trust.

In an effort to solve its problems, Bluegrass Ford–Mercury, on April 9, 1981, obtained a loan in the principal amount of $250,000 from Farmers National Bank. The Small Business Administration (SBA) guaranteed this loan. The proceeds of this loan were deposited into Bluegrass Ford–Mercury's account at Farmers. A note for this amount, payable to the bank, was executed by Bluegrass Ford–Mercury. A security agreement was simultaneously executed and filed as a financing statement. This agreement is dated March 27, 1981. The security agreement stated that it was given to secure the $250,000 loan and listed specific types of collateral as security, including "all inventory, raw materials, work in process, returned goods, and supplies now owned or hereafter acquired." Additionally, the security agreement enumerated other items as collateral, such as machinery, equipment, furniture and fixtures, and accounts receivable.

---

2. The phrase "sale out of trust" refers to sales by a borrower who has not paid off the loan against the units sold. The trust terminology is a holdover from the Trust Receipts Act of the 1930s, which provided the legal foundation for floor plan financing.

Farmers' security interest in the SBA loan was perfected when it filed a combined financing statement and security agreement in the Harrison County Court Clerk's Office on April 9, 1981.

The SBA authorization and loan agreement identified the collateral as a "[s]ecurity interest, under the Uniform Commercial Code on: all machinery, equipment (excluding licensed motor vehicles), furniture and fixtures; all inventory, excluding any floor-planned vehicles . . ." and all accounts receivable.

On October 8, 1981, Farmers filed a financing statement in the Harrison County Court Clerk's Office showing Farmers as the secured party, and Bluegrass Ford–Mercury as the debtor, covering "[a]ll new & Used vehicles in the inventory of Bluegrass Ford Merc., Inc." By this time, Bluegrass Ford–Mercury had become indebted to Farmers in the amount of $230,985.53 on licensed and floor plan vehicles.

On January 5, 1982, Bluegrass filed a Chapter 11 bankruptcy petition. During the 89–day period between the October 8, 1981, filing of the financing statement securing the inventory and the filing of the bankruptcy petition on January 5, 1982, the debtor made principal payments of $91,950.31 and interest payments of $10,545.54 on the floor plan note debt incurred before October 8, 1981. As of January 5, 1982, Bluegrass owed a balance of $139,035.22 on floor plan loans originated before October 8, 1981. Vehicles financed pursuant to these notes (executed before October 8, 1981), which were in inventory on January 5, 1982, were sold in the Chapter 11 proceeding. The proceeds of this sale, $23,938.87, were paid to the defendant.

Also during this period the bank loaned an additional $109,733.61 to purchase more vehicles under the floor plan. Bluegrass executed notes for these loans as well. Of this debt, $29,877.88 had been repaid at the time of the bankruptcy filing, leaving $79,855.73 unpaid. After the bankruptcy filing, an additional $8,635.89 was paid on these loans. The vehicles, the subject of the post-October 8, 1981, loans, were sold for $31,810.95. These proceeds were held in escrow.

Additionally, Bluegrass Ford–Mercury made three payments of $4,667 on the SBA loan within 90 days of filing the Chapter 11 proceeding. After it filed the petition, Bluegrass made two further payments of $4,667 each. Thus, the total payments made on the SBA loan, within the 90–day period before filing and after the Chapter 11 filing, were $23,335.

Bluegrass, as debtor in possession, brought this proceeding to recover certain payments it made to Farmers as preferential. The bankruptcy court held in favor of Bluegrass. * * *

Farmers first argues that it is a perfected, secured creditor and, thus, the payments Bluegrass made could not be avoided as preferences. A preference is "a transfer that enables a creditor to receive payment of a greater percentage of his claim against the debtor than he would have received if the transfer had not been made and he had participated in the distribution of the assets of the bankrupt estate." H.R. Rep. No. 595, 95th Cong., 1st Sess. 177 (1977) (hereinafter House Report). * * *

The determination of whether and when a security interest is perfected is determined by Kentucky law. Kentucky Revised Statutes § 355.9–303(1) provides the following:

> (1) A security interest is perfected when it has attached and when all of the applicable steps required for perfection have been taken. Such steps are specified in KRS 355.9–302, 355.9–304, 355.9–305 and 355.9–306. If such steps are taken before the security interest attaches, it is perfected at the time when it attaches

Kentucky Revised Statutes § 355.9–302(1) specifies that "[a] financing statement must be filed to perfect all security interests...." Farmers argues that both a financing statement filed in 1977, which references Bluegrass' predecessor, and another financing statement filed in 1981, served to perfect its interest in Bluegrass Ford–Mercury's inventory. Thus, the central question for appellate review is whether either of these financing statements perfected Farmers' security interest in Bluegrass Ford–Mercury's inventory. * * *

The corresponding UCC provision does not differ in any material respect from Kentucky's Code. A recent commentary restated the comparable UCC provision as follows: "Section 9–306(2) states the general rule that a security interest in collateral is not terminated upon a disposition of the collateral and can be enforced against the collateral in the hands of the transferee." Permanent Editorial Board Commentary on the Uniform Commercial Code No. 3 Sections 9–306(2) and 9–402(7) 9 (1990) (hereinafter Commentary). This provision makes it clear that a debtor cannot avoid or nullify a security interest in property by sale or transfer.

This provision also contains an exception to this general rule, however. If a secured party authorizes the disposition of its collateral and, additionally, the secured party has, "by agreement or otherwise, [authorized the disposition of the property] *free and clear of the security interest*," *id.* at 10, then the transferee will acquire the property free of the security interest.

In the present case, the record is unclear as to whether Farmers authorized the transfer, and, if it did, whether it authorized the transfer only subject to its continuing security interest. The district court concluded that "the bank would seem to have known of the transfer and accepted it." Although the bank was indisputably aware of the transfer, no evidence was presented regarding the conditions, if any, to the transfer. We will assume that the bank's security interest in the inventory continued after the transfer of the inventory to Bluegrass Ford–Mercury. Despite this assumption in the bank's favor, the bank still does not prevail in its argument that it had a security interest in all of the inventory of Bluegrass Ford–Mercury.

After assuming that Farmers' security interest continued, we must next determine whether its security interest was perfected. Kentucky Revised Statutes § 355.9–402 enumerates the requirements for an effective financing statement. Specifically, at issue here is the interpretation of subsection (7). Kentucky Revised Statutes § 355.9–402(7) provides:

> (7) A financing statement sufficiently shows the name of the debtor if it gives the individual, partnership or corporate name of the debtor, whether or not it adds other trade names or the names of partners. Where the debtor so changes his name or in the case of an organization its name, identity or corporate structure that a filed financing statement becomes seriously misleading, the filing is not effective to perfect a security interest in collateral acquired by the debtor more than four (4) months after the debtor notifies the secured party in writing of the change, unless a new appropriate financing statement is filed before the expiration of that time. A filed financing statement remains effective with respect to collateral transferred by the debtor even though the secured party knows of or consents to the transfer.

Again, we note that the corresponding UCC provision, § 9–402(7), is nearly identical.

The last sentence in section 9–402(7) is particularly applicable to the facts before us. "A filed financing statement remains effective with respect to collateral transferred by the debtor even though the secured party knows of or consents to the transfer." *Id.* Thus, this sentence, when read together with section 9–306(2), supports the following interpretation.

> If the secured party does not authorize the disposition or if the secured party authorizes the disposition subject to the security interest, the security interest will continue in the collateral following the disposition (§ 9–306(2)) and no new financing statement or amendment to the existing financing statement will be required in order to continue the perfected status of the security interest in the collateral following the disposition (§ 9–402(7)).

Commentary at 12. Thus, any collateral transferred from Bluegrass to Bluegrass Ford–Mercury would be subject to Farmers' security interest, which was perfected by the 1977 financing statement. The issue is whether Farmers' security interest included those vehicles acquired by Bluegrass Ford–Mercury after Bluegrass Ford's transfer of inventory.

Because the financing agreement covered all inventory, *i.e.*, as written it would include the cars that Bluegrass Ford acquired after the financing statement was filed, Farmers argues that its security interest, including "all inventory of Bluegrass[,] remained valid." We disagree. We note that the third sentence of UCC section 9–402(7), Ky. Rev. Stat. § 355.9–402, operates with respect "to collateral transferred by the debtor...." Ky. Rev. Stat. § 355.9–402(7). We do not interpret this language to encompass collateral not yet acquired by the transferee debtor. * * *

Farmers also argues that, even if it is an unsecured and unperfected creditor, Bluegrass failed to prove all of the elements of a preferential transfer pursuant to 11 U.S.C. § 547(b). Thus, the payments Bluegrass made to Farmers during the preference period do not have to be refunded. Farmers asserts that Bluegrass failed to prove that it was insolvent during the preferential period and that the transfers allowed Farmers to receive more than it would have under a Chapter 7 liquidation.

Title 11 U.S.C. § 547(b)(3) enables the trustee, in this case Bluegrass, to avoid any transfers made while the debtor was insolvent. Section 547(f) of the same title provides that, "for the purposes of this section, the debtor is presumed to have been insolvent on and during the 90 days immediately preceding the date of the filing of the petition." 11 U.S.C. § 547(f). Thus, to prevail, *Farmers* was required to present evidence to rebut this presumption.

Farmers argues that it introduced monthly financial statements filed by the debtor during this period, which the debtor submitted to Ford Motor Company. Farmers asserts that these documents demonstrate that Bluegrass was solvent because they show that total assets exceeded liabilities. At trial, Bluegrass' owner testified that these financial statements were misleading because they included personal assets, as well as personal liabilities, of the owners. The bankruptcy court concluded that if the financial statements were adjusted to reflect only Bluegrass' corporate assets, Bluegrass' liabilities exceeded its assets for each month during the preference period. This inference is further supported by Bluegrass' 1980 tax return, which showed a net loss of approximately $95,000.

The bankruptcy court's findings of fact with regard to Bluegrass' assets and liabilities during the preference period can be reversed only if clearly erroneous. In light of the testimony and supporting documentation demonstrating the misleading nature of the financial statements submitted to Ford, we cannot conclude that the bankruptcy court's determination was clearly erroneous. * * *

NOTE

Another way to raise working capital is by the practice of assigning or selling account receivables. Historically a basis for finance in the textile industry, but also used elsewhere including the furniture industry, was a practice called "factoring" in which notice of the assignment is given to the debtors on the account receivables. See Corn Exchange National Bank & Trust Co. v. Klauder, 318 U.S. 434, 438, n. 9, 63 S.Ct. 679, 87 L.Ed. 884 (1943) (describing factoring). The account receivables are purchased by the factor at a discount. If it is non-recourse factoring, the factor bears the risk of any defaulting account receivable purchased. Mr. Furniture Warehouse, Inc.

v. Barclays American/ Commercial Inc., 919 F.2d 1517 (11th Cir.1990), cert. denied, 502 U.S. 815, 112 S.Ct. 68, 116 L.Ed.2d 43 (1991).

BOULDER FRUIT EXPRESS v. TRANSPORATION FACTORING, INC.

251 F.3d 1268 (9th Cir.2001), cert. denied, 534 U.S. 1133, 122 S.Ct. 1077, 151 L.Ed.2d 978 (2002).

SILVERMAN, CIRCUIT JUDGE

This case concerns the Perishable Agricultural Commodities Act (PACA), 7 U.S.C. § 499a–499t (2000). Appellants are growers of fresh fruits and vegetables. From April 1996 to April 1997, appellant growers sold perishable goods to Certified Organics on credit. Certified was in the business of purchasing fresh agricultural produce from growers for resale. Certified resold the produce and invoiced its customers, creating accounts receivable. Certified then sold its accounts receivable to Transportation Factoring, Inc. (Transfac) pursuant to a factoring agreement. Under that agreement, Transfac purchased the accounts from Certified for 80% of their face value.

When Certified defaulted in its payments to the growers, the growers sued not only Certified but also Transfac. Why Transfac? The growers allege that Certified's factoring of its accounts to Transfac breached a statutory trust created by PACA for the benefit of the growers. They allege that Certified was to have held the accounts receivable in trust for the growers until the growers were paid for their produce. They allege that in factoring Certified's accounts receivable, Transfac acquired "trust assets"—the receivables—in breach of the trust and must disgorge them to the growers, unless Transfac can prove that it was a bona fide purchaser for value without notice of the breach. The growers also sued Capital Resource Funding, Inc., another factoring company that referred Certified's business to Transfac.

On motion for summary judgment, the district court granted summary judgment for Transfac and Capital Funding. The court ruled that because Transfac had paid Certified more for the accounts ($3.297 million) than Transfac collected on them ($3.278 million), albeit less than the face value of the accounts ($4.7 million), Certified's factoring of its accounts did not breach the trust. In other words, because Transfac bought the accounts for at least what they were worth, maybe more, the factoring arrangement did not dissipate trust assets, and therefore, Transfac cannot be found to have acquired the accounts in breach of the trust.

The district court entered judgment in favor of Transfac and Capital Resource Funding pursuant to Fed.R.Civ.P. 54(b). Other claims against Certified and John Messing, Certified's principal, were not resolved by the summary judgment motion.

We have jurisdiction under 28 U.S.C. § 1291, and review the district court's grant of summary judgment de novo. *Balint v. Carson City,* 180 F.3d 1047, 1050 (9th Cir.1999) (en banc). We affirm.

Congress enacted PACA in 1930 to prevent unfair business practices and promote financial responsibility in the fresh fruit and produce industry. *See Sunkist Growers, Inc. v. Fisher,* 104 F.3d 280, 282 (9th Cir.1997) (citing *Farley & Calfee, Inc. v. USDA,* 941 F.2d 964, 966 (9th Cir.1991)). In 1984, Congress amended PACA "to remedy [the] burden on commerce in perishable agricultural commodities and to protect the public interest" caused by accounts receivable financing arrangements that "encumber or give lenders a security interest" in the perishable agricultural commodities superior to the growers. 7 U.S.C. § 499e(c)(1). Section 499e(c) created the PACA trust:

> Perishable agricultural commodities received by a commission merchant, dealer, or broker in all transactions, and all inventories of food or other products derived from perishable agricultural commodities, and any receivables or proceeds from the sale of such commodities or products, shall be held by such commission merchant, dealer, or broker in trust for the benefit of all unpaid suppliers or sellers of such commodities or agents involved in the transaction, until full payment of the sums owing in connection with such transactions has been received by such unpaid suppliers, sellers, or agents.

Id. at § 499e(c)(2); *see also* 7 C.F.R. § 46.46 (2000). As explained by the Second Circuit:

> This provision imposes a "non-segregated floating trust" on the commodities and their derivatives, and permits the commingling of trust assets without defeating the trust. Through this trust, the sellers of the commodities maintain a right to recover against the purchasers superior to all creditors, including secured creditors.

Endico Potatoes, Inc. v. CIT Group/Factoring, Inc., 67 F.3d 1063, 1067 (2d Cir.1995) (citations omitted).

By the express language of PACA, the trust applies to receivables generated by the sale of commodities, just as it does to the commodities themselves. 7 U.S.C. § 499e(c)(2); 7 C.F.R. § 46.46. It is designed to protect commodity producers against secured lenders. In the ordinary case, here is how it works: Farmer sells oranges on credit to Broker. Broker turns around and sells the oranges on credit to Supermarket, generating an account receivable from Supermarket. Broker then obtains a loan from Bank and grants Bank a security interest in the account receivable to secure the loan. Broker goes bankrupt. Under PACA, Broker is required to hold the receivable in trust for Farmer until Farmer was paid in full; use of the receivable as collateral was a breach of the trust. Therefore, Farmer's rights in the Supermarket receivable are superior to Bank's. In fact, as a trust asset, the Supermarket receivable is not even part of the bankruptcy estate.

That's the easy case. The issue today concerns factoring, the commercial practice of converting receivables into cash by selling them at a discount. BLACK'S LAW DICTIONARY (7th ed.1999). The question before us is whether Certified breached the PACA trust by selling its accounts to Transfac pursuant to the factoring agreement.

We apply general trust principles to questions involving the PACA trust, unless those principles directly conflict with PACA. *Sunkist,* 104 F.3d at 282. The Restatement of Trusts defines a breach of trust as "a violation by the trustee of any duty which as trustee he owes to the beneficiary." RESTATEMENT (SECOND) OF TRUSTS § 201 (1959). Federal regulations set forth a PACA trustee's primary duty:

> Commission merchants, dealers and brokers are required to maintain trust assets in a manner that such assets are freely available to satisfy outstanding obligations to sellers of perishable agricultural commodities. Any act or omission which is inconsistent with this responsibility, including dissipation of trust assets, is unlawful and in violation of [PACA].

7 C.F.R. § 46.46(d)(1). The regulations further define "dissipation" as "any act or failure to act which could result in the diversion of trust assets or which could prejudice or impair the ability of unpaid suppliers, sellers, or agents to recover money owed in connection with produce transactions." *Id.* § 46.46(a)(2).

In this case, the growers argue that factoring agreements per se breach the PACA trust because, by definition, they contemplate the sale of trust receivables at less than their face value. However, nothing in PACA or the regulations prohibits PACA trustees from attempting to turn receivables into cash by factoring. To the contrary, a commercially reasonable sale of accounts for fair value is entirely consistent with the trustee's primary duty under PACA and 7 C.F.R. § 46.46(d)(1)—to maintain trust assets so that they are "freely available to satisfy outstanding obligations to sellers of perishable commodities." The goal of PACA, after all, is not the perpetuation of unliquidated commercial paper, but to assure that growers are paid for their commodities. H.R.Rep. No. 98–543, at 3 (1983), *reprinted in* 1983 U.S.C.C.A.N. 405, 406; *Sunkist,* 104 F.3d at 282. Of course, whether a particular factoring arrangement is commercially reasonable will depend upon its terms. A PACA trustee who sells accounts for pennies on the dollar, just to turn a quick buck, might well have breached the PACA trust, while a trustee who factors accounts at a commercially reasonable rate would not. *Cf. E. Armata, Inc. v. Platinum Funding Corp.,* 887 F.Supp. 590, 593 (S.D.N.Y.1995) (accounts receivable factored at 60 to 65% of face value were not factored for value). We hold that factoring agreements do not, per se, violate PACA.

Our view that factoring agreements do not per se violate the PACA trust is consistent with general trust principles. Generally, a trustee can sell trust assets *unless* the sale breaches the trust. RESTATEMENT (SECOND) OF TRUSTS § 190. Whether a transferee of trust assets is a bona fide purchaser becomes relevant only as a defense after it has been determined that a breach of trust has occurred. (citations omitted).

Appellant growers argue in the alternative that, even if factoring agreements do not per se violate PACA, the factoring agreement in this case breached the trust by dissipating the trust assets because Transfac did not pay face value for the receivables. Transfac responds that the factoring arrangement here actually enhanced the trust because it was commercially reasonable. We agree with Transfac.

The factoring agreement allowed Certified to convert invoices that were not payable for 30 days (including uncollectible and invalid invoices) into cash that Certified could have used to immediately pay growers. Far from dissipating assets, Certified actually received from Transfac $18,482 more for the accounts than the accounts would prove to be worth. In any case, a factoring discount of 20% was never shown to be commercially unreasonable.

The growers argue that Certified necessarily admitted a breach of the trust when it admitted that it was unable to pay its growers and suppliers of produce. The growers confuse breach of contract with breach of trust. The only question in this case is whether Certified breached its duty as a trustee when it sold the accounts receivable to Transfac. Certified's *contractual* obligation to pay is not in issue. To the extent that the growers argue that Transfac, as a transferee of trust assets, is strictly liable to the growers because Certified, the transferor, has failed to pay, we already have held that third parties are not guarantors of the PACA trust. They are liable only if they had some role in causing the breach or dissipation of the trust. *Sunkist,* 104 F.3d at 283; *see also Consumers Produce,* 16 F.3d at 1381–82. To reiterate, in this case, Transfac paid Certified more for trust assets than those assets were worth.

Finally, we agree with the district court that the growers never proved that the trust funds were misapplied in the first place. The growers conceded that they did not know how Certified spent the funds it received from Transfac. If, for example, the funds were used to pay off *other* perishable commodities producers, no breach of the trust would have occurred. This is because the PACA trust, by definition, is a non-segregated floating trust in which assets of other growers can be commingled. 7 U.S.C. § 499e(c).

In summary, we hold that factoring does not, per se, breach a PACA trust. We also hold that the particular factoring arrangement in this case was commercially reasonable and did not breach or otherwise dissipate the trust. The judgment of the district court in favor of Transfac and Capital Resource Funding is AFFIRMED.

Bankers' Acceptances

A bankers' acceptance is a negotiable instrument in the form of a "draft," which is simply an order to pay a stated amount of money to the holder of the draft on a specified day. The draft is drawn on, and accepted by, a bank. The accepting bank assumes responsibility to pay the draft at maturity. The Federal Reserve Act of 1913 sought to create a bankers' acceptance market in the United States in order to promote exports and trade.

A bankers' acceptance may be a "sight" draft that is payable on presentation. More frequently, the bankers' acceptance is a "time" draft payable a specific number of days after acceptance by a bank. A bankers' acceptance is redeemed at maturity for face value by the accepting bank. Maturities on bankers' acceptances vary but typically are one, three and six months.

Once accepted by a bank, a draft becomes a bankers' acceptance and is a negotiable instrument. It may be sold (discounted) by the party receiving the instrument upon endorsement and delivery, or the bankers' acceptance may be held until maturity. Bankers' acceptances are issued at a discount determined by current interest rates and the time to maturity. Since they are accepted by a bank, the risk of a default is low, making these instruments a desirable investment for short terms. A bankers' acceptance may be eligible for discount or purchase by the Federal Reserve Board. This further enhances their liquidity. The eligibility requirements for bankers' acceptances that may be purchased by the Federal Reserve Board are found at 12 C.F.R. § 250.165.

Bankers' acceptances are also a means to finance a sale of goods, as described in the footnote in the next case.

UNITED STATES v. DOUGHERTY

763 F.2d 970 (8th Cir.1985).

HENRY WOODS, DISTRICT JUDGE.

After a jury trial, the appellant, Richard A. Dougherty, was found guilty of twenty-five counts of misapplying $14,500,000 in funds of the First National Bank of St. Paul, Minnesota, and falsifying the bank's books and records. The nine counts of misapplication dealt with the improper issuance of bankers' acceptances in violation of 18 U.S.C. § 656. The remaining sixteen counts charged a violation of 18 U.S.C. § 1005 in that appellant willfully failed to record these transactions. Appellant was given concurrent sentences of a year and a day on three counts, five years of probation, and a $15,000 fine on the remaining counts by the trial judge. Appellant challenges the sufficiency of the evidence and the correctness of the jury instructions. We affirm the convictions.

Appellant was a vice president in charge of the International Banking Division of the third largest bank in the Ninth Federal Reserve District. The offenses charged were mainly related to the financial difficulties of a seafood processing venture by Transalaska Fisheries Corporation (Transalaska). Based in Seattle, the company proposed to convert a ship into a floating seafood processor and to harvest mainly king crab. In April, 1979,

Dougherty secured approval of the bank's loan committee for a $3,500,000 advance for which Transalaska gave a term note. Conversion of the ship ran into delays and cost overruns, with the result that the ship was not ready for the 1979 king crab harvest. The 1980 season fell far below expectations. During conversion in September, 1979, Dougherty disbursed $350,000 beyond the approved limit, documenting the excess amount in a memo to the bank's president and in comments placed in the Transalaska credit file. Transalaska's financial difficulties worsened, and its officers began calling on Dougherty for more financing. He complied by using the device of unapproved bankers' acceptances.[3] The First National Bank of St. Paul required approval of its senior loan committee for loans and credit extensions in excess of $100,000. Dougherty sat on the senior loan committee and participated in its weekly discussion and decisions on lending. He presented none of the bankers' acceptances for Transalaska to the loan committee for approval. Nor were they posted in the bank's general ledger. Proceeds of the acceptances were deposited into the company's checking account. On maturity date Dougherty paid off the maturing acceptance with a new one, in an amount equal to or greater than the maturing acceptance, since the customer was unable to meet the obligation on its due date. An overdraft would have resulted if he had allowed the account to be charged on the due dates. When a customer's account suffers an overdraft of $1,000 for five days, a computerized printout automatically goes to the loan review personnel. This pattern of roll-overs prevented what would have been a series of overdraft reports from coming to the attention of the loan review committee.

The same system of bankers' acceptances and concealment was used by Dougherty to finance the operation of David Noland, who was engaged in the restaurant business in the Minneapolis–St. Paul area. Dougherty extended Noland more than $400,000 in bankers acceptances during 1979 and 1980, none of which were paid. These advances were made in spite of the fact that Noland was a very poor credit risk. If anything, bankers'

---

3. A bankers acceptance is a negotiable instrument, governed by 12 U.S.C. § 372 and applicable regulations and rulings of the Federal Reserve Board, which define and interpret the "eligibility" of the financing instrument. An "eligible" bankers acceptance is one which the Federal Reserve has authority to purchase. Eligible bankers' acceptances ordinarily, and for purposes of this case, are used to finance shipments of goods between foreign countries. The typical transaction involves an exporter who proves in some manner to the bank that he has a given amount of product which will be shipped to a foreign country. He must have goods or a firm contract at least equal to the amount of financing. The shipment must be consummated in 180 days or less. The bank may then agree to finance for whatever period of time the shipment will require by taking the exporter's promise to pay in the form of a written draft. The bank stamps the word "accepted" on the draft, and the authorized officer signs or initials the item. The document will provide for a given sum to be due on a given date, correlating with the completion of the shipment. An authorized officer then places on the face of the instrument an eligibility clause, describing the international transaction in goods which is represented by the acceptance. The proceeds of the shipment then are to be used to liquidate the transaction, without expectation of resorting to collateral or other security. The bank may choose to hold the acceptance until maturity, at which time the customer pays the bank. More commonly, however, the bank sells acceptances at a discount on the secondary market, with the bank paying the holder in the face amount upon maturity. The market maintains a high interest in the instrument because it is a secure, no-risk investment due to the bank's absolute obligation to pay upon maturity, regardless of the customer's ability to pay the proceeds from the transaction.

acceptances were more inappropriate in Noland's case than in the advances to Transalaska Fisheries[4] Although the Transalaska and Noland transactions were not recorded in the bank ledger, Dougherty maintained a private desk drawer accounting of the transactions.

When it appeared that an audit in progress would uncover the concealed multi-million dollar losses of the bank, Dougherty went to the bank president and confessed that he had issued the unauthorized acceptances. Four days later he tendered his resignation. There is no evidence that appellant personally profited from any of these transactions or that he had any type of special relationship with the officers of Transalaska Fisheries Corporation or David Noland. * * *

Note

The Federal Reserve Board has noted that an excellent non-technical definition of a banker's acceptance is:

> A banker's acceptance is a time bill of exchange (frequently called a time draft) drawn on and accepted by a banking institution. By accepting the draft the bank signifies its commitment to pay the face amount at maturity to anyone who presents it for payment at that time. In this way the bank provides its name and credit and enables its customer, who pays a commission to the accepting bank for this accommodation, to secure financing readily and at a reasonable interest cost. For investors, bankers' acceptances represent short-term private paper with a maximum degree of safety and liquidity, comparable to that enjoyed by Treasury bills.

> Bankers' acceptances have been utilized in the United States and abroad in part to finance domestic transactions but primarily in transactions related to international trade. Buyers and sellers engaged in foreign transactions are apt to be less well known to each other and the shipping time is longer than is usually the case in domestic transactions.

Board of Governors of the Federal Reserve System. Lending Functions of the Federal Reserve Banks: A History 55–57 (1973) (citation omitted).

---

4. In sum, the prerequisites to an eligible bankers' acceptance are:

(a) that there be a specific transaction involving the shipment of goods usually between foreign countries;

(b) that there be actual goods or a firm contract for sale of the goods, in either case, representing at least the face value of the acceptance; (Anderson 26, 29);

(c) that the transaction take no longer than 180 days, to correlate to the time set forth on the acceptance; and

(d) that the acceptance be paid upon maturity with the proceeds of the transaction.

Letters of Credit

Letters of credit are instruments are instruments issued by banks that act as a guarantee of payment for goods or services.

CENTRIFUGAL CASTING MACHINE CO. v. AMERICAN BANK AND TRUST CO.

966 F.2d 1348 (10th Cir.1992).

SEYMOUR, CIRCUIT JUDGE.

The United States appeals from the judgment entered in one of two consolidated diversity actions involving a letter of credit and a standby letter of credit. The letters were issued in connection with a contract between plaintiff-appellee Centrifugal Casting Machine (CCM) and State Machinery Trading Company (SMTC), an agency of the Iraqi government, under which CCM was to provide cast ductile iron pipe plant equipment to SMTC for a total contract price of $27,390,731. The contracting parties agreed that the payment mechanism from SMTC to CCM was to be an irrevocable letter of credit for the benefit of CCM in the contract amount, out of which CCM was entitled to draw ten percent as a down payment. This letter was issued by Central Bank of Iraq and confirmed by defendant-appellee Banca Nazionale del Lavoro (BNL).

The parties further agreed that a standby letter of credit in the amount of the $2.7 million down payment would be issued on behalf of CCM for the benefit of an agent of SMTC, and would be available to repay SMTC the amount of the down payment upon the requisite proof that CCM had not performed under the contract.[5] This standby letter was issued by BNL to defendant-appellee American Bank of Tulsa (ABT), CCM's bank, as account party, and made payable to Rafidain Bank, which in turn issued a $2.7 million guarantee to SMTC. CCM drew its down payment under the letter of credit and deposited that amount with ABT as security to protect ABT against any obligation it might incur on the standby letter of credit. Although an attempt was subsequently made on behalf of SMTC to draw on the standby letter of credit, the attempt was not accompanied by proof of nonperformance by CCM, and was not honored before the expiration date set out in that letter.

The suits below involved claims to the $2.7 million down payment by CCM, ABT, and BNL, the bank that had confirmed the letter of credit in favor of CCM and had issued the standby letter of credit in favor of SMTC. The United States intervened, asserting that Iraq had a property interest in the down payment and therefore in the money deposited by CCM in ABT. The United States claimed that the bank account was a

---

5. "The essential function of [a letter of credit] is to assure a party to an agreement that he will receive the benefits of his performance." Wood v. R.R. Donnelley & Sons Co., 888 F.2d 313, 317 (3d Cir.1989). "A variation on this arrangement is present where, as here, the bank issues a 'stand-by' letter of credit. The beneficiary of an ordinary letter may draw upon it simply by presenting documents that show that the beneficiary has performed and is entitled to the funds. In contrast, a 'stand-by' letter requires documents that show that the customer has defaulted on some obligation, thereby triggering the beneficiary's right to draw down on the letter." Id.

blocked account under the regulations implementing the Executive Orders freezing assets of the Iraqi government. * * *

Following Iraq's invasion of Kuwait on August 2, 1990, the President issued two Executive Orders blocking any transfer of property in which Iraq holds an interest. *See* Exec. Order No. 12,722, 55 Fed.Reg. 31,803 (1990); Exec. Order 12,724, 55 Fed.Reg. 33,089 (1990). These orders are implemented by regulations promulgated by the Secretary of the Treasury, through the Office of Foreign Assets Control. *See* 31 CFR §§ 575.201–.806 (1991). Under these regulations, "no property or interests in property of the Government of Iraq that are in the United States ... may be transferred, paid, exported, withdrawn or otherwise dealt in." *Id.* § 575.201(a).

The United States contends on appeal that the freeze of Iraq's assets furthers national policy to punish Iraq by preventing it from obtaining economic benefits from transactions with American citizens, and by preserving such assets both for use as a bargaining chip in resolving this country's differences with Iraq and as a source of compensation for claims Americans may have against Iraq. We agree that these policy considerations are compelling and that we are therefore required to construe Iraqi property interests broadly. However, we are not persuaded these policies would be furthered by construing the circumstances here to give rise to a property interest on behalf of Iraq that would not otherwise be cognizable under governing legal principles. Iraq would not be punished if denied use of an asset in which it could not claim a property interest in any event. Likewise, compensation and bargaining through use of such an asset would not be to Iraq's detriment.

We perceive the gist of the United States's argument to be that the asset at issue is a down payment Iraq made on a contract that CCM has not performed. Therefore, it is argued, Iraq has a property interest in this asset on the basis of a purported breach-of-contract claim under principles of rescission and restitution. This analysis, however, runs directly contrary to the legal principles governing the financial mechanisms chosen by the contracting parties to facilitate payments under the contract.

We begin by observing that CCM received the funds at issue by drawing on an irrevocable letter of credit. We must therefore determine the particular characteristics of that financial instrument and ascertain the nature of the interest that it conveys. Because the term "letter of credit" is not defined in either the Executive Orders or the implementing regulations, we give it the meaning ordinarily attributed to it by courts and parties dealing with this document. *See Propper v. Clark,* 337 U.S. 472, 480, 69 S.Ct. 1333, 1338, 93 L.Ed. 1480 (1949).

> "[A] letter of credit involves three parties: (1) an issuer (generally a bank) who agrees to pay conforming drafts presented under the letter of credit; (2) a bank customer or 'account party' who orders the letter of credit and dictates its terms; and (3) a beneficiary to whom the

letter of credit is issued, who can collect monies under the letter of credit by presenting drafts and making proper demand on the issuer."

Arbest Const. Co. v. First Nat'l Bank & Trust Co., 777 F.2d 581, 583 (10th Cir.1985). A letter of credit thus involves three legally distinct relationships, that "between the issuer and the account party, the issuer and the beneficiary, and the account party and the beneficiary (this last relationship being the underlying business deal giving rise to the issuance of the letter of credit)." *Id.* In this case, CCM was the beneficiary of the letter which was issued by Central Bank of Iraq to fund the contract, BNL was the confirming bank which then became directly liable to CCM,[6] and SMTC was the bank customer or account party.

Two interrelated features of the letter of credit provide it with its unique value in the marketplace and are of critical importance in our consideration of the United States's claim here. First, "[t]he simple result [of a letter of credit] is that the issuer substitutes its credit, preferred by the beneficiary, for that of the account party." *Id.; see also Republic Nat'l Bank v. Fidelity & Deposit Co.,* 894 F.2d 1255, 1258 (11th Cir.) (letter gives beneficiary irrevocable right to payment, not from account party, who might become insolvent or refuse to pay, but from bank), *cert. denied,* 498 U.S. 926, 111 S.Ct. 308, 112 L.Ed.2d 261 (1990); *Airline Reporting Corp. v. First Nat'l Bank,* 832 F.2d 823, 826 (4th Cir.1987) (issuer replaces customer's promise to pay with its own promise to pay); *Pringle–Associated Mortgage Corp. v. Southern Nat'l Bank,* 571 F.2d 871, 874 (5th Cir.1978) (beneficiary's claim based on letter of credit, not on agreement between issuer and account party and not on the underlying contract). The issuing bank thus pays the beneficiary *out of its own funds,* and then must look to the account party for reimbursement. *See generally Republic Nat'l Bank,* 894 F.2d at 1257–58; Okla.Stat. tit. 12A, § 5–114(3) (issuer which has honored demand for payment entitled to immediate reimbursement).

Second, the issuer's obligation to pay on a letter of credit is completely independent from the underlying commercial transaction between the beneficiary and the account party. *See Ward Petroleum Corp. v. FDIC,* 903 F.2d 1297, 1299–1300 (10th Cir.1990). Significantly, the issuer must honor a proper demand even though the beneficiary has breached the underlying contract, *see id.* at 1299; Okla.Stat.Ann. tit. 12A, § 5–114 Okla. comment (1); even though the insolvency of the account party renders reimbursement impossible, *see Wood v. R.R. Donnelley & Sons Co.,* 888 F.2d 313, 318 (3d Cir.1989); and notwithstanding supervening illegality, impossibility, war or insurrection, *see KMW Int'l v. Chase Manhattan Bank, N.A.,* 606 F.2d 10, 16 (2d Cir.1979). This principle of independence is universally viewed as essential to the proper functioning of a letter of credit and to

---

6. "A 'confirming bank' is a bank which engages either that it will itself honor a credit already issued by another bank or that such a credit will be honored by the issuer or a third bank." Okla.Stat. tit. 12A, § 5–103(1)(f). Here, BNL agreed to honor the credit itself. "A confirming bank by confirming a credit becomes directly obligated on the credit to the extent of its confirmation as though it were its issuer and acquires the rights of an issuer." § 5–107(2).

its particular value, *i.e.,* its certainty of payment. *See, e.g., Ward Petroleum,* 903 F.2d at 1299; *Wood,* 888 F.2d at 318; *Tradax Petroleum Am., Inc. v. Coral Petroleum, Inc. (In re Coral Petroleum),* 878 F.2d 830, 834 (5th Cir.1989); *FDIC v. Bank of San Francisco,* 817 F.2d 1395, 1398 (9th Cir.1987); *KMW Int'l,* 606 F.2d at 16. "Parties to a contract may use a letter of credit in order to make certain that contractual disputes wend their way towards resolution with money in the beneficiary's pocket rather than in the pocket of the contracting party." *Itek Corp. v. First Nat'l Bank,* 730 F.2d 19, 24 (1st Cir.1984); *see also Ward Petroleum,* 903 F.2d at 1299.

This assurance of payment gives letters of credit a central role in commercial dealings, *see Bank of San Francisco,* 817 F.2d at 1398–99, and gives them a particular value in international transactions, "in which sophisticated investors knowingly undertake such risks as political upheaval or contractual breach in return for the benefits to be reaped from international trade," *Enterprise Int'l, Inc. v. Corporacion Estatal Petrolera Ecuatoriana,* 762 F.2d 464, 474 (5th Cir.1985). "Law affecting such an essential instrument of the economy must be shaped with sensitivity to its special characteristics." *Bank of San Francisco,* 817 F.2d at 1399; *see Pringle–Associated Mortgage,* 571 F.2d at 874. Accordingly, courts have concluded that the whole purpose of a letter of credit would be defeated by examining the merits of the underlying contract dispute to determine whether the letter should be paid. *Andy Marine, Inc. v. Zidell, Inc.,* 812 F.2d 534, 537 (9th Cir.1987); *Itek,* 730 F.2d at 24 (resort to underlying contract dispute risks depriving beneficiary "of the very advantage for which he bargained, namely that the dispute would be resolved while he is in possession of the money").

Because of the nature of a letter of credit, we conclude that Iraq does not have a property interest in the money CCM received under the letter. The United States contends in essence that Iraq has a property interest in this money because it was allegedly a contract payment made by Iraq, which Iraq should recover because CCM breached the contract. In so arguing, the United States makes a breach of contract claim on behalf of Iraq that Iraq has never made, creates a remedy for the contracting parties in derogation of the remedy they themselves provided, and, most importantly, disregards the controlling legal principles with respect to letters of credit. * * *

In rejecting the United States's position, we reiterate our recognition that blocked Iraqi property interests are to be broadly construed so as to effectuate the purposes underlying the blocking orders. We nonetheless are not at liberty to restructure the essential characteristics of a letter of credit in order to create a property interest that would not be recognized under the rules applicable to that internationally recognized financing instrument. Because those rules do not establish that Iraq has a legally cognizable property interest in the payment made to CCM under the letter of credit, the policies underlying the blocking of Iraqi assets are simply not implicated. The national interest is not furthered by creating a property interest out of conditions that would not otherwise generate such an interest, particularly when we must do so at the expense of a critical and unique device of international trade.

AFFIRMED.

———————

FEDERAL DEPOSIT INSURANCE CORP.
v. PHILADELPHIA GEAR CORP.

476 U.S. 426, 106 S.Ct. 1931, 90 L.Ed.2d 428 (1986).

JUSTICE O'CONNOR delivered the opinion of the Court.

We granted certiorari to consider whether a standby letter of credit backed by a contingent promissory note is insured as a "deposit" under the federal deposit insurance program. We hold that, in light of the longstanding interpretation of petitioner Federal Deposit Insurance Corporation (FDIC) that such a letter does not create a deposit and, in light of the fact that such a letter does not entrust any noncontingent assets to the bank, a standby letter of credit backed by a contingent promissory note does not give rise to an insured deposit.

Orion Manufacturing Corporation (Orion) was, at the time of the relevant transactions, a customer of respondent Philadelphia Gear Corporation (Philadelphia Gear). On Orion's application, the Penn Square Bank, N.A. (Penn Square) issued a letter of credit for the benefit of Philadelphia Gear in the amount of $145,200. The letter of credit provided that a draft drawn upon the letter of credit would be honored by Penn Square only if accompanied by Philadelphia Gear's "signed statement that [it had] invoiced Orion Manufacturing Corporation and that said invoices have remained unpaid for at least fifteen (15) days." Because the letter of credit was intended to provide payment to the seller only if the buyer of the invoiced goods failed to make payment, the letter of credit was what is commonly referred to as a "standby" or "guaranty" letter of credit. See, e.g., 12 CFR § 337.2(a), and n. 1 (1985) (defining standby letters of credit and mentioning that they may " 'guaranty' payment of a money obligation"). A conventional "commercial" letter of credit, in contrast, is one in which the seller obtains payment from the issuing bank without looking to the buyer for payment even in the first instance. See ibid. (distinguishing standby letters of credit from commercial letters of credit). See also Verkuil, Bank Solvency and Guaranty Letters of Credit, 25 Stan.L.Rev. 716, 717–724 (1973); Arnold & Bransilver, The Standby Letter of Credit— The Controversy Continues, 10 U.C.C.L.J. 272, 277–279 (Spring 1978).

On the same day that Penn Square issued the standby letter of credit, Orion executed an unsecured promissory note for $145,200 in favor of Penn Square. The purpose of the note was listed as "Back up Letter of Credit." Ibid. Although the face of the note did not so indicate, both Orion and Penn Square understood that nothing would be considered due on the note, and no interest charged by Penn Square, unless Philadelphia Gear presented drafts on the standby letter of credit after nonpayment by Orion. 751 F.2d 1131, 1134 (CA10 1984).

On July 5, 1982, Penn Square was declared insolvent. Petitioner FDIC was appointed its receiver. Shortly thereafter, Philadelphia Gear presented drafts on the standby letter of credit for payment of over $700,000 for goods delivered before Penn Square's insolvency. The FDIC returned the drafts unpaid. 751 F.2d, at 1133–1134.

Philadelphia Gear sued the FDIC in the Western District of Oklahoma. Philadelphia Gear alleged that the standby letter of credit was an insured deposit under the definition of "deposit" set forth at 12 U.S.C. § 1813(*l*)(1), and that Philadelphia Gear was therefore entitled to $100,000 in deposit insurance from the FDIC. See 12 U.S.C. § 1821(a)(1) (setting forth $100,000 as the maximum amount generally insured by the FDIC for any single depositor at a given bank). In apparent hopes of obtaining additional funds from the FDIC in the latter's capacity as receiver rather than as insurer, respondent also alleged that terms of the standby letter of credit allowing repeated reinstatements of the credit made the letter's total value more than $145,200. * * *

Title 12 U.S.C. § 1813(*l*)(1) provides:

"The term 'deposit' means—(1) the unpaid balance of money or its equivalent received or held by a bank in the usual course of business and for which it has given or is obligated to give credit, either conditionally or unconditionally, to a commercial ... account, or which is evidenced by ... a letter of credit or a traveler's check on which the bank is primarily liable: *Provided,* That, without limiting the generality of the term 'money or its equivalent,' any such account or instrument must be regarded as evidencing the receipt of the equivalent of money when credited or issued in exchange for checks or drafts or for a promissory note upon which the person obtaining any such credit or instrument is primarily or secondarily liable...."

Philadelphia Gear successfully argued before the Court of Appeals that the standby letter of credit backed by a contingent promissory note constituted a "deposit" under 12 U.S.C. § 1813(*l*)(1) because that letter was one on which the bank was primarily liable, and evidenced the receipt by the bank of "money or its equivalent" in the form of a promissory note upon which the person obtaining the credit was primarily or secondarily liable. The FDIC does not here dispute that the bank was primarily liable on the letter of credit. Nor does the FDIC contest the fact that the backup note executed by Orion is, at least in some sense, a "promissory note." The FDIC argues rather that it has consistently interpreted § 1813(*l*)(1) not to include standby letters of credit backed only by a contingent promissory note because such a note represents no hard assets and thus does not constitute "money or its equivalent." Because the alleged "deposit" consists only of a *contingent* liability, asserts the FDIC, a standby letter of credit backed by a contingent promissory note does not give rise to a "deposit" that Congress intended the FDIC to insure. Under this theory, while the note here may have been labeled a promissory note on its face and may have been a promissory note under state law, it was not a promissory note for purposes of the federal law set forth in 12 U.S.C. § 1813(*l*)(1). * * *

When Congress created the FDIC, the Nation was in the throes of an extraordinary financial crisis. See generally F. Allen, Since Yesterday: The Nineteen–Thirties in America 98–121 (1940); A. Schlesinger, The Crisis of the Old Order 474–482 (1957). More than one-third of the banks in the United States open in 1929 had shut their doors just four years later. Bureau of the Census, Historical Statistics of the United States: Colonial Times to 1970, pt. 2, pp. 1019, 1038 (1976). In response to this financial crisis, President Roosevelt declared a national banking holiday effective the first business day after he took office. 48 Stat. 1689. Congress in turn responded with extensive legislation on banking, including the laws that gave the FDIC its existence.

Congress' purpose in creating the FDIC was clear. Faced with virtual panic, Congress attempted to safeguard the hard earnings of individuals against the possibility that bank failures would deprive them of their savings. Congress passed the 1933 provisions "[i]n order to provide against a repetition of the present painful experience in which a vast sum of *assets and purchasing power* is 'tied up.'" S.Rep. No. 77, 73d Cong., 1st Sess., 12 (1933) (emphasis added). The focus of Congress was therefore upon ensuring that a deposit of "hard earnings" entrusted by individuals to a bank would not lead to a tangible loss in the event of a bank failure. * * *

Congress' focus in providing for a system of deposit insurance—a system that has been continued to the present without modification to the basic definition of deposits that are "money or its equivalent"—was clearly a focus upon safeguarding the assets and "hard earnings" that businesses and individuals have entrusted to banks. Congress wanted to ensure that someone who put tangible assets into a bank could always get those assets back. The purpose behind the insurance of deposits in general, and especially in the section defining deposits as "money or its equivalent," therefore, is the protection of assets and hard earnings entrusted to a bank.

This purpose is not furthered by extending deposit insurance to cover a standby letter of credit backed by a contingent promissory note, which involves no such surrender of assets or hard earnings to the custody of the bank. Philadelphia Gear, which now seeks to collect deposit insurance, surrendered absolutely nothing to the bank. The letter of credit is for Philadelphia Gear's benefit, but the bank relied upon Orion to meet the obligations of the letter of credit and made no demands upon Philadelphia Gear. Nor, more importantly, did Orion surrender any assets unconditionally to the bank. The bank did not credit any account of Orion's in exchange for the promissory note, and did not treat its own assets as increased by its acceptance of the note. The bank could not have collected on the note from Orion unless Philadelphia Gear presented the unpaid invoices and a draft on the letter of credit. In the absence of a presentation by Philadelphia Gear of the unpaid invoices, the promissory note was a wholly contingent promise, and when Penn Square went into receivership, neither Orion nor Philadelphia Gear had lost anything except the ability to use Penn Square to reduce Philadelphia Gear's risk that Philadelphia Gear would go unpaid for a delivery of goods to Orion.

Congress' actions with respect to the particular definition of "deposit" that it has chosen in order to effect its general purpose likewise lead us to believe that a standby letter of credit backed by a contingent promissory note is not an insurable "deposit." In 1933, Congress amended the Federal Reserve Act to authorize the creation of the FDIC and charged it "to insure . . . the deposits of all banks which are entitled to the benefits of [FDIC] insurance." § 8, Banking Act of 1933, ch. 89, 48 Stat. 168. Congress did not define the term "deposit," however, until the Banking Act of 1935, in which it stated:

> "The term 'deposit' means the unpaid balance of money or its equivalent received by a bank in the usual course of business and for which it has given or is obligated to give credit to a commercial, checking, savings, time or thrift account, or which is evidenced by its certificate of deposit, and trust funds held by such bank whether retained or deposited in any department of such bank or deposited in another bank, together with such other obligations of a bank as the board of directors [of the FDIC] shall find and shall prescribe by its regulations to be deposit liabilities by general usage. . . ." § 101, Banking Act of 1935, ch. 614, 49 Stat. 684, 685–686. * * *

Accordingly, the judgment of the court below is reversed, and the case is remanded for further proceedings consistent with this opinion.

JUSTICES MARSHALL, BLACKMUN and REHNQUIST, dissent * * *.

NOTES

1. The "independence principal" associated with letters of credit prevents a bank from examining the goods that is the subject of the transaction to see if they conform to the contract of sale between the buyer and seller. Instead, the bank pays against documents. If the documents conform to their description in the letter of credit, the bank must pay upon presentation of those documents and a draft (order to pay) from the seller. How could a buyer protect itself from non-conforming goods?

2. An exception to the requirement that a bank pay when documents conform even if the goods do not is where there is fraud. The fraud exception is based on the maxim noted by Lord Diplock in an English letter of credit case: *ex turpi causa non oritur actio* or "fraud unravels all." United City

Merchants (Investments) Ltd. v. Royal Bank of Canada, 2 W.L.R. 1039, 2 All E. R. Rep. 720 (House of Lords 1982) (declining to apply fraud exception to fraud by third party). See Sztejn v. J. Henry Schroder Banking Corp., 177 Misc. 719, 31 N.Y.S.2d 631 (1941) (applying fraud exception).

3. A standby letter of credit is sometimes referred to as a "suicide letter" because the issuer of the credit loses control of the ability to block payment even when payment is not actually due. This became a problem during the Iranian crisis when American diplomatic personnel were seized as hostages, American assets were then appropriated, and standby letters of credit called without justification. For a discussion of those events and the solutions imposed by the courts see American Bell International v. Islamic Republic of Iran, 474 F.Supp. 420 (S.D.N.Y.1979), and Harris Corp. v. National Iranian Radio and Television, 691 F.2d 1344 (11th Cir.1982).

4. Consider the following set of circumstances: An American businessman ("Joe") is approached by a group of Russian traders. They offer to buy large cargoes of sugar at a premium well above world market prices. They will provide a letter of credit from a reputable bank to assure their payment when the shipping documents are presented. However, they ask Joe for a standby letter of credit to assure his performance. Should Joe go through with this deal? What happens if he delivers the sugar and the Russians draw down on the standby letter of credit? Remember, if it is too good to be true it is too good to be true. Why would the Russians pay a premium over market if they have the credit to buy at market prices?

Certificates of Deposit

Certificates of deposit can be used by corporations, as well as individuals, as a means to earn interest on excess cash. The Federal Deposit Insurance Corporation insured payment by the bank issuing the certificate of deposit for up to $100,000 at the time of the following case, since increased to $250,000. This amount, however, is often too small for corporations dealing in large amounts of funds, making them unsecured creditors for amounts in excess of the insured amount. Consider the following effort to solve that problem.

GARY PLASTIC PACKAGING CORP. v. MERRILL LYNCH, PIERCE, FENNER & SMITH, INC.

756 F.2d 230 (2d Cir.1985).

CARDAMONE, CIRCUIT JUDGE

On this appeal we must determine whether a program devised by defendants Merrill, Lynch, Pierce, Fenner & Smith, Inc. (Merrill Lynch) and its wholly-owned subsidiary, Merrill Lynch Money Markets, Inc. (Money Markets), to sell bank certificates of deposit (CDs) is within the compass of the federal securities law. In *Marine Bank v. Weaver*, 455 U.S. 551, 71 L.Ed.2d 409, 102 S.Ct. 1220 (1982), the Supreme Court held that a conventional CD purchased from an issuing bank is not a security under the antifraud provisions of the federal securities laws. Nonetheless, the Court stated that each transaction must be analyzed on the content of the particular instrument involved and the factual setting as a whole. The possibility that in certain circumstances a CD might be a security within the scope of the federal securities laws was specifically left open. *Id.* at 560 n.11, 102 S.Ct. at 1225 n. 11.

The complaint alleges that defendants publish the Money Market Information Bulletin, which tells prospective customers that Merrill Lynch has available negotiable, insured, and liquid $100,000 CDs, for which they will maintain a secondary market. Defendants advertise that they screen daily a large group of quality banks to provide their customers with CDs with ''competitive'' yields from a variety of issuers. They represent that they will monitor the creditworthiness of issuing banks on a regular basis, and they discourage potential customers from seeking to deal directly with those banks. If the allegations of plaintiff's amended complaint are true, this sales message might be characterized as artful, but certainly not candid.

Plaintiff, who purchased 12 of the $100,000 CDs, claims that these certificates are not those regularly available at the issuing banks. Instead, plaintiff asserts that these CDs are specially created, issued and sold only to Merrill Lynch customers. Most significantly, plaintiff alleges that the rates of interest on the Merrill Lynch CDs were lower than the rates paid by the banks on their ordinarily issued CDs and that defendants pocketed the difference between the rates as an undisclosed commission. From the gold that flows through a broker's hands, a small shaving may be taken as commission. Yet, credibility and confidence in the market may demand that the amount of this shaving be revealed to investors. At this early stage of the litigation, before any discovery, it is difficult to discern if there is merit to plaintiff's claims against these defendants. It is sufficient to say that in our view plaintiff's complaint states a cause of action and should not have been dismissed on defendants' motion for summary judgment.
* * *

In its Money Market Information Bulletin, Merrill Lynch described its CD Program involving bank certificates of deposit[7] issued by both commercial and savings and loan institutions (referred to as banks) as follows:

---

7. As defined in federal regulations,

the term ''time certificate of deposit'' means a deposit evidenced by a negotiable or nonnegotiable instrument which provides on its face that the amount of such deposit is payable to bearer or to any specified person or to his order: (1) On a certain date, specified in the instrument, not less than 30 days after the date of the deposit, or (2) At the expiration of a certain specified time not less than 30 days after the date of the instrument, or (3) Upon notice in writing which is actually required to be given not less than 30 days before the date of repayment, and, (4) In all cases only upon presentation and surrender of the instrument.

12 C.F.R. § 217.1(c) (1951).

A certificate of deposit is a receipt for the deposit of funds in a bank of which there are two classes, demand and time. Demand certificates of deposit are payable on demand, and time certificates of deposit are payable on a specified date, or so many days after date, upon proper

FULLY INSURED $100,000 NEGOTIABLE CERTIFICATES OF DEPOSIT Merrill Lynch Money Markets Inc. (MLMMI) is offering its customers a unique opportunity to purchase $100,000 *negotiable* certificates of deposit that are fully *insured* and *liquid.*

INSURANCE COVERAGE his opportunity, for individuals or corporate investors with $100,000 or more to invest, has been made possible as a result of recent changes in Federal Deposit Insurance Corporation (FDIC) and Federal Savings and Loan Insurance Corporation (FSLIC) regulations dealing with deposit insurance coverage. In essence, both the FDIC and FSLIC have raised their deposit insurance coverage to $100,000 from $40,000 per depositor per institution.

SIGNIFICANCE The extended coverage will enable an investor to purchase a $100,000 certificate of deposit from an FDIC or FSLIC insured commercial bank or savings and loan association and have the total principal amount of the investment covered by Federal deposit insurance. Carrying this a step further, one could distribute investible funds in $100,000 increments among a number of banks to ensure Federal deposit insurance coverage of the total amount. Investors can now purchase $100,000 negotiable certificates of deposit and enjoy the benefits of having their entire deposit insured by a Federal agency and at the same time take advantage of the exemption from interest rate ceilings that Regulation Q provides for certificates of deposit that are $100,000 or larger.

A NEW OPPORTUNITY MLMMI will provide its investors with an opportunity to take advantage of this regulatory change by offering, on a daily basis, a broad selection of fully insured $100,000 certificates of deposit issued by domestic commercial banks and savings and loan associations in a range of maturities. Each of the issuers whose certificates of deposit are offered has been reviewed and approved by the MLPF & S Corporate Credit Department and is monitored on a regular basis. Credit reports that provide an historical analysis on each issuer will be readily available through your MLPF & S Account Executive.

LIQUIDITY The $100,000 certificates of deposit that MLMMI is offering enjoy a high degree of liquidity since they are in negotiable bearer form and are fully insured by a Federal agency. In addition, MLMMI fully intends to maintain a secondary market for its customers which would enable them to sell their certificates of deposit back to MLMMI at prevailing market rates without the significant interest rate penalties Federal banking regulations require banks to impose on the early redemption of their certificates of deposit.

---

indorsement. These time certificates are similar to savings deposits, but have a definite maturity, and are evidenced by a certificate instead of a passbook entry. Time certificates of deposit may bear interest, and are, therefore, a convenient means of investing temporarily idle funds, which otherwise would be unemployed.

G. MUNN. ENCYCLOPEDIA OF BANKING OF FINANCE 178–79 (F. L. Garcia rev. ed. 1973).

ALTERNATIVES The more popular alternatives would include *Treasury Bills, Federal Agency Securities* and *Money Market Funds*. With the increase in deposit insurance coverage, an investor now has the opportunity to purchase Federally insured certificates of deposit, an investment which usually carries higher yields than Treasury Bills and Federal Agency Securities. While money market funds do enjoy liquidity, they are not Federally insured and cannot guarantee a future rate of return.

WHY MLMMI Some investors may seek to purchase $100,000 certificates of deposit directly from a bank or savings and loan association. However, they can only call a few local banks at most, their alternatives are critically limited. You have no way of knowing if the banks you are calling are in the market trying to raise money at a competitive rate or if they are quoting a rate just to accommodate a depositor. Our specialized bank liability trading staff talks to a large group of pre-screened, quality banks daily before offering certificates of deposit to investors enabling MLMMI to provide the investor with certificates of deposit with competitive yields from a variety of issuers. The interest rate penalties for early redemption imposed under Federal Banking regulations do not apply to certificates of deposit sold back to MLMMI. They do apply if you redeem your certificates of deposit prior to maturity at the issuing bank. MLMMI intends to maintain a secondary market in these negotiable bearer certificates of deposit for its customers providing them with a source of liquidity at prevailing market rates. In addition to the safety factor of having Federal insurance for these deposits, the highly professional MLPF & S Corporate Credit Department is monitoring, on a regular basis, those issuers whose certificates of deposit MLMMI offers and will provide a written credit analysis on each. For additional information on this new program, contact your local Merrill Lynch Account Executive.

When, in 1982, plaintiff ordered 12 CDs from Merrill Lynch, Money Markets contacted financial institutions in various parts of the country, and purchased the CDs. For each certificate of deposit purchased, Gary Plastic received an order ticket and a confirmation slip from Merrill Lynch. The actual CDs were held by the "delivery agent," Manufacturers Hanover Trust Company, and when they matured Gary Plastic received all principal and interest due it under the terms of the confirmation slips.

On May 20, 1983, plaintiff brought this action. The gravamen of the complaint was that the interest rates shown on the customer confirmation slips were lower than the interest rates actually paid by the banks according to the terms of the deposit certificates. The complaint further asserted that while defendants in the Money Market Information Bulletin purported to perform its services free of charge, they actually retained the difference between the rate shown on the confirmation slip and the actual certificate of deposit rate as an "excessive, undisclosed commission." Plaintiff further charged that the Bulletin omitted and misrepresented material facts in violation of the antifraud provisions of the 1933 and 1934

Acts and that in violation of § 5(a) of the 1933 Act, defendants sold the CDs when no registration statement was in effect.

On April 17, 1984 plaintiff's counsel met informally with Merrill Lynch employees and, for the first time, learned how Merrill Lynch operated its CD Program. Although the information plaintiff obtained during that meeting was far from complete, plaintiff realized that some of the factual assumptions upon which its complaint was based were incorrect. The complaint's premise that the confirmation slips and the certificates of deposit stated different rates of interest was inaccurate. In its proposed amended complaint plaintiff has set forth the facts that came to light during the meeting. Essentially, Merrill Lynch determines on a given day the lowest interest rate it can market (the "competitive" rate) and has its subsidiary Money Markets purchase CDs in bulk from various banks at that rate. The banks specially create these CDs for Money Markets and Merrill Lynch market them to its customers. Money Markets pays a commission to Merrill Lynch for the sale. Merrill Lynch furnishes its customer with a confirmation slip indicating that it acted as agent on its customer's behalf.

Plaintiff claims that the wrong in all of this is that Merrill Lynch never informed customers that the issuing bank was actually paying on its regularly issued CDs a rate of interest higher than the rate set on the instruments created for and marketed by Merrill Lynch. For example, plaintiff introduced evidence that Pacific Federal offered 15% interest to customers who purchased CDs directly from it, as compared to the 13.8% interest paid plaintiff on the CD it bought through Merrill Lynch. Similarly, State Savings Stockton was offering 16.1%, while plaintiff received only 14.5%, and Northern California Savings was offering 14.75%, while plaintiff earned only 13.8%. Money Markets collects the difference between the rates a bank agrees to pay on its regular CDs and the lesser amount it pays on CDs marketed by Merrill Lynch. Thus, plaintiff claims Merrill Lynch pooled funds and used its market power not to obtain the best rates available that day for its customers, as its literature implied, but instead to advance its own economic advantage.

Just one week after their informal meeting in April 1984, the parties appeared at a hearing before the district judge. Plaintiff told the court that it had new information on the operation of the CD Program and that the program's operation was based on a "factual pattern" that was "slightly different from that that [plaintiff] had envisioned" when drafting the complaint 11 months earlier. On April 30 defendants submitted portions of the confirmation slips and an affidavit explaining that the rates stated on the confirmation slips matched the rates on the certificates of deposit. Defendants' documents confirmed what plaintiffs had already conceded, that the original complaint was based upon an incorrect factual predicate. * * *

In dismissing the complaint, the trial court concluded that the factual predicate of the complaint—that the interest rates stated on the confirmation slips were less than the interest rates stated on the certificates of deposit—was not correct. Merrill Lynch's unrefuted evidence showed that the interest rates stated on the certificates of deposit purchased by Gary Plastic were identical to the rates shown on the corresponding confirmations. Plaintiff had learned at the April 17 meeting that this factual predicate was incorrect. Instead of continuing to argue plaintiff's initial position, counsel informed the district court that new facts had come to light and sought leave to amend the complaint. Dismissal of the case at that point, without further opportunity to conduct discovery, was an abuse of discretion. With the exception of one informal meeting and a few incomplete "audit trail" documents, plaintiff has not obtained information from a single Merrill Lynch officer or bank officer. Thus, it has been forced to proceed without knowledge of many material facts. For example, plaintiff has yet to learn important details of the operation of the CD Program, such as the precise amount and derivation of the commissions Merrill Lynch received, the specific roles played by Merrill Lynch and its subsidiaries, and the exact nature of the dealings between Merrill Lynch and the various banking institutions. That the district judge had some knowledge of plaintiff's inability to obtain information is clear from the fact that he ordered Merrill Lynch to file confirmation slips and other documentary evidence of the transactions with its customers. To resolve this dispute, Merrill Lynch's relationship with its customers and the banks should be further explored. Plaintiff should have the opportunity to incorporate its newly obtained facts into its amended complaint to correct the factual predicate of its original complaint.

In its amended complaint plaintiff will charge that defendants have violated Sections 5 (a) and 17 of the 1933 Act, 15 U.S.C. §§ 77e(a), 77q, and Section 10(b) of the 1934 Act, 15 U.S.C. § 78j(b), and SEC Rule 10b–5 promulgated thereunder, 17 C.F.R. § 240.10b–5 (1984). Section 5 of the 1933 Act prohibits the sale of a "security" unless a registration statement is in effect. Section 17(a) of the 1933 Act and Section 10(b) of the 1934 Act are the antifraud provisions of the securities acts, prohibiting the use of any scheme to obtain money by means of an untrue statement or omission to state a material fact or of any manipulative or deceptive device in connection with the purchase or sale of any "security." Hence, as a threshold matter, in the application of both federal acts, plaintiff must show that the transactions involved a "security." Plaintiff argues that the CDs sold through the CD Program are "securities" within the meaning of the Acts. We undertake now to resolve that important issue. * * *

In *Marine Bank v. Weaver*, the Supreme Court ... for an instrument to be a security the investor must risk loss. The Court held that a conventional certificate of deposit was not a security under the federal securities acts because federal banking regulations and the FDIC eliminate all risk of loss to the investor. The court below concluded that the CDs in this case are not different from those in *Marine Bank* and that neither the CDs nor the CD Program is a security under federal law. We disagree.

In *Marine Bank* plaintiffs purchased a $50,000 six-year certificate of deposit from defendant Marine Bank, a federally regulated Pennsylvania bank. Plaintiffs pledged the CD to Marine Bank to guarantee a loan made by the bank to Columbus Packing Co. In consideration for guaranteeing the loan, the Weavers contracted with the owners of Columbus to receive $100 per month, 50% of Columbus' net profits, and the use of a barn and pasture. They also were given the right to veto future borrowing by Columbus. When Columbus failed and the bank prepared to claim the CD, plaintiffs sued the bank, alleging, *inter alia*, that the bank had violated the antifraud provisions of the 1934 Act, 15 U.S.C. § 78j(b). Plaintiffs claimed that the bank had told them that Columbus would use the loan as working capital, but instead the loan was immediately applied by the bank against Columbus' overdue obligations. 455 U.S. at 553. The Supreme Court rejected the Third Circuit's conclusion that this certificate of deposit is similar to any other long-term debt obligation commonly found to be a security and held that the CD was not a security. In a footnote the Court added the following caveat:

> It does not follow that a certificate of deposit ... invariably falls outside the definition of a "security" as defined by the federal statutes. Each transaction must be analyzed and evaluated on the basis of the content of the instruments in question, the purposes intended to be served, and the factual setting as a whole.

Id. at 560 n.11. The crux of the *Marine Bank* decision is that federal banking regulations and federal deposit insurance eliminate the risk of loss to the investor, thereby obviating the need for the protection of the federal securities laws. *Id.* at 558–59. In addition, the Court held that the private agreement between plaintiffs and the owners of Columbus, negotiated one-on-one, was not a security because of its unique character and highly personal terms. The CDs issued by Merrill Lynch present an entirely different picture. * * *

The result we reach is consonant with the comprehensive financial regulatory plan enacted by Congress in 1933 and 1934. The Glass–Steagall Act separated large private banks, whose chief business was investment, from deposit banks. *See* 77 Cong. Rec. 3730 (1933). *See generally* Note, *Bank Certificate of Deposit: Notes not in Tune with Securities Regulation*, 10 *Fordham Urban L.J.* 469, 476–77 (1982). The CDs sold through the CD Program represent essentially a joint effort between the issuer of the CD, the deposit bank, and Merrill Lynch as the market maker, the investment bank. Investors put their money and confidence in the financial and managerial expertise of both institutions. They receive returns from both: interest payments from the deposit bank and services such as credit checks and negotiability from the investment bank. The banking laws protect investors from the abuses and misrepresentations of the former. The securities acts regulate the latter.

In *Marine Bank*, the reason for exempting certificates of deposit from the securities acts was to eliminate double coverage when the Glass–Steagall Act and the securities acts overlap. Were we to find the CDs sold through this CD Program not to be covered by the federal securities laws, a gap would exist in the regulatory scheme that would strip the investor of needed federal protection. The "content of the instruments in question, the purposes intended to be served, and the factual setting as a whole" make this an appropriate case for finding these instruments to be within the definitions of "security." *See Marine Bank*, 455 U.S. at 560 n.11. *See also* H.R. No. 626(I), 97th Cong., 2d Sess. 9–10, *reprinted in* 1982 U.S. Code Cong. & Ad. News 2780, 2788 (*Marine Bank* left "open the question of whether a certificate of deposit could be a security in another context"). Therefore, we hold that the certificates of deposit issued and sold pursuant to defendant Merrill Lynch's CD Program are "securities" for purposes of the antifraud provisions of both Acts. * * *

Accordingly, the judgment of the district court is reversed and the case is remanded with directions to reinstate the complaint, as amended, and for further proceedings consistent with this Opinion.

Notes

1. Deposit brokers became adept at placing millions of dollars of funds for clients at several banks in order to maximize FDIC coverage. The bank regulators sought to halt that practice and the brokering of funds described in the Gary Plastic Packing case by adopting a rule that limited coverage to $100,000 per broker per institution for all funds deposited by the broker for third parties. The District of Columbia Court of Appeals, however, struck down that regulation. FAIC Securities, Inc. v. United States, 768 F.2d 352 (D.C.Cir.1985). Congress later acted to restrict banks that were not well capitalized from excess dependence on brokered deposits. 12 U.S.C. § 1831f(a). This did little to stop the use of brokered deposits. The amount of brokered deposits grew from $47.7 billion in 1994 to $193 billion in 2000.

2. Certificates of deposit, usually in larger denominations, may be negotiable, which means that they may be sold to a third party. Most certificates of deposit purchased by consumers are non-negotiable, which means they cannot be sold to a third party. Penalties may also attach for early withdrawal of funds, making the nonnegotiable certificate of deposit somewhat illiquid. If negotiable, however, such penalties may be avoided by selling the instrument.

Commercial Paper

THE COMMERCIAL PAPER MARKET AND THE SECURITIES ACTS

39 University of Chicago Law Review 362, 363–64 (1972).

Commercial paper consists of unsecured, short-term promissory notes issued by sales and personal finance companies; by manufacturing transportation, trade, and utility companies; and by the affiliates and subsidiaries of commercial banks. The notes are payable to the bearer on a stated maturity date. Maturities range from one day to nine months, but most paper carries an original maturity between thirty and ninety days. When the paper becomes due, it is generally rolled over—that is, reissued—to the same or a different investor at the market rate at the time of maturity.

Commercial paper notes are of two types, discount notes without interest and nondiscount notes with interest. Their face denominations range from approximately $2,500 to $1 million or more. Placement of commercial paper is made either directly with the investor by the issuer (direct paper) or indirectly through a dealer who in most cases acts as principal (dealer paper). Because the notes are unsecured, the issuers have generally consisted of large, well-known companies whose financial positions have been assumed to be above question. Largely because of the financial reputation of these issuers, commercial paper has been considered by many relatively riskless, bearing interest rates just above those on Treasury bills and bankers' acceptances.

SANDERS v. JOHN NUVEEN & CO., INC.

463 F.2d 1075 (7th Cir.), cert. denied 409 U.S. 1009,
93 S.Ct. 452, 34 L.Ed.2d 303 (1972).

SPRECHER, CIRCUIT JUDGE.

* * * Plaintiff, Henry T. Sanders, filed his complaint on March 12, 1970, against John Nuveen & Co., Inc., a broker-dealer in securities, one of its registered representatives, and its directors and controlling persons. The complaint charged defendants with a scheme and artifice to defraud plaintiff and others in his class by selling to them short-term commercial paper issued by Winter & Hirsch, Inc. but owned by Nuveen. Plaintiff's claim was based on the Securities Act of 1933, 15 U.S.C. § 77a, the Securities Exchange Act of 1934, 15 U.S.C. § 78a, Rule 10b–5, 17 C.F.R. § 240.10b–5, and the Rules of Fair Practice of the National Association of Securities Dealers.

On May 18, 1970, the defendants moved to strike certain allegations of the complaint and expressly attacked the class-action aspects of the complaint. They also challenged the jurisdiction of the court under the

1934 act on the ground that the short-term commercial paper involved was not a "security." The district court denied the motion to strike on October 8, 1970. * * *

Federal securities legislation enacted for the purpose of avoiding frauds is to be construed "not technically and restrictively, but flexibly to effectuate its remedial purposes." S.E.C. v. Capital Gains Research Bureau, Inc., 375 U.S. 180 (1963).

Particularly, the definition of a security "embodies a flexible rather than a static principle, one that is capable of adaptation to meet the countless and variable schemes devised by those who seek the use of the money of others on the promise of profits." S.E.C. v. W.J. Howey Co., 328 U.S. 293, 299 (1946). "[I]n searching for the meaning and scope of the word 'security' in the [Securities Exchange] Act [of 1934], form should be disregarded for substance and the emphasis should be on economic reality." Tcherepnin v. Knight, 389 U.S. 332, 336 (1967).

The Supreme Court has sanctioned, in interpreting the definition of a security in the 1934 act, recourse to the definitions of security in the Securities Act of 1933 (*Tcherepnin* at 335–336, 338) and in the "companion legislative enactments." Affiliated Ute Citizens v. United States, 406 U.S. 128 (1972).

An examination of the six basic federal securities acts is relevant and revealing.

The Securities Act of 1933, The Trust Indenture Act of 1939, the Investment Company Act of 1940, and the Investment Advisers Act of 1940, all define a security as follows: "The term 'security' means any note, . . . evidence of indebtedness, . . . investment contract, . . . or, in general, any interest or instrument commonly known as a 'security'. . . ." The Public Utility Holding Company Act of 1935 definition differs slightly: " 'Security' means any note, . . . investment contract, . . . or, in general, any instrument commonly known as a 'security'. . . ."

In none of these five acts does there appear any language limiting in any way the broad definitions of "security" or of "note," "evidence of indebtedness," "investment contract" or "instrument commonly known as a security." Therefore *any* note, regardless of its nature, terms or conditions, is fully subject to whatever antifraud provisions are included in the five acts.

Only in the Securities Exchange Act of 1934 is there an exception to the broad definition of a security; it reads:[8]

> "The term 'security' means any note, . . . investment contract, . . . or in general, any instrument commonly known as a 'security'; . . . but shall not include currency or any note, draft, bill of exchange, or banker's acceptance which has a maturity at the time of issuance of not exceeding nine months, exclusive of days of grace, or any renewal thereof the maturity of which is likewise limited."

---

8.   Section 3(a)(10). 15 U.S.C. § 78c(a) (10).

Therefore only in the 1934 act is a note with a maturity not exceeding nine months withdrawn from the application of the antifraud provisions of the act, section 10(b) and Rule 10b–5. Since the same note is subject to the antifraud provisions of all the other securities acts, it becomes important to determine just what Congress intended to be exempt from the operation of the 1934 act.

Although all notes are subject to the antifraud provisions of the other acts, some of those acts exempt short-term commercial paper from registration or other requirements. Plaintiff urges that the meaning given to short-term obligations in other securities legislation, particularly the 1933 act, be applied to the definition found in the 1934 act. The 1933 act exempts from registration, but not from antifraud sanctions, "[a]ny note, draft, bill of exchange, or banker's acceptance which arises out of a current transaction or the proceeds of which have been or are to be used for current transactions," and which has a maturity not exceeding nine months.

The Securities and Exchange Commission has interpreted the 1933 act's exemption of short-term commercial paper as embodying four requirements:[9]

> "The legislative history of the Act makes clear that section 3(a) (3) applies only to (1) prime quality negotiable commercial paper (2) of a type not ordinarily purchased by the general public, that is, (3) paper issued to facilitate well recognized types of current operational business requirements and (4) of a type eligible for discounting by Federal Reserve banks."

Although no evidence has been heard in this case, the record shows that the commercial paper purchased by the plaintiff was dated January 30, 1970, and that "Winter & Hirsch was engaged in the business of making loans until in or about February 1970, when it advised its creditors of its precarious financial condition and ceased to make any further payments on any of its obligations for borrowed money." At that time it had assets of $12.5 million and liabilities of more than $36 million. Thus, because of the company's insolvency, it seems highly unlikely that the paper purchased by the plaintiff and members of his class is either prime quality or issued to facilitate current transactions or eligible for discounting by Federal Reserve banks.

The record further shows that the commercial paper purchased by the plaintiff was "placed through John Nuveen & Co." and bought by 42 purchasers, including the plaintiff, in the aggregate face amount of

---

9. Release No. 33–4412, 17 C.F.R. § 231.4412 (1961) (numerals added). The release emphasized the prime quality of the paper intended to be exempted and stated that the exempted items are "composed of assets easily convertible into cash and are comparable to liquid inventories of an industrial or mercantile company." During the hearings on the 1933 act, commercial paper discountable by Federal Reserve banks was described as having "a record of safety only second to Government bonds" and as being the basis of our currency. Hearings on S. 875 Before the Senate Comm. on Banking and Currency, 73rd Cong., 1st Sess. at 94, 95 (1933). It is significant that section 3(a)(10) of the 1934 act exempts "currency" from the definition of security. 15 U.S.C. § 78c(a)(10).

$1,661,500. The paper was therefore obviously offered and sold to the general public; indeed, it was characterized in the issuer's financial statements as "short term open market" paper.[10] The notes fail to meet any of the S.E.C.'s four requirements for exemption.

If, as the Supreme Court has admonished, "form should be disregarded for substance" and economic reality emphasized, it is reasonably clear that plaintiff and his class purchased the kind of "security" in regard to which the securities acts were intended to offer protection against fraud, misrepresentation and non-disclosure. Five of those acts expressly did so. We believe Congress intended to protect against fraud the purchasers of securities such as those involved here under the 1934 act as well. * * *

In other words, when Congress spoke of notes with a maturity not exceeding nine months, it meant commercial paper, not investment securities. When a prospective borrower approaches a bank for a loan and gives his note in consideration for it, the bank has purchased commercial paper. But a person who seeks to invest his money and receives a note in return for it has not purchased commercial paper in the usual sense. He has purchased a security investment. *Cf.* City National Bank v. Vanderboom, 290 F.Supp. 592, 608 (W.D.Ark.1968), aff'd, 422 F.2d 221 (8th Cir.), cert. denied, 399 U.S. 905 (1970). * * *

NOTES

1. Justice Powell dissented (a dissent in which Justice Rehnquist joined) to the denial of the petition for a writ of certiorari in the Sanders case. In the course of that dissent, he defined commercial paper as follows:

> Commercial paper, for example, normally is issued for periods of 30 to 90 days, and in no event more than 270 days. It is useful for borrowers with fluctuating temporary cash needs. Dealers such as petitioner buy commercial paper from issuers and resell it to investors. A dealer's compensation is the "spread" between the price at which he buys the paper from the issuer and the price charged the investor. Comment, The Commercial Paper Market and the Securities Acts, 39 U. Chi. L. Rev. 362, 367–368 (1972). The dealer's "spread" historically has been relatively small. Id., at 368. The additional expense and legal exposure made necessary by the Court of Appeals' decision will increase the "spread," and hence also the cost of borrowing.

John Nuveen & Co., Inc. v. Sanders, 450 U.S. 1005, 1011, n. 6, 101 S.Ct. 1719, 68 L.Ed.2d 210 (1981). Do you agree with his concern that the efficiency of the commercial paper market will be impaired by the application of the federal securities laws?

---

10. H.R.Rep.No.85, 73rd Cong., 1st Sess., 15 (1933) stated in discussing the bill, which became the Securities Act of 1933, "Paragraph (3) exempts short-term paper of the type available for discount at a Federal Reserve bank and of a type which rarely is bought by private investors."

Issuers of commercial paper often roll it over on maturity, which some-times has the effect of creating a long term credit line. Is this consistent with the use of such paper? Consider the following description of commercial paper by the Federal Reserve Board:

> A basic concept underlying the discount provisions of the Federal Reserve Act was that commercial paper admitted to discount should be self-liquidating paper. In a published statement, the Board recognized this concept. It stated that paper eligible for discount was limited to "liquid paper," that is, paper which is issued or drawn under such circumstances that in the normal course of business there will automatically come into existence a fund available to liquidate each piece of paper, that fund being the final proceeds of the transaction out of which the paper arose.

Board of Governors of the Federal Reserve System. Lending Functions of the Federal Reserve Banks: A History 31 (1973) (citation omitted).

2. In *Securities Industry Association v. Board of Governors of the Federal Reserve System*, 468 U.S. 137, 104 S.Ct. 2979, 82 L.Ed.2d 107 (1984), the Supreme Court held that even commercial paper that was exempt from the registration requirements of the federal securities law was still a security for purposes of then existing restrictions against banks dealing in securities. What then is commercial paper, a security or something else? For a discussion of the family resemblance test and when notes may fall under the securities laws, see Reves v. Ernst & Young, 494 U.S. 56, 110 S.Ct. 945, 108 L.Ed.2d 47 (1990), which is included in Chap. 4.

3. Commercial paper is generally thought to be a low risk investment because of its short term nature and the high credit ratings of the issuers accepted by the market. Nevertheless, there have been defaults by highly rated issuers. When this occurs there is usually a sharp contraction in the market until lenders are reassured that the problem is not systemic. That situation arose during the financial crisis between 2007–2009, causing liquidity problems for commercial paper issuers The Federal Reserve Board created Commercial Paper Funding Facility to facilitate liquidity. The Fed described that facility as follows:

> Commercial paper is a critical source of funding for many businesses. In the fall of 2008, the commercial paper market was under considerable strain as money market mutual funds and other investors—themselves often facing liquidity pressures—became increasingly reluctant to purchase commercial paper. As a result, the volume of outstanding commercial paper fell, interest rates on longer-term commercial paper increased significantly, and an increasingly high percentage of outstanding commercial paper needed to be refinanced each day. This restriction in the availability of credit made it more difficult for businesses to obtain credit during a critical period of economic stress.

> To address these strains, the Federal Reserve established the Commercial Paper Funding Facility (CPFF) to provide liquidity to U.S. issuers of commercial paper in the event that credit was not available in the market. By providing liquidity to the commercial paper market, the CPFF encouraged investors to resume lending in the market.

Under the program, the Federal Reserve Bank of New York (FRBNY) provided three-month loans to the CPFF LLC, a specially created limited liability company (LLC) that used the funds to purchase commercial paper directly from eligible issuers. The commercial paper that was eligible for purchase was highly rated, U.S. dollar-denominated, unsecured and asset-backed commercial paper with a three-month maturity. To manage its risk, the Federal Reserve required issuers whose commercial paper was purchased by the CPFF LLC to pay fees at the time of each purchase. Additionally, at the time of the initial registration, each issuer was required to pay a facility fee equal to 10 basis points of the maximum amount of commercial paper that it could issue to the CPFF LLC. A total of $849 million in fees were collected by the CPFF LLC. The FRBNY's loan to the CPFF LLC was secured by all of the LLC's assets, including its commercial paper holdings, accumulated fees, and proceeds from investments.

http://www.federalreserve.gov/newsevents/reform_cpff.htm. Interestingly, five of the top ten users of this facility were foreign financial institutions, a recognition of the globalization of finance, but also raising the question of whether the U.S. government should be committing taxpayer funds to rescue foreign institutions. What do you think?

4. Consider the following discussion on the interrelationship of lines of credit and commercial paper that arose after a large default:

While banks have lost their primary position as direct lenders to large corporations, they continue to serve as "standby sources of liquidity" for large firms. Most large companies maintain lines of credit with banks. The typical line of credit agreement permits the borrower to draw against a specified credit facility during the term of the contract. Lines of credit are usually granted on a relatively short-term basis. The lending bank therefore has frequent opportunities to decide whether to renew the credit line based on the borrower's current financial condition.

Lines of credit provide borrowers with a qualified assurance of liquidity during adverse credit market conditions. When financial markets are subject to unusual stress, even large, well-established firms may find it difficult to issue commercial paper or other debt securities on reasonable terms. In such circumstances, a firm can meet its funding needs by drawing on an established bank line of credit, as long as the firm's financial position has not deteriorated enough to breach a covenant in the governing agreement. Banks are particularly well situated to provide this emergency liquidity service, because (i) banks usually receive a substantial inflow of deposits during financial market disruptions, when investors shift funds from risky securities into the "safe haven" of bank deposits, and (ii) banks can further expand their lending capacity by borrowing from the interbank federal funds market and the FRB's discount window.

The Penn Central bankruptcy of 1970, the stock market crash of 1987, and the Russian debt crisis of 1998 demonstrate the crucial role of banks as emergency suppliers of liquidity to large firms and the capital markets during financial crises. In 1970, the commercial paper market was virtually frozen by Penn Central's default on more than $200 million of its

> short-term notes. The FRB [Federal Reserve Board] urged major banks to provide credit to large firms that were unable to roll over their commercial paper, and the banks responded by lending over $2 billion during a three-week period. The FRB supported the banks by providing almost $600 million of discount window advances and taking other steps to reduce short-term interest rates. Since the Penn Central crisis, most large companies have relied on bank lines of credit or other credit enhancements to support their commercial paper issues. These standby arrangements are attractive to banks because they provide fee income and enable banks to maintain long-term relationships with large corporations.

Arthur E. Wilmarth, Jr., The Transformation of the U.S. Financial Services Industry 1975–2000: Competition, Consolidation, and Increased Risks, 2002 U. Ill. L. Rev. 215, 235–236.

4. Short term financing may take other forms as observed by a law firm's description of a "multiple Option Financing Facility":

> ... Bank—International Limited [acts] as agent in connection with their Multiple Option Financing Facilities, which combine fairly standard revolving credit or term loans with a variety of different funding options for the borrower. For example, the borrower might be given the option to request bankers' acceptances or issue Euro-commercial paper as well as draw down advances in a range of convertible currencies. The MOF transactions are documented under New York law and the borrowers are generally large U.S. corporations....

> After the documents have been negotiated and agreed between the borrower and Bank, copies are sent to each of the banks which have been invited ... to join the syndicate of lenders. The bank syndicate is made up of major U.S., European and Japanese financial institutions and, depending on the amount of the loan, may include anywhere from ten to fifty participants. The next stage of the transaction involves negotiations with the bank group, which generally requires fairly extensive discussions with each of the banks regarding their questions and concerns about the structure of the deal and the draft documentation.

Rogers & Wells, Client Newsletter (1991).

SECTION 3. EVOLVING REGULATORY APPROACHES TO CREDIT RATING AGENCIES

FRANK PARTNOY
THE SISKEL AND EBERT OF FINANCIAL MARKETS? TWO THUMBS DOWN FOR THE CREDIT RATINGS AGENCIES

77 Wash. U. L. Q. 619 (1999).

* * * The precursors to twentieth-century credit rating agencies were mercantile credit agencies, and their history seems to fit the above view of ratings and reputational capital. During the seventeenth and eighteenth centuries, colonial importers customarily extended up to a year of credit to their retail customers, shopkeepers, and general stores. Payments were often late, and it was difficult for sellers to gather credible information about the reputation of buyers: letters of reference were faked or forged, detailed financial data were not available, and the process was tediously slow. As markets and trade evolved during the nineteenth century, it became clear that there were economies of scale associated with gathering and disseminating credit information in a systematic, organized way.

One of the victims of the crisis of 1837 was Lewis Tappan who operated a substantial silk business with his brother. Fortunately for the Tappans, they kept detailed credit information about current and prospective customers, which included many large commercial enterprises. When the silk business collapsed, that customer information proved valuable to other merchants, and in 1841, Tappan formed The Mercantile Agency, the first mercantile credit agency.

As Tappan and other mercantile credit raters thrived during the late 1800s, other raters began to copy Tappan's idea, particularly in rating investments in stocks and bonds. By 1890, Poor's Publishing Company (S & P's predecessor) was publishing Poor's Manual, an analysis of various types of investments, including bonds. By the early 1900s, various American firms were classifying bonds, primarily railroad bonds, into groups according to quality, and there was at least one bond rating system in Europe.

John Moody, a Wall Street analyst during the early 1900s, observed the success of mercantile credit ratings and became interested in applying this simple rating methodology to bonds. In his words, "[s]omebody, sooner or later, will bring out an industrial statistical manual, and when it comes, it will be a gold mine." By 1907, several analysts had issued reports on the railroad industry, with elaborate statistics and detailed operating and financial data. Moody believed that if he could synthesize the complex data in these reports into a single rating symbol for each bond, he could make his fortune selling such ratings to the public. Other bankers opposed Moody's plan, saying Moody could earn superior returns by using such "inside information" to trade, instead of publicly flaunting it. Moody ignored these protestations, persevered, and in 1909 published the first rating scheme for bonds, in a book entitled Analysis of Railroad Investments. Moody's Investors Service was incorporated in 1914 and created a formal rating department in 1922. By 1924 Moody's ratings covered nearly 100 percent of the U.S. bond market.

Within a few years after Moody published his first ratings, three other credit rating organizations entered the market. Poor's Publishing Company was the second rating agency; it began rating stocks and bonds in 1916. Standard Statistics Company, Inc. followed in 1922. Fitch Publishing Company began publishing ratings in 1924. * * *

Rating agencies continued to accumulate reputational capital during the 1920s because they were able to gather and synthesize valuable information. During this time, ratings were financed entirely by subscription fees paid by investors, and the rating agencies competed to acquire their respective reputations for independence, integrity, and reliability. In a market with low barriers to entry, a rating agency issued inaccurate ratings at its peril. Every time an agency assigned a rating, that agency's name, integrity, and credibility were subject to inspection and critique by the entire investment community. Reputational considerations would have been especially acute in such an environment.

There is evidence that rating agencies continued to accumulate reputational capital during the 1930s. Rating agencies and ratings became much more important to both investors and issuers during this period. In the years following the stock market crash of 1929, demand for credit ratings increased, as investors became concerned about high bond default rates and credit risk. By the end of the 1920s, the U.S. bond market included approximately 6,000 bond issues with a total face amount of more than $26 billion; the vast majority of those bond issues were rated by the rating agencies. * * *

The credit ratings systems and scales were well established by 1929. Ratings were divided into categories, based on the credit quality of the rated financial instrument. Generally, a bond rating was intended to indicate the likelihood of default or delayed payment for that bond. As with many ratings, the practice was to assign the letter A or the number 1 to the highest grade, with A1 signifying a high, if not the highest, grade. Relative rankings, in descending order, would be B or 2, then C or 3, and so on.

The agencies' scales were similar, with each agency employing both ordinal (e.g., A,B,C) and cardinal (e.g., Aaa, Aa, A) ratings. Each agency used three subcategories for each broad rating category (e.g., three levels of "As," three levels of "Bs"). By 1930, it was possible to match each agency's rating symbols one-for-one with each of the other agency's symbols.

Moreover, although the agencies did not agree on every rating, ratings were loosely correlated and there was a certain amount of rating "inflation" evident in each of the agency's scales. For example, the vast majority of ratings were in the A category. Very few bonds were rated C or lower.

Following the stock market crash of 1929, numerous ratings were lowered, as the rating agencies, along with most individuals and institutions, failed to anticipate the rapid decline in the prices of hundreds of bond issues. For example, the Chicago, Rock Island & Pacific 4s–1988, was rated Aaa, or the equivalent highest rating, by all four agencies in 1929, was only rated Aa, or the equivalent rating, for another five years thereafter, and by 1934 was in default.

Notwithstanding the large number of ratings changes (mostly downgrades) in the early 1930s and the considerable lag between the time market prices incorporated negative information about bonds and the time credit ratings incorporated such information, ratings continued to be a respected and important institution in the bond market. The preface to Moody's 1931 Manual of Industrials stated that "[t]he fundamental thought back of the system of rating investment securities ... has been to furnish an authoritative key to the relative security and stability, from an investment standpoint, of all types of bonds and stocks." Moody's and other agencies apparently were able to retain this "authority" during the 1930s, despite the obvious decline in the accuracy of their ratings. * * *

As quickly as credit rating agencies were able to accumulate reputational capital during their meteoric rise of the early 1930s, they just as quickly squandered such capital during the following years. As a result, credit rating agencies did not remain important or influential for long. Following their heyday in the 1920s and 1930s, the agencies experienced austerity and contraction during the 1940s and 1950s. During this period, bond prices were not volatile, the economy was healthy, and few corporations defaulted. As a consequence, both the demand for and the supply of relevant credit information dwindled. The rating agencies were struggling when John Moody died in 1958. According to the reputational capital view, the decline of the rating agencies would have been a response to their inability to generate accurate and valuable information after the early 1930s.

During the Vietnam War, bond price volatility increased somewhat, as did issuance of commercial paper, and borrowers faced a severe credit contraction. Demand for credit information increased during this period, but the agencies remained relatively small and not obviously important as a source of information to issuers or investors. At the time, the rating agencies employed only a few analysts each and generated revenues primarily from the sale of published research reports. The market did not place great value on those research reports, presumably, according to the reputational capital view, because rating agencies had lost a large portion of their reputational capital. Moreover, as the commercial paper market expanded rapidly during the 1960s, investors were not very precise in assessing credit quality. In the fallout of the 1970 Penn Central default on $82 million of commercial paper, investors began demanding more sophisticated levels of research. The rating agencies, still relatively small and without substantial reputational capital, were not in a position to satisfy this demand.

One study of 207 corporate bond rating changes from 1950 to 1972 found that rating agencies' changes generated information of little or no value; instead, such changes merely reflected information already incorporated into stock market prices of the companies whose ratings were changed approximately one-and-one-half years previously. In other words, the lag between the change in stock market price due to new information and the corresponding change in bond rating was more than a year. Concern about the failure of the rating agencies to generate accurate and reliable information, especially during a time of crisis, led to public arguments for regulation of the credit rating industry. * * *

From the mid–1970s to today, credit rating agencies have exploded in size. The modern credit rating agency is more influential and more profitable than at any time this century, despite the fact that the rating system hasn't changed in any substantial way since the 1930s. The rating scales also are similar to those used during the 1930s. The number of credit rating agency employees has multiplied more than ten-fold during the past decade. In 1980, there were thirty professionals working in the S & P Industrials group; by 1986, there were only forty. By 1995, S & P had 800 analysts and a total staff of 1,200; Moody's has expanded at a similar rate and in 1995 employed 560 analysts and a total staff of 1,700.

The number of rated issuers has increased by the same order of magnitude. In 1975, 600 new bond issues were rated, increasing the number of outstanding rated corporate bonds to 5,500. Today, Moody's rates 20,000 public and private issuers in the U.S., and about 1,200 non-U.S. issuers, both corporations and sovereign states; S & P rates slightly fewer in each category. Moody's rates $5 trillion worth of securities; S & P rates $2 trillion. Moody's and S & P thus dominate the world business of rating government and corporate debt.

In the mid–1980s, credit rating agencies limited their coverage to predominantly U.S. corporations and the debt of fifteen sovereign states. As of 1981, for example, S & P rated only thirteen countries, all AAA, and by 1993, S & P rated the debt of forty-three countries, including many so-called emerging markets countries, which received low ratings. By 1995, half of the fifty-two countries rated by Moody's and S & P were in the emerging markets category. * * *

[B]oth Moody's and S & P make rating determinations in secret. The agencies never describe their terms or analysis precisely or say, for example, that a particular rating has a particular probability of default, and they stress that the ratings are qualitative and judgmental. * * *

Perhaps the most important change in the credit rating agencies' approach since the mid–1970s has been their means of generating revenue. Today, issuers, not investors, pay fees to the rating agencies. Ninety-five percent of the agencies' annual revenue is from issuer fees, typically two to three basis points of a bond's face amount. Moody's and S & P have aggressively expanded and now receive most of their revenue from the corporations they rate. Duff & Phelps and Fitch IBCA also charge fees to issuers. * * *

NOTES

1. Dun, Boyd & Co., was another credit information agency that was operating before the Civil War. It later combined with the Bradstreet Agency to become Dun & Bradstreet. The firm used a network of some 10,000 correspondents to gather information on businessmen and companies in order

to assess their creditworthiness. Its correspondents included several future presidents, U.S. Grant, William McKinley, Grover Cleveland and Abraham Lincoln. Rating agencies soon proved their fallibility. One correspondent reported that John D. Rockefeller, later to be the head of the most successful business in the world, was "not much of a businessman." Julie Flaherty, A Good Credit History Indeed, Opening the Books on American Business, 1841–1891, N.Y. Times, Aug. 21, 1999, at B1. Dun & Bradstreet acquired Moody's Investors Services in 1962, but spun that operation off into a separate entity in 1996 and placed its commercial credit service in another company.

2. The collapse of the Penn Central Railroad was unexpected and unpredicted by the agencies. *See* Mallinckrodt Chemical Works v. Goldman, Sachs & Co., 420 F.Supp. 231 (S.D.N.Y.1976) (dismissing claims against rating agency for giving Penn Central a high credit rating on which a creditor of the railroad relied). Both Mood's and Standard & Poor's gave their highest ratings to Orange County California before it declared bankruptcy. SEC v. Dain Rauscher, Inc., 254 F.3d 852 (9th Cir.2001).

SECURITIES AND EXCHANGE COMMISSION REPORT ON THE ROLE AND FUNCTION OF CREDIT RATING AGENCIES IN THE OPERATION OF THE SECURITIES MARKETS AS REQUIRED BY SECTION 702(B) OF THE SARBANES–OXLEY ACT OF 2002

(January 2003).

* * * In essence, a credit rating reflects agency's opinion, as of a specific date, of the creditworthiness of a particular company, security, or obligation. For almost a century, credit rating agencies have been providing opinions on the creditworthiness of issuers of securities and their financial obligations. During this time, the importance of these opinions on the securities markets, have increased significantly. This is due in part to the increase in the number of issuers and the advent of new and complex financial products, such as asset-backed securities and credit derivatives. The globalization of the financial markets also has served to expand the role of credit ratings to countries other than the United States, where the reliance on credit ratings largely was confined for the first half of the twentieth century. Today, credit ratings affect securities markets in many ways, including an issuer's access to capital, the structure of transactions, and the ability of fiduciaries and others to make particular investments.

During the past 30 years, regulators, including the [Securities and Exchange] Commission, have increasingly used credit ratings to help monitor the risk of investments held by regulated entities, and to provide an appropriate disclosure framework for securities of differing risks. Since 1975, the Commission has relied on ratings by market-recognized credible rating agencies for distinguishing among grades of creditworthiness in various regulations under the federal securities laws. These "nationally recognized statistical rating organizations," or "NRSROs," are recognized as such by Commission staff through the no-action letter process. * * * Although the Commission originated the use of the term "NRSRO" in regulation, ratings by NRSROs today are widely used as benchmarks in federal and state legislation, rules issued by financial and other regulators, foreign regulatory schemes, and private financial contracts.

In another report,[11] the SEC notes that:

* * *

In recent years, the credit ratings issued by agencies that are recognized as nationally recognized statistical rating agencies ("NRSROs") have attained an increased level of importance within the context of the Commission's rules and regulations. The Commission looks to the credit ratings issued by NRSROs in a variety of contexts, and for different purposes, to distinguish among various grades of debt and other rated securities.

The increasing utilization of credit ratings as a component in Commission rules, in turn, has prompted a number of domestic and foreign rating agencies to seek NRSRO status. Currently, the Commission's rules do not define the term "NRSRO," nor is there a formal mechanism for monitoring the activities of agencies that have been recognized as NRSROs. * * *

In 1975, the Commission adopted the uniform net capital Rule, Rule 15c3–1 under the Securities Exchange Act of 1934 ("Exchange Act"), which in part also incorporated the use of ratings issued by NRSROs in connection with certain provisions of the net capital rule. Rule 15c3–1 requires broker-dealers, when computing net capital, to deduct from net worth certain percentages of the market value ("haircuts") of their proprietary securities positions. Haircuts serve as a safeguard against the risks associated with fluctuations in the price of each broker-dealer's proprietary securities. Broker-dealers' proprietary positions in commercial paper, nonconvertible debt securities and nonconvertible preferred stock are accorded preferential treatment under the net capital rule, in the form of reduced haircuts, if the instruments are rated investment grade by at least two NRSROs. The Commission did not attempt to define the term in the context of the net capital rule and, in using the term subsequently in other regulatory contexts, the Commission generally has stated that the term should have the same meaning as it does for purposes of the net capital rule.

Over time, the NRSRO concept has been incorporated into other areas of the federal securities laws and Congress itself employed the

---

11. Securities Exchange Act Release No. 34616 (1994).

term "NRSRO" in the definition of "mortgage related security." Pursuant to Section 3(a)(41) of the Exchange Act, which was added by the Secondary Mortgage Market Enhancement Act of 1984 a mortgage related security must, among other things, be rated in one of the two highest rating categories by at least one NRSRO. Although Congress did not define what it meant by an NRSRO, its reliance on the term used in Commission rules is significant because it reflects a congressional recognition that the "term has acquired currency as a term of art."

In addition, several regulations issued pursuant to the Securities Act of 1933 ("Securities Act"), the Exchange Act, and the Investment Company Act of 1940 ("Investment Company Act") have incorporated the term "NRSRO" as it is used in the net capital rule. For example, the Commission employs NRSRO ratings as a basis for distinguishing between certain types of securities that may be issued using simplified registration procedures under the Securities Act. NRSRO ratings also are employed in connection with investment restrictions applicable to money market funds. Rule 2a–7 under the Investment Company Act requires a money market fund to limit its investments to securities that are "Eligible Securities," which, among other things, are securities rated in one of the two highest rating categories for short-term debt by the requisite number of NRSROs. * * *

Rating agencies and other organizations have developed ratings of open-end and other types of investment companies. These ratings serve a number of purposes. Three rating agencies, Fitch Investors Service, Inc. ("Fitch"), Standard & Poor's Corporation ("Standard & Poor's"), and Moody's Investors Service, Inc. ("Moody's"), issue ratings that assess the safety of principal invested in a money market mutual fund. These rating agencies also have begun to rate different characteristics of bond funds. For example, Fitch, Standard & Poor's, and Moody's each issue bond fund ratings designed to identify the degree of credit risk in a bond fund's underlying investments. Fitch and Standard & Poor's also issue bond fund "stability" or "market risk" ratings that purport to quantify the potential volatility of the market value of bond fund shares, based on an analysis of interest rate risk, spread risk, currency risk, and the fund's use of derivatives. Other organizations issue mutual fund risk ratings that are designed to quantify different types of investment risk. These ratings may provide investors with information that may be useful in assessing the risks of investing in a mutual fund; however, they also may create expectations of investment performance that may not be achieved, notwithstanding disclaimers that they are not projections of future results. * * *

In reaching a decision regarding whether to provide no-action assurances to rating agencies regarding NRSRO designation, the Division staff undertakes an informal examination of the agency's operations, its position in the marketplace, as well as considering other factors. If the Division staff determines that no-action assurances are appropriate, the staff prepares a letter stating that it will not recommend enforcement action to the Commission if the rating agency is considered to be an NRSRO for purposes of applying the relevant subdivisions of the net capital rule.

In determining whether a rating agency possesses the characteristics of an NRSRO, the staff considers a number of criteria. The Division believes that the single most important criterion is that the rating agency is in fact nationally recognized by the predominant users of ratings in the United States as an issuer of credible and reliable ratings. Consistent with this standard of national recognition is a minimum level of operational capability and reliability of ratings. Therefore, the staff also assesses, among other factors: (a) the agency's organizational structure; (b) the agency's financial resources (to determine, among other things, whether it is able to operate independently of economic pressures); (c) the size and quality of the agency's staff (to determine if the entity is capable of thoroughly and competently evaluating an issuer's credit); (d) the agency's independence from the companies it rates and its reputation for integrity in the marketplace; (e) the agency's rating procedures (to determine whether it has systematic procedures designed to ensure credible and accurate ratings); and (f) the agency's establishment and compliance with internal procedures to prevent misuses of non-public information.

NOTES

1. The SEC was traditionally wary of the ratings agencies. It was not until 1981 that the SEC changed its policy of prohibiting disclosure of a company's credit rating in prospectuses and other disclosure documents filed with the agency. The role of the rating agencies was expanded with the creation of federal insurance for customers of bankrupt broker-dealers (SIPC). The SEC adopted a "net capital" rule to assure broker-dealer liquidity and to act as a protective device to cut losses in the event of insolvency. This net capital rule is complex beyond comprehension but includes a requirement for a reduction in value (a "haircut") on bonds held in inventory based on their rating by a rating agency designated as a NRSRO. Regulators relied on ratings from the rating agencies for other regulatory requirements. Money market funds were restricted in their ability to invest in bonds other than those rated in the highest categories. In addition, bank regulators used ratings to define valuation standards for so called Type III securities which must be at least investment grade to be held in a bank portfolio. Securitizations held by banks were risk weighted for capital requirements based on their credit ratings, and a proposed revision in bank capital requirements would do the same for corporate loans.

Some have argued that reliance by federal agencies on private rating companies was giving those rating agencies a quasi-governmental role and creating an artificial demand for rating agency services. The oligarchic nature of the ratings business added further criticism. Like the accountants, rating agencies were paid by the companies they rated for their services. This created the appearance of a conflict of interest, which critics were quick to point out whenever a highly rated company failed. Frank Partnoy, *The Siskel and Ebert of Financial Markets? Two Thumbs Down for the Credit Rating Agencies*, 77 Wash. U. L. Q. 619 (1999).

2. The rating agencies were severely criticized for not predicting the demise of the Enron Corporation. See *Testimony of Frank Partnoy, Prof. of L. U. San Diego School of Law Before the Senate Committee on Governmental Affairs*, 107th Cong.2d Sess., at 58 (January 24, 2002). The Sarbanes–Oxley Act of 2002, Pub. L. No. 107–204 at § 702, required the SEC to conduct a study of the NRSROs and to report to Congress on any deficiencies, raising the possibility that the NRSROs would be subject to regulation in the future. The SEC conducted that study and advised Congress that further examination was needed on these issues. SEC, Report on the Role and Function of Credit Rating Agencies in the Operation of the Securities Markets As Required by Section 702(b) of the Sarbanes–Oxley Act of 2002 (Jan. 2003). The SEC later issued a concept release asking for public comment on how NRSROs should be treated for regulatory purposes. Securities Exchange Act Release No. 47972 (June 4, 2003). Subsequently, the Credit Rating Agency Reform Act of 2006 (109 P.L. 291; 120 Stat. 1327, codified at 15 USCS § 78o–7) required NRSROs to register with the SEC. As a part of that application, the NRSRO must disclose its performance measurement statistics, its rating methodologies, whether it has a code of ethics and financial statements were required to be supplied to the SEC periodically. NRSROs were required to adopt procedures for the prevention of the misuse of inside information and procedures for dealing with conflicts of interest such as payment by the entity being rated for the rating. The SEC was also given rule making authority to deal with conflicts. Tying practices such as requiring payment for additional services in order to obtain or retain a rating were prohibited.

In Europe, the German parliament called for IOSCO (the International Organization of Security Commissions) to create an international code of conduct for the ratings agencies that would allow issuers to appeal ratings they think are unfair. IOSCO published a report in 2004 on the ratings agencies and principles they should follow. It was also working on a code of conduct. The European Parliament passed a resolution asking the ratings agencies to improve the transparency of their ratings and to avoid conflicts of interest.

3. Should NRSROs be liable for giving a high credit rating to a firm that fails before the rating is changed? Is this constitutionally protected speech if the rating is too low and causes a borrower to pay a higher interest rate or lose the ability to sell a bond issue? The court in Jefferson County School District No. R–1 v. Moody's Investor's Services, Inc., 175 F.3d 848 (10th Cir.1999) held such speech was constitutionally protected. In In re Fitch, 330 F.3d 104 (2d Cir.2003), however, the court of appeals ruled that a rating

agency could not claim a privilege from third party subpoenas available under New York law to news gathering organizations.

4. The subprime crisis that arose between 2007 and 2009 resulted in renewed criticism of the rating agencies.[12] A popular form of securitization for subprime mortgages was the collateralized debt obligation (CDO). These were simply packaged subprime mortgage pools that were securitized and sold off to investors who bought participation certificates that entitled them to some portion of the proceeds from the pooled mortgages. Subprime CDO participation certificates were broken up into separate tranches. The less secure tranches were required to absorb any larger than expected losses from mortgage defaults, providing a cushion from loss for the most secure tranches, called the "Super–Seniors."

As a result of this credit enhancement feature, the Super–Seniors were considered to be more credit-worthy than the underlying subprime mortgages themselves. The credit rating agencies often gave the Super Seniors their highest triple-A rating. This was the same credit rating enjoyed by the federal government. The rating agencies bestowed their triple A rating on over 64,000 structured finance instruments, while only twelve operating companies in the world had such a rating.[13] Tens of thousands of other such instruments were given investment grade ratings just below triple A.

This was a very lucrative business for the ratings agencies. Moody's rated nine out of every ten dollars raised through structured instruments. In 2005, its structured finance ratings resulted in revenues of $715 million, which was over forty percent of Moody's total revenues. Moody's charged over $200,000 to rate a $350 million mortgage-backed offering, while a municipal bond offering in the same amount would generate fees of only $50,000. Standard & Poor's and Moody's revenues grew from $3 billion in 2002 to over $6 billion in 2007 as a result of structured finance ratings. Moody's had the highest profit margin of any company in the S & P 500 for five straight years.

The high ratings given to the Super Seniors signaled to the world that a default on those Super Senior tranches was highly unlikely. Unfortunately, the rating agencies' risk models for awarding the triple-A rating on CDOs did not take into account the possibility of a major downturn in the real estate market. That flaw was not spotted until the subprime crisis arose. The high credit ratings given to the Super Senior tranches posed another problem. These securities were hard to market due to their lower interest rates, which was a function of their triple-A rating. That problem was solved after bank regulators in the United States allowed favorable capital treatment of Super Seniors on bank balance sheets, provided that the Super Senior had a high credit rating.[14]

---

12. For a further discussion of the role of the rating agencies during the subprime crisis see Jerry W. Markham, A Financial History of the United States, From the Subprime Crisis to the Great Recession (2010).

13. *See Heard on the Street*, WALL ST. J., Apr. 11, 2009, at B8.

14. *See* Tett, *supra*, note 48, 63–64.

This regulatory blessing removed any residual concerns on the part of the banks of undue risk from Super–Seniors and created a demand for the Super Seniors by banks here and abroad. As a result, a large portion of the Super Senior tranches were held on the books of many major commercial and investment banks such as Citigroup, Merrill Lynch, UBS AG and Lehman Brothers. The twenty-five largest banks were also holding $13 trillion in CDS notionals on their books in March 2008.[15]

The flaw in thee ratings for these instruments became apparent in 2008. During that year the rating agencies downgraded over 221,000 tranches of asset-backed securities, and banks experienced over $500 billion in losses on subprime mortgages. A credit down grade at the American International Group, Inc. (AIG) in September 2008 raised concerns that large losses would be experienced in the financial community if AIG defaulted on its $500 billion CDS portfolio. This spurred the federal government to mount a $183 billion rescue of that firm.[16]

A study released by the SEC in July 2008 found that the rating agencies had been careless in their approach to rating CDOs and other structured mortgage instruments. The SEC found that the rating agencies were understaffed and overwhelmed by the large number of subprime securitized offerings. The analysts employed by the rating agencies were also found to have considered the risk of losing business if they did not give instruments the ratings sought by the issuer. The risks of the subprime securitizations were often not fully measured by the rating agencies. Moody's discovered in February 2007 that it had committed a computer error in giving a triple-A rating to so-called "constant proportion debt obligations" (CPDO), a form of synthetic debt security that was widely sold in Europe. Although it became aware of the error shortly after the issuance of the securities, Moody's did not correct the rating for more than a year.

Some $300 billion of CDOs were in default by February 2009. Banks in the European Union had been badly damaged by the triple-A rated Super–Seniors. Their governments turned on the rating agencies, finding them to be a convenient scapegoat. The European Commission proposed legislation in November 2008 that would regulate credit rating agencies through its Committee of European Securities Regulators. In the United States, Treasury Secretary Henry J. Paulson stated that he would be seeking additional regulation of the rating agencies, including different ratings categories for mortgage-backed securities, the disclosure of conflict of interest, and explanation of the basis for their reviews. He also wanted the rating agencies to assume a more aggressive regulatory role over loan originators. The President's Working Group on Financial Markets endorsed this plan. In response to that pressure, Moody's announced in

15. *See* Janet Morrissey, *Credit Default Swaps: The Next Crisis*, TIME, Mar. 17, 2008, *available at* http://www.time.com/time/business/article/0,8599,1723152,00.html.

16. *See* Lauren Silva Laughlin, *Is the A.I.G. Rally a Little Early?* N.Y. TIMES, Sept. 8, 2009, at B2.

March 2010 that it was changing its ratings to use a single scale for municipal and corporate bonds.

Connecticut Attorney General Richard Blumenthal filed suit in July 2008 against the rating agencies, claiming that they had systematically and intentionally given lower ratings to states and municipalities than to corporations and other entities with higher default rates. The rating agencies entered into an agreement with New York State Attorney General Andrew Cuomo on June 5, 2008, pursuant to which they agreed to strengthen their independence and ensure that critical loan data was available before they rated loan pools. The rating agencies further agreed to increase their transparency in connection with their ratings for the residential mortgage-backed securities market. In order to restrict shopping for ratings, the settlement required the ratings firms to be paid for their reviews, even if they were not hired to rate the transaction. The theory was that the rating agencies would be less inclined to provide the desired rating merely in order to get paid. In addition, the rating agencies agreed to review due diligence reports on loans being securitized and to establish criteria for assessing the reliability of loan originators.

The SEC also jumped on the rating agencies once again. An SEC staff study in July 2008 discovered what the staff believed were significant flaws in the rating processes at the larger credit rating agencies. The SEC was proposing to require credit rating firms to make more disclosures about how they rated securities and to provide special classifications for securitized instruments. The SEC was also proposing to prohibit rating agencies from rating instruments that they designed, leaving them little incentive to develop new products, hardly a desirable economic goal. In addition, executives at rating agencies negotiating fees would be prohibited from involvement with the rating of the company's securities. Under the SEC proposals, employees of rating agencies involved in advising on rating methodologies would be prohibited from receiving a gift of more than $25 per meeting on the issue. More significantly, the rating agencies would have to publish the performance of their ratings over one, three and ten-year periods, including upgrades and downgrades. The SEC also proposed to change its rules to remove some references to NRSROs as value determiners, and it cautioned investors that a credit rating was only the first step in considering whether to make an investment.

The SEC decided in December 2008 to defer action on the proposal to require the rating agencies to differentiate between bonds and structured investments in their rating methodologies. The agency also deferred action on its proposal to require the rating firms to disclose all underlying information about debt offerings being rated. The SEC did adopt some changes that required the rating agencies to take additional steps to mitigate conflicts of interest, to require more disclosures on their rating processes, and to disclose the performance of their ratings.

This did not satisfy rating agency critics, and the Obama administration proposed in July 2009 that a special office be created in the SEC to monitor rating agencies and that the rating agencies separate ratings of structured finance from other debt offerings. Additional disclosures would also be required. The SEC went a step further in April 2010 proposing a rule that would remove recognition of the rating agencies as an official evaluator of mortgage and other asset backed securities. Instead, the return on the bonds would have to be vouchsafed by the CEO of the issuer and the issuer would have to invest its own funds in at least five percent of the issue. This was a radical departure from the view that investors accepted the risks of an investment and that issuers could not guarantee returns.

5.   The Dodd–Frank Wall Street Reform and Consumer Protection Act of 2010 ("Dodd–Frank" (§§ 931–939H) addressed the regulation of rating agencies. The legislation stated that regulation was justified because the ratings agencies are financial "gatekeepers" and should be subject to same standards of liability and oversight as auditors, securities analysts, and investment bankers. The legislative justification statement also noted that the mis-rating of structured products had contributed substantially to the subprime crisis. Among other things, rating agencies were, in a Sarbanes–Oxley like provision, required to strengthen their internal controls and attest to their effectiveness.

The SEC was ordered to establish an Office of Credit Ratings and the SEC was to conduct examinations of credit rating agencies at least once a year. The SEC was directed to adopt rules governing the procedures and methodologies, including qualitative and quantitative data and models, used by the rating agencies. Disclosure of rating methodologies was also required. At least 50 percent of the directors of the rating agencies were required to be independent directors. The rating agencies were required to report any violations of the federal securities laws that they might observe in the course of gathering information for a rating. Ratings analysts will be required to pass qualifying exams and have continuing education.

The rating agencies were also subjected to liability under the federal securities laws for the failure of their ratings. This caused all three of the rating agencies to suspend the use of their ratings for asset-backed bonds, which then had the effect of freezing that $1.2 trillion dollar market. The SEC then acted to allow bond offerings to be made without credit ratings for a period of six months.

CHAPTER FOUR

MEDIUM AND LONG TERM OBLIGATIONS

■ ■ ■

Chapter objectives

- To see that stockholders and bondholders can have opposing interests as to how a corporation invests in assets, finances itself, and issues dividends.

- To understand the federal securities laws that apply to debt issuance, including the Trust Indenture Act.

- To appreciate the range of medium-and long-term debt instruments issued by corporations.

SECTION 1. INSTRUMENT DESIGN

Corporate debt is classified on the balance sheet as long term (with a maturity of more than 10 years), medium term (with a maturity of one year to ten years) and short-term as described in the preceding chapter. *See generally* In re Bevill, Bresler & Schulman Asset Management Corp., 67 B.R. 557, 567 (D.N.J.1986) (describing debt with differing maturities). This section will focus on medium and long-term debt.

Other Long Term Debt

There are many forms of long-term debt. The English government issued "consols" in 1751, which was debt that had no maturity date. These loans remained outstanding in the twentieth century. The French government issued a similar device called the "rent perpetuelle." Corporations may also issue bonds with extraordinarily long maturity dates. One hundred year bonds were issued by railroads in the nineteenth century. See Schickler v. Santa Fe Southern Pacific Corp., 229 Ill.App.3d 291, 171 Ill.Dec. 141, 593 N.E.2d 961 (1992) (gold payment clauses in 100–year bond issued in 1895 negated by action taken by federal government in 1933 declaring such clauses void). IBM made a $850 million offering of 100 year bonds in 1996. They paid a coupon rate of 7.22 percent.

United States firms may seek to raise funds abroad. The Euro dollar market has been a popular source of such borrowings. These are United States dollars that are held abroad. Foreign firms may also borrow money in the United States through "Yankee" bonds, which are dollar denominated.

Long-term borrowing may take many complex forms. Corporate bonds may be secured or unsecured. If secured, a particular piece of property acts as collateral for the loan, and the creditor has priority over that property. Utility and railroad bonds may be issued as mortgage bonds or equipment trust certificates that have secured interests in specific assets. A collateral trust bond is secured by securities or other assets that are pledged to the trustee for payment of the bonds in event of default. If unsecured (as are most debentures), the only security is the general credit of the company and in liquidation the debenture will share with other creditors in the disposition of the assets of the corporation. Bond principal repayments may be funded by "sinking funds" that periodically retire a portion of the outstanding bond issue.

Zero Coupon Bonds

Consider the following variation on a typical corporate note:

Liquid Yield Option Notes ("LYONs") were developed by Merrill lynch and first offered to investors in early 1985. To create LYONs, Merrill Lynch redesigned the standard convertible bond in two important respects: (1) the bonds were reconfigured as zero coupon instruments which are offered at a deep discount to their face amount; and (2) investors were given a put option which is exercisable at one or more future dates at a price equal to the original offering price of the LYONs plus the interest that accrues to the date of the put.

Merrill Lynch's primary objective in creating LYONs was to reduce the downside risk of the security while, at the same time, retaining the equity participation characteristics of traditional convertible bonds. By early 1989, LYONs accounted for between 5% and 6%, in terms of market value, of all convertible bonds issued by U.S. corporations. That figure has grown substantially; LYONs now constitute 29% of the $46 billion in total market value of all outstanding U.S. dollar denominated convertible bonds of U.S. issuers. Merrill Lynch has now underwritten 44 different LYONs issues-including an "Index LYON", the principal amount of which is keyed to the performance of the NYSE Composite Index. The total cash proceeds raised from the sale of these LYONs amounted to $10.7 billion. Since Merrill Lynch developed LYONs, other firms have offered a total of twelve convertible bond issues with a structure similar to LYONs. The total cash proceeds from the sale of these ten issues amounted to $2.9 billion. LYONs are gaining a proportionately greater share of the convertible securities market not only because they constitute an increasing percentage of new convertible issues; but also because the prospect of the early redemption of a LYONs issue is less likely than for a traditional convertible, all else being equal. * * *

LYON's, like other convertibles, contain elements of both equity and fixed income securities. Depending upon the price of a LYON in relation to that of its underlying stock, conversion premium and yield as well as terms specific to a given issue, a LYON may be primarily equity or primarily fixed income in terms of its investment characteristics. Different issues will, therefore, provide opportunities to different groups of investors. Our analysis focuses not only on present prices and relationships but also on theoretical future prices and rates of return as calculated using the Merrill Lynch Theoretical Valuation Model. * * *

Merrill Lynch, LYONS (April 1992).

The LYON is a "zero coupon" bond. This means that it is sold at a discount and does not make periodic interest rate payments. The reference to a zero coupon is to indicate that there is no coupon interest paid, i.e., in earlier times coupons were attached to the bond and were clipped off and sent in to the issuer to claim the periodic interest payment. A "coupon clipper" was someone living off the interest on their investments, clipping and sending in the coupons for their income. A zero coupon bond has no coupons. Instead, the interest is computed on the discount between the amount paid for the instrument and the amount due on maturity. Zero coupon bonds of extended maturity sell at a sharp discount to their principal payment amount, once again evidencing the time value of money.

A disadvantage to the zero coupon bond is its taxation. The Internal Revenue Service taxes the holder as if they were in fact receiving the interest payment imputed from the discount each year, an amount referred to as "original issue discount" ("OID"). *See* United States v. Midland–Ross Corp., 381 U.S. 54, 85 S.Ct. 1308, 14 L.Ed.2d 214 (1965) (OID was ordinary income and not a capital gain). This is undesirable because the taxpayer is paying taxes out-of-pocket without any corresponding income to make the payment. Rather, the holder will not receive that income until the bond is paid at maturity. The zero coupon bond is still attractive, however, to tax advantaged situations such as a retirement account that is not taxed until the money is actually paid out to the owner.

NOTES

1. Another Merrill Lynch product was the "Corporate U.S. Dollar Bond Index Linked Securities" or "Dollar BILS." Merrill Lynch & Co., Inc., Dollar BILS Prospectus, dated August 21, 1998. These instruments were issued in face amount certificates of $100,000 with a 10–year maturity. They were non-redeemable senior securities sold under a trust indenture agreement. The holder received no periodic interest payments. Rather, on maturity, the holder received the principal amount plus an interest payment calculated on the

basis of any increases or decreases in the value of a specified portfolio of bonds. The value of the portfolio was calculated on the total return of the component bonds from interest payments and any increase or decrease in the market value of those bonds. What would the effect be on the value of the Dollar BIL if defaults occurred on the bonds in the portfolio or if interest rates rise sharply? What would be the effect of a decrease in interest rates? Do these instruments serve an economic function other than speculation?

2.   Salomon Brothers developed the Continuously Offered Longer–Term Securities ("COLTS") for the World Bank with maturities ranging from three to thirty years. The continuous offering and the range of maturities provide flexibility in meeting funding needs. The World Bank sold some $1.4 billion in these securities over a two-year period. World Bank Seeks New Agent Firms, N.Y. Times, March 30, 1998, at D19.

3.   Bond offerings may offer returns in addition to conventional interest rates. For example, Citibank N.A. arranged a bond offering for Bulgaria that based the amount of interest payments on increases in the country's GDP. Robert J. Shiller, The New Financial Order, Risk in the 21st Century 124–125 (2003). For other examples of unconventional offerings see Chapter 12.

Warrants

Warrants may also be attached to a bond. The warrant usually is an option on the common stock of the company exercisable at a price above its current market price. This requires some market appreciation before the warrant will provide a profit if exercised. The warrant may be detachable from the bond and, if so, may trade separately from the bond.

As always, there is no free lunch on Wall Street. A warrant will carry a price. Usually, that means that the interest rate on a bond with a warrant attached will be less than the rate paid by a comparable bond without such a feature.

Warrants may provide an option on items other than the stock of the company. Consider the following:

The Notes and Warrants are being offered and sold separately, and not in units.

The Notes will bear interest from July 15, 1988, payable semi-annually on January 15 and July 15, commencing January 15, 1989. The Notes will mature on July 15, 1991, and will not be redeemable prior to maturity.

Each Warrant will entitle the holder thereof to receive from Ford Motor Credit Company ("Ford Credit") the cash value in U.S. dollars of the right to purchase U.S.$50 at a price of ¥6989, which represents an exchange rate of ¥139.78 per U.S.$1.00. The Warrants will be exercisable immediately upon issuance and until 3:00 p.m., New York City time, on the fifth New York Business Day (as hereinafter defined, preceding their expiration on July 15, 1991 or earlier expiration upon delisting from, or permanent suspension of trading on, the American Stock Exchange unless, at the same time, the Warrants are accepted for listing on another national securities exchange. Any Warrant not exercised at or before 3:00

p.m., New York City time on the fifth New York Business Day preceding its expiration date will be deemed automatically exercised on such expiration date. A Warrant holder may exercise no fewer than 2,000 Warrants at any one time, except in the case of automatic exercises, including at expiration).

The Warrants involve a high degree of risk, including foreign exchange risks and the risk of expiring worthless if the U.S. dollar does not appreciate or depreciates against the Japanese Yen. Investors therefore should be prepared to sustain a total loss of the purchase price of their Warrants.

Prospectus, Ford Motor Credit Company, $100,000,000 8.95% Notes Due 1991, 2,000,000 Currency Exchange Warrants (CEWs), Expiring July 15, 1991.

4. As with any option (see Chapter 11), the value of a warrant, will hinge on a number of factors, including the length of time to expiration, the strike price, and the volatility of the stock.

5. Issues may arise as to the exact expiration date of a warrant. In Swiss Bank Corp. v. Dresser Industries, Inc., 141 F.3d 689 (7th Cir.1998), the court held that a warrant requiring exercise "prior to" a date five years from its issuance was not properly exercised where notice was not sent until the first business day after the expiration of the five year period. The court rejected a claim that notice was proper because the last expiration date was a holiday and the issuer's offices were closed.

6. Berkshire Hathaway, a company managed by the legendary investor Warren Buffett, sold negative interest bonds that paid three percent interest and were coupled with five year warrants to buy Berkshire Hathaway stock at a fifteen percent premium over its present stock price. The investor, however, had to pay 3.75 percent each year to maintain the right to exercise the warrant. This would result in a net negative rate of 0.75 percent if the warrant did not become valuable. Buffett's Negative–Interest Issues Sell Well, N.Y. Times, May 23, 2002, at C2.

THE PRUDENTIAL INSURANCE COMPANY OF AMERICA v. COMMISSIONER OF INTERNAL REVENUE

882 F.2d 832, 836–838 (3d Cir.1989).

GIBBONS, CHIEF JUDGE.

* * * The value of a debt instrument varies inversely with increases and decreases in the market interest rate for instruments of similar credit risk. *See W. Meigs & R. Meigs, Financial Accounting* 488–491 (4th ed. 1983); T. Maness, *Introduction to Corporate Finance* 154–56 (1988). The value of a debt instrument equals the present value of its expected cash flows, interest payments, plus principal payments. *Id.* As market interest rates decrease, the value of the obligation increases. An instrument which is generating a higher than market income stream because its interest rates are higher than the current market rate will be more highly valued. Because this higher value depends upon the higher income stream, the value decreases as the obligation nears maturity and the life of the income stream is reduced.

When interest rates increase relative to a debt instrument, the value of such a debt instrument decreases. The borrower realizes benefit because he is able to pay back the monetary obligation at less than the prevailing market interest rate. He receives the use of the money without bearing the current cost of borrowing.

When interest rates decrease relative to a debt instrument, whether the lender receives the benefit of the higher valued instrument depends upon the prepayment terms. If no prepayment is allowed, the lender may receive the benefit of his higher valued instrument in the form of higher than market interest receipts. Alternatively, he may sell the instrument at its appreciated value. * * *

Conversely, if the instrument allows prepayment at any time without penalty, the lender will generally not receive the benefit from a significant drop in interest rates. The borrower will simply refinance the obligation at the prevailing lower interest rate. The borrower will borrow money at the lower rate and pay off the debt instrument which has the higher interest rate. The lender will not receive the higher than market interest receipts. Moreover, the lender is not able to sell the instrument at a higher value because of the probability of prepayment.

A prepayment charge is a middle course between no prepayment and prepayment at will. To a limited extent, it preserves the lender's right to receive the benefit of appreciation in value of the debt instrument resulting from a drop in the prevailing interest rates. The prepayment charge acts as a ceiling on the amount of appreciated value that the lender will receive. At the point where prevailing interest rates have dropped far enough to result in an increase in value of the instrument which exceeds the prepayment charge, the borrower will pay the prepayment charge and refinance the debt.

As previously stated, the value of an instrument with a higher than market interest rate decreases as the obligation nears maturity because there are fewer higher than market interest payments to be received. Frequently, prepayment charges decrease as an obligation nears maturity as a corollary to this fact. * * *

Mortgages

Another long-term obligation is the mortgage. This means that the lender is given a security interest in a particular piece of property. You may be familiar with this concept in financing the purchase of your own home. The repayment of principal may be amortized over the life of the loan. This usually involves a fixed payment each month that is part principal and part interest. The amount of interest in that monthly fixed payment will decrease as principal is paid down. Charts are available that identify the amount of a mortgage payment amortized over varying periods (usually 15 or 30 years) for specific amounts borrowed at specific interest rates.

Bonds are typically sold at par on initial issuance. This term is conceptually different than when used in reference to stock. See Chapter 6. In the context of bonds, this term refers to the principal amount of the bond. A $1,000 par bond means that the holder has loaned the borrower $1,000 and agrees to pay interest on that amount and return that principal on maturity. Bonds may be bought at a premium or discount over par to reflect changes in interest rates. Those changes are expressed in increments called "basis" points (bps). There are 100 basis points in each dollar change in premium or discount from par.

> Par value is the official ("parity") value of a bond or other financial instrument. The par value of bonds is the principal that the bond represents. Prices for bonds are expressed as a percentage of this value, so that when dealing in bonds prices par means 100%. Prices are generally expressed simply as numbers rather than percentages; that is, a price of 80 means 80% of par value. (Shares also have par values, but their prices are not generally expressed in this way.)

James MacDonald, The Financial Roots of Democracy, A Free Nation Deep in Debt 76 (2003).

A secondary market may exist in corporate bonds. That is, once the bonds are initially sold, they may be resold by the holder to a third party, providing liquidity for the investment. This market is a broad one and is important to the economy. One aspect of the long-term corporate debt market is the high yield debenture or what are sometimes derisively referred to as "junk bonds." These are simply bonds paying high rates of interest because of a higher risk of default. These high yield securities may be "fallen angels," i.e., previously rated investment grade bonds that have had a drop in their ratings. This was what happened in the Metropolitan Life Insurance case. In other instances, corporations with less than investment grade ratings will sell junk bonds as an original issue. They are willing to pay the high interest rates demanded by creditors for incurring higher default risks. The issuer assumes that it will be able to obtain a higher rate of return from its investment of those funds than will be required for the debt service.

Junk bonds became a popular means to raise funds by aggressive companies for use in takeover attempts and to expand their businesses during the 1980s. That market was developed by Michael Milken, a bond salesman at the firm of Drexel Burnham Lambert, who claimed that junk bonds were paying interest rates in excess of their default risk. The following is a description of his much criticized activities:

> This case arises from the ashes of what is regarded by some as the most spectacular scam of the 1980s. The complaint alleges that early

in that decade, Michael Milken of Drexel Burnham Lambert Group, Inc. began to successfully tout high risk, high yield "junk" bonds as a way to finance growth for otherwise under-capitalized companies. For a while the junk market flourished. Eventually, however, it became apparent that the market comprised, not arm's-length participants, but primarily a group of Milken clients. These people depended on him to sell their high risk bonds to a so-called "daisy chain" of other Milken controlled clients with proceeds from their own (typically over-financed) junk offerings. The whole pyramid fell apart when the market realized that junk debt carried a much higher default rate than had been advertised. The initiation of criminal and civil enforcement proceedings against Milken and Drexel exacerbated the matter. In January 1989, Drexel pleaded guilty to, inter alia, federal securities fraud, and agreed to pay $650 million in fines and restitution. In April 1990, Milken followed suit by pleading guilty to, inter alia, securities fraud, and agreeing to pay $600 million in fines and restitution.

Goldberger v. Integrated Resources, 209 F.3d 43 (2d Cir. 2000). Despite this harsh condemnation, the junk bond recovered by the year 2000. Symposium, The Direction of Corporate Law: The Scholars' Perspective, 25 Del. J. Corp. L. 79, 83 (2000) ("The junk bond market is as big now as ever"). The market then took another dive. Christopher O'Leary, Wanted: New Junk Bond, Investment Dealers Digest, January 27, 2003. The junk bond market experienced another recovery at the beginning of 2002. Gregory Zuckerman, Junk Bonds Seem Poised to Leap Back to Top of the Heap, Wall St. J., Jan. 14, 2002, at C1. It was also rallying in 2010 after recovering from the financial crisis.

In any event, it should be noted that, as pointed out by Milken's attorney, high yield security owners must be paid in full before shareholders receive anything in liquidation. Yet, no one calls common stock "junk stock." Arthur L. Liman, Lawyer: A Life of Counsel and Controversy 268 (1998).

SECTION 2. MARKET STRUCTURE

Medium Term Financing

Corporations also use medium term financing to conduct business. Medium-term notes, those with maturities from nine months to ten years vary from the simple to the complex, and it has been a growing market. "The outstanding amount of medium-term notes issued by U.S. corporations in the domestic market rose from less than $1 billion in 1981 to $299 billion in 1999." Arthur E. Wilmarth, Jr., The Transformation of the U.S. Financial Services Industry 1975–2000: Competition, Consolidation, and Increased Risks, 2002 U. Ill. L. Rev. 215, 231, n. 50 (citation omitted).

Medium term notes may be continuously offered at varying interest rates and maturity dates. These notes may also be sold under a trust indenture, which usually provides for interest to be paid on a fixed payment date regardless of the interest rate or maturity date.

LELAND E. CRABBE
ANATOMY OF THE MEDIUM–TERM NOTE MARKET

79 Fed. Res. Bull. 751 (1993).

Over the past decade, medium-term notes (MTNs) have emerged as a major source of funding for U.S. and foreign corporations, federal agencies, supra-national institutions, and sovereign countries. U.S. corporations have issued MTNs since the early 1970s. At that time, the market was established as an alternative to short-term financing in the commercial paper market and long-term borrowing in the bond market; thus the name "medium term." Through the 1970s, however, only a few corporations issued MTNs, and by 1981 outstandings amounted to only about $800 million. In the 1980s, the U.S. MTN market evolved from a relatively obscure niche market dominated by the auto finance companies into a major source of debt financing for several hundred large corporations. In the 1990s, the U.S. market has continued to attract a diversity of new borrowers, and outside the United States, the Euro–MTN market has grown at a phenomenal rate. By year-end 1992, outstanding MTNs in domestic and international markets stood at an estimated $283 billion.
* * *

Most MTNs are noncallable, unsecured, senior debt securities with fixed coupon rates and investment-grade credit ratings. In these features, MTNs are similar to investment-grade corporate bonds. However, they have generally differed from bonds in their primary distribution process. MTNs have traditionally been sold on a best-efforts basis by investment banks and other broker-dealers acting as agents. In contrast to an underwriter in the conventional bond market, an agent in the MTN market has no obligation to underwrite MTNs for the issuer, and the issuer is not guaranteed funds. Also, unlike corporate bonds, which are typically sold in large, discrete offerings, MTNs are usually sold in relatively small amounts either on a continuous or on an intermittent basis.

Borrowers with MTN programs have great flexibility in the types of securities they may issue. As the market for MTNs has evolved, issuers have taken advantage of this flexibility by issuing MTNs with less conventional features. Many MTNs are now issued with floating interest rates or with rates that are computed according to unusual formulas tied to equity or commodity prices. Also, many include calls, puts, and other options. Furthermore, maturities are not necessarily "medium term"—they have ranged from nine months to thirty years and longer. Moreover, like corporate bonds, MTNs are now often sold on an underwritten basis, and offering amounts are occasionally as large as those of bonds. Indeed, rather than denoting a narrow security with an intermediate maturity, an MTN is more accurately defined as a highly flexible debt instrument that can easily be designed to respond to market opportunities and investor preferences. The emergence of the MTN market has transformed the way that corporations raise capital and that institutions invest. In recent years, this transformation has accelerated because of the development of derivatives markets, such as swaps, options, and futures, that allow investors and borrowers to transfer risk to others in the financial system who have different risk preferences. * * *

General Motors Acceptance Corporation (GMAC) created the MTN market in the early 1970s as an extension of the commercial paper market. To improve their asset-liability management, GMAC and the other auto finance companies needed to issue debt with a maturity that matched that of their auto loans to dealers and consumers. However, underwriting costs made bond offerings with short maturities impractical, and maturities on commercial paper cannot exceed 270 days. The auto finance companies therefore began to sell MTNs directly to investors. In the 1970s, the growth of the market was hindered by illiquidity in the secondary market and by securities regulations requiring approval by the Securities and Exchange Commission (SEC) of any amendment to a registered public offering. The latter, in particular, increased the costs of issuance significantly because borrowers had to obtain the approval of the SEC each time they changed the posted coupon rates on their MTN offering schedule. To avoid this regulatory hurdle, some corporations sold MTNs in the private placement market. In the early 1980s, two institutional changes set the stage for rapid growth of the MTN market. First, in 1981 major investment banks, acting as agents, committed resources to assist in primary issuance and to provide secondary market liquidity. By 1984, the captive finance companies of the three large automakers had at least two agents for their MTN programs. The ongoing financing requirements of these companies and the competition among agents established a basis for the market to develop. Because investment banks stood ready to buy back MTNs in the secondary market, investors became more receptive to adding MTNs to their portfolio holdings. In turn, the improved liquidity and consequent reduction in the cost of issuance attracted new borrowers to the market.

Second, the adoption by the SEC of Rule 415 in March 1982 served as another important institutional change. Rule 415 permits delayed or continuous issuance of so-called shelf registered corporate securities. Under shelf registrations, issuers register securities that may be sold for two years after the effective date of the registration without the requirement of another registration statement each time new offerings are made. Thus, shelf registration enables issuers to take advantage of brief periods of low interest rates by selling previously registered securities on a moment's notice. In contrast, debt offerings that are not made from shelf registrations are subject to a delay of at least forty-eight hours between the filing with the SEC and the subsequent offering to the public.

The ability of borrowers to sell a variety of debt instruments with a broad range of coupons and maturities under a single prospectus supplement is another advantage of a shelf-registered MTN program. Indeed, a wide array of financing options have been included in MTN filings. For example, MTN programs commonly give the borrower the choice of issuing fixed-or floating-rate debt. Furthermore, several "global" programs allow for placements in the U.S. market or in the Euro-market. Other innovations that reflect the specific funding needs of issuers include MTNs collateralized by mortgages issued by thrift institutions, equipment trust certificates issued by railways, amortizing notes issued by leasing companies, and subordinated notes issued by bank holding companies. Another significant innovation has been the development of asset-backed MTNs, a form of asset securitization used predominantly to finance trade receivables and corporate loans. This flexibility in types of instruments that may be sold as MTNs, coupled with the market timing benefits of shelf registration, enables issuers to respond readily to changing market opportunities.

In the early and mid–1980s, when finance companies dominated the market, most issues of MTNs were fixed rate, noncallable, and unsecured, with maturities of five years or less. In recent years, as new issuers with more diverse financing needs have established programs, the characteristics of new issues have become less generic. For example, maturities have lengthened as industrial and utility companies with longer financing needs have entered the market. Indeed, frequent placements of notes with thirty-year maturities have made the designation "medium term" something of a misnomer.

The process of raising funds in the public MTN market usually begins when a corporation files a shelf registration with the SEC. Once the SEC declares the registration statement effective, the borrower files a prospectus supplement that describes the MTN program. The amount of debt under the program generally ranges from $100 million to $1 billion. After establishing an MTN program, a borrower may enter the MTN market continuously or intermittently with large or relatively small offerings. Although underwritten corporate bonds may also be issued from shelf registrations, MTNs provide issuers with more flexibility than traditional underwritings in which the entire debt issue is made at one time, typically with a single coupon and a single maturity. The registration filing usually includes a list of the investment banks with which the corporation has arranged to act as agents to distribute the notes to investors. Most MTN programs have two to four agents. Having multiple agents encourages competition among investment banks and thus lowers financing costs. The large New York-based investment banks dominate the distribution of MTNs.

Through its agents, an issuer of MTNs posts offering rates over a range of maturities: for example, nine months to one year, one year to eighteen months, eighteen months to two years, and annually thereafter. Many issuers post rates as a yield spread over a Treasury security of comparable maturity. The investment banks disseminate this offering rate information to their investor clients. When an investor expresses interest in an MTN offering, the agent contacts the issuer to obtain a confirmation of the terms of the transaction. Within a maturity range, the investor has the option of choosing the final maturity of the note sale, subject to agreement by the issuing company. The issuer will lower its posted rates once it raises the desired amount of funds at a given maturity. The issuer might lower its posted rate for MTNs with a five-year maturity to 40 basis points over comparable Treasury securities after it sells the desired amount of debt at this maturity. Of course, issuers also change their offering rate scales in response to changing market conditions. Issuers may withdraw from the market by suspending sales or, alternatively, by posting narrow offering spreads at all maturity ranges. The proceeds from primary trades in the MTN market typically range from $1 million to $25 million, but the size of transactions varies considerably. After the amount of registered debt is sold, the issuer may "reload" its MTN program by filing a new registration with the SEC. * * *

Although MTNs are generally offered on an agency basis, most programs permit other means of distribution. For example, MTN programs usually allow the agents to acquire notes for their own account and for resale at par or at prevailing market prices. MTNs may also be sold on an underwritten basis. In addition, many MTN programs permit the borrower to bypass financial intermediaries by selling debt directly to investors.

In deciding whether to finance with MTNs or with bonds, a corporate borrower weighs the interest cost, flexibility, and other advantages of each security. The growth of the MTN market indicates that MTNs offer advantages that bonds do not. However, most companies that raise funds in the MTN market have also continued to issue corporate bonds, suggesting that each form of debt has advantages under particular circumstances.

The amount of the offering is the most important determinant of the cost differential between the MTN and corporate bond markets. For large, standard financings (such as $300 million of straight debt with a ten-year maturity) the all-in interest cost to an issuer of underwritten corporate bonds may be lower than the all-in cost of issuing MTNs. This cost advantage arises from economies of scale in underwriting and, most important, from the greater liquidity of large issues. As a result, corporations that have large financing needs for a specific term usually choose to borrow with bonds. From an empirical point of view, the liquidity premium, if any, on small offerings has yet to be quantified. Nevertheless, the sheer volume of financing in the MTN market suggests that any liquidity premium that may exist for small offerings is not a significant deterrent to financing. According to market participants, the interest cost differential between the markets has narrowed in recent years as liquidity in the MTN market has improved. Many borrowers estimate that the premium is now only about 5 to 10 basis points. Furthermore, many borrowers believe that financing costs are slightly lower in the MTN market because its distribution process allows borrowers to price discriminate. Consider a stylized example of a company that needs to raise $100 million. With a bond offering, the company may have to raise the offering yield significantly, for example, from 6 percent to 6.25 percent, to place the final $10 million with the marginal buyer. In contrast, with MTNs the company could raise $90 million by posting a yield of 6 percent; to raise the additional $10 million, the company could increase its MTN offering rates or issue at a different maturity. Consequently, because all of the debt does not have to be priced to the marginal buyer, financing costs can be lower with MTNs.

Even if conventional bonds enjoy an interest cost advantage, this advantage may be offset by the flexibility that MTNs afford. Offerings of investment-grade straight bonds are clustered at standard maturities of two, three, five, seven, ten, and thirty years. Also, because the fixed costs of underwritings make small offerings impractical, corporate bond offerings rarely amount to less than $100 million. These institutional conventions impede corporations from implementing a financing policy of matching the maturities of assets with those of liabilities. By contrast, drawdowns from MTN programs over the course of a month typically amount to $30 million, and these drawdowns frequently have different maturities and special features that are tailored to meet the needs of the borrower. This flexibility of the MTN market allows companies to match more closely the maturities of assets and liabilities.

The flexibility of continuous offerings also plays a role in a corporation's decision to finance with MTNs. With MTNs, a corporation can "average out" its cost of funds by issuing continuously rather than coming to market on a single day. Therefore, even if bond offerings have lower average yields, a risk-averse borrower might still elect to raise funds in the MTN market with several offerings in a range of $5 million to $10 million over several weeks, rather than with a single $100 million bond offering. The flexibility of the MTN market also allows borrowers to take advantage of funding opportunities. By having an MTN program, an issuer can raise a sizable amount of debt in a short time; often, the process takes less than half an hour. Bonds may also be sold from a shelf registration, but the completion of the transaction may be delayed by the arrangement of a syndicate, the negotiation of an underwriting agreement, and the "pre-selling" of the issue to investors. Furthermore, some corporations require that underwritten offerings receive prior approval by the president of the company or the board of directors. In contrast, a corporate treasurer may finance with MTNs without delay and at his or her discretion.

———————

The following excerpt from a prospectus for medium term notes to be continuously issued by the Kingdom of Spain is illustrative of the form these notes may take:

> The Kingdom of Spain ("Spain") may offer from time to time up to U.S. $1,000,000,000 aggregate principal amount, or the equivalent in one or more foreign currencies or currency units, of its Medium–Term Notes (the "Notes"). Each Note will mature on any Business Day from or exceeding nine months from its date of issue, as selected by the purchaser and agreed to by Spain. Unless otherwise indicated in

the applicable Pricing Supplement to this Prospectus Supplement (a "Pricing Supplement"), the Notes may not be redeemed by Spain prior to maturity and will be issued in fully registered form in denominations of U.S. $100,000 or in multiples of U.S. $1,000 in excess thereof. If the Notes are to be denominated in a foreign currency or currency unit, then the provisions with respect thereto will be set forth in a foreign currency supplement hereto (a "Multi–Currency Prospectus Supplement").

The interest rate, if any, or interest rate formula applicable to each Note and other variable terms of the Notes as described herein will be established by Spain at the date of issuance of each Note. . . . Unless otherwise indicated . . . , the Notes will bear interest at a fixed rate ("Fixed Rate Notes") or at floating rates ("Floating Rate Notes") determined by reference to the Certificate of Deposit Rate, Commercial Paper Rate, Federal Funds Rate, LIBID, LIBOR, Prime Rate or Treasury Rate, as adjusted by any Spread or Multipler applicable to such notes . . . Notes may also be issued at original issue discounts and such notes may or may not bear interest. * * *

The rate of interest on each Floating Rate Note will be reset daily, weekly, monthly, quarterly, semi-annually or annually (each an Interest Reset Period) as specified in the applicable Pricing Supplement.

U.S. $1,000,000,000, Kingdom of Spain Medium–Term Notes, Prospectus Supplement to Prospectus dated Nov. 29, 1988.

Medium term notes may be issued in series with varying rights as shown by the following SEC filing:

Citigroup Inc., a Delaware corporation (the "Company"), confirms its agreement with the Agent . . . with respect to the issue and sale by the Company of its Medium–Term Senior Notes, Series E, Due Nine Months or More from the Date of Issue (the "Senior Notes") and its Medium–Term Subordinated Notes, Series E, Due Nine Months or More from the Date of Issue (the "Subordinated Notes" and, together with the Senior Notes, the "Notes"). The Senior Notes are to be issued under an Indenture dated as of March 15, 1987, as supplemented by the First Supplemental Indenture dated as of December 15, 1988, the Second Supplemental Indenture dated as of January 31, 1991, the Third Supplemental Indenture dated as of December 9, 1992 and the Fourth Supplemental Indenture dated as of November 2, 1998 (as so supplemented or as it may from time to time be further supplemented or amended by one or more indentures supplemental thereto, the "Senior Debt Indenture"), between the Company and The Bank of New York, as trustee (the "Senior Debt Trustee"). The Subordinated Notes are to be issued under an Indenture dated as of March ___, 2001 (as so supplemented or as it may from time to time be further supplemented or amended by one or more indentures supplemental thereto, the "Subordinated Debt Indenture" and, together with the Senior Debt Indenture, the "Indentures"), between the Company and Bank One Trust Company, N.A., as trustee (the "Subordinated Debt Trustee" and, together with the Senior Debt Trustee, the "Trustees"). The Notes will have the maturities, interest rates (whether fixed or floating), redemption provisions and other terms set forth in pricing supplements to the Prospectus.... The Notes may be denominated in U.S. dollars, foreign currencies or foreign composite currency units (the "Specified Currency") as may be specified in the applicable pricing supplement.

Citigroup Inc., Medium–Term Senior Notes, Series E Medium–Term Subordinated Notes, Series E Due Nine Months or More from the Date of Issue Distribution Agreement (2001).

The types of medium term notes expanded to include notes with varying features such as floating or fixed rates, payment in varying currencies, multiple tranches, exchangeable, puttable (notes that can be sold back at a specified price), and secured by mortgages.

NOTES

1. Are medium term notes effectively being used as an alternative to a line of credit, especially when sold as floating rate notes?

2. What are the characteristics of the Kingdom of Spain offering that makes it a desirable investment?

Auction Rate Securities

An auction rate security (ARS) is a form of money market investment that is essentially a hybrid-term instrument that utilizes periodic auctions to reset the interest rate on the instrument at market rates:

In other words, ARS are long-term bonds whose interest rates are based on short-term market interest rates. The interest rates for ARS are typically set at a dutch auction, which are held at seven, twenty-eight, thirty-five, and forty-nine day intervals.... ARS are issued as either bonds or preferred stock and are designed to serve as money market-type instruments. Also, it is important to note that ARS have long-term maturity or no maturity at all. They have been marketed to rich individuals (for tax exemption purposes) and corporate treasuries (for liquid cash on corporate balance sheets, however taxable) as an alternative to money market funds.[1]

Municipalities and not-for-profit institutions issued many of these auction rate securities. There was also an active auction rate market for

1. Amod Choudhary, "Auction Rate Securities = Auction Risky Securities," 11 Duq. Bus. L. J. 11, 24–25 (2008).

student loans that many individual investors used for their short-term investments. Minimum investments were set at around $25,000. The auction rate market had about $330 billion in outstanding obligations in February 2008. More than 400 companies had large exposures from such investments in the first quarter of 2008.

Auction rate securities typically paid one percent more than money market funds, which made them attractive to large investors seeking a place to invest funds for a short-term with the assurance of liquidity. Liquidity, however, depended upon the success of the auctions that allowed investors to sell out their positions and reset interest rates for new participants.

Auctions for about $80 billion of auction rate securities failed in the second week of February 2008 as a result of the liquidity crisis that arose during the subprime crisis. In April 2008, over 500 auctions were scheduled during a single day for $27 billion of ARS, but they too failed. Under the terms of many auction rate securities, if an auction failed, the holder would receive an interest rate below Libor until the auctions could be resumed. This meant that the holder would have to either sell at a large discount or accept a very low interest rate. As a result of the auction failures, ARS securities posed an unexpected liquidity problem for the holder. However, it was a liquidity issue, not a default on payments, ever how low the interest payments might be after an auction freeze. The liquidity problem could be met in part by using the ARS as collateral for a margin loan until they were refinanced.

The auction rate market was slowly thawing out in May 2008. By then, about twenty-five percent of the market had been refinanced. The most problematic were the student loan auction rate notes, which reset at very low rates, even zero in some instances, when an auction failed. As a consequence, there was no incentive on the part of the issuer to refinance those notes. Indeed, many of those issuers were suffering losses in the student loan market, and this was a way for them to ease those problems.

After coming under pressure from regulators and threats of investor lawsuits, several investment banking firms agreed to buy back the ARS they had underwritten. Bank of America agreed to buy back $4.5 billion of ARS from investors in September 2008; Morgan Stanley agreed to repurchase $4.5 billion. Citigroup announced plans to buy back more than $7 billion of ARS. Citigroup also agreed to pay a fine of $100 million to state regulators from forty-nine other states, who were charging misrepresentations had been made in connection with the ARS auctions. UBS agreed to buy back more than $41 billion in auction rate securities as a part of a settlement with various regulators. UBS also agreed to pay a $150 million fine. Wachovia agreed to repay investors more than $8.5 billion in a settlement with state regulators concerning its ARS sales. Wachovia and Citigroup agreed to pay California investors $4.7 billion over auction rate claims, plus over $12 million to regulators. Bank of America reached a settlement with the State of California to repurchase $3 billion of ARS sold in that state. In another settlement, Morgan Stanley repaid its ARS investors $4.5 billion plus penalties of $35 million. J.P. Morgan agreed to return $3 billion to ARS investors and pay penalties of $25 million. Merrill Lynch agreed to buy back $10 to $12 billion in auction rate securities. Goldman Sachs agreed to buy back $1.5 billion of auction rate securities from retail investors and pay a $22.5 million penalty. Deutsche Bank agreed to buy back $1 billion of those securities and pay a $15 million fine.

In total, state regulators forced brokerage firms to repurchase $60 billion in ARS. Still, some 400 businesses holding over $20 billion in ARS remained locked into those investments because they were not protected by these settlements.

Capital Leasing of Equipment

Equipment leasing is another popular form of corporate finance that is usually conducted on a medium or long-term basis. *See* Michael I. Tsai, A Unified Treatment of Finance Lessees' Revocation of Acceptance Under the Uniform Commercial Code, 137 U.Pa. L. Rev. 967, 1004–1005 (1989) (describing growth of equipment leasing industry). The use of this form of finance requires knowledge and application of the Uniform Commercial Code's provisions so that the lessor's security interest in the equipment is protected from the claims of other creditors.

How is an equipment lease different from a secured loan on the same property? Tax implications may help answer that question.

LEE A. SHEPARD
NEWS ANALYSIS: EQUIPMENT LEASING SHELTERS FOR CORPORATE CUSTOMERS

66 Tax Notes 1591 (1995).

The standard equipment lease starts with the Lessee, who needs a particular piece of equipment, like a computer or an airplane, but either does not need the tax benefits that go with ownership or wants to be able to put the equipment back to the Lessor when it is no longer needed. The Lessee's ability to make lease payments is usually not in doubt. The Lessor is usually in the business of leasing. Lessee and Lessor work with the manufacturer of the equipment to design a lease according to the Lessee's needs.

The Lessor finances the purchase of the desired equipment with a nonrecourse loan from the Lender, plus some cash and a small negotiable note. The Lender takes a security interest in the equipment and an assignment of the rents due under the lease, which payments are to be applied to the loan. The Lessor may have sold the equipment to Investors operating as a limited partnership, and re-leased the equipment from them. The term of the lease between Lessor and Lessee is shorter than the term of the lease between Investors and Lessor; the difference is called the re-lease period. The Investors are deemed to pay down their debt to the Lessor with funds they are deemed to collect from the Lessor under its lease of the equipment from them. No money ever changes hands; these circular payments are simply credited on the books of the Lender. It is for this reason that this sale-leaseback arrangement is called a 'wrap' lease; it wraps around the real deal.

The point of the new corporate equipment leasing shelter is that the circularity of the wrap lease payments is broken in a way that allows net operating losses to be used. A second limited partnership is formed in which the Lessor is a 1–percent general partner and a Loss Corporation is a 99–percent limited partner. This Loss Corporation Limited Partnership will buy out the Lessor at a negotiated price based on the anticipated tax benefits and what are called the residuals. The residuals represent the re-lease period, which allows the equipment to be re-let for the remaining term of the loan. The partnership replaces the Lessor in the deal. The partnership then sells the right to receive rents from the Lessee to an unrelated third-party lease factoring company, which usually pays for these rights by assuming the debt to the Lender. Or the partnership uses the cash proceeds of the sale to retire the debt to the Lender.

Alternatively, instead of being owned at the outset by an Investor limited partnership, the equipment could be owned by a Loss Corporation Limited Partnership in which the Lessor is a 1–percent general partner, and a Loss Corporation is a 99–percent limited partner. This partnership would engage in the same type of sale-leaseback transaction described for the Investor partnership. Then an unrelated third-party lease factoring company purchases the stream of rents due from the partnership to the Lessor by assuming the partnership's debt to the Lessor.

In either case, the factoring company has entered the circle and broken it, though the real deal involving the Lessee is largely unaffected. The factoring company's purchase of the right to rent payments is thought to have the effect of accelerating the lease income into the period in which the assumption of the debt occurred, under Schlude v. Commissioner, 372 U.S. 128 (1963), allowing the Loss Corporation limited partner to use the income to freshen its expiring net operating losses. If the Loss Corporation Limited Partnership enters the deal in place of the Lessor, the losses are regenerated through deductions for rent paid to the Investor partnership. If the Loss Corporation Limited Partnership enters the deal in the position of the Investor partnership, the losses are regenerated through continuing depreciation deductions on the equipment. (One participant at the ABA meeting interjected that the proposed neutral cost recovery system now being considered by the House Ways and Means Committee would enable corporations to get inflation-adjusted net operating loss carryovers.)

Instead of the Loss Corporation, the recipient of the big slug of income could be a partnership of nonresident aliens or someone else who is functionally tax-exempt. After that exempt person or group recognized the big income item from the factoring of the lease, the limited partnership would contribute the equipment to a new corporation. Because the equipment now represents a stream of deductions, the shares of the new corporation would then be peddled to a large domestic corporation in need of deductions; this corporate customer may come in by participating in the section 351 transaction. These leasehold interest deduction schemes have been marketed to many Fortune 500 corporations. 'The numbers on these deals are scary,' Mackles commented. 'Some promoters won't even talk to you unless you're talking about $30 million and up, and some deals have even more zeroes.'

Bond Trading

Corporate bonds may be bought and traded like stocks, providing liquidity when such trading is active in a particular bond or note. Many large broker-dealers have "fixed income" departments and trading floors where this activity takes place. Bonds were once widely traded on the stock exchanges as well but that business has migrated to the over-the-counter ("OTC") market. The NASD, the self-regulator for the OTC market, has created a reporting program that requires that the trading prices of particular bonds be publicly disclosed *albeit* on a delayed basis. The number of bond issues subject to that requirement was expanded to from 500 to 4,200 in February 2003. Steven Vames, NASD Sets Date For Expansion of Price Disclosure, Wall St. J., Feb. 21, 2003, at C13. There were uncertainties over whether this increased transparency will add further liquidity to the market. Steven Vames, NASD Expands Bond–Price Reports, Wall St. J., March 4, 2003, at C15.

The price of a fixed income instrument such as a bond or note will vary with changes in interest rates, all other things being equal. Say you own a 30–year bond in the principal amount of $1,000 that pays a fixed annual five percent rate of interest. Assume that interest rates in the market increase by one percent one year after you bought the note. You would now like to sell the bond. To do so, you will have to accept a discount on the principal amount because the purchaser will not lend you $1,000 for an instrument paying one percent less interest than comparable notes being issued at the increased market rate. Of course, you could hold the note to maturity and receive all your principal back, but you will have forgone the higher available interest rate. The converse is true for bond prices when interest rates in the market drop. Where a bond is bought at a premium or discount, the yield to maturity will reflect that factor as well as the periodic interest payments from the corporation.

As seen in Chapter 3, there are several factors in addition to interest rates that affect bond prices, including counter party risk. The more risk, the higher the rate of interest required. The yield curve must also be considered. Normally, the longer the term of a fixed income instrument, the higher the interest rate. This is a reflection of several factors including inflation and increased risk of a default over longer terms. The yield curve encourages "carry" trades in which an investor or bank borrows funds short term and then lends those funds to a borrower for a longer term at a higher fixed rate. The investor continually rolls over the short term borrowing in order to maintain the longer-term loan. This sounds like a good way to print money but poses substantial dangers when short term rates increase, because the investor will be required to roll over the short term loans at the higher rate but will not be able to pass that increase on to the party given the long-term fixed rate loan. Many banks and financial institutions incurred massive losses from their carry trades during the financial crisis in 20007–2009. Carry trades also raise liquidity risk concerns because short-term financing may dry up during a credit crunch, precluding a rollover of the short-term loans in the carry trade.

Leveraged Loans

During the bull market in credit leading up to the 2007 crash, an asset class developed that combined the major features of loan and bonds: leveraged loans.

JOSÉ GABILONDO
LEVERAGED LIQUIDITY: BEAR RAIDS AND JUNK LOANS IN THE NEW CREDIT MARKET

34 Iowa J. Corp. L. 447, 495 (2009).

... Leveraged loans are secured, floating-rate loans (typically priced off LIBOR) that are syndicated between commercial banks and nonbank lenders such as hedge funds and investment banks. Corporate borrowers may seek these loans for many reasons. Start-up companies may be unable to secure investment-grade ratings. Or cyclical businesses may need capital during a low point in their operations. Firms exiting bankruptcy or "fallen angels"—formerly investment-grade issuers that have been notched down—may be relegated here until the issuer's financial prospects improve. Leveraged loan issuance is cyclical in the direction that Minsky predicted—increasing during economic expansion and risk-taking. Issuance also correlates with trends in mergers and acquisitions and recapitalizations, two common forms of "shareholder-friendly" upstreaming.

Like the junk bonds that financed the takeovers of the 1980s, leveraged loans rest on the assumption that lending at a subinvestment grade (albeit at a floating rate) is fine, so long as the rate reflects the default risk and is diversified in a portfolio. How borrowers, lenders, traders, and brokers came to think about leveraged loans reflects the semantic shifts that come with financial euphoria. The financial prefix "leverage" came to substitute for the harsher sounding "subinvestment grade" or, worse still, "junk" before the word "loan." Rather than thinking in terms of "credit supply" and borrower "demand for credit," the loans became "supply" for which (leveraged) investment demand competed, completing the semantic shift thanks to the growth of secondary markets. Indeed, even global financial regulators have adopted the custom of using "leveraged" as a substitute for "subinvestment grade" when it comes to these loans. These loans are another example of the kind of financial innovation that, according to Minsky, "regulates the pace of movement out of hedge and into speculative finance," and, presumably, Ponzi finance too. Much as the petro-liquidity of the 1970s led to this type of investment demand, this last leverage wave led to increasingly complex products that were further removed from their underlying cash flows.

In 2006, the leveraged loan market represented about one-fifth of the overall corporate loan market and equaled about one-half of overall bond issuance.... Leveraged loans have their own trade group—the Loan Syndications & Trading Association (LSTA). LSTA promotes standardization of loan and settlement documentation, credit ratings for loans, Committee on Uniform Securities Identification Procedures (CUSIP) numbers for loans, and benchmark indices. Credit rating agencies helped to promote these loans by rating them, beginning with S & P in 2000. Within a few years, specialized recovery ratings had developed to supplement the projected default rate with estimates of how much an investor would recover in the event of default....

The arranger of the leveraged loan gets a fee of 1.5%–2.5% for putting the loan together, more than the fees charged for investment-grade loans, which may have no arranger fees. Initially, leveraged loans included a revolving credit line and an amortizing term loan—so called "pro rata" tranches that bank investors preferred. While banks prefer to hold pro rata tranches, nonbank investors have tended to prefer junior tranches that did not amortize, had longer terms, and often lower security. So it has tended to be nonbank institutional investors who provided the riskier financing, a trend borne out by a finding in a 2006 federal review of syndicated lending that generally the credit quality of syndicated loans held by banks increased while that held by nonbanks decreased. Indeed, nonbank investors have become so dominant in these loans that "by early 2002, most [leveraged] loans were structured without an amortizing term loan component, and while the typical structure still included a revolver, it was usually a much smaller share of the overall package than would have been the norm in the past."

The Loan Pricing Corporation classifies as leveraged those loans with BB, BB/B, and B or lower ratings. Others use the loan's spread over a reference rate at the time the loan is made, typically a spread of between 125 to 275 basis points over a reference rate. Not surprisingly, leveraged loans correlate most closely as an asset class to high-yield (junk) bonds, despite formal differences between the two. For example, most leveraged loans may be prepaid without penalty while high-yield bonds may not be callable by the issuer at all, or only occasionally, and then subject to a premium. These loans generally have a shorter term than high-yield bonds. These loans may also have more financial covenants than do high-yield bonds....

Between June and August 2007, leveraged loans faced their first major market liquidity crisis: origination dried up, loan products traded at a discount in the secondary market, and traders shorted loan indices. As activity slowed in the secondary market, these loans became stranded on the books of originating lenders, including banks....

In the secondary market for leveraged loans, buyers and sellers deal in previously-issued loans, sometimes at a discount over the loan's par value based on changes in interest rates or the borrower's creditworthiness. The secondary market for these loans grew during the past decade....

As in the origination market, in the secondary market nonbank investors are more active than banks. As this market grew, investment banks that had traded these loans as brokers for the accounts of others began to take more proprietary positions in the loans. The same seems to be true for hedge funds that specialize in the credit market exposures.

Investment vehicles called "collateralized loan obligations" (CLO) played a key role in the secondary market by buying leveraged loans to collateralize the issuance of their own securities. Such CLOs may have accounted for over one-fifth of all secondary market demand for the loans. Compared with other forms of asset-backed securities like mortgage-backed securities and collateralized-debt obligations, CLOs tend to contain a more diverse set of receivables whose prepayment characteristics are harder to predict....

Repackaging leveraged loans into CLOs changes the total amount of leverage built into the product, hence increasing the product's exposure (and contribution) to financial instability. To begin with, the CLO is itself leveraged, typically at a debt-to-equity ratio of 10:1 to 12:1. The CLO uses these leveraged resources to acquire leveraged loans issued by a borrower that is itself already leveraged, i.e., to the extent of any debt issued by the leveraged borrower. With these leveraged loans as collateral, the CLO then issues securities that may be more or less leveraged than the underlying leveraged loan collateral. And the investor who purchases a security issued by the CLO may borrow (through margin or other form of credit) to invest in the security. Each of the three different leverage "points" in the transaction—the debt burden of the leveraged loan issuer, the borrowing of the CLO, and the margin (or other) debt of the investor in the CLO—props up the price of the ultimate investment asset, i.e., the interest held by the investor in the CLO. Aggregate leverage supports the market liquidity for the product while, at the same time, exposing three borrowers to funding liquidity risk: the leveraged loan borrower, the CLO, and the leveraged investor. It is easy to see, then, how a product with so many layers of leverage can lose value quickly when speculative and Ponzi euphoria slows down.

SECTION 3.   STOCKHOLDER–BONDHOLDER CONFLICT

METROPOLITAIN LIFE INS. CO. v. RJR NABISCO, INC.

716 F.Supp. 1504 (S.D.N.Y.1989).[2]

WALKER, DISTRICT JUDGE:

The corporate parties to this action are among the country's most sophisticated financial institutions, as familiar with the Wall Street investment community and the securities market as American consumers are with the Oreo cookies and Winston cigarettes made by defendant RJR Nabisco, Inc. (sometimes "the company" or "RJR Nabisco"). The present action traces its origins to October 20, 1988, when F. Ross Johnson, then the Chief Executive Officer of RJR Nabisco, proposed a $17 billion leveraged buy-out ("LBO") of the company's shareholders, at $75 per share. Within a few days, a bidding war developed among the investment group led by Johnson and the investment firm of Kohlberg Kravis Roberts & Co. ("KKR"), and others. On December 1, 1988, a special committee of RJR Nabisco directors, established by the company specifically to consider the competing proposals, recommended that the company accept the KKR proposal, a $24 billion LBO that called for the purchase of the company's outstanding stock at roughly $109 per share.

The flurry of activity late last year that accompanied the bidding war for RJR Nabisco spawned at least eight lawsuits, filed before this Court, charging the company and its former CEO with a variety of securities and common law violations. The Court agreed to hear the present action—filed even before the company accepted the KKR proposal—on an expedited basis, with an eye toward March 1, 1989, when RJR Nabisco was expected to merge with the KKR holding entities created to facilitate the LBO. On that date, RJR Nabisco was also scheduled to assume roughly $19 billion of new debt. After a delay unrelated to the present action, the merger was ultimately completed during the week of April 24, 1989.

Plaintiffs now allege, in short, that RJR Nabisco's actions have drastically impaired the value of bonds previously issued to plaintiffs by, in effect, misappropriating the value of those bonds to help finance the LBO and to distribute an enormous windfall to the company's shareholders. As a result, plaintiffs argue, they have unfairly suffered a multimillion dollar loss in the value of their bonds.[3] * * *

Although the numbers involved in this case are large, and the financing necessary to complete the LBO unprecedented, the legal princi-

---

2. This decision was reversed in part on other points. *Metropolitan Life Ins. Co. v. RJR Nabisco, Inc.*, 906 F.2d 884 (2d Cir. 1990).

3. Agencies like Standard & Poor's and Moody's generally rate bonds in two broad categories: investment grade and speculative grade. Standard & Poor's rates investment grade bonds from "AAA" to "BBB." Moody's rates those bonds from "AAA" to "Baa3." Speculative grade bonds are rated either "BB" and lower, or "Ba1" and lower, by Standard & Poor's and Moody's, respectively. *See, e.g., Standard and Poor's Debt Rating Criteria* at 10–11. No one disputes that, subsequent to the announcement of the LBO, the RJR Nabisco bonds lost their "A" ratings.

ples nonetheless remain discrete and familiar. Yet while the instant motions thus primarily require the Court to evaluate and apply traditional rules of equity and contract interpretation, plaintiffs do raise issues of first impression in the context of an LBO. At the heart of the present motions lies plaintiffs' claim that RJR Nabisco violated a restrictive covenant—not an explicit covenant found within the four corners of the relevant bond indentures, but rather an *implied* covenant of good faith and fair dealing—not to incur the debt necessary to facilitate the LBO and thereby betray what plaintiffs claim was the fundamental basis of their bargain with the company. The company, plaintiffs assert, consistently reassured its bondholders that it had a "mandate" from its Board of Directors to maintain RJR Nabisco's preferred credit rating. Plaintiffs ask this Court first to imply a covenant of good faith and fair dealing that would prevent the recent transaction, then to hold that this covenant has been breached, and finally to require RJR Nabisco to redeem their bonds.

RJR Nabisco defends the LBO by pointing to express provisions in the bond indentures that, *inter alia,* permit mergers and the assumption of additional debt. These provisions, as well as others that could have been included but were not, were known to the market and to plaintiffs, sophisticated investors who freely bought the bonds and were equally free to sell them at any time. Any attempt by this Court to create contractual terms *post hoc,* defendants contend, not only finds no basis in the controlling law and undisputed facts of this case, but also would constitute an impermissible invasion into the free and open operation of the marketplace.

For the reasons set forth below, this Court agrees with defendants. There being no express covenant between the parties that would restrict the incurrence of new debt, and no perceived direction to that end from covenants that are express, this Court will not imply a covenant to prevent the recent LBO and thereby create an indenture term that, while bargained for in other contexts, was not bargained for here and was not even within the mutual contemplation of the parties. * * *

Metropolitan Life Insurance Co. ("MetLife"), incorporated in New York, is a life insurance company that provides pension benefits for 42 million individuals. According to its most recent annual report, MetLife's assets exceed $88 billion and its debt securities holdings exceed $49 billion. MetLife is a mutual company and therefore has no stockholders and is instead operated for the benefit of its policyholders. MetLife alleges that it owns $340,542,000 in principal amount of six separate RJR Nabisco debt issues, bonds allegedly purchased between July 1975 and July 1988. Some bonds become due as early as this year; others will not become due until 2017. The bonds bear interest rates of anywhere from 8 to 10.25 percent. MetLife also owned 186,000 shares of RJR Nabisco common stock at the time this suit was filed.

Jefferson–Pilot Life Insurance Co. ("Jefferson–Pilot") is a North Carolina company that has more than $3 billion in total assets, $1.5

billion of which are invested in debt securities. Jefferson–Pilot alleges that it owns $9.34 million in principal amount of three separate RJR Nabisco debt issues, allegedly purchased between June 1978 and June 1988. Those bonds, bearing interest rates of anywhere from 8.45 to 10.75 percent, become due in 1993 and 1998.

RJR Nabisco, a Delaware corporation, is a consumer products holding company that owns some of the country's best known product lines, including LifeSavers candy, Oreo cookies, and Winston cigarettes. The company was formed in 1985, when R.J. Reynolds Industries, Inc. ("R.J. Reynolds") merged with Nabisco Brands, Inc. ("Nabisco Brands"). In 1979, and thus before the R.J. Reynolds–Nabisco Brands merger, R.J. Reynolds acquired the Del Monte Corporation ("Del Monte"), which distributes canned fruits and vegetables. From January 1987 until February 1989, co-defendant Johnson served as the company's CEO. KKR, a private investment firm, organizes funds through which investors provide pools of equity to finance LBOs.

The bonds implicated by this suit are governed by long, detailed indentures, which in turn are governed by New York contract law. No one disputes that the holders of public bond issues, like plaintiffs here, often enter the market after the indentures have been negotiated and memorialized. Thus, those indentures are often not the product of face-to-face negotiations between the ultimate holders and the issuing company. What remains equally true, however, is that underwriters ordinarily negotiate the terms of the indentures with the issuers. Since the underwriters must then sell or place the bonds, they necessarily negotiate in part with the interests of the buyers in mind. Moreover, these indentures were not secret agreements foisted upon unwitting participants in the bond market. No successive holder is required to accept or to continue to hold the bonds, governed by their accompanying indentures; indeed, plaintiffs readily admit that they could have sold their bonds right up until the announcement of the LBO. Instead, sophisticated investors like plaintiffs are well aware of the indenture terms and, presumably, review them carefully before lending hundreds of millions of dollars to any company.

Indeed, the prospectuses for the indentures contain a statement relevant to this action:

> The Indenture contains no restrictions on the creation of unsecured short-term debt by [RJR Nabisco] or its subsidiaries, no restriction on the creation of unsecured Funded Debt by [RJR Nabisco] or its subsidiaries which are not Restricted Subsidiaries, and no restriction on the payment of dividends by [RJR Nabisco].

Further, as plaintiffs themselves note, the contracts at issue "[do] not impose debt limits, since debt is assumed to be used for productive purposes."

A typical RJR Nabisco indenture contains thirteen Articles. At least four of them are relevant to the present motions and thus merit a brief review.

Article Three delineates the covenants of the issuer. Most important, it first provides for payment of principal and interest. It then addresses various mechanical provisions regarding such matters as payment terms and trustee vacancies. The Article also contains "negative pledge" and related provisions, which restrict mortgages or other liens on the assets of RJR Nabisco or its subsidiaries and seek to protect the bondholders from being subordinated to other debt.

Article Five describes various procedures to remedy defaults and the responsibilities of the Trustee. In seven of the nine securities at issue, a provision in Article Five prohibits bondholders from suing for any remedy based on rights in the indentures unless 25 percent of the holders have requested in writing that the indenture trustee seek such relief, and, after 60 days, the trustee has not sued. * * *

Article Nine governs the adoption of supplemental indentures. It provides, *inter alia,* that the Issuer and the Trustee can

> add to the covenants of the Issuer such further covenants, restrictions, conditions or provisions as its Board of Directors by Board Resolution and the Trustee shall consider to be for the protection of the holders of Securities, and to make the occurrence, or the occurrence and continuance, of a default in any such additional covenants, restrictions, conditions or provisions an Event of Default permitting the enforcement of all or any of the several remedies provided in this Indenture as herein set forth . . .

Article Ten addresses a potential "Consolidation, Merger, Sale or Conveyance," and explicitly sets forth the conditions under which the company can consolidate or merge into or with any other corporation. It provides explicitly that RJR Nabisco "may consolidate with, or sell or convey, all or substantially all of its assets to, or merge into or with any other corporation," so long as the new entity is a United States corporation, and so long as it assumes RJR Nabisco's debt. The Article also requires that any such transaction not result in the company's default under any indenture provision.[4]

In its Amended Complaint, MetLife lists the six debt issues on which it bases its claims. Indentures for two of those issues—the 10.25 percent Notes due in 1990, of which MetLife continues to hold $10 million, and the 8.9 percent Debentures due in 1996, of which MetLife continues to hold $50 million—once contained express covenants that, among other things, restricted the company's ability to incur precisely the sort of debt involved in the recent LBO. In order to eliminate those restrictions, the

---

4. The remaining Articles are not relevant to the motions currently before the Court. Article One contains definitions; Article Two contains mechanical terms regarding, for instance, the issuance and transfer of the securities; Article Four concerns such mechanical matters as securityholders' lists and annual reports; Article Six addresses the rights and responsibilities of the Trustee; Article Seven contains mechanical provisions concerning the securityholders; Article Eight concerns procedural matters such as securityholders' meetings and consents; Article Eleven deals with the satisfaction and discharge of the indenture; Article Twelve sets forth various miscellaneous provisions; and Article Thirteen includes provisions regarding the redemption of securities and sinking funds.

parties to this action renegotiated the terms of those indentures, first in 1983 and then again in 1985.

MetLife acquired $50 million principal amount of 10.25 percent Notes from Del Monte in July of 1975. To cover the $50 million, MetLife and Del Monte entered into a loan agreement. That agreement restricted Del Monte's ability, among other things, to incur the sort of indebtedness involved in the RJR Nabisco LBO. In 1979, R.J. Reynolds—the corporate predecessor to RJR Nabisco—purchased Del Monte and assumed its indebtedness. Then, in December of 1983, R.J. Reynolds requested MetLife to agree to deletions of those restrictive covenants in exchange for various guarantees from R.J. Reynolds. A few months later, MetLife and R.J. Reynolds entered into a guarantee and amendment agreement reflecting those terms. Pursuant to that agreement, and in the words of Robert E. Chappell, Jr., MetLife's Executive Vice President, MetLife thus "gave up the restrictive covenants applicable to the Del Monte debt ... in return for [the parent company's] guarantee and public covenants."

MetLife acquired the 8.9 percent Debentures from R.J. Reynolds in October of 1976 in a private placement. A promissory note evidenced MetLife's $100 million loan. That note, like the Del Monte agreement, contained covenants that restricted R.J. Reynolds' ability to incur new debt. In June of 1985, R.J. Reynolds announced its plans to acquire Nabisco Brands in a $3.6 billion transaction that involved the incurrence of a significant amount of new debt. R.J. Reynolds requested MetLife to waive compliance with these restrictive covenants in light of the Nabisco acquisition.

In exchange for certain benefits, MetLife agreed to exchange its 8.9 percent debentures—which *did* contain explicit debt limitations—for debentures issued under a public indenture—which contain no explicit limits on new debt. An internal MetLife memorandum explained the parties' understanding:

> [MetLife's $100 million financing of the Nabisco Brands purchase] had its origins in discussions with RJR regarding potential covenant violations in the 8.90% Notes. More specifically, *in its acquisition of Nabisco Brands, RJR was slated to incur significant new long-term debt, which would have caused a violation in the funded indebtedness incurrence tests in the 8.90% Notes.* In the discussions regarding [MetLife's] willingness to consent to the additional indebtedness, *it was determined that a mutually beneficial approach to the problem* was to 1) agree on a new financing having a rate and a maturity desirable for [MetLife] and 2) modify the 8.90% Notes. The former was accomplished with agreement on the proposed financing, while the latter was accomplished by [MetLife] agreeing to substitute RJR's public indenture covenants for the covenants in the 8.90% Notes. In addition to the covenant substitution, RJR has agreed to "debenturize" the 8.90% Notes upon [MetLife's] request. This will permit [MetLife] to sell the 8.90% Notes to the public. (emphasis added).

Other internal MetLife documents help frame the background to this action, for they accurately describe the changing securities markets and the responses those changes engendered from sophisticated market participants, such as MetLife and Jefferson–Pilot. At least as early as 1982, MetLife recognized an LBO's effect on bond values. In the spring of that year, MetLife participated in the financing of an LBO of a company called Reeves Brothers ("Reeves"). At the time of that LBO, MetLife also held bonds in that company. Subsequent to the LBO, as a MetLife memorandum explained, the "Debentures of Reeves were downgraded by Standard & Poor's from BBB to B and by Moody's from Baal to Ba3, thereby lowering the value of the Notes and Debentures held by [MetLife]."

MetLife further recognized its "inability to force any type of payout of the [Reeves'] Notes or the Debentures as a result of the buy-out [which] was somewhat disturbing at the time we considered a participation in the new financing. However," the memorandum continued,

> our concern was tempered since, as a stockholder in [the holding company used to facilitate the transaction], we would benefit from the increased net income attributable to the continued presence of the low coupon indebtedness. The recent downgrading of the Reeves Debentures and the consequent "loss" in value has again raised questions regarding our ability to have forced a payout. *Questions have also been raised about our ability to force payouts in similar future situations, particularly when we would not be participating in the buy-out financing.*

Id. (emphasis added). In the memorandum, MetLife sought to answer those very "questions" about how it might force payouts in "similar future situations."

> *A method of closing this apparent "loophole," thereby forcing a payout of [MetLife's] holdings, would be through a covenant dealing with a change in ownership.* Such a covenant is fairly standard in financings with privately-held companies ... It provides the lender with an option to end a particular borrowing relationship via some type of special redemption (emphasis added).

A more comprehensive memorandum, prepared in late 1985, evaluated and explained several aspects of the corporate world's increasing use of mergers, takeovers and other debt-financed transactions. That memorandum first reviewed the available protection for lenders such as MetLife:

> Covenants are incorporated into loan documents to ensure that after a lender makes a loan, the creditworthiness of the borrower and the lender's ability to reach the borrower's assets do not deteriorate substantially. *Restrictions on the incurrence of debt,* sale of assets, mergers, dividends, restricted payments and loans and advances to affiliates *are some of the traditional negative covenants that can help protect lenders in the event their obligors become involved in undesirable merger/takeover situations....*

Because almost any industrial company is apt to engineer a takeover or be taken over itself, *Business Week* says that investors are beginning to view debt securities of high grade industrial corporations as Wall Street's riskiest investments. In addition, *because public bondholders do not enjoy the protection of any restrictive covenants,* owners of high grade corporates face substantial losses from takeover situations, if not immediately, then when the bond market finally adjusts.... [T]here have been 10–15 merger/takeover/LBO situations where, *due to the lack of covenant protection, [MetLife] has had no choice but to remain a lender to a less creditworthy obligor....* The fact that the quality of our investment portfolio is greater than the other large insurance companies ... may indicate that we have negotiated better covenant protection than other institutions, thus generally being able to require prepayment when situations become too risky ... [However,] a problem exists. And *because the current merger craze is not likely to decelerate* and because there exist vehicles to circumvent traditional covenants, the problem will probably continue. Therefore, *perhaps it is time to institute appropriate language designed to protect Metropolitan from the negative implications of mergers and takeovers.* (emphasis added).

Indeed, MetLife does not dispute that, as a member of a bondholders' association, it received and discussed a proposed model indenture, which included a "comprehensive covenant" entitled "Limitations on Shareholders' Payments." As becomes clear from reading the proposed—but never adopted—provision, it was "intend[ed] to provide protection against all of the types of situations in which shareholders profit at the expense of bondholders." *Id.* The provision dictated that the "[c]orporation will not, and will not permit any [s]ubsidiary to, directly or indirectly, make any [s]hareholder [p]ayment unless ... (1) the aggregate amount of all [s]hareholder payments during the period [at issue] ... shall not exceed [figure left blank]." The term "shareholder payments" is defined to include "restructuring distributions, stock repurchases, debt incurred or guaranteed to finance merger payments to shareholders, etc."

Apparently, that provision—or provisions with similar intentions—never went beyond the discussion stage at MetLife. That fact is easily understood; indeed, MetLife's own documents articulate several reasonable, undisputed explanations:

While it would be possible to broaden the change in ownership covenant to cover any acquisition-oriented transaction, *we might well encounter significant resistance in implementation with larger public companies* ... With respect to implementation, we would be faced with the task of imposing a non-standard limitation on potential borrowers, *which could be a difficult task in today's highly competitive marketplace. Competitive pressures notwithstanding, it would seem that management of larger public companies would be particularly opposed to such a covenant since its effect would be to increase the cost of an acquisition* (due to an assumed debt repayment), a factor that could well lower the price of any tender offer (thereby impacting shareholders). The November 1985 memorandum explained that [o]bviously, our ability to implement methods of takeover protection will vary between the public and private market. In that public securities do not contain any meaningful covenants, it would be very difficult for [MetLife] to demand takeover protection in public bonds. Such a requirement would effectively take us out of the public industrial market. A recent *Business Week* article does suggest, however, that there is increasing talk among lending institutions about requiring blue chip companies to compensate them for the growing risk of downgradings. *This talk, regarding such protection as restrictions on future debt financings, is met with skepticism by the investment banking community which feels that CFO's are not about to give up the option of adding debt and do not really care if their companies' credit ratings drop a notch or two* (emphasis added).

The Court quotes these documents at such length not because they represent an "admission" or "waiver" from MetLife, or an "assumption of risk" in any tort sense, or its "consent" to any particular course of conduct—all terms discussed at even greater length in the parties' submissions. Rather, the documents set forth the background to the present action, and highlight the risks inherent in the market itself, for any investor. Investors as sophisticated as MetLife and Jefferson–Pilot would be hard-pressed to plead ignorance of these market risks. Indeed, MetLife has not disputed the facts asserted in its own internal documents. Nor has Jefferson–Pilot—presumably an institution no less sophisticated than MetLife—offered any reason to believe that its understanding of the securities market differed in any material respect from the description and analysis set forth in the MetLife documents. Those documents, after all, were not born in a vacuum. They are descriptions of, and responses to, the market in which investors like MetLife and Jefferson–Pilot knowingly participated. * * *

Solely for the purposes of these motions, the Court accepts various factual assertions advanced by plaintiffs: first, that RJR Nabisco actively solicited "investment grade" ratings for its debt; second, that it relied on descriptions of its strong capital structure and earnings record which included prominent display of its ability to pay the interest obligations on its long-term debt several times over, and third, that the company made express or implied representations not contained in the relevant indentures concerning its future creditworthiness. In support of those allegations, plaintiffs have marshaled a number of speeches made by co-defendant Johnson and other executives of RJR Nabisco.[5] In addition, plaintiffs

5. *See, e.g.,* Address by F. Ross Johnson, November 12, 1987, P.Exh. 8, at 5 ("Our strong balance sheet is a cornerstone of our strategies. It gives us the resources to modernize facilities, develop new technologies, bring on new products, and support our leading brands around the world."); Remarks of Edward J. Robinson, Executive Vice President and Chief Financial Officer, February 15, 1988, P.Exh. 6, at 1 ("RJR Nabisco's financial strategy is ... to enhance the strength of the balance sheet by reducing the level of debt as well as lowering the cost of existing

rely on an affidavit sworn to by John Dowdle, the former Treasurer and then Senior Vice President of RJR Nabisco from 1970 until 1987. In his opinion, the LBO "clearly undermines the fundamental premise of the [c]ompany's bargain with the bondholders, and the commitment that I believe the [c]ompany made to the bondholders ... I firmly believe that the company made commitments ... that require it to redeem [these bonds and notes] before paying out the value to the shareholders." * * *

The indentures[6] at issue clearly address the eventuality of a merger. They impose certain related restrictions not at issue in this suit, but no restriction that would prevent the recent RJR Nabisco merger transaction. The indentures also explicitly set forth provisions for the adoption of new covenants, if such a course is deemed appropriate. While it may be true that no explicit provision either permits or prohibits an LBO, such contractual silence itself cannot create ambiguity to avoid the dictates of the parole evidence rule, particularly where the indentures impose no debt limitations.

Under certain circumstances, however, courts will, as plaintiffs note, consider extrinsic evidence to evaluate the scope of an implied covenant of good faith. *See Valley National Bank v. Babylon Chrysler–Plymouth, Inc.,* 53 Misc.2d 1029, 1031–32, 280 N.Y.S.2d 786, 788–89 (Sup.Ct. Nassau), *aff'd,* 28 A.D.2d 1092, 284 N.Y.S.2d 849 (2d Dep't 1967) (Relying on custom and usage because "[w]hen a contract fails to establish the time for performance, the law implies that the act shall be done within a reasonable time ...". However, the Second Circuit has established a different rule for customary, or boilerplate, provisions of detailed indentures used and relied upon throughout the securities market, such as those at issue. Thus, in *Sharon Steel Corporation v. Chase Manhattan Bank, N.A.,* 691 F.2d 1039 (2d Cir.1982), Judge Winter concluded that

> [b]oilerplate provisions are ... not the consequences of the relationship of particular borrowers and lenders and do not depend upon particularized intentions of the parties to an indenture. There are no adjudicative facts relating to the parties to the litigation for a jury to find and the meaning of boilerplate provisions is, therefore, a matter of law rather than fact. Moreover, uniformity in interpretation is important to the efficiency of capital markets ... Whereas participants in the capital market can adjust their affairs according to a uniform interpretation, whether it be correct or not as an initial proposition, the creation of enduring uncertainties as to the meaning of boilerplate provisions would decrease the value of all debenture issues and greatly impair the efficient working of capital markets ... Just such uncertainties would be created if interpretation of boiler-

debt."); Remarks by Dr. Robert J. Carbonell, Vice Chairman of RJR Nabisco, June 3, 1987 ("We will not sacrifice our longer-term health for the sake of short term heroics.").

6. A "debenture" is a long-term, unsecured debt security. An "indenture" is a contract between the issuing corporation and indenture trustee pursuant to which debentures are issued. The "indenture trustee" is the person or institution named in the indenture who is responsible for carrying out its terms. Black's Law Dictionary 401, 770 (6th ed. 1990).

> plate provisions were submitted to juries sitting in every judicial
> district in the nation.

Id. at 1048. *See also Morgan Stanley & Co. v. Archer Daniels Midland Co.,*
570 F.Supp. 1529, 1535–36 (S.D.N.Y.1983) (Sand, J.) ("[Plaintiff concedes
that the legality of [the transaction at issue] would depend on a factual
inquiry ... This case-by-case approach is problematic ... [Plaintiff's
theory] appears keyed to the subjective expectations of the bondholders
... and reads a subjective element into what presumably should be an
objective determination based on the language appearing in the bond
agreement.]"); *Purcell v. Flying Tiger Line, Inc.,* No. 84–7102, at 5, 8
(S.D.N.Y. Jan. 12, 1984) (CES) ("The Indenture does not contain any such
limitation [as the one proposed by plaintiff].... In light of our holding
that the Indenture unambiguously permits the transaction at issue in this
case, we are precluded from considering any of the extrinsic evidence that
plaintiff offers on this motion ... It would be improper to consider
evidence as to the subjective intent, collateral representations, and either
the statements or the conduct of the parties in performing the contract.")
(citations omitted). * * *

In their first count, plaintiffs assert that [d]efendant RJR Nabisco
owes a continuing duty of good faith and fair dealing in connection with
the contract [i.e., the indentures] through which it borrowed money from
MetLife, Jefferson–Pilot and other holders of its debt, including a duty not
to frustrate the purpose of the contracts to the debtholders or to deprive
the debtholders of the intended object of the contracts—purchase of
investment-grade securities.

> In the "buy-out," the [c]ompany breaches the duty [or implied cove-
> nant] of good faith and fair dealing by, *inter alia,* destroying the
> investment grade quality of the debt and transferring that value to
> the "buy-out" proponents and to the shareholders.

> In effect, plaintiffs contend that express covenants were not necessary
because an *implied* covenant would prevent what defendants have now
done. * * *

In contracts like bond indentures, "an implied covenant ... derives
its substance directly from the language of the Indenture, and 'cannot give
the holders of Debentures any rights inconsistent with those set out in the
Indenture.' *[Where] plaintiffs' contractual rights [have not been] violated,
there can have been no breach of an implied covenant." Gardner &
Florence Call Cowles Foundation v. Empire Inc.,* 589 F.Supp. 669, 673
(S.D.N.Y.1984), *vacated on procedural grounds,* 754 F.2d 478 (2d Cir.1985)
(quoting *Broad v. Rockwell,* 642 F.2d 929, 957 (5th Cir.) (*en banc*), *cert.
denied,* 454 U.S. 965 (1981)) (emphasis added).

Thus, in cases like *Van Gemert v. Boeing Co.,* 520 F.2d 1373 (2d Cir.),
cert. denied, 423 U.S. 947 (1975) ("*Van Gemert I*"), and *Pittsburgh
Terminal Corp. v. Baltimore & Ohio Ry. Co.,* 680 F.2d 933 (3d Cir.), *cert.
denied,* 459 U.S. 1056 (1982)—both relied upon by plaintiffs—the courts
used the implied covenant of good faith and fair dealing to ensure that the

bondholders received the benefit of their bargain as determined from the face of the contracts at issue. In *Van Gemert I,* the plaintiff bondholders alleged inadequate notice to them of defendant's intention to redeem the debentures in question and hence an inability to exercise their conversion rights before the applicable deadline. The contract itself provided that notice would be given in the first place. *See, e.g., id.* at 1375 ("A number of provisions in the debenture, the Indenture Agreement, the prospectus, the registration statement . . . and the Listing Agreement . . . dealt with the possible redemption of the debentures . . . and the notice debenture-holders were to receive . . ."). Faced with those provisions, defendants in that case unsurprisingly admitted that the indentures specifically required the company to provide the bondholders with notice. *See id.* at 1379. While defendant there issued a press release that mentioned the possible redemption of outstanding convertible debentures, that limited release did not "mention even the tentative dates for redemption and expiration of the conversion rights of debenture holders." *Id.* at 1375. Moreover, defendant did not issue any general publicity or news release. Through an implied covenant, then, the court fleshed out the full extent of the more skeletal right that appeared in the contract itself, and thus protected plaintiff's bargained-for right of conversion. As the court observed,

> What one buys when purchasing a convertible debenture in addition to the debt obligation of the company . . . is principally the expectation that the stock will increase sufficiently in value that the conversion right will make the debenture worth more than the debt . . . *Any loss* occurring to him from failure to convert, as here, *is not from a risk inherent in his investment but rather from unsatisfactory notification procedures. Id.* at 1385 (emphasis added, citations omitted).

I also note, in passing, that *Van Gemert I* presented the Second Circuit with "less sophisticated investors." *Id.* at 1383. Similarly, the court in *Pittsburgh Terminal* applied an implied covenant to the indentures at issue because defendants there "took steps to prevent the Bondholders from receiving information which they needed *in order to receive the fruits of their conversion option should they choose to exercise it." Pittsburgh Terminal,* 680 F.2d at 941 (emphasis added).

The appropriate analysis, then, is first to examine the indentures to determine "the fruits of the agreement" between the parties, and then to decide whether those "fruits" have been spoiled—which is to say, whether plaintiffs' contractual rights have been violated by defendants.

The American Bar Foundation's *Commentaries on Indentures* ("the *Commentaries*"), relied upon and respected by both plaintiffs and defendants, describes the rights and risks generally found in bond indentures like those at issue:

> The most obvious and important characteristic of long-term debt financing is that the holder ordinarily has not bargained for and does not expect any substantial gain in the value of the security to compensate for the risk of loss . . . [T]he significant fact, *which*

accounts in part for the detailed protective provisions of the typical long-term debt financing instrument, is that *the lender (the purchaser of the debt security) can expect only interest at the prescribed rate plus the eventual return of the principal.* Except for possible increases in the market value of the debt security because of changes in interest rates, the debt security will seldom be worth more than the lender paid for it . . . It may, of course, become worth much less. Accordingly, the typical investor in a long-term debt security is primarily interested in every reasonable assurance that the principal and interest will be paid when due. . . . Short of bankruptcy, *the debt security holder can do nothing to protect himself against actions of the borrower which jeopardize its ability to pay the debt unless he . . . establishes his rights through contractual provisions set forth in the debt agreement or indenture. Id.* at 1–2 (1971) (emphasis added).

A review of the parties' submissions and the indentures themselves satisfies the Court that the substantive "fruits" guaranteed by those contracts and relevant to the present motions include the periodic and regular payment of interest and the eventual repayment of principal. . . . According to a typical indenture, a default shall occur if the company either (1) fails to pay principal when due; (2) fails to make a timely sinking fund payment; (3) fails to pay within 30 days of the due date thereof any interest on the date; or (4) fails duly to observe or perform any of the express covenants or agreements set forth in the agreement. Plaintiffs' Amended Complaint nowhere alleges that RJR Nabisco has breached these contractual obligations; interest payments continue and there is no reason to believe that the principal will not be paid when due.

It is not necessary to decide that indentures like those at issue could never support a finding of additional benefits, under different circumstances with different parties. Rather, for present purposes, it is sufficient to conclude what obligation is *not* covered, either explicitly or implicitly, by these contracts held by these plaintiffs. Accordingly, this Court holds that the "fruits" of these indentures do not include an implied restrictive covenant that would prevent the incurrence of new debt to facilitate the recent LBO. To hold otherwise would permit these plaintiffs to straightjacket the company in order to guarantee their investment. These plaintiffs do not invoke an implied covenant of good faith to protect a legitimate, mutually contemplated benefit of the indentures; rather, they seek to have this Court create an additional benefit for which they did not bargain.

Although the indentures generally permit mergers and the incurrence of new debt, there admittedly is not an explicit indenture provision to the contrary of what plaintiffs now claim the implied covenant requires. That absence, however, does *not* mean that the Court should imply into those very same indentures a covenant of good faith so broad that it imposes a new, substantive term of enormous scope. This is so particularly where, as here, that very term—a limitation on the incurrence of additional debt—has in other past contexts been expressly bargained for; particularly where the indentures grant the company broad discretion in the management of its affairs, as plaintiffs admit, particularly where the indentures explicitly set forth specific provisions for the adoption of new covenants and restrictions, and *especially* where there has been no breach of the parties' bargained-for contractual rights on which the implied covenant necessarily is based. While the Court stands ready to employ an implied covenant of good faith to ensure that such bargained-for rights are performed and upheld, it will not, however, permit an implied covenant to shoehorn into an indenture additional terms plaintiffs now wish had been included. *See also Broad v. Rockwell International Corp.,* 642 F.2d 929 (5th Cir.) (*en banc*) (applying New York law), *cert. denied,* 454 U.S. 965, 102 S.Ct. 506, 70 L.Ed.2d 380 (1981) (finding no liability pursuant to an implied covenant where the terms of the indenture, as bargained for, were enforced). * * *

In the final analysis, plaintiffs offer no objective or reasonable standard for a court to use in its effort to define the sort of actions their "implied covenant" would permit a corporation to take, and those it would not. Plaintiffs say only that investors like themselves rely upon the "skill" and "good faith" of a company's board and management, and that their covenant would prevent the company from "destroy [ing] ... the legitimate expectations of its long-term bondholders." As is clear from the preceding discussion, however, plaintiffs have failed to convince the Court that by upholding the explicit, bargained-for terms of the indenture, RJR Nabisco has either exhibited bad faith or destroyed plaintiffs' *legitimate, protected* expectations. * * *

Third, [P]laintiffs advance a claim that remains based, their assertions to the contrary notwithstanding, on an alleged breach of a fiduciary duty. Defendants go to great lengths to prove that the law of Delaware, and not New York, governs this question. Defendants' attempt to rely on Delaware law is readily explained by even a cursory reading of *Simons v. Cogan,* 549 A.2d 300, 303 (Del.1988), the recent Delaware Supreme Court ruling which held, *inter alia,* that a corporate bond "represents a contractual entitlement to the repayment of a debt and does not represent an equitable interest in the issuing corporation necessary for the imposition of a trust relationship with concomitant fiduciary duties." Before such a fiduciary duty arises, "an existing property right or equitable interest supporting such a duty must exist." *Id.* at 304. A bondholder, that court concluded, "acquires no equitable interest, and remains a creditor of the corporation whose interests are protected by the contractual terms of the indenture." *Id.* Defendants argue that New York law is not to the contrary, but the single Supreme Court case they cite—a case decided over fifty years ago that was not squarely presented with the issue addressed by the *Simons* court—provides something less than dispositive support. *See Marx v. Merchants' National Properties, Inc.,* 148 Misc. 6, 7, 265 N.Y.S. 163, 165 (1933). For their part, plaintiffs more convincingly demonstrate that New York law applies than that New York law recognizes their claim. * * *

[T]his Court finds *Simons* persuasive, and believes that a New York court would agree with that conclusion. In the venerable case of *Meinhard v. Salmon*, 249 N.Y. 458, 164 N.E. 545 (1928), then Chief Judge Cardozo explained the obligations imposed on a fiduciary, and why those obligations are so special and rare:

> Many forms of conduct permissible in a workaday world for those acting at arm's length, are forbidden to those bound by fiduciary ties. A trustee is held to something stricter than the morals of the market place. Not honesty alone, but the punctilio of an honor the most sensitive, is then the standard of behavior. As to this there has developed a tradition that is unbending and inveterate. Uncompromising rigidity has been the attitude of courts of equity when petitioned to undermine the rule of undivided loyalty ... Only thus has the level of conduct for fiduciaries been kept at a level higher than that trodden by the crowd.

Id. at 464 (citation omitted). Before a court recognizes the duty of a "punctilio of an honor the most sensitive," it must be certain that the complainant is entitled to more than the "morals of the market place," and the protections offered by actions based on fraud, state statutes or the panoply of available federal securities laws. This Court has concluded that the plaintiffs presently before it—sophisticated investors who are unsecured creditors—are not entitled to such additional protections.

Equally important, plaintiffs' position on this issue—that "A Company May Not Deliberately Deplete its Assets to the Injury of its Debtholders,"—provides no reasonable or workable limits, and is thus reminiscent of their implied covenant of good faith. Indeed, many indisputably legitimate corporate transactions would not survive plaintiffs' theory. With no workable limits, plaintiffs' envisioned duty would extend equally to trade creditors, employees, and every other person to whom the defendants are liable in any way. Of all such parties, these informed plaintiffs least require a Court's equitable protection; not only are they willing participants in a largely impersonal market, but they also possess the financial sophistication and size to secure their own protection.

Finally, plaintiffs cannot seriously allege unconscionability, given their sophistication and, at least judging from this action, the sophistication of their legal counsel as well. Under the undisputed facts of this case, this Court finds no actionable unconscionability. * * *

For the reasons set forth above, the Court grants defendants summary judgment on Counts I and V, judgment on the pleadings for certain of the securities at issue in Count III, and dismisses for want of requisite particularity Counts II, III, and IX. All remaining motions made by the parties are denied in all respects. Plaintiffs shall have twenty days to replead.

SO ORDERED.

LORENZ v. CSX CORP.

1 F.3d 1406 (3d Cir.1993).

COWEN, CIRCUIT JUDGE.

Prior to December 13, 1977, the plaintiffs in these two related actions purchased convertible debentures issued by the defendant Baltimore and Ohio Railroad Company ("B & O"). At that time, 99.63% of the B & O's shares were owned by defendant Chesapeake and Ohio Railway Company, which in turn was a wholly-owned subsidiary of Chessie Systems, Inc., the corporate predecessor to defendant CSX Corporation ("CSX"). The indenture trustee was defendant Chase Manhattan Bank. Plaintiffs allege that the defendants defrauded them from 1977 to 1986 by failing to disclose material information which would have enabled them to convert their debentures into B & O common stock and receive a lucrative dividend.
* * *

The plaintiffs were holders of debentures in the B & O Railroad as of December 13, 1977. The debentures were convertible into B & O common stock at any time before maturing in the year 2010. To avoid Interstate Commerce Commission regulations hindering the development of non-rail assets owned by railroads, B & O devised a plan to segregate its rail and non-rail assets. Non-rail assets were transferred to a wholly owned subsidiary, Mid Allegheny Corporation ("MAC"), and MAC common stock was distributed as a dividend on a share-for-share basis to B & O shareholders. B & O sought to avoid the registration of its shares with the Securities and Exchange Commission ("SEC"), a time-consuming process which would have required appraisals of the transferred assets. Because B & O had few shareholders, the company thought that the SEC would issue a "no-action" letter excusing the registration of MAC stock. This plan would have been foiled if large numbers of B & O debenture holders exercised their conversion option in order to receive the MAC dividend.

To avoid this occurrence, B & O transferred its non-rail assets to MAC on December 13, 1977 and declared the dividend in MAC stock on the same date, without prior notice. As a result, the debenture holders could not convert their shares in time to receive the MAC dividend. Some of the debenture holders brought actions, later consolidated, under section 10(b) of the '34 Act against B & O, C & O, and Chessie Systems. This suit is known as the PTC/Guttmann litigation. In 1978 and 1979, B & O and Chase Manhattan Bank entered into a series of letter agreements, whereby B & O agreed that if the PTC/Guttmann plaintiffs prevailed or obtained a settlement, debenture holders would be allowed to participate equally in that judgment or settlement regardless of whether they had converted their debentures. * * *

On May 8, 1984, the district court granted plaintiffs the opportunity to convert their debentures into shares and receive the MAC dividend plus dividend income accruing since December 13, 1977. Pittsburgh Terminal

Corp. v. Baltimore & Ohio R.R. Co., 586 F.Supp. 1297, 1304–05 (W.D.Pa. 1984), aff'd, 760 F.2d 257 (3d Cir.), cert. denied, 474 U.S. 919, 106 S.Ct. 247, 88 L.Ed.2d 256 (1985). * * *

The plaintiffs in the present actions are those persons who are outside the scope of the PTC/Guttmann remedy. They held debentures on December 13, 1977 but subsequently sold them without having ever converted them into stock. On July 25, 1986, plaintiff Ethel B. Savin filed her complaint in the United States District Court for the Southern District of New York on behalf of a class of similarly situated former B & O debentureholders. The case was transferred to the Western District of Pennsylvania because of the related litigation there. On April 23, 1987, the Lorenz plaintiffs filed their complaint in the United States District Court for the Western District of Pennsylvania on behalf of a class of similarly situated former B & O debentureholders. * * *

The district court dismissed plaintiffs' claims against the indenture trustee Chase Manhattan Bank for breach of the implied covenant of good faith and fair dealing, allegedly arising from the bank's failure to inform them of the MAC dividend, the letter agreements with B & O, and the PTC/Guttmann judgment. Because the indenture specifies that the liability of the trustee shall be determined under New York law, we will apply New York law.

The courts of New York consistently have held that the duties of an indenture trustee, unlike those of a typical trustee, are defined exclusively by the terms of the indenture. The sole exception to this rule is that the indenture trustee must avoid conflicts of interest with the debenture holders. See United States Trust Co. v. First Nat'l Bank, 57 A.D.2d 285, 295–96, 394 N.Y.S.2d 653, 660–61 (1st Dep't 1977), aff'd, 45 N.Y.2d 869, 410 N.Y.S.2d 580, 382 N.E.2d 1355 (1978); Elliott Associates, 838 F.2d at 71, 73.

The plaintiffs specifically claim that Chase Manhattan Bank violated the implied covenant of good faith and fair dealing which, under New York law, is contained in every contract. Rowe v. Great Atl. & Pac. Tea Co., 46 N.Y.2d 62, 68, 412 N.Y.S.2d 827, 830, 385 N.E.2d 566, 569 (1978). The implied covenant prohibits either party from doing anything which would prevent the other party from receiving the fruits of the contract. Kirke La Shelle Co. v. Paul Armstrong Co., 263 N.Y. 79, 87, 188 N.E. 163, 167 (1933). The covenant, however, cannot be used to insert new terms that were not bargained for. A covenant is implied only when it is consistent with the express terms of the contract. Sabetay v. Sterling Drug, Inc., 69 N.Y.2d 329, 335, 514 N.Y.S.2d 209, 212, 506 N.E.2d 919, 922 (1987).

An indenture is, of course, a contract. Unless the indenture trustee has deprived the debenture holders of a right or benefit specifically provided to them in the indenture, there is no violation of the implied covenant of good faith and fair dealing. See Broad v. Rockwell Int'l Corp., 642 F.2d 929, 957–58 (5th Cir.) (in banc) (applying New York law), cert. denied, 454 U.S. 965, 102 S.Ct. 506, 70 L.Ed.2d 380 (1981); cf. Metropolitan Life Ins. Co. v. RJR Nabisco, Inc., 716 F.Supp. 1504, 1517–22 (S.D.N.Y.1989) (no breach of implied covenant under New York law where corporation's incurrence of debt to fund leveraged buyout depleted the value of its debentures, as the indenture lacked any terms prohibiting the transaction). We therefore will consider whether the indenture in this case contains provisions which entitled the debenture holders to receive notice of the MAC dividend, the letter agreements with B & O, or any of the remedies in the PTC/Guttmann action.

The indenture contains no provisions which explicitly require the trustee to provide notice of any kind to the debenture holders. Plaintiffs cite two provisions which they claim implicitly require notice. First, the indenture states:

> The Indenture permits the amendment thereof and the modification or alteration, in any respect, of the rights and obligations of the Company and the rights of the holders of the Debentures ... at any time by the concurrent action of the Company and of the holders of 66 2/3% in principal amount of the Debentures then outstanding affected by such amendment, modification or alteration (including, in the case of a modification of the terms of conversion of this Debenture into common stock of the Company or of payment of the principal of, or the premium or interest on, this Debenture, the consent of the holder hereof), all as more fully provided in the Indenture.

Plaintiffs claim that the letter agreements between B & O and Chase Manhattan Bank altered their rights under the Indenture. Those agreements provided that the debentureholders would be allowed to participate equally in any judgment against B & O or any settlement regardless of whether they converted their debentures to common stock. Because the quoted language gives the debenture holders the right to vote regarding any change in their or the company's rights and obligations under the indenture, the plaintiffs argue that they were entitled to notice of the letter agreements.

Second, the indenture provides:

> At any meeting at which there shall be a quorum the holders of the Affected Debentures shall have the power by resolution adopted as hereinafter provided:
>
> > (a) to authorize the Trustee to join with the Company in making any modification, alteration, repeal of or addition to any provision of this Indenture or of the Debentures, and any modification of or addition to the rights and obligations of the Company or the rights of the holders of the Debentures ... under this Indenture or under the Debentures....

The plaintiffs claim that the letter agreements between B & O and Chase Manhattan Bank were supplemental indentures which modified or added to their rights under the indenture. Because the debenture holders have the right to vote on whether to permit the indenture trustee and company to execute a supplemental indenture, the plaintiffs argue that they were entitled to notice.

Both provisions cited by plaintiffs provide debenture holders with the right to vote, and arguably therefore to receive notice, only if there is some modification of the debenture holders' rights or the company's obligations under the indenture. We agree with the district court that the letter agreements did not affect their rights under the indenture and cannot be characterized as supplemental indentures. The agreements pertained only to the scope of a possible remedy under the federal securities laws in the PTC/Guttmann litigation, in the event of a judgment against the defendant corporations or a settlement. The plaintiffs' contractual rights under the indenture itself, including rights regarding conversion of shares, were never modified.

It would have been advantageous for the plaintiffs to have been informed of the letter agreements and thus of potential violations of securities laws committed by B & O. They may have sued the defendant corporations years earlier. However, so long as an indenture trustee fulfills its obligations under the express terms of the indenture, it owes the debenture holders no additional, implicit duties or obligations, except to avoid conflicts of interest. Elliott Associates, 838 F.2d at 71. There is no provision in the indenture which obligated the trustee Chase Manhattan Bank to inform the debenture holders that they possibly had rights against B & O and its parent companies under the federal securities laws. Because the bank did not deprive the plaintiff of any right under the indenture, the bank could not have breached the implied covenant of good faith and fair dealing.

Plaintiffs rely heavily on Van Gemert v. Boeing Co., 520 F.2d 1373 (2d Cir.) (Van Gemert I), cert. denied, 423 U.S. 947, 96 S.Ct. 364, 46 L.Ed.2d 282 (1975). In that case, debentures on their face required the company to provide notice before exercising its option to redeem them. The indenture provided that such notice could be by publication in a newspaper. The court concluded that because the debentures did not specify the kind of notice that would be provided, the debenture holders were entitled to expect reasonable notice of the redemption call. Id. at 1383–85. Though the company complied with the terms of the indenture by publishing notice in a newspaper, the court held that it failed to provide fair and reasonable notice to the debenture holders. Id. at 1383. In a subsequent opinion, the court stated that the defendant was liable because it violated the implied covenant of good faith and fair dealing. Van Gemert v. Boeing Co., 553 F.2d 812, 815 (2d Cir.1977) (Van Gemert II).

Van Gemert indicates that when a debenture or indenture expressly requires notice, the implied covenant of good faith and fair dealing requires the defendant to provide notice which is reasonably calculated to enable the debenture holders to obtain the benefit of their contract. In the present case, however, the indenture does not have any provision which required the bank to provide notice regarding B & O's alleged violations of securities laws and the resulting litigation. To infer such a requirement would, in effect, add a new term to the indenture, and the implied covenant can never be used for that purpose. The district court correctly dismissed the claims against Chase Manhattan Bank for breach of the implied covenant of good faith and fair dealing.

Plaintiffs claim that defendants CSX and C & O, as controlling shareholders of B & O, breached a fiduciary duty to disclose material information. The district court concluded that the defendants owed no duties to the plaintiff debenture holders aside from those specified in the indenture. Finding no breach of the indenture, the district court dismissed the breach of fiduciary duty claims.

It is well-established that a corporation does not have a fiduciary relationship with its debt security holders, as with its shareholders. The relationship between a corporation and its debenture holders is contractual in nature. See Broad, 642 F.2d at 958–59 (applying New York law); Metropolitan Sec. v. Occidental Petroleum Corp., 705 F.Supp. 134, 141 (S.D.N.Y.1989) (same); Simons v. Cogan, 549 A.2d 300, 303 (Del.1988); American Bar Foundation, Commentaries on Indentures 2–3 (1971). Just as an indenture trustee's duties are strictly defined by the indenture, see, e.g., Hazzard, 159 Misc. at 80–81, 287 N.Y.S. at 566–67, a corporation is under no duty to act for the benefit of its debenture holders, or to refrain from action which dilutes their interest, except as provided in the indenture. Parkinson v. West End St. Ry. Co., 173 Mass. 446, 448, 53 N.E. 891, 892 (1899) (Holmes, J.); Commentaries, supra, at 527. Even if the debentures are convertible, the debenture holder is merely a creditor who is owed no fiduciary duty until conversion takes place. In re Will of Migel, 71 Misc.2d 640, 642–43 336 N.Y.S.2d 376, 379 (Sur. Ct. Orange County 1972); Simons, 549 A.2d at 303–04.

As we stated ... with respect to the indenture trustee's liability, the indenture contains no provisions which entitled the debenture holders to receive notice of the Hochwarth Stipulation, the letter agreements between B & O and Chase Manhattan Bank, or events in the PTC/Guttmann litigation. Plaintiffs have not identified, nor have we found, any additional provisions which impose upon B & O or its controlling shareholders a duty to disclose such information. The district court, therefore, correctly dismissed the breach of fiduciary duty claims. * * *

NOTES

1.   The rights of bondholders are set forth in the trust indenture. The rights of bondholders differ from those of common stockholders. Common stockholders usually have voting rights that allow them to elect directors and vote on important matters affecting the company. Bondholders usually do not have such rights, except possibly in reorganization or on default. Common stockholders are also protected by fiduciary duties, which are not available to

creditors. Does this mean that a board of directors has a fiduciary duty to protect shareholders at the expense of creditors. *See* Revlon v. MacAndrews & Forbes Holdings, Inc., 506 A.2d 173 (Del.Supr.1986) (when auctioning off a company, board of directors had to obtain best price for shareholders even if a competing bid would provide a slightly lower price but protect bondholders who had been a crucial part of management's efforts to obtain a higher price for the common stock than first offered in a hostile bid) *and* North American Catholic Educational Programming Foundation v. Gheewalla, 930 A.2d 92 (Del. 2007) (a creditor of a corporation in the zone of insolvency is owed no fiduciary duties by the board of the corporation, overruling a contrary decision by a lower court).

2.   Convertible debentures have some features of common stock, in that they are convertible into that equity security. When will fiduciary duties apply to the holder? In Simons v. Cogan, 549 A.2d 300, 304 (Del.1988) the court stated that:

> Until the debenture is converted into stock the convertible debenture holder acquires no equitable interest, and remains a creditor of the corporation whose interests are protected by the contractual terms of the indenture.

3.   Why do corporations offer a conversion feature on their bonds, and what is the advantage of this hybrid creature to its holders? The conversion feature is sought by the purchasers of the debenture because it allows them to capture the corporation's capital appreciation in the event the stock price moves more than the interest rate return on the debenture. Usually, the conversion price will be above the market price at the time of issue, so that some material amount of appreciation is required in the common stock price before this feature becomes valuable. There is, of course, no free lunch on Wall Street. The debenture holders will receive a lower interest rate on a convertible debenture than a comparable bond that is not convertible. Conversion will also relieve the corporation of repaying the principal and future interest payments but conversion will dilute the ownership of other common stockholders. In other words, if stock prices rise, the corporation simply issues new stock to the bondholders converting, but this will dilute the percentage of ownership of existing shareholders.

4.   In February 2003, Deutsche Telekom issued $2.3 billion in "mandatory convertible bonds." These bonds paid interest but were subject to mandatory conversion into the company's common stock at the end of three years. This avoided the necessity of repaying principal in cash and was designed to boost the company's credit rating. Matthew Karnitschnig & Silvia Ascarelli, Deutsche Telekom Sets Bond Deal, Wall St. J., Feb. 20, 2003, at C13. What are the advantages of such an instrument to an investor? In July 2003, a German bank issued a record $5.66 billion in convertible bond shares. Those shares were convertible into the shares of another company whose stock it held. David Reilly & Silvia Ascarelli, History Is Made (Again) in Convertible Boom, Wall St. J., July 9, 2003, at C1. What are the advantages to the issuer of such bonds? Another innovation arose during the subprime crisis were contingent convertible bonds ("CoCos") that allow banks to convert bonds to equity when a financial crisis occurs and a bank's capital is impaired. This has

the dual effect of reducing debt and increasing capital, a highly desirable goal in a crisis. See Nicholas & Hugo Dixon, New Fangled Bank Capital, N.Y. Times, November 12, 2009.

5. The Lehman Brothers investment-banking firm conducted an offering of Premium Income Exchangeable Securities ("PIES") for the MediaOne Group in 1999. These were notes paying seven percent interest with a conversion feature that allowed them to be converted into American Depository Receipts ("ADRs") for the ordinary shares of Vodafone AirTouch. ADRs are special accounts holding foreign shares. These certificates may be sold in the United States without requiring the registration of the foreign company. *See* IES Industries, Inc. v. United States, 253 F.3d 350 (8th Cir.2001) ("ADRs are publicly traded securities, or receipts, fully negotiable in U.S. dollars, that represent shares of a foreign corporation held in trust by a U.S. bank …")

6. The court in the Metropolitan Life Insurance case references the use of "negative covenants" to protect bondholders. Such restrictive measures may be used to restrict the amount of additional debt the corporation may subsequently incur. These restrictions may use complex formulas to determine maximum debt to asset ratios, or they may restrict the payment of dividends if certain conditions are not met.

7. Before its spectacular bankruptcy, the Enron Corporation created something called "credit sensitive notes" that paid higher rates of return in the event the company's credit rating was lowered by the credit rating agencies or lower rates in the event of an upgrade. Loren Fox, Enron, The Rise and Fall 66 (2002). Several other large companies followed Enron's lead and issued such notes. Should the plaintiffs in the Metropolitan case have negotiated for notes with such terms? Are these credit sensitive notes cannibalistic? After all, a credit downgrade suggests that debt costs are too high. If the downgrade causes a higher rate to be paid, this only worsens the financial condition of the company. The Enron offering may not be all that novel. Around the beginning of the twentieth century income bonds were used to finance troubled firms. These instruments were given a debtor's preference on assets but paid a return based on the company's earnings. Jonathan Barron Baskin & Paul J. Miranti, Jr., A History of Corporate Finance 155–56 (1997).

8. A corporation may have several classes of bonds outstanding. Those issues may be junior or senior. If junior, the creditor is subordinated to other specified classes of debt. Creditors must be careful to assure that more senior debt may not be subsequently issued because they will be pushed further back in line for their claims in the event of bankruptcy. Debentures may be sold under a "master" indenture agreement that allows the corporation to issue additional debt at a future date with varying terms, including debentures payable in foreign currency, with varying interest rates and other additional features.

––––––––––

The Trust Indenture Act of 1939

Trust indentures are master agreements that govern the terms and conditions of debentures (bonds) issued by corporations. Initially, trust indentures were used for mortgage bonds but were later extended to unsecured bonds. The bond or debenture itself is a simple document, but the trust indenture is a long, complex instrument. The trust indenture spells out the rights of bond holders. It also designates a trustee to make sure that the issuer's obligations are met and that the bondholders' rights are respected.

An SEC investigation and hearings by Congress during the 1930's determined that trustees often failed to assure that issuers met their obligations under the trust indenture agreement. Indenture agreements were often favorable to the issuing companies and sought to limit or disclaim all liability on the part of the trustees administering the terms of indenture agreements. The SEC and Congress found that indenture trustees seldom provided bondholders with basic information concerning default under the indenture agreement. Congress was particularly concerned with "ostrich clauses," which allowed indenture trustees to assume that there was no default until they received notice from at least ten percent of the security holders. The trustee was allowed to make this assumption even if the trustee had actual knowledge of a default. In addition, Congress discovered that trustees often had financial interests that conflicted with the interests of bondholders.

The Trust Indenture Act of 1939 was enacted to clarify the role of trustees and to lessen conflicts between trustees and bondholders. The Act sought to provide full disclosure for issues of bonds, notes, and debentures. It requires the rights of debenture holders and the duties of the trustees to be specified in the indenture agreement and requires trustees to provide reports to debenture holders.

HARRIET & HENDERSON YARNS, INC. v. CASTLE

75 F.Supp.2d 818 (W.D.Tenn.1999).

DONALD, DISTRICT JUDGE.

Before the court are Plaintiffs' motion for partial summary judgment and Defendant's motion for summary judgement. Plaintiff's Amended Complaint includes six counts and plaintiffs have moved for partial summary judgment on the issue of liability as to four of those counts. For the reasons stated herein, Plaintiffs motion is denied in its entirety. Defendants have moved for summary judgment as to the entire case. For the reasons stated herein, Defendants motion is granted in part and denied in part.

This is a complex case, featuring multiple parties and multiple claims. It arises out of the creation in 1995 of Star Hosiery, Inc. ("Star"). FLR Hosiery ("FLR") and Lora Lee Knitting ("Lora Lee") were two pre-existing Tennessee hosiery companies, both experiencing financial difficulties in early 1995. Both companies were heavily indebted to trade creditors, most of whom supplied them with raw materials. Together they owed approximately $3,000,000, much of it to Plaintiffs. Plaintiff RDC, Inc. was

FLR's landlord. Plaintiffs Harriet & Henderson Yarns, Inc., Thomaston Mills, Inc., Unifi, Inc., McMichael Mills, Jefferson Mills, Inc., Mount Vernon Mills, Inc., Huskey Knitting Mills, Jacob Textile Sales, Jones Textile, Kings Mountain Hosiery Mills, Inc., Merlin Creel Systems, Inc., O'Mara, Inc., Pharr Yarns, Inc., and Ruppe Hosiery, Inc. were suppliers of yarn or textile services. Brookfield & Company ("Brookfield"), an investment banking firm, became involved with FLR and Lora Lee, assisting in the two companies' attempt to secure additional financing. Brookfield arranged a deal whereby FLR and Lora Lee would contribute substantially all their combined assets to form a new company, Star. Brookfield arranged for Congress Financial ("Congress") to finance the new company. Brookfield also engaged the Defendant law firm Wolff Ardis, P.C. ("Wolff Ardis") to represent Star during its creation, incorporation, and loan deal from Congress. Defendant Renee Castle ("Castle") was a shareholder in Wolff Ardis, and was the lead attorney for the Star transactions.

In order for Star to obtain financing from Congress, Brookfield advised that much of the pre-existing FLR and Lora Lee debt should be restructured into subordinated, convertible debenture notes ("Debenture Notes").[7] The Debenture Notes were to be paid by Star over three years. To induce the existing creditors to accept the Debenture Notes, the creditors were granted a second lien in Star's machinery and equipment to secure the Debenture Notes, behind a first lien held by Congress. The creditors were also told that the Star merger and financing plan would improve the likelihood that the current debt would be paid off. As the creditors were informed about the proposed creation of Star, they were asked to sign confidentiality agreements, which prevented the creditors from sharing information or discussing the proposal.

Brookfield had Castle prepare the necessary documents. Castle drafted the Debenture Note based on a form given her by Brookfield. She also drafted the Indenture Agreement, based on a form in the Wolff Ardis computer files. The Debenture Notes provided that Star promised to pay various amounts to the different Debenture holders. They also named Wolff Ardis as trustee. Other relevant parts of the Debenture Notes included the following:

1. *Payment of Principal.* The total obligation of Star to all Debenture Holders is set forth in the Indenture Agreement dated as of December 1, 1995, by and between Star and Wolff Ardis P.C., as Trustee for the Debenture Holders (the "Indenture Agreement")....

5. *Indenture Agreement.* This Debenture is one of several debentures of Star issued pursuant to the Indenture Agreement, the provisions of which are hereby incorporated by reference and made a part of this Debenture. All the Debentures issued pursuant to that Indenture Agreement are equally secured by a second lien and security interest

---

7. A subordinated, convertible debenture note is a promissory note that is subordinated to other debt and that is convertible to stock at the holder's option. *See Pittsburgh Terminal Corp. v. Baltimore & Ohio R. Co.,* 680 F.2d 933 (3rd Cir.1982).

in certain of Star's equipment, as more fully described in the Indenture Agreement. Reference is hereby made to the Indenture Agreement for a more detailed description of the property in which the Trustee holds a security interest, the nature and extent of the security interest, the rights and obligations of the Debenture Holder and other debenture holders, of Star, and of the Trustee.

6. *Events of Default.* One or more of the following events shall be deemed "Events of Default": (a) If any payment of principal and interest on this Debenture is not paid when due; provided that the Debenture Holder shall give Star written notice of such default and Star shall have sixty (60) days from receipt of such notice within which to cure such default;....

The Indenture Agreement stated, in relevant part:

This Indenture Agreement between Star Hosiery, Inc., a Tennessee corporation (the "Company" or "Star") and Renee E. Castle of Wolff Ardis, P.C. having an address of 6055 Primacy Parkway, Suite 360, Memphis, TN 38119 (the "Trustee"), dated as of this 12th date of December, 1995 is for the benefit of certain holders of Debenture Notes ("Noteholders") who hold Debenture Notes issued pursuant to this Indenture. Such Debenture Notes are collectively referred to herein as the "Debentures." The terms of the Debentures include those stated in the Note Debentures and those made part of the Note Debentures by reference to the Trust Indenture Act of 1939 (the "Trust Indenture Act") as in effect on the date of the Debentures....

Security. The Debenture Notes shall be secured by a subordinate lien on all equipment owned by the Company. This lien shall extend on a pro rata basis to each Noteholder. It shall have a second priority (inferior to the liens securing Senior Indebtedness) on all equipment with the exception of the equipment presently encumbered by liens in favor of GECC, Speizman and Nations Bank, in which case the lien shall have a third priority....

Events of Default. One or more of the following events shall be deemed "Events of Default": (a) If any payment of principal and interest on this Debenture is not paid when due; provided that the Debenture Holder shall give the Company written notice of such default and the Company shall have sixty (60) days from receipt of such notice within which to cure such default;....

The Trustee. The Trustee shall be under no obligation to exercise any of its rights or powers under this Indenture relating to any issue of Debentures at the request of any of the holders thereof, unless they shall have offered to the Trustee security and indemnity satisfactory to it....

The Debenture Notes prepared by Castle were sent to each Plaintiff in November, 1995 by FLR and Lora Lee, each for a varying amount. The Indenture Agreement was presented to Plaintiffs by their debtors as the best chance for them to recover the money owed them, and they were urged by FLR and Lora Lee to sign the Debenture Notes. Each Plaintiff did sign and return its Debenture Note. Once all Notes had been returned, Castle prepared the final Indenture Agreement, which stated that the total sum owed to the holders of the Debenture Notes pursuant to the Notes was $2,322,973.42.

The closing of the transactions occurred on December 12, 1995. At the closing were Defendant Castle and representatives of FLR, Lora Lee, Star, Congress, and Brookfield. None of the Plaintiffs had an attorney or other representative present. After the closing, copies of the signed Debenture Notes were sent to Plaintiffs, and the original Debenture Notes were kept in the offices of Wolff Ardis.

Castle had received instructions from Congress regarding the execution and filing of UCC–1 financing statements to perfect Congress' first lien in Star's equipment. Those financing statements, executed by Star in favor of Congress, were duly recorded with the Tennessee Secretary of State. However, there was never any discussion among any of the parties to the transaction about preparing or filing financing statements in favor of Plaintiffs. No UCC–1 financing statements were prepared, executed, or filed with regard to Plaintiffs' lien in Star's equipment. Because no financing statement was filed, the Debenture holders' lien was never properly perfected under Tennessee law.

Star made the required payments from January to June, 1996. However, it then stopped making payments, and on August 16, 1996, Star filed for Chapter 11 bankruptcy. Shortly thereafter, Plaintiffs learned that no financing statements had been filed on their behalf. Because the lien was unperfected, each Plaintiff was treated as an unsecured creditor in Star's bankruptcy case. Star's assets were sold in bankruptcy, resulting in full repayment to Congress, but only approximately a 3% dividend to Plaintiffs and other unsecured creditors. Plaintiffs contend that they would have received all or most of the debt owed to them under the Debenture Notes if their security interest in Star's equipment had been properly perfected. * * *

The crux of this suit is Plaintiffs' claim that Defendants had the responsibility to perfect Plaintiffs' security interests, or to ensure that the interests were perfected. * * *

Plaintiffs ... allege that by not perfecting Plaintiffs' security interests, Defendants breached a state common law fiduciary duty owed to Plaintiffs. Defendants filled the role of trustee in this case, and Plaintiffs were the trust beneficiaries. Under Tennessee law, a trustee owes a duty of loyalty to the trust beneficiary. *Smail v. Smail,* 617 S.W.2d 889 (Tenn.1981). A trustee also has a duty to act in good faith, with due diligence, and with care and skill. *Branum v. Akins,* 978 S.W.2d 554, 557 (Tenn.Ct.App.1998). Plaintiffs contend that Defendants had a fiduciary duty to ensure that Plaintiffs' interests under the Indenture Agreement and Debenture Notes were protected. Plaintiffs argue that Defendants breached this duty by failing to perfect the liens.

This case does not deal with the duty of an ordinary trustee, but with the obligations of an indenture trustee. In arguing over the scope of those duties, the parties look primarily to caselaw from the state of New York, out of which most of the important cases on this topic have issued. The leading authorities make clear that, unlike those of an ordinary trustee, the duties of an indenture trustee are generally defined by and limited to the terms of the indenture. *See, e.g., Elliott Assocs. v. J. Henry Schroder Bank & Trust Co.*, 838 F.2d 66, 71 (2nd Cir.1988). *See also LNC Inv., Inc. v. First Fidelity Bank*, 935 F.Supp. 1333, 1346 (S.D.N.Y.1996) ("Under New York law, the pre-default duties of an indenture trustee, unlike those of an ordinary trustee, generally are limited to the duties imposed by the indenture"); *Lorenz v. CSX Corp.*, 1 F.3d 1406, 1415 (3rd Cir.1993) ("The courts of New York consistently have held that the duties of an indenture trustee, unlike those of a typical trustee, are defined exclusively by the terms of the indenture"); *Meckel v. Continental Resources Co.*, 758 F.2d 811, 816 (2nd Cir.1985) ("Unlike the ordinary trustee, who has historic common-law duties imposed beyond those in the trust agreement, an indenture trustee is more like a stakeholder whose duties and obligations are exclusively defined by the terms of the indenture agreement."); Hazen, *The Law of Securities Regulation* § 16.5, p. 154, n. 5 (West 1995) ("Despite some earlier cases that held that trustees may have pre-default liability beyond that put forth in the indenture, [it] is now well established that prior to default the trustee's responsibilities (and hence his/or her liability) are determined solely under the terms of the indenture agreement."); *First Interstate Bank of Denver, N.A. v. Pring*, 969 F.2d 891 (10th Cir.1992); *Shawmut Bank, N.A. v. Kress Assocs.*, 33 F.3d 1477 (9th Cir.1994).

That limits are imposed on the duties of an indenture trustee is not arbitrary, but reasonably based on the difference between the role of an indenture trustee and an ordinary trustee. One difference is that the rights and duties of an ordinary trustee arise from the common law, whereas the duties of an indenture trustee arise out of, and thus are limited to, a contract. *Lorenz v. CSX Corp.*, 736 F.Supp. 650, 656 (W.D.Pa. 1990) (aff'd. by 1 F.3d 1406 (3rd Cir.1993)). Another reason for the difference is that an indenture trustee must consider the interests of the issuer of the debenture as well as the beneficiaries. *In re E.F. Hutton Southwest Properties II, Ltd.*, 953 F.2d 963, 972 (5th Cir.1992). And a third reason is that "the purchaser of such debt is offered, and voluntarily accepts, a security whose myriad terms are highly specified. Broad and abstract requirements of a 'fiduciary' character ordinarily can be expected to have little or no constructive role to play in the governance of such a negotiated, commercial relationship." *Simons v. Cogan*, 542 A.2d 785, 786 (Del.Ch.1987).

The Indenture Agreement in this case said nothing about a duty of Defendants to perfect Plaintiffs' liens. Courts, however, have found two narrow exceptions to the general rule that the duties of an indenture trustee are strictly defined by the indenture agreement. One of these is that after default, "the loyalties of an indenture trustee no longer are divided between the issuer and the investors, and as a consequence ... the limits on an indenture trustee's duties before an event of default ... do not apply after an event of default ..." *LNC Inv.*, 935 F.Supp. at 1347. *See also Beck v. Manufacturers Hanover Trust Co.*, 218 A.D.2d 1, 632 N.Y.S.2d 520, 527 (N.Y.App.Div.1995) ("[E]ven if the responsibilities of an indenture trustee may be significantly more narrowly defined than those of an ordinary trustee while the obligation that it is the indenture's purpose to secure remains current, subsequent to the obligor's default ... the indenture trustee's obligations come more closely to resemble those of an ordinary fiduciary ..."). This post-default exception does not apply to the case at bar, in which the alleged breach of duty occurred prior to Star's default. Once Star had defaulted, it was already too late for the security interests to be effectively perfected.

Plaintiffs contend that the other exception to the limits of an indenture trustee's duties applies here. That exception is the requirement that even indenture trustees have an obligation to avoid a conflict of interest. *See, e.g., LNC Inv.*, 935 F.Supp. at 1347 ("an indenture trustee must avoid conflicts of interest and discharge its obligations with absolute singleness of purpose") (internal quotations omitted); *Lorenz*, 1 F.3d at 1415 ("The sole exception to this rule [that the duties of an indenture trustee are defined exclusively by the terms of the indenture] is that the indenture trustee must avoid conflicts of interest with the debentureholders."); *Elliott*, 838 F.2d at 71 ("[S]o long as the trustee fulfills its obligations under the express terms of the indenture, it owes the debenture holders no additional, implicit pre-default duties or obligations except to avoid conflicts of interests.").

Plaintiffs argue that by assuming the role of trustee, Defendants created a conflict of interest, and thereby breached the fiduciary duty they owed to Plaintiffs. However, the existing legal authority in this area does not support Plaintiffs' argument that this dual role sufficed to impart additional fiduciary duties. In *In re E.F. Hutton*, the Fifth Circuit stated that "heightened fiduciary duties ... are not activated until a conflict arises where it is evident that the indenture trustee may be sacrificing the interests of the beneficiaries in favor of its own financial position. There must be a clear possibility of this evident from the facts of the case, e.g., where the indenture trustee is a general creditor of the obligor, who is in turn in financial straits. A mere hypothetical possibility that the indenture trustee might favor the interests of the issuer merely because the former is an indenture trustee does not suffice." 953 F.2d at 972. Similarly, the Second Circuit found no conflict of interest in *Elliott* when it found that "except for bald assertions of conflict of interest, [the plaintiff] presents no serious claim that [the indenture trustee] personally benefitted in any way ..." 838 F.2d at 70. In the case before the court, Plaintiffs likewise have done no more than make bald assertions of a conflict of interest.

Plaintiffs accurately point out that many of the cases finding no implied duties for indenture trustees involved indenture agreements containing clauses specifically excusing the trustee of any duty outside of those made explicit in the agreement. *see, e.g., Eldred v. Merchants Nat'l Bank of Cedar Rapids,* 468 N.W.2d 221, 223 (Iowa 1991). This at least suggests that in the absence of such a clause, an indenture trustee could be held to a higher fiduciary standard. There was no such clause in the Indenture Agreement in this case. However, Plaintiffs are unable to direct the court to a single case in which, in the absence of such a disclaimer, a court has found that an indenture trustee has the same fiduciary duty as an ordinary trustee.

Plaintiffs also attempt to distinguish this case by virtue of the fact that the Defendants were the attorneys of the debenture issuer, as opposed to the financial institutions which served as trustees in many of the cited cases. Plaintiffs argue that where the trustees are attorneys of an obligor who will benefit at the expense of the trust beneficiaries, the trustees have a conflict of interest which violates their fiduciary duty. However, Plaintiffs again are unable to produce any legal authority to back their argument, and there is no evidence to suggest that Defendants could have personally benefitted from the failure to file the financing statements.

Plaintiffs can successfully distinguish this case from any of the other individual cases on the fiduciary duties of indenture trustees. But what Plaintiffs ultimately ask this court to do is to find a new exception to well-settled law. This the court is unwilling to do. As a general rule, the duties of indenture trustees are strictly defined by the indenture agreement. There is no reason in this case not to follow that rule. The governing documents did not impose on the trustees the duty to perfect the security interests. * * *

Plaintiffs' sixth and final complaint is that Defendants' failure to ensure that Plaintiffs' liens were perfected violated a provision of the Trust Indenture Act of 1939 ("Trust Indenture Act"). Before discussing that claim, the court must resolve the preliminary dispute over whether that Act applies to this case at all.

Plaintiffs contend that the Indenture Agreement incorporates by reference the Trust Indenture Act. Indeed, the Indenture Agreement states:

> The terms of the Debentures include those stated in the Note Debentures and those made part of the Note Debentures by reference to the Trust Indenture Act of 1939 (the "Trust Indenture Act") as in effect on the date of the Debentures.

The Debenture Notes, however, make no reference to the Trust Indenture Act. Defendants argue that the Trust Indenture Act therefore was not incorporated. Defendants claim that "the clear meaning" of the Indenture Agreement provision is that "[b]ecause there are no references to the Indenture Act contained in the debenture notes ... no Indenture

Act provisions were incorporated by reference into the indenture transaction."

Defendants may find the meaning of this provision "clear," but the court does not. The language of a contract is ambiguous if its meaning is susceptible to more than one reasonable interpretation. *Farmers–Peoples Bank,* 519 S.W.2d at 805. If the terms are ambiguous, then the intended meaning of the contract becomes a question for the finder of fact. *Tenn. Consol. Coal Co.,* 416 F.2d at 1198. It is also true that where the language of the contract is ambiguous, it will be construed against the party responsible for the drafting (in this case, Defendants). *Hanover Ins. Co. v. Haney,* 221 Tenn. 148, 425 S.W.2d 590, 592 (1968).

Despite Defendants' contention to the contrary, the one thing that is clear about this provision is that it is ambiguous. Therefore, at the very least, the meaning should be left to be determined by the finder of fact. However, due to the court's ultimate disposition of this issue on another basis, it is unnecessary to decide this question. Instead, the court will assume arguendo that the Trust Indenture Act was incorporated into the Indenture Agreement.

Plaintiffs state that the Trust Indenture Act requires an indenture trustee to review the filing and effectiveness of any lien intended to be created by the Debenture Notes. According to Plaintiffs, this duty is imposed by 15 U.S.C.A. § 77nnn(b). Putting it simply, Plaintiffs either misunderstand or misrepresent the duty imposed by that section of the Trust Indenture Act. That section imposes two duties upon Star, the *obligor* of the indenture agreement. Furthermore, the duties imposed are for the benefit of the indenture trustee, i.e. Defendants. And finally, the duty it imposes is not to actually file the indenture, but merely to furnish an opinion of counsel as to whether the indenture has been properly recorded and filed. 15 U.S.C.A. § 77nnn(b). This section clearly does not impose a duty on indenture trustees to ensure that liens are perfected for the benefit of the debenture holders. Therefore the question of whether the Trust Indenture Act is incorporated into the Indenture Agreement is irrelevant. Because the Trust Indenture Act does not provide Plaintiffs with a cause of action under the facts of this case, Defendants' Motion for Summary Judgment on this count is GRANTED, and Plaintiffs' Motion for Summary Judgment is DENIED. * * *

NOTES

1. The provisions of the Trust Indenture Act of 1939 were described as follows by the court in *Zeffiro v. First Pennsylvania Banking and Trust Co.,* 623 F.2d 290, 292–94 (3d Cir.1980), *cert. denied,* 456 U.S. 1005, 102 S.Ct. 2295, 73 L.Ed.2d 1299 (1982):

Before proceeding to a discussion of the merits, it may be useful to briefly outline the structure and background of the Trust Indenture Act. A study was conducted by the Securities Exchange Commission (SEC) in 1936 which revealed widespread abuses in the issuance of corporate bonds under indentures.[8] The main problems identified by the study were that the indenture trustee was frequently aligned with the issuer of the debentures and that the debenture holders were widely dispersed, thereby hampering their ability to enforce their rights. Furthermore, courts frequently enforced broad exculpatory terms of the indenture inserted by the issuer, which offered the investors less protection than the traditional standards of fiduciary duty.

Rather than allow the SEC direct supervision of trustee behavior and thereby provide for a more overt intrusion into capital markets, the Act establishes a standard of behavior indirectly by refashioning the form of the indenture itself. The Act is structured so that before a debt security non-exempted from the Act may be offered to the public, the indenture under which it is issued must be "qualified" by the SEC. The indenture is deemed "qualified" when registration becomes effective. Before registration of the debenture is declared effective it must be qualified under the following conditions: (1) the security has been issued under an indenture; (2) the person designated as trustee is eligible to serve; and (3) the indenture conforms to the requirements of §§ 310–318, 15 U.S.C. §§ 77jjj–77rrr. Judge Bechtle aptly described the operative provisions of the Act, §§ 310–318, as follows.

Sections 310 through 318 form the core of the Act in that they outline the substantive duties that the indenture must impose on the trustee. These sections are of three types. The first type is proscriptive in nature, prohibiting certain terms. For example, § 315, 15 U.S.C. § 77ooo (d), prohibits provisions in the indenture which would relieve or exculpate the trustee from liability for negligence. The second type of section is merely permissive in nature. An example of this type of section is § 315(a), 15 U.S.C. § 77ooo (a)(1), which states that the indenture may contain a provision relieving the trustee of liability except for the performance of such duties as are specifically set out in such indenture.

The third type of section, and the most important for our purposes, is mandatory and prescriptive in nature. These sections begin with the phrase "indenture to be qualified shall provide" or "shall require." An example of this type of section is § 311, 15 U.S.C. § 77kkk, which states that the indenture shall require the trustee to establish certain accounts for the benefit of bond holders in the event the trustee also becomes a creditor of the issuer and the issuer defaults on the bonds.

473 F.Supp. at 206. The SEC has no enforcement authority over the terms of the indenture once the registration statement becomes effective, and it cannot issue a stop order for violation of indenture provisions by the indenture trustee. After the effective date of the indenture the SEC's role is limited to general rulemaking and investigation. 15 U.S.C. §§ 77ddd(c), (d), (e);

---

8. See Securities and Exchange Commission Report on the Study and Investigation of the Work, Activities, Personnel and Functions of Protective and Reorganization Committees, Part IV, Trustees Under Indentures (1937); See also Hearings on H.R. 10292 Before a Subcommittee of the Committee on Interstate and Foreign Commerce, 75th Cong., 3d Sess. 20 (1938).

77eee(a), (c); 77ggg; 77sss; 77ttt. The Act contains criminal liability for certain willful violations and misrepresentations and express civil liability for any omission or misstatement in the filing documents.

———————

Redemption features in corporate bonds affect their value. Such a right allows the corporation to repay the principal at an early date. The corporation may call or redeem the bonds if interest rates decline, allowing the corporation to refund its loans at a lower cost. This is not desirable to bondholders. Consequentially, the call or redemption provision is subject to restrictions or the redemption price is usually set at a premium over par so that only a substantial interest rate decrease would justify a redemption.

MUTUAL SAVINGS LIFE INSURANCE CO. v. JAMES RIVER CORP.

716 So.2d 1172 (Ala.1998).

HOOPER, CHIEF JUSTICE.

* * * The plaintiffs alleged that James River, with the knowing assistance and active encouragement of Merrill Lynch, wrongfully, fraudulently, and prematurely called, retired and refunded with lower-rate debt its $250,000,000 issue of 10.75% debentures. The company issued these 30–year bonds in 1988, and the tender took place in 1992. James River bought back the tendered bonds with the proceeds of a sale of $200,000,000 in notes at 6.75%. The bonds that were not tendered were redeemed with the proceeds of an issuance of preferred stock. The investors claim that this retiring of the bonds violated a clause in their contract known in the bond market as a "non-refund covenant."

A brief explanation of the financial terminology used in this case will be helpful. The plaintiffs invested in 10.75% debentures, also known as bonds. A contract known as an indenture governs a bond issuance. One of the key provisions of an indenture defines the ability of the issuer to buy back the bond before the latest possible maturity date. The most common way this is done is through a call and redemption. A redemption occurs when the issuer of a bond compels the bondholder to sell back the bond at a specified price. The indenture defines the call price—the price at which the redemption takes place.

However, certain limitations exist. The indenture in this case (as in most all indentures) prohibited the issuer from paying for the redeemed bonds with money borrowed at an interest rate lower than that of the bond—10.75% in this case. The issuer must pay for the redeemed bonds with qualified funds (also known as "clean cash"). Thus, the money used to redeem the bonds must be from a qualified source. Callable bonds may be called and redeemed at any time as long as they are paid with qualified funds.

An issuer of bonds also is entitled to make a tender offer at any time for the bonds. Unlike a call and redemption, a tender offer is *not* governed by the indenture. A company may make a tender offer for noncallable bonds. Because a tender offer is not governed by the indenture, there are no restrictions on the type of funds that an issuer may use to buy back tendered bonds. In other words, an issuer can use lower-rate borrowed money to pay for tendered bonds. Also, when a tender offer is made, the issuer must pay a premium to the bondholder that it would not have to pay if it called the bonds. For example, the call price in this case was $1,086.00 per $1,000 par value, and the tender price was $1,093.75 per $1,000 par value. Therefore, a tender offer is different from a call and redemption.

When a tender offer is made, the bondholder may accept or hold. By holding, the bondholder rejects the tender offer. In this case, James River made a tender offer to buy back its 30–year 10.75% bonds. In the letter notifying bondholders of the tender offer, James River expressed its intention to call any bonds that were not tendered. On the day that the tender offer expired, James River called all of the bonds. Ninety-eight percent of the bondholders accepted the tender offer, while the other 2% of the bondholders chose to have their bonds called. James River paid the bondholders who accepted the tender offer with the proceeds from the sale of $200,000,000 worth of 6.75% medium-term notes. Thus, James River bought back the tendered bonds with money that was borrowed at a rate lower than 10.75%. James River then redeemed the remaining 2% of the bonds. It paid for the redeemed bonds with qualified funds—the proceeds of the issuance of preferred stock. The investors claim that the process of retiring these bonds violated the redemption clause in the indenture because James River replaced the debt with lower-rate debt.

This case involves the interpretation of one paragraph in the contract between James River and the investors regarding redemption of the bonds. That paragraph reads:

"Prior to October 1, 1998, no *redemption* of Debentures due October 1, 2018, may be made directly or indirectly, in whole or in part, from or in anticipation of the proceeds (or any part of the proceeds) of any moneys borrowed by or for the account of the Company which have an effective interest cost to the Company (calculated in accordance with generally accepted financial practice) of less than 10.75% per annum."

(Emphasis added.) We interpret this paragraph to mean that James River cannot *redeem* the bonds before the date specified by using money borrowed at a rate lower than the rate at which it had issued the bonds—10.75%.

The plaintiff investors claimed that James River, with the assistance of Merrill Lynch, breached its contract with them by refunding its bonds in violation of the redemption clause. They also made several tort claims based on the defendants' failure to inform them that the company did not have sufficient qualified funds and on James River's failure to fully disclose its plan to retire the bonds. The investors also made a claim under the Trust Indenture Act ("TIA"), which provides a cause of action when an issuer of bonds has defaulted in payments of interest or principal. The investors also made a separate claim against Merrill Lynch alleging tortious interference with a business relation. The trial court certified a class for the breach-of-contract claim. However, the trial court denied class certification on the tort claims because the laws of each investor's home state would control the claims. * * *

[After considering the facts, the court upheld summary judgment in favor of the defendants] * * *

SECTION 4. FEDERAL SECURITIES LAW ISSUES

The issuance of notes or other indebtedness may raise the issue of whether the instrument is a security and whether the instrument must be registered under the provisions of the Securities Act of 1933, 15 U.S.C. § 77a *et seq.* Issues may also arise concerning the application of other provisions of the federal securities laws, including those of the Williams Act.

Registration Requirements for Notes

REVES v. ERNST & YOUNG

494 U.S. 56, 110 S.Ct. 945, 108 L.Ed.2d 47 (1990).

Justice Marshall delivered the opinion of the Court.

This case presents the question whether certain demand notes issued by the Farmers Cooperative of Arkansas and Oklahoma (Co–Op) are "securities" within the meaning of § 3(a)(10) of the Securities Exchange Act of 1934. We conclude that they are.

The Co–Op is an agricultural cooperative that, at the time relevant here, had approximately 23,000 members. In order to raise money to support its general business operations, the Co–Op sold promissory notes payable on demand by the holder. Although the notes were uncollateralized and uninsured, they paid a variable rate of interest that was adjusted monthly to keep it higher than the rate paid by local financial institutions. The Co–Op offered the notes to both members and nonmembers, marketing the scheme as an "Investment Program." Advertisements for the notes, which appeared in each Co–Op newsletter, read in part: "YOUR CO–OP has more than $11,000,000 in assets to stand behind your investments. The Investment is not Federal [*sic*] insured but it is ... Safe ... Secure ... and available when you need it." App. 5 (ellipses in original).

Despite these assurances, the Co–Op filed for bankruptcy in 1984. At the time of the filing, over 1,600 people held notes worth a total of $10 million.

After the Co–Op filed for bankruptcy, petitioners, a class of holders of the notes, filed suit against Arthur Young & Co., the firm that had audited the Co–Op's financial statements (and the predecessor to respondent Ernst & Young). Petitioners alleged, *inter alia,* that Arthur Young had intentionally failed to follow generally accepted accounting principles in its audit, specifically with respect to the valuation of one of the Co–Op's major assets, a gasohol plant. Petitioners claimed that Arthur Young violated these principles in an effort to inflate the assets and net worth of the Co–Op. Petitioners maintained that, had Arthur Young properly treated the plant in its audits, they would not have purchased demand notes because the Co–Op's insolvency would have been apparent. On the basis of these allegations, petitioners claimed that Arthur Young had violated the antifraud provisions of the 1934 Act as well as Arkansas' securities laws. * * *

This case requires us to decide whether the note issued by the Co–Op is a "security" within the meaning of the 1934 Act. Section 3(a)(10) of that Act is our starting point:

> "The term 'security' means any note, stock, treasury stock, bond, debenture, certificate of interest or participation in any profit-sharing agreement or in any oil, gas, or other mineral royalty or lease, any collateral-trust certificate, preorganization certificate or subscription, transferable share, investment contract, voting-trust certificate, certificate of deposit, for a security, any put, call, straddle, option, or privilege on any security, certificate of deposit, or group or index of securities (including any interest therein or based on the value thereof), or any put, call, straddle, option, or privilege entered into on a national securities exchange relating to foreign currency, or in general, any instrument commonly known as a 'security'; or any certificate of interest or participation in, temporary or interim certificate for, receipt for, or warrant or right to subscribe to or purchase, any of the foregoing; but shall not include currency or any note, draft, bill of exchange, or banker's acceptance which has a maturity at the time of issuance of not exceeding nine months, exclusive of days of grace, or any renewal thereof the maturity of which is likewise limited." 48 Stat. 884, as amended, 15 U.S.C. § 78c(a)(10).

The fundamental purpose undergirding the Securities Acts is "to eliminate serious abuses in a largely unregulated securities market." *United Housing Foundation, Inc. v. Forman,* 421 U.S. 837, 849, 95 S.Ct. 2051, 2059, 44 L.Ed.2d 621 (1975). In defining the scope of the market that it wished to regulate, Congress painted with a broad brush. It recognized the virtually limitless scope of human ingenuity, especially in the creation of "countless and variable schemes devised by those who seek the use of the money of others on the promise of profits," *SEC v. W.J.*

Howey Co., 328 U.S. 293, 299, 66 S.Ct. 1100, 1103, 90 L.Ed. 1244 (1946), and determined that the best way to achieve its goal of protecting investors was "to define 'the term "security" in sufficiently broad and general terms so as to include within that definition the many types of instruments that in our commercial world fall within the ordinary concept of a security.' " *Forman, supra,* 421 U.S., at 847–848, 95 S.Ct., at 2058–2059 (quoting H.R.Rep. No. 85, 73d Cong., 1st Sess., 11 (1933)). Congress therefore did not attempt precisely to cabin the scope of the Securities Acts. Rather, it enacted a definition of "security" sufficiently broad to encompass virtually any instrument that might be sold as an investment.

Congress did not, however, "intend to provide a broad federal remedy for all fraud." *Marine Bank v. Weaver,* 455 U.S. 551, 556, 102 S.Ct. 1220, 1223, 71 L.Ed.2d 409 (1982). Accordingly, "[t]he task has fallen to the Securities and Exchange Commission (SEC), the body charged with administering the Securities Acts, and ultimately to the federal courts to decide which of the myriad financial transactions in our society come within the coverage of these statutes." *Forman, supra,* 421 U.S., at 848, 95 S.Ct., at 2059. In discharging our duty, we are not bound by legal formalisms, but instead take account of the economics of the transaction under investigation. See, *e.g., Tcherepnin v. Knight,* 389 U.S. 332, 336, 88 S.Ct. 548, 553, 19 L.Ed.2d 564 (1967) (in interpreting the term "security," "form should be disregarded for substance and the emphasis should be on economic reality"). Congress' purpose in enacting the securities laws was to regulate *investments,* in whatever form they are made and by whatever name they are called.

A commitment to an examination of the economic realities of a transaction does not necessarily entail a case-by-case analysis of every instrument, however. Some instruments are obviously within the class Congress intended to regulate because they are by their nature investments. In *Landreth Timber Co. v. Landreth,* 471 U.S. 681, 105 S.Ct. 2297, 85 L.Ed.2d 692 (1985), we held that an instrument bearing the name "stock" that, among other things, is negotiable, offers the possibility of capital appreciation, and carries the right to dividends contingent on the profits of a business enterprise is plainly within the class of instruments Congress intended the securities laws to cover. *Landreth Timber* does not signify a lack of concern with economic reality; rather, it signals a recognition that stock is, as a practical matter, always an investment if it has the economic characteristics traditionally associated with stock. Even if sparse exceptions to this generalization can be found, the public perception of common stock as the paradigm of a security suggests that stock, in whatever context it is sold, should be treated as within the ambit of the Acts. *Id.,* at 687, 693, 105 S.Ct., at 2302, 2305.

We made clear in *Landreth Timber* that stock was a special case, explicitly limiting our holding to that sort of instrument. *Id.,* at 694, 105 S.Ct., at 2304. Although we refused finally to rule out a similar *per se* rule for notes, we intimated that such a rule would be unjustified. Unlike "stock," we said, " 'note' may now be viewed as a relatively broad term that encompasses instruments with widely varying characteristics, depending on whether issued in a consumer context, as commercial paper, or in some other investment context." *Ibid.* (citing *Securities Industry Assn. v. Board of Governors of Federal Reserve System,* 468 U.S. 137, 149–153, 104 S.Ct. 2979, 2985–88, 82 L.Ed.2d 107 (1984)). While common stock is the quintessence of a security, *Landreth Timber, supra,* 471 U.S., at 693, 105 S.Ct., at 2305, and investors therefore justifiably assume that a sale of stock is covered by the Securities Acts, the same simply cannot be said of notes, which are used in a variety of settings, not all of which involve investments. Thus, the phrase "any note" should not be interpreted to mean literally "any note," but must be understood against the backdrop of what Congress was attempting to accomplish in enacting the Securities Acts.

Because the *Landreth Timber* formula cannot sensibly be applied to notes, some other principle must be developed to define the term "note." A majority of the Courts of Appeals that have considered the issue have adopted, in varying forms, "investment versus commercial" approaches that distinguish, on the basis of all of the circumstances surrounding the transactions, notes issued in an investment context (which are "securities") from notes issued in a commercial or consumer context (which are not). See, *e.g., Futura Development Corp. v. Centex Corp.,* 761 F.2d 33, 40–41 (CA1 1985); *McClure v. First Nat. Bank of Lubbock, Texas,* 497 F.2d 490, 492–494 (CA5 1974); *Hunssinger v. Rockford Business Credits, Inc.,* 745 F.2d 484, 488 (CA7 1984); *Holloway v. Peat, Marwick, Mitchell & Co.,* 879 F.2d 772, 778–779 (CA10 1989), cert. pending No. 89–532.

The Second Circuit's "family resemblance" approach begins with a presumption that *any* note with a term of more than nine months is a "security." See, *e.g., Exchange Nat. Bank of Chicago v. Touche Ross & Co.,* 544 F.2d 1126, 1137 (CA2 1976). Recognizing that not all notes are securities, however, the Second Circuit has also devised a list of notes that it has decided are obviously not securities. Accordingly, the "family resemblance" test permits an issuer to rebut the presumption that a note is a security if it can show that the note in question "bear[s] a strong family resemblance" to an item on the judicially crafted list of exceptions, *id.,* at 1137–1138, or convinces the court to add a new instrument to the list, see, *e.g., Chemical Bank v. Arthur Andersen & Co.,* 726 F.2d 930, 939 (CA2 1984).

In contrast, the Eighth and District of Columbia Circuits apply the test we created in *SEC v. W.J. Howey Co.,* 328 U.S. 293, 66 S.Ct. 1100, 90 L.Ed. 1244 (1946), to determine whether an instrument is an "investment contract" to the determination whether an instrument is a "note." Under this test, a note is a security only if it evidences "(1) an investment; (2) in a common enterprise; (3) with a reasonable expectation of profits; (4) to be derived from the entrepreneurial or managerial efforts of others." 856 F.2d, at 54 (case below). Accord, *Baurer v. Planning Group, Inc.,* 215 U.S.App.D.C. 384, 391–393, 669 F.2d 770, 777–779 (1981). See also *Under-*

hill v. Royal, 769 F.2d 1426, 1431 (CA9 1985) (setting forth what it terms a "risk capital" approach that is virtually identical to the *Howey* test).

We reject the approaches of those courts that have applied the *Howey* test to notes; *Howey* provides a mechanism for determining whether an instrument is an "investment contract." The demand notes here may well not be "investment contracts," but that does not mean they are not "notes." To hold that a "note" is not a "security" unless it meets a test designed for an entirely different variety of instrument "would make the Acts' enumeration of many types of instruments superfluous," *Landreth Timber,* 471 U.S., at 692, 105 S.Ct., at 2305, and would be inconsistent with Congress' intent to regulate the entire body of instruments sold as investments, see *supra,* at 949–950.

The other two contenders—the "family resemblance" and "investment versus commercial" tests—are really two ways of formulating the same general approach. Because we think the "family resemblance" test provides a more promising framework for analysis, however, we adopt it. The test begins with the language of the statute; because the Securities Acts define "security" to include "any note," we begin with a presumption that every note is a security. We nonetheless recognize that this presumption cannot be irrebuttable. Congress was concerned with regulating the investment market, not with creating a general federal cause of action for fraud. In an attempt to give more content to that dividing line, the Second Circuit has identified a list of instruments commonly denominated "notes" that nonetheless fall without the "security" category. See *Exchange Nat. Bank, supra,* at 1138 (types of notes that are not "securities" include "the note delivered in consumer financing, the note secured by a mortgage on a home, the short-term note secured by a lien on a small business or some of its assets, the note evidencing a 'character' loan to a bank customer, short-term notes secured by an assignment of accounts receivable, or a note which simply formalizes an open-account debt incurred in the ordinary course of business (particularly if, as in the case of the customer of a broker, it is collateralized)"); *Chemical Bank, supra,* at 939 (adding to list "notes evidencing loans by commercial banks for current operations").

We agree that the items identified by the Second Circuit are not properly viewed as "securities." More guidance, though, is needed. It is impossible to make any meaningful inquiry into whether an instrument bears a "resemblance" to one of the instruments identified by the Second Circuit without specifying what it is about *those* instruments that makes *them* non-"securities." Moreover, as the Second Circuit itself has noted, its list is "not graven in stone," 726 F.2d, at 939, and is therefore capable of expansion. Thus, some standards must be developed for determining when an item should be added to the list.

An examination of the list itself makes clear what those standards should be. In creating its list, the Second Circuit was applying the same factors that this Court has held apply in deciding whether a transaction involves a "security." First, we examine the transaction to assess the motivations that would prompt a reasonable seller and buyer to enter into it. If the seller's purpose is to raise money for the general use of a business enterprise or to finance substantial investments and the buyer is interested primarily in the profit the note is expected to generate, the instrument is likely to be a "security." If the note is exchanged to facilitate the purchase and sale of a minor asset or consumer good, to correct for the seller's cash-flow difficulties, or to advance some other commercial or consumer purpose, on the other hand, the note is less sensibly described as a "security." See, *e.g., Forman,* 421 U.S., at 851, 95 S.Ct., at 2060 (share of "stock" carrying a right to subsidized housing not a security because "the inducement to purchase was solely to acquire subsidized low-cost living space; it was not to invest for profit"). Second, we examine the "plan of distribution" of the instrument, *SEC v. C.M. Joiner Leasing Corp.,* 320 U.S. 344, 353, 64 S.Ct. 120, 124, 88 L.Ed. 88 (1943), to determine whether it is an instrument in which there is "common trading for speculation or investment," *id.,* at 351, 64 S.Ct., at 123. Third, we examine the reasonable expectations of the investing public: The Court will consider instruments to be "securities" on the basis of such public expectations, even where an economic analysis of the circumstances of the particular transaction might suggest that the instruments are not "securities" as used in that transaction. Compare *Landreth Timber,* 471 U.S., at 687, 693, 105 S.Ct., at 2302, 2305 (relying on public expectations in holding that common stock is always a security), with *id.,* at 697–700, 105 S.Ct., at 2307–2308 (Stevens, J., dissenting) (arguing that sale of business to single informed purchaser through stock is not within the purview of the Acts under the economic reality test). See also *Forman, supra,* at 851, 95 S.Ct., at 2060. Finally, we examine whether some factor such as the existence of another regulatory scheme significantly reduces the risk of the instrument, thereby rendering application of the Securities Acts unnecessary. See, *e.g., Marine Bank,* 455 U.S., at 557–559, and n. 7, 102 S.Ct., at 1224–1225, and n. 7.

We conclude, then, that in determining whether an instrument denominated a "note" is a "security," courts are to apply the version of the "family resemblance" test that we have articulated here: A note is presumed to be a "security," and that presumption may be rebutted only by a showing that the note bears a strong resemblance (in terms of the four factors we have identified) to one of the enumerated categories of instrument. If an instrument is not sufficiently similar to an item on the list, the decision whether another category should be added is to be made by examining the same factors.

Applying the family resemblance approach to this case, we have little difficulty in concluding that the notes at issue here are "securities." Ernst & Young admits that "a demand note does not closely resemble any of the Second Circuit's family resemblance examples." Nor does an examination of the four factors we have identified as being relevant to our inquiry suggest that the demand notes here are not "securities" despite their lack of similarity to any of the enumerated categories. The Co–Op sold the notes in an effort to raise capital for its general business operations, and purchasers bought them in order to earn a profit in the form of interest. Indeed, one of the primary inducements offered purchasers was an interest rate constantly revised to keep it slightly above the rate paid by local banks and savings and loans. From both sides, then, the transaction is most naturally conceived as an investment in a business enterprise rather than as a purely commercial or consumer transaction.

As to the plan of distribution, the Co–Op offered the notes over an extended period to its 23,000 members, as well as to nonmembers, and more than 1,600 people held notes when the Co–Op filed for bankruptcy. To be sure, the notes were not traded on an exchange. They were, however, offered and sold to a broad segment of the public, and that is all we have held to be necessary to establish the requisite "common trading" in an instrument. See, *e.g., Landreth Timber, supra* (stock of closely held corporation not traded on any exchange held to be a "security"); *Tcherepnin,* 389 U.S., at 337, 88 S.Ct., at 553 (nonnegotiable but transferable "withdrawable capital shares" in savings and loan association held to be a "security"); *Howey,* 328 U.S., at 295, 66 S.Ct., at 1101 (units of citrus grove and maintenance contract "securities" although not traded on exchange).

The third factor—the public's reasonable perceptions—also supports a finding that the notes in this case are "securities." We have consistently identified the fundamental essence of a "security" to be its character as an "investment." The advertisements for the notes here characterized them as "investments," and there were no countervailing factors that would have led a reasonable person to question this characterization. In these circumstances, it would be reasonable for a prospective purchaser to take the Co–Op at its word.

Finally, we find no risk-reducing factor to suggest that these instruments are not in fact securities. The notes are uncollateralized and uninsured. Moreover, unlike the certificates of deposit in *Marine Bank, supra,* at 557–558, which were insured by the Federal Deposit Insurance Corporation and subject to substantial regulation under the federal banking laws, and unlike the pension plan in *Teamsters v. Daniel,* 439 U.S. 551, 569–570, 99 S.Ct. 790, 801–802, 58 L.Ed.2d 808 (1979), which was comprehensively regulated under the Employee Retirement Income Security Act of 1974, 88 Stat. 829, 29 U.S.C. § 1001 *et seq.* (1982 ed.), the notes here would escape federal regulation entirely if the Acts were held not to apply. * * *

Relying on the exception in the statute for "any note . . . which has a maturity at the time of issuance of not exceeding nine months," 15 U.S.C. § 78c(a)(10), respondent contends that the notes here are not "securities," even if they would otherwise qualify. Respondent cites Arkansas cases standing for the proposition that, in the context of the state statute of limitations, "[a] note payable on demand is due immediately." See, *e.g.,*

McMahon v. O'Keefe, 213 Ark. 105, 106, 209 S.W.2d 449, 450 (1948) (statute of limitations is triggered by the date of issuance rather than by date of first demand). Respondent concludes from this rule that the "maturity" of a demand note within the meaning of § 3(a)(10) is immediate, which is, of course, less than nine months. Respondent therefore contends that the notes fall within the plain words of the exclusion and are thus not "securities."

Petitioners counter that the "plain words" of the exclusion should not govern. Petitioners cite the legislative history of a similar provision of the 1933 Act, 48 Stat. 76, 15 U.S.C. § 77c(a)(3), for the proposition that the purpose of the exclusion is to except from the coverage of the Acts only commercial paper—short-term, high quality instruments issued to fund current operations and sold only to highly sophisticated investors. See S.Rep. No. 47, 73d Cong., 1st Sess., 3–4 (1933); H.R.Rep. No. 85, 73d Cong., 1st Sess., 15 (1933). Petitioners also emphasize that this Court has repeatedly held (see *supra,* at 948–950) that the plain words of the definition of a "security" are not dispositive, and that we consider the economic reality of the transaction to determine whether Congress intended the Securities Acts to apply. Petitioners therefore argue, with some force, that reading the exception for short-term notes to exclude from the Acts' coverage investment notes of less than nine months' duration would be inconsistent with Congress' evident desire to permit the SEC and the courts flexibility to ensure that the Acts are not manipulated to investors' detriment. If petitioners are correct that the exclusion is intended to cover only commercial paper, these notes, which were sold in a large scale offering to unsophisticated members of the public, plainly should not fall within the exclusion.

We need not decide, however, whether petitioners' interpretation of the exception is correct, for we conclude that even if we give literal effect to the exception, the notes do not fall within its terms. * * *

For the foregoing reasons, we conclude that the demand notes at issue here fall under the "note" category of instruments that are "securities" under the 1933 and 1934 Acts. We also conclude that, even under respondent's preferred approach to § 3(a)(10)'s exclusion for short-term notes, these demand notes do not fall within the exclusion. Accordingly, we reverse the judgment of the Court of Appeals and remand the case for further proceedings consistent with this opinion.

So ordered.

JUSTICE STEVENS, concurring. * * *

CHIEF JUSTICE REHNQUIST filed an opinion concurring in part and dissenting in part, in which JUSTICES WHITE, O'CONNOR and SCALIA joined.

NOTES

1. Keep the Reves decision in mind when considering the application of the Securities Act of 1933 in Chapter 8 to investments that have the characteristics of stocks.

2. Note that an accounting firm in the Reves case was a deep pocket defendant in this action. As you will recall from Chapter 2, this is often the case in security law claims.

An alternative to registration is a private placement with an institution. Such transactions, if properly qualified, are exempt from the registration requirements of the Securities Act of 1933. Consider the following excerpt from the Bank of America website describing the activities of one of its affiliates.

As the market leader in private placements, Banc of America Securities consistently ranks first among placement agents for straight corporate debt private placements. Since 1997, Banc of America Securities has placed approximately $5144 billion in debt private placements.

Debt private placements allow the issuer to avoid the time and expense of SEC registration by placing securities directly with institutional investors. As such, a private placement is a very efficient instrument for raising capital.

The private placement market is attractive to issuers who require long term debt for a variety of purposes, including diversifying funding sources, adding a more permanent layer of fixed rate capital, ratings arbitrage or refinancing. In addition, the private placement market is ideally suited to meet an issuer's confidentiality requirements.

Investors are primarily insurance companies that typically utilize a buy and hold investment strategy. Other investors include pension funds, mezzanine and equity funds, investment managers, banks and finance companies.

Product Strengths

- Longer maturities.
- Defers required principal amortization.
- Diversifies sources of capital.
- Debt requirements smaller than the public market minimum.
- Privacy of the issuer's financial situation maintained.
- More permanent layer of debt capital.
- Ability to issue notes without formal credit ratings.

bankofamerica.com, visited February 6, 2003.

NOTES

1. Consider the following description of the private placement market:

The typical borrower in the private placement market is a medium-sized corporation. Large firms tend to issue in the public bond market, and small firms generally borrow only in the bank loan market. For a sample of nonfinancial corporations, the median value of assets for those borrowing in the private market was $0.5 billion in 1989, whereas the median for those borrowing in the public market was $1.5 billion. Because issues are smaller in the private market, issue sizes are also smaller on average than in the public market: Nearly two-thirds of the number of all private placements in 1989 were between $10 million and $100 million, whereas more than 85 percent of the public issues were in excess of $100 million. For the same year, the median issue size of private placements was $34 million, and the median for public bonds was $150 million.

An interaction among issue size, issuing costs, and yields is often thought to be the major reason that medium-sized firms tend to offer their securities in the private rather than in the public market. Issuance costs are lower for a private placement than for a public offering, in part because the issuer does not have to incur the considerable expense of registering the issue with the SEC. Also, most private placements, especially the smaller issues, are not underwritten and thus typically have lower distribution expenses than do public bonds, which are almost always underwritten. In contrast, for those few public and private issues that are of comparable size and quality, yields are generally higher on private placements than on public bonds. The total cost of borrowing for comparable medium-sized issues is thus generally lower in the private market because any higher coupon rate that must be paid there is offset by lower fixed costs of issuance. Total costs for comparable large issues are generally lower in the public market because fixed costs are a smaller percentage of large issues. According to market participants, the break-even point between the two markets is at issue sizes between $75 million and $100 million.

Issue size, however, is not the main reason that medium-sized companies borrow in the private rather than in the public market. A more important reason is that lenders must perform extensive credit evaluations of such companies before loans can be extended to them. In any credit transaction, public or private, the lender must determine the financial condition and prospects of the borrower. For large, well-known companies, this task is facilitated by the ready availability of information from many sources. In contrast, for other, less well known companies, a lender cannot obtain information as easily and must collect the necessary information on its own. Moreover, the lender must continue in this effort after the credit is extended in order to adequately monitor the borrower's ability to make timely payment of interest and principal. Because of the information problems that less well known companies present to lenders, they are sometimes referred to as information-problematic borrowers.

Mark Carey, Recent Developments in the Market for Privately Placed Debt, 79 Fed. Res. Bull. No. 2, at 77 (Feb. 1993).

2. "The private placement market is a well established and well recognized securities market. It is typically used to place, usually through an investment[banker] ..., debt securities with institutional investors. It is not uncommon for persons accepting private placements to negotiate regarding some of the terms. Offering investments as private placements is a means of ensuring exemption from the registration requirements of the federal securities laws." Crocker Nat'l Bank v. Rockwell International Corp., 555 F.Supp. 47 (N.D.Cal.1982). Why do you think pension funds and insurance companies are interested in loaning funds in a private placement? The stringent regulation imposed by SEC regulations has caused many issuers to seek capital raises through private placements rather than public offerings. In 2006, private placements raised more capital than did offerings listed on the major exchanges in the U.S. Jerry W. Markham, A Financial History of the United States, From Enron Era Scandals to the Subprime Crisis (2004–2006), 80 (2010).

PIPEs (private investments in public equity) have become a popular tool for raising private equity. In such transactions, institutional investors purchase the stock of a public company at a substantial discount. These transactions may also include warrants and debt. These transactions are used where the expense of a public offering or other concerns make the private equity market more attractive. PIPE transactions raised nearly $20 billion in 2004. See generally, George L. Majoros, Jr., Comment: The Development of "PIPEs" in Today's Private Equity Market, 51 Case W. Res. 493 (2001) (describing losses from PIPEs). For more on private placements see Chapter 8, Section 3. The SEC has uncovered abuses in which PIPE purchasers anticipating a drop in the price of the stock, sell short and cover with their PIPE shares. Floyd Norris, A Troubling Finance Tool for Companies in Trouble, N.Y. Times, March 15, 2006, at C4. See also SEC v. Cuban, 620 F.3d 551 (5th Cir. 2010). (court reverses dismissal of complaint against Mark Cuban, the owner of the Dallas Mavericks, charging insider trading in connection with a PIPE transaction).

3. Mezzanine finance is subordinated debt. Howell E. Jackson, The Expanding Obligations of Financial Holding Companies, 107 Harv. L. Rev. 509, 597 (1994). In other words, it is debt located between senior debt and common equity. *See generally* John R. Willis & David A. Clark, Introduction to Mezzanine Finance and Private Equity, in New Developments in Commercial Banking 323 (Donald Chew ed., 1991). A related concept is "mezzanine capital" that "contains characteristics of both equity and liability, and hence is classified somewhere in between." KA Invs. LDC v. Number Nine Visual Tech. Corp., 2002 WL 31194865 (D.Mass.2002)

The Williams Act

If an instrument denominated as 'debt' has enough elements of an equity security, tender offers involving the instrument may trigger the reporting requirements of the Williams Act, as alleged (unsuccessfully) by the plaintiff in the case below.

ERICKSON v. WHEATLEY VENTURES

1997 WL 119849 (N.D.Cal.1997).

MARILYN HALL PATEL, DISTRICT COURT JUDGE.

Plaintiff Deanne R. Erickson, trustee of the Kaufman Family 1981 Trust, dated October 21, 1981, brought this action on behalf of herself and all others similarly situated against defendants Wheatley Ventures, Inc., et al. ("Wheatley"), Montgomery Realty Company–80, et al. ("Fox") and Northern Trust Bank of California, N.A. ("Northern Trust") alleging (1) four causes of action for failure to comply with the disclosure requirements for tender offers under Section 14(d) of the Williams Act, Securities Exchange Act of 1934 (the "1934 Act"), as amended, 15 U.S.C. § 78(n), and Regulation 14D, 17 C.F.R. § 240.14d–1 to § 240.14d–101 promulgated thereunder, and (2) violation of Section 315(c) of the Trust Indenture Act of 1939 (the "Trust Indenture Act"), 15 U.S.C. § 77ooo(c), and a trust indenture (the "Indenture") qualified under the Trust Indenture Act. * * *

Northern Trust is the trustee under the Indenture governing the terms and provisions of nonrecourse promissory notes (the "Notes") issued by Preferred Properties Fund–80 (the "Partnership"), the target of the challenged tender offer. Wheatley, a Georgia corporation, acquired the Notes from the plaintiff class (the "Noteholders") in the challenged tender offer. Fox represents the management of the Partnership in this action, including Montgomery Realty Company–80, a California limited partnership and the general partner of the Partnership. * * *

The Partnership issued the Notes under the Indenture, dated January 31, 1980, and registered the Notes as Section 12(g) securities in 1981. The Partnership sold the Notes to the public in 1980, at the same time that it sold its limited partnership interests to the public. In addition to repayment of principal and interest, the Noteholders were also entitled to residual proceeds from the sale of the Partnership's properties (the "residual interest").[10] Erickson does not allege that the Notes conferred any voting or other participatory rights other than the right to remove the trustee and to nominate a successor under the Indenture.

---

10. The Notes bore interest at the rate of 10% per annum, payable on the Notes quarterly, with the principal amount due and payable on June 30, 1994. Interest not paid was added to the principal and compounded at the rate of 10% per annum. The Notes were secured by deeds of trust and other security instruments on each of the real properties owned by the Partnership. The Noteholders were entitled to residual interest after a payment of certain preferential returns to the limited and general partners of the Partnership. The Notes could be redeemed prior to June 30, 1994.

Chapter Five

Preferred Stock

■ ■ ■

Chapter objectives

- To understand how preferred stock combines elements of both debt and equity.

- To appreciate the wide range of features—including liquidation preferences—that preferred stock can include.

- To see the conflicts between preferred shareholders and common shareholders over fundamental corporate decisions that affect firm value.

SECTION 1. INSTRUMENT DESIGN

Moving down the right hand of the balance sheet past liabilities, equity securities appear as a source of capital for the corporation. Equity connotes an ownership interest, as opposed to a loan that is to be repaid in the form of principal and interest. The equity holder is an owner of the corporation and will be allowed to elect directors to oversee management of the corporation.

In its purest sense, an equity owner shares in aliquot portion in the liquidation of the corporation of any assets after payment of liabilities. The equity owner will also share in the profits of the corporation, provided that the board of directors authorizes such a distribution in the form of a dividend.

In actual practice, an equity security may not have all of the attributes associated with ownership. Preferred stock, for example, may be limited in the amount it will receive in liquidation. Although preferred stock is carried on the balance sheet as equity, it has characteristics of both debt and equity. It is debt in the sense that the preferred dividend approximates an interest rate and its liquidation value will approximate its purchase price (usually with a premium). Therefore, its pricing may be more related to a debt security than an equity security. That is, the preferred stock price may be more responsive to interest rates than to the capital appreciation of the company.

253

Preferred stocks are often redeemable, usually at their liquidation value. As noted, the liquidation value is often set at some amount over the purchase price, providing some redemption protection. Nevertheless, the holder of a redeemable, non-convertible preferred may have the worst of both worlds. The holder of a preferred share must stand in line behind debt holders in liquidation and is denied an opportunity to participate in capital appreciation. If interest rates fall, the preferred may be redeemed and will have to reinvest at a lower rate of return.

Preferred shares usually must receive dividends before common shareholders. Nevertheless, the dividend is not assured. It is up to the board of directors to determine whether a dividend will be declared, and the preferred shareholders have no right to the dividend until declared. Preferred shares may be cumulative. This means that the common shareholders will receive no dividends until arrearages (missed dividends) are paid to the preferred. Adding a cumulative feature pushes it more toward a debt obligation because the obligation continues. Preferred shares may also be "participating," which means that they may share in dividends with the common shareholders in some amount above the preset preferred dividend.

Preferred shares usually have limited voting rights. For example, preferred shareholders may not be allowed to vote unless some event that is adverse to their interests occur, such as missing dividends for specified periods. In Santa Fe Gaming Corp. v. Hudson Bay Partners, L.P., 49 F.Supp.2d 1178 (D.Nev.1999), the court held that preferred shares were not voting securities that were subject to the protections of the disclosure requirements of the Williams Act, which governs corporate takeover activities. The preferred shares in that case could vote only in the event of certain triggering events such as missing a total of four dividends. This again suggests that preferred stock will be treated more like debt than equity in determining the rights of such holders. See also Koppers Co., Inc. v. American Express Co., 689 F.Supp. 1408, 1411 (W.D.Pa.1988) ("true" preferred stock, as distinguished from misnamed debt securities, is not stock that is subject to margin restrictions under the Securities Exchange Act of 1934).

Consider the following history and description of preferred stock:

> From the inception of its usage in England in the 1840s, preferred stock began a metamorphosis from functioning as a true equity security to a fixed-income instrument that could effectively supplement bonds in a corporation's financing mix.

> Preferred stock was developed as a financial innovation in Britain.... It was designed partially to overcome shareholder objections to the issuance of additional stock, which diluted the equity of the original owners. The New preference shares usually combined the features of both fixed-income and equity securities. It provided a ... [set] dividend rate and, if the shares were participating, could also receive dividends in excess of the ... [set] rate, thus in some ways

resembling common stock. Moreover, a corporation could not be forced into receivership if dividends, unlike bond interest, fell in arrears.

Jonathan Barron Baskin & Paul J. Miranti, Jr., A History of Corporate Finance 152–53 (1997).

Some preferred stock is convertible into common, which allows the holder to participate (in the amount of any increase above the conversion level) in capital appreciation. There being no free lunch on Wall Street, however, a convertible preferred will pay a lower dividend than a comparable preferred without such a feature.

Convertible features may be quite exotic as shown by the following reference:

> Defendants were granted the right to convert their Preferred Stock into Common Stock at a fixed discount to market at the time of conversion. Plaintiff states that this type of Preferred Stock, which is based on a "floating" conversion ratio, is known as "floorless convertible," "toxic convertible," or "death spiral convertible." According to Plaintiff, the lower the market price of the common stock at the time of conversion, the greater the number of shares Defendants would receive upon conversion of Preferred Stock.

Log On America, Inc. v. Promethean Asset Management L.L.C., 223 F.Supp.2d 435, 439, n. 3 (S.D.N.Y.2001). Such securities are susceptible to abuse:

> In general, plaintiffs allege that this short-selling activity was part of a larger strategy that defendants have repeatedly employed to manipulate the stock price of companies in which they have invested. According to plaintiffs, defendants Hicks, Pickett, and Valentine are seasoned practitioners of "death spiral" funding schemes in which they provide financing to a target company and proceed to aggressively short-sell its stock in the hope that such short sales will drive down its price. This price drop, in turn, enables the defendants to obtain more shares of common stock upon conversion by virtue of an arrangement known as a "toxic convertible" that allows the company's preferred stock to be converted at a discount to the present market value of the common stock issuable upon conversion. Defendants then use the additional shares obtained upon conversion to cover their short positions, profiting handsomely from the difference between the price at which the stock was sold short and at which it was converted. There are even times, according to plaintiffs, when defendants need not cover at all, typically when they have succeeded in driving down the stock price of the target company practically to zero. Moreover, the defendants use the stock from the conversion to push the stock price still lower, hence the characterization "death spiral." Plaintiffs have listed over 25 other companies in their Amended Consolidated Complaint that they believe have been the victims of

toxic convertible or similar financing schemes orchestrated by defendants.

Internet Law Library, Inc. v. Southridge Capital Management, LLC, 223 F.Supp.2d 474, 479 (S.D.N.Y.2002).

TIMOTHY J. HARRIS
MODELING THE CONVERSION DECISIONS OF
PREFERRED STOCK

58 Bus. Law. 587 (2003).

For many years, convertible preferred stock has been the predominant vehicle for startup companies raising venture capital. Venture capital investors negotiate the rights, privileges, and preferences of such convertible preferred stock in the hopes of realizing returns on their investment by disposing of their shares in or following an initial public offering by the company or pursuant to an acquisition of the company. In the case of an initial public offering, venture capital investors usually convert their preferred stock into common stock because initial public offerings of startup companies typically only create public markets for common stock. In the case of an acquisition, however, a venture capital investor is faced with a "conversion decision," the choice of either converting its preferred stock into common stock and sharing in the acquisition proceeds as a common shareholder, or retaining its preferred stock position and sharing in the acquisition proceeds as a preferred shareholder.

An acquisition has always been a much more likely liquidity event to be achieved by venture capital investors than an initial public offering. Since the downturn in the public equity markets that began in the second quarter of 2000, the initial public offering has practically become a hypothetical liquidity event for venture capital investors. With the resulting increased emphasis on acquisitions as an exit strategy, venture capital investors will face conversion decisions with increasing frequency.

Convertible preferred stock usually entitles the holder to convert its shares of preferred stock into common stock at any time, at the option of the holder. When a venture capital investor converts its preferred stock into common stock, it loses all of the rights, privileges, and preferences that accrue to the benefit of the holders of such preferred stock pursuant to the terms of the charter documents that authorize the preferred stock. Notwithstanding this loss of rights, privileges, and preferences, venture capital investors will choose to convert their preferred stock into common stock in the event of an acquisition if, as common shareholders, they would receive a larger portion of the acquisition proceeds than they would as preferred shareholders.

One of the hallmark preferences of convertible preferred stock issued to venture capital investors is the liquidation preference. The liquidation preference is the right of a preferred shareholder to receive certain distributions in respect of its preferred stock before distributions are made to the common shareholders in the event of a liquidation of the company. Oddly, this preference is expressed in terms of distributions made to shareholders upon liquidation of the company, although provisions in the charter documents make clear that a liquidation is deemed to be occasioned by the customary acquisition transaction structures (e.g., mergers, reorganizations, stock or asset purchases, or any transaction or series of related transactions in which the company's shareholders prior to such transaction do not hold a majority of the voting power of the resulting or surviving entity after such transaction). In this light, the liquidation preference would more appropriately be referred to as the "acquisition proceeds preference" because the liquidation preference directs the manner in which acquisition proceeds are distributed to the preferred shareholders and common shareholders.

The liquidation preference is the amount which must be distributed to the preferred shareholders before any amount may be distributed to the common shareholders. Liquidation preferences are typically expressed in multiples of the original issue price of the preferred stock. For example, suppose a venture capital investor invests $10 million in a startup company in exchange for preferred stock with a "1x liquidation preference." In the event of an acquisition, the venture capital investor is entitled to the return of its original $10 million investment before the common shareholders are entitled to receive anything.

After satisfying the liquidation preference of any outstanding preferred stock, the remaining acquisition proceeds must be distributed to shareholders. But the question is whether the remaining proceeds are to be distributed solely among the common shareholders or whether the remaining proceeds are to be distributed among the common shareholders *and* the preferred shareholders.

If a series of preferred stock is not entitled to participate in the distribution of the remaining proceeds, it is referred to as "non-participating preferred." The conversion decision of non-participating preferred is an easy one: the venture capital investor will only convert if the venture capital investor's share of the acquisition proceeds as a common shareholder would exceed its liquidation preference as a preferred shareholder. If a venture capital investor invests $10 million in a startup company in exchange for non-participating preferred stock with a "1x liquidation preference" that represents a number of shares of common stock equal to fifty percent of the company on an as-converted basis, then the venture capital investor will only convert if the acquisition price is greater than $20 million because only at acquisition prices greater than $20 million will the venture capital investor's fifty percent share of the acquisition proceeds as a common shareholder be greater than its $10 million liquidation preference as a preferred shareholder.

If a series of preferred stock is entitled to participate in the distribution of remaining proceeds, it is referred to as "participating preferred." After satisfying the liquidation preferences of any outstanding preferred stock, the remaining proceeds are distributed among the participating preferred shareholders and common shareholders in a pro rata fashion based on the number of shares of common stock held by such shareholders assuming full conversion of the preferred stock.

The participation of a series of participating preferred may be unlimited (so-called fully participating preferred or participating preferred without a cap). The conversion decision of fully participating preferred is an easy one: the venture capital investor will never convert. If the acquisition proceeds are less than the venture capital investor's liquidation preference, then all of the acquisition proceeds are distributed to the venture capital investor. If the acquisition proceeds are more than the venture capital investor's liquidation preference, then the venture capital investor will take its liquidation preference and then share in the remaining proceeds with the common shareholders based upon its percentage ownership interest on an as-converted basis.

The participation of a series of participating preferred may be limited to a maximum amount, or a "cap." For example, if a venture capital investor invests $10 million in a startup company in exchange for preferred stock with a "1x liquidation preference" and is "participating subject to a 3x cap," the venture capital investor would be entitled to participate in the distribution of the remaining proceeds with the common shareholders until the venture capital investor has received three times its original $10 million investment. So, if the company is acquired for $60 million, and assuming that the preferred stock represents a number of shares of common stock equal to fifty percent of the company on an as-converted basis, the first $10 million is distributed to the venture capital investor as its liquidation preference, the next $40 million is distributed half to the venture capital investor and half to the common shareholders (so that the venture capital investor has received a total of $30 million), and the remaining $10 million is distributed to the common shareholders.

The conversion decision of participating preferred subject to a cap can be difficult. If the amount of acquisition proceeds that it would receive as a common shareholder are greater than the amount of acquisition proceeds that it would receive as a preferred shareholder, then the venture capital investor will convert. If, in the example discussed in the prior paragraph, the company is acquired for $70 million, the venture capital investor will convert because it would receive $30 million as a preferred shareholder ($10 million liquidation preference, plus fifty percent of the next $40 million at which point the 3x cap on participation is reached) or $35 million as a common shareholder (fifty percent of $70 million).

In each of the above examples, a simple capital structure with a single series of preferred stock has been assumed. As the capital structure of a company becomes more complicated, the calculations required to make economically rational conversion decisions become quite difficult because the decisions of preferred shareholders become interdependent. The conversion decision of a series of preferred stock can be mooted by an investor-favored provision in the charter documents that provides for the automatic conversion of shares of preferred stock immediately prior to the consummation of an acquisition as the result of which the aggregate distributions to the holders of common stock issued upon conversion of such preferred stock would exceed the aggregate distributions to the holder of such preferred stock if not otherwise converted.

SECTION 2. LIQUIDATION PREFERENCES

ROTHSCHILD INTERN. CORP.
v. LIGGETT GROUP, INC.

474 A.2d 133 (Del.1984).

HORSEY, JUSTICE.

This appeal is from a summary judgment Order of the Court of Chancery dismissing a purported class action filed by the owners of 7% cumulative preferred stock in Liggett Group, Inc. ("Liggett"), a Delaware corporation. The suit arises out of a combined tender offer and reverse cash-out merger whereby the interests of the 7% preferred shareholders were eliminated for a price of $70 per share, an amount $30 below the liquidation preference stated in Liggett's certificate of incorporation. Plaintiff-appellant asserts claims for breach of contract and breach of fiduciary duty based on the non-payment of the $30 premium.

Plaintiff, Rothschild International Corp., filed a class action in the Court of Chancery on behalf of 7% cumulative preferred stockholders of Liggett against defendants Liggett, Grand Metropolitan Limited ("GM"), a corporation of England, GM Sub Corporation ("GM Sub"), a Delaware corporation formed for the purpose of acquiring Liggett, and GM Sub II, a wholly-owned Delaware subsidiary of GM. The class was to consist of those 7% shareholders who tendered their preferred stock for $70 per share in response to GM's tender offer and those who did not so tender and were cashed out for the same per share price in the subsequent merger of GM Sub II into Liggett.

On motion by defendants, GM was dismissed as a party to the action for lack of personal jurisdiction; similarly, the case against GM Sub II was dismissed as GM Sub II had ceased to exist by virtue of its merger into Liggett in August, 1980. After such dismissal, but during the pendency of plaintiff's motion for class certification, both sides moved for summary judgment on the merits of plaintiff's claims. Upon consolidation of the motions and presentation of oral argument, the Court granted defendants' motion for summary judgment.

On appeal, plaintiff contends that the takeover of Liggett via the combined tender offer and merger in essence effected a liquidation of the company thus warranting payment to the holders of the 7% preferred stock of the $100 liquidation value set forth in Liggett's charter. Plaintiff's breach of contract and breach of fiduciary duty claims are premised on a single assertion—that GM's plan of acquisition was equivalent to a liquidation. However, as we view the record, the transaction did not involve a liquidation of Liggett's business. Hence, we must affirm.

There is no dispute of facts. Liggett's certificate of incorporation provided that "[i]n the event of any liquidation of the assets of the Corporation (whether voluntary or involuntary) the holders of the 7% Preferred Stock shall be entitled to be paid the par amount of their 7% Preferred shares and the amount of any dividends accumulated and unpaid thereon...."[1] Under the terms of Liggett's charter, each share of the 7% security carried a $100 par value. Plaintiff makes two interrelated arguments: (1) that the economic effect of the merger was a liquidation of Liggett's assets "just as if [Liggett] were sold piece meal to Grand Met"; and (2) that any corporate reorganization that forcibly liquidates a shareholder's *interests* is tantamount to a liquidation of the *corporation* itself. From this, plaintiff argues that it necessarily follows that defendants' failure to pay the preferred shareholders the full liquidation price constituted a breach of Liggett's charter. We cannot agree with either argument.

Preferential rights are contractual in nature and therefore are governed by the express provisions of a company's certificate of incorporation. Stock preferences must also be clearly expressed and will not be presumed.

Liggett's charter stated that the $100 liquidation preference would be paid only in the event of "any liquidation of the assets of the Corporation." The term "liquidation", as applied to a corporation, means the "winding up of the affairs of the corporation by getting in its assets, settling with creditors and debtors and apportioning the amount of profit and loss." W. Fletcher, *Corporations* § 7968 (1979). *See Sterling v. Mayflower Hotel Corp.,* Del.Supr., 93 A.2d 107, 112 (1952).

Our view of the record confirms the correctness of the Chancellor's finding that there was no "liquidation" of Liggett within the well-defined meaning of that term. Clearly the directors and shareholders of Liggett determined that the company should be integrated with GM, not that the corporate assets be liquidated on a "piece meal" basis. The fact is that Liggett has retained its corporate identity. Having elected this plan of reorganization, the parties had the right to avail themselves of the most effective means for achieving that result, subject only to their duty to deal fairly with the minority interests.

Thus, we must construe Liggett's liquidation provision as written and conclude that the reverse cash-out merger of Liggett did not accomplish a "liquidation" of Liggett's assets. Only upon a liquidation of its assets would Liggett's preferred shareholders' charter rights to payment of par

---

1. The certificate also provided that its 7% Cumulative Preferred stock could not be redeemed, called or converted into any other security. The stock also guaranteed a fixed 7% return per annum.

value "spring into being." *Rothschild International Corp. v. Liggett Group,* Del.Ch., 463 A.2d 642, 647 (1983).

Sterling v. Mayflower Hotel Corp., supra is in point on this issue. There, this Court held that a merger is not equivalent to a sale of assets. In so holding, the Court followed the well-settled principle of Delaware Corporation Law that "action taken under one section of that law is legally independent, and its validity is not dependent upon, nor to be tested by the requirements of other unrelated sections under which the same final result might be attained by different means." *Orzeck v. Englehart,* Del.Supr., 195 A.2d 375, 378 (1963).

It is equally settled under Delaware law that minority stock interests may be eliminated by merger. And, where a merger of corporations is permitted by law, a shareholder's preferential rights are subject to defeasance. Stockholders are charged with knowledge of this possibility at the time they acquire their shares. *Federal United Corp. v. Havender,* Del. Supr., 11 A.2d 331, 338 (1940). *Accord, Langfelder v. Universal Laboratories, Inc.,* D.Del., 68 F.Supp. 209 (1946), *aff'd,* 3rd Cir., 163 F.2d 804, 806–807 (1947); *Hottenstein v. York Ice Machinery Corp.,* 3rd Cir., 136 F.2d 944, 950 (1943).

Plaintiff claims that reliance on *Sterling* and *Havender* for a finding that Liggett was not liquidated is misplaced. To support this claim, plaintiff variously argues: (1) that as *Sterling* and *Havender* pre-dated cash mergers, they are not dispositive as to whether a Liggett-like takeover could constitute a liquidation; (2) that the relied-on authorities viewed a merger as contemplating the continuance of a stockholder's investment in the corporate enterprise; and (3) that because of the *Sterling/Havender* view of a merger and the unique features of the 7% preferred stock, the 7% shareholders could reasonably expect to be paid the $100 liquidation preference in any circumstance effecting a total elimination of their investment in Liggett.

The short answer to plaintiff's arguments is that, as a matter of law, stock issued or purchased prior to the Legislature's authorization of cash mergers does not entitle the stockholder to any vested right of immunity from the operation of the cash merger provision. *Coyne v. Park & Tilford Distillers Corp.,* Del.Supr., 154 A.2d 893 (1959). Further, it is settled that the State has the reserved power to enact laws having the effect of amending certificates of incorporation and any rights arising thereunder. *Id.* at 897. As plaintiff is charged with knowledge of the possible defeasance of its stock interests upon a merger, *Singer v. Magnavox Co.,* Del.Supr., 380 A.2d 969, 978 (1977), plaintiff cannot successfully argue for relief on the basis of the uniqueness of the 7% stock and the stockholders' "reasonable expectations" theory.

Plaintiff also claims that Liggett and GM, acting through its subsidiary GM Sub, breached their fiduciary duties to accord to the 7% shareholders fair and equitable terms of conversion. Simply stated, plaintiff argues that, irrespective of whether a de facto liquidation occurred, "[a]ny payment less than the full liquidation price was not 'entirely fair' to the 7% Preferred stockholders."

We agree with the Chancellor that plaintiff's "fairness" argument presumes a *right* of the 7% shareholders to receive full liquidation value and does not *per se* raise the issue of the intrinsic fairness of the $70 price offered at the time of the tender offer and merger. However, even assuming *arguendo* that plaintiff did present a fairness issue, it is well settled that "the stockholder is entitled to be paid for that which has been taken from him, *viz.*, his proportionate interest in a going concern." *Tri-Continental Corp. v. Battye*, Del.Supr., 74 A.2d 71, 72 (1950). Moreover, the measure of "fair value" is not "liquidation value." Rather, the 7% shareholders were entitled only to an amount equal to their proportionate interests in Liggett as determined by "all relevant factors." 8 *Del.C.* § 262; *Weinberger v. UOP, Inc.*, Del.Supr., 457 A.2d 701 (1983); *Tri-Continental Corp. v. Battye, supra.*

Thus, having reviewed the transaction, we find that the Chancellor did not err as a matter of law in granting defendants' motion for summary judgment.

IN THE MATTER OF THE APPRAISAL OF FORD HOLDINGS, INC. PREFERRED STOCK

698 A.2d 973 (Del.Ch.1997).

ALLEN, CHANCELLOR.

This is an appraisal proceeding under Section 262 of the Delaware General Corporation Law. It arises from a merger in which Ford Holdings, Inc. ("Holdings"), a subsidiary of Ford Motor Company, merged with Ford Holdings Capital Corporation, its own wholly owned subsidiary. The effect of the merger was to cash-out various types and series of Holdings' preferred stock. In each instance, the holders of preferred were paid the liquidation value of their security, plus a "merger premium" if the certificate creating the preferred called for it, plus any accumulated and unpaid dividends. Holdings asserts that under the various documents creating these securities that is exactly what the holders of the preferred stock are entitled to in the event of a merger. Plaintiffs in this appraisal action are certain holders of preferred stocks of Holdings. They seek a judicial appraisal of the "fair value" of their shares at the time of the merger, which they contend is higher than the amount Holdings calculated as due to them. * * *

Holdings was incorporated in 1989 to engage in the business of consumer and commercial lending, insurance underwriting, and equipment leasing. All of its common stock is held, directly or indirectly, by Ford Motor Company. Between October 1990 and June 1995, Holdings issued twenty series of preferred stock to the public. The preferred shares were of two different types: (1) Flexible Rate Auction Series A through P ("Auction Preferred"), and (2) Cumulative Preferred Series A through D ("Cumulative Preferred"). The specific terms of each series of preferred stock were contained in its Certificate of Designations ("Designations"). All series were nonconvertible and nonredeemable, had cumulative dividends, and had liquidation preferences equal to par plus any accumulated and unpaid dividends. The Certificates of Designations setting forth the terms, preferences, and limitations of the stock were not identical.

The Cumulative Preferred stock bore a stated dividend, payable quarterly. The returns on the Auction Preferred were determined in a more complex fashion. Initially these shares had a set dividend rate for a specified period. At the end of a period, initially forty-nine days, a designated agent (the "Term Selection Agent") would reset the term and announce whether the shares would also carry any "merger premium". (A merger premium is defined as *any amount of money above the stated liquidation preference paid to holders of the Auction Preferred in the event of a merger or consolidation*). Once the length of the period or term of the continuing investment was set by the Term Selection Agent and the existence of a merger premium was established, investors entered bids in a Dutch auction stating the interest or dividend rate that they would require to invest or continue their investment and how much they wanted to invest at that level. The company, thus, could refinance the whole of the issue (or series) at the lowest cost that the market (auction market) would permit. Those holders who demanded a return higher than the rate that the auction generated for the security for the next period would then sell the security to those willing to invest at that rate. They would get the liquidation value (par) plus any unpaid dividend. If the bidders at the new yield were insufficient to take all current holders out of the security who wanted to exit the investment, Holdings was precluded from altering the terms of the shares for the next period. In this situation, the period would be the minimum, forty-nine days, and the dividend rate would be set at a high rate according to a formula in the Certificate of Designations. This financing technique is designed to afford the issuer access to capital, through an equity instrument, that bears a resettable rate of interest.

Bancorp purchased 100 shares of Auction Preferred Series D shares on February 14, 1995 in the secondary market. The terms of these shares at that time included a five year period and no merger premium. Later that year, on October 16, 1995, Holdings' board of directors approved a plan to merge Holdings with Ford Holdings Capital Corporation. The merger was effectuated on December 20, 1995. In the merger, all of Holdings' preferred stock was eliminated and converted to a right to receive cash.

As a holder of Auction Preferred Series D, Bancorp did not accept the merger consideration; it dissented and filed this suit seeking an adjudication of the fair value of its shares. Certain holders of the Cumulative Preferred joined Bancorp's action seeking appraisal rights. Holdings then filed a motion for summary judgment asserting that it is clear from the language of the Designations that the holders of the preferred shares are entitled in the event of a merger to consideration fixed in those documents and not to any other amount. * * *

Delaware's General Corporation Law, like most general laws of incorporation in the twentieth century U.S., is an *enabling statute*. That is, the philosophy that underlies it is that the public good is advanced by the provision of an inexpensive mechanism that allows all individuals to achieve the benefits that the corporate form provides (most importantly, centralized management and entity status, with its characteristics of indefinite duration and separately salable share interests) through establishing management and governance terms that appear advantageous to those designing the organization. Thus, unlike the corporation law of the nineteenth century, modern corporation law contains few mandatory terms; it is largely enabling in character. It is not, however, bereft of mandatory terms. Under Delaware law, for example, a corporation is required to have an annual meeting for the election of directors; is required to have shareholder approval for amendments to the certificate of incorporation; must have appropriate shareholder concurrence in the authorization of a merger; and is required to have shareholder approval in order to dissolve. Generally, these mandatory provisions may not be varied by terms of the certificate of incorporation or otherwise.

Among these mandatory provisions of Delaware law is Section 262, the appraisal remedy. That Section provides in part:

(a) Any stockholder of a corporation of this State who holds shares of stock on the date of a demand pursuant to subsection (d) ... who continuously holds such shares through the effective date of the merger ..., who has otherwise complied with subsection (d) ... and who has [not] voted in favor of the merger ... *shall be entitled to an appraisal ... of the fair value of his stock* ... (Emphasis added).

It is this provision upon which petitioners rely. They satisfy each of the statutory conditions to an appraisal of the "fair value" of their shares, they say. They have evidence, they say, that the market price of their securities was greater than the merger consideration. They add that they have a right to present that evidence and for the court to determine the "fair value" of their shares in light of it and other indicia of value as of the merger date.

Defendant asserts that the Designations of the Cumulative Preferred and the Auction Preferred limit the appraisal rights of holders of these shares. Specifically, defendant contends that the Designations define the consideration to which the holders are entitled in the event of a merger. According to defendant, while shareholders may be statutorily entitled to an appraisal of fair value, the instrument creating their security fixes that value.

One question to be resolved then, is whether purchasers of preferred stock can, in effect, contract away their rights to seek judicial determination of the fair value of their stock, by accepting a security that explicitly provides either a stated amount or a formula by which an amount to be received in the event of a merger is set forth. This question is a specification of the general question—which has received a great deal of scholarly attention—whether, as a matter of sound policy, mandatory provisions are ever desirable in corporation law. *See generally Symposium: Contractual Freedom in Corporate Law,* 89 Colum.L.Rev. 1395 *et seq.* (1989). While this question is of general interest, we need not hazard any speculation on whether mandatory terms are efficient in general, because this case deals only with the appraisal remedy for preferred stock and preferred stock is a very special case. As is well understood, preferred stock can have characteristics of both debt and equity. To the extent it possesses any special rights or powers and to the extent it is restricted or limited in any way, the relation between the holder of the preferred and the corporation is contractual. *Ellingwood v. Wolf's Head Oil Refining Co.,* Del.Supr., 38 A.2d 743 (1944); *H.B. Korenvaes Investments, LP, et al. v. Marriott Corp., et al.,* Del. Ch., C.A. No. 12922, Allen, C., 1993 WL 205040 (June 9, 1993) ("rights of preferred stock are primarily but not exclusively contractual in nature.") While, as part of that contract, an issuer will owe the limited duty of good faith that one contractual party always owes to the other, with respect to those special preferences, etc., the issuer owes no duty of loyalty to the holders of the preferred. *E.g., H.B. Korenvaes, supra,* at 5; *Jedwab v. MGM Grand Hotels, Inc.,* Del. Ch., 509 A.2d 584 (1986).

All of the characteristics of the preferred are open for negotiation; that is the nature of the security. There is no utility in defining as forbidden any term thought advantageous to informed parties, unless that term violates substantive law. Particularly, there is no utility in forbidding the parties *creating* a preferred stock (the issuer, its advisors and counsel, and the underwriter and its counsel) from establishing a security that has a stated value (or a value established by a stated formula) in the event of stated contingencies.

The general rule applies as with all contracting parties: that which is a valid contract will be enforced either specifically or through a damages action, unless the contract violates positive law or its non-performance is excused. I cannot conclude that a provision that establishes the cash value of a preferred stock in the event of a cash-out merger would violate the public policy reflected in Section 262, given the essentially contractual nature of preferred stock. Thus, the relevant question in this case is whether the instruments establishing the rights and preferences of these various series of preferred stocks do contractually limit the right of a holder to seek judicial appraisal in the event of a cash-out merger.

I start with a preliminary generality. Since Section 262 represents a statutorily conferred right, it may be effectively waived in the documents creating the security only when that result is quite clearly set forth when interpreting the relevant document under generally applicable principles of construction. *See Red Clay Educ. Ass'n v. Bd. of Educ. of Red Clay Consol. Sch. Dist.,* Del. Ch., C.A. No. 11958, Chandler, V.C., 1992 WL 14965 at *7 (Jan. 16, 1992), 1992 Del. Ch. LEXIS 9 at *20. Secondly, I note that ambiguity in these matters ought to be construed against the issuer who, as the analysis below certainly indicates, had it within its power clearly to establish the result for which it here contends. *Kaiser Alum. Corp. v. Matheson*, Del.Supr., 681 A.2d 392 (1996).

The rights of stockholders of the Cumulative Preferred in the event of a merger are clearly stated in the Designations. Paragraph 4(b) of the Designations states:

> 4. *Rights on Liquidation or Cash–Out Merger.*
>
> (b) In any merger ... of [Holdings] with or into any other corpora-tion ... which ... provides for the payment of only cash to the holders ... each holder ... shall be entitled to receive an amount equal to the liquidation preference [which is defined in paragraph 4(a) as $100,000 per share] of shares ... held by such holder, plus an amount equal to accumulated and unpaid dividends on such shares ..., and no more in exchange for such shares of Series D Preferred Stock....

This provision specifically identifies the consideration that preferred shareholders will receive upon a cash-out merger of the type which occurred between Holdings and Ford Holdings Capital Corporation on December 31, 1995. It states explicitly that shareholders will be paid the liquidation preference—a specific, pre-determined dollar amount—and ac-crued and unpaid dividends—also a specifically determinable amount. The last phrase of the provision, stating that the holder is entitled to the consideration specified "and no more", reinforces the conclusion that the shareholders are not entitled to anything additional.

It is my judgment, then, that the terms of the Designations of the Cumulative Preferred clearly describe an agreement between the share-holders and the company regarding the consideration to be received by the shareholders in the event of a cash-out merger. There is no ambiguity in paragraph 4 regarding the value to be paid to shareholders if they are forced to give up their shares in a cash-out merger. The shareholders can not now come to this court seeking additional consideration in the merger through the appraisal process. Their security had a stated value in a merger which they have received.

The rights of the Auction Preferred Series D shareholders in the event of a cash-out merger are not as clearly expressed as those of the Cumulative Preferred shares. Most notably, there is no provision specifi-cally governing (and limiting) "Rights on ... Cash-out Merger." There are two interrelated provisions in the Designations which the corporation claims bear upon the rights of the shareholders to receive money in a cash-out merger.

The provisions state in relevant part:

> 3. *Dividends.*
>
> (b)(viii) [T]he Term Selection Agent *may give ... notice* [shortly before an auction is held to set the terms of the shares for the next

period] *specify [ing]* the [length of the] next succeeding Dividend Period ... and *whether such shares shall be entitled under the circumstances set forth in paragraph 5(d)(iii) to a premium upon ... [the] merger of [Holdings]* with or into any other corporation ("Merger Premium").... (Emphasis added)

Preferred Section 5(d)(iii) deals with voting rights. It provides in pertinent part:

Voting Rights ...

(d) *Right to Vote in Certain Events. ...*

(iii) Without the affirmative vote of the holders of a majority of the Outstanding shares of all series of Auction Preferred, Voting Preferred and Parity Preferred, voting as a single class, ... [Holdings] may not ... merge with or into any other corporation unless, in the case of a ... merger, each holder of shares of Auction Preferred, Voting Preferred and Parity Preferred shall receive, upon such ... merger, an amount in cash equal to the liquid preference, Merger Premium, if any, and accumulated and unpaid dividends....

Under Holding's interpretation of the Designations, the merger consideration is fixed by the operation of these provisions, just as it was in the case of the Cumulative Preferred shares. I cannot agree, although that may have been the imperfectly expressed intention of the drafter.

Paragraph 5(d)(iii) assures that the preferred shareholders will be able *to vote as a class* to prevent the corporation from engaging in a merger that a majority of holders find disadvantageous, but that the class *loses that power if* the preferred receive specified consideration—the liquidation preference ($100,000), a merger premium, if any is authorized, and accumulated and unpaid dividends. Thus, the provision implies that the class has no need for class vote protection—no risk of exploitation—if the preferred receives in the merger consideration equal to the liquidation value, etc. Such an implication would of course be consistent with an understanding that that consideration was all that the preferred was entitled to receive. While this implication is possible, it is not clear or compelled. The voting provisions are, in the end, voting provisions. The stipulated absence of a class vote is too frail a base upon which to rest the claim that there has been a contractual relinquishment of rights under Section 262 or, to state it differently, that the consideration that acts to remove the rights to a class vote also is conclusively established to be the "fair value."

Clear and direct drafting, of the type found in Section 4 of the Designation of the Cumulative Preferred, can implement a term conclusively fixing merger consideration of preferred. But the court may not cut stockholders off from a statutory right by the level of indirection that the company's argument requires.

Two principles mentioned above support the determination that the "fair value" of Series D Preferred is not contractually limited by the terms of the Designation. The first is the principle that statutory rights should ordinarily be waived only by clear affirmative words or actions. *See Red Clay Educ. Ass'n v. Bd. of Educ. of Red Clay Consol. Sch. Dist.,* Del. Ch., C.A. No. 11958, Chandler, V.C., 1992 WL 14965 at *7 (Jan. 16, 1992). The second is the principle that holds that ambiguity in a contractual document should be construed against the party that had the power to avoid the ambiguity. *See Kaiser Alum. Corp. v. Matheson,* Del.Supr., 681 A.2d 392 (1996). * * *

NOTES

1. In Rauch v. RCA Corp., 861 F.2d 29 (2d Cir.1988), the court held in applying Delaware law that a cash out merger payment of $40 to a class of preferred shareholders did not trigger a provision requiring a payment of $100 in the event the preferred shares were redeemed. Does this encourage sharp business practices in order to evade preferred shareholder rights?

2. For another case considering whether a corporate reorganization triggered preferred shareholder liquidation preferences see Quadrangle Offshore (Cayman) LLC v. Kenetech Corp., 1999 WL 893575 (Del.Ch.), aff'd, 751 A.2d 878 (Del.Supr.2000).

SECTION 3. PREFERRED AND COMMON SHAREHOLDER CONFLICTS

The rights of preferred shareholders sometimes conflict with efforts by common shareholders to reorganize a corporation experiencing financial difficulties. There is often tension in such instances because saving the corporation may result in a reduction of the liquidating or other preferences of the preferred stockholders. In considering such claims, the courts often try to save the corporation even at the expense of the preferred shareholders' interests. Conflicts over corporate actions may also develop between different classes of preferred shareholders.

EQUITY–LINKED INVESTORS, L.P. v. ADAMS
705 A.2d 1040 (Del.Ch.1997).

ALLEN, CHANCELLOR.

The case now under consideration involves a conflict between the financial interests of the holders of a convertible preferred stock with a liquidation preference, and the interests of the common stock. The conflict arises because the company, Genta Incorporated, is on the lip of insolvency and in liquidation it would probably be worth substantially less than the $30 million liquidation preference of the preferred stock. Thus, if the liquidation preference of the preferred were treated as a liability of Genta, the firm would certainly be insolvent now. Yet Genta, a bio-pharmaceutical company that has never made a profit, does have several promising technologies in research and there is some ground to think that the value of products that might be developed from those technologies could be very great.[2] Were that to occur, naturally, a large part of the "upside" gain would accrue to the benefit of the common stock, in equity the residual owners of the firm's net cash flows. (Of course, whatever the source of funds that would enable a nearly insolvent company to achieve that result would also negotiate for a share of those future gains—which is what this case is about). But since the current net worth of the company would be put at risk in such an effort—or more accurately would continue at risk—if Genta continues to try to develop these opportunities, any loss that may eventuate will in effect fall, not on the common stock, but on the preferred stock.

As the story sketched below shows, the Genta board sought actively to find a means to continue the firm in operation so that some chance to develop commercial products from its promising technologies could be achieved. It publicly announced its interest in finding new sources of capital. Contemporaneously, the holders of the preferred stock, relatively few institutional investors, were seeking a means to cut their losses, which meant, in effect, liquidating Genta and distributing most or all of its assets to the preferred. The contractual rights of the preferred stock did not, however, give the holders the necessary legal power to force this course of action on the corporation. Negotiations held between Genta's management and representatives of the preferred stock with respect to the rights of the preferred came to an unproductive and somewhat unpleasant end in January 1997.

Shortly thereafter, Genta announced that a third party source of additional capital had been located and that an agreement had been reached that would enable the corporation to pursue its business plan for a further period. The evidence indicates that at the time set for the closing of that transaction, Genta had available sufficient cash to cover its operations for only one additional week. A Petition in Bankruptcy had been prepared by counsel.

This suit by a lead holder of the preferred stock followed the announcement of the loan transaction. Plaintiff is Equity–Linked Investors, L.P. (together with its affiliate herein referred to as Equity–Linked), one of the institutional investors that holds Genta's Series A preferred stock. Equity–Linked also holds a relatively small amount of Genta's common stock, which it received as a dividend on its preferred. The suit challenges the transaction in which Genta borrowed on a secured basis some

---

2. Were one highly confident that all available information about those prospects was widely available and that non-public capital markets were highly efficient, one would be skeptical that a disjunction between liquidation value and management's envisioned long-term value could exist. Very good information about these research properties is not publicly available, however, and the market for bank loans or small private placements is surely imperfectly efficient. In all events the law admits of the possibility of such disjunction.

$3,000,000 and received other significant consideration from Paramount Capital Asset Management, Inc., a manager of the Aries Fund (together referred to as "Aries") in exchange for a note, warrants exercisable into half of Genta's outstanding stock, and other consideration. The suit seeks an injunction or other equitable relief against this transaction.

While *from a realistic or finance perspective,* the heart of the matter is the conflict between the interests of the institutional investors that own the preferred stock and the economic interests of the common stock, *from a legal perspective,* the case has been presented as one on behalf of the common stock, or more correctly on behalf of all holders of equity securities. The legal theory of the case, as it was tried, was that the Aries transaction was a "change of corporate control" transaction that placed upon Genta special obligations—"Revlon duties"—which the directors failed to satisfy.

While the facts out of which this dispute arises indisputably entail the imposition by the board of (or continuation of) economic risks upon the preferred stock which the holders of the preferred did not want, and while this board action was taken for the benefit largely of the common stock, those facts do not constitute a breach of duty. While the board in these circumstances could have made a different business judgment, in my opinion, it violated no duty owed to the preferred in not doing so. The special protections offered to the preferred are contractual in nature. *See Ellingwood v. Wolf's Head Oil Refining Co.,* Del.Supr., 38 A.2d 743, 747 (1944). The corporation is, of course, required to respect those legal rights. But, aside from the insolvency point just alluded to, generally it will be the duty of the board, where discretionary judgment is to be exercised, to prefer the interests of common stock—as the good faith judgment of the board sees them to be—to the interests created by the special rights, preferences, *etc.,* of preferred stock, where there is a conflict. *See Katz v. Oak Industries, Inc.,* Del. Ch., 508 A.2d 873, 879 (1986). The facts of this case, as they are explained below, do not involve any violation by the board of any special right or privilege of the Series A preferred stock, nor of any residual right of the preferred as owners of equity.

As I have said, that is, I think, the heart of this matter. But the case has been presented, not as a preferred stock case, but as a "Revlon" case. The plaintiff now purports to act as a holder of common stock. In effect, the plaintiff says: "Certainly the board can raise funds to try to realize its long-term business plan of developing commercial products from the company's research, (even though we holders of preferred stock are bearing the risk of it), but if the financing it arranges constitutes a 'change in corporate control,' then it must proceed in a way that satisfies the relevant legal test". Relying upon the teachings of *Paramount Communications v. QVC Network,* Del.Supr., 637 A.2d 34 (1993), plaintiff argues that the board did not satisfy the relevant legal test because, it says, defendants did not search for the best deal. Specifically, the board did not ask the holders of the preferred stock what they would have paid for the consideration given by Genta to Aries. The preferred, plaintiff says, would have "paid more" and that *would have benefited the common or all equity.*

For the reasons set forth below, ... I conclude that the directors of Genta were independent with respect to the Aries transaction, acted in good faith in arranging and committing the company to that transaction, and, in the circumstances faced by them and the company, were well informed of the available alternatives to try to bring about the long-term business plan of the board. In my opinion, they breached no duty owed to the corporation or any of the holders of its equity securities. Moreover, if tested judicially by a standard other than the "business judgment rule," the board's actions continue to appear sound. That is, in the circumstances, the board's actions appear reasonable in relation to the board's goal of achieving its valid business plan. While the board had no legally enforceable means to assure that the Aries transaction would achieve that goal, that transaction offered several attributes that permitted the board reasonably to conclude that it was the only available alternative. Indeed, in my opinion, given the history of the parties as of January 1997, it would be perfectly reasonable to conclude that any proposal that the plaintiff might make would be aimed at achieving, not the business plan the board legitimately sought to facilitate, but the dismantling of the company. While certainly some corporations at some points ought to be liquidated, when that point occurs is a question of business judgment ordinarily and in this instance. * * *

As of January 28, 1997, the capital structure of Genta comprised 39,991,626 shares of common stock; 528,100 shares of Series A preferred stock; and 1,424 shares of Series C preferred stock outstanding. The original investment by the common stock had been about $58 million. The Series A preferred had originally invested $30 million. Something less than $10 million had been raised from later classes of preferred, much of which had subsequently been converted to common stock.

The Series A preferred stock was issued in 1993 at $50 per share. It carries a $50 per share liquidation premium ($30 million in total). It had a dividend paid in common stock for the first two years and earns a $5 per share cumulative dividend, payable if, as, and when declared for subsequent years. In the event of a "fundamental change," holders of Series A preferred stock would have an option to have their shares redeemed by the company at $50 per share, plus accrued dividends. Among events that would constitute a "fundamental change" would be a delisting of Genta stock on the Nasdaq.[3] More important for this case, Genta was contractually obligated to redeem the Series A shares on September 23, 1996 with cash or common stock and, if common stock, to use its best efforts to

---

3. A fundamental change would occur if there were a change in voting power of the company greater than 60%, a merger or transfer of the joint venture, or a substantial reduction of the public market for Genta common stock, as would occur in the event of a delisting from Nasdaq. An occurrence of a fundamental change due to a delisting from Nasdaq became a realistic threat as of December 1996. In the event of a fundamental change, the Series A shareholders would become creditors of the company and could potentially require the company to enter into bankruptcy proceedings.

arrange a public underwriting of the common stock. This obligation, and the factors which prevented the redemption from occurring, occasioned the long negotiation with the holders of the preferred stock discussed below.

In addition to the foregoing, the preferred had certain governance rights. For example, the holders were entitled to notice of board meetings and were to be given rights to inspect corporate books and visit and observe board meetings.

The lack of a product that generates substantial positive cash flows, coupled with an active research and development agenda, has led to a notable (later, a somewhat desperate) search for sources of new investment capital. Genta engaged in a series of small equity placements in 1995 and 1996. In December 1995, it placed a $3 million Regulation S offering of Series B convertible preferred stock. In March 1996, it issued $6 million of Series C convertible preferred stock. Finally, on September 17, 1996, it placed a $2 million Regulation S offering of convertible debentures.[4]

By the spring of 1996, it became quite apparent that as of September the company would have insufficient cash to redeem the preferred with cash and, that while common stock would be available, the company's good faith efforts to arrange a firm commitment underwriting of that stock would in all likelihood have no reasonable prospect of success. Genta's board retained Alex. Brown & Sons Incorporated ("Alex.Brown") to advise and assist the company in dealing with its inability to provide either cash or an assured underwriting of its common stock. In addition, the company asked Alex. Brown to attempt to locate potential sources of equity financing for Genta and to participate in negotiations with Skye-Phanna. In June 1996, Genta retained an additional firm, Henson/Montrose, to assist it in locating potential equity investors in Asia.

In July 1996, plaintiff and five other investors holding Series A stock created the Series A Preferred Ad Hoc Committee to act as a bargaining agent with the company. The Committee was intensely interested in getting some return on the Series A and, no doubt, was interested in slowing or stopping the losses that the holders were implicitly realizing as the company continued to lose money.

At the first meeting between the committee and the company (July 1996), Alex. Brown proposed for discussion a three part restructuring. Two elements of that proposal involved the sale of the antisense and JBL businesses. The third part of the proposal involved the sale of a *controlling block* of Genta stock to SkyePharma, in exchange for SkyePharma's interest in the joint venture. Under this proposal, the obligation to the preferred stock would be satisfied and the common stock would continue to have an equity interest in Genta, which would continue to develop the intellectual property in the joint venture.

---

4. Only 1,424 shares of the Series C preferred stock remain outstanding, the rest of the shares issued in these offerings having been converted into common stock.

On August 14, 1996, Genta issued a press release disclosing its difficult cash situation and its search for financing alternatives, including a potential restructuring or an equity investment that would permit it to continue its operations. The press release stated that:

The Company is in discussions with potential corporate partners and other sources regarding collaborative agreements, restructurings and other financing arrangements and is actively seeking additional equity financing ... If such funding is unavailable, the Company will deplete its cash in September 1996 and will be forced to license or sell certain of its assets and technology, scale back or eliminate some or all of its development programs and further reduce its workforce and spending. If such measures are not successfully completed, the Company will be required to discontinue its operations.

On August 19, 1996, the three part restructuring proposal was formally presented to the Series A committee by Alex. Brown. As discussed above, the plan included the sale or spin-off of the two businesses and the SkyePharma proposal, in which the Series A holders would convert their shares into a minority block of Genta's common stock, with SkyePharma becoming Genta's controlling shareholder. The proportionate interest of the pre-existing Genta common stockholders would be severely diluted as a result. The Series A holders did not accept this proposal.

The prospect of bankruptcy thus was discussed. According to a later Alex. Brown report to the Genta board, the Series A committee took the position that the preferred would "wait and see if [Genta would] run out of money and then get [delisted]...." A delisting would give the preferred stock the legal right to the liquidation preference, allowing them to place the company into bankruptcy.* * *

In September, Genta gave the Series A holders an option to convert their shares into common stock, but could provide no underwriting in any event. Genta offered to effectuate the conversion or to permit the preferred stock simply to remain outstanding for the time. Due to the low market price of Genta's common stock, (less than $1 per share) an immediate conversion into common stock was not an economically attractive option. Only 10% of the Series A stockholders elected to convert into common stock without an underwriting. The remaining Series A shareholders continued to negotiate with Genta concerning its restructuring proposal. * * *

Recognizing that Genta would not have sufficient cash for its payroll due on February 1, Genta's bankruptcy lawyers had begun preparing the necessary papers to file for bankruptcy on January 29. At this juncture, faced with an imminent decision, Dr. Adams informed the board that he opposed the restructuring proposal in its present form. Further, Dr. Adams reported to the board that he had told Mr. Gineris that the current Series A proposal was unacceptable. * * *

Pursuant to a January 28 letter of intent, Genta and Aries agreed to enter into a two step financing on the following terms. The first step, which by the time of trial of this case had already occurred, involved Aries loaning Genta $3 million in cash. In exchange, Aries received convertible secured bridge notes with a $3 million face value, 7.8 million Class A warrants with a $.001 per share exercise price, and 12.2 million Class B warrants with a per share exercise price of $.55. The bridge notes are immediately convertible into 600,000 shares of Series D convertible preferred stock with a $10 stated value per share. In the event that Aries converts this preferred stock, Aries would receive 20 million shares of Genta common stock. Together the transaction offers Aries the right to acquire 40 million shares of Genta common stock—a controlling interest in the company.

In addition to this consideration in the form of debt and equity, Aries received an immediate contractual right to require the Genta board to cause a sufficient number of its designees to be added to the board so as to constitute a majority of the board. In the event that Aries does not satisfy its future obligations to raise additional capital (the second tier financing), however, this right will terminate. * * *

Immediately prior to the hearing in this action, Equity Linked delivered a proposal to Genta that offered to extend a $3.6 million loan to Genta on the same terms as those reflected in the Aries transaction. This offer appears to have been an attempt by plaintiff to demonstrate that it would have been willing to do the same deal on terms at least as favorable as those offered by Aries.

The broad question is whether the foregoing facts constitute a breach of duty by the directors of Genta. The theory of the original complaint was that the Aries transaction represented a bad faith exercise of corporate power; that the purpose of the transaction was simply to protect the employment of the incumbent officers; and that a sweetheart deal with Dr. Rosenwald's entity was arranged in order to do that. Indeed, the discovery here showed that Rosenwald was very much an arm's length negotiator and that there was no comfort offered to (or sought by) existing management. Rather, the evidence tends to show that the majority of the Genta board was motivated by a desire to see the enterprise finally pay-off by developing or participating in a portion of the development of some of its intellectual properties.

In all events, at trial, plaintiff's theory was no longer that the transaction represented an effort to protect management. The legal theory that plaintiff advanced at trial does not really acknowledge the true nature of the financial conflict at the heart of the matter. Rather, plaintiff's trial theory acts as if plaintiff were simply like any other holder of *common stock* and sought a corrective order so that a higher price for the common could be achieved in a sale.

The claim now is that the board "transferred control" of the company and that in such a transaction it is necessary that the board act reasonably to get the highest price, which this board did not do. Plaintiff urges that the special duty recognized in *Revlon, Inc. v. MacAndrews & Forbes*

Holdings, Inc., Del.Supr., 506 A.2d 173 (1986), arose here because (1) Aries has a contract right to designate a majority of the Genta board and (2) Aries acquired warrants that if exercised would give it the power to control any election of the Genta board. Thus, this transaction is seen as similar to the noted case of *Paramount Communications Inc. v. QVC Network Inc.,* Del.Supr., 637 A.2d 34 (1993). Plaintiff claims that the board hid the fact that control might be for sale, instead of announcing it and creating price competition respecting it. In support of the assertion that the board could have done better for common stockholders, like themselves, plaintiff points to the litigation produced alternative proposal of the Series A preferred stock. The idea is that this alternative is financially a little better and that if the directors would have met their "Revlon duty" then, this or another better alternative would have come to light. In this way, plaintiff claims the interests of all holders of equity securities would have been better off because Genta would have gotten greater value.

Based upon a preponderance of the admissible, credible testimony, it is my opinion ... that the Genta board fully satisfied its obligations of good faith and attention with respect to the Aries transaction. The directors of Genta did not, therefore, breach a fiduciary duty owed to the corporation or any of its equity security holders. I conclude that with respect to this transaction, the board was independent; it was motivated throughout by a good faith attempt to maximize long-term corporate value; and that the board and senior management were appropriately informed of alternatives available *to implement the business plan that the directors sought to achieve.* Moreover, if reviewed under a reasonableness criterion, I conclude that the board acted in an entirely reasonable way to achieve its goal and that its goal, although obviously one that reasonable minds could disagree about—was not one that was impermissible. * * *

The charge of failure to search appropriately for alternatives that would have been more beneficial to the owners of the company's equity securities is deeply unconvincing on the evidence. The evidence is completely inconsistent with the notion that some other (third) party, who was unknown, would have offered a better deal to Genta. The board, with the advice and assistance of professional advisors, had thoroughly explored that possibility. The more plausible supposition is that if the board had gone back to the Series A preferred stock once its deal with Aries was substantially negotiated, the preferred would likely have authorized a proposal like the one that the holders ultimately put forth in the litigation, which I will assume is in certain respects superior. Nevertheless, I conclude that the board's failure to afford the preferred stock an opportunity to meet or exceed the Aries proposal was quite reasonable in the circumstances (some reasonable minds may have thought it likely to be futile and wasteful). * * *

Moreover, the Series A knew that management was looking for financing. There were press releases to that effect. Yet they were unwilling to put in more money. The preferred is of course not to be criticized for that. They have every right to send no good dollars after bad ones. Indeed, they had the right to withhold necessary consents to salvage plans unless their demands were satisfied. But when plaintiff now contends that the Genta board was required by fiduciary duty to the company's common stockholders to go back to the Series A preferred after finding an investor willing to do what the Series A sought to prevent, I cannot agree. Delaware law cannot sensibly criticize the Genta board of directors for recognizing the practical reality with which they were faced and acting on their permissible vision of their duty.

It was quite reasonable for the Genta board to conclude that, if the policy of the board was to try to find a way to finance further research and development in order to attempt to benefit the residual owners of the firm, that any proposal that transferred corporate control or potential control to the preferred stock was a highly dubious way to achieve *that goal.* * * *

Thus, I conclude in the circumstances disclosed by the balance of the credible evidence, that the Genta board concluded in good faith that the corporation's interests were best served by a transaction that it thought would maximize potential long-run wealth creation and that in the circumstances, including the potential insolvency of the company and the presence of a $30 million liquidation preference, the board acted reasonably in pursuit of the highest achievable *present* value of the Genta common stock, by proceeding as it did.

Judgment will be granted for defendants and against plaintiff. Each party to bear its own costs.

ELLIOTT ASSOCIATES, LP v. AVATEX CORP.

715 A.2d 843 (Del.1998).

VEASEY, CHIEF JUSTICE:

In this case of first impression, we hold that certain preferred stockholders have the right to a class vote in a merger where: (1) the certificate of incorporation expressly provides such a right in the event of any "amendment, alteration or repeal, whether by merger, consolidation or otherwise" of any of the provisions of the certificate of incorporation; (2) the certificate of incorporation that provides protections for the preferred stock is nullified and thereby repealed by the merger; and (3) the result of the transaction would materially and adversely affect the rights, preferences, privileges or voting power of those preferred stockholders. In so holding, we distinguish prior Delaware precedent narrowly because of the inclusion by the drafters of the phrase, "whether by merger, consolidation or otherwise."

Defendant Avatex Corporation ("Avatex") is a Delaware corporation that has outstanding both common and preferred stock. The latter includes two distinct series of outstanding preferred stock: "First Series Preferred" and "Series A Preferred." Plaintiffs in these consolidated cases are all preferred stockholders of defendant Avatex. The individual defendants are all members of the Avatex board of directors.

Avatex created and incorporated Xetava Corporation ("Xetava") as its wholly-owned subsidiary on April 13, 1998, and the following day announced its intention to merge with and into Xetava. Under the terms of the proposed merger, Xetava is to be the surviving corporation. Once the transaction is consummated, Xetava will immediately change its name to Avatex Corporation. The proposed merger would cause a conversion of the preferred stock of Avatex into common stock of Xetava. The merger will effectively eliminate Avatex' certificate of incorporation, which includes the certificate of designations creating the Avatex preferred stock and setting forth its rights and preferences.[5] The terms of the merger do not call for a class vote of these preferred stockholders. Herein lies the heart of the legal issue presented in this case.

Plaintiffs filed suit in the Court of Chancery to enjoin the proposed merger, arguing, among other things, that the transaction required the consent of two-thirds of the holders of the First Series Preferred stock. Defendants responded with a motion for judgment on the pleadings, which the Court of Chancery granted, finding that the provisions governing the rights of the First Series Preferred stockholders do not require such consent.

The plaintiffs allege that, because of Avatex' anemic financial state, "all the value of Avatex is [currently] in the preferred stock." By forcing the conversion of the preferred shares into common stock of the surviving corporation, however, the merger would place current preferred stockholders of Avatex on an even footing with its common stockholders. In fact, the Avatex preferred stockholders will receive in exchange for their preferred stock approximately 73% of Xetava common stock, and the common stockholders of Avatex will receive approximately 27% of the common stock of Xetava.

Under the terms of the Avatex certificate of incorporation, First Series stockholders have no right to vote except on:

> (a) any "amendment, alteration or repeal" of the certificate of incorporation "whether by merger, consolidation or otherwise," that
>
> (b) "materially and adversely" affects the rights of the First Series stockholders.

The text of the terms governing the voting rights of the First Series Preferred Stock is set forth in the certificate of designations as follows:

---

5. When certificates of designations become effective, they constitute amendments to the certificate of incorporation so that the rights of preferred stockholders become part of the certificate of incorporation. Accordingly, we will use the term "certificate" to refer to the certificate of designations as integrated into the certificate of incorporation. *See Kaiser Aluminum Corp. v. Matheson*, Del. Supr., 681 A.2d 392, 394 n.3 (1996) (citing 8 Del. C. §§ 102(a)(4), 151(g)).

Except as expressly provided hereinafter in this Section (6) or as otherwise ... required by law, the First Series Preferred Stock shall have no voting rights....

So long as any shares of First Series Preferred Stock remain outstanding, the *consent* of the holders of at least two-thirds of the shares of the *First Series Preferred Stock* outstanding at the time (voting separately as a class ...) ... *shall be necessary to permit, effect or validate* any one or more of the following: ...

> (b) *The amendment, alteration or repeal, whether by merger consolidation or otherwise, of any of the provisions of the* Restated *Certificate* of Incorporation or of [the certificate of designations] *which would materially and adversely affect any right, preference, privilege or voting power of the First Series Preferred Stock* or of the holders thereof ...

These are the operative terms of Section 6 of the certificate of designations (with emphasis supplied) setting forth the rights and preferences of the First Series Preferred stock that became effective March 18, 1983. On September 14, 1983 a new certificate of designations became effective with respect to the Second Series Preferred stock. There is, however, no Second Series Preferred stock outstanding. Unlike the First Series certificate, Section 6 of the Second Series certificate expressly provides the Second Series Preferred stock with a right to vote on any consolidation or merger (with certain exceptions not relevant here) to which Avatex is a party:

> So long as any shares of the Second Series Preferred Stock remain outstanding, the consent of the holders of at least a majority of the shares of the Second Series Preferred Stock outstanding at the time ... shall be necessary to permit or approve any of the following: ...
>
> (b) The consolidation or merger of the Corporation with or into any other corporation unless....

* * * Delaware law permits corporations to create and issue stock that carries no voting power. Professor Buxbaum, in his seminal article on preferred stock nearly 45 years ago, noted, among many other cogent observations, that: (a) statutes often permit alteration of preferred stock rights and preferences by merger; (b) the merger may be with a "paper subsidiary created for that purpose with no independent business validity"; (c) "corporate articles [often] require consent of two-thirds (or a majority) of the preferred shareholders as a class for the consummation of any merger...."; and (d) courts have struggled with "controls in the name ... of 'fairness' and generally abandoned them [, which] is as it should be [since the] issue is one of corporate power."

The Avatex certificate of incorporation provides that Avatex preferred shares have no right to vote except on matters set forth therein or required by law. This denial of the right to vote is subject to an exception carved out for any "amendment, alteration or repeal" of the certificate "whether by merger, consolidation or otherwise" that "materially and adversely" affects the rights of the preferred stockholders. Such an event requires the consent of two-thirds of the First Series Preferred stockholders voting as a class.

This appeal, then, reduces to a narrow legal question: whether the "amendment, alteration or repeal" of the certificate of incorporation is caused "by merger, consolidation or otherwise" thereby requiring a two-thirds class vote of the First Series Preferred stockholders, it being assumed for purposes of this appeal that their rights would be "materially and adversely" affected. The Court of Chancery answered this question in the negative. Although we respect that Court's craftsman like analysis, we are constrained to disagree with its conclusion.

Relying primarily on *Warner Communications Inc. v. Chris–Craft Industries, Inc.,* [583 A.2d 962 (Del.)] the Court of Chancery held that it was only the *conversion* of the stock as a result of the merger, and not the *amendment, alteration or repeal* of the certificate, that would adversely affect the preferred stockholders. It is important to keep in mind, however, that the terms of the preferred stock in *Warner* were significantly different from those present here, because in *Warner* the phrase "whether by merger, consolidation or otherwise" was not included. The issue here, therefore, is whether the presence of this additional phrase in the Avatex certificate is an outcome-determinative distinction from *Warner.*

In *Warner,* the question was whether the Series B preferred stock of Warner Communications, Inc. had the right to a class vote on a proposed merger of Warner with Time, Inc. (renamed Time Warner Inc.) and TW Sub, its wholly-owned subsidiary. As the first step in a two-step transaction, Time had acquired approximately 50% of Warner's common stock in a tender offer. The second step was the "back-end" merger in which TW Sub was merged into Warner, which survived as a wholly-owned subsidiary of Time. The Warner common stock not held by Time was converted into cash, securities and other property. In the merger, the Warner Series B preferred would be converted into Time Series BB preferred stock. The parties stipulated that the Warner Series B stockholders would thereby be adversely affected.

The Chancellor held that the drafters of the Warner Series B certificate of designations did not intend for two-thirds of the Series B stockholders to have a veto over every merger in which their interest would be adversely affected because the right to vote was conferred expressly (as it must under Delaware law), and "only in narrowly defined circumstances ... not present here." * * *

Plaintiffs here argue that *Warner* is distinguishable for three reasons: (1) the fact that the words "whether by merger, consolidation or otherwise" were not present in the Warner Series B certificate; (2) in *Warner,* unlike here, the preferred stockholders did not remain as stockholders of the surviving corporation, whose certificate arguably was amended and on which the preferred stockholders in *Warner* were relying for a right to a class vote; and (3) in *Warner,* unlike here, the merger was not an attempt simply to change the rights of the preferred stock, but rather there was economic and business substance to that transaction beyond an effort to do indirectly what could not be done directly.

In our view, only the first reason is valid in this appeal. The third reason cited is not before us because we do not examine the economic quality of the merger for purposes of this appeal. The second reason strikes us as a distinction without a difference. Here the First Series Preferred stock of Avatex is converted to common stock of the surviving corporation, Xetava, a newly formed corporation admittedly a wholly owned subsidiary of Avatex created for the sole purpose of effecting this merger and eliminating the rights of the Avatex First Series Preferred. In *Warner,* the Warner Series B Preferred also received a new security— Time Series BB Preferred—a senior security issued by the surviving corporation, Time (renamed Time Warner). This was accomplished by using TW Sub, Time's wholly-owned subsidiary, as the merger partner of Warner. Since we do not reach the question of the economic quality of the transaction, it makes no difference for purposes of this analysis (as plaintiffs argue) that in *Warner* there were two distinct acts that operated independently—that the substitution of charters was between Warner and TW Sub and the exchange of shares was between Warner and Time. The operative events here are that the proposed downstream merger of Avatex into Xetava results in the conversion of Avatex stock to Xetava stock and the elimination "by merger" of the certificate protections granted to the Avatex First Series Preferred. Thus, it is *both* the stock conversion *and* the repeal of the Avatex certificate that causes the adverse effect to the First Series Preferred. In *Warner,* it was only the stock conversion that caused the adverse effect because the phrase, "whether by merger, consolidation or otherwise" was not present. * * *

Articulation of the rights of preferred stockholders is fundamentally the function of corporate drafters. Construction of the terms of preferred stock is the function of courts. This Court's function is essentially one of contract interpretation against the background of Delaware precedent. These precedential parameters are simply stated: Any rights, preferences and limitations of preferred stock that distinguish that stock from common stock must be expressly and clearly stated, as provided by statute.[6] Therefore, these rights, preferences and limitations will not be presumed or implied.[7] The other doctrine states that when there is a hopeless

---

6. *See* 8 Del. C. § 151(a), which provides, in pertinent part:

  (a) Every corporation may issue 1 or more classes of stock or 1 or more series of stock within any class thereof, any or all of which classes may be of stock with par value or stock without par value and which classes or series may have such voting powers, full or limited, or no voting powers, and such designations, preferences and relative, participating, optional or other special rights, and qualifications, limitations or restrictions thereof, *as shall be stated and expressed* in the certificate of incorporation or of any amendment thereto, or in the resolution or resolutions providing for the issue of such stock adopted by the board of directors pursuant to authority expressly vested in it by the provisions of its certificate of incorporation. . . .

7. *Rothschild Int'l Corp. v. Liggett Group Inc.,* Del Supr., 474 A.2d 133, 136 (1984). *See also Waggoner v. Laster,* Del. Supr., 581 A.2d 1127, 1134–35 (1990). In *Waggoner,* the term "strictly

ambiguity attributable to the corporate drafter that could mislead a reasonable investor, such ambiguity must be construed in favor of the reasonable expectations of the investor and against the drafter. This latter doctrine is not applicable here because there is no ambiguity.

In our view, the rights of the First Series Preferred are expressly and clearly stated in the Avatex certificate. The drafters of this instrument could not reasonably have intended any consequence other than granting to the First Series Preferred stock the right to consent by a two-thirds class vote to any merger that would result in the elimination of the protections in the Avatex certificate if the rights of the holders of that stock would thereby be adversely affected. The First Series Preferred stock rights granted by the corporate drafters here are the functional equivalent of a provision that would expressly require such consent if a merger were to eliminate any provision of the Avatex certificate resulting in materially adverse consequences to the holders of that security. * * *

The path for future drafters to follow in articulating class vote provisions is clear. When a certificate (like the Warner certificate or the Series A provisions here) grants only the right to vote on an amendment, alteration or repeal, the preferred have no class vote in a merger. When a certificate (like the First Series Preferred certificate here) adds the terms "whether by merger, consolidation or otherwise" and a merger results in an amendment, alteration or repeal that causes an adverse effect on the preferred, there would be a class vote. When a certificate grants the preferred a class vote in any merger or in any merger where the preferred stockholders receive a junior security, such provisions are broader than those involved in the First Series Preferred certificate. We agree with plaintiffs' argument that these results are uniform, predictable and consistent with existing law relating to the unique attributes of preferred stock. * * *

The judgment of the Court of Chancery is reversed and the matter is remanded for further proceedings consistent with this Opinion.

---

construed" was used when describing the judicial approach to determining stock preferences in a case where the holding was that a general reservation clause in a certificate of incorporation was insufficient to expressly reserve authority in the board to establish preferences. We continue to approve that holding, but we do not approve the continued use of the term "strict construction" as appropriately describing the judicial process of analyzing the existence and scope of the contractual statement of preferences in certificates of incorporation or certificates of designations. We believe that the appropriate articulation of that analysis was set forth in our opinion in *Rothschild:* "Preferential rights are contractual in nature and therefore are governed by the express provisions of a company's certificate of incorporation. Stock preferences must also be clearly expressed and will not be presumed." 474 A.2d at 136. The term "strict construction" (as contrasted to "liberal construction") is often used to describe the approach to statutes in derogation of common law, *see Waggoner*, 581 A.2d at 1135 n.9, or to certain contracts *(e.g.,* forfeitures, penalties and restrictive covenants, *see* 4 WALTER H.E. JAEGER, WILLISTON ON CONTRACTS § 602A (3d ed. 1961)). In light of other doctrines, continued use of the term "strict construction" as a substitute for, or gloss on, the *Rothschild* formulation is problematic.

BENCHMARK CAPITAL PARTNERS IV, L.P. v. VAGUE

2002 WL 1732423 (Del.Ch.2002).

NOBLE, VICE CHANCELLOR

This is another one of those cases in which sophisticated investors have negotiated protective provisions in a corporate charter to define the balance of power or certain economic rights as between the holders of junior preferred stock and senior preferred stock. These provisions tend to come in to play when additional financing becomes necessary. One side cannot or will not put up more money; the other side is willing to put up more money, but will not do so without obtaining additional control or other diminution of the rights of the other side. In short, these cases focus on the tension between minority rights established through the corporate charter and the corporation's need for additional capital.

In this case, Plaintiff Benchmark Capital Partners IV, L.P. ("Benchmark") invested in the first two series of the Defendant Juniper Financial Corp.'s ("Juniper") preferred stock. When additional capital was required, Defendant Canadian Imperial Bank of Commerce ("CIBC") was an able and somewhat willing investor. As a result of that investment, Benchmark's holdings were relegated to the status of junior preferred stock and CIBC acquired a controlling interest in Juniper by virtue of ownership of senior preferred stock. The lot of a holder of junior preferred stock is not always a happy one. Juniper's Fifth Amendment and Restated Certificate of Incorporation (the "Certificate") contains several provisions to protect the holders of junior preferred stock from abuse by the holder of senior preferred stock. Two of those provisions are of particular importance here. The Certificate grants the junior preferred stockholders a series vote on corporate actions that would "materially adversely change the rights, preferences and privileges of the [series of junior preferred stock]." In addition, the junior preferred stockholders are entitled to a class vote before Juniper may "authorize or issue, or obligate itself to issue, any other equity security . . . senior to or on a parity with the [junior preferred stock]."

The Certificate provides that those provisions protecting the rights of the junior preferred stockholders may be waived by CIBC. CIBC may not, however, exercise this power "if such amendment, waiver or modification would . . . diminish or alter the liquidation preference or other financial or economic rights" of the junior preferred stockholders or would shelter breaches of fiduciary duties.

Juniper now must seek more capital in order to satisfy regulators and business requirements, and CIBC, and apparently only CIBC, is willing to provide the necessary funds. Juniper initially considered amending its charter to allow for the issuance of another series of senior preferred stock. When it recognized that the protective provisions of the Certificate could be invoked to thwart that strategy, it elected to structure a more complicated transaction that now consists principally of a merger and a sale of Series D Preferred Stock to CIBC. The merger is scheduled to occur on July 16, 2002 with a subsidiary merging with and into Juniper that will leave Juniper as the surviving corporation, but with a restated certificate of incorporation that will authorize the issuance of a new series of senior preferred stock and new junior preferred stock with a reduced liquidation preference and will cause a number of other adverse consequences or limitations to be suffered by the holders of the junior preferred. As part of this overall financing transaction, Juniper, after the merger, intends to issue a new series of preferred, the Series D Preferred Stock, to CIBC in exchange for a $50 million capital contribution. As the result of this sequence of events, the equity holdings of the junior preferred stockholders will be reduced from approximately 29% to 7%. Juniper will not obtain approval for these actions from the holders of the junior preferred stock. It contends that the protective provisions do not give the junior preferred stockholders a vote on these plans and, furthermore, in any event, that CIBC has the right to waive the protective provisions through the Series C Trump.

Benchmark, on the other hand, asserts that the protective provisions preclude Juniper's and CIBC's heavy-handed conduct and brings this action to prevent the violation of the junior preferred stockholder's fundamental right to vote on these corporate actions as provided in the Certificate and to obtain interim protection from the planned evisceration of its equity interest in Juniper. Because of the imminence of the merger and the issuance of the new senior preferred stock, Benchmark has moved for a preliminary injunction to stop the proposed transaction. This is the Court's decision on that motion.

Benchmark, a Delaware limited partnership based in Menlow Park, California, is a venture capital firm specializing in preferred stock investments. It manages more than $2 billion and has made approximately 50 preferred stock investments in the preceding 5 years.

Juniper is a Delaware corporation with its principal place of business in Wilmington, Delaware, where it has more than 300 employees. It is a financial services enterprise with the issuance of credit cards as its core business. Juniper Bank is Juniper's wholly-owned state-chartered banking subsidiary.

CIBC is a Canadian bank based in Toronto and controls Juniper through a subsidiary as the result of a $145 million investment in 2001.
* * *

Certificates of incorporation define contractual relationships not only among the corporation and its stockholders but also among the stockholders. Thus, the Certificate defines, as a matter of contract, both the relationship between Benchmark and Juniper and the relative relationship between Benchmark, as a holder of junior preferred stock, and CIBC, as the holder of senior preferred stock. For these reasons, courts look to general principles of contract construction in construing certificates of incorporation.

[A court's function in ascertaining the rights of preferred stockholders] is essentially one of contract interpretation against the background of Delaware precedent. These precedential parameters are simply stated: Any rights, preferences and limitations of preferred stock that distinguish that stock from common stock must be expressly and clearly stated, as provided by statute. Therefore, these rights, preferences and liquidations will not be presumed or implied.[8]

These principles also apply in construing the relative rights of holders of different series of preferred stock. * * *

Benchmark looks at the Series D Preferred financing and the merger that is integral to that transaction and concludes that the authorization of the Series D Preferred Stock and the other revisions to the Juniper certificate of incorporation accomplished as part of the merger will materially adversely affect the rights, preferences, and privileges of the junior preferred shares. Among the adverse affects to be suffered by Benchmark are a significant reduction in its right to a liquidation preference, the authorization of a new series of senior preferred stock that will further subordinate its interests in Juniper, and a reduction in other rights such as dividend priority. These adverse consequences will all be the product of the merger. Benchmark's existing Series A Preferred and Series B Preferred shares will cease to exist as of the merger and will be replaced with new Series A Preferred Stock, new Series B Preferred Stock, warrants, common stock, and a small amount of cash. One of the terms governing the new junior preferred stock will specify that those new junior preferred shares are not merely subordinate to Series C Preferred Stock, but they also will be subordinate to the new Series D Preferred Stock. Thus, the harm to Benchmark is directly attributable to the differences between the new junior preferred stock, authorized through the merger, and the old junior preferred stock as evidenced by the planned post-merger capital structure of Juniper.

Benchmark's challenge is confronted by a long line of Delaware cases which, in general terms, hold that protective provisions drafted to provide a class of preferred stock with a class vote before those shares' rights, preferences and privileges may be altered or modified do not fulfill their apparent purpose of assuring a class vote if adverse consequences flow from a merger and the protective provisions do not expressly afford protection against a merger. This result traces back to the language of 8 *Del. C.* § 242(b)(2), which deals with the rights of various classes of stock to vote on amendments to the certificate of incorporation that would "alter or change the powers, preferences, or special rights of the shares of such class so as to affect them adversely." That language is substantially the same as the language ("rights, preferences and privileges") of Sections C.6.c(ii) & C.6.d(ii). Where the drafters have tracked the statutory language relating to charter amendments in 8 *Del. C.* § 242(b), courts have been reluctant to expand those restrictions to encompass the separate

---

8. *Elliott Assocs., L.P. v. Avatex Corp.*, 715 A.2d 843, 852–53 (Del.1998) (footnotes omitted). *See* 8 Del. C. § 151. The Supreme Court in *Avatex* further noted that "strict construction" as an analytical methodology is "problematic" in interpreting such provisions in corporate charters. *See id.* 715 A.2d at 853 n.46.

process of merger as set forth in 8 *Del. C.* § 251, unless the drafters have made clear the intention to grant a class vote in the context of a merger. * * *

In short, to the extent that the merger adversely affects the rights, preferences and privileges of either the Series A Preferred or Series B Preferred Stock, those consequences are the product of a merger, a corporate event which the drafters of the protective provision could have addressed, but did not. Accordingly, I am satisfied that Benchmark has not demonstrated a reasonable probability of success on the merits of its claim that Sections C.6.c(ii) and C.6.d(ii) require a series vote on the merger contemplated as part of the Series D Transaction. * * *

Benchmark complains of the harm which will occur because of alterations to Juniper's capital structure resulting from modifications of the certificate of incorporation emerging from the merger. General language alone granting preferred stockholders a class vote on certain changes to the corporate charter (such as authorization of a senior series of stock) will not be read to require a class vote on a merger and its integral and accompanying modifications to the corporate charter and the corporation's capital structure. To reach the result sought by Benchmark, the protective rights " 'must * * * be clearly expressed and will not be presumed.' " Unfortunately for Benchmark, the requirements of a class vote for authorization of a new senior preferred stock through a merger was not "clearly expressed" in the Certificate. Against this background, I am reluctant both to presume that protection from a merger was intended and, perhaps more importantly, to create uncertainty in a complex area where *Avatex* has set down a framework for consistency. * * *

Under Section C.6.a(i), Juniper is also required to obtain class approval, unless effectively waived by CIBC, from its junior preferred holders before it can issue or obligate itself to issue a senior preferred stock. Juniper plans to issue its Series D Preferred Stock after the merger and at a time when the new Series A Preferred shares and the new Series B Preferred shares will be outstanding. The shares will not be issued as the result of the merger, but instead will be issued pursuant to the Purchase Agreement between CIBC and Juniper. Because the merger is not implicated by the issuance of the shares, there is no "background" precedent against which this act must be evaluated in the same sense as the case law addressing the consequences of mergers. These facts bring Juniper's proposed issuance of its Series D Preferred Stock squarely within the scope of the restrictions imposed by Section C.6.a(i) of the post-merger certificate. Specifically, to paraphrase that provision, so long as any shares of the new Series A Preferred or Series B Preferred are outstanding, Juniper may not, without the class vote or class consent of the new Series A Preferred and Series B Preferred stockholders, issue any senior equity security. While the restrictions of Section C.6.a(i) may be subject to the Series C Trump and, thus, may yet not prevent the issuance of the Series D Preferred Stock without the approval of the holders of the junior preferred stock, I am satisfied that Section C.6.a(i) applies, from the plain and unambiguous language of its text, to the issuance of Series D Preferred Stock when and as planned by Juniper. * * *

All of the class voting rights conferred upon the junior preferred holders by Section C.6.a(i) are subject to waiver by CIBC through the proper exercise of its Series C Trump. The Series C Trump is broad and (for present purposes) is restricted in application only if the corporate action for which the class vote is waived would "diminish or alter the liquidation preference or other financial or economic rights" of the holders of the junior preferred stock. Issuance of the Series D Preferred Stock will not "diminish or alter" Benchmark's liquidation preference—that was accomplished through the merger. The question thus becomes one of whether the issuance of a previously authorized senior preferred security "diminish[es] or alter[s]" the junior preferred shares' "financial or economic rights." * * *

The meaning to be given to the exception to Series C Trump or waiver is not free of ambiguity. There is no ambiguity in the actual grant of the Series C Trump to CIBC. Both sides agree that the Series C Trump, absent the exception, would provide CIBC with the authority it claims. Accordingly, the effectiveness of any exercise of the Series C Trump in this context depends upon the scope to be given to the exception. Benchmark suffers, in this context, because it must rely on the exception; terms of preferred shareholders' protective provisions "must ... be clearly expressed and will not be presumed"; and it bears the burden as the moving party on its motion for a preliminary injunction.

No words of explicit import clearly express the voting right the plaintiffs claim exists in this case. No positive evidence supports the claim that the drafters intended to create such a right. Although one might argue (as the plaintiffs do) that that right exists by implication, it does not exist by necessary implication. To adopt the plaintiff's position would amount to presuming a preferential voting right. In the present case, however, where (at least) an ambiguity exists, our law requires that it be resolved against creating the preference.

A preliminary injunction necessarily involves an initial determination on less than complete record and that limitation precludes a detailed consideration of extrinsic evidence. In light of the foregoing, I conclude that Benchmark has not demonstrated a reasonable probability of success on the merits of its claim that the waiver should not be available to CIBC. * * *

Therefore, for the foregoing reasons, Benchmark's motion for a preliminary injunction is denied. An order will be entered in accordance with this memorandum opinion.

DOPPELT v. PERINI CORP.

2002 WL 392289 (S.D.N.Y.2002), aff'd 53 Fed.Appx. 174 (2d Cir.2002).

McKENNA, DISTRICT JUDGE.

Frederick Doppelt ("Doppelt"), Arthur I. Caplan ("Caplan") and Michael Miller ("Miller") (collectively, "plaintiffs") commenced this action on behalf of themselves and other holders of Depository Convertible Exchangeable Preferred Shares ("Senior Preferred Stock") of Perini Corporation ("Perini") alleging breach of contract against defendant Perini and breach of fiduciary duty against the individually named directors (collectively, "individual defendants") of Perini. * * * For the reasons set forth below, the motions are granted and the case is dismissed.

Perini is a construction corporation organized and existing under the laws of the Commonwealth of Massachusetts. Its principal place of business is in Massachusetts but it maintains an office in New York and is registered in New York as a foreign corporation authorized to do business in the state.

In June 1987, Perini filed a prospectus and registration statement with the Securities and Exchange Commission ("SEC") in connection with the initial public offering of the Senior Preferred Stock. Thereafter, Perini sold 1,000,000 shares of the Senior Preferred Stock to the public at the price of $25.00 per share. According to plaintiffs, each share was entitled to receive annual cash dividends of $2.125. Under the heading "Description of Preferred Stock," the prospectus states, in relevant part, that:

> Dividends on the Preferred Stock will be cumulative from the date of original issue and shall be payable to the holder of record on the record date fixed for such payment. * * * Unless full cumulative dividends on the Preferred Stock have been paid or declared and funds therefore set apart for such payment, no cash dividends shall be declared or paid or other distribution made upon the Common Stock of the Company or any other stock of the Company ranking junior to or on a parity with the Preferred Stock as to dividends.

The prospectus generally provides that:

> [the] summary of terms ... contained in this Prospectus does not purport to be complete and is subject to, and qualified in its entirety by, the provisions of the Company's Restated Articles and the Certificate of Vote of Directors Establishing a Series of a Class of Stock fixing the relative rights and preferences of the Preferred Stock.

The Certificate of Vote of Director's Establishing a Series of a Class of Stock ("Certificate of Vote"), which was filed with the SEC along with the prospectus and registration statement provides, in relevant part, that:

> in no event (so long as any [Senior Preferred Stock] shall remain outstanding) shall any cash dividends whatsoever be declared or paid upon, nor shall any cash distribution be made upon, the Common

Stock, or any other stock of the corporation ranking junior to or on a parity with the [Senior Preferred Stock] as to dividends unless full cumulative dividends on all outstanding shares of [Senior Preferred Stock] for all dividend payment periods terminating on or prior to the date of the payment of such dividends shall have been paid or declared and funds therefore set apart for such payments.

According to plaintiffs, Perini paid cash dividends to the holders of Senior Preferred Stock from 1987 through 1995 but ceased making such payments on or about February 22, 1996 when Perini amended its revolving credit agreements with its banks. Under the modified credit agreements, Perini could no longer pay any dividends on any of its equity securities until, among other things, the credit line was repaid. (Id. P 35.) Thus, at that point, the unpaid dividends began to accrue despite alleged statements by Perini that it intended to continue making dividend payments to the Senior Preferred Stockholders once it satisfied the terms of its credit agreements. Plaintiffs claim that Perini refused to resume paying dividends to the Senior Preferred Stockholders despite paying the credit line. Moreover, according to plaintiffs, Perini's annual report for the year 2000 states that the company does not foresee ever resuming such payments or paying the amounts that have accrued.

On or about January 17, 1997, Perini sold an aggregate of 150,150 shares of Series B Cumulative Convertible Preferred Stock (the "Junior Preferred Stock") in a private offering to an investment group, in which Perini received approximately $30,000,000 in total compensation. These stockholders were junior in rank to the Senior Preferred Stockholders, both as to priority for the payment of dividends and liquidation preference. Because the Junior Preferred Stock was not registered, the stockholders could not freely trade their shares on a stock exchange or national market.

Subsequently, on March 29, 2000 Perini engaged in two transactions which form the basis for this lawsuit. First, Perini authorized the holders of the Junior Preferred Stock to exchange their shares for 7,490,417 shares of Perini's liquid Common Stock at $5.50 per share, an approximate 43% discount from the current conversion price of 9.68 per share. Perini received over $41,000,000 from this exchange, $11,000,000 more than the original $30,000,000 Perini received when the Junior Preferred Stock was initially sold. Plaintiffs allege that the $11,000,000 difference represents the payment of "cash dividends" or "other distribution" to the Junior Preferred Stockholders in violation of the Senior Preferred Stock's prospectus or a "cash distribution" in violation of the Senior Preferred Certificate of Vote.

Second, Perini sold 9,411,765 shares of its Common Stock to a different investment group at $4.25 per share, raising an additional $40,000,000 in capital. One member of this investment group was the Tutor–Saliba Corporation in which defendant Ronald Tutor, a director of Perini, is the Chairman, President, CEO and sole shareholder.

The two transactions were jointly approved by the Board of Directors. The transactions were not brought to the Senior Preferred Stockholders for approval. As a result of these transactions, Perini announced that it had satisfied its credit agreements with its banks. According to plaintiffs, at this time, the accumulated dividend arrears on the Senior Preferred Stock were approximately $9,562,500. Plaintiffs claim that "no payment in whole or in part for the accumulated dividend arrears was made to the holders of the Senior Preferred Stock on March 29, 2000 or at any time thereafter, despite repeated demands for such payment by the holders of the Senior Preferred Stock."

Plaintiff Doppelt, a current director of Perini, owns 63,900 shares of the Senior Preferred Stock and has owned shares since August 22, 1991. Plaintiff Caplan, a director of Perini during the relevant period of this lawsuit, owns 2,500 shares of the Senior Preferred Stock and has owned shares since February 20, 1996. Plaintiff Miller owns 2000 shares of the Senior Preferred Stock which he has owned since September 19, 1996. The individual defendants are either former or current directors of Perini.

Plaintiffs initially commenced this action in state court but defendants removed it to federal court. Plaintiffs' first cause of action is for breach of contract against Perini. Plaintiffs' second cause of action is for breach of fiduciary duty against the individual defendants. * * *

Plaintiffs claim that when Perini engaged in the transactions described above and approved of the exchange of Junior Preferred Stock for Perini Common Stock:

Perini breached the covenant contained in the prospectus which guaranteed to the holders of the Senior Preferred Stock that no cash dividends would be declared or paid, or other distribution of any kind made, upon any other stock of the Company ranking junior to the Senior Preferred Stock, while there were accumulated unpaid dividends due to the Senior Preferred Stockholders.

Defendants move to dismiss this claim on the grounds that the Certificate of Vote, not the prospectus, was the controlling contract between the Senior Preferred Stockholders and Perini, and that none of the transactions violated the terms of the Certificate of Vote.

The two documents differ in that the prospectus states that no "cash dividends shall be declared or paid or *other distribution* made," whereas the Certificate of Vote states that no "cash dividends whatsoever [will] be declared or paid upon, nor shall any *cash distribution* be made." (emphasis added.) Thus, the critical issues in evaluating this breach of contract claim are: (1) which document (or documents) is controlling and (2) whether the transactions described above violate the terms of that document.

Massachusetts law applies in this diversity action because that is the state in which Perini is incorporated. Guttmann v. Illinois Cent. R. Co., 91 F.Supp. 285, 292 (E.D.N.Y.1950) (finding Illinois law applicable in diversity action for the determination of plaintiff's dividend rights where defendant was incorporated in Illinois). Under Massachusetts law, contract interpretation is generally a matter of law and when the language in the contract is unambiguous, the court will interpret the contract according to its plain terms. Den Norske Bank AS v. First Nat'l Bank of Boston, 75 F.3d 49, 52 (1st Cir.1996).

The Court finds that the Certificate of Vote is the controlling document in this case. The prospectus clearly states that it is only a summary of terms and that it "does not purport to be complete and is subject to, and qualified in its entirety by, the provisions of" the Certificate of Vote. With such explicit qualifying language, the Court must apply the terms of the Certificate of Vote in analyzing whether plaintiff's breach of contract allegations have any merit. In the Matter of Discon Corp., 346 F. Supp. 839, 843 (S.D.Fla.1971) (resolving conflict between documents where prospectus included such qualifying language). While it is true that a party may challenge the terms of the prospectus as containing false or misleading statements under the securities laws, plaintiffs' action in this case is for breach of contract. E.g. Discon Corp., 346 F.Supp. at 844 ("the purpose of the registration statement and prospectus is to prevent fraud by fully and fairly disclosing the nature and finances of the company to investors...."); Hassett v. S.F. Iszard Co., 61 N.Y.S.2d 451, 455 (N.Y.Sup. Ct.1945) (prospectus might be evidence in action in fraud by a purchaser of stock). Although plaintiffs claim that they reviewed and relied only upon the prospectus when they decided to purchase shares of Senior Preferred Stock, the plain language of the prospectus would have made them aware of the Certificate of Vote.

The terms in the provision of the Certificate of Vote at issue here are unambiguous. Because the terms "dividends" and "distribution" are modified in this provision by the word "cash," Perini would have violated the terms of the Certificate of Vote only if it declared or paid "cash" dividends or made a "cash" distribution before it paid or declared full cumulative dividends on the outstanding shares of Senior Preferred Stock.

Thus, the only remaining issue is whether the transactions plaintiffs complain of involved cash dividends or a cash distribution to any shareholder junior to the Senior Preferred Shareholder. Defendants argue that the transactions resulted in the issuance of stock to the Junior Preferred Stockholders, not cash, and therefore did not violate the Certificate of Vote.

In opposition, plaintiffs principally argue that by authorizing the conversion of Junior Preferred Stock into freely tradeable Perini Common Stock, Perini violated the terms of the Certificate of Vote because the common stock was a form of "cash distribution." As a result, according to plaintiffs, "Perini has, in effect, made a cash equivalent distribution to the Junior Preferred Stockholders while unpaid dividend arrearages due to holders of the Senior Preferred Stock were outstanding."

Plaintiffs have failed to convince the Court that the transaction in which the Junior Preferred Stockholders exchanged their Junior Preferred Stock for Perini common stock was either a "cash dividend" or "cash distribution." As a result of the exchange, the Junior Preferred Stockholders did not receive cash. In fact, the Junior Preferred Stockholders actually paid cash to the company. Plaintiffs' argument that the receipt of freely tradeable common stock is a functional equivalent of cash is without merit. Thus, as a matter of law, plaintiffs' breach of contract claim fails and must be dismissed. * * *

HB KORENVAES INVESTMENTS LP v. MARRIOTT CORP.

1993 WL 257422 (Del.Ch.1993).

ALLEN, CHANCELLOR

In this action holders of Series A Cumulative Convertible Preferred Stock of Marriott Corporation seek to enjoin a planned reorganization of the businesses owned by that corporation. The reorganization involves the creation of a new corporate subsidiary, Marriott International, Inc., ("International"), the transfer to International of the greatest part of Marriott's cash-generating businesses, followed by the distribution of the stock of International to all of the holders of Marriott common stock, as a special dividend.

Plaintiffs assert that the proposed special dividend would leave the residual Marriott endangered by a disproportionate debt burden and would deprive them of certain rights created by the certificate of designation that defines the special rights, etc., of the preferred stock. More particularly, they claim: (1) that the proposed transaction, taken together with a recently declared intention to discontinue the payment of dividends on the preferred stock, constitutes coercive action designed wrongfully to force them to exercise their conversion privilege and thus surrender their preference rights; (2) that the planned payment of cash dividends on International's common stock, while plaintiffs' preferred dividend will have been suspended, violates the preferred stock's dividend preference; (3) that the authorization by the directors of Marriott of the spin-off transaction, without the affirmative vote of the holders of preferred stock, violates the voting rights of the preferred conferred by the certificate of designation; and (4) that the distribution of the dividend will violate the provisions of Section 5(e)(iv) of the certificate of designation of the preferred stock. Section 5(e)(iv) is designed to protect the economic interests of the preferred stock in the event of a special dividend. Finally, plaintiffs allege (5) that defendants have made false statements upon which they have relied in buying preferred stock in the market and that defendants are liable for fraud.

The Series A Cumulative Convertible Preferred Stock is Marriott's only outstanding issue of preferred stock. Plaintiffs are four institutional investors who have acquired more than 50% of the preferred stock. They present their case as one involving manipulation, deception and a legalistic interpretation of rights, which, if permitted and generalized will impose a material future cost on the operation of capital markets.

Defendants assert that the reorganization, and more particularly the special dividend, constitutes a valid, good faith attempt to maximize the interests of Marriott's common stockholders. Marriott asserts the right to deal with the preferred stock at arm's length, to afford them their legal rights arising from the certificate of designation, but also to take steps not inconsistent with those rights to maximize the economic position of Marriott's common stock. It claims that this is what the proposed special dividend does. Defendants also deny that they have intentionally misled plaintiffs. * * *

Marriott Corporation, as presently constituted, is in the business (1) of owning and operating hotels, resorts, and retirement homes, (2) of providing institutional food service and facilities management, and (3) of operating restaurants and food, beverage and merchandise concessions at airports, tollway plazas and other facilities. Its common stock has a present market value of approximately $2.6 billion. In December 1991 Marriott issued $200,000,000 face amount of convertible preferred stock bearing an 8 1/4% cumulative dividend, the stock owned by plaintiffs. Marriott has substantial debt, including Liquid Yield Option Notes ("LYONS") with an accreted value of $228 million;[9] and long-term debt of $2.732 billion. According to its proxy statement, the book value of Marriott's assets is $6.560 billion.

In the fiscal year ending January 1, 1993 Marriott's sales were $8.722 billion; earnings before interest, taxes, depreciation and amortization (EBITDA) was $777 million; earnings before interest and corporate expenses was $496 million; and net income was $85 million. Each common share has received an annual cash dividend of $0.28 per share and the preferred stock dividends have been paid over its short life.

The preferred stock is entitled to an 8 1/4% cumulative dividend and no more. It ranks prior to the common stock with respect to dividends and distribution of assets. It has in total, a face amount of $200,000,000 and that, plus the amount of any unpaid cumulated dividends, "and no more" is the amount of its liquidation preference. The corporation may, at its option, redeem any or all of the preferred stock after January 15, 1996, at prices set forth in the certificate.

The preferred stock is convertible at the option of the holder into common stock at a conversion price set forth in the certificate. Generally

---

9. A leading finance text notes that "a liquid yield option note (LYON) is a callable and retractable, convertible zero coupon bond (and you can't get much more complicated than that)." An example set forth in that text explains the security. See Richard A. Brealey and Stewart C. Myers, Principles of Corporate Finance, 3d ed. (1988) at p. 586.

that means that every $50.00 face amount share of preferred stock may be converted into 2.87 shares of common stock. The certificate provides a mechanism to adjust the conversion price "in case the Corporation shall, by dividend ... distribute to all holders of Common Stock ... assets (including securities)...." Certificate of Designation § 5(e)(iv).

The value of the right to convert is protected by a notice provision. The certificate provides that "in the event the Corporation shall declare a dividend ... on its Common Stock payable otherwise than in cash or out of retained earnings," the Corporation shall give written notice to the holders of the preferred stock 15 days in advance of the record date. Certificate of Designation § 5(k).

There are no express restrictions on the payment of dividends other than the requirement that the quarterly dividend on the preferred must be paid prior to the distribution of dividend payments to common stock.[10]

On October 5, 1993, Marriott announced a radical rearrangement of the legal structure of the Company's businesses. The restructuring was said to be designed to separate Marriott's "ownership of real estate ... and other capital intensive businesses from its management and services businesses." (Proxy Statement at 19). The latter constitute Marriott's most profitable and fastest growing business segments. As indicated above, following this transfer Marriott intends to "spin-off" this new subsidiary by distributing all its stock as a dividend to Marriott's common stockholders.

Marriott International is anticipated to be highly profitable from its inception and to be well positioned for future growth. It is expected to pay to its common stockholders the same dividend that has been paid to Marriott's common stock. Marriott's proxy statement describes International's proposed business activities as follows:

> Pursuant to existing long-term management, lease and franchise agreements with hotel owners, and [similar] ... agreements to be entered into with Host Marriott with respect to lodging facilities and senior living properties to be owned by Host Marriott, Marriott international will operate or franchise a total of 242 Marriott full service hotels, 207 Courtyard by Marriott hotels, 179 Residence Inns, 118 Fairfield Inns and 16 senior living communities. Marriott International will also conduct the Company's food and facilities management businesses, as well as the Company's vacation timesharing operations.

According to its pro forma balance sheet for the quarter ending March 26, 1993, after the distribution * * * International will have assets of

---

10. *See* Richard M. Buxbaum, Preferred Stock—Law and Draftsmanship, 42 Calif. L. Rev. 243, 255–56 (1954) (review of possible protective provisions in preferred stock designation). *See also* Morey W. McDaniel, Bondholders and Corporate Governance, 41 Bus. Law. 413, 424–26 (1986); William W. Bratton, Jr., Corporate Debt Relationships, *1989 Duke L. J. 92, 139–42 (1989)* (both of which comment upon the "disappearance" in the last twenty years of dividend covenants in bond indentures).

$3.048 billion, long-term debt of $902 million, and shareholders equity of $375 million.

Had International, with all the assets it will hold, been operated as a separate company in 1992, it would have had sales of $7.787 billion, earnings before interest and corporate expenses of $331 million and net income of $136 million. Marriott's adviser, S.G. Warburg & Company, has estimated that in 1993 International will have sales of $8.210 billion, and EBIT of $368 million.

Marriott's remaining assets will consist of large real estate holdings and Marriott's airport and tollway concession business. Marriott will be renamed Host Marriott ("Host"). The assets retained by Host have a value of several billion dollars but will be burdened with great debt and produce little cash-flow after debt service.

> Host Marriott will retain [ownership of] most of the Company's [Marriott's] existing real estate properties, including 136 lodging and senior living properties. Host Marriott will also complete the Company's existing real estate development projects and manage the Company's holdings of undeveloped real estate. Host Marriott will seek to maximize the cash flow from ... its real estate holdings ... Host Marriott ... will also be the leading operator of airport and toll-road food and merchandise concessions in the U.S., holding contracts at 68 major airports and operating concessions at nearly 100 toll-road units.

Assuming the Exchange Offer is effectuated, after the special dividend Host will have, according to its pro forma balance sheet as of March 26, 1993, assets of $3.796 billion, long-term debt of 2.130 billion and shareholders' equity of $516 million. (Marriott Proxy Statement at 70). Host's pro forma income statement for the fiscal year ending January 1, 1993, would reflect sales of $1.209 billion, earnings before corporate expenses and interest of $152 million, interest expense of $196 million, corporate expenses of $46 million, and a net loss of $44 million. * * *

Since the preferred stock is convertible at the option of the holder into 2.87 shares of Marriott common stock and bears a dividend of 8 1/4% on its stated (liquidation) value of $50 per share, the market value of a share of preferred stock includes two possible components of value: the value of the conversion right and the value of the preferences. The presence of a presently exercisable conversion right will assure that the market value of the preferred will not fail below the market value of the security or property into which the preferred might convert, in this case 2.87 shares of common stock (less transaction costs of the conversion). The stated dividend, the dividend preference and the liquidation preference and other features of the preferred will ordinarily assure that the preferred trades at some premium to the value of the conversion right.

In this instance plaintiffs have acquired a majority of the shares of the preferred stock. Plaintiffs, however, did not simply acquire preferred stock. The record shows that each of the plaintiffs, except one, have hedged their risk by entering short sales contracts with respect to Marriott common stock. In this way plaintiffs have isolated their risk to that part of the preferred stock trading value represented by that stock's preference rights. Any change in the market price of the preferred stock caused by movement in the value of the underlying common stock will in their case be offset by change in the extent of their obligations under the short sales contracts.

The prices of both Marriott common stock and Marriott preferred stock have increased substantially since the announcement of the special dividend. On the last trading day before the announcement of the transaction Marriott's common stock closed at $17.125 per share. The day of the announcement the price increased to $19.25 and by June 4, 1993 it had reached $25.75, for a total increase of approximately 50.3%.

The price of Marriott preferred stock closed on the last trading day before the announcement at $62.75, which represented a premium of $13.54 over the value of the 2.8736 common shares into which each preferred share could convert. The day of the announcement the preferred stock increased to $68.875. On June 4, 1993 the price of the preferred stock closed at $77.00 per share, an increase of 22.8% over the pre-announcement market price. The premium that the preferred stock commanded over the common into which it could convert (i.e., the market value of the preferences) however, had by June 4th, shrunk, to $3.00.

Thus while both common stock and preferred stock have experienced substantial increases in the market value of their securities, because of the impact of their hedging strategy, plaintiffs are in a different position than are non-hedged holders of preferred stock. The reduction of the premium at which the preferred stock trades has resulted in losses on their short sales, leading some plaintiffs, as of June 4, 1993, to net unrealized losses on their investments.

For example, plaintiff, The President and Fellows of Harvard College, ("Harvard") as of June 4, 1993 owned 480,300 shares of preferred stock, which were purchased for $33,580,108 and which had a market value on that day of $37,724,801. Thus, this plaintiff has an unrealized profit of $4,144,693 on its investment in the preferred stock. Harvard also entered into short sales of 1,338,300 shares of Marriott common stock, approximately 2.8 times the number of preferred shared it purchased. It received $30,949,383 on these short sales. The cost to cover these short sales, however, has increased to $34,609,056, or $3,659,673 more than was received on the sales, representing an unrealized loss in that amount. Thus, as of June 4, 1993, although the value of the preferred stock owned by this plaintiff has increased in value by over $4 million, the total value of its investment position has increased by only $485,020. * * *

The pertinent foundational inquiry here is whether there is a duty arising from the contract (the certificate) not to transfer substantial assets out of Marriott. The answer clearly is that there is no such duty. The certificate explicitly provides for such special dividends in Section 5. It is impossible to say that the payment of such a dividend is unauthorized.

Does the large size of the planned distribution render it an evasion of the rights set forth in Sections 1, 2 or 6? Plainly, in my opinion, it does not. * * *

A related claim is that the suspension of dividends constitutes wrongful coercion designed to force plaintiffs to convert to common stock. Plainly the discontinuation of current dividend payments on the preferred stock will tend to make conversion into Marriott common stock prior to the special dividend more attractive. Plaintiffs call the effect coercion and assert that in this context, it is a wrong.

This court has on occasion enjoined as inequitable and inconsistent with an applicable fiduciary duty, corporate action designed principally to coerce stockholders in the exercise of a choice that the applicable certificate of incorporation, bylaws or statute confers upon them. See, e.g., AC Acquisitions Corp. v. Anderson, Clayton & Co., supra; Lacos Land Co. v. Arden Group, Inc., Del. Ch., 517 A.2d 271 (1986); Kahn v. U.S. Sugar Co., Del. Ch., C.A. No. 7313, Hartnett, V.C., Del. J. Corp. L. 908 (1986); Eisenberg v. Chicago Milwaukee Corp., 537 A.2d 1051 (1987). These cases are premised upon the existence of a fiduciary duty on the part of the corporate directors with respect to the transaction under review. The last of them involved preferred stockholders to whom a tender offer had been extended by the Company. As an alternative holding this court held that a gratuitous statement by the Company concerning a plan to seek delisting of the preferred, constituted an inappropriate effort to coerce acceptance of the Company's offer. See Eisenberg, 537 A.2d at 1062. Plaintiffs rely upon this precedent to argue that the announcement of the discontinuation of preferred stock dividends has an analogous effect and is analogously a breach of duty.

Plaintiffs are, I believe, incorrect in this. The critical differences between this case as it now appears and Eisenberg are several. First, that case was treated as a fiduciary duty case, not as a case involving, as this one does, the construction and interpretation of rights and duties set forth in the certificate of designation. In this instance Marriott has a right to suspend dividend payments and in the event that that should happen, the preferred's protections are in the contract and are several: most importantly, the dividends are cumulative and enjoy a liquidation preference; in addition, the redemption price is adjusted to include unpaid dividends; and prolonged suspension of dividends gives the preferred the right to elect two directors. Finally, the preferred may, in all events, be converted into common stock; and, as I construe the certificate, there is necessarily implied a restriction on the proportion of net worth that may be distributed by special dividend. These contractual protections are a recognition of the risk that dividends might not be paid currently. These protections are substantial. The correlative of the fact that Marriott has a duty to respect them is the conclusion that it has a right to discontinue dividends when it observes them.

Secondly, unlike Eisenberg it cannot persuasively be urged, at this stage, that the discontinuation of dividends is not itself a prudent, business-driven decision. Thus, assuming that a corporation owes to the holders of its preferred stock the same implied duty of good faith that is present in every contractual relationship, as I believe to be the case, the circumstances as they appear could not be construed as justifying the preliminary conclusion that the suspension of dividend payments is not a good faith business decision. Host is expected to have no net income, even though it will have substantial assets. Plaintiffs' suggestion that Host could, in the circumstances, borrow money to pay preferred dividends presents a classic business judgment issue; that such a possibility may exist does not constitute a persuasive argument that the suspension of dividend payments was itself undertaken in bad faith.

Thus, while the suspension of dividends may exert a powerful influence upon the decision whether holders of preferred stock will exercise rights to convert or not, I can see in that effect, at this time, no violation of any implied right to that degree of good faith that every commercial contractor is entitled to expect from those with whom she contracts.

I turn now to to analysis of that which I regard as the centrally important certificate provision, Section 5(e)(iv). That section affords protection against dilution of the conversion component of the market value of the preferred stock by providing an adjustment to the conversion price when the corporation declares a dividend of assets, including securities. The principle that appears embedded in Section 5(e)(iv) is that when the assets of the Firm are depleted through a special distribution to shareholders, the preferred will be protected by the triggering of a conversion price adjustment formula. Under Section 5(e)(iv) the number of shares into which the preferred can convert will be proportionately increased in order to maintain the value of the preferred's conversion feature. The principle seems clear enough; the realization of it will inevitably involve problems.

> (a) Section 5(e)(iv) of the certificate of designation requires Marriott, when effectuating a special dividend, to leave sufficient net assets in the corporation to permit that Section to function as intended to protect the predisposition value of the preferred stock.

The language of the certificate of designation is as follows:

5.   Conversion Rights. The holders of shares of Convertible Preferred Stock shall have the right at their option, to convert such shares into shares of Common Stock on the following terms and conditions:

> (a) Shares of Convertible Preferred Stock shall be convertible at any time into fully paid and nonassessable shares of Common Stock at a conversion price of $17.40 per share of Common Stock (the "Conversion Price").

* * * (e) The conversion Price shall be adjusted from time to time as follows:

> (iv) In case the Corporation shall, by dividend or otherwise, distribute to all holders of its Common Stock ... assets (includ-

ing securities . . .), the Conversion Price shall be adjusted so that the same shall equal the price determined by multiplying the Conversion Price in effect immediately prior to the close of business on the date fixed for the determination of stockholders entitled to receive such distribution by a fraction of which the numerator shall be the current market price per share (determined as provided in subsection (vi) below) of the Common Stock on the date fixed for such determination less the then fair market value (as determined by the Board of Directors, whose determination shall be conclusive and shall be described in a statement filed with the transfer agent for the Convertible Preferred Stock) of the portion of the evidences of indebtedness or assets so distributed applicable to one share of Common Stock and the denominator shall be such current market price per share of the Common Stock, such adjustment to become effective immediately prior to the opening of business on the day following the date fixed for the determination of stockholders entitled to receive such distribution. (emphasis added).

Thus, stated simply, whenever Marriott distributes assets to its common stockholders this provision protects the value of the preferred conversion right by reducing the conversion price. Protection of this type may be important to the buyer of preferred stock and presumably its inclusion will permit an issuer to arrange the sale of preferred stock on somewhat more advantageous terms than would otherwise be available. What is intuitively apparent is that in a narrow range of extreme cases, a dividend of property may be so large relative to the corporation's net worth, that following the distribution, the firm, while still solvent,[11] will not represent sufficient value to preserve the pre-dividend value of the preferred's conversion right. * * *

Section 5(e)(iv) operates to prevent the confiscation of the value of the preferred conversion right through a special dividend. By necessary implication it limits the board's discretion with respect to the size of special dividends. But that limitation is one that has its effect when it is respected by the board of directors at the time it takes corporate action to declare the dividend. If, when declared, the dividend will leave the corporation with sufficient assets to preserve the conversion value that the preferred possesses at that time, it satisfies the limitation that such a protective provision necessarily implies. That is, Section 5(e)(iv) does not, in my opinion, explicitly or by necessary implication grant the preferred a right to assurance that any increase in the value of their conversion rights following the authorization of a special dividend be maintained. * * *

---

11. Traditionally preferred stockholders have not been treated as creditors for the amount of the liquidation preference and the preference does not count as a "claim" for fraudulent conveyance purposes. See Fletcher's Cyc. Corp., § 5293 (Perm. ed. 1986); Compare Model Bus. Corp. Act, § 6.40(c)(2) (Supp.1989).

NOTES

1. Efforts to provide preferred shareholders with extraordinary powers may meet judicial resistance. In Waggoner v. Laster, 581 A.2d 1127 (Del. 1990), the court held that the certificate of incorporation did not allow the issuance of preferred shares with supermajority voting rights.

2. Strict construction was often used to undermine preferred shareholders protections. See e.g., Bernstein v. Canet, 1996 WL 342096 (Del.Ch. 1996) (conversion of preferred into common stock did not trigger anti-dilution measure). Will the decision in Elliot Associates broaden the protection given to preferred shareholders?

3. In Dart v. Kohlberg, Kravis, Roberts & Co., 1985 WL 11566 (Del.Ch. 1985), the court denied summary judgment to defendants on claims by preferred shareholders that a leveraged buyout impaired their interests because of the large amount of debt assumed by the corporation as a part of that transaction. The buyout involved a "going private" transaction for the common shareholders, but the preferred remained publicly held. The transaction impaired the assets of the corporation and raised the danger that the preferred shareholders would not be paid their dividends. The court stated:

> Although everything done by defendants may have been in strict compliance with the letter of Delaware law, it is possible that the totality of actions resulted in an impermissible inequity to the holders of the preferred stock. The difficulty with the challenged transaction is that it was highly leveraged and a majority of the preferred stockholders ended up still owning their shares although they preferred to be bought out. The assets of the corporation were used as sole security for the loans obtained for the purpose of buying out the common stock and the public preferred stockholders were left holding their shares in a corporation which, as a result of the transaction, has a much greater debt and therefore perhaps a lessened ability to pay preferred dividends. Such a leveraged buy-out calls for judicial scrutiny to prevent possible abuse. On the present record, therefore, which does not contain the fruits of full discovery, it can be at least reasonably inferred that plaintiff has a cause of action, however imperfectly stated and however speculative, as to the allegations which attack the leveraged buy-out and its effect on the preferred stockholders.

Does this suggest a fiduciary duty of some kind is owed to the preferred shareholders?

SECTION 4. CUMULATIVE PREFERRED DIVIDENDS

BOVE v. COMMUNITY HOTEL CORP. OF NEWPORT, R.I.

105 R.I. 36, 249 A.2d 89 (1969).

JOSLIN, JUSTICE.

This civil action was brought in the superior court to enjoin a proposed merger of The Community Hotel Corporation of Newport, Rhode Island, a defendant herein, into Newport Hotel Corp. Both corporations were organized under the general corporation law of this state and are hereinafter referred to respectively as "Community Hotel" and "Newport." No oral testimony was presented and a trial justice sitting without a jury decided the case on the facts appearing in the exhibits and as assented to by the parties in the pretrial order. The case is here on the plaintiffs' appeal from a judgment denying injunctive relief and dismissing the action.

Community Hotel was incorporated on October 21, 1924, for the stated purpose of erecting, maintaining, operating, managing and leasing hotels; and it commenced operations in 1927 with the opening of the Viking Hotel in Newport. Its authorized capital stock consists of 6,000 shares of $100 par value six per cent prior preference cumulative preferred stock, and 6,000 shares of no par common stock of which 2,106 shares are issued and outstanding. The plaintiffs as well as the individual defendants are holders and owners of preferred stock, plaintiffs having acquired their holdings of approximately 900 shares not later than 1930. At the time this suit was commenced, dividends on the 4,335 then-issued and outstanding preferred shares had accrued, but had not been declared, for approximately 24 years, and totaled about $645,000 or $148.75 per share.

Newport was organized at the instance and request of the board of directors of Community Hotel solely for the purpose of effectuating the merger which is the subject matter of this action. Its authorized capital stock consists of 80,000 shares of common stock, par value $1.00, of which only one share has been issued, and that to Community Hotel for a consideration of $10.

The essentials of the merger plan call for Community Hotel to merge into Newport, which will then become the surviving corporation. Although previously without assets, Newport will, if the contemplated merger is effectuated, acquire the sole ownership of all the property and assets now owned by Community Hotel. The plan also calls for the outstanding shares of Community Hotel's capital stock to be converted into shares of the capital stock of Newport upon the following basis: Each outstanding share of the constituent corporation's preferred stock, together with all accrued dividends thereon, will be changed and converted into five shares of the $1.00 par value common stock of the surviving corporation; and each share of the constituent corporation's no par common stock will be changed and converted into one share of the common stock, $1.00 par value, of the surviving corporation.

Consistent with the requirements of G.L.1956, § 7–5–3, the merger will become effective only if the plan receives the affirmative votes of the stockholders of each of the corporations representing at least two-thirds of the shares of each class of its capital stock. For the purpose of obtaining the required approval, notice was given to both common and preferred stockholders of Community Hotel that a special meeting would be held for the purpose of considering and voting upon the proposed merger. Before the scheduled meeting date arrived, this action was commenced and the meeting was postponed to a future time and place. So far as the record before us indicates, it has not yet been held.

The plaintiffs argue that the primary, and indeed, the only purpose of the proposed merger is to eliminate the priorities of the preferred stock with less than the unanimous consent of its holders. Assuming that premise, a preliminary matter for our consideration concerns the merger of a parent corporation into a wholly-owned subsidiary created for the sole purpose of achieving a recapitalization which will eliminate the parent's preferred stock and the dividends accumulated thereon, and whether such a merger qualifies within the contemplation of the statute permitting any two or more corporations to merge into a single corporation.

It is true, of course, that to accomplish the proposed recapitalization by amending Community Hotel's articles of association under relevant provisions of the general corporation law[12] would require the unanimous vote of the preferred shareholders, whereas under the merger statute, only a two-third vote of those stockholders will be needed. Concededly, unanimity of the preferred stockholders is unobtainable in this case, and plaintiffs argue, therefore, that to permit the less restrictive provisions of the merger statute to be used to accomplish indirectly what otherwise would be incapable of being accomplished directly by the more stringent amendment procedures of the general corporation law is tantamount to sanctioning a circumvention or perversion of that law.

The question, however, is not whether recapitalization by the merger route is a subterfuge, but whether a merger which is designed for the sole purpose of cancelling the rights of preferred stockholders with the consent

---

12. Section 7–2–18, as amended, provides that a corporation may " * * * from time to time when and as desired amend its articles of association * * * " and § 7–2–19, as amended, provides that "Unless otherwise provided in the articles of association, every such amendment shall require the affirmative vote of the following proportion of the stockholders, passed at a meeting duly called for the purpose:

'(a) * * *

'(b) Where the amendment diminishes the stipulated rate of dividends on any class of stock or the stipulated amount to be paid thereon in case of call or liquidation, the unanimous vote of the stockholders of such class and the vote of a majority in interest of all other stockholders entitled to vote.' "

of less than all has been authorized by the legislature. The controlling statute is § 7–5–2. Its language is clear, all-embracing and unqualified. It authorizes any two or more business corporations which were or might have been organized under the general corporation law to merge into a single corporation; and it provides that the merger agreement shall prescribe " * * * the terms and conditions of consolidation or merger, the mode of carrying the same into effect * * * *as well as the manner of converting the shares of each of the constituent corporations into shares or other securities of the corporation resulting from or surviving such consolidation or merger*, with such other details and provisions as are deemed necessary."[13] (italics ours) Nothing in that language even suggests that the legislature intended to make underlying purpose a standard for determining permissibility. Indeed, the contrary is apparent since the very breadth of the language selected presupposes a complete lack of concern with whether the merger is designed to further the mutual interests of two existing and nonaffiliated corporations or whether alternatively it is purposed solely upon effecting a substantial change in an existing corporation's capital structure.

Moreover, that a possible effect of corporate action under the merger statute is not possible, or is even forbidden, under another section of the general corporation law is of no import, it being settled that the several sections of that law may have independent legal significance, and that the validity of corporate action taken pursuant to one section is not necessarily dependent upon its being valid under another. Hariton v. Arco Electronics, Inc., 40 Del.Ch. 326, 182 A.2d 22, aff'd, 41 Del.Ch. 74, 188 A.2d 123; Langfelder v. Universal Laboratories Inc., D.C., 68 F.Supp. 209, aff'd, 3 Cir., 163 F.2d 804.

We hold, therefore, that nothing within the purview of our statute forbids a merger between a parent and a subsidiary corporation even under circumstances where the merger device has been resorted to solely for the purpose of obviating the necessity for the unanimous vote which would otherwise be required in order to cancel the priorities of preferred shareholders. Federal United Corp. v. Havender, supra; Hottenstein v. York Ice Machinery Corp., 3 Cir., 136 F.2d 944; 7 Fletcher, Cyclopedia of Corporations, chap. 43, § 3696.1, page 892.

A more basic problem, narrowed so as to bring it within the factual context of this case, is whether the right of a holder of cumulative preferred stock to dividend arrearages and other preferences may be cancelled by a statutory merger. That precise problem has not heretofore been before this court, but elsewhere there is a considerable body of law on the subject. There is no need to discuss all of the authorities. For illustrative purposes it is sufficient that we refer principally to cases involving Delaware corporations. That state is important as a state of incorporation, and the decisions of its courts on the precise problem are

---

13. The quoted provision is substantially identical to the Delaware merger statute (Del.Rev. Code (1935) C. 65, § 2091) construed in Federal United Corp. v. Havender, 24 Del.Ch. 318, 11 A.2d 331.

not only referred to and relied on by the parties, but are generally considered to be the leading ones in the field.

The earliest case in point of time is Keller v. Wilson & Co., 21 Del.Ch. 391, 190 A. 115 (1936). Wilson & Company was formed and its stock was issued in 1925 and the law then in effect protected against charter amendments which might destroy a preferred shareholder's right to accumulated dividends. In 1927 that law was amended so as to permit such destruction, and thereafter the stockholders of Wilson & Company, by the required majorities, voted to cancel the dividends which had by then accrued on its preferred stock. In invalidating that action the rationale of the Delaware court was that the right of a holder of a corporation's cumulative preferred stock to eventual payment of dividend arrearages was a fixed contractual right, that it was a property right in the nature of a debt, that it was vested, and that it could not be destroyed by corporate action taken under legislative authority subsequently conferred, without the consent of all of the shareholders.

Consolidated Film Industries, Inc. v. Johnson, 22 Del.Ch. 407, 197 A. 489 (1937), decided a year later, was an almost precisely similar case. The only difference was that Consolidated Film Industries, Inc. was not created until after the adoption of the 1927 amendment, whereas in the earlier case the statutory amendment upon which Wilson & Company purported to act postdated both its creation and the issuance of its stock. Notwithstanding the Keller rationale that an investor should be entitled to rely upon the law in existence at the time the preferred stock was issued, the court in this case was " * * * unable to discover a difference in principle between the two cases." In refusing to allow the proposed reclassification, it reasoned that a shareholder's fixed contractual right to unpaid dividends is of such dignity that it cannot be diminished or eliminated retrospectively even if the authorizing legislation precedes the issuance of its stock.

Two years elapsed before Federal United Corp. v. Havender, supra, was decided. The issue was substantially the same as that in the two cases which preceded. The dissenting stockholders had argued, as might have been expected, that the proposed corporate action, even though styled a "merger," was in effect a Keller type recapitalization and was entitled to no different treatment. Notwithstanding that argument, the court did not refer to the preferred stockholder's right as "vested" or as "a property right in the nature of a debt." Neither did it reject the use of Keller-type nomenclature as creating "confusion" or as "substitutes for reason and analysis" which are the characterizations used respectively in Davison v. Parke, Austin & Lipscomb, Inc., 285 N.Y. 500, 509, 35 N.E.2d 618, 622; Meck, Accrued Dividends on Cumulative Preferred Stocks; The Legal Doctrine, 55 Harv.L.Rev. 7, 76. Instead, it talked about the extent of the corporate power under the merger statute; and it held that the statute in existence when Federal United Corp. was organized had in effect been written into its charter, and that its preferred shareholders had thereby been advised and informed that their rights to accrued dividends might be extinguished by corporate action taken pursuant thereto.

Faced with a question of corporate action adjusting preferred stock dividends, and required to apply Delaware law under Erie R.R. v. Tompkins, 304 U.S. 64, it is understandable that a federal court in Hottenstein v. York Ice Machinery Corp., 3 Cir., 136 F.2d 944, 950, found Keller, Johnson and Havender irreconcilable and said,

> "If it is fair to say that the decision of the Supreme Court of Delaware in the Keller case astonished the corporate world, it is just to state that the decision of the Supreme Court in Havender astounded it, for shorn of rationalization the decision constitutes a repudiation of principles enunciated in the Keller case and in Consolidated Film Industries v. Johnson, supra." at 950.

With Keller's back thus broken, *Hottenstein* went on to say that under Delaware law a parent corporation may merge with a wholly-owned inactive subsidiary pursuant to a plan cancelling preferred stock and the rights of holders thereof to unpaid accumulated dividends and substituting in lieu thereof stock of the surviving corporation.

Only four years intervened between *Keller* and *Havender*, but that was long enough for Delaware to have discarded "vested rights" as the test for determining the power of a corporation to eliminate a shareholder's right to preferred stock dividend accumulation, and to have adopted in its stead a standard calling for judicial inquiry into whether the proposed interference with a preferred stockholder's contract has been authorized by the legislature. The *Havender* approach is the one to which we subscribed as being the sounder, and it has support in the authorities. Davison v. Parke, Austin & Lipscomb, Inc., supra; Langfelder v. Universal Laboratories, Inc., 3 Cir., 163 F.2d 804; Western Foundry Co. v. Wicker, supra, note 4; Anderson v. International Minerals & Chemical Corp., 295 N.Y. 343, 67 N.E.2d 573; Hubbard v. Jones & Laughlin Steel Corp., D.C., 42 F.Supp. 432; Donohue v. Heuser, 239 S.W.2d 238 (Ky).

The plaintiffs do not suggest, other than as they may have argued that this particular merger is a subterfuge, that our merger statute will not permit in any circumstances a merger for the sole reason that it affects accrued, but undeclared, preferred stock dividends. Rather do they argue that what should control is the date of the enactment of the enabling legislation, and they point out that in *Havender*, Federal United Corp. was organized and its stock was issued subsequent to the adoption of the statute authorizing mergers, whereas in this case the corporate creation and the stock issue preceded adoption of such a statute. That distinguishing feature brings into question what limitations, if any, exist to a state's authority under the reserved power to permit by subsequent legislation corporate acts which affect the preferential rights of a stockholder. More specifically, it raises the problem of whether subsequent legislation is repugnant to the federal and state constitutional prohibitions against the passage of laws impairing the obligations of contracts, because it permits elimination of accumulated preferred dividends by a lesser vote than was required under the law in existence at the time of the incorporation and when the stock was issued.

The mere mention of the constitutional prohibitions against such laws calls to mind Trustees of Dartmouth College v. Woodward, 17 U.S. 518, 4 Wheaton 518, 4 L.Ed. 629, where the decision was that a private corporation charter granted by the state is a contract protected under the constitution against repeal, amendment or alteration by subsequent legislation. Of equal significance in the field of corporation law is Mr. Justice Story's concurring opinion wherein he suggested that application of the impairment clause upon acts of incorporation might be avoided if a state legislature, coincident with granting a corporate charter, reserved as a part of that contract the right of amendment or repeal. With such a reservation, he said, any subsequent amendment or repeal would be pursuant, rather than repugnant, to the terms of the contract and would not therefore impair its obligation.

Our own legislature was quick to heed Story's advice, and in the early part of the 19th century, when corporations were customarily created by special act, the power to alter, amend, or revoke was written directly into each charter. Later, when the practice changed and corporations, instead of being created by special enactment, were incorporated under the general corporation law, the power to amend and repeal was reserved in an act of general application, and since at least as far back as 1844 the corporation law has read in substance as it does today viz., " * * * The charter or articles of association of every corporation hereafter created may be amended or repealed at the will of the general assembly." Section 7–1–13.

The language in which the reserved power is customarily stated is not, however, self-explaining, and the extent of the legislative authority under it has frequently been a source of difficulty. Recognizing that problem, but not answering it, the United States Supreme Court said in a frequently quoted passage:

> "The authority of a state under the so-called reserve power is wide; but it is not unlimited. The corporate charter may be repealed or amended, and, within limits not now necessary to define, the interrelations of state, corporation and stockholders may be changed; but neither vested property rights nor the obligation of contracts of third persons may be destroyed or impaired." Coombes v. Getz, 285 U.S. 434.

* * * On the basis of our own precedents we conclude that the merger legislation, notwithstanding its effect on the rights of its stockholders, did not necessarily constitute an improper exercise of the right of amendment reserved merely because it was subsequent.

In addition to arguing that the proposed plan suffers from a constitutional infirmity, plaintiffs also contend that it is unfair and inequitable to them, and that its consummation should, therefore, be enjoined. By that assertion they raise the problem of whether equity should heed the request of a dissenting stockholder and intervene to prevent a merger notwithstanding that it has received the vote of the designated proportions of the various classes of stock of the constituent corporations.

In looking to the authorities for assistance on this question, we avoided those involving recapitalization by charter amendment where a dissident's only remedy against allegedly unfair treatment was in equity. In those situations the authorities generally permit equitable intervention to protect against unfair or inequitable treatment. Kamena v. Janssen Dairy Corp., 133 N.J.Eq. 214, 31 A.2d 200, aff'd, 134 N.J.Eq. 359, 35 A.2d 894. They are founded on the concept that otherwise there might be confiscation without recompense. The same rationale, however, is not available in the case of a merger, because there the dissenting stockholders usually can find a measure of protection in the statutory procedures giving them the option to compel the corporation to purchase their shares at an appraised value. This is a significant difference and is ample reason for considering the two situations as raising separate and distinct issues. Anderson v. International Minerals & Chemical Corp., supra.

This case involves a merger, not a recapitalization by charter amendment, and in this state the legislature, looking to the possibility that there might be those who would not be agreeable to the proposed merger, provided a means whereby a dissatisfied stockholder might demand and the corporation be compelled to pay the fair value of his securities. G.L.1956, §§ 7-5-8 through 7-5-16 inclusive. Our inquiry then is to the effect of that remedy upon plaintiff's right to challenge the proposed merger on the ground that it is unfair and inequitable because it dictates what shall be their proportionate interests in the corporate assets. Once again there is no agreement among the authorities. Vorenberg, 'Exclusiveness of the Dissenting Stockholder's Appraisal Right,' 77 Harv.L.Rev. 1189. See also Annot. 162 A.L.R. 1237, 1250. Some authorities appear to say that the statutory remedy of appraisal is exclusive. Beloff v. Consolidated Edison Co., 300 N.Y. 11, 87 N.E.2d 561; Hubbard v. Jones & Laughlin Steel Corp., D.C., 42 F.Supp. 432. Others say that it may be disregarded and that equity may intervene if the minority is treated oppressively or unfairly, Barnett v. Philadelphia Market Co., 218 Pa. 649, 67 A. 912; May v. Midwest Refining Co., 1 Cir., 121 F.2d 431, cert. denied 314 U.S. 668, 62 Sup.Ct. 129, 86 L.Ed. 534, or if the merger is tainted with fraud or illegality, Adams v. United States Distributing Corp., 184 Va. 134, 147, 34 S.E.2d 244, 250, 162 A.L.R. 1227; Porges v. Vadsco Sales Corp., 27 Del.Ch. 127, 32 A.2d 148. To these differing views must also be added the divergence of opinion on whether those in control or those dissenting must bear the burden of establishing that the plan meets whatever the required standard may be. Vorenberg, supra; 77 Harv.L.Rev. 1189, 1210-1215.

In this case we do not choose as between the varying views, nor is there any need for us to do so. Even were we to accept that view which is most favorable to plaintiffs we still would not be able to find that they have been either unfairly or inequitably treated. The record insofar as it relates to the unfairness issue is at best sparse. In substance it consists of the corporation's balance sheet as of September 1967, together with supporting schedules. That statement uses book, rather than the appraised, values, and neither it nor any other evidentiary matter in any way indicates, except as the same may be reflected in the surplus account, the corporation's earning history or its prospects for profitable operations in the future.

Going to the figures we find a capital and surplus account of. $669,948 of which $453,000 is allocable to the 4,530 issued and outstanding shares of $100 par value preferred stock and the balance of $216,948 to surplus. Obviously, a realization of the book value of the assets in the event of liquidation, forced or otherwise, would not only leave nothing for the common stockholders, but would not even suffice to pay the preferred shareholders the par value of their stock plus the accrued dividends of $645,000.

If we were to follow a rule of absolute priority, any proposal which would give anything to common stockholders without first providing for full payment of stated value plus dividend accruals would be unfair to the preferred shareholders. It could be argued that the proposal in this case violates that rule because an exchange of one share of Community Hotel's preferred stock for five shares of Newport's common stock would give the preferred shareholders securities worth less than the amount of their liquidation preference rights while at the same time the one to one exchange ratio on the common would enrich Community Hotel's common stockholders by allowing them to participate in its surplus.

An inherent fallacy in applying the rule of absolute priority to the circumstances of this case, however, is its assumption that assets would be liquidated and that nothing more than their book value will be realized. But Community Hotel is not in liquidation. Instead it is a going concern which, because of its present capitalization, cannot obtain the modern debt-financing needed to meet threatened competition. Moreover, management, in the call of the meeting at which it was intended to consider and vote on the plan, said that the proposed recapitalization plan was conceived only " * * * after careful consideration by your Board of Directors and a review of the relative values of the preferred and common stocks by the independent public accountants of the Corporation. The exchange ratio of five new common shares for each share of the existing preferred stock was determined on the basis of the book and market values of the preferred and the inherent value of the unpaid preferred dividends." Those assertions are contained in a document admitted as an exhibit and they have testimonial value.

When the varying considerations—both balance sheet figures and management's assertions—are taken into account, we are unable to conclude, at least at this stage of the proceedings, that the proposed plan is unfair and inequitable, particularly because plaintiffs as dissidents may avail themselves of the opportunity to receive the fair market value of their securities under the appraisal methods prescribed in § 7–5–8 through § 7–5–16 inclusive. * * *

For the reasons stated, the judgment appealed from is affirmed.

NOTES

1. Was this merger fair to the preferred shareholders? Consider the fact that their dividends were in arrears for twenty-four years. As the result of the merger, those arrearages would be lost, as they probably were as a practical matter in any event. In exchange for giving up those arrearages, the old preferred shareholder would own over ninety percent of the new corporation, while the old common shareholders would own less than ten percent. The old common shareholders thus had to give up most of their equity interest to the preferred in order for the corporation to have a new start and possibly make profits for all.

2. Another method for eliminating accrued cumulative dividends is to offer to exchange a new class of prior preferred stock for the old cumulative preferred. There is an element of coercion in such an offer because the old cumulative preferred will not receive dividends until the prior preferred are paid, if at all. In *Patterson v. Durham Hosiery Mills*, 214 N.C. 806, 200 S.E. 906 (1939), the court held that such a plan was coercive even though the old preferred shareholders were also given a new preferred share and two shares of common stock for each old preferred. Ninety eight percent of the shareholders approved the exchange. The court described the nature of cumulative dividends as follows:

> Dividends on common stock are not segregated from the assets of the corporation, so as to become the property of the stockholder, or a debt recoverable by action at law, until declared. In the absence of statute or charter provision requiring distribution, they may be passed into the surplus, remain undivided profits, or be reinvested in the corporate enterprise, at the sound discretion of the directors. While the preferred stockholder is not a creditor of the corporation until the dividend is declared, his right to that dividend stands upon a somewhat different footing. While as a matter of law the right to receive dividends, even on preferred stock, is made to depend on the actual existence of earnings, he has, in appropriate cases, a remedy in equity to compel the payment of his dividends; and we think, meantime, the right to their equitable protection. Dividends are cumulative under plaintiffs' stock, and the right to receive them out of earnings does not abate because they were not promptly declared. The right of the plaintiffs to receive dividends at the expiration of stated periods during which they are earned, and the maturing of the dates upon which the premiums were due, created a definite obligation on the part of the corporation to pay such dividends, out of appropriate funds, of course, which must be considered a vested

property right, although circumstances might intervene to postpone or prevent its enjoyment.

200 S.E. at 908–909. *See also* Barrett v. Denver Tramway Corp., 53 F.Supp. 198 (D.Del.1943), *aff'd*, 146 F.2d 701 (3d Cir.1944) (exchange of new non-cumulative preferred for old cumulative preferred objectively unfair but not fraudulent and was permissible).

Cumulative preferred stock that is in arrears on dividends will usually trade at a discount. This provides an opportunity for the corporation to buy up those shares at a price less than their liquidating value and accrued dividends or to otherwise avoid those preferences.

IN RE SUNSTATES CORP. SHAREHOLDER LITIGATION
788 A.2d 530 (Del.Ch.2001).

LAMB, VICE CHANCELLOR.

* * *The pertinent facts are easily stated. Sunstates Corporation is a Delaware corporation having a number of subsidiaries incorporated in various jurisdictions. Article IV, Section 4.3 of the Sunstates certificate of incorporation creates the $3.75 Preferred Stock. Paragraph 3 thereof specifies the dividend rights of that stock and provides that, unless Sunstates is current in its payment of dividends on the Preferred Stock:

> [t]he Corporation shall not (i) declare or pay or set apart for payment any dividends or distributions on any stock ranking as to dividends junior to the $3.75 Preferred Stock (other than dividends paid in shares of such junior stock) or (ii) *make any purpose . . . of . . . any stock ranking as to dividends junior or* pari passu *to the $3.75 Preferred Stock . . .*

(emphasis added). Paragraph 4(e) of section 4.3 similarly proscribes all non-pro rata purchases of shares of Preferred Stock when dividends are in arrears, as follows:

> [I]n the event that any semiannual dividend payable on the $3.75 Preferred Stock shall be in arrears and until all such dividends in arrears shall have been paid or declared and set apart for payment, the Corporation shall not . . . purchase or otherwise acquire any shares of $3.75 Preferred Stock except in accordance with a purchase offer made by the Corporation on the same terms to all holders of record of $3.75 Preferred Stock for the purchase of all outstanding shares thereof.

Article I, section 1.1 of the certificate defines the "Corporation" to mean Sunstates Corporation. Nothing in the certificate expressly provides that the "Corporation" includes anything but Sunstates Corporation.

In 1991, Sunstates fell into arrears in the payment of the Preferred Stock dividend. Over the next two years, subsidiary corporations controlled, directly or indirectly, by Sunstates bought shares of both common stock and Preferred Stock. The Preferred Shares were not acquired in compliance with the "any and all" tender offer requirement of paragraph 4(e). According to plaintiffs' brief, the repurchases of common stock amounted, over a three year period, to nearly 70 percent of the total outstanding common stock. The Preferred Stock repurchased equaled nearly 30 percent of the total number outstanding.

Plaintiffs point to evidence from which it may be inferred that the decisions to make all these purchases were made by a single person, Clyde Engle. Engle is Sunstates's Chairman and also served as the Investment Officer for Coronet Insurance Company, one of Sunstates's indirect, wholly-owned subsidiaries. Engle controls Sunstates through his owner-ship control over Telco Capital Corporation, the owner, directly or indi-rectly, of a majority of Sunstates's common stock. Engle conducted the share repurchase program through Crown Casualty Company and Suns-tates Equities, Inc., wholly-owned subsidiaries of Coronet Insurance Com-pany, and through Sew Simple Systems, Inc. and National Assurance Indemnitee Corp., indirect, wholly-owned subsidiaries of Sunstates.* * *

Section 151(a) of the Delaware General Corporation Law allows Delaware corporations to issue stock having such "special rights, and qualifications, limitations or restrictions" relating thereto "as shall be stated and expressed in the certificate of incorporation or of any amend-ment thereto...." Thus, the law recognizes that the existence and extent of rights of preferred stock must be determined by reference to the certificate of incorporation, those rights being essentially contractual in nature. As was said by this court more than 70 years ago:

> It is elementary that the rights of stockholders are contract rights. The mere word "preferred" unless it is supplemented by a definition of its significance conveys no special meaning. The holder of preferred stock must, therefore, refer to the appropriate language of the corpo-rate contract for the ascertainment of his rights. The nub of the present controversy is—where may such appropriate language be found? The exceptants say in the certificate of incorporation and nowhere else. In this I think they are right.[14]

Moreover, the law is settled that, while courts "will employ principles of contract interpretation, and read the Certificate in its entirety to arrive at the intended meaning of the words employed in any specific provision," stock preferences are to be strictly construed and nothing is to be presumed in their favor. "[A]ny ambiguity must be resolved against granting the challenged preferences, rights or powers."

Plaintiffs advance no construction of the certificate of incorporation that would permit me to read the word "Corporation" to refer to any corporation other than Sunstates. This is hardly surprising since the language at issue is clear in its meaning and there is nothing within the four corners of the certificate suggesting a broader or different interpreta-

---

14. *Gaskill v. Gladys Belle Oil Co.*, Del.Ch., 146 A. 337, 339 (1929).

tion. Thus, as a matter of simple contract interpretation, there is no basis on which to apply the special limitation against share repurchases to any entity other than Sunstates.

As earlier mentioned, plaintiffs do make several other arguments that require discussion. First, they argue that the subsidiary corporations making the share purchases were acting as mere agents for Sunstates and, for that reason, the court should treat their acts as those of Sunstates. Second, they argue that the repurchases violated the implied covenant of good faith and fair dealing. I will address these now.

Plaintiffs' agency theory is both factually and legally flawed. Factually, the record suggests that the repurchases were made to further the interests of Engle, the person who (through several layers of intermediary corporations) controlled Sunstates, and not Sunstates's own interests. Plaintiffs' brief states as follows:

> In committing so much money to these repurchases, Engle had two overriding purposes: to prop up the price of Sunstates' common stock, which was the sole asset of Sunstates' parent companies ... and which was the collateral those companies had used for their loans; and to assemble a large enough block of preferred stock to assure that, in the event that the preferred stockholders ever forced an annual meeting and attempted to exercise their rights to elect half the directors, those shares could be used to block any effort by the class members to secure representation on the Sunstates board [and] assure that [Engle's] hand-picked cronies were re-elected.

Thus, the factual predicate necessary to argue that the purchasing subsidiaries were acting as Sunstates's agents is weak or missing.

The legal flaw in the agency argument is more fundamental. For the purposes of the corporation law, the act of one corporation is not regarded as the act of another merely because the first corporation is a subsidiary of the other, or because the two may be treated as part of a single economic enterprise for some other purpose. Rather, to pierce the corporate veil based on an agency or "alter ego" theory, "the corporation must be a sham and exist for no other purpose than as a vehicle for fraud."

Plaintiffs' brief simply ignores this more difficult standard—offering no record evidence from which I might infer that any of the four corporations making the share repurchases was a sham or existed merely to perpetrate a fraud. On the contrary, the record shows that each of those entities was engaged in substantial business operations and was formed or acquired by Sunstates for purposes relating to the pursuit of normal business operations. In the circumstances, it is clear to me that there is no basis in the record or the law of corporate veil-piercing from which I might infer that the program of share repurchases by those subsidiaries should be treated as though Sunstates, itself, was the buyer. * * *

In the final analysis, plaintiffs' arguments run counter to both the doctrine of strict construction of special rights, preferences and limitations relating to stock and the doctrine of independent legal significance. The situation is not unlike that confronted in *Rothschild Int'l Corp. v. Liggett Group, Inc.*[15] There, the plaintiffs owned preferred shares that were entitled to a liquidation preference. To avoid paying this preference, the defendant companies structured a combined tender offer and reverse cash-out merger that eliminated the preferred shares for a price substantially lower than the liquidation preference. Construing the charter provision strictly, the Supreme Court concluded that the charter provision only operated in the case of a liquidation and that there had been no liquidation. Applying the doctrine of independent legal significance, the Supreme Court reiterated "that 'action taken under one section of [the DGCL] is legally independent, and its validity is not dependent upon, nor to be tested by the requirements of other unrelated sections under which the same final result might be attained by different means.'"

For these reasons, the defendants' motion for partial summary judgment as to Count II of the Amended Complaint will be granted.

SECTION 5. REMARKETED PREFERRED STOCK

In order to make preferred more flexible, financial engineers developed something called remarketed preferred stock. This is a preferred stock that pays a floating rate dividend. The dividend is reset periodically, and the purchaser may tender the security on the remarketing date for a price at which those shares can be remarketed at their liquidation value. A variation on this security is the auction rate preferred stock that has a floating rate dividend. That dividend is reset at specified intervals through an auction in which bidders set the rate at a level that allows the security to sell at its liquidation value. These securities were popular in certain tax-advantaged situations (such as for corporate investors that had a partial dividend exclusion from income advantage) and in certain regulatory situations where preferred stock was more advantageous to the issuer than debt.

> The following is a description in the prospectus of one such offering:
>
> First Federal Capital Funding IV, Inc. (the "Company") is a newly formed Delaware corporation organized for the sole purpose of issuing the shares of RP ["Exchangeable Remarketed Preferred Stock"] and managing Eligible Assets consisting of cash, FHLMC Certificates, FNMA Certificates, GNMA Certificates, Conventional Mortgage Pass-through Certificates, U.S. Treasury Securities, Short–Term Money Market Instruments and certain Other Securities as described in this Prospectus. The principal business of the Company will be to purchase, acquire, own, hold, invest in, sell, trade and exchange such

---

15.   Del.Supr., 474 A.2d 133 (1984).

Eligible Assets and to use the income generated by such Eligible Assets to pay dividends and to acquire additional Eligible Assets and to conduct activities incidental thereto. All of the Company's outstanding Common Stock is owned by First Federal Savings and Loan Association of Rochester (the "Association" or "First Federal"), Rochester, New York. See "The Company," "Management" and "Management Discussion and Analysis of Financial Condition and Results of Operations."

The Company is offering 1,500 shares of RP at a purchase price of $100,000 per share. At the election of the Company, subject to certain conditions, the shares of RP are exchangeable in whole for Notes, in the event of certain changes in tax law or on or after the first anniversary of the Date of Original Issue.... * * *

Dividends on the shares of RP are cumulative from the Date of Original Issue and are payable when, as and if declared by the Board of Directors of the Company, commencing on August 22, 1988, in the case of 500 shares of RP, commencing on August 29, 1988 with respect to an additional 500 shares of RP, and commencing on September 12, 1988, in the case of the remaining 500 shares of RP (each, an "Initial Dividend Payment Date") and thereafter on the Business Day following the last of each successive 7–day Dividend Period or 49–day Dividend Period, as the case may be (normally a Monday), subject to certain exceptions (a "Dividend Payment Date"). On the Tender Date with respect to each share of RP, the holder of such share can elect either to tender such share of RP at a price of $100,000 per share, or to hold such share at the new Applicable Dividend Rate and elect either a 7–day Dividend Period or a 49–day Dividend Period with respect thereto. The Applicable Dividend Rate for the Initial Dividend Period ending on August 21, 1988 will be 6.05% per annum, for the Initial Dividend Period ending on August 28, 1988 will be 6.05% per annum, and for the Initial Dividend Period ending on September 11, 1988 will be 6.10% per annum. For each Dividend Period after the corresponding Initial Dividend Period, dividends on each share of RP will accrue at the Applicable Dividend Rate per annum as determined by the Remarketing Agent in its sole judgment (which judgment will be conclusive and binding on all holders).... * * *

Prospectus $150,000,000 First Federal Capital Funding IV, Inc. Exchangeable Remarketed Preferred Stock ["RP"] 1,500 Shares—Liquidation Preference $100,000 Per Share.

NOTES

1. A tax play on dividends made the First Federal program possible. Do you think that such securities should be treated as debt or equity on the

balance sheet? Is this program really an equity investment or simply a way to profit on the spread between the dividend payment and the lower interest on the remarketed preferred that is tax advantaged? For a discussion of the tax aspects of adjustable rate preferred stock see American Bar Association Section of Taxation Comm. On Financial Transactions Sub Comm. on Asset Securitizations, 46 Tax L. Rev. 299, 322–325 (1991).

2.   The Internal Revenue Code was amended in 2003 to reduce the tax on dividends to 15 percent. Will this encourage offerings of remarketed preferred to individuals since the top rate for income from debt instruments is more than twice that amount?

3.   How does a remarketed security differ from the auction rate security discussed in Chapter 4?

SECTION 6.   PREFERRED STOCK VARIATIONS

TODD H. EVESON
FINANCIAL AND BANK HOLDING COMPANY ISSUANCE OF TRUST PREFERRED SECURITIES

6 N.C. Banking Institute 315–317 (2002).

Since the first issuance of a "trust preferred" type security in 1993,[16] the aggregate offering price of all trust preferred securities issued annually in the United States has steadily increased, while the same period has been characterized by a corresponding decrease in the aggregate offering price of all traditional preferred securities issued. This trend exists, in spite of the higher transaction costs associated with an issuance of trust preferred securities as compared to those associated with an issuance of traditional preferred shares, because of the primary advantages of trust preferred securities: (1) they do not involve the direct issuance of equity and do not therefore dilute earnings per share or return on equity of the

---

16.   Texaco, Inc. is usually cited as the first issuer of a trust preferred security. See George Benston, Paul Irvine, Jim Rosenfield & Joseph F. Sinkey, Jr., Federal Reserve Bank of Atlanta, Bank Capital Structure, Regulatory Capital and Securities Innovations, 6 (Oct. 2000) (working paper series). In October 1993, Texaco issued a hybrid security called 6–7/8% Cumulative Guaranteed Monthly Income Preferred Shares ("Mips"). Form 10–K of Texaco, Inc., as filed with the Securities and Exchange Commission on March 28, 1994, at http://www.sec.gov (last visited Feb. 8, 2002). This security was the prototype for today's trust preferred shares. Texaco's hybrid involved the issuance of preferred shares by a limited liability company organized under the laws of the Turks & Caicos Islands, British West Indies. The proceeds from the sale of these securities were then loaned to Texaco, Inc. In this manner, Texaco was able to deduct from income the interest payments made to service the debt owed to the limited liability company. Texaco cited this advantage in its annual report for 1993. Id. Texaco, Inc. also effected a second issuance of its "Cumulative Guaranteed Monthly Income Preferred Shares" in September 1994. See Preliminary Prospectus Summary of Texaco, Inc. and Texaco Capital, LLC, as filed with the Securities and Exchange Commission on June 3, 1994 at http://www.sec.gov (last visited Feb. 22, 2002). Trust preferred securities are known by various acronyms, including TruPS ("trust preferred securities" or "trust pass-through securities"), Quics ("quarterly income capital securities"), Quips ("quarterly income preferred shares"), Skis ("subordinated capital income shares"), Toprs ("trust originated preferred shares"), and Mips ("monthly income preferred shares").

issuer; and (2) the disbursements paid by the issuer of a trust preferred security, unlike dividends paid on traditional preferred stock, are typically tax deductible.

Trust preferred securities achieve these advantages because they are "hybrid" securities, possessing favorable characteristics of both equity and debt. The "hybrid" nature of trust preferred securities derives from the fact that their issuance actually involves two offerings: first, the issuance of subordinated debt to a specially formed subsidiary of the issuer; and second, the issuance of equity, by that subsidiary, to investors. This subsidiary is typically a trust and the equity it issues is typically preferred stock, thus the name "trust preferred."

Trust preferred securities have become increasingly popular with financial holding companies and bank holding companies precisely because they are hybrid securities, possessing the favorable characteristics of both equity and debt. Until 1996, however, it was not clear whether trust preferred securities had enough equity characteristics to qualify as Tier 1 capital of a holding company. As a result, the utility of these securities was limited, at least from the standpoint of a bank holding company. All of this changed on October 21, 1996, when the Board of Governors of the Federal Reserve System ruled that the proceeds of trust preferred securities would, subject to certain limitations, qualify as Tier 1 capital of a holding company. Since the date of the Federal Reserve's ruling, trust preferred securities have become increasingly popular with holding companies, including many community bank holding companies, as a tool for generating Tier 1 capital. * * *

The Board of Governors of the Federal Reserve System has established certain capital measures to assist in the assessment of the capital adequacy of holding companies. In order to ensure that these measures are meaningful, the Federal Reserve mandates precise methods for calculating an institution's qualifying total capital. Qualifying total capital is the sum of two distinct components: Tier 1 capital and Tier 2 capital.

Tier 1 capital is a crucial measure for two reasons. First, Tier 1 capital is the only form of capital which factors into the calculus of an institution's Tier 1 leverage ratio. Second, Tier 1 capital limits the amount of Tier 2 capital that may be included in qualifying total capital. While Tier 1 capital is a component of qualifying total capital, it is itself composed of four elements. "These elements are common stockholders' equity, qualifying non-cumulative perpetual preferred stock (including related surplus), qualifying cumulative perpetual stock (including related surplus) and minority interests in the equity accounts of consolidated subsidiaries."

Common stockholders' equity is comprised of common stock, related surplus and retained earnings, including associated capital reserves, less certain deductions. A holding company may not, however, take into account treasury shares in its computation of common stockholders' equity.

Common stockholders' equity is the form of Tier 1 capital most favored by regulatory agencies, because it is the source of capital with the purest equity characteristics. The form of Tier 1 capital most favored from a regulatory standpoint is not, however, necessarily the form most favored by holding companies. Hybrid instruments, the proceeds of which meet the qualifications for Tier 1 treatment, may be preferable from the standpoint of an issuing holding company because they allow the issuing holding company to take a deduction for the associated dividend/interest disbursements and because they do not involve the direct issuance of equity by the issuer, and do not, therefore, dilute earnings per share or return on equity.

The second element of Tier 1 capital is "perpetual preferred stock." Perpetual preferred stock, as the term suggests, is simply preferred stock that is not associated with any redemption or maturity feature and that is not callable by the holder. The Federal Reserve's regulations draw a distinction between two sub-types of perpetual preferred stock: non-cumulative perpetual preferred stock and cumulative preferred stock. Each sub-type allows for the deferral of dividends, but in the case of cumulative perpetual preferred stock, dividends that are deferred continue to add up; whereas in the case of non-cumulative perpetual preferred stock, the issuer has the right to eliminate the payment of dividends altogether. Because non-cumulative perpetual preferred stock has characteristics that more closely resemble pure equity, the Federal Reserve places no limit on the amount of non-cumulative perpetual preferred stock that can qualify as Tier 1 capital of a holding company. Cumulative perpetual preferred stock, on the other hand, is not accorded the same regulatory treatment because the issuer of cumulative perpetual preferred stock cannot totally eliminate the payment of dividends. This trait places cumulative perpetual preferred stock farther away from pure equity and closer to the middle of the debt/equity continuum. As a result, the Federal Reserve permits the inclusion of the proceeds of cumulative perpetual preferred stock in Tier 1 capital, but it limits the amount that may qualify as Tier 1 capital to one quarter of total Tier 1 capital.

NOTES

1. The Tier 1 capital reference in the above excerpt is to a requirement that banks maintain a minimum amount of equity capital on their balance sheets in order to prevent the bank from becoming over-leveraged. Is that goal furthered by recognizing trust preferred as Tier 1 capital? The widespread use of trust preferred securities during the subprime crisis that arose between 2007 and 2009 as a means to boost bank capital caused concerns. A last minute amendment to the Dodd–Frank Wall Street Reform and Consumer Protection Act of 2010 phased out the use of trust preferred securities as Tier 1 capital for larger banks. A proposed alternative to trust preferred securities

are "contigent capital" securities called "CoCos." These securities are issued as debt but convert to equity securities when the issuing bank's capital ration falls below a specified level. This conversion then boosts the bank's capital and provides further protection to more conventional debt and depositors. Section 115 of the Dodd–Frank Act of 2010 directed the newly created Financial Stability Oversight Council to conduct a study and report to Congress on the elements of these instruments and their value in bank capital structures.

2.   The Enron Corp. created another way to turn debt into equity by creating an entity called Whitewing that borrowed $1 billion from Citigroup, Inc. and then used the proceeds to buy Enron preferred stock. Bethany McLean & Peter Elkind, The Smartest Guys in the Room, The Amazing Rise and Scandalous Fall of Enron 155 (2003).

3.   General Motors has offered several forms of preferred stock, including a perpetual preferred that was to be an alternative to a money fund investment. It also issued something called preferred equity redemption cumulative stock ("PERCS") that required redemption in three years through an exchange for the company's common stock but placed a cap on the possible appreciation gain of 35 percent over par. GM had another class of preferred that had contingent voting rights that management thought could be used to challenge their control, and that class was retired through a payment of $120 for each $5 preferred share. III Jerry W. Markham, A Financial History of the United States, From the Age of Derivatives to the New Millennium (1970–2001) 214 (2002).

4.   Hybrid preferred stock may also be used to leverage through debt under the Investment Company Act of 1940. See Chapter 13.

5.   In 1918, the Ford Motor Company issued "Ford Motor Certificates" to its employees. These instruments paid a rate of return that was based on company profits but with a minimum interest payment of six percent. Douglas Brinkley, Wheels for the World 280 (2003). Is this a debt instrument or a form of preferred stock?

6.   At the end of the twentieth century, the Enron Corp. was issuing "equity certificates," which was stock that paid a fixed return to investors. Bethany McLean & Peter Elkind, The Smartest Guys in the Room, The Amazing Rise and Scandalous Fall of Enron 249 (2003).

CHAPTER SIX

STOCK SUBSCRIPTIONS, PREEMPTIVE RIGHTS, DIVIDENDS, AND OTHER DISTRIBUTIONS

■ ■ ■

Chapter objectives

- To understand the different legal theories used to provide an equity capital cushion for the benefit of a corporation's creditors.

- To see how common law and statutory preemptive rights protect a shareholder from dilution of value as a result of subsequent share issuance by the corporation.

- To understand both common law and contemporary restrictions on dividend distributions to shareholders.

- To identify when a corporation's distributions to shareholders may expose the corporate directors or shareholder-distributees to liability.

SECTION 1.   INTRODUCTION

Equity ownership raises a broad range of questions in the context of corporate finance. A threshold issue that arises during the issuance of corporate shares is whether an investor has given adequate value for these shares. Even when share issuance is adequately funded, existing shareholders may enjoy a property right to keep their interest in the corporation from being diluted when additional shares are issued to new owners. To varying degrees, corporate law also protects the creditors of a corporation by limiting the extent to which a corporation can upstream value to its owners if doing so would interfere with satisfying corporate debts. Both a corporation's managers and its owners may become liable when dividends are improperly distributed. Finally, closely-held corporations present special issues regarding the need to protect minority shareholders and the enforceability of redemption agreements.

318

SECTION 2. STOCK SUBSCRIPTIONS

Promoters of a corporation often sell stock to potential investors in advance of the formation of the corporation, as well as after. Such sales are made under subscription agreements that promise issuance of the stock to the subscriber upon formation of the corporation. State statutes may regulate the terms of stock subscriptions. For example, New York makes stock subscriptions irrevocable for a period of three months unless certain conditions are met. In addition, the subscription must be in writing in order to be enforceable. N.Y. Bus. Corp. L. § 503. *See generally* Estate of Purnell v. LH Radiologists, P.C., 90 N.Y.2d 524, 664 N.Y.S.2d 238, 686 N.E.2d 1332 (Ct.App.1997) (agreement to form a corporation was not a subscription agreement that was subject to the terms of § 503(b)).

Other issues that arise under subscription agreements are the adequacy and validity of the consideration paid for the stock and whether creditors of the corporation can enforce a subscription agreement when the corporation becomes insolvent. State statutes also require directors to value consideration given for shares to prevent the issuance of "watered" stock.

BING CROSBY MINUTE MAID CORP. v. EATON

46 Cal.2d 484, 297 P.2d 5 (1956).

SHENK, JUSTICE.

The plaintiff appeals from an order granting a new trial after judgment in its favor. The defendant appeals from the judgment.

As a judgment creditor of a corporation the plaintiff brought this action against a shareholder of the corporation to recover the difference between the par value of stock issued to him and the fair value of the consideration he paid for the stock. At the conclusion of the trial, the court, sitting without a jury, made findings of fact and conclusions of law and entered judgment for the plaintiff. In support of his motion for a new trial the defendant assigned certain alleged defects in the findings as errors of law.

The defendant formed a corporation to acquire his going frozen foods business. The Commissioner of Corporations issued a permit authorizing the corporation to sell and issue not more than 4,500 shares of $10 par value stock to the defendant and other named individuals in consideration of the transfer of the business. The permit provided that 1,022 shares be deposited in escrow and not be transferred without the written consent of the Commissioner, and that the escrowed shares not be sold or issued until the prospective shareholders named in the permit waived certain rights to dividends and to participation in any distribution of assets.

The defendant transferred his business to the corporation. The corporation placed 1,022 shares in escrow in his name pursuant to the provisions of the permit. The remaining 3,478 shares were issued outright to the defendant and after three years were transferred to the other persons named in the permit. Although the 1,022 shares were listed on the corporate records as held by the defendant (accompanied by the notation "escrowed"), they were never released from escrow. The corporation had financial difficulties and executed an assignment of its assets for the benefit of creditors to a credit association. The plaintiff recovered a judgment against the corporation for $21,246.42. A writ of execution on the judgment was returned unsatisfied.

The trial court found that the value to the corporation of the consideration from the defendant was $34,780.83; that 4,500 shares of stock having a par value of $10 each were issued to the defendant and he became the owner of those shares; that subsequent to the issue of the shares the corporation purchased merchandise from the plaintiff and has not yet paid for all of it; that some $15,000 of the judgment the plaintiff recovered from the corporation remains unsatisfied, and that the corporation is insolvent.

The judgment for the plaintiff was for $10,219.17—approximately the par value of the 1,022 shares of stock placed in escrow. The judgment was based on the trial court's conclusion that the defendant was liable for the difference between the par value of the 4,500 shares and the value of the consideration the defendant paid for them.

The plaintiff contends that the trial court's findings of fact were supported by the evidence and required a judgment in its favor, and therefore that it was error to grant a new trial. The defendant contends that the order granting a new trial was proper because (1) the finding that he was the owner of 4,500 shares was unsupported by the evidence, and (2) the trial court failed to make a finding on a material issue raised by his answer.

In this state a shareholder is ordinarily not personally liable for the debts of the corporation; he undertakes only the risk that his shares may become worthless. See repeal of Cal.Const. Art. XII, § 3, at general election, nov. 4, 1930; repeal of former Civ.Code section 322, Stats.1931, ch. 257, p. 444; Kaysser v. McNaughton, 6 Cal.2d 248, 251–255, 57 P.2d 927. There are, however, certain exceptions to this rule of limited liability. For example, a subscriber to shares who pays in only part of what he agreed to pay is liable to creditors for the balance. Corp. Code, §§ 1300, 1306. Although the trial court in the present case found that the defendant had agreed to pay par value for the 4,500 shares registered in his name, the record on appeal discloses no evidence supporting this finding. Therefore, the defendant's liability cannot be predicated upon the theory that a subscribing shareholder is liable for the full consideration agreed to be paid for the shares.

The plaintiff seeks to base its recovery on the only other exception to the limited liability rule that the record could support, namely, liability for holding watered stock, which is stock issued in return for properties or services worth less than its par value. Accordingly, this case calls for an analysis of the rights of a creditor of an insolvent corporation against a holder of watered stock. Holders of watered stock are generally held liable to the corporation's creditors for the difference between the par value of the stock and the amount paid in.

The defendant's first contention is that because of the escrow he never became an owner of the 1,022 shares and that he therefore never acquired such title to the 1,022 shares as would enable a creditor to proceed against him for their par value. Section 25508 of the Corporations Code authorizes the Commissioner of Corporations to require that shares be placed in escrow has frequently been exercised for the protection of the public. The escrow in the present case permitted the defendant to retain some, but not all, of the incidents of ownership in the 1,022 shares. Although he could not transfer the shares, it appears that despite the escrow he was entitled to count them in determining the extent of his rights to vote and to participate in dividends and asset distributions. The critical feature of the escrow of purposes of the present case is the absence of any restriction on representations that the escrowed shares were outstanding and fully paid. Although the escrow contained provisions designed to protect future stockholders, it afforded no special protection to future creditors of the corporation. Therefore, the escrow did not affect the rights of future creditors and it would appear that despite the escrow the defendant acquired sufficient title to the 1,022 shares to permit the plaintiff to proceed against him for their par value.

The defendant's second contention is that the trial court failed to make a finding on a material issue raised by his answer.

The liability of a holder of watered stock has been based on one of two theories: the misrepresentation theory or the statutory obligation theory. The misrepresentation theory is the one accepted in most jurisdictions. The courts view the issue of watered stock as a misrepresentation of the corporation's capital. Creditors who rely on this misrepresentation are entitled to recover the "water" from the holders of the watered shares. See cases collected in Ballantine, Corporations, rev. ed. 1946, sec. 350; Dodd and Baker, Cases and Materials on Corporations, 2d ed. 1951, pp. 786–789; 11 Fletcher, Cyclopedia of the Law of Private Corporations, rev. and perm. ed. 1932, sec. 5232, p. 568, n. 64, sec. 5233, pp. 577–579; Bonbright, "Shareholders' Defenses Against Liability to Creditors on Watered Stock." 1925, 25 Col.L.Rev. 408, 412, 420–421.

Statutes expressly prohibiting watered stock are commonplace today. See statutes collected in 11 Fletcher, Cyclopedia of the Law of Private Corporations, rev. and perm. ed. 1932, sec. 5209. In some jurisdictions where they have been enacted, the statutory obligation theory has been applied. See cases collected in 7 A.L.R. 983–986; Dodd and Baker, cases and Materials on Corporations, 2d ed. 1951, p. 795, n. 7. Under that theory the holder of watered stock is held responsible to creditors whether or not they have relied on an overvaluation of corporate capital.

In his answer the defendant alleged that in extending credit to the corporation the plaintiff did not rely on the par value of the shares issued, but only on independent investigation and reports as to the corporation's current cash position, its physical assets and its business experience. At the trial the plaintiff's district manager admitted that during the period when the plaintiff extended credit to the corporation, (1) the district manager believed that the original capital of the corporation amounted to only $25,000, and (2) the only financial statement of the corporation that the plaintiff ever saw showed a capital stock account of less than $33,000. These admissions would be sufficient to support a finding that the plaintiff did not rely on any misrepresentation arising out of the issuance of watered stock. The court made no finding on the issue of reliance. If the misrepresentation theory prevails in California, that issue was material and the defendant was entitled to a finding thereon. Code Civ.Proc. § 632; see Edgar v. Hitch, 46 Cal.2d 309, 294 P.2d 3. If the statutory obligation theory prevails, the fact that the plaintiff did not rely on any misrepresentation arising out of the issuance of watered stock is irrelevant and accordingly a finding on the issue of reliance would be surplusage.

It is therefore necessary to determine which theory prevails in this state. The plaintiff concedes that before the enactment of section 1110 of the Corporations Code (originally Civ. Code, § 299) in 1931, the misrepresentation theory was the only one available to creditors seeking to recover from holders of watered stock. See Clark v. Tompkins, 205 Cal. 373, 270 P. 946; Spencer v. Anderson, 193 Cal. 1, 6, 222 P. 355, 35 A.L.R. 822; Rhode v. Dock–Hop Co., 184 Cal. 367, 194 P. 11, 12 A.L.R. 437. However, he contends that the enactment of that section reflected a legislative intent to impose on the holders of watered stock a statutory obligation to creditors to make good the "water." Section 1110 provides that "The value of the consideration to be received by a corporation for the issue of shares having par value shall be at least equal to the par value thereof, except that: (a) A corporation may issue par value shares, as fully paid up, at less than par, if the board of directors determines that such shares cannot be sold at par. * * *" The statute does not expressly impose an obligation to creditors. Most jurisdictions having similar statutes have applied the misrepresentation theory obviously on the ground that creditors are sufficiently protected against stock watering schemes under that theory. See cases collected in Ballantine, Corporations, rev. ed. 1946, sec. 351, pp. 809–812; Dodd and Baker, Cases and Materials on Corporations, 2d ed. 1951, pp. 785–786; 11 Fletcher, Cyclopedia of the Law of Private Corporations, rev. and perm. ed. 1932, sec. 5209; Bonbright, "Shareholders' Defenses Against Liability to Creditors on Watered Stock," 1925, 25 Cal.L.Rev. 408, 414–416, 422. In view of the cases in this state prior to 1931 adopting the misrepresentation theory, it is reasonable to assume that the Legislature would have used clear language expressing an intent to broaden the basis of liability of holders of watered stock had it entertained such an intention. In this state the liability of a holder of watered stock may only be based on the misrepresentation theory.

The plaintiff contends that even under the misrepresentation theory a creditor's reliance on the misrepresentation arising out of the issuance of watered stock should be conclusively presumed. This contention is without substantial merit. If it should prevail, the misrepresentation theory and the statutory obligation theory would be essentially identical. This court has held that under the misrepresentation theory a person who extended credit to a corporation (1) before the watered stock was issued, Clark v. Tompkins, supra, 205 Cal. 373, 270 P. 946, or (2) with full knowledge that watered stock was outstanding, Sherman v. S. K. D. Oil Co., 185 Cal. 534, 197 P. 799; Sherman v. Harley, 178 Cal. 584, 174 P. 901, 7 A.L.R. 950. See also Spencer v. Anderson, supra, 193 Cal. 1, 6, 222 P. 355; Rhode v. Dock–Hop Co., supra, 184 Cal. 367, 378, 194 P. 11; R. H. Herron Co. v. Shaw, 165 Cal. 668, 671–672, 133 P. 488, cannot recover from the holders of the watered stock. These decisions indicate that under the misrepresentation theory reliance by the creditor is a prerequisite to the liability of a holder of watered stock. The trial court was therefore justified in ordering a new trial because of the absence of a finding on that issue. It is unnecessary to further consider the defendant's appeal from the judgment.

The order granting the new trial is affirmed. The appeal from the judgment is dismissed.

GIBSON, C. J., and CARTER, TRAYNOR, SCHAUER, SPENCE and McCOMB, JJ., concur.

NOTES

1. The concern associated with the failure to pay full price (at least par value) for stock issued by a corporation is that creditors will be misled. Courts may apply various theories to provide that protection, including a trust fund theory (*i.e.*, the stated capital of the company is a trust fund for creditors), a misrepresentation theory (*i.e.*, the stated capital is a representation to creditors that there is at least that much paid in capital) and a fiduciary duty to other shareholders to pay full consideration. In *Hospes v. Northwestern Mfg. & Car Co.*, 48 Minn. 174, 50 N.W. 1117 (1892), the court found flaws in the trust fund theory where a creditor failed to pay for subscribed stock that was issued before the plaintiff became a creditor, *i.e.*, no trust fund had actually been created for non-existent creditors. Instead, the court adopted a type of fraud on the market theory in which the court presumed a general reliance by the community on a company's financial statements. This meant that a creditor would not have to prove actual reliance on the company's financial statements in claiming that the value of its capital and assets were misrepresented. This presumption could be rebutted by a showing of actual knowledge on the part of the creditor that the stock was watered. *See* Handley v. Stutz,

139 U.S. 417, 11 S.Ct. 530, 35 L.Ed. 227 (1891) (describing the basis for the trust fund theory as an implied promise to pay for their stock when called on by the creditors of an insolvent corporation). The reliance requirement in *Bing Crosby* comports more closely with reality because creditors will take the necessary steps to protect their interests by examining the books and records of the company, credit reports, or by obtaining express representations concerning the assets or cash flow that will assure repayment. Alternatively, creditors may take a security interest in particular property that will give them priority over other creditors.

2. A traditional way to water stock was to issue common stock for property in amounts far in excess of the value of the property. The property was then carried on the books and records of the company at the inflated value, misleading creditors and subsequent stock purchasers as to the value of the company. *See* Old Dominion Copper Mining & Smelting Co. v. Lewisohn, 210 U.S. 206, 28 S.Ct. 634, 52 L.Ed. 1025 (1908) and Old Dominion Copper Mining & Smelting Co. v. Bigelow, 203 Mass. 159, 89 N.E. 193 (1909), *aff'd,* 225 U.S. 111, 32 S.Ct. 641, 56 L.Ed. 1009 (1912).

3. How do you appraise property given in exchange for stock to see if its value is inflated? Delaware statutes require shares with par value to be issued for consideration having a value not less than par. 8 Del. Corp. L. § 153. In the absence of fraud, however, the judgment of the board of directors as to value is conclusive. 8 Del. Corp. L. § 152. Cf., Pipelife Corp. v. Bedford, 150 A.2d 319 (Del.Ch.1959) (valuation of non-exclusive license given for shares was based on bad faith valuation and shares were canceled). *See also* Model Bus. Corp. Act § 6.21(c) (decision of board of directors is conclusive as to adequacy of that consideration paid for shares).

4. In Bissias v. Koulovatos, 761 A.2d 47 (Me.2000), the court held that a Maine statute requiring that consideration be given for shares required the board of directors to assure that the shares had "some" value but that the board need not assign a specific valuation to the property. Does this assure that watered stock will not be issued?

5. Shares are considered to be fully paid and non-assessable when the required consideration is paid into the corporation in the form of cash, services rendered, personal or real property or leases of real property. 8 Del. Corp. L. § 152.

6. Traditionally, some states did not allow stock to be issued for future services or for promissory notes. Section 6.21 of the Model Bus. Corp. Act, however, now recognizes such consideration as valid for the payment of securities. The Official Comments to this section note that, since the Act does away with the concept of par value, there can be no watered stock, leaving only a concern with the dilution of the other shareholders securities.

7. Under Delaware law, certificates for partly paid shares must note that they are not fully paid, and such shares are entitled to dividends only on the basis of the percentage paid for the shares. 8 Del. Corp. L. § 152.

8. New York law prohibits the issuance of shares for less than par value. N.Y. Bus. Corp. L. § 504. That provision, however, does not apply to the

resale of the stock in secondary market transactions. Torres v. Speiser, 268 A.D.2d 253, 701 N.Y.S.2d 360 (App.1st Dept.2000).

SECTION 3.   PREEMPTIVE RIGHTS

The common law concept of preemptive rights sought to protect existing shareholders from dilution of their stock ownership through subsequent stock offerings to a few existing shareholders or to new ones. To illustrate, assume that the ABC Corp. has authorized 100,000 shares of common stock, of which 10,000 shares are outstanding. You own 4,000 of the outstanding shares or forty percent of the company. The board of directors, thereafter, votes to sell the remaining 90,000 shares of previously unissued shares to a third party. This will reduce your percentage of ownership to just four percent. Even if the purchaser has paid full value for the shares—avoiding the watered stock problem from the previous section—your proportional amount of control has been reduced dramatically. This will affect every aspect of your voting, dividend and other rights. Although some statutes have reduced common law preemptive rights, anti-dilution provisions may be established in a certificate of incorporation or through provisions in the security itself.

STOKES v. CONTINENTAL TRUST CO. OF THE CITY OF NEW YORK

186 N.Y. 285, 78 N.E. 1090 (1906).

* * * This action was brought by a stockholder to compel his corporation to issue to him at par such a proportion of an increase made in its capital stock as the number of shares held by him before such increase bore to the number of all the shares originally issued, and in case such additional shares could not be delivered to him for his damages in the premises. The defendant is a domestic banking corporation in the city of New York, organized in 1890, with a capital stock of $500,000, consisting of 5,000 shares of the par value of $100 each. The plaintiff was one of the original stockholders, and still owns all the stock issued to him at the date of organization, together with enough more acquired since to make 221 shares in all. On the 29th of January, 1902, the defendant had a surplus of $1,048,450.94, which made the book value of the stock at that time $309.69 per share. On the 2nd of January, 1902, Blair & Co., a strong and influential firm of private bankers in the city of New York, made the following proposition to the defendant:

> "If your stockholders at the special meeting to be called for January 29th, 1902, vote to increase your capital stock from $500,000 to $1,000,000 you may deliver the additional stock to us as soon as

issued at $450 per share ($100 par value) for ourselves and our associates, it being understood that we may nominate ten of the 21 trustees to be elected at the adjourned annual meeting of stockholders."

The directors of the defendant promptly met and duly authorized a special meeting of the stockholders to be called to meet on January 29, 1902, for the purpose of voting upon the proposed increase of stock and the acceptance of the offer to purchase the same. Upon due notice a meeting of the stockholders was held accordingly, more than a majority attending either in person or by proxy. A resolution to increase the stock was adopted by the vote of 4,197 shares, all that were cast. Thereupon the plaintiff demanded from the defendant the right to subscribe for 221 shares of the new stock at par, and offered to pay immediately for the same, which demand was refused. A resolution directing a sale to Blair & Co. at $450 a share was then adopted by a vote of 3,596 shares to 241. The plaintiff voted for the first resolution, but against the last, and before the adoption of the latter he protested against the proposed sale of his proportionate share of the stock, and again demanded the right to subscribe and pay for the same, but the demand was refused. On the 30th of January, 1902, the stock was increased, and on the same day was sold to Blair & Co. at the price named, although the plaintiff formerly renewed his demand for 221 shares of the new stock at par, and tendered payment therefor, but it was refused upon the ground that the stock had already been issued to Blair & Co. owing in part to the offer of Blair & Co. which had become known to the public, the market price of the stock had increased from $450 a share in September, 1901, to $550 in January, 1902, and at the time of the trial, in April, 1904, it was worth $700 per share. Prior to the special meeting of the stockholders, by authority of the board of directors, a circular letter was sent to each stockholder, including the plaintiff, giving notice of the proposition made by Blair & Co. and recommending that it be accepted. Thereupon the plaintiff notified the defendant that he wished to subscribe for his proportionate share of the new stock, if issued, and at no time did he waive his right to subscribe for the same. Before the special meeting, he had not been definitely notified by the defendant that he could not receive his proportionate part of the increase, but was informed that his proposition would 'be taken under consideration.' After finding these facts in substance, the trial court found, as conclusions of law, that the plaintiff had the right to subscribe for such proportion of the increase, as his holdings bore to all the stock before the increase was made; that the stockholders, directors, and officers of the defendant had no power to deprive him of that right, and that he was entitled to recover the difference between the market value of 221 shares on the 30th of January, 1902, and the par value thereof, or the sum of $99,450, together with interest from said date. * * *

VANN, J. (after stating the facts).

* * * [T]he question presented for decision is whether according to the facts found the plaintiff had the legal right to subscribe for and take

the same number of shares of the new stock that he held of the old? The subject is not regulated by statute, and the question presented has never been directly passed upon by this court, and only to a limited extent has it been considered by courts in this state. Miller v. Illinois Central R. R. Co., 24 Barb. 312; Matter of Wheeler, 2 Abb. Pr. [N. S.] 361; Currie v. White, 45 N. Y. 822. In the first case cited judgment was rendered by a divided vote of the General Term in the first district. The court held that the plaintiff was entitled to no relief because he did not own any shares when the new stock was issued but only an option, and that he could not claim to be an actual holder until he had exercised his right of election. The court further said, however, that if he was the owner of shares at the time of the new issue he had no absolute right as such owner to a distributive allotment of the new stock. Matter of Wheeler was decided by Judge Mason at Special Term, and, although the point was not directly involved, the learned judge said: "As I understand the law all these old stockholders had a right to share in the issuing of this new stock in proportion to the amount of stock held by them. And if none of the stock was to be apportioned to the old stockholders, they had certainly the right to have the new stock sold at public sale, and to the highest bidder, that they might share in the gains arising from the sale. In short, the old stockholders, as this was good stock and above par, had a property in the new stock, or a right at least to be secured the profits to be derived from a fair sale of it if they did not wish to purchase it themselves; and they have been deprived of this by the course which these directors have taken with this new stock by transferring or issuing it to themselves and others in a manner not authorized by law." In Currie v. White the point was not directly involved, but Judge Folger, referring to the rights acquired under a certain contract, said: "One of these rights was to take new shares upon any legitimate increase of the capital stock, which right attaches to the old shares, not as profit or income, but as inherent in the shares in their very creation," citing Atkins v. Albree, 12 Allen (Mass.) 359; Brander v. Brander, 4 Ves. 800, and notes, Sumner Ed. While this was said in a dissenting opinion, Judge Rapallo, who spoke for the court, concurred, saying, "As to the claim for the additional stock, I concur in the conclusions of my learned Brother Folger." The fair implication from both opinions is that if the plaintiff had preserved his rights, he would have been entitled to the new stock.

In other jurisdictions the decisions support the claim of the plaintiff with the exception of Ohio Insurance Co. v. Nunnemacher, 15 Ind. 294, which turned on the language of the charter. The leading authority is Gray v. Portland Bank, decided in 1807 and reported in 3 Mass. 364, 3 Am. Dec. 156. In that case a verdict was found for the plaintiff, subject, by the agreement of the parties, to the opinion of the court upon the evidence in the case whether the plaintiff was entitled to recover, and, if so, as to the measure of damages. The court held that stockholders who held old stock had a right to subscribe for and take new stock in proportion to their respective shares. As the corporation refused this right to the plaintiff he was permitted to recover the excess of the market value above the par value, with interest. In the course of its argument the court said: "A share in the stock or trust when only the least sum has been paid in is a share in the power of increasing it when the trustee determines or rather when the cestuis que trustent agree upon employing a greater sum. * * * A vote to increase the capital stock, if it was not the creation of a new and disjointed capital, was in its nature an agreement among the stockholders to enlarge their shares in the amount or in the number to the extent required to effect that increase. * * * If from the progress of the institution and the expense incurred in it any advance upon the additional shares might be obtained in the market, this advance upon the shares relinquished belonged to the whole, and was not to be disposed of at the will of a majority of the stockholders to the partial benefit of some and exclusion of others." This decision has stood unquestioned for nearly a hundred years and has been followed generally by courts of the highest standing. It is the foundation of the rule upon the subject that prevails, almost without exception, throughout the entire country.

In Way v. American Grease Company, 60 N. J. Eq. 263, 269, 47 Atl. 44, the headnote fairly expresses the decision as follows: "Directors of a corporation, which is fully organized and in the active conduct of its business, are bound to afford to existing stockholders an opportunity to subscribe for any new shares of its capital, in proportion to their holdings, before disposing of such new shares in any other way." In Eidman v. Bowman, 58 Ill. 444, 447, 11 Am. Rep. 90, it was said: "When this corporation was organized, the charter and all of its franchises and privileges vested in the shareholders, and the directors became their trustees for its management. The right to the remainder of the stock, when it should be issued, vested in the original stockholders, in proportion to the amount each held of the original stock, if they would pay for it, and was as fully theirs as was the stock already held and for which they had paid." In Dousman v. Wisconsin, etc., Co., 40 Wis. 418, 421, it was held that a court of equity would compel a corporation to issue to every stockholder his proportion of new stock on the ground that "he has a right to maintain his proportionate interest in the corporation, certainly as long as there is sufficient stock remaining undisposed of by the corporation." In Jones v. Morrison, 31 Minn. 140, 152, 16 N. W. 854, it was said: "When the proposition that a corporation is trustee of the corporate property for the benefit of the stockholders in proportion to the stock held by them is admitted (and we find no well-considered case which denies it), it covers as well the power to issue new stock as any other franchise or property which may be of value, held by the corporation. The value of that power, where it has actual value, is given to it by the property acquired and the business built up with the money paid by the subsisting stockholders."

It happens not infrequently that corporations, instead of distributing their profits in the way of dividends to stockholders, accumulate them till a large surplus is on hand. No one would deny that, in such case, each stockholder has an interest in the surplus which the courts will protect.

No one would claim that the officers, directors or majority of the stockholders, without the consent of all, could give away the surplus, or devote it to any other than the general purposes of the corporation. But when new stock is issued, each share of it has an interest in the surplus equal to that pertaining to each share of the original stock. And if the corporation, either through the officers, directors or majority of stockholders, may dispose of the new stock to whomsoever it will, at whatever price it may fix, then it has the power to diminish the value of each share of old stock by letting in other parties to an equal interest in the surplus and in the good will or value of the established business.

In Real Estate Trust Co. v. Bird, 90 Md. 229, 245, 44 Atl. 1048, the court said: "There can be no doubt that the general rule is that when the capital stock of a corporation is increased by the issue of new shares, authorized by the charter, the holders of the original stock are entitled to the new stock in the proportion that the number of shares held by them bears to the whole number before the increase." In all these cases, as well as many others, Gray v. Portland Bank, supra, is followed without criticism or question. In some cases the same result is reached without citing that case. Thus in Jones v. Concord & Montreal R. R. Co., 67 N. H. 119, 38 Atl. 120, it was declared, as stated in the headnote, that "an issue of new shares of stock in an increase of the capital of a corporation is a partial division of the common property, which can be taken from the original shareholders only by their consent or by legal process." * * *

The elementary writers are very clear and emphatic in laying down the same rule. Thus in 2 Beach on Private Corporations, § 473, the learned author says: "A stockholder of the old stock, at the time of the vote to augment the capital of a company, has a right in the new stock, in proportion to the amount of his interest in the old, of which he cannot be rightfully deprived by other stockholders. When the capital stock of a corporation is increased by the issue of new shares, each holder of the original stock has a right to offer to subscribe for and to demand from the corporation such a proportion of the new stock as the number of shares already owned by him bears to the whole number of shares before the increase. This pre-emptive right of the shareholders in respect to new stock is well recognized. * * * The corporation cannot compel the old stockholders upon their subscription for a new stock to pay more than par value therefor. They are entitled to it without extra burden or price beyond the regular par value. An attempt to deprive the stockholder of this right will be enjoined in the absence of laches or acquiescence. The courts go very far in protecting the right of stockholders to subscribe for new stock. It is often a very important right." 1 Cook on Corporations (4th Ed.) 286. "Each shareholder, it has been held, has a right to the opportunity to subscribe for and take the new or increased stock in proportion to the old stock held by him; so that a vote at a shareholders' meeting, directing the new stock to be sold, without giving to each shareholder such an opportunity, is void as to any dissenting shareholder." 10 Cyc. 543. "Those who are shareholders when an increase of capital stock is effected enjoy the right to subscribe to the new stock in proportion to their original holdings and before subscriptions may be received from outsiders." 26 Am. & Eng. Enc. (2d Ed.) 947. See, also, 2 Thompson's Commentaries, § 2094; Angell & Ames on Corporations, § 430; Morawetz on Corporations, § 455.

If the right claimed by the plaintiff was a right of property belonging to him as a stockholder, he could not be deprived of it by the joint action of the other stockholders, and of all the directors and officers of the corporation. What is the nature of the right acquired by a stockholder through the ownership of shares of stock? What rights can he assert against the will of a majority of the stockholders, and all the officers and directors? While he does not own and cannot dispose of any specific property of the corporation, yet he and his associates own the corporation itself, its charter, franchises, and all rights conferred thereby, including the right to increase the stock. He has an inherent right to his proportionate share of any dividend declared, or of any surplus arising upon dissolution, and he can prevent waste or misappropriation of the property of the corporation by those in control. Finally, he has the right to vote for directors and upon all propositions subject by law to the control of the stockholders, and this is his supreme right and main protection. Stockholders have no direct voice in transacting the corporate business, but through their right to vote they can select those to whom the law entrusts the power of management and control. A corporation is somewhat like a partnership, if one were possible, conducted wholly by agents where the copartners have power to appoint the agents, but are not responsible for their acts. The power to manage its affairs resides in the directors, who are its agents, but the power to elect directors resides in the stockholders. This right to vote for directors, and upon propositions to increase the stock or mortgage the assets, is about all the power the stockholder has. So long as the management is honest, within the corporate powers, and involves no waste, the stockholders cannot interfere, even if the administration is feeble and unsatisfactory, but must correct such evils through their power to elect other directors. Hence, the power of the individual stockholder to vote in proportion to the number of his shares is vital, and cannot be cut off or curtailed by the action of all the other stockholders, even with the co-operation of the directors and officers.

In the case before us the new stock came into existence through the exercise of a right belonging wholly to the stockholders. As the right to increase the stock belonged to them, the stock when increased belonged to them also, as it was issued for money and not for property or for some purpose other than the sale thereof for money. By the increase of stock the voting power of the plaintiff was reduced one-half, and while he consented to the increase he did not consent to the disposition of the new stock by a sale thereof to Blair & Co. at less than its market value, nor by sale to any person in any way except by an allotment to the stockholders. The increase and sale involved the transfer of rights belonging to the stockholders as part of their investment. The issue of new stock and the sale thereof to Blair & Co. was not only a transfer to them of one-half the voting power of the old stockholders, but also of an equitable right to one-half the surplus which belonged to them. In other words, it was a partial division of the property of the old stockholders. The right to increase stock is not an asset of the corporation any more than the original stock when it was issued pursuant to subscription. The ownership of stock is in the nature of an inherent but indirect power to control the corporation. The stock when issued ready for delivery does not belong to the corporation in the way that it holds its real and personal property, with power to sell the same, but is held by it with no power of alienation in trust for the stockholders, who are the beneficial owners, and become the legal owners upon paying therefor.

The corporation has no rights hostile to those of the stockholders, but is the trustee for all including the minority. The new stock issued by the defendant under the permission of the statute did not belong to it, but was held by it the same as the original stock when first issued was held in trust for the stockholders. It has the same voting power as the old, share for share. The stockholders decided to enlarge their holdings, not by increasing the amount of each share, but by increasing the number of shares. The new stock belonged to the stockholders as an inherent right by virtue of their being stockholders, to be shared in proportion upon paying its par value or the value per share fixed by vote of a majority of the stockholders, or ascertained by a sale at public auction. While the corporation could not compel the plaintiff to take new shares at any price, since they were issued for money and not for property, it could not lawfully dispose of those shares without giving him a chance to get his proportion at the same price that outsiders got theirs. He had an inchoate right to one share of the new stock for each share owned by him of the old stock, provided he was ready to pay the price fixed by the stockholders. If so situated that he could not take it himself, he was entitled to sell the right to one who could, as is frequently done. Even this gives an advantage to capital, but capital necessarily has some advantage.

Of course, there is a distinction when the new stock is issued in payment for property, but that is not this case. The stock in question was issued to be sold for money and was sold for money only. A majority of the stockholders, as part of their power to increase the stock, may attach reasonable conditions to the disposition thereof, such as the requirement that every old stockholder electing to take new stock shall pay a fixed price therefor, not less than par, however, owing to the limitation of the statute. They may also provide for a sale in parcels or bulk at public auction, when every stockholder can bid the same as strangers. They cannot, however, dispose of it to strangers against the protest of any stockholder who insists that he has a right to his proportion. Otherwise the majority could deprive the minority of their proportionate power in the election of directors and their proportionate right to share in the surplus, each of which is an inherent, pre-emptive, and vested right of property. It is inviolable, and can neither be taken away nor lessened without consent, or a waiver implying consent. The plaintiff had power, before the increase of stock, to vote on 221 shares of stock, out of a total of 5,000, at any meeting held by the stockholders for any purpose. By the action of the majority, taken against his will and protest, he now has only one-half the voting power that he had before, because the number of shares has been doubled while he still owns but 221. This touches him as a stockholder in such a way as to deprive him of a right of property. Blair & Co. acquired virtual control, while he and the other stockholders lost it. We are not discussing equities, but legal rights, for this is an action at law, and the plaintiff was deprived of a strictly legal right. If the result gives him an advantage over other stockholders, it is because he stood upon his legal rights, while they did not.

The question is what were his legal rights, not what his profit may be under the sale to Blair & Co., but what it might have been if the new stock had been issued to him in proportion to his holding of the old. The other stockholders could give their property to Blair & Co., but they could not give his. A share of stock is a share in the power to increase the stock, and belongs to the stockholders the same as the stock itself. When that power is exercised, the new stock belongs to the old stockholders in proportion to their holding of old stock, subject to compliance with the lawful terms upon which it is issued. When the new stock is issued in payment for property purchased by the corporation, the stockholders' right is merged in the purchase, and they have an advantage in the increase of the property of the corporation in proportion to the increase of stock. When the new stock is issued for money, while the stockholders may provide that it be sold at auction or fix the price at which it is to be sold, each stockholder is entitled to his proportion of the proceeds of the sale at auction, after he has had a right to bid at the sale, or to his proportion of the new stock at the price fixed by the stockholders.

We are thus led to lay down the rule that a stockholder has an inherent right to a proportionate share of new stock issued for money only and not to purchase property for the purposes of the corporation or to effect a consolidation, and while he can waive that right, he cannot be deprived of it without his consent except when the stock is issued at a fixed price not less than par, and he is given the right to take at that price in proportion to his holding, or in some other equitable way that will enable him to protect his interest by acting on his own judgment and using his own resources. This rule is just to all and tends to prevent the tyranny of majorities which needs restraint, as well as virtual attempts to blackmail by small minorities which should be prevented.

The remaining question is whether the plaintiff waived his rights by failing to do what he ought to have done, or by doing something he ought not to have done. He demanded his share of the new stock at par, instead of at the price fixed by the stockholders, for the authorization to sell at $450 a share was virtually fixing the price of the stock. He did more than this, however, for he not only voted against the proposition to sell to Blair & Co. at $450, but, as the court expressly found, he 'protested against the proposed sale of his proportionate share of the stock, and again demanded the right to subscribe and pay for the same which demands were again refused,' and 'the resolution was carried notwithstanding such protest and demands.' Thus he protested against the sale of his share before the price was fixed, for the same resolution fixed the price, and directed the sale, which was promptly carried into effect. If he had not attended the meeting, called upon due notice to do precisely what was done, perhaps he would have waived his rights, but he attended the meeting and, before the price was fixed, demanded the right to subscribe for 221 shares at par, and offered to pay for the same immediately. It is true that after the price was fixed he did not offer to take his share at that price, but he did not acquiesce in the sale of his proportion to Blair & Co., and unless he acquiesced the sale as to him was without right. He was under no obligation to put the corporation in default by making a demand.

The ordinary doctrine of demand, tender, and refusal has no application to this case. The plaintiff had made no contract. He had not promised to do anything. No duty of performance rested upon him. He had an absolute right to the new stock in proportion to his holding of the old, and he gave notice that he wanted it. It was his property, and could not be disposed of without his consent. He did not consent. He protested in due time, and the sale was made in defiance of his protest. While in connection with his protest he demanded the right to subscribe at par, that demand was entirely proper when made, because the price had not then been fixed. After the price was fixed it was the duty of the defendant to offer him his proportion at that price, for it had notice that he had not acquiesced in the proposed sale of his share, but wanted it himself. The directors were under the legal obligation to give him an opportunity to purchase at the price fixed before they could sell his property to a third party, even with the approval of a large majority of the stockholders. If he had remained silent, and had made no request or protest he would have waived his rights, but after he had given notice that he wanted his part and had protested against the sale thereof, the defendant was bound to offer it to him at the price fixed by the stockholders. By selling to strangers without thus offering to sell to him, the defendant wrongfully deprived him of his property, and is liable for such damages as he actually sustained.

The learned trial court, however, did not measure the damages according to law. The plaintiff was not entitled to the difference between the par value of the new stock and the market value thereof, for the stockholders had the right to fix the price at which the stock should be sold. They fixed the price at $450 a share, and for the failure of the defendant to offer the plaintiff his share at that price we hold it liable in damages. His actual loss, therefore, is $100 per share, or the difference between $450, the price that he would have been obliged to pay had he been permitted to purchase, and the market value on the day of sale, which was $550. This conclusion requires a reversal of the judgment rendered by the Appellate Division and a modification of that rendered by the trial court.

The order appealed from should be reversed and the judgment of the trial court modified by reducing the damages from the sum of $99,450, with interest from January 30, 1902, to the sum of $22,100, with interest from that date, and by striking out the extra allowance of costs, and as thus modified the judgment of the trial court is affirmed, without costs in this court or in the Appellate Division to either party.

HAIGHT, J. (dissenting). [omitted]

CULLEN, C. J., and WERNER and HISCOCK, JJ., concur with VANN, J.; WILLARD BARTLETT, J., concurs with HAIGHT, J.; O'BRIEN, J., absent.

Ordered accordingly.

———

NOTES

1.   The common law rule expressed in *Stokes v. Continental Trust Co.*, recognizing shareholder preemptive rights was changed by statute. Delaware, for example, denies preemptive rights unless they are specified in the certificate of incorporation. 8 Del. Corp. § 102(b)(3). Model Bus. Corp. Act § 6.30 contains a similar provision but defines the extent of preemptive rights when generally elected in the articles of incorporation, *viz.*,

> The shareholders of the corporation have a preemptive right granted on uniform terms and conditions prescribed by the board of directors to provide a fair and reasonable opportunity to exercise the right, to acquire proportional amounts of the corporation's unissued shares upon the decision of the board of directors to issue them.

Model Bus. Corp. Act § 6.30(b)(1).

2.   Most publicly held corporations have not elected to include preemptive rights in their charters because such a right would impair and delay their ability to raise further capital in the market. Preemptive rights issues in large corporations may arise where certain shareholders are given preference over share issues. *Compare Clarendon Group, Ltd. v. Smith Laboratories, Inc.*, 741 F.Supp. 1449 (S.D.Cal.1990) (provision in articles of corporation that rejected preemptive rights did not bar poison pill (a "flip-in" rights plan) that gave certain shareholders preferential right to purchase stock in the event of a takeover threat), *with*, Bank of New York Co. v. Irving Bank Corp., 142 Misc.2d 145, 536 N.Y.S.2d 923 (Sup.1988) (provision in certificate of incorporation that rejected preemptive rights did authorize poison pill (a "flip-in" rights plan) that gave certain shareholders preferential right to purchase stock in the event of a takeover threat; but such a provision was discriminatory among shareholders and violated New York law provision against discrimination among shareholders of a single class of stock).

3.   Although rejected by most publicly owned corporations, minority shareholders in close corporations may find preemptive rights desirable, as discussed in Section 7 of this Chapter on closely-held corporations.

———

As the case below illustrates, corporate securities other than equity shares may also enjoy anti-dilution protections.

LOHNES v. LEVEL 3 COMMUNICATIONS, INC.

272 F.3d 49 (1st Cir.2001).

SELYA, CIRCUIT JUDGE.

The primary issue raised in this appeal is whether the terms "capital reorganization" and/or "reclassification of stock," as used in a stock warrant, encompass a stock split. Asserting the affirmative of this proposition, a warrantholder, plaintiff-appellant Paul R. Lohnes, claims that a stock split effectuated by defendant-appellee Level 3 Communications, Inc. (Level 3) triggered an antidilution provision in the warrant that automatically increased the number of shares of stock to which he was entitled. Level 3 resists this claim. * * *

The appellant is both a trustee and a beneficiary of C.E.M. Realty Trust (the Trust). In February of 1998, the Trust leased 40,000 square feet of commercial space to XCOM Technologies, Inc. (XCOM). The details of the lease transaction need not concern us, save for the fact that, as part of the consideration, XCOM issued a stock warrant to the appellant. The parties negotiated the principal terms of the warrant—the number of shares, the exercise price, and the expiration date—and XCOM's lawyer then drafted the document. The warrant specified that its exercise would be governed by Massachusetts law. It empowered the holder to purchase, at his discretion but within a fixed period, 100,000 shares of XCOM common stock at $0.30 per share. Unbeknownst to the appellant, XCOM's days as an independent entity were numbered.

Shortly after the appellant executed the lease and accepted the warrant, Level 3 acquired XCOM in a stock-for-stock transaction and converted XCOM into a wholly-owned subsidiary. As part of this transaction, Level 3 agreed to assume XCOM's warrant obligations and satisfy them with shares of Level 3's common stock (using a designated share exchange formula). Following this paradigm, the appellant's unexercised warrant for XCOM shares was duly converted into a warrant to purchase 8,541 shares of Level 3's common stock. The appellant does not challenge this conversion (which took effect in April of 1998).

The next significant development occurred on July 14, 1998. On that date, Level 3's board of directors authorized a two-for-one stock split, to be effectuated in the form of a stock dividend granting common shareholders one new share of stock for each share held.[1] The board set the record

---

1. A corporation effects a "stock split" by increasing the number of shares outstanding without changing the proportional ownership interests of each shareholder. Companies typically execute a stock split by issuing a "stock dividend" to current shareholders, i.e., "paid in stock expressed as a percentage of the number of shares already held by a shareholder." *Black's Law Dict.* 493 (7th ed.1999) (cross-referencing definition of "dividend"). Stock splits lower the price per share, thereby fostering increased marketability and wider distribution of shares. Technically, not all stock dividends are stock splits, and the two may, in limited instances, receive different

date as July 30, 1998. On July 20, Level 3 issued a press release announcing the stock split, but it did not provide the appellant with personalized notice.

The split occurred as scheduled. Adhering to generally accepted accounting practices, Level 3 adjusted its balance sheet to account for the split by increasing its common stock account in the amount of $1,000,000 and reducing paid-in-capital by a like amount. These accounting entries had no net effect on either the retained earnings or the net equity of the company.

Despite the sharp reduction in the share price that accompanied the stock split, the appellant paid no heed until approximately three months after the record date. When his belated inquiry revealed what had transpired, the appellant contacted Level 3 to confirm that the stock split had triggered a share adjustment provision, thus entitling him to 17,082 shares (twice the number of shares specified in the warrant). Level 3 demurred on the ground that the warrant did not provide for any share adjustment based upon the occurrence of a stock split effected as a stock dividend.

Dissatisfied by Level 3's response, the appellant exercised the warrant and received 8,541 shares of Level 3's common stock. He then sued Level 3 in a Massachusetts state court alleging breach of both the warrant and the implied duty of good faith and fair dealing. Citing diversity of citizenship and the existence of a controversy in the requisite amount, Level 3 removed the action to the federal district court. *See* 28 U.S.C. §§ 1332(a), 1441.

We begin our analysis by outlining the legal framework that governs our review. Next, we apply well-worn principles of contract interpretation to resolve the appellant's contention that the terms "capital reorganization" and "reclassification of stock" encompass a stock split implemented as a stock dividend. In this endeavor, our principal task is to determine the ambiguity *vel non* of the disputed terms. Thus, we investigate whether either term is reasonably susceptible to the interpretation urged by the appellant. As part of this exercise, we consider (and reject) the appellant's belated attempt to introduce expert testimony bearing on this question. We conclude by addressing the appellant's claim that Level 3 breached the implied duty of good faith and fair dealing inherent in the warrant. * * *

A stock warrant is an instrument that grants the warrant holder an option to purchase shares of stock at a fixed price. *See Black's Law Dict.* 1441 (7th ed.1999); II James Cox et al., *Corporations* § 18.15 (1995 & 1999 Supp.); 6A William Meade Fletcher, *Fletcher Cyclopedia of the Law of Private Corps.* § 2641 (perm. ed.1997); *see also Tribble v. J.W. Greer Co.,* 83 F.Supp. 1015, 1022 (D.Mass.1949) (holding, under Massachusetts law, that a stock warrant is "a contract by which the corporation gives an irrevocable option to the holder to purchase authorized corporate stock

---

accounting treatment. In the instant matter, however, "stock split" and "stock dividend" are two sides of the same coin, and we use the terms interchangeably.

within a period of time at a price and upon terms specified in the contract"). * * *

The warrant at issue here contained a two-paragraph anti-dilution provision which, upon the occurrence of certain described events, automatically adjusted the number of shares to which the warrant holder would be entitled upon exercise of the warrant. In all, share adjustments were engendered by five separate contingencies: capital reorganization, reclassification of common stock, merger, consolidation, and sale of all (or substantially all) the capital stock or assets. However, the warrant did not explicitly provide for an adjustment of shares in the event of a stock split. The appellant attempts to plug this lacuna by equating a stock split with a capital reorganization and/or a reclassification of stock. This argument brings the following paragraph of the antidilution provision into play:

> *Reorganizations and Reclassifications.* If there shall occur any capital reorganization or reclassification of the Common Stock, then, as part of any such reorganization or reclassification, lawful provision shall be made so that the Holder shall have the right thereafter to receive upon the exercise hereof the kind and amount of shares of stock or other securities or property which such Holder would have been entitled to receive if, immediately prior to any such reorganization or reclassification, such Holder had held the number of shares of Common Stock which were then purchasable upon the exercise of this Warrant.

Building upon the premise that either "capital reorganization" or "reclassification of stock" encompasses a stock split, the appellant concludes that Level 3's stock split activated the share adjustment mechanism set forth in the quoted paragraph. * * *

Since the warrant does not elaborate upon the meaning of "capital reorganization," we turn to other sources. Massachusetts law offers no discernible guidance. Outside of Massachusetts, the closest case is *Prescott, Ball & Turben v. LTV Corp.,* 531 F.Supp. 213 (S.D.N.Y.1981). There, the plaintiffs owned debentures, issued pursuant to a trust indenture, which were convertible into common stock of LTV Corp. (LTV). LTV's board ratified a spin-off proposal calling for the distribution of all the shares of a wholly-owned LTV subsidiary to LTV's common stockholders on a pro rata basis. The distribution stood to reduce LTV's stated capital and retained earnings by $62.4 million and $30.3 million, respectively. *Id.* at 215. The plaintiffs argued that the proposed distribution of the subsidiary's stock entailed a capital reorganization that triggered an antidilution provision contained in the trust indenture. The defendants countered that the spin-off was merely a dividend, and, therefore, did not trigger the share adjustment machinery established in the antidilution provision.

The *Prescott* court sided with the defendants. It noted that the "only way" the defendants could prevail was if the terms of the trust indenture made it unambiguously clear that the parties did not intend to treat the spin-off as a capital reorganization. *Id.* at 217. Finding the terms of the trust indenture to be unambiguous, the court ruled that:

> The plain language of the Trust Indenture contemplates an exchange or alteration in the existing ownership form of the interest held by LTV common shareholders before a particular transaction can be classified as a capital reorganization for purposes of the Trust Indenture. No such exchange or alteration is involved in the proposed distribution of the [LTV subsidiary's] stock. The proposed distribution therefore does not activate the [antidilution adjustment provision in] the Trust Indenture. *Id.* at 219–20. * * *

Moving beyond the case law, the meaning of the term "capital reorganization" in common legal parlance seemingly belies the appellant's ambitious definition. The preeminent legal lexicon defines "reorganization," in pertinent part, as a "[g]eneral term describing corporate amalgamations or readjustments occurring, for example, when one corporation acquires another in a merger or acquisition, a single corporation divides into two or more entities, or a corporation makes a substantial change in its capital structure." *Black's Law Dict.* 1298 (6th ed.1990). The first two prongs of this definition are clearly inapposite here. That leaves only the question of whether a stock split entails a "substantial change in [a corporation's] capital structure." We think not.

First and foremost, the accounting mechanics that accompany a stock split are mere window dressing. *See generally* Robert S. Anthony & James S. Reece, *Accounting Principles* 37–39 (7th ed.1995). To be sure, a stock split effected through the distribution of shares in the form of a stock dividend results in an increase in the common stock at par account and an offsetting decrease in additional paid-in capital, *id.,* but this subtle set of entries has no effect on total shareholder equity or on any other substantive aspect of the balance sheet. *See* FASB, Accounting Research Bulletin No. 43; *see also* III Cox, *supra* § 20.20 ("A share split-up does not, however, make any representations as to any accumulation of earnings or surplus or involve any increase of the legal capital."). Because a stock split does not entail a substantial change in a corporation's capital structure, the unelaborated term "capital reorganization" cannot plausibly include a stock split effected as a stock dividend.

We turn next to the phrase "reclassification of stock." Two Massachusetts cases seem worthy of mention. In the first, a corporation took advantage of a new statute authorizing the issuance of preferred stock and amended its charter to divide its previously undifferentiated stock into common and preferred shares. *Page v. Whittenton Mfg. Co.,* 211 Mass. 424, 97 N.E. 1006, 1007–08 (1912). The Massachusetts Supreme Judicial Court approved the corporation's actions. It held that a corporation could classify stock into common and preferred shares (providing preferred shareholders with cumulative dividends and a liquidation preference) so long as that classification was effected through a charter amendment. *Id.* at 1007. Although *Page* uses the verb "classify," we view what transpired as a reclassification. *See* XIII *Oxford English Dict.* 339 (2d ed.1989) (defining "reclassify" as "[t]o classify again; to alter the classification of").

In *Boston Safe Deposit & Trust Co. v. State Tax Comm'n*, 340 Mass. 250, 163 N.E.2d 637 (Mass.1960), the court considered the tax implications of a reclassification of stock. The reclassification in question involved the partial substitution of redeemable, convertible, cumulative, nonvoting shares for nonredeemable, nonconvertible, noncumulative, voting shares. *Id.* at 642. The court held that the reclassification constituted a taxable event under Massachusetts law. *Id.* at 643. Our reading of the Massachusetts cases leads us to conclude that the sine qua non of a reclassification of stock is the modification of existing shares into something fundamentally different. At the end of the day, the stockholders in *Page* held a different class of shares, while the stockholders in *Boston Safe* gained some privileges while losing the right to vote. Thus, *Page* and *Boston Safe,* respectively, illustrate two ways in which a security can be altered fundamentally: (a) by changing the class of stock, or (b) by modifying important rights or preferences linked to stock. Stock splits effected as stock dividends do not entail any such fundamental alteration of the character of an existing security. For example, Level 3's stock split in no way altered its shareholders' proportionate ownership interests, varied the class of securities held, or revised any of the attributes associated with the stock. What is more, the stock split did not have a meaningful impact on either the corporation's balance sheet or capital structure. For those reasons, we perceive no principled basis on which to stretch the definition of "reclassification of stock" to encompass a stock split.

A rule promulgated by the Securities and Exchange Commission confirms our intuition. This rule extends the protections of the Securities Act of 1933 to shareholders who are offered securities in a business combination and are required to decide "whether to accept a new or different security in exchange for their existing security." SEC Rule 145, 17 C.F.R. § 230.145 (preliminary note). While the rule extends to reclassifications of stock, it explicitly exempts stock splits from the reclassification rubric. *See* SEC Rule 145, 17 C.F.R. § 230.145. The upshot of this carve-out is unmistakable: the SEC does not consider shares received in conjunction with a stock split to constitute a "new or different security."

To cinch matters, while no Massachusetts statute defines the term "reclassification of stock," two states have enacted pertinent statutes. Under Louisiana law, a reclassification of stock is defined as amendment of the articles to change the authorized number of shares of an existing class or series; to authorize shares of a new class or series; to change the designation, par value (including change of par-value shares to shares without par value or vice versa), preferences, limitations or relative rights, including cancellation or modification of the right to receive accumulated dividends which have not been declared, or variations in relative rights, of the issued, and authorized but unissued, shares of any existing class or series; or to change the issued shares of any existing class or series into a greater or smaller number of shares of the same class or series (subject to such changes as the reclassification may make in the designation, par value, preferences, limitations or relative rights or variations in relative rights, thereof) or of another class or series, and to cancel any issued shares in connection with a reduction in the number thereof. La.Rev.Stat. Ann. § 12:1 (West 2000). The stock split effected by Level 3 implicates none of the categories established by the Louisiana legislature.

Pennsylvania's statutory definition goes one step further; it expressly provides that the term "reclassification" excludes "a stock dividend or split effected by distribution of [the company's] own previously authorized shares pro rata to the holders of shares of the same or any other class or series pursuant to action solely of the board of directors." 15 Pa. Con. Stat. Ann. § 1103 (West 2001).

Although this case must be decided under Massachusetts law, we regard these statutes and rules as relevant and informative. *Cf. Ambrose v. New Engl. Ass'n of Schs. & Colls., Inc.*, 252 F.3d 488, 497–98 (1st Cir.2001) (noting that, in exercising diversity jurisdiction, a federal court should consult case law from other jurisdictions when the forum state's highest court has not yet spoken). Moreover, they afford enlightenment as to common usage and as to what a reasonable person would (or would not) consider to be encompassed within the ambit of a particular term. So viewed, these statutes and rules reinforce our intuition that the term "reclassification of stock" does not encompass a stock split. * * *

We need go no further. In light of the appellant's inability to show that a reasonable person plausibly could construe either "capital reorganization" or "reclassification of stock" to include stock splits, we conclude that these terms, as they appear in the warrant, were unambiguous and did not cover the contingency of a stock split effected as a stock dividend. It follows that the stock split in question here did not trip the warrant's antidilution provision. By like token, Level 3 did not breach the implied covenant of good faith and fair dealing by neglecting to give special notice beyond what the warrant itself required. The bottom line, then, is that the district court was correct in granting Level 3's motion for summary judgment.

Affirmed.

SECTION 4. LEGAL CAPITAL: RESTRICTIONS ON CORPORATE DISTRIBUTIONS TO OWNERS

State corporate laws govern the conditions under which a corporation may make a distribution to owners, commonly called "dividends." The board of directors has the discretion to declare dividends only if those statutory conditions are met. State corporate statutes variously require dividends to be paid out of retained earnings (profits) or prohibit payment of dividends out of stated capital (the par value of the company's stock) *See e.g.*, Cal. Gen. Corp. Law § 500 (limiting dividends from retained earnings); 8 Del. §§ 154 & 170 (dividends payable out of excess of net assets (assets minus liabilities) over stated capital); N.Y. Business Corp. L. § 510 (net assets must equal stated capital after payment of dividend). States using these tests viewed payments to shareholders from sources other than surplus as a liquidation of at least a part of the company. Such liquidating distributions could affect the rights of creditors, as well as varying classes of shareholders. *See generally* Wood v. Dummer, 30 Fed. Cas. 435 (D.Me.1824) (the capital of a corporation "is deemed a pledge or trust fund for the payment of debts"). In employing these tests, however, the valuation of assets and the manipulation of the capital accounts allow a great deal of leeway for distributions by companies that are losing money.

RANDALL v. BAILEY

288 N.Y. 280, 43 N.E.2d 43 (1942).

CONWAY, JUDGE.

The plaintiff, as trustee, seeks in this action to recover from directors and executors of deceased directors dividends declared and paid between 1928 and 1932, alleging that they were paid from capital in violation of section 58 of the Stock Corporation Law.

The corporation involved is the Bush Terminal Company, hereinafter called Terminal, which was organized in 1902. It owns and operates a great ocean terminal. The land in Brooklyn which it and its wholly owned subsidiary, Bush Terminal Buildings Company, hereinafter called Buildings, purchased between 1902 and 1905, increased in value with the passing years. Until 1915 Terminal and Buildings carried that land at its original cost. In 1915 and again in 1919 they committed to their books a portion of the increase in value of that land. It has not since been increased. The trial court found that its value during the years 1928 to 1932 was greater than the value to which it had been increased upon the corporate books. Those findings have been unanimously affirmed. Even apart from that affirmance, which concludes us, there is no claim that the findings are not correct. Moreover, there is no allegation in the complaint that any director acted fraudulently, in bad faith or negligently in valuing the land or in voting the dividends. The question presented, therefore, is solely one of law and involves the construction of section 58 of the Stock Corporation Law. We are concerned only with the legislative prohibition as evidenced in section 58 as enacted in 1923. If the directors of Terminal were permitted to include among the corporate assets the value of the land at the amount at which it was valued on the books from 1919 onward there was a surplus for the payment of dividends and no recovery may be had in this action. If it must be carried at cost then the directors unjustifiably declared and paid the dividends which plaintiff seeks to recover. The question presented, therefore, is: may unrealized appreciation in value of fixed assets held for use in carrying on a corporate enterprise be taken into consideration by directors in determining whether a corporate surplus exists from which cash dividends may be paid to stockholders. * * *

The appellant contends that the first sentence of section 58 of the Stock Corporation Law should be divided into two parts; that the first twenty-six words should be applicable to the payment of what he terms regular or ordinary dividends and that the remaining portion of the sentence should be applicable to such dividend as may be declared in connection with a reduction of capital. That construction makes the clause commencing "unless the value of its assets' modify only the second portion."

The appellant points out that in 1912 the Legislature authorized the issuance of stock without par value and provided in section 20 of the Stock Corporation Law, with reference to such a corporation, "No such corporation shall declare any dividend which shall reduce the amount of its capital below the amount stated in the certificate as the amount of capital with which the corporation will carry on business," L.1912, ch. 351, § 20; and that in 1921 that section was amended to read, "No such corporation shall declare or pay any dividend which shall reduce the amount of its stated capital." Thus immediately prior to 1923, corporations having only par value stock were governed by the "surplus profits" language while those having stock without par value were governed by the "amount of stated capital" language. Appellant then contends that the Legislature intended to eliminate the variation of terminology and the overlapping provisions contained in sections 20 and 28 and accomplished that elimination by the enactment of the first twenty-six words in the first sentence of the new section (§ 58) by simply providing that no business stock corporation should distribute dividends which should "impair its capital or capital stock," although the Legislature was in reality continuing the "surplus profits" test of former section 28; that the terminology "surplus profits" and "impairment of capital" were used to express the same test. He contends that the surplus from which cash dividends may be distributed must be based upon actual profits and realized gains, over and above the capital investment, after provision has been made in respect of all losses, which, however, must be treated as realized or accrued, although conceding that dividends may properly be paid from paid-in surplus.

We shall first consider appellant's division of the first sentence of section 58 into two parts. Assuming that there may be some justification for that construction as a matter of syntax and statutory history, it seems to us that an equally strong argument may be made to the contrary. The words any dividend are contained in both portions of the sentence. Any is an all-exclusive word. When repeated in the same sentence one would reasonably assume that the two words bore the same meaning each time. Those two words tie together by repetition the first and second portions of the sentence or so it might well be urged. They must mean a dividend of any kind or character and both portions of the sentence must be read in that light. They must mean that no dividend may be declared or paid which shall impair capital or capital stock nor unless the value of the corporate assets "remaining after the payment of such dividend, or after such distribution of assets, as the case may be, shall be at least equal to the aggregate amount of its debts and liabilities including capital or capital stock as the case may be."

That reasonable men may differ upon the syntax of the sentence under discussion is made apparent by an allegation contained in each of the causes of action in the plaintiff's complaint. It reads as follows: "The declaration and payment of said dividends impaired the capital and capital stock of Terminal; and the value of the assets of Terminal remaining after said payment was less, by an amount in excess of such payment, than the aggregate amount of the debts and liabilities of Terminal including its capital or capital stock; and, both at the time such dividends were declared and at the time they were paid, the capital and capital stock of Terminal was impaired and the declaration and payment of said dividends further impaired said capital and capital stock * * *."

There is other evidence, well nigh conclusive, that the Legislature intended to drop the "surplus profits" test, apart from the internal evidence contained in section 58 itself. In 1924 two subdivisions of section 664 of the Penal Law were amended. Prior to that year the Penal Law, Consol. Laws 1909, c. 40, provided that a director was guilty of a misdemeanor who concurred in any vote: "1. To make a dividend, except from the surplus profits arising from the business of the corporation, and in the cases and manner allowed by law * * *." In 1924 that subdivision was amended to read: "1. To make a dividend, except from surplus, and in the cases and manner allowed by law * * *."

Subdivision 5 of the same section had read: "To apply any portion of the funds of such corporation, except surplus profits, directly or indirectly, to the purchase of shares of its own stock." That subdivision was amended in 1924 to read: "To apply any portion of the funds of such corporation, except surplus, directly or indirectly, to the purchase of shares of its own stock."

Again, we are concerned with the legislative will as written in the statute. We should construe the statutory language as the average business man would read and understand it. He is the one who must bear the burden civilly and criminally. If the Legislature had intended to continue the "surplus profits" test it would have said so clearly and unmistakably rather than by using the words "impair its capital or capital stock." While it is true that punctuation is no part of a writing, it also may not be amiss to point out that there is no semicolon separating the two portions of the sentence in question. We think that a fair reading of the sentence is that the valuation test is applicable to both portions and that it applies to the declaration and payment of regular or ordinary dividends, so termed by appellant.

Finally, as some indication of how the Legislature viewed its own language in section 58, as enacted in 1923, it is interesting to note an amendment of section 58 in 1939. The amendment was not retroactive by express provision of the amending act. It provided, however, in substance, that directors should have an affirmative defense if able to show that they had "reasonable grounds to believe, and did believe, that such dividend or distribution would not impair the capital of such corporation." Quite clearly, in 1939 the Legislature believed that in the enactment of 1923 it had used impairment of capital terminology and the "value of its assets" terminology interchangeably.

Let us now consider section 58 with the applicable sections which preceded it. We are concerned primarily with the meaning of the words "impair its capital or capital stock." In the statute of 1825 neither the word value nor the word impair was used. In the statute of 1890 there was a definition of impairment of capital stock. It read: "The capital stock of a stock corporation shall be deemed impaired when the value of its property and assets after deducting the amount of its debts and liabilities, shall be less than the amount of its paid up capital stock. No dividends shall be declared or paid by any stock corporation, except from the surplus profits of its business, nor when its capital stock is or will be impaired thereby, * * *." That was a clear definition of impairment in terms of value. The "surplus profits" terminology was retained from the act of 1825. In 1892 the statute was amended. It retained the "surplus profits" provision but omitted that word "impair." Instead it returned to the "reduce its capital stock" terminology. Having omitted the word impair the Legislature naturally omitted the definition of impairment. The Legislature did not necessarily, as appellant contends, "reject" the definition of impairment as contained in the 1890 statute. There was no need for it since the word "impair" was not used. The Legislature continued its use of the "surplus profits" and "reduce its capital stock" terminology down to 1923.

When the Legislature in 1923 wrote into the first sentence the words "impair its capital or capital stock, nor while its capital or capital stock is impaired," and in the same sentence used words almost identical with those in the definition of impairment contained in the 1890 statute, it is more reasonable than not to assume that the Legislature was returning to its former definition of impairment of capital and at the same time abandoning the "surplus profits" test. The courts had consistently applied the value of assets rule in determining surplus, surplus profits or impairment of capital without distinction, and the Legislature clarified the language of the statute so as to remove any doubt as to the fact that value was the test. In fact appellant concedes that the determination of the courts below is correct if in drafting the provisions of section 58 in 1923 the Legislature changed the then existing law as to illegal dividends and reinstated the definition of impairment of capital which it had omitted when enacting the statute of 1892. It seems to us that a fair reading of the statute in the light of its language and historical development clearly indicates that that is exactly what the Legislature intended to accomplish.

To say that in the one sentence there were different tests of liability for directors of business corporations, one involving "surplus profits," although those words were not there, and the other involving value of assets, regardless of surplus profits, would be to depart from the authorities, the plain words of the statute and its historical implications. It has always been the rule that where an act amends an existing statute "so as to read as follows," thereupon enacting a new and substituted provision, all of the former statute omitted from the act as amended is repealed. In reality, therefore, appellant is basing his construction of the statute upon the continuance therein of a provision repealed by the act of 1923. * * *

The Legislature having declared that dividends may be paid when there is no impairment of capital or capital stock caused thereby and when the value of the corporate assets remaining after the payment of such dividends is at least equal to the aggregate amount of its debts and liabilities including capital or capital stock as the case may be, Stock Corporation Law, § 58, in other words from its surplus, our inquiry turns to the question whether surplus may consist of increases resulting from a revaluation of fixed assets. Surplus has been well defined as follows in Edwards v. Douglas, 269 U.S. 204, 214, 46 S.Ct. 85, 88, 70 L.Ed. 235, Brandeis J.: "The word 'surplus' is a term commonly employed in corporate finance and accounting to designate an account on corporate books. * * * The surplus account represents the net assets of a corporation in excess of all liabilities including its capital stock. This surplus may be 'paid-in surplus,' as where the stock is issued at a price above par; it may be 'earned surplus,' as where it was derived wholly from undistributed profits; or it may, among other things, represent the increase in valuation of land or other assets made upon a revaluation of the company's fixed property."

The decision below was correct and the judgment should be affirmed, with costs.

LEHMAN, C. J., and LOUGHRAN, FINCH, RIPPEY, LEWIS, and DESMOND, JJ., concur.

Judgment affirmed.

NOTES

1. The New York legislature revised the state's dividend provision in 1961, but the drafting committee asserted that dividends could still be paid out of unrealized appreciation. N.Y. Business Corp. L. § 510 (Revision Notes). The Official Comments to the Model Bus. Corp. Act § 6.40 also state that, in valuing assets, the corporation may use a "fair valuation or other method that is reasonable under the circumstances." The approach allowed by the court in *Randall v. Bailey* does not conform to GAAP, and some states refused to follow the New York rule, concluding that unrealized appreciation was not

appropriate for dividends. *See* Commissioner v. Hirshon Trust, 213 F.2d 523, 527 (2d Cir.1954). Why do you suppose those states took that view?

2. Additional techniques have been used to free up capital for dividends, including decreasing the amount of required stated capital by reducing the par value of outstanding stock. Such action will usually require a shareholder vote and possibly a charter amendment. Another method is to buy up shares and cancel those treasury shares, which will reduce the corporation's stated capital. Delaware broadly allows such changes. 8 Del Corp. L. § 244 (allowing reduction of capital by share purchases). *See also* 8 Del Corp. L. § 242(a)(3) (permits changes in par value through amendment of certificate of incorporation).

3. Another technique called a "quasi-reorganization" is used to reduce or eliminate an earned surplus deficit by applying capital surplus to the deficit. Such action will usually require a shareholder vote. Concern has been expressed that this account juggling, without proper disclosures, may mislead subsequent purchasers of the stock of the corporation because the company's history of operating losses has now been removed. *See generally James D. Cox, Thomas Lee Hazen & F. Hodge O'Neal, Corporations,* § 21.18 (1995) (discussing quasi-reorganizations).

4. Restrictions on dividends may be imposed by loan covenants or shareholder agreements. A lender may thus want to assure that earnings are applied to debt reduction or service before being distributed to shareholders. Complex formulas are often employed in debt covenants that, for example, prohibit dividends where working capital (current assets less current liabilities) or net worth would be reduced.

5. *Leveraged dividends*: During the bull credit market leading up to the 2007 crash, some firms funded dividends to private equity investors by borrowing, often at floating rates. Robert McNatt & Frank Benassi, The Dividend Recap Game: Credit Risk vs. the Allure of Quick Money, Standard & Poor's, Aug. 7, 2006, http://www2.standardandpoors.com/portal/ site/sp/en/us/ page.article/2,1,1,0,1145848227253.html (giving the example of a $1 billion leveraged dividend which returned half of the capital investment of a private equity group). By one estimate, the annual volume of these 'drive by' dividends increased from under five billion in 2000 to between 20 and 40 billion in 2004–2006. Id. Borrowing to fund a dividend increases the firm's leverage and, at the same time, reduces its asset liquidity by upstreaming value to shareholders.

State laws impose restrictions on dividends beyond capital based tests. One unique provision adopted by California requires that the assets of the corporation (exclusive of goodwill and certain other intangible assets) equal at least 1¼ the amount of liabilities. Current assets must also at least equal current liabilities (increased to 1¼ times current liabilities in some instances). Cal. Gen. Corp. Law § 500. Most other state corporate laws preclude distributions that would render the corporation insolvent.

See e.g., N.Y. Business Corp. L. § 510 (dividends prohibited if corporation would be rendered insolvent).

States may use various tests for insolvency. The so-called bankruptcy test prohibits dividends if liabilities exceed assets after the distribution. An equity test precludes a dividend if the corporation will be unable to meet its liabilities as they come due. The Model Bus. Corp. Act § 6.40(c) adopts both a bankruptcy and equity test as the bases for restricting dividends. In adopting a bankruptcy test, the Model Bus. Corp. Act treats any liquidating preferences for senior securities the same as debt in determining whether assets exceed liabilities. The Official Comments to this section liken this to a balance sheet test.

Special dividend provisions may be created for closely held corporations. North Carolina has adopted the following statute:

(i) As used in this subsection, net profits shall mean such net profits as can lawfully be paid in dividends to a particular class of shares after making allowance for the prior claims of shares, if any, entitled to preference in the payment of dividends. If during its immediately preceding fiscal period a corporation having less than 25 shareholders on the final day of said period has not paid to any class of shares dividends in cash or property amounting to at least one-third of the net profits of said period allocable to that class, the holder or holders of twenty percent (20%) or more of the shares of that class may, within four months after the close of said period, make written demand upon the corporation for the payment of additional dividends for that period. After a corporation has received such a demand, the directors shall, during the then current fiscal period or within three months after the close thereof, either (i) cause dividends in cash or property to be paid to the shareholders of that class in an amount equal to the difference between the dividends paid in said preceding fiscal period to shareholders of that class and one-third of the net profits of said period allocable to that class, or in such lesser amount as may be demanded, or (ii) give notice pursuant to subsection (j) of this section to all shareholders making such demand. Such corporation shall not, however, be required to pay dividends pursuant to such demand insofar as (i) such payment would exceed fifty percent (50%) of the net profits of the current fiscal period in which such demand is made, or (ii) the net profits are being retained to eliminate a deficit, or (iii) the payment of dividends would be a breach of a bona fide agreement between the corporation and its creditors restricting the payment of dividends, or (iv) the directors of the corporation can show that its earnings are being retained to meet the reasonably anticipated needs of the business and that such retention of earnings is not inequitable in light of all the circumstances. Upon receipt of such a demand a corporation may elect to treat any dividend previously paid in the current fiscal period as having been paid in the preceding fiscal period, in which event the corporation shall so notify all shareholders. If a dividend is paid in satisfaction of a demand made in accordance with this subsection it shall be deemed to have been paid in the period for which it was demanded, and all shareholders shall be so informed concurrently with such payment.

(j) Upon receipt of a demand from the holders of twenty percent (20%) or more of the shares of any class of shares pursuant to subsection (i) of this section, the corporation receiving such demand may, during the then fiscal period or within three months after the close thereof, give written notice to each shareholder making such written demand that the corporation elects to redeem all shares held by such shareholder in lieu of the payment of dividends as provided in subsection (i) of this section and shall pay to such shareholder the fair value of his shares as of the day preceding the mailing or otherwise reasonably dispatching of the notice. * * *

N.C.G.S. 55–6–40. Does such a provision protect minority shareholders in a closely held corporation from a freeze out by the majority?

MORRIS v. STANDARD GAS & ELEC. CO.

63 A.2d 577 (Del.Ch.1949).

SEITZ, VICE-CHANCELLOR.

Plaintiff seeks a preliminary injunction to prevent the defendant corporation from paying dividends declared on certain classes of its preferred stock on the ground that such action would violate the General Corporation Law of Delaware.

Section 34 of the General Corporation Law of Delaware [now § 170] sets forth the circumstances under which the directors of a Delaware corporation shall have the power to declare and pay dividends. Insofar as pertinent, Section 34 provides:

"The directors * * * shall have power to declare and pay dividends * * * either (a) out of its net assets in excess of its capital as computed in accordance with the provisions of Sections * * * or (b), in case there shall be no such excess, out of its net profits for the fiscal year then current and/or the preceding fiscal year; provided, however, that if the capital of the corporation computed as aforesaid shall have been diminished by depreciation in the value of its property, or by losses, or otherwise, to an amount less than the aggregate amount of the capital represented by the issued and outstanding stock of all classes having a preference upon the distribution of assets, the directors of such corporation shall not declare and pay out of such net profits any dividends upon any shares of any classes of its capital stock until the deficiency in the amount of capital represented by the issued and outstanding stock of all classes having a preference upon the distribution of assets shall have been repaired."

Under the power purportedly given by Section 34(b), the directors of the defendant corporation on December 20, 1948 declared a regular quarterly dividend on the $7 and the $6 prior preference cumulative stock to be paid on January 25, 1949. Shortly thereafter, plaintiff filed this action to enjoin the payment of the dividends on the ground that the requirements of Section 34(b) had not been met because the net value of the assets was less than the aggregate amount of the capital represented by the issued and outstanding stock of all classes having a preference upon the distribution of assets. This is the decision on the application for a preliminary injunction which was heard entirely on affidavits.

The defendant is a Delaware corporation and a public utility holding company. It has outstanding 368,348 shares of prior preference stock $7 cumulative, and 100,000 shares of prior preference stock $6 cumulative. Each of the series mentioned is entitled to cumulative dividends payable quarterly at the annual rate indicated before any dividend may be paid on any other class of stock. In the event of liquidation or dissolution, each share of both series is entitled to a $100 preference over the shares of any other class, plus all dividend arrearages. No dividends have been paid on either series since 1934 and as of September 30, 1948 the $7 series had a per share arrearage of $102.90, and the $6 series an arrearage of $88.20, or an aggregate arrearage on both series of $46,723,009.20.

Defendant also has outstanding 757,442 shares of $4 cumulative preferred stock. This stock has a yearly cumulative dividend preference of $4 per share over the common stock. Subject to the rights of the prior preference stock, this class is entitled to receive $50 per share, plus arrearages in the event of liquidation or dissolution before any distribution is made on the common stock. No dividends have been declared on this stock since 1933, and as of September 30, 1948, the arrearages on the class aggregated $47,213,884.67.

Defendant has outstanding 2,162,607 shares of common stock.

The defendant's board consists of 9 directors, 3 are elected by the holders of the $6 and $7 shares voting as a class, 2 by the $4 shareholders voting as a class, and 4 by the common stockholders voting as a class.

The facts surrounding the declaration of the dividend can best be presented in chronological order. The defendant by an agreement dated December 21, 1945, as amended, had borrowed $51,000,000 from a group of banks. Under this agreement the defendant was prohibited from paying any dividends so long as any of the notes issued under the agreement remained unpaid. In order to clear the way for the declaration of a dividend, the defendant negotiated a new bank loan agreement dated November 26, 1948, under which about $11,600,000 was secured to liquidate the balance of the 1945 obligation. The new agreement permitted the defendant to declare current quarterly dividends on its prior preference stock, provided the amount of the dividends so paid does not exceed the dividend income received by the defendant after September 30, 1948.

Once the defendant was assured that the new bank loan agreement would be signed, its directors met to consider the possibility of declaring the regular quarterly dividend on the $6 and $7 prior preference stock. At a directors' meeting held on November 17, 1948, the minutes recite that all the directors discussed at length various considerations arising in connection with the question of the declaration of current quarterly dividends on the company's prior preference stock. The directors were advised that the Rules of the S.E.C. prohibit a registered holding company from paying dividends out of unearned surplus or capital without the permission of the Commission. The minutes recite:

> "* * * that the Company had on its balance sheet an item designated 'Earned Surplus since December 31, 1937,' the amount of which at October 31, 1948, was $25,602,663.61; and that in view of the qualification by the independent accountants of the Company to the effect that the investments of the Company are subject to such adjustment as may be required in the completion of the corporate simplification program under the Public Utility Holding Company Act of 1935 [15 U.S.C.A. § 79 et seq.], it appeared desirable that the Company obtain from the Securities and Exchange Commission, before the declaration by the Board of current quarterly dividends on the Prior Preference Stock, authority to declare and pay those dividends, which would be charged to that item."

After a discussion by the directors, a resolution was passed authorizing the officers of the defendant to file with the Commission such papers as in their judgment would be necessary or advisable in respect to the proposed declaration of a dividend on the prior preference stock.

About November 24, 1948, the defendant filed an application with the Commission requesting authority to pay current quarterly dividends on its prior preference stock. The application made it clear that the defendant corporation did not concede that the payment would be out of capital.

On December 7, 1948, the directors met, and reference was made to the possibility mentioned at the November 17, 1948 meeting that a dividend might be declared on the prior preference stock. The meeting was advised that an application had been made to the Commission for authority to pay such dividend. The chairman advised the meeting that consideration had been given to the Delaware statute and that in order that the company might have evidence of its compliance with the Delaware statute, W. C. Gilman and Company, at his request, prepared an appraisal of the assets to determine whether in its judgment the assets less the liabilities exceeded $88,500,000—this figure is the approximate total of the aggregate capital represented by the $7, $6, and $4 preferred, plus the sum required to pay a quarterly dividend on the prior preference stock ($87,-350,943.35 plus $794,609). It is not denied that W. C. Gilman and Company possesses expert competence in appraisal matters and is familiar with the defendant's assets by reason of having been engaged to study them for other purposes. The factual appraisal made by Gilman and

Company and submitted to the meeting was necessarily somewhat general. This appraisal discussed the values of the various stocks owned by the defendant by reference to market value, past, present, and future earnings, percentage of stock owned and knowledge based on other studies and sources of information. The report concluded that the net assets of the defendant had a fair value substantially in excess of $88,500,000. The meeting also heard a report made by G. W. Knourek, Vice–President and Treasurer of the defendant corporation. Mr. Knourek was eminently qualified both in education and experience to make such a valuation. His complete familiarity with the defendant's assets is clearly demonstrated. This report dated December 6, 1948, also discussed the value of the stocks and concluded that the fair value of the defendant's net assets substantially exceeded $88,500,000. In this report Mr. Knourek stated that in appraising the assets he gave consideration to market prices, capitalization of current dividends, capitalization of average earnings for the two years nine months ending September 30, 1948, appraisals made in 1943 in connection with the defendant's recapitalization, and the recent orders of the S. E. C. with respect to Louisville Gas and Electric Co. (Del.) and a sale of Oklahoma Gas and Electric Co. stock. The chairman made a statement to the meeting that he had examined the Gilman and Company report and the statement by Mr. Knourek, and that in his opinion a fair value of the net assets was in excess of $88,500,000. He explained to the meeting the methods he used in his study and valuation.

The chairman also stated that since this was the first time this matter had come before the board in many years, he had obtained opinions from two Delaware attorneys and one Chicago attorney as to whether a dividend might legally be declared under the Delaware statute. The opinion, which was read to the meeting, stated that based on the assumptions contained therein the company might legally pay the dividend under the Delaware law.

The minutes recite that the board made numerous inquiries and discussed the asset value problem generally. A balance sheet of the company as of October 31, 1948, and a statement of its income for the twelve months ending that date were presented to the meeting. The chairman suggested an adjournment of the meeting with the hope that in the the interim a Commission order would be entered permitting the proposed dividend declaration to become effective.

A public hearing was held by the Commission at which hearing the present plaintiff appeared and objected to the defendant's proposal. After considering the record, a memorandum by the present plaintiff opposed and a memorandum of the prior preference protective committee in support of the proposal the Commission by order dated December 17, 1948, permitted the proposed dividend to become effective forthwith, but provided, inter alia, that the stockholders be advised "that the Commission permitted the declaration to become effective without determining whether the payment is being made out of capital".

The Commission's opinion contains the following language:

"* * * David Morris & Co. has attacked the valuation and the witnesses who testified in support of it. Although we are not convinced that this issue raised by the objecting stockholder is relevant to these proceedings, nevertheless we have considered the record and are not persuaded that the objection is well founded in fact. However, it should be clearly understood that we are expressing no opinion as to whether this valuation should be accepted for any purpose other than that for which it was presented."

In the light of the Commission's conclusion that the dividend would be allowed without deciding whether the dividend payment would be out of capital, it is apparent that the quoted factual conclusion was in the nature of a "factual dictum" by an administrative body. In view of my approach to the problem presented, it is unnecessary to consider what weight should be given to the Commission's remark.

The directors met on December 20, 1948, and having been advised of the Commission's approval of the proposed dividend, and after discussion, unanimously adopted a resolution providing for a dividend of $1.75 per share on the $7 and a dividend of $1.50 per share on the $6 cumulative preference stock to be paid January 25, 1949 out of the net profits of the defendant corporation accumulated since January 1, 1947, and to be charged to the earned surplus account.

On December 28, 1948, plaintiff filed this action seeking a temporary injunction against the payment of the dividend. As permanent relief, plaintiff requested that the defendant be enjoined from paying any dividend on its stock until the court determined that any such dividend would not constitute a payment out of capital or unearned surplus in violation of the Delaware law. Has plaintiff made out a case for interlocutory relief?

Plaintiff says that when the dividend was declared the capital of the defendant (its assets less its liabilities) was not equal to the aggregate amount of the capital represented by the issued and outstanding stock of all classes having a preference upon distribution. The defendants, of course, take a contrary view. I am not persuaded that the contention and the denial pose the precise issue this court must decide because it assumes that one objective value exists and is capable of being determined.

The defendant corporation concedes that the power to pay the proposed dividend must be found under Section 34(b) of the General Corporation Law of Delaware. It is clear that the net profits of the defendant corporation for the then current and/or the preceding fiscal year are more than sufficient to cover the proposed dividend, and it is clear that the proposed dividend will be charged to the earned surplus account. The sole question then is whether the conditions of the proviso contained in Section 34(b) have been met. Otherwise stated, at the time the board of directors declared the dividend in question were they entitled to conclude that the net assets of the defendant were at least equal to the aggregate amount of the capital represented by the issued and outstanding stock of all classes having a preference upon distribution? Stated with relation to the present facts, were the net assets worth at least $88,145,552.35—being the amount of capital represented by the outstanding stock having a preference on distribution, plus the proposed quarterly dividend.

The problem is one of valuation which is surpassed in difficulty only in the domestic relations law. The numerous and varied standards applied in the legal, accounting and business fields have mapped a wavering course for one required to resolve a substantial problem of valuation. Here the governing statute has declared that the capital must—roughly speaking—be valued at its dollar equivalent before a dividend can be declared out of net profits for a designated period. This duty falls to the directors. What legal standard will be applied in determining whether the directors have valued the corporate assets in a manner deemed sufficient to comply with the requirements of Section 34(b)?

The plaintiff's attorney stated at the oral argument that he did not charge that the directors were guilty of any fraud or bad faith in valuating the capital assets at a dollar value which would satisfy the provisions of Section 34(b). He appeared to take the position that based on the standards he would apply in evaluating the assets, they were not sufficient to comply with the requirements of the statute, and hence the action of the directors violated the statute. He also took the position that nothing short of an actual appraisal of the assets in the underlying companies whose stock was owned by the defendant would be sufficient. Let us consider the second problem first.

Initially, of course, reasonable men can differ as to what constitutes an appraisal. If by an appraisal plaintiff means that all the assets had to be viewed and evaluated separately by the directors or experts in a manner similar to a valuation for purposes of a reorganization of the type currently popular at least in the utility field, then I conclude that the statute imposes no such requirement on the directors as a prerequisite to the employment of the power granted in Section 34(b). In large companies, especially those such as the defendant, an appraisal of the type suggested by plaintiff would mean that as a practical matter the provisions of Section 34(b) would be unavailable. See generally II Bonbright, Valuation of Property, pp. 973–974. I prefer the view expressed in the following language of the New York Supreme Court in Randall v. Bailey, Sup., 23 N.Y.S.2d 173, 184, affirmed 288 N.Y. 280, 43 N.E.2d 43:

> "I see no cause for alarm over the fact that this view [taking assets at actual value] requires directors to make a determination of the value of the assets at each dividend declaration. On the contrary, I think that is exactly what the law always has contemplated that directors should do. That does not mean that the books themselves necessarily must be altered by write-ups or write-downs at each dividend period, or that formal appraisals must be obtained from professional appraisers or even made by the directors themselves. That is obviously impossible in the case of corporations of any considerable size."

In concluding that a formal appraisal of the type mentioned is not required, I do not mean to imply that the directors are not under a duty to evaluate the assets on the basis of acceptable data and by standards which they are entitled to believe reasonably reflect present "values". It is not practical to attempt to lay down a rigid rule as to what constitutes prior evidence of value for the consideration of directors in declaring a dividend under Section 34(b). The factors considered and the emphasis given will depend upon the case presented. At the expense of brevity, let us consider what the directors of the defendant corporation actually did in connection with the declaration of the dividend under attack and then evaluate that action.

Since no dividend had been declared for a great many years, the directors proceeded with some caution. Having seen that the current net assets were more than sufficient to meet the dividend requirements of the $6 and $7 preferred stock, the directors considered the possibility of paying such dividends. The first obstacle to such payment was removed by negotiating a new bank loan. Plaintiff points out that defendant corporation was apparently required to pledge or restrict practically its entire portfolio for this loan of $11,600,000, callable on three days' notice for default. Plaintiff argues that the very fact that the banks required the defendant to pledge or restrict assets which the defendant values at over $100,000,000 to secure a loan of $11,600,000, is evidence that the assets were not worth anything near the value placed on them by the board of directors for dividend purposes. Nothing appears in the papers before me which would throw any light on the question as to why assets of the value alleged were pledged or restricted. Lacking particulars, I do not feel that I should give any particular weight to this argument advanced by the plaintiff. Moreover, plaintiff concedes that the assets are worth upwards of $50,000,000, yet there is no explanation as to why the banks would require a pledge or restriction on assets even at the value placed on them by plaintiff, which is many times the value of the loan.

The directors considered the value factor at three meetings and had available and personally studied the reports concerning the defendant's assets prepared by admitted experts in the field. They had the balance sheets and profit and loss statements. Moreover, evidence as to value became available through the hearing before the S. E. C. even though the issue there presented was not the one now before this court.

That then is what was done before directors representing all classes of stock unanimously declared the dividend now under attack. Let us examine the case presented by plaintiff.

Plaintiff relied on his sworn complaint and his two affidavits. Since October 27, 1947, plaintiff has been the holder of record of 100 shares of the defendant's $4 cumulative preferred stock. In his complaint the plaintiff sets forth his 'opinion' of the value of defendant's assets and arrives at a gross value of $82,109,858. After deducting liabilities of $11,242,729, the plaintiff determines the defendant's net worth to be

$70,863,829. The complaint merely sets forth plaintiff's opinion of the value of each asset owned by the defendant, plus the following allegation:

"Complainant in arriving at the total of $82,109,858. used the figures shown on the left side of Exhibit 'B'. While recently 100 shares of Philadelphia Co. stock sold for $9.75 per share, he feels that a large block could not be sold at such price. Wisconsin Public Service stock pays 20 cents dividend, or 5% on a value of $1.00 [sic] Stocks just as sound, if not better, are yielding 7% and 8%. It has no market value. The stock showing 'no value' are considered valueless and have no market value. The other stocks are valued at market prices."

Plaintiff's first affidavit recites once again his opinion of the value of the defendant's assets with one remarkable change. In his affidavit he states that "Thru a clerical error, the value of Wisconsin Public Service was erroneously listed in Exhibit 'B' to the injunction bill at $1.00 per share, instead of $10.00 per share." This error is the more remarkable because it amounted to an error of $12,375,000, and meant that in drawing his complaint plaintiff by his own statement under-estimated the value of the defendant's assets by that amount. Plaintiff in his first affidavit also revised his net asset value in several respects, but principally to correct the clerical error. After these revisions, plaintiff arrived at a figure of $81,728,640 which he designated as "(Net Assets Appraised)". He then proceeded to deduct the sum of $25,244,457 from this figure and arrived at the sum of $56,484,183 which he describes as "net assets with safety margin". This item is explained by a note which says:

"Less for safety margin 33 1/3% of $50247900 Phila stock and 20% of 42475785 other operating utility stock or total deduction of $25 244 457."

The plaintiff's affidavit supplies plaintiff's explanation of the 'safety margin' deduction. It reads:

"At the moment we are, in my opinion, at a critical point in an inflated economy. Conditions are highly uncertain. Earnings are now high. If our economy contracts, stocks can go lower. I do not think that it would be prudent for a company like the respondent with relatively little cash, to pay a cash dividend at this time without allowing a margin of safety for its investments. I think that a fair margin for safety would be 33–1/3% for a utility holding company like the Philadelphia Company herein mentioned and 20% for the other operating utility companies such as Oklahoma Gas & Electric Co. and the others mentioned in Exhibit 'D'."

Plaintiff appraises the net assets at about $82,000,000 before his "safety margin" deduction. There is no justification under Section 34(b) for requiring an arbitrary deduction from present value before ascertaining the value of the net assets. The safety factor mentioned by plaintiff actually is an element in present value, but there is no justification under the statute for determining present value, and then making an arbitrary deduction. This "safety margin" deduction is actually an attack on the wisdom of the directors in declaring a dividend at the present time. Indeed, in attempting to justify his argument for a deduction plaintiff speaks of what is "prudent". Where, as here, the only question is one of compliance with the statute, and there is no suggestion that the directors have been guilty of fraud or bad faith in attempting to comply therewith, I do not believe this court can substitute its concept of wisdom for that of the directors.

Plaintiff's affidavit indicates that he arbitrarily applied a ten times earnings formula as a standard for valuing the principal assets of the defendant. Defendant's assets consist of the ownership of various stock interests in public utility companies providing gas, electricity, transportation and other services in at least seven states. Certainly this test may be one standard by which the value of such assets are weighed, but it is most assuredly not the only standard to be applied. Indeed, the assets sought to be valued may have such a factual background that the application of such a rule would be misleading and even fraudulent. Although a certain picked class of utility stocks may have an average value of ten times earnings, nevertheless, as counsel for the stockholders' committee pointed out, it is only an average. The values of the utilities chose to determine an average may vary widely. Consequently, plaintiff's assumption that this standard of valuing the assets is the only one to be applied is fallacious. The defendant corporation does not say that this arbitrary standard should not be considered. It merely says that it is only one criterion of value to be considered. I am in accord with the defendant's position. Compare generally In re General Realty & Utilities Corporation, Del.Ch., 52 A.2d 6.

We are left then with plaintiff's opinion that the net assets are worth about $82,000,000. This is about $6,500,000 less than the value admittedly necessary if a dividend is to be legally declared under Section 34(b). The plaintiff gives only his opinion of the value of the assets. As a basis for qualifying himself to give such opinion, plaintiff mentions his experiences in the investment field. His college education was in the business field, and for about 15 years he has operated an investment business in Wall Street, New York City. He holds official positions in the New York Security Dealers Association. He states that it is his business to know the value of securities, although he overlooked a 'clerical error' of $12,375,000, and confused a worthless stock in the defendant's portfolio with stock of another class having a value of about $600,000. Indeed, there is nothing in the plaintiff's papers to show any real familiarity with the corporations whose stocks are owned by the defendant. Plaintiff speaks of the stocks as though the defendant's business was trading in utility stocks. Such is not the case, and in consequence plaintiff loses sight of the value inherent in holding certain blocks of stock which give the defendant working control of such corporations.

Plaintiff also contends that the appraisals relied on by the defendant's directors erroneously took into consideration such factors as the future earnings and prospects of the stocks owned by the defendant. He urges that such elements may not be considered in determining present value under Section 34(b). I am unable to agree with plaintiff's contention. The factors mentioned certainly form elements to be considered in determining the present value of stock in a going concern. It is indeed common knowledge that future prospects often constitute a most important factor where present value is sought to be determined.

Plaintiff points out that the reputable accountants who prepared the defendant's balance sheet stated that the value of the defendant's assets was subject to such adjustment as might be required under a simplification program called for by the Public Utility Holding Company Act of 1935. From this and other statements plaintiff implies that the accountants were suggesting that the capital assets were overvalued. In my opinion, the statements made by the accountants merely constituted a caveat for their own protection and did not purport to go further. Nor in my opinion does the fact that the defendant applied to the S.E.C. for permission to declare the dividend constitute persuasive evidence that the directors felt that the value of the assets was such that the dividend would actually be paid out of capital.

Thus we have a situation where plaintiff seeks a preliminary injunction to prevent the directors from paying a dividend under Section 34(b) because he alone values the net assets at about $6,500,000 below the required value, while the defendant's directors have declared the dividend after having been presented with substantial data as to value compiled by admitted experts in the field. This data, along with the corporate records, indicate that the net assets are substantially in excess of the statutory requirement. I purposely refrain from placing too much reliance upon the more elaborate statements contained in defendant's affidavits showing the justification for the action of the directors because I prefer to evaluate the information presented to and the action taken by the directors prior to or at the time the dividend was declared. The information presented to and the action taken by the directors, when contrasted with plaintiff's case, permits of but one reasonable answer. The plaintiff has failed utterly to make out a showing which would entitle him to a preliminary injunction.

Plaintiff's case comes down to a disagreement with the directors as to value under circumstances where the directors took great care to obtain data on the point in issue, and exercised an informed judgment on the matter. In such a situation, I am persuaded that this court cannot substitute either plaintiff's or its own opinion of value for that reached by the directors where there is no charge of fraud or bad faith. As stated, the process of valuation called for by Section 34(b) of necessity permits of no one objective standard of value. Having in mind its function, the directors must be given reasonable latitude in ascertaining value. Such being the case, I conclude that the action of the directors in determining that the net assets were worth at least the aggregate amount of the capital represented by the issued and outstanding stock of all classes having preference upon the distribution of assets cannot be disturbed on the showing here made. Consequently, plaintiff is not entitled to a preliminary injunction restraining the payment of the dividend.

An order accordingly will be advised on notice.

NOTES

1. The "nimble dividend" provision in the Delaware Code (§ 170), which allows a dividend to be paid in a profitable year even where there is no surplus, has been the subject of much criticism. *See James D. Cox, Thomas Lee Hazen & F. Hodge O'Neal, Corporations*, § 20.17 (1995) (discussing the appropriateness of nimble dividends). *Compare* Weinberg v. Baltimore Brick Co., 114 A.2d 812 (Del.1955) (charter provision for dividends from "net earnings" did not preclude nimble dividend for preferred shareholders from current earnings even though there was a cumulative capital deficit), *with*, Jones v. First National Bldg. Corp., 155 F.2d 815 (10th Cir.1946) (charter provision providing for dividend payments out of surplus precluded nimble dividends where capital was impaired).

2. As you will recall from your Business Associations class, stockholders generally do not have the power to require the board of directors to declare a dividend. *See e.g.*, Dodge v. Ford Motor Co., 204 Mich. 459, 170 N.W. 668 (1919) (board of directors has broad, although not unlimited, discretion in declaring dividends). Once declared, however, the dividend becomes a debt obligation of the corporation. *See e.g.*, Fidelity & Columbia Trust Co. v. Louisville Railroad, 265 Ky. 820, 97 S.W.2d 825 (1936).

3. Four separate dates determine who has a right to a dividend. The dividend *declaration date* is when the company announces to the market that a dividend will be paid. One of the terms of this announcement is the *record date*, which refers to when the company's master security holder's file is checked to determine the set of current shareholders with a right to receive the dividend. Another term included in the announcement is when the company actually disburses the dividend, i.e., the *payment date*. Since ownership of the corporation's shares may change between the declaration date and the payment date, the market establishes a cutoff time before which purchasers of the security take the dividend (because their ownership is recorded in the master security holder's file the record date) and after which the dividend accrues to the previous owners. This cutoff date is known as the *ex-date* because after it the security trades without, i.e., *ex*, the dividend. Typically, the ex-date is three days before the record date.

SECTION 5.   OTHER DISTRIBUTIONS

KAMIN v. AMERICAN EXPRESS CO.

86 Misc.2d 809, 383 N.Y.S.2d 807 (Sup.), aff'd, 54 A.D.2d 654, 387 N.Y.S.2d 993 (1976).

EDWARD J. GREENFIELD, JUSTICE:

In this stockholders' derivative action, the individual defendants, who are the directors of the American Express Company, move for an order dismissing the complaint for failure to state a cause of action pursuant to CPLR 3211(a)(7), and alternatively, for summary judgment pursuant to CPLR 3211(c).

The complaint is brought derivatively by two minority stockholders of the American Express Company, asking for a declaration that a certain dividend in kind is a waste of corporate assets, directing the defendants not to proceed with the distribution, or, in the alternative, for monetary damages. The motion to dismiss the complaint requires the Court to presuppose the truth of the allegations. It is the defendants' contention that, conceding everything in the complaint, no viable cause of action is made out. After establishing the identity of the parties, the complaint alleges that in 1972 American Express acquired for investment 1,954,418 shares of common stock of Donaldson, Lufken and Jenrette, Inc. (hereafter DLJ), a publicly traded corporation, at a cost of $29.9 million. It is further alleged that the current market value of those shares is approximately $4.0 million. On July 28, 1975, it is alleged, the Board of Directors of American Express declared a special dividend to all stockholders of record pursuant to which the shares of DLJ would be distributed in kind. Plaintiffs contend further that if American Express were to sell the DLJ shares on the market, it would sustain a capital loss of $25 million, which could be offset against taxable capital gains on other investments. Such a sale, they allege, would result in tax savings to the company of approximately $8 million, which would not be available in the case of the distribution of DLJ shares to stockholders. It is alleged that on October 8, 1975 and October 16, 1975, plaintiffs demanded that the directors rescind the previously declared dividend in DLJ shares and take steps to preserve the capital loss which would result from selling the shares. This demand was rejected by the Board of Directors on October 17, 1975.

It is apparent that all the previously-mentioned allegations of the complaint go to the question of the exercise by the Board of Directors of business judgment in deciding how to deal with the DLJ shares. The crucial allegation which must be scrutinized to determine the legal sufficiency of the complaint is paragraph 19, which alleges: "19. All of the defendant Directors engaged in or acquiesced in or negligently permitted the declaration and payment of the Dividend in violation of the fiduciary duty owed by them to Amex to care for and preserve Amex's assets in the same manner as a man of average prudence would care for his own property."

Plaintiffs never moved for temporary injunctive relief, and did nothing to bar the actual distribution of the DLJ shares. The dividend was in fact paid on October 31, 1975. Accordingly, that portion of the complaint seeking a direction not to distribute the shares is deemed to be moot, and the Court will deal only with the request for declaratory judgment or for damages.

Examination of the complaint reveals that there is no claim of fraud or self-dealing, and no contention that there was any bad faith or oppressive conduct. The law is quite clear as to what is necessary to ground a claim for actionable wrongdoing. "In actions by stockholders, which assail the acts of their directors or trustees, courts will not interfere unless the powers have been illegally or unconscientiously executed; or unless it be made to appear that the acts were fraudulent or collusive, and destructive of the rights of the stockholders. Mere errors of judgment are not sufficient as grounds for equity interference, for the powers of those entrusted with corporate management are largely discretionary." Leslie v. Lorillard, 110 N.Y. 519, 532, 18 N.E. 363, 365. See also, Winter v. Anderson, 242 App.Div. 430, 432, 275 N.Y.S. 373, 374; Rous v. Carlisle, 261 App.Div. 432, 434, 26 N.Y.S.2d 197, 200, affd. 290 N.Y. 869, 50 N.E.2d 250; 11 New York Jurisprudence, Corporations, Section 378.

More specifically, the question of whether or not a dividend is to be declared or a distribution of some kind should be made is exclusively a matter of business judgment for the Board of Directors. " * * * Courts will not interfere with such discretion unless it be first made to appear that the directors have acted or are about to act in bad faith and for a dishonest purpose. It is for the directors to say, acting in good faith of course, when and to what extent dividends shall be declared * * * The statute confers upon the directors this power, and the minority stockholders are not in a position to question this right, so long as the directors are acting in good faith * * * " Liebman v. Auto Strop Co., 241 N.Y. 427, 433–4, 150 N.E. 505, 506. Accord: City Bank Farmers Trust Co. v. Hewitt Realty Co., 257 N.Y. 62, 177 N.E. 309; Venner v. Southern Pacific Co., 2 Cir., 279 F. 832, cert. denied 258 U.S. 628.

Thus, a complaint must be dismissed if all that is presented is a decision to pay dividends rather than pursuing some other course of conduct. Weinberger v. Quinn, 264 App.Div. 405, 35 N.Y.S.2d 567, affd. 290 N.Y. 635, 49 N.E.2d 131. A complaint which alleges merely that some course of action other than that pursued by the Board of Directors would have been more advantageous gives rise to no cognizable cause of action. Courts have more than enough to do in adjudicating legal rights and devising remedies for wrongs. The directors' room rather than the courtroom is the appropriate forum for thrashing out purely business questions which will have an impact on profits, market prices, competitive situations, or tax advantages. As stated by Cardozo, J., when sitting at Special Term, the substitution of someone else's business judgment for that of the directors "is no business for any court to follow." Holmes v. St. Joseph Lead Co., 84 Misc. 278, 283, 147 N.Y.S. 104, 107, quoting from Gamble v. Queens County Water Co., 123 N.Y. 91, 99, 25 N.E. 201, 208.

It is not enough to allege, as plaintiffs do here, that the directors made an imprudent decision, which did not capitalize on the possibility of using a potential capital loss to offset capital gains. More than imprudence or mistaken judgment must be shown.

"Questions of policy of management, expediency of contracts or action, adequacy of consideration, lawful appropriation of corporate funds to advance corporate interests, are left solely to their honest and unselfish decision, for their powers therein are without limitation and free from restraint, and the exercise of them for the common and general interests of the corporation may not be questioned, although the results show that what they did was unwise or inexpedient." Pollitz v. Wabash Railroad Co., 207 N.Y. 113, 124, 100 N.E. 721, 724.

Section 720(a)(1)(A) of the Business Corporation Law permits an action against directors for "the neglect of, or failure to perform, or other violation of his duties in the management and disposition of corporate assets committed to his charge." This does not mean that a director is chargeable with ordinary negligence for having made an improper decision, or having acted imprudently. The "neglect" referred to in the statute is neglect of duties (i.e., malfeasance or nonfeasance) and not misjudgment. To allege that a director "negligently permitted the declaration and payment" of a dividend without alleging fraud, dishonesty or nonfeasance, is to state merely that a decision was taken with which one disagrees.

Nor does this appear to be a case in which a potentially valid cause of action is inartfully stated. The defendants have moved alternatively for summary judgment and have submitted affidavits under CPLR 3211(c), and plaintiffs likewise have submitted papers enlarging upon the allegations of the complaint. The affidavits of the defendants and the exhibits annexed thereto demonstrate that the objections raised by the plaintiffs to the proposed dividend action were carefully considered and unanimously rejected by the Board at a special meeting called precisely for that purpose at the plaintiffs' request. The minutes of the special meeting indicate that the defendants were fully aware that a sale rather than a distribution of the DLJ shares might result in the realization of a substantial income tax saving. Nevertheless, they concluded that there were countervailing considerations primarily with respect to the adverse effect such a sale, realizing a loss of $25 million, would have on the net income figures in the American Express financial statement. Such a reduction of net income would have a serious effect on the market value of the publicly traded American Express stock. This was not a situation in which the defendant directors totally overlooked facts called to their attention. They gave them consideration, and attempted to view the total picture in arriving at their decision. While plaintiffs contend that according to their accounting consultants the loss on the DLJ stock would still have to be charged against current earnings even if the stock were distributed, the defendants' accounting experts assert that the loss would be a charge against earnings only in the event of a sale, whereas in the event of distribution of the stock as a dividend, the proper accounting treatment would be to charge the loss only against surplus. While the chief accountant for the SEC raised some question as to the appropriate accounting treatment of this transaction, there was no basis for any action to be taken by the SEC with respect to the American Express financial statement.

The only hint of self-interest which is raised, not in the complaint but in the papers on the motion, is that four of the twenty directors were officers and employees of American Express and members of its Executive Incentive Compensation Plan. Hence, it is suggested, by virtue of the action taken earnings may have been overstated and their compensation affected thereby. Such a claim is highly speculative and standing alone can hardly be regarded as sufficient to support an inference of self-dealing. There is no claim or showing that the four company directors dominated and controlled the sixteen outside members of the Board. Certainly, every action taken by the Board has some impact on earnings and may therefore affect the compensation of those whose earnings are keyed to profits. That does not disqualify the inside directors, nor does it put every policy adopted by the Board in question. All directors have an obligation, using sound business judgment, to maximize income for the benefit of all persons having a stake in the welfare of the corporate entity. See, Amdur v. Meyer, 15 A.D.2d 425, 224 N.Y.S.2d 440, appeal dismissed 14 N.Y.2d 541, 248 N.Y.S.2d 639, 198 N.E.2d 30. What we have here as revealed both by the complaint and by the affidavits and exhibits, is that a disagreement exists between two minority stockholders and a unanimous Board of Directors as to the best way to handle a loss already incurred on an investment. The directors are entitled to exercise their honest business judgment on the information before them, and to act within their corporate powers. That they may be mistaken, that other courses of action might have differing consequences, or that their action might benefit some shareholders more than others presents no basis for the superimposition of judicial judgment, so long as it appears that the directors have been acting in good faith. The question of to what extent a dividend shall be declared and the manner in which it shall be paid is ordinarily subject only to the qualification that the dividend be paid out of surplus (Business Corporation Law Section 510, subd. b). The Court will not interfere unless a clear case is made out of fraud, oppression, arbitrary action, or breach of trust.

Courts should not shrink from the responsibility of dismissing complaints or granting summary judgment when no legal wrongdoing is set forth. As stated in Greenbaum v. American Metal Climax, Inc., 27 A.D.2d 225, 231–2, 278 N.Y.S.2d 123, 130: "It is well known that derivative actions by stockholders generally involve extensive pretrial procedures, including lengthy examinations before trial, and then, finally, prolonged trials; and that they also entail large litigation costs, including the probability of a considerable liability upon the corporation for the defense costs of defendant officers. Such actions are a heavy burden upon the courts and litigants. Consequently, the summary judgment remedy should be fully utilized and given due effect to challenge such an action which appears to be in the nature of a strike suit or otherwise lacks apparent merit * * * (plaintiffs) are bound to bear in mind that matters depending on business judgment are not actionable (Cf. Steinberg v. Carey, 285 App.Div. 1131, 140 N.Y.S.2d 574). They are required to set forth something more than vague general charges of wrongdoing; the charges must be supported by factual assertions of specific wrongdoing; conclusory allegations of breaches of fiduciary duty are not enough." In this case it clearly appears that the plaintiffs have failed as a matter of law to make out an actionable claim. Accordingly, the motion by the defendants for summary judgment and dismissal of the complaint is granted.

NOTES

1. Do you agree with the court that that a corporation's board of directors may properly forgo an $8 million tax benefit in order to dress up the company's earnings and allow the board to avoid acknowledging that it made a bad investment?

2. For subsequent developments in the ownership of Donaldson, Lufkin & Jenrette, including its issuance of tracking stock for its online trading operations, see Sedighim v. Donaldson, Lufkin & Jenrette, Inc., 167 F.Supp.2d 639 (S.D.N.Y.2001).

3. Another form of the distribution is the stock dividend in which existing shareholders are given additional stock as a dividend. This distribution is to be distinguished from a stock split in which existing shares are merely divided into smaller units, diluting all shares equally. The stock dividend may have a similar effect on dilution, but in balance sheet states surplus capital must be set aside to support the stated capital or par value of the stocks issued as a dividend. See 8 Del. Corp. L. § 173. This will reduce the ability of the company to pay cash dividends because the amount of capital surplus will be less. Model Bus. Corp. Act. § 1.40(6), however, excludes stock dividends from the act's restrictions on cash dividends and other distributions in Model Bus. Corp. Act § 6.40. Generally accepted accounting principles may still require a reduction of retained earnings to reflect the stock dividend. *See James D. Cox, Thomas Lee Hazen & F. Hodge O'Neal, Corporations,* § 20.21 (1995).

4. Dividends and distributions may take other forms. One of the more exotic dividends is the payment-in-kind ("PIK") used for some preferred shares or even debentures as an interest payment. For a PIK Preferred, the dividend is paid initially in additional shares of the preferred, and in later years cash dividends are paid. Richard B. Tyler, "Other Constituency Statutes," 59 Mo. L. Rev. 373, 397, n. 121 (1994). *See generally* Mezzonen, S.A. v. Wright, Fed Sec. L. Rep. (CCH) ¶ 90,704 (S.D.N.Y.1999) (dividends ranging from 15% to 25% paid on preferred shares in the form of "payments in kind" of additional shares of preferred stock).

STRASSBURGER v. EARLY

752 A.2d 557 (Del.Ch.2000).

JACOBS, VICE CHANCELLOR.

In August, 1994, at a time when it was desperately short of cash, Ridgewood Properties, Inc., a Delaware corporation ("Ridgewood" or "the

Company'') repurchased 83% of its outstanding common stock from its two largest stockholders—Triton Group, Ltd. (''Triton'') and Hesperus Limited Partners (''Hesperus''). To finance those repurchases, Ridgewood had to sell its principal operating assets. At issue in this post-trial Opinion is whether those repurchases constituted a breach of the fiduciary duty of loyalty owed by Ridgewood's board of directors to the Company and its minority stockholders.

The plaintiff, who is a Ridgewood stockholder suing derivatively, claims that the repurchases constituted a breach of fiduciary duty because they had no purpose other than to benefit one person—N. Russell Walden (''Walden'')—Ridgewood's President, a director, and the Company's third large stockholder—by increasing Walden's stock ownership interest from 6.9% to a 55% position of absolute majority control. The plaintiff also claims that those transactions were highly unfair to Ridgewood's remaining stockholders and also a waste of corporate assets. * * *

The plaintiff seeks the invalidation of the Triton and Hesperus stock repurchases on the ground that they constituted three distinct breaches of the Ridgewood directors' fiduciary duty of loyalty. The first claim is that because the two repurchases were components of a unitary transaction approved by self-interested directors, those directors must carry the burden of demonstrating that the transaction was entirely fair to Ridgewood and its minority public stockholders. The plaintiff contends that the directors have not carried that burden, as the evidence shows that the repurchases were the product of unfair dealing and an unfair purchase price. The second fiduciary claim is that the share repurchases constituted an improper expenditure of corporate funds for the purpose of placing and perpetuating Walden in a position of corporate control. The third claim is that the repurchases were a waste of corporate assets. * * *

The defendants assiduously dispute these claims, and resist the relief that plaintiff seeks. * * *

Although arms length negotiations between Triton and Ridgewood did take place, they were not conducted by an independent committee acting on behalf of the Ridgewood minority. The negotiations were conducted by Walden, an interested party, and Triton, another interested party on the ''other side of the table.'' Walden was serving his own personal interest in negotiating a transaction he intended as part of a larger plan to confer control upon himself. His ''vigorous negotiation'' focused only on one term—the purchase price that Ridgewood would pay. While that negotiation process did protect *one* of the minority stockholder's interests, it did not protect them all, because Walden's interests were antagonistic to the minority's *other* significant interests. As negotiated, the repurchases would afford only two stockholders—Triton and Hesperus—an opportunity to liquidate their investment, and they would give a third stockholder (Walden) voting control—all at corporate expense. The only benefit the minority would receive from these transactions was an arithmetic boost in the book value of their stock, but in all other respects they would be worse off. The minority would end up holding illiquid investments in a company now having no significant productive assets and now controlled by a stockholder-executive with strong incentives to continue paying himself annual compensation at a six figure level, but with weak incentives to part with control in any transaction (such as, for example, a sale of the company) that would enable the minority to realize on their investment. In these circumstances, the minority's predominate interest would be for these transactions not to take place at all—at least in the form of a company-financed repurchase of control.

To be relieved of their exacting burden of proof, the defendants would have to establish that the minority's true interests were adequately represented by advocates committed to their cause. There were no such advocates and there was no adequate representation.

Even the defendants cannot bring themselves to argue that Mr. Henderson, acting as a one man independent committee, effectively performed that advocacy function. Henderson conducted no negotiations, and although he did conclude that the Triton repurchase was in the best interests of Ridgewood and its minority stockholders, Henderson based that conclusion on an investigation that he was required to conduct practically blindfolded. Henderson's assignment and investigation was restricted solely to the Triton repurchase. It did not include any assessment of the combined Triton–Hesperus transaction. The narrow scope of Henderson's assignment was highly significant, because the effectuation of the Triton repurchase alone would not give Walden absolute control, but the combined Triton and Hesperus repurchases would. Consequently, and with all due respect for Henderson's acumen as a businessman and his good intentions, his independent committee role could not and did not provide meaningful protection for the Ridgewood minority.

For these reasons the Triton and Hesperus repurchase transactions must be evaluated under the entire fairness standard with the burden of proof resting upon the defendants. * * *

The legal principles that govern this claim are well-established and undisputed. By statute, a Delaware corporation has the power to repurchase its own shares. [368 Del. C § 160]. The corporation may, moreover, lawfully repurchase shares of particular stockholders selectively, without being required to offer to repurchase the shares of all stockholders generally. The exercise of this power is constrained only by the board's fiduciary duties.

The limiting fiduciary principle upon which plaintiff relies is that it is improper to cause the corporation to repurchase its stock for the sole or primary purpose of maintaining the board or management in control. In such a case the purchase is deemed unlawful even if the purchase price is fair. * * *

In this case all elements of this claim but one are conceded. It is undisputed that the Ridgewood stock held by Triton and Hesperus was repurchased with corporate funds. It also is undisputed that the effect of the repurchase was to put Walden into a position of absolute control. The only issue is whether the sole or primary purpose of those repurchases was to entrench Walden into that control position. That issue is factual, and requires the Court to resolve a conflict between the defendants' testimony and the objective evidence.

The defendants' testimony incants a consistent choral refrain: they caused the Company to repurchase Triton's Ridgewood stock because (a) some solution was needed to protect against the potential threat implicit in Triton's plan to liquidate its investment in Ridgewood, and (b) after considering all available alternatives, the board determined that a repurchase was the best solution. In addition to the reasons previously discussed, a repurchase would be at an advantageous, below-book-value price that would benefit all stockholders equally. The defendants further contend that the Hesperus repurchase represented a second opportunity—unrelated to Triton but serendipitously timed—to buy another significant block at the same equally favorable price.

The defendants concede that the repurchases elevated Walden's stock ownership level from 6.9% to absolute control, but insist that that was only the transactions' incidental effect, not their purpose. Indeed, defendants assert that Walden did not actually even obtain board control, because the newly issued Preferred Stock entitled Triton to designate two of Ridgewood's four directors. Moreover, defendants claim, if Walden's motive was to serve his personal interests at Ridgewood's expense, he would have advocated a cash dividend, that would have netted him $1.2 million personally while enabling him to continue on as Ridgewood's CEO.

If credible, that testimony would constitute a valid defense to the entrenchment claim. The difficulty is that the testimony is not credible, not only because it is self-serving but also because it does not square with the objective facts. * * *

In the Spring of 1994, Ridgewood was so desperately in need of cash that it had to sell assets and also borrow $500,000 from Triton just to pay expenses. In those straitened circumstances, for Ridgewood's board to sell off the mobile home parks—Ridgewood's then-crown jewel—and then use a significant part of the proceeds to repurchase the control block, would strike any prudent businessman striving to serve the interests of all shareholders as an extravagance. That would be not unlike an unemployed person whose savings account is depleted, deciding to sell his family's only valuable asset (the house) and use the proceeds to buy a luxury car. From a business standpoint, to sell Ridgewood's remaining productive assets (the mobile home parks) to purchase a nonproductive asset (Ridgewood stock) even at below book value, would diminish, not enhance, Ridgewood's prospects for future growth and profit. In these circumstances, only a crisis that threatened the ongoing viability of the Company, and that was so grave as to outweigh these negative business concerns, might arguably justify a repurchase of control.

Had the board voted to repurchase *only* the Triton shares, that at least would have been consistent with defendants' claim that they were motivated only by a desire to protect the Company and its minority stockholders from "bone pickers." But the repurchase of Hesperus's shares fatally undercuts this rationale, because Hesperus held only 9% of Ridgewood's stock. It did not own control and it did not pose any threat to the enterprise. There was no need to buy back Hesperus's stock to eliminate a potentially threatening controlling stockholder. The buyout of Triton's shares was sufficient to accomplish that. Given Ridgewood's shaky financial condition, a prudent businessman-fiduciary would spend not one penny more than was necessary to acquire Triton's controlling interest. Once Triton's control block was acquired, a further expenditure of $1.45 million to acquire Hesperus's 9% block would accomplish nothing except to further deplete Ridgewood's badly needed working capital. I conclude, for these reasons, that a repurchase of Hesperus's shares could further only one purpose—to confer absolute control on Walden. * * *

In short, I find that the defendants have not met their burden of proving that the repurchase of the Ridgewood shares owned by Triton and Hesperus was "primarily in the corporate interest." * * *

The facts that invalidate the Triton/Hesperus repurchases under the "entrenchment-motivated repurchase" doctrine are equally invalidating under conventional "entire fairness" analysis. Indeed, any different result would be hard to fathom, since it cannot be supposed that a stock repurchase paid for with corporate assets to install a fiduciary-director in control would be a breach of fiduciary duty under one well-settled doctrine, yet still be "entirely fair" to minority shareholders under another doctrine that is closely related. In this case the "entrenchment purpose" and "entire fairness" analyses conflate, and for that reason alone the legal discussion could conclude at this point. Nonetheless, I proceed to scrutinize the repurchases through the separate and analytically different lens of "entire fairness," because that perspective illuminates the analysis of the problematic issue of the appropriate remedy.

For reasons previously discussed, this case implicates only the "fair dealing" aspect of entire fairness. The analysis of fair dealing "embraces questions of when the transaction was timed, how it was initiated, structured, negotiated, disclosed to the directors, and how the approvals of the directors and the stockholders were obtained."

Here, the board's decision to repurchase the Triton and Hesperus stock was triggered by Triton's announcement of its plan to exit its investment. The board's response to that announcement—the repurchases—was initiated by Walden, whose intense self interest in making that happen guided his conduct. To assure that the board would arrive at the specific outcome (structure) he desired, Walden subtly assumed control of the decision making process—a feat that was not difficult to carry off because the remaining directors trusted Walden and followed his lead. In that sense the three relevant fair dealing factors—initiation, structure and negotiation—converged. The board, at Walden's initiation and urging, approved a transaction structure that would benefit only Walden and the two largest shareholders whose holdings were to be repurchased. Walden then negotiated with those two shareholders to obtain favorable price and other terms. Missing from the negotiating process and the board decision making process, however, was any independent representation of the interests of Ridgewood's minority public stockholders. In those circumstances, there was no fair dealing, because there was no advocate committed to protect the minority's interests, and because the players were either indifferent, or had objectives adverse, to those interests.

This failure of process explains, at least in part, why the Ridgewood board did not observe its duty to assure that the repurchases were fair to the corporation and its minority shareholders. The transactions were the functional equivalent of Ridgewood (a) purchasing the control block of its own stock for $8 million and then (b) transferring the repurchased block to a single shareholder without receiving any consideration in return. The fiduciary duty implications of such a transaction should have been apparent had the board members straightforwardly acknowledged that they were about to approve a gratis transfer of corporate control to a single stockholder—Walden—and as a result, leave the minority stockholders worse off than they were before.

I therefore conclude that the repurchases are invalid for the additional reason that the defendants have not demonstrated that those transactions were entirely fair to Ridgewood or its minority stockholders. * * *

NOTE

Stock redemption agreements and other share purchases represent in effect a partial liquidation of the company. If the redemption is extended to less than all shareholders in a closely held corporation, the excluded shareholders are being denied a market for their stock. As you may recall from your Business Association classes, this concern is ever present in closely held corporations.

SECTION 6. LIABILITY FOR WRONGFUL DISTRIBUTIONS

PROTOCOMM CORP. v. NOVELL, INC.

171 F.Supp.2d 459 (E.D.Pa.2001).

LOWELL A. REED, JR., SENIOR DISTRICT JUDGE.

Two motions are presently before this Court in this third generation lawsuit which sprung from a breach of contract dispute between plaintiff

ProtoComm Corporation ("ProtoComm") and Fluent, Inc., ("Fluent"), now Novell Advanced Services ("Novell"). Defendants Technology for Information and Publishing, L.P., David L. Nelson, Cornelius A. Ferris, and Premkumar Uppaluru (collectively referred to as "Former Fluent Shareholders") filed a motion for summary judgment (Document No. 67), pursuant to Federal Rule of Civil Procedure 56, and ProtoComm and remaining defendants Aenas Venture Corporation, ASCII Corporation, Cirrus Logic, Inc., FIP Associates Ltd. and FIP II, Ltd., and Intel Corporation (collectively referred to as "settling defendants") filed a joint motion to dismiss with prejudice all claims of plaintiff against such defendants (Document No. 76), pursuant to Federal Rule of Civil Procedure 41(a)(2) to which the Former Fluent Shareholders (also referred to as "non-settling defendants") object.

Upon consideration of the motions, responses and replies thereto, and for the reasons set forth below, I will deny in part and grant in part the motion for summary judgment and grant the joint motion to dismiss.

This lawsuit has its roots in a case brought by ProtoComm against Fluent which alleged a breach of a contract to develop a video server software. ("ProtoComm I"). On July 24, 1996, a jury returned a verdict in favor of ProtoComm and against Fluent for $12.5 million. The Court of Appeals for the Third Circuit affirmed the verdict on October 29, 1997. The details of ProtoComm I and the suit which followed, ProtoComm II, have been detailed at length by this Court and will not be repeated here. The following background is relevant to this case, ProtoComm III, which involves at its core a complex transaction whereby Novell acquired Fluent while the ProtoComm I case was pending. In or around January, 1993, Novell began investigating the possibility of investing in Fluent. In February, 1993, Novell appeared "positive" toward making such an investment. This investment would go into Fluent's treasury. The ProtoComm I suit was filed on January 29, 1993. Upon discovering the lawsuit, Novell told Fluent that the investment activities would cease until the suit was settled.

On March 19, 1993, David Bradford ("Bradford"), Novell's Senior Vice President and General Counsel, sent a draft letter of intent to Cornelius Ferris ("Ferris"), Fluent's President; the letter contemplated that the acquisition would take the form of an asset purchase. On April 28, 1993, Bradford sent a letter of intent to Ferris; the letter contemplated that the acquisition would take the form of a stock sale in which Fluent would become a wholly owned subsidiary of Novell. The letter of intent required as a condition precedent to the acquisition that "the lawsuit with ProtoComm be provided for to Novell's satisfaction."

Where the April 28, 1993 letter of intent had included the language that Novell would acquire "all of the business, assets, and obligations of Fluent," the actual agreement, dated June 4, 1993, excluded such language. The agreement did retain language providing that the ProtoComm litigation "shall have been resolved to the satisfaction of Fluent and

Novell." The proxy statement furnished to Fluent's stockholders in connection with the solicitation of proxies by Fluent's Board approving the agreement, introduces the acquisition as a "merger" constituting "a liquidation of the Company under the Charter." On July 2, 1993, Paul Desjourdy, Fluent's attorney, sent a letter to Betty Depaola at Novell, detailing the disbursement of payments as a result of the acquisition. The payment included, *inter alia,* employee bonus payments and noteholder payments. Neither Bradford nor Cameron Read, Fluent's counsel for the transaction, could recall at their depositions why the acquisition evolved into a cash-for-stock transaction.

The ProtoComm I lawsuit was discussed during at least three Board meetings. The files of Read contained the complaint and the underlying agreement, as well as other ProtoComm related documents. Ferris originally testified at his deposition that at the final hours before the deal, Bradford requested that the deal be redone to set aside money for the potential judgment in the ProtoComm I suit. Ferris pleaded with Bradford not to make this change, and Bradford acquiesced. Ferris later recanted this testimony. In June, 1993, Rob Hicks, an associate counsel at Novell, sent a fax to Dan Heist, President of ProtoComm, proposing a settlement in the ProtoComm I litigation. David Smith, on behalf of ProtoComm, sent a counter proposal. A second proposal was then made by Novell.

On July 7, 1993, the acquisition occurred. Novell paid $18.5 million and assumed $3 million in liabilities. The litigation had not ended at the time of the closing. On August 9, 1993, Ernst & Young sent Novell an asset valuation study of Fluent, in which the assets were valued at $21.55 million. Eventually, Fluent's assets, including, *inter alia,* Fluent's intellectual property and technology patents, as well as Fluent employees, were transferred to Novell. It is unclear to this Court when the transfer began. It seems that at least some employees were transferred onto the Novell payroll soon after the closing. It appears the technology assets were transferred by May, 1994.

ProtoComm's claim is essentially as follows: Although defendants called Novell's acquisition of Fluent a stock purchase, in reality, it was an asset sale designed to leave Fluent an empty shell and ProtoComm holding an uncollectible judgment. Fluent's assets were conveyed to Novell, and the purchase price was paid out either as a fraudulent conveyances or illegal dividends or both to Fluent's shareholders. Fluent was then left with nothing but obligations to ProtoComm.

The Former Fluent Shareholders essentially contend the following: On July 7, 1993, Novell purchased all of the outstanding stock of Fluent from the Fluent shareholders. After the stock sale occurred, Fluent became a wholly owned subsidiary of Novell and the stock sale ownership of Fluent passed to Novell. It was only after Novell's sales of Fluent's products were deemed disappointing that steps were taken to consolidate Fluent with Novell and to transfer the assets. * * *

The claim for fraudulent conveyances is brought under the Pennsylvania Uniform Fraudulent Conveyances Act ("PAUFCA"). 39 P.S. § 351 *et seq.*[2] The purpose of fraudulent transfer law is to prevent a debtor from transferring valuable assets for inadequate consideration if such transfer leaves the debtor with insufficient assets to pay honest creditors. *See In re Bay Plastics, Inc.*, 187 B.R. 315, 322 (Bkrtcy.C.D.Cal.1995). The uniform statute was established upon the recognition that debtors often try to avoid payment of legitimate debts by concealing or transferring property. *See In re Lease-A-Fleet, Inc.*, 155 B.R. 666, 672–73 (Bkrtcy.E.D.Pa.1993). Conveyance is defined by statute as "every payment of money, assignment, release, transfer, lease, mortgage, or pledge of tangible or intangible property, and also the conveyance of any lien or incumbrance." 39 P.S. § 351. Stocks are thus absent from this definition. A claim may be brought under this Act by a future creditor, i.e., by a party which has not yet received a judgment on a legal claim at the time of the transfer in question. *See Stauffer v. Stauffer*, 465 Pa. 558, 576, 351 A.2d 236, 245 (1976).

In my prior opinion, I concluded, *inter alia*, that ProtoComm could establish a claim for fraudulent conveyances upon showing that the stock transaction between the Former Fluent Shareholders and Novell was only part of a complex transaction that transferred assets of Fluent to Novell, paid money to the shareholders and left Fluent insolvent. *ProtoComm III*, 55 F.Supp.2d at 327–28. Analogizing to Leveraged Buyout ("LBO") cases, I concluded that upon such a showing, this Court would be convinced to treat the transactions among the Former Fluent Shareholders, Fluent and Novell as one integrated transaction for the purposes of ProtoComm's claim of fraudulent conveyances. *See id.* at 328.

In *U.S. v. Tabor Court Realty Corp.*, 803 F.2d 1288 (3d Cir.1986), *cert. denied*, 483 U.S. 1005, the Court of Appeals for the Third Circuit applied PAUFCA to LBOs for the first time. As articulated by the Court, a typical LBO involves the following:

> [A] company is sold to a small number of investors, typically including members of the company's management, under financial arrangements in which there is a minimum amount of equity and a maximum amount of debt. The financing typically provides for a substantial return of investment capital by means of mortgages or high risk bonds, popularly known as "junk bonds."

Id. at 1292. *Tabor* involved an incredibly complex LBO in which the court "collapsed" separate transactions for the purposes of the claims brought under PAUFCA. *See id.* at 1302. In summary, the President of Raymond Group ("Raymond"), James Durkin ("Durkin"), received an option to buy Raymond from its shareholders for $8.5 million. *See id.* After failed attempts to secure financing, Durkin and investors incorporated a holding

---

2. This statute was later repealed and replaced by, 12 Pa.Cons.Stat. § 5101 *et. seq.;* however, because of when this lawsuit was filed, the older statute governs this case. *See ProtoComm III*, 55 F.Supp.2d at 323 n. 1.

company, Great American, to which the option was assigned. *See id.* To effectuate the buy-out, Great American, a seemingly empty company, received a loan commitment from Institutional Investors Trust ("ITT") for $8.5 million. *See id.* The loan was structured to divide Raymond into borrowing companies and guarantor companies and was secured by mortgages on assets of both groups of companies. *See id.*

The loan arrangement occurred in two stages. "The loan proceeds went from ITT to the borrowing Raymond Group companies, which immediately turned the funds over to Great American, which used the funds for the buy-out." *Id.* at 1302. The Court in *Tabor* upheld the district court finding that the ITT loan proceeds merely passed through the borrowers to Great American and in the end to the selling stockholders and could not be deemed consideration received by the borrowing companies. *See id.* Other courts have applied fraudulent conveyance to the LBO context and collapsed the transactions for the purposes of fraudulent conveyance law. *See, e.g. In re Bay Plastics, Inc.,* 187 B.R. 315; *MFS/Sun Life Trust–High Yield Series v. Van Dusen Airport Serv. Co.,* 910 F.Supp. 913 (S.D.N.Y., 1995). *See also Lease–A–Fleet,* 155 B.R. at 676 (applying *Tabor's* collapsing method to case outside LBO). In essence, courts look "past the form of a transaction to its substance" and evaluate the transactions on a whole to determine whether a fraudulent conveyance has occurred. *MFS/Sun Life Trust,* 910 F.Supp. at 933. Thus while each transaction in isolation may appear kosher, the full transaction is examined to determine whether fraudulent conveyance law has been violated.

Former Fluent Shareholders argue that no asset sale occurred and that ProtoComm is unable to show that the stock sale was but one occurrence in a series of interdependent steps. ProtoComm counters that genuine issues of material fact exist as to both issues. At the motion to dismiss stage, ProtoComm appeared to rely solely on the collapsing theory. In other words, plaintiff sought to establish that the stock sale and the asset transfer which followed should be viewed as one transaction. Plaintiff now brings forth evidence which it argues raises a genuine dispute as to whether the initial transaction actually constituted an asset transfer. ProtoComm essentially relies on the same evidence for these alternative theories which in reality do not differ significantly because the end result is the same: ProtoComm needs to show that an asset transfer, as opposed to a stock sale, took place.[3]

---

3. A brief review of basic corporate law principles may be helpful to the discussion here. There are three principal acquisition methods used to effectuate a corporate acquisition, two of which are relevant here: acquisition of assets and acquisition of stock. *See* Eleanor M. Fox & Byron E. Fox, 1 *Corporate Acquisitions and Mergers* § 5A.01, at 5A–4 (Matthew Bender 2001). In an acquisition of assets, the acquiring corporation acquires "all or part of the assets of the transferor corporation either in exchange for shares of its stock, securities, cash or other property." *Id.* at 5A–5. The transaction can be molded by the parties at their own choosing, "so long as appropriate safeguards are provided for the interests of corporate shareholders and creditors." *Id.* at § 5A.03, at 5A–11–12. In other words, the acquisition cannot be in the form of a fraudulent transfer. After the sale, the transferor can choose to engage in active business, or pay creditors, liquidate, and formally dissolve. *See id.* In an acquisition of stock, "the acquiring corporation purchases the shares owned by the individual shareholders of the transferor corporation for cash, stock,

ProtoComm's expert witness, Michael Pakter ("Pakter"), characterizes the acquisition as an asset sale. In addition to Pakter's expert opinion, ProtoComm points to the following evidence, *inter alia,* to demonstrate that genuine issues of material fact exist concerning what type of transition occurred. According to Novell's 10–K the acquisition cost $21.5 million. Instead of distributing cash on a pro rata basis to the Former Fluent Shareholders, the cash was distributed at the direction of Fluent's Board and included monies for employee bonuses and reimbursements for bridge loans. The Ernst & Young Report, while admittedly conducted *after* the stock transaction occurred, valued the assets of Fluent at approximately the same price as the acquisition cost. ProtoComm also relies on the fact that early in the negotiations, an asset sale was considered and then the structure changed without explanation. In the backdrop of the transaction was the looming potential judgment from the ProtoComm I litigation. Thus, under ProtoComm's theory defendants knew that if the deal was in the structure of an asset transfer, they would potentially be liable under fraudulent transfer law. I conclude based on the foregoing that ProtoComm has raised a genuine issue of material fact as to the predicate issue of whether the stock transfer was actually an asset sale. Plaintiff has established evidence under which a reasonable trier of fact could find either that the initial transaction in June, 1993, was actually an asset sale, or, alternatively, that the initial transaction was not complete until the assets were physically transferred.

I now turn to whether plaintiff raises genuine issues of material fact with respect to the specific provisions of PAUFCA. Four sections of the Act detail situations in which a conveyance will be deemed fraudulent. Sections 354 and 355 are the constructive intent provisions of the Act.[4] Both provisions require that the conveyance occur without "fair consideration" which occurs "when property of a fair equivalent is transferred in good faith." *Buncher Co. v. Official Comm. of Unsecured Creditors of GenFarm Ltd. P'ship IV,* 229 F.3d 245, 251 (3d Cir.2000) (citing section 353). "[K]nowledge of insolvency is a rational interpretation of the statutory language of lack of 'good faith.'" *Tabor,* 803 F.2d at 1296. Section 354 provides that a conveyance is fraudulent where the debtor was left insolvent at the time of the transfer or becomes insolvent thereby.[5] The statute encompasses insolvency both in the bankruptcy sense, i.e., a negative net worth and in the equity sense, i.e., inability to pay existing

securities or other property." *Id.* at § 5A.01 at 5A–5. The acquiring corporation or one of its subsidiaries becomes a shareholder of the acquired corporation. *See id.* at § 5A.04 at 5A–16.

4.   This Court recognizes that in its prior ruling it observed that Section 356 was also a constructive intent provision. It appears that most courts place this section or its equivalent in that category. *See, e.g., In re Bay Plastics, Inc.,* 187 B.R. at 322; *MFS/Sun Life,* 910 F.Supp. at 936. The Court of Appeals for the Third Circuit, however, has construed this section as an actual intent provision. *See Moody v. Security Pacific Bus. Credit. Inc.,* 971 F.2d 1056, 1063–64 (3d Cir.1992). I must be guided accordingly by this holding.

5.   Section 354 provides: "Every conveyance made and every obligation incurred by a person who is or will be thereby rendered insolvent, is fraudulent as to creditors, without regard to his actual intent, if the conveyance is made or the obligation is incurred without a fair consideration."

debt as they mature. *See Buncher,* 229 F.3d at 251. Section 355 provides that a conveyance is fraudulent where the debtor was left with unreasonably small capital after the transfer which indicates "a financial condition short of equitable insolvency."[6] *Moody v. Security Pacific Bus. Credit, Inc.,* 971 F.2d 1056, 1064 (3d Cir.1992). The test is one of "reasonable foreseeability." *Id.* at 1073. The main inquiry under the constructive intent provision is "whether there is a link between the challenged conveyance and the debtor's insolvency." *Id.*

If insolvency or unreasonably small capital is established, the burden shifts to the transferees, the Former Fluent Shareholders, to show by clear and convincing evidence either that the transferor was then solvent, not rendered insolvent, not left with unreasonably small capital or that the assets were transferred for fair consideration. *See Elliott v. Kiesewetter,* 98 F.3d 47, 56–57 (3d Cir.1996) (citations omitted); (*Moody,* 971 F.2d at 1065 n. 2) (noting belief that Pennsylvania Supreme Court would apply insolvency standard to adequacy of capital standard; standard determined in dicta because court concluded that clear and convincing standard had been met). Thus, the first question is whether ProtoComm has raised a genuine issue of material fact as to either Fluent's solvency at the time of the transfer or as a result of the transfer, as required under section 354, or as to whether the transfer left Fluent with unreasonably small capital, as required under section 355. These issues are in large part dependent on how the fact finder characterizes the acquisition. For example, the trier of fact could reasonably find that a legitimate stock-for-cash transaction took place which had no impact on Fluent's assets, or it could reasonably find that an asset sale occurred which was structured to deplete Fluent's treasury. Thus, I conclude that a genuine issue of material fact has been raised as to the required elements of sections 354 and 355.

Sections 356 and 357 are the actual intent provisions of the Act. Section 356 also requires that the conveyance be made without fair consideration; it provides that a conveyance is fraudulent where the debtor intends or believes that it was unable to pay future debts as they became due as a consequence of the transfer. Again, the issue raised by this provision turns in large part on how the fact finder sees the acquisition. For example, if it is found to be a exchange for stock and that Fluent's assets were transferred only after Fluent's products did not reach expectations, then the requisite intent and unfair consideration may be unfounded. If, however, an asset transfer is found, then the structure of the acquisition could reasonably be seen as a transfer made without proper consideration to Fluent's treasury and with the intent or belief that creditors could not be satisfied. Thus, I conclude that a genuine issue of material fact has been raised as to the required elements of section 356.

---

6. Section 355 provides: "Every conveyance made without fair consideration, when the person making it is engaged, or is about to engage, in a business or transaction for which the property remaining in his hands after the conveyance is an unreasonably small capital, is fraudulent as to creditors, and as to other persons who become creditors during the continuance of such business or transaction, without regard to his actual intent."

The final question under PAUFCA concerns section 357 which provides that a conveyance is fraudulent where the conveyance was made with the actual intent to hinder, delay or defraud present or future creditors. Such intent must be proven by clear and convincing evidence. *See Moody v. Security Pacific Bus. Credit Inc.*, 127 B.R. 958, 990 (W.D.Pa. 1991), *aff'd*, 971 F.2d 1056 (1992). The existence of actual intent is a question of fact. *See Tabor*, 803 F.2d at 1304. Direct evidence is not required; actual intent may be inferred from the totality of the circumstances. *See Moody*, 971 F.2d at 1075 (citing *Tabor*, 803 F.2d at 1304).

Thus this Court must ask whether ProtoComm has raised a genuine issue of material fact in showing by clear and convincing evidence that defendants intentionally structured the acquisition to defraud creditors. This question of fact, though ProtoComm will face a higher burden of proof, overlaps with the aforementioned provisions because under Pennsylvania law, intent may be inferred when transfers are made without fair consideration and where the parties to the transfer have knowledge of the claims of creditors and know that such creditors cannot be paid. *See Tabor*, 803 F.2d at 1304. *See also, Lease–A–Fleet*, 155 B.R. at 674 (reciting "badges of fraud" which may indicate actual intent). As explained above, genuine disputes remain concerning these questions. Thus, I conclude that ProtoComm has met its burden in raising a triable issue. I therefore conclude that defendants are not entitled to judgment on the PAUFCA claim as a matter of law.

Plaintiffs bring the wrongful dividend claim under 8 Del. C. § 174, which holds directors, but not shareholders, liable for wilfully or negligently paying dividends in violation of the general corporate law chapter of the Delaware Code.[7] ProtoComm brings this cause of action against those Former Fluent Shareholders who served as Directors. There are times when upon consideration of a summary judgment motion, cases are reevaluated in light of the facts presented and determinations previously made by a court are reconsidered as well. This is one of those times. This Court concluded in its prior opinion that ProtoComm had standing to pursue this claim. *ProtoComm*, 55 F.Supp.2d at 330. This Court now concludes, for the reasons which follow, that plaintiff lacks such standing.

The Delaware Supreme Court's decision in *Johnston v. Wolf*, 487 A.2d 1132 (Del.1985), governs standing under section 174. The facts of *Johnston* are as follows. Allied Artists Pictures Corporation ("Allied") entered into a complex reorganization plan and agreement which provided, *inter alia*, that Allied would merge with another corporation. *See id.* at 1134. As part of the plan, Allied redeemed its preferred stock prior to the merger. *See id.* Under the agreement, as well as under Delaware law, creditors of

---

7. Section 174 provides in pertinent part: "In case of any wilful or negligent violation of § 160 or 173 of this title, the directors under whose administration the same may happen shall be jointly and severally liable." Section 173 provides in pertinent part: "No corporation shall pay dividends except in accordance with this chapter." Section 170 provides in pertinent part: "The directors of every corporation ... may ... pay dividends upon the shares of its capital stock ... either (1) out of its surplus, as defined in and computed in accordance with §§ 154 and 244 of this title, or (2) in case there shall be no such surplus, out of its net profits."

Allied became creditors of the post-merger corporation. *See id.* Plaintiffs alleged that the redemption violated the Delaware Code. *See id.*

Two plaintiffs filed suit after the merger occurred and, obviously, therefore had not secured a judgment before the merger occurred. *See id.* at 1136. One plaintiff had brought his claim prior to the merger, but had not obtained a judgment until after the merger. *See* id. The court denied standing as to all three plaintiffs under section 174, holding that all three were creditors of the post-merger corporation only. *See id.* Thus, unlike PAUFCA, section 174 provides no protection to future creditors. Accordingly, I conclude that plaintiff cannot proceed with its claim against these defendants under section 174 because ProtoComm did not receive its judgment until after the acquisition of Fluent had occurred.

In this Court's prior ruling, it turned to *Pinellas County v. Great Am. Indus. Group Inc.,* No. 90 C 5254, 1991 WL 259020 (N.D.Ill. Dec. 2, 1991). There, the plaintiff had obtained a $25,000,000 judgment against defendant Madison. Before the judgment against it, Madison had engaged in two corporate acts which rendered it insolvent. *See id.* In the first act, Madison paid a $5 million dividend to its sole shareholder, GAIG. *See id.* Plaintiff claimed that the dividend payment should be voided. *See id.* The court acknowledged that under *Johnston,* only current creditors had standing to sue under section 174. The court then noted that section 174 would not have application even if standing were not problematic because the plaintiff was suing a shareholder and not a director. The court then turned to 8 Del.C. § 325 which provides:

> (a) When the officers, directors or stockholders of any corporation shall be liable *by the provisions of this chapter* to pay the debts of the corporation, or any part thereof, any person to whom they are liable may have an action, at law or in equity, against any 1 or more of them, and *the complaint shall state the claim against the corporation, and the ground on which the plaintiff expects to charge the defendants personally.*

> (b) No suit shall be brought against any officer, director or stockholder for any debt of a corporation of which such person is an officer, director or stockholder, *until judgment be obtained therefor against the corporation and execution thereon returned unsatisfied.*

(emphasis added). Thus, section 325 allows for a suit to be brought against officers, directors or stockholders when, under the provisions of the general corporate law chapter of the Delaware Code, they are liable to pay the debts of the corporation. And, such suit may not be brought until judgment is obtained and returned unsatisfied. The court in *Pinellas* determined that section 325 could not provide a cause of action to the plaintiff before it because Delaware statutory corporate law provided no means for holding shareholders liable for corporate debts. *See Pinellas,* 1991 WL 259020, at *3. The court then acknowledged that section 325 does not work to restrict causes of action traditionally available to creditors independent of corporate law. *See id.* (citing *Lone Star Indus., Inc. v. Redwine,* 757 F.2d 1544, 1554 (5th Cir.1985)).

The court observed that under Delaware common law, where a corporation distributes assets to its shareholders while leaving creditors unsatisfied, those creditors are entitled to recovery directly from the shareholders, without resort to fraudulent conveyance law and without having to first obtain a prior judgment against the corporate debtor. *See id.* The court ultimately concluded that because the complaint alleged that the dividend payment occurred at a time when Madison was technically bankrupt, and thus constituted substantially all of Madison's assets, the allegations were sufficient to sustain the claim to void the dividend payment. *See id.*

Thus, the court in *Pinellas* did not determine that section 325 could be used to provide standing for a claim brought under section 174. Rather, the court essentially provided that the cause of action be brought under the common law fraudulent conveyance claim. Accordingly, while it may be that ProtoComm would have a common law claim under Delaware law, which presumably would require a similar showing to the claim brought under PAUFCA, ProtoComm does not have a claim against these defendants under section 174, which is the law invoked by plaintiff. * * *

IN THE MATTER OF MUNFORD, INC.

97 F.3d 456 (11th Cir.1996).

HATCHETT, CHIEF JUDGE.

In this corporate leveraged-buy-out merger case, we affirm the district court's ruling that Georgia's stock distribution and repurchase statutes apply.

In May 1988, the Panfida Group offered to purchase Munford, Inc., a public company on the New York Stock Exchange, through a leverage buy out (LBO) structured as a reverse triangle merger for $18 per share. Under the terms of the proposed merger agreement, the Panfida Group agreed to create Alabama Acquisition Corporation (AAC) and a subsidiary, Alabama Merger Corporation (AMC), and through AAC or AMC deposit the funds necessary to purchase Munford, Inc.'s outstanding stock with Citizens & Southern Trust Company. As evidence of its commitment to purchase Munford, Inc., the Panfida Group bought 291,100 of Munford, Inc.'s stock. In June 1988, the Panfida Group also told Munford, Inc.'s board of directors that it, upon the sale of Munford, Inc., intended to put additional capital into Munford, Inc. but would only invest as much as Citibank required to finance the proposed merger.

After consulting its lawyers and financial experts at Shearson Lehman Brothers (Shearson), the board of directors accepted the Panfida Group's offer pending shareholder approval of the purchase agreement.

Prior to the directors seeking shareholder approval, the Panfida Group learned that Munford, Inc. had potential environmental liability. Consequently, the Panfida Group reduced the purchase price from $18.50 a share to $17 a share. On October 18, 1988, the shareholders approved the merger plan. On November 29, 1988, the sale of Munford, Inc. to the Panfida Group closed. Pursuant to the purchase agreement, the LBO transaction converted each share of common stock into the right to receive the merger price of $17 per share and extinguished the shareholders' ownership in Munford, Inc. On January 2, 1990, thirteen months after the merger, Munford, Inc. filed for Chapter 11 proceedings in bankruptcy court.

On June 17, 1991, Munford, Inc. brought an adversary proceeding in bankruptcy court in the Northern District of Georgia on behalf of itself and unsecured creditors pursuant to 11 U.S.C. §§ 544(b) and 1107(a) (1988), seeking to avoid transfers of property, disallow claims and recover damages against former shareholders, officers, directors, and Shearson. In Count III of its complaint, Munford, Inc. asserted that the directors violated legal restrictions under Georgia's distribution and share repurchase statutes in approving the LBO merger. Specifically, Munford, Inc. asserts that the LBO transaction constituted a distribution of corporate assets that rendered Munford, Inc. insolvent. The directors moved for summary judgment contending that the Georgia distribution and repurchase statutes did not apply to LBO mergers. * * *

Georgia's capital surplus distribution statute provides, in pertinent part:

> (a) The board of directors of a corporation may from time to time distribute to shareholders out of capital surplus of the corporation a portion of its assets in cash or property subject to the following [provision]:

>> (1) No such distribution shall be made at a time when the corporation is insolvent or when such distribution would render the corporation insolvent[.]

O.C.G.A. § 14–2–91 (1988).Similarly, Georgia's stock repurchasing statute prohibits directors of a corporation from repurchasing the corporation's shares when such purchase would render the corporation insolvent. O.C.G.A. § 14–2–92(e) (1982).[8] Under both statutes, directors who vote for or assent to a corporate distribution or stock repurchase in violation of these statutes are jointly and severally liable for the amount distributed or paid to the extent the payments violated the restrictions. O.C.G.A. § 14–2–154(a)(1), (2) (1982).

The directors appeal the district court's denial of summary judgment contending that Georgia's distribution and share repurchase statutes do not apply to LBO mergers. The directors argue that Georgia's distribution and repurchase statutes only apply in circumstances where the directors

---

8. On July 1, *1989,* O.C.G.A. § 14–2–640 superseded O.C.G.A. §§ 14–2–91 and 14–2–92(e).

take assets of the corporation and either distribute them to shareholders or use them to repurchase shares. In both cases, the directors assert, control of the company does not change hands and the directors determine the source of the assets used. The directors note that in this case the Panfida Group owned Munford, Inc. at the completion of the LBO merger and thereafter ran the company. The directors therefore argue that only Georgia's merger statutes apply to this transaction.

The district court denied the directors' motion for summary judgment adopting the reasoning of the bankruptcy court. The bankruptcy court, in analyzing the LBO merger, considered the substance of the transaction and equated the LBO merger to a stock distribution or repurchase, disregarding the fact that Munford, Inc. had new owners and stockholders as a result of the merger at the time the shareholders received the LBO payments. The bankruptcy court specifically found that: (1) the directors "approved or assented to the underlying [m]erger [a]greement which structured and required payment to the shareholders"; (2) the merger agreement contemplated the Panfida Group's pledging of "virtually all of Munford[, Inc.]'s assets as collateral" for the loan that funded the LBO payments made to the shareholders; and (3) the directors knew or should have known "the source, purpose, or use of" Munford, Inc.'s assets prior to or at the time the directors approved the merger plan. Based on these findings, the bankruptcy court concluded that a reasonable jury could conclude that the merger rendered Munford, Inc. insolvent in violation of Georgia's distribution and stock repurchase statutes.

In reaching its conclusion, the bankruptcy court rejected a Fourth Circuit case that refused to apply Virginia's corporate distribution statute to recapture payments made to shareholders pursuant to an LBO merger. *See C–T of Virginia, Inc. v. Barrett,* 958 F.2d 606 (4th Cir.1992).

In *C–T of Virginia,* the Fourth Circuit held that the LBO merger did not constitute a distribution within the meaning of Virginia's share repurchase and distribution statutes reasoning that Virginia's distribution statute

> [was] not intended to obstruct an arm's-length acquisition of an enterprise by new owners who have their own plans for commercial success. The reason for this distinction is simple: a corporate acquisition, structured as a merger, is simply a different animal from a distribution.

C–T of Virginia, 958 F.2d at 611. The court in *C–T of Virginia* further reasoned that because such distribution statutes derive from the regulation of corporate dividends courts should limit their restriction to situations in which shareholders after receiving the transfer from the corporation retain their status as owners of the corporation.

The bankruptcy court, in this case, rejected this line of reasoning, reasoning that the legislature enacted the distribution and share repurchase statutes of the Georgia Code to protect creditors "by prohibiting transfers at a time when a corporation is insolvent or would be rendered insolvent." Such intent, the bankruptcy court noted, "furthers the long-standing principle that creditors are to be paid before shareholders." We agree with the district court and the reasoning of the bankruptcy court and decline to join the Fourth Circuit in holding that "[a] corporate acquisition, structured as a merger, is simply a different animal from a distribution." *C–T of Virginia, Inc.*, 958 F.2d at 611.

We note that the LBO transaction in this case did not merge two separate operating companies into one combined entity. Instead, the LBO transaction represented a "paper merger" of Munford, Inc. and AMC, a shell corporation with very little assets of its own. To hold that Georgia's distribution and repurchase statutes did not apply to LBO mergers such as this, while nothing in these statutes precludes such a result, would frustrate the restrictions imposed upon directors who authorize a corporation to distribute its assets or to repurchase shares from stockholders when such transactions would render the corporation insolvent. We therefore affirm the district court's ruling that Georgia's restrictions on distribution and stock repurchase apply to LBO.

In the alternative, the directors argue that their approval of the LBO merger should not subject them to liability under the distribution and repurchase statutes because they approved the merger in good faith and with the advice of legal counsel. Because we are not aware of any Georgia courts that recognize good faith or reasonable reliance on legal counsel's advice as an affirmative defense to liability under Georgia's distribution and repurchase statutes, we reject this argument.

For the reasons stated above, we affirm the district court's denial of the directors' motion for summary judgment on Munford, Inc.'s stock distribution and repurchase claim.

IN RE COLOR TILE, INC.

2000 WL 152129 (D. Del.2000).

SUE L. ROBINSON, DISTRICT JUDGE.

* * * Plaintiff seeks restoration to the estate of approximately $10,077,500 in dividends that Color Tile paid to holders of its Class B, Series A, Senior Increasing Rate Preferred Stock ("preferred shares"). In 1992, Color Tile issued 2,200,000 shares of the preferred stock, the proceeds of which it used to retire approximately $47,700,000 in debt associated with Color Tile's Senior Notes. The terms governing the preferred shares were outlined in a June 24, 1992 Private Placement Memorandum and in an August 7, 1992 supplement thereto. The sale of the preferred shares replaced the existing debt on Color Tile's Senior Notes with a new obligation redeemable after ten years, at an amount equal to the purchase price of the preferred shares plus any unpaid and accrued dividends. The preferred shares carried a lower stated dividend

than the interest carried on the Senior Notes. The dividend payments began on or about January 1, 1994.

On January 24, 1996, Color Tile filed voluntary petitions for relief under Chapter 11 of the Bankruptcy Code. On January 15, 1998, plaintiff commenced this action against the Blackstone defendants and the other recipients of the dividends. The complaint asserts claims under the Delaware Fraudulent Transfer Act, 6 Del. C. § 1301 et seq. (the "DFTA"), and 11 U.S.C. §§ 544(b) and 548(a)(2). In essence, the complaint alleges that the preferred stock dividends were fraudulent transfers under the DFTA because they left Color Tile with unreasonably small capital and caused it to incur debts beyond its ability to pay. Plaintiff seeks to avoid these transfers under 11 U.S.C. § 544. The complaint also seeks recovery under 11 U.S.C. § 548(a)(2) for transfers that occurred within one year prior to the petition date. With respect to these payments, the complaint alleges that Color Tile received less than reasonably equivalent value in exchange for these dividends and that it was insolvent on the date of the dividend payments or became insolvent because of such payments.

Defendants seek dismissal of the complaint on several grounds. First, they allege that the DFTA is inapplicable to plaintiff's claims because "its application would improperly nullify the Delaware General Corporation Law ["DGCL"] remedial statutory scheme, which specifically addresses the recovery of unlawful dividends from shareholders." Second, defendants argue that the court must dismiss the DFTA claim because plaintiff fails to allege that defendants knew the dividend payments were unlawful. Third, even if the DFTA claim were viable, defendants contend that plaintiff cannot establish that the payments constituted fraudulent transfers because defendants provided Color Tile with reasonably equivalent value for the dividends and because the dividends were payments in satisfaction of antecedent debt.

Defendants argue that § 174 of the DGCL trumps the DFTA and that, therefore, plaintiff's sole remedy is to proceed under the DGCL and recover the dividend payments from the directors of Color Tile rather than from the preferred shareholders. Defendants do not cite a single case supporting this proposition. Instead, defendants rely on general principles of statutory construction. Specifically, they argue that when two acts touch upon the same subject, the general statute (here the DFTA) should not prevail over the more specific statute (allegedly the dividend recovery provisions of the DGCL). Otherwise, defendants argue, the DFTA would nullify the DGCL.

Upon closer inspection, however, the two statutes serve distinct purposes and provide different remedies. Section 1305(a) n3 of DFTA provides, in pertinent part, that:

> A transfer made or obligation incurred by a debtor is fraudulent as to a creditor whose claim arose before the transfer was made or the obligation was incurred if the debtor made the transfer or incurred the obligation without receiving a reasonably equivalent value in

exchange for the transfer or obligation and the debtor was insolvent at that time or the debtor became insolvent as a result of the transfer or obligation.

6 Del. C. § 1305(a). Once a transfer is found to be fraudulent, § 1307 of the DFTA enables a creditor to avoid the transfer to the extent necessary to satisfy the creditor's claim. The DFTA thus focuses on ensuring that creditors recover fraudulent transfers to third parties. Section 174 of the DGCL, on the other hand, imposes liability on corporate directors for approving unlawful dividend payments. Unlike the DFTA's avoidance provision, the DGCL provides for damages against corporate directors. Because it makes directors (rather than the recipients of the dividends) primarily liable, § 174 is designed to discourage directors from depleting a corporation's ability to repay its debts. Section 174 focuses on deterrence rather than on returning fraudulent payments to creditors. Thus, contrary to defendants' assertion, the DGCL and the DFTA serve different purposes.

The DFTA's focus on ensuring the equitable distribution of assets to a debtor's rightful creditors also makes it the more appropriate statute in the context of a bankruptcy proceeding. Indeed, the DFTA looks to the economic effects of the transfer on a debtor's creditors rather than to the debtor's mere compliance with corporate governance rules. See China Resource Prods. (U.S.A.) Ltd. v. Fayda Int'l, Inc., 788 F.Supp. 815, 818 (D.Del.1992) (noting that Delaware's fraudulent transfer act "judges a transaction by its effect on the debtor's unsecured creditors"). Moreover, statutes like § 170 of the DGCL lack the DFTA's "equity-oriented, purposive concept of capital, which is much more relevant to the question of risk actually posed to creditors." See Robert Charles Clark, The Duties of the Corporate Debtor to its Creditors, 90 Harv. L. Rev. 505, 556 (1977); see also 1 R. Franklin Balotti et al., The Delaware Law of Corporations & Business Organizations § 5.22, at 5–48 n.309 (3d ed. 1999).

For instance, the DFTA requires proof only of inequivalent value in exchange for the payment and the debtor's resulting or contemporaneous insolvency. On the other hand, to state a cause of action under § 174, a creditor first must prove that the corporation depleted its surplus in paying the dividend. See 8 Del. C. § 170(a)(1). The directors, however, have almost unfettered discretion in defining the extent of the corporation's surplus. The Delaware Code defines surplus as the value of net assets over the par value of the stock. See 8 Del. C. § 154; 1 David A. Drexler et al., Delaware Corporation Law and Practice § 20.03[2], at 20–9–11 (1999). In determining the value of net assets, the directors are not tied to any formal financial appraisal of their assets. They need only "evaluate the assets on the basis of acceptable data and by standards which they are entitled to believe reasonably reflect present 'values.' " Morris v. Standard Gas & Elec. Co., 31 Del. Ch. 20, 63 A.2d 577, 582 (Del.Ch.1949); see also Klang v. Smith's Food & Drug Centers, Inc., 702 A.2d 150, 152 (Del.1997). By manipulating the value of net assets, directors can skew the calculation of surplus and thereby render "lawful" (in a strictly formalistic sense) dividend payments that otherwise would qualify as fraudulent transfers under the DFTA. The easy manipulation of a corporation's surplus has prompted one commentator to note that statutes prohibiting payments of dividends out of surplus are "virtually meaningless." See Clark, supra, at 556. This conclusion is buttressed by the fact that directors can easily insulate themselves from liability under § 170 of the DGCL by demonstrating that they relied on the reports of employees, committees of the board, or experts "selected with reasonable care by or on behalf of the corporation" as to the availability of surplus. See 8 Del. C. § 172.

For these reasons, plaintiff may proceed under the DFTA against defendants. Plaintiff is not required to proceed against Color Tile's directors under the DGCL simply because the allegedly fraudulent transfers took the form of dividend payments. See Stanley v. Brock (In re Kettle Fried Chicken of Am., Inc.), 513 F.2d 807, 814 (6th Cir.1975) (explaining that the Delaware legislature, in providing a specific remedy against corporate directors, "in no way intended to relieve shareholders of liability").

Quoting the DGCL, defendants also argue that plaintiff's DFTA claim is invalid because the complaint does not allege that defendants received the dividends with knowledge that they were unlawful. See D.I. B26 at 12 (quoting 8 Del. C. § 174(c)). The DGCL has no bearing on the pleading requirements under the DFTA. The DFTA requires only that a plaintiff plead and prove (1) a transfer, (2) made without receiving reasonably equivalent value in exchange, and (3) resulting or contemporaneous insolvency. See 6 Del. C. §§ 1304(a), 1305(a); Corporate Property Assocs. 8, L.P. v. Amersig Graphics, Inc., 1994 Del. Ch. LEXIS 45, Civ. A. No. 13241, 1994 WL 148269, at *2 (Del. Ch. Mar. 31, 1994) (construing the Delaware Fraudulent Conveyances Act, 6 Del. C. § 1304). Knowledge of the fraudulent transfer on the part of the recipient is not an element of a DFTA claim.

Defendants next argue that the purchase of the preferred shares was tantamount to a $52 million loan to Color Tile and that the dividends were payments in satisfaction of this antecedent debt. Construed as such, the dividend payments could not have been fraudulent transfers. See 6 Del. C. § 1303(a) ("Value is given for a transfer or an obligation if, in exchange for the transfer or obligation, ... an antecedent debt is secured or satisfied...."). At issue, then, is whether the purchasers of the preferred shares held equity or debt in Color Tile.

Whether a security constitutes equity or debt depends on the interpretation of the contract between the corporation and the security holders. See Wolfensohn v. Madison Fund, Inc., 253 A.2d 72, 75 (Del. 1969); accord Drexler, supra, at 17–5 n.8. In interpreting the contract, courts consider numerous factors, including: (1) the name given to the instrument; (2) the intent of the parties; (3) the presence or absence of a fixed maturity date; (4) the right to enforce payment of principal and interest; (5) the presence or absence of voting rights; (6) the status of the contribution in relation to regular corporate contributors; and (7) certainty of payment in the event of the corporation's insolvency or liquidation. See Slappey Drive Indus. Park v. United States, 561 F.2d 572, 581–82 (5th Cir.1977); Moore v. American Fin. & Secs. Co., 31 Del.Ch. 335, 73 A.2d 47, 48 (Del.Ch.1950); Drexler, supra, at 17–5 n.8.

In light of these standards, there is little doubt that the preferred shares and their accompanying Private Placement Memorandum (the "Memorandum") contemplated an equity interest in Color Tile. The instrument, itself, is denoted as "Series A Senior Increasing Rate Preferred Stock." Although the dividend and redemption dates were projected, the very first page of the Memorandum warns purchasers that, "the Company's ability to pay dividends on the Shares and to redeem or repurchase the Shares is subject to the satisfaction of certain covenants and restrictions under the Company's credit facilities, the Company's Certificate of Incorporation and the Delaware General Corporation Law." This caveat is repeated elsewhere in the Memorandum. For instance, the terms of the Memorandum limit the payment of dividends to "funds legally available therefor." (D.I. B27 at 7) The Memorandum also states that, "pursuant to the terms of its Senior Credit Agreement, its Certificate of Incorporation and the DGCL under certain circumstances the Company will be restricted from repurchasing the Shares." (D.I. B27 at 9) More tellingly, the "Investment Considerations" section of the Memorandum warns that Color Tile is "substantially leveraged" and that, due to

> the degree to which the Company is leveraged, the need to apply a substantial portion of the Company's cash flow from operations to pay principal of and interest on indebtedness, and the operating and financial restrictions contained in the agreements governing the Company's credit facilities could have important consequences to holders of the Shares, including the following: (1) the Company's ability to pay dividends, including dividends on the [Preferred] Shares, may be restricted. . . .

Thus, the Memorandum explicitly distinguishes between Color Tile's "credit facilities," which enjoy priority, and its preferred shareholders, whose interests are junior to such secured creditors.

If there were any doubt as to the true nature of the preferred shareholders' interest, it is dispelled by the Memorandum's description of the liquidation preference: "Holders of the [Preferred] Shares will be entitled to be paid out of the assets of the Company available to its stockholders an amount in cash equal to $25.00 for each Share outstanding." In other words, the preferred shareholders enjoy priority only with respect to the funds available to stockholders, whose interests as a class are junior to the corporation's secured creditors in the context of liquidation. Thus, there is no certainty of payment of accrued dividends or of redemption of the shares upon liquidation. Where such certainty of payment is missing, the security is equity, not debt. See Moore, 73 A.2d at 48.

The fact that the preferred shareholders held equity is further evidenced by the fact that the Memorandum accorded shareholders voting rights if Color Tile failed to pay dividends for six consecutive quarters or if it failed to redeem the shares in 2003. In discussing the tax ramifications of the security, the Memorandum also states that, "the Company believes that the [Preferred] Shares will constitute equity for Federal income tax purposes and that distributions on the Shares ... will constitute dividends."

Despite defendants' vehement protestations to the contrary, the preferred shares constituted equity, not debt. Therefore, their attempt to characterize the dividend payments as payments in satisfaction of antecedent debt is unavailing. Equally unavailing is defendants' attempt to characterize the declaration of the dividend as creating a debt, the payment of which constitutes "fair consideration" under the DFTA. Under Delaware law, a declaration of a dividend gives rise to a debt only if the dividends are lawfully declared. See Anadarko Petroleum Corp. v. Panhandle Eastern Corp., 545 A.2d 1171, 1175 (Del.1988) (noting that "upon a valid declaration of a dividend the corporation becomes indebted to the stockholder") (emphasis added). Construed broadly, the complaint alleges that Color Tile lacked legally available funds at the time of the dividend declaration. For purposes of this motion only, the court shall presume that the dividends were not validly declared and that, therefore, they did not constitute payment of an antecedent debt. * * *

For the aforementioned reasons, the court shall deny defendants' motions to dismiss. An appropriate order shall issue.

NOTES

1. The Uniform Fraudulent Transfer Act has been adopted by some twenty states, while eight others adopted the Uniform Fraudulent Conveyance Act. *James D. Cox & Thomas Lee Hazen Corporations*, § 7.20 (2d ed.2003). The concern with fraudulent conveyances is an ancient one. In colonial times, such transfers were a frequent means of protecting assets from creditors. After the Revolution and before the adoption of bankruptcy laws, the penalty for failing to pay creditors was debtors' prison. See generally Bruce H. Mann, Republic of Debtors, Bankruptcy in the Age of American Independence (2002).

2. For cases holding that distributions to shareholders were subject to fraudulent conveyance acts see Schall v. Anderson's Implement, Inc., 240 Neb. 658, 484 N.W.2d 86 (1992); Spanier v. U.S. Fidelity and Guaranty Co., 127 Ariz. 589, 623 P.2d 19 (App.1980).

3. The difference between state corporate statutes restricting dividends and bankruptcy and fraudulent conveyance statutes has been explained as follows:

The revised Model Business Corporation Act establishes the validity of distributions from the corporate law standpoint under section 6.40 and determines the potential liability of directors for improper distributions under sections 8.30 and 8.33. The federal Bankruptcy Act and state fraudulent conveyance statutes, on the other hand, are designed to enable the trustee or other representative to recapture for the benefit of creditors funds distributed to others in some circumstances. In light of these diverse purposes, it was not thought necessary to make the tests of section 6.40 identical with the tests for insolvency under these various statutes.

Official Comments, Rev. Model Bus. Corp. Act § 6.40.

JOHN A. ROEBLING'S SONS CO. v. MODE

43 A. 480, 17 Del. 515 (Super.1899).

LORE, C. J.

By an action on the case in this suit, the plaintiff seeks to hold the defendant individually liable for a judgment due to the plaintiff from the Kent Iron & Hardware Co., an insolvent corporation of the state of Delaware, upon the ground that the defendant was one of the directors of the said corporation, and participated in an illegal dividend which was declared and paid, not out of the net earnings or surplus of the company, but in diminution of its capital stock. The declaration of the plaintiff contains four counts, all of which are substantially the same. The declaration sets forth, in substance, that the directors of the Kent Iron & Hardware Company, an insolvent corporation of the state of Delaware, on the 1st day of July, 1891, declared and paid a dividend of $9,000, being 6 per cent. on the capital stock of $150,000, not out of its net earnings, but in diminution of its capital stock; that the defendant was one of the directors who made and participated in the dividend; that thereby he became liable, under the statutes of this state, to pay to the plaintiff, a judgment creditor of the said corporation, the full amount of his claim, being the sum of $630.60, with interest from March 10, 1894, with the costs of obtaining the judgment against the corporation. * * *

* * * The action is based upon section 7, c. 147, 17 Laws Del., [now 8 Del. Corp. L. § 174] entitled "An act concerning private corporations," and is as follows:

"Sec. 7. It shall not be lawful for the directors of any bank or moneyed or manufacturing corporation in this state, or any corporation created under this act, to make dividends, except from the surplus or net profits arising from the business of the corporation, nor to divide, withdraw, or in any way pay to the stockholders, or any of them, any part of the capital stock of said corporation, or to reduce the said capital stock, except according to this act, without the consent of the legislature; and in case of any violation of the provisions of this section, the directors, under whose administration the same may happen, shall, in their individual capacities, jointly and severally, be liable at any time within the period of six years after paying any such dividend to the said corporation, and to the creditors thereof in the event of its dissolution or insolvency, to the full amount of the dividend made or capital stock so divided, withdrawn, paid out or reduced, with legal interest on the same from the time such liability accrued."

* * * This section contemplates the recovery and restoration to the capital of the corporation of the entire amount thus illegally withdrawn, and, to that end, each director is made individually liable for such amount. When so recovered and restored, whether at the instance and in the name of the corporation primarily, or in the name and at the instance of the creditors, it becomes at once a part of the capital stock again, to be held and disposed of as such for the benefit of all concerned. Manifestly this would be so if the amount was recovered by the corporation itself, before dissolution or insolvency. Of necessity, it would then go into the common funds. No other construction seems tenable, if, on the other hand, the recovery should be at the instance of the creditors after the dissolution or insolvency of the corporation. Under this view, each creditor would be entitled to his proportionate share thereof, and any action for the recovery of such illegal dividends or abstracted capital must contemplate such proportionate distribution. It cannot be maintained that this declaration contemplates any such distribution. It demands the plaintiff's entire debt out of the alleged illegal $9,000 dividend, without respect to any of the other creditors. It is equally plain that under this declaration the plaintiff cannot recover a proportionate share of the said dividend, inasmuch as that share must depend upon the correct ascertainment and adjustment of the claims of all other creditors entitled. Recovery in this action of such proportionate share would be an attempt to determine the rights of such other creditors without any day given to them in court, and without any opportunity to be heard, either as to their own claims, or those of the plaintiff and others.

* * * If this be a common fund, the remedy would be by proceedings in equity, where all persons interested would be made parties, and the rights and liabilities of each one could be fully considered and equitably adjusted. * * *

We conclude, therefore, that the remedy by action on the case * * * does not apply to cases arising under section 7, and that the provisions of section 7 can only adequately and properly be enforced by proceedings in equity. It follows, therefore, that this declaration is not sufficient in law to support the plaintiff's claim, and that, under the demurrer, judgment should be entered against the plaintiff. * * * Let judgment be entered against the plaintiff.

REILLY v. SEGERT

31 Ill.2d 297, 201 N.E.2d 444 (1964).

SCHAEFER, JUSTICE.

Prior to the enactment of the Business Corporation Act of 1933, it was settled that a shareholder of a corporation who sold his stock to the corporation while it was insolvent was liable to an injured creditor of the corporation for the amount paid to the shareholder for his stock. (Singer v. Hutchinson, 183 Ill. 606, 56 N.E. 388; Johnson v. Canfield–Swigart Co., 292 Ill. 101, 126 N.E. 608.) This liability was based upon the adverse effect of the transaction upon creditors, and not upon the guilt or innocence of the shareholder, who was held liable even though there was no evidence of fraud. (Clapp v. Peterson, 104 Ill. 26, 31.) The question for decision in this case is whether or not this liability was repealed by section 42 of the Business Corporation Act. (Ill.Rev.Stat.1959, chap. 32, par. 157.–42.) The circuit court of Lake County held that it was, the Appellate Court affirmed (44 Ill.App.2d 343, 194 N.E.2d 544), and we allowed leave to appeal.

The plaintiffs are George L. Reilly, the receiver of Deerfield Lumber & Fuel Co., Inc. and three creditors of that company. The defendants are the directors of the company and five shareholders. The complaint alleged that the directors authorized purchases of stock from the defendant shareholders at a time when the corporation was insolvent and had no earned surplus. The directors defaulted, and judgments were entered against them for the amounts paid to the defendant shareholders for their stock. No appeal was taken from the judgments so entered, and we are not concerned with them.

Those counts of the complaint, however, that asserted liability against the defendant shareholders, were dismissed upon motion, and final judgments were entered against the plaintiffs on those counts. The judgments thus entered were based upon the proposition that section 42 of the Business Corporation Act (Ill.Rev.Stat.1959, chap. 32, par. 157.42) affords the only remedy available, and that it does not authorize an action directly against shareholders.

The portions of section 42 that are relied upon to support the judgment are as follows:

"In addition to any other liabilities imposed by law upon directors of a corporation:

"(a) Directors of a corporation who vote for or assent to the declaration of any dividend or other distribution of the assets of a corporation to its shareholders shall be jointly and severally liable to the corporation for the amount of such dividend which is paid or the value of such assets which are distributed if, at the time of such payment or distribution, the corporation is insolvent or its net assets are less than its stated capital.

"(b) The directors of a corporation who vote for or assent to the declaration of any dividend or other distribution of assets of a corporation to its shareholders which renders the corporation insolvent or reduces its net assets below its stated capital shall be jointly and severally liable to the corporation for the amount of such dividend which is paid or the value of such assets which are distributed, to the extent that the corporation is thereby rendered insolvent or its net assets are reduced below its stated capital.

"Any director against whom a claim shall be asserted under or pursuant to this section for the improper declaration of a dividend or other distribution of assets of a corporation and who shall be held liable thereon, shall be entitled to contribution from the shareholders who knowingly accepted or received any such dividend or assets, in proportion to the amounts received by them respectively."

In our opinion section 42 does not preclude this action against the shareholders. Even as to the liability of directors, its language makes it clear that it was not designed to provide an exclusive remedy, for the liability with which it deals are expressly stated to be "(i)n addition to any other liabilities imposed by law upon directors of a corporation." In the absence of this specific disclaimer, the result would be the same. "Where a liability is imposed upon an officer of (sic) a director by a state statute, his common-law liability for misfeasance and negligence in the performance of his duties is not thereby excluded." 3 Fletcher, Cyclopedia of Corporations, sec. 993.

In this case, moreover, we are concerned with the direct liability of shareholders, a subject with which section 42 does not purport to deal. The existence of a statutory provision dealing with the liability of directors does not preclude a non-statutory liability on the part of shareholders. When Clapp v. Peterson, 104 Ill. 26, and other decisions dealing with the liability here asserted were decided, statutes which provided specific liabilities for particular misconduct of directors were in effect. Yet those provisions of the Corporation Act of 1872 and the General Corporation Act of 1919 did not bar the creditor's common law action against shareholders who sold their stock to the corporation while it was insolvent.

A further word is appropriate to prevent misapprehension as to our understanding of section 42. Both parties appear to have assumed that the section applies to purchases by a corporation of its own stock at a time when the corporation is insolvent, and we have dealt with the case on that assumption. The section does not, however, expressly mention such transactions, and it can apply to them only if a "distribution" of assets is construed to include payment by the corporation to a shareholder for his stock. From the language of section 42 it seems likely that it pertains to outright distributions of corporate assets to all shareholders, by dividend or otherwise, and questionable whether it includes as a corporate "distribution" a corporation's purchase of its stock from a particular shareholder. That question has not been argued, however, and we express no opinion concerning it. But see Precision Extrusions, Inc. v. Stewart, 36 Ill.App.2d 30, 43, 183 N.E.2d 547.

The judgment of the Appellate Court is reversed, and the cause is remanded to the circuit court of Lake County for further proceedings not inconsistent with this opinion.

AJAY SPORTS, INC. v. CASAZZA

1 P.3d 267 (Colo.App.2000).

Opinion by JUDGE PIERCE.

Defendant, Michael S. Casazza, appeals a judgment entered against him on a jury verdict finding him liable to plaintiff, Ajay Sports, Inc. (ASI), for damages resulting from a creditor claim of wrongful distribution of assets. We affirm.

Ajay Leisure Products, Inc. (Ajay Leisure), a subsidiary of ASI, is a manufacturer of golf products. In 1991, Pro–Mark, Inc. (PMI), a Delaware corporation, was formed to market golf equipment manufactured by Ajay Leisure. PMI also marketed other sporting goods trademarked under the "MacGregor" brand name and manufactured by another corporation, Sports Acquisition Corporation (MacGregor). Defendant was a director of PMI and a director and officer of MacGregor,

Through a private offering of stock, PMI raised approximately $700,000. PMI and Ajay Leisure entered a purchase agreement whereby PMI paid Ajay Leisure $300,000 plus one million shares of PMI common stock for all rights to Ajay Leisure's trademarked "Double Eagle" brand name and all existing Double Eagle inventory. PMI also paid MacGregor $300,000 to acquire the right to market sporting goods under MacGregor's brand name.

It was later determined that Ajay Leisure had used the Double Eagle trademark as collateral for certain bank loans, and could not transfer the brand name as contemplated by the purchase agreement. Accordingly, the parties entered into a marketing agreement whereby PMI was granted the exclusive license to market products under the Double Eagle name. This agreement provided for PMI's previous payment of $300,000, but made no mention of the one million shares of stock that had been previously transferred.

PMI marketed products under the Double Eagle brand name for almost two years. During this time, PMI incurred marketing, administrative, and manufacturing expenses for services performed by Ajay Leisure. PMI was unsuccessful in marketing the equipment and ceased business operations by the end of 1992.

PMI then attempted to recoup the loss sustained by its original private offering investors. Because MacGregor had never allowed PMI to use the MacGregor brand name in exchange for the $300,000 it had received, defendant negotiated an agreement between PMI and MacGregor. Under the agreement, MacGregor would provide 150,000 shares of its common stock to PMI in exchange for PMI's release of all claims against MacGregor.

After the receipt of this stock, PMI's directors met and authorized the distribution of the MacGregor stock to PMI's original investors. Defendant maintained that Russell Casement was elected a director of PMI at this meeting. However, Casement denied participating in the meeting or being a director of PMI.

In addition to the MacGregor stock distribution, defendant also distributed stock options in an unrelated company to some of the original investors, and defendant received liability releases from some of these investors. It is uncontested that Ajay Leisure never received any part of PMI's distribution.

ASI initiated this lawsuit against defendant, as well as against Casement and other directors, claiming that PMI was insolvent at the time of the distribution, that the distribution was unlawful, and therefore, that the directors were personally liable to ASI for damages. ASI asserted its claims both as a creditor and a shareholder of PMI. The creditor claim was based on money owed for the services ASI claimed to have provided to PMI during the course of its operations. * * *

ASI's creditor claim was premised upon defendant's alleged violation of a Delaware statute, and at trial, the court ruled that Delaware law applied to the liability issues. On appeal, the parties similarly rely on Delaware authority in addressing the liability issues.

Under the Delaware code, directors of a corporation are liable to creditors of the corporation for an illegal distribution if the directors authorize such distribution while the corporation is dissolved or insolvent. Del. Code Ann. tit. 8, § 174(a) (1998); see Geyer v. Ingersoll Publications Co., 621 A.2d 784 (Del.Ch.1992). * * *

* * * An insolvent corporation is one whose asset value has decreased to less than the amount of its debts. Geyer v. Ingersoll Publications Co., supra.

At trial, ASI's expert testified that PMI was insolvent when the distribution occurred. The expert based this opinion on PMI's financial statements for the two years preceding the year in which the distribution occurred, and on notes in ASI's consolidated financial statement. The financial statements were admitted, and although defendant presented conflicting evidence on the issue of insolvency, the jury was free to determine the weight of the evidence and the credibility of witnesses in the manner it deemed appropriate. * * *

Under Delaware law, the business judgment rule is the offspring of the fundamental principle that the business and affairs of a corporation are managed by or under its board of directors. In carrying out their managerial roles, directors are charged with a fiduciary duty to the corporation and its shareholders. Smith v. Van Gorkom, 488 A.2d 858 (Del.1985).

The business judgment rule exists to protect and promote the full and free exercise of the managerial power granted to directors. The rule establishes a presumption that in making a business decision, the directors of a corporation acted on an informed basis, in good faith, and in the honest belief that the action taken was in the best interests of the company. Smith v. Van Gorkom, supra; Aronson v. Lewis, 473 A.2d 805 (Del.1984).

However, the protections of the business judgment rule can only be claimed by disinterested directors whose conduct otherwise meets the tests of business judgment. As the Delaware Supreme Court explained in Aronson v. Lewis, supra, 473 A.2d at 812:

> Directors can neither appear on both sides of a transaction nor expect to derive any personal financial benefit from it in the sense of self-dealing, as opposed to a benefit which devolves upon the corporation or all stockholders generally.

To invoke the protection of the business judgment rule, directors have a duty to inform themselves, before making a business decision, of all material information reasonably available to them. They must then act with requisite care in the discharge of their duties. Aronson v. Lewis, supra, 473 A.2d at 812 ("While the Delaware cases use a variety of terms to describe the applicable standard of care, ... under the business judgment rule director liability is predicated upon concepts of gross negligence."). * * *

In order to prevail on its unlawful dividend and breach of fiduciary duty claims, the plaintiff must rebut the presumption by a preponderance of the evidence that in authorizing the distribution by [PMI] of the [MacGregor] shares at issue, the defendants acted on an informed basis, in good faith and in the honest belief that the action taken was in the best interests of [PMI].

The trial court refused to give the tendered instruction to the jury, but it sent another instruction to the jury stating that:

> It is presumed that directors act reasonably, but this presumption can be overcome by a showing of gross negligence.... Gross negligence means reckless indifference to or a deliberate disregard of a corporation's stockholders or actions which are without the bounds of reason; it is a higher level of negligence representing an extreme departure from the ordinary standard of care. If you find that the defendants derived any personal financial benefit or were on both sides of the transaction, then the business judgment rule has no application as a defense.

Although the court's instruction may not have given as much detail on the business judgment rule as defendant's tendered instruction, nevertheless, all applicable elements of the defense were embodied in the instruction given. Further, in reaching its verdict, the jury necessarily determined that the business judgment defense was unavailable to defendant. We thus perceive no error. * * *

Finally, defendant contends that the award of exemplary damages must be set aside because the jury found defendant liable to ASI for $70,140 in exemplary damages, but found Casement liable for $35,070 in exemplary damages, a different amount. We conclude that it is proper to permit a jury to apportion exemplary damages among multiple defendants.

Although exemplary damages are governed by statute, see § 13–21–102, there is no Colorado statutory or case law to guide us on the apportionment issue. Nevertheless, the majority of jurisdictions that have addressed the issue have upheld the apportionment of exemplary damages among multiple defendants under many differing factual situations.

The basic rationale is set forth as follows:

> Many states ... have adopted the rule that punitive damages may be apportioned between wrongdoers either by providing varying amounts of such award or by levying exemplary damages against some of the defendants but not others. In our view, this is the most sensible approach to the subject, for punitive damages, in order to be fair and effective, must relate to the degree of culpability exhibited by a particular defendant.... Punitive damages, in essence, represent a civil fine, and as such, should be imposed on an individual basis.

Embrey v. Holly, 293 Md. 128, 141–42, 442 A.2d 966, 973 (1982). See also Davidson v. Dixon, 386 F.Supp. 482, 489 (D.Del.1974) (recognizing that defendants' liability for compensatory damages was joint and several, but holding that "separate awards for [exemplary] damages may be made against different defendants."); Fredeen v. Stride, 269 Ore. 369, 525 P.2d 166 (1974)(reversing award of exemplary damages against one defendant but upholding award of exemplary damages against other defendant); Annot., 20 A.L.R. 666 (1968).

We adopt this reasoning and similarly conclude that in an action involving multiple defendants, as here, "exemplary damages may be awarded against one or more of the defendants and not others, depending ... upon the differing degree of culpability or the existence or nonexistence of malice on the part of the defendants." Exxon Corp. v. Yarema, 69 Md.App. 124, 137, 516 A.2d 990, 997 (1986)(further concluding that the Uniform Contribution Among Tortfeasors Act does not apply to punitive damages, only to compensatory damages). Cf. § 13–50.5–102, C.R.S. 1999 (stating that there is "no right of contribution in favor of any tortfeasor who has intentionally, willfully, or wantonly caused or contributed to [an] injury or wrongful death"). * * *

Accordingly, we conclude the trial court did not err in permitting the jury to apportion the exemplary damages.

Judgment affirmed.

JUDGE JONES and JUDGE ROTHENBERG concur.

NOTES

1. Model Bus. Corp. Act § 8.33 imposes personal liability on a director not using due care in declaring a dividend in violation of Model Bus. Corp. Act § 6.40. State corporate statutes impose varying standards for imposing liability on directors for wrongfully declared dividends. As seen in the prior case, Delaware imposes liability on directors for any willful or negligent violation of the provisions in Delaware corporate law restricting payments of dividends. Each director is jointly or severally liable for declaring an unlawful dividend, unless they voted against the declaration. 8 Del. Corp. L. § 174.

2. Model Bus Corp. Act §§ 8.30 and 8.33 allow directors to rely reasonably on reports of accountants in absolving themselves of negligently or willfully declaring a wrongful dividend. Delaware has a similar provision. 8 Del Corp. L. § 172.

WOOD v. NATIONAL CITY BANK

24 F.2d 661 (2d Cir.1928).

* * * The amended bill set forth the following facts: At some undisclosed time the District Court for the Eastern District of Kentucky appointed a receiver for the Stanton Oil Company, a Delaware corporation, and later the plaintiff was appointed ancillary receiver "by an order entered in the District Court of the United States for the Southern District of New York." The nature of neither suit was disclosed. From July 16, 1917, to April 1, 1919, the defendants were stockholders of the corporation, between which dates they had received certain dividends from its assets. At the time when all these dividends were paid, the corporation "was in debt, and was in fact insolvent and unable to pay its debts, and had not then, nor had it ever had, any reserve over and above its capital stock, or any surplus or net profits of any kind, and each and all of the said dividends were paid wholly from and out of the capital of said corporation." Claims had been "filed" against the corporation, amounting to more than $100,000, and receiver's certificates issued in the sum of $25,000.

L. HAND, CIRCUIT JUDGE (after stating the facts as above).

It is impossible from the bill to learn just what the plaintiff meant to allege. On the one hand, he may have meant only that, when the dividends were paid, the corporate assets did not equal its debts together with the aggregate amount of its corporate shares, considered as a liability, and that the payments left the assets insufficient to pay the shares in full. On the other hand, he may have meant that the assets were not at those times enough to pay the debts; that is, that the corporation was insolvent, as that word is used in the Bankruptcy Act (11 USCA). Considering the liberal attitude which courts now take towards pleadings, we think that some of the language is susceptible of being understood in the second sense. "Unable to pay its debts" certainly says more than that the corporation has failed to pay them in due course. It more naturally means that the assets were not enough for that purpose. We must, it is true, confess to a complete inability to understand the relevancy of the remainder of the third article of the bill, in which these words appear. They strongly suggest that the gist of the suit was the receipt of dividends paid in depletion of capital, without regard to whether the corporation was solvent or insolvent. However that may be, if there is a sufficient allegation of insolvency, as we think, the bill is at worst only indefinite and ambiguous, and the proper remedy was to move under rule 20 for a better statement, not to dismiss it under rule 29.

Such being a permissible construction of the complaint, the question of its sufficiency depends upon the law of stockholders' liability. We have not to do with the liability commonly imposed by statute, because, whatever that may be in Delaware, the plaintiff does not invoke it here. He depends upon the fact that the directors have paid, and the defendants received, dividends when the corporation was insolvent. Merely because this impairs the capital stock, it is commonly regarded as a wrong to creditors on the directors' part, and it is often made such by statute. We may, without discussion, assume that it would be a wrong in the case at bar. Even so, it is primarily only the wrong of those who commit it, like any other tort, and innocent participants are not accomplices to its commission. Hence it has been settled, at least for us, that, when the liability is based merely on the depletion of the capital, a stockholder must be charged with notice of that fact. McDonald v. Williams, 174 U.S. 397, 19 S.Ct. 743, 43 L.Ed. 1022. This has become a thoroughly fixed principle in the federal courts. Lawrence v. Greenup (C.C.A. 6) 97 F. 906; New Hampshire Savings Bank v. Richey (C.C.A. 8) 121 F. 956; Great Western, etc., Co. v. Harris (C.C.A. 2) 128 F. 321; Ratcliff v. Clendenin (C.C.A. 8) 232 F. 61; Atherton v. Beaman (C.C.A. 1) 264 F. 878.

It is apparent that this result could not have been reached if the capital of the corporation were regarded as a trust fund for its creditors, because a stockholder is not a purchaser, but a donee, and his bona fides would not protect him, in the absence of some further equity, in retaining the proceeds of a trust. So it became necessary to decide that the capital was not such a fund, and McDonald v. Williams did expressly so decide. The so-called "trust fund" doctrine had, indeed, earlier been repudiated by the Supreme Court, especially in Hollins v. Brierfield, etc., Co., 150 U.S. 371; but it was a hardy weed and would not die at the first uprooting. It is apparent, therefore, that the bill does not set forth a cause of suit based upon the impairment of the capital, because the stockholders are not alleged to have been privy to the directors' tort. This is not a defense which must be pleaded, like that of bona fide purchaser; it is necessary positively to allege the stockholders' complicity in the wrong to set forth any case at all.

However, there is quite another theory, and quite another liability, if the payments not only impair the capital, but are taken out of assets already too small to pay the existing debts. The situation then strictly is not peculiar to corporation law, but merely an instance of a payment from an insolvent estate. Since, as we have said, a stockholder is a donee, he receives such payments charged with whatever trust they were subject to in the hands of the corporation. In that situation it can indeed be said with some truth that the corporate assets have become a "trust fund." Wabash, etc., Ry. v. Ham, 114 U.S. 587, 594. Hence it has never been doubted, so far as we can find, at least in any federal court, that if the dividends are paid in fraud of creditors the stockholder is so liable. Hayden v. Thompson (C.C.A. 8) 71 F. 60; Hayden v. Williams (C.C.A. 2) 96 F. 279. The defendants, who suppose that there has been an inconsistency in the decisions of the Eighth Circuit (and they might have added in our own), have failed to distinguish the quite independent bases of the two liabilities.

If the bill be regarded as presenting only an instance of a payment in fraud of creditors, the question arises whether it is enough merely to allege that the payment was made while the corporation was insolvent. It is agreed with substantial unanimity that, when an insolvent makes a voluntary payment out of his assets, it is regarded as at least presumptively in fraud of his creditors, Hume v. Central Washington Bank, 128 U.S. 195; Kehr v. Smith, 20 Wall. 31; Parich v. Murphree, 13 How. 92, 99; Klinger v. Hyman, 223 F. 257 (C.C.A. 2); Hessian v. Patten, 154 F. 829, 832 (C.C.A. 8); Cole v. Tyler, 65 N.Y. 73; Smith v. Reid, 134 N.Y. 568, 31 N.E. 1082; Lehrenkrauss v. Bonnell, 199 N.Y. 240, 246, 92 N.E. 637. We shall assume, for argument, in accordance with the language of some of the foregoing decisions, that such a transfer is fraudulent per se. In Hayden v. Williams no more is mentioned than that the corporation was insolvent, and apparently no more was thought necessary. Even so, the bill is bad, because, when the invalidity of the gift depends only upon the fact of the donor's insolvency, regardless of his intent, it is voidable only at the demand of creditors existing when it is made. Horbach v. Hill, 112 U.S. 144, 149 (semble); Ratcliff v. Clendenin, 232 F. 61 (C.C.A. 8) (semble); Church v. Chapin, 35 Vt. 223; Sheppard v. Thomas, 24 Kan. 780; Eckhart v. Burrell Mfg. Co., 236 Ill. 134, 86 N.E. 199; Crowley v. Brower, 201 Iowa, 257, 207 N.W. 230. Hummell v. Harrington (Fla.) 109 So. 320, if holding otherwise, is an exception; it probably meant no more than that, if there be actual intent to defraud subsequent creditors, they also may avoid the gift. Day v. Cooley, 118 Mass. 524. In the case at bar the bill does not allege that any of the creditors in existence when the receiver was appointed were creditors when the dividends were declared. Only in case the bill had alleged this, would the question arise whether insolvency per se avoids the gift. For this reason, and this alone, the decree was right.
* * *

Decree affirmed.

NOTE

Current Delaware law allows a director found liable for declaring an unlawful dividend to seek contribution from shareholders for their pro rata distribution, if they knew the distribution was unlawful. 8 Del. Corp. L. § 174(c). Model Bus. Corp. Act § 8.33 has a similar provision. Directors held severally liable may seek also contribution from other directors. 8 Del. Corp. L. § 174.

SECTION 7. CLOSELY–HELD CORPORATIONS

ROSS TRANSPORT v. CROTHERS

185 Md. 573, 45 A.2d 267 (1946).

MARBURY, CHIEF JUDGE.

This is a derivative suit by a stockholder of a Maryland corporation, acting on his own behalf as well as for other stockholders who might join and be made parties, brought after demand had been made on the corporation to institute such a proceeding, which demand was neglected and refused. The original plaintiff was Charles T. Crothers, and he was subsequently joined by another stockholder, his brother Edmund W. Crothers, who was made an additional party plaintiff by order of court. The defendants (appellants here) are the corporation, Ross Transport, Inc., Wallace Williams, F. DuPont Thomson, James W. Hughes and William B. Ross, directors, and Elizabeth B. Williams, Lois Williams Young and Corrine Williams, stockholders. The purpose of the suit is to set aside the issuance of 40 shares of stock to Elizabeth B. Williams, 100 shares of stock to Corrine Williams, 100 shares of stock to Lois Williams Young and 125 shares of stock to William B. Ross. The defendants all answered, testimony was taken and the court passed a decree granting the relief prayed, and directing the four stockholders named to repay to the corporation the dividends received by them on the stock declared to be illegally issued, and ordered cancelled. From this decree, all the defendants appealed.

It appears from the record that the corporation was organized on January 19, 1942 to operate a fleet of buses to transport employees of Triumph Explosives, Inc. to and from its plant at Elkton, Maryland. The incorporators were Wallace Williams, William B. Ross and Gervase R. Sinclair who later died. These three and F. DuPont Thomson and James W. Hughes were the directors. At the organization meeting of the directors, Williams was named as President and Ross as General Manager. The authorized stock was 5000 shares of no par value. At the organization meeting a resolution was passed authorizing the sale of this stock at $20 a share, and providing that stock to the value of $30,000 be offered for sale. This limited the stock to be issued to 1500 shares. The stock records of the company showed the original subscriptions to stock, all in March and April 1942, to be as follows:

March 25th— To Wallace Williams	50 shares	
" " Wallace Williams, Jr.	100 "	
" " Elizabeth B. Williams	200 "	
" " Edmund W. Crothers	100 "	
" " William B. Ross	25 "	
" " James W. Hughes	150 "	
April 2nd F. DuPont Thomson	150 "	
" " Bessie F. Whitelaw	10 "	
April 20th Charles T. Crothers	50 "	
April 27th Gervase R. Sinclair	50 "	
" " Jean W. Sinclair	150 "	
Total	1035	

In the latter part of July 1942, after the death of Mr. Sinclair, Charles T. Crothers purchased the Sinclair stock, 200 shares, at $20 and 5% interest from the date of issuance. This did not, of course, increase the amount of stock outstanding. On August 26, 1942, the stock complained of was issued to the wife and daughters of Wallace Williams and to William B. Ross, totaling 365 shares in all, and increasing the outstanding stock to 1400 shares. All of this stock was issued at the set price of $20.00 a share. The stock issued to the Williams family was paid by Mr. Williams' check for $4800. Mr. Ross paid the company $2500 for his stock.

As a result of these purchases by Williams and Ross the stock books showed that the Williams family had 590 shares, Ross had 150 shares, Hughes had 150 shares, Thomson had 150 shares, Whitelaw had 10 shares, Edmund W. Crothers had 100 shares and Charles T. Crothers had 250 shares. Williams and Ross, therefore, had the controlling interest in the company. Mr. Williams testified that all of the stock in the company was sold by him personally under the directors' resolution. He said that all the stock in dispute was definitely promised in the beginning, except 40 shares to Mrs. Williams. This, he said, he put in to round out an even 1400 shares, holding back 100 shares which he thought Hughes or Thomson might like to take. He never called any other directors meeting to authorize any of the sales made after the original subscriptions and none of the other stockholders were given an opportunity to buy. He told Mr. Ross and Mr. Hughes how he was going to divide it. Mr. Ross did not testify.

The sale of this additional stock to a director and to the family of the president and director without any further authority than the original resolution, and without opportunity to buy given to other stockholders, is sought to be justified on the ground that it was originally planned, and that the money was needed to purchase additional buses at a cost of about $16,000. The facts, however, show no such need. The company was an immediate financial success. It was engaged in a special business, of which it had a monopoly, and in which it could not help making money so long as Triumph Explosives continued to operate its large plant, employing the workmen the Transport Corporation hauled. The loan of $3000 by Triumph Explosives, made in March, was paid in June. The record shows the following figures during the first five months of its existence.

On August 7th, the directors authorized salary payments dating back to February 1, 1942, $3915 to Mr. Williams, $2875 to Mr. Ross and $2025 to Mr. Hughes who was Secretary and Treasurer of the company which had started business a few months before with a paid in capital of $20,700, and which had bought its operating equipment, i.e. the buses, on conditional sales contracts, and had borrowed $3000 to pay for its licenses. Prosperity continued. On November 27, 1942, a dividend of $5 a share was declared. On December 17, 1942 one of $15 (called a return of capital, but not authorized by the stockholders, Code, Article 23, Sec. 32). On the same date, another dividend of $5 a share was declared payable June 30, 1943. The defendants, Williams and Ross, who were operating the company, knew on August 26, 1942, that they were about to receive large sums in dividends in addition to the salaries they were getting. The benefit of these dividends would not only increase the value of the stock, but the first two would pay back all the subscribers had invested, leaving any future earnings and distributions pure profit. Under these circumstances, they took the opportunity they thought they had to increase their investment, and in fact received in December the full amount they invested in August, leaving them with the additional stock on which to receive such further dividends as were obviously in sight.

The appellants contend that the company was not in the claimed good financial condition in August, because no allowance had been made for income and profits taxes. But if we reduce the book surplus of $25,000 on August 16, 1942, by allowing for a 40% tax (the limit unless the earnings increased), we still find the company with a net surplus of $15,000, 75% of the original investment. The stock had no "market value," but it must be obvious that it was worth much more than $20 a share on August 26th.

	Surplus above liabilities and invested capital	Outstanding obligations on conditional sales contract	Cash Bank balance
April 25	$8,459.77	$50,372.22	$ 9,092.65
May 23	13,295.38	45,712.34	13,811.80
June 21	20,214.53	42,144.63	14,154.62
July 19	26,414.74	31,154.69	12,842.81
Aug. 16	25,057.73	28,997.68	8,970.83

The appellees give two reasons for their contention that the stock sales of August 26th were void: First, because they deprive them and the other original stockholders of their preemptive rights to purchase a proportionate amount of the remaining shares, and, second, because, in selling to themselves and their nominees, Williams and Ross have abused their trust as officers and directors. They claim to be injured in two ways.

Their voting powers have been proportionately lessened, and the control of the company has passed to Williams and Ross. And the amount paid in dividends has to be divided among 365 more shares of stock to the consequent financial loss of the holders of the original shares.

Before discussing these legal questions, the outline of the case may be completed by quoting from the appellants' brief certain facts about the plaintiffs (appellees) which appellants claim are pertinent. The original plaintiff, Charles T. Crothers, was an employee of the corporation as well as a stockholder. Edmund W. Crothers had no position in the corporation, but he furnished it part of the buses that were bought at the inception of the business. The appellants' brief states:

"The 365 shares complained of were issued on August 26th, 1942. Charles T. Crothers learned of that fact two or three weeks thereafter; and his brother, Edmund W. Crothers learned about it three or four weeks after said Stock was issued. Charles T. Crothers understood from the first that the Sale of 1,500 Shares had been authorized; and no one had ever represented to him that no more than 1,035 Shares would be issued. In July, 1942, Charles T. Crothers refused to turn over half of the Sinclair Stock, then purchased by him, to Ross, and assigned for his reason the fact that Ross could buy more Stock from the Corporation; and he also attempted to buy the remaining 100 of the authorized 1,500 Shares for himself. On February 1st, 1943, at a Meeting of Stockholders, Charles T. Crothers was elected a Director and served for one year. At that Meeting the Treasurer's Report was accepted on a motion seconded by Edmund W. Crothers. At that Meeting of the Stockholders a Resolution was adopted, expressing to the Management and Employees the appreciation of the Stockholders for the manner in which the operation of the Corporation had been conducted during the previous year. The minutes show that Edmund W. Crothers seconded this Resolution. Charles T. Crothers was then present. and testified that he does not know whether he voted for this Resolution, but he did not object to it. Edmund W. Crothers testified that he did not second the Resolution of Approbation and that he objected to the Minutes on the following year (after this suit was instituted by his brother, but before he, Edmund W. Crothers, had become a party thereto), and that he assigned as his reason for his protest that he was just reserving his decision. On September 13th, 1943, Charles T. Crothers, then a Director, seconded and voted for the Declaration of a Dividend on all 1,400 Shares of Stock. No protest was made to the Corporation about the issuance of the 365 Shares until a letter of protest was written by counsel for Charles T. Crothers on October 27th, 1943, which was after he had been 'fired,' to use his own words, by the Corporation, in October, 1943. Charles T. Crothers, by his own testimony, never made any objection to the 365 Shares complained of having been issued at any meeting of the Corporation."

Charles T. Crothers testified that he protested to Mr. Hughes and to Mr. Thomson shortly after he learned of the stock issues of August 26th. Mr. Hughes said he was told by Mr. Thomson in "the latter part of the summer, or the early summer of 1942" that Edmund Crothers had spoken to him about it. Edmund Crothers said he got in touch with Mr. Thomson when he learned of the transaction, and also talked to Mr. Hughes, and at one time had "quite a little argument" with Mr. Williams and the latter said "Wouldn't you do it, if you could get away with it." Charles Crothers gave as a reason for not bringing up the matter at a directors meeting "They were just a matter of form. Mr. Williams was the boss of the company. He owned the company."

The doctrine known as the preemptive right of shareholders is a judicial interpretation of general principles of corporation law. Existing stockholders are the owners of the business, and are entitled to have that ownership continued in the same proportion. Therefore, when additional stock is issued, those already having shares, are held to have the first right to buy the new stock in proportion to their holdings. This doctrine was first promulgated in 1807 in the case of Gray v. Portland Bank, 3 Mass. 364, 3 Am.Dec. 156. At that time, corporations were small and closely held, much like the one before us in this case. But in the succeeding years, corporations grew and expanded. New capital was frequently required. New properties had to be acquired for which it was desirable to issue stock. Companies merged, and new stock in the consolidation was issued. Stock was issued for services. Different kinds of stock were authorized—preferred without voting power but with prior dividend rights—preferred with the right to convert into common—several classes of both common and preferred with different rights. Some stock had voting rights. Other stock did not. Bonds were issued, convertible into stock. All of these changes in the corporate structure made it impossible always to follow the simple doctrines earlier decided. Exceptions grew, and were noted in the decisions.

Only one of these exceptions is involved in the present case. It has been held that pre-emptive rights do not exist where the stock about to be issued is part of the original issue. This exception is based upon the fact that the original subscribers took their stock on the implied understanding that the incorporators could complete the sale of the remaining stock to obtain the capital thought necessary to start the business. But this gives rise to an exception to the exception, where conditions have changed since the original issue. The stock sold the Williams family and Ross was part of the original issue, and it is claimed by the appellants that it comes within the exception, and the appellees and the other stockholders have no pre-emptive rights. Balto. Ry. Co. v. Hambleton, 77 Md. 341, 26 A. 279; Real Estate Trust Co. v. Bird, 90 Md. 229, 44 A. 1048; Thom v. Baltimore Trust Co., 158 Md. 352, 148 A. 234; Yasik v. Wachtel, Del. Ch., 17 A.2d 309; 40 Mich.L.Rev. 115. The appellees, on the other hand, contend, and the chancellors found, that changed conditions made it unnecessary to use the remaining unsold stock to obtain capital, and pre-emptive rights exist in it just as they would exist in newly authorized stock. Hammer v. Werner, 239 App.Div. 38, 265 N.Y.S. 172, Dunlay v. Avenue etc. Co., 253 N.Y. 274, 170 N.E. 917, 43 Harvard L.Rev. 586, 602–603.

It is unnecessary for us to decide which of these two conflicting points of view applies to this case, because another controlling consideration enters. The doctrine of pre-emptive right is not affected by the identity of the purchasers of the issued stock. What it is concerned with is who did not get it. But when officers and directors sell to themselves, and thereby gain an advantage, both in value and in voting power, another situation arises, which it does not require the assertion of a pre-emptive right to deal with.

It has long been the law in this State that trustees cannot purchase at their own sale, and trustees, in this sense, include directors of corporations. This principle of the law was discussed by Chief Judge LeGrand in the first of the cases involving the dealings of Sherman with the Cumberland Coal and Iron Company, Hoffman Coal Company v. Cumberland C. & I. Co., 16 Md. 456 at pages 507–508, 77 Am.Dec. 311. This case referred to the earlier case of Richardson v. Jones, 3 Gill & J. 163, 22 Am.Dec. 293. As authority for the general policy of the law forbidding a trustee to become a purchaser, either directly or indirectly, at his own sale, and stating, "if he does, such sale may, and will be set aside, on the proper and reasonable application of the parties interested." The same statement is repeated in the second Sherman case, Cumberland C. & I. Co. v. Sherman, 20 Md. 117, pages 133, 134. This would lead to the conclusion that such a transaction is entirely voidable at the option of a party interested. In the third case involving the same company, Cumberland Coal and Iron Co. v. Parish, 42 Md. 598, Judge Alvey, speaking for this Court said: "The affairs of corporations are generally intrusted to the exclusive management and control of the board of directors; and there is an inherent obligation, implied in the acceptance of such trust, not only that they will use their best efforts to promote the interest of the shareholders, but that they will in no manner use their positions to advance their own individual interest as distinguished from that of the corporation, or acquire interests that may conflict with the fair and proper discharge of their duty." After some other observations on the subject, the opinion then states: "The transaction may not be ipso facto void, but it is not necessary to establish that there has been actual fraud or imposition practiced by the party holding the confidential or fiduciary relation;—the onus of proof being upon him to establish the perfect fairness, adequacy, and equity of the transaction; and that too by proof entirely independent of the instrument under which he may claim." This last quotation indicates that such a transaction is not absolutely voided at the option of the interested parties, but shifts the burden of proof upon the directors to establish its fairness. This last view was again stated by Judge Alvey in the case of Booth v. Robinson, 55 Md. 419, at pages 441–442, and his words in the last case are quoted by this Court in the case of Penn. R. Co. v. Minis, 120 Md. 461, at page 486, 87 A. 1062. See also Macgill v. Macgill, 135 Md. 384 and cases cited on page 394,

109 A. 72. Coffman v. Publishing Co., 167 Md. 275, 173 A. 248, and Williams v. Messick, 177 Md. 605, 11 A.2d 472, 129 A.L.R. 1035.

It is not necessary for us to determine in this case whether the sale of stock to the Williams family and Ross is voidable merely upon the application of some of the other stockholders, or whether proof of such sale merely makes it necessary for these appellants to show the complete equity of the transaction. If we take the latter view, which is that most favorable to these appellants, we must hold that the burden placed upon the two directors has not been met. They have not shown that the company needed the money so badly and was in such a financial condition that the sale of the additional stock to themselves was the only was the money could be obtained. On the contrary, the corporation appears to have been in a very good financial condition. It is probable that any necessary financing of any buses could easily have been arranged through some financial institution, and Williams and Ross benefited greatly by their action in selling the stock to themselves. Nor is there any corroboration of Williams' statement that it was all arranged in the beginning, who was to get this additional stock. None of the other incorporators or directors were called to testify about this, and Ross himself, as we have noted, did not testify at all. We conclude, therefore, that the sale must be set aside as a constructive fraud upon the other stockholders. * * *

The decree will be affirmed.

NOTES

1. Maryland amended its corporate statutes in 1995 to provide:

    § 2–205. Preemptive rights

    (a) Circumstances in which preemptive rights do not accrue.—Unless the charter expressly grants such rights to the stockholder, a stockholder does not have any preemptive right to subscribe to:

       (2) Any additional issue of stock; or

       (3) Any security convertible into an additional issue of stock.

    (b) Waiver.—

       (1) A stockholder to whom a preemptive right has been granted may waive the preemptive right.

       (2) A written waiver of a preemptive right is irrevocable even though it is not supported by consideration.

2. Dilution concerns in a closely held corporation may arise in subsequent financings. To illustrate: a small corporation is in need of further funds. Some of the owners are willing to contribute more funds to the struggling company but only on terms more favorable than the initial offering. Those owners not willing to participate will be effectively diluted, raising concerns with conflicts of interests on the part of those participating in the new

offering. See Richard L. Dickson & David A. Bell, Dilutive Venture Capital Financings of Distressed Companies, 36 Securities & Commodities Regulation 36 (March 12, 2003).

KATZOWITZ v. SIDLER

24 N.Y.2d 512, 301 N.Y.S.2d 470, 249 N.E.2d 359 (1969).

KEATING, JUDGE.

Isador Katzowitz is a director and stockholder of a close corporation. Two other persons, Jacob Sidler and Max Lasker, own the remaining securities and, with Katzowitz, comprise Sulburn Holding Corp.'s board of directors. Sulburn was organized in 1955 to supply propane gas to three other corporations controlled by these men. Sulburn's certificate of incorporation authorized it to issue 1,000 shares of no par value stock for which the incorporators established a $100 selling price. Katzowitz, Sidler and Lasker each invested $500 and received five shares of the corporation's stock.

The three men had been jointly engaged in several corporate ventures for more than 25 years. In this period they had always been equal partners and received identical compensation from the corporations they controlled. Though all the corporations controlled by these three men prospered, disenchantment with their inter-personal relationship flared into the open in 1956. At this time, Sidler and Lasker joined forces to oust Katzowitz from any role in managing the corporations. They first voted to replace Katzowitz as a director of Sullivan County Gas Company with the corporation's private counsel. Notice of directors' meetings was then caused to be sent out by Lasker and Sidler for Burnwell Gas Corporation. Sidler and Lasker advised Katzowitz that they intended to vote for a new board of directors. Katzowitz at this time held the position of manager of the Burnwell facility.

Katzowitz sought a temporary injunction to prevent the meeting until his rights could be judicially determined. A temporary injunction was granted to maintain the status quo until trial. The order was affirmed by the Appellate Division (Katzowitz v. Sidler, 8 A.D.2d 726, 187 N.Y.S.2d 986).

Before the issue could be tried, the three men entered into a stipulation in 1959 whereby Katzowitz withdrew from active participation in the day-to-day operations of the business. The agreement provided that he would remain on the boards of all the corporations, and each board would be limited to three members composed of the three stockholders or their designees. Katzowitz was to receive the same compensation and other fringe benefits which the controlled corporations paid Lasker and Sidler. The stipulation also provided that Katzowitz, Sidler and Lasker were "equal stockholders and each of said parties now owns the same number of shares of stock in each of the defendant corporations and that such shares of stock shall continue to be in full force and effect and unaffected by this stipulation, except as hereby otherwise expressly provided." The stipulation contained no other provision affecting equal stock interests.

The business relationship established by the stipulation was fully complied with. Sidler and Lasker, however, were still interested in disassociating themselves from Katzowitz and purchased his interest in one of the gas distribution corporations and approached him with regard to the purchase of his interest in another.

In December of 1961 Sulburn was indebted to each stockholder to the extent of $2,500 for fees and commissions earned up until September, 1961. Instead of paying this debt, Sidler and Lasker wanted Sulburn to loan the money to another corporation which all three men controlled. Sidler and Lasker called a meeting of the board of directors to propose that additional securities be offered at $100 per share to substitute for the money owed to the directors. The notice of meeting for October 30, 1961 had on its agenda "a proposition that the corporation issue common stock of its unissued common capital stock, *the total par value which shall equal the total sum of the fees and commissions now owing by the corporation to its * * * directors*". (Emphasis added.) Katzowitz made it quite clear at the meeting that he would not invest any additional funds in Sulburn in order for it to make a loan to this other corporation. The only resolution passed at the meeting was that the corporation would pay the sum of $2,500 to each director.

With full knowledge that Katzowitz expected to be paid his fees and commissions and that he did not want to participate in any new stock issuance, the other two directors called a special meeting of the board on December 1, 1961. The only item on the agenda for this special meeting was the issuance of 75 shares of the corporation's common stock at $100 per share. The offer was to be made to stockholders in "accordance with their respective preemptive rights for the purpose of acquiring additional working capital". The amount to be raised was the exact amount owed by the corporation to its shareholders. The offering price for the securities was 1/18 the book value of the stock. Only Sidler and Lasker attended the special board meeting. They approved the issuance of the 75 shares.

Notice was mailed to each stockholder that they had the right to purchase 25 shares of the corporation's stock at $100 a share. The offer was to expire on December 27, 1961. Failure to act by that date was stated to constitute a waiver. At about the same time Katzowitz received the notice, he received a check for $2,500 from the corporation for his fees and commissions. Katzowitz did not exercise his option to buy the additional shares. Sidler and Lasker purchased their full complement, 25 shares each. This purchase by Sidler and Lasker caused an immediate dilution of the book value of the outstanding securities.

On August 25, 1962 the principal asset of Sulburn, a tractor trailer truck, was destroyed. On August 31, 1962 the directors unanimously voted to dissolve the corporation. Upon dissolution, Sidler and Lasker each received $18,885.52 but Katzowitz only received $3,147.59.

The plaintiff instituted a declaratory judgment action to establish his right to the proportional interest in the assets of Sulburn in liquidation less the $5,000 which Sidler and Lasker used to purchase their shares in December, 1961.

Special Term (Westchester County) found the book value of the corporation's securities on the day the stock was offered at $100 to be worth $1,800. The court also found that "the individual defendants * * * decided that in lieu of taking that sum in cash (the commissions and fees due the stockholders), they preferred to add to their investment by having the corporate defendant make available and offer each stockholder an additional twenty-five shares of unissued stock." The court reasoned that Katzowitz waived his right to purchase the stock or object to its sale to Lasker and Sidler by failing to exercise his pre-emptive right and found his protest at the time of dissolution untimely.

The Appellate Division (Second Department), two Justices, dissenting, modified the order of Special Term 29 A.D.2d 955, 289 N.Y.S.2d 324. The modification was procedural. The decretal paragraph in Special Term's order was corrected by reinstating the complaint and substituting a statement of the parties' rights. On the substantive legal issues and findings of fact, the Appellate Division was in agreement with Special Term. The majority agreed that the book value of the corporation's stock at the time of the stock offering was $1,800. The Appellate Division reasoned, however, that showing a disparity between book value and offering price was insufficient without also showing fraud or overreaching. Disparity in price by itself was not enough to prove fraud. The Appellate Division also found that the plaintiff had waived his right to object to his recovery in dissolution by failing to either exercise his pre-emptive rights or take steps to prevent the sale of the stock.

The concept of pre-emptive rights was fashioned by the judiciary to safeguard two distinct interests of stockholders—the right to protection against dilution of their equity in the corporation and protection against dilution of their proportionate voting control. (Ballantine, Corporations (rev. ed., 1946), § 209.) After early decisions (Gray v. Portland Bank, 3 Mass. 364; Stokes v. Continental Trust Co., 186 N.Y. 285, 78 N.E. 1090, 12 L.R.A., N.S., 969), legislation fixed the right enunciated with respect to proportionate voting but left to the judiciary the role of protecting existing shareholders from the dilution of their equity (e.g., Stock Corporation Law, § 39, now Business Corporation Law, Consol. Laws, c. 4, § 622; see Drinker, The Preemptive Right of Shareholders to Subscribe to New Shares, 43 Harv. L. Rev. 586; Frey, Shareholders' Pre-emptive Rights, 38 Yale L.J. 563).

It is clear that directors of a corporation have no discretion in the choice of those to whom the earnings and assets of the corporation should be distributed. Directors, being fiduciaries of the corporation, must, in issuing new stock, treat existing shareholders fairly. [citations omitted]. Though there is very little statutory control over the price which a corporation must receive for new shares (Stock Corporation Law §§ 12, 27, 69, 74; Business Corporation Law § 504) the power to determine price must be exercised for the benefit of the corporation and in the interest of all the stockholders (see, e.g., Bodell v. General Gas & Elec. Corp., 15 Del.Ch. 119, 132 A. 442, affd. 15 Del.Ch. 420, 140 A. 264; Minn.Stat. § 301.16 (1953)).

Issuing stock for less than fair value can injure existing shareholders by diluting their interest in the corporation's surplus, in current and future earnings and in the assets upon liquidation. Normally, a stockholder is protected from the loss of his equity from dilution, even though the stock is being offered at less than fair value, because the shareholder receives rights which he may either exercise or sell. If he exercises, he has protected his interest and, if not, he can sell the rights, thereby compensating himself for the dilution of his remaining shares in the equity of the corporation (Schramme v. Cowin, 205 App.Div. 20, 23, 199 N.Y.S. 98, 100; Noble v. Great Amer. Ins. Co., 200 App.Div. 773, 778–779, 194 N.Y.S. 60, 65–66).[9]

On rare occasions stock will be issued below book value because this indicia of value is not reflective of the actual worth of the corporation. The book value of the corporation's assets may be inflated or the company may not be glamorous to the public because it is in a declining industry or the company may be under the direction of poor management. In these circumstances there may be a business justification for a major disparity in issuing price and book value in order to inject new capital into the corporation. (See, e.g., Conklin v. United Constr. & Supply Co., 166 App.Div. 284, 151 N.Y.S. 624, affd. 219 N.Y. 555, 114 N.E. 1063.)

When new shares are issued, however, at prices far below fair value in a close corporation or a corporation with only a limited market for its shares, existing stockholders, who do not want to invest or do not have the capacity to invest additional funds, can have their equity interest in the corporation diluted to the vanishing point. (2 Hornstein, Corporation Law and Practice, § 624, pp. 152–153.)

The protection afforded by stock rights is illusory in close corporations. Even if a buyer could be found for the rights, they would have to be sold at an inadequate price because of the nature of a close corporation. Outsiders are normally discouraged from acquiring minority interests after a close corporation has been organized. Certainly a stockholder in a close corporation is at a total loss to safeguard his equity from dilution if no rights are offered and he does not want to invest additional funds.

---

9. There is little justification for issuing stock far below its fair value. The only reason for issuing stock below fair value exists in publicly held corporations where the problem of floating new issues through subscription is concerned. The reasons advanced in this situation is that it insures the success of the issue or that it has the same psychological effect as a dividend (Guthman and Dagell, Corporate Financial Policy (3d ed., 1955), p. 369).

Though it is difficult to determine fair value for a corporation's securities and courts are therefore reluctant to get into the thicket, when the issuing price is shown to be markedly below book value in a close corporation and when the remaining shareholder-directors benefit from the issuance, a case for judicial relief has been established. In that instance, the corporation's directors must show that the issuing price falls within some range which can be justified on the basis of valid business reasons. (See Borden v. Guthrie, 23 A.D.2d 313, 260 N.Y.S.2d 769 (concurring opn. of Breitel, J.P.), affd. 17 N.Y.2d 571, 268 N.Y.S.2d 330, 215 N.E.2d 511; Steven v. Hale–Haas Corp., 249 Wis. 205, 23 N.W.2d 620, 768.) If no such showing is made by the directors, there is no reason for the judiciary to abdicate its function to a majority of the board or stockholders who have not seen fit to come forward and justify the propriety of diverting property from the corporation and allow the issuance of securities to become an oppressive device permitting the dilution of the equity of dissident stockholders.

The defendant directors here make no claim that the price set was a fair one. No business justification is offered to sustain it (Blaustein v. Pan Amer. Petroleum & Transpt. Co., 293 N.Y. 281, 303–304, 56 N.E.2d 705, 715–716; Pollitz v. Wabash R.R. Co., 207 N.Y. 113, 124, 100 N.E. 721, 723). Admittedly, the stock was sold at less than book value. The defendants simply contend that, as long as all stockholders were given an equal opportunity to purchase additional shares, no stockholder can complain simply because the offering dilutes his interest in the corporation.

The defendants' argument is fallacious.

The corollary of a stockholder's right to maintain his proportionate equity in a corporation by purchasing additional shares is the right not to purchase additional shares without being confronted with dilution of his existing equity if no valid business justification exists for the dilution. (Bennett v. Breuil Petroleum Corp., 34 Del.Ch. 6, 99 A.2d 236; Steven v. Hale–Haas Corp., 249 Wis. 205, 23 N.W.2d 620, 768, Supra; Gord v. Iowana Farms Milk Co., 245 Iowa 1, 60 N.W.2d 820; Borwning v. C & C Plywood Corp., 248 Or. 574, 434 P.2d 339; see Tashman v. Tashman, 13 Misc.2d 982, 174 N.Y.S.2d 482; Berle, Corporate Powers as Powers in Trust, 44 Harv.L.Rev. 1049, 1055–1060; Berle, Corporate Devices for Diluting Stock Participations, 31 Col.L.Rev. 1239, 1241–1243, 1257–1260; Morawetz, The Preemptive Right of Shareholders, 42 Harv.L.Rev. 186, 188.)

A stockholder's right not to purchase is seriously undermined if the stock offered is worth substantially more than the offering price. Any purchase at this price dilutes his interest and impairs the value of his original holding. "A corporation is not permitted to sell its stock for a legally inadequate price at least where there is objection. Plaintiff has a right to insist upon compliance with the law whether or not he cares to exercise his option. He cannot block a sale for a fair price merely because he disagrees with the wisdom of the plan but he can insist that the sale price be fixed accordance with legal requirements." (Bennett v. Breuil Petroleum Corp., Supra, 34 Del.Ch. pp. 14–15, 99 A.2d p. 241.) Judicial review in this area is limited to whether under all the circumstances, including the disparity between issuing price of the stock and its true value, the nature of the corporation, the business necessity for establishing an offering price at a certain amount to facilitate raising new capital, and the ability of stockholders to sell rights, the additional offering of securities should be condemned because the directors in establishing the sale price did not fix it with reference to financial considerations with respect to the ready disposition of securities.

Here the obvious disparity in selling price and book value was calculated to force the dissident stockholder into investing additional sums. No valid business justification was advanced for the disparity in price, and the only beneficiaries of the disparity were the two director-stockholders who were eager to have additional capital in the business.

It is no answer to Katzowitz' action that he was also given a chance to purchase additional shares at this bargain rate. The price was not so much a bargain as it was a tactic, conscious or unconscious on the part of the directors, to place Katzowitz in a compromising situation. The price was so fixed to make the failure to invest costly. However, Katzowitz at the time might not have been aware of the dilution because no notice of the effect of the issuance of the new shares on the already outstanding shares was disclosed (Gord v. Iowana Farms Milk Co., Supra, 245 Iowa p. 18, 60 N.W.2d 820). In addition, since the stipulation entitled Katzowitz to the same compensation as Sidler and Lasker, the disparity in equity interest caused by their purchase of additional securities in 1961 did not affect stockholder income from Sulburn and, therefore, Katzowitz possibly was not aware of the effect of the stock issuance on his interest in the corporation until dissolution.

No reason exists at this time to permit Sidler and Lasker to benefit from their course of conduct. Katzowitz' delay in commencing the action did not prejudice the defendants. By permitting the defendants to recover their additional investment in Sulburn before the remaining assets of Sulburn are distributed to the stockholders upon dissolution, all the stockholders will be treated equitably. Katzowitz, therefore, should receive his aliquot share of the assets of Sulburn less the amount invested by Sidler and Lasker for their purchase of stock on December 27, 1961.

Accordingly, the order of the Appellate Division should be reversed, with costs, and judgment granted in favor of the plaintiff against the individual defendants.

BURKE, SCILEPPI, BERGAN, BREITEL and JASEN, JJ., concur with KEATING, J.

FULD, C.J., dissents and votes to affirm on the opinion at the Appellate Division.

NOTES

1. In *Schwartz v. Marien*, 37 N.Y.2d 487, 373 N.Y.S.2d 122, 335 N.E.2d 334 (1975), ownership and control in a closely held corporation with a four-member board was equally divided between two families. One member died, and the other family filled his vacancy, giving that family control of the board. The controlling family then approved a sale of treasury stock to themselves, which also gave them voting control and assured future control of the board. The New York Court of Appeals held that, even though preemptive rights did not apply to treasury shares and even if corporate charter did not provide for preemptive rights, the members of the board were required to justify the sale of treasury stock by showing a bona fide business purpose that could not have been achieved by other means. Such action would otherwise be a breach of fiduciary duties to the other shareholders.

2. Do you think that a preemptive rights provision should be included in the charter of a closely held corporation? What happens where the board of directors authorizes the issuance of more shares at a fair price, but the minority is unable to exercise their preemptive right because the cost is too great? Has the minority lost anything?

NEIMARK v. MEL KRAMER SALES, INC.

102 Wis.2d 282, 306 N.W.2d 278 (App.1981), *review denied*, 324 N.W.2d 825 (Wis.1982).

DECKER, CHIEF JUDGE.

This appeal questions whether the trial court erred in this shareholder's derivative action by ordering specific performance of a stock redemption agreement upon death of the principal shareholder of defendant corporation. We vacate the judgment and remand with directions.

Plaintiff seeks specific performance of an agreement for the redemption of stock owned by the late Mel Kramer (Kramer), founder and majority shareholder of Mel Kramer Sales, Inc. (MKS). MKS is a closely-held Wisconsin corporation engaged in the business of selling automotive parts and accessories. The interests of the shareholders are:

Shareholder	Number of Shares	Percentage
Mel Kramer/ Estate of Mel Kramer	1,020	51
Delores Kramer	200	10
Jack Neimark	580	29
Jerome Sadowsky	200	10

Kramer died on December 5, 1976. On May 9, 1977, Delores Kramer, Kramer's widow, was appointed personal representative of his estate. Delores Kramer is president and a director of MKS. Jack Neimark is vice-president and a director. Directors David Gutkin and Sara Lee Begun are relatives of Delores Kramer.

On June 22, 1976, a stock redemption agreement was executed by MKS and its stockholders. The agreement requires MKS to purchase, and a deceased shareholder's estate to sell, all of the deceased shareholder's stock in MKS at $400 per share, less a specified credit.[10] The agreement also provided Delores Kramer with the option to sell her shares to MKS in the event of Kramer's death.

Under the agreement, Kramer's 1,020 shares were to be redeemed by MKS within thirty days after the appointment of his estate's personal representative, Delores Kramer, in the following manner. The redemption price of $408,000, less a specifically provided $50,000 credit, constituting a net price of $358,000, was to be paid in installments of $100,000 at the closing, and the balance in five consecutive annual installments. The first installment after the closing was to be $43,200, with four remaining installments of $53,700, plus interest at 6%. If Delores Kramer elected to redeem her shares, her stock was to be purchased at the same per-share price payable in two installments of $40,000, on the sixth and seventh anniversaries of the closing, plus interest at 6% after five years.

The agreement provided that the $100,000 payment for Kramer's shares was to be funded by a life insurance policy on Kramer's life. Upon Kramer's death, MKS received the $100,000 proceeds from the life insurance policy, and it was reflected in MKS's retained earnings as of December 31, 1976.

The agreement also provided that if MKS did not have sufficient surplus or retained earnings to purchase the deceased shareholder's stock, the parties would contribute the necessary capital to enable MKS to lawfully redeem the decedent's shares. It was also agreed that the parties would be entitled to specific performance of the agreement.

After Kramer's death, Delores Kramer indicated a reluctance to have MKS redeem the shares owned by her husband's estate. Neimark insisted that MKS redeem the estate's shares, and on May 23, 1977, the board of directors met to consider Neimark's demand. The MKS attorney who was the author of the stock redemption agreement was present at this meeting and explained to the board that redemption of the stock by MKS would violate sec. 180.385(1), Stats.[11] The board voted 3–1 not to purchase the Kramer estate's shares. Neimark, of course, cast the losing vote.

---

10. The $50,000 credit was funded by a group life insurance policy paid to Kramer's beneficiary.

11. Section 180.385(1), Stats., provides:

180.385 Right of corporation to acquire and dispose of its own shares.

On November 30, 1978, Neimark commenced an action for specific performance of the 1976 agreement and alternatively, sought monetary damages. The first claim was derivative on behalf of MKS, pursuant to sec. 180.405, Stats; the second claim was personal.

Subsequently, a third party offered to purchase the business for $1,000,000. Neimark conditioned his approval of the sale on the requirement that Delores Kramer and the Kramer estate receive proceeds equal only to the redemption price of the shares which was substantially less than the tendered per-share price. The defendants counterclaimed in Neimark's action and sought an order declaring that Neimark was entitled to receive only his ratable share of the proceeds of any sale of the business, which denied him the redemption agreement benefits. The trial court dismissed Neimark's personal claim, but ordered specific performance of the stock redemption agreement under the derivative claim. The counterclaim was dismissed.

Defendants present three issues for our consideration:

(1) did the failure to perform the stock redemption agreement cause injury to the corporation sufficient to provide a basis for the shareholder's derivative claim;

(2) did the trial court correctly conclude that MKS could lawfully redeem the estate's shares under secs. 180.385(1), 180.02(11), and 180.02(14), Stats; and

(3) would specific performance of the redemption agreement be inequitable?

A fundamental requirement of a stockholder's derivative action is an injury or wrong to the corporation. Shelstad v. Cook, 77 Wis.2d 547, 553, 253 N.W.2d 517, 521 (1977); Rose v. Schantz, 56 Wis.2d 222, 229, 201 N.W.2d 593, 598 (1972). In the context of this case, we view the existence of injury or wrong to MKS as a question of mixed fact and law. The trial court found that the failure of MKS to perform its agreement to redeem the Mel Kramer stock constituted an injury to MKS, because such conduct neglected to take advantage of a $50,000 credit upon the purchase price of

---

2. (1) Unless otherwise provided in the articles of incorporation, a corporation shall have the right to purchase, take, receive, or otherwise acquire, hold, own, pledge, transfer, or otherwise dispose of its own shares; provided that no such acquisition, directly or indirectly, of its own shares for a consideration other than its own shares of equal or subordinate rank shall be made unless all of the following conditions are met:

(a) At the time of such acquisition the corporation is not and would not thereby be rendered insolvent;

(b) The net assets of the corporation remaining after such acquisition would be not less than the aggregate preferential amount payable in the event of voluntary liquidation to the holders of shares having preferential rights to the assets of the corporation in the event of liquidation; and

(c) 1. Such acquisition is authorized by the articles of incorporation or by the affirmative vote or the written consent of the holders of at least a majority of the outstanding shares of the same class and of each class entitled to equal or prior rank in the distribution of assets in the event of voluntary liquidation; or

(2) Such acquisition is authorized by the board of directors and the corporation has unreserved and unrestricted earned surplus equal to the cost of such shares . . . . .

the stock, and hazarded the prospect of acquisition of the stock by outsiders. We observe that such omission also sacrificed the utilization of the financial advantage to MKS of acquisition of the stock over a five-year period at a low interest rate.

The trial court's findings are basically grounded upon the terms of the stock redemption agreement. Since that evidence is undisputed and not in conflict with other evidence, we need not accord special deference to those findings. Nonetheless, we are in complete agreement with the trial court's conclusion that failure to perform the agreement resulted in economic injury to the corporation.

Section 180.385(1), Stats., prohibits, inter alia, acquisition by a corporation of its own stock if the corporation would thereby be rendered insolvent. "Insolvent" is defined in sec. 180.02(14) as the "inability of a corporation to pay its debts as they become due in the usual course of its business." The purpose of prohibiting own stock acquisition by a corporation if it would thereby be rendered insolvent is to protect the creditors, preferred security holders, and in some cases, common stockholders whose stock is not acquired, from director action which would strip funds from the corporation and create a distributive preference to the stockholder whose stock is acquired.

In the context of this case, we view the question of whether MKS would be rendered insolvent by performance of the stock redemption agreement as a mixed question of law and fact. To the extent that the evidence with respect to factual matters is in conflict, we defer to the factual determination by the trial court unless we find it contrary to the great weight and clear preponderance of the evidence. Zapuchlak v. Hucal, 82 Wis.2d 184, 192, 262 N.W.2d 514, 518 (1978).

The trial court's finding of fact, that performance of the stock redemption agreement would not render the corporation insolvent, is supported by ample evidence, and is not contrary to the great weight and clear preponderance of the evidence. The evidence establishes the fact that the corporation had the ability to pay its debts as they became due. In arriving at that conclusion, the trial court is not restricted to analyzing the cash and cash-equivalent assets of the corporation. The flow of cash to maintain solvency can be generated by a multitude of means other than cash generated solely from sales.

In this case, MKS had a $275,000 line of credit with a local bank. Its annual financial statements for 1976, 1977, and 1978, and the May 31, 1979, financial statement, disclose no inability of MKS to pay its debts as they became due if the redemption agreement had been performed.

Upon Kramer's death, it became the obligation of MKS to redeem his stock, provided the corporation could comply with sec. 180.385(1), Stats., with respect to solvency. We agree with the trial court's finding of fact that it could. To the extent that the finding also constitutes a conclusion of law, we also agree.

Contrary to the English rule, American courts at common law generally permit a corporation to acquire its own shares. The American rule has undergone harsh criticism because of the opportunity it affords to prefer selected stockholder/sellers and strip funds from the corporation to the disadvantage of preferred security interest holders, other common stockholders, and creditors. The rule sought protection for those persons by vaguely requiring that the purchase be "without prejudice" to their interests. Steven v. Hale–Haas Corp., 249 Wis. 205, 231, 23 N.W.2d 620, 632 (1946); Koeppler v. Crocker Chair Co., 200 Wis. 476, 480–81, 228 N.W. 130, 132 (1930). Additional statutory restrictions resulted and culminated in the two major restraints (for the purposes of this case): the purchase must be made out of earned surplus and cannot be made if insolvency, in the equity sense, is present or would result. "(I)nsolvency in the equity sense has always meant an inability of the debtor to pay his debts as they mature. Under the Bankruptcy Act it means an insufficiency of assets at a fair valuation to pay the debts." Finn v. Meighan, 325 U.S. 300, 303, 65 S.Ct. 1147, 1149, 89 L.Ed. 1624 (1945). The surplus and insolvency tests were incorporated in § 6 of the Model Business Corporation Act which formed the basis of the revision of the Wisconsin Business Corporation Law in the early 1950's. Section 180.385, Stats., adopts surplus and insolvency tests. Purchase of shares is permitted if: "At the time of such acquisition the corporation is not and would not thereby be rendered insolvent." Sec. 180.385(1)(a), Stats.

The self-evident applicability of the insolvency test at the time of acquisition of the stock is not equally self-evident in the case of an installment purchase. Considerations of "corporate flexibility" in the acquisition of its stock for legitimate purposes, balanced by "protection for creditors," led the majority of American courts to apply the insolvency test contemporaneously with each installment payment. The Model Business Corporation Act § 6 has been amended to specifically so provide. Although that specific change has not been incorporated in sec. 180.385(1)(a), Stats., we agree with the reasoning of the majority of American courts that the protection of the corporation's creditors requires that the insolvency limitation be applied both at the time of purchase and when each installment payment is made pursuant to the purchase agreement. When the payment is actually made, the assets leave the corporation and concomitantly the loss of financial protection occurs. If insolvency results or would result, the purchase may constitute a fraudulent conveyance. In any event, the hazard of fraud to creditors is too great to permit the insolvency test to be applied at times remote to payment for the share repurchase.

Section 180.385(1)(a), Stats., recognized the problem inherent in the single application of the insolvency test and achieved flexibility by prohibiting a purchase resulting in a corporation that "is" insolvent or "would ... be" rendered insolvent. Thus, flexibility is achieved by the statute in its application of the insolvency test to each purchase payment.

When applying the insolvency test at the stage of each payment for a stock repurchase to achieve creditor protection, consistency suggests that the amount of each payment, not the total purchase price, should be a component of the determination of solvency. The weight of authority has so applied the tests and we adopt that method of application. That method is in accord with the equity sense insolvency test expressly prescribed by secs. 180.02(11) and 180.385(1)(a), Stats.

Defendants have not demonstrated insolvency in the equity sense to the trial court or to us. Our review of the corporate financial statements in evidence discloses no arguable claim of insolvency in the equity sense. The only claim of MKS's insolvency made by defendants is premised upon a deduction of the total stock redemption purchase price from the corporate assets, thereby creating a balance sheet negative net worth, although the installment payments of the purchase price are spread over five years. We reject the argument because it applies a bankruptcy rather than equity insolvency test, and is contrary to secs. 180.02(11) and 180.385(1)(a), Stats.[12]

The second limitation upon the corporate repurchase of its stock pertinent to this case is the restriction that "the corporation has unreserved and unrestricted earned surplus equal to the cost of such shares." Sec. 180.385(1)(c)2., Stats. In this respect, the Wisconsin Business Corporation Law generally follows its paradigm, the Model Business Corporation Act. Earned surplus is defined in sec. 180.02(11).[13] In this case, the parties do not dispute the amount of earned surplus.

Our review of the record again establishes the following undisputed evidence with respect to paid-up capital stock, retained earnings, and total stockholders' equity.

	12/31 1976	12/31 1977	12/31 1978	5/31 1979
Paid-up Capital Stock	69,400	69,400	69,400	69,400
Retained Earnings	246,409	276,073	317,586	317,584
Current Earnings		31,575		
Stockholders' Equity	315,809	345,473	386,986	418,559

We subtract projected payments pursuant to the stock redemption agreement.

Retained and Current Earnings Adjusted to Reflect Deducted Installment Payments	276,073	217,586	205,961	

12.　The modernized corporation statutes of Maryland, North Carolina, and Texas apply a bankruptcy insolvency test in addition to an equity insolvency test.

13.　For the purpose of this case, earned surplus can be considered to be the retained earnings of the corporation.

Installment Payments Without Interest	100,000	43,200	53,700
Net Retained Earnings	176,073	174,386	152,261
Credit	50,000		

Historically, the statutory insolvency cutoff test evolved from the "no prejudice to creditors" rule. Dissatisfaction with the limited effectiveness of that test resulted in the formulation of the surplus cutoff test to be applied in conjunction with the insolvency cutoff test.

The same problem arose with the application of the surplus cutoff test that developed in applying the insolvency cutoff test: in the case of an installment purchase, should the surplus test be applied at the time of purchase or at the time cash payment is made? Most cases demonstrate little effort to distinguish between the methods of applying both tests and resolve the question by the easier and more convenient method of applying both tests in the same fashion.

For example, the effect of the Fourth Circuit Court of Appeals' holding in Mountain State Steel Foundries, Inc. v. Commissioner, 284 F.2d 737 (1960), was to treat an installment repurchase transaction as if each successive installment constituted an independent purchase transaction by applying the surplus test at the time of each payment. In re Matthews Construction Co., 120 F.Supp. 818 (S.D.Cal.1954), also involved application of the surplus cutoff test and like Mountain State, indiscriminately applied the reasoning found in Robinson v. Wangemann, 75 F.2d 756 (5th Cir.1935), that a contract of sale was executory until each payment was made in cash, and therefore applied the surplus cutoff test to each installment payment.

Professor Herwitz discusses a number of reasons for applying the surplus to the time of purchase rather than at each installment payment. We agree with his view that the statutory surplus cutoff rule should be applied only once, and at the time of purchase, for the following reasons:

(1) unlike the equity insolvency test, a surplus test does not center upon current liabilities;

(2) unlike the application of the insolvency test, the surplus test is analogous to a purchase for cash and a loan of the unpaid cash price back to the corporation;

(3) installment application of the surplus test could bar performance of a valid obligation of the corporation to the selling stockholder but permit the corporation to disburse funds to current stockholders;

(4) the statutory requirement that surplus be restricted by such a purchase agreement could be frustrated by a construction that would require restriction only on an installment-by-installment basis and permit distributions to shareholders even though the surplus was insufficient to consummate the purchase agreement;

(5) in the manner described in (4), a limited amount of surplus could be used to justify the purchase of an unlimited amount of stock;

(6) when applied to installment payments, the surplus test could be continued indefinitely with current stockholders receiving distributions, putting the selling stockholder in limbo without the status of either creditor or stockholder;

(7) if a default in an installment is compelled by the surplus test, the selling stockholder could possibly obtain a windfall return of all of stock, including the part for which payment had already been made;

(8) a creditor with knowledge of the purchase agreement could be unprotected by installment application of the statutory surplus test limitation, Atlanta & Walworth Butter & Cheese Ass'n v. Smith, 141 Wis. 377, 123 N.W. 106 (1909);

(9) if interest has been deducted in computing corporate net income, application of the surplus test upon an installment basis to the interest on the purchase price is unsupportable because it would take interest into account twice;

(10) the unpaid selling stockholder is given no consideration, at least to the extent of undistributed surplus, over the other stockholders who are the beneficiaries of the stock purchase; and

(11) the application of the surplus cutoff test at the outset of an installment purchase would in no way hamper or alter the installment application of the equity insolvency test.

We consider it a futile exercise to attempt to ground our decision upon the subtleties and nuances of semantic lexicography in defining "purchase," "acquisition," and the other acquisitory words of transfer used in the statute. The above reasons persuade us that the application of the surplus cutoff test is required to be timed to the purchase rather than the payment of cash. Such a construction comports with the need for corporate flexibility in acquiring its own stock for legitimate purposes and the protection of creditors and holders of other securities of the corporation.

The Minnesota and Texas Supreme Courts, and the Ninth Circuit Court of Appeals, have taken similar views in Tracy v. Perkins–Tracy Printing Co., 278 Minn. 159, 153 N.W.2d 241 (1967); Williams v. Nevelow, 513 S.W.2d 535 (Tex.1974); and Walsh v. Paterna, 537 F.2d 329 (9th Cir.1976). Although differing state statutory formulations were involved, like Wisconsin's, the statutes do not specifically resolve the issues presented there or here.

Although it is apparent from the MKS financial statements that application of the surplus cutoff test upon an installment basis would not have precluded specific performance as ordered by the trial court, application of the test at the outset will preclude specific performance upon the basis of the facts as presented to us. However, we note that the stock redemption agreement provides:

(f) Insufficient Corporate Surplus. If the Corporation does not have sufficient surplus or retained earnings to permit it to lawfully purchase all of such shares, each of the parties shall promptly take such measures as are required to reduce the capital of the Corporation or to take such other steps as may be necessary in order to enable the Corporation to lawfully purchase and pay for the Decedent's shares.

We vacate the judgment of the circuit court and remand for further proceedings consistent with this opinion. The circuit court is directed to apply the surplus cutoff test to the time of specific performance of the stock redemption agreement if it concludes that the evidence justifies specific performance. Because we adopt an application of the statute which has not heretofore been explicated, we think it fair to permit the parties to offer current financial data with respect to MKS and the ability of the parties to the redemption agreement to take the necessary steps to enable the corporation to lawfully purchase and pay for the redeemed stock. Such evidence will enable a current evaluation of the propriety of specific performance. In the event the trial court deems specific performance appropriate, it shall make the necessary findings and requirements with regard to providing sufficient earned surplus and assuring solvency as a condition to specific performance.

We reject the defendants' claim of applicability of the business judgment rule to the facts of this case. That rule accords judicial deference to a business judgment but is generally applicable to acquisition of a corporation's own stock where the board of directors has authorized the acquisition without approval of the stockholders, unlike the present circumstance where all of the stockholders consented and bound themselves to the stock redemption agreement.

Defendant Delores Kramer claims that enforcement of the stock redemption agreement would be inequitable. We disagree. The requirement of adequate surplus at purchase will provide a restricted surplus account to the extent of the unpaid balance of the purchase price. It is true that she becomes a creditor of the corporation and is subject to the hazard of a business failure. She also received the benefit of a compelled market for her stock, had she desired to liquidate her interest in MKS. Her predecessor owner executed the agreement which expressly provided for specific performance. The transaction by its terms made the seller a creditor of the business. Obviously Mel Kramer thought the agreement fairly balanced the corporate obligation to acquire the stock with the owner's opportunity to liquidate an investment in a corporation whose majority stockholder and principal officer had died.

Judgment vacated and cause remanded for further proceedings consistent with this opinion.

NOTE

Several other cases have considered whether redemption agreements were enforceable under state dividend tests. *See generally* Wolff v. Heidritter Lumber Co., 112 N.J.Eq. 34, 163 A. 140 (N.J.Ch.1932) (selling shareholder had a valid claim in bankruptcy where corporation became insolvent before completing installment payments); Williams v. Nevelow, 513 S.W.2d 535 (Tex.1974) (selling shareholder could execute on notes where at the time of the exchange of the corporation's secured note for its stock, the corporation was solvent and had unrestricted earned surplus in excess of the amount of the note and where the exchange did not cause the bankruptcy of the corporation). *But see* Mountain State Steel Foundries v. Commissioner, 284 F.2d 737 (4th Cir.1960) (West Virginia Statute required surplus test be met when each installment is paid).

CHAPTER SEVEN

MERGER FINANCING, APPRAISAL RIGHTS, AND VALUATION

■ ■ ■

Chapter objectives

- To understand how appraisal rights protect dissenting shareholders and to identify the transactional contexts in which minority shareholder may exercise these rights.

- To identify and apply the standards of review used by state courts to evaluate appraisal remedies.

- To appreciate the alternative methods used to value a corporation and the range of issues presented by these methods, including the difference between going concern and liquidation values.

SECTION 1. MERGER FINANCING

A key part of the merger and acquisition process is funding of the acquisition. In larger acquisitions, hundreds of millions, or even billions, of dollars may be required. Even the smallest acquisition of a closely held corporation will usually focus on the financing requirements, once the price is settled. The financial arrangements for the acquisition may involve a number of sources, ranging from a simple cash purchase to a complicated exchange of stock and other securities.

If a cash acquisition is being made, the purchaser must have a source of funds for the payment. This may require incurring additional debt that will affect the viability of the surviving corporation. If an exchange of stock is used, the parties must decide on the ratio at which stock will be exchanged, taking into account that the price of the stock will fluctuate between the time the merger is negotiated and the actual exchange is made. Often, complex merger agreements are used to set the exchange ratios because the respective stock prices of the merging entities may fluctuate during the period required for shareholder approval and regulatory review. The merger agreement may include a "walkaway" provision that will allow either party to cancel the merger if the stock prices of the merging companies become so disparate that the deal is no longer economically viable.

Some shareholders may object to a merger or its financing terms by seeking an alternative appraisal of the value of the target company from a state court. Appraisal rights may also be triggered by amendments to the articles of incorporation that modify the fundamental rights of shareholders. The appraisal rights of these dissenting shareholders raise many questions about the valuation methods used when exercising these rights.

SECTION 2. VALUING EXCHANGES OF STOCK OR OTHER SECURITIES

IN RE RJR NABISCO, INC. SHAREHOLDERS LITIGATION

Fed. Sec. L. Rep. (CCH) ¶ 94,194 (Del.Ch.1989).

WILLIAM T. ALLEN, CHANCELLOR.

* * * RJR is a Delaware corporation formed following the 1985 merger of RJ Reynolds Tobacco Company and Nabisco Brands, Inc. The Company's principal offices are now in Atlanta, Georgia. Through its subsidiaries, which include RJ Reynolds, Nabisco Brands, Inc., Del Monte Corporation and Planters Life Savers Company, the Company holds leading positions in the tobacco, food and consumer products industries. The Company has 225,519,911 shares of common stock and 1,251,904 shares of preferred stock issued and outstanding. Immediately prior to the events here in question, RJR's common stock was trading on the New York Stock Exchange in the mid 50's.

At an October 19, 1988 RJR board of directors meeting, F. Ross Johnson, speaking on behalf of the Management Group, informed the board that that group was seeking to develop a transaction to take the Company private by means of a leveraged buyout. He suggested a price of $75 per share. Mr. Charles E. Hugel, the Chairman of RJR's board but not an officer of the Company, had had some advance notice that this subject would be brought up at the meeting and had prepared for it to the limited extent of having invited Peter Atkins, Esquire, an attorney with experience with transactions of the type proposed, present.

On October 20, 1988, the board issued a press release announcing the proposed transaction. It also announced the appointment of a special committee of the board comprising Charles E. Hugel as Chairman, John D. Macomber as Vice Chairman, Martin S. Davis, William S. Anderson and Albert L. Butler, Jr. The Special Committee immediately retained two financial advisors, Dillon, Read & Co. (the Company's regular investment banker) and Lazard Freres, Inc. The Committee also retained Mr. Atkins' firm, Skadden, Arps, Slate, Meagher & Flom, to render legal advice to the

Committee and to the Company's outside directors. The Delaware firm of Young, Conaway, Stargatt & Taylor was retained as special legal counsel to the Company.

On October 24, KKR, who had purportedly earlier been rebuffed in an effort to entice management to join it in a leveraged buyout, informed the Special Committee that it was planning to extend an offer to acquire the Company for $90 per share in cash and securities. On October 27, KKR commenced a tender offer at $90 per share cash for up to 87% of the Company's stock. The offer stated that the balance of RJR's shares were to be exchanged for new securities in a second step merger.

On November 2, the Special Committee issued a press release announcing that it was interested in receiving proposals to acquire the Company. On November 7, the Committee disseminated Rules and Procedures for Submission of Proposals. This provided, inter alia, for a deadline of 5:00 p.m. November 18, 1988 for the final submission of bids. The rules specified that "[t]he rules and procedures outlined above are intended to constitute a single round of bidding. Any Proposal should reflect the potential purchasers highest offer." The Special Committee also stated that it "encourage[d] proposals that provided to current RJR shareholders a prospect for a substantial common stock related interest in the purchasing entity."

Three bids were in the hands of the Special Committee on the appointed deadline of November 18. The Management Group bid was valued by the Management Group at $100 per share, consisting of $90 in cash, $6 preferred stock and an equity interest of $4. KKR's bid came in at a claimed $94 per share, ($75 in cash, $11 in preferred stock and $8 in convertible debt which would convert into 25% of the purchasing entity's equity). The third bidder was the First Boston Corporation. Its proposal, while not fully developed, was in some respects the most interesting. It contemplated an acquisition of the Company's tobacco business in 1989 for approximately $15.75 billion in cash and warrants, and an installment sale of the Company's food businesses immediately (by year end 1988), with the proceeds of such sale to be held for the account of the Company's shareholders. The total value of the First Boston Group proposal, if it could be realized, was estimated to be in the range of $98 to $110 in cash and cash equivalents, securities valued at $5, and warrants valued at $2–$3. The warrants would entitle RJR shareholders to acquire up to 20% of the Company's tobacco business.

The First Boston approach was innovative, appealing and problematic. Its primary appeal lay in the fact that the installment sale mechanism would provide tax advantages estimated to be as high as $3 billion. There were two difficulties, however, with this proposal. First, its terms were not fully worked out. Second, impending changes in the tax code created time constraints which placed the realization of those tax benefits at risk.

In view of the fact that the First Boston Group's proposal was at this point potentially the most attractive, and that more time was necessary to develop it further, the Committee decided to extend the bidding until November 29. In its press release announcing the terms of the extension, it also published the terms of the three bids it had received, including the percentage of potential equity participation each contemplated.

The Special Committee met with the three bidders at various times during the week of November 21. Bids were actively solicited by the Committee's investment bankers, and there is testimony that the bidders were reminded that the Committee was concerned that a significant equity component be provided to shareholders.

At 5:00 p.m. November 29, the Committee again received three bids. The Management Group raised its bid only minimally; it valued its new bid at $101 per share ($88 cash; $9 preferred stock; $4 convertible preferred). It was the lowest of the three bids. KKR's bid jumped appreciably to a claimed value of $106 ($80 cash; $17 preferred stock; $8 automatically converting debenture), the First Boston Group's bid was said to be in a range from $103 to $115.

The Special Committee concluded early on that the First Boston Group's bid, while attractive, was subject to too much uncertainty to be practicable. Between the remaining bids, KKR's bid plainly appeared to be the higher if the securities included in the bids were worth what the bidders claimed. The Committee determined that before it would choose between these two bids it would seek to assure that KKR's higher bid was worth what it claimed. Accordingly, it directed its lawyers and investment bankers to negotiate concerning the terms of the securities and the details of a merger agreement. This was done during the course of the evening of the 29th and the morning of the 30th.

Some time late in the evening of November 29, the Management Group learned of these talks, apparently from a newspaper reporter. The Management Group apparently realized that it had made a tactical error in raising its bid only $1 when, as later events show, it was willing to pay substantially more. It attempted to recoup by advising the Committee that it had yet to submit its best bid. It requested an opportunity to do so. This request was not responded to before the Management Group pressed ahead late in the following morning to present another bid.

The Special Committee reconvened at 7:45 a.m. on November 30, together with its financial advisors and six independent outside directors of RJR. Once convened, this group, with a few recesses, remained in session throughout the day.

The independent directors were first informed that the terms of the merger agreement with KKR were essentially complete, but that KKR had expressed displeasure because of its suspicion that its bid had been leaked to the press and from there to the Management Group. In light of its fears, KKR had requested, first informally and then by letter, that its bid be acted upon that day. The letter required action on the bid by 1:00 p.m November 30. This assertedly created concern in the minds of some of the directors that the KKR bid might be withdrawn if not acted upon in a timely manner.

At some time early on in the meeting on November 30, before the Committee turned to its consideration of the competing bids, the meeting was informed that a letter had been hand-delivered from the Management Group protesting the board's negotiation the night before of the KKR bid as a final offer. The letter stated the Management Group's willingness to discuss all aspects of its proposals. The Committee agreed to waive the terms of the rules and procedures and consider new bids from both parties should such bids be forthcoming. It did not, however, invite or encourage further bidding. Further bidding did, however, eventuate; before describing it, I turn to a brief outline of the alternatives before the Committee on the morning of the 30th.

The KKR proposal of $106, made on the night of November 29, consisted of $80 in cash, $17 in cumulative exchangeable pay-in-kind preferred stock and $8 in face value senior converting debentures, which KKR valued at $9 because of the conversion feature.

The terms of the KKR PIK preferred eventually agreed to were designed to achieve the aim that the security would trade at par at some point following distribution.[1] The concern was that a massive public sale of securities, anticipated in order to refinance the bridge loans used to fund the purchase of RJR shares, would push down the value of the preferred stock. This problem was addressed by a provision to reset the rate after the market had absorbed the securities needed to pay off the bridge loans. The Committee also sought to achieve as brief an interval as possible in which the yield on the preferred would float. KKR eventually agreed to reset the rate at the earlier of one year following the refinancing of the bridge loan or two years after the tender offer closed. In light of these agreements, the Committee's investment advisors informed the Committee of their view that the securities should trade at close to their face value of $17 per share.

The senior converting debentures were to convert automatically into common stock of the Company at the end of three years unless the holder "opts out" during a two week option period which then arises. If none of the debenture holders were to opt out, the debenture holders as a class would own 25% of the equity of the Company at the end of four years. These securities were to pay interest in kind for the first ten years following their issuance, and generate cash distributions thereafter. The

---

1. The terms of the pay-in-kind preferred are as follows: Initially, that is, for the first six years, the stock pays dividends "in kind." The dividend rate would initially be a floating rate set at 5 1/2% over a basket of interest rates (defined as the highest of (i) the three month Treasury bill rate, (ii) the 10 year Treasury bond rate, and (iii) the 30 year Treasury bond rate), subject to a ceiling of 16 5/8% and a floor of 12 5/8%. The dividend rate is subject to a reset mechanism that will reset the rate at a fixed rate within one year of any refinancing of the bridge loans used to finance the transaction or two years after consummation of the tender offer. The fixed rate is to be set in an arbitration proceeding among the advisors to KKR, the advisors to the Company, and, if necessary, a third party investment banker. The hope is to permit the security to trade at par at the time the fixed rate is determined.

interest rate was to float initially, subject to a reset identical to the preferred stock reset. The rate initially would be approximately 14.5%.

On the morning of the 30th, before the Management Group presented further proposals, the Special Committee also considered the apparently lower bid, the Management Group's November 29 bid of $101, consisting of $88 per share in cash, $9 cumulative PIK preferred stock, and $4 face amount 13% junior convertible exchangeable preferred stock.

At the time of submission,the terms of the cumulative PIK preferred stock were not final. The other security proposed—the 13% junior convertible exchangeable preferred stock—would initially accrue, but not pay, dividends calculated at a rate of 13%. By its terms, this stock could be converted at any time into a maximum of 15% of the fully diluted stock of the surviving tobacco entity. The stock, however, had a "call" feature that allowed the Company to redeem it at any time at par plus accrued and unpaid dividends. RJR's investment advisors were of the view that this unrestricted call provided the issuer with the ability to destroy the equity aspects of the security before it would make financial sense to exercise them. This was said to deprive Managements convertible preferred of any premium value in addition to its value as a straight debt instrument. This security remained unchanged in the final bid and was assigned a value of $2–$2.50.

In addition to the two bids before it on the morning of November 30, the Special Committee and the outside directors also analyzed the value of a recapitalization of the Company. They concluded that neither a breakup nor a recapitalization would yield value to shareholders in excess of the $106 being offered by KKR.

Having reviewed the three alternatives, the Special Committee invited Messrs. Kravis and Roberts to make a presentation to the meeting concerning their plans should they acquire the Company. Following the presentation, which took place around 11:00 a.m., Mr. Hugel asked Mr. Roberts to extend the 1:00 p.m. deadline for consideration of KKR's bid. Mr. Roberts gave no assurances that the deadline would be extended.

Following a brief recess, the meeting was reconvened at about 12:30 p.m. A representative of the Management Group then reported to the Committee orally that the Management Group was raising its bid to $108 per share consisting of $84 cash, $20 in PIK preferred stock, and $4 in convertible preferred (i.e., $4 less cash and $11 more preferred stock than the bid of the prior evening). No terms for the component securities were given, but it was stated that the Management Group was willing to negotiate all terms, including price, with the Committee.

With this in mind, the Special Committee told KKR that another bid had been received and again requested an extension of the 1:00 p.m. deadline. This time an extension until 2:00 p.m. was granted.[2] The

---

2. In consideration, KKR got the Company to agree to reimburse KKR's expenses up to $.20 per share in the event that no merger agreement was signed between the Company and KKR.

minutes of the November 30 board meeting reflect that the Management Group had been asked to make its highest and best bid shortly after 1:00 p.m. Mr. Hugel testified that the directors discussed the need to obtain their highest and best bid and agreed that this was to be relayed to the Management Group. James A. Stern, an officer of Shearson Lehman involved in the process, testified that the Management Group was told about 1:00 p.m. or 1:30 p.m. to "[s]harpen your pencils and put your best bid on the table." In response to which the Management Group "reached back and submitted a final proposal, final bid that again had $84 a share in cash, a $24 a share of PIK preferred and the same 15% equity interest via the convertible preferred."

The Management Group's last proposal was submitted to the Committee shortly before 1:30 p.m. The Management Group asserted it to be worth $112; the additional $4 of value was all additional preferred stock, raising the face amount of the PIK preferred securities from $20 to $24. Like the previous bid, Management's $112 offer left open certain significant terms, including provisions of the PIK preferred stock and the convertible preferred. As it had done the previous evening with KKR's $106 bid, the Special Committee began negotiating with the Management Group to determine if it could achieve terms for the securities offered which would allow them to trade at their stated value.

In view of KKR's actions in extracting assurance of $.20 per share expense reimbursement provision before it agreed to an extension, the Special Committee and its advisors assert that they were concerned that KKR might simply withdraw its bid altogether at this point. This would, it is said, have left the Committee in a markedly worse negotiating position than the position it was in with competing bids on the table.

Assertedly in order to protect the shareholders from the risk of losing the bird in hand, after receiving the Management Group's face value $112 proposal, the Committee offered to KKR to enter into the now fully negotiated merger agreement with it at $106 per share, subject to a $1 topping fee should the Company accept another offer within seven days, but with the agreement that no further expenses would be paid. It also offered KKR the opportunity to bid again prior to the acceptance of any other offer. In response to the Committee's offer to enter into a contract, KKR declined but delivered a revised bid which it claimed to be worth $108 per share. The new bid, which was not subject to a deadline, consisted of $80 per share in cash, $18 PIK preferred and converting debentures which KKR valued at $10. The terms of the PIK preferred remained the same as those of the previous bid, but the conversion period for the other security, the automatically converting debentures, was extended another year which was the basis for KKR's assertion that the same face amount of converting debt was now worth $1 per share more.

KKR agreed, on its part, to reduce the topping fee provision in its proposed merger agreement from $1 to $.75 per share.

The Committee's advisors gave their preliminary opinion that the revised KKR bid was worth between $107 and $108 per share.

There were no on-going discussions with KKR for the remainder of the afternoon of November 30; during that time, the Special Committee's investment advisors negotiated with the Management Group in an attempt to improve the terms of the Management Group's securities. Specifically, there was an attempt to get the Management Group to agree to tie the length of the reset period on its PIKs to the refinancing of the bridge loans used to finance the stock acquisition. The Management Group declined to do so. Its PIK preferred had the potential, indeed the likelihood, of not being reset to the market for almost three years.

Attempts to increase the lower rate on Management's PIK were unavailing. The Management Group also declined to put a reset mechanism on its convertible preferred.

By about 6:00 p.m., when the Special Committee reconvened to confer concerning the discussions with the Management Group, it was reported to the Special Committee that no significant progress had been made with respect to the terms of the Management Group's securities. It was further reported by the Committee's investment advisors that in its view, the securities were unlikely to trade at the values assigned them by the Management Group. The Committee apparently decided to return to both bidders one last time. * * *

... KKR responded to this further invitation after receiving reassurances that the members of the Management Group would not be in attendance at any board meeting at which the offers were considered. It submitted a merger agreement with its final bid of $109; $1 more in cash. This final bid consisted of $81 in cash, $18 PIK preferred, and $10 converting debentures. KKR placed a 30–minute fuse on this offer when it was submitted.

The Management Group replied to a last communication from the Committee that "they had our final proposal." It is possible, however, that an imperfect communication occurred at this point. The Committee's advisors had been negotiating with the Management Group concerning the reset provision of the preferred stock. The communication at about 5:00 p.m. or 6:00 p.m. on November 30 may have been thought to relate only to that subject or may have been thought to relate to all subjects concerning the bids. * * *

The Special Committee's investment advisors, Lazard Freres and Dillon Read, met with the Special Committee after both "final" bids were received. It estimated the Management Group's proposal to be worth between $108.50 and $109 per share, based on its conclusions that (1) the Management Group's PIK preferred stock should be discounted approximately $2 per share because of the longer term of its reset provisions, its below market dividend rate, and its weaker yield curve protections; and (2) that the Management Group's convertible preferred should be discounted from $4 to $2.50 because it had no reset mechanism, also carried a low dividend rate and was callable at any time. The fluctuating rate on the Management Group security was pegged to LIBOR (London Inter–Bank Offering Rate) which is a short term rate, as opposed to the "basket" of rates against which the KKR security was measured. By opting for the highest of several rates with different maturities to fix the current interest rate, as opposed to a single rate, an investor is offered greater protection against market changes with respect to different maturities.

The advisors only discounted the KKR PIK preferred stock between $.50 and $1. With respect to the KKR converting debentures, they advised the Special Committee that they should trade at their estimated value of $10 and determined as a result that the KKR bid was worth approximately $108 to $108.50 per share.

Based on these valuations, the unprecedented size of the debt offerings of high yield securities involved, and the inherent limitations of predicting future markets, the investment advisors concluded that the bids were substantially equivalent. Both investment bankers advised the Committee that, in their view, the Committee could exercise sound business judgment in recommending either offer, and that they were prepared to give fairness opinions on either transaction.

According to the minutes of the meeting (which are attacked as post hoc creations by lawyers for use in litigation), the Committee then reviewed the following factors:

1. the risk that further negotiating with either the management group or KKR could result in the withdrawal of either party from the bidding process;

2. the 15% equity interest in the management group proposal as contrasted with the 25% equity interest in the KKR proposal;

3. the fact that the KKR structure contemplated that the tobacco and a substantial part of the food businesses would remain going forward versus the tobacco only business contemplated by the management group proposal;

4. the greater amount of permanent equity in the KKR proposal;

5. the fact that the amount of PIK securities in both proposals was unprecedented and that there would be an additional $1.5 billion in PIK securities issued in the management group transaction;

6. the fact that the management group proposal provided for $84 in cash per share of common stock while the KKR proposal provided for $81 in cash per share of common stock.

7. the potential issues arising under the Company's debt indentures in connection with the management group's proposal but not in connection with the KKR proposal; and

8. that KKR (but not the management group) was willing to provide for the presentation of benefits for employees whose jobs were terminated as the result of business divestitures.

Based on these considerations, and without attempting to seek a higher bid from either party, the Committee elected to recommend the KKR bid and the board shortly thereafter authorized the execution of the KKR merger agreement that had been negotiated. * * *

The requested preliminary relief importantly involves a preliminary injunction against KKR, although no claim is made that KKR has itself violated any duty that it owed to the RJR shareholders. Nor does the amended complaint contain any allegations that a conspiracy exists which joins KKR in a breach of duties owed by the directors of the Company to the shareholders. The briefs of plaintiffs, inspired no doubt by recent history, now claim that KKR was tipped by the agents of the Special Committee concerning the Committee's desire for an equity participation in the range of 25%–35%. But the record at this stage makes any such claim appear far too flimsy to support provisional acceptance of it for these purposes. Thus, I must treat this application as one in which no reasonable probability has been shown that plaintiffs will be able to prove that KKR has itself committed or participated in a wrong. * * *

In assessing the probability of success of plaintiffs' various claims, I first note that this action constitutes an attack upon a decision made by an apparently disinterested board in the exercise of its statutory power to manage the business and affairs of the corporation. That being apparently the case, the appropriate format or structure for judicial review of the action under attack would be provided by the business judgment rule, Pogostin v. Rice, Del Supr., 480 A.2d 619 (1984) * * *

In reviewing, with respect to bona fides, the Special Committee's decision to accept one of the proposals in the early evening of November 30, two circumstances must be first noted. First, the consideration offered in both proposals contained complex securities not susceptible to intuitive evaluation. Sophisticated and effective business generalists of the type likely to be found on the board of such companies as RJR will seldom have the specialized skills useful to most accurately value such securities. Our law, of course, recognizes the appropriateness of directors relying upon the advice of experts when specialized judgment is necessary as part of a business judgment. See 8 Del. C. § 141(e). In this instance, the Committee did receive the advice of Lazard Freres and of Dillon Read that when the respective securities were appropriately valued, they regarded the bids as substantially equivalent.

Plaintiffs spend a good deal of effort in attacking this judgment. The effort (as it relates to this theory of liability) is to show that the opinion was not only incorrect but was implausible. From this plaintiffs would infer a motive to favor KKR (the unspoken link being the assumption that the bankers detected a preference by the Committee and fell in with it). I have reviewed the competing affidavits by the investment bankers. I cannot conclude that plaintiffs have shown the Lazard Freres or Dillon Read work to be flawed. Briefly, that is because it is quite apparent, even to one with modest sophistication in techniques of financial analysis, that the value of the reset provision for the interest rate of a subordinated security issued in these circumstances (when very large amounts of senior debt is shortly to be issued) is of great importance to the value of the security. It is plausible (more than that really, but I need go no further) that the KKR reset provision made its convertible debentures relatively more valuable than was the Management Group's analogous convertible preferred. This fact, together with the higher rate that the converting debentures were to bear and the fact that the convertibility feature of the Management Group's preferred stock could be mooted by exercise of a call provision at any time (thus diminishing the value of the prospect of a later equity participation), provides quite sufficient bases to conclude that the opinions of the Special Committee's advisors concerning prospective value of the respective packages (which largely reduced to quite different assessments of the relative values of the converting debentures and the convertible preferred) were competent and reached in good faith.

Thus, the fact that the board was faced with what it could reasonably believe were bids that were essentially equivalent from a financial point of view is a relevant circumstance in assessing its good faith n acting as it did.

The second especially relevant circumstance with respect to the Committee's decision to act when it did relates to the fact that the Committee had been place under severe time constraints by KKR in submitting its final proposal—the Committee was given thirty minutes to accept the bid on pain of its being withdrawn. Of course, this may have been an empty threat. I suppose that few thought the chances of such a withdrawal very high but no one, of course, was in a position to assure that it would not happen.

Were it to have happened, it is plain that the recap option would have provided a poor substitute at the range of values the bidding had been driven to. Thus, the Committee would have been left with the Management Group's proposal of substantially equivalent value but with some important terms that were plainly less appealing. * * *

I cannot conclude that plaintiffs have demonstrated a reasonable likelihood that this theory of liability will be sustained. In connection with it, their burden of course will be to establish at final hearing that in electing to sign the KKR proposed merger agreement, the directors were grossly negligent. Aronson v. Lewis, Del. Supr., 473 A.2d 805 (1984); Smith v. Van Gorkom, Del. Supr., 488 A.2d 858 (1985). * * *

SECTION 3. APPRAISAL RIGHTS

Dissenters' appraisal rights developed in response to statutory abrogation of the common law rule that fundamental modifications of shareholder rights required unanimous approval.

"Dissenters' rights statutes were enacted in response to the common-law rule that required unanimous consent from shareholders to make fundamental changes in a corporation. See *Hansen v. 75 Ranch Co.*, 288 Mont. 310, 957 P.2d 32, 37 (1998). Under this rule, minority shareholders could block corporate change by refusing to cooperate in hopes of establishing a nuisance value for their shares... To protect the interests of minority shareholders, the statutes generally permitted a dissenting minority to recover the appraised value of its shares. See *id*. Most recent statutes allow dissenting shareholders to demand that the corporation buy back shares at fair value.

"The basic concept of fair value under a dissenters' rights statute is that the stockholder is entitled to be paid for his or her 'proportionate interest in a going concern.' ... The focus of the valuation 'is not the stock as a commodity, but rather the stock only as it represents a proportionate part of the enterprise as a whole.' *McLoon Oil*, 565 A.2d at 1004. Thus, to find fair value, the trial court must determine the best price a single buyer could reasonably be expected to pay for the corporation as an entirety and prorate this value equally among all shares of its common stock. See *id*. Under this method, all shares of the corporation have the same fair value. See *id*.

"A dissenting shareholder is not in the position of a willing seller, however, and thus, courts have held that fair value cannot be equated with 'fair market value.' See, e.g., *McLoon Oil*, 565 A.2d at 1005; *Hansen*, 957 P.2d at 41. Accordingly, methods of stock valuation used in tax, probate or divorce cases to determine fair market value are inapposite to the determination of 'fair value' under the dissenters' rights statute... A shareholder who disapproves of a proposed merger gives up the right of veto in exchange for the right to be bought out at 'fair value,' not at market value. See *Hansen*, 957 P.2d at 41."

In re 75,629 Shares of Common Stock of Trapp Family Lodge, Inc., 169 Vt. 82, 725 A.2d 927 (1999).

The Model Business Corporation Act § 13.02(a) sets forth the situations in which appraisal rights exist:

    i. merger (except where surviving corporation increases its shares by less than 20%);

    ii. share exchange to which corporation is a party; appraisal rights exist for shareholders whose shares are to be exchanged;

iii. Sale of substantially all of the assets not in the regular course of business;

iv. Amendments to the articles of incorporation which affect certain shareholder fundamental rights:

    a. altering or abolishing preferential rights;

    b. creating, abolishing, or altering redemption rights (including sinking funds);

    c. altering or abolishing preemptive rights;

    d. excluding or limiting shareholder voting rights;

v. Any other matter where the right to dissent is given by the articles, bylaws, or directors' resolution.

The shareholder seeking an appraisal is entitled only to the fair value of the stock. Model Bus. Corp. Act § 13.01 defines fair value in terms of the value immediately before the transaction in question, discounting any change in value due to anticipation of the transaction. The appraiser may thus exclude any appreciation or decrease in value of the shares due to anticipation of the transaction. In essence, fair value is defined in such as way as to defer to the case law. Most of the case law on appraisal rights arose in Delaware. For years, the Delaware "block method" was used.

Valuation of shares under the block method is a numerical computation consisting of three factors. The appraiser then assigns a relative weight to each of the factors in order to calculated a weighted average. The "blocks" of the method are:

1. *Earnings value.* The earnings value is based on past performance and then multiplying annual earnings by a multiple which reflects comparable companies. There is considerable discretion in selecting the multiplier

2. *Market value.* If there is a market for the securities, then the market value will be considered in the appraisal formula. Note that the market is not the sole determinant of the preacquisition value of the securities. Where there is a public market operating with the full disclosure, the Efficient Capital Market Hypothesis would suggest that market value be given a heavy weight in the weighting process. Delaware provides an exception from the right to dissent for shares that are listed on a national securities exchange. Del § 262(b). Presumably, the rationale is that the efficient market exists for a shareholder who does not like the transaction.

3. *Asset value.* The third factor is the assignment of an asset value to the shares. The selection of asset value raises the issue of whether book value (historical cost) or some other valuation such as replacement value, going concern value or liquidation value should be applied. Should the appraiser consider goodwill?

GONSALVES v. STRAIGHT ARROW PUBLISHERS, INC.

701 A.2d 357 (Del.1997).

WALSH, JUSTICE:

* * * The underlying appraisal dispute involves the value of 2,000 shares of the common stock of the respondent Straight Arrow Publishers, Inc. ("SAP") owned by the petitioner, Laurel Gonsalves ("Petitioner"). SAP was founded in 1967 to publish *Rolling Stone,* a magazine focused on pop culture and rock and roll music. Petitioner acquired her shares, 2.3% of SAP's total outstanding, in 1971, while she was employed by SAP. In the late 1970s, a decline in advertising revenue generated by *Rolling Stone* prompted SAP, in 1981, to implement a repositioning plan. This plan was designed to increase the revenue and earnings of *Rolling Stone,* SAP's primary source of earnings at that time and through the time of the merger. In the early 1980s, SAP also became involved in other business ventures, most of which generated losses, and which were discontinued prior to the merger.

In the fall of 1985, Straight Arrow Publishers Holding Company, Inc., a company wholly owned by SAP's founder and majority stockholder, Jann Wenner, made a first step $100 cash tender offer that closed on November 11, 1985. Contemporaneous with the tender offer, Martin Whitman, SAP's expert witness in this action, issued a fairness opinion, concluding that $100 was a fair price. Whitman's opinion was not based on SAP's earnings for the second half of 1985, which were not known at the time. On January 8, 1986, Straight Arrow Publishers Holding Company, Inc. was merged with and into SAP. In the merger, all of SAP's shares were converted into the right to receive $100 per share or were canceled. The merger did not result in a change in corporate control.

* * * At a brief trial conference held on August 21, 1996, the Chancellor advised counsel that it was "[his] inclination and [his] temperamental approach ... to want to accept one expert or the other hook, line and sinker." The court also commented that, if the court engages in "detailed financial analysis," it creates incentives for the parties' experts to "create plausible bargaining ranges" and "drive litigants to the most extreme positions." The Chancellor indicated that in past cases he had made "a few adjustments to the one who I accepted, but I don't want to."

When the matter proceeded to trial it became obvious that the range of difference in the valuation views of the respective experts was quite large. James Kobak, petitioner's expert, valued SAP at the time of the merger at $1,059.37 per share, a figure over ten times the merger price. This calculation was based solely on the value of *Rolling Stone,* which, he concluded, was SAP's sole operating asset, accounting for substantially all of its revenue and earnings. In Kobak's opinion, a magazine is best characterized as an intangible business with relatively few fixed assets and, therefore, should be valued using an earnings capitalization valuation method. Kobak made several adjustments to *Rolling Stone's* reported pre-tax earnings to account for one time expenditures and deferred subscription income. Relying on *Rolling Stone's* adjusted earnings before taxes, Kobak arrived at an earnings base for SAP of $6,002,000. In capitalizing SAP's earnings base, Kobak chose a price/earnings multiple of 14, derived from comparisons of sales of similar magazines and companies. Kobak selected a multiple of 14, which was the highest in the range for the middle 50% for such sales, because, in his view, *Rolling Stone* was well positioned to enjoy increasing profitability as of the merger.

Martin Whitman, respondent's expert, in calculating SAP's earnings base, used a method similar to the Delaware Block Method, analyzing SAP's yearly earnings value, asset value, and market or trading value. The latter two "blocks" were given a weight of 10% each because there was no active market for SAP stock and because, like Kobak, Whitman believes that magazines are essentially intangible businesses whose tangible assets do not reflect the essential value of the company.

Rather than rely solely on the 1985 earnings of *Rolling Stone* to arrive at the value of the "earnings block," Whitman used SAP's five year earnings, ending December 31, 1985.[3] Accordingly, Whitman arrived at an earnings bases of $1,372,755, reflecting earnings before interest and taxes ("EBIT"), and $1,523,846, reflecting earnings before interest, taxes, depreciation and amortization ("EBITDA"). In selecting multiples of 9.5, based on EBIT, and 8.5 based on EBITDA, Whitman analyzed implied capitalization rates of comparable companies with publicly traded stocks, instead of magazine purchases and sales as had Kobak. Whitman believes that these multiples, which are lower than the median multiples for the selected comparable companies, are appropriate due to SAP's relatively small size, dependence on a single print publication, low EBIT and EBITDA margins, volatile operating profits, low level of capital reinvestment, speculative use of its excess cash, non-dividend paying policy, and contingent liabilities, as well as *Rolling Stone's* lower-than-median readership demographics.

Turning to the less weighted components of the analysis, Whitman estimated SAP's trading value by examining the purchases of SAP stock from 1981 to June 1984, which totaled only six. All of these purchases were corporate repurchases at prices ranging between $15 to $20, and none occurred during the 20 months directly preceding the merger. In April 1984, however, 1,000 shares of SAP were sold to the company at a price of $20 per share. With respect to the asset value of SAP, Whitman averaged the value produced by two different methods. First, using the book value method, he concluded that SAP had an asset value of $156.56 per share at the time of the merger. Using a theoretical takeover value method, Whitman concluded that SAP's asset value was $244.79 per share. Thus, he concluded that, on average, SAP had an asset value of

---

3. The five year pattern reflected significant fluctuation: 1981—$458,600; 1982—$698,000; 1983—$2,255,000; 1984—$804,000; 1985—$3,470,000.

$200 per share at the time of the merger. Accordingly, Whitman concluded that SAP's fair value as of the time of the merger was $131.60 per share.

SAP also presented, on rebuttal, the testimony of Daniel McNamee, III, an expert in the magazine publishing field. McNamee supported Whitman's opinion on several issues, specifically, the use of a five-year earnings base and multipliers, as calculated. McNamee criticized Kobak's opinion on his conclusion concerning *Rolling Stone's* market positioning at the time of the merger and for the use of: (i) a 1985 earnings base rather than a five-year earnings base; (ii) adjustments to earnings made for deferred subscription income; and (iii) selection of a high price/earnings multiple.

In his post-hearing opinion, the Chancellor prefaced his findings by noting that the case presented a typical appraisal trial in which the dynamics of the judicial process "tend to produce evidence of absurdly differing values." The court noted that, while there was a wide variation in the fair value estimate of the two experts, eighty percent of the difference resulted from the selection of the base used for earnings capitalization. In the Chancellor's view, because the earnings multiple selected by Whitman (13) was "rather close to the 14 multiple employed by Mr. Kobak," the critical determination facing the court was whether to accept the five year base advanced by Whitman or the one year base selected by Kobak.

Petitioner argues that the Chancellor's adoption of a five year earnings base, compounded by the acceptance of every adjustment to earnings and assets made by Whitman, was inconsistent with the Court of Chancery's "affirmative duty to consider the nature of the enterprise as an element of its valuation" set forth in this Court's decision in *Rapid–American Corp. v. Harris,* Del.Supr., 603 A.2d 796, 799 (1992). SAP responds that, in discharging its appraisal function, the Court of Chancery is afforded wide discretion and, in view of SAP's "historic earnings validity and low profit margin," the selection of a five year base was within the Chancellor's discretion. Moreover, SAP argues the Chancellor's finding that Whitman's opinion was "accurate and reliable" is, in all respects, "the product of a logical and deductive process and is binding for purposes of appeal."

We begin our analysis by addressing the standard of review. The Court of Chancery's determination under the appraisal statute, 8 *Del.C.* § 262(h), has traditionally been granted "a high level of deference" by this Court. *In re Appraisal of Shell Oil Co.,* Del.Supr., 607 A.2d 1213, 1219 (1992). This deference reflects a recognition that appraisal cases tend to be factually intensive and often involve competing valuation methodologies. The Court of Chancery's fact-finding role in appraisal cases often requires the court to cope with "widely divergent views reflecting partisan positions" in value-fixing tasks. *Id.* at 1222–23. But the deference standard also assumes that the court will employ its own acknowledged expertise, which is essential to the appraisal task.

The modern appraisal process presumes a sophisticated judge who exercises independence in determining the value of corporation in a contested proceeding. The role of the Court of Chancery has undergone significant change, however, since the appraisal remedy was created in 1899. *See* Calio, Joseph Evan, *New Appraisals of Old Problems: Reflections on the Delaware Appraisal Proceeding,* 32 Am.Busn.L.J. 1, 12 n. 44 (1994). In the original 1899 appraisal proceeding, value was determined by three disinterested appraisers: one chosen by the directors, one chosen by the dissenting shareholder, and one chosen by those selected above. *Id.* (citing 21 *Del. Laws* 273, § 56 (1899)). The value determined by these appraisers was conclusive proof of the share's value. *Id.*

In 1943, the General Assembly reduced the number of appraisers to one. 44 *Del. Laws* 125, § 6 (1943). The 1943 DGCL provided:

> the Court shall determine the shareholders who have complied with the provisions of this section and become entitled to the valuation of and payment for their share, and *shall appoint an appraiser* to determine such value.

Id. (emphasis added). Under the 1943 version of § 262, the Appraiser had the same "powers and authority as may be conferred upon the Masters by the Rules of the Court of Chancery or by the order of his appointment." *Id.* The Court of Chancery was to determine its own value for the corporation's shares after hearing the exceptions based on law and fact to the Appraisers' report. *Id.* Thus, the Appraiser's value was no longer considered conclusive proof of the value, but was accorded "some weight." *In re General Realty & Utilities Corp.,* Del.Ch., 52 A.2d 6, 11 (1947). *See also Charlip v. Lear Siegler, Inc.,* Del.Ch., No. 5178, Brown, V.C., 1984 WL 8248 (Nov. 27, 1984), slip op. at 8 ("I do not deem it proper, in considering exceptions taken from the report of a master or an appraiser, to ignore his findings and review the entire evidentiary record anew."). If the Appraiser was known in the community, however, as "highly-reputable" and was a longstanding member of the Delaware Bar with considerable experience in corporate matters, the Court might accept the Appraiser's value uncritically and *in toto. Charlip,* slip op. at 9.

In 1976, the General Assembly eliminated the role of the Appraiser by enacting a new version of DGCL § 262, which provided "the *court* shall appraise the shares. . . ." 60 *Del.Laws* 371, § 7 (1976) (emphasis supplied). The legislative synopsis for the bill proposing this change recites that "[e]xperience has shown this two-step procedure to be wasteful of time and money." Comm. to H.R. 916, 128th G.A., 2d Sess. (1976) (enacted). Thus, the modification in the procedure was intended to "provide for the streamlining of the appraisal process by the elimination of the appraiser. The action will now be heard by the Court of Chancery in the first instance." *Id.*

The role of the Court of Chancery has evolved over time to the present requirement that the court independently determine the value of the shares that are the subject of the appraisal action. *See In re Shell Oil,*

607 A.2d at 1221; *Weinberger v. UOP, Inc.,* Del.Supr., 457 A.2d 701, 713–14 (1983). Even though today a Chancellor may be faced with widely divergent values presented by the parties' experts, the acceptance of one expert's value, *in toto,* creates the risk that the favored expert will be accorded a status greater than that of the now-eliminated master.

This is not to say that the selection of one expert to the total exclusion of another is, in itself, an arbitrary act. The testimony of a thoroughly discredited witness, expert or lay, is subject to rejection under the usual standards which govern receipt of such evidence. *See Security First Corp. v. U.S. Die Casting and Dev. Co.,* Del.Supr., 687 A.2d 563, 569 (1997).

The nub of the present appeal is not merely that the Chancellor made an uncritical acceptance of the evidence of SAP's appraiser but that he announced in advance that he intended to choose between absolutes. True, the Chancellor did not, nor could he, indicate which side he would favor, but the evidentiary construct he established for the subsequent trial created a standard for value determination which is at odds with Section 262's command that the Court "shall appraise" fair value.

Thus, while we recognize the deference due a judicial determination on the mixed fact/law question of fair value under Section 262, we believe the valuation approach of the Chancellor in this case presents a question of law. That question, as we pose it, is whether the Court of Chancery may adopt an expert's valuation views under a previously announced "hook, line and sinker" rationale in the face of significant arguable considerations advanced by both sides of the dispute.

The Chancellor was confronted with divergent views by the two principal experts in several areas of valuation, but he focused upon the earnings base as an "either-or" determination, which, in large part, dictated the result. There is justification for the Chancellor's rejection of a one year earnings base despite Kobak's insistence that 1985 was the best indication of SAP's potential since SAP's Repositioning Plan was put into effect that year. As the Chancellor noted, under Delaware decisional law, a one year earnings base in appraisal cases has met sparing approval. But there is also support for Petitioner's argument that 1985 was a precursor year and indicative of post-merger growth.

Rejection of a one year earnings base, however, does not, *ipso facto,* require acceptance of Whitman's alternative five year base. SAP experienced fluctuating earnings in each of the years from 1981 to 1985. If the 1985 earnings were deemed aberrational, it could be argued that they were much more reflective of current prospects than the 1981 earnings of $458,000. The inclusion of that figure, the lowest of any of the figures in the five year earnings base, could be said to equally distort the pattern of going concern value. Whether such a rejection is warranted is of course a matter for the Court of Chancery to determine in the first instance, but its selection or rejection should not spring from an "all or nothing" mind-set reached at the beginning of the analysis.

We do not suggest that the selection of an alternative earnings base, *e.g.,* a two year or three year period, was required in this case. But consideration of alternative earnings bases, other than the two choices advanced by the experts, was clearly within the court's discretion had the court not adopted a hook-line-and-sinker approach. Moreover, a determination of alternative earning bases is subject to easy calculation on the stipulated data. As this Court stated in *Cede & Co. v. Technicolor, Inc.,* the Court of Chancery may "select one of the parties' valuation modes as its general framework, *or fashion its own.*" Del.Supr., 684 A.2d 289, 299 (1996) (emphasis supplied). * * *

Notes

1.   The Chancery court in the *Gonsalves* case initially valued the stock in question at $131.60. After another appeal and a further remand, the chancellor retained a neutral expert and concluded that the fair value of the stock was $262.96 per share. Gonsalves v. Straight Arrow Publishers, Inc., 2002 WL 31057465. Does such a wide disparity suggest that the valuation process is a highly subjective one, or was the first decision simply wrong in accepting an exaggerated appraisal from one party? If the latter, is the use of an independent expert the only way to assure balanced appraisal evidence?

2.   The dynamics of the appraisal process is important. Under our adversary system, each party selects their own appraisers who appraise the company in the light most favorable to their client. Some European countries do not allow partisan experts in judicial proceedings. Rather, the courts there independently appoint experts. What happens in such a case if that expert is incompetent or just wrong? Would a hybrid model in which the parties' experts comment on the report of an independent expert appointed by the court provide greater assurance of accuracy? Would an even better approach be for the independent expert to comment on the parties' expert reports? Do you think the original Delaware law had it right in having an appraiser appointed by each party and one by the court?

SECTION 4. SCOPE OF APPRAISAL REMEDIES

As reflected below, litigation over appraisal remedies raises several issues over the scope of the remedy, including the relative weight to be given alternative valuation factors, the role of cash flow discounting in valuation, whether a going concern valuation of a corporation should consider its hypothetical liquidation value or its future value, and how to account in the valuation for control premiums, minority discounts, and liquidity discounts.

In *Santa Fe Industries v. Green*, 430 U.S. 462, 97 S.Ct. 1292, 51 L.Ed.2d 480 (1977), the Supreme Court held that SEC Rule 10b–5 is a disclosure-based remedy and therefore a claim that a grossly unfair transaction amounted to equitable fraud was not sufficient to state a claim. The Court there further pointed out that, since the defendant had complied with the Delaware appraisal statute, it would not be appropriate for federal law to impose additional requirements regarding this state law procedure. In that case, Santa Fe was conducting a short form merger that entitled the remaining shareholders to seek an appraisal proceeding if they were unsatisfied with the $150 offered by Santa Fe. Some shareholders sued under Rule 10b–5 claiming that the offer was misleading. As noted, the Supreme Court dismissed that claim, but other shareholders did seek an appraisal under Delaware law in the following case.

BELL v. KIRBY LUMBER CORP.

413 A.2d 137 (Del.1980).

McNEILLY, JUSTICE:

This is an appeal and cross-appeal from the Vice–Chancellor's denial of exceptions taken by certain minority stockholders (stockholders) and by the surviving corporation, Kirby Lumber Company (Kirby) to the appraiser's final report following a short form merger (8 Del.C. § 253). Alfred Folweiler, another stockholder, appeals from the rejection by the Vice–Chancellor of his timely letter addressed to Kirby which the Vice–Chancellor ruled was inadequate to constitute a demand for appraisal.

The factual and historical background leading to the merger and cash out of Kirby's minority stockholders by Santa Fe Industries, Inc. (Santa Fe) are detailed throughout the Vice–Chancellor's opinion. 395 A.2d 730 (1978). Reference is made to the Vice–Chancellor's opinion here to avoid unnecessary repetition.

During the fall of 1973 Santa Fe, then owner of approximately 95% of the outstanding stock of Kirby, in contemplation of acquiring the remaining stock of Kirby, commissioned W. D. Davis of the firm of Appraisal Associates to make an appraisal of Kirby's business and assets, and retained the investment banking firm of Morgan Stanley & Company, Incorporated (Morgan Stanley) to furnish an opinion of the fair market value of the Kirby minority stock, approximately 25,000 shares of a total outstanding of 500,000. The Davis appraisal of assets as of December 31, 1973, was $320,000,000, and the Morgan Stanley opinion of the per share fair market value of the Kirby minority stock was $125. Based upon these reports and related data Santa Fe determined that a cash out of the Kirby minority was feasible and proceeded to effect the 8 Del.C. § 253 short form merger as of July 31, 1974. The owners of approximately 5000 Kirby shares dissented and properly demanded an appraisal under 8 Del.C. § 262. The appointed appraiser concluded the per share value of the Kirby minority stock to be $254.40, based upon an earnings value of $120, assets value of $456 with assigned weight of 60% to earnings and 40% to assets.

Basically the greatest area of disagreement between the parties lies in the appraisers' valuation of assets and the weight assigned to assets and earnings in arriving at the fair value per share of Kirby minority stock on the date of merger. The entire fairness and strict judicial scrutiny rule of Sterling v. Mayflower Hotel Corp., Del.Supr., 93 A.2d 107 (1952); Singer v. Magnavox Company, Del.Supr., 380 A.2d 969 (1977); and Tanzer v. International General Industries, Inc., Del.Supr., 379 A.2d 1121 (1977), as it applies to the merger itself is not before the Court in this appeal. The fiduciary duty aspect of this merger has been litigated in the federal courts, but there is no issue here involving a violation of any fiduciary duty owed the minority by the majority in effecting the merger. Therefore, the assessment of damages does not include consideration by the Vice-Chancellor of possible rescission, monetary damages based upon factors beyond the scope of statutory appraisal, or other relief deemed appropriate in the discretion of the Court under Singer. Of primary consideration here is our inquiry into fair price within the context of entire fairness under the appraisal statute in assessing damages to be paid the minority as a result of their being cashed out. The stockholders contend that the entire fairness, close judicial scrutiny rule in this parent/subsidiary merger requires the Court to assess damages on the basis of a per share value of the stock as negotiated in a hypothetical third party arms length transaction in which the vast natural resource assets of Kirby would control. Kirby on the other hand would have earnings control on the traditional appraisal going concern basis, contending that the value of the shares depends upon the success of Kirby's manufacturing and marketing of lumber, plywood and other wood products for which the timber acreage provides a sustained yield.

The stockholders' first argument is that because Santa Fe controlled the decision to cash out the minority stockholders of Kirby, the Vice-Chancellor erred by permitting appraisal under the short form merger statute to be used by the parent company as an instrument to avoid its fiduciary duty of entire fairness to the stockholders under Sterling v. Mayflower Corp., supra; Singer v. Magnavox Company, supra; and Tanzer v. International General Industries, Inc., supra. Kirby does not contest the applicability of the fiduciary duty of entire fairness by the parent to the minority, but does contend that to follow a standard of damages based upon an amount all shareholders would have received in a third party sale negotiated at arms length, is an unwarranted expansion of the appraisal remedy. Kirby claims this calls for an aliquot valuation of shares based upon a sale or liquidation rather than upon a determination of stock value in a going concern which is the traditional standard established by Tri-Continental Corp. v. Battye, Del.Supr., 74 A.2d 71 (1950) and its progeny.

Santa Fe, as the holder of 95% of Kirby's outstanding stock, had the power to do with Kirby whatever it chose. Based upon the Davis appraisal of assets it could have liquidated Kirby and realized approximately $670 per share for each stockholder. It could have negotiated a merger with an unrelated corporation; or it could have permitted the minority to continue in the corporation for better or for worse. Instead Santa Fe chose to cash out the minority because the price of the minority stock was as low as Santa Fe management could anticipate under existing market conditions. The stockholders claim this to be a forced sale at a distress price, at a time immediately following a period of rapid increase in the value of Kirby's assets, and prior to the time of a period of contemplated "phenomenal" growth. This argument is appealing from the stockholder's viewpoint because the majority engineered the transaction at a time when it appeared to Santa Fe management that it was unlikely that the price of the Kirby minority shares would ever be less than it was at that time. The stockholders were effectively locked in. Aside from a tender offer for $65 per share and isolated transactions in the area of $85–95 the Kirby stock had no market but paid $3 per share dividends. In such a situation there is substantial likelihood that the takeout transaction may result in a low value appraisal. See Jonathan H. Holman, 1978 Ann. Survey of American Law, 279, 296 (1978); Brudney & Chirelstein, Fair Shares In Corporate Mergers and Takeovers, 88 Harv.L.Rev. 297, 304 (1974).

The stockholders argue also that the application of the arms length standard urged by them would not result in a wholesale change in the mechanics of arriving at value by appraisal but could be accomplished by a reevaluation of weighting the traditional value factors, assigning controlling weight to asset value and negligible weight to earnings. The stockholders suggest in this case 90% to assets and 10% to earnings, something only slightly less than full liquidation. Kirby would weigh earnings over assets.

In Tri–Continental Corp. v. Battye, supra, this Court said:

"Section 61 of the General Corporation Law Code 1935, § 2093, provides that upon the merger of a corporation, stockholders who object to the merger and who fulfill the statutory requirements to register their objection shall be paid the value of their stock on the date of the merger, exclusive of any element of value arising from the expectation or accomplishment of the merger."

"The basic concept of value under the appraisal statute is that the stockholder is entitled to be paid for that which has been taken from him, viz., his proportionate interest in a going concern. By value of the stockholder's proportionate interest in the corporate enterprise is meant the true or intrinsic value of his stock which has been taken by the merger. In determining what figure represents this true or intrinsic value, the appraiser and the courts must take into consideration all factors and elements which reasonably might enter into the fixing of value. Thus, market value, asset value, dividends, earning prospects, the nature of the enterprise and any other facts which were known or which could be ascertained as of the date of merger and which throw any light on future prospects of the merged corporation are not only pertinent to an inquiry as to the value of the dissenting stockholders' interest, but must be considered by the agency fixing the value."

"The rule as stated requires that certain obvious conclusions be drawn. Thus, since intrinsic or true value is to be ascertained, the problem will not be settled by the acceptance as the sole measure of only one element entering into value without considering other elements. For example, as was specifically held in Chicago Corporation v. Munds, (20 Del.Ch. 142, 172 A. 452) supra, market value may not be taken as the sole measure of the value of the stock. So, also, since value is to be fixed on a going-concern basis, the liquidating value of the stock may not be accepted as the sole measure."

"A great deal of argument in this cause has turned around the phrase 'net asset value'" which is simply a mathematical figure representing the total value of the assets of General less the prior claims. The net asset value of the common stock of General could be determined as of any date by computing the total market value of the securities in the portfolio, adding to that sum the cash in the company's possession, deducting the total of the outstanding liabilities, debentures and preferred stock, and dividing the final result by the number of common shares outstanding."

However, since the value of dissenting stock is to be fixed on a going-concern basis, the taking of the net asset value as the appraisal value of the stock obviously is precluded by the rule. This is so because, primarily, net asset value is a theoretical liquidating value to which the share would be entitled upon the company going out of business. Its very nature indicates that it is not the value of stock in going concern." 74 A.2d at 72–74.

In Application of Delaware Racing Association, Del.Supr., 213 A.2d 203, 207–208 (1965) this Court said:

"In substance, the rule as to scope of review is as it has always been, that it is our duty to review the evidence to test the propriety of the findings below. When the evidence consists primarily of depositions, documents, or the report of a master or appraiser, we may make our own conclusions, if the requirement of doing justice requires it and if the findings below are clearly wrong. Furthermore, when we are concerned with findings arising from deductions, processes of reasoning, or logical inferences, it is our duty to review them and, if the requirement of doing justice requires it and if the findings below are clearly wrong, then to draw our own inferences and reach our own conclusions. This is not to say, however, that we may ignore the findings below. On the contrary, when they are supported by the record and are the product of an orderly and logical deductive process, we, in the exercise of judicial restraint, accept them, even though independently we might have reached opposite conclusions. This, we think, is the rule this Court has followed in the past, and it is the rule it will continue to follow for the future."

"The argument of the stockholders that the fact that they are being forced out of a going concern and being paid off in cash should lead to a measure of value which would give them that which they would have received in the event of dissolution, while perhaps superficially appealing, is more properly addressed to the General Assembly which enacted the law as we have found it."

Applying the rules laid down by these authorities, the Vice–Chancellor rejected the stockholders' arms length standard because it "presupposes an acquisition value based upon the very fact that the company will not continue in business on the same basis that existed immediately prior to the merger. It introduces another element, namely the value another would place upon it as a price for merger as opposed to the corporation's independent value as a going concern."

We find nothing in the record to persuade us that the Vice–Chancellor erroneously exercised his judgment in rejecting the stockholders' arms length standard in favor of the traditional going concern standard under established Delaware law.

The stockholders' second argument is that natural resource companies like Kirby cannot be, and are not valued properly by following traditional standards. They contend that natural resource companies must be appraised on the basis of the value inherent in the corporation's assets. On the other hand, Kirby argues that the Vice–Chancellor erred in accepting the weight assigned to assets by the Appraiser. Kirby contends that this Court should substitute a weighting scheme which gives controlling weight to earnings adjusted for the lack of a market for Kirby stock.

> The Court of Chancery has weighted assets value from zero in Gibbons v. Schenley Industries, Inc., Del.Ch., 339 A.2d 460 (1975), to 100%; In re Creole Petroleum Corp., Del.Ch., C.A.No. 4860 (Jan. 11, 1978). In Swanton v. State Guaranty Corp., Del.Ch., 215 A.2d 242 (1965) the Chancellor weighted assets at 60%, in Levin v. Midland–Ross Corp., 194 A.2d 50 (1963) and In re General Realty & Utilities Corp., Del.Ch., 52 A.2d 6 (1947) at 50%, 40% in Sporborg v. City Specialty Stores, Del.Ch., 123 A.2d 121 (1956) and Adams v. R. C. Williams & Co., Del.Ch., C.A.Nos. 978, 993, (Feb. 21, 1961), 25% in In re Olivetti Underwood Corp., Del.Ch., 246 A.2d 800 (1968), and 20% in Felder v. Anderson, Clayton & Co., Del.Ch., 159 A.2d 278 (1960) and Heller v. Munsingwear, Inc., Del.Ch., 98 A.2d 774 (1953).

This Court also affirmed 12½% in *Universal City Studios, Inc. v. Francis I. duPont & Co.*, Del.Supr., 334 A.2d 216 (1975). It is thus apparent that no rule of thumb is applicable to weighting; rather, the rule becomes one of entire fairness and sound reasoning in the application of traditional standard and settled Delaware law to the particular facts of each case.

Asset value represents a judgment as to the fair market value of the assets based upon the price that would be agreed upon by a willing seller and a willing buyer under no compulsion to sell or buy, but the weighting of those assets with other available factors is left to the Court. Poole v. N. V. Deli Maatschappij, Del.Supr., 243 A.2d 67 (1968). As a result, appraisals involving different corporate structures have resulted in different weighting of factors for varying reasons. * * *

The stockholders contend that historically Kirby has been engaged in the production of low margin wood products but recently has made significant changes in its production and marketing strategies which will not be reflected in earnings until the new Bon Weir plywood plant and new particle-board plant are in operation. They contend that since the traditional approach eschews the use of projected earnings value in appraising assets, it thus becomes appropriate to give greater than usual weight to asset value. The stockholders also contend that * * * the thing making Kirby unique is its vast timberland, not its management or its manufacturing facilities. They rely upon the growth rate of the Kirby forest, rapid appreciation in value and saleability. * * *

Kirby on the other hand contends that to approach weighting of assets from the stockholders' viewpoint would be to assign heavy weight to a theoretical liquidating value proscribed by settled Delaware law, which Kirby stockholders had no foreseeable possibility of receiving. The stockholders respond to this contention by saying they are not seeking a liquidation value but that they are seeking to be treated on a par with Santa Fe.

The stockholders attack the weight assigned to earnings value which was computed by applying a multiplier of 15.2 to Kirby's average earnings of $7.92 for the five year period prior to the merger. The stockholders' attack is not directed to the earnings' multiplier, but to the use of historical earnings which they claim are unrealistic in view of the future earnings' projection and should be disregarded or recalculated. Kirby contends the earnings' value determined by the Appraiser and accepted by the Vice–Chancellor is an accurate reflection of the fair value of Kirby stock if it is discounted for lack of a market.

The Appraiser in arriving at his conclusions as to the weight he assigned to assets and earnings stated:

"A factor which casts a shadow on this appraisal is the fact that the disparity between market value of assets and earnings value (or for that matter reconstructed market) was not at the time unique to Kirby. Indeed such a disparity existed at the same time in many natural resource companies including Morgan Stanley's comparables. I deduce from this that at the time of the merger, the market prices were depressed and therefore the price earnings multiple derived from comparables used in determining earnings value was lower than one might hope for on the average. Sporborg v. City Specialty Stores, 123 A.2d at 127. Compare Chicago Corporation v. Munds, Del.Ch., 172 A. 452, 454 (1934). It is at such times some say, that companies have a tendency to buy out their minorities and thus turn the disparity of value between assets and capitalized earnings into a bargain for the parent. Townsend testified accurately, I believe, that minority stockholders could, at such a time, take their lesser price, reduced by market forces and buy into other equally depressed situations. That seems fair enough, but there are unknown tax and transaction costs to be considered and there is also the recognition that the corporation may have obtained a bargain at the expense of its stockholders; although, I suppose on the same logic as above, other bargains besides the Kirby minority's stock would have been available to the parent on the market place. Fortunately, I need not go extensively into this area because the present weighting of assets takes care of whatever disparity may exist.

Therefore, considering the peculiar nature of natural resource companies, the inferences of saleability of the assets and the disparity between asset and earnings value, I conclude that this case is more like Levin or Sporborg, than it is like Schenley. I, therefore, weight assets at 40% and capitalized earnings at 60%."

The Vice–Chancellor accepted the Appraiser's 40/60% assignment of weight, and we are not persuaded from our review of the record and arguments of counsel to rule otherwise. Kirby's assets at the time of the merger were appreciating in value, appeared to be saleable on the open market although no sale or liquidation was contemplated, and the forest utilization on a sustained-yield basis was readily available to generate an anticipated increase in earnings. Therefore, as in Swanton, asset value is entitled to substantial weight. However, earnings value and reconstructed market value also must be accorded substantial weight. . . . The earnings value gives effect to Kirby's future prospects to the value of its assets, and to what Kirby stockholders should derive as the value of their stock on the date of merger. We feel as the Vice–Chancellor that the 40% weight assigned to asset value, which represents $182.40, or 71%, of the total value of $254.40 per share assigned to the Kirby stock, and the 60% weight assigned to earnings value, "fairly capture the situation", as will appear from our response to the substantive and evidentiary attacks on the appraisals and rulings of the Appraiser in his acceptance and rejection of evidence offered at the hearing before the Appraiser.

In considering the parties' respective positions on the Morgan Stanley evaluation of earnings value we find the testimony of Charles C. Townsend (Townsend) most helpful. Townsend as managing director of Morgan Stanley was the person responsible for the opinion rendered Santa Fe as to the value of Kirby stock for purposes of the contemplated merger. Preliminarily Townsend and his staff inspected the Kirby forests and manufacturing facilities, and made a comparative analysis of other companies in the industry including a review of factors such as revenues, income from sales, return on equity, timber acreage, earnings per share, market price, price earnings ratios, and dividend yield. Based upon these observations Morgan Stanley concluded that Kirby was among the higher quality companies in the field, and that it deserved a higher than average price/earnings ratio which they figured should be about ten times earnings. Townsend also testified that the $125 reconstructed market value was the value Morgan Stanley thought a share would trade at in the market whether it was a single share owned by Santa Fe or a single share owned by the stockholders.

Early in their work Townsend and his team met with a group from Santa Fe to review a timber volume analysis, from which they concluded that Kirby was managing its forests in a manner to support its business and there was no excess timber. For that reason it was decided that Kirby needed its timber assets to support its ability to earn and pay dividends. They also thought it either proper or appropriate to add any increment of value for timber that either was not necessary or Kirby could not use in another manner. On this point Townsend testified that the $125 per share opinion would not have been changed materially by accepting either the $320,000,000 dollar Davis appraisal of assets or the $230,000,000 Nichols appraisal because both were so large, as compared to their conclusion of what market value (reconstructed) would be, that either would have caused them to bias their conclusion on price-earnings ratio substantially upwards.

In opining that the reconstructed market value on the date of merger would have been $125 per share, Morgan Stanley assumed that the Kirby shares were widely distributed and freely traded such that willing buyers and sellers could readily effect transactions. Townsend explained this assumption, knowing that such was not the fact, because stock which is broadly distributed and freely traded is more valuable, requiring here a built-in discount rate to bring the stock into the category of being marketably attractive.

In considering Kirby's dividend policy in connection with earnings value, Townsend testified that a comparison with other companies was made for the period 1969 through 1973. Kirby's earnings payout or dividend payout for that period was 38.1 percent. Among the other companies, six paid out less, three the same, and three more. Based upon this comparison it was concluded that Kirby's dividend payout was not unreasonable.

Townsend testified that Kirby's capital expansion program and its five year projection of increased earnings entered into their utilization of comparables and the price/earnings ratios of comparable companies because a number of other forest companies were in a very expansionary mode of planning new facilities. Townsend further testified that expansion and increased earnings was a very positive factor in the minds of his appraisal team. He indicated that they looked at historical earnings as compared to other companies in the business and determined that there were no extraordinary factors related to historical earnings which were not apparent in the industry as a whole.

In calculating earnings value, average payout ratios of comparables were considered, as were historical and projected earnings, Kirby's partially completed capital program, Kirby's appraised asset value, and Kirby's aggressive management. A ratio of 15.2 was selected, which when multiplied by five years average earnings of $7.92 per share, resulted in an earnings value of $120 per share.

On the basis of our review of the Townsend testimony we are satisfied that the Morgan Stanley appraisal is the product of an orderly and logical deductive process in accordance with approved methodology properly accepted by the Appraiser and the Vice–Chancellor.

Kirby would have the earnings value determined by the Appraiser and the Vice–Chancellor, adjusted for lack of a market. The Appraiser stated that he was aware of no Delaware authority for discounting earnings and declined to do so. We agree.

The stockholders claim the Appraiser and the Court of Chancery erred in rejecting the Davis valuation of assets and in accepting the Nichols valuation of assets, in rejecting the testimony of Charles H. Carpenter, and also in rejecting their estoppel argument.[4]

Both Davis and Nichols based upon their years of experience and their professional credentials were well qualified to appraise the assets of Kirby. Their appraisals compare as follows:

	Davis	Nichols
Land	103,898,515.50	66,424,000.00
Stumpage (growing timber)	207,268,000.00	125,000,000.00
Construction in Progress	8,695,380.52	21,657,000.00
Improvements	20,000,000.00	14,673,000.00
Total	339,861,986.02	227,754,000.00
Less 4% Discount for Size	320,000,000.00	N/A

At the outset of his report Davis stated that the purpose of the appraisal was to estimate the market value of the land, exclusive of minerals, buildings, equipment belonging to Kirby based upon "the price which the property would bring when it is offered for sale by one who desires but is not obligated to sell and is bought by one who is under no necessity of buying it. (State v. Carpenter et al., 126 Texas 604, 89 S.W.2d 194)." This basis purports to be on the "willing seller/willing buyer" as required by Poole v. N. V. Deli Maatschappij, supra. Our review of the record, however, leads us to the same conclusion as the Appraiser and the Vice–Chancellor that the report is a going concern appraisal based largely on two sales transactions, the Temple Time merger and the Crown Zellerbach/Lehman purchase of Tremont, without making any adjustment from going concern value to liquidation of assets i.e., the willing sell-

---

4. The Davis $320,000,000 valuation of assets is the equivalent of $640 per share, whereas the Nichols' $227,754,000 valuation accepted by the Appraiser and after certain adjustments made by the Appraiser, amounts to $456 per share.

er/buyer standard of Poole. The Davis appraisal is very thorough and detailed, covering 300 pages of text. But our review of the record leads us to agree with the Appraiser and the Vice–Chancellor in their reliance upon the Nichols' report which we find to be in conformity with the methodology approved in Poole v. N. V. Deli Maatschappij, supra.

In arriving at his final asset value Davis followed three approaches: (1) the cost approach which he described on deposition as a piece by piece sale; (2) the earnings approach in which he capitalized earnings at 2%; and (3) the direct sales approach which he described as an entire package sale and the best approach. In computing asset value under the direct sales approach Davis analogized, adjusted and compared his analysis of the Temple and Tremont transaction with Kirby appraisal figures because "they were the only two sales of any size in the vicinity and were therefore the best guide as to the whole of the Kirby property in my judgment." From our review of the Davis report and the Davis deposition it appears that in his allocation of values in the Temple and Tremont transactions Davis based his allocations upon what he thought the buyers intended and not upon allocation of amounts taken from the actual transactions. Because of his discussions with Mr. Temple of the Temple company, Davis did have more information about Temple than about Tremont, but it does not appear that his information included actual allocations of amounts. There are many questionable details in the Davis report in addition to the errors therein emphasized in the Vice–Chancellor's opinion which we find unnecessary to discuss because of our approval of the Nichols report. * * *

Acting pursuant to 8 Del.C. § 262(h), the Vice–Chancellor awarded interest on the fair value of Kirby stock at the rate of 7% per annum from the date of merger to the date of payment. Kirby does not quarrel with the rate of interest accruing between the date of merger and the date of judgment, but contends the post judgment rate should have been no more than the legal rate of 6%.

Kirby's contention is without merit. The purpose of interest is to fairly compensate the stockholders for their inability to use the money during the entire period in question. The amount of interest awarded pursuant to 8 Del.C. s 262(h) is discretionary. We cannot independently find an abuse of discretion in the Vice–Chancellor's award of 7% simple interest from the date of merger to date of payment. Universal City Studios, Inc. v. Francis I. duPont & Co., supra; Felder v. Anderson, Clayton & Co., Del.Ch., 159 A.2d 278 (1960).

The stockholders contend the Vice–Chancellor erred in holding the letter of Alfred Folweiler insufficient to constitute a demand for appraisal under 8 Del.C. § 262(b). They also dispute Kirby's contention that the appeal of Folweiler had to be filed within 30 days of the entry of the order dismissing his claim, rather than within 30 days of the entry of the final order of the Court below.

In the absence of an express determination that there is no reason to delay and an express entry of judgment against a party, Chancery Court Rule 54(b) provides that any order adjudicating fewer than all the claims of all the parties in an action is subject to revision at any time prior to the entry of judgment adjudicating all such claims. That express determination and express entry of judgment do not appear in the record. Consequently, the order dismissing Folweiler's claim was not final at the time it was issued, and his appeal is timely. See Lightburn v. Delaware Power & Light Co., Del.Supr., 158 A.2d 919, 922 (1960).

The Vice–Chancellor improperly rejected the Folweiler letter to Kirby as a demand for an appraisal under under 8 Del.C. § 262(b). Folweiler's letter referred to Kirby's offer of $150.00 per share and further stated:

> "Inasmuch as I regard the offered price as inadequate, based on the data that accompanied the offer, I am not submitting my stock certificate for 25 shares.

> "It is my opinion that the stock has a value of $601/share. Upon request, data will be presented to support my opinion concerning the value of the stock."

In Raab v. Villager Industries, Inc., Del.Supr., 355 A.2d 888, 891 (1976) this Court said:

> "The requirements of § 262(b) are to be liberally construed for the protection of objecting stockholders, within the boundaries of orderly corporate procedures and the purpose of the requirement."

Realistically, the explicit rejection of the $150.00 offer was a demand for the only available alternative, appraisal under § 262. The language reasonably informed Kirby that Folweiler wanted an appraisal. The letter can, "by fair implication, be read as being (a) written demand(s) for payment." Carl Marks & Co. v. Universal City Studios, Inc., Del.Supr., 233 A.2d 63, 64 (1967); and the Vice–Chancellor erred in determining otherwise. We hold that Mr. Folweiler's letter met the requirements of 8 Del.C. § 262(b) and that he should have been allowed to remain as a plaintiff in this action.

Affirmed, in part; reversed, in part.

QUILLEN, JUSTICE, concurring * * *

NOTE

It has not been uncommon for courts to award more in appraisal proceedings than offered by the acquirer. *See, e.g.*, M.G. Bancorporation, Inc. v. Le Beau, 737 A.2d 513 (Del.1999) (offer was for $41 but court awards $85); In the Matter of Shell Oil Co., 607 A.2d 1213 (Del.1992) (offer was for $58, but court awards $71.20 per share); Rapid–American Corp. v. Harris, 603 A.2d 796 (Del.1992) (offer valued at $28, but court awards $51, which was 200%

over market price; remanded for consideration of control premium and an additional $22.29 awarded in an unreported decision); Kahn v. Household Acquisition Corp., 591 A.2d 166 (Del.1999) (offer was for $6.00, but court awarded $7.27 as a "quasi-appraisal" remedy; valuation was dominated by asset value technique); Alabama By–Products Corp. v. Neal, 588 A.2d 255 (Del.1991) (offer was for $75.60, but court awards $180.67 per share plus 12.5% prejudgment interest); Cavalier Oil Corp. v. Harnett, 564 A.2d 1137 (Del.1989) (offer was $93,950, but court awarded $347,000 for shareholder's stock).

WEINBERGER v. UOP, INC.

457 A.2d 701 (Del.1983).

MOORE, JUSTICE.

* * * In considering the nature of the remedy available under our law to minority shareholders in a cash-out merger, we believe that it is, and hereafter should be, an appraisal under 8 *Del.C.* § 262 as hereinafter construed. We therefore overrule *Lynch v. Vickers Energy Corp.*, Del. Supr., 429 A.2d 497 (1981) (*Lynch II*) to the extent that it purports to limit a stockholder's monetary relief to a specific damage formula. *See Lynch II*, 429 A.2d at 507–08 (McNeilly & Quillen, JJ., dissenting). But to give full effect to section 262 within the framework of the General Corporation Law we adopt a more liberal, less rigid and stylized, approach to the valuation process than has heretofore been permitted by our courts. While the present state of these proceedings does not admit the plaintiff to the appraisal remedy per se, the practical effect of the remedy we do grant him will be co-extensive with the liberalized valuation and appraisal methods we herein approve for cases coming after this decision. * * *

Turning to the matter of price, plaintiff also challenges its fairness. His evidence was that on the date the merger was approved the stock was worth at least $26 per share. In support, he offered the testimony of a chartered investment analyst who used two basic approaches to valuation: a comparative analysis of the premium paid over market in ten other tender offer-merger combinations, and a discounted cash flow analysis.

In this breach of fiduciary duty case, the Chancellor perceived that the approach to valuation was the same as that in an appraisal proceeding. Consistent with precedent, he rejected plaintiff's method of proof and accepted defendants' evidence of value as being in accord with practice under prior case law. This means that the so-called "Delaware block" or weighted average method was employed wherein the elements of value, i.e., assets, market price, earnings, etc., were assigned a particular weight and the resulting amounts added to determine the value per share. This procedure has been in use for decades. *See In re General Realty & Utilities Corp.*, Del.Ch., 52 A.2d 6, 14–15 (1947). However, to the extent it excludes other generally accepted techniques used in the financial community and the courts, it is now clearly outmoded. It is time we recognize this in appraisal and other stock valuation proceedings and bring our law current on the subject.

While the Chancellor rejected plaintiff's discounted cash flow method of valuing UOP's stock, as not corresponding with "either logic or the existing law" (426 A.2d at 1360), it is significant that this was essentially the focus, i.e., earnings potential of UOP, of Messrs. Arledge and Chitiea in their evaluation of the merger. Accordingly, the standard "Delaware block" or weighted average method of valuation, formerly employed in appraisal and other stock valuation cases, shall no longer exclusively control such proceedings. We believe that a more liberal approach must include proof of value by any techniques or methods which are generally considered acceptable in the financial community and otherwise admissible in court, subject only to our interpretation of 8 *Del.C.* § 262(h), *infra*. *See also* D.R.E. 702–05. This will obviate the very structured and mechanistic procedure that has heretofore governed such matters. *See Jacques Coe & Co. v. Minneapolis–Moline Co.,* Del.Ch., 75 A.2d 244, 247 (1950); *Tri–Continental Corp. v. Battye,* Del.Ch., 66 A.2d 910, 917–18 (1949); *In re General Realty and Utilities Corp., supra.*

Fair price obviously requires consideration of all relevant factors involving the value of a company. This has long been the law of Delaware as stated in *Tri–Continental Corp.,* 74 A.2d at 72:

> The basic concept of value under the appraisal statute is that the stockholder is entitled to be paid for that which has been taken from him, viz., his proportionate interest in a going concern. By value of the stockholder's proportionate interest in the corporate enterprise is meant the true or intrinsic value of his stock which has been taken by the merger. In determining what figure represents this true or intrinsic value, the appraiser and the courts must take into consideration all factors and elements which reasonably might enter into the fixing of value. Thus, market value, asset value, dividends, earning prospects, the nature of the enterprise and any other facts which were known or which could be ascertained as of the date of merger and which throw any light on *future prospects* of the merged corporation are not only pertinent to an inquiry as to the value of the dissenting stockholders' interest, but *must be considered* by the agency fixing the value. (Emphasis added.)

This is not only in accord with the realities of present day affairs, but it is thoroughly consonant with the purpose and intent of our statutory law. Under 8 *Del.C.* § 262(h), the Court of Chancery:

> shall appraise the shares, determining their *fair* value exclusive of any element of value arising from the accomplishment or expectation of the merger, together with a fair rate of interest, if any, to be paid upon the amount determined to be the *fair* value. In determining such *fair* value, the Court shall take into account *all relevant factors* ... (Emphasis added)

See also Bell v. Kirby Lumber Corp., Del.Supr., 413 A.2d 137, 150–51 (1980) (Quillen, J., concurring).

It is significant that section 262 now mandates the determination of "fair" value based upon "all relevant factors". Only the speculative elements of value that may arise from the "accomplishment or expectation" of the merger are excluded. We take this to be a very narrow exception to the appraisal process, designed to eliminate use of *pro forma* data and projections of a speculative variety relating to the completion of a merger. But elements of future value, including the nature of the enterprise, which are known or susceptible of proof as of the date of the merger and not the product of speculation, may be considered. When the trial court deems it appropriate, fair value also includes any damages, resulting from the taking, which the stockholders sustain as a class. If that was not the case, then the obligation to consider "all relevant factors" in the valuation process would be eroded. We are supported in this view not only by *Tri–Continental Corp.,* 74 A.2d at 72, but also by the evolutionary amendments to section 262.

Prior to an amendment in 1976, the earlier relevant provision of section 262 stated:

> (f) The appraiser shall determine the value of the stock of the stockholders ... The Court shall by its decree determine the value of the stock of the stockholders entitled to payment therefor ...

The first references to "fair" value occurred in a 1976 amendment to section 262(f), which provided:

> (f) ... the Court shall appraise the shares, determining their fair value exclusively of any element of value arising from the accomplishment or expectation of the merger....

It was not until the 1981 amendment to section 262 that the reference to "fair value" was repeatedly emphasized and the statutory mandate that the Court "take into account all relevant factors" appeared [section 262(h)]. Clearly, there is a legislative intent to fully compensate shareholders for whatever their loss may be, subject only to the narrow limitation that one can not take speculative effects of the merger into account.

Although the Chancellor received the plaintiff's evidence, his opinion indicates that the use of it was precluded because of past Delaware practice. While we do not suggest a monetary result one way or the other, we do think the plaintiff's evidence should be part of the factual mix and weighed as such. Until the $21 price is measured on remand by the valuation standards mandated by Delaware law, there can be no finding at the present stage of these proceedings that the price is fair. Given the lack of any candid disclosure of the material facts surrounding establishment of the $21 price, the majority of the minority vote, approving the merger, is meaningless.

The plaintiff has not sought an appraisal, but rescissory damages of the type contemplated by *Lynch v. Vickers Energy Corp.,* Del.Supr., 429

A.2d 497, 505–06 (1981) (*Lynch II*). In view of the approach to valuation that we announce today, we see no basis in our law for *Lynch II*'s exclusive monetary formula for relief. On remand the plaintiff will be permitted to test the fairness of the $21 price by the standards we herein establish, in conformity with the principle applicable to an appraisal—that fair value be determined by taking "into account all relevant factors" [*see* 8 *Del.C.* § 262(h), *supra*]. In our view this includes the elements of rescissory damages if the Chancellor considers them susceptible of proof and a remedy appropriate to all the issues of fairness before him. To the extent that *Lynch II,* 429 A.2d at 505–06, purports to limit the Chancellor's discretion to a single remedial formula for monetary damages in a cash-out merger, it is overruled.

While a plaintiff's monetary remedy ordinarily should be confined to the more liberalized appraisal proceeding herein established, we do not intend any limitation on the historic powers of the Chancellor to grant such other relief as the facts of a particular case may dictate. The appraisal remedy we approve may not be adequate in certain cases, particularly where fraud, misrepresentation, self-dealing, deliberate waste of corporate assets, or gross and palpable overreaching are involved. *Cole v. National Cash Credit Association,* Del.Ch., 156 A. 183, 187 (1931). Under such circumstances, the Chancellor's powers are complete to fashion any form of equitable and monetary relief as may be appropriate, including rescissory damages. Since it is apparent that this long completed transaction is too involved to undo, and in view of the Chancellor's discretion, the award, if any, should be in the form of monetary damages based upon entire fairness standards, i.e., fair dealing and fair price.

Obviously, there are other litigants, like the plaintiff, who abjured an appraisal and whose rights to challenge the element of fair value must be preserved. Accordingly, the quasi-appraisal remedy we grant the plaintiff here will apply only to: (1) this case; (2) any case now pending on appeal to this Court; (3) any case now pending in the Court of Chancery which has not yet been appealed but which may be eligible for direct appeal to this Court; (4) any case challenging a cash-out merger, the effective date of which is on or before February 1, 1983; and (5) any proposed merger to be presented at a shareholders' meeting, the notification of which is mailed to the stockholders on or before February 23, 1983. Thereafter, the provisions of 8 *Del.C.* § 262, as herein construed, respecting the scope of an appraisal and the means for perfecting the same, shall govern the financial remedy available to minority shareholders in a cash-out merger. Thus, we return to the well established principles of *Stauffer v. Standard Brands, Inc.,* Del.Supr., 187 A.2d 78 (1962) and *David J. Greene & Co. v. Schenley Industries, Inc.,* Del.Ch., 281 A.2d 30 (1971), mandating a stockholder's recourse to the basic remedy of an appraisal. * * *

NOTE

Despite the acceptance of the discounted cash flow valuation method by the Delaware court, a study of court decisions valuing acquisitions found that only about a third of the cases were using that methodology. Rutherford B. Campbell, Jr., The Impact of Modern Finance Theory in Acquisition Cases, 53 Syracuse L. Rev. 1 (2003).

The Time Value of Money

The discounted cash flow method accepted by the court in *Weinberger* sought to ascertain the present value of the shareholder's stock based on the expected cash flows of the company. This methodology involves an essential part of corporate (and personal) finance, *i.e.*, the time value of money. Whenever funds are not invested ("sitting idle"), money is lost on the forgone interest. Each investment must also be assessed to determine if the rate of return is worth the risk. This assessment is often done by comparing the investment being analyzed with the amount of money that could be earned on an alternate investment.

The time value of money has several aspects. One is compounding of interest. Interest will itself earn interest. One dollar invested at a 6 percent interest rate will double within 12 years and that amount will double again in another twelve years. This has several applications. In your personal finance, your retirement funds will grow more the longer you invest, so start early. Imagine that the amount saved each year for retirement is $20,000, rather than the dollar in the example just given, and that you have a work life of 35 years. The compounded amount when you retire would supply a nice nest egg. What if you did not start saving until you are fifty? Your retirement in that case may be a bit bleak.

The present value of a dollar that you receive five years from now would be presently worth about 62 cents if we assume an interest rate of ten percent. In other words, you could invest 62 cents today at ten percent and you would have a dollar in five years from the principal and accumulated interest. What is the future value of a dollar held today? If invested at twelve percent, it would be worth about $1.76 in five years.

These present and future value concepts have many applications. What is an asset producing X dollars for X years worth to you if purchased with a lump sum today. This will require an interest calculation on the lump sum that would return the X dollars for X years. This is essentially how the lottery values its lump sum payouts. Say you win a $1 million lottery. You do not really win $1 million. Rather, you will receive say $50,000 for twenty years or you may elect a lump sum, an up front cash payout of say $500,000 (before taxes a sum that will be determined by an imputed interest rate that would return a total of $1 million in principal and interest over twenty years).

In the case of an annuity, you pay a lump sum amount that will provide a lifetime stream of income that will be based on the amount of the lump payment, an assumed interest rate and your life expectancy. You can value a corporation similarly by determining what lump sum will be equal to the income produced by a corporation over its expected earnings based on a rate of return you believe is desirable based on the risks of the investment and current and projected interest rates. If the corporation will cost you more than what you could earn on a United States government guaranteed bond, why would you pay such an amount for a business and incur the uncompensated risk?

Future and present value may also be used to value cash flows. Say you want to buy a corporation that sells athletic shoes. It has a single store and had total assets of $150,000, including inventory and some computers. The corporation has $125,000 in debts, including its lease. What would you pay for this corporation? Would your answer change, if you discovered that the company turned its inventory over weekly and was making profits of $75,000 a month? Would your answer change if there was a lawsuit against the corporation making a tort claim and seeking $25 million in damages? Would your answer change if the corporation had insurance to cover the claim or if a lawyer advised that the claim was without merit? Would your answer change if you discovered that the corporation's shoe line was becoming less fashionable? These are just a few considerations that arise in seeking to value an ongoing business.

Remember that determining fair value is really a set of educated guesses. It is not a science. No matter how objective some valuation models appear, no amount of math or complex formulas assure that the value they reach is a correct one. Only the market is able to truly value a business, and that valuation changes constantly, as evidenced by the constant fluctuations in prices for stocks traded on the markets.

Consider the following:

Petitioner and its expert Mr. Gelfond contend that an independent investor would be satisfied with the 43.82 percent compounded annual rate of return they calculate was enjoyed through the year ended July 31, 1996, on that investor's initial $10,000 investment in the corporation. Mr. Gelfond computed this 43.82 percent compounded annual rate by using a present-value-future-value formula where: Present value equals $10,000 (the shareholder initial investment); future value equals $378,542 (the company's stated "equity" or net book asset value at the end of the 1996 fiscal year before consideration of its deferred payment obligation to Mr. Myers and Mrs. Myers); and N (the number of years over which that investment is annually compounded) equals 10.

B & D Foundations, Inc. v. Commissioner of Internal Revenue, T.C. Memo 2001–262, at 49–50 (Tax Ct. 2001).

"The value, referred to as the present value or the capital value of periodic payments, is computed by means of a mathematical formula which takes into account the interest rate at which a given amount invested now would grow for any specified period of time." In re Williams, 3 B.R. 728, 732 (Br. N.D. Ill. 1980). The formula for computing present value has been described as follows:

$$v = a (1 - 1/(1 + i)n/i)$$

where:

v is the present value of the series of future payments;

a is the amount of each payment;

i is the interest rate per period, and

n is the number of periods over which payments are made.

The formula given here is an adaptation of formulas published in Financial Compound Interest and Annuity Tables (5th ed., Financial Publishing Co. 1970).

Present and future value be easily computed on many pocket calculators or you could you use tables that compute such values.

Financial theorists have developed some complicated methods for determining the value of stocks. The Capital Asset Pricing Model ("CAPM") seeks to use a mathematical formula for determining the return on an investment that an investor should require in pricing the investment. "The required return is equal to the return you could earn on a riskless asset plus a market risk premium adjusted by beta." Stanley G. Eakins, Finance, Investments, Institutions, Management 198 (2d ed. 2002). The "beta" is a measure of how movements in the stock's price correlates to the entire market.

CAPM may be stated as follows:

r-r[f] = beta (r[m]-r[f]),

where:

r is the expected return on any stock;

beta is the covariance of the stock in the market portfolio;

r[f] is the risk-free interest rate;

r[m] is the expected return on the market;

r-r[f] is the expected risk premium; and

r[m]-r[f] is the expected market risk premium.

Return is essentially an investment's expected profitability, which turns on the likelihood of any given performance scenario. For example, if there is a 50% chance that a particular investment will return 10% this year and also a 50% chance that it will return only 5%, then the expected return is: .5(10%) + .5(5%) = 7.5%. Risk is a measure of the uncertainty or standard deviation of the return. This means that the value of any potential investment will depend on the future return the investor expects to receive, as well as on the likelihood that the return will be realized.

Maria O'Brien Hylton, "Socially Responsible" Investing: Doing Good Versus Doing Well in an Efficient Market, 42 Am. U. L. Rev. 1, 16 (1992).

CAPM has weaknesses and has been "much criticized." Hylton, Id. at n. 63. As one author notes:

> As with any model, there are assumptions to be made with CAPM. First, we assume that capital markets are highly efficient, investors are well informed, transaction costs are zero, there are negligible restrictions on investment, there are no taxes, and no investor is large enough to affect the market price of the stock. We also assume that investors are in agreement about the likely performance and risk of individual securities and that their return expectations are based on a common investment time holding period of, say, one year. Under this set of hypothetical conditions, all investors will perceive the opportunity set of risky securities in the same way, and they will draw their efficient investment frontiers in the same place.

Robert F. Reilly, Value and Cents, The Use and Misuse of CAPM, 14 Am. Bankrup. Instit. 2824 (1994).

Do you think CAPM can be used to value stock in appraisal actions? CAPM measurements will depend on the assumptions inputted into the model. Does this make it susceptible to manipulation favoring one party over the other?

CEDE & CO. v. TECHNICOLOR, INC.

684 A.2d 289 (Del.1996).

HOLLAND, JUSTICE.

This appeal is from a final judgment of the Court of Chancery in an appraisal action. The proceeding arises from a cash-out merger of the minority shareholders of Technicolor Incorporated ("Technicolor"), a Delaware corporation. With the approval from a majority of Technicolor's shareholders, MacAndrews & Forbes Group Incorporated ("MAF") merged its wholly-owned subsidiary, Macanfor Corporation ("Macanfor"), into Technicolor. The only defendant-appellee in this appraisal action is Technicolor, the surviving corporation of the merger. The plaintiffs-appellants are Cinerama, Incorporated, the beneficial owner of 201,200 shares of Technicolor common stock, and Cede & Company, the record owner of those shares (collectively "Cinerama.").

Cinerama contends, *inter alia,* that the Court of Chancery erred, as a matter of law, in appraising the fair value of its Technicolor shares. According to Cinerama, that legal error was a refusal to include in the valuation calculus "MAF's new business plans and strategies for Technicolor, which the [C]ourt [of Chancery] *found* were not speculative but had been developed, adopted and implemented" between the date of the merger agreement and the date of the merger. That contention is correct and dispositive of this appeal. *Weinberger v. UOP, Inc.,* Del.Supr., 457 A.2d 701 (1983). Accordingly, the appraisal action will be remanded for further proceedings in accordance with this opinion. Cinerama's other contentions are addressed only to the extent they are relevant to the remand.* * *

Technicolor engaged in a number of distinct businesses through separate operating units. Technicolor's Professional Services Group was its main source of revenue and profit. The Videocassette Duplicating Division operated one of the largest duplicating facilities in the world. The Consumer Services Group operated film processing laboratories ("Consumer Photo Processing Division" or "CPPD"), which provided film processing services to other photofinishers. CPPD also operated the Standard Manufacturing Company ("Standard"), which manufactured film splicers and associated equipment. The Government Services Group ("Government Services") provided photographic and non-photographic support and management services under contract to governmental agencies. Technicolor's Gold Key Entertainment Division ("Gold Key"), licensed motion pictures and other programs for television exhibition. The Audio Visual Division ("Audio Visual") distributed film and video equipment.

Morton Kamerman ("Kamerman"), Technicolor's Chief Executive Officer and Board Chairman, concluded that Technicolor's principal business, theatrical film processing, did not offer sufficient long-term growth for Technicolor. Kamerman proposed that Technicolor enter the field of rapid processing of consumer film by establishing a network of stores across the country offering one-hour development of film. The business, named One Hour Photo ("OHP"), would require Technicolor to open approximately 1,000 stores over five years and to invest about $150 million.

In May 1981, Technicolor's Board of Directors approved Kamerman's plan. The following month, Technicolor announced its ambitious venture with considerable fanfare. On the date of its OHP announcement, Technicolor's stock had risen to a high of $22.13.

In the months that followed, Technicolor fell behind on its schedule for OHP store openings. The few stores that did open reported operating losses. At the same time, Technicolor's other major divisions were experiencing mixed, if not disappointing, results.

As of August 1982, Technicolor had opened only twenty-one of a planned fifty OHP retail stores. Its Board was anticipating a $5.2 million operating loss for OHP in fiscal 1983. On August 25, 1982, the Technicolor Board "authorized the company's officers to seek a buyer for Gold Key." During 1982, Technicolor also decided to terminate the Audio Visual Division. Nevertheless, Kamerman remained committed to OHP. In Technicolor's Annual Report, issued September 7, 1982, Kamerman stated, "We remain optimistic that the One Hour Photo business represents a significant growth opportunity for the Company."

Technicolor's September 1982 financial statements, for the fiscal year ending June 1982, reported an eighty percent decline of consolidated net income—from $17.073 million in fiscal 1981 to $3.445 million in 1982. Profits had declined in Technicolor's core business, film processing. Technicolor's management also attributed the decline in profits to write-offs for losses in its Gold Key and Audio Visual divisions, which had already been targeted for sale. By September 1982, Technicolor's stock had reached a new low of $8.37 after falling by the end of June to $10.37 a share. * * *

The merger was accomplished on January 24, 1983. The parties agree that the appraised value of Technicolor must be fixed as of that date. *See Alabama By–Products Corp. v. Neal,* Del.Supr., 588 A.2d 255, 256–57 (1991). There is a fundamental disagreement between the litigants, however, concerning the nature of the enterprise to be appraised.

Cinerama argues that the Court of Chancery should have valued Technicolor as it existed on the date of the merger and, in particular, with due regard for the strategies that had been conceived and implemented following the merger agreement by MAF's controlling shareholder, Ronald O. Perelman ("Perelman Plan"). Technicolor argues that the Court of Chancery properly considered Technicolor without regard to the Perelman Plan and only as it existed on or before October 29, 1982, with the then extant strategies that had been conceived and implemented by Technicolor's Chairman, Morton Kamerman ("Kamerman Plan"). According to Cinerama:

> Reduced to its simplest form, the dispute was whether the trial court should value Perelman's Technicolor—a company whose business plans and strategies focused on the processing and duplication of film and videotape and the provision of services to the United States Government and which planned and expected to generate $50 million in cash during 1983 from the sale of unwanted and/or unsuccessful businesses, namely, OHP, CPPD, Gold Key and Audio Visual; or Kamerman's Technicolor—a company whose business plans and strategies assumed diversification away from a concentration on film processing and videotape duplication for the professional market toward consumer oriented businesses, especially OHP.

The economic experts for both parties used a form of discounted cash flow methodology to value Technicolor. Cinerama's expert was John Torkelsen ("Torkelsen"), a financial analyst with Princeton Venture Research, Inc. Technicolor's primary expert witness was Alfred Rappaport ("Rappaport"), a professor at Northwestern University Graduate Business School and a consultant with The Alcar Group ("Alcar"). The fundamental nature of the disagreement between the parties about the Perelman

Plan and the Kamerman Plan, however, resulted in different factual assumptions by their respective experts. * * *

An appraisal proceeding is a limited statutory remedy. *Technicolor I,* 542 A.2d at 1186. Its legislative purpose is to provide equitable relief for shareholders dissenting from a merger on grounds of inadequacy of the offering price. *Id.* The appraisal statute affords the dissenters the right to a judicial determination of the fair value of their shareholdings. *Id.* (citing *Weinberger v. UOP, Inc.* Del.Supr., 457 A.2d 701, 714 (1983)); *accord Cavalier Oil Corp. v. Harnett,* Del.Supr., 564 A.2d 1137, 1142 (1989). We summarized the nature of the proceeding in *Technicolor I,* as follows:

> in a section 262 appraisal action the only litigable issue is the determination of the value of the appraisal petitioners' shares on the date of the merger, the only party defendant is the surviving corporation and the only relief available is a judgment against the surviving corporation for the fair value of the dissenters' shares.

Technicolor I, 542 A.2d at 1187.

The seminal decision by this Court regarding an appraisal proceeding is *Weinberger v. UOP, Inc.,* Del.Supr., 457 A.2d 701 (1983). In *Weinberger,* this Court broadened the process for determining the "fair value" of the company's outstanding shares by including all generally accepted techniques of valuation used in the financial community. *Weinberger v. UOP, Inc.,* 457 A.2d at 712–13; *see Technicolor I,* 542 A.2d at 1186–87. The result of that expansion was the holding in *Weinberger* that "the standard 'Delaware block' or weighted average method of valuation, formerly employed in appraisal and other stock valuation cases, shall no longer exclusively control such proceedings." *Weinberger v. UOP, Inc.,* 457 A.2d at 712–13.

> The Delaware appraisal statute provides that the Court of Chancery: shall appraise the shares, determining their fair value exclusive of any element of value arising from the accomplishment or expectation of the merger or consolidation, together with a fair rate of interest, if any, to be paid upon the amount determined to be the fair value. In determining such fair value, the Court shall take into account all relevant factors.

8 *Del.C.* § 262(h). In *Weinberger,* this Court construed the appraisal statute. That construction required this Court to reconcile the dual mandates of Section 262(h) which direct the Court of Chancery to: determine "fair" value based upon "all relevant factors;" but, to exclude "any element of value arising from the accomplishment or expectation of the merger." In making that reconciliation, the *ratio decidendi* of this Court was, as follows:

> *Only the speculative elements of value that may arise from the "accomplishment or expectation" of the merger are excluded. We take this to be a very narrow exception to the appraisal process,* designed to eliminate use of *pro forma* data and projections of a speculative

variety relating to the completion of a merger. But elements of future value, including the *nature of the enterprise,* which are known or susceptible of proof as of the date of the merger and not the product of speculation, may be considered. When the trial court deems it appropriate, fair value also includes any damages, resulting from the taking, which the stockholders sustain as a class. If that was not the case, then the obligation to consider "all relevant factors" in the valuation process would be eroded. We are supported in this view not only by [*Tri–Continental Corp. v. Battye,* Del.Supr., 74 A.2d 71, 72 (1950)], but also by the evolutionary amendments to section 262.

Weinberger v. UOP, Inc., 457 A.2d at 713 (emphasis added).

After examining the evolution of the statutory text in Section 262(h), this Court concluded "there is a legislative intent to fully compensate shareholders for whatever their loss may be, *subject only to the narrow limitation that one can not take speculative effects of the merger into account.*" *Id.* at 714 (emphasis added). Therefore, in *Weinberger,* this Court held that the more liberal methodology we had just authorized in appraisal and other stock valuation cases "*must* include proof of value by any techniques or methods which are generally considered acceptable in the financial community and otherwise admissible in court, *subject only to our [narrow] interpretation of [the exclusionary language in] 8 Del.C. § 262(h),*" *i.e.,* requiring that only speculative elements of value, which may arise from the accomplishment or expectation of the merger, be disregarded. *Weinberger v. UOP, Inc.,* 457 A.2d at 713 (emphasis added); *see also Kahn v. Household Acquisition Corp.,* Del.Supr., 591 A.2d 166, 174 (1991); *Rosenblatt v. Getty Oil Co.,* Del.Supr., 493 A.2d 929, 940 (1985).

This Court's final holding in *Weinberger* was to overrule the trilogy of cases that had adopted the business purpose test for mergers. *Weinberger v. UOP, Inc.,* 457 A.2d at 715. We explained that the final holding followed logically from the entire fairness test, the expanded appraisal remedy being made available to dissenting shareholders, and the Court of Chancery's broad discretion to fashion equitable relief. *Id.* Consequently, we concluded that no "additional meaningful protection is afforded minority shareholders by the business purpose requirement." *Id.* Accordingly, the majority may now cash-out the minority by a merger without a business purpose, but must pay the dissenters fair value for "*whatever* their loss may be, subject only to the narrow limitation that one can not take speculative effects of the merger into account." *Id.* at 714 (emphasis added).

The underlying assumption in an appraisal valuation is that the dissenting shareholders would be willing to maintain their investment position had the merger not occurred. *Cavalier Oil Corp. v. Harnett,* Del.Supr., 564 A.2d 1137, 1145 (1989). Accordingly, the Court of Chancery's task in an appraisal proceeding is to value what has been taken from the shareholder, *i.e.,* the proportionate interest in the going concern.

Id. at 1144 (citing *Tri–Continental Corp. v. Battye,* Del.Supr., 74 A.2d 71, 72 (1950)). To that end, this Court has held that the corporation must be valued as an operating entity. *Id.* We conclude that the Court of Chancery did not adhere to this principle.

The Court of Chancery determined that Perelman "had a fixed view of how [Technicolor's] assets would be sold before the merger and had begun to implement it" prior to January 24, 1983. Consequently, the Court of Chancery found that the Perelman Plan for Technicolor was the operative reality on the date of the merger. Nevertheless, the Court of Chancery held that Cinerama was not entitled to an appraisal of Technicolor as it was actually functioning on the date of the merger pursuant to the Perelman Plan.

The Court of Chancery reached that holding by applying its majority acquiror principle and correlative proximate cause exception. The Court of Chancery excluded any value that was admittedly part of Technicolor as a going concern on the date of the merger, if that value was created by substituting new management or redeploying assets during the transient period between the first and second steps of this two-step merger, *i.e.,* Perelman's Plan. The Court of Chancery reasoned that valuing Technicolor as a going concern, under the Perelman Plan, on the date of the merger, would be tantamount to awarding Cinerama a proportionate share of a control premium, which the Court of Chancery deemed to be both economically undesirable and contrary to this Court's holding in *Bell v. Kirby Lumber Corp.,* Del.Supr., 413 A.2d 137, 140–42 (1980). *See also Rapid–American Corp. v. Harris,* Del.Supr., 603 A.2d 796, 805–07 (1992). Thus, the Court of Chancery concluded "that value [added by a majority acquiror] is not ... a part of the 'going concern' in which a dissenting shareholder has a legal (or equitable) right to participate."

In *Kirby* and its progeny, including *Technicolor I,* this Court has explained that the dissenter in an appraisal action is entitled to receive a proportionate share of fair value in the *going concern* on the date of the merger, rather than value that is determined on a liquidated basis. *Bell v. Kirby Lumber Corp.,* 413 A.2d at 142; *see also In re Shell Oil Co.,* Del.Supr., 607 A.2d 1213, 1219 (1992). Thus, the company must first be valued as an operating entity. *Cavalier Oil Corp. v. Harnett,* 564 A.2d at 1144. In that regard, one of the most important factors to consider is the "nature of the enterprise" that is the subject of the appraisal proceeding. *Rapid–American Corp. v. Harris,* 603 A.2d at 805; *see Weinberger v. UOP, Inc.,* 457 A.2d 701, 713 (1983).

In a two-step merger, to the extent that value has been added following a change in majority control before cash-out, it is still value attributable to the going concern, *i.e.,* the extant "nature of the enterprise," on the date of the merger. *See Rapid–American Corp. v. Harris,* 603 A.2d at 805. The dissenting shareholder's proportionate interest is determined only after the company has been valued as an operating entity on the date of the merger. *Cavalier Oil Corp. v. Harnett,* 564 A.2d at 1144;

cf. Walter W.B. v. Elizabeth P.B., Del.Supr., 462 A.2d 414, 415 (1983). Consequently, value added to the going concern by the "majority acquiror," during the transient period of a two-step merger, accrues to the benefit of all shareholders and must be included in the appraisal process on the date of the merger. *See Rapid–American Corp. v. Harris*, 603 A.2d 796; *Cavalier Oil Corp. v. Harnett*, 564 A.2d 1137; *cf. Walter W.B. v. Elizabeth P.B.*, 462 A.2d at 415.

In this case, the question in the appraisal action was the fair value of Technicolor stock on the date of the merger, January 24, 1983, as Technicolor was operating pursuant to the Perelman Plan. The Court of Chancery erred, as a matter of law, by determining the fair value of Technicolor on the date of the merger "but for" the Perelman Plan; or, in other words, by valuing Technicolor as it was operating on October 29, 1982, pursuant to the Kamerman Plan. By failing to accord Cinerama the *full proportionate value of its shares in the going concern on the date of the merger,* the Court of Chancery imposed a penalty upon Cinerama for lack of control. *Cavalier Oil Corp. v. Harnett*, 564 A.2d at 1145; *accord Rapid–American Corp. v. Harris*, 603 A.2d at 805–07; *Bell v. Kirby Lumber Corp.*, 413 A.2d at 140–42.

The "accomplishment or expectation" of the merger exception in Section 262 is very narrow, "designed to eliminate use of *pro forma* data and projections of a speculative variety relating to the completion of a merger." *Weinberger v. UOP, Inc.*, 457 A.2d at 713. That narrow exclusion does not encompass known elements of value, including those which exist on the date of the merger because of a majority acquiror's interim action in a two-step cash-out transaction. *Cf. In re Shell Oil Co.*, 607 A.2d at 1218–19. "[O]nly the *speculative* elements of value that may arise from the 'accomplishment or expectation' of the merger" should have been excluded from the Court of Chancery's calculation of fair value on the date of the merger. *Weinberger v. UOP, Inc.*, 457 A.2d at 713 (emphasis added); *cf. In re Shell Oil Co.*, 607 A.2d at 1219.

The Court of Chancery's determination not to value Technicolor as a going concern on the date of the merger under the Perelman Plan, resulted in an understatement of Technicolor's fair value in the appraisal action. That result was inevitable when the Court of Chancery valued Technicolor pursuant to a discounted cash flow model with the negative factual input and assumptions from the Kamerman Plan rather than the Perelman Plan. Consequently, the Court of Chancery permitted MAF to "reap a windfall from the appraisal process by cashing out a dissenting shareholder [Cinerama]," for less than the fair value of its interest in Technicolor as a going concern on the date of the merger. *Cavalier Oil Corp. v. Harnett*, 564 A.2d at 1145.

Cinerama has asked this Court to make an appraisal of the fair value of its Technicolor shares on the date of the merger, rather than remand this protracted litigation to the Court of Chancery. This Court will not make an independent determination of value on appeal. *Rapid–American*

Corp. v. Harris, 603 A.2d at 799. This appraisal action will be remanded to the Court of Chancery for a recalculation of Technicolor's fair value on the date of the merger. *See id.*

Upon remand, it is within the Court of Chancery's discretion to select one of the parties' valuation models as its general framework, or fashion its own, to determine fair value in the appraisal proceeding. *See Rapid–American Corp. v. Harris,* 603 A.2d at 804. The Court of Chancery has properly recognized that its choice of a framework does not require it to adopt any one expert's model, methodology, or mathematical calculations *in toto. See id.* The undervaluation in this appraisal proceeding resulted from negative factual assumptions that originated from an erroneous legal theory, not from either the valuation framework selected or adaptions to it by the Court of Chancery. In that regard, however, we have concluded that the Court of Chancery's erroneous majority acquiror principle and proximate cause exception permeated its factual assumptions so pervasively, that the Court of Chancery's attribution of only a $4.43 per share value difference between the Perelman Plan and the Kamerman Plan should not be considered the law of this case upon remand. * * *

NOTES

1. The statutory appraisal remedy is designed to determine the dissenter's *proportionate* value of the firm. *See,* e.g., Advanced Communication Design, Inc. v. Follett, 615 N.W.2d 285, 290 (Minn.2000) ("fair value" means pro rata value of corporation's value as a going concern); First Western Bank Wall v. Olsen, 621 N.W.2d 611, 617 (S.D.2001) ("fair value" means value of dissenters' shares as proportionate interest in going concern; appraisal proceeding should not focus on stock as a commodity). What exactly does proportionate value mean?

2. Is the insistence on valuation as a going concern unfair to dissenting shareholders? After all, they are effectively being forced to liquidate their ownership interests through no fault of their own.

PASKILL CORP. v. ALCOMA CORP.

747 A.2d 549 (Del.2000).

HOLLAND, JUSTICE.

This appeal relates to a stock appraisal proceeding that was initiated in the Court of Chancery by the petitioner-appellant, Paskill Corporation ("Paskill"), a 14.6% minority shareholder of Okeechobee, Inc. ("Okeechobee"), a Delaware corporation. The impetus for Paskill's petition for an appraisal was Okeechobee's merger with and into Okeechobee, LLC, a Delaware limited liability company wholly owned by Alcoma Corporation

("Alcoma"). Prior to the merger, Alcoma owned approximately 54% of Okeechobee's outstanding stock. * * *

On November 12, 1997, Okeechobee, was merged into a wholly-owned subsidiary of Alcoma Corporation. Alcoma is wholly-owned by The Heckscher Foundation for Children, Inc., a not-for-profit corporation. Immediately prior to the merger, Alcoma held 54%, and Paskill's ownership constituted 14%, of the outstanding stock of Okeechobee.

The Okeechobee stockholders were advised that, pursuant to the proposed Okeechobee/Alcoma merger, the minority stockholders of Okeechobee would receive in cash the "net asset value" of their stock and that Alcoma would receive "the equivalent per-share amount but in kind—the remaining assets after the cash paid to the minority shareholders." Alcoma described how it would calculate "net asset value":

> The net asset value would be determined by valuing the marketable stocks and bonds held by Okeechobee at their trading values on the New York Stock Exchange (or other public markets in which such securities are traded) shortly prior to the effective date of the merger. Any mortgages held by Okeechobee would be valued at full face value. The real estate of Okeechobee would be valued by an independent qualified real estate appraiser. The total of such assets at their fair market values would then be reduced by the liabilities of Okeechobee, *including capital gains tax that would be paid on the unrealized appreciation when such appreciation is realized.* Thus, the full fair market values of the net assets of Okeechobee as described above would be reflected by the net asset value of the shares. (emphasis added).

A special meeting of the stockholders of Okeechobee was held on November 6, 1997, to vote upon the proposed Okeechobee/Alcoma merger. Prior to the vote on the proposed merger, Paskill delivered a written demand for an appraisal of its shares pursuant to 8 *Del.C.* § 262(d)(1) of the Delaware General Corporation Law. Paskill voted its 140.625 shares against the proposed merger. Nevertheless, the merger was approved. Thereafter, Paskill perfected its right to appraisal under Section 262.

In a notice dated November 6, 1997, the Okeechobee's minority stockholder's shares were valued at $9,480.50 per share. The calculation of net asset value was set forth in a "Consolidated Statement of Net Assets" which was attached to the November 6 notice.

According to that Consolidated Statement, Okeechobee had "assets" of $256,909 and "investments" of $7,402,114. The investments were: marketable securities consisting of stock and cash equivalents equal to $5,670,878; an operating parking garage in New York City valued at $6,270,000; unimproved land in Florida valued at $34,100; and a mortgage receivable relating to a Nashua, New Hampshire property valued at $1,098.014. The total value of the two properties and the mortgage receivable as of the valuation date was $7,402,114. The total value of Okeechobee's assets and investments equaled $13,329,901.

According to the same Consolidated Statement of Net Assets, Okee-chobee had two liabilities as of the valuation date. Those liabilities consisted of "taxes payable-current" of $87,000 and "accrued expenses-operations" of $36,706. In addition to these two liabilities, Alcoma deduct-ed "additional expenses" that totaled $3,725,700 and consisted of: $568,700 for the "estimated closing costs on sales-commissions, environ-mental issues, legal, etc." regarding the sale of the New York parking garage and unimproved land in Florida; $569,000 for the "deferred feder-al, state and other taxes" on the estimated unrealized capital gain on the securities held by Okeechobee; $2,338,000 for the "deferred taxes" on the estimated unrealized gain on the New York City parking garage; $240,000, for the "deferred taxes" on the mortgage receivable; and $10,000 for the "deferred taxes" on the unimproved land in Florida.

The Court of Chancery appraised Okeechobee exclusively on the basis of its net asset value. At the time of its merger with Alcoma, Okeechobee's investment assets were not for sale. Under those circumstances, the Court of Chancery determined that Alcoma's deduction of the estimated ex-penses that Alcoma attributed to those uncontemplated sales of appreciat-ed investment assets was improper. Nevertheless, the Court of Chancery held that it was appropriate to compute Okeechobee's net asset value by deducting the estimated future tax liabilities attributed to those uncon-templated asset sales on the basis of the investment assets' appreciated value. The Court of Chancery distinguished its *allowance* of deductions for possible future tax liabilities from its *disallowance* of deductions for possible future sales expenses as follows:

> First, sales expenses occur only when and if sale of an asset occurs. They are not an accrued, deferred liability such as capital gains tax. Sales expenses represent transaction costs associated with one possi-ble use of an investment. It is a cost difficult to quantify because the seller may be able to reduce or eliminate the expenses. Okeechobee's investments were not sold, but retained by its acquirer at the time of the merger; therefore, sales expenses had not been incurred and the minority shareholders should not front a portion of a cost that might (or might not) be incurred down the road. Instead, the minority are entitled to shareholders' *pro rata* share of the assets' value as a held investment.

The record reflects that a sale of its appreciated investment assets was not part of Okeechobee's operative reality on the date of the merger.[5] Therefore, the Court of Chancery should have excluded any deduction for the speculative future tax liabilities that were attributed by Alcoma to those uncontemplated sales. Conversely, the Court of Chancery properly denied any deduction from Okeechobee's net asset value for speculative expenses relating to future sales that were not contemplated on the date

---

5. *Paskill Corp. v. Alcoma Corp.*, Del.Ch., C.A. 16221, Steele, V.C. (June 16, 1999) Mem.Op. at 4–5, 1999 WL 438832 at *3. Compare *Cede & Co. v. Technicolor, Inc.*, Del.Supr., 684 A.2d 289, 298 (1996) (fixed view of selling certain assets was the operative reality on the date of the merger).

of the merger. The Court of Chancery erred by attempting to appraise Okeechobee exclusively on the basis of its net asset value, however, even if Okeechobee's net asset value had been calculated correctly. Our reasoning is set forth in the balance of this opinion.

An appraisal proceeding is a limited statutory remedy. Its legislative purpose is to provide equitable relief for shareholders dissenting from a merger on grounds of inadequacy of the offering price. Several eminent legal scholars have developed theories in an attempt to explain appraisal statutes. The most recent is Professor Peter Letsou's "preference reconciliation" theory of appraisal, which he explains as follows:

> ... when shareholders lack effective access to capital markets, risk-altering transactions (particularly those that alter the firm's market risk) can make some shareholders better off while leaving others worse off. Appraisal rights require the corporation to compensate shareholders who may be harmed by such transactions and place the net costs of providing that compensation on shareholders who otherwise gain. As a result, shareholders who otherwise gain from appraisal-triggering transactions will only vote in favor of those transactions if their gains more than offset the net costs of compensating objectors. Appraisal rights therefore decrease the probability of risk-altering transactions that result in net losses to shareholders, causing *all* shares to trade at higher prices *ex ante*.

The Delaware appraisal statute affords dissenting minority stockholders the right to a judicial determination of the fair value of their shareholdings. The statutory mandate directs the Court of Chancery to determine the value of the shares that qualify for appraisal by:

> ... determining their fair value, exclusive of any element of value arising from the accomplishment or expectation of the merger or consolidation, together with a fair rate of interest, if any, to be paid upon the amount determined to be the fair value. In determining such fair value, the Court shall take into account all relevant factors. 8 *Del.C.* § 262(h).

In *Tri–Continental Corp. v. Battye,* 74 A.2d 71 (1950) this Court explained the concept of value contemplated by the statutory mandate:

> ... that the stockholder is entitled to be paid for that which has been taken from him, *viz.*, his proportionate interest in a going concern. By value of the stockholder's proportionate interest in the corporate enterprise is meant the true or intrinsic value of his stock which has been taken by the merger.

The underlying assumption in an appraisal valuation is that the dissenting shareholders would be willing to maintain their investment position had the merger not occurred. Consequently, this Court has held that the corporation must be valued as an operating entity. Accordingly, the Court of Chancery's task in an appraisal proceeding is to value what has been taken from the shareholder, *i.e.,* the proportionate interest in the going concern.

In the briefs filed with this Court, Alcoma contends that its proposed net asset valuation constituted the fair value appraisal of Okeechobee's shares because the minority shareholders received "precisely the *same* value as [they] would" if "Okeechobee could have sold all of its assets, paid the applicable tax on the appreciation realized on the sale, and distributed the net cash proceeds after taxes to all shareholders." Alcoma's argument demonstrates a fundamental misunderstanding of Delaware's appraisal jurisprudence. It also conclusively establishes that the Court of Chancery did not properly determine the fair value of Paskill's shares in Okeechobee as a going concern.

In *Tri–Continental,* the phrase "net asset value" was defined as "simply a mathematical figure representing the total value of the assets of [the corporation] less the prior claims." Accordingly, in *Tri–Continental,* this Court characterized "net asset value" as the "theoretical liquidating value to which the share would be entitled upon the company going out of business." In footnote 2, we acknowledged that theoretical liquidating net asset value could never be obtained in an actual liquidation because of the attendant expenses, *e.g.,* sales costs and taxes.

The seminal importance of *Tri–Continental* is readily apparent fifty years later when the principles it established are applied to the appraisal case *sub judice.* First, "the value of dissenting stock is to be fixed on a going concern basis." Second, "the basic concept of value under the appraisal statute is that the stockholder is entitled to be paid for what has been taken from him, *viz,* his proportionate interest in a going concern." Third, "net asset value is a theoretical liquidating value to which the share would be entitled upon the company going out of business." Fourth, because "the value of dissenting stock is to be fixed on a going concern basis, the taking of the net asset value as the appraisal value of the stock is obviously precluded by the [going-concern] rule." Fifth, since "net asset value is, in reality, a liquidating value, it cannot be made the *sole* criterion of the measure of the value of the dissenting stock."

The Court of Chancery erred, as a matter of law, by relying upon the net asset value as the *sole* criterion for determining the fair value of Okeechobee's stock. It compounded that error when it deducted the speculative future tax liabilities from its net asset value calculation. That deduction was inconsistent with the theoretical nature of the liquidating value that this Court ascribed to the term "net asset value" in *Tri–Continental* and converted Okeechobee's theoretical net asset value into an actual liquidation value. Since it is impermissible to appraise a corporation on the sole basis of its theoretical liquidation net asset value, *a fortiori,* a statutory appraisal can never be made solely on the basis of an actual liquidation net asset value.

The dissenter in an appraisal action is entitled to receive a proportionate share of fair value in the *going concern* on the date of the merger, rather than value that is determined on a liquidated basis. Therefore, the corporation must first be valued as an operating entity. Consequently, one of the most important factors to consider is the "nature of the enterprise" that is the subject of the appraisal proceeding.

According to Alcoma, Okeechobee was a closed-end investment company. We have assumed the *bona fides* of that contention for the purposes of this appeal. In *Tri–Continental,* one of Delaware's seminal appraisal cases, this Court considered the valuation of a regulated closed-end investment company with leverage that was engaged in the business of investing in a cross-section of the stock market.

Tri–Continental was decided at a time when the Delaware Block Method was the exclusive basis for calculating the value of a corporation in an appraisal proceeding. "The Delaware Block Method actually is a combination of three generally accepted methods for valuation: the asset approach, the market approach, and the earnings approach." Under the Delaware Block Method, the asset, market and earnings approach are each used separately to calculate a value for the entire corporation. A percentage weight is then assigned those three valuations on the basis of each approach's significance to the nature of the subject corporation's business. The appraised value of the corporation is then determined by the weighted average of the *three* valuations.

In *Tri–Continental,* this Court held that in determining what figure represents this true or intrinsic value of the corporation being appraised, the Court of Chancery:

> must take into consideration all factors and elements which reasonably might enter into the fixing of value. Thus, market value, asset value, dividends, earning prospects, the nature of the enterprise, and any other facts which were known or which could be ascertained as of the date of merger and which throw any light on future prospects of the merged corporation are not only pertinent to an inquiry as to the value of the dissenting stockholders' interest, but must be considered by the agency fixing the value.

That holding has become one of the bedrock principles of Delaware's appraisal jurisprudence over the last fifty years. * * *

The combined argot of law and economics requires periodic explication. *Tri–Continental* has been construed by this Court as standing for the proposition that an appraisal valuation must take into consideration the unique nature of the enterprise. In *Tri–Continental,* this Court held that the Court of Chancery had the authority to discount asset values at the corporate level, in appropriate circumstances, as a means of establishing the fair value of the entire corporation as a going concern. Read in the proper context, *Tri–Continental* was an acknowledgment that the Court of Chancery was vested with the authority to make a discount of the subject corporation's fair asset value at the corporate level because it constituted a proper application of an accepted methodology for arriving at the proper valuation of the unique corporate enterprise, *i.e.,* in *Tri–Continental,* the

Delaware Block Method was applied to value a regulated closed-end investment company with leverage that was engaged in investing in a cross-section of the stock market. Similarly, this Court recently upheld the Court of Chancery's conclusion that a corporate level comparative acquisition approach to valuing a company, which included a control premium for a majority interest in a subsidiary, was a relevant and reliable methodology to use in an appraisal proceeding to determine the fair market value of shares in a holding company.

Once the entire corporation has been fairly valued as an operating entity, however, the Delaware appraisal process requires the Court of Chancery to determine the fair value that has been taken from the dissenting shareholder who was forced out of the corporate enterprise, i.e., a proportionate interest in the entire going concern. In *Weinberger,* this Court broadened the process for determining the "fair value" of the company's outstanding shares by including all generally accepted techniques of valuation used in the financial community. As a result of that holding in *Weinberger,* the standard "Delaware block" or weighted average method of valuation, formerly employed in appraisal valuation cases, no longer exclusively controls such proceedings.

The *ratio decidendi* in *Weinberger* was based upon the evaluation of the Delaware appraisal statute and this Court's prior holding in *Tri–Continental Corporation.* Last year, this Court adopted the holdings of *Daubert*[6] and *Carmichael*[7] as the correct interpretation of Delaware Rule of Evidence 702 generally and for the admission of expert testimony in the specific context of determining the acceptability of a valuation theory or technique in an appraisal proceeding. In *Bancorporation,*[8] however, we once again held that, after the entire corporation has been valued as a going concern by applying an appraisal methodology that passes judicial muster, there can be no discounting at the shareholder level.

We emphasize the last point because this matter will be remanded for another determination of fair value. In arguing that its liquidated valuation was fair, Alcoma noted that it did not seek a reduction for "the discount normally applied to unmarketable shares not registered with the Securities and Exchange Commission or traded on any public market." Such a discount would have constituted an improper discount at the shareholder level.

Upon remand, the Court of Chancery must ascertain the exact nature of Okeechobee as an enterprise. It must then determine Okeechobee's fair value as a going concern on the date of the merger by any admissible valuation technique that is based on reliable and relevant record evidence. Paskill is then entitled to receive the fair value of its proportionate

---

6. *Daubert v. Merrell Dow Pharmaceuticals, Inc.,* 509 U.S. 579, 113 S.Ct. 2786, 125 L.Ed.2d 469 (1993).

7. *Kumho Tire Co. v. Carmichael,* 526 U.S. 137, 119 S.Ct. 1167, 143 L.Ed.2d 238 (1999).

8. *M.G. Bancorporation, Inc. v. Le Beau,* Del.Supr., 737 A.2d 513 (1999).

interest in that operating entity at the time of the merger without any discount at the shareholder level.

NOTES

1. The court in the *Paskill* case notes the use of comparable premiums in other mergers is an appropriate valuation method. Is that really true? Are not most mergers unique, sometimes driven by the ego of participants in the battle? What if the purchaser in another merger overpaid and is now bankrupt? How much weight should that premium be given?

2. *Minority discount.* The majority of the more recent decisions have emphasized that the appraisal statutes call for a value of the shareholder's proportionate interest in the firm, not simply their shares, so that it is inappropriate to deduct a minority discount. *See* Swope v. Siegel–Robert, Inc., 243 F.3d 486, 495–496 (8th Cir.2001) (applying Missouri law; minority status of stock is irrelevant in appraisal proceeding); Pueblo Bancorporation v. Lindoe, Inc., 37 P.3d 492 (Colo.App.2001) (reversing trial court's use of minority discount); Cavalier Oil Corp. v. Harnett, 564 A.2d 1137 (Del.1989); Blitch v. Peoples Bank, 246 Ga.App. 453, 540 S.E.2d 667 (2000) (rejecting minority discount in appraisal); In re Valuation of Common Stock of McLoon Oil Co., 565 A.2d 997 (Me.1989); Richton Bank & Trust Company v. Bowen, 798 So.2d 1268, 2001 WL 1336458 (Miss.2001); MT Properties Inc. v. CMC Real Estate Corp., 481 N.W.2d 383 (Minn.Ct.App.1992); Rigel Corp. v. Cutchall, 245 Neb. 118, 511 N.W.2d 519 (1994); First Western Bank Wall v. Olsen, 621 N.W.2d 611, 619 (S.D.2001); Robblee v. Robblee, 68 Wash.App. 69, 841 P.2d 1289 (1992) (minority discount inappropriate in close corporation); HMO–W, Inc. v. SSM Health Care System, 234 Wis.2d 707, 611 N.W.2d 250 (2000), *affirming in relevant part* 228 Wis.2d 815, 598 N.W.2d 577 (App.1999) (reversing trial court's use of minority discount). *See also,* e.g., Friedman v. Beway Realty Corp., 87 N.Y.2d 161, 638 N.Y.S.2d 399, 661 N.E.2d 972 (1995) (though a discount for the lack of marketability of shares in closely held corporation is appropriate, for public policy reasons there should be no minority discount); Model Business Corp. Act § 13.01(4)(iii) (no minority discount). As explained by the Delaware Supreme Court:

> The application of a discount to a minority shareholder is contrary to the requirement that the company be viewed as a "going concern." Cavalier's argument, that the only way Harnett would have received value for his 1.5% stock interest was to sell his stock, subject to market treatment of its minority status, misperceives the nature of the appraisal remedy. Where there is no objective market data available, the appraisal process is not intended to reconstruct a *pro forma* sale but to assume that the shareholder was willing to maintain his investment position, however slight, had the merger not occurred. Discounting individual share holdings injects into the appraisal process speculation on the various factors which may dictate the marketability of minority shareholdings. More important, to fail to accord to a minority shareholder the full proportionate value of his shares imposes a penalty for lack of control, and unfairly

enriches the majority shareholders who may reap a windfall from the appraisal process by cashing out a dissenting shareholder, a clearly undesirable result.

Cavalier Oil Corp. v. Harnett, 564 A.2d 1137, 1145 (Del.1989). The 1999 amendments to the Model Business Corporation Act provide that fair value in appraisal is to be determined on a proportionate basis without considering a minority discount. Model Business Corporation Act § 13.01(4).

3. *Marketability discount.* Once a value is arrived at should the appraiser consider a marketablility discount for illiquid shares? A number of courts have disapproved the application of a marketability discount. Swope v. Siegel–Robert, Inc., 243 F.3d 486, 493 (8th Cir.2001) (applying Missouri law; marketability discount is incompatible with purpose of appraisal-i.e., to enable dissenting shareholders to recapture their complete investment when they are unwillingly subjected to substantial corporate changes); Paskill Corp. v. Alcoma Corp., 747 A.2d 549, 557 (Del.2000) (reduction for discount applied to unmarketable shares not registered with SEC or traded on any public market would constitute improper discount at the shareholder level); Arnaud v. Stockgrowers State Bank of Ashland, Kan., 268 Kan. 163, 992 P.2d 216, 220–221 (1999) (marketability discount is not appropriate when purchaser is either majority shareholder or the corporation itself, or when fractional share resulted from reverse stock split intended to eliminate minority shareholder's interest); Richton Bank & Trust Company v. Bowen, 798 So.2d 1268 (Miss. 2001) (rejecting marketability discount); Lawson Mardon Wheaton, Inc. v. Smith, 160 N.J. 383, 734 A.2d 738, 749 (1999) (marketability discounts generally should not be applied in determining fair value of dissenting shareholder's stock in appraisal action); Balsamides v. Protameen Chems., Inc., 160 N.J. 352, 734 A.2d 721, 734 (1999) (same); DiLuglio v. Providence Auto Body, Inc., 755 A.2d 757, 774 (R.I.2000) (even in close corporation, marketability discount is inappropriate if sale of stock to known and qualified buyer is certain); First Western Bank Wall v. Olsen, 621 N.W.2d 611, 619 (S.D.2001) (since appraisal process merely values business as a whole and divides up that value proportionately, the fact that dissenting shareholders would have a difficult time selling their shares is irrelevant). *See also* Model Business Corp. Act § 13.01(4)(iii) (no marketability discount). The 1999 amendments to the Model Business Corporation Act provide that the appraiser should not take into account a marketability discount. Model Bus. Corp. Act § 13.01(4).

COOPER v. PABST BREWING CO.

1993 WL 208763 (Del.Ch., 1993).

[Former minority shareholders of Pabst Brewing Company ("Pabst") sought a fair value appraisal of their shares before the corporation's merger into G. Heileman Brewing Company ("Heileman"). Heileman acquired Pabst through a front-loaded, two-tier tender offer in which up to 3.75 million Pabst shares would be purchased at $32.00 per share in cash,

Pabst would be merged into Heileman, and the minority Pabst shares would be converted into a $24 subordinated debenture. Of the 6.7 million Pabst shares tendered during the first phase of the merger, Heileman accepted 5.6 million shares for payment at $32 per share and executed the merger. Petitioners did not tender their shares and, instead, commenced this appraisal action. As discussed in the following excerpt, the Court found the fair value of petitioners' shares at the time of the merger to be $27 per share which is less than the $45.72 to $51.71 per share value claimed by petitioners but more than the $20 per share value asserted by respondent.]

* * *

Where there is an established market for a corporation's stock, market value must be considered in appraising the value of the corporation's shares. In re Application of Delaware Racing Association, 42 Del. Ch. 406, 213 A.2d 203, 211 (1965); Cede & Co. v. Technicolor, Inc., 1990 Del. Ch. LEXIS 259, *101, Del. Ch., C.A. No. 7129–NC, Allen, C. (Oct. 19, 1990). Compare also 8 Del. C. § 262(b)(1)(i). However, the market price following the announcement of a tender offer is often an unreliable guide to the true market value because it may reflect a control premium and other factors connected with the acquiror's intentions but unrelated to the value of the firm as a going concern. Bell v. Kirby Lumber Corp., Del. Supr., 413 A.2d 137, 140–42 (1980); Cede & Co. v. Technicolor, Inc., 1990 Del. Ch. LEXIS 259, *71, Del. Ch., C.A. No. 7129–NC, Allen, C. (Oct. 19, 1990); Salomon Brothers Inc. v. Interstate Bakeries Corp., 1992 Del. Ch. LEXIS 100, *16, Del. Ch., C.A. No. 10,054–NC, Berger, V.C. (May 1, 1992). Therefore, Pabst argues, to the extent market value is considered, it should be based upon the approximate $14 per share that Pabst traded at just prior to Schmidt's initial tender offer in March 1982, one year prior to the date of the evaluation.

Camp's report, however, indicated that the high market price for Pabst's shares during 1982 was $31.50 per share. Pabst is probably correct in indicating that this is not an accurate reflection of Pabst's market value as a going concern. For various reasons, including the length of time between Schmidt's initial offer and the merger following Heileman's ultimately successful tender offer—a period in excess of one year—Pabst's share price in the period just prior to Schmidt's initial offer does not reflect its market value at the time of the merger.

Ordinarily, the value of any commodity in a competitive market is what a willing buyer would pay a willing seller for that commodity. Compare 8 Del. C. § 262(b)(1)(i). There is no question, in light of the number of bidders for Pabst in 1982, that there was a competitive market for its shares and that the value to the bidders exceeded $29. Therefore, under conventional principles of economics, the results of the auction for Pabst might be expected to provide a reasonable indication of Pabst's value that this Court can consider in light of the parties' failure to satisfactorily provide a persuasive measure of value using other techniques.

Delaware courts in the past, however, have been unwilling to consider just the results of an "auction" between competing tender offerors as evidence of a firm's value because such offers ordinarily contain a control premium unrelated to the value of the firm as a going concern. Bell v. Kirby Lumber Corp., Del. Supr., 413 A.2d 137, 140–42 (1980); Cede & Co. v. Technicolor, Inc., 1990 Del. Ch. LEXIS 259, *70, Del. Ch., C.A. No. 7129–NC, Allen, C. (Oct. 19, 1990); Salomon Brothers Inc. v. Interstate Bakeries Corp., 1992 Del. Ch. LEXIS 100, *15–16, Del. Ch., C.A. No. 10,054–NC, Berger, V.C. (May 1, 1992). To allocate a pro rata share of a premium to dissenting shareholders would, in effect, make the deal price a "floor" for the appraisal value. Technicolor, 1990 Del. Ch. LEXIS 259, *70, n.41. By making the deal price a "floor" for the appraised value, minority shareholders would be presented with a "no-lose" situation if they seek an appraisal and dissents from mergers would therefore be encouraged. Id.

The blended price of $29.50 here necessarily does not include much of a control premium. In a two-tiered tender offer such as this, the front-end of the offer—which would enable the offeror to exert control over the corporation—would incorporate any control premium (while the back-end would reflect a minority discount). The blended price in a two-tiered offer therefore, in this case, comes fairly close to reflecting the true market value of the firm. Therefore, while it would not be appropriate to consider Heileman's $32 per share offer for a majority of Pabst's shares (or Kalmonovitz's $40 per share offer for a majority of Pabst's shares) as a measure of Pabst's value because of the inclusion of the control premium, the $29.50 blended price does come close to representing Pabst's market value. At most the control premium did not exceed $2.50 per share and therefore the fair value range is $27–$28 per share.

"When a court is faced with a lack of reliable direct evidence of value, or when doubt exists as to the accuracy of its findings, it is appropriate for the court, as a factfinder, to test its conclusions against other evidence in the record before it." Matter of Shell Oil Co., Del. Supr., 607 A.2d 1213, 1220 (1992). Therefore, in order to see if the $27–$28 per share price accurately reflects Pabst's intrinsic value, that price should be compared with the price reached using other techniques.

As indicated above, petitioners' expert, Dr. Stanley J. Liebowitz, testified on cross-examination that under his present value of projected earnings methodology, the value of petitioners' shares would be approximately $27 per share if one assumed a 3.0% return on sales and annual sales volume growth of 1.5%. While both of these assumptions reflect somewhat higher profitability and sales growth than Pabst had experienced for the six years preceding the merger, they appear to be reasonable assumptions.

Pabst's return on sales for that period was depressed to some extent by $39 million in non-recurring costs arising out of the closing of its Peoria plant. There were two recessions during that period—the 1979–80 recession and the 1982–83 recession, which was the deepest recession since the Great Depression. These recessions undoubtedly affected Pabst's sales and profitability during the years immediately preceding the merger.

Finally, as Dooley acknowledged, Pabst "had gone through an unsettled period" following the death of James Windham, its CEO and that Pabst had "decided on a management team" just at the time when Pabst became the subject of takeover attempts. The unsettled situation following Windham's death likely exacerbated the declining levels of profitability and volume growth experienced by Pabst as a result of industry-wide changes during the years immediately preceding the merger. Dr. Liebowitz may have been over-optimistic as to the extent to which Windham's death contributed to Pabst's declining performance and the prospects of its profitability being restored to the levels of the early 1970s. However, some improvement in Pabst's performance could reasonably have been expected as a result of its achieving stable management and the better economic climate.

In light of these factors, assumptions of a 3.0% return on sales and 1.5% annual sales volume growth appear to be reasonable notwithstanding that Pabst's' actual performance had not reached those levels during the years immediately preceding the merger. The $27 per share value reached using these assumptions provides corroboration of a $27 per share value based on Pabst's market value. After considering all the evidence, the fair value is therefore found to be $27 per share. * * *

Notes

1. Assumptions must be made as to what cash flows will be in the future when using a discounted cash flow or similar analysis for valuation. Such analysis is often based on historical data, but is that an accurate measure of future returns? After all businesses grow, decline, recover and often stagnate in maturity. Competitors enter and leave. New products appear that make your company's offerings obsolete. How do you account for such eventualities in an appraisal of the present value based on future earnings shorn of merger value?

2. A corporation may have several lines of business that produce revenue unevenly. Should each revenue source be identified? What role do unnecessary expenses play in assessing the cash flow of the company? What if the merger results in a layoff of large amounts of workers who were unneeded even at the old firm? What if a prudent manager should have sold off a division that was losing large sums? What if such a plan was already underway before the merger? Should an efficient management assumption be imputed into the formula?

3.   Another assumption used in a discounted cash flow valuation is an assumed rate of return. Is that accurate? Interest rates change frequently, sometimes dramatically in a short period of time. Does a high interest rate at the present time (or conversely a low one) distort the valuation process?

———————

IN RE 75,629 SHARES OF COMMON STOCK OF TRAPP FAMILY LODGE, INC.

169 Vt. 82, 725 A.2d 927 (1999).

JOHNSON, J.

This is a dissenters' rights case in which Trapp Family Lodge, Inc., (TFL) appeals from a decision of the Lamoille County Superior Court that determined the fair value of the corporation's stock to be $63.44 per share.
* * *

The facts as found by the trial court are as follows. TFL was incorporated in Vermont in 1962 as a holding company for certain assets of the von Trapp family. TFL's assets include the Trapp Family Lodge, located in Stowe, Vermont. The Trapp Family Lodge is a resort hotel complex consisting of a hotel, two residential dwellings, and a cross-country skiing complex, all located on approximately 100 acres of land. In addition to the lodge facility, TFL owns approximately 2,200 acres of additional land. At the time of the merger that spawned this dispute, in January 1995, TFL also owned a timeshare facility known as the Trapp Family Guest Houses. Timeshare unit owners had exercised an option to purchase part of this facility, and the remaining $4,517,000 was payable to TFL in June 1995. Finally, TFL owns some royalty rights from which it receives annual income. As of the date of the merger, TFL's long term debt totaled approximately $6,430,700.

In September 1994, TFL gave notice to its shareholders of a special meeting to be held to consider a proposed merger of TFL into a new corporation. Prior to the meeting, TFL received notice from the dissenting shareholders indicating their intent to vote against the merger and to demand the payment of fair value for their shares. The merger was duly approved by the shareholders on October 17, 1994 at the special meeting. Prior to December 1, 1994, the dissenting shareholders, holding 75,629 of the corporation's 198,000 outstanding shares, tendered their shares and submitted forms demanding payment for them.

On January 28, 1995, TFL notified the dissenting shareholders that the merger had been completed, and paid the dissenting shareholders $33.84 per share, which the TFL board of directors estimated to be the fair value of each share based on a valuation completed by its expert Arthur Haut. On February 24, 1995, the dissenting shareholders filed demands with TFL for additional payments for their shares, claiming each share to be worth $61.00. On March 31, 1995, TFL commenced this action under 11A V.S.A. § 13.30 to determine the fair value of its stock as of the date of the merger.

The trial court concluded that the dissenting shareholders had complied with all statutory requirements necessary to entitle them to receive fair value for their shares. The court fixed the per share value of TFL on January 28, 1995, the date of merger, at $63.44 based on a valuation by the dissenters' expert Howard Gordon. TFL appeals, arguing that the court erred in determining the fair value of TFL shares.

Vermont's Business Corporation Act was amended effective January 1, 1994. See 11A V.S.A. §§ 1.01–20.16; 1993, No. 85, § 7. This case brings the new dissenters' rights chapter of this Act before us for the first time. See 11A V.S.A. §§ 13.01–13.31. Under the new statute, a shareholder of a Vermont corporation who dissents from certain enumerated corporate actions, including consummation of a plan of merger, is entitled to obtain from the corporation payment of the "fair value" of his or her shares. See 11A V.S.A. § 13.02(a)(1). Section 13.01(3) defines "fair value" to mean "the value of the shares immediately before the effectuation of the corporate action to which the dissenter objects, excluding any appreciation or depreciation in anticipation of the corporate action unless exclusion would be inequitable." See *id.* § 13.01(3). This definition mirrors the definition of "fair value" in the Model Business Corporation Act. See Model Bus.Corp.Act § 13.01 (1978). The official comment to the Model Act indicates that this broad definition "leaves untouched the accumulated case law" on the various methods of determining fair value. Model Bus.Corp.Act § 13.01 cmt. (3). * * *

TFL first argues that the trial court's valuation was clearly erroneous because it relied on the testimony of the dissenters' expert, Gordon, and rejected the testimony of TFL's expert, Haut. Although we do not find it necessary to detail the valuations by each expert to address the legal issues presented, an overview of the two approaches provides some context for our discussion. The dissenters' expert, Gordon, a certified financial analyst, conducted his appraisal using a net-asset-value approach; he used different methods to arrive at the values for individual assets, which were the lodge, the guest house option, the other guest house subsidiary assets, the royalties, and the excess land. Gordon used two methods to determine the value of the lodge. First, he used a discounted-cash-flow method; the value of the lodge added to the value of TFL's other assets resulted in a share value of $64.00. Second, Gordon recalculated the net assets value using a prior real estate appraisal by Frank Bredice for the lodge; the Bredice value of the lodge added to the other TFL assets resulted in a share value of $62.67. Averaging these results, Gordon determined that the fair value of TFL was $63.44 per share.

TFL's expert, Haut, a certified public accountant, separated TFL's assets into three separate groups: the lodge facility and related operations, the excess land, and the guest house option. He used a capitalized-cash-flow method to value the lodge facility, relied upon the Bredice appraisal to determine the value of the excess land, and valued the guest house option by discounting the option price to a present value. Using these methods, Haut valued TFL in its entirety at $6,700,000, which yields a per share value of $33.84.

The trial court held that the fair value of TFL was $63.44 per share, as established by Gordon. The court rejected Haut's appraisal for several reasons, including (1) Haut's valuation lacked the thoroughness and credibility of Gordon's valuation and the Bredice appraisal, (2) Haut unreasonably assumed TFL's earnings would not grow, (3) Haut valued the lodge operations at $7,300,00 in 1992, $7,000,000 in 1993, but then at only $4,748,000 for 1994, and (4) Haut overstated income taxes reducing after-tax cashflows.

On appeal, TFL argues that the court erred by adopting one expert's valuation wholesale and completely rejecting the valuations of the other experts. TFL relies on *Gonsalves v. Straight Arrow Publishers, Inc.,* 701 A.2d 357, 362 (Del.1997), which reversed the trial court's fair-value determination because the court had relied upon the valuation of one expert to the total exclusion of the valuation by the other expert. *Gonsalves* is distinguishable for two reasons. First, in *Gonsalves,* the court was presented with two widely divergent values: $1,059.37 and $131.60 per share. Here, the evidence included Gordon's lodge valuation ($9,355,000) and the Bredice lodge appraisal ($9,982,000), which was remarkably close to Gordon's valuation. On the other hand, Haut's valuation ($4,748,000) differed significantly from Gordon's valuation, the Bredice appraisal and even Haut's valuations for the two previous years ($7,300,000 in 1992 and $7,000,000 in 1993). Thus, the court here was not faced with the either-or evidence the court faced in *Gonsalves.* Second, essential to the court's reversal in *Gonsalves* was that the trial court had announced prior to trial that it intended to choose one expert's valuation in total. The Supreme Court of Delaware concluded that the court's either-or approach conflicted with its statutory obligation to engage in an independent valuation. See *id.* at 361–62. Here, there was no pretrial decision to adopt such an approach.

TFL presents five specific reasons why Gordon's valuation was unreliable. First, TFL claims that the court abused its discretion by adopting Gordon's discounted-cash-flow-valuation method because it is highly speculative as it is based on future financial performance rather than historical financial data. Under the dissenters' rights statute, however, a valuation may be based on any method generally considered acceptable in the financial community and otherwise admissible in court. See *McLoon,* 565 A.2d at 1003; *Weinberger,* 457 A.2d at 713. Here, three experts testified that the discounted-cash-flow-valuation method was considered acceptable in the financial community; thus, the court's decision to accept this method of valuation for the lodge operations was within its discretion. See *Waller,* 167 Vt. at 394, 706 A.2d at 463 (weight to be given to particular method of valuation is within sound discretion of court); see also *In re Radiology Assocs., Inc.,* 611 A.2d 485, 490 (Del.Ch.1991) (Delaware courts have affirmed validity of discounted-cash-flow method of valuation repeatedly). And contrary to TFL's claim, the court did not rely exclusively on the discounted-cash-flow method of valuation. Gordon's valuation of the lodge operations was based on averaging his discounted-cash-flow valuation of $9,355,000 and Bredice's fair-market-value appraisal of $9,982,000. The latter value was also comparable to national hotel industry sales data.

Second, TFL maintains that the trial court erred by adopting Gordon's three-percent growth rate because it was not supported by credible evidence and was not reasonable. The three-percent growth rate was supported by (1) TFL's comptroller's testimony that TFL's revenue increased three and one-half percent from 1993 to 1994, (2) a memorandum from TFL management to stockholders prior to the merger projecting substantial growth in the future, (3) a report submitted to shareholders with the memorandum indicating an expected growth rate of four percent for 1994 and further improvement expected based on national trends for 1995, and (4) Gordon's analysis of historical and projected revenue rates for the lodge and national hotel industry statistics. Based on this evidence, the court found that a three-percent growth rate was reasonable. We agree. See *Rubin v. Sterling Enterprises, Inc.,* 164 Vt. 582, 588, 674 A.2d 782, 786 (1996) (factual findings will be upheld on appeal unless there is no credible evidence to support finding).

Third, TFL argues that the evidence does not support Gordon's use of a discount rate of 8.6 percent. TFL relies primarily on material submitted to this Court with its brief in appendix IV. The dissenters have moved to strike the appendix on the ground that the material contained therein was not admitted into evidence before the trial court and, therefore, is not part of the record. We agree and strike appendix IV. See V.R.A.P. 10(a); *State v. Brown,* 165 Vt. 79, 82, 676 A.2d 350, 352 (1996) (documents not on file in trial court cannot be part of record on appeal). The record indicates that the 8.6 percent discount rate was derived from methods generally accepted in the financial community for valuing businesses. Moreover, despite TFL's claims that Gordon's discount rate was inappropriately low, the evidence indicated that Gordon's discount rate did not differ significantly from Haut's capitalization rate. Most of the difference in their lodge valuations stemmed from Haut applying a zero growth rate and failing to account for depreciation in a generally accepted method.

Fourth, TFL maintains that the court's reliance on the Bredice appraisal was clearly erroneous because the court rejected the capitalized-cash-flow method used by Haut, but accepted the Bredice appraisal using the same method. Gordon explained, however, his limited use of the Bredice appraisal. According to Gordon, if the liquidation value of the business is greater than the operating value, then the liquidation value should prevail. Consequently, Gordon reviewed the Bredice real estate appraisal, determined that it was reliable, and considered it as the lodge liquidation value against which he could check his operation value. Because the two values were so close, he gave equal weight to each by averaging the two values. Haut, on the other hand, used a valuation method that the court found less appropriate than Gordon's method, but more importantly, the court found that Haut did not use the method accurately. There was no error in using a valid real estate appraisal as a check on the discount-cash-flow-method valuation, while rejecting a valuation made solely on an inaccurate and unreasonable application of the capitalized-cash-flow method.

Fifth, TFL contends that the trial court erred by accepting Gordon's valuation and expense adjustments. The court found that Gordon eliminated extraordinary, nonrecurring expenses from his calculation, which is a generally-accepted adjustment for business valuation. This finding is supported by the record. See *Waller,* 167 Vt. at 395, 706 A.2d at 464 (recognizing that adjustments to income statement are often necessary to show an accurate profit picture). Indeed, Haut also made some adjustments to the income statements, such as adding back payments made to family members. TFL has submitted a list of other alleged errors made by Gordon. Although referencing Gordon's testimony in the record, TFL provides no support for most of its claims that the statements were erroneous. The court made an adjustment for the single error that was acknowledged by Gordon. To the extent that the other statements to which TFL objects reflected on Gordon's credibility, the trial court was in the better position to make this evaluation. See *Bruntaeger v. Zeller,* 147 Vt. 247, 252, 515 A.2d 123, 126 (1986) (it is province of trial court to determine credibility of witnesses and weigh persuasive effect of evidence).

We conclude, therefore, that the trial court's finding setting the fair value of TFL's stock at $63.44 is supported by the evidence and is not clearly erroneous.

TFL next contends that the court erred as a matter of law by failing to consider the tax consequences of a potential sale. According to TFL, a potential buyer of a corporation would consider the potential tax consequences of the purchase, and therefore, the trial court should have considered the tax consequences of a liquidation of the corporation's assets. TFL points to appendices I, II and III submitted in support of its brief to illustrate the tax consequences of a sale of TFL assets. The dissenters move to strike the appendices because these documents were not admitted into evidence at trial. We do not consider the appendices on appeal because we conclude that the trial court correctly determined that no tax consequences of a sale of corporate assets should be considered where no such sale is contemplated.

Under the dissenters' rights statute, the court is required to value the corporation as "a going concern." *Weinberger,* 457 A.2d at 713. Accordingly, courts have generally rejected any tax discount "unless the corporation is undergoing an actual liquidation." *Hansen,* 957 P.2d at 42; see also *Bogosian v. Woloohojian,* 882 F.Supp. at 266 (only when corporation has committed to sale of assets may tax impact, if any, be considered). Here, there was no evidence that TFL was undergoing liquidation on the valuation date. Indeed, the evidence indicated that TFL was a going concern. Thus, the trial court correctly declined to consider the tax consequences of the sale of any assets.

TFL maintains that it will have to sell assets in order to pay the dissenters for their shares, and that therefore the tax consequences of the sale should be considered in the valuation. Under the dissenters' rights statute, however, the dissenters are entitled to a pro rata share of the fair value of the corporation immediately before the merger. See 11A V.S.A. § 13.01(3) (value shares immediately before effectuation of corporate action to which dissenter objects). "Thus, if costs are incurred after effectuation of the exchange, those costs should not be assessed against the dissenting shareholders." *Hansen*, 957 P.2d at 43. Accordingly, it would be inappropriate to consider a future sale of assets to determine the fair value prior to merger. See *id.* (rejecting tax discount in fair value determination where corporation is not undergoing liquidation); see also *Bogosian v. Woloohojian Realty Corp.*, 973 F.Supp. 98, 107 (D.R.I.1997) (rejecting similar tax-consequences argument by corporation because it would be inequitable to order dissenter to reimburse corporation for tax consequences of buy-out where dissenter undoubtedly would also face tax consequences).

TFL next contends that the trial court erred as a matter of law by refusing to consider certain "agreed values" determined pursuant to a shareholders' restriction agreement. Under the agreement, a shareholder who desired to transfer shares to anyone other than ascendants or lineal descendants was required to offer the shares first to TFL. If TFL declined to purchase them, then the shareholder was required to offer the shares to the remaining shareholders. The purchase price for the shares was determined by an "agreed value" established by the stockholders of at least seventy-five percent of the outstanding shares. In the absence of an "agreed value," the stock price was set by "book value" calculated pursuant to the procedures in the agreement. The agreed value under the stock restriction agreement for 1992 was $28.78 and for 1993 was $30.92. The trial court found that the agreed values were based upon the fair market value for minority interest shares and were not timely representations of the "fair value" of the shares in January 1995. TFL claims it was reversible error to accord no weight to the "agreed values."

In close corporations, "shareholders' agreements restricting the manner in which shareholders may dispose of their shares are quite common." *Hansen*, 957 P.2d at 37. Such an agreement does not apply, however, to a fair value determination pursuant to the dissenters' rights statute unless the agreement so provides. See *id.* (rejecting shareholders' agreement in determining fair value because agreement did not contemplate a fundamental change in corporate form such as merger); see also *In re Pace Photographers, Ltd.*, 71 N.Y.2d 737, 530 N.Y.S.2d 67, 525 N.E.2d 713, 718 (1988) (fair value under minority buy-out statute not determined by shareholders' agreement concerning voluntary sale of stock). The shareholders' objective in establishing an agreed value for voluntary sale of shares may be very different than the court's objective in determining fair value in a dissenters' rights case. See *id.* at 719.

Similarly, the restriction agreement here is not applicable because it did not contemplate establishing share values for a corporate merger. Moreover, the agreed values for 1992 and 1993 were not indicative of the fair value in January 1995 because they were untimely in the sense that they were no longer in effect, and because they were based on fair market value of a minority interest. The court weighed these factors and was not persuaded that the agreed values provided any basis for the fair value in January 1995. It was within the court's discretion to determine the weight to be given any particular evidence. See *Waller,* 167 Vt. at 394, 706 A.2d at 463.

TFL next argues that the trial court's application of a thirty-percent control premium was clearly erroneous. Gordon testified that, in applying the discounted-cash-flow-method to value the lodge, he relied on figures derived from publicly traded companies and that the per share value of a share on the public market is a minority interest value. Thus, even if this value is multiplied by the number of outstanding shares, the total reflects an accumulation of minority interests; it does not reflect the value of a controlling interest. A controlling interest is of greater value than a minority interest because the controlling shareholder has control over operation of the corporation. Because Gordon's valuation was based on publicly-traded minority interest values, he applied a control premium to account for the value of control in owning the lodge as a whole. For the same reason, Haut also applied a control premium in his valuation. Based on this evidence, the trial court applied a control premium in deciding fair value.

Under the circumstances presented here, there was no legal error in applying a control premium to adjust a valuation that reflected publicly traded minority interests. See *Rapid–American Corp. v. Harris,* 603 A.2d 796, 806 (Del.1992) (reversing trial court's valuation for failing to apply a control premium where corporation had one hundred percent interest in three subsidiaries and valuation of subsidiaries was based on publicly traded value, which represented discounted minority values). TFL relies on appendices IV and V to contest application of a control premium. Again, this material was not admitted into evidence at trial, and thus, we do not consider it here on appeal. The expert testimony at trial supported the court's use of a control premium.

TFL further argues that even if a control premium is appropriate, there is no evidence in the record to support the trial court's finding that a thirty-percent premium is reasonable, if not somewhat conservative. Gordon testified, however, that the average control premium for the hotel and motel industry was forty-six percent. Haut applied a fifteen-percent control premium. Gordon applied a thirty-percent control premium and stated that this figure was on the conservative side. The court's findings are supported by the evidence. See *Wyatt v. Palmer,* 165 Vt. 600, 601, 683

A.2d 1353, 1356 (1996) (court's findings upheld if supported by reasonable evidentiary basis).

Affirmed.

M.P.M. ENTERPRISES, INC. v. GILBERT

731 A.2d 790 (Del.1999).

Veasy, Chief Justice.

In this appeal of a statutory appraisal action under 8 *Del.C.* § 262, we consider whether the Court of Chancery committed legal error or, alternatively, abused its discretion by applying an appraisal analysis that accorded no weight to the terms of the merger giving rise to the appraisal action or to the terms of two prior offers for equity stakes in the subject corporation. We further consider whether the Court of Chancery erred in refusing to consider the dilutive effect of alleged obligations incurred by the company to non-stockholder employees. We affirm the judgment of the Court of Chancery on the ground that under well-established precedent of this Court, the Court of Chancery did not commit legal error or abuse its discretion in its choice and application of appraisal methods.

Petitioner below-appellee, Jeffrey D. Gilbert instituted a statutory appraisal action as the sole dissenting stockholder of respondent below-appellant, M.P.M. Enterprises, Inc. ("MPM"), following MPM's merger into a subsidiary of Cookson Group, PLC ("Cookson") a London-based industrial concern, on May 2, 1995.

Prior to the merger, MPM was a Delaware corporation, headquartered in Franklin, Massachusetts. It was engaged in the design, manufacture and distribution of screen printers.[9] Business was very good in the 1980s and early 1990s. In fact, according to MPM's consolidated financial statements, in fiscal years 1991–94, MPM's sales increased from $13.5 million to $55.5 million and MPM's net income increased from $8,300 to $6.5 million. In March 1995, MPM and Cookson signed an Agreement of Merger that provided for immediate payments by Cookson of $65 million upon consummation of the merger, with contingent earn-out payments up to an additional $73.635 million.[10] On May 2, 1995, the parties consummated the merger.

---

9. Screen printers are one form of machine used in the surface mount technology industry to attach electronic components to circuit boards. Screen printers use a squeegee to push solder paste through a stencil onto specific points on circuit boards where components need to be attached.

10. The contingent earn-out depended on MPM's average annual earnings between June 1, 1995 and June 30, 1998. If the average annual earnings met or exceeded $35 million, the entire contingent payout became due. If the average annual earnings fell between $14 million and $35 million, some contingent payout less than the maximum became due. If the average annual earnings fell below $14 million, no contingent payout became due.

Gilbert owned 600 shares of MPM's common stock and 200 shares of MPM's preferred stock, giving him an ownership stake in MPM of 7.273% on a fully diluted basis. Under the terms of the merger, Gilbert would have received $4.56 million (minus transactional costs) and the opportunity to receive contingent payments of up to an additional $5.36 million if MPM reached the earn-out goals set forth in the Merger Agreement. Apparently believing that these sums did not reflect MPM's going concern value at the date of the merger, Gilbert chose to exercise his statutory appraisal right, pursuant to 8 *Del.C.* § 262(a), and filed an action in the Court of Chancery.

In the appraisal action, MPM presented expert testimony concerning MPM's going concern value at the date of the merger from William A. Lundquist and Advest, Inc. (collectively "Lundquist"). In response, Gilbert presented expert testimony from Kenneth W. McGraw and Patricof & Co. (collectively "McGraw"). As is often the case in such actions before the Court of Chancery, these experts came up with widely divergent appraisal values. Lundquist, focusing on a supposedly gloomy outlook for MPM and its industry, placed MPM's going concern value at $81.7 million. In contrast, McGraw focused on a particularly rosy outlook for MPM and its industry, placing MPM's going concern value at $357.1 million.

Lundquist arrived at his appraisal value through two separate discounted cash flow ("DCF") analyses along with a comparable public companies analysis. He constructed both a "sell-side" DCF (representing the transaction from MPM's point of view) and a "buy-side" DCF (representing the transaction from a buyer's point of view). The buy-side analysis, representing the price at which all of the synergies from the transaction go to the seller, resulted in the highest price a reasonable buyer would pay for MPM. As part of his analysis, Lundquist compared the values derived from the buy-side analysis to the terms of the merger, as well as two earlier offers for equity interests in MPM from Dover Technologies and TA Associates, Inc. (the "prior offers"). In his comparable public companies analysis, Lundquist compared MPM's EBITDA, EBIT and P/E ratios to those of comparable public companies to determine a fair market value for MPM.

After examining the data, Lundquist concluded that the comparable public companies approach was problematic because MPM was not in a position to go public, rendering comparison unhelpful. He also concluded, based on the sell-side DCF, that MPM's equity value at the time of the merger was $90.5 million. He then discounted this amount by 8.8% (the amount of alleged obligations to non-stockholder employees) and again by 1% (the transaction costs borne by approving stockholders) to arrive at a fair market value for MPM at the date of the merger of $81.7 million. Assuming that this last figure included some synergies from the merger (disallowed by § 262), Lundquist pegged it as the highest possible going concern value for MPM at the date of the merger.

McGraw performed two analyses: a DCF analysis and a comparative public companies analysis. McGraw took the values from each of these approaches, weighted them equally, and arrived at a fair market value for MPM's equity at the date of the merger of $357.1 million.

In evaluating the various approaches, the Court of Chancery settled on a DCF analysis as the best method for discerning MPM's going concern value at the date of the merger. It first noted that it could not consider Lundquist's buy-side DCF analysis because this method approached the value from the buyer's perspective, rather than valuing the company as a going concern, as required by § 262. In addition, the Court of Chancery stated that it would not use Lundquist's proffer of previous offers to invest in MPM because "[t]hese figures represent nothing more than offers to purchase, which were surely based on the value of MPM to a particular entity." Finally, the Court discarded the opposing comparative public company analyses as being relatively weak in comparison to the DCF analyses. Finding that the DCF analysis conducted by McGraw, Gilbert's expert, was the more "thorough and convincing approach to the determination of the discount rate," the Court accepted Gilbert's framework as a starting point.

The first step in the Court of Chancery's manipulation of this framework was to determine revenue growth projections. The Court found that, although MPM management had predicted 1995 sales of $108 million in April 1995, it was apparent by the date of the merger that MPM would have a very difficult time meeting this projection. Therefore, the Court based the cash flow forecast on the assumption that MPM's 1995 revenues would be lower than the April projection.

Also included in the April management projection were projected revenue growth rates of 38.9% for 1996, 20% for 1997 and 22.2% for 1998. At the date of the merger, MPM had recently developed a new product. Gilbert argued that, at the date of the merger, this product was expected to revolutionize the screen printing industry and, therefore, the Court of Chancery should adjust the growth rates upward. MPM, on the other hand, noted that this new product was experiencing serious development problems at the date of the merger and, therefore, the trial court should adjust the growth rates downward. The Court rejected both attempts to adjust the growth rates, finding no way to conclude that the April 1995 projection had not incorporated both of these claims. For the same reason, it refused to adjust the April 1995 projection for research and development expenses.

Assuming a five year DCF projection, the next step was to determine the terminal value of MPM at the end of fiscal year 2000. Both experts used comparable public companies to make this determination. Finding that Lundquist, MPM's expert, had "convincingly demonstrated the appropriateness of [his] selection [of comparable companies]" the Court of Chancery used the terminal value multiple of 7.5 provided by MPM.

The Court of Chancery next moved to the determination of the proper discount rate. It approved of McGraw's methods, but disapproved of the comparable companies McGraw used in applying these methods. It solved this problem by holding that "MPM's discount rate shall be that rate determined through use of [McGraw's] CAPM model except that the comparable beta employed shall be based on the *average beta of [MPM's] comparable companies.*"

As a final matter, the Court of Chancery considered MPM's claim that Gibson's ownership percentage in MPM should be diluted by 8.8%, or the amount of obligations it claimed to have outstanding to non-stockholder employees. It found that MPM had failed to provide any evidence that these obligations existed, or that litigation had been threatened over them. Accordingly, the Court refused to allow a dilution of Gibson's ownership percentage based on these alleged obligations.

The opinion of the Court of Chancery left some issues unanswered, as it never provided the actual discount rate that the parties should apply. On April 24, 1998, the Court issued a second opinion, in which it determined several components of the discount rate: the cost of debt (9.6%); the debt to total capital ratio (5%); the source of "raw" beta data (Bloomberg); and a small company premium (2.87%). On May 22, 1998, the Court issued a final order and judgment, in which it determined that MPM's equity value at the date of the merger was $156,331,000. On a per share basis, this translated into a value of $14,211.91, or a total of $11,369,528 for Gilbert's 800 shares.

MPM appealed to this Court, challenging the decision of the Court of Chancery on two grounds. First, MPM claimed that the Court erred in failing to consider the terms of the merger or the terms of the prior offers in its determination of fair value. Second, MPM challenged the Court's conclusion that there was no evidence of record to support the dilution of Gilbert's ownership share due to obligations owed to non-stockholder employees.

From the language in the opinions of the Court of Chancery, we were unable to discern why the Court did not use the values derived from the merger and the prior offers in its determination of fair value. We could not determine whether it accorded these values no weight after admitting them into evidence, or whether it refused to admit them into evidence as inconsistent with legally acceptable methods of valuation under § 262. We remanded this matter to the Court of Chancery for clarification so that it could provide a better explanation of its analysis with respect to both the merger and the prior offers. In the event its determination was factual and not legal, we further asked the Court to recite the facts it relied on in according zero weight to these values.

In its remand opinion, the Court of Chancery clarified its position with respect to the merger and the prior offers. The Court stated that it did not mean to imply that § 262 barred consideration of specific offers for a company, and that it did, in fact, consider the relevance of each of these offers to the fair value of MPM at the date of the merger. It explained that, while potentially relevant, the evidence with respect to both the merger and the prior offers was of only marginal utility and therefore received no weight in the final analysis. The Court further explained that, rather than relying on specific evidence supporting its decision to accord zero weight to these offers, it relied on the absence of any credible evidence provided by MPM that established a nexus between the values derived from the offers at issue and the going concern value of MPM at the date of the merger. * * *

In this case, the Court of Chancery did not err in its decision regarding the admissibility of the terms of the merger and of the prior offers. It did admit all of these offers into evidence, although it did not dwell on them and ultimately chose not to accord them any weight. Therefore, the inquiry must shift to whether the Court abused its discretion in refusing to give any weight to the terms of the merger and of the prior offers in its appraisal of Gilbert's shares.

Section 262(h) requires the trial court to "appraise the shares, determining their fair value exclusive of any element of value arising from the accomplishment or expectation of the merger or consolidation." Fair value, as used in § 262(h), is more properly described as the value of the company to the stockholder as a going concern, rather than its value to a third party as an acquisition. We have long recognized that failure to value a company as a going concern may result in an understatement of fair value.

In *Weinberger v. UOP*, 457 A.2d 701 (1983) and its progeny, we elucidated the extent of the discretion of the Court of Chancery in choosing a method of valuation in a statutory appraisal. *Weinberger* acknowledged the Court's discretion to use "any techniques or methods which are generally considered acceptable in the financial community and otherwise admissible in court, subject to our interpretation of 8 *Del.C.* § 262(h)." Assuming the variables applied by the trial court are proper, a DCF analysis is one such technique or method of determining going concern value that is within the trial court's discretion to use.

In this appeal, MPM does not challenge the DCF analysis employed by the Court of Chancery or the specific variables used in the analysis. Instead, MPM focuses on other language in § 262(h) requiring the trial court to "take into account all relevant factors" when determining the fair value of a petitioner's shares. MPM contends that the figures derived from the merger and the prior offers are "relevant factors" that the trial court impermissibly ignored in its determination of fair value. According to MPM, if the trial court had considered these "real world" values, it would have realized that the results of the DCF analysis did not accurately reflect the going concern value of MPM at the date of the merger.

The initial determination by the Court of Chancery of the variables the parties should employ in the DCF analysis was a well-reasoned use of discretion. The Court certainly acted as an independent appraiser of

MPM, using its judgment to discern which facets of the experts' competing analyses correctly set forth the assumptions necessary for a proper DCF analysis. The only question remaining is whether the Court abused its discretion in refusing to compare the figures derived from this properly-applied DCF analysis to the merger value and the valuations implicit in the prior offers. Values derived in the open market through arms-length negotiations offer better indicia of reliability than the interested party transactions that are often the subject of appraisals under § 262. But the trial court, in its discretion, need not accord any weight to such values when unsupported by evidence that they represent the going concern value of the company at the effective date of the merger or consolidation.

In this case, MPM proffered evidence of the merger and the prior offers only as part of Lundquist's buy-side DCF. The Court of Chancery properly rejected this DCF approach because it focused on the elements of value that would arise from the merger, rather than on the going concern value of MPM without any consideration of such synergistic values. As noted, section 262(h) explicitly states that the trial court "shall appraise the shares, determining their fair value *exclusive of any element of value arising from the accomplishment or expectation of the merger or consolidation....*" By determining the highest price at which all synergies devolved to the seller, this buy-side analysis was undoubtedly proscribed by § 262(h).

Irrespective of that fact, MPM contends that the Court of Chancery still should have considered the terms of the merger and the prior offers in its final appraisal decision. To support this contention, MPM points to *Van de Walle v. Unimation Inc.*, 1991 WL 36477 (1991) where the Court of Chancery found that such transactions are the most reliable indicia of fair value, even more reliable than expert testimony concerning DCF analyses. But *Van de Walle* differs from this case in a very significant respect. In *Van de Walle*, certain minority stockholders claimed that the target company's board of directors had breached its fiduciary duties in accepting an unfair merger price. In essence, the stockholders argued that the board of directors had failed to obtain the best price available in executing a merger. In this case, a dissenting stockholder petitioned the Court of Chancery to determine the fair value of his shares. Under section 262, the fairness of the price on the open market is not the overriding consideration. Instead section 262(h) requires that the Court of Chancery discern the going concern value of the company irrespective of the synergies involved in a merger. A fair merger price in the context of a breach of fiduciary duty claim will not always be a fair value in the context of determining going concern value.

We agree with the general statement made by the Court in *Van de Walle*. A merger price resulting from arms-length negotiations where there are no claims of collusion is a very strong indication of fair value. But in an appraisal action, that merger price must be accompanied by evidence tending to show that it represents the going concern value of the company rather than just the value of the company to one specific buyer.

In this case, MPM failed to present this additional evidence with respect to either the merger or the prior offers.[11] This led the Court of Chancery to decide that these values were of only marginal relevance, if any. In our view, this determination was not an abuse of discretion. * * *

At trial, MPM provided two forms of evidence to prove that it was obliged to provide equity to non-stockholder management. This consisted of three written employment agreements and the live testimony of Thomas Bagley, MPM's President and Chief Executive Officer.

The three written employment agreements each include a section entitled "Long–Term Incentive." According to this section, the specified employees *"will be* granted an option, *subject to rules, regulations, and restrictions* as determined by the Board of Directors of the Company in their sole discretion to acquire ... stock in the company." This section goes on to define the specific number of shares that the employee "shall possibly have the right to acquire...." The Court of Chancery did not have before it a later agreement showing that these contingent obligations actually vested, and in what amount they vested. Also, MPM's financial statements prior to the merger did not contain any indication of these options. The trial court did not err in finding that the employment agreements alone did not provide sufficient proof of the alleged obligations.

Bagley's testimony could have provided the extra element lacking in the employment agreements. He testified that MPM made oral commitments to the non-stockholder management. When asked how MPM determined that payments would be made to non-stockholders, Bagley answered that "[w]e had in all of these instances with all of these people had discussions with them. In some cases we had written commitments to them to provide them with equity participation in the organization, in MPM." The trial court was not convinced by this testimony and found that MPM had failed to provide sufficient evidence to prove that these payments of equity actually were legal obligations of MPM rather than merely costs of the merger. As we have stated, "[w]hen the determination of facts turns on a question of credibility and the acceptance or rejection of 'live' testimony by the trial judge, [the trial court's] findings will be approved on review."

The Court of Chancery's appraisal of Gilbert's shares in MPM is affirmed in all respects

---

SECTION 5. DE FACTO MERGERS

There may be a variety of alternatives for structuring a corporate combination to achieve the desired result. Frequently a transaction will be

---

11. The prior offers suffered from flaws that made them marginally useful in an appraisal under *section 262*, under the best of circumstances. Both were remote in time from the date of the merger and neither was actually consummated.

structured so as to invoke a statutory form that avoids appraisal rights that would be afforded to the transaction if the parties selected a straight merger. The argument has been made that, where a transaction is structured in a manner to deprive a constituency of their appraisal rights, it should be treated as a de facto merger, thus giving the shareholders the appraisal remedy that would apply under the merger statute.

In Farris v. Glen Alden Corp., 393 Pa. 427, 143 A.2d 25 (1958), the court held that a transaction that was structured as a sale of assets, which did not have appraisal rights, was actually a de facto merger that required such protection. The Pennsylvania legislature, however, repudiated the de facto merger doctrine. See Penn. Stat. C. A. § 1904. In *Terry v. Penn Central Corp.*, 668 F.2d 188 (3d Cir. 1981), the plaintiff claimed that the de facto merger doctrine should be invoked to grant statutory appraisal rights to the shareholders of the parent corporation in a triangular merger of the target company into a subsidiary:

> Appellants argue that Penn Central is nevertheless brought into the amalgamation by the de facto merger doctrine as set out in Pennsylvania law in Farris v. Glen Alden Corp., 393 Pa. 427, 143 A.2d 25 (1958). Farris was the penultimate step in a pas de deux involving the Pennsylvania courts and the Pennsylvania legislature regarding the proper treatment for transactions that reached the same practical result as a merger but avoided the legal form of merger and the concomitant legal obligations. In the 1950s the Pennsylvania courts advanced the doctrine that a transaction having the effect of an amalgamation would be treated as a de facto merger. See, e.g., Bloch v. The Baldwin Locomotive Works, 75 Pa.D. & C. 24 (1950). The legislature responded with efforts to constrict the de facto merger doctrine. Farris, addressing those efforts, held that the doctrine still covered a reorganization agreement that had the effect of merging a large corporation into a smaller corporation. In a 1959 response to Farris, the legislature made explicit its objection to earlier cases that found certain transactions to be de facto mergers. The legislature enacted a law, modifying inter alia Sections 311 and 908, entitled in part:

>> An Act ... changing the law as to ... the acquisition or transfer of corporate assets, the rights of dissenting shareholders, ... abolishing the doctrine of de facto mergers or consolidation and reversing the rules laid down in Bloch v. Baldwin Locomotive Works, 75 D & C 24, and Marks v. The Autocar Co., 153 F.Supp. 768, ... Act of November 10, 1959 (P.L. 1406, No. 502). * * *

> In the absence of any explicit guidance to the contrary by the Pennsylvania courts, we conclude that the language of the legislature in 1959 precludes a decision that the transaction in this case constitutes a de facto merger sufficient to entitle Penn Central shareholders to dissent and appraisal rights. We therefore hold that appellants do

not possess such rights if a transaction such as the one involved here is consummated.

In *Heilbrunn v. Sun Chemical Corp.*, 150 A.2d 755 (Del.1959) the Delaware Supreme Court rejected application of the de fact merger doctrine. In that case, shareholders of the corporation making the asset purchase, were seeking an appraisal. More broadly, the Delaware court rejected a de facto merger claim in circumstances described as follows:

> A sale of assets is effected under § 271 in consideration of shares of stock of the purchasing corporation. The agreement of sale embodies also a plan to dissolve the selling corporation and distribute the shares so received to the stockholders of the seller, so as to accomplish the same result as would be accomplished by a merger of the seller into the purchaser.

Hariton v. Arco Electronics, Inc., 188 A.2d 123 (Del.1963). The court based its decision under its "equal dignity" doctrine that recognizes that an act taken legally under one statute cannot be found to be illegal merely because it conflicts with the goal of another statute.

Other courts have embraced the de facto merger doctrine. Rath v. Rath Packing Co., 257 Iowa 1277, 136 N.W.2d 410 (1965) (recognizing the *de facto* merger doctrine); Pratt v. Ballman–Cummings Furniture Co., 261 Ark. 396, 549 S.W.2d 270 (1977) (applying de facto merger doctrine to invoke statutory appraisal rights); Arnold Graphics Industries, Inc. v. Independent Agent Center, Inc., 775 F.2d 38 (2d Cir.1985) (applying de facto merger doctrine to establish successor corporation liability); Marks v. Minnesota Mining & Manufacturing Co., 187 Cal.App.3d 1429, 232 Cal. Rptr. 594 (1986) (same). The court in Applestein v. United Board & Carton Corp., 60 N.J.Super. 333, 159 A.2d 146 (Ch. 1960), aff'd 33 N.J. 72, 161 A.2d 474 (1960) also applied a de facto merger doctrine. The New Jersey legislature, thereafter, adopted the result in Applestein. N.J. Stat. Ann. § 14A:10–12. The doctrine also received legislative approval in California. *See* Cal. Corp. Code §§ 168, 1101, 1200 & 1300 (West 1990).

NOTE

As described earlier in this chapter, the appraisal remedy is often disadvantageous to corporations in cash out mergers because the Delaware courts may place substantially higher values on the stock being cashed out than was offered to the shareholders by the corporation. Is an appraisal proceeding needed to keep management honest in an asset purchase, or will the arms-length nature of the transaction assure that result? Are assets sales always arms-length?

CHAPTER EIGHT

PUBLICLY TRADED STOCKS— SEC REGULATION

■ ■ ■

Chapter objectives

- To understand the major federal securities laws that apply to the primary and secondary capital markets.

- To see why many firms prefer to raise capital through a private placement of securities rather than through a public offering.

- To appreciate the role played by underwriters in the issuance of securities.

- To understand the role of self-regulatory organizations as both markets and enforcers of securities laws.

SECTION 1.   INTRODUCTION—THE FEDERAL SECURITIES LAWS

Corporate lawyers will devote much of their time to compliance with the federal securities laws and rules adopted by the Securities and Exchange Commission ("SEC"). The following is a description of the background that led to the creation of the SEC:

The SEC's foundation was laid in an era that was ripe for reform. Before the Great Crash of 1929, there was little support for federal regulation of the securities markets. This was particularly true during the post-World War I surge of securities activity. Proposals that the federal government require financial disclosure and prevent the fraudulent sale of stock were never seriously pursued.

Tempted by promises of "rags to riches" transformations and easy credit, most investors gave little thought to the dangers inherent in uncontrolled market operation. During the 1920s, approximately 20 million large and small shareholders took advantage of post-war prosperity and set out to make their fortunes in the stock market. It is estimated that of the $50 billion in new securities offered during this period, half became worthless.

When the stock market crashed in October 1929, the fortunes of countless investors were lost. Banks also lost great sums of money in the Crash because they had invested heavily in the markets. When people feared their banks might not be able to pay back the money they had in their accounts, a "run" on the banking system caused many bank failures.

With the Crash and ensuing depression, public confidence in the markets plummeted. There was a consensus that for the economy to recover, the public's faith in the capital markets needed to be restored. Congress held hearings to identify the problems and search for solutions.

Based on the findings in these hearings, Congress passed the Securities Act of 1933 and the Securities Exchange Act of 1934. These laws were designed to restore investor confidence in our capital markets by providing more structure and government oversight. The main purposes of these laws can be reduced to two common-sense notions:

Companies publicly offering securities for investment dollars must tell the public the truth about their businesses, the securities they are selling, and the risks involved in investing.

People who sell and trade securities—brokers, dealers, and exchanges—must treat investors fairly and honestly, putting investors' interests first.

Monitoring the securities industry requires a highly coordinated effort. Congress established the Securities and Exchange Commission in 1934 to enforce the newly-passed securities laws, to promote stability in the markets and, most importantly, to protect investors. President Franklin Delano Roosevelt appointed Joseph P. Kennedy, President John F. Kennedy's father, to serve as the first Chairman of the SEC.

SEC Website visited on Jan. 9, 2011: www.sec.gov/about/whatwedo. shtml# create.

The core of the federal securities laws are six statutes enacted between 1933 and 1940. They are:

Securities Act of 1933. This statute regulates public offerings of securities and prohibits offers and sales of securities which are not registered with the Securities and Exchange Commission. Certain securities, such as municipal bonds, are exempted from those registration requirements. The statute and SEC regulations specify the contents of the registration statement and prospectus. This legislation requires the disclosure of material information about companies that sell their stock to the public. This legislation was based on the theory propounded by Justice Louis Brandeis. He stated that "publicity is justly commended as a remedy for social and industrial diseases. Sun light is said to be the best of disinfectants; electric light the most efficient policeman." *Louis Brandeis, Other People's Money and How the Brokers Use It* 4 (1932). The Securities Act of 1933 sought to bring full disclosure to securities sales as a way of exposing and deterring abuses. It added "to the ancient rule of caveat emptor, the further doctrine 'let the seller also beware.'" H.R. Rep. No. 85, 73d Cong., 1st Sess. 2 (1934). The Securities Act did not seek to "guarantee the present soundness or the future value of any security. The investor must still, in the final analysis, select the security which he deems appropriate for investment." S. Rep. No. 1455, 73d Cong., 2d Sess. 153 (1934). The act sought to assure that the investor has "complete and truthful information from which he may intelligently appraise the value of a security. . . . *Id.* The Securities Act of 1933 required a twenty-day waiting period between the filing of the registration statement with the SEC and the offer of the stock to the public. This allowed investors time to asses the information being disclosed and to make an informed unhurried investment decision."

Securities Exchange Act of 1934. This act extended federal regulation to trading in securities which are already issued to the public. Section 13 of the Securities Exchange Act of 1934 now requires public companies to report periodically on their financial condition. Another section of the Securities Exchange Act, Section 14, regulates the solicitation of proxies from holders of such securities. Still another provision regulates take-over bids, tender offers and purchases by companies of their own shares. Section 16 of the Securities Exchange Act, restricts the ability of insiders to make short-term profits by trading in their company's stock, and Section 10 prohibited manipulation of securities prices and imposes a broad antifraud prohibits in connection with the purchase and sale of stocks and other securities.

Public Utility Holding Company Act of 1935. This act was designed to correct abuses in the financing and operation of electric and gas public utility holding company systems, and to achieve physical integration and corporate simplification of those systems. This legislation was passed in response to a report by the Federal Trade Commission that totaled over 100 volumes. That study found that holding company structures were used to create pyramid structures that controlled hundreds of companies and vast empires in electricity generation and transmission. This legislation was adopted in particular response to the collapse of a public utility holding company controlled by Samuel Insull in Chicago. Through that structure, Insull controlled 250 operating companies that provided more than 10 percent of the electrical power of the United States. Investors lost hundreds of millions of dollars when this empire collapsed during the great depression. The Public Utility Holding Company Act of 1935 was repealed by the Energy Policy Act of 2005.

Trust Indenture Act of 1939. This act applies generally to public issues of debt securities in excess of $1,000,000. Trust indentures are master agreements that govern the terms and conditions of general obligation corporate bonds (debentures) that are offered to the public. See Chapter 4. The trust indenture covering the securities is also subject to the Trust Indenture Act of 1939, which defines standards of independence and responsibility on the indenture trustee and requires other provisions for the protection of the debenture holders in the event of a default.

Investment Company Act of 1940. This statute resulted from an SEC study directed by Congress in the Public Utility Holding Company Act. This legislation granted the SEC regulatory authority over investment companies, which include the mutual funds that are so popular today. The mutual fund is simply a pool of money collected from investors and then invested by an advisor to the fund in various securities. See Chapter 13. The investor may have his or her interest in the mutual fund liquidated at any time by the mutual fund at the net asset value of the investor's share of the fund. The mutual fund is continuously offering its shares to the public. The Investment Company Act of 1940 is said to be "the most intrusive financial legislation known to man or beast." *Clifford E. Kirsch, The Financial Services Revolution: Understanding the Changing Role of Banks, Mutual Funds, and Insurance Companies* 382 (1997). Among other things, this legislation regulates the composition of the management of investment companies, their capital structure, approval of their advisory contracts and changes in investment policy.

Investment Advisers Act of 1940. This statute requires the registration and regulation of investment advisers after an SEC study of their operations found abuses. This act prohibits fraud by investment advisers and restricted performance fees that rewarded the investment adviser on the basis of profits made by the adviser. The SEC found that such agreements were a "heads I win, tails you lose" proposition because the advisers had nothing to lose if they were unsuccessful and large rewards if they engaged in high risk investments that could provide large profits. *SEC, Report Pursuant to Special Study of the Public Utilities Holding Company Act of 1935 on Investment Trusts, and Investment Companies (Investment Counsel, Investment Management, Investment Future Prices, and Investment Advisory Services* (1939)).[1]

The Securities and Exchange Commission (SEC) is an independent federal agency that is charged with responsibility for the enforcement and administration of the federal securities laws. The SEC is composed of five members appointed by the President, with the advice and consent of the

---

1. This underscores a very basic premise of the securities markets—"risk vs. reward." The higher the risk the greater the profits, but also the more likely and the larger the losses. This principle is best illustrated by the lottery or the gambling casino. The rewards from such activities can be great but the risk of loss is equally great, and the vast majority of gamblers lose rather than make money. Still, "no guts, no glory."

Senate, for five-year terms (the term of one Commissioner expires each year), not more than three of whom shall be members of the same political party. Much of the SEC's work is carried out through its staff, most of whom are housed at the SEC's headquarters in Washington, D.C. The SEC, however, also maintains several regional offices across the country, the largest of which is located in New York City.

The SEC's headquarters staff is divided into four "divisions" and a number of separate "offices." The Division of Corporation Finance reviews the various disclosure documents filed by corporations and other issuers to assure full disclosure and compliance with SEC requirements. The Division of Enforcement is responsible for investigations of violations and prosecutes administrative and court proceedings against alleged violators. The Division of Trading and Markets is responsible for developing regulatory policy over the markets and broker-dealers. The Division of Investment Management is responsible for administering the regulation of investment companies (including mutual funds) and investment advisers. A new Division of Risk, Strategy and Financial Innovation (Risk Fin) was created after the financial crisis of 2007–2009 to assess financial risks. The Office of General Counsel advises the SEC and its Divisions on questions of law, and represents the SEC in appellate court proceedings. The Office of Chief Accountant develops policy on accounting questions and presents the SEC's positions on accounting issues to the standard-setting bodies in the accounting profession. Numerous other offices have also been created by the SEC, including an Office of Investor Education and Advocacy and an Office of International Affairs. The following diagram describes the SEC structure:

SECTION 2. AN INTRODUCTION TO THE SECURITIES ACT OF 1933

TREATISE ON THE LAW OF SECURITIES REGULATION THOMAS LEE HAZEN

Vol. 1 § 16[1] (5th ed. 2005).

What do the following have in common: scotch whiskey, self-improvement courses, cosmetics, earthworms, beavers, muskrats, rabbits, chinchillas, animal feeding programs, cattle embryos, fishing boats, vacuum cleaners, cemetery lots, coin operated telephones, master recording contracts, pooled litigation funds, and fruit trees? The answer is that they have all been held to be securities within the meaning of federal or state securities statutes. The vast range of such unconventional investments that have fallen within the ambit of the securities laws' coverage is due to the broad statutory definition of a "security," section 2(a)(1) of the Securities Act of 1933 is representative:

The term "security" means any note, stock, treasury stock, bond, debenture, evidence of indebtedness. Certificate of interest or participation in any profit-sharing agreement, collateral-trust certificate, pre-organization certificate or subscription, transferable share, investment contract, voting-trust certificate, certificate of deposit for a security, fractional undivided interest in oil, gas, or other mineral rights, any put, call, straddle, option, or privilege on any security, certificate of deposit, or group or index of securities (including any interest therein or based on the value thereof), or any put, call, straddle, option, or privilege entered into on a national securities exchange relating to foreign currency, or, in general, any interest or instrument commonly known as a "security", or any certificate of interest or participation in, temporary or interim certificate for, receipt for, guarantee of, or warrant or right to subscribe to or purchase, any of the foregoing. . . . * * *

In determining the basic coverage of the securities laws, the slightly different definitions of a security in the 1933 and 1934 Acts are to be treated as "virtually identical," according to the Supreme Court. The statutory language is expansive and has been interpreted accordingly. The broadly drafted statutory definition has continued to give the courts problems in providing predictable guidelines. Nevertheless, an attorney's failure to advise a client of the possibility of an investment offering being classified as a security can constitute legal malpractice. Furthermore, it is not necessary to establish that the defendant knew that the instrument he or she was marketing was a security.

Notwithstanding the broad statutory definition, not every fraud based on the payment of money is a security. In order to establish a violation of the securities laws, the plaintiff must first establish that a security was involved.

S.E.C. v. W. J. HOWEY CO.

328 U.S. 293, 66 S.Ct. 1100, 90 L.Ed. 1244 (1946).

MR. JUSTICE MURPHY delivered the opinion of the Court.

This case involves the application of § 2(1) of the Securities Act of 1933 to an offering of units of a citrus grove development coupled with a contract for cultivating, marketing and remitting the net proceeds to the investor.

The Securities and Exchange Commission instituted this action to restrain the respondents from using the mails and instrumentalities of interstate commerce in the offer and sale of unregistered and nonexempt securities in violation of § 5(a) of the Act. The District Court denied the injunction, 60 F.Supp. 440, and the Fifth Circuit Court of Appeals affirmed the judgment, 151 F.2d 714. We grant certiorari on a petition alleging that the ruling of the Circuit Court of Appeals conflicted with other federal and state decisions and that it introduced a novel and unwarranted test under the statute which the Commission regarded as administratively impractical.

Most of the facts are stipulated. The respondents, W. J. Howey Company and Howey-in-the-Hills Service Inc., are Florida corporations under direct common control and management. The Howey Company owns large tracts of citrus acreage in Lake County, Florida. During the past several years it has planted about 500 acres annually, keeping half of the groves itself and offering the other half to the public "to help us finance additional development." Howey-in-the-Hills Service, Inc., is a service company engaged in cultivating and developing many of these groves, including the harvesting and marketing of the crops.

Each prospective customer is offered both a land sales contract and a service contract, after having been told that it is not feasible to invest in a grove unless service arrangements are made. While the purchaser is free to make arrangements with other service companies, the superiority of Howey-in-the-Hills Service, Inc., is stressed. Indeed, 85% of the acreage sold during the 3–year period ending May 31, 1943, was covered by service contracts with Howey-in-the-Hills Service, Inc.

The land sales contract with the Howey Company provides for a uniform purchase price per acre or fraction thereof, varying in amount only in accordance with the number of years the particular plot has been planted with citrus trees. Upon full payment of the purchase price the land is conveyed to the purchaser by warranty deed. Purchases are usually made in narrow strips of land arranged so that an acre consists of a row of 48 trees. During the period between February 1, 1941, and May 31, 1943, 31 of the 42 persons making purchases bought less than 5 acres each. The average holding of these 31 persons was 1.33 acres and sales of as little as 0.65, 0.7 and 0.73 of an acre were made. These tracts are not separately fenced and the sole indication of several ownership is found in small land marks intelligible only through a plat book record.

The service contract, generally of a 10–year duration without option of cancellation, gives Howey-in-the-Hills Service, Inc., a leasehold interest and "full and complete" possession of the acreage. For a specified fee plus the cost of labor and materials, the company is given full discretion and authority over the cultivation of the groves and the harvest and marketing of the crops. The company is well established in the citrus business and maintains a large force of skilled personnel and a great deal of equipment, including 75 tractors, sprayer wagons, fertilizer trucks and the like. Without the consent of the company, the land owner or purchaser has no right of entry to market the crop; thus there is ordinarily no right to specific fruit. The company is accountable only for an allocation of the net profits based upon a check made at the time of picking. All the produce is pooled by the respondent companies, which do business under their own names.

The purchasers for the most part are non-residents of Florida. They are predominantly business and professional people who lack the knowledge, skill and equipment necessary for the care and cultivation of citrus trees. They are attracted by the expectation of substantial profits. It was represented, for example, that profits during the 1943–1944 season amounted to 20% and that even greater profits might be expected during the 1944–1945 season, although only a 10% annual return was to be expected over a 10–year period. Many of these purchasers are patrons of a resort hotel owned and operated by the Howey Company in a scenic section adjacent to the groves. The hotel's advertising mentions the fine groves in the vicinity and the attention of the patrons is drawn to the groves as they are being escorted about the surrounding countryside. They are told that the groves are for sale; if they indicate an interest in the matter they are then given a sales talk.

It is admitted that the mails and instrumentalities of interstate commerce are used in the sale of the land and service contracts and that no registration statement or letter of notification has ever been filed with the Commission in accordance with the Securities Act of 1933 and the rules and regulations thereunder.

Section 2(1) of the Act defines the term 'security' to include the commonly known documents traded for speculation or investment.[2] This definition also includes 'securities' of a more variable character, designated by such descriptive terms as 'certificate of interest or participation in any profit-sharing agreement' 'investment contract' and "in general, any interest or instrument commonly known as a 'security'." The legal issue

2. "The term 'security' means any note, stock, treasury stock, bond, debenture, evidence of indebtedness, certificate of interest or participation in any profit-sharing agreement, collateral-trust certificate, preorganization certificate or subscription, transferable share, investment contract, voting-trust certificate, certificate of deposit for a security, fractional undivided interest in oil, gas, or other mineral rights, or, in general, any interest or instrument commonly known as a 'security,' or any certificate of interest or participation in, temporary or interim certificate for, receipt for, guarantee of, or warrant or right to subscribe to or purchase, any of the foregoing."

in this case turns upon a determination of whether, under the circumstances, the land sales contract, the warranty deed and the service contract together constitute an "investment contract" within the meaning of § 2(1). An affirmative answer brings into operation the registration requirements of § 5(a), unless the security is granted an exemption under § 3(b), 15 U.S.C.A. § 77c(b). The lower courts, in reaching a negative answer to this problem, treated the contracts and deeds as separate transactions involving no more than an ordinary real estate sale and an agreement by the seller to manage the property for the buyer.

The term "investment contract" is undefined by the Securities Act or by relevant legislative reports. But the term was common in many state "blue sky" laws in existence prior to the adoption of the federal statute and, although the term was also undefined by the state laws, it had been broadly construed by state courts so as to afford the investing public a full measure of protection. Form was disregarded for substance and emphasis was placed upon economic reality. An investment contract thus came to mean a contract or scheme for "the placing of capital or laying out of money in a way intended to secure income or profit from its employment." State v. Gopher Tire & Rubber Co., 146 Minn. 52, 56, 177 N.W. 937, 938. This definition was uniformly applied by state courts to a variety of situations where individuals were led to invest money in a common enterprise with the expectation that they would earn a profit solely through the efforts of the promoter or of some one other than themselves.

By including an investment contract within the scope of § 2(1) of the Securities Act, Congress was using a term the meaning of which had been crystallized by this prior judicial interpretation. It is therefore reasonable to attach that meaning to the term as used by Congress, especially since such a definition is consistent with the statutory aims. In other words, an investment contract for purposes of the Securities Act means a contract, transaction or scheme whereby a person invests his money in a common enterprise and is led to expect profits solely from the efforts of the promoter or a third party, it being immaterial whether the shares in the enterprise are evidenced by formal certificates or by nominal interests in the physical assets employed in the enterprise. Such a definition necessarily underlies this Court's decision in Securities & Exch. Commission v. C. M. Joiner Leasing Corp., 320 U.S. 344, and has been enunciated and applied many times by lower federal courts. It permits the fulfillment of the statutory purpose of compelling full and fair disclosure relative to the issuance of "the many types of instruments that in our commercial world fall within the ordinary concept of a security." H.Rep.No.85, 73rd Cong., 1st Sess., p. 11. It embodies a flexible rather than a static principle, one that is capable of adaptation to meet the countless and variable schemes devised by those who seek the use of the money of others on the promise of profits.

The transactions in this case clearly involve investment contracts as so defined. The respondent companies are offering something more than fee simple interests in land, something different from a farm or orchard coupled with management services. They are offering an opportunity to contribute money and to share in the profits of a large citrus fruit enterprise managed and partly owned by respondents. They are offering this opportunity to persons who reside in distant localities and who lack the equipment and experience requisite to the cultivation, harvesting and marketing of the citrus products. Such persons have no desire to occupy the land or to develop it themselves; they are attracted solely by the prospects of a return on their investment. Indeed, individual development of the plots of land that are offered and sold would seldom be economically feasible due to their small size. Such tracts gain utility as citrus groves only when cultivated and developed as component parts of a larger area. A common enterprise managed by respondents or third parties with adequate personnel and equipment is therefore essential if the investors are to achieve their paramount aim of a return on their investments. Their respective shares in this enterprise are evidenced by land sales contracts and warranty deeds, which serve as a convenient method of determining the investors' allocable shares of the profits. The resulting transfer of rights in land is purely incidental.

Thus all the elements of a profit-seeking business venture are present here. The investors provide the capital and share in the earnings and profits; the promoters manage, control and operate the enterprise. It follows that the arrangements whereby the investors' interests are made manifest involve investment contracts, regardless of the legal terminology in which such contracts are clothed. The investment contracts in this instance take the form of land sales contracts, warranty deeds and service contracts which respondents offer to prospective investors. And respondents' failure to abide by the statutory and administrative rules in making such offerings, even though the failure result from a bona fide mistake as to the law, cannot be sanctioned under the Act.

This conclusion is unaffected by the fact that some purchasers choose not to accept the full offer of an investment contract by declining to enter into a service contract with the respondents. The Securities Act prohibits the offer as well as the sale of unregistered, non-exempt securities. Hence it is enough that the respondents merely offer the essential ingredients of an investment contract.

We reject the suggestion of the Circuit Court of Appeals, 151 F.2d at page 717, that an investment contract is necessarily missing where the enterprise is not speculative or promotional in character and where the tangible interest which is sold has intrinsic value independent of the success of the enterprise as a whole. The test is whether the scheme involves an investment of money in a common enterprise with profits to come solely from the efforts of others. If that test be satisfied, it is immaterial whether the enterprise is speculative or non-speculative or whether there is a sale of property with or without intrinsic value. See S.E.C. v. C. M. Joiner Leasing Corp., supra, 320 U.S. 352. The statutory policy of affording broad protection to investors is not to be thwarted by unrealistic and irrelevant formulae.

Reversed.

MR. JUSTICE JACKSON took no part in the consideration or decision of this case.

MR. JUSTICE FRANKFURTER dissenting. [omitted]

S.E.C. v. SG LTD.

265 F.3d 42 (1st Cir.2001).

SELYA, CIRCUIT JUDGE.

These appeals—procedurally, there are two, but for all practical purposes they may be treated as one—require us to determine whether virtual shares in an enterprise existing only in cyberspace fall within the purview of the federal securities laws. SG Ltd., a Dominican corporation, and its affiliate, SG Trading Ltd. (collectively, "SG" or "defendants"), asseverate that the virtual shares were part of a fantasy investment game created for the personal entertainment of Internet users, and therefore, that those shares do not implicate the federal securities laws. The Securities and Exchange Commission ("the SEC"), plaintiff below and appellant here, counters that substance ought to prevail over form, and that merely labeling a website as a game should not negate the applicability of the securities laws. The district court accepted the defendants' view and dismissed the SEC's complaint. SEC v. SG Ltd., 142 F.Supp.2d 126 (D.Mass.2001). Concluding, as we do, that the SEC alleged sufficient facts to state a triable claim, we reverse. * * *

The underlying litigation was spawned by SG's operation of a "Stock-Generation" website offering on-line denizens an opportunity to purchase shares in eleven different "virtual companies" listed on the website's "virtual stock exchange." SG arbitrarily set the purchase and sale prices of each of these imaginary companies in biweekly "rounds," and guaranteed that investors could buy or sell any quantity of shares at posted prices. SG placed no upper limit on the amount of funds that an investor could squirrel away in its virtual offerings.

The SEC's complaint focused on shares in a particular virtual enterprise referred to by SG as the "privileged company," and so do we. SG advised potential purchasers to pay "particular attention" to shares in the privileged company and boasted that investing in those shares was a "game without any risk." To this end, its website announced that the privileged company's shares would unfailingly appreciate, boldly proclaiming that "the share price of [the privileged company] is supported by the owners of SG, this is why its value constantly rises; on average at a rate of 10% monthly (this is approximately 215% annually)." To add plausibility to this representation and to allay anxiety about future pricing, SG published prices of the privileged company's shares one month in advance.

While SG conceded that a decline in the share price was theoretically possible, it assured prospective participants that "under the rules governing the fall in prices, [the share price for the privileged company] cannot fall by more than 5% in a round." To bolster this claim, it vouchsafed that shares in the privileged company were supported by several distinct revenue streams. According to SG's representations, capital inflow from new participants provided liquidity for existing participants who might choose to sell their virtual shareholdings. As a backstop, SG pledged to allocate an indeterminate portion of the profits derived from its website operations to a special reserve fund designed to maintain the price of the privileged company's shares. SG asserted that these profits emanated from four sources: (1) the collection of a 1.5% commission on each transaction conducted on its virtual stock exchange; (2) the bid-ask spread on the virtual shares; (3) the "skillful manipulation" of the share prices of eight particular imaginary companies, not including the privileged company, listed on the virtual stock exchange; and (4) SG's right to sell shares of three other virtual companies (including the privileged company). As a further hedge against adversity, SG alluded to the availability of auxiliary stabilization funds which could be tapped to ensure the continued operation of its virtual stock exchange.

SG's website contained lists of purported "big winners," an Internet bulletin board featuring testimonials from supposedly satisfied participants, and descriptions of incentive programs that held out the prospect of rewards for such activities as the referral of new participants (e.g., SG's representation that it would pay "20, 25 or 30% of the referred player's highest of the first three payments") and the establishment of affiliate websites.

At least 800 United States domiciliaries, paying real cash, purchased virtual shares in the virtual companies listed on the defendants' virtual stock exchange. In the fall of 1999, over $4,700,000 in participants' funds was deposited into a Latvian bank account in the name of SG Trading Ltd. The following spring, more than $2,700,000 was deposited in Estonian bank accounts standing in the names of SG Ltd. and SG Perfect Ltd., respectively.

In late 1999, participants began to experience difficulties in redeeming their virtual shares. On March 20, 2000, these difficulties crested; SG unilaterally suspended all pending requests to withdraw funds and sharply reduced participants' account balances in all companies except the privileged company. Two weeks later, SG peremptorily announced a reverse stock split, which caused the share prices of all companies listed on the virtual stock exchange, including the privileged company, to plummet to 1/10,000 of their previous values. At about the same time, SG stopped responding to participant requests for the return of funds, yet continued to solicit new participants through its website. * * *

These appeals turn on whether the SEC alleged facts which, if proven, would bring this case within the jurisdictional ambit of the federal securities laws. Consequently, we focus on the type of security that the SEC alleges is apposite here: investment contracts.

The applicable regulatory regime rests on two complementary pillars: the Securities Act of 1933, 15 U.S.C. §§ 77a–77aa, and the Securities Exchange Act of 1934, 15 U.S.C. §§ 78a–78mm. These statutes employ nearly identical definitions of the term "security." See Securities Act of 1933 § 2(a)(1), 15 U.S.C. § 77b(a)(1); Securities Exchange Act of 1934 § 3(a)(10), 15 U.S.C. § 78c (a)(10). Congress intended these sweeping definitions, set forth in an appendix hereto, to encompass a wide array of financial instruments, ranging from well-established investment vehicles (e.g., stocks and bonds) to much more arcane arrangements. SEC v. C. M. Joiner Leasing Corp., 320 U.S. 344, 351 (1943). Included in this array is the elusive, essentially protean, concept of an investment contract.

Judicial efforts to delineate what is—and what is not—an investment contract are grounded in the seminal case of SEC v. W. J. Howey Co., 328 U.S. 293 (1946). The Howey Court established a tripartite test to determine whether a particular financial instrument constitutes an investment contract (and, hence, a security). This test has proven durable. Under it, an investment contract comprises (1) the investment of money (2) in a common enterprise (3) with an expectation of profits to be derived solely from the efforts of the promoter or a third party. Id. at 298–99. This formulation must be applied in light of the economic realities of the transaction. United Hous. Found., Inc. v. Forman, 421 U.S. 837, 851–52 (1975); Tcherepnin v. Knight, 389 U.S. 332, 336 (1967); Futura Dev. Corp. v. Centex Corp., 761 F.2d 33, 39 (1st Cir.1985). In other words,

> substance governs form, and the substance of an investment contract is a security-like interest in a "common enterprise" that, through the efforts of the promoter or others, is expected to generate profits for the security holder, either for direct distribution or as an increase in the value of the investment.

Rodriguez v. Banco Cent. Corp., 990 F.2d 7, 10 (1st Cir.1993) (citations omitted).

The Supreme Court has long espoused a broad construction of what constitutes an investment contract, aspiring "to afford the investing public a full measure of protection." Howey, 328 U.S. at 298. The investment contract taxonomy thus "embodies a flexible rather than a static principle, one that is capable of adaptation to meet the countless and variable schemes devised by those who seek the use of the money of others on the promise of profits." Id. at 299.

The Howey test has proven to be versatile in practice. Over time, courts have classified as investment contracts a kaleidoscopic assortment of pecuniary arrangements that defy categorization in conventional financial terms, yet nonetheless satisfy the Howey Court's three criteria. See, e.g., id. (holding that sale of citrus groves, in conjunction with service contract, qualifies as an investment contract); Teague v. Bakker, 35 F.3d 978, 981, 990 (4th Cir.1994) (same re purchase of life partnership in evangelical community); Long v. Shultz Cattle Co., 881 F.2d 129, 132 (5th Cir.1989) (same re cattle-feeding and consulting agreement); Miller v. Cent. Chinchilla Group, 494 F.2d 414, 415, 418 (8th Cir.1974) (same re chinchilla breeding and resale arrangement). * * *

The first component of the Howey test focuses on the investment of money. The determining factor is whether an investor "chose to give up a specific consideration in return for a separable financial interest with the characteristics of a security." Daniel, 439 U.S. at 559. We conclude that the SEC's complaint sufficiently alleges the existence of this factor.

To be sure, SG disputes the point. It argues that the individuals who purchased shares in the privileged company were not so much investing money in return for rights in the virtual shares as paying for an entertainment commodity (the opportunity to play the StockGeneration game). This argument suggests that an interesting factual issue may await resolution—whether participants were motivated primarily by a perceived investment opportunity or by the visceral excitement of playing a game. Nevertheless, this case comes to us following a dismissal under Rule 12(b)(6), and the SEC's complaint memorializes, inter alia, SG's representation that participants could "firmly expect a 10% profit monthly" on purchases of the privileged company's shares. That representation plainly supports the SEC's legal claim that participants who invested substantial amounts of money in exchange for virtual shares in the privileged company likely did so in anticipation of investment gains. Given the procedural posture of the case, no more is exigible to fulfill the first part of the Howey test.

The second component of the Howey test involves the existence of a common enterprise. Before diving headlong into the sea of facts, we must dispel the miasma that surrounds the appropriate legal standard.

Courts are in some disarray as to the legal rules associated with the ascertainment of a common enterprise. See generally II Louis Loss & Joel Seligman, Securities Regulation 989–97 (3d ed. rev. 1999). Many courts require a showing of horizontal commonality—a type of commonality that involves the pooling of assets from multiple investors so that all share in the profits and risks of the enterprise. Other courts have modeled the concept of common enterprise around fact patterns in which an investor's fortunes are tied to the promoter's success rather than to the fortunes of his or her fellow investors. [citations omitted] This doctrine, known as vertical commonality, has two variants. Broad vertical commonality requires that the well-being of all investors be dependent upon the promoter's expertise. See Villeneuve v. Advanced Bus. Concepts Corp., 698 F.2d 1121, 1124 (11th Cir.1983), aff'd en banc, 730 F.2d 1403 (11th Cir.1984); SEC v. Koscot Interplanetary, Inc., 497 F.2d 473, 478–79 (5th Cir.1974). In contrast, narrow vertical commonality requires that the investors' fortunes be "interwoven with and dependent upon the efforts and success of those seeking the investment or of third parties." SEC v. Glenn W. Turner Enters., 474 F.2d 476, 482 n.7 (9th Cir.1973).

Courts also differ in the steadfastness of their allegiance to a single standard of commonality. Two courts of appeals recognize only horizontal commonality. See Wals, 24 F.3d at 1018; Curran, 622 F.2d at 222, 224. Two others adhere exclusively to broad vertical commonality. See Ville-neuve, 698 F.2d at 1124; Koscot, 497 F.2d at 478–79. The Ninth Circuit recognizes both horizontal commonality and narrow vertical commonality. See Hocking v. Dubois, 885 F.2d 1449, 1459 (9th Cir.1989) (en banc). To complicate matters further, four courts of appeals have accepted horizontal commonality, but have not yet ruled on whether they also will accept some form of vertical commonality. See Infinity Group, 212 F.3d at 187 n.8; Life Partners, 87 F.3d at 544;; Teague, 35 F.3d at 986 n.8; Revak, 18 F.3d at 88. At least one of these courts, however, has explicitly rejected broad vertical commonality. See Revak, 18 F.3d at 88.

Thus far, neither the Supreme Court nor this court has authoritatively determined what type of commonality must be present to satisfy the common enterprise element. We came close in Rodriguez, in which we hinted at a preference for horizontal commonality. There, promoters selling parcels of land made "strong and repeated suggestions that the surrounding area would develop into a thriving residential community." 990 F.2d at 11. Although we held that the financial arrangement did not constitute a security, we implied that an actual commitment by the promoters to develop the community themselves, coupled with the buyers' joint financing of the enterprise, could constitute a common enterprise. See id.

The case at bar requires us to take a position on the common enterprise component of the Howey test. We hold that a showing of horizontal commonality—the pooling of assets from multiple investors in such a manner that all share in the profits and risks of the enterprise—satisfies the test. This holding flows naturally from the facts of Howey, in which the promoter commingled fruit from the investors' groves and allocated net profits based upon the production from each tract. See Howey, 328 U.S. at 296. Adopting this rule also aligns us with the majority view and confirms the intimation of Rodriguez. Last, but surely not least, the horizontal commonality standard places easily ascertainable and predictable limits on the types of financial instruments that will qualify as securities.

Here, the pooling element of horizontal commonality jumps off the screen. The defendants' website stated that: "The players' money is accumulated on the SG current account and is not invested anywhere, because no investment, not even the most profitable one, could possibly fully compensate for the lack of sufficiency in settling accounts with players, which lack would otherwise be more likely." Thus, as the SEC's complaint suggests, SG unambiguously represented to its clientele that participants' funds were pooled in a single account used to settle participants' on-line transactions. Therefore, pooling is established.

Of course, horizontal commonality requires more than pooling alone; it also requires that investors share in the profits and risks of the enterprise. The SEC maintains that two separate elements of SG's operations embody the necessary sharing. First, it asserts that SG was running a Ponzi or pyramid scheme dependent upon a continuous influx of new money to remain in operation,[3] and argues that such arrangements inherently involve the sharing of profit and risk among investors. Second, the SEC construes SG's promise to divert a portion of its profits from website operations to support the privileged company's shares as a bond that ties together the collective fortunes of those who have purchased the shares. While we analyze each of these theories, we note that any one of them suffices to support a finding of commonality.

We endorse the SEC's suggestion that Ponzi schemes typically satisfy the horizontal commonality standard. In Infinity Group, investors contributed substantial sums of money to a trust established by the defendants and received in exchange a property transfer agreement guaranteeing stupendous annual rates of return. 212 F.3d at 184–85. The economic guarantees were based upon the trust's purported performance experience, financial connections, and ability to pool large amounts of money. Id. at 185. Participants were promised that investing in the trust was a risk-free proposition, and that their cash infusions would be repaid in full upon demand. Id. at 184–85. Expected profits were a function of the number of "capital units" held pursuant to the contract with the trust; in turn, the number of capital units allocated to each investor was directly proportional to the size of his or her investment. Id. at 188–89. On these facts, the Third Circuit held that horizontal commonality existed, emphasizing that under the plan's terms each investor was entitled to receive returns directly proportionate to his or her investment stake. Id. at 188. * * *

The final component of the Howey test—the expectation of profits solely from the efforts of others—is itself divisible. We address each sub-element separately.

The Supreme Court has recognized an expectation of profits in two situations, namely, (1) capital appreciation from the original investment, and (2) participation in earnings resulting from the use of investors' funds. Forman, 421 U.S. at 852. These situations are to be contrasted with transactions in which an individual purchases a commodity for personal use or consumption. Id. at 858. The SEC posits that SG's guarantees created a reasonable expectancy of profit from investments in the privileged company, whereas SG maintains that participants paid money not to

___

3. While the terms "Ponzi" and "pyramid" often are used interchangeably to describe financial arrangements which rob Peter to pay Paul, the two differ slightly. In Ponzi schemes—named after a notorious Boston swindler, Charles Ponzi, who parlayed an initial stake of $150 into a fortune by means of an elaborate scheme featuring promissory notes yielding interest at annual rates of up to 50%—money tendered by later investors is used to pay off earlier investors. In contrast, pyramid schemes incorporate a recruiting element; they are marketing arrangements in which participants are rewarded financially based upon their ability to induce others to participate. The SEC alleges that SG's operations aptly can be characterized under either appellation.

make money, but, rather, to acquire an entertainment commodity for personal consumption. Relying heavily on Forman, the district court accepted SG's thesis. SEC v. SG Ltd., 142 F.Supp.2d at 130–31. We do not agree.

In Forman, apartment dwellers who desired to reside in a New York City cooperative were required to buy shares of stock in the nonprofit cooperative housing corporation that owned and operated the complex. Based on its determination that "investors were attracted solely by the prospect of acquiring a place to live, and not by financial returns on their investments," the Forman Court held that the cooperative housing arrangement did not qualify as a security under either the "stock" or "investment contract" rubrics. 421 U.S. at 853. The Court's conclusion rested in large part upon an Information Bulletin distributed to prospective residents which stressed the nonprofit nature of the cooperative housing endeavor. Id. at 854 (emphasizing that "nowhere does the Bulletin seek to attract investors by the prospect of profits resulting from the efforts of the promoters or third parties").

We think it noteworthy that the Forman Court contrasted the case before it with Joiner. In that case, economic inducements made by promoters in conjunction with the assignment of oil well leases transformed the financial instrument under consideration from a naked leasehold right to an investment contract. 320 U.S. at 348, 64 S.Ct. 120. The Joiner Court found dispositive advertising literature circulated by the promoters which emphasized the benefits to be reaped from the exploratory drilling of a test well. Id. ("Had the offer mailed by defendants omitted the economic inducements of the proposed and promised exploration well, it would have been a quite different proposition.").

The way in which these cases fit together is instructive. In Forman, the apartment was the principal attraction for prospective buyers, the purchase of shares was merely incidental, and the combination of the two did not add up to an investment contract. 421 U.S. at 853, 95 S.Ct. 2051. In Joiner, the prospect of exploratory drilling gave the investments "most of their value and all of their lure," the leasehold interests themselves were no more than an incidental consideration in the transaction, and the combination of the two added up to an investment contract. 320 U.S. at 349, 64 S.Ct. 120. This distinction is crucial, see Forman, 421 U.S. at 853 n. 18, 95 S.Ct. 2051, and it furnishes the beacon by which we must steer.

Seen in this light, SG's persistent representations of substantial pecuniary gains for privileged company shareholders distinguish its Stock-Generation website from the Information Bulletin circulated to prospective purchasers in Forman. While SG's use of gaming language is roughly analogous to the cooperative's emphasis on the nonprofit nature of the housing endeavor, SG made additional representations on its website that played upon greed and fueled expectations of profit. For example, SG flatly guaranteed that investments in the shares of the privileged company would be profitable, yielding monthly returns of 10% and annual returns of 215%. In our view, these profit-related guarantees constitute a not-very-subtle form of economic inducement, closely analogous to the advertising representations in *Joiner*. In the same way that the prospect of profitable discoveries induced investors to buy oil well leases, the prospect of a sure-fire return lured participants to buy shares in the privileged company (or so it can be argued).

This is not to say that SG's gaming language and repeated disclaimers are irrelevant. SG has a plausible argument, forcefully advanced by able counsel, that no participant in his or her right mind should have expected guaranteed profits from purchases of privileged company shares. But this argument, though plausible, is not inevitable. In the end, it merely gives rise to an issue of fact (or, perhaps, multiple issues of fact) regarding whether SG's representations satisfy *Howey*'s expectation-of-profit requirement.

We turn now to the question of whether the expected profits can be said to result solely from the efforts of others. The courts of appeals have been unanimous in declining to give literal meaning to the word "solely" in this context, instead holding the requirement satisfied as long as "the efforts made by those other than the investor are the undeniably significant ones, those essential managerial efforts which affect the failure or success of the enterprise." *Turner Enters.*, 474 F.2d at 482; *accord Rivanna Trawlers Unlimited v. Thompson Trawlers, Inc.*, 840 F.2d 236, 240 n. 4 (4th Cir.1988) (adopting this holding and listing eight other circuits which have held to like effect). This liberal interpretation of the requirement seemingly comports with the Supreme Court's restatement of the *Howey* test. *See Forman*, 421 U.S. at 852, 95 S.Ct. 2051 (explaining that "the touchstone is the presence of an investment in a common venture premised on a reasonable expectation of profits to be derived from the entrepreneurial or managerial efforts of others").

We need not reach the issue of whether a lesser degree of control by a promoter or third party suffices to give rise to an investment contract because SG's alleged scheme meets the literal definition of "solely." According to the SEC's allegations, SG represented to its customers the lack of investor effort required to make guaranteed profits on purchases of the privileged company's shares, noting, for example, that "playing with [the] privileged shares practically requires no time at all." SG was responsible for all the important efforts that undergirded the 10% guaranteed monthly return. As the sole proprietor of the StockGeneration website, SG enjoyed direct operational control over all aspects of the virtual stock exchange. And SG's marketing efforts generated direct capital investment and commissions on the transactions (which it pledged to earmark to support the privileged company's shares).

SG's payment of referral bonuses to participants who introduced new users to the website does not require a different result. Even if a participant chose not to refer others to the StockGeneration website, he or she still could expect, based on SG's profit-related guarantees, to reap monthly profits from mere ownership of the privileged company's shares. Accordingly, the SEC's complaint makes out a triable issue on whether participants expected to receive profits derived solely from the efforts of others.

We need go no further. Giving due weight to the economic realities of the situation, we hold that the SEC has alleged a set of facts which, if proven, satisfy the three-part *Howey* test and support its assertion that the opportunity to invest in the shares of the privileged company, described on SG's website, constituted an invitation to enter into an investment contract within the jurisdictional reach of the federal securities laws. Accordingly, we reverse the order of dismissal and remand the case for further proceedings consistent with this opinion. The preliminary injunction and asset freeze shall remain in force pending conclusion of the proceedings below.

Reversed and remanded.

NOTE

As described in Chapter 4, the Supreme Court adopted a "family resemblance" test in determining whether notes are securities subject to SEC regulation. See Reves v. Ernst & Young, 494 U.S. 56, 110 S.Ct. 945, 108 L.Ed.2d 47 (1990). How would that test apply to SG's operations in the preceding case?

Derivatives as "Securities"

The proliferation of new hybrid investment instruments has led to increasing jurisdictional tension between the SEC and Commodity Futures Trading Commission (CFTC). Futures contracts that are derivative of securities are regulated by the CFTC. In 1989, securities exchanges authorized the listing of index participation units (the value of which depended upon an underlying stock index which is computed according to the value of a designated "basket" of securities). Clearly, these index participation units more closely resemble securities than commodities. However, as discussed in chapter 11 below, the Seventh Circuit held that these derivative investments were subject to the exclusive jurisdiction of the CFTC. Chicago Mercantile Exchange v. SEC, 883 F.2d 537 (7th Cir.1989), *cert. denied* 496 U.S. 936, 110 S.Ct. 3214, 110 L.Ed.2d 662 (1990). The Jurisdictional battle between the SEC and CFTC continued. In adopting the Commodity Futures Modernization Act of 2000 (Pub. Law No. 106–554, 114 Stat. 2763) (Dec. 21, 2000), Congress clarified many of the issues that had been fought over for decades when it adopted the Dodd–Frank Act in 2010. As described in Chapter 12, that legislation drew a distinction between security-based swaps, non-security-based swaps and swaps with mixed elements of both securities and non-securities and allocated jurisdiction on that basis between the SEC and CFTC. This allocation has left many questions open, including the effect of this legislation on end-users of swaps.

SECTION 3.   PRIVATE PLACEMENTS

The decision to go public is often tempting for small companies seeking to expand or to provide a market for their owner's stock. That decision should not be lightly made. The burden of filing the financial reports is considerable and expensive. Further, the company's operations will be subject to continuous scrutiny by the SEC and investors. Serious penalties may be imposed by the SEC for violations and criminal prosecutions are not uncommon. Public companies are also often the subject of expensive and sometimes frivolous lawsuits brought by investors under the federal securities laws. An alternative is for a corporation to seek financing through a private placement that is exempt from the SEC registration and periodic reporting requirements.

NON–PUBLIC OFFERING EXEMPTION

Securities Act Release No. 4552 (Nov. 6, 1962).

The [Securities and Exchange] Commission today announced the issuance of a statement regarding the availability of the exemption from the registration requirements of Section 5 of the Securities Act of 1933 afforded by the Section 4(2) of the Act for "transactions by an issuer not involving any public offering," the so-called "private offering exemption." Traditionally, Section 4(2) has been regarded as providing an exemption from registration for bank loans, private placements of securities with institutions, and the promotion of a business venture by a few closely related persons. However, an increasing tendency to rely upon the exemption for offerings of speculative issues to unrelated and uninformed persons prompts this statement to point out the limitations on its availability.

Whether a transaction is one not involving any public offering is essentially a question of fact and necessitates a consideration of all surrounding circumstances, including such factors as the relationship between the offerees and the issuer, the nature, scope, size, type and manner of the offering.

The Supreme Court in S.E.C. v. Ralston Purina Co., 346 U.S. 119, 124, 125 (1953), noted that the exemption must be interpreted in the light of the statutory purpose to "protect investors by promoting full disclosure of information thought necessary to informed investment decisions" and held that "the applicability of Section 4[(2)] should turn on whether the particular class of persons affected need the protection of the Act." The Court stated that the number of offerees is not conclusive as to the availability of the exemption, since the statute seems to apply to an offering "whether to few or many." However, the Court indicated that "nothing prevents the Commission, in enforcing the statute, from using some kind of numerical test in deciding when to investigate particular exemption claims." It should be emphasized, therefore, that the number of persons to whom the offering is extended is relevant only to the question whether they have the requisite association with and knowledge of the issuer which make the exemption available.

Consideration must be given not only to the identity of the actual purchasers but also to the offerees. Negotiations or conversations with or general solicitations of an unrestricted and unrelated group of prospective purchasers for the purpose of ascertaining who would be willing to accept an offer of securities is inconsistent with a claim that the transaction does not involve a public offering even though ultimately there may only be a few knowledgeable purchasers.

A question frequently arises in the context of an offering to an issuer's employees. Limitation of an offering to certain employees designated as key employees may not be a sufficient showing to qualify for the exemption. As the Supreme Court stated in the *Ralston Purina* case: "The exemption as we construe it, does not deprive corporate employees, as a class, of the safeguards of the Act. We agree that some employee offerings may come within Section 4(2), e.g., one made to executive personnel who because of their position have access to the same kind of information that the Act would make available in the form of a registration statement. Absent such a showing of special circumstances, employees are just as much members of the investing 'public' as any of their neighbors in the community." The Court's concept is that the exemption is necessarily narrow. The exemption does not become available simply because offerees are voluntarily *furnished* information about the issuer. Such a construction would give each issuer the choice of registering or making its own voluntary disclosures without regard to the standards and sanctions of the Act.

The sale of stock to promoters who take the initiative in founding or organizing the business would come within the exemption. On the other hand, the transaction tends to become public when the promoters begin to bring in a diverse group of uninformed friends, neighbors and associates.

The size of the offering may also raise questions as to the probability that the offering will be completed within the strict confines of the exemption. An offering of millions of dollars to non-institutional and non-affiliated investors or one divided, or convertible, into many units would suggest that a public offering may be involved.

When the services of an investment banker, or other facility through which public distributions are normally effected, are used to place the securities, special care must be taken to avoid a public offering. If the investment banker places the securities with discretionary accounts and other customers without regard to the ability of such customers to meet the tests implicit in the *Ralston Purina* case, the exemption may be lost.

Public advertising of the offerings would, of course, be incompatible with a claim of a private offering. Similarly, the use of the facilities of a securities exchange to place the securities necessarily involves an offering to the public.

An important factor to be considered is whether the securities offered have come to rest in the hands of the initial informed group or whether the purchasers are merely conduits for a wider distribution. Persons who act in this capacity, whether or not engaged in the securities business, are deemed to be "underwriters" within the meaning of Section 2(11) of the Act. If the purchasers do in fact acquire the securities with a view to public distribution, the seller assumes the risk of possible violation of the registration requirements of the Act and consequent civil liabilities. * * *

A determination whether an offering is public or private would also include a consideration of the question whether it should be regarded as a part of a larger offering made or to be made. The following factors are relevant to such question of integration: whether (1) the different offerings are part of a single plan of financing, (2) the offerings involve issuance of the same class of security, (3) the offerings are made at or about the same time, (4) the same type of consideration is to be received, (5) the offerings are made for the same general purpose.

What may appear to be a separate offering to a properly limited group will not be so considered if it is one of a related series of offerings. A person may not separate parts of a series of related transactions, the sum total of which is really one offering, and claim that a particular part is a non-public transaction. Thus, in the case of offerings of fractional undivided interests in separate oil or gas properties where the promoters must constantly find new participants for each new venture, it would appear to be appropriate to consider the entire series of offerings to determine the scope of this solicitation.

As has been emphasized in other releases discussing exemptions from the registration and prospectus requirements of the Securities Act, the terms of an exemption are to be strictly construed against the claimant who also has the burden of proving its availability. Moreover, persons receiving advice from the staff of the Commission that no action will be recommended if they proceed without registration in reliance upon the exemption should do so only with full realization that the tests so applied may not be proof against claims by purchasers of the security that registration should have been effected. Finally, Sections 12(2) and 17 of the Act, which provide civil liabilities and criminal sanctions for fraud in the sale of a security, are applicable to the transactions notwithstanding the availability of an exemption from registration.

The SEC has adopted regulations defining various offerings that need not be registered under the Securities Act of 1933. They include Regulation A and Regulation D.

SUBCOMMITTEE ON ANNUAL REVIEW FEDERAL REGULATION OF SECURITIES: REGULATORY DEVELOPMENTS

48 Bus. Law. 997 (1993).

REGULATION A

The SEC increased the dollar amount of securities that may be sold under Regulation A and adopted a series of specific procedural and timing requirements for Regulation A offerings. The SEC adopted Regulation A under the authority of section 3(b) of the 1933 Act to exempt from registration issues of up to $5 million.

Up to $5 million of securities may now be sold under Regulation A in any twelve month period, including up to $1.5 million of non-issuer resales. [Rule 251(b)]. In determining the amount of securities that may be sold under this exemption, the amount of securities sold under other small issues exemptions, such as the rule 504 exemption, generally are not taken into consideration. [Rule 251(c)].

The Regulation A exemption now has been made available to qualifying Canadian issuers. [Rule 251(a)(1)]. While the exemption continues to be available to partnerships and other entities organized to invest in properties, commodities, and other investment vehicles, it will not be available to "blank check companies." The exemption also remains unavailable if the issuer, a controlling person for the issuer, or an underwriter involved in the offering is subject to one or more specific legal sanctions. [Rule 251(a)(6)].

An issuer can offer securities under Regulation A after it has filed a prescribed offering statement with the SEC. [Rule 251(d)(1); Form 1–A]. Sales may not be made until the offering statement is qualified by the SEC. [Rule 251(d)(2)]. As in the case of registered public offerings, an offering statement will be deemed qualified twenty calendar days after filing, unless a delaying procedure is used by the issuer. [Rule 252(g)(1)]. After an offering statement is filed, written offers may only be made by means of a preliminary or final offering circular. A preliminary or final offering circular must be delivered at least forty-eight hours prior to any confirmation of sale. [Rule 251(d)(2)(i)(B)]. An offering circular must be revised annually during the term of a continuous offering and whenever the information it contains has become false or misleading, material developments have occurred, or there has been a fundamental change in the information initially presented. [Rule 253(e)].

The issuer must file Form 2–A with information about the distribution and use of proceeds from the offering. [Rule 257]. While the failure to file a Form 2–A can lead to an administrative suspension of the Regulation A exemption, it will not cause the exemption to be lost. [Rule 258(a)(1)]. The suspension of the exemption will not in and of itself affect the exempt status of prior offers and sales.

The failure to comply with a requirement of Regulation A will not result in the loss of an exemption for the sale to an investor if the requirement was not intended to protect the investor, the violation was not material to the offering as a whole, and the issuer made a good faith attempt to comply with all of the requirements of Regulation A. [Rule 260]. This "substantial and good faith compliance" provision will not preserve the Regulation A exemption if the issuer did not meet the issuer qualification requirements failed to file an offering statement, or exceeded the specified dollar limitation.

A significant and novel feature of the SEC amendments to Regulation A permits issuers intending to engage in a Regulation A offering to circulate written solicitations of intent before commencing the offering. [Rule 254]. Any such written solicitation must be filed with the SEC at the time of first use. [Rule 254(b)(1)].

While the issuer has broad latitude with respect to the contents of a written solicitation of interest, the solicitation must state that no money is being solicited, no money will be accepted, no sales can be made until delivery and qualification of an offering circular, and that an indication of interest does not constitute an obligation or commitment of any kind. [Rule 254(b)(2)(i)–(iii)]. The writing must also include a brief, general identification of the issuer's business, products, and chief executive officer. [Rule 254(b)(2(iv)]. When the solicitation of interest material is filed with the SEC, the issuer is required to provide the name and telephone number of a person who will respond to questions about the material. [Rule 254(b)(1)].

The written solicitation of interest material may be delivered to prospective investors or published in the print and broadcast media. [Rule 254(a)]. Oral communications with prospective investors may be made after the written solicitation of interest has been filed with the SEC.

Once the Regulation A offering statement is filed with the SEC, the solicitation of interest materials can no longer be used. [Rule 254(b)(3)]. The issuer must wait at least twenty days after the last use of the materials or any broadcast before it may sell any securities under the Regulation A exemption. [Rule 254(b)(4)]. An issuer that has filed and used written solicitation of interest materials in preparation for a Regulation A offering may later elect to proceed with a registered public offering and still have the written solicitations exempt under Rule 254, if the issuer waits at least thirty calendar days after the last use of such materials before filing a registration statement. [Rule 254(d)].

The failure to file solicitation of interest materials with the SEC, the failure to include the required statements in the materials, and the use of the materials after the filing of an offering statement will not result in the loss of the Regulation A exemption, but can serve as a basis for the administrative suspension of the exemption. [Rule 258].

NOTE ON REGULATION D[4]

In 1982, the Commission took a major step in simplifying and coordinating the exemptions for limited offerings by repealing Rules 146, 240 and 242, and adopting in their place a new Regulation D, composed of Rules 501 through 506. The following summary and overview of Regulation D will help guide you through the applicable rules.

Definitions. Rule 501 defines the terms used in Regulation D. The most important of these is the term "accredited investor," which is defined to include (1) any bank, savings and loan association, credit union, insurance company, investment company, or employee benefit plan, (2) any business development company, (3) any charitable or educational institution with assets of more than $5 million, as well as corporations, partnerships, and business trusts with more than $5 million in assets, (4) any director, executive officer or general partner of the issuer, (5) any person with a net worth of more than $1 million, and (6) any person with an annual income of more than $200,000 (or annual joint spousal income of $300,000). Section 413 of the Dodd–Frank Wall Street Reform and Consumer Protection Act of 2010 mandated that the SEC's net worth standard for an accredited investor be increased to $1 million, *excluding the value of the person's primary residence.*

General Conditions. Rule 502 sets forth certain conditions applicable to all offerings under Regulation D. Those conditions are summarized directly below.

Integration. Offerings that are separated in time by more than six months are not deemed to be parts of a single offering. Whether offerings within six months of each other will be considered part of a single offering depends on application of the five factors traditionally employed by the SEC: whether the offerings (1) are part of a single plan of financing, (2) involve the same class of security, (3) are made at or about the same time, (4) involve the same type of consideration, and (5) are made for the same general purpose.

Information. If an issuer sells securities under Rule 504 or to accredited investors only, there are no specific requirements for furnishing information to offerees or purchasers. If securities are sold to non-accredited purchasers under Rule 505 or 506, specified information must be furnished to them. If the issuer is not subject to the 1934 Act periodic reporting requirements, it must furnish non-financial information that would be required by Part II of Form 1–A (for issuers qualified to use Regulation A). Rule 502(b)(2)(I)(A). Issuers who would not qualify for Regulation A must furnish non-financial information as would be required by Part I of the registration from under the 1933 Act for which the issuer would qualify. Id. There are three different levels of disclosure of financial information of issuers not subject to the 1934 Act reporting requirements. For offerings up to $2 million, the issuer must provide the information required in Item 310 of Regulation S–B, but only the balance sheet need be audited. Rule 502(b)(2)(B)(*1*). For offerings of more than $2 million and up to $7.5 million, the issuer must supply the information

4. This note is adapted from Thomas L. Hazen, The Law of Securities Regulation (5th ed. 2005).

required by Form SB–2 except that if the obtaining of audited financials would result in unreasonable expense, only the balance sheet need be audited. Rule 502(b)(2)(B)(*2*). For offerings over $7.5 million, the issuer must provide the financial information that would be required by a registration form for which the issuer would qualify. Rule 502(b)(2)(B)(*3*). Issuers subject to the 1934 Act reporting requirements must make available specified information from the 1934 Act annual and other reports. Rule 502(b)(2).

Formerly, the Commission required that the private placement memorandum be furnished to *all* purchasers if there were *any* unaccredited purchasers. In deleting the express requirement that accredited investors in such an offering receive the memorandum, the SEC nevertheless included a note in the rule recommending use of the memorandum in light of the securities laws' antifraud provisions. Note to Rule 502(b)(1).

Manner of Offering and Limitations on Resale. No general solicitation or general offering is permitted. Securities sold pursuant to Regulation D are considered to have been purchased in a non-public offering and cannot be resold without registration unless an exemption is available under § 4(1) or Rule 144. The issuer must take certain specified precautions to insure that the purchasers do not make resales.

Notice. Under Rule 503, notices of any sales pursuant to Regulation D must be filed with the Commission. Rule 507 renders Regulation D unavailable if the issuer, its predecessors, or affiliates have been subject to a court order or decree for noncompliance with Rule 503's notice requirement. Rule 507(b) permits the Commission to waive this disqualification. Failure to file Rule 503 notices will not by itself destroy the exemption.

Rule 504. Under Rule 504, as liberalized in 1992, an issuer may sell an aggregate of $1 million of securities in any twelve-month period to any number of purchasers, accredited or unaccredited. No disclosure document is required, and the Rule 502 restrictions on the manner of offering and resales by purchasers do not apply. The exemption is unavailable to investment companies, companies registered under the 1934 Act, and "blank check" companies (companies which issue stock without any stated business plans for using the proceeds). In 1998, the SEC proposed amending Rule 504 so as to classify securities offered under the exemption as "restricted" and therefore subject to the one-year holding period of Rule 144. The stated purpose behind this proposal was to help reduce fraud in the offer and sale of low priced or "microcap" securities. In 1999, the Commission amended Regulation D to implement this proposal so that now securities issued under Rule 504 are restricted securities unless (1) the transaction is registered under a state securities law that requires public filing and delivery of a substantive disclosure document or (2) the offering is made only to accredited investors (as that term is defined in Regulation D) under a state law exemption that permits a general solicitation. At the same time the SEC amended Rule 504 to preclude general solicitations in Rule 504 offerings. Thus, general solicitations in Rule 504 offerings may occur only under very limited circumstances—namely those offerings mentioned directly above.

Rule 505. Under Rule 505, an issuer can sell up to $5 million of securities in any 12–month period to any number of accredited investors and up to 35 other purchasers. If there are any non-accredited purchasers, the information prescribed by Rule 502 must be furnished to them. The exemption is available to any issuer except an investment company or an issuer that would be disqualified by Rule 262 from using Regulation A.

Rule 506. Under Rule 506, an issuer can sell an unlimited amount of securities to any number of accredited investors and up to 35 other purchasers. Prior to the sale, the issuer must reasonably believe that each non-accredited investor, or his "purchaser representative" (a term defined in Rule 501) has such knowledge or experience in financial and business matters that he is capable of evaluating the merits and risks of the prospective investment. If there are any non-accredited purchasers, the information prescribed by Rule 502 must be furnished to them. The exemption is available to all issuers. In addition to the distinction between accredited and unaccredited investors, Rule 506 contains a suitability requirement which derives from the statutory exemption. The issuer trying to establish a Rule 506 exemption carries the burden of showing that it had reasonable grounds to believe that each purchaser was in fact suitable.

"No harm, no foul"—Rule 508. Rule 508 provides that "insignificant deviations" from Regulation D's requirements will not destroy the exemption so long as the issuer made a reasonable and good faith effort to comply and the deviation did not pertain to a term or condition designed to protect the complaining party.

Section 4(6). The Commission also adopted a new Rule 215, defining the term "accredited investor" for purposes of § 4(6) to include the various categories of purchasers listed in Rule 501. Section 4(6) is thus an alternative exemption for an offering of up to $5 million made solely to accredited investors.

Relationship to other exemptions. Note that offerings complying with Rule 504 or 505 are exempted from registration pursuant to § 3(b) of the Act, while offerings complying with Rule 506 (which may amount to more than $5 million) are deemed to be transactions not involving any public offering within the meaning of § 4(2). Also note that Rule 506 is not the exclusive method of complying with § 4(2); offerings which do not meet all of the Rule's requirements may still be exempt under § 4(2) as interpreted by the courts and the SEC.

In 1996, Congress enacted § 18(b) of the 1933 Act, which preempts state law registration requirements for certain offerings, including offerings pursuant to SEC rules adopted under authority of § 4(2), i.e. Rule 506. Accordingly, states cannot impose their own registration requirements or conditions on a Rule 506 offering; all they can do is to require a notification of reliance on the federal exemption. In contrast, offerings exempted under Rule 505 are not subject to the preemption provision, since Rule 505 was issued under authority of § 3(b).

In that same year, the Commission, in a novel move, adopted a rule providing a federal exemption conditioned on qualification for an exemption under state law. Under authority of § 3(b), the Commission adopted Rule 1001, exempting from federal registration offerings of up to $5 million that qualify for exemption under § 25102(n) of the California Corporations Code.

This new rule is significant, since California § 25102(n) does not contain the prohibitions on general solicitation and advertising found in Rules 505 and 506. The Commission indicated that it would be prepared to adopt additional exemptions based on comparable exemptions adopted in other states.

NOTE ON RULES 144 AND 144A

Rule 144 applies to sales of securities by an "affiliate" of the issuer (i.e., a person who controls or is controlled by the issuer) and any sale of "restricted securities" (i.e., securities acquired from the issuer in a nonpublic transaction). To be exempted from registration, the seller must comply with the following requirements:

(1) A person's sales under Rule 144 during any three-month period may not exceed the greater of (a) 1% of the total number of units of the security outstanding and (b) the average weekly trading volume for the preceding four weeks.

(2) If the person acquired the securities from the issuer or affiliate of the issuer in a non-public transaction, he or she must have held them for at least six months if the issuer is a publicly-held corporation and one year otherwise before reselling them. (Securities are not considered fungible for this purpose; securities held for more than two years may be sold, even if the seller has recently acquired additional securities of the same class from the issuer.) In 1990, the Commission amended rule 144 to provide that the holding period runs from the time the securities were purchased from the issuer or an affiliate of the issuer. Accordingly, there now is a tacking of holding periods for nonaffiliates who purchase securities from a nonaffiliate.

(3) The issuer must be subject to, and in current compliance with, the periodic reporting requirements of the 1934 Act, or there must otherwise be publicly available information comparable to that which would be found in such reports.

(4) The securities must be sold in ordinary brokerage transactions, or transactions directly with a "market maker," not involving any special remuneration or solicitation.

(5) A notice of each sale must be filed with the SEC at the time the order is placed with the broker.

In 1998, the SEC moved to expand the types of securities covered by Rule 144. It included securities issued in off-shore offerings under Regulation S in the definition of "restricted securities." See Rules 903(b)(3), 905. In 1999, the Commission amended Rule 144 to include in the definition of restricted securities most securities issued under Rule 504's exemption for offerings up to $1 million. Thus, securities issued in Rule 504 offerings will be restricted unless either (1) the transaction is registered under a state securities law that requires public filing and delivery of a substantive disclosure document or (2) the offering is made only to accredited investors (as that term is defined in Regulation D) under a state law exemption that permits a general solicitation.

A significant liberalization of the Rule took place October 1983, when the Commission amended paragraph (k) to remove all of the restrictions of the Rule from resales of restricted securities by any person who has held those securities for at least three years and has not been an affiliate of the issuer for at least three months. This liberalization enabled investors who have provided venture capital to a closely-held company to resell all of their securities publicly after a three-year holding period, even though the company has not made any information publicly available under either the 1933 or the 1934 Act. When the SEC reduced the holding period for restricted securities from two years to one, it also amended paragraph (k) to provide that all restrictions on resales by nonaffiliates terminate after two years rather than three.

Still another exemption to the registration requirement is available to institutional investors. Rule 144A classifies certain offers and sales as not involving a distribution requiring registration, so that persons participating in such offers and sales are not considered "underwriters." Essentially, the exemption covers any sale to a "qualified institutional buyer," which is defined as any institution (including insurance companies, investment companies, employee benefit plans, banks, and savings and loan associations) that owns more than $100 million worth of securities of unaffiliated issuers and, in the case of banks and savings and loans, has a net worth of at least $25 million.

In addition to direct transactions among these classes of institutions, the Rule also permits securities dealers to participate in transactions, either as purchasers for their own account, provided they themselves own at least $10 million worth of securities of unaffiliated issuers, or as agents for qualified institutions. Indeed, the Rule contemplates the formation of an active trading market in Rule 144A securities, in which qualified institutions and dealers can enter bids and offers. Simultaneously with the adoption of Rule 144A, the SEC approved the establishment by the National Association of Securities Dealers (NASD) of a screen-based computer and communication system called PORTAL (Private Offerings, Resales and Trading through Automated Linkages) to facilitate secondary trading of Rule 144A securities.

Rule 144A only applies to sales of securities of a class that is *not* listed on a U.S. stock exchange or traded in the NASDAQ system. With respect to securities issued by companies subject to the 1934 Act reporting requirements, or by foreign issuers, use of the Rule is not conditioned on the provision or availability of any information about the issuer. With respect to securities of other issuers, however, the Rule is only available if the prospective purchaser has received from the issuer a brief statement of the nature of the issuer's business and certain specified financial statements. * * *

The adoption of Rule 144A and the establishment of the PORTAL system create the potential for an active trading market in foreign securities and in unregistered debt and equity issues of domestic issuers, limited to a designated class of large institutions and dealers. The SEC has also indicated that it will consider expanding the availability of the Rule as experience is gained about its operation.

SECTION 4.   THE UNDERWRITING PROCESS

A key aspect of an investment in securities is liquidity. Stock in a closely held corporation is illiquid, thereby trapping its investors in the corporation. Equity or notes obtained in a private placement may also be difficult to sell, making them illiquid. How does a security become liquid? The principle method used to create liquidity is to develop a public market in the security. Frequently, some percentage of the company is sold to the public through an initial public offering, or "IPO" in Wall Street terms. This will require the services of an underwriter.

UNITED STATES v. MORGAN

118 F.Supp. 621 (S.D.N.Y.1953).

MEDINA, CIRCUIT JUDGE.

[In dismissing antitrust claims against several investment banking firms, the court provided the following description of the growth and operation of underwriting syndicates in America].

* * * It would be difficult to exaggerate the importance of investment banking to the national economy. The vast industrial growth of the past fifty years has covered the United States with a network of manufacturing, processing, sales and distributing plants, the smooth functioning of which is vital to our welfare as a nation. They vary from huge corporate structures such as the great steel and automobile companies, railroads and airlines, producers of commodities and merchandise of all kinds, oil companies and public utilities, down to comparatively small manufacturing plants and stores. The variety and usefulness of these myriad enterprises defy description. They are the result of American ingenuity and the will to work unceasingly and to improve our standard of living. But adequate financing for their needs is the life blood without which many if not most of these parts of the great machine of business would cease to function in a healthy, normal fashion. * * *

The present method for issuing and distributing new security issues thus has its roots in the latter part of the nineteenth century. It is the product of a gradual evolution to meet specific economic problems created by demands for capital, which arose as the result of the increasing industrialization of the country and the growth of a widely dispersed investor class. It was born in large part because of, and gradually adapted itself to, conditions and needs which are peculiar to the business of raising capital. * * *

The evolution of the investment banking industry in the United States is illustrated by the early phases of the development of two of the defendant investment banking firms, Goldman, Sachs & Co. and Lehman Brothers.

Goldman, Sachs & Co. traces its origin back to the year 1869, when Marcus Goldman started a small business buying and selling commercial paper. In the year 1882, he was joined in that business by Samuel Sachs, and at that time the firm, which had been known as Marcus Goldman, became M. Goldman & Sachs. In the year 1885, when additional partners joined the firm, the firm became Goldman, Sachs & Co., and has continued as such from then on to today. At that time, it was very difficult for small manufacturers and merchants to get capital with which to operate, so Goldman, Sachs & Co. developed the business of buying their short-term promissory notes, thus furnishing them with needed capital, and selling these notes to banks or other investors. * * *

After the beginning of this century, as family corporations grew larger and needed more capital for expansion, or when the head of a family died and money was needed to pay inheritance taxes, it became increasingly apparent that commercial paper, which was short-term money, was insufficient to meet the capital requirements of those small enterprises. At about this time, Goldman, Sachs & Co., desirous of entering the business of underwriting securities, conceived the idea of inducing privately owned business enterprises to incorporate and to launch public offerings of securities. In the early 1900's it was considered undignified to peddle retail store securities, but Goldman, Sachs & Co. believed that, with the growth in size of family corporations and other privately owned business enterprises, there would be a market on a national basis for their security issues. The problems involved in offering securities to the public, where no securities were previously outstanding in the hands of the public, were new and difficult of solution, and different from the problems involved in the underwriting of bonds of a well known railroad. The sale of retail or department store securities required a different market.

When the opportunity arose in the year 1906 for Goldman, Sachs & Co. to underwrite the financing of United Cigar Manufacturers, it was unable to undertake the entire commitment alone, and could not get the additional funds which it needed to underwrite from commercial banks or other underwriters, as they would not at that time underwrite this type of securities. Henry Goldman prevailed upon his friend Philip Lehman of Lehman Brothers to divert some of his capital from the commodity business and to take a share in the underwriting. The result was that the two firms, Goldman, Sachs & Co. and Lehman Brothers, became partners in the underwriting of the financing of United Cigar Manufacturers. When the opportunity arose in that same year for Goldman, Sachs & Co. to underwrite the financing of Sears, Roebuck & Co., it was perfectly natural for it again to turn to Lehman Brothers for assistance, and the two firms became partners in that enterprise. * * *

In the period from the year 1906 to the year 1917, Goldman, Sachs & Co. and Lehman Brothers together underwrote the financings of many enterprises which had a small and humble beginning, but which later grew to very great size, among them being United Cigar Manufacturers, Sears, Roebuck & Co., B. F. Goodrich Company, May Department Stores

Company and F. W. Woolworth Company. Many of the business concerns whose securities were underwritten by Goldman, Sachs & Co. and Lehman Brothers during this period were houses with which Goldman, Sachs & Co. had previously had commercial paper transactions. As Goldman, Sachs & Co. and Lehman Brothers were better known at the time than many of the business enterprises whose securities they underwrote, investors bought the securities to some extent in reliance on their reputation. * * *

There was then no network of securities dealers throughout the country, such as there is at the present time. In or about the year 1905 or 1906, there were only about five investment banking houses which had a national distribution system for securities: Lee Higginson & Co.; N. W. Harris & Co.; N. W. Halsey & Co.; Kidder, Peabody & Co.; and William Salomon & Co. Investment banking houses such as J. P. Morgan & Co., Kuhn, Loeb & Co., and William A. Read & Co. were underwriters of securities primarily in the New York market. Up to about the year 1912 or 1915, there were approximately only two hundred and fifty securities dealers in the entire United States, most of whom were concentrated in the eastern and middle eastern parts of the country. It was not until the time of the launching of the Liberty Loan in the year 1917 that we find a large number of independent dealers engaged in the business of distributing securities throughout the country. * * *

In the period under discussion, it was common for an investment banker to purchase an entire issue directly from the issuer at stated price, and that banker alone would sign the purchase contract with the issuer. Generally, the investment banker's agreement to purchase represented a firm obligation. This investment banker would then immediately organize a larger group, composed of a limited number of investment banking firms, which was sometimes called a "purchase syndicate," whereby he would, in effect, sub-underwrite his risk by selling the securities which he had purchased alone from the issuer to this larger group, at an increase or "step-up" in price. The investment banker who purchased the entire issue directly from the issuer was known as the "originating banker" or "house of issue." The originating banker became a member and the manager of the "purchase syndicate." Goldman, Sachs & Co. is said to be one of the first investment banking firms to develop this method of underwriting securities; and, although this method may have been developed to underwrite the securities of the smaller, less well-known industrial enterprises and of the family concerns which were for the first time launching securities for sale to the public, other investment bankers used the same method to underwrite the securities of large industrial enterprises, railroads and utilities. As business enterprises in this country grew in size, and as the amounts of capital required by these enterprises became larger, sometimes a second group, more numerous than the "purchase syndicate," would be formed in order to spread still wider the risk involved in the purchase and sale of the securities. The "purchase syndicate" would then sell the securities which it had purchased at an increase in price from the originating banker to this second larger group, which was sometimes called a "banking syndicate," at another increase or "step-up" in price. The originating banker and the other investment banking firms, which were members of the "purchase syndicate," usually became members of the "banking syndicate" and the originating banker became its manager. The transfer of the securities to the "purchase syndicate" and then to the "banking syndicate" was practically simultaneous with the original purchase of the securities from the issuer by the originating banker. * * *

From all the above it is evident that the various steps which were taken, including use of the purchase and banking groups above described, were all part of the development of a single effective method of security underwriting and distribution, with such features as maintenance of a fixed price during distribution, stabilization and direction by a manager of the entire coordinated operation of originating, underwriting and distributing the entire issue.

This evolution of the syndicate system was in no sense a plan or scheme invented by anyone. Its form and development were due entirely to the economic conditions in the midst of which investment bankers functioned. No single underwriter could have borne alone the underwriting risk involved in the purchase and sale of a large security issue. No single underwriter could have effected a successful public distribution of the issue. The various investment bankers combined and formed groups, and pooled their underwriting resources in order to compete for business. * * *

The number of underwriters in the syndicates increased [after World War I], in order both to spread the risk and to effect a widespread and rapid distribution of the securities to the public. Even so the problems of distribution became so complicated that it became customary to form an additional group called a "selling syndicate" or "selling group." The new "selling syndicate" was much larger and more widely dispersed than the purchase and banking groups had been.

There were three types of these selling syndicates throughout this period. While they represented successive steps in the development of investment banking, and while there were shifts in the type that was most extensively used, all three were used throughout the 1920's.

The first type was known as the "unlimited liability selling syndicate." In this group, each member agreed to take a pro rata share in the purchase of the security issue by the selling syndicate from the previous group, at a stated price, and to take up his share of any unsold securities, which remained in the syndicate at the time of its expiration. The syndicate agreement stated the terms upon which the offering to the public was to be made. Each member was given the right to offer securities to the public, and he received a stated commission on all confirmed sales. However, regardless of the amount of securities which he sold, he still retained his liability to take up his proportionate share of unsold securities. The undivided syndicate combined selling with the assumption of risk; therefore, both houses with distributing ability and houses with financial capacity, but without distributing ability, were included in the syndicate. Usually, a banking group was not organized where this type of selling syndicate was to be used. The purchase group sold the security issue directly to the selling syndicate.

The dealers who did the actual selling of the securities objected to the "unlimited liability selling syndicate," as they were compelled to take up in their proportionate shares the securities, which the other dealers, who were members of the selling syndicate, were unable to sell. Consequently, the second type of selling syndicate, which was known as the "limited liability selling syndicate," subsequently was developed. This syndicate operated in much the same manner as the undivided syndicate, except that the obligation of each member was limited to the amount of his commitment, and, when he distributed that amount, he was relieved of further liability. Each member retained his proportionate liability for the costs of carrying the securities, shared in the profits or losses of the trading account, and was liable for such other expenses as occurred after the purchase from the purchase or banking group. A banking group was usually organized where the "limited liability selling syndicate" was to be used.

The "limited liability selling syndicate" gradually evolved into the third type of selling syndicate, which was simply known as the "selling group." The "selling group" differed from the "limited liability selling syndicate" in that its members relieved themselves of all liability for carrying costs, the trading account and other expenses. Each member of the "selling group" was concerned only with expenses connected with the actual retail distribution of securities. The financial liability of the member was restricted to selling or taking up the amount of securities for which he subscribed. Usually, a large banking group was organized where the "selling group" was to be used. The banking group took over the liability for carrying costs, the trading account and other expenses.

The size and makeup of the selling syndicates varied with the circumstances of the particular security issue. Among the important factors, which were considered in the selection of dealers, were the size of the security issue, the type and quality of the security, the size and nature of the class of investors to whom the distribution was to be made, and the ability of a dealer to distribute securities of a particular type. All of these factors were considered in the selection of underwriters and dealers for the formation of the underwriting syndicates and selling groups.

In all of these types of selling syndicates, the members acted as principals, and not as agents of the manager, in distributing securities to the public. The syndicate agreement specified the price at which the securities were to be sold, and it was a violation of the agreement for a member to sell at any other price. The manager traded in the open market during the period of distribution in order to maintain the public offering price. Through such stabilizing operations, the manager sought to prevent any securities, which had been sold by dealers, from coming back into the market in such a manner as to depress the public offering price. It was felt that with respect to the securities which appeared in the market, the members of the selling syndicate had not performed their function of "placing" with investors, for which they were paid a selling commission; and, consequently, "repurchase penalties" were provided for, whereby the manager had the right to cancel the selling commission on the sale of those securities which he purchased in the market at or below the public offering price. Under most agreements, the manager had the option of either canceling the selling commission on the sale of the securities, or of requiring the member who sold the securities to take them up at their cost to the trading account. Records of the serial numbers of securities were kept, and the securities which appeared in the market were thus traced to the dealers who sold them. Stabilizing operations and the repurchase penalty were used in all of the three types of selling syndicates which prevailed throughout this period. However, where a "selling group" was used, it became more and more common practice to restrict the re-purchase penalty to the cancellation of commissions.

The operations of the "selling syndicate" like those of the pre-war withdrawing subscribers, dealers and selling agents, were directed by the manager whose general supervisory function over the whole machinery of purchase and distribution was continued. Even in the earlier period provisions for maintenance of the public offering price by persons to whom title had passed had been included in some agreements. * * *

As the amounts of capital required by business enterprises became larger, and the number and size of securities issues greatly increased, the problems with which investment bankers were confronted, in connection with the underwriting of security issues, multiplied. Extensive investigations had to be conducted into the affairs of a business enterprise, and studies made of its financial structure and capital needs, at considerable expense to the investment banker, before that banker would undertake the risk and underwrite the securities of that enterprise. In this connection, investment banking firms were compelled to bring into their organizations individuals who had new types of specialized knowledge and experience; so that they gradually built up teams of specialists, who were experts in the different fields in which their respective investment banking firms underwrote securities. * * *

More important than any of the other developments between World War I and the passage of the Securities Act of 1933 was the effect of the unprecedented era of expansion upon the participation of the great banking institutions and their affiliates. As the need for vast amounts of new capital for expansion, plant construction and the establishment of thousands of new enterprises made increasing demands for new money, the banks and their affiliates became increasingly interested in managing and participating in the various underwritings. While the evidence in this case relative to the pre-Securities Act period is far from complete, there is ample documentary evidence to show that many of the banks became directly interested through their bond departments and many others formed affiliates, as above stated. J. P. Morgan & Co., the First National Bank and the Bankers Trust Company and many others in New York City, as well as large banking institutions in Chicago, Cleveland and other cities did a large investment banking business. The National City Company, the Guaranty Company and Chase Securities Corporation, affiliates of the National City Bank, the Guaranty Trust Company of New York and the Chase National Bank were in the investment banking business in a big way. The National City Company as of December 31, 1929, had a capital of $110,000,000. On the same date the capital of the Chase Securities Corporation was over $101,000,000. The economic power of these huge aggregations of capital vis-a-vis the relatively small capital of issuers was a factor of no mean significance in the period just before the great depression. There was an additional leverage in the multiplicity of banking functions which could be placed at the disposal of issuers. Added to this was the vast influence and prestige which must have made itself felt in a variety of ways. Issuers were dependent upon these great banking institutions in a way which finds no parallel in the relations between issuers and investment bankers in the period subsequent to the passage of the Banking and Securities Acts.

Before it became necessary by law to choose between commercial banking on the one hand and investment banking on the other, many of these great banking institutions were private banking houses under no statutory duty to make the disclosures required of national banks and others and this, coupled with the lack of legal requirements for disclosure of relevant facts connected with security issues, helped to make the period under discussion what has been described in the trial as an era of "dignity and mystery." * * *

Following the Armstrong Insurance investigation in 1905 and Governor Hughes' Committee Report in 1909 there had been other investigations which covered activities of investment bankers. The Pujo investigation was conducted in 1912 and 1913, the Utility Corporation inquiry by the Federal Trade Commission started in 1928; and these were followed by a long series of hearings, under the auspices of various committees of the Congress, which resulted in the Banking Act of 1933 (known also as the Glass–Steagall Act), the Securities Act of 1933 and the Securities Exchange Act of 1934. From December 10, 1931 through February 1932 the Senate Committee on Finance pursuant to the Johnson Resolution undertook to investigate the flotation of foreign bonds and other securities in the United States. Perhaps the most important of these investigations was the Gray–Pecora investigation of the Senate Committee on Banking and Currency which began on April 11, 1932 and continued through May 4, 1934.

In this chronological survey of the history and development of the investment banking business it will suffice to say that these statutes, together with the Public Utility Holding Company Act of 1935 and the Maloney Act, effective June 25, 1938, which added Section 15A to the

Securities Exchange Act of 1934, and authorized the organization of the National Association of Securities Dealers, Inc. (NASD), under the supervision of the SEC, which followed, effected changes of the most radical and pervasive character; and these changes were made with a complete and comprehensive understanding by the Congress of current methods of operation in common use in the securities issue business, such information having been made available in the course of the investigations to which reference has just been made.

Institutions which had previously engaged both in commercial and deposit banking on the one hand and investment banking on the other were required to elect prior to June 16, 1934, which of the two functions they would pursue to the exclusion of the other. This resulted in the complete elimination of the commercial banks and trust companies from the investment banking business; and the various bank affiliates were dissolved and liquidated.

The elaborate procedures which now became necessary in connection with the sale of new issues of securities were at first implemented by the Federal Trade Commission and then, upon the creation of the Securities and Exchange Commission, transferred to it. The regulation of the securities business which followed with such salutary and beneficial results has been one of the significant developments of our time. The era of "dignity and mystery" was over.

When we come to discuss the syndicate system and its operation, it will be appropriate to treat in some detail the various applicable provisions of the Securities Act of 1933 and the Securities Exchange Act of 1934, with their respective amendments, and also the numerous regulations, interpretations and releases of the SEC relative thereto. For the sake of continuity and clarity, however, this brief recital of the development of the investment banking business will be continued in order to furnish general background. * * *

Due largely to the impact of the income and inheritance tax laws, the importance of the individual as an investor diminished and there was an extraordinary and continued growth in the size and investment needs of large institutional investors such as life and casualty companies, savings banks, investment trusts, pension funds, universities, hospitals and fraternal orders.

Perhaps the most significant change of all was caused by the withdrawal from the field of investment banking of the capital funds of the commercial banks and their affiliates, which had previously been among the foremost managers and underwriters of security issues. * * *

The form in which underwriting transactions commonly took place from the passage of the Banking and Securities legislation up to the present time is that of a purchase or "underwriting agreement" between the issuer and the underwriters represented by the manager, and an "agreement among underwriters."

The substance of the entire transaction is substantially what it was before. The manager, like the originating banker or manager in the previous periods, handles the negotiations with the issuer and supervises the whole process of underwriting and distribution. The management for of today is not a new development either in form or in purpose after the Securities Act of 1933, but is the direct equivalent of the management fee paid by the members of the syndicate to the manager for his services in pre–1933 financings, where the syndicate either purchased directly from the issuer or from a prior "original purchaser."

Dealer and group sales are still made, under the authority of the manager who directs the entire process of distribution. But the change in the character of the investing public and especially the development of institutional investors on such a large scale and the impact of regulation by the SEC and of the Securities Act of 1933, the Securities Exchange Act of 1934 and the organization and functioning of the NASD, brought about a gradual decrease in the use of selling group agreements, especially in issues of the higher grades of debt financing and preferred stock. It is worthy of note that in performing his function of making sales for the accounts of the underwriters both to dealers and to institutions the manager sells "out of the pot." In other words, he does not allocate particular bonds to particular underwriters but simply sells "bonds" and does not allocate numbers to any participant until the time comes for delivery of securities to the purchasers.

In accordance with the trend of the previous period spreads are gradually becoming smaller and smaller; and the maximum life of the syndicates is now 15, 20 or 30 days, although in some cases the maximum period may be longer, and it is not unusual to find clauses authorizing the manager to extend the period with or without the consent of a certain proportion of the underwriters. Price restrictions may, however, be removed earlier than the actual termination date of the syndicate, and as a practical matter they are generally terminated within a few days after the offering.

Stabilization provisions have become commonplace pursuant to statutory provisions and administrative regulations and interpretations relating to their use. While the authority to stabilize is generally given, it is only in relatively few cases that the authority has been exercised.

The use of "penalty clauses" has varied and the same is true of the use of price maintenance clauses.... But it is well to bear in mind throughout that the entire pattern of the statutory scheme above referred to, as implemented by the various rules and regulations of the SEC and the rules of Fair Practice of the National Association of Securities Dealers, Inc., approved by the SEC pursuant to legislative authority, contemplates the sale of each security issue at the public offering price proposed in the prospectus and set forth in the registration statement as finally made effective by the SEC. Having proposed and tendered a security issue to the public at the public offering price, it is not strange that those who propose to sell the entire issue at this public offering price should be required to make a bona fide attempt to do so. Otherwise, the elaborate statutory provisions relative to "the public offering price" would be meaningless. Nor, under these circumstances, should one wonder that some investment banking houses continued to use price maintenance clauses while others did not. * * *

Due in part to the registration provisions of the Securities Act of 1933, but also in large measure to the increase in the number of institutional investors and their particular requirements, private placements grew by leaps and bounds. * * *

Where the services of an investment banker are used, the typical transactions are even more varied. The principal ones are:

1. A negotiated underwritten public offering.

2. An underwritten public offering awarded on the basis of publicly invited sealed bids, an investment banker having been retained on a fee basis to shape up the issue.

3. A negotiated underwritten offering to existing security-holders. Here the investment banker enters into a commitment to 'stand by' until the subscription or exchange period has expired, at which time the investment banker must take up the securities not subscribed or exchanged.

4. An underwritten offering to existing security-holders awarded on the basis of publicly invited sealed bids, an investment banker having been retained on a fee basis to render the necessary assistance.

5. A non-underwritten offering to existing security-holders, with an investment banker acting as agent of the seller on a negotiated basis.

6. A private placement with an investment banker acting as agent of the seller on a negotiated basis.

There are many and sundry variations of the types of transactions just described, depending on the designing of the plan, the amount of risk-taking involved and the problems of distribution; and these variations are reflected in the amount of compensation to be paid to the investment banker, which is always subject to negotiation. * * *

The actual design of the issue involves preparation of the prospectus and registration statement, with supporting documents and reports, compliance with the numerous rules and regulations of the SEC or ICC or FPC and the various Blue Sky Laws passed by the several States. In view of the staggering potential liabilities under the Securities Act of 1933 this is no child's play, as is known only too well by the management of issuers.

This hasty and far from complete recital of available alternatives will suffice to indicate the milieu in which the investment banker demonstrates his skill, ingenuity and resourcefulness, to the extent and to the extent only that an issuer wishes to avail itself of his services. It is always the hope of the investment banker that the issuer will use the full range of the services of the investment banker, including the design and setting up of the issue, the organization of the group to underwrite the risk and the planning of the distribution. If he cannot wholly succeed, the investment banker will try to get as much of the business as he can. Thus he may wind up as the manager or co-manager, or as a participant in the group of underwriters with or without an additional selling position; or he may earn a fee as agent for a private placement or other transaction without any risk-bearing feature. Or someone else may get the business away from him.

Thus we find that in the beginning there is no "it." The security issue which eventuates is a nebulous thing, still in future. Consequently the competition for business by investment bankers must start with an effort to establish or continue a relationship with the issuer. That is why we hear so much in this case about ingenious ways to prevail upon the issuers in particular instances to select this or that investment banking house to work on the general problem of shaping up the issue and handling the financing. This is the initial step; and it is generally taken many months prior to the time when it is expected that the money will be needed. It is clear beyond any reasonable doubt that this procedure is due primarily to the wishes of the issuers; and one of the reasons why issuers like this form of competition is that they are under no legal obligation whatever to the investment banker until some document such as an underwriting agreement or agency contract with the investment banker has actually been signed.

Sometimes an investment banking house will go it alone at this initial stage. At times two or three houses or even more will work together in seeking the business, with various understandings relative to the managership or co-managership and the amount of their underwriting participations. These are called nucleus groups. Occasionally one comes across documents pertaining to such nucleus groups which seem to contemplate the continuance of the group for future business, only to find that in a few weeks or less the whole picture has changed and some realignment of forces has taken place.

The tentative selection of an investment banker to shape up the issue and handle the financing has now been made; and there ensues a more or less prolonged period during which the skilled technicians of the investment banker are working with the executive and financial advisers of the issuer, studying the business from every angle, becoming familiar with the industry in which it functions, its future prospects, the character and efficiency of its operating policies and similar matters. Much of this information will eventually find its way in one form or another into the prospectus and registration statement. Sometimes engineers will be employed to make a survey of the business. The investment banker will submit a plan of the financing, often in writing; and this plan and perhaps others will be the subject of discussions. Gradually the definitive plan will be agreed upon, or perhaps the entire matter will be dropped in favor of a private placement, without the services of an investment banker. Often, and after many months of effort on the part of the investment banker, the issuer will decide to postpone the raising of the money for a year or two.

In the interval between the time when the investment banker is put on the job and the time when the definitive product begins to take form, a variety of other problems of great importance require consideration. The most vital of these, in terms of money and otherwise, is the timing of the issue. It is here, with his feel and judgment of the market, that the top-notch investment banker renders what is perhaps his most important service. The probable state of the general security market at any given future time is a most difficult thing to forecast. Only those with ripe trading experience and the finest kind of general background in financial affairs and practical economics can effectively render service of this character.

At last the issue has been cast in more or less final form, the prospectus and registration statement have been drafted and decisions relative to matters bearing a direct relation to the effective cost of the money, such as the coupon or dividend rate, sinking fund, conversion and redemption provisions and serial dates, if any, are shaped up subject to further consideration at the last moment. The work of organizing the syndicate, determining the participation positions of those selected as underwriters and the making up of a list of dealers for the selling group or, if no selling group is to be used, the formulation of plans for distribution by some other means, have been gradually proceeding, practically always in consultation with the issuer, who has the final say as to who the participating underwriters are to be. The general plans for distribution of the issue require the most careful and expert consideration, as the credit of the issuer may be seriously affected should the issue not be successful. Occasionally an elaborate campaign of education of dealers and investors is conducted.

Thus, if the negotiated underwritten public offering route is to be followed, we come at last to what may be the parting of the ways between the issuer and the investment banker—negotiation relative to the public offering price, the spread and the price to be paid to the issuer for the securities. These three are inextricably interrelated. The stating point is and must be the determination of the price at which the issue is to be offered to the public. This must in the very nature of things be the price at which the issuer and the investment banker jointly think the security can be put on the market with reasonable assurance of success; and at times the issuer, as already indicated in this brief recital of the way the investment banker functions, will for good and sufficient reasons not desire the public offering price to be placed at the highest figure attainable.

Once agreement has been tentatively reached on the public offering price, the negotiation shifts to the amount of the contemplated gross spread. This figure must include the gross compensation of all those who participate in the distribution of the issue: the manager, the underwriting participants and the dealers who are to receive concessions and re-allowances. Naturally, the amount of the spread will be governed largely by the nature of the problems of distribution and the amount of work involved. The statistical charts and static data indicate that the amount of the contemplated gross spreads is smallest with the highest class of bonds and largest with common stock issues, where the actual work of selling is at its maximum. While no two security issues are precisely alike and they vary as the leaves on the trees, it is apparent that the executive and financial officers of issuers may sit down on the other side of the bargaining table confidently, and without apprehension of being imposed upon, as data relating to public offering prices, spreads, and net proceeds to issuers from new security issues registered under the Securities Act of 1933 are all public information which are publicized among other means by the wide distribution of the prospectuses for each issue.

And so in the end the 'pricing' of the issue is arrived at as a single, unitary determination of the public offering price, spread and price to the issuer. * * *

NOTE

In Friedman v. Salomon Smith Barney, Inc., 313 F.3d 796 (2d Cir. 2002), cert. denied, 540 U.S. 822, 124 S.Ct. 152, 157 L.Ed.2d 43 (2003), the Second Circuit held that broker-dealers are immune from antitrust liability in their underwriting activities because the application of antitrust laws would conflict with the federal securities laws. The complaint had charged that the practice of restricting resales of stock distributed in an initial public offering (anti "flipping" provisions) for specified time periods was an anticompetitive activity. As will be seen in the following materials, the SEC has extensive regulations covering underwriting activities. See also Credit Suisse Securities (USA) v. Billing, 551 U.S. 264, 127 S.Ct. 2383, 168 L.Ed.2d 145 (2007) (held aftermarket IPO purchase agreements were protected from the reach of the antitrust laws by SEC regulations).

23A JERRY W. MARKHAM & THOMAS LEE HAZEN BROKER–DEALER REGULATION UNDER SECURITIES AND COMMODITIES LAWS
§ 9:9 to § 9:14 (2002).

One of the most critical periods in which manipulative activities can affect securities prices is the period surrounding a distribution of securities. Even prior to the creation of the SEC, underwriters commonly entered into stabilizing transactions to support the price of a stock during a distribution. Penalties were imposed on underwriting participants that sold below the offering price set by the lead underwriter. Market prices were often quite volatile during the offering period as the market sought to price and adjust to the new offering. The underwriters sometimes artificially stimulated prices in order to boost the offering and to profit from their own holdings. These activities included transactions that were designed to create the appearance of artificial demand in order to inflate the value of the offering. This encouraged unsuspecting investors to purchase the securities at inflated values and enabled insiders to sell their holdings at an artificial price.

The federal securities laws and the SEC have sought to restrict distributions into a market that has been artificially stimulated by the activities of persons that have an interest in the distribution. However, the SEC did not wish to ban all trading by participants during a distribution. A complete ban would have stopped necessary and desirable activities such as transactions by underwriters in the regular course of their business for customer accounts. A complete ban would further prevent an underwriter from engaging in legitimate stabilizing activity, which could facilitate an orderly market. As the SEC noted in 1940, stabilizing activities were an "integral part of the American system of fixed price security distribution." Stabilizing trades were designed to facilitate an orderly market during a distribution. They sought to prevent, or at lessen, a decline in the price of the securities being distributed. These activities were often needed when new stock was being brought into the market, as well as when there was an existing market for the securities. The issuance of new or additional securities into an existing market could have a downward effect on prices, and securities values could be diluted unnecessarily. * * *

The SEC's first efforts at regulating trading activities by participants during a distribution were informal. They expressed "the fundamental principle that a stabilizing transaction is one which is effected for the *limited purpose* of preventing or retarding a decline in the market price of a security in contemplation of or during its distribution." Underwriters agreed not to trade for their own account during a distribution, except for necessary stabilizing activities. Underwriters also, as a matter of practice, refrained from recommending a security being distributed to customers. In 1939, the SEC concluded that more affirmative regulation was needed to supplement these voluntary practices. Initially, this meant the adoption of Rule 426 that required the public to be advised that the underwriters were supporting the market in the security during a distribution. This disclosure was made in SEC required prospectuses and informed investors that stabilizing transactions might be conducted in connection with the distribution of securities covered by the prospectus. Reporting requirements were also imposed where such trading activities were being conducted.

In 1955, the SEC concluded that additional regulations were needed to govern the trading activities of participants in a distribution. It then adopted Rules 10b–6, 10b–7 and 10b–8. Rule 10b–6 was designed to regulate trading by participants in a distribution, Rule 10b–7 governed stabilizing transactions, and Rule 10b–8 dealt with rights offerings. * * *

In 1994, the SEC issued a concept release that sought comment on the need to revise its trading practice rules. As a result of those comments, and its own studies, the SEC concluded that revision was needed. In proposing such changes, the SEC noted that since the adoption of its trading practices rules the markets and their participants had significantly changed. Regulators and broker-dealers had also developed sophisticated surveillance capabilities, enabling them to monitor market activity on a real-time basis. In light of this capability, the SEC concluded that its trading practice rules could be narrowed and simplified without sacrificing investor protection. Accordingly, a new Regulation M [17 C.F.R. Part 242] was adopted to replace the prior trading practice rules. * * *

Regulation M replaces Rules 10b–6, 10b–6A, 10b–7, 10b–8 and 10b–21. Regulation M sought to simplify and reduce the burden imposed by its former trading practice rules. "Regulation M exemplifies the Commission's efforts to relax restrictions in cases where either the risk of manipulation is small or the costs of the restrictions are disproportionate to the purposes they serve." However, it remains a complex provision.

Regulation M consists of six rules that apply to:

> (1) Activities by underwriters or other persons who are participating in a distribution and affiliated purchasers;

> (2) Activities by the issuer or selling security holder and their affiliated purchasers;

> (3) Nasdaq passive market making;

> (4) Stabilizing transactions to cover syndicate short positions and penalty bids; and

> (5) Short selling in advance of a public offering.

In principal, Regulation M is a set of rules that govern participants' trading activities during a distribution. But it also imposes restrictions on issuers or selling security holders and their affiliated purchasers. Passive market making is regulated, as are stabilizing transactions and short selling in advance of a public offering. Regulation M replaced the former trading practice rules and rescinded Rule 10b–8, which previously regulated rights offerings. * * *

The general anti-fraud provisions of Rule 10b–5 and the anti-manipulation provisions of Section 9 of the Securities Exchange Act of 1934 continue to apply to offering participants. Regulation M [17 C.F.R. Part 242] does not affect the application of the registration and prospectus delivery requirements under the Securities Act of 1933. In addition, Regulation M is not a "safe harbor" that will allow activities other than those specified in the Regulation. Rather, it is a mandatory regime for trading practices and offerings.

NYSE/NASD IPO Advisory Committee, Report and Recommendations of a Committee Convened by the New York Stock Exchange, Inc. and NASD at the Request of the U.S. Securities and Exchange Commission 1–2 (May 2003).

Fairness, integrity and efficiency make the U.S. Capital markets the most successful in the world. In the past decade, more than 5,600 domestic and foreign enterprises raised an aggregate of over $500 billion through IPOs in U.S. markets. These IPOs served as an engine for corporate growth and active participation by all sectors of the investment community, from venture capitalists to large institutions and individual investors.

In recent years, however, public confidence in the integrity of the IPO process has eroded significantly. Investigations have revealed that certain underwriters and other participants in IPOs at times engaged in misconduct contrary to the best interests of investors and our markets; at least some of this misconduct was unlawful. Instances of this behavior became more frequent during the IPO "bubble" of the late 1990s and 2000, a period in which an unusually large number of offerings traded at extraordinary and immediate aftermarket premiums. These large first-day price increases in turn affected the allocation process by creating a pool of instant profits for underwriters to distribute. Some did so improperly—in exchange for a share of these profits, or perhaps for a promise of future business. In turn, some institutional investors were willing to participate in improper arrangements in order to receive the essentially guaranteed profit that "hot" IPOs came to represent. Among the most harmful practices that have given rise to public concern are:

"Spinning" Certain underwriters allocated "hot" IPO shares to directors and/or executives of potential investment banking clients in exchange for investment banking business.

Artificial Inflation of Aftermarket Prices: Some underwriters engaged in inequitable or unlawful tactics to support aftermarket prices and boost aftermarket demand. These included, for example, (1) allocating IPO shares based on a potential investor's commitment to purchase additional shares in the aftermarket at specified prices and (2) imposing penalties on retail brokers in connection with immediate "flipping" by retail IPO investors but not by other categories of IPO participants (such as institutions).

Unlawful Quid Pro Quo Arrangements: Underwriters unlawfully allocated IPO shares based on a potential investor's agreement to pay excessive commissions on trades of unrelated securities.

Biased Recommendations by Research Analysts: With their compensation and promotion tied to the success of their firms' investment banking business, some research analysts apparently agreed to issue and maintain "buy" recommendations on certain stocks despite aftermarket prices that jumped to multiples of their IPO prices.

Exacerbating the loss of confidence in our IPO process is the widespread perception that IPOs are parceled out disproportionately to a few, favored investors, be they large institutions, powerful individuals or "friends and family" of the issuer.

SECTION 5. AFTER THE IPO— THE SECONDARY MARKET

U.S. CONGRESS, OFFICE OF TECHNOLOGY ASSESSMENT ELECTRONIC BULLS & BEARS: U.S. SECURITIES MARKETS AND INFORMATION TECHNOLOGY

(1990).[5]

What happens when you visit or call a stock backer to buy or sell stock? The following description traces the chain of events that results in a transaction by a small investor.

A. When you decide to buy or sell stock, an Account Executive writes an order ticket, filling in the details—whether to buy or sell, the name of the security, how many shares, whether the order is to be executed at the market price or is a limit order (an order to buy or sell when the price reaches a specified level). The market order is passed to a teletype operator who keyboards the information and sends it immediately to an electronic system linking the broker to the various exchanges and over-the-counter dealers.

B. If the order involves an exchange-listed stock and there are not special instructions routing it to another market center, the order will enter the Common Message Switch, an electronic pathway linking brokerage firms and trading floors. This is the beginning of a journey that could carry the order to several alternative destinations.

C. Most orders in NYSE-listed stocks are routed to the NYSE's SuperDOT 240 system, where orders of fewer than 2,000 shares are executed. These orders can go either to the specialist's post on the floor of the exchange, or to the brokerage firm's floor booth (although with a small order, that is unlikely).

What happens next depends on the timing. On a typical day, between 15 and 20 percent of all orders are executed at the market opening. Through SuperDOT *market orders* to buy or sell, routed to the specialist post prior to the market opening, are automatically paired with opposing orders. The specialist, after matching buy and sell market orders and checking outstanding *limit orders* and larger opening orders, sets an opening price for the stock. The specialist then executes all paired orders at one price and sends confirmation notices to originating brokers within seconds of the market opening, through the Opening Automated Reporting System (OARS).

---

5. Adapted from "The Saga of a Stock Transaction," *The Individual Investor* vol. 3, No. 3, June–July 1983 (American Association of Individual Investors).

Orders that arrive at the specialist's post through SuperDOT after the opening can be filled in several ways. Orders of up to 2,099 shares are usually filled at the best quoted price or better in the Intermarket Trading System (ITS). This system connects NYSE, AMEX, five regional exchanges, and NASD's Computer Assisted Execution System (CAES). ITS quotes are displayed at the NYSE specialist's post for all floor traders to see. An order sent to ITS will be filled within 1 or 2 minutes at the best price among any of these markets.

For larger orders, or when a wide spread exists between bid and asked prices, the specialist will execute a SuperDOT order in the traditional way (see D). He can also execute the trades from limit orders in his "book." The specialist is obligated to get the best price available at that moment for the client.

D.   Some orders are not handled electronically but rather by the broker firm's floor broker. Wire orders reach floor brokers when they are too large for SuperDOT (see C above) or are larger than the broker's chosen parameters for direct routing through SuperDOT.

At the broker's floor booth, these orders are translated into floor tickets containing the essential buy/sell information necessary to make the trade. Floor clerks pass the details to floor brokers by hard copy (or through hand signals at the AMEX). The floor broker then presents the order at the specialist's post. There the stock is traded with another brokerage firm, or with the specialist, who may be acting as agent for a client on his books, or who may be acting for his own account. Or the floor broker may execute the trade on another exchange, if there is a better price posted on the ITS screen over the specialist's post. The above applies to exchange-traded stock.

E.   If the stock is traded over the counter, and the quantity is more than 1,000 shares, the wire order goes to one of the broker's OTC traders at its main office. There, a computer on the OTC trader's desk displays the identities of all market-makers for that stock and their current bids and asked prices. The trader telephones the market-maker with the best price, and executes the trade.

If the brokerage firm itself makes a market in that stock, and the broker's OTC trader is willing to match the best price shown on NASDAQ, the trader can buy or sell its as principal. In either case, or the press of a button on the trader's keyboard, the trade is executed and a confirmation notice is sent to the originating office.

If the OTC order is for 1,000 shares or less, and the stock is listed on NASD's "National Market System." It will be automatically routed via NASDAQ's Small Order Executive System (SOES) to the market-maker with the best price at the time of order (If the stock is not on the National Market System, it must be for 500 shares maximum to go through this system.) Trades executed through SOES take less than 90 seconds from order wire to confirmation.

F. What happens next is "after the trade" activities, and the process depends on whether the trade was executed manually or electronically. Generally, the trade confirmation is sent back to the broker through the same pathway by which the order arrived, and the broker calls the customer to confirm the transaction.

Executed trades are also reported immediately to the brokerage firm's purchase and sales department and to the exchange, so that the transaction will go on the Consolidated Ticker Tape. Once on the tape it is visible to the investor community, and to the exchange's and regulatory agency's surveillance analysts.

G. On or before the day following a trade, the brokerage firm sends its customer a written confirmation showing the details of the transaction. The customer has five business days from the trade date to pay for purchases delivery (i.e., to settle). About 95 percent of trades are settled through the National Securities Clearing Corp.

The Depository Trust Company (DTC) stores stock and other certificates and maintains records of ownership for brokerage firms and banks. Under normal circumstances, your stock certificate will be registered in DTC's nominee name "held in street name"—for you as the "beneficial" or real owner. Or you may choose to request physical delivery of the stock to you.

For customers who want physical possession of their stock certificates, these shares are registered in the customer's name by the transfer agent of the issuer. Errors and delays can occur in the paperwork trail from brokerage firm to NSCC, NSCC to DTC, DTC to transfer agent, transfer agent back to DTC, DTC to brokerage firm, brokerage firm to customer. For this reason (and other good reasons) there is considerable interest in eliminating paper certificates ("dematerialization") and replacing these with electronic records, as some countries have already done.

IN THE MATTER OF CERTAIN MARKET MAKING ACTIVITIES ON NASDAQ

1998 WL 919673 (1998).

* * *The Respondents are entities registered with the Commission as broker-dealers pursuant to Section 15(b) of the Exchange Act and individuals who, at relevant times, were associated with such entities or their predecessors. During the relevant time period, all of the entity Respondents or their predecessors were market makers in Nasdaq securities. All of the individual Respondents were at relevant times employed at Nasdaq market-making firms as traders or assistant traders making markets in Nasdaq stocks, institutional or retail salespeople dealing in Nasdaq stocks, or supervisors of Nasdaq trading and sales.

The Nasdaq Stock Market, Inc. ("Nasdaq") is an electronic interdealer quotation system owned and operated by the National Association of

Securities Dealers, Inc. ("NASD"), a national securities association registered with the Commission under Section 15A of the Exchange Act. The Nasdaq market is a dealer market, in which a number of broker-dealers make markets in the same security and execute trades. Making a market consists of standing ready to buy and sell a security at prices and quantities displayed on Nasdaq's computerized quotation system which links the market makers. The market makers in Nasdaq are required simultaneously to quote two prices: a "bid" price, at which they are willing to buy the security, and an "ask" price, at which they are willing to sell the security. The "inside bid" is the highest prevailing bid price in a stock at any given time, while the "inside ask" is the lowest prevailing asked price. Together, the inside bid and inside ask represent the "inside market." The difference between the inside bid and the inside ask is commonly referred to as the "spread" or "inside spread." As noted in the Commission's Report Pursuant to Section 21(a) of the Securities Exchange Act of 1934 Regarding the NASD and Nasdaq Market, Exchange Act Release 37542 (hereinafter referred to as the "21(a) Report"), most customer orders during the time period in question were executed by market makers at the inside bid or ask. Trades in the Nasdaq market can be executed in a variety of ways, including, without limitation, through telephone calls to other dealers, the Instinet trading system, and certain electronic order delivery and execution systems owned and operated by Nasdaq (such as SOES, SelectNet and ACES). The time, price and volume of most transactions must be reported to Nasdaq, which in turn disseminates this information publicly through its electronic network.

On August 8, 1996, the Commission issued the 21(a) Report, which described, among other things, coordination among market makers of quotations and trades that may have advanced or protected their proprietary interests, in a manner that may have been contrary to the best interests of their customers, and that may have created a false or misleading appearance of trading activity in the Nasdaq market. After the issuance of the 21(a) Report, the Commission's investigation of market making activities in the Nasdaq market continued, and these proceedings result from the continuation of the investigation.

The investigation uncovered a number of anticompetitive and improper practices by Nasdaq market makers during 1994 which violated certain provisions of the federal securities laws. Nasdaq market making firms and their traders coordinated their trading and other activities with other market makers to create false or misleading appearances in, or otherwise artificially influence, the market for various Nasdaq stocks. This coordination was primarily accomplished the one market maker asking another to move its quoted prices in order to create a different appearance to the market from which the requesting market maker could benefit, and violated the antifraud provisions of Section 15(c)(1) of the Exchange Act and Rule 15c1–2 thereunder, and the prohibition against fictitious quotations provided in Section 15(c)(2) of the Exchange Act and Rule 15c2–7 thereunder. Nasdaq market makers also engaged in other violations related to their trading of Nasdaq stocks, including failing to provide the best execution of customer orders, intentionally delaying trade reports, failing to honor their quoted prices on Nasdaq, failing to create or maintain required books and records and failing reasonably to establish and enforce policies and procedures to supervise Nasdaq trading personnel with a view to preventing violations of law. Market maker misconduct was typically, but not always, limited in duration and scope to intraday violations relating to particular stocks, but cumulatively had a detrimental impact on the fairness and efficient functioning of the Nasdaq market. Most of the conduct described herein was intended to increase the market makers' trading profits or otherwise advance their proprietary interests, often at the expense of their customers and other market participants. The following section summarizes the violative practices uncovered and discusses the manner in which the conduct violated the federal securities laws.

The most common form of violative activity uncovered by the staff's investigation was the coordinated entry of bid and/or ask quotations by market makers into the Nasdaq system for the purpose of artificially affecting the price of subsequent transactions. This behavior typically consisted of one market maker soliciting the agreement of a second market maker to change the Nasdaq quotations disseminated by one or both market makers. Although the specific reasons for the coordination of quote movement requests varied from transaction to transaction, all involved obtaining an unfair trading advantage for the participating market makers. These arrangements, which changed the inside spread or harmed customers or other market participants, were not disclosed by the market makers involved in the scheme to other market participants or the Nasdaq market. Such coordinated activity constituted market manipulation in violation of the antifraud provisions of Section 15(c)(1) of the Exchange Act and Rule 15c1–2 thereunder, and the prohibition on the entry of fictitious quotations provided in Section 15(c)(2) of the Exchange Act and Rule 15c2–7 thereunder.

Market makers coordinated quote movements in order to create a false or misleading appearance of change in the supply or demand for a particular Nasdaq stock. The coordinated quote movements often involved one market maker moving one of its quotations to or from the inside quotes in order to change the number of market makers at the inside quote, which other market participants could reasonably perceive as an apparent change in the level of buying or selling interest. For example, a market maker needing to buy stock because of a customer order to purchase stock, or a short inventory position, would ask another market maker to move his quote downwards to join the inside ask. The purpose of the requested quote movement was to signal a downward price trend and the apparent addition of supply at the inside ask, thus misleading potential sellers on Nasdaq or Instinet into reducing their price expectations. After the quote movement, the requesting market maker would purchase stock on Nasdaq or Instinet at a reduced price, at the expense of the seller. The same strategy was also employed when the requesting market maker held a customer sell order, or had a long position in its inventory account. In such instances, the request was usually for the other market maker to join the inside bid, in order to signal an upward movement in price. In some instances, market makers entered large orders to buy stock on Instinet that created the appearance of rising demand for the stock, in connection with requesting a quote move from another market maker, in order to induce other market participants to buy the stock on the Nasdaq market (or vice versa to induce other market participants to sell).

At times, market makers also asked other market makers to move their quotes in a manner designed to create a new inside bid or ask price for a particular security in order to allow the requesting market maker to execute existing or anticipated customer orders at the new price levels, which benefitted the requesting market maker and disadvantaged its customer(s). In some instances where a customer had submitted a market order to buy stock, a trader would ask a lone market maker on the inside ask to move its ask quotation upwards. This quote movement created a higher inside ask, and the requesting market maker would then sell stock to its customer at the new, higher price. Additionally, institutional investors frequently transacted at prices between the inside bid and ask by a process of negotiation with market makers. Both institutional investors and market makers viewed the prices quoted at the inside spread as benchmarks for these negotiations, and the movement of the inside quotes upwards or downwards tended to move the ultimate transaction price in the direction of the quote move. Thus, changes in the inside quotes allowed market makers in some instances to influence the price even with respect to negotiated trades that were executed between the inside spread.

The undisclosed collaboration among market makers was detrimental to the interests of investors. By coordinating quote movements to move the quoted price of a stock up or down, traders facilitated trades at prices that were more favorable for the market makers, often at the expense of their customers or other market participants. Where customer orders were executed at prices detrimental to the customers, the coordinated misconduct also breached market makers' obligation to provide best execution and deal fairly with their customers. The undisclosed arrangements to move quotations also distorted the appearance of supply and demand in the Nasdaq market, potentially undermining investor confidence and the integrity of widely disseminated trading and market data. * * *

The coordinated entry of Nasdaq quotes for the purpose of altering the inside market, painting a deceptive picture of market conditions, or inducing another market participant into buying or selling at an artificial price constitutes an "arrangement" as that term is used in Rule 15c2–7. Since there was no disclosure of such arrangements to Nasdaq or other market participants, such quotations violated Section 15(c)(2) of the Exchange Act and Rule 15c2–7 thereunder. * * *

The investigation uncovered instances in which certain market makers entered into explicit agreements to delay reporting significant trades, and other scenarios where market makers unilaterally failed to report significant trades. This practice of intentionally delaying trade reports typically occurred when a timely report of a significant trade could have moved prices in a direction adverse to the market maker's interests. For example, a market maker that purchased a large amount from a customer selling stock would, either singly or in concert with other market makers, deliberately delay reporting the trade. The purpose of holding the trade report was to avoid the natural downward price movement that would reasonably be expected to result from the report of a large sale of stock by a customer. In order to reduce the long position resulting from its purchase from the customer, the relevant market maker would then sell stock in the open market at a price unaffected by the information contained in the withheld trade report. These market sales were typically executed at higher prices than would have been available if the customer's trade had been properly reported, to the detriment of the market as a whole, as well as the parties who purchased stock from the market maker. The delay of trade reports under such circumstances was manipulative and resulted in market makers obtaining an unfair and unlawful informational advantage in the market. * * *

The investigation uncovered a number of instances in which Nasdaq market makers failed to provide best execution for their customers' orders. The duty of best execution has generally been defined as the obligation of the broker-dealer to seek to obtain the most favorable terms reasonably available under the circumstances for a customer's order. When a broker-dealer acting with scienter fails to seek the most favorable price reasonably available under the circumstances for a customer order, the broker has failed to meet its obligation of best execution in violation of the antifraud provisions of Section 15(c) of the Exchange Act and Rule 15c1–2 thereunder.

During the relevant time period, best execution violations occurred in a number of different situations. A common denominator in such scenarios was the favoring by the market maker of its own interests, or those of a cooperating market maker, over the interests of its customers. First, in many instances, market makers' coordination of quotations allowed them to execute customer orders at artificial prices unfavorable to the customer. In other instances, market makers in the process of executing customer orders sometimes suggested to cooperating market makers on the inside bid or ask that they move away from the inside quote without executing a trade, thereby depriving the customer of a more favorable execution. On occasion, market makers did not execute or cancelled customer trades at advantageous prices in order to maintain good relations with other market makers. Market makers also sometimes entered into "print-splitting" arrangements with other market makers, by which they agreed to share any executions. If a market maker was holding a customer order at the time which was left unfilled as a result of the print-splitting arrangement, the failure to fill the order as promptly as possible violated its best execution obligations. Other violations occurred when market makers sometimes traded with customers at prices outside of the inside spread, with no apparent justification. In certain instances, market makers delayed the execution of large customer orders in order to trade first for their own account at more favorable prices, e.g., by selling stock for their own account first, while delaying the execution of a customer sell order, and later purchasing the customer's stock at market prices that had been depressed by the market maker's earlier sales for its own account. Finally, market makers sometimes traded with cooperating market makers at a particular price without filling customer limit orders at the same price, and without advance disclosure of and consent by their customers to their limit order policies.

Under the Commission's "firm quote" rule, a market maker is required to execute any order presented to it to buy or sell a security at a price at least as favorable to the buyer or seller as the market maker's published bid or offer and up to its published quotation size. On certain occasions, Nasdaq traders failed to honor the quotations that they disseminated. Market makers backed away from orders presented to them by firms whose trading practices they disliked or for other improper reasons. The failure of Nasdaq market makers to honor their quotations prevented investors from accessing the best advertised price, and reduced liquidity in the market. * * *

Under Section 15(b)(4) of the Exchange Act, the Commission may sanction a broker-dealer for failing reasonably to supervise a person under its supervision. Supervision is an essential function of broker-dealers. The Commission has made it clear that it is critical for investor protection that a broker-dealer establish and enforce procedures reasonably designed to supervise its employees. In large organizations in particular, it is imperative that the system of internal control be adequate and effective. A firm's failure to establish such procedures is symptomatic of a failure to supervise reasonably.

The frequency of the violations described herein raised serious questions concerning the adequacy of supervision by the respondent firms of their Nasdaq traders, and the investigation uncovered supervisory deficiencies at numerous of the respondent firms. Most of the respondent firms failed reasonably to supervise with a view to preventing or detecting these violations, in that they did not have adequate policies or procedures.... In addition, some respondent firms' policies and procedures were inadequately documented, promulgated and enforced. * * *

Each Respondent has submitted an Offer of Settlement which, as set forth in the accompanying Orders Making Findings and Imposing Sanctions, the Commission has determined to accept.

By the Commission. Jonathan G. Katz, Secretary

NOTE

The Nasdaq market makers' collusive actions were taken in many instances in response to the trading of so-called "SOES Bandits." The development of that phenomenon is described in the following excerpt:

> The NASD developed the SOES in 1984 in order to allow automatic execution of small trades at prices advertised on the *National Association of Securities Dealers Automated Quotation System (NASDAQ)*. See *56 Fed.Reg. 52092 (Oct. 17, 1991)* ("SOES was designed to provide the benefits of automatic execution to retail customer orders of limited size for securities quoted on the [NASDAQ] System"). Using the SOES, a broker-dealer can instantly execute a trade for a customer at the "inside market"—the best bid or ask price offered by any firm making a market in the relevant security. Because the order is executed on the NASDAQ computer, the OTC market maker whose offer is accepted does not know about the SOES trade until just after it has been executed.
>
> In June 1988 the NASD began requiring that each market maker automatically execute at its quoted price orders aggregating five times the maximum order size (200, 500, or 1,000 shares, depending upon the security) for every security in which it makes a market. It soon emerged, however, that an attentive trader using the SOES could exploit even a momentary disparity among the prices being offered by the firms making a market in a particular security; traders would closely track movements in the price of a volatile stock and, if one market maker was the least bit behindhand in repricing the stock, lock in an arbitrage profit at no risk. The traders would also monitor news developments constantly and use the instantaneous execution feature of the SOES to purchase shares before the market makers—who frequently handle many stocks—could adjust their quotations to reflect the new information. By executing within a few seconds as many as five orders for up to 1,000 shares each and liquidating the position shortly afterward at the new market price, a trader could profit handsomely at the expense of the market maker.

Timpinaro v. SEC, 2 F.3d 453 (D.C.Cir.1993). The NASD sought to exclude SOES Bandits from its automated execution system, but they morphed into something called "day traders," i.e., semi-professional traders using online systems at brokerage firms to try and beat the Nasdaq market makers. The NASD subsequently replaced SOES with a program called SuperMontage, which operates as an electronic communications network. See Section 7 of this chapter.

***

Nasdaq. The Nasdaq market is what we traditionally called the "over-the-counter" market where brokers simply trade among themselves. At an earlier date, these brokers would learn of each others interest in a particular stock through trading in the streets (the "curb" market) and later through something called the "pink sheets." These were simply reports of trading interest that were printed on pink colored paper by the publisher of those quotations. A broker wanting to purchase a stock quoted in the pink sheets for himself or a customer would call the dealer making the quote and negotiate a purchase and sale. Nasdaq automated that process. As described in the SEC's decision above, this is an electronic network in which broker-dealers post their stock quotations in a central computer so that other brokers may see them on computer screens located in their offices. This allows broker-dealers to post competing quotations or to call the broker-dealer posting the quotation and negotiate a purchase or sale of the stock. A key element in the Nasdaq market is the "market-maker," actually there are several market-makers for many of the more actively traded stocks. These are simply dealers who stand ready to buy and sell particular stocks for their own account as principal. They include many of the large brokerage firms. Their "bids" and "offers" will be listed on the Nasdaq computer screen for particular stocks. Market makers are required to make a continuous two-sided market in that security by both bidding to buy the stocks in which they make a market and offering to sell it. The concept of a continuous two-sided market is critical to the liquidity of your investment in a stock. Market-makers must both buy and sell the stock at any time during trading hours in a minimum quantity at the price posted on the Nasdaq computer screen. This means that, if you want to buy the stock, the market-maker stands ready to sell it to you. Conversely, if you want to sell that same stock, the market-maker will buy it back from you. This provides liquidity. It allows you to buy and sell easily at the best available price for that stock, as determined by competing market-makers and other investors interested in that stock.

There are limitations on liquidity. Quotations by market-makers on Nasdaq are good only up to a limited number of shares. Small orders up to that minimum are executed automatically at the best quoted prices through Nasdaq's Small Order Execution System ("SOES"). Larger orders must be negotiated and executed with the market-makers by your broker-dealer over the telephone. For amounts greater than that minimum, the price will have to be negotiated directly with the market-maker. Market-makers may also change their quotations at any time before receiving an order even for the minimum amount they are required to trade, possibly resulting in a less favorable price. One rule that every investor must know is that there is no free lunch on Wall Street. This liquidity is being made available to you at a price. The market-makers are not providing this service *gratis*. They may profit in several ways. First, they may profit from the "spread." This means that the market-makers quotes for the prices at which they will buy and sell your stock will not be the same. The price at which they will buy the stock from you will be lower than the price at which they will sell it to you. The market-makers seek to profit from that spread. As a hypothetical example, assume that Dot.Com. Inc. stock is being quoted by market-makers at $9.25 and $9.50. This means that the market-makers will buy the stock from you at $9.25 and sell it to you for $9.50. All things being equal, they stand to make $.25

on each share of stock they buy and sell. So if you bought and sold the stock immediately, and there was nothing that would otherwise affect its price, you would lose $.25 per share. The width or amount of the spread will depend on a number of factors. To over simplify a bit, the more competition, the narrower the spread. A sign of an illiquid security is a wide spread between the bid and offer price.

Further consideration of a hypothetical trade for Dot.com, Inc. may simplify this whole process for you. Let us suppose that you were not an original investor in that company. But you have been reading about its product and think that it will increase in value. You call your stock broker and ask for its current price. She tells you that it is a NASDAQ stock and that the best current quote bid for the stock is $9.25 and the offer is $9.50. You enter an order to buy 10 shares, and the order is executed at the quoted price. This means that you will pay $95.00 for the ten shares. You will also have to pay a commission on the shares if your broker was acting as agent on the transaction. That amount could vary widely from broker to broker. If the stock is owned by your broker-dealer, and it is being sold from its own account, you will be charged a markup. Under Nasdaq rules this amount is limited to less than 5% of the transaction price. Now what would happen if you immediately resold your stock and no changes have occurred in its price? You would be paid $92.50 by the market-makers, a loss of $2.50, plus another commission or markdown. Assuming that the total markups and markdowns on the round-turn buy and sell transactions were 10 percent, your loss on the transaction would be $21.25. That is a pretty hefty loss on a $95 investment. But that is the cost of liquidity. You hope to offset those costs through an increase in the value of the stock if the company becomes successful.

More on NASDAQ. The NASD was reorganized following the SEC's finding that the NASD failed to police its market-makers. A separate subsidiary called NASD Regulation, Inc. was created to police the activities of NASD members. Another subsidiary, NASD Dispute Resolution, Inc. was created to conduct arbitrations, including those involving customer claims brought against broker-dealers. In 2007, NASD Regulation merged with the New York Stock Exchange enforcement division to become the Financial Industry Regulatory Authority, Inc. ("FINRA").

The Nasdaq market operates as a separate entity that is divided into three basic tiers. The National Market System ("NMS") is a grouping of the most heavily capitalized and actively traded stocks listed on NASDAQ. NMS stocks have several market-makers that compete with each other, which usually means that these stocks are highly liquid, have narrow spreads and are efficiently priced. NMS stocks include such established corporate giants as Microsoft and Budweiser. A second tier of NASD securities are the so-called "small-cap" securities. These are generally stocks issued by small start up companies. They are often thinly capitalized and sometimes speculative in nature. The number of market-makers for each stock will vary from several to a few. Some of these stocks may not be highly liquid, may have wider spreads and be less efficiently priced than the NMS stocks. Some of the companies issuing these securities will become successful and join the NMS system. Traders are always looking to invest in the small-cap stocks they believe will be successful. A third tier is the "Bulletin Board." This is a group of stocks that are not actively traded. Market-makers will post indications of interest in these securities. Your broker-dealer will have to contact the market-makers in these securities and negotiate a price to execute an order. These stocks are usually illiquid and may be speculative in nature.

What is a broker-dealer? It is simply the technical name for a stockbroker that may execute trades for customers and for its own account. The broker-dealer may buy or sell stock for you as your agent by purchasing or selling it to some third party. In that agency role, the firm is acting as a "broker," and you will be charged a commission for that service. The broker-dealer may also buy and sell stock to you that it has purchased for its own account. In that role, the broker-dealer is acting as a "principal," or in Wall Street terms as a "dealer." Instead of a commission, you will be charged a mark-up for the stock purchased from a dealer.

NOTE

The role of the market maker has been described as follows:

A market maker is a dealer who places his own capital at risk by buying and ... options for his own account. He is expected to contribute to price continuity on the Exchange. For instance, a public investor might wish to sell a given quantity of a security at a certain price at a time when there is no other public investor wanting to buy the stated quantity at the given price. When this occurs, a market maker is expected to buy for his own account. In return for undertaking these special obligations to the market, market makers enjoy advantages not available to others. One principal advantage is that Federal Reserve Board rules exempt market makers from "margin" rules that limit the amount one may borrow in order to finance trading activity. Compare 12 C.F.R. § 220.4(g) (1981) with id. § 220.8(f).

Clement v. Securities and Exchange Commission, 674 F.2d 641 (7th Cir. 1982).

SECTION 6. THE NEW YORK STOCK EXCHANGE

SILVER v. NEW YORK STOCK EXCHANGE
373 U.S. 341, 83 S.Ct. 1246, 10 L.Ed.2d 389 (1963).

MR. JUSTICE GOLDBERG delivered the opinion of the Court.

We deal here today with the question, of great importance to the public and the financial community, of whether and to what extent the federal antitrust laws apply to securities exchanges regulated by the Securities Exchange Act of 1934. More particularly, the question is whether the New York Stock Exchange is to be held liable to a nonmember broker-dealer under the antitrust laws or regarded as impliedly immune therefrom when, pursuant to rules the Exchange has adopted under the Securities Exchange Act of 1934, it orders a number of its members to remove private direct telephone wire connections previously in operation between their offices and those of the nonmember, without giving the nonmember notice, assigning him any reason for the action, or affording him an opportunity to be heard.

The facts material to resolution of this question are not in dispute. Harold J. Silver, who died during the pendency of this action, entered the securities business in Dallas, Texas, in 1955, by establishing the predecessor of petitioner Municipal Securities (Municipal) to deal primarily in municipal bonds. The business of Municipal having increased steadily, Silver, in June 1958, established petitioner Municipal Securities, Inc. (Municipal, Inc.), to trade in corporate over-the-counter securities. Both firms are registered broker-dealers and members of the National Association of Securities Dealers, Inc. (NASD); neither is a member of the respondent Exchange.

Instantaneous communication with firms in the mainstream of the securities business is of great significance to a broker-dealer not a member of the Exchange, and Silver took steps to see that this was established for his firms. Municipal obtained direct private telephone wire connections with the municipal bond departments of a number of securities firms (three of which were members of the Exchange) and banks, and Municipal, Inc., arranged for private wires to the corporate securities trading departments of 10 member firms of the Exchange, as well as to the trading desks of a number of nonmember firms.

Pursuant to the requirements of the Exchange's rules, all but one of the member firms which had granted private wires to Municipal, Inc., applied to the Exchange for approval of the connections. During the summer of 1958 the Exchange granted "temporary approval" for these, as well as for a direct teletype connection to a member firm in New York City and for stock ticker service to be furnished to petitioners directly from the floor of the Exchange.

On February 12, 1959, without prior notice to Silver, his firms, or anyone connected with them, the Exchange's Department of Member Firms decided to disapprove the private wire and related applications. Notice was sent to the member firms involved, instructing them to discontinue the wires, a directive with which compliance was required by the Exchange's Constitution and rules. These firms in turn notified Silver that the private wires would have to be discontinued, and the Exchange advised him directly of the discontinuance of the stock ticker service. The wires and ticker were all removed by the beginning of March. By telephone calls, letters, and a personal trip to New York, Silver sought an explanation from the Exchange of the reason for its decision, but was repeatedly told it was the policy of the Exchange not to disclose the reasons for such action.

Petitioners contend that their volume of business dropped substantially thereafter and that their profits fell, due to a combination of forces all stemming from the removal of the private wires—their consequent inability to obtain quotations quickly, the inconvenience to other traders in calling petitioners, and the stigma attaching to the disapproval. As a result of this change in fortunes, petitioners contend, Municipal, Inc., soon ceased functioning as an operating business organization, and Municipal has remained in business only on a greatly diminished scale. * * *

The fundamental issue confronting us is whether the Securities Exchange Act has created a duty of exchange self-regulation so pervasive as to constitute an implied repeal of our antitrust laws, thereby exempting the Exchange from liability in this and similar cases.

It is plain, to begin with, that removal of the wires by collective action of the Exchange and its members would, had it occurred in a context free from other federal regulation, constitute a per se violation of § 1 of the Sherman Act. The concerted action of the Exchange and its members here was, in simple terms, a group boycott depriving petitioners of a valuable business service which they needed in order to compete effectively as broker-dealers in the over-the-counter securities market. Unlike listed securities, there is no central trading place for securities traded over the counter. The market is established by traders in the numerous firms all over the country through a process of constant communication to one another of the latest offers to buy and sell. The private wire connection, which allows communication to occur with a flip of a switch, is an essential part of this process. Without the instantaneously available market information provided by private wire connections, an over-the-counter dealer is hampered substantially in his crucial endeavor—to buy, whether it be for customers or on his own account, at the lowest quoted price and sell at the highest quoted price. Without membership in the network of simultaneous communication, the over-the-counter dealer loses a significant volume of trading with other members of the network which would come to him as a result of his easy accessibility. These important business advantages were taken away from petitioners by the group action of the Exchange and its members. Such "concerted refusals by traders to deal with other traders * * * have long been held to be in the forbidden category," Klor's, Inc. v. Broadway–Hale Stores, Inc., 359 U.S., at 212 of restraints which "because of their inherent nature or effect * * * injuriously restrained trade," United States v. American Tobacco Co., 221 U.S. 106, 179. Hence, absent any justification derived from the policy of another statute or otherwise, the Exchange acted in violation of the Sherman Act. In this case, however, the presence of another statutory scheme, that of the Securities Exchange Act of 1934, means that such a conclusion is only the beginning, not the end, of inquiry.

The difficult problem here arises from the need to reconcile pursuit of the antitrust aim of eliminating restraints on competition with the effective operation of a public policy contemplating that securities exchanges will engage in self-regulation which may well have anti-competitive effects in general and in specific applications.

The need for statutory regulation of securities exchanges and the nature of the duty of self-regulation imposed by the Securities Exchange Act are properly understood in the context of a consideration of both the economic role played by exchanges and the historical setting of the Act. Stock exchanges perform an important function in the economic life of this country. They serve, first of all, as an indispensable mechanism through which corporate securities can be bought and sold. To corporate enterprise such a market mechanism is a fundamental element in facilitating the successful marshaling of large aggregations of funds that would otherwise be extremely difficult of access. To the public the exchanges are an investment channel which promises ready convertibility of stock holdings into cash. The importance of these functions in dollar terms is vast— in 1962 the New York Stock Exchange, by far the largest of the 14 exchanges which are registered with the Securities and Exchange Commission, had $47.4 billion of transactions in stocks, rights, and warrants (a figure which represented 86% of the total dollar volume on registered exchanges). Report of the Special Study of Securities Markets (1963), c. IB, p. 6. Moreover, because trading on the exchanges, in addition to establishing the price level of listed securities, affects securities prices in general, and because such transactions are often regarded as an indicator of our national economic health, the significance of the exchanges in our economy cannot be measured only in terms of the dollar volume of trading. Recognition of the importance of the exchanges' role led the House Committee on Interstate and Foreign Commerce to declare in its report preceding the enactment of the Securities Exchange Act of 1934 that "The great exchanges of this country upon which millions of dollars of securities are sold are affected with a public interest in the same degree as any other great utility." H.R.Rep. No. 1383, 73d Cong., 2d Sess. 15 (1934).

The exchanges are by their nature bodies with a limited number of members, each of which plays a certain role in the carrying out of an exchange's activities. The limited-entry feature of exchanges led historically to their being treated by the courts as private clubs, Belton v. Hatch, 109 N.Y. 593, 17 N.E. 225 (1888), and to their being given great latitude by the courts in disciplining errant members, see Westwood and Howard, Self–Government in the Securities Business, 17 Law and Contemp. Prob. 518–525 (1952). As exchanges became a more and more important element in our Nation's economic and financial system, however, the private-club analogy became increasingly inapposite and the ungoverned self-regulation became more and more obviously inadequate, with acceleratingly grave consequences. This impotency ultimately led to the enactment of the

1934 Act. The House Committee Report summed up the long-developing problem in discussing the general purposes of the bill:

> "The fundamental fact behind the necessity for this bill is that the leaders of private business, whether because of inertia, pressure of vested interests, lack of organization, or otherwise, have not since the war been able to act to protect themselves by compelling a continuous and orderly program of change in methods and standards of doing business to match the degree to which the economic system has itself been constantly changing * * *. The repetition in the summer of 1933 of the blindness and abuses of 1929 has convinced a patient public that enlightened self-interest in private leadership is not sufficiently powerful to effect the necessary changes alone—that private leadership seeking to make changes must be given Government help and protection." H.R.Rep. No. 1383, supra, at 3, 17 N.E. 225.

It was, therefore, the combination of the enormous growth in the power and impact of exchanges in our economy, and their inability and unwillingness to curb abuses which had increasingly grave implications because of this growth, that moved Congress to enact the Securities Exchange Act of 1934. S.Rep. No. 792, 73d Cong., 2d Sess. 2–5 (1934); H.R.Rep. No. 1383, supra, at 2–5.

The pattern of governmental entry, however, was by no means one of total displacement of the exchanges' traditional process of self-regulation. The intention was rather, as Mr. Justice Douglas said, while Chairman of the S.E.C., one of "letting the exchanges take the leadership with Government playing a residual role. Government would keep the shotgun, so to speak, behind the door, loaded, well oiled, cleaned, ready for use but with the hope it would never have to be used." Douglas, Democracy and Finance (Allen ed. 1940), 82. Thus the Senate Committee Report stressed that "the initiative and responsibility for promulgating regulations pertaining to the administration of their ordinary affairs remain with the exchanges themselves. It is only where they fail adequately to provide protection to investors that the Commission is authorized to step in and compel them to do so." S.Rep. No. 792, supra, at 13. The House Committee Report added the hope that the bill would give the exchanges sufficient power to reform themselves without intervention by the Commission. H.R.Rep. No. 1383, supra, at 15. See also 2 Loss, Securities Regulation (2d ed. 1961), 1175–1178, 1180–1182.

Thus arose the federally mandated duty of self-policing by exchanges. Instead of giving the Commission the power to curb specific instances of abuse, the Act placed in the exchanges a duty to register with the Commission, § 5, 15 U.S.C. § 78e, and decreed that registration could not be granted unless the exchange submitted copies of its rules, § 6(a)(3), 15 U.S.C. § 78f(a)(3), and unless such rules were "just and adequate to insure fair dealing and to protect investors," § 6(d), 15 U.S.C. § 78f(d). The general dimensions of the duty of self-regulation are suggested by § 19(b) of the Act, 15 U.S.C. § 78s(b), which gives the Commission power to order changes in exchange rules respecting a number of subjects, which are set forth in the margin.[6]

One aspect of the statutorily imposed duty of self-regulation is the obligation to formulate rules governing the conduct of exchange members. The Act specifically requires that registration cannot be granted 'unless the rules of the exchange include provision for the expulsion, suspension, or disciplining of a member for conduct or proceeding inconsistent with just and equitable principles of trade * * *,' § 6(b), 15 U.S.C. § 78f(b). In addition, the general requirement of § 6(d) that an exchange's rules be "just and adequate to insure fair dealing and to protect investors' has obvious relevance to the area of rules regulating the conduct of an exchange's members."

The § 6(b) and § 6(d) duties taken together have the broadest implications in relation to the present problem, for members inevitably trade on the over-the-counter market in addition to dealing in listed securities, and such trading inexorably brings contact and dealings with nonmember firms which deal in or specialize in over-the-counter securities. It is no accident that the Exchange's Constitution and rules are permeated with instances of regulation of members' relationships with nonmembers including nonmember broker-dealers. A member's purchase of unlisted securities for itself or on behalf of its customer from a boiler-shop operation creates an obvious danger of loss to the principal in the transaction, and sale of securities to a nonmember insufficiently capitalized to protect customers' rights creates similar risks. In addition to the potential financial injury to the investing public and Exchange members that is inherent in these transactions as well as in dealings with nonmembers who are unreliable for any other reason, all such intercourse carries with it the gravest danger of engendering in the public a loss of confidence in the Exchange and its members, a kind of damage which can significantly impair fulfillment of the Exchange's function in our economy. Rules which regulate Exchange members' doing of business with nonmembers in the over-the-counter market are therefore very much pertinent to the aims of self-regulation under the 1934 Act. Transactions with nonmembers under the circumstances mentioned can only be described as "inconsistent with just and equitable principles of trade," and rules regulating

---

6. "The Commission is * * * authorized * * * to alter or supplement the rules of * * * (an) exchange * * * in respect of such matters as (1) safeguards in respect of the financial responsibility of members and adequate provision against the evasion of financial responsibility through the use of corporate forms or special partnerships; (2) the limitation or prohibition of the registration or trading in any security within a specified period after the issuance or primary distribution thereof; (3) the listing or striking from listing of any security; (4) hours of trading; (5) the manner, method, and place of soliciting business; (6) fictitious or numbered accounts; (7) the time and method of making settlements, payments, and deliveries and of closing accounts; (5) the reporting of transactions on the exchange and upon tickers maintained by or with the consent of the exchange, including the method of reporting short sales, stopped sales, sales of securities of issuers in default, bankruptcy or receivership, and sales involving other special circumstances; (9) the fixing of reasonable rates of commission, interest, listing, and other charges; (10) minimum units of trading; (11) odd-lot purchases and sales; (12) minimum deposits on margin accounts; and (13) similar matters."

such dealing are indeed "just and adequate to insure fair dealing and to protect investors."

The Exchange's constitutional provision and rules relating to private wire connections are unquestionably part of this fulfillment of the § 6(b) and § 6(d) duties, for such wires between members and nonmembers facilitate trading in and exchange of information about unlisted securities, and such contact with an unreliable nonmember not only may further his business undesirably, but may injure the member or the member's customer on whose behalf the contract is made and ultimately imperil the future status of the Exchange by sapping public confidence. In light of the important role of exchanges in our economy and the 1934 Act's design of giving the exchanges a major part in curbing abuses by obligating them to regulate themselves, it appears conclusively—contrary to the District Court's conclusion—that the rules applied in the present case are germane to performance of the duty, implied by § 6(b) and § 6(d), to have rules governing members' transactions and relationships with nonmembers. The Exchange's enforcement of such rules inevitably affects the nonmember involved, often (as here) far more seriously than it affects the members in question. The sweeping of the nonmembers into the currents of the Exchange's process of self-regulation is therefore unavoidable; the case cannot be disposed of by holding as the district judge did that the substantive act of regulation engaged in here was outside the boundaries of the public policy established by the Securities Exchange Act of 1934.

But, it does not follow that the case can be disposed of, as the Court of Appeals did, by holding that since the Exchange has a general power to adopt rules governing its members' relations with nonmembers, particular applications of such rules are therefore outside the purview of the antitrust laws. Contrary to the conclusions reached by the courts below, the proper approach to this case, in our view, is an analysis which reconciles the operation of both statutory schemes with one another rather than holding one completely ousted.

The Securities Exchange Act contains no express exemption from the antitrust laws or, for that matter, from any other statute. This means that any repealer of the antitrust laws must be discerned as a matter of implication, and "(i)t is a cardinal principle of construction that repeals by implication are not favored." Repeal is to be regarded as implied only if necessary to make the Securities Exchange Act work, and even then only to the minimum extent necessary. This is the guiding principle to reconciliation of the two statutory schemes. * * *

The final question here is, therefore, whether the act of self-regulation in this case was so justified. The answer to that question is that it was not, because the collective refusal to continue the private wires occurred under totally unjustifiable circumstances. Notwithstanding their prompt and repeated requests, petitioners were not informed of the charges underlying the decision to invoke the Exchange rules and were not afforded an appropriate opportunity to explain or refute the charges against them.

Given the principle that exchange self-regulation is to be regarded as justified in response to antitrust charges only to the extent necessary to protect the achievement of the aims of the Securities Exchange Act, it is clear that no justification can be offered for self-regulation conducted without provision for some method of telling a protesting non-member why a rule is being invoked so as to harm him and allowing him to reply in explanation of his position. No policy reflected in the Securities Exchange Act is, to begin with, served by denial of notice and an opportunity for hearing. Indeed, the aims of the statutory scheme of self-policing—to protect investors and promote fair dealing—are defeated when an exchange exercises its tremendous economic power without explaining its basis for acting, for the absence of an obligation to give some form of notice and, if timely requested, a hearing creates a great danger of perpetration of injury that will damage public confidence in the exchanges. The requirement of such a hearing will, by contrast, help in effectuating antitrust policies by discouraging anticompetitive applications of exchange rules which are not justifiable as within the scope of the purposes of the Securities Exchange Act. In addition to the general impetus to refrain from making unsupportable accusations that is present when it is required that the basis of charges be laid bare, the explanation or rebuttal offered by the nonmember will in many instances dissipate the force of the ex parte information upon which an exchange proposes to act. The duty to explain and afford an opportunity to answer will, therefore, be of extremely beneficial effect in keeping exchange action from straying into areas wholly foreign to the purposes of the Securities Exchange Act. And, given the possibility of antitrust liability for anti-competitive acts of self-regulation which fall too far outside the scope of the Exchange Act, the utilization of a notice and hearing procedure with its inherent check upon unauthorized exchange action will diminish rather than enlarge the likelihood that such liability will be incurred and hence will not interfere with the Exchange's ability to engage efficaciously in legitimate substantive self-regulation. Provision of such a hearing will, moreover, contribute to the effective functioning of the antitrust court, which would be severely impeded in providing the review of exchange action which we deem essential if the exchange could obscure rather than illuminate the circumstances under which it has acted. Hence the affording of procedural safeguards not only will substantively encourage the lessening of anticompetitive behavior outlawed by the Sherman Act but will allow the antitrust court to perform its function effectively.

Our decision today recognizes that the action here taken by the Exchange would clearly be in violation of the Sherman Act unless justified by reference to the purposes of the Securities Exchange Act, and holds that that statute affords no justification for anti-competitive collective action taken without according fair procedures. Congress in effecting a scheme of self-regulation designed to insure fair dealing cannot be thought to have sanctioned and protected self-regulative activity when carried out in a fundamentally unfair manner. The point is not that the antitrust laws impose the requirement of notice and a hearing here, but rather that, in acting without according petitioners these safeguards in response to their request, the Exchange has plainly exceeded the scope of its authority under the Securities Exchange Act to engage in self-regulation and therefore has not even reached that threshold of justification under that statute for what would otherwise be an antitrust violation. * * *[7]

The judgment is reversed and remanded for further proceedings consistent with this opinion.

It is so ordered.

MR. JUSTICE CLARK concurs in the result on the grounds stated in the opinion of the District Court, and the dissenting opinion in the Court of Appeals.

MR. JUSTICE STEWART, whom MR. JUSTICE HARLAN joins, dissenting. [omitted]

The elimination of fixed commission rates had several significant effects on Wall Street. Discount brokers appeared that offered bare bones execution services at cheap prices, while the traditional ("full service") firms continued to charge high commissions that they justified on the basis of the services they provided including research on stocks they recommended to you. The discount brokers received a boost in popularity with the advent of online trading through the Internet. This allowed even cheaper commissions, which encouraged the day traders. These were simply individuals trading online that sought to make short-term profits through quick in-and-out transactions. Unfortunately, most of those traders lost money. One survey found that more than ninety percent of day traders lost money. Nevertheless, the online brokers were eroding the customer base of the more traditional broker-dealers firms. The full service firms were also affected by the institutional traders who could negotiate low commissions because, after all, a trade for 1,000 shares requires about as much work as one for 5,000 shares. This declining revenue base from commissions led many broker-dealers to change their business plan and they themselves became institutional investors trading for their own account, as well as executing customer orders.

---

7. [eds. note: "After *Silver* was decided, Congress amended the Exchange Act to require the SEC to take competition, among other things, into account in rulemaking and when reviewing rules of exchanges." *Friedman v. Salomon/Smith Barney*, 313 F.3d 796 (2d Cir. 2002). See also *Credit Suisse Securities (USA) LLC v. Billing*, 127 S.Ct. 2383 (2007): "Unlike *Silver*, there is here no question of the existence of appropriate regulatory authority, nor is there doubt as to whether the regulators have exercised that authority. Rather, the question before us concerns the third condition: Is there a conflict that rises to the level of incompatibility?" Such a conflict was found.]

The NYSE trades the stocks of many of the larger and better established corporate businesses. The system for trading stocks on the NYSE varies from the system used on Nasdaq. Historically, the NYSE uses "specialists" rather than market-makers to maintain a continuous two sided market in listed stocks. Each stock is assigned a specialist, and that specialist has the duty to maintain a fair and orderly market in that stock. This means that the specialist must be buying when the market is going down and selling when it is going up in order to provide some stability and liquidity. Note that the specialist has a monopoly on this trading. There are no competing market-makers on the floor of the NYSE such as those found in the Nasdaq system. Which system is better? There has been much debate over that question, but no real definitive answer.

The NYSE specialist will be quoting a two-sided market with a spread, as in the case of the Nasdaq market makers. Because the specialist has the duty to maintain a continuous market, NYSE securities are usually highly liquid. The quotes are good for only stated amounts of the stock and may be changed at any time. Small orders are executed automatically at the specialist's quoted price through the NYSE Super-DOT system. The following is a description of how orders my be executed on the floor of the NYSE:

> Stock exchange specialists act as both brokers and dealers. As brokers, specialists buy and sell for the public, by executing limit orders that are brought to them on behalf of customers by floor brokers; they also execute market orders that reach them through the automated order routing system, Super DOT. (A limit order specifies the price at which an investor is willing to buy or sell. Limit orders are put in the specialist's "book" until they can be executed at the designated price or a better price. A market order is an order to buy or sell immediately, at the prevailing price.) Specialists are prohibited by law from handling customer orders other than limit orders. The specialist's book was once a loose leaf notebook but now it is, for most NYSE stocks, a computer screen. * * *

> As dealers, specialists buy and sell for their own account. They have an "affirmative obligation" to do so when it is necessary to provide liquidity. Specialists provide liquidity by buying or selling when there are no other bidders or offerers at or near the market price. The specialist tries to keep prices from making big jumps by make a bid or offer that acts as a bridge when there is a wide gap between bids and offers. The specialist also has a "negative obligation," not to trade for his own account when there are already customers wanting to trade at or near the market place.

> Specialists participate in a substantial portion of NYSE trades. * * *

U.S. Congress, Office of Technology Assessment, Electronic Bulls & Bears: U.S. Securities Markets and Information Technology 42 (1990).

Price Changes. The Nasdaq and NYSE seek to provide a liquid market for the stocks they list. That does not, however, assure that you will receive any particular price for your stock. The Nasdaq market-makers and the NYSE specialists are constantly adjusting their quotations to reflect any changes in the value of your stock. That means the value of your stock can change rapidly before you are able to enter a buy or sell order. Further, the specialist and market-maker quotations are only for limited amounts. This means that, even if you are able to enter your order before the quotation is changed, the amount of stock available at that price may be limited. Another thing to consider is that during periods of extreme market stress, market-makers and specialists may not be able to provide liquidity. This occurred during the Stock Market Crash of 1987. Many investors trying to sell their stocks discovered that their stocks were not trading during that event. The markets have tried to correct those problems, but the danger remains.

Large "block" trades in NYSE stocks (*i.e.*, a transaction consisting of 10,000 or more shares or one with a market value of more than $200,000) may be arranged "upstairs" by block positioners at large securities firms. The terms of the sale are reported on the floor of the exchange. This prearrangement is needed because most specialists do not have adequate capital to conduct business of that size with any frequency. Trades of block size have become common with the growth of the institutional investor. U.S. Congress, Office of Technology Assessment, *Electronic Bulls & Bears: U.S. Securities Markets and Information Technology* 50–51 (1990).

Regional exchanges. The American Stock Exchange (now NYSE Amex Equities) and other regional exchanges such as the Chicago Stock Exchange and the Philadelphia Stock Exchange (later acquired by NASDAQ) also made markets in securities, including options. Their trading may included smaller cap stocks, as well as those listed on the NYSE. To facilitate trading of NYSE stocks on the regional exchanges there is an Intermarket Trading System that links the exchanges. This linkage seeks to assure that customers receive the best price available for jointly traded stock. That linkage was required by the SEC's "trade through" rule, which requires that investors be given the "best execution" available on any market for jointly traded stocks. The result was to keep most trading in dually listed stocks on the NYSE. The SEC extended this rule to other markets in 2005. See generally Jonathan R. Macey and Maureen O'Hara, "From Markets to Venues: Securities Regulation in an Evolving World," 58 Stan. L. Rev. 563, 586–588 (2005) (discussing controversial nature of the trade through rule).

MFS SECURITIES CORP. v. NEW YORK STOCK EXCHANGE, INC.

277 F.3d 613 (2d Cir.), cert. denied, 536 U.S. 924,
122 S.Ct. 2592, 153 L.Ed.2d 781 (2002).

CALABRESI, CIRCUIT JUDGE.

* * * In the 1990s, floor brokers on the NYSE participated in a trading practice known as stock "flipping." Flipping stocks, also known as "trading for eights," involves the purchase or sale of a security for a customer followed by the sale or purchase of the same security for a profit of one-eighth of a point, the then-spread between the bid and ask prices. Through this practice, the floor broker for the transaction not only received a commission for the trade but also obtained profits, which were typically shared with the customer. In 1993, two MFS Securities Corp. floor brokers, Mark Savarese and John Savarese, sons of plaintiff Marco Savarese, began flipping stocks.

According to MFS, the NYSE was aware, as early as 1991, that floor brokers participated in flipping stocks and were sharing in the resulting profits gained by their customers. MFS alleged that the NYSE supported and encouraged this activity, both because it increased daily trading volume on the NYSE, which in turn augmented the allure of the Exchange, and because it created higher profits for the NYSE, which collected fees from brokers based on total commissions.

Under Section 11(a) of the Securities Exchange Act of 1934 (the "Exchange Act"), 15 U.S.C. § 78k(a)(1), and Securities and Exchange Commission ("SEC" or "Commission") Rule 11a 1, 17 C.F.R. § 240.11a–1, however, it is illegal for floor brokers to trade on the NYSE for their own accounts or for accounts in which they have an interest. Accordingly, because the stock-flipping floor brokers shared in the profits, the practice violated Section 11(a) and Rule 11a–1.

The Exchange Act delegates substantial authority to the securities exchanges to regulate their own conduct and that of their members. *See* 15 U.S.C. §§ 78o–3(b),–3(h), 78s(g). MFS contended that the NYSE was able to permit stock flipping by interpreting Rule 11a–1 in an obviously incorrect manner, namely by excluding profit sharing arrangements from the definition of "interest in an account." MFS also maintained that the NYSE's support for flipping was surreptitious; thus the Exchange took various steps, such as declining to issue official statements on its policy with respect to stock flipping, in order to avoid attention and ultimate responsibility for the persistence of the practice.

In late 1997, the SEC and the United States Attorney's Office for the Southern District of New York began an investigation of stock flipping. MFS claimed that when senior NYSE officials met with the investigators, the Exchange officials attempted to cover up NYSE practices and curry favor with the investigators by scapegoating MFS. This was done by providing false information about MFS and by concealing relevant information, for instance, as to the extent of stock flipping that was occurring on the Exchange.

On February 25, 1998, the Savarese brothers were arrested on a charge that they had violated Section 11(a) by flipping stocks. Shortly thereafter, the SEC began an action against the Savarese brothers and against MFS. On the same day as the arrests, the NYSE expelled MFS from Exchange membership and cut MFS's phone lines on the Exchange floor. According to MFS, these actions violated both the Exchange Act and the rules of the NYSE, because each requires notice and an opportunity to be heard before a member's privileges can be revoked. MFS, in fact, did not receive a pre-termination hearing before the NYSE. In addition, according to MFS, because the NYSE did not proceed according to its disciplinary rules, MFS was barred from seeking SEC review of the NYSE's termination of MFS's Exchange membership. MFS, therefore, was allegedly left without any recourse from, or source of review of, the Exchange's actions.

On July 27, 2000, MFS brought this suit alleging both a group boycott in violation of the Sherman Act, 15 U.S.C. § 1, and a breach of contract. MFS claimed that the termination of its Exchange membership, occurring as it did without notice and without an opportunity to be heard, amounted to participation by the NYSE in a group boycott. And, because MFS's membership contract required the NYSE fairly and accurately to advise MFS of the rules of the Exchange, MFS argued that the NYSE's failure so to inform MFS, with respect to the rule that outlaws stock flipping, meant that the Exchange had breached its contract with MFS. * * *

In dismissing MFS's contract claim, the district court relied on *D'Alessio v. New York Stock Exch., Inc.,* 125 F.Supp.2d 656 (S.D.N.Y. 2000). Since the district court's decision in the instant case, we have affirmed the lower court in *D'Alessio. See D'Alessio v. New York Stock Exch., Inc.,* 258 F.3d 93 (2d Cir.2001), *cert. denied,* 534 U.S. 1066, 122 S.Ct. 666, 151 L.Ed.2d 580 (2001).

D'Alessio's claim arose out of a set of events similar to those in this case. D'Alessio had participated in stock flipping and had sued the NYSE alleging that it had failed accurately to interpret Section 11(a) and, in turn, had failed to monitor D'Alessio's compliance with the Act. We agreed with the district court's dismissal of the suit and held that the "NYSE is immune from liability for claims arising out of the discharge of its duties under the Exchange Act." Specifically, we found that the "NYSE's alleged misconduct falls within the scope of quasi-governmental powers delegated to the NYSE pursuant to the Exchange Act and, therefore, ... absolute immunity precludes D'Alessio from recovering money damages in connection with his claims." *Id.* at 106.

As both sides recognize, our decision in *D'Alessio* controls MFS's contract claim. Accordingly, we affirm the district court's dismissal of that claim. * * *

Section 6(b)(7) of the Exchange Act requires national exchanges, such as the NYSE, to "provide a fair procedure for ... the prohibition or limitation by the exchange of any person with respect to access to services offered by the exchange or a member thereof." 15 U.S.C. § 78f(b)(7). Section 6(d)(1) of the Act requires notice and a hearing for any such disciplinary action. 15 U.S.C. § 78f(d)(1). Though the Act provides for summary proceedings in certain circumstances-in which case notice and a hearing will not occur—it does also require that "[a]ny person aggrieved by any such summary action shall be promptly afforded an opportunity for a hearing by the exchange in accordance with [§ 78f(d)(1)–(2)]." 15 U.S.C. § 78f(d)(3). Moreover, the NYSE's rules, enacted in accordance with this section of the Exchange Act, impose similar requirements. *See* NYSE Rule 475. And, the Exchange Act mandates that the national exchanges comply with their own rules. 15 U.S.C. § 78s(g).

Furthermore, Section 19 of the Exchange Act provides for SEC review of disciplinary actions taken by the NYSE. 15 U.S.C. § 78s(d)–(e). [FN5] Through this review, the SEC can affirm the sanctions imposed by the Exchange or lift them, impose various other sanctions, and/or remand for any further proceedings as necessary. *See* 15 U.S.C. § 78s(e)–(f). Of special significance to the instant case is the fact that, in conducting this review, the SEC must consider the effects on competition that the disciplinary action of the Exchange might have had. And, these effects are meant to affect the SEC's determination of whether the sanctions imposed were appropriate. *See* 15 U.S.C. § 78s(f). Finally, a party aggrieved by the decision of the SEC can seek review of that ruling in a court of appeals. 15 U.S.C. § 78y(a)(1). * * *

The NYSE's revocation of MFS's membership and its actions to cut off phone service manifestly limited MFS's access to services. Accordingly, SEC review was available to MFS. Given that availability, MFS cannot, by denying its existence, and hence failing to seek it, create the very procedural deficiency (in its membership termination) as to which it now complains. That is not to say, of course, that MFS's termination by the Exchange complied with the procedural requirements of the Exchange Act or of the NYSE rules. Indeed, whether the membership revocation contravened the Act and the rules is precisely the question that the SEC, in reviewing MFS's termination, could consider. Moreover, under the Exchange Act, the decision of the SEC as to the propriety of that termination is itself directly reviewable in a court of appeals. 15 U.S.C. § 78y(a)(1). * * *

NOTES

1. Criminal charges were also brought against the floor brokers involved in "flipping" on the New York Stock Exchange. Were they doing anything that a specialist is allowed to do., i.e., profit on the spread between the bid and ask quotes? The charges against those individuals were later dropped or reduced.

2.   Do you think that stocks are a good investment? Most financial analysts will point out that stocks will outperform all other investments over the long term. Remember, however, that it was not until November of 1954 that the stock market was able to exceed the high it reached just before the stock market crash of 1929.

SECTION 7.   ELECTRONIC COMMUNICATIONS NETWORKS

Trading in common stocks has been increasingly dominated by "institutional investors"—principally pension funds, mutual funds, bank trust departments, and insurance companies—with small individual investors accounting for a continually decreasing percentage of trading volume. The distinctive trading practices of institutions, and the types of services they require and do not require, have put serious strains on the traditional market mechanisms and compensation structures. There has also been increased off-exchange trading of exchange-listed securities, which means that many transactions in exchange-listed securities do not take place on the floor of the exchange or through Nasdaq. The NYSE for years had a rule (Rule 390) that prohibited its members from trading NYSE listed stock other than through the exchange. That restriction was avoided by institutions through a "third market" maintained by broker-dealers that were not NYSE members or in a "fourth market" that involved transactions directly between institutional traders that were not members of the NYSE. Rule 390 was widely criticized as being anti-competitive, and the NYSE eventually eliminated it.

The computer and communication technology, which enables buyers and sellers in all parts of the country to be in instantaneous and continuous communication with one another with respect to any security, has revolutionized the securities markets and has raised serious questions about the necessity and desirability of a physical exchange "floor." The NYSE and Nasdaq are the principal markets used by small investors, but there are other alternatives available to large institutional traders. These alternate markets are often Electronic Communications Networks ("ECNs") that link large traders by computer and allow them to post or negotiate transactions with each other.

23A   JERRY W. MARKHAM & THOMAS LEE HAZEN BROKER–DEALER REGULATION UNDER SECURITIES AND COMMODITIES LAWS

§ 13:1 to § 13:3 (2002).

The development of computers and their linkage through the Internet has had an effect on Wall Street that equals or exceeds earlier electronic innovations in the markets such as those caused by the telegraph and the telephone. The computer and the growth of the Internet have given rise to electronic trading and the creation of alternate electronic marketplaces that are threatening traditional exchange and over-the-counter markets. This revolution has also raised regulatory concerns. * * *

Interconnected with these developments was the SEC's endorsement of the concept of a "central market system" in its 1971 study on the role of institutional investors. The SEC envisioned the creation of a central market that would encompass a network of broker-dealers linked together by electronic communications. The SEC wanted this centralized system to include securities on the exchanges and in the over-the-counter market. The SEC issued a statement on the future structure of the securities markets in 1972 that contended that a central market would better assure that customers were receiving the best executions in any market, the NYSE, the over-the-counter, or the third market.

The central market system was a somewhat amorphous and uncertain concept. The SEC did pressure the exchanges to develop the composite last sale price reporting system as a step in the development of a central market The SEC soon lost interest in the central market system concept. It did propose a "universal message switch" that would have required the exchanges to create a system whereby customer orders would be automatically routed to the market with the best quotation price. This was objected to by the industry. The alternative developed by the exchanges was the Intermarket Trading System, which allowed orders to be executed by specialists at the best price available on any exchange. The Intermarket Trading System was an electronic link among the NYSE, the AMEX, and the regional exchanges. The Intermarket Trading System did not require an order to be executed on the market quoting the best price. Instead, the specialist receiving an order could execute the order, as long as the execution was done at the best quoted price on any exchange.

The computer was soon making other inroads on Wall Street by allowing access to databases, information processing services and market models. Another development in electronic trading was the electronic network for institutional trading created by the Institutional Network Corporation in 1969 (Instinet). "It was composed of a network of computer terminals that permitted broker-dealers and their institutional customers to indicate their interest in securities listed on exchanges and traded in the over-the-counter market. The system allowed the execution of trades and provided trading reports. Clearing and settlement functions could be effected through the Instinet system, although not entirely. Pricing in the system used various sources including trading on the NYSE." Instinet developed rapidly in part because it provided a private market. Orders in its system were not publicly disclosed or accessible to public investors. This protected the identity of the institution in the trade. "It also allowed institutions to avoid intermediation on the NYSE and that exchange's Rule 390 prohibition on off-exchange transactions-in listed securities."

Instinet was successful and provided an alternative market to institutions. It was the largest electronic communications network for trading at the end of the century and was processing 170 million shares per day. Twenty million of those trades were executed after traditional trading hours. "Instinet was partnering with online brokers such as E*Trade Group to increase its trading."

By the end of the century, Instinet and other so-called electronic communications networks (ECNs) were posing a threat to the traditional securities markets. ECNs and other alternative trading systems were then handling more than 20 percent of the orders for securities listed on Nasdaq and almost 4 percent of orders on exchange listed securities. The SEC concluded that alternative trading systems were threatening to become the primary market for some securities.

A number of ECNs were operating in the market. They included Wit Capital, OptiMark, and Easdaq, Instinet Corp., the Island System, the TONTO System, which became Archipelago, Bloomberg Tradebook, the REDI System operated by Spear, Leeds & Kellogg, the Attain System, the BRUT System, the Strike System, and the Trading System. Goldman Sachs, Merrill Lynch & Co., Salomon Smith Barney, Morgan Stanley Dean Witter and Bernard L. Madoff Investment Securities formed Primex Trading N.A. It was an electronic trading system for stocks listed on the NYSE, the AMEX, and Nasdaq. Primex priced stocks in an auction market using decimals. This system was to be available for broker-dealers, institutional investors, market makers and exchange specialists. Primex was to be used to obtain securities at prices better than those posted prices in other markets.

Charles Schwab, Fidelity Investments, DLJdirect, and Spear, Leeds & Kellogg developed MarketXT, Inc. It was offering an evening trading session in August 1999 for the 200 largest stocks on the NYSE and Nasdaq. Bridge Trader was providing for Internet institutional order entry and allowed orders to be routed to multiple brokers through its trading network. This information system was also providing quotes, watch lists, and order book market data. In June 1999, J.P. Morgan & Co. announced that it was investing in an electronic trading network. Another electronic communication network GFINet System provided quotations on national market securities that were also American Depository Receipts. Still another ECN was the MarketXT. The BRASS Utility System was an ECN that provided automatic execution, clearance and settlement of trades in Nasdaq National Market System and Small–Cap stocks. Subscribers were broker-dealers, but their institutional customers could be given direct access to the system.

The Attain superTM System was an ECN that provided an alternative method by which market makers could handle their requirements to display customer limit orders to the public pursuant to the SEC's order handling rules. It also allowed matching of orders of subscribers as well as displaying a book of orders on Nasdaq. The system sought to provide matching without unnecessary intermediation by market makers. Spear, Leeds & Kellogg was operating a routing and execution DOT interface electronic communications network called the REDI System that was designed to process mixed-lot orders directed to it by SelectNet (another ECN) and from customer terminals. The system was designed to match mixed-lot orders. The remaining odd lot portions of a mixed lot order were to be executed against orders in odd lots or the odd lot portions of other mixed-lot orders. * * *

The increasing availability of computer linkages renewed some long held concerns that such systems could be used to divert volume from public exchanges, reduce market transparency, cause fragmentation of markets and result in disparate execution prices. The SEC issued a concept release seeking the public's views on how the market should be structured in light of the availability of alternate electronic trading systems and whether fragmentation was a threat to competitive executions. "Congress was also conducting hearings on whether legislation was needed to protect investors from market fragmentation resulting from the creation of more and more ECNs." Electronic trading allowed trading to continue past normal trading hours on the exchanges. This too raised concerns. An SEC staff study revealed wide price disparities in transactions conducted in after hours trading.

ECNs were reducing the market share of both the New York Stock Exchange and Nasdaq by the end of the last century. ECNs were handling over twenty percent of Nasdaq volume in 1999. Nasdaq responded to this threat by developing its own electronic system. This was to be done through Optimark Technologies, Inc., which was owned by several Wall Street firms, including Dow Jones & Co. Optimark had a supercomputer that was being used to match orders automatically. In addition, Nasdaq was considering whether it should develop an Internet trading system and was meeting with Instinet to discuss centralizing the trading of Nasdaq stocks. Nasdaq also announced in December 1999 that it was entering into an agreement with Primex Trading to adopt an electronic auction market system to trade its issues and those listed on the stock exchanges Nasdaq planned to expand its systems to allow the display of quotes from electronic communication networks so that investors would have more information on available prices. The Nasdaq market thereafter began competing with the ECNs through an electronic trading program called SuperMontage.

ECNs and Internet trading were also causing an upheaval at the stock exchanges. The SEC also recognized that traditional exchanges were under competitive pressure from the ECNs. It, therefore, allowed the exchanges to restructure themselves as for profit organizations. Traditionally, the exchanges had been operated as not-for-profits. This change was intended to allow the exchanges to raise capital and compete with the electronic markets. Demutualization was in progress on many of the exchanges. The NYSE was among the exchanges that were considering demutualizing. This would permit the exchange to raise capital and provide a better structure to meet competition. Nasdaq also announced similar plans, as did the Chicago Board of Trade and the London Stock Exchange. The NASD announced that it planned to sell a portion of its interest in the Nasdaq Stock Market through a private placement. This restructuring was intended to make the Nasdaq market more competitive and provide greater access to the markets for capital. The exchange, however, has been slow to actually demutualize.

Archipelago, a rapidly growing ECN, agreed to form a fully electronic stock market with the Pacific Exchange. The latter was the fourth largest stock exchange in the United States on the basis of trading volume. The new market planned to match customer buy and sell orders. The Pacific Exchange planned to close its trading floors in San Francisco and Los Angeles, but continue its options market. Archipelago was a success, so much so that the New York Stock Exchange merged with it in 2005. At that time, Archipelago was executing about twenty-five percent of volume in Nasdaq stocks. This move was intended to provide the NYSE with competitive access to Nasdaq stocks and allow it to enter the market for electronic executions. The merged entity was named NYSE Group Inc., and it became a public company. The NYSE then merged with Euronext, a combination of five European electronic exchanges that trade stocks and derivatives. In order to close that deal, the NYSE had to surrender half of its board seats to the Europeans, thus giving up control by Americans of one of the oldest most venerated of the country's financial institutions. George Ceron, "NYSE to Split Board Evenly With Euronext," Wall St. J., Nov. 22, 2006, at C3. The NYSE was then being transformed into an electronic exchange that was rapidly shutting down the trading floor. The NYSE sought to enhance liquidity through new market makers called "Liquidity Providers". The SEC and European regulators entered into a Memorandum of Understanding to coordinate their regulation of the merged entity. The merger was also structured in a fashion that essentially allows the European exchanges to be removed from the merged entity if there is any effort to apply U.S. laws to those exchanges.

A seat on the Chicago Stock Exchange sold for $135,000 in February 1999. The previous high price for a seat on that exchange had been $110,000 in August 1929. The Chicago Stock Exchange had, in the interim, evolved into the Midwest Stock Exchange, which then changed its name back to the Chicago Stock Exchange. That exchange was enjoying success because it was trading NYSE, AMEX and Nasdaq listed stocks through the Internet. This was attracting business from Online brokers. The Chicago Stock Exchange announced in August 1999 that it planned to begin two-hour evening sessions in several NYSE and Nasdaq stocks. The Chicago Stock Exchange was then trading about 50 million shares a day. Nasdaq, thereafter, disclosed that it was expanding its trading hours to allow evening trading sessions. Like other exchanges, the Chicago Stock Exchange dropped its not-for-profit status and became a for-profit, shareholder owned corporation.

NOTES

1. Trading on an ECN is order driven. This means there is no designated market-maker or specialist that is maintaining a two-sided market in the security being traded. Liquidity depends entirely on the ability to find a willing buyer or seller that has entered an opposing order or quote. Finding a counter party through a posted bid or offer in actively traded security may be easy, but in less actively traded securities that task is considerably more difficult. See generally, Jerry W. Markham & Daniel J. Harty, For Whom the Bell Tolls: the Demise of Exchange Trading Floors and the Growth of ECNs, 33 J. Corp. L. 865 (2008) (describing growth of electronic trading).

2. The SEC requires registration of stock exchanges and imposes pervasive regulation over their activities, but ECNs are only lightly regulated because they are simply order executing mechanisms. There is no designated specialist or market-maker that has a particular time and place advantage in trading for their own account that needs regulation. Do you think this is fair to the exchanges or the market-makers on Nasdaq? Do you think ECNs should be subject to greater regulation?

3. The SEC adopted Regulation ATS (17 C.F.R. § 242.300 et seq.) that imposed some limited regulation on ECNs. Basically, they may operate without registering as a national securities exchange as long as they do not dominate trading in a security. Access must also be generally open in instances where certain volume levels are met.

4. The Cincinnati Stock Exchange, which was founded in 1885, was one of the first traditional stock exchanges that turned from open outcry trading by traders on a centralized floor to electronic trading that matches orders by algorithmic equations. The transformation to electronic trading at the Cincinnati Stock Exchange began in the 1976 and was led by Bernard Madoff, who was later sentenced to 150 years in prison for running a giant Ponzi scheme through his hedge funds.[8] That exchange changed its name in 1995 to the National Stock Exchange, Inc. and moved to Chicago.

Electronic trading platforms also fostered the use of high speed, high volume trading that is driven by algorithmic programs, which seek to take advantage of even minute price disparities. By 2009 "[m]ore than two-thirds of stock-market volume comes from high-frequency traders, who can buy or sell in less than 400 microseconds, or nearly a thousand times faster than you can blink your eye." Jason Zweig, The Intelligent Investor: Staying Calm in a World of Dark Pools, Dark Doings, Wall St. J., Oct. 24, 2009, at B1.

This growth in high frequency trading soon caused concerns at the SEC. One concern was "flash" orders used by high frequency traders. These are orders that are cancelled immediately upon communication or

---

8. Madoff also introduced the concept of "payment for order flow" that paid brokerage firms to direct customer order flow to a particular firm or exchange. See Jerry W. Markham, A Financial History of the United States, From Enron Era Scandals to the Subprime Crisis (2004–2006), 249 (2010).

which are withdrawn if not executed immediately after entry. See, Securities Exchange Act Release No. 34–60684, 74 Fed. Reg. 48632 (Sept. 23, 2009). These orders are also called "quote stuffing." Tom Lauricella & Jenny Strasburg, SEC Probes Cancelled Trades, Wall St. J., Sept. 2, 2010, at A1. An earlier SEC rule had allowed exchanges to exclude such orders from publicly available consolidated quotation data because they were not viewed to be material. However, electronic traders began using flash orders for a variety of purposes and in large amounts. Among other things, "[f]or those seeking liquidity, the flash mechanism may attract additional liquidity from market participants who are not willing to display their trading interest publicly." See 74 Fed. Reg., *supra*, at 48637. The SEC sought public comment in September 2009 on whether its exception from quotation for flash orders should be continued. Among other things, the SEC was concerned with the fact that flash orders provide professional short-term traders an advantage over long-term investors.

In January 2010, the SEC proposed another rule that would restrict "naked access" by high frequency traders to exchange electronic operated electronic trading platforms. The SEC was concerned that broker-dealers were allowing these traders to directly access ("naked" or "sponsored access" as it is sometimes called) electronic trading platforms operated by the exchanges without broker-dealer intermediation or supervision, allowing the possibility of abuses by the traders given such access. See, Risk Management Controls for Brokers or Dealers With Market Access 2010 SEC LEXIS 359 (Jan. 19, 2010).

The SEC also issued a concept release in January 2010 that launched a broad based review of the current equity market structure to determine whether the agency's rules had kept pace with the growth of electronic trading, including the role of flash orders. 75 Fed. Reg. 3594 (Jan. 21, 2010). Another concern raised in the concept release were the so-called "dark" liquidity pools, which were trading platforms that did not publicly disclose their trading activity as is required for traditional exchanges. The SEC described these dark pools as follows:

> Dark pools can vary quite widely in the services they offer their customers. For example, some dark pools, such as block crossing networks, offer specialized size discovery mechanisms that attempt to bring large buyers and sellers in the same NMS stock together anonymously and to facilitate a trade between them. The average trade size of these block crossing networks can be as high as 50,000 shares. Most dark pools, though they may handle large orders, primarily execute trades with small sizes that are more comparable to the average size of trades in the public markets, which was less than 300 shares in July 2009. These dark pools that primarily match smaller orders (though the matched orders may be "child" orders of much larger "parent" orders) execute more than 90% of dark pool trading volume. The majority of this volume is executed by dark pools that are sponsored by multi-service broker-dealers. These broker-

dealers also offer order routing services, trade as principal in the sponsored . . . [dark pool], or both.

75 Fed. Reg., *supra*, at 3599 (footnotes omitted). The SEC also proposed another rule that sought to track high frequency traders by assigning them codes and requiring them to report their trading to the agency when requested. See, Large Trader Reporting System, Securities Exchange Act Release No. 61908 (April 23, 2010).

The SEC's concerns with high frequency traders seemed justified after the "flash crash" that occurred on May 6, 2010, an event that saw the Dow Jones Industrial Average drop by almost 1,000 points in just a few minutes. The market recovered quickly and there was no immediate apparent reason for this crash, but it raised grave concerns that high frequency traders were responsible. See, Tom Lauricella & Scott Patterson, Legacy of the Flash Crash: Enduring Worries of Repeat, Wall St. J., Aug. 6. 2010, at A1.

The staffs of the SEC and CFTC mounted an intensive investigation of the flash crash and issued a preliminary report on May 18, 2010[9] and a final joint report on September 30, 2010.[10] The final report found that on May 6, 2010 at 2:32 p.m., a large mutual fund complex (Waddell & Reed Financial Inc.) entered an automated algorithm order to sell 75,000 E–Mini futures contracts valued at over $4 billion in order to hedge an existing position. The algorithm dictated an execution rate of 9 percent of trading volume without regard to time or price. High frequency traders ("HFTs") then quickly responded to the order, thereby increasing volume and the rate of execution of this massive order. The joint report then describes the results:

> The combined selling pressure from the Sell Algorithm, HFTs and other traders drove the price of the E–Mini down approximately 3% in just four minutes from the beginning of 2:41 p.m. through the end of 2:44 p.m. During this same time cross-market arbitrageurs who did buy the E–Mini, simultaneously sold equivalent amounts in the equities markets, driving the price of SPY also down approximately 3%.

> Still lacking sufficient demand from fundamental buyers or cross-market arbitrageurs, HFTs began to quickly buy and then resell contracts to each other—generating a "hot-potato" volume effect as the same positions were rapidly passed back and forth. Between 2:45:13 and 2:45:27, HFTs traded over 27,000 contracts, which accounted for about 49 percent of the total trading volume, while buying only about 200 additional contracts net.

> At this time, buy-side market depth in the E–Mini fell to about $58 million, less than 1% of its depth from that morning's level. As

---

9. Report of the Staffs of the CFTC & SEC to the Joint Advisory Committee on Emerging Regulatory Issues, Preliminary Findings Regarding the Market Events on May 6, 2010, Comm. Fut. L. Rep. (CCH) ¶ 31,569 (May 18, 2010).

10. Report of the Staffs of the CFTC & SEC to the Joint Advisory Committee on Emerging Regulatory Issues, Findings Regarding the Market Events on May 6, 2010 (Sept. 30, 2010).

liquidity vanished, the price of the E–Mini dropped by an additional 1.7% in just these 15 seconds, to reach its intraday low of 1056. This sudden decline in both price and liquidity may be symptomatic of the notion that prices were moving so fast, fundamental buyers and cross-market arbitrageurs were either unable or unwilling to supply enough buy-side liquidity. . . .

Between 2:32 p.m. and 2:45 p.m., as prices of the E–Mini rapidly declined, the Sell Algorithm sold about 35,000 E–Mini contracts (valued at approximately $1.9 billion) of the 75,000 intended. During the same time, all fundamental sellers combined sold more than 80,000 contracts net, while all fundamental buyers bought only about 50,000 contracts net, for a net fundamental imbalance of 30,000 contracts. This level of net selling by fundamental sellers is about 15 times larger compared to the same 13–minute interval during the previous three days, while this level of net buying by the fundamental buyers is about 10 times larger compared to the same time period during the previous three days.[11]

This selloff then spread to the equities markets for individual stocks.[12]

The Staff report noted that:

One key lesson is that under stressed market conditions, the automated execution of a large sell order can trigger extreme price movements, especially if the automated execution algorithm does not take prices into account. Moreover, the interaction between automated execution programs and algorithmic trading strategies can quickly erode liquidity and result in disorderly markets. As the events of May 6 demonstrate, especially in times of significant volatility, high trading volume is not necessarily a reliable indicator of market liquidity.[13]

The final report also pointed to the important effect of the inter-connectedness of the derivatives and securities markets,[14] a factor that was focused on after the Stock Market Crash of 1987.[15] The exchanges involved in the flash crash announced that trades executed at a price of more than sixty percent below the share prices at the time of the flash crash would be cancelled. This displeased traders with large profits from the fall. At the request of the SEC, the exchanges agreed to adopt circuit breakers to interrupt trading when such a sharp downturn begins.[16]

---

11. Id. at 3–4.

12. Id. at 4–5.

13. Id. at 6.

14. Id.

15. Jerry W. Markham & Rita McCloy Stephanz, The Stock Market Crash of 1987—The United States Looks at New Recommendations, 76 Georgetown Law Journal 1993, 2010 (1988).

16. Jerry W. Markham, A Financial History of the United States, From the Subprime Crisis to the Great Recession (2006–2009) 690 (2010). See also Tom Lauricella & Scott Patterson, Legacy of the Flash Crash: Enduring Worries of Repeat, Wall St. J., Aug. 6. 2010, at A1.

Sarbanes–Oxley Effects on Capital Markets

The Sarbanes–Oxley Corporate Reform Act of 2002 (107 Pub. L. 204, 116 Stat. 745 (2002).) that was enacted after the Enron and WorldCom scandals caused public companies to incur massive costs. These onerous burdens were threatening the premium for the listing of foreign firms on U.S. markets. Only one of the top 20 global initial public offerings in 2006 was listed in the United States, down from 60 percent of such offerings five years earlier. The U.S. raised only 28 percent of global equity raised in leading markets in 2006, down from 41 percent in 1995. "Is Wall Street Losing Its Competitive Edge?" Wall St. J., Dec. 2–3, 2006, at A6. As one critic has noted:

> Between 1996 and 2001, the New York Stock Exchange averaged 50 new non-U.S. listings annually; in 2005, it was 19. In the same year, the London Stock Exchange, including its small company affiliate, the Alternative Investment Market, gained 139 new listings while Nasdaq attracted 19. Since the end of 2004, 30 foreign companies have left the NYSE and Nasdaq. Financial capital—the kind that finances mergers, acquisitions and new business formation—is also increasingly finding a more comfortable home abroad. Large offerings by Chinese, Korean and Russian companies—involving billions of dollars—have occurred in Hong Kong and London; meanwhile, large new foreign offerings this year by Russian aluminum producers and Kazakhstan oil and copper companies are planning to list in London.

Peter J. Wallison, "Capital Punishment," Wall St. J., Nov. 4, 2006 at A7. More directly, SEC regulations impose a compliance cost of an estimated $25 billion each year. Underwriting costs abroad are less than half of those in the United States.[17]

The *Wall Street Journal* has noted that venture capital funds traditionally "used the IPO market as their exit strategy ... Today, however, nearly 90% of those venture-capital-backed startups are sold to strategic buyers in private transactions." "Capital Flight," Wall St.J., Dec. 2–3, 2006, at A8. *See also* Kit Roane, "The New Face of Capitalism," U.S. News & World Rep., Dec. 4, 2006, at 49 (describing the private equity buying binge). Another indication of the growing disaffection with SEC regulation was the fact that in 2006 the amount of money raised in private placements exceeded the amount of funds raised in initial public offerings.

There has been some recognition that this regulation had gone awry. Treasury Secretary Henry Paulson has warned that the country was "creating a thicket of regulation that impedes competitiveness." Even politicians normally in favor of more, rather than less, regulation were recognizing that things had gone too far. New York Senator Chuck Schumer co-authored an Op-ed piece in the *Wall Street Journal* with New

---

17. One study showed that the premium for listing on a U.S. exchange had declined, but another study disagreed with that conclusion and found that a U.S. listing still carries a 17 percent premium over foreign listings. Greg Ip, Maybe U.S. Markets are Still Supreme, Wall St. J., April 27, 2007, at C1.

York Mayor Michael Bloomberg that called for a study to determine if New York was losing its position as the world's leading financial center because of over-regulation and abusive shareholder litigation. The resulting study called for a repeal of some of the worst Sarbanes–Oxley provisions and limits on class action lawsuits. There was some reason for this sudden concern with over-regulation. The securities industry accounts for 20.7 percent of total wages in New York City and 18.7 percent of total tax receipts in New York State.

The SEC indicated that it will be backing off some of the more onerous provisions in Sarbanes–Oxley, at least for small companies. The Public Company Accounting Oversight Board ("PCAOB") has sought to ease the most expensive and controversial provision in Sarbanes–Oxley concerning the adequacy of internal accounting controls. PCAOB reduced its rule for accountants making that assessment from 180 to 65 pages. This reform of the reforms was further spurred by a report of a blue ribbon Committee on Capital Markets that recommended that excessive regulation was hurting the securities markets and making foreign markets more competitive.

This deregulatory effort was derailed by the subprime crisis that arose between 2007–2009. The Dodd–Frank Act of 2010, a statute 2,300 pages in length, added much new regulation to nearly all areas of finance, including the stock markets.

CHAPTER NINE

THE GOVERNMENT SECURITIES MARKET

■ ■ ■

Chapter objectives

- To understand the role and structure of the government securities markets

- To appreciate the special liquidity and regulatory functions served by the repurchase market for government securities.

- To identify the range of government securities products offered by the Department of the Treasury and private issuers.

- To understand the role played by the municipal securities offered by governments and instrumentalities other than the federal government.

SECTION 1.   INTRODUCTION

The United States government debt market is the largest and most efficient securities market in the world. As such, it is an important market for the investment of corporate and private funds. This market is also the benchmark for corporate interest rates.

The government securities market has a long history. Our Revolution was funded with the Continental dollar and other scrip that were simply a borrowing on an unfunded promise to pay in the future. After the Revolution, Congress agreed to assume responsibility for that debt, which had generally been viewed too be worthless. This gave rise to our first insider trading scandal as congressmen and their cohorts bought up the Revolutionary debt from unsuspecting holders at sharp discounts. The speculators were then paid at par when Congress assumed the debt.

Debt became the means for funding wars in which the United States became engaged. The War of 1812 involved large loans to the government. The Civil War was of even greater proportions. Both the Union and the Confederacy borrowed to fund their operations. The creation of the Greenback was a part of that process. That conflict also witnessed the first widespread securities sales. Jay Cooke, an investment banker was commissioned by the Union government to sell its bonds, and he did so through the use of 2,500 salesmen and widespread newspaper advertisements. At one point, his salesmen were selling over $5 million in bonds each day.

World War I saw another massive marketing operation as Liberty Bonds were sold to investors across the country. The Victory Loans of World War II served a similar purpose. After that last conflict, the government became more and more dependant on the government securities market to fund its daily and long term operations. In so doing, the government offered debt obligations of varying maturities and payment terms. The three most important for corporate finance being Treasury Bills ("T–Bills"), Treasury Notes and Bonds.

SECTION 2.   THE TREASURY MARKET

THE BASICS OF TREASURY SECURITIES

WWW.U.S.TreasuryDirect (Feb. 2003).

What are U.S. Treasury securities?

U.S. Treasury securities are debt instruments. The U.S. Treasury issues securities to raise the money needed to operate the Federal Government and to pay off maturing obligations—its debt, in other words.

Why should I buy a Treasury security?

Treasury securities are a safe and secure investment option because the full faith and credit of the United States government guarantees that interest and principal payments will be paid on time. Also, most Treasury securities are liquid, which means they can easily be sold for cash. * * *

What are Treasury bills?

Treasury bills (or T-bills) are short-term securities that mature in one year or less from their issue date. You buy T-bills for a price less than their par (face) value, and when they mature we pay you their par value. Your interest is the difference between the purchase price of the security and what we pay you at maturity (or what you get if you sell the bill before it matures). For example, if you bought a $10,000 26–week Treasury bill for $9,750 and held it until maturity, your interest would be $250.

What are Treasury notes and bonds?

Treasury notes and bonds are securities that pay a fixed rate of interest every six months until your security matures, which is when we pay you their par value. The only difference between them is their length until maturity. Treasury notes mature in more than a year, but not more than 10 years from their issue date. Bonds, on the other hand, mature in more than 10 years from their issue date. You usually can buy notes and bonds for a price close to their par value. * * *

What is the minimum purchase amount for Treasury securities?

The minimum amount that you can purchase of any given Treasury bill or note is $1,000. Additional amounts must be in multiples of $1,000.
* * *

IN THE MATTER OF BIELFELDT

T.C. Memo. 1998–394, aff'd, 231 F.3d 1035 (7th Cir.2000), cert.
denied, 534 U.S. 813, 122 S.Ct. 38, 151 L.Ed.2d 11 (2001).

The Treasury securities cash market consists of bills, notes, and bonds issued by the Department of the Treasury (Treasury). Treasury bills (T-bills) are issued in 3–month, 6–month, or 1–year maturities. T-bills are non-interest-bearing obligations that are issued below face value and redeemed at maturity at face value. Treasury notes (T-notes) are issued in 2, 3, 4, 5, 7, or 10–year maturities. T-notes are issued at or near face value, and they are redeemed at maturity at face value. T-notes bear a fixed rate of interest, which is payable semiannually, and most T-notes are noncertificated; i.e., they do not exist in physical form but trade through an electronic system known as the Federal Reserve Bank book entry system. Treasury bonds (T-bonds) mature 10 or more years after issuance. T-bonds are issued at or near face value, and they are redeemed at maturity at face value. T-bonds bear interest, which is payable semiannually, and most new T-bonds are noncertificated. The interest rate on new T-bonds is set at auctions held by the Federal Reserve Bank of New York (the Fed).

Treasury securities are rarely listed on an organized exchange, and the volume of trading of Treasury securities on organized exchanges is minimal. Virtually all trading of Treasury securities occurs over the counter or at auctions which the Treasury holds to sell the securities initially. Auction bidders tender competitive or noncompetitive bids. Competitive bids generally represent the price that bidders offer to buy the securities, and noncompetitive bids generally represent the bidders offers to buy the securities at the average of the successful competitive bids. Bidders, other than primary dealers (as defined below), must deposit 10 percent of any competitive bid tendered, and these deposits are held without interest for days or weeks until the auction purchase settles. In practice, only primary dealers submit competitive bids directly to the Treasury; they do so for their own accounts as well as on behalf of others.

After Treasury securities are issued through the auction process, they are generally traded over the counter in direct transactions between the buyer and the seller or through interdealer brokers (as defined below).[1]

---

1. Between the announcement of an upcoming auction and the issuance of the securities following the auction, new issues of Treasury securities also are traded over the counter on a "when-issued" (WI) basis for a period that may last from several days to approximately 2 weeks.

Prices are quoted as bids (the price that a buyer is willing to pay) and offers or asks (the price at which a seller is willing to sell). A transaction is effectuated when a buyer or seller accepts a bid or offer, respectively, or when they negotiate a different price. Over-the-counter trading of Treasury securities is usually effectuated over the telephone on the basis of established business relationships.

"Primary dealers" are the 35 to 40 firms which have been recognized as such by the Fed to deal with it directly in the Treasury securities market.[2] In designating primary dealers, the Fed applies the following criteria: (1) The firm must have adequate capital relative to the positions it assumes; (2) the firm must participate consistently and meaningfully in Treasury auctions of new securities and must submit bids in every auction; (3) the firm must file periodic reports with the Fed setting forth certain market information; and (4) the firm must be an effective market maker.

Primary dealers trade Treasury securities for their own accounts (proprietary trading) or for the accounts of customers pursuant to customer directives (customer trading). These two types of trading are not mutually exclusive. A primary dealer may accept a customer's bid or offer for a particular security as part of the dealer's proprietary trading strategy, or it may initiate trades to improve its proprietary position. Primary dealers frequently trade Treasury securities with other primary dealers either directly (trader to trader) or indirectly through interdealer brokers. Primary dealers frequently sell to other primary dealers the Treasury securities that they purchase at auction. When a primary dealer and a counterparty agree on a transaction, a trade ticket is prepared which states the terms of the transaction. The primary dealer uses the information on the trade ticket to prepare a confirmation slip that is sent to the counterparty.

Interdealer brokers are brokerage firms that facilitate trades between counterparties who are mainly primary dealers; interdealer brokers do not hold positions in Government securities themselves. The principal interdealer brokers are RMJ, Fundamental Brokers, Inc., Garban, Liberty, and Cantor Fitzgerald (CF). CF is the only interdealer broker that trades for customers other than primary dealers. CF's customers include banks, fund managers, and investment funds. Approximately 30 percent of CF's volume of trading in Treasury securities is for customers who are not primary dealers.

Interdealer brokers provide their customers with CRT terminals (screens) on which the customers may view in their offices the best bids and offers made by the broker's subscribers. The customers telephone bids and offers to their broker, and the broker electronically posts these bids

---

The purchaser of WI securities must pay for the securities on or before the date that the securities are issued.

2. Dealers in the Treasury securities market who are not primary dealers are known informally as "secondary dealers". The Treasury securities market has many secondary dealers.

and offers on its screens without identifying the customers who are tendering the bids or offers. When a person accepts a bid or an offer listed with the broker, the broker effectuates the transaction and indicates on its screens that the bid or offer was accepted. The broker sends confirmation to the buyer and seller showing the broker itself as the counterparty; neither the person quoting the price nor the person accepting the price knows the identity of the counterparty.[3] The broker earns a commission, which is paid by the person who accepted the bid or offer. * * *

Dealers try to be available regularly to satisfy customer requests, and the normal function of a Government securities trading desk at a primary dealer is to try to buy and sell securities all the time. Primary dealers typically engage in Government securities trading daily, and they seldom fail to respond to a customer request to do a transaction or to make a market.[4]

NOTES

1.   The pricing of the Treasury auctions is a complicated process:

"When-issued" trading occurs during the period between the time a new Treasury issue is announced and the time it is actually issued. During this period, various market participants may purchase or sell the new issue, an activity which facilitates the distribution process for Treasury securities and helps determine the price of the new issue by providing a gauge of market demand. Deliveries on when-issued trading occur at the time of issue of the new Treasury securities on the auction settlement day.

H. R. Rep. No. 102–722, pt. 1 (1992).

2.   The Treasury Department also offers savings bonds. Unlike Treasury bills, notes, and bonds, however, savings bonds are not negotiable. This means there is no secondary market in savings bonds.

3.   Treasury securities sales play a role in the monetary policy of the United States. The Federal Reserve Bank of New York carries out the monetary policies of the Reserve Board's Federal Open Market Committee by conducting open market operations with the primary dealers. Those operations often involve buying or selling government securities from dealers and thereby increasing or decreasing the money supply.

4.   One of the more popular Treasury instruments was the 30–year "long bond." The Treasury stopped issuing that instrument in October 2001 because surpluses were reducing the need for such long-term borrowing. The Treasury's decision to discontinue the 30–year bond resulted in an insider trading scandal. Peter J. Davis, who had attended an "embargoed" Treasury

---

3.   For this reason, inter-dealer brokers are known as "blind brokers".

4.   Making a market means providing a simultaneous bid and offer on the same security pursuant to a customer request.

press conference describing the change, phoned the information to a Senior Economist at Goldman Sachs, John M. Youngdahl, twenty-five minutes before the embargo on disclosure of the information was lifted, but only eight minutes before a Treasury official inadvertently posted the announcement online. In that period, Goldman Sachs bought $84 million in thirty-year bonds and bond futures covering another $233 million, resulting in profits of $3.8 million. Youngdahl pled guilty to charges of insider trading and other misconduct for misuse of this information. He was sentenced to two years and nine months in prison and paid the SEC a civil penalty of $240,000. Goldman Sachs agreed to pay $9.3 million to settle charges brought by the SEC. Ironically, the government returned the 30–year "long" Treasury bond to the market in February 2006.

5.   Treasury securities are said to be free of default risk. As long as the flag is flying, payment is said to be assured. There are, however occasional budget crises where that claim is called into question. In 1995, wrangling over the budget in Congress nearly resulted in a default. Agreement was reached in time to avoid that result, which would have unhinged credit markets around the world. III Jerry W. Markham, A Financial History of the United States: From the Age of Derivatives Into the New Millennium (1970–2001) 265 (2002). The Treasury Department borrowed forty billion dollars from government employees' pension funds during that crisis to avoid default. The federal government was raiding government pension funds again in May of 2002 in order to meet expenses, a need that had been brought about with a renewed deficit. The Debt Limit Pension Raid, Wall St. J., June 13, 2002, at A16.

IN THE MATTER OF JOHN H. GUTFREUND ET AL.

Securities Exchange Act of 1934, Release No. 34–
31554, 51 S.E.C. 93 (December 3, 1992).

* * * In anticipation of the institution of these administrative proceedings, [John H.] Gutfreund, [Thomas W.] Strauss, and [John W.] Meriwether have each submitted Offers of Settlement which the Commission has determined to accept. Solely for the purposes of these proceedings and any other proceedings brought by or on behalf of the Commission or to which the Commission is a party, prior to a hearing pursuant to the Commission's Rules of Practice, and without admitting or denying the facts, findings, or conclusions herein, Gutfreund, Strauss, and Meriwether each consent to entry of the findings, and the imposition of the remedial sanctions, set forth below. * * *

Salomon Brothers Inc ("Salomon") is a Delaware corporation with its principal place of business in New York, New York. At all times relevant to this proceeding, Salomon was registered with the Commission as a broker-dealer pursuant to Section 15(b) of the Exchange Act. Salomon has been a government-designated dealer in U.S. Treasury securities since 1939 and a primary dealer since 1961.

John H. Gutfreund was the Chairman and Chief Executive Officer of Salomon from 1983 to August 18, 1991. He had worked at Salomon since 1953.

Thomas W. Strauss was the President of Salomon from 1986 to August 18, 1991. During that time period, Strauss reported to Gutfreund. He had worked at Salomon since 1963.

John W. Meriwether was a Vice Chairman of Salomon and in charge of all fixed income trading activities of the firm from 1988 to August 18, 1991. During that period, Meriwether reported to Strauss. During the same period, Paul W. Mozer, a managing director and the head of Salomon's Government Trading Desk, reported directly to Meriwether.

Donald M. Feuerstein was the chief legal officer of Salomon Inc and the head of the Legal Department of Salomon until August 23, 1991. From 1987 until August 23, 1991, the head of Salomon's Compliance Department reported directly to Feuerstein.

In late April of 1991, three members of the senior management of Salomon—John Gutfreund, Thomas Strauss, and John Meriwether—were informed that Paul Mozer, the head of the firm's Government Trading Desk, had submitted a false bid in the amount of $3.15 billion in an auction of U.S. Treasury securities on February 21, 1991. The executives were also informed by Donald Feuerstein, the firm's chief legal officer, that the submission of the false bid appeared to be a criminal act and, although not legally required, should be reported to the government. Gutfreund and Strauss agreed to report the matter to the Federal Reserve Bank of New York. Mozer was told that his actions might threaten his future with the firm and would be reported to the government. However, for a period of months, none of the executives took action to investigate the matter or to discipline or impose limitations on Mozer. The information was also not reported to the government for a period of months. During that same period, Mozer committed additional violations of the federal securities laws in connection with two subsequent auctions of U.S. Treasury securities.

The Respondents in this proceeding are not being charged with any participation in the underlying violations. However, as set forth herein, the Commission believes that the Respondents' supervision was deficient and that this failure was compounded by the delay in reporting the matter to the government.

For a considerable period of time prior to the February 21, 1991 auction, the Treasury Department had limited the maximum bid that any one bidder could submit in an auction of U.S. Treasury securities at any one yield to 35% of the auction amount. On February 21, 1991, the Treasury Department auctioned $9 billion of five-year U.S. Treasury notes. Salomon submitted a bid in its own name in that auction at a yield of 7.51% in the amount of $3.15 billion, or 35% of the auction amount.[5] In

---

5. The Treasury Department adopted the 35% limitation in July of 1990 after Salomon submitted several large bids in amounts far in excess of the amount of securities to be auctioned.

the same auction, Salomon submitted two additional $3.15 billion bids at the same yield in the names of two customers: Quantum Fund and Mercury Asset Management. Both accounts were those of established customers of Salomon, but the bids were submitted without the knowledge or authorization of either customer. Both bids were in fact false bids intended to secure additional securities for Salomon. Each of the three $3.15 billion bids was prorated 54% and Salomon received a total of $5.103 billion of the five-year notes from the auction, or 56.7% of the total amount of securities sold at that auction. * * *

In the February 21, 1991 five-year note auction, S.G. Warburg, a primary dealer in U.S. Treasury securities, submitted a bid in its own name in the amount of $100 million at a yield of 7.51%. The 7.51% yield was the same yield used for the unauthorized $3.15 billion Mercury bid submitted by Salomon. At the time the bids were submitted, S.G. Warburg and Mercury Asset Management were subsidiaries of the same holding company, S.G. Warburg, PLC. Because the unauthorized Mercury bid was for the maximum 35% amount, the submission of the $100 million bid in the name of S.G. Warburg meant that two bids had apparently been submitted by affiliated entities in an amount in excess of 35% of the auction.

The submission of the bids was noticed by officials of the Federal Reserve Bank of New York and brought to the attention of officials of the Treasury Department in Washington, D.C. The Treasury Department officials did not know that one of the bids had been submitted by Salomon without authorization from Mercury. Because the bids were to be significantly prorated, officials of the Treasury Department decided not to reduce the amount of either bid for purposes of determining the results of the February 21, 1991 auction. The Treasury Department began to review whether the relationship between S.G. Warburg and Mercury Asset Management was such that the bids should be aggregated for determination of how the 35% limitation should be applied to those entities in future auctions.

After reviewing facts concerning the corporate relationship between Mercury Asset Management and S.G. Warburg, the Treasury Department determined to treat the two firms as a single bidder in future auctions of U.S. Treasury securities. The Treasury Department conveyed that decision in a letter dated April 17, 1991 from the Acting Assistant Commissioner for Financing to a Senior Director of Mercury Asset Management in

Prior to July of 1990, the Treasury Department had not placed limitations on the amount of bids that could be submitted but had limited the maximum amount that any single bidder could purchase in an auction to 35% of the auction amount. The Salomon bids which led to the adoption of the 35% bidding limitation were submitted at the direction of Paul Mozer. Mozer was angered by the adoption of the new bidding limitation and he expressed his disagreement with the decision to adopt the new rule to officials at the Treasury Department and in several news articles. Mozer also registered his anger through his bidding activity in the Treasury auction the following day. In an auction for $8 billion of seven-year U.S. Treasury notes on July 11, 1990, Mozer entered 11 bids at the maximum 35% amount at successive yields between 8.60% and 8.70%. The successful bids in the auction were between 8.55% and 8.58%, and the bids submitted by Mozer were intended as protest bids.

London. The April 17 letter noted that a $3.15 billion bid had been submitted by Salomon on behalf of Mercury Asset Management in the five-year U.S. Treasury note auction on February 21, 1991, and that S.G. Warburg had also submitted a bid in the same auction, at the same yield, in the amount of $100 million. The letter noted that Mercury Asset Management and S.G. Warburg were subsidiaries of the same holding company and stated that the Treasury Department would thereafter "treat all subsidiaries of S.G. Warburg, PLC as one single entity for purposes of the 35 percent limitation rule." Copies of the letter were sent to Mozer and to a managing director of S.G. Warburg in New York.

Mozer received the April 17 letter during the week of April 21, 1991. On April 24, he spoke with the Senior Director at Mercury Asset Management who had also received the April 17 letter. Mozer told the Senior Director that the submission of the $3.15 billion bid in the name of Mercury Asset Management was the result of an "error" by a clerk who had incorrectly placed the name of Mercury on the tender form. Mozer told the Senior Director that he was embarrassed by the "error," which he said had been "corrected" internally, and he asked the Senior Director to keep the matter confidential to avoid "problems." The Senior Director indicated that such a course of action would be acceptable. The Mercury Senior Director was not aware that the submission of the bid was an intentional effort by Salomon to acquire additional securities for its own account.

Mozer then went to the office of John Meriwether, his immediate supervisor, and handed him the April 17 letter. When Meriwether was finished reading the letter, Mozer told him that the Mercury Asset Management bid referred to in the letter was in fact a bid for Salomon and had not been authorized by Mercury. After expressing shock at Mozer's conduct, Meriwether told him that his behavior was career-threatening, and he asked Mozer why he had submitted the bid. Mozer told Meriwether that the Government Trading Desk had needed a substantial amount of the notes, that there was also demand from the Government Arbitrage Desk for the notes, and that he had submitted the false bid to satisfy those demands.

Meriwether then asked Mozer if he had ever engaged in that type of conduct before or since. Mozer responded that he had not. Meriwether told Mozer that he would have to take the matter immediately to Thomas Strauss. Mozer then told Meriwether of his conversation with the Mercury Senior Director in which he had told that individual that the bid was an "error" and had asked him to keep the matter confidential. Meriwether listened to Mozer's description of the conversation, but did not respond. He then gave the letter back to Mozer and Mozer left the office. * * *

After Mozer's disclosure of one unauthorized bid on April 24, 1991, he submitted two subsequent unauthorized bids in auctions of U.S. Treasury securities.

On April 25, 1991, the U.S. Treasury auctioned $9 billion of five-year U.S. Treasury notes. Salomon submitted a bid in that auction for $3 billion, just under the maximum 35% amount of $3.15 billion. Salomon also submitted a $2.5 billion bid in the name of Tudor Investment Corporation ("Tudor"). A bid of only $1.5 billion had been authorized by Tudor, however, and the tender form submitted by Salomon was thus false in the amount of $1 billion. The bid by Salomon in its own name and the unauthorized portion of the Tudor bid totaled $4 billion, or 44.4% of the auction amount.

The $2.5 billion bid on behalf of Tudor was prorated 84% and $2.1 billion of five-year notes was awarded in response to the bid. Trade tickets were written providing the entire $2.1 billion auction allocation to Tudor after the auction. At Mozer's instruction, a trade ticket was then written "selling" $600 million of the notes back to Salomon on the auction day at the auction price. The five-year notes were "sold" from Tudor to Salomon at the auction price even though the price of the notes had risen above that price by the time of the transaction.

On May 22, 1991, the U.S. Treasury auctioned $12.255 billion of two-year U.S. Treasury notes. Salomon submitted a $2 billion bid in that auction on behalf of Tiger Management Corporation ("Tiger"). A bid of only $1.5 billion had been authorized by Tiger, and the tender form submitted by Salomon was thus false in the amount of $500 million.

The $2 billion bid submitted on behalf of Tiger was accepted in full. After the auction results were announced, Tiger was provided with $1.5 billion of the $2 billion allocation provided in response to its bid. The remaining $500 million was not provided to Tiger but was transferred internally to a proprietary trading account on the Government Trading Desk at Salomon.

Prior to the auction on May 22, 1991, Mozer had decided that the firm should accumulate a long position in the two-year notes prior to the auction. He communicated that decision to the individual then trading two-year notes on the Government Trading Desk. Consistent with that trading decision, at 12:30 p.m. on May 22, 1991, Salomon had a net long position in the two-year notes of $485 million. Salomon failed to disclose that position, however, on its tender form submitted in the auction, as required by the auction rules. The tender form falsely stated that Salomon had a net position of less than $200 million in the notes as of 12:30 p.m. on the auction day.

With the securities received in response to its own bid, the $500 million of notes received in response to the unauthorized portion of the Tiger bid, and the extra $485 million received as a result of the failure accurately to disclose the firm's net long position, Salomon received a total of $5.185 billion of the two-year notes from the auction, or 42.3% of the auction amount. * * *

There was no disclosure to the government of the false bid in the February 21, 1991 auction prior to August 9, 1991, when the results of the internal investigation were first made public. * * *

In early July, Salomon retained a law firm to conduct an internal investigation of the firm's role in the May 22, 1991 two-year note auction. On July 2, a lawyer with that law firm had received a call from the general counsel of a brokerage firm who indicated that an FBI agent and a representative from the Antitrust Division of the Department of Justice had made a request to speak with representatives of the firm about the May two-year note auction. Before agreeing to be retained by the firm, the lawyer indicated that he wished to determine whether Salomon, which was a regular client of the firm, also wanted representation in connection with the matter. The lawyer then spoke with employees of Salomon and was told that Salomon might wish to be represented in connection with the matter and that the firm should hold itself available. Prior to that time, in late June of 1991, Salomon had received inquiries from the Commission and from another government agency concerning activities in the two-year U.S. Treasury notes auctioned on May 22, 1991. Several days after the lawyer contacted Salomon, Feuerstein decided to retain the law firm and directed that it begin an internal investigation of the firm's activities in the May 22, 1991 two-year note auction. * * *

During the review that was conducted between July 15 and early August, the law firm discovered a $1 billion false bid in the December 27, 1990 auction of four-year U.S. Treasury notes, a second $3.15 billion false bid in the February 21, 1991 auction, a $1 billion false bid in the February 7, 1991 auction of thirty-year U.S. Treasury bonds,[6] the failure to disclose the $485 million when-issued position in the May 22, 1991 auction, and questions concerning customer authorization for the bid submitted in the name of Tudor in the April 25, 1991 auction.[7] The results of the internal investigation were reported to Feuerstein on August 6 and to other members of senior management of Salomon, including Gutfreund, Strauss, and Meriwether, on August 7.

On August 9, 1991, after consultation with and review by outside counsel, Salomon issued a press release stating that it had "uncovered irregularities and rule violations in connection with its submission of bids in certain auctions of Treasury securities." The release described several of the violations and stated that Salomon had suspended two managing directors on the Government Trading Desk and two other employees.

---

6. The bid submitted by Salomon in the February 7, 1991 auction was the result of a failed practical joke which employees of the firm had intended to play against a sales manager in the San Francisco office of Salomon who was scheduled to retire on the day after the auction.

7. As with the false bids submitted in the February 21, 1991 auction, the false bids in the December 27, 1990 and February 7, 1991 auctions were accompanied by fictitious sales of auction allocations received in response to the false bids to accounts in the names of customers and then back to Salomon, all at the auction price. In addition, in each of those instances, the normal procedures of Salomon were also overridden and confirmations for the fictitious transactions were not sent to the customers.

In telephone conversations on August 9, 1991 in which they reported on the results of the internal investigation, Gutfreund and Strauss disclosed to government officials for the first time that the firm had known of a false bid in a U.S. Treasury auction since late April of 1991. On August 14, 1991, Salomon issued a second press release which publicly disclosed for the first time that Gutfreund, Strauss and Meriwether had been "informed in late April by one of the suspended managing directors that a single unauthorized bid had been submitted in the February 1991 auction of five-year notes."

On Sunday, August 18, at a special meeting of the Board of Directors of Salomon Inc, Gutfreund and Strauss resigned their positions with Salomon and Salomon Inc, and Meriwether resigned his position with Salomon. On August 23, 1991, Feuerstein resigned his position as Chief Legal Officer of Salomon.

Following an intensive investigation, on May 20, 1992, the Commission filed a complaint in U.S. District Court for the Southern District of New York charging Salomon and its publicly-held parent, Salomon Inc, with numerous violations of the federal securities laws. Among other things, the complaint charged that Salomon had submitted or caused to be submitted ten false bids in nine separate auctions for U.S. Treasury securities between August of 1989 and May of 1991. The false bids alleged in the complaint totalled $15.5 billion and resulted in the illegal acquisition by Salomon of $9.548 billion of U.S. Treasury securities. The complaint alleged that submission of the bids allowed Salomon repeatedly to circumvent the limitations imposed by the Treasury Department on the amount of securities any one person or entity may obtain from auctions of U.S. Treasury securities.[8]

Simultaneously with the filing of the action, Salomon and Salomon Inc consented, without admitting or denying the allegations of the complaint, to the entry of a Final Judgment of Permanent Injunction and Other Relief. The Judgment required, among other things, that Salomon pay the amount of $290 million, representing a payment of $190 million to the United States Treasury as civil penalties and asset forfeitures and a payment of $100 million to establish a civil claims fund to be administered by a Fund Administrator appointed by the Court.

On May 20, 1992, the Commission also instituted and settled, pursuant to an Offer of Settlement submitted by Salomon, an administrative

8. The Commission's complaint also charged that Salomon and Salomon Inc had engaged in a number of other violations of the federal securities laws. The complaint alleged that the August 9, 1991 press release failed to state material facts by not disclosing that members of senior management had known of the false bid in the February 21, 1991 auction since late April, that Salomon had engaged in prearranged trades in U.S. Treasury securities in 1986 with other firms to create the false appearance that the firm had sustained approximately $168 million of trading losses for income tax purposes, that Salomon had engaged in a practice of overstating the amount of customer orders for debt securities of certain government-sponsored enterprises ("GSEs") in discussions with representatives of the GSEs prior to the primary distributions of those securities, and that the firm had engaged in a practice of purchasing medium term notes from corporate issuers as principal while representing to those issuers that the notes had been purchased as agent for a customer.

proceeding against the firm pursuant to Section 15(b) of the Exchange Act. In that proceeding, the Commission found that Salomon had failed, in connection with the facts described in this Order, reasonably to supervise a person subject to its supervision with a view to preventing violations of the federal securities laws.

Section 15(b)(4)(E) of the Exchange Act authorizes the Commission to impose sanctions against a broker-dealer if the firm has: failed reasonably to supervise, with a view to preventing violations [of federal securities laws], another person who commits such a violation, if such person is subject to his supervision.

Section 15(b)(6) of the Exchange incorporates Section 15(b)(4)(E) by reference and authorizes the Commission to impose sanctions for deficient supervision on individuals associated with broker-dealers.

The principles which govern this proceeding are well-established by the Commission's cases involving failure to supervise. The Commission has long emphasized that the responsibility of broker-dealers to supervise their employees is a critical component of the federal regulatory scheme. * * *

The supervisory obligations imposed by the federal securities laws require a vigorous response even to indications of wrongdoing. Many of the Commission's cases involving a failure to supervise arise from situations where supervisors were aware only of "red flags" or "suggestions" of irregularity, rather than situations where, as here, supervisors were explicitly informed of an illegal act.

Even where the knowledge of supervisors is limited to "red flags" or "suggestions" of irregularity, they cannot discharge their supervisory obligations simply by relying on the unverified representations of employees. Instead, as the Commission has repeatedly emphasized, "[t]here must be adequate follow-up and review when a firm's own procedures detect irregularities or unusual trading activity...." Moreover, if more than one supervisor is involved in considering the actions to be taken in response to possible misconduct, there must be a clear definition of the efforts to be taken and a clear assignment of those responsibilities to specific individuals within the firm.

As described above, in late April of 1991 three supervisors of Paul Mozer—John Meriwether, Thomas Strauss, and John Gutfreund—learned that Mozer had submitted a false bid in the amount of $3.15 billion in an auction of U.S. Treasury securities. Those supervisors learned that Mozer had said that the bid had been submitted to obtain additional securities for another trading area of the firm. They also learned that Mozer had contacted an employee of the customer whose name was used on the bid and falsely told that individual that the bid was an error. The supervisors also learned that the bid had been the subject of a letter from the Treasury Department to the customer and that Mozer had attempted to persuade the customer not to inform the Treasury Department that the bid had not been authorized. The supervisors were also informed by

Salomon's chief legal officer that the submission of the false bid appeared to be a criminal act. * * *

The need to take prompt action was all the more critical in view of the fact that the potential unlawful conduct had taken place in the market for U.S. Treasury securities. The integrity of that market is of vital importance to the capital markets of the United States, as well as to capital markets worldwide, and Salomon occupied a privileged role as a government-designated primary dealer. The failure of the supervisors to take vigorous action to address known misconduct by the head of the firm's Government Trading Desk caused unnecessary risks to the integrity of this important market. * * *

NOTES

1. Mozer's purchases were squeezing other dealers in the market who had sold the Treasury securities short. They had to pay Salomon Brothers higher prices when it came time for them to buy-in those securities because Mozer controlled a substantial portion of the supply for those issues. Mozer was fined $1.1 million and imprisoned. *See generally* Martin Mayer, Nightmare on Wall Street, Salomon Brothers and the corruption of the Marketplace (1993) (describing these events).

2. John Meriwhether went on to more infamy when Long Term Capital Management LP, a large hedge fund he headed, nearly collapsed in 1998. See Chapter 12.

3. Following the Mozer scandal, the Treasury changed its auction system and began using "Dutch auctions." In such an auction, the bidders will receive notes that all pay the same interest rate at the highest rate that will fill bids sufficient to dispose of the entire issue. Pursuant to authority in the Government Securities Act of 1993, the Treasury also adopted regulations in 1996 that required government securities dealers to report on their trading to the Department on demand. This allows the Treasury to determine the source and nature of bids in its auctions.

4. Cantor Fitzgerald LP, a large U.S government bond dealer, created an electronic network to trade those securities. It was competing with BrokerTec Global LLC, an electronic bond trading network. Cantor Fitzgerald lost 658 of its 960 employees in the September 11 attack on the World Trade Center, but the firm managed to survive. Tom Barbash, On Top of the World, Cantor Fitzgerald, Howard Lutnick, & 9/11 (2003); Gregory Zuckerman, Cantor, Hardest Hit, Is Able to Repair Itself, Relations with Families, Wall St. J., Mar. 8, 2002, at C1. In 2001, the firm conducted $45 trillion in transactions for over 700 institutional customers. www.cantor.com. Less successful was an electronic exchange for trading Treasury bond futures contracts created in a joint venture between Cantor Fitzgerald and the New York Board of Trade. Terzah Ewing, Slow U.S. Mix for Electronics and Derivatives, Wall St. J., Nov. 16, 1998, at C1.

5. The Treasury Department had further problems with its auctions in 2002. A bidder exceeded the limits for individual investors by placing a bid for one billion dollars in treasury securities and then defaulted on payment. Greg Ip & Gregory Zuckerman, U.S. Officials Investigate Bids Made for Bonds, Wall St. J., Feb. 20, 2002, at C1.

SECTION 3. REPOS AND REVERSE REPOS

Government securities also play a key role in specialized financing transactions called repurchase and reverse repurchase agreements. As described in the following case about repurchase agreements, a government security can serve as collateral for a cash loan. Later in the chapter we describe the reverse situation, in which it is the cash that serves as the collateral for a loan of the government securities. (Equity securities can also have value as collateral through securities lending operations.)

SECURITIES AND EXCHANGE COMMISSION v. MILLER

495 F.Supp. 465 (S.D.N.Y.1980).

CANNELLA, DISTRICT JUDGE.

After a bench trial, the Court finds that the plaintiff has failed to prove its entitlement to an injunction against the defendant pursuant to 15 U.S.C. § 77t(b), and, accordingly, judgment is entered for the defendant.

Jurisdiction is based upon the federal securities laws. 15 U.S.C. § 77t(b).

This is a Rule 10b–5 case involving allegations of deceptive conduct in connection with a highly specialized type of securities transaction, one which is used exclusively by a relatively small class of sophisticated investors. It is therefore essential to develop an understanding of the nature and purposes of such transactions, the market in which they occur, and the expectations of the persons and institutions that engage in them.

The transaction is commonly known as a "repurchase agreement," or "repo" for short.... It involves two parties, who, for reasons that may become clearer, may be deemed the "borrower" and "lender." Each agreement may also be viewed as comprising two distinguishable transactions, which, although agreed upon simultaneously, are performed at different times: (1) the borrower agrees to sell, and the lender agrees to buy, upon immediate payment and delivery, specified securities at a specified price; and (2) the borrower agrees to buy and the lender agrees to sell, with payment and delivery at a specified future date or, if the agreement is "open," on demand the same securities for the same price plus interest on the price. The parties customarily provide that any interest accruing on the securities between the dates of the initial purchase and subsequent "repurchase" remains the borrower's property.

From a purely economic perspective, therefore, a repo is essentially a short-term collateralized loan, and the parties to these transactions tend to perceive them as such.[9] The element of the transaction over which the most bargaining usually occurs is the interest rate. The parties customarily refer to the underlying securities as "collateral," and the risk of a change in the value of the collateral remains with the borrower, even though the lender "owns" it for the term of the agreement.

Why, then, are these deals structured as sales and repurchases rather than straight loans? The answer appears to be threefold: (1) certain regulations of the Federal Reserve Bank (the "Fed"), which treat repos differently from ordinary loans; (2) a desire to circumvent the U.C.C. requirements and other legal obstacles to using ordinary collateralized loans; and (3) market convention.

In order to understand the repo market, a brief discussion of the "federal funds" market may be helpful, since the development of repos is by and large related to that of federal funds transactions, which they resemble considerably. Since the early days of the Fed, member banks have traded reserve balances[10] as a means of allowing those with reserves below their legal requirements to borrow reserves from those with reserves in excess of their legal requirements. This enables the borrowing bank to meet its reserve requirements without having to sell securities from its portfolio, and at relatively lost cost. Since reserve deficits and surpluses can often be brief, most member banks prefer to borrow or lend reserves for relatively short periods, usually overnight, which is possible since such loans are effected over the federal wire. These transactions also benefit the lending banks, since any reserves in excess of their legal requirements are unnecessarily idle assets. And because of their short duration, they do not significantly impair the lending banks' liquidity. As with repos, such transactions are referred to as sales and purchases rather than loans. A borrowing of reserve balances which came to be known as "federal funds" or "fed funds" is usually characterized as a "purchase"

---

9. "The essence of a repo transaction is not that securities are being sold, it is that secured loans and borrowings are being made. Thus the securities 'sold' should be thought of simply as collateral." This does not mean, however, that a security interest under the U.C.C. is created thereby. * * *

10. Regulation D of the Federal Reserve Bank, 12 C.F.R. §§ 204.1–204.5 (1980), requires member banks to retain a certain specified percentage of their deposits as "reserves," which means, in essence, as uninvested funds. Reserves may be maintained in two forms, either as deposits by the member bank in its non-interest bearing reserve account at the Fed, or as currency and coin held by the member bank. 12 C.F.R. § 204.2 (1980). Since failure to maintain adequate reserves to meet requirements will subject a bank to penalties, id. § 204.3(b), (d), whereas reserves in excess of requirements constitute unnecessarily idle assets, banks generally aim to meet their requirements as closely as possible. Bank deposits fluctuate, however, and member banks often find themselves with an unanticipated reserve surplus or deficit. In order to make short-term adjustments to their reserve positions, therefore, banks developed the practice of trading reserve balances. To effect such a trade, a bank simply instructs the Fed to transfer funds from its reserve account to that of another member. These transfers, which are usually overnight loans, are commonly known as "fed funds" transactions.

with an agreement to resell, and a loan as a "sale" with an agreement to repurchase. * * *

Repos are different from federal funds transactions in essentially only two ways. First, fed funds by definition can be traded only by institutions whose unsecured loans to member banks are exempt from reserve requirements, whereas repos can be done by anyone with enough money. Second, a fed funds transaction is essentially an unsecured loan, whereas a repo is essentially a secured loan. In all other respects, however, they are identical. Both are for very short duration, usually overnight. Both are settled in immediately available funds. And since one day's interest is a rather small fraction, both are done only for large amounts of money. Nevertheless, because of the speed with which they must be concluded, they are both done on the basis of an oral contract subject to a written confirmation. * * *

Repos also contain provisions for the treatment of collateral, which, of course, need not be included in fed funds agreements. Repos customarily provide for a right of substitution, which means that the lender need not resell the identical securities purchased, but may substitute different securities of the same issue. Thus, the lender is not required to safekeep the collateral, but may sell, pledge, use or dispose of it in any manner for any purpose, so long as he resells acceptable securities on the repurchase date. Repos also customarily give added protection to the lender against fluctuation in the value of the collateral, by providing a "margin," that is, a spread between the value of the collateral and the amount of the loan. In other words, the lender will usually demand as collateral securities that are worth more than the amount of the loan.

For repos that last longer than a day, the lender may receive even further protection. "Term repos," which are those for a definite period longer than a day, and "open" repos, which are indefinite and may be terminated by either party on demand, customarily give the lender a right to demand additional collateral if the value of the original collateral declines significantly. In the event the borrower fails to honor such a demand, the lender may unilaterally terminate the agreement, sell the collateral on the open market, and hold the borrower liable for any difference between the amount of the loan plus interest and the recovery from the sale.

As noted above, the types of collateral most commonly used in repos are government and agency securities. One advantage of this is that the risk that the issuer will dishonor them is presumed to be nonexistent, and hence their value does not fluctuate significantly in periods of steady interest rates. Of course, like any other fixed-rate security, their value does fluctuate generally in relation to interest rates: when interest rates rise, their value declines; when interest rates decline, their value rises.

Another advantage of using government and agency securities is their ease of transfer. Most of them are not held in the form of certificates, but rather as bookkeeping entries at the Fed. Thus, they can be transferred without any physical deliveries. If a member bank wishes to transfer securities it owns to another bank, it simply wires instructions to the Fed, which debits one account and credits another. No certificates are necessary. Since the regional Federal Reserve Banks are all linked by wire, these transfers can be made almost instantaneously between member banks anywhere in the nation. And since immediately available funds may be transferred the same way, repos may be cleared very quickly. Regardless of the parties' locations, therefore, the funds and securities may be exchanged almost simultaneously shortly after they come to an agreement.

It is worth noting the different participants in the repo market. Most banks participate, both to adjust short-term cash and reserve positions, and as a continuing source of either funds or brief, highly liquid investments. Even the Federal Reserve Bank participates but only for the purpose of making short-term adjustments to the nation's money supply.

Among the important lenders in the repo market are large corporations and state and local governments. These institutions regularly find themselves with vast amounts of idle cash for brief, often indefinite periods of time. At one time, they would simply have kept such assets in a checking account as demand deposits, which earn no interest. Within the last ten or fifteen years, however, they have grown much more sophisticated about managing their liquid cash positions, and have increasingly turned to short-term instruments such as Treasury bills, commercial paper, negotiable certificates of deposit, and repos as a means of earning profit on them.

Of all of these short-term instruments, repos are by far the most flexible. They can be structured as overnight deals and "rolled over" to whatever extent the money is not needed. Or they can be set up as open agreements. In either case they provide exactly what a money manager needs most: liquidity; security in the form of collateral; and a good return. Consequently, they have come to be viewed by many as "income-generating substitutes for demand deposits at commercial banks."

Among the significant net borrowers in the repo market are government securities dealers, who use repos to finance their holdings. Their activities warrant a somewhat detailed treatment, since the defendant in this case was operating as a dealer in government and agency securities. Most dealers run highly leveraged operations, which means that their investment positions in the securities they hold are significantly larger than their net capital. In other words, the dealers tend to borrow a very high percentage of the money they invest. According to one source, dealers as a whole "borrow 95 cents or more of every dollar used to buy securities, pledging the securities bought as collateral." According to another, "(t)he typical dealer is running a highly levered operation in which securities held in position may total 500 or 600 times capital."

Repos are a very convenient way to leverage capital in order to take large positions in a security. And it is easy to see how a repo can be used to borrow against either a long or short position. Simply stated, "long" means taking the risks of owning, while "short" means taking the risks of owing. When a dealer wants to leverage long, he can buy a large amount of a security and finance nearly all of its purchase price by immediately "hanging it out" on repo in other words, by borrowing the money and using the securities as collateral. Using repos to leverage short is slightly more complicated. The dealer sells securities he does not own, then lends the proceeds of the sale in a repo, receiving as collateral the same type of securities he has sold.[11] He then delivers the collateral to the initial purchaser to complete the transaction. Since all the parts of these transactions can be cleared over the federal wire, it is possible to arrange to have everything clear nearly simultaneously, thus enabling the dealer to avoid tying up much of his own money for long.

Leveraging is nothing untoward or unusual, since it is, in effect, the way even banks make money. It is a means of increasing the potential net return on capital. A major source of dealer profits comes from correctly predicting market trends and then taking a highly leveraged position in accordance with that prediction. If the prediction proves accurate, the profits can be huge. If it proves wrong, however, so can the losses.

There are two other significant sources of dealer profit. One is known as "carry," which is the difference between the yield of a security and the interest rate charged on the money borrowed to purchase it. Short-term rates are often below long-term rates; consequently, when a dealer purchases government or agency securities and finances them by hanging them out on repo, he can earn the difference between the securities' yield and the repo rate.

The other source of dealer profit is a trading differential or "mark-up" similar to that of any wholesaler or middleman, which arises from the dealers' ability to buy more cheaply than they sell. The reason dealers can do this is that as they become known, and as they build up the volume of their business, their clients expect them to make a market in repos that is, to be ready to participate as either borrower or lender. Their position as market-makers enables them to command better rates on both sides of the transaction. Thus, a well-established dealer could make a profit by running a "matched book" that is, without taking a position long or short by, in effect, lending at higher rates than he borrows.

Of course, these sources of profit entail risks, an understanding of which is essential to this case. The principal risks to anyone trading in securities are: (1) a "credit risk" that one's trading partner will prove uncreditworthy; (2) a "price risk" that the securities involved will change

11. Market participants usually distinguish between "repos" and "reverse repos," or "reverses," but they are actually the same transactions viewed from different perspectives. Viewed from the position of the borrower, who first sells then "repurchases," the transaction is commonly called a "repurchase agreement" or "repo." Viewed from the perspective of the lender, who purchases then resells, the transaction is commonly called a "reverse repurchase agreement," or simply a "reverse." "Reversing securities in" means lending money and receiving the securities as collateral. Thus, using repos to leverage short is commonly called "reversing" or "running a reverse book." * * *

in value against one's expectations; and (3) a "liquidity risk" that one will need cash at a time when it is difficult or disadvantageous to sell the securities or borrow money. These are not rules of law, but of the market.

As to credit risk, the best way to minimize it is to deal only with persons you know, either through prior experience or good reputation, and by contractual protections such as margin where possible. One protects oneself against liquidity risk by prudently tending one's own garden, and by paying attention to the various indicators of trends in the cost and availability of money.

Price risk is more difficult to minimize, because it depends entirely on prognostication. As noted above, for government and agency securities, the price risk is essentially the risk that interest rates will change. In general, once a fixed-rate debt security has been issued, its market value will vary inversely to changes in interest rates.

A highly leveraged position is very exposed to price risk. For example, if a dealer is leveraged long at 100 times capital in a particular security, a 1% drop in value will wipe out his equity in that position. To illustrate, if a dealer has used $10,000 of his own money and $990,000 of borrowed money to purchase $1 million of a bond at par 100, he can sustain no more than a one point loss without having to put up additional capital: if the price drops to 99, the bonds will be worth only $990,000, precisely what he has borrowed on them, so that his $10,000 would be gone. For short positions, the computations are similar, except that losses arise when the securities' value increases.

"Carry" is also susceptible to the risk of a change in interest rates, but in a different way. As noted above, short-term rates are often below long-term rates. They are also more volatile, however, and often rise above long-term rates. When this happens, the carry is said to be negative, and anyone who has hung securities out on repo will suffer a daily net loss, since the yield on them will be below the rate of interest he has to pay for the money borrowed to buy them. There are roughly similar, although inverse risks to anyone who has taken a short position using repos.

Both of the effects of interest rate fluctuations just described can quickly drain a dealer's operating liquid assets. This is compounded by the likelihood that when interest rates rise, parties that have lent to the dealer will demand additional collateral on their loans, and when interest rates fall, those who have borrowed from him will demand additional money for their collateral.

Among dealers in government and agency securities are three special categories that are pertinent to this case. Certain dealers are known as "primary dealers," which the Fed describes as "institutions which buy new government securities directly from the Treasury and are ready to buy or sell outstanding U.S. government and agency securities." These, then, are the major marketmakers. Approximately thirty of these primary dealers regularly report their trading activities and positions to the Federal Reserve Bank of New York, and are therefore known as "reporting dealers." Finally, there is a group whom market participants call "recognized dealers," which are those reporting dealers with whom the Fed trades when it wishes to buy and sell government securities and do repos as part of its open market operations.

According to the Fed, any dealer, upon becoming a "significant" market participant, may "contact the New York Fed and begin reporting activity and positions informally." Thereafter, if it is satisfied with the dealer's capitalization, trading volume and management, it will add the dealer to its regular reporting list, and may subsequently establish a trading relationship. Today, as well as in 1975, when the events underlying this action transpired, nearly all of the "recognized dealers" had their principal offices within whispering distance of the New York Fed. The defendant in this action had his there as well, although he was not a primary dealer, and hence neither a reporting nor recognized dealer either. * * *

The Commission's theory of the instant case is that Miller and Financial failed to keep accounting records that would have enabled them to ascertain Financial's net assets and liabilities, and that such failure, and their failure to disclose that fact to their repo customers, constitute violations of section 10(b) and Rule 10b–5. The Court finds, however, that Miller's records were sufficient to enable him to monitor all of Financial's assets and liabilities, and determine its financial position, on any given day. * * * [Although the court did find some misrepresentations, it concluded an injunction was not justified]

The daily trading volume for repo transactions grew to be six times greater than that of the underlying Treasury securities. H. R. Rep. No. 102–722, pt. 1 (1992). There were, however, serious problems in the repo market that led to the enactment of the Government Securities Act of 1986 ("GSA"), Pub. L. No. 99–571, 100 Stat. 3208 (Oct. 28. 1986):

> Prior to passage of the GSA, the regulations of the government securities market was largely limited to the rules governing Treasury auctions pursuant to the Liberty Bond Act of 1917 and the general antifraud provisions of the federal securities laws. The Liberty Bond Act granted authority to the Treasury to issue securities and administer the federal debt. Treasury was also given authority to prescribe terms and conditions for the issuance and sale of these securities and to enforce these rules. In addition, Section 10(b) of the Exchange Act and Section 17(a) of the Securities Act, which apply to "any person," proscribe manipulative or deceptive devices or contrivances in connection with transactions in any security.

> Prior to 1986, only those dealers in government securities who also dealt in non-exempt securities were regulated by the [Securities & Exchange] Commission. Banks dealing in government securities were

regulated by the appropriate bank regulatory authorities. However, dealers who traded only in government securities were not subject to any direct regulatory oversight.

The failure of several unregulated government securities dealers in the early 1980s demonstrated that the minimal regulation of the government securities market that then existed provided inadequate protections to investors. Between 1977 and 1985, 10 government securities dealers failed, causing substantial investor losses and shaking public confidence in the integrity of the market. As a result of the failure of one of these firms, ESM Government Securities Inc. of Fort Lauderdale, Florida, investors lost an estimated $300 million, triggering a run on 71 Ohio thrifts. The temporary closing of these financial institutions in turn precipitated a sharp rise in the price of gold and a decline in the value of the dollar. The failures of these government securities dealers and the absence of regulatory oversight with respect to such dealers led the Congress to enact the GSA.

As a result of enactment of the GSA, for the first time, all brokers and dealers engaged in government securities transactions were subject to a limited scheme of government regulation. To carry out the mandate of the GSA to lessen the potential for dealer failures, and to protect customers funds and securities in the event of a failure, Treasury was authorized to promulgate rules with respect to capital adequacy standards for government securities dealers, the acceptance of custody and use of customers securities, the carrying and use of customers deposits or credit balances, and the transfer and control of government securities subject to repurchase agreements and similar transactions. In furtherance of this limited regulatory scheme, Treasury was authorized to promulgate rules concerning recordkeeping, financial reporting, and auditing of government securities brokers and dealers. Many of these rules were designed specifically to improve the safety of repo and hold-in-custody repo transactions.

The rules promulgated by Treasury pursuant to this authority provided by the GSA duplicated or were very similar to certain rules already in place for financial institutions and registered brokers and dealers. Thus, the GSAs greatest practical impact was that it applied a limited regulatory scheme to the previously unregistered brokers and dealers (i.e., those who dealt exclusively in government securities).

In addition, the GSA required previously unregistered government securities brokers and dealers to register with the [Securities and Exchange] Commission and join a self-regulatory organization (SRO). Firms already registered with the Commission as general securities brokers or dealers under Section 15 of the Exchange Act or as municipal securities brokers or dealers under Section 15B of the Exchange Act were required to notify the Commission if they were conducting government securities transactions. Likewise, financial institutions that engaged in government securities broker or dealer activities were required to notify their appropriate regulatory agencies. Certain specific enforcement responsibilities were assigned to those federal agencies that had existing authority over entities participating in the government securities market (the Commission for registered brokers and dealers and the bank regulators for financial institutions). The Commission also was assigned authority for the previously unregulated dealers.

In addition, the GSA provided to the National Association of Securities Dealers, Inc. (NASD) authority to adopt rules pertaining to advertising practices by its members who are government securities brokers and dealers, and it added to the Commissions general authority over clearing agencies under Section 17A of the Exchange Act authority over clearing organizations that clear transactions in government securities. Finally, the GSA expressly left intact the Commissions general antifraud authority over government securities transactions by any person.

H. R. Rep. No. 102–722, pt. 1 (1992).

———————

The ESM failure mentioned in the above House report shook confidence in the banking system and other failures caused concern. Drysdale Government Securities, Inc. was found to have been running a complex Ponzi scheme using the accrued coupon interest on securities sold under reverse repos. That interest was not reflected in the original sale and was used by Drysdale to meet preexisting obligations and for speculation. The result was $300 million in losses to customers. Manufacturers Hanover Trust Co. v. Drysdale Securities Corp., 801 F.2d 13 (2d Cir. 1986), cert. denied, 479 U.S. 1066, 107 S.Ct. 952, 93 L.Ed.2d 1001 (1987). The failure of Bevell, Bresler & Schulman Asset Management Corp. caused another $235 million in losses. It had entered into repos without proper collateralization in order to cover large trading losses of an affiliate. Regulation of the Government Securities Market, Report by the Securities & Exchange Commission to the House Subcommittee on Telecommunications, Consumer Protection and Finance of the Committee on Energy and Commerce 12 (June 20, 1985).

———————

Reverse Repurchase Agreements

Sometimes the economic logic of a transaction runs the other way—a market participant wants to hold a particular government security and is willing to induce the holder of such a security to part with it by collateralizing the loan of that security with cash. In the context of government securities, this is called a reverse repurchase agreement and is engaged in most frequently by primary dealers. Typically, the reason that a primary dealer develops demand for a particular government security is because, having sold the security short, the dealer must now settle with its purchaser but does not want to buy the security outright, perhaps because its price has not declined as expected. Just as in a repurchase agreement, the two parties enter into back-to-back purchase and sale agreements, for a term of at least one day. The time between starting and unwinding the arrangement is the term of the "loan." The primary dealer offers to collateralize the "loan" of the security during this term with cash.

Ordinarily, the cash lender would demand a market rate of interest on this cash collateral. To induce a holder of the desired security to part with it, however, the cash lender accepts a below-market rate of interest on the cash collateral, the so called repurchase rate. This financing spread sweetens the deal from the point of view of the cash-lender, securities-borrower. At the end of the deal, the cash lender returns the principal of the cash loan with the discounted amount of interest. When dealing with equity securities, where it also occurs due to short-selling, this practice is referred to as securities lending.

FEDERAL RESERVE BANK OF NEW YORK IT'S 8:00 A.M. DO YOU KNOW WHERE YOUR COLLATERAL IS? BASIC INFORMATION ON REPURCHASE TRANSACTIONS.

Repurchase Agreements . . .

Repurchase agreements (or "repos") have become a popular cash management tool for investors looking to earn a return on idle cash. In a repo, an investor purchases a government security from a dealer (usually a bank or securities firm) which in turn promises to repurchase the obligation after a specified period of time. When repurchasing the security, the dealer pays the investor the original price plus an agreed-upon return.

Overnight or other short-term repos provide both liquidity and a market rate of return But repos have their potential dangers as well, if not used carefully. Some investors have lost their money, or its use for a time, when a dealer has defaulted or declared bankruptcy. Prudent business practices are necessary to reduce the transaction's risk to an acceptable level.* * *

A Bird in Hand . . .

An investor who exchanges money for securities should have control over the securities.

You or your custodian should not pay for a repurchase agreement until the securities are received.

Custody of the securities should be with someone in whom you have full confidence. Many investors prefer that custody be with someone besides the seller, such as their custodian bank* * *

A Stitch In Time . . .

Consider carefully how much margin each transaction warrants.

In most cases, the market value of the securities you receive should exceed the cash you provide—that is, you should take "margin." Receiving securities with a market value (including accrued interest) equal to the purchase price looks adequate on the surface, but it leaves no room for a drop in market prices or protection of the higher payment due on the repurchase date.* * * *

Here Today, Gone ...

Develop standards for choosing your trading partners and review their performance regularly.

Know the people you are dealing with and gather credit information about their firm. This should include information about the background of the firm and the capabilities of its management. Check references and seek advice from experienced professionals.

Sometimes dealer firms have a number of affiliates, some with greater financial strength than others. Be sure of exactly who your counterparty is.

Request reports about the financial condition of the firm on a regular basis and certification of conformity with accepted capital standards. Make sure you have annual audited statements of the firm which is your counterparty* * *

The Pen Is Mightier ...

Have a written repurchase agreement.

Get experienced legal advice.

A written agreement should describe the nature of the transaction, the terms and conditions of the contracts and the rights of all the parties. The industry is currently working toward development of a standard repo contract.

Your agreement should include provisions that give you, the investor, control of the securities during the term of the repo.

Include the formula to be sued for calculating the value of the transaction, taking into account accrued interest on the underlying securities and accrued interest on the repo.

Adjustments in terms and conditions for coupon payments that occur prior to the termination of the repo are appropriate.

If the market value of the securities falls, the contract should require the dealer firm to put up more margin and should permit you to sell the securities if your counterparty does not meet such a margin call or defaults on other terms of the contract.* * *

NOTES

1. A variation on the repo is the "dollar roll":

Dollar rolls, which are a form of collateralized short-term financing where the collateral consists of mortgage securities, perform a function analogous to that provided by the repo (repurchase agreement) market..... Unlike a reverse repurchase agreement, which generally requires redelivery of exactly the same securities that are delivered during the first leg of the transaction, a dollar roll is a simultaneous purchase and sale of substantially similar ... securities for different settlement dates. The dealer, who is said to "roll in" the securities received, is not required to deliver the identical securities, only securities that meet the Good Delivery Guidelines. Thus, the investor may assume some risk because the characteristics of the [securities] ... delivered to the investor may be less favorable than the [securities] ... the investor delivered to the dealer.

SEC, Dept. Treasury & Office of Fed. Housing Enterprise Oversight, Staff Report: Enhancing Disclosures in the Mortgage Backed Securities Market, pt. E.4 (Jan. 2003).

2. A fraudulent practice in the securities area is parking, which has some appearances of a repo transaction. In a case involving "parking" to obtain false tax losses, the Second Circuit defined "parking" as:

[A] purported transfer of ownership in securities combined with a secret agreement providing the "seller" with the right to repurchase them at a later date. The "seller" receives the tax benefits of a loss realized by the "sale"; the "buyer" is compensated for the "cost of carrying" the securities. Since the agreement to resell ensures that the "seller" never loses control of the securities, the government considers "parking" a form of tax and securities fraud.

Yoshikawa v. SEC, 192 F.3d 1209, 1214 (9th Cir.1999) (describing the holding of the court in, United States v. Jones, 900 F.2d 512, 515 (2d Cir.), *cert. denied*, 498 U.S. 846, 111 S.Ct. 131, 112 L.Ed.2d 99 (1990)). "Parking" has also been described by the SEC as "the sale of securities subject to an agreement or understanding that the securities will be repurchased by the seller at a later time and at a price which leaves the economic risk on the seller." *In re Barlage,* 63 S.E.C. 1060, 1996 WL 733756, at 1 n. 2 (S.E.C.1996), noted *supra* in Yoshikawa v. SEC, 192 F.3d 1209, 1214 (9th Cir. 1999). The Court in *Yoshikawa* held that securities "parking" is, at a minimum, comprised of the following elements:

(1) a pre-arrangement to sell and then buy back securities (to conceal true ownership);

(2) on the same, or substantially the same, terms (thus keeping the market risk entirely on the seller);

(3) for a bad-faith purpose, accomplished through a sham transaction in which nominal title is transferred to the purported buyer while the economic incidents of ownership are left with the purported seller.

192 F.2d at 1214 (footnote omitted). A key distinction between parking and a legitimate repo transaction is the third element listed by the court.

3. The Treasury market was again hit by concerns of manipulation in 2006 after some controversial trading involving repos by the primary dealers. All of the twenty-two primary dealers were then called before the Interagency Working Group on Market Surveillance that includes representatives from the Federal Reserve Board, the SEC, the CFTC, and the Treasury Department to discuss that concern. The New York Federal Reserve Bank subsequently announced that no primary dealer would be allowed to hold more than 35 percent of any single Treasury issue. Katie Benner, A Whiff of Scandal Threatens the Treasury Repurchase Market, Fortune Magazine, Dec. 11, 2006, at p. 40.

4. The two major kinds of repo activity are specials trading and a general collateral matched book. A particular security is said to go on 'special' when demand for it increases, typically due to short sale activity in that security that creates demand to cover by borrowing the security. A borrower of a security on special will charge less then a market rate of interest on the cash used to collateralize the securities loan. In contrast, most repo activity consists of more generic collateral in which a dealer keeps a matched book of loans and borrowing that permit for substitution of collateral from among a basket of comparable securities. See generally Frank J. Fabozzi, ed., Securities Lending & Repurchase Agreements (Fabozzi, 1997).

5. The repo market was a key concern during the financial crisis in 2007–2009. Bear Stearns, a systemically important broker-dealer failed in March 2008 after its overnight funding in the repo market dried up because of concerns over its liquidity. The firm was rescued through the combined efforts of the federal government and JPMorgan Chase. More spectacularly, another giant firm, Lehman Brothers, failed in September 2008, touching off a market panic. The Lehman Brothers bankruptcy examiner found that:

> Lehman's business model was not unique; all of the major investment banks that existed at the time followed some variation of a high risk, high leverage model that required the confidence of counterparties to sustain. Lehman maintained approximately $700 billion of assets, and corresponding liabilities, on capital of approximately $25 billion. But the assets were predominantly long term, while the liabilities were largely short term. Lehman funded itself through the short term repo markets and had to borrow tens or hundreds of billions of dollars in those markets each day from counterparties to be able to open for business. Confidence was critical. The moment that repo counterparties were to lose confidence in Lehman and decline to roll over its daily funding, Lehman would be unable to fund itself and continue to operate.

> [That is what happened to Lehman Brothers in September 2008 and it became the largest ever bankruptcy]. So too with the other investment banks, had they continued business as usual. It is no coincidence that no major investment bank still exists with that model.

In re Lehman Brothers Holdings, Inc., 08–13555 (JMP) Bank. (S.D.N.Y.) report of Anton R. Valukas, Examiner, March 11, 2010, at p. 3.

SECTION 4. STRIPPED SECURITIES— TIGRS & CATS

ZERO COUPON TREASURY INVESTMENT GROWTH RECEIPTS SERIES 14 SERIAL TIGRS DUE SEMIANNUALLY FEBRUARY 15, 1985–AUGUST 15, 2004. PRINCIPAL TIGRS DUE AUGUST 15, 2004.

Offering Circular Supplement (to Offering Circular dated March 13, 1984).

Treasury Investment Growth Receipts, Series 14 ("TIGR's") evidence ownership of future interest and principal payments on United States Treasury 13 ¾% Bonds due August 15, 2004 (the "Bonds"), held or to be held by Manufacturers Hanover Trust Company (the "custodian") for the benefit of TIGR owners. TIGR's will be offered from time to time on a continuous basis in amounts and at prices determined at the time of sale. Prior to the delivery of any TIGR's offered hereby, the aggregate principal amount of Bonds relating thereto will be deposited with the Custodian. It is anticipated that, prior to the termination of this offering, at least $100,000,000 principal amount of Bonds will be deposited with the Custodian and the TIGR's relating thereto delivered.

The obligor with respect to TIGR's is The United States of America.

Separate maturities of TIGR's (the "Serial TIGR's") are offered with respect to each semiannual interest payment on the Bonds up to and including August 15, 2004, when the Bonds mature. The Serial TIGR's offered hereby have 40 separate maturities due semiannually from February 15, 1985 to August 15, 2004. The Serial TIGR's due February 15, 1985 evidence ownership of an interest payment on the Bonds for a long coupon period and therefore will be in an aggregate face amount in excess of the other 39 maturities of Serial TIGR's. The principal of the Bonds is offered separately (the "Principal TIGR's"). The Principal TIGR's offered hereby mature on August 15, 2004. There will not be any payments on TIGR's prior to their maturities. The TIGR's will not be redeemable prior to their maturities. See "Summary and Supplemental Information" herein and "Description of Treasury Investment Growth Receipts" in the accompanying Offering Circular dated March 13, 1984 (the "Offering Circular"), of which this Offering Circular Supplement forms a part.

The face amount of each TIGR will be the payment to be received thereon. The TIGR's are being offered at substantial discounts from their face amounts. See "Income Tax Consequences" in the Offering Circular for a discussion of the United States tax treatment of TIGR's, including the implications of original issue discount, and for a discussion of state and local taxation of TIGR's.

Treasury Investment Growth Receipts and TIGR's are trademarks of Merrill Lynch & Co., Inc.

The TIGR's are being offered by the undersigned in face amount denominations of $1,000 and integral multiples of $1,000 at varying prices which will be determined at the time of sale based upon market conditions at such time. In addition, TIGR's may be offered and sold to certain dealers at prices less selling concessions to be determined by the undersigned.

Merrill Lynch, Pierce, Fenner & Smith Incorporated intends to maintain markets for TIGR's but is not obligated to do so. * * *

Each series of Treasury Investment Growth Receipts ("TIGR's") will evidence ownership of future interest and principal payments on the specific United State Treasury obligations (the "Bonds") referred to in the Supplement relating to such series. Such Bonds will be held in a custody account by the Custodian pursuant to the terms of a custody agreement, as amended or supplemented from time to time (the "Custody Agreement"), between the Custodian and Merrill Lynch, Pierce, Fenner & Smith Incorporated ("Merrill Lynch"), for itself and as representative of other purchasers of the Bonds relating to such series, if any, as set forth in the Supplement relating to such series.

The TIGR's will be issued as Serial TIGR's and either as Principal or Callable TIGR's, depending on whether the Bonds relating to such series of TIGR's are subject to redemption by the United States prior to their maturity. Payment with respect to each maturity of Serial TIGR's will consist of the interest payment due on the Bonds on the maturity date of such Serial TIGR's. There will not be any payments on Serial TIGR's prior to their respective maturities. Payment with respect to any Principal TIGR will consist of the principal payment due on the Bonds to which such Principal TIGR relates. Payment with respect to any Callable TIGR will commence on the first semiannual interest payment date following the first optional redemption date of the Bonds to which such Callable TIGR relates and will consist of all interest payments subsequent to such first optional redemption date and the principal payment due on the Bonds to which such Callable TIGR relates. The face amount of each TIGR will be the payment or payments to be received thereon.

Owners of TIGR's will have all the rights and privileges of owners of the underlying Bonds, except that, in the absence of a default on such Bonds by the United States of America, the Custodian will be required to hold the Bonds on behalf of TIGR holders. Each TIGR holder, as the real party in interest, will have the right upon default on the underlying Bonds to proceed directly and individually against the United States in whatever manner is deemed to be appropriate. In such event the holder will not be required to act in concert with other holders of TIGR's or with the Custodian. The Custodian will not be authorized to assert the rights and privileges of TIGR holders and will have no duty to do so.

The sole obligor with respect to TIGR's will be the United States of America, the issuer of the Bonds. Neither the Custodian nor Merrill Lynch nor any other firms named in the accompanying Supplement, if any, will be responsible for the payments due on the TIGR's, except that the Custodian must apply all payments received in respect of the Bonds to the TIGR;s to which they relate, without making any deduction for its own fees or expenses.

The TIGR's

The TIGR's will be issued as Serial TIGR's and either as Principal or Callable TIGR's. The TIGR's of each series will be available only in registered form in the face amount denominations set forth in "Form and Denominations" under "Summary and Supplemental Information" in the Supplement relating to such series. The TIGR's will be transferable and exchangeable as provided in "Transfer and Exchange of TIGR's".

Serial TIGR's. Each Serial TIGR evidences ownership of a direct interest in one of the semiannual interest payments due on the Bonds to which such series relates up to and including the first optional redemption date in the event the underlying Bonds are subject to redemption, or up to and including the maturity of the Bonds in the event the underlying Bonds are not subject to redemption. There will be any payments on Serial TIGR's nor will Serial TIGR's be redeemable prior to their maturities. At maturity each holder will receive a single payment of the face amount of such TIGR.

Principal TIGR's. Principal TIGR's will be issued only in connection with a series of TIGR's with respect to which the underlying Bonds are not subject to redemption prior to their maturity. Principal TIGR's evidence ownership of the principal of such Bonds. At maturity each holder of Principal TIGR's will receive a single payment of the face amount of such TIGR.

Callable TIGR's. Callable TIGR's will be issued only in connection with a series of TIGR's with respect to which the underlying Bonds are subject to redemption prior to their maturity. Callable TIGR's evidence ownership of the principal of such Bonds payable at maturity and each of the seminannual interest payments due on such Bonds commencing on the first interest payment date following the first optional redemption date. The face amount of each Callable TIGR will be the aggregate of all such payments to be received thereon unless such Callable TIGR is redeemed.

If Callable TIGR's are redeemed, their holders will receive a payment equal to the principal portion of the face amount of such Callable TIGR's plus any interest payment represented by such Callable TIGR's maturing on the date of redemption. The redemption prices as percentages of face amount outstanding and yields to each redemption date for such Callable TIGR's will be set forth in the Supplement with respect to any series in which Callable TIGR's are issued.

If the Bonds underlying any series of TIGR's are called for redemption prior to their maturity, the Callable TIGR's of such series will be redeemed as nearly as practicable on the same terms. See "The Bonds".

In such event, the Callable TIGR's will be redeemed, in whole or in part as applicable, on not less than 90 nor more than 120 days' prior notice. In the event of partial redemption, the Custodian will, unless otherwise specified in the Supplement, select Callable TIGR's for redemption, or portions thereof, in such manner as the Custodian deems fair and appropriate and which will provide for redemption of portions of Callable TIGR's not smaller than the smallest authorized denomination; provided, however, if any of the Bonds selected for redemption are in certificate form to which particular TIGR's relate, such TIGR's will be designated by the Custodian for redemption prior to selection of other TIGR's for redemption.

NOTES

1. The 13.75 percent interest rate on the above TIGR was a reflection of inflation concerns at time the government bonds were issued. Since the TIGR is a zero coupon bond, the Internal Revenue Service will tax the holders as if they were in fact receiving the interest payment imputed from the discount each year, an amount referred to as "original issue discount" ("OID"). See Chapter 4. The TIGR is still attractive for tax advantaged situations such as a retirement account.

2. A product similar to the he Merrill Lynch TIGR was the Certificate of Accrual on Treasury Securities ("CAT") developed by Salomon Brothers, Inc. The Treasury Department also began offering its own Separate Trading of Registered Interest and Principal of Securities ("STRIPS"):

> STRIPS, also known as zero-coupon securities, are Treasury securities that don't make periodic interest payments. Market participants create STRIPs by separating the interest and principal parts of a Treasury note or bond. For example, a 10–year Treasury note consists of 20 interest payments—one every six months for 10 years—and a principal payment payable at maturity. When this security is "stripped," each of the 20 interest payments and the principal payment become separate securities and can be held and transferred separately. STRIPS can only be bought and sold through a financial institution, broker, or dealer and held in the commercial book-entry system.

The Basics of Treasury Securities, WWW.U.S.TreasuryDirect (Feb. 2003). By allowing the payment of principal and interest components of U.S. Treasury bonds to be registered separately, STRIPS facilitated the TIGR and CAT programs. Merrill Lynch and Salomon Brothers profit from these transactions by the difference between the price they pay for the U.S. government bonds and the price received from the sale of the TIGRS and CATs plus expenses. TIGRS and CATs are negotiable and may be bought and sold in a secondary market maintained by Merrill Lynch, Salomon Brothers and others. David J. Gilberg, Regulation of New Financial Instruments Under the Federal Securities and Commodities Laws, 39 Vand. L. Rev. 1599, 1667–1668 (1986). As demonstrated by the next case, that secondary market offers another opportunity to profit.

ETTINGER v. MERRILL LYNCH, PIERCE, FENNER & SMITH, INC.

835 F.2d 1031 (3d Cir.1987).

SEITZ, CIRCUIT JUDGE.

In May and June 1984, Ettinger purchased from Merrill Lynch several zero-coupon bonds, which Merrill Lynch calls TIGR's.[12] It is undisputed that Merrill Lynch is a market maker in these securities.[13] After selling these securities several months later, Ettinger filed this action in the district court alleging that Merrill Lynch charged excessive and unconscionable mark-ups on the sale of these zero-coupon bonds and failed to disclose this compensation in violation of section 10(b) of the Securities Exchange Act of 1934, 15 U.S.C. § 78j(b) (1982), and Rule 10b–5 promulgated thereunder, 17 C.F.R. § 240.10b–5 (1984). * * *

We first address Merrill Lynch's contention that its compliance with the disclosure requirements of Rule 10b–10, 17 C.F.R. § 240.10b–10 (1984), exempted it from liability under section 10(b) and Rule 10b–5. Section 10(b) of the Securities Exchange Act of 1934 makes it unlawful to utilize "any manipulative or deceptive device or contrivance" in connection with the purchase or sale of securities. * * *

The SEC has established through its enforcement actions the principle that charging undisclosed excessive commissions constitutes fraud. "This fraud is avoided only by charging a price which bears a reasonable relation to the prevailing price or disclosing such information as will permit the customer to make an informed judgment upon whether or not he will complete the transaction." *In re Duker & Duker,* 6 S.E.C. 386, 388–89 (1939). The SEC has continually adhered to this position, *see, e.g., In re Associated Secs. Corp.,* 40 S.E.C. 10, 14 (1960), which has also received judicial approval. *Charles Hughes & Co. v. Securities & Exch. Comm'n,* 139 F.2d 434, 437 (1943), *cert. denied,* 321 U.S. 786, 64 S.Ct. 781, 88 L.Ed. 1077 (1944). Although these cases were proceedings to revoke broker-dealers' registrations taken by the SEC pursuant to section 15(b) of the Securities Exchange Act of 1934, 15 U.S.C. § 78o (b), we

---

12. Zero-coupon bonds are debt securities on which no interest is paid prior to maturity. At maturity, a one-time payment incorporating the principal repayment and accrued interest is made. These securities are therefore sold at a discount from face value. TIGR's (Treasury Investment Growth Receipts) are a proprietary product of Merrill Lynch. TIGR's consist of United States Treasury bonds that have been repackaged by Merrill Lynch into zero-coupon securities. Specifically, a TIGR is a receipt that evidences ownership of a future payment of interest or principal on Treasury bonds which are purchased by Merrill Lynch and are held by a custodian for the benefit of the TIGR holder.

13. A market maker is defined as a dealer "who, with respect to a security, holds himself out ... as being willing to buy and sell such security for his own account on a regular or continuous basis." 15 U.S.C. § 78c(a)(38) (1982).

believe that they illuminate the SEC's view as to what constitutes fraud. They therefore have applicability in the context of private actions brought under the anti-fraud provisions of Rule 10b–5.

Thus, we have no doubt that, at least prior to the enactment of Rule 10b–10 in 1977, the alleged fraudulent actions of Merrill Lynch would have been actionable under section 10(b) and Rule 10b–5.

This brings us to Merrill Lynch's contention, accepted by the district court, that the language and history of Rule 10b–10 show an intention to exempt brokers from liability under Rule 10b–5 for not disclosing allegedly excessive mark-ups in transactions by market makers in debt securities, such as Merrill Lynch's sale of TIGR's to Ettinger. Rule 10b–10 was first proposed by the SEC in 1976 and was adopted in slightly revised form in 1977. Rule 10b–10 is entitled "Confirmation of Transactions" and sets forth various disclosures that a broker or dealer must make to customers in writing at or before the completion of certain transactions.[14] In its release announcing the adoption of this rule, the SEC stated:

> The rule does not attempt to set forth all possible categories of material information to be disclosed by broker-dealers in connection with a particular transaction in securities. Rule 10b–10 only mandates the disclosure of information which can generally be expected to be material. Of course, in particular circumstances, additional information may be material and disclosure may be required.

Securities Exchange Act Release No. 13,508 [1977–1978 Decisions] Fed. Sec.L.Rep. (CCH) ¶ 81,143, at 87,930 n. 28 (May 5, 1977).

Subsequent to the initial adoption of Rule 10b–10, the SEC released various proposed amendments to the rule and adopted some of these amendments in modified form in light of public comments. In 1978, the SEC brought within the rule dealers acting as "riskless principals" (only dealers acting as agents were covered originally) in transactions involving equity securities; the SEC specifically deferred a decision on the applicability of the rule to transactions in debt securities. Securities Exchange Act

---

14. In 1984 when the transactions at issue in this case occurred, Rule 10b–10 provided in pertinent part:

(a) It shall be unlawful for any broker or dealer to effect for or with the account of a customer any transaction in, or to induce the purchase or sale by such customer of, any security (other than U.S. Savings Bonds or municipal securities) unless such broker or dealer, at or before completion of such transaction, gives or sends to such customer written notification disclosing:

. . .

(4) In the case of a transaction in a debt security effected exclusively on the basis of dollar price: (i) The dollar price at which the transaction was effected, and (ii) The yield to maturity calculated from the dollar price. . . .

(5) In the case of a transaction in a debt security effected on the basis of yield: (i) The yield at which the transaction was effected including the percentage amount . . . (ii) The dollar price calculated from the yield at which the transaction was effected. . . .

(8) If he is acting as principal for his own account: (i) The amount of any mark-up, mark-down, or similar remuneration received in a transaction in an equity security if he is not a market maker in that security . . . (ii) In the case of a transaction in an equity security, whether he is a market maker in that security. . . .

Release No. 15,219 [1978 Decisions] Fed.Sec.L.Rep. (CCH) ¶ 81,746 (Oct. 6, 1978). The SEC noted,

> [A] market maker may often engage in transactions that effectively offset one another, giving the appearance of being "riskless" principal transactions, even though the market maker did not structure any particular pair of transactions as offsetting, "riskless" principal transactions. As a result, the problem of identifying when a "riskless" principal disclosure might have to be made could create substantial practical and interpretive difficulties for a bona fide market maker. For that reason, the [SEC] has determined to provide an exemption from the riskless principal disclosure requirement for ... market makers....

Id. at 80,974. The limited scope of this exemption from the strictures of Rule 10b–10 for market makers is highlighted by *In re Alstead, Dempsey & Co.,* Securities Exchange Act Release No. 20,805 [1984 Decisions] Fed.Sec.L.Rep. (CCH) ¶ 83,607 (Apr. 5, 1984). In this disciplinary proceeding against a broker-dealer who charged excessive commissions in over 300 transactions in equity securities in which he acted as a market maker, the SEC concluded that the market maker "violated the antifraud provisions of Section 17(a)(1) of the Securities Act *and* Section 10(b) of the Securities Exchange Act and Rule 10b–5 thereunder." *Id.* at 86,742 (emphasis added).

In 1982, the SEC withdrew a proposed amendment to Rule 10b–10 that it had published in 1978. Securities Exchange Act Release No. 15,220 [1978 Decisions] Fed.Sec.L.Rep. (CCH) ¶ 81,747 (Oct. 6, 1978). The amendment would have required broker-dealers (other than market makers) engaging in "riskless principal" transactions in non-municipal debt securities to disclose the mark-ups. *Id.* at 80,980. In announcing the withdrawal of the proposal, the SEC stated that the amendment "would not achieve the purposes [of deterring pricing abuse] at an acceptable cost and that there are alternative ways of achieving the same goals with fewer adverse side effects." Securities Exchange Act Release No. 18,987 [1982 Decisions] Fed.Sec.L.Rep. (CCH) ¶ 83,245 at 85,259 (Aug. 20, 1982). The Commission, however, stressed that it would "maintain close scrutiny to prevent excessive mark-ups and take enforcement actions where appropriate." *Id.*

On the same day, the SEC proposed an amendment to Rule 10b–10 requiring the disclosure of yield information. Securities Exchange Act Release No. 18,988 [1982 Decisions] Fed.Sec.L.Rep. (CCH) ¶ 83,246 (Aug. 20, 1982). The SEC labeled this proposal "a means of discouraging potentially deceptive practices." *Id.* at 85,264. Finally, in 1983, the SEC adopted the requirement that yield be disclosed and indicated that "[y]ield has been characterized as the single most important piece of information to an investor in the context of a transaction in debt securities." Securities

Exchange Act Release No. 19,687 [1982–1983 Decisions] Fed.Sec.L.Rep. (CCH) ¶ 83,341, at 85,893 (April 18, 1983).[15]

Merrill Lynch argues from the foregoing that over this period the SEC specifically considered and rejected various proposals that would have brought the transactions at issue here under the mark-up disclosure requirements of Rule 10b–10. From this, it asserts that it is shielded from liability under the anti-fraud provisions of Rule 10b–5.

First of all, we think Merrill Lynch's formulation of the approach to the impact of Rule 10b–10 is faulty. Since we have decided that Ettinger would have stated a claim under Rule 10b–5 prior to the adoption of Rule 10b–10, Merrill Lynch must show that the Commission intended to abrogate such a claim in its actions relating to Rule 10b–10. We turn to that issue.

Throughout the process of adopting and amending Rule 10b–10, the SEC has maintained that "additional information may be material and disclosure may be required"; the SEC narrowly construed the exemption for market makers in its enforcement actions. Although it did not mandate disclosure of mark-ups in transactions of debt securities, the SEC stressed that it would "also maintain close scrutiny to prevent excessive mark-ups and take enforcement actions where appropriate"; similarly, although it noted that yield may be "the single most important piece of information" in debt transactions, the SEC never indicated that yield is the exclusive datum required or even that yield by itself is sufficient to permit a customer to make an informed investment decision.

We believe that these statements by the SEC, the noticeable lack of any reference in SEC documents to the exclusivity of the provisions of Rule 10b–10, and, finally, but of decisive significance, the absence of any language in Rule 10b–10 carving out a limitation to the traditional actions under Rule 10b–5 for fraud of this nature negate the contention advanced by Merrill Lynch. We hold that a broker-dealer's compliance with the disclosure requirements of Rule 10b–10 does not, as a matter of law, shield it from possible liability under Rule 10b–5. * * *

NOTES

1. For a discussion of the existing requirements of SEC Rule 10b–10 see 23 Jerry W. Markham & Thomas L. Hazen, Broker–Dealer Operations Under Securities and Commodities Law § 6.13 (2d ed. 2002).

2. Should the SEC be in the role of regulating markups and commissions. Is this really a fraud issue or one for negotiation. For more on markups

---

15. Because the transactions at issue in this case occurred in 1984, we need not consider SEC actions in 1985 in which all broker-dealers were required to disclose in transactions in "reported securities" the "trade price" (prevailing market price), the price to the customer, and the difference, if any, between the two. See Securities Exchange Act Release 22,397 [1985–1986 Decisions] Fed.Sec.L.Rep. (CCH) ¶ 83,912 (Sept. 11, 1985).

and NASD limitations on the size of markups see 23A Jerry W. Markham & Thomas L. Hazen, Broker–Dealer Operations Under Securities and Commodities Law § 10.23 (2d ed. 2002).

SECTION 5. OTHER FORMS OF U.S. GOVERNMENT SECURITIES

There are other forms of United States government securities available from time-to-time in the marketplace. For example, the Treasury sells Treasury Inflation Protected Securities ("TIPS"). These are inflation-indexed notes and bonds. The principal value of these notes is adjusted semi-annually to reflect inflation or deflation as measured by the Consumer Price Index. The fixed rate semiannual interest payments are then made based on the inflation or deflation-adjusted principal value of the security. Iris L. Blasi & Frank Byrt, TIPS Are Finally Getting Respect, Wall St. J., July 11, 2002, at D9.

TIPS are a popular product in periods of inflation, acting as a hedge against that investment risk. As always, however, there is no free lunch on Wall Street. The initial interest rate paid on TIPS will be less than the rate paid on Treasury securities with the same maturity but without this feature. What happens to this investment if there is a period of deflation?

In 1978, the United States began issuing "Carter bonds," which were treasury securities denominated in foreign currency. The goal in issuing these securities was to bring back dollars to the United States and strengthen the dollar. Similar instruments were used during the Kennedy Administration. They were then called Roosa Bonds, which were named after Robert Roosa, the Undersecretary of the Treasury. W. Carl Biben, Jimmy Carter's Economy, Policy in an Age of Limits 170 (2002). In that regard, the stability of our government and its guarantee of performance have resulted in a large number of foreign purchases of Treasury securities. Investors in Great Britain and Japan, the largest foreign holders, owned collectively almost $600 billion in these securities in 1998. III Jerry W. Markham, A Financial History of the United States: From the Age of Derivatives Into the New Millennium (1970–2001) 265 (2002). Foreign governments also owned enormous amounts of U.S. Treasury Securities, reaching $2.6 trillion in 2010. China held over $900 billion of that amount.

The United States also participates occasionally in international financings that are then marketed to the public. Brady Bonds (which were named after the Secretary of the Treasury, Nicholas Brady who fostered these plans) were used to refinance the sovereign debt of defaulting nations. For example, in 1989, Mexico restructured its defaulted debt by discounting that debt in exchange for Brady Bonds that it issued. Those Brady Bonds were backed by United States government securities. Those securities were supplied by the United States with the involvement of the

International Monetary Fund ("IMF"). See Ross P. Buckley, The Facilitation of the Brady Plan: Emerging Markets Debt Trading From 1989 to 1993, 21 Fordham Int'l L. J. 1802 (1998); Ross P. Buckley, The Transformative Potential of a Secondary Market: Emerging Markets Debt Trading from 1983 to 1989, 21 Fordham Int'l L.J. 1152 (1998). (describing Brady Bonds).

Another earlier issue of U.S. government securities were called "flower" bonds:

> Treasury bonds in general and Flower Bonds in particular are issued under the authority given Congress in Article I, Section 8, Clause 2, of the Constitution "to borrow Money on the credit of the United States." Flower Bonds derive from the Second Liberty Bond Act, 31 U.S.C. § 752, and more particularly Section 20 of the Act, 31 U.S.C. § 754b, which was amended, 56 Stat. 189 (1942), so as to permit "under such regulations and upon such terms and conditions as the Commissioner of Internal Revenue with the approval of the Secretary of the Treasury may prescribe (bonds to) be receivable by the United States in payment of . . . taxes." Regulations were adopted to permit certain bonds issues to be redeemed at par for purposes of paying federal estate tax. These issues are called Flower Bonds because in effect they bloom at the time of the death of the owner, prior to which, particularly because they bear low interest, they sell at a substantial discount on the open market. The Treasury Department could not issue Flower Bonds after March 3, 1971, because of a statutory repeal, 31 U.S.C. § 757c–4, but a number of issues made in the 1940s and '50s with maturity dates in the 1970s, '80s and '90s are outstanding, purchasable on the open market and ready to 'bloom' upon the owner's death." In connection with each issue here involved, the Treasury's Bureau of the Public Debt issued "offering circulars" that set forth the conditions for the redemption of the bonds. Although the language of each of the offering circulars varies somewhat, they all require ownership or actual ownership by the decedent at the time of his death. The circulars incorporate the regulations now appearing at 31 C.F.R. § 306.28, which also set forth, Subparagraph (b), as the requirements for redemption of bonds under this section that (1) the decedent must have owned the bonds at the time of his death, and (2) the bonds must constitute a part of his estate.

Estate of Watson v. Blumenthal, 586 F.2d 925, 927 (2d Cir.1978).

Government created corporations and agencies may also issue debt instruments. Those instruments are described in Chapter 10.

SECTION 6.   MUNICIPAL SECURITIES

Another aspect of the government securities market is the obligations of the various state and municipal subdivisions. At the end of the last century, that market included some 1.5 million issues valued in excess of $1.2 trillion. Those securities were issued by some 50,000 state and local government units. Although it is a market popular with individuals (because of the tax advantages described below) municipal securities have some considerable importance to corporate finance. Corporations hold a significant amount of that debt, and municipal financing may be used to aid corporate projects.

As with other financial instruments, municipal financing has a history. The colonies had issued "bills of credit" (promises to pay) to finance their operations, and those bills passed as money in the colonies. This was an uncertain currency and values fluctuated wildly. A London publication, the American Negotiator, set forth "exchange rates between sterling and all the indigenous currencies of the American colonies." Jackson Goodwin, Greenback, The Almighty Dollar and the Invention of America 61 (2003).

The practice of issuing bills of credit continued through the Revolution. Congress assumed that debt, as well as the debts incurred by the Continental Congress after the Revolution. Article I, § 10 of the Constitution, however, prohibited the states from further issuing bills of credit that would act as legal tender. Craig v. Missouri, 29 U.S. (4 Pet.) 410, 7 L.Ed. 903 (1830). This prohibition did not prevent the states from borrowing money, which they soon did through bond sales which, for many years, were referred to as "stock." See Poindexter v. Greenhow, 114 U.S. 270, 5 S.Ct. 903, 29 L.Ed. 185 (1885) (coupons for state bonds not prohibited bills of credit).

The proceeds of state loans were often devoted to internal improvements such as canal and railroad building. The states and municipal governments sought to attract railroads by helping finance their construction through state bond sales. One railroad was found to have zigzagged its way across upstate New York in search of such bonds. Charles Sellers, The Market Revolution: Jacksonian America 1815–1846 44 (1991). Some of the states defaulted on bonds following the Panic of 1837, many of which were sold in London. That caused consternation in that city and mockery. Scrooge in Charles Dicken's *Christmas Carol* had a nightmare in which his investments were turned into a "mere United States security." Further defaults occurred after Reconstruction.

Those defaults gave rise to concerns that state debts might be unstable and lack integrity. The states were, however, able to regain their credibility. Even during the Great Depression in the 1930s, only some 16 percent of municipal bonds defaulted. Those defaults were for about $1.35 billion as compared to about $7 billion in corporate bond defaults. Moreover, most of the municipal debt defaults were eventually cured with payment of both principal and interest arrearages. *See generally* Paul S. Maco, Building a Strong Subnational Debt Market: A Regulator's Perspective 2 Rich. J. Global L. & Bus. 1, 12 (2001) (describing depression era defaults). This would take some time for a few municipal issues. A default by the City of Detroit on $400 million in debt was not cured until 1963. III Jerry W. Markham, A Financial History of the United States: From the Age of Derivatives Into the New Millennium (1970–2001) 229 (2002). Chicago was another city in temporary default. I Allan H. Meltzer, A History of the Federal Reserve (1913–1951) 368 (2003).

This record of stability helped shield municipal securities from federal regulation. For example, the Glass–Steagall act prohibitions on bank underwriting did not include municipal securities, allowing commercial banks to remain engaged in this activity. The registration provisions of the Securities Act of 1933 and the reporting requirements of the Securities Exchange Act of 1934 were not applied to municipal debt securities. Nevertheless, municipal securities were subject to the antifraud provisions of those securities statutes.

The exemplary record of the municipal securities markets continued for many years. Only about .025 percent of municipal debt defaulted between 1945 and 1974, and most of those defaults were eventually cured. Municipal expenditures began to grow, however, more than doubling between 1966 and 1973. This resulted in increased borrowing, and the municipal securities market was soon comparable in size to that of the securities market. The secondary market in municipal securities also expanded with the growth of these issues. That growth caused concern.

Fiscal problems arose in New York City, which had more than tripled its budget between 1965 and 1975. The City encountered difficulty in selling one of its bond issues in 1974, and the banks conducting the City's underwriting had to absorb the balance of the issue. Those banks advised the City that they would no longer take down unsold offerings for their own accounts. The City's credit was then running out. It could only sell half of a $900 million issue in 1975. The SEC conducted an investigation of the City's bond sales and issued a report asserting that the City had misled bond purchasers in failing to disclose the full extent of the City's financial problems. This report played into the Mayoral race then underway, unseating the incumbent mayor, Abraham D. Beame. In an effort to bail out the City, the New York legislature created the Municipal Assistance Corporation ("Big MAC") for the purpose of issuing new bonds on the City's behalf. It too encountered difficulties and was forced to raid State and City pension funds by selling them its bonds. See generally Tron v. Condello, 427 F.Supp. 1175 (S.D.N.Y.1976) (describing MAC and pension raid). The federal government at first refused aid, but after a famous newspaper headline in the New York Daily News (President "Ford to City: Drop Dead"), aid was given. Problems spread to State bonds as well, but recovery was eventually effected. III Jerry W. Markham, A Financial History of the United States: From the Age of Derivatives Into the New Millennium (1970–2001) 48 (2002).

Municipal securities woes spread to other jurisdictions. A default of a stunning size occurred 1982 when the Washington Public Power Supply System ("WPPS") defaulted on $2.25 billion in bonds it had issued to build the last two of five nuclear power plants. In re Washington Public Power Supply System Securities Litigation, 823 F.2d 1349 (9th Cir. 1987). Another massive default occurred in 1994 when Orange County, California announced large losses from speculative trading by its Treasurer. It was the largest municipal bankruptcy in history. Losses amounted to almost $1,000 for every man, woman and child in the county. Frank Partnoy, F.I.A.S.C.O., Blood in the Water on Wall Street 94 (1999). The Orange County Treasurer, Robert Citron, was jailed. His early success had caused other municipal units to allow him to invest their funds. This is a not uncommon practice, often carried out through Local Government Investment Pools ("LGIPs"):

> LGIPs are established by state or local governmental entities as trusts that serve as vehicles for the pooled investment of public moneys of participating governmental entities. Participating units of governments purchase interests in the trust and trust assets are invested according to the trust's stated investment objectives. Many LGIPs engage investment management firms to manage the investment of trust assets, although many also rely on government employees to undertake such management. In a limited number of cases, broker-dealers have been engaged to market interests in LGIPs to local governments.

Msrb.org (visited February 23, 2003). A LGIP in Florida experienced a run on its assets due to the subprime crisis and redemptions were halted.

A large secondary market exists for municipal bonds. By the 1970s, there were some 900 dealers engaging in municipal bond transactions. Nevertheless, not all municipal securities were liquid because dealers do not make a market in every issue. Moreover, not all of those dealers were scrupulous. The "bond daddies." located in Little Rock, Arkansas and other southern cities during the early part of the 1970s were operating high pressure boiler rooms selling municipal securities without disclosing large markups in their prices while "churning" those accounts with constant sales in order to charge more markups or commissions. Bond Daddies: The Birth of the Memphis Blues, Institutional Investor 155, 156 (June 1997). The SEC brought several enforcement actions against those firms using the antifraud provisions of the federal securities laws. Paul S. Maco, Building a Strong Subnational Debt Market: A Regulator's Perspective, 2 Rich. J. Global L. & Bus.1, 19 (2001). Additional legislation soon followed.

Until the subprime crisis that began in 2007, state and municipal governments were able to substantially reduce their funding costs by obtaining high ratings from the rating agencies. This was possible because

(1) the default rate was low on such debt and (2) so-called monoline insurance companies provided insurance against any defaults that might occur. See Jerry W. Markham, A Financial History of the United States, From the Subprime Crisis to the Great Recession (2006–2009) 403 (2011). This system worked well until the monoline insurance companies sought to branch out and began insuring collateralized debt obligations (CDOs) against default.

The insured CDOs consisted largely of subprime residential mortgages that had been securitized. The CDOs upper level tranches were given investment grade ratings, in part, due to the monoline insurance, making the CDOs highly marketable. However, the insured CDOs were sharply downgraded during the subprime crisis. Those downgrades triggered the monoline insurers' payment obligations. Unfortunately, the monolines did not have sufficient reserves to cover their obligations. This shortfall in reserves also endangered the monolines' ability to meet their state and municipal debt coverage obligations. The monoline insurers eventually settled most of their CDO obligations at steeply discounted prices, but not before the state and municipal bond market was thrown into turmoil. Those problems were compounded by a drop in municipal revenues as a result of the Great Recession during 2007–2009.

ANN JUDITH GELLIS
MUNICIPAL SECURITIES MARKET:
SAME PROBLEM, NO SOLUTION

21 Delaware Journal of Corporation Law 427 (1996).

[Before 1975], the municipal securities market was unregulated and virtually unknown. Although the dollar volume of municipal bonds issued each year was more than substantial, the workings of the market attracted little attention other than from underwriters and legal counsel who specialized in municipal bond finance. A standard municipal bond issue was a public offering of general obligation bonds, sold by a syndicate of underwriters who had been chosen by competitive bidding. Disclosure was not required and nonexistent. Those who purchased municipal securities were well defined and included commercial banks, property and fire casualty insurance companies, and wealthy individuals. These groups were able to take advantage of the federal income tax exemption of interest paid on municipal bonds.

Then came the near default of New York in 1975 on $600 million of debt, followed by the default of the Washington Public Power Supply System (WPPSS) on $2.5 billion of outstanding bonds in 1988. Furthermore, for the first six months of 1995, the market was anticipating the default of bankrupt Orange County, California on $800 million of short-term debt due in the summer of 1995. Orange County managed to renegotiate a one-year extension of the debt and avoided payment default.

In recent months, stories of widespread corruption in the municipal securities market have made headlines in major newspapers, prompting a number of investigations and criminal indictments. The front page of The Bond Buyer, a daily trade newspaper, often reads like a local crime beat column.

Today the municipal securities industry barely resembles the pre-New York City crisis market. The types of securities issued and the nature of investors and other participants have changed and expanded in number. Municipal securities mutual funds and municipal bond insurance, each a major factor in today's market, were virtually non-existent before 1974. Finally, the regulatory environment has changed significantly, so much so, that the ... Chairman of the Securities and Exchange Commission (SEC), Arthur Levitt, has made the oversight of the municipal securities market the primary focus of his tenure at the SEC. * * *

The New York City fiscal crisis was a wake-up call to both the securities market and Congress that the staid municipal securities market had changed. The old rule of no rules had to be reexamined. For the first time, questions were raised about the serious inadequacies in market information, particularly in light of the growth in the types of municipal issuers, the types of securities being sold, and the number and types of investors. New York City's close call with default raised the basic question of how an issuer, the magnitude of New York City, could get to the brink of bankruptcy without the market's knowledge?

In reaction, Congress took its first tentative step to regulate the municipal securities market. It rejected legislative efforts to simply eliminate the section 3(a) exemption for municipal issuers from the registration provisions of the Securities Act of 1933 (1933 Act), which would have resulted in municipal and corporate securities issuers being treated the same in terms of public primary offerings of securities. As a compromise, Congress created a regulatory body, the Municipal Securities Rulemaking Board (MSRB or Board), to establish fair practices for underwriting and trading of municipal securities. Congress also required brokers and dealers of municipal securities to register with the SEC. But, through the Securities Acts Amendments of 1975, Congress specifically prohibited the imposition of any pre-issuance filing requirements, by either the SEC or the newly-created MSRB, on municipal issuers in connection with the issuance, sale, or distribution of securities. Congress also prevented the MSRB from getting around this prohibition by forbidding any requirement that brokers and dealers furnish documents related to an issuer unless such information is generally available from other sources. These amendments to section 15B of the 1934 Act are known collectively as the Tower Amendment.

The Tower Amendment forms the structural foundation of the current municipal securities regulatory scheme in that directives as to market practices and procedures, including any requirements for disclosure, are imposed on municipal securities dealers alone. As a result, regulations as to information disclosure are primarily procedural. The SEC has shied away from any content regulation because of the prohibitions of the Tower Amendment. Any affirmative obligation on the part of municipal issuers to provide information to investors is imposed indirectly through application of the antifraud provisions of the securities laws to municipal issuers, and interpretation of those provisions by the SEC as they relate to the offering of municipal securities to the public.

The inability to regulate the market behavior of municipal issuers, except indirectly, has resulted in a skewed regulatory scheme where the interests of issuers are underrepresented, and the public's interest in getting accurate and timely information is still dependent on voluntary compliance by the issuers. It is perhaps too early to know, but the startling bankruptcy of Orange County may suggest that this reliance is ill-founded.

There were two significant changes in the Securities Acts Amendments of 1975 concerning municipal securities. Section 3(a)(9) of the 1934 Act was added to clarify that municipal issuers could be sued under section 10(b), and section 15B was added to create the MSRB. The MSRB is a hybrid organization, a combination of a government regulatory body— a mini-SEC for municipal securities—and a self-regulatory body, comparable to the New York Stock Exchange (NYSE) and the National Association of Securities Dealers (NASD) for corporate securities. The Board, located in Washington, D.C., is by statute dominated by dealers and banks, who, as the underwriters and traders of municipal securities offerings, are the subjects of the Board's regulations. The Board has five members from investment banking firms, five members from commercial banks, and five representatives of the public which includes a minimum of one representative of issuers and one representative of investors.

Much of the regulatory efforts of the MSRB has focused on standardizing municipal securities trading practices. For example, Rule G–8 (books and records); Rule G–15 (confirmation, clearance, and settlement); G–17 (conduct of municipal securities business); and G–30 (prices and commissions), to name a few. In this respect, given the type of regulation and the makeup of the Board, the MSRB resembles the other self-regulatory organizations (SROs). But, its powers are defined by statute and its rules have the force of law. All rules, however, require the approval of the SEC, as is true of the other SROs. Enforcement of the MSRB rules is left to the SEC, the NASD, and with respect to bank municipal securities dealers, the bank regulatory agencies: Comptroller of the Currency, the Federal Reserve Board, and the Federal Deposit Insurance Corporation.

A number of the rules of the MSRB are aimed at promoting disclosure and better distribution of information to the market. For example, Rule G–32 requires dealers to provide to their customers copies of official statements, voluntarily supplied by an issuer. Rule G–36 requires that copies of final official statements be filed with the MSRB. Rule G–19, the "suitability rule," requires dealers to have "reasonable grounds" for believing that the recommendation of a sale to a customer is suitable for that customer, and such belief is to be founded on reasonable investigation. * * *

The WPPSS default ..., however, made it apparent that the MSRB rules and market forces alone were not sufficient to correct the informational problems of the municipal bond market. There had been major improvements in disclosure of information, including more uniformity, with much credit going to the efforts of the GFOA. However, the behavior of issuers, underwriters and counsel, as evidenced by the WPPSS official statements, continued to fall short in terms of adequate disclosure.

In 1989, after an investigation of the WPPSS securities transactions, the SEC stepped in to directly regulate the primary offerings of municipal securities with the adoption of Rule 15c2–12. Rule 15c2–12 was issued pursuant to the authority given to the SEC under the antifraud provisions of sections 10 and 15 of the 1934 Act. As discussed above, the prohibitions contained in the Tower Amendment do not permit direct disclosure regulation of issuers, at least in terms of imposing any pre-filing requirement. Thus, Rule 15c2–12 indirectly regulates issuers by regulating the activities of underwriters of municipal securities.

Rule 15c2–12 basically requires underwriters (1) to obtain and review a "deemed final official statement of the issuer" prior to bidding for, offering, or selling municipal securities in a primary offering; and (2) to distribute copies of the official statement to potential purchasers, who so request, within ninety days of the end of the underwriting period.

The Rule also introduces the concept of Nationally Recognized Municipal Securities Information Repositories (NRMSIRs), as a key to the distribution of information in the marketplace. Unlike the scheme for corporate securities regulation, there are no requirements to file any documents with the SEC either for review or, simply, as an informational filing. Rather, the Rule contemplates filing with private entities set up to provide the public with access to information about municipal issuers and their securities. To encourage the use of NRMSIRs, the filing of a copy of the final official statement with a NRMSIR shortens the period in which an underwriter is obligated to distribute copies of the official statement to purchasers from ninety to twenty-five days from the end of the underwriting period. The end of the underwriting period is defined as the later of such time as "(i) the issuer of municipal securities delivers the securities to the Participating Underwriters or (ii) the Participating Underwriter does not retain, directly or as a member of an underwriting syndicate, an unsold balance of the securities for sale to the public." At the time of the Rule's adoption, there were no NRMSIRs in existence. The MSRB had proposed to set up a central filing system under its aegis. The SEC, however, rejected the Board's centralized filing proposal in favor of the competitive private sector system of NRMSIRs.

Accompanying the SEC's Rule 15c2–12 was an interpretive release, setting forth the Commission's views on the duty of underwriters to make investigations prior to commencing an offering. The SEC acknowledged that the creation of the MSRB in 1975, and the increased use of the GFOA's disclosure guidelines following the New York City crisis, had not had the influence expected on underwriters' behavior with respect to their obligations to investigate statements contained in the official statement. The SEC recognized that the reasonableness of an investigation necessary to avoid liability under the antifraud provisions depends on, among other things, whether the offering is competitively bid or negotiated. However, the test is the same, the underwriter must have a reasonable basis for belief in the bulk of key representations in the official statements prepared by the issuer. The release specifically addressed the practical difficulties in performing due diligence investigations in competitively bid offerings.

Thus, by 1991, there was a system of federal regulation which essentially required new offerings to be accompanied by a final official statement of the issuer, and provided for the distribution of the official statements to the market either through the NRMSIRs or the MSRB. The content of the official statements, however, as it related to the issuer, remained unregulated. * * *

The municipal securities secondary market for trading is characterized by mystery. There has been little information about the secondary market in terms of the volume and makeup of the participants in the market. The traditional view has been that most investors, including to some extent the banks and insurance companies, hold municipal securities until maturity. To date, trading has not been significant. Small trades are expensive and discouraged. Those people who do trade tend to be sophisticated financial entities, trading in large blocks of securities. The average trading block is estimated to be $25,000 for individuals and $100,000 for institutions. As a consequence, individuals, even wealthy ones, are not active traders.

In a report on the municipal securities market issued in September 1993, the SEC staff emphasized the need for greater price information to facilitate trading. To this end, the Commission proposed a rule in March 1994 which would have required disclosure of mark-ups in riskless principal transactions in municipal securities. Meanwhile, at the SEC's urging, the MSRB began a pilot program to improve price transparency for trades between dealers, with the hope that the information reported by dealers would enable the MSRB to make price information for municipal securities transactions publicly available on a next day basis. Phase one of the program covered reported information on those issues that traded four or more times a day. The MSRB estimated that somewhere between 80 and 350 issues may trade four or more times a day, with 180 issues as an average. At the time, there were an estimated 1.5 million municipal issues outstanding.

Phase two of the program requires dealers to report daily to the MSRB all inter-dealer transactions. Citing the MSRB pilot program and other efforts to enhance price transparency by the Public Securities Association (PSA), the SEC in November 1994 postponed its mark-up proposal for six months. No action has yet been taken. On February 28, 1995, the MSRB also amended a number of its rules to require trades to be settled within three business days of the trade date, known as T + 3. This rule parallels SEC's Rule 15c6–1 under the 1934 Act, which mandates T + 3 settlement with respect to the settlement of trades in the corporate securities market.

Finally, but certainly not least of all, in November 1994, the SEC amended Rule 15c2–12 to add the new paragraphs (b)(5) and (c), requiring continuous disclosure by issuers of municipal securities. Like the regulation of disclosure in the primary market, the amended Rule regulates issuers indirectly. Dealers are prohibited from underwriting the securities of any issuer who does not agree in writing to provide to the secondary market annual financial information and timely disclosure of certain material events.

Carrying through with the structure of disseminating information through multiple channels, the new provisions call for annual financial information and operating data [hereinafter referred to collectively as "annual financial information"] to be provided to each NRMSIR, as well as to any state information depository (SID) that may exist in the state in which the issuer is located. Annual financial information need not be filed with the MSRB or the SEC. [Notices of any of the enumerated "material events" required by the provisions of paragraph (b)(5)(i)(C) are to be given to either each NRMSIR or the MSRB and to any SID. Industry participants differ as to which route issuers will take, filing with the NRMSIRs or with the MSRB. * * *]

Notes

1.   Section 976 of the Dodd–Frank Act of 2010 directed that a study be conducted by the Government Accountability Office (GAO) to determine whether the Tower amendment should be repealed.

2.   Another concern in the regulation of the municipal securities markets is clearing and settlement of transactions. The MSRB has sought to automate that process as much as possible. Depositories, like those used for common stocks, were created. About one-half of all municipal securities were held in those depositories by 1987. The T + 3 (3 day settlement) requirement greatly assisted in modernizing the settlement process. The GAO was directed by Section 977 of the Dodd–Frank Act to conduct an analysis of the mechanisms for trading, quality of trade executions, market transparency, trade reporting, price discovery, settlement clearing, and credit enhancements.

BLOUNT v. SECURITIES & EXCHANGE COMMISSION

61 F.3d 938 (D.C.Cir.1995), cert. denied, 517 U.S. 1119,
116 S.Ct. 1351, 134 L.Ed.2d 520 (1996).

WILLIAMS, CIRCUIT JUDGE.

In late 1993, regulators of the municipal securities markets began to investigate reports that brokers and dealers were engaging in a variety of ethically questionable practices in order to secure underwriting contracts. These practices, often lumped together under the label "pay to play", include as a paradigmatic example the making of political contributions to state and local officials who may influence the choice of underwriter. Concerned that such practices were becoming more prevalent and were undermining the integrity of the $250 billion municipal securities market, the Municipal Securities Rulemaking Board ("MSRB" or "Board") drafted several new rules, which were then approved by the Securities and Exchange Commission. Among these was Rule G–37, the rule challenged in this case. See SEC Release No. 34–33868 (April 7, 1994) (order approving proposed rule change) ("SEC Approval Order").

The two principal sections of Rule G–37, (b) and (c), together restrict the ability of municipal securities professionals to contribute and to solicit contributions to the political campaigns of state officials from whom they obtain business. Section (d) serves as a loophole-closer, prohibiting indirect violations of the restrictions in (b) or (c). We describe each in turn.

Contributions. Section (b) prohibits any "broker, dealer, or municipal securities dealer" who has contributed "to an official of [an] issuer" from "engaging in municipal securities business with [that] issuer" for a period of two years after the contribution.[16] Contributions by a "municipal finance professional associated" with the broker or dealer are treated as equivalent to contributions by the broker or dealer itself; as are contributions by a political action committee "controlled" either by the broker or dealer or by "any municipal finance professional" whatsoever. The two-year restriction on business is not triggered, however, by any of these various parties' contribution of up to $250 per official per election to an official for whom that party is entitled to vote.

Solicitations. Section (c) prohibits brokers, dealers, and municipal securities dealers—as well as their associated municipal finance professionals—from soliciting or coordinating contributions to officials of any issuer with whom the broker, etc., is "engaging or is seeking to engage in municipal securities business."

Loophole-closer. Section (d) prohibits brokers, dealers, municipal securities dealers, and municipal finance professionals in general from "directly or indirectly" doing anything that would "result in a violation of sections (b) or (c). . . ."

---

16. "Municipal securities business" is defined for most purposes as excluding issues based on competitive bids. See Rule G–37(g)(vii).

The petitioner, William B. Blount, is the chairman of the Alabama Democratic Party and a registered broker and dealer of municipal securities. He challenges the SEC's order approving Rule G–37, claiming that each of the three sections of the rule we have described impermissibly infringes his First Amendment rights; that section (d) is, in addition, unconstitutionally vague; and that the rule as a whole violates the Tenth Amendment. The SEC rebuts each of these claims, and the MSRB, as intervenor, raises two defenses not urged by the SEC: that Blount does not have standing under the Exchange Act to pursue his claim and that the rule is not the product of government action and thus cannot violate either the First or Tenth Amendments. We find that Blount has standing to sue and that Rule G–37 is government action. We therefore meet all of Blount's arguments on the merits, though ultimately we reject them and deny the petition for review. * * *

The Board maintains that it is a private organization and that Rule G–37 is a private rule. As such, the Board asserts, the rule cannot be found to violate the First or Tenth Amendments, since the Constitution is "a restraint on government action, not that of private persons", *CBS v. Democratic Nat'l Comm.*, 412 U.S. 94, 114, 36 L.Ed.2d 772, 93 S.Ct. 2080 (1973) (plurality opinion).

We put to one side the Board's questionable assertion that it is a purely private organization even though it was created by an act of Congress and directed by Congress to "propose and adopt rules to effect the purposes of [the Exchange Act]" within specified constraints, § 78o–4(b)(2). Cf. *Lebron v. National R.R. Passenger Corp.*, 130 L.Ed.2d 902, 115 S.Ct. 961, 973 (1995) (fact that Amtrak was created by federal law to accomplish federal governmental objectives points toward classification as federal actor). What is critical here is that MSRB Rule G–37 operates not as a private compact among brokers and dealers but as federal law. Under § 15B of the Exchange Act, a broker or dealer may not engage in interstate trade in municipal securities unless he registers under § 15B itself or under § 15 of the Exchange Act. See 15 U.S.C. § 78o–4(a)(1) (forbidding dealers to use "instrumentality of interstate commerce" to effect or solicit transactions in municipal securities unless registered as a broker or dealer in accordance with § 15 or § 15B, 15 U.S.C. § 78o or § 78o–4). If he violates an MSRB rule, he may be sanctioned by revocation or suspension of his license to deal in municipal securities. See *id.* § 78o–4(c)(1) (forbidding brokers and dealers from contravening the rules of the MSRB in effecting or soliciting interstate transactions in municipal securities); § 78o(b)(4)(D) (authorizing the Commission to suspend or revoke the registration of any broker or dealer who "has willfully violated" or "is unable to comply with" any of the applicable rules, including those of the MSRB); § 78o–4(c)(2) (similar authority as to municipal securities dealers). Dealers who violate Rule G–37 and who persist in securities dealing after any resulting Commission suspension or revocation of their licenses are subject to federal criminal penalties. 15 U.S.C. § 78ff(a) (providing for criminal penalties up to $1,000,000 and 10–year imprisonment for natural persons who willfully violate rules). As a government-enforced condition to any participation in a municipal securities career, Rule G–37 constitutes government action of the purest sort.

We turn now to the central issue in this case, petitioner's claim that Rule G–37 violates his First Amendment rights to free speech and free association. * * *

> Congress has charged the Commission and the MSRB to create rules
>
> to prevent fraudulent and manipulative acts and practices, to promote just and equitable principles of trade, ... to remove impediments to and perfect the mechanism of a free and open market ..., and not ... to permit unfair discrimination between ... municipal securities brokers, or municipal securities dealers....

15 U.S.C. § 78o–4(b)(2)(C). The Commission claims that Rule G–37 supports two interests encompassed within this mandate: (1) protecting investors in municipal bonds from fraud and (2) protecting underwriters of municipal bonds from unfair, corrupt market practices. Both of these interests are not only substantial, see *Turner Broadcasting,* 114 S.Ct. at 2470 ("The Government's interest in eliminating restraints on fair competition is always substantial....") (citing cases), but, we think, compelling. The Supreme Court has said that "preventing corruption or the appearance of corruption" is "the only legitimate and compelling government interest[ ] thus far identified for restricting campaign finances." *FEC v. National Conservative PAC,* 470 U.S. 480, 496–97, 84 L.Ed.2d 455, 105 S.Ct. 1459 (1985). * * *

[T]he link between eliminating pay-to-play practices and the Commission's goals of "perfecting the mechanism of a free and open market" and promoting "just and equitable principles of trade" is self-evident. The Commission explained:

> "Pay to play" practices raise artificial barriers to competition for those firms that either cannot afford or decide not to make political contributions. Moreover, if "pay to play" is the determining factor in the selection of an underwriting syndicate, an official may not necessarily hire the most qualified underwriter for the issue.... "Pay to play" practices undermine [just and equitable] principles [of trade] since underwriters working on a particular issuance may be assigned similar roles, and take on equivalent risks, but be given different allocations of bonds to sell—resulting in differing profits—based on their political contributions or contacts.

See *SEC Approval Order* at 29–30. Moreover, there appears to be a collective action problem tending to make the misallocation of resources persist. As beneficiaries of the practice, politicians vying for state or local office may be reluctant to stop it legislatively; some, of course, may seek to exploit their rivals' cozy relation with bond dealers as a campaign issue, but if they refuse to enter into similar relations, their campaigns will be financially handicapped. Bond dealers are in a still worse position to initiate reform: individual firms that decline to pay will have less chance to play, and may even be the object of explicit boycott if they do. See "Politicians Are Mobilizing to Derail Ban on Muni Underwriters", *Wall St. J.*, Dec. 27, 1993, at C16 (reporting that Florida Association of Counties called for a boycott of 17 firms that had voluntarily banned political contributions). * * *

Because Rule G–37 withstands all of Blount's challenges, the petition for review is *Denied.*

NOTES

1. For a description of pay-to-play practices and their regulation see Jon B. Jordan, The Regulation of "Pay–To–Play" and the Influence of Political Contributions in the Municipal Securities Market, 1999 Colum. Bus. L. Rev. 489. Section 975 of the Dodd–Frank Act of 2010 makes it unlawful for "a municipal advisor to provide advice to or on behalf of a municipal entity or obligated person with respect to municipal financial products or the issuance of municipal securities, or to undertake a solicitation of a municipal entity or obligated person, unless the municipal advisor is registered." Dodd–Frank also adopted an antifraud provision for municipal advisors and states that municipal advisors have a fiduciary duty to any municipal entity for whom such municipal advisor acts as a municipal advisor.

2. Although usually handled privately, the underwriting process for municipal securities has varied from that for stocks and corporate bonds. As all ready noted, banks were permitted to underwrite municipal securities even after the adoption of the Glass–Steagall Act in the 1930s. Many municipal securities issues were also put to auction as the means for their underwriting, a method the SEC required for public utility securities and advocated for other private underwritings. The auction process, however, never became popular in the private underwritings. An action under the antitrust laws designed to force competitive bidding was dismissed. United States v. Morgan, 118 F.Supp. 621 (S.D.N.Y.1953). Municipalities also often viewed underwriting placements as a form of patronage for financial supporters. Rule G–37 sought to change that practice. How should municipalities select their underwriting placements? Will competitive bidding assure the best price and placement?

3. Could the Internet change the underwriting process for municipal securities?

The Internet continues to change the traditional distribution methods for primary issues of municipal bonds. For example, in the year 2000, municipal issuers completed fourteen percent of all competitive municipal bond sales electronically. MuniAuction, an online auction company, promotes itself as the first Internet website to conduct auctions of municipal debt securities. The company employs a system whereby municipalities can directly auction new issues through the Internet allowing bidders to inspect the offering documents online before bidding for the issue. Several municipalities have successfully used, and continue to utilize, this system. Most notably, in November 1997, MuniAuction assisted the City of Pittsburgh in conducting what appears to be the first online auction of a new municipal bond issue. Subsequently, in November 1999, the City of Pittsburgh bypassed traditional underwriters and became the first municipality to offer bonds directly to institutional investors. MuniAuction received a patent for its system in December 2000 and changed its name to Grant Street Group in February of 2001 to exemplify the company's expansion into other product lines, such as software tailored to support institutional sales of municipal bonds and other fixed income instruments.

Taylor J. Hart, Distributing Debt Securities in Cyberspace: How the Internet May Permanently Alter the Role of Underwriters, 35 Suffolk L. Rev. 395, 417–418 (2001).

4. Some municipal offerings can be massive. In 1998 an offering of $7 billion and was used to finance the takeover of the Long Island Lighting Co. by the State of New York. Are there any limits on the size of municipal borrowings in your state?

CITY OF NEW ORLEANS v. SMITH BARNEY, INC.

1999 WL 288797 (E.D.La.1999).

STANWOOD R. DUVAL, UNITED STATES DISTRICT COURT JUDGE.

Before the Court is a Motion to Dismiss filed by Smith Barney Inc. ("Smith Barney") and BT Alex. Brown Inc. ("Alex Brown"). This suit arises out of the defendants' allegedly having engaged in a practice known as "yield burning" during the issuance of the "$179,880,829.25 City of New Orleans, Louisiana General Obligation Refunding Bonds Series 1991" ("1991 G.O. Refunding Bonds") which has allegedly placed in jeopardy the tax-exempt status of those bonds. The City of New Orleans ("the City") and the Board of Liquidation, City Debt of the City of New Orleans ("the Board") have filed the instant parallel suits seeking declaratory judgments that the defendants are "100% responsible for any determination by the Internal Revenue Service ('IRS') to deny the Bonds' tax-exempt status and, therefore, should be ordered to indemnify, hold harmless, and defend the City from any and all potential claims occasioned thereby." * * *

From time to time the City issues General Obligation Bonds ("G.O.Bonds") as a way to finance capital improvements in the City. The Board, which was specifically established to control and direct all matters relating to the bonded debt of the City, directs the issuance of these bonds. The principal marketing feature of such bonds is that interest payments to G.O. Bond investors are exempted from federal and state income taxes. (26 U.S.C. § 103(a)).

Periodic reductions in the interest rate can occasionally present an opportunity to refinance the City's outstanding G.O. Bonds at lower interest rates resulting in overall debt service savings to the City. The Board is directed by law to act as the "governing authority" for the City when outstanding G.O. Bonds are refinanced. La. Rev. Stat. 39:1034(F). The Board selects an investment banking firm to serve as "senior managing underwriter" in compliance with the provisions of La. Rev. Stat. 39:1037.

When the G.O.Bonds to be refinanced are not yet callable and thus cannot be redeemed, the Board utilizes an "advanced refunding". New "refunding bonds" are issued and sold publicly to refinance or "defease" the "refunded bonds." In an "advanced refunding" the proceeds from the "refunding bonds" are used to purchase a portfolio of U.S. government securities which are then placed in an escrow account which is managed so that the proceeds from the securities purchased with the "refunding bonds" are disbursed as they are needed to pay the debt service on the refunding bonds and to redeem the refunded bonds as they mature.

Advance refunding escrow funds are subject to arbitrage regulations of the IRS (26 U.S.C. § 103(b)(2) and § 148). U.S. treasury securities put in the escrow account must be purchased at their fair market values, and their yield in the escrow account must not exceed the yield of the "refunding bonds." If the IRS determines that the structure or yield of an advance refunding escrow violates its arbitrage rules it can declare the refunding bonds to be taxable arbitrage bonds. For instance, where there has been a substantial mark-up on the escrow securities over and above the fair market value the IRS can find these rules violated. This marking-up practice is known as "yield burning" and occurs when the underwriters and dealers sell portfolios of U.S. treasury securities to local governments for advanced refunding open market escrow accounts at artificially high prices in order to keep the yields low enough to meet federal arbitrage requirements, which creates allegedly excessive and undisclosed profits to the dealers. As stated by one commentator:

> Such yield burning wrongly diverts to the investment provider positive arbitrage that would otherwise be owed to the federal Treasury. As a result, overpricing of positive arbitrage refunding escrows directly damage the federal Treasury. In addition, in negative arbitrage cases (i.e., where the escrow's yield is below the restricted rate) investment overpricing is paid directly by the issuer.

J. Phillips, M.L. Cohen, E. Kelton, "Overpricing of Municipal Escrow Purchases: Yield Burning Issues and Potential Liabilities" 1033 PLI/Corp 551, 554 (Feb. 1998) (hereinafter "Overpricing of Municipal Escrow Purchases"). When the IRS determines that the tax-exempt status is thus destroyed, it can require the owner of the refunding bonds to file amended tax returns and pay unexpected income tax on the interest payments.

Apparently, this practice of yield burning has spawned significant controversy and potential revenue for the IRS. There exists a "closing agreement program" for issuers to protect the tax-exempt status of advance refunding bond issues affected by escrow overpricing. In essence, the IRS collects the difference between the amount paid for the Treasury securities and the spot price for the Treasury securities, plus interest. Arbitrage Prop. Regs. "Target Excessive Purchase Prices for Treasury Securities", 85 J. Tax'n 187 (Sept. 1997). By doing so, the tax-exempt status of the bonds is maintained and the issuer avoids "the risk that their advance refunding bonds will be declared taxable arbitrage bonds. Revocation of tax exemption would, in turn, expose public agencies to even greater potential liabilities to bondholders." * * *

The 1991 G.O. Refunding Bonds, the subject bonds, were used as an advanced refunding to refinance approximate $180,000,000 of outstanding G.O.Bonds. The Board hired Alex. Brown as the Senior Managing Under-writer, and Smith Barney sold the portfolio of treasury securities placed in the open market escrow by Smith Barney. It is alleged that these two companies had the duty to advise the Board and the City and insure that the escrow account was funded in compliance with applicable IRS arbi-trage regulations, including particularly the requirement that the escrow securities be purchased at fair market value.

At the time of the delivery of the 1991 G.O. Refunding Bonds, Smith Barney apparently provided a sworn certification dated September 17, 1991 that the treasury securities were sold to the City at a price which was "equal to or lower than the mean bid and offered price" of the established market and that "no amount was paid by the City to reduce the yield." However, on June 16, 1997, the City allegedly received a subpoena issued by the IRS concerning the 1991 G.O. Refunding Bonds arising out of its apparently nationwide yield burning investigation. Alleg-edly, Alex. Brown admitted to the IRS in a letter dated November 18, 1996 that a "markup charge of between $1,460,000 and $1,590,000 had been paid by the City with respect to the transaction involving the Bonds."

On August 21, 1997 and again on September 15, 1997, the District Director of the Internal Revenue Service issued letters to the City inform-ing it that the IRS had made a "preliminary determination" that the 1991 G.O. Refunding Bonds did not meet the IRS requirements for tax-exempt bonds, based upon the IRS having concluded that securities purchased for the 1991 G.O. Refunding Bonds defeasance escrow fund were excessively marked up. The plaintiffs contend that the IRS informed the City and the Board that Smith Barney and Alex Brown apparently had a private agreement to share these "excessive mark-ups" without the knowledge of the City or Board, and "therefore the 1991 G.O. Refunding Bonds were arbitrage bonds that that the interest paid to bondholders is not likely to be excludable income."

While not part of the allegations of the Amended Complaints, the August 21, 1997 letter includes an allegation that the City of New Orleans may have had knowledge that securities were excessively marked-up. Indeed, the IRS continues in that letter:

In addition, we have found some evidence that fees paid to subordinate underwriters and bond counsel could have been excessive. Some of these parties made political contributions to persons in a position to influence the issuance. While we have not fully developed this area, it could also be an issue affecting the taxability of bond interest. We would certainly be willing to discuss these concerns with you.

Under the Internal Revenue Code, if the requirements for tax-exempt bonds are not met, interest received on the bonds must be included in the gross income of the bondholders. Accordingly, if a final determination is made that the interest on the name bond issue is not excludable, it is our responsibility under the law to recover any unpaid tax on the interest from the holders of the bonds. We are issuing this letter now to give you the earliest possible notification of a potential problem.

The writer continues by offering to discuss a "closing agreement"; however, he also opines that the examination will not be suspended during any negotiations.

The September 15, 1997 letter is identical to the August letter; however, the following indicates some change in the IRS's perception of the situation:

The markups do not appear to be consistent with any reasonable assessment of risk. It also appears that the lead underwriter, Alex Brown, had what may have been a private agreement with the escrow provider, Smith Barney, to share in these excessive markups. Alex Brown received sixty percent (60%) of the markups.

Testimony reveals that the Board of Liquidation may not have been aware of this arrangement.

Consequently, we have concluded that the bonds are arbitrage bonds and that the interest paid to bondholders is not likely to be excludable from income. * * *

The core of plaintiffs' request for relief is premised on the IRS making a final determination that the 1991 G.O.Refunding Bonds are subject to taxation as gross income. The extent of the damages as to each claim cannot be determined until such a determination is made. The Court recognizes from the pleadings and letters provided that indeed it would appear imminent and likely that the IRS will do so. However, while the IRS has rattled its saber mightily, it has not issued that final determination. Although there are apparent wrongs that need to be addressed, they are not ripe at this time.

Without the final determination and the IRS's reasons for such a determination, the Court would be placed in a similar position as in the Texas case. On the other hand, if the plaintiffs are convinced that the ostensible perfidy committed by Smith Barney and Alex. Brown resulted in the 1991 G.O.Refunding Bonds being arbitrage bonds and thus subject to taxation, it would appear that perhaps the plaintiffs would be well advised to enter into a closing agreement in order to mitigate their damages. Certainly at that point, this matter would be ripe for adjudication as concrete damage to the plaintiffs would have occurred.

Nonetheless, the Court recognizes that many of plaintiffs' claims might be jeopardized by the running of prescription. For instance, any claim grounded in tort might be lost if the Court were to dismiss this case. Therefore, the Court will not do so Instead, it will stay this matter and statistically close it, pending a resolution with regard to whether the 1991 G.O.Refunding Bonds are generate taxable income or the City enters into a closing agreement. Upon the reopening of this suit, the Court will then address dismissing any of the individual counts based on the legal merits thereof.

Accordingly,

IT IS ORDERED that the motion to dismiss is DENIED

A key element in municipal securities is the fact that their interest payments are free from federal tax. The state in which a municipal security in issued also does not usually tax the issue, but other states often do. This means that residents will be inclined to municipal securities issued in their own state in order to avoid state as well as federal taxes. A Kentucky court held that such discrimination violated the commerce clause. The Supreme Court reversed. Department of Rev. of Ky. v. Davis, 553 U.S. 328, 128 S.Ct. 1801, 170 L.Ed.2d 685 (2008). The favorable tax treatment given to municipal securities has traditionally meant that municipal securities pay a lower interest rate than other comparable debt obligations, thereby reducing state funding costs. On occasion, municipal security yields may approach that of federal security yields. For example in early 2003, long-term municipal securities were paying 4.81 percent, while long term U.S. Treasury securities were paying only 4.80 percent. There was, however, an increased risk of default as municipal finances were experiencing difficulties from a recession and attending drop in revenues. Russell Pearlman, Muni Bonds Look Cheap, Raleigh News & Observer, Feb. 23, 2003, at 8E.

An investor must be in a sufficiently high tax bracket to take advantage of the lack of taxation. This means that, if the reduced yield on a municipal security is not offset by its tax advantage, the investor should (all other things being equal) choose an alternative investment. The reduced yield on a municipal security also make them less desirable for tax advantaged situations, including retirement accounts. Capital gains from municipal securities are taxable and the alternative minimum tax may include municipal security income in its computation.

Municipal bonds vary in the nature of their repayment obligations. Some such securities are backed by the full faith and credit of the state in which they are issued. This offers substantial assurance of performance in that the state is pledging the full extent of it tax payments and other resources in promising repayment. Municipalities may issue general obligation bonds that are backed by their full taxing authority. Other municipal securities, such as revenue and industrial development bonds, are backed by lesser security.

PAUL S. MACO
BUILDING A STRONG SUBNATIONAL DEBT MARKET:
A REGULATOR'S PERSPECTIVE

2 Rich. J. Global L. & Bus. 1, 12 (2001).

The Revenue Bond

No financing structure has been of greater importance to growth of the U.S. municipal market than the revenue bond. Of the $226.6 billion in long-term bonds issued in the United States in 1999, $156.4 billion were revenue bonds and $70.2 billion were general obligation bonds. The turning point from general obligation to revenue bonds as the preferred tool of municipal finance occurred in 1976. The concept of self-supporting municipal infrastructure financing existed a century before this turning point. Double-barreled revenue bonds, paid from fees collected from users of a facility but also secured by general obligation of the government issuer, had been used in the 1800s to finance water supply systems. The first "pure" revenue bond, with principal and interest derived exclusively from a project's earnings, was issued by Wheeling, West Virginia in 1885 to finance a water and gas plant. Today, revenue bonds finance airports, toll roads, housing, health care, educational and environmental facilities as well as traditional municipal utilities.

Observers have called the 1921 Act of the New York and New Jersey legislatures, copied from the 300–year old Port of London Authority, creating the Port Authority of New York and New Jersey, "the most important development in the history of the revenue bond." The Port Authority was the first major user of the public authority device in the United States. Unlike earlier authorities in the United States, the Port Authority financed multiple projects. The creation of the Port Authority and the Triborough Bridge and Tunnel Authority also clearly established that the debt of special district governments with wide functional and territorial jurisdictions as well as political subdivisions was entitled to exemption from federal income taxation. By the 1950s, almost every state had enabling legislation for revenue bond financing. Among other attributes, revenue bonds issued by authorities are considered by bond counsel to be outside many of the restrictive limits on debt earlier added to state constitutions. Debt financing for large infrastructure projects was now available without the hurdle of voter approval by means of the authority issued revenue bond. Numerous permutations of the basic structure of capturing project revenues under a trust agreement or indenture to provide for costs of operation, maintenance and repair as well as for payment of principal and interest have developed, adapting to the needs of specific situations. Some modern revenue bond structures use surplus revenues to support projects unrelated to the original facilities, such as bridge toll revenues providing additional security to subway and light rail transportation bonds. The flexibility of enabling legislation in many instances permits creativity in structuring revenue bond issues. Revenue bonds are now the financing mainstay for modern infrastructure development in the United States.

There are three basic types of revenue bonds commonly used worldwide: stand alone enterprise, supplement-supported enterprise, and government-guaranteed enterprise. In the stand-alone enterprise revenue bond, payment of all costs of operation, maintenance and payments on bonds is derived exclusively from revenues of an enterprise. This is the classic revenue bond structure. The enterprise is an operation or facility, such as a toll bridge or water treatment plant. The cost of constructing and acquiring the enterprise is provided by the money raised through selling the bonds. Following completion of the project, fees are charged and collected for use of the service offered by the enterprise, such as bridge tolls or water or electric bills, and the collected fees are used to pay down principal and interest on the bonds.

Because the revenues provide debt service, the term of the debt may be as long as the expected life of the toll bridge or water plant. In some markets, this period may significantly exceed the maturities available in the market for the general obligation of the local government. The project may be owned by the local government or by an authority. If owned by the local government, revenues of the enterprise are segregated from other revenues of the government legally and in the financial statements of the local government. Use of authorities such as the Port Authority and Triborough Bridge and Tunnel Authority has become the preferred structure in the United States, although some local governments still issue revenue bonds.

If a stand-alone enterprise cannot collect sufficient revenues to cover costs of operation and maintenance and repay bonds, the classic revenue bond structure may be modified with the addition of a second revenue source. This second revenue source may be a subsidy or grant from the local, regional or national government or a surplus in revenues collected by the local government entirely independent of the enterprise.

If the stand-alone enterprise is unable to collect sufficient revenues to cover costs of operation and maintenance, and repayment of bonds and circumstances do not present an opportunity to add a supplemental revenue source, the local government may choose to guarantee bond payments out of its general funds, creating a double-barreled bond. In some circumstances where the local government has a very strong credit, the choice may be made to add such a guarantee even though the enterprise revenues are adequate to meet needs, because of savings in interest rates achieved by the resulting stronger credit.

As the number of authorities and use of revenue bonds grew in the first half of the twentieth century, so did variations in structure. The use of an authority to blend the revenue streams and credits of several issuers into one debt obligation through the revenue bond structure has proven particularly useful. Many subnational governments with modest needs are placed at a financial disadvantage by the fixed costs of selling securities in the public market on one hand and the higher interest rates charged by banks on the other. The costs of a public offering may exceed savings in interest rates over bank loans. For small, first time issuers, interest rate savings may be insufficient because the market is unfamiliar with the credit of the local government. Either or both conditions may make the public bond markets an unrealistic alternative to bank financing for small local governments. To address this problem, many States have created special government agencies, usually called bond banks or bond pools, to assist small units of local government to obtain capital more cheaply. The cost savings come from two sources: efficiencies of scale achieved through combination of the fixed costs of many smaller financings into the fixed costs of a single large financing, and lower interest rates achieved through blending of risks and issuer familiarity in the marketplace than would otherwise be available to individual small financings.

A bond bank issues its own debt securities and re-lends the proceeds to various units of local government with smaller needs. In exchange for a part of the proceeds of the bond bank's securities offering, each local government delivers its own debt instrument to the bond bank bearing interest at the same rate as the bond bank's securities. In some circumstances, the local governments pay a slightly higher interest rate to cover operating expenses of the bond bank or to fund reserves providing additional security for repayment of the bond bank's debt.

Bond banks may be used for many different public purposes. For example, the Indiana Bond Bank annually assists nearly all of the primary and secondary public schools in the state (i.e. province) to borrow for working capital each year because the timing of receipt of revenues and need to make expenditures is not coordinated. By keeping costs low, the Bond Bank ensures that more funds will be available to pay for educational costs instead of interest and financing costs. The Illinois Health Facilities Financing Authority operates a bond bank program to assist charity hospitals to borrow for new equipment purchases. The resulting reduced equipment costs ultimately provide lower costs to health care consumers than would bank financing or individual borrowing by each hospital. In many states, bond bank programs provide below-market rate financing (because of the federal income tax-exemption for interest on the bond banks debt) to sectors of particular policy or economic importance, such as small business assistance or blighted area development.

NOTES

1.   The special facility revenue bond is issued by municipal airports but is backed by an airline using the airport. Some of these bonds are secured by particular revenue streams from the facilities, but others are unsecured. The financial troubles of the airlines have raised concern with the viability of some of those bonds. Karen Damato, Airline–Backed Munis Take a Toll, Wall St. J., March 26, 2003, at D7.

2.   The "moral obligation" municipal bond was developed in New York in order to avoid mandated limits. Those bonds are not supported by the full faith and credit of the state and are not subject to those debt limits. The promise to repay is only a moral obligation of the state. If the state fails to meet that obligation, however, it will have difficulty selling future issues. In another innovation, New York issued Tax Anticipation Notes ("TANs"), Bond Anticipation Notes ("BANs") and a Revenue Anticipation Notes ("RANs"). These were simply borrowings made in anticipation of future tax receipts, proceeds from a future issue or revenue from a particular source. This allowed the government to spend money in advance of its receipt. Is that a sound budgeting practice?

3.   New York had been issuing TANs since at least 1914. The federal government had also resorted to such devices. In World War I, it issued tax anticipation certificates that were to be retired from Liberty Loan sales. I Allan H. Meltzer, A History of the Federal Reserve (1913–1951) 77, n. 26, 86 (2003). Tax anticipation notes have appeared elsewhere. In the seventeenth century, for example, the English government issued Exchequer tallies that were wooden sticks reflecting a promise to pay future revenues from the government. Jonathan Barron Baskin & Paul J. Miranti, Jr., A History of Corporate Finance 101 (1997).

4.   Certificates of Participation are borrowings by municipal units, such as school boards, to avoid referendum requirements for new bond issues. People Who Care v. Rockford Bd. of Educ., 111 F.3d 528, 539 (7th Cir.1997). What limitations are imposed on such borrowings? Industrial development bonds are another form of municipal security. These issues are used to raise money for private developers and may not be exempt from taxation. A municipality issues such bonds in order to increase employment and to increase its tax base. These bonds are usually not backed by the credit of the municipality. Related in concept is the Tax Incremental Finance bond, or Tax Allocation bonds as they are sometimes called. These bonds are issued through special development authorities and are funded through increased property taxes from an area being redeveloped by private initiatives. See Janice Griffith, The Preservation of Community Green Space: Is Georgia Ready to Combat Sprawl With Smart Growth? 35 Wake Forest L. Rev. 563, 592 (2000) (describing tax allocation bonds).

5.   More exotic offerings by municipalities were appearing in the 1990s. Municipalities were selling their shares in the massive tobacco litigation settlements they reached with the major tobacco companies. Continuing litigation against the tobacco companies, however, was threatening the collect-

ability of those instruments. Ruth Simon, A Safe Investment Gets Less Safe, Wall St. J., April 3, 2003, at D1. Lottery bonds were being sold that were secured by revenue from future state lotteries. The municipal "multiplier" is a municipal bond that pays a coupon rate but the coupon is reinvested and paid at maturity with the principle, reducing concerns with the reinvestment risk for the coupon payments. A "mini-coupon" municipal security pays an interest rate lower than the rate for comparable bonds but is issued at a discount, thereby increasing its yield to maturity. A "stepped coupon" municipal bond pays an increased interest rate on bonds in a redeemable offering that are not called under the redemption schedule. Municipalities also issued "super sinkers." The latter is a housing revenue bond backed by single-family mortgages. The holder may suffer a loss of principal if this security is purchased at a premium and is redeemed before maturity. An "option tender" bond allows the holder to cash in a bond at face value after a specified waiting period. This provides a measure of liquidity.

6. State and municipal governments were also facing large shortfalls in revenues as a result of the subprime crisis. California was issuing IOUs in 2009 to meet obligations, and it had a massive budget deficit. The Illinois governor was seeking a fifty percent increase in income taxes in order to close a budget shortfall. Philadelphia simply stopped paying its bills. As will be described below, the states were also exposed to enormous shortfalls in their state employee pension plans.

7. State and municipal governments are building up large amounts of retirement obligations to their employees that are under-funded. Jerry W. Markham, A Financial History of Modern U.S. Corporate Scandals, From Enron to Reform 645 (2006). Some states have been accused of trying to cover up the amount of those obligations. A Stanford University study concluded that in 2008 the three largest California pension funds were underfunded by $500 billion, rather than the $55 billion they claimed. Pension Bomb Ticks Louder, Wall St. J., April 27, 2010, at A16.The SEC sued the State of New Jersey for misrepresenting in its bond offerings the status of the underfunding of its pension plans. Steve Malanga, How States Hide Their Budget Deficits, Wall St. J., Aug. 23, 2010, at A15. The Governmental Accounting Standards Board ("GASB") is the body responsible for assuring that the states use uniform accounting practices that fully disclose such obligations. Its counterpart in the private sector is the Financial Accounting Standards Board ("FASB"). Texas has passed legislation that would permit the state to deviate from the accounting standards set by GASB, allowing it to avoid disclosing the true extent of its pension and other obligations. In 2007, the governor of Connecticut vetoed similar legislation passed by the legislature in that state. Mary Williams Walsh, S.E.C. Chief Seeks New Clout for Board Overseeing States, N.Y. Times, July 18, 2007, at C3. Section 978 of the Dodd–Frank Act requires the GAO to conduct a study of the role and importance of the GASB and made provisions for the funding of the GASB.

CHAPTER TEN

STRUCTURED FINANCE AND SECURITIZATION

■ ■ ■

Chapter objectives

- To understand how securitization creates asset-backed securities by repackaging existing financial instruments.
- To understand asset-backed securities collateralized by residential mortgage obligations in greater detail.
- To appreciate the wide range of structured finance products created through securitization vehicles.

SECTION 1. SECURITIZATION TECHNIQUES AND OBJECTIVES

The world of corporate finance changed dramatically during the last quarter of the twentieth century. Finance had once been a staid and placid money raising function involving mostly bank loans, bonds and stocks, but during this period it witnessed the dramatic introduction of a host of new products ranging from structured finance to exotic derivative instruments. This chapter focuses on structured finance and "asset securitization," a technique that transformed the organization of financial markets.

STRUCTURED FINANCING TECHNIQUES COMMITTEE ON BANKRUPTCY AND CORPORATE REORGANIZATION OF THE ASSOCIATION OF THE BAR OF THE CITY OF NEW YORK

50 Bus. Law. 527 (1995).

Although relatively new, the use of structured financing techniques has grown rapidly and now accounts for $450 billion per year of financings in the United States alone. There is nearly $2 trillion of mortgage and asset-backed financings outstanding in the United States. The possibilities seem limitless. This Report explores structured financings—their history, structural elements and underlying legal basis. It is hoped this Report will provide a background and an analytical framework for counsel and others involved in this significant and growing financing technique.[1]

Structured financings are based on one central, core principle—a defined group of assets can be structurally isolated, and thus serve as the basis of a financing that is independent as a legal matter, from the bankruptcy risks of the former owner of the assets. Additionally, by isolating assets, structured financings can facilitate access to the capital markets, vastly expanding the sources of available funding.

The parties involved in a structured financing typically include:

- An entity that has financing needs and that also has assets capable of serving as the basis for a structured financing. This entity parts absolutely with ownership of the assets in the structured financing and is typically referred to as the "originator," "transferor" or "party benefiting from the financing."

- One or more entities specially created for the structured financing. These entities, which acquire ownership of the transferred assets and/or issue securities, are typically referred to as "special purpose vehicles," "SPVs" or "issuers." The securities that are issued by these entities are sometimes referred to as "asset-backed securities."

- One or more financial institutions that provide credit enhancement for the transferred assets or for the asset-backed securities directly. These entities are referred to as "credit enhancers."

- An entity that monitors the assets, collects their cash flow, and ensures that the cash flow is properly distributed. This entity is referred to as the "servicer." The cash flow is generally applied to the payment of the asset-backed securities or, in some transactions of a "revolving" nature, to acquire ownership for the issuer of additional assets from the originator (for a specified period of time so long as no default or other specified event exists).

- An entity that supports the structured financing by providing liquidity to avoid mismatches between the receipt of cash flow from the assets and the payment dates on the asset-backed securities. This entity is referred to as the "liquidity provider." Sometimes the servicer is also the liquidity provider.

- Where the asset-backed securities are being distributed in the public capital markets, one or more underwriters that purchase and distribute the securities issued in the structured financing.

- One or more nationally recognized credit rating agencies that rate the asset-backed securities on the basis of the credit quality of the

---

1. Lawyers and other professionals involved in structured financing require expertise in relevant principles of secured transactions (e.g., perfection requirements and priority rules); bankruptcy law (e.g., the existence of the automatic stay, the avoidance of preferences and fraudulent conveyances, and the right to reject executory contracts and leases); and commercial law (e.g., the differences between senior and subordinated debt).

assets (in many cases, as supported by credit enhancement) and the structural elements of the financing.

- Investors that acquire the asset-backed securities.

An entity may have difficulty raising funds. It may be new or it may be experiencing credit difficulties. Alternatively, an entity may have a number of financing opportunities but finds them expensive or it may want to expand its investor base. Structured financing may provide an option. Structured financing can also play a role in debt restructurings, debtor in possession financings, and confirmation financings. The reason for using structured financings in each of these situations is the same—to reduce concern about the credit risk of the entity benefiting from the financing.

The key is the existence of assets that can be segregated for purposes of the financing. If an entity has assets that can be segregated as a legal matter, it may be able to use structured financing techniques to obtain financing it would not otherwise be able to obtain or at a cost that would not otherwise be available to it. * * *

One of the principal benefits from structured financings is a reduction in the cost of financing (e.g., interest rate). Not only is the credit rating of the financing likely to be enhanced, but also the cost of the financing in the capital markets may be less than the cost of comparable financing in the bank or insurance company private placement market. The availability of funds in the U.S. capital markets is not as limited as in the private markets and certain issues encountered in the private markets, such as the lending limits of a particular financing institution, do not arise in the capital markets.

Structured financings also permit tremendous flexibility. Discrete pools or revolving pools of assets may be used, and asset-backed securities may be constructed having cash flow and maturity characteristics that differ from those of the assets in the pool(s). Covenants and other terms in structured financings are generally less restrictive in relation to the party benefiting from the financing than those in private market transactions. Moreover, structured financings may permit off-balance sheet financing—both the assets and the source of funding are removed from the balance sheet—and thus a structured financing transaction may be a possible method of financing in some circumstances where a secured financing would be prohibited by pre-existing restrictions in outstanding credit documents of the party benefiting from the financing or where the benefitted party for other reasons (such as capital requirements) does not want to undertake on-balance sheet financing. Structured financings of receivables also can accelerate the receipt of cash flows, allowing the quicker redeployment of the proceeds of those assets.

The process of issuing securities backed by assets in structured financings is sometimes called "securitization" because assets are, in a sense, turned into securities—they are monetized, not through traditional secured borrowings or factoring, but through the issuance of asset-backed securities. The assets that can be securitized through structured financings are virtually limitless.

COMPTROLLER OF THE CURRENCY ASSET SECURITIZATION, COMPTROLLER'S HANDBOOK
(Nov. 1997).

For Originators

Securitization improves returns on capital by converting an on-balance sheet lending business into an off-balance sheet fee income stream that is less capital intensive. Depending on the type of structure used, securitization may also lower borrowing costs, release additional capital for expansion or reinvestment purposes, and improve asset/liability and credit risk management.

For Investors

Securitized assets offer a combination of attractive yields (compared with other instruments of similar quality), increasing secondary market liquidity, and generally more protection by way of collateral overages and/or guarantees by entities with high and stable credit ratings. They also offer a measure of flexibility because their payment streams can be structured to meet investors' particular requirements. Most important, structural credit enhancements and diversified asset pools free investors of the need to obtain a detailed understanding of the underlying loans. This has been the single largest factor in the growth of the structured finance market.

For Borrowers

Borrowers benefit from the increasing availability of credit on terms that lenders may not have provided had they kept the loans on their balance sheets For example, because a market exists for mortgage-backed securities, lenders can now extend fixed rate debt, which many consumers prefer over variable rate debt, without exposing themselves to interest rate risk. Credit card lender can originate very large loan pools for a diverse customer base at lower rates than if they had to fund the loans on their balance sheet. * * *

SECURITIES INDUSTRY ASSOCIATION v. CLARKE
885 F.2d 1034 (2d Cir.1989), cert. denied, 493 U.S. 1070, 110 S.Ct. 1113, 107 L.Ed.2d 1021 (1990).

MESKILL, CIRCUIT JUDGE.

* * * Mortgage pass-through certificates are used by banks as a mechanism for selling mortgage loans. A number of mortgage loans

previously originated by a bank are placed in a pool. The bank then transfers the pool to a trust. In exchange for the pool, the trustee transfers to the bank pass-through certificates. These certificates represent fractional undivided interests in the pool of mortgage loans. The certificates may then be sold publicly or privately.

After sale of the certificates, the mortgage loans are often serviced by the originator-bank. In such a case, the bank collects the loan payments and "passes through" the principal and interest on a pro rata basis to the certificate holders. In doing so, the bank may deduct service or other fees.

Use of this mechanism has important benefits for banks, benefits that have resulted in its increasing popularity and use. Because residential mortgage loans typically are of long duration, banks traditionally have bought and sold the loans to facilitate management of their assets and liabilities. Use of the pass-through certificate mechanism makes the sale of these loans easier. Individual loans do not have to be sold separately, and buyers may find it more efficient and less risky to purchase interests in a pool of mortgages instead of single mortgages.

A Prospectus and Prospectus Supplement dated January 23, 1987 described the offering of approximately $194 million of Security Pacific Mortgage Pass–Through Certificates, Series 1987–B.

The Prospectus provided for the creation of a pool consisting of conventional, fixed-rate residential mortgage loans. "Each Mortgage Loan [would] be selected by [SPN Bank] for inclusion in the Mortgage Pool from among those originated by [SPN Bank] in the ordinary course of [SPN Bank's] lending activities as carried on in its offices in California." Certain characteristics of the mortgages to be selected were specified.

The Prospectus provided that, at the time of issuance of the series, "[SPN Bank] will assign the Mortgage Loans in the Mortgage Pool evidenced by that series to the Trustee.... The Trustee will, concurrently with such assignment, authenticate and deliver Certificates evidencing such series to [SPN Bank] in exchange for the Mortgage Loans." The freely transferable certificates would represent fractional undivided interests in the Trust Fund.

Limited credit support for the issue was to be provided either by (1) an irrevocable letter of credit issued by SPN Bank, (2) a limited guaranty issued by an entity other than SPN Bank, or (3) third-party mortgage insurance purchased by SPN Bank in its role as servicer of the mortgage loans. If SPN Bank provided its own letter of credit, the coverage was to be no more than ten percent of the initial aggregate principal balance of the mortgage pool. Any risk of delinquency or default not covered by these mechanisms of credit support would be borne by the certificate holders.

The Prospectus provided for distribution of the certificates by any of three methods: "1. By negotiated firm commitment underwriting and public reoffering by underwriters; 2. By placements by [SPN Bank] with institutional investors through agents; and 3. By direct placements by [SPN Bank] with institutional investors."

After the sale of the certificates, SPN Bank was to continue to service the mortgage loans on behalf of the certificate holders for a contractually specified fee. As part of its ongoing responsibilities, SPN Bank would "monthly distribute[] to certificate holders the payments received from the mortgagors (net of its servicing fee) based on their pro rata interest in the mortgage loans."

The Prospectus Supplement for Series 1987–B described various characteristics of the mortgages selected for inclusion in the pool for that particular issue. The Supplement also specified that the trustee was to be Union Bank, a California bank. Credit support was to be provided by SPN Bank's parent, Security Pacific Corporation, in the form of a limited guaranty of no more than ten percent of the aggregate principal balance of the mortgage loans. With respect to distribution of this issue, the Supplement provided, in pertinent part:

> Subject to the terms and conditions of [an] Underwriting Agreement ... among [SPN Bank, its parent Security Pacific Corporation and Kidder, Peabody & Co., Inc.], under which [SPN Bank] and Kidder Peabody ... will act as [the Underwriters] ..., the Certificates are being purchased from [SPN Bank] by the Underwriters upon issuance. Distribution of the Certificates is being made by the Underwriters from time to time in negotiated transactions or otherwise at varying prices to be determined at the time of sale.

On February 23, 1987, the sale of certificates for Series 1987–B closed and the certificates were delivered to their purchasers. [The court holds that the banking laws did not prevent banks from engaging in such activities].

NOTE

The private mortgage back process has been described in more detail as follows:

> The two largest originators of mortgage loans are mortgage bankers and savings and loan associations. Mortgage bankers are frequently affiliates of financial institutions. Savings and loan associations historically have supplied funds for housing and remain the primary suppliers of mortgage credit to home owners. Their chief assets, mortgage loans, traditionally had maturities of thirty years and had fixed rates of interest. By contrast, sixty-five percent of a typical saving and loan association's liabilities are time and savings deposits that will mature in less than one year. Thus, an association's liabilities could be renegotiated at higher rates as interest rates increased, while its assets, mortgage loans, remained fixed. To avoid the problems that mismatching the maturities of assets and liabilities can

cause, and to increase the amount of new funds available to finance housing, savings and loan associations and other depository institutions have introduced adjustable rate mortgages and have also sought to pass the investment and interest rate risk to private investors through the sale of whole loans and mortgage securities.

Creation of the most common form of mortgage security, the mortgage pass-through security, begins with the formation of a pool of mortgages. The mortgages may be originated by the issuer, or purchased from other lenders that meet the issuer's eligibility standards. When loans are purchased from other lenders, they must generally conform with the issuer's underwriting standards. Mortgage pools are typically formed by savings and loan associations, commercial banks, mortgage bankers or other mortgage lenders, including developers, who may desire to obtain a fixed return on their loans and to avoid subjecting themselves to interest rate risk. In order to hedge against changes in interest rates while the pools are being formed, the originator may enter into forward commitments, in which investors contract to purchase, at a fixed price, interests in the pool of mortgage loans that the originator expects to produce in the future.

When a pool of mortgage loans has been gathered, the loans are transferred to a trustee. The trustee, in turn, typically will deliver certificates evidencing beneficial ownership in the pool. If the certificates have been sold pursuant to forward commitments, the trustee will give the certificates to an underwriter for distribution to investors. The certificates also may be placed directly with a small number of institutional investors.

Once the pool of mortgages has been transferred to the trust, the originator frequently will act as "servicer" of the pool, collecting mortgage payments on behalf of investors in the trust and performing other duties comparable to those of a lender including foreclosing on defaulted mortgage notes. These duties are set forth in a contract between the servicer and the trustee. The servicer receives a fee equal to a percentage of the total principal amount of mortgages in the pool, which is deducted from the interest payments collected from the mortgagors.

Edward L. Pittman, Economic and Regulatory Developments Affecting Mortgage Related Securities, 64 Notre Dame L. Rev. 497, 501–502 (1989).

Credit enhancement

An important aspect of the securitization process is credit enhancement, which allows an originator to obtain funds at a lower rate than its credit might not otherwise support. Consider the following letter to the staff of the Securities and Exchange Commission:

> * * * Econo Lodges of America, Inc. ("Econo Lodges") and Econo Lodges Receivables Funding Corp. ("Funding Corp."), an indirect, wholly-owned subsidiary of Econo Lodges, . . . request advice from the

Staff of the Commission that no enforcement action will be recommended if Econo Lodges implements a reorganization of its operations and Funding Corp. issues certain indebtedness without Funding Corp.'s registering under the Investment Company Act of 1940 (the "1940 Act"). Econo Lodges proposes to cause certain franchise fee receivables generated by the hotel and motel franchise business of Econo Lodges to be contributed to Funding Corp. Funding Corp. in turn proposes to issue and sell, pursuant to a private placement exempt from registration under the Securities Act of 1933, as amended (the "Securities Act"), notes secured by a security interest in the franchise fee receivables so contributed to Funding Corp. (the "Notes"). The net proceeds from the sale of the Notes by Funding Corp. will from time to time be loaned to Econo Lodges for use in general corporate purposes on an as-needed basis. * * *

Econo Lodges is a large national lodging chain whose business is currently conducted exclusively through franchising and franchising-related activities. On September 15, 1989, there were 543 Econo Lodges facilities, all of which were franchised and none of which were owned by Econo Lodges. Econo Lodges intends to pursue its future growth through franchising activities, although it may decide to purchase and/or construct additional hotels in limited number that it may ultimately sell to franchisees. Econo Lodges is not an investment company within the meaning of the 1940 Act.

Econo Lodges' standard form of franchise agreement provides for initial fees payable upon execution of the franchise agreement, and royalty fees and advertising and advance reservation system fees payable on a weekly basis after a franchised unit is opened for business (collectively, the "Franchise Fees"). In essence, the franchise agreements represent the sale by Econo Lodges to the franchisees of membership in the "Econo Lodges System," a package of trademarks, know-how, advertising, reservation, consulting and other services which are made available by Econo Lodges to its franchisees and which, taken as an integrated whole, comprises the hotel and motel franchising business of Econo Lodges. Under the current form of franchise agreement, Econo Lodges performs the following services for its franchisees in exchange for their payment of Franchise Fees: (1) Econo Lodges promotes national advertising campaigns and provides advertising assistance; (2) Econo Lodges provides training in the form of franchisee orientation and manager training courses conducted for the franchisees and the managers of the facilities under franchise; (3) Econo Lodges shares know-how by loaning periodically updated systems-standards confidential manuals to franchisees and periodically publishing newsletters and operational bulletins that set forth policies and procedures for the management of Econo Lodges; (4) Econo Lodges provides and affords access to a nation-wide advertising and advance reservation service at a fee of up to 2 1/2% of gross room receipts (beyond which there is no extra cost); (5) Econo Lodges makes available its logos and other trademarks; (6) Econo Lodges reviews and inspects facilities and consults with franchisees in respect of construction, renovation, or substantial improvements of physical plant; (7) Econo Lodges conducts frequent quality assurance inspections of the facilities; (8) Econo Lodges consults with and advises franchisees regarding the required remodeling and alterations necessary to insure compliance with company standards; (9) Econo Lodges provides franchisees with a bulk purchasing service for, as well as information as to sources for the purchase of, approved furniture, equipment, signs, and supplies; and (10) Econo Lodges issues a semi-annual directory for distribution among motel guests and other travelers, advertising Econo Lodges motels in good standing. The franchise agreements which are entered into between Econo Lodges and the franchisee typically are for a term of five years and are automatically renewed for up to three additional five-year periods unless a notice of non-renewal is given by either the franchisee or Econo Lodges within specified time periods at the end of each such five-year period.

The proposed transaction involves the following steps: (1) Econo Lodges will contribute as a capital contribution franchise agreements covering various Econo Lodges hotel sites (the "Franchise Agreements") to Econo Lodges Receivables Holding Corp., to be organized as a wholly-owned subsidiary of Econo Lodges ("Holding Corp."); (2) Holding Corp. will contribute as a capital contribution the royalty fee receivables (the "Receivables") under the Franchise Agreements to Funding Corp., to be organized as a wholly-owned subsidiary of Holding Corp.; (3) Holding Corp. and Econo Lodges will enter into an agreement (the "Franchise Management Agreement") under which Econo Lodges will assume, as the agent of Holding Corp., responsibility for carrying out Holding Corp.'s obligations under the Franchise Agreements contributed to Holding Corp.; (4) Econo Lodges will assign as a capital contribution to Holding Corp., which will assign as a capital contribution to Funding Corp., rights with respect to various trademarks and other intellectual property rights (collectively, the "Marks"), subject to licenses to Econo Lodges and Holding Corp. for certain limited purposes (and in particular with respect to the application of the Marks to the hotel sites covered by the Franchise Agreements); (5) Funding Corp. will issue the Notes and will grant to the holders of the Notes a security interest in the Receivables and the Marks (subject to the licenses referred to above); and (6) Funding Corp. will loan the proceeds of the sale of the Notes to Econo Lodges, which will use such proceeds for general corporate purposes. It is possible that not all of such proceeds will be immediately required by Econo Lodges, in which case Funding Corp. will invest such proceeds on an interim basis in U.S. government securities, high-grade corporate paper or other Eligible Investments (as such term is defined in the Indenture governing the Notes). Funds not immediately required by Econo Lodges will be loaned by Funding Corp. to Econo Lodges on an as-needed basis. Loans from Funding Corp. to Econo Lodges will be evidenced by a long-term note or notes which may or may not require any regularly scheduled principal payments prior to maturity.

Funding Corp. will conduct no business other than as described in the preceding paragraph. As part of the transaction, Funding Corp. will grant to the Trustee under the Indenture governing the Notes (the "Trustee") for the benefit of the holders of the Notes a security interest in the following collateral: (1) Funding Corp.'s rights to the Receivables; (2) Funding Corp.'s rights with respect to the Marks; (3) Funding Corp.'s rights under a licensing agreement to be entered into between Funding Corp. and Holding Corp. pursuant to which Funding Corp. will grant Holding Corp. exclusive rights to license the Marks solely in connection with the Franchise Agreements; and (4) any proceeds from any of the foregoing. Thus, substantially all of Funding Corp.'s assets (other than the net proceeds from the sale of the Notes and the note or notes evidencing loans thereof from Funding Corp. to Econo Lodges) will serve as collateral to secure performance by Funding Corp. of its obligations under the Notes and the Indenture.

The precise flow of the funds to be paid over by franchisees under the Franchise Agreements will operate in the following manner. Sums due under the Franchise Agreements will be collected by Econo Lodges as agent under the Franchise Management Agreement for Funding Corp. and Holding Corp. Funds so collected by Econo Lodges will be deposited upon receipt directly into one or more segregated accounts (the "Deposit Account") in the name of Econo Lodges, Funding Corp., Holding Corp. and the Trustee.[2] Promptly after the funds are deposited into the Deposit Account, Econo Lodges will transfer the Receivables (net of certain amounts owed to Econo Lodges by Funding Corp. pursuant to the Franchise Management Agreement) to a bank account maintained by or for the benefit of the Trustee (the "Collection Account"). Econo Lodges will remit certain other funds collected under the Franchise Agreements to Holding Corp. Payments of principal and interest on the Notes will be made from the Collection Account by the Trustee. After appropriate provision for debt service requirements, the balance of funds remaining in the Collection Account will either be (1) transferred into a segregated reserve account (the "Reserve Account") if necessary to establish or maintain a reserve for Funding Corp. is future debt service requirements in the event of any future revenue shortfall from the Receivables; (2) transferred from the Collection Account to Econo Lodges in payment of a service fee due from Funding Corp. under the Franchise Management Agreement; or (3) transferred from the Collection Ac-

---

2. The Notes will be issued by Funding Corp. under an Indenture to be entered into between Funding Corp. and the Trustee. It is expected that the Trustee will be a banking association unaffiliated with any of the various Econo Lodges entities.

count by the payment of dividends by Funding Corp. to Holding Corp. (which dividends may ultimately be paid to Econo Lodges). In summary, funds due under the Franchise Agreements will be (1) initially deposited into the Deposit Account (net of monies owed to Econo Lodges by Funding Corp.), (2) transferred to the Collection Account (net of monies paid to Holding Corp.), (3) transferred to the Reserve Account (net of debt service on the Notes) and/or (4) transferred to Holding Corp. or Econo Lodges (net of debt service on the Notes) in payment of Funding Corp.'s obligations or as dividends.

The transaction is designed to reduce Econo Lodges' overall financing costs. By organizing and financing Holding Corp. and Funding Corp. as described above, Econo Lodges believes that it can borrow at a lower effective interest cost due to the greater security afforded to the creditors of Funding Corp. by means of the security interest granted in the Receivables to support the Notes, and because the assets of Holding Corp. and Funding Corp. (which are structured to be "bankruptcy remote" entities) will not be subject to the claims of Econo Lodges' creditors. Econo Lodges is seeking to have the Notes rated as investment grade securities by Standard & Poor's Corporation.

Letter from John J. Huber, Latham & Watkins, Attorneys at Law, Washington, D.C. to W. John McGuire, Special Counsel, Office of Chief Counsel, Division of Investment Management, Securities and Exchange Commission, Washington, D.C. dated October 11, 1989.

SECTION 2. INSTRUMENT DESIGN AND TRADING MARKETS

The "securitization" of cash flows of corporations has been a popular form of structured finance. This is not a completely new process. Factors for many years advanced funds on or bought accounts receivables of businesses. See Chapter 3. Securitization, however, is distinctive in placing a set of cash flows into a separate bankruptcy remote "special purpose" vehicle or entity (an "SPV" or "SPE" as they are often called). The SPE's only assets are these cash flows or perhaps additional collateral or guarantees. The SPE then sells ownership interests itself that entitles the holder to their aliquot portion of the cash flow. These interests are sometimes called asset-backed securities.

One early such transaction was developed for the mortgage market by the Government National Mortgage Association ("GNMA" or "Ginnnie Mae"), a United States Government corporation lodged in the Department of Housing and Urban Development. GNMA helped create a secondary market in mortgages. The first step in that process started in 1934 with the creation of the Federal Housing Administration, a federal agency that insured the performance of qualifying mortgages. That effort was expanded with similar provisions for mortgage loans to veterans. This removed the default risk concern for qualifying loans, aiding the resale of those mortgages.

The Federal National Mortgage Association (now known as Fannie Mae), a government entity created in 1938 (and privatized in 1968), was authorized to create a secondary market in government insured mortgages. Before the financial crisis in 2008, it is one of the largest corporations in America, and its shares traded on the New York Stock Exchange. Fannie Mae purchases mortgages guaranteed by the Veterans Administration and the Federal Housing Authority. Another entity, the Federal Home Loan Mortgage Corporation (now known as Freddie Mac) that was chartered in 1970 buys conventional mortgages from banks and other federally insured deposit institutions. See generally American Bankers Mortgage Corp. v. Federal Home Loan Mortgage Corp., 75 F.3d 1401 (9th Cir.) cert. denied, 519 U.S. 812, 117 S.Ct. 58, 136 L.Ed.2d 21 (1996) (describing Freddie Mac's mortgage operations). Fannie Mae and Freddie Mac were supervised by the Office of Federal Housing Enterprise Oversight within the Department of Housing and Urban Development. It was replaced by the Federal Housing Finance Authority in July 2008 as concerns mounted over the operations and losses being experienced by Fannie Mae and Freddie Mac during the financial crisis.

These two bodies facilitated the ability of financial institutions to originate mortgages and then sell those mortgages to investors. This process was greatly aided by the creation of "pass-through" certificates by GNMA in 1970. That entity sought to increase the funds available for home mortgages through the sale of these certificates. A GNMA certificate is in effect an ownership interest in a pool or "package" of home mortgages. The holder of a GNMA will receive an aliquot portion of all interest and principal payments of the mortgages in that pool of mortgages. These mortgages are often associated with other government programs guaranteeing certain mortgage lending such as those obtained through the Veterans Administration and the Federal Housing Authority.

The following is a description of the process for originating GNMA pass-through certificates:

> The mortgage pool would be formed by a [private] mortgage company, ... such as Jefferson, which had originated or bought the necessary FHA and VA mortgages, closed the loans, and would place the mortgage documents in the custody of a supervised lender, usually a commercial bank. The custodian bank would certify to GNMA that it had physical possession of the proper documentation for all loans in the pool and would forward a list of the loans to GNMA with other required forms. GNMA would approve the issue, assign a pool number and a series of certificate numbers, and prepare the certificates. The certificates could be issued in the name of the issuer or in a street name. The issuer, under contractual arrangement with GNMA, would be responsible for servicing and administering the mortgages forming the pool and would receive monthly remuneration for these functions.

First National Bank of Chicago v. Jefferson Mortgage Co., 576 F.2d 479, n.1 (3d Cir.1978).

The GNMA certificate was further described by the Supreme Court in the following case.

ROCKFORD LIFE INSURANCE CO. v. ILLINOIS DEPT. OF REVENUE

482 U.S. 182, 107 S.Ct. 2312, 96 L.Ed.2d 152 (1987).

JUSTICE STEVENS delivered the opinion of the Court.

This case involves financial instruments commonly known as "Ginnie Maes." These instruments are issued by private financial institutions, which are obliged to make timely payment of the principal and interest as set forth in the certificates. The Government National Mortgage Association (GNMA) guarantees that the payments will be made as scheduled. * * *

The instruments involved here are standard securities bearing the title "Mortgage Backed Certificate Guaranteed by Government National Mortgage Association." True to that title, the instruments contain a provision in which GNMA pledges the "full faith and credit of the United States" to secure the timely payment of the interest and principal set forth in the instrument. The purpose of the guarantee, and the function of GNMA, which is a wholly owned government corporation within the Department of Housing and Urban Development, is to attract investors into the mortgage market by minimizing the risk of loss.[3] See 12 U.S.C. § 1716(a). There is uncontradicted evidence in the record supporting the conclusion that GNMA's guarantee is responsible for the ready marketability of these securities. That guarantee is not the primary obligation described in the instrument, however. The duty to make monthly payments of principal and interest to the investors falls squarely on the issuer of the certificate.

The issuer of the certificate is a private party, generally a financial institution, that possesses a pool of federally guaranteed mortgages.[4] Those individual mortgages are the product of transactions between individual borrowers and private lending institutions. It is this pool of private obligations that provides the source of funds, as well as the

---

3. "The Mortgage–Backed Securities Program provides a means for channeling funds from the Nation's securities markets into the housing market. The U.S. Government full faith and credit guaranty of securities makes them widely accepted in those sectors of the capital markets that otherwise would not be likely to supply funds to the mortgage market. The funds raised through the securities issued are used to make residential and other mortgage loans. Through this process, the program serves to increase the overall supply of credit available for housing and helps to assure that this credit is available at reasonable interest rates." Dept. of Housing and Urban Development, Handbook GNMA 5500.1 Rev. 6, GNMA I Mortgage Backed Securities Guide 1–1 (1984) (hereinafter GNMA Guide).

4. The issuer must satisfy various financial requirements imposed by the Federal Housing Authority (FHA) and GNMA. See 24 CFR § 390.3 (1986). In addition each of the individual mortgages in the pool must be guaranteed by the FHA, the Veterans Administration, or another Government agency. Ibid.

primary security, for the principal and interest that the issuer promises to pay to the order of the holder of the instrument. After a pool of qualified mortgages is assembled by a qualified issuer, the issuer enters into an agreement with GNMA authorizing the issuer to sell one or more certificates, each of which is proportionately based on and backed by all the mortgages in the designated pool, and each of which is also guaranteed by GNMA. The issuer thereafter may sell the "mortgage-backed certificates" to holders such as Rockford. The issuer administers the pool by collecting principal and interest from the individual mortgagors and remitting the amounts specified in the certificates to the holders. GNMA's costs for the regulatory duties is covered by a fee charged to the issuer. Unless the issuer defaults in its payments to the holder of a certificate, no federal funds are used in connection with the issuance and sale of these securities, the administration of the pool of mortgages, or the payments of principal and interest set forth in the certificates.

Under the type of Ginnie Maes involved in this case, the issuer is required to continue to make payments to the holders even if an individual mortgage in the pool becomes delinquent. In such event, the issuer may pursue its remedies against the individual mortgagor, or the guarantor of the mortgage, but the issuer does not have any rights against GNMA. GNMA's guarantee is implicated only if the issuer fails to meet its obligations to the holders under the certificates. In that event the holder proceeds directly against GNMA, and not against the issuer. But the risk of actual loss to GNMA is minimal because its guarantee is secured not only by the individual mortgages in the pool but also by the separate guarantee of each of those mortgages, and by a fidelity bond which the issuer is required to post. See 24 CFR § 390.1 (1986). * * * [The court then holds that GNMA certificates are not immune from state taxation].

NOTES

1. The securitization process seems to be a "win-win" situation for borrowers and lenders for GNMA pass-through securities. The borrower has better access to funds for a mortgage at a favorable rate because of the government guarantee. The lender need not concern itself with defaults and a secondary market makes the loan liquid. Do you see any faults in the concept? Who bears the risk of loss from defaults?

2. Another government corporation, the Federal Agricultural Mortgage Corporation ("Farmer Mac"), was created in 1988 to establish a secondary market in farm loans. It buys and guarantees farm loans in order to make them saleable. Farmer Mac is overseen by the Farm Credit Administration. Alison L. Cowan, One Man Stands Watch on Billions in Farm loans, N.Y. Times, June 20, 2002, at C1.

3. The Student Loan Marketing Association ("Sallie Mae") provided finance to banks making student loans under the federal Guaranteed Student

Loan Program. Sallie Mae purchased student loans in the secondary market and securitized some of those loans. See Student Loan Marketing Association v. Riley, 104 F.3d 397 (D.C.Cir.), cert. denied, 522 U.S. 913, 118 S.Ct. 295, 139 L.Ed.2d 227 (1997) (describing this process). Do you understand how this process made additional funds available for student loans? Much of the private sector student loan business was taken over by the government in 2010.

Private Mortgage Backed Securities

Private banks also entered the mortgage backed security market. They were aided by some additional legislation:

> On February 24, 1985, President Reagan signed into law the Secondary Mortgage Market Enhancement Act ("SMMEA"), which was designed to increase the flow of funds to housing by facilitating the participation of the private sector in the secondary mortgage market. In order to encourage private firms to enter the secondary mortgage market, SMMEA amended several provisions of the Securities Exchange Act of 1934 ("Exchange Act") and designated privately issued "mortgage related securities" as "legal investments" for state and federally regulated financial institutions. Through these amendments, Congress intended to place privately sponsored mortgage securities on similar footing, under federal and state laws, with the mortgage securities issued or guaranteed by the government or government sponsored agencies.
>
> Since the adoption of SMMEA, the market for mortgage securities has increased dramatically. Already, the market for all mortgage securities, including privately sponsored securities, has reached that of municipal and corporate bonds. From 1984 through 1988, the total amount of private mortgage securities offered yearly increased from ten billion dollars to over seventy-one billion dollars. Moreover, in 1988, over one-third of all non-governmental offerings were mortgage securities.

Edward L. Pittman, Economic and Regulatory Developments Affecting Mortgage Related Securities, 64 Notre Dame L. Rev. 497 (1989).

The SMMEA legislation was needed to assure that financial institutions purchasing these instruments did not run afoul of prudential investment standards for fiduciaries. The prudent man rule created by the decision of the court in Harvard College v. Amory, 26 Mass. (9 Pick.) 446, 454 (1830) required fiduciaries in their investments to act in the same manner as "men of prudence, discretion and intelligence manage their own affairs, not in regard to speculation, but in regard to the permanent disposition of their funds, considering the probable income as the probable safety of the capital to be invested." This standard was uncertain in scope and many states adopted "legal lists" specifying what securities were appropriate for investment by trustees. SMMEA sought to assure that mortgage-backed securities were on the legal list for the institutions affected by that legislation.

Private lenders packaging loans do not have a government guarantee or backing and the loans in the pool may not be guaranteed by the government. To offset that disadvantage, the conventional mortgage pools may be over-collateralized or have a guarantee or other security arrangement from a large financial institution to provide better protection from default on the underlying mortgages.

Fannie Mae and Freddie Mac have been criticized for the unfair advantage they have in acting as governmental corporations. Among other things, they were not subject to the same accounting and disclosure requirements imposed on private issuers, and they were dropping their lending standards and increasing the likelihood of defaults. III Jerry W. Markham, A Financial History of the United States: From the Age of Derivatives Into the New Millennium (1970–2001) 347 (2002). A government report suggested that more disclosures were needed. SEC, Dept. Treasury & Office of Fed. Housing Enterprise Oversight, Staff Report: Enhancing Disclosures in the Mortgage Backed Securities Market, pt. E.4 (Jan. 2003). Freddie Mac was at the center of a scandal in 2003 over accounting errors it made in its own financial statements to the tune of about $5 billion. Kathleen Day & David Hilzenrath, Analyst's Question Freddie's New CEO On His Role in Deals; Parseghian Says He Got Bad Advice, Wash. Post, Aug. 7, 2003, at EO2. Congress began considering legislation to enhance regulatory oversight. Fannie Mae had also been incorrectly accounting for its operations, overstating its revenues by $9 billion. The Office of Federal Housing Enterprise Oversight (OFHEO), an independent entity within the Department of Housing and Urban Development was the designated regulator for Fannie Mae and Freddie Mac. OFHEO stepped up its regulatory efforts after these revelations. Critics of Fannie Mae and Freddie Mac have urged that they be stripped of their quasi-governmental status. Peter J. Wallison, *Privatizing Fannie Mae, Freddie Mac, and the Federal Investment Risks and CMOs.*

The Subprime Crisis

Critics of Fannie Mae and Freddie Mac had been warning for some time that their huge portfolios and risk exposures posed systemic risk. Fannie Mae for example had purchased or guaranteed some $270 billion in subprime mortgages between 2005 and 2008.[5] Efforts by the George W. Bush administration to regulate Fannie Mae and Freddie Mac as banks were blocked in congress.[6] Fannie Mae and Freddie Mac suffered enormous losses as the subprime crisis worsened in 2008. In July 2008, the government announced that Freddie and Fannie were technically insolvent. The Housing and Economic Recovery Act was then passed. It created the Federal Housing Finance Agency as the new regulator for Fannie and Freddie, taking over the duties of OFHEO and the Federal Housing Finance Board. That legislation also created an unlimited credit line for Fannie and Freddie.[7] Losses continued at Fannie and Freddie and on September 8, 2008, the Treasury Department seized control of both of those entities and they were placed into conservatorship. The government injected about $150 billion into Fannie and Freddie in order to keep them operating. The Federal Reserve Board was authorized to purchase $1.25 trillion in Fannie and Freddie assets.[8]

---

5. Jerry W. Markham, A Financial History of the United States, From the Subprime Crisis to the Great Recession (2006–2009) 399 (2011).

6. Id. at 401.

7. Id. at 522–523.

8. Id. at 709.

A former executive at Fannie Mae testified before congress in December 2008 that Fannie Mae and Freddie Mac were then guaranteeing or holding 10.5 million subprime loans covering $1.6 trillion in debt, or one in three subprime loans. They also held two-thirds of outstanding Alt–A mortgages, which were those rated just above subprime. He predicted that mortgages held by Fannie and Freddie would result in 8 million foreclosures.[9] Fannie and Freddie had been given quotas by the federal government before the subprime crisis that had required them to commit to keeping at least half of their portfolio in subprime loans.[10] Those quotas and lax lending standards led to the disaster at Fannie and Freddie.

Interestingly, the massive Dodd–Frank financial services reform legislation that was passed in July 2010 did nothing to reform Fannie and Freddie. Rather it called only for a study of their operations.[11] By that time, most private mortgage issuers had cut back their lending and Fannie and Freddie were making or guarantying most residential mortgages. However, the new Fannie and Freddie regulator announced on September 2, 2010 that they would no longer be allowed to buy mortgages in order to meet affordable housing goals.[12]

Investment Risks and CMOs

Pass-through certificate programs are in effect selling the mortgages originated by private financial institutions to the investors purchasing the pool certificates. The proceeds of that sale are then available to be used to make more mortgages, thereby continually increasing the amount and sources of funds available for home mortgages and increasing home ownership. These certificates traditionally paid higher rates than other government issued securities.

The high rates of interest and low default risk made pass through securities a desirable investment. There are, however, some unique aspects of these certificates that raise some investment concerns. These pass through certificates pay both principal and interest from the pooled mortgages to the holder of the certificate. Monthly mortgage payments conventionally contain both a principal and interest component. This raises a "reinvestment risk," *i.e.*, the principal and interest received by the certificate holder must be reinvested in another instrument that may pay a lower interest rate than was received under the certificate.

A related concern is the "prepayment risk." This is a reference to the fact that mortgages may be prepaid before their maturity date. In such event, those principal repayments will be passed through the pool to the certificate holder and will have to be reinvested.

---

9. Id. at 590.

10. Id. at 704.

11. Dodd–Frank Wall Street Reform and Consumer Protection Act of 2010 at § 1074.

12. Nick Timiraos, Regulator Issues Rules on Purchases of Mortgages, Wall St. J., Sept. 3, 2010, at C3.

Because the trustee for a mortgage pass-through security was forced to play a passive role for tax purposes, all prepayments of principal on the underlying mortgage loans were passed through to investors, resulting in cash flow problems. Although a pool of mortgages may call for payment over the course of thirty years, excess payments or prepayments resulting from the sale, refinancing, or foreclosure of mortgaged property are proportionately distributed to the investors as soon as they are received by the trust. Since it is difficult to forecast the changes in interest rates and other conditions that might cause early payment of mortgage loans, investors risked unexpected increases in income during periods when the tax consequences may have been adverse. Moreover, the ability of the mortgagor to refinance his loan during periods when interest rates have decreased, exposes the investor in a mortgage pass-through security to "reinvestment risk," since he or she may be unable to reinvest the money being distributed by the trust in investments of comparable quality bearing the same yield.

The yield that an investor receives on a debt security is a function of current interest rates, any premium or discount paid for the security, and the expected maturity date. As suggested above, there is no way to accurately anticipate the amount of prepayments that will result from changes in interest rates or other economic conditions, so that investors in a pass-through security cannot be sure of their actual yield. However, barometers have been developed to gauge the prepayment speed of mortgage pools. Detailed records of the past prepayment experience of pools of mortgages allow dealers to forecast yields based upon historical patterns. Generally, premium coupon securities prepay faster than lower coupon securities, because the value of the mortgagors' "refinance option" is greater. Nevertheless, the actual prepayment experience of each pool may differ from the models developed by the industry because of the geographic location of the mortgages, the interest rate of the mortgages, the age of the mortgage pool, and the type of mortgages, among other factors. Moreover, the prepayment experience of a particular pool only shows the reaction of mortgagors in previous interest rate environments. Consequently, the investor must still try to predict the impact that changes in interest rates will have on historical prepayment patterns.

Edward L. Pittman, Economic and Regulatory Developments Affecting Mortgage Related Securities, 64 Notre Dame L. Rev. 497, 503–505 (1989).

Collateralized Mortgage Obligations

In times of declining interest rates, mortgage owners often refinance their homes at a lower rate, resulting in massive prepayments that will be passed through to the certificate holder who will have to reinvest those funds at the lower prevailing interest rates. A new instrument was created by Freddie Mac to deal with the prepayment risk—the collateralized mortgage obligation ("CMO"). That instrument was given a boost by the

Tax reform Act of 1986 that provided tax advantages to real estate mortgage investment conduits ("REMICs"). *See* Thomas A Kasper & Les Parker, Understanding Collateralized Mortgage Obligations, 1987 Colum. Bus. L. Rev. 139 (describing CMOs and their use by REMICs).

The CMO sought to even out the cash flow from the mortgages in the pass through pool. This was done by selling tranches or strips in the pool of mortgages with differing maturity dates. The tranche with the shortest maturity date is the first to receive principal payments from the mortgages. Once that tranche is paid off, the next tranche begins receiving the mortgage principal payments and so on until all tranches are paid off. The result is that the tranches receiving mortgage principal payments last have longer average lives than those first receiving that principal. This helps defer the concern with prepayment for those tranches receiving principal last.

The use of several tranches in a CMO allows greater flexibility on the part of investors seeking differing maturity dates. They also add a great deal of complexity to this investment. For example, in order to further stabilize the cash flow from the pool of mortgages, another tranche was created that in effect was a zero coupon bond. This "Z" bond tranche does not make periodic interest or principal payments. Rather, the bond is paid off when the other classes are retired. The Z bond in a CMO has no definite maturity date, making it difficult to price.

CMOs may also use floating rate securities that pay interest on the basis of some specified interest index rate, but are often capped because the underlying mortgages will not support too great of an increase. Inverse floaters may also be used. These are certificates that pay less when interest rates increase and more when rates decrease. Inverse floaters can be used to offset the effects of the floating rate tranche.

All in all, CMOs are very complicated instruments. Consider the following excerpt from a prospectus filed with the Securities and Exchange Commission.

> OFFERED SECURITIES REMIC Pass–Through Certificates, Series 1999–1, consisting of:
>
>> One Class of Senior Class A CitiCertificates, which is subdivided into ten Subclasses, of which nine Subclasses are being offered hereby,
>>
>> One Class of Senior Subordinated Class M CitiCertificates and
>>
>> One Class of Subordinated Class B CitiCertificates, which is subdivided into five Subclasses, of which two Subclasses (Class B–1 and Class B–2) are being offered hereby.
>
> The securities listed above and offered hereby are collectively called the "Offered CitiCertificates".
>
> In addition to the Offered CitiCertificates, the Trust will issue one interest-only Subclass of Senior Class A CitiCertificates (the "Class

A–IO CitiCertificates''), three Subclasses of Subordinated Class B–3, Class B–4 and Class B–5 CitiCertificates and one class of residual certificates. None of these CitiCertificates or residual certificates are offered hereby.

The Class A–9 CitiCertificates are principal-only CitiCertificates and do not accrue interest. The Class B–1 and Class B–2 CitiCertificates are the "Offered Class B CitiCertificates", and each is an "Offered Class B Subclass".

On the Closing Date, the total principal amount of CitiCertificates will equal the total principal amount of mortgage loans in the Trust, as measured on the Cut–Off Date.

The ratio of (a) the total outstanding principal amount of a Class or Subclass of CitiCertificates and (b) the total outstanding principal amount of the mortgage loans, is called the "Beneficial Percentage" of that Class or Subclass. The Beneficial Percentage of a Class or Subclass reflects its proportionate undivided beneficial interest in the assets of the Trust. On the Closing Date,

The Class A Beneficial Percentage will be from 95% to 97%,

The Class M Beneficial Percentage will be from 1.40% to 2.40%,

The Class B Beneficial Percentage will be from 1.60% to 2.60%,

The Class B–1 Beneficial Percentage will be from 0.65% to 1.05% and

The Class B–2 Beneficial Percentage will be from 0.25% to 0.65%.

The Class A–IO CitiCertificates are interest-only certificates and, therefore, their Beneficial Percentage is zero.

> Each Class A CitiCertificate offered hereby and each Class M CitiCertificate will qualify at issuance as a "mortgage related security" within the meaning of the Secondary Mortgage Market Enhancement Act of 1984. The Class B–1 and Class B–2 CitiCertificates will not so qualify. * * *

The mortgage loans will be divided into two groups. The first group, having a total principal balance of approximately $12,155,027, will comprise all loans having a net note rate of less than 6.50% per annum. This group is called the "Discount Loan" group. The second group, having a total principal balance of approximately $288,845,752, will comprise all loans having a net note rate equal to or greater than 6.50% per annum. This group is called the "Premium Loan" group. The "net note rate" or "NNR" for a particular mortgage loan is the per annum rate at which interest accrues on the outstanding principal amount of the mortgage loan, minus the servicing fee of 0.25% per annum.

RATIO STRIPPING This transaction uses a structuring technique known as "ratio stripping". This technique converts a pool of mortgage loans with varying interest rates into a pool with a single fixed interest rate, or target rate. This is achieved by dividing the loans into one group of Premium Loans with NNRs equal to or greater than the target rate and one group of Discount Loans with NNRs less than the target rate. Then,

> For each Premium Loan, the interest accruing and paid in excess of that at the target rate is stripped off from that loan and applied to make payments on an interest-only class of securities.

> For each Discount Loan, a portion of the principal of such loan is stripped off and applied to create a principal-only class of securities. This stripping-off of principal is done in order to cause the effective yield on the Discount Loan to equal the target rate. The lower the net note rate on a loan, the greater the portion of principal stripped off. The portion of principal stripped off from each Discount Loan is equal to: (target rate minus NNR)/target rate. This ratio, expressed as a percentage, is called the "PO Percentage" for that Discount Loan. The PO Percentage is zero for all Premium Loans.

> For each mortgage loan, all or a portion of the principal of such loan is applied to create the other Classes and Subclasses of CitiCertificates entitled to receive principal payments. The portion of each loan so applied is equal to 100% minus the PO Percentage for such loan. This percentage is called the "Non–PO Percentage". The Non–PO Percentage is 100% for each Premium Loan and ranges from 86.5% to 98.1% for the Discount Loans.

In order to preserve the allocation of the principal of the mortgage loans between the principal-only class created from the Discount Loans and all other CitiCertificates, in the event a principal loss is realized on a mortgage loan, the PO Percentage of the principal loss on that loan is allocated solely to that principal-only class and the Non–PO Percentage of such principal loss is allocated solely to the other CitiCertificates. . . .

The "target rate" for this transaction is 6.50% per annum. You should note that the Certificate Rate for the majority of the interest-bearing Offered CitiCertificates (as well as the Class B–3, Class B–4 and Class B–5 CitiCertificates not offered hereby) is equal to the target rate. The principal-only Subclass created by stripping off the PO Percentage of principal from the Discount Loans is the Class A–9 CitiCertificates. The interest-only Subclass created by stripping off the interest on the Premium Loans in excess of the target rate is the Class A–IO CitiCertificates.

DISTRIBUTION DATES The 25th day of each month, commencing in April 1999. Distribution Dates are the monthly dates on which payments of interest and principal are made on the Classes and Subclasses of CitiCertificates. If the 25th day of a month is not a business day, then the Distribution Date will be the next business day.

SOURCE OF FUNDS FOR PAYMENTS Monies received on the mortgage loans will be the source of essentially all funds available to make payments on the CitiCertificates. This source of funds includes monthly payments of principal and interest by borrowers and principal prepayments by borrowers, as well as monies received upon foreclosure and sale of properties securing defaulted mortgage loans and any proceeds of insurance policies. These funds also include any advances made due to delinquent monthly payments, as described under "Advances" below in this Summary.

Prospectus Supplement (to Prospectus Dated March 25, 1999) $298,592,684 (Approximate) Citicorp Mortgage Securities, Inc. (Packager and Servicer) REMIC Pass–Through Certificates, Series 1999–1.

Extending Securitization to Other Cash Flows

The securitization technique was extended to a broad range of other cash flows. Consider the following description in a preliminary prospectus of the securitization of credit card receivables by a bank:

> Interest at the Certificate Rate of ___% per annum will be distributed to holders of the ... Asset Backed Certificates (the "Certificates") on the 15th day of each month (or the next business day) (the "Distribution Date"), commencing ___ 15, 1987. Principal will be distributed to holders of the Certificates on each Distribution Date commencing on ___ 15, 1988. . . .
>
> Each Certificate will represent a specified percentage of an undivided interest in the California Credit Card Trust 1986–A (the "Trust") to be formed by Bank of America National Trust and Savings Association (the "Bank"). The property of the Trust will include a portfolio of Classic VISA credit card receivables (the "Receivables") generated or to be generated by the Bank in its ordinary course of business, all monies due in payment of the Receivables and the benefits of a letter of credit. The Bank will own the remaining undivided interest in the Trust not represented by the Certificates and will continue to service the Receivables.
>
> There currently is no secondary market for the Certificates and there is no assurance that one will develop.

Preliminary Prospectus, Bank of America National Trust and Savings Association, $250,000,000 California Credit Card Trust 1986–A-% Asset Backed Certificates.

The securitization of short term receivables did not fit exactly into the GNMA pass through mold:

> The typically short lives of receivables associated with revolving loan products (credit cards, home equity lines, etc.) require issuers to modify the structures used to securitize the assets. For example, a static portfolio of credit card receivables typically has a life of between five months and ten months. Because such a life is far too short for

efficient security issuance, securities backed by revolving loans are structured in a manner to facilitate management of the cash flows. Rather than distributing principal and interest to investors as received, the securities distribute cash flows in stages-a revolving phase followed by an amortization phase. During the revolving period, only interest is paid and principal payments are reinvested in additional receivables as, for example, customers use their credit cards or take additional draws on their home equity lines. At the end of the revolving period, an amortization phase begins, and principal payments are made to investors along with interest payments. Because the principal balances are repaid over a short period of time, the life of the security is largely determined by the length of the revolving period.

Comptroller of the Currency, Asset Securitization, Comptroller's Handbook 7 (Nov. 1997).

_____

NOTES

1. Collateralized Automobile Receivables ("CARS") were used to securitize automobile loans. What exactly are you receiving when you purchase such an investment? How long will the investment last? What will the effect be on the investment if interest rates change?

2. Note the advantage to the seller of credit card receivables. It obtains cash that allows it to extend more credit on its credit cards.

3. Commercial mortgage loans may also be securitized. A credit crunch in 1998, however, caused some losses as rising interest rates diminished the value of the certificates when they were issued. Commercial Mortgage Backed Securitization: A Review of the Market in Europe and the United States, 6 International Securitization & Structured Finance Report, No. 2, at 1 (Jan. 31, 2003). Commercial asset-backed securities also experienced difficulties during the financial crisis in 2007–2008. The Federal Reserve Board created a Term Asset–Backed Securities Lending Facility (TALF):

> TALF is a funding facility that will help market participants meet the credit needs of households and small businesses by supporting the issuance of asset-backed securities (ABS) collateralized by loans of various types to consumers and businesses of all sizes. Under the TALF, the Federal Reserve Bank of New York (FRBNY) will lend up to $200 billion on a non-recourse basis to holders of certain AAA-rated ABS backed by newly and recently originated consumer and small business loans. The FRBNY will lend an amount equal to the market value of the ABS less a haircut and will be secured at all times by the ABS. The U.S. Treasury Department—under the Troubled Assets Relief Program (TARP) of the Emergency Economic Stabilization Act of 2008—will provide $20 billion of credit protection to the FRBNY in connection with the TALF.

http://www.federalreserve.gov/monetarypolicy/talf.htm. TALF extended some $70 billion under this program as loans, may of which were repaid before maturity as the market strengthened.

4. In 1989, the British Petroleum Co. p.l.c. ("BP") was offering interest in the BP Prudhoe Bay Royalty Trust that was entitled to receive royalties on certain amounts of BP's production in Prudhoe Bay. Can you think of other revenue streams that could be securitized?

5. The American Stock Exchange created something called "TRACERS" that were interests in a trust that held a basket of fifteen or more investment grade fixed-income securities. The interest and principal in those securities was passed on to the holders of the trust participation certificates. What advantage does such an investment offer to investors? Exchanges were also offering ABS (Asset Backed Security) certificates that provided similar pass-through features. These instruments were likened to equity linked notes ("ELNs") that provided cash flow from a basket of equity securities.

6. The SEC has adopted a Regulation AB to govern the registration of asset backed securities and required disclosures in offerings of such securities. In adopting that regulation, the SEC noted that:

> Asset-backed securities are securities that are backed by a discrete pool of self-liquidating financial assets. Asset-backed securitization is a financing technique in which financial assets, in many cases themselves less liquid, are pooled and converted into instruments that may be offered and sold in the capital markets. In a basic securitization structure, an entity, often a financial institution and commonly known as a 'sponsor,' originates or otherwise acquires a pool of financial assets, such as mortgage loans, either directly or through an affiliate. It then sells the financial assets, again either directly or through an affiliate, to a specially created investment vehicle that issues securities 'backed' or supported by those financial assets, which securities are 'asset-backed securities.' Payment on the asset-backed securities depends primarily on the cash flows generated by the assets in the underlying pool and other rights designed to assure timely payment, such as liquidity facilities, guarantees or other features generally known as credit enhancements. The structure of asset-backed securities is intended, among other things, to insulate ABS investors from the corporate credit risk of the sponsor that originated or acquired the financial assets.

> The ABS market is fairly young and has rapidly become an important part of the U.S. capital markets. One source estimates that U.S. public non-agency ABS issuance grew from $46.8 billion in 1990 to $416 billion in 2003. Another source estimates 2003 new issuance closer to $800 billion. ABS issuance is on pace to exceed corporate debt issuance in 2004. While residential mortgages were the first financial assets to be securitized, non-mortgage related securitizations have grown to include many other types of financial assets, such as credit card receivables, auto loans and student loans.

Asset Backed Securities, Securities Act Release No. 8518 (SEC, December 12, 2004) (citations and footnotes omitted).

Consider the following securitization arrangement described in another letter to the SEC staff:

Ambassador Capital Corporation ("ACC"), a wholly-owned subsidiary of J. H. Holdings Corporation, which is wholly-owned by The Class of 1960 Trust settled by members of the Harvard College class of 1960 for the benefit of Harvard College, proposes to purchase, at a discount, some of the air travel credit card program accounts receivable (the "Receivables") of a major U.A. air carrier (the "Airline"). ACC will finance 90% of its purchases of Receivables with the proceeds of secured negotiable promissory notes (the "Notes") issued from time to time under a revolving underwriting facility (the "Facility") arranged by an investment bank (the "Bank"). 10% of ACC's purchases will be financed with the proceeds of secured advances (the "Funding Advances") made by the Facility's participants, all of which are financial institutions (the "Managers").

The Notes will have terms of one, two or three months, at ACC's option, will yield LIBOR plus 1/2% per annum, will be issued in denominations of $500,000 and will be secured by the Receivables. The Bank will offer the Notes to third-party investors. The Notes will not be offered or sold in the United States or to United States persons (except, under certain circumstances, to foreign branches of United States banks) and will be legended to restrict their offering, sale or resale in the United States or to United States persons. In addition, each Note will contain a representation that the holder thereof is not a United States person and does not hold the Note on behalf of any United States person. Any Notes not placed by the Bank with third-party investors will be allocated to the Managers, who must either purchase the unplaced Notes or make secured advances to ACC in an amount equal to the principal amount of such Notes (the "Allocation Advances"), in either case pro rata to their respective underwriting commitments.

The Funding Advances will be subordinate in priority of payment to the Notes and the Allocation Advances, such that no payments of principal of or interest on the Funding Advances may be made until all principal of and interest on the Notes and Allocation Advances has been paid in full. In the event that any of the Funding Advances are not paid when due, the Managers shall be required to make certain subordinated credit advances (the "Credit Advances"), pro rata to their several underwriting commitments to cover such shortfall. The Credit Advances shall mature at the termination of the Facility (December 31, 1988).

ACC will engage in no other business other than as described above. All of the payments on the Receivables will be made directly to lockboxes owned by ACC, and it is anticipated that the collection period will range from seven to ninety days after billing, with approximately 90% of the Receivables collected within thirty to forty-five days after billing. ACC will purchase Receivable with the proceeds of such collections to the extent that the Airline offers additional Receivables to ACC and the conditions precedent to such purchase are satisfied. The remainder of the proceeds will be invested temporarily in short-term money market obligations until applied, along with the proceeds of such temporary investments, to purchases of additional Receivables or to pay maturing Notes. Because Receivables are expected to liquidate prior to the maturity of the Notes (generally, it is expected that 40% of the Receivables will be paid within 20 days of billing and Receivables will be purchased within 15 days of billing), if Airline does not offer additional Receivables to ACC, the temporary investment of what would otherwise be idle, nonearning cash collections of Receivables pending maturity of the Notes will be necessary to produce sufficient cash to pay interest on the Notes. Airline will pay ACC an annual purchase fee and will cover the costs of the revolving underwriting facility, and ACC will pay J. H. Holdings Corporation an annual fee for various administrative services. ACC will have no assets other than cash, Receivables (and the proceeds thereof) and the temporary money market investments.

Letter from Marc Weitzen of Gordon Hurwitz Butowsky Weitzen Shalov & Wein, New York, NY to Office of Chief Counsel, Division of Investment Management, Securities and Exchange Commission, Washington, D.C. dated August 8, 1986.

NOTES

1. What exactly was the Harvard trust and the airlines accomplishing with the above arrangement? Were the airlines accelerating cash flow?

2. The above inquiries involved requests that the SEC staff would not view these arrangements to involve the Investment Company Act of 1940 that regulates mutual funds and other investment companies. If applicable, that statute would preclude the operation of these programs. See Chapter 13.

3. The isolation of receivables into an SPE (special purpose entity) protects those assets from the claims of general creditors of the firm originating the cash flow. Is this fair to those creditors? Why is such an act not subject to state fraudulent conveyance statutes? The short answer is that fair value has been given for those assets by the SPE.

NICOLE CHU
BOWIE BONDS: A KEY TO UNLOCKING THE WEALTH OF INTELLECTUAL PROPERTY

21 Hastings Comm. & Ent. L. J. 469 (1999).

On January 31, 1997, David Bowie broke a new frontier in financing by selling $55 million in bonds backed by future music royalty payments and copyrights. Music royalties and copyrights had never previously been securitized due to the uncertainty in predicting future cash flows. David Bowie's bond offering represents a "brand new beat," a novel and innovative financing method for any individual or entity who owns intellectual property rights. The concept of intellectual property securitization resolves the dilemma of inexpensively raising a large amount of money, while still retaining ownership in the underlying intellectual property.

The concept of securitizing David Bowie's catalogue of recordings and song copyrights developed during a casual conversation between William L. Zysblat, Mr. Bowie's business manager, and investment banker David Pullman, a managing director at Fahnestock & Co. Mr. Zysblat mentioned that because Mr. Bowie's recording and distribution deal was about to expire, he was looking for possible financing vehicles. Mr. Bowie wanted to raise money for two primary reasons: 1) to buy out his former manager, who owned a minority of the rights to his music, and 2) to get a significant amount of cash up-front before returning to United Kingdom residency. Mr. Pullman, known for securitizing exotic asset-backed securities (or as he calls them, "financial tech"), saw the immediate potential in Mr. Bowie's music catalogues—Mr. Bowie owned all of his music catalogues and rights dating back to the 1960's, cash flow was predictable with sales consistently over $1 million annually, there was no bad debt, and there was little risk involved. Richard Rudder, a partner at Willkie, Farr & Gallagher, was brought in to handle all the legal aspects of the transaction.

The David Bowie securities ("Bowie bonds"), offer a 7.9% interest rate with a 10–year average life and a 15–year maturity. The bonds are backed by royalties on a twenty-five album catalogue consisting of about 300 songs of Bowie's recordings and song copyrights. EMI Music provided the credit enhancement necessary for the securitization, resulting in an A3 investment grade by Moody's Investors Service. The bonds were "snapped up" by Prudential Insurance in a traditional private placement. As a result of this deal, David Bowie has topped the charts as the richest British rock star with an estate worth an estimated $917 million.

Asset securitization of intellectual property touches upon copyright, bankruptcy, tax, and securities law, as well as being impacted by the Uniform Commercial Code. This securitization technique raises new possibilities for unlocking the wealth contained in intellectual property. The long-term acceptance of intellectual property securitization will impact artists and similarly situated people and companies. This note will provide a brief overview of the securitization structure, previous securitizations, the legal and policy areas involved in creating "Bowie-style bonds," and suggest future applications not only to other musicians, but also to other entities owning intellectual property rights. * * *

In theory securitization of intellectual property is no different from typical securitizations involving credit card receivables, mortgages, and auto loans if a constant predictable cash flow exists. Intellectual property has previously been used as collateral to secure credit for start-up and financing ventures. For example, in 1995, Steven Spielberg, Jeffrey Katzenberg, and David Geffen founded Dreamworks, SKG. The one billion dollar loan used to fund the studio was arranged by Chemical Bank and secured largely by intellectual property holdings of the creators.

However, the unpredictability of the cash flow and the difficulty in finding the necessary credit enhancement for intellectual property collateral greatly increases the risk associated with the financing method of securitization. The uncertainty stems from certain event risks, for example, if no one buys the income-producing assets for six months, or if there is a lawsuit, or if the company merges with another, etc. Due diligence is generally designed to cover these type of risks for mainstream asset-backed deals, but not for intellectual property asset-backed deals. If one can overcome both the uncertainty in cash flow and find the credit enhancement, the risk is reduced and you can apply the basic securitization structure.

Applying the basic securitization structure to "Bowie bonds," David Bowie's assets are a twenty-five album catalogue, roughly 300 songs, of Bowie's recordings and song copyrights. There are several revenue sources supporting the bonds. The two main sources are record royalties and publishing revenues. Since David Bowie actually owns his own record masters, all record royalties go to him. As for publishing revenues, there are mechanical royalties, synchronical usage (e.g. films, commercials), sheet music, air play, Muzak, voice mail, live performances and tours by Bowie. So there was a predictable cash flow with a measurable history dating back three decades. The credit enhancement was a third party guarantee given by EMI Music, which entered into a 15–year licensing deal for the singer's back catalogue. The licensing deal was the collateral put up for the investor, Prudential Insurance. After 15 years, ownership of the master tapes reverts back to David Bowie. The Moody's Investors Service gave the Bowie bonds a higher rating than entities, like New York State, because of the diversity or variety of royalty sources.

David Bowie assigned these assets over to a special purpose trust, another version of a SPV. Next, the trust issued debt securities backed by the assets, which were in turn purchased by Prudential Insurance in a private placement. The proceeds from the sale were transferred back to David Bowie. As the assets generate royalties, the royalties are used to service the debt.

The Bowie Bond deal is just a hint of the possible potential of the securitization of intellectual property rights. Applications can be envisioned beyond just entertainers, to novelists, screenwriters, playwrights, inventors, sports stars, music recording and publishing companies, and patents.

NOTES

1.　Other performers have issued Bowie style bonds including Ron Isley, Rod Stewart, Dusty Springfield and James Brown. George Forman, the retired boxer, sold his name and likeness for $137.5 million to one buyer. III Jerry W. Markham, A Financial History of the United States: From the Age of Derivatives Into the New Millennium (1970–2001) 259 (2002) The Bowie Bond concept did have limitations:

> Maintaining control over his intellectual property was one of the driving forces behind Bowie's decision to securitize his assets: Bowie used some of the money he made on the deal to buy back the rights to some of his music owned by a former manager. Control of one's intellectual property is obviously a key factor in a Bowie bond issuance because it is necessary for one to own the assets that one wishes to securitize. Consequently, since the Bowie bond deal was announced, only the very top artists in the recording industry have managed to arrange a similar type of offering. This state of affairs has led some experts to speculate that only artists with "an existing catalogue of work[,] . . . one that has been in existence for a number of years[,] . . . [with a] track record you can document" are capable of executing a Bowie bond offering. David Bowie's catalogue of music had consistently sold in excess of one million recordings each year, generating the earning power and steady performance that motivated Prudential to buy the bonds. Another reason that the Bowie offering was so appealing to Prudential was the "credit enhancement" that the bonds received as a result of the fifteen year, global distribution deal that Bowie reached with his label, EMI recording. Furthermore, this credit enhancement directly affected the bond rating that Bowie received from Moody's. Although the Bowie bond deal was a private offering, the fact that Moody's gave the Bowie bond a AAA rating, the highest rating reserved only for the strongest and safest of bonds, still served an important purpose.

Adam Grant, Ziggy Stardust Reborn: A Proposed Modification of the Bowie Bond, 22 Cardozo L. Rev. 1291 (2001).

The Bowie Bonds did have one downside. Downloading on the Internet resulted in a plunge in royalties from song sales, causing the credit rating agencies to review the ratings on Bowie bonds. Jenny Wiggins, Bowie Diamonds May Turn Into Dogs, Financial Times (London), May 28, 2003, at 1.

2.　Could a movie star securitize royalties from a future movie? What other assets are susceptible to securitization? Consider the following:

In April of 1999, a federal court judge ordered the federal government to pay Glendale Federal Bank the amount of $908.9 million. That bank was owned by Golden State Bancorp, which was controlled by Ronald Perelman [the corporate raider]. That judgment followed a Supreme Court decision that held that the government had improperly changed the accounting standards retroactively for thrift associations, causing them to incur large losses. It was estimated that the Supreme Court's ruling could add another $30 billion to the total cost of the banking crisis [that occurred in the 1980s]. . . . Golden State Bancorp did not await collection from the government. It began selling litigation participation certificates that allowed investors to receive a portion of the expected award in these suits. Another S & L was issuing litigation participation certificates that were called contingent payment rights.

III Jerry W. Markham, A Financial History of the United States: From the Age of Derivatives Into the New Millennium (1970–2001) 173–174 (2002). As noted in Chapter 9, various states have also been selling interests in their tobacco litigation settlements and in lottery proceeds. The tobacco companies paid the states $6.2 billion in 2004 as a part of their $246 billion settlement with the states that was to be paid over a twenty-five year period. The states securitized about $20 billion of that settlement through bond sales. Altria Group, the former Phillip Morris companies, was hit with a $12 billion judgment in a tobacco suit. The company was required to post a bond in that amount in order to appeal that verdict but had difficulty raising the money. Some thirty states then passed statutes limiting the amount required to be posted on bond for appeals, fearing that such large bonds could bankrupt the tobacco companies and cost the states their settlements. Another threat to the settlement was a massive action brought by the federal government against the tobacco companies seeking $280 billion. The federal government, however, was encountering some difficulty in prosecuting that claim. United States v. Philip Morris USA, Inc., 396 F.3d 1190 (D.C.Cir. 2005).

3. In England, funeral home operators were securitizing their cash flows. Henry J. Pulizzi, Funeral Company Plans Bond Issue Backed by Assets, Wall St. J., March 19, 2003, at B4A. What happens to those flows if someone discovers a fountain of youth?

————————

Structured financial arrangements were extended to other areas to provide tax and accounting advantages.

Synthetic Leases

THOMAS R. FILETI & CARL R. STEEN
SYNTHETIC LEASE FINANCING FOR THE ACQUISITION AND CONSTRUCTION OF POWER GENERATION FACILITIES IN A CHANGING U.S. ENERGY ENVIRONMENT

24 Fordham Int'l L. J. 1083 (2001).

During the past two years, several leading players in the power generation industry have used "synthetic" leases to finance both the construction and acquisition of power generation assets, as well as bulk purchases of combustion turbines. Synthetic leases can offer a tax and balance sheet efficient alternative for the acquisition and construction of a power generation facility and related equipment (collectively referred to in this Essay as a "power generation facility"). A synthetic lease (also known by other names such as "off-balance sheet financing" or "tax oriented operating lease") is a financing transaction structured through a lease that satisfies the requirements for characterization of a lease as an operating lease set forth in the Financial Accounting Standards Board ("FASB") Statement 13 ("SFAS 13") and related accounting rules. 16 Because a synthetic lease allows a project sponsor to enjoy operating lease accounting treatment and avoid depreciation charges attributable to the leased asset, power producers employing this technique may obtain tangible economic advantages in the current market-driven environment. Synthetic lease financing may also allow a project sponsor greater financial flexibility to participate in a number of large scale projects and equipment purchases while mitigating the adverse credit impact of any particular project or transaction. The execution of synthetic leasing transactions in the power generation industry by leading players during the past two years may encourage others in the industry to consider such innovative approaches. * * *

Starting in the 1990s, public companies in the high-tech and biotech fields financed the acquisition of manufacturing plants, headquarters buildings, corporate campuses, and other "strategic" real estate assets using synthetic lease financing. Other public companies involved in manufacturing, retail, and other lines of business have also used this technique. * * *

The benefits of off-balance sheet financing to the lessee, as compared to traditional debt arrangements, are several-fold. These benefits primarily result from differences in how leases are characterized for tax purposes under the Internal Revenue Code and for book purposes under the standards of the Financial Accounting Standards Board ("FASB"). In general, and as discussed more fully below, for tax purposes, the lessee of an asset that is financed under a synthetic lease is treated as the owner of the asset for tax purposes and the lease is viewed as a financing for tax purposes. Thus, the lessee will enjoy the cash flow benefits of tax depreciation deductions on the leased asset and can deduct the interest component of the rent it pays under the lease. However, for accounting purposes, the lessee is viewed not as the owner, but merely as a lessee renting an asset. In its income statement, the lessee thus avoids the reduction of earnings that would be attributable to book depreciation of the leased asset. Both the leased asset and the liability of the lessee under the lease remain off the lessee's balance sheet, the book depreciation of the asset remains off the lessee's income statement, and the lessee's rental payments will be reflected as operating expenses on its income statement. (However, the transaction may be footnoted in the lessee's financial statement and, if the lessee is a reporting company, it may have certain disclosure obligations relating to the transaction under the Securities Exchange Commission rules if the lease represents a material transaction.) In addition to these tax and accounting benefits, a synthetic lease, like other lease financing transactions, represents an opportunity to finance one hundred percent of acquisition or construction costs.

The tax and accounting benefits of synthetic lease transactions can be very attractive to "balance sheet-sensitive" companies, particularly those that can make efficient use of the tax benefits of the asset. A public company or a company that is seeking to go public and that has entered into a synthetic lease will be able, when it sells its stock, to avoid the depressive effects on its earnings of book depreciation of the leased asset, and thereby enhance book income and the price that it may obtain for its stock, since that price is usually expressed as a multiple of earnings.

Companies (whether public or private) that are subject to financial covenants in indentures or credit agreements (e.g., such as requirements for minimum net worth, maximum ratio of debt to net worth, minimum profitability, or a minimum ratio of earnings to fixed charges or of liquid assets to current liabilities) also find synthetic leases attractive. They may be able to engage in a synthetic lease financing without running afoul of such covenants, whereas a financing that would be regarded as a liability under generally accepted accounting principles ("GAAP") might result in a violation of those covenants or "use up" capacity under those covenants, since those covenants are usually constructed based on GAAP classification of earnings, assets, and liabilities. In addition, companies seeking to preserve their corporate cash or revenues for their core lines of business will benefit from the one hundred percent financing features of the transaction.

These transactions are not without disadvantages, however. The typical synthetic lease is a medium-term financing, and financing a long-term asset such as a power generation facility with a medium-term liability flies in the face of conventional wisdom that a long-term asset should be financed with a long-term liability. Additionally, synthetic leases can involve high up-front advisory, accounting, and legal fees and other transaction costs. Structuring a synthetic lease for construction of a power generation facility requires compliance with a myriad of accounting rules, which can make underwriting the transaction difficult from the financing sources viewpoint. Further, because a synthetic lease (especially one in which real estate improvements, rather than equipment, form the primary asset) can involve relatively low amortization, the lessee may need to seek to "refinance" a substantial balance upon the expiration of its term. Although this feature in certain respects is not substantially different from the need to refinance the unpaid balance of a financing at its maturity, certain accounting challenges and additional transaction costs can be encountered in refinancing or unwinding a synthetic lease that would not necessarily arise in traditional financings, especially if the lessee seeks to preserve the off-balance sheet treatment of the asset in a new transaction. * * *

NOTES

1.   The authors of the above excerpt have noted that structuring of synthetic leases for off-balance sheet treatment has been made more difficult as the result of accounting changes made in the aftermath of the Enron scandal. See Financial Interpretations Nos. 45 & 46. For more on synthetic leasing see Donald J. Weidner, Synthetic Leases: Structured Finance Financial Accounting and Tax Ownership, 25 J. Corp. L. 445 (2000).

2.   The use of synthetic leases came under criticism in the wake of the collapse of the Enron Corp. in October 2001. Enron had aggressively used a number of off-balance sheet investments to conceal its true financial condition including synthetic leases. Loren Fox, Enron The Rise and Fall, 120 (2003).

PERLS

One exotic structured note is the "Multicurrency PERLS" described as follows:

> Interest on the Multicurrency Principal Exchange Rate Linked Securities (Multicurrency PERLS) offered hereby (the "Notes") will be payable in U.S. dollars based on the face amount of the Notes, semiannually in arrears on each June 14 and December 14, commencing June 14, 1990. The Notes will mature and be payable on December 14, 1992 (the "Maturity Date"). Principal in respect of each U.S. $1,000 face amount of the Notes will be payable at maturity in an amount equal to U.S. $1,000 plus the U.S. dollar equivalent of [Australian] A$1,276,30, minus the U.S. dollar equivalent of T143,000, in each case as determined by the average of the exchange rate quotations furnished by three reference dealers for Australian dollars and Yen, respectively, on the second business day prior to the Maturity Date. Accordingly, ... Noteholders would receive at maturity an amount of principal greater than, less than (to a minimum of zero) or equal to the face amount of the Notes, depending on the relative exchange rates of the U.S. dollar to the Australian dollar and of the Yen to the U.S. dollar at maturity.

Student Loan Marketing Association (SallieMae) 12% Multicurrency Principal Exchange Rate Linked Securities (Multicurrency PERLS) Due December 14,

1992 Information Statement Supplement (To Information Statement dated October 31, 1989).

Are PERLS really notes or are they something else, perhaps an investment in currency values? Consider the following somewhat pejorative description of these instruments:

PERLS stands for Principal Exchange Rate Linked Security, so named because the trade's principal repayment is linked to various foreign exchange rates, such as British pounds or German marks. PERLS look like bonds and smell like bonds. In fact, they *are* bonds-an extremely odd type of bond, however, because they behave like leveraged bets on foreign exchange rates. They are issued by reputable companies (DuPont, General Electric Credit) and U.S. government agencies (Fannie Mae, Sallie Mae), but instead of promising to repay the investor's principal at maturity, the issuers promise to repay the principal amount multiplied by some formula linked to various foreign currencies.

For example, if you paid $100 for a normal bond, you would expect to receive interest and to be repaid $100 for PERLS and expected to receive $100 at maturity, in most cases you would be wrong. Very wrong. In fact, if you bought PERLS and expected to receive exactly your principal at maturity, you either did not understand what you were buying, or you were a fool.

PERLS are a kind of bond called a structured note, which is simply a custom-designed bond. Structured notes are among the derivatives that have caused the most problems for buyers. If you own a structured note, instead of receiving a fixed coupon and principal, your coupon or principal-or both-may be adjusted by one or more complex formulas. If you haven't heard of structured notes, just wait. They are one of the largest and fastest growing markets in the world. Estimates of the size of the market range from hundreds of millions to more than $1 *trillion*-almost $10,000 for every working American.
* * *

One of the ironic selling points of PERLS ... was that the most a buyer could lose was everything.

Frank Partnoy, F.I.A.S.C.O., Blood in the Water on Wall Street 55–56 (1997). For a critical analysis of that author's disparagement of PERLS see Jonathan R. Macey, Wall Street Versus Main Street: How Ignorance, Hyperbole, and Fear Lead to Regulation, 65 U. Chi. L. Rev. 1487, 1489–1493 (1998).

The PERL may be a variation on an instrument issued by the Confederacy during the Civil War. These "Erlanger" bonds were offered in Europe on behalf of the Confederate states by Emile Erlanger & Co. in Paris and J. Henry Schroeder & Co. in London. The bond stated in part that:

> The Holder of the Bond ... will have the option of converting the same at its nominal amount into Cotton, at the rate of sixpence sterling per pound—say 4,000 lbs. of Cotton in exchange for a Bond of 100 pounds—at any time not later than six months after the ratification of a Treaty of Peace between the present belligerents. Notice of the intention of converting Bonds into Cotton to be given to the representatives of the Government in Paris or London, and sixty days after such notice the Cotton will be delivered, if peace, at the ports of Charleston, Savannah, Mobile, or New Orleans; if war, at a point in the interior within 10 miles of a railroad or stream navigable to the ocean.... The quality of the Cotton to be the standard of New Orleans middling. If any Cotton is of superior or inferior quality, the difference in value shall be settled by two Brokers, one to be appointed by the Government, the other by the Bondholder: whenever these two Brokers cannot agree on the value, an Umpire is to be chosen, whose decision shall be final.

7 Percent Cotton Loan Confederate States of America, quoted in Jerry W. Markham, "Confederate Bonds," "General Custer," and the Regulation of Derivative Financial Instruments, 25 Seton Hall L. Rev. 1, 7, n.17 (1994). The Erlanger bonds thus allowed the holder to speculate on the price relationships among cotton, French francs or the British pound.[14]

NOTES

1. Do you see an economic purpose for PERLS or is it an entirely speculative instrument?

2. There have been variations on these instruments including Reverse PERLS that measures the amount of principal return based on how well the U.S. dollar performs against the Japanese Yen. Whose economy are you betting on in such an instrument, the United States or Japan?

---

14. The lower denominations of the Erlanger bonds were tri-valued at 500£, 1250ff or 20,000 pounds of cotton. Although defaulted, this is roughly the value of those bonds today as a collector's item. As a measure of the time value of money, however, if the original purchaser had purchased an alternate investment that returned on average a compounded six percent per year, that individual would have a substantial fortune today.

Collateralized Debt Obligations and the Subprime Crisis

JERRY W. MARKHAM
REGULATING CREDIT DEFAULT SWAPS IN THE WAKE OF THE SUBPRIME CRISIS

A Working Paper Prepared for the International Monetary Fund Seminar on Current
Developments in Monetary and Financial Law
Washington, D.C., Dec. 2, 2009.

The amount of securitized subprime mortgages grew from about $11 billion in 1994 to over $100 billion in 2002. Bear Stearns made its first subprime securitization offering in 1997 for mortgages totaling $385 million, and it underwrote an additional $1.9 billion in securitizations over the next ten months. "By 2005, almost 68 percent of home mortgage originations were securitized."[15] The FDIC noted, in 2006, that:

> A significant development in the mortgage securities market is the recent and dramatic expansion of 'private-label, [mortgage-backed securities] MBS ... Total outstanding private-label MBS represented 29 percent of total outstanding MBS in 2005, more than double the share in 2003. Of total private-label MBS issuance, *two thirds comprised non-prime loans in 2005*, up from 46 percent in 2003.[16]

The securitization process was carried out through collateralized debt obligations (CDOs) that were distributed through "warehouse" operations, in which mortgages were purchased from non-bank originators by investment banks and then resold through securitizations. These warehousing operations became a part of an unregulated "shadow banking" system.[17] A shareholder report by UBS AG described its CDO facility as follows:

> In the initial stage of a CDO securitization, the [CDO] desk would typically enter into an agreement with a collateral manager. UBS sourced residential mortgage backed securities ('RMBS') and other securities on behalf of the manager. These positions were held in a CDO Warehouse in anticipation of securitization into CDOs. Generally, while in the Warehouse, these positions would be on UBS's books with exposure to market risk. Upon completion of the Warehouse, the securities were transferred to a CDO special-purpose vehicle, and structured into tranches. The CDO desk received structuring fees on the notional value of the deal, and focused on Mezzanine ('Mezz') CDOs, which generated fees of approximately 125 to 150 bp (compared with high-grade CDOs, which generated fees of approximately 30 to 50 bp)....

---

15. FDIC, *Breaking New Ground in U.S. Mortgage Lending* FDIC Outlook 21 (Summer 2006) (emphasis supplied).

16. *Id.*

17. These warehousing operations often involved the purchase on non-bank subprime mortgage originations by investment banks like Bear Stearns and Merrill Lynch. *See* PAUL MUOLO & MATHEW PADILLA, CHAIN OF BLAME (2008) (describing these warehousing operations).

Under normal market conditions, there would be a rise and fall in positions held in the CDO Warehouse line as assets were accumulated ('ramped up') and then sold as CDOs. There was typically a lag of between 1 and 4 months between initial agreement with a collateral manager to buy assets, and the full ramping of a CDO Warehouse.[18]

Subprime CDOs were broken up into separate tranches. The less secure tranches were required to absorb any larger than expected losses from mortgage defaults, providing a cushion from loss for the most secure tranche, called the "Super–Senior." As a result of this credit enhancement feature, the Super–Seniors were considered to be more credit-worthy than the underlying subprime mortgages themselves. The use of multiple payment stream tranches for a securitization was not a novel concept. "Collateralized mortgage obligations" (CMOs), also known as "real estate mortgage investment conduits" (REMICs), was a product that [as described below] divided principal and interest payments from the mortgages placed in the pool into different payment streams. * * *

A risk model developed by David Li did for CDOs what the Black–Scholes model did for options. Seemingly, it allowed a supposed precise mathematical computation of the risks posed by CDOs. That and other Gaussian Copula risk models failed, however, to predict the massive losses sustained by commercial banks in the United States, and Europe, from their exposures to subprime CDOs.[19] Fail they did, but there was no cabal using a secret formula to deceive investors. Moody's actually published its CDO risk assessment model (CDOROM), which became the industry standard, on the Internet in 2004. The whole world was free to discover its flaws but, except for a few naysayers, the model went pretty much unchallenged.

The mathematical model used to rate CDOs proved to be badly flawed. Critics charged that these models were defective because they relied on historical prices generated by a rising market. That Pollyanna approach overlooked the possibility of a hundred-year, "perfect" storm, which arrived in the form of the subprime crisis. The possibility of such an unusual event was called a "fat tail" or "outlier." They were also called "black swans," as a metaphor for the widely held belief that there was no such thing as a black swan, until explorers reached Australia and found just such a bird.[20] The probability of an outlier was considered so small that they were ignored by the credit assessors. Lloyd Blankfein, the CEO at Goldman Sachs, also asserted that many financial institutions had erred in outsourcing their risk management to the rating agencies. He believed that the rating agencies had diluted their triple-A rating by giving

---

18. UBS AG, SHAREHOLDER REPORT ON UBS's WRITE-DOWNS § 4.22 (2008).

19. These risk models were created by high IQ quants, but as Warren Buffett warned, "beware of Geeks ... bearing models." Vincent Ryan, *Shiller to CFOs: Quick Action Needed to Avert "D-word,"* CFO.COM, Mar. 9, 2009, http://www.cfo.com/article.cfm/13257035?f=related (last visited Nov. 12, 2009).

20. *See* NASSIM NICHOLAS TALEB, THE BLACK SWAN: THE IMPACT OF THE HIGHLY IMPROBABLE (2007).

that rating to over 64,000 structured finance instruments, while only twelve operating companies in the world had such a rating.

The high credit ratings given to the Super Senior tranches posed another problem. These securities were hard to market due to their lower interest rates, which was a function of their triple-A rating. That problem was solved after bank regulators in the United States allowed favorable capital treatment of Super Seniors on bank balance sheets, provided that the Super Senior had a high credit rating. This regulatory blessing removed any residual concerns on the part of the banks of undue risk from Super–Seniors and created a demand for the Super Seniors by banks here and abroad. As a result, a large portion of the Super Senior tranches were held on the books of many major investment banks such as Citigroup, Merrill Lynch, UBS AG and Lehman Brothers. The twenty-five largest banks were also holding $13 trillion in CDS notionals on their books in March 2008.[21] * * *

As Peter Wallison, an American Enterprise Institute Fellow, noted in the midst of the subprime crisis:

> As losses mounted in subprime mortgage portfolios in mid–2007, lenders demanded more collateral. If the companies holding the assets did not have additional collateral to supply, they were compelled to sell the assets. These sales depressed the market for mortgage-backed securities (MBS) and also raised questions about the quality of the ratings these securities had previously received. Doubts about the quality of ratings for MBS raised questions about the quality of ratings for other asset-backed securities (ABS). Because of the complexity of many of the instruments out in the market, it also became difficult to determine where the real losses on MBS and ABS actually resided. As a result, trading in MBS and ABS came virtually to a halt and has remained at a standstill for almost a year. Meanwhile, continued withdrawal of financing sources has compelled the holders of ABS to sell them at distressed or liquidation prices, even though the underlying cash flows of these portfolios have not necessarily been seriously diminished. As more and more distress or liquidation sales occurred, asset prices declined further, and these declines created more lender demands for additional collateral, resulting in more distress or liquidation sales and more declines in asset values as measured on a mark-to-market basis. A downward spiral developed and is still operating.[22]

"The difficulty in putting a value on loans, securities, and exotic financial instruments banks were carrying on their books became one of the most debilitating features of the Great Panic" in 2008.[23] Critics of fair value accounting charged that, because liquidity in subprime investments

---

21. *See* Janet Morrissey, *Credit Default Swaps: The Next Crisis*, TIME, Mar. 17, 2008, *available at* http://www.time.com/time/business/article/0,8599,1723152,00.html.

22. *Id.*

23. WESSEL, *supra* note 62, at 128.

had dried up as the subprime crisis blossomed, the only prices available for "fair value" accounting were fire sale prices from desperate sellers.[24] Those prices in no way reflected the actual value of the Super Seniors as measured by their cash flows or defaults.[25] * * *

The SEC gave some interpretative relief on September 23, 2008. The Emergency Economic Stabilization Act passed on October 3, 2008 required the SEC to conduct a study of mark-to-market accounting and authorized suspension of that requirement. However, a debate arose over whether a suspension was appropriate, and the SEC subsequently announced that it had decided not to suspend mark-to-market accounting. Its staff stated that: "Rather than a crisis precipitated by fair value accounting, the crisis was a 'run on the bank' at certain institutions, manifesting itself in counterparties reducing or eliminating the various credit and other risk exposures they had to each firm."[26] * * *

At the end of the first quarter in 2009, the delinquency rate for subprime mortgages, *i.e.*, those with payments more than sixty days overdue, was sixteen percent, but CDOs had been sold for as little as twenty-one cents on the dollar. This defies explanation. Fifty percent or more of the value of the sixteen percent of homes foreclosed should be recovered in foreclosure proceedings. Moreover, the Super Seniors were modeled to withstand a loss in foreclosure of four percent or more, plus many Super Seniors had four percent or more in CDS coverage.[27] Even adding in a big risk discount for the new junk bond status of these once triple-A Super Seniors does not justify the steep discounts at which these instruments were dumped on the market.

This analysis is, admittedly, over-simplistic, but it does seem to suggest that the massive write-downs of the Super Seniors were driven by panic and had no ties to the actual value of many of these securities.

NOTES

1. The Dodd–Frank Wall Street Reform and Consumer Protection Act of 2010 contains several provisions imposing regulation of originators of residen-

24. *Accounting Principles*, 40 SEC. REG. & L. REP. (BNA) 1767 (2008).

25. Holman W. Jenkins, Jr., *Buffett's Unmentionable Bank Solution*, WALL ST. J., Mar. 11, 2009, at A13. As one author noted:

> The argument against fair value is a compelling one: volatile markets make securities valuation difficult and undermine investors' confidence, forcing companies to mark down values, leading to greater illiquidity and further markdowns. The more the markdowns impair capital, the greater the loss of investor confidence, and the faster the churn of the self-reinforcing cycle.

Todd Davenport. *Fair Value: Few Fans, But Fewer Alternatives; Despite Widespread Frustration, Changes Don't Seem Likely*, 173 AM. BANKER 1 (Mar. 24, 2008).

26. SEC OFFICE OF THE CHIEF ACCOUNTANT, DIVISION OF CORPORATE FINANCE, REPORT AND RECOMMENDATIONS PURSUANT TO SECTION 133 OF THE EMERGENCY ECONOMIC STABILIZATION ACT OF 2008: STUDY ON MARK-TO-MARKET ACCOUNTING 3 (2008).

27. *See* UBS AG, SHAREHOLDER REPORT ON UBS's WRITE-DOWNS (2008).

tial mortgage loans that are securitized. For example, Dodd–Frank (§ 941) seeks to require some of the risk (not less than five percent) from asset-backed securities to be retained by originators and securitizers. It was thought that by requiring these entities to have some "skin in the game" they would have an incentive to more carefully vet securitized mortgages for default risk. "Qualified residential mortgages" were exempt from this risk retention requirement. Such qualified mortgages may not allow balloon payments, negative amortization, prepayment penalties, interest-only payments, and other features that have been demonstrated to exhibit a higher risk of borrower defaults.

2. Dodd–Frank (§ 1403) also prohibits financial incentives, including yield spread premiums, that would provide an incentive to steer consumers to higher cost abusive mortgages. Dodd–Frank (§ 1100) authorizes the new Bureau of Consumer Financial Protection (BCFP) to set minimum net worth or surety bond requirements for mortgage loan originators.

SECTION 3.   LIABILITY AND REGULATORY ISSUES

IN RE NATIONAL MORTGAGE EQUITY CORP. MORTGAGE POOL CERTIFICATES SECURITIES LITIGATION

636 F.Supp. 1138 (C.D.Cal.1986).

A. WALLACE TASHIMA, UNITED STATES DISTRICT JUDGE

This multidistrict litigation involves allegations of massive fraud in connection with the sale of mortgage pool certificates to numerous savings banks and savings and loan associations ("Investor Institutions"). Before the Court are several defendants' motions to dismiss the complaints in four of these actions, as well as two plaintiffs' motions to dismiss certain counterclaims.

The complaints under attack are those of Riverhead Savings Bank ("Riverhead"), Missouri Savings Association ("Missouri"), FirstFederal Savings and Loan Association ("First Federal"), and Bank of America ("B of A" or the "Bank"). B of A's complaint differs significantly from the other three. It not only asserts claims which the Bank brings in its own right, but also claims which B of A purports to bring as the assignee of nineteen Investor Institutions that are alleged to be victims of the fraud.
* * *

Defendant David A. Feldman ("Feldman"), promoted, organized and managed defendant National Mortgage Equity Corporation ("NMEC"). Beginning in 1981, NMEC organized pools of real estate loans secured by first or second deeds of trust on residential real property, located primarily in California and Texas. Riverhead, Missouri and First Federal allege that defendants Wells Fargo Bank ("Wells Fargo") and Advance Mortgage Corporation ("Advance") also played a role in promoting the formation of certain of the pools during 1981 and 1982. In connection with these mortgage pools, NMEC marketed "Mortgage Pass–Through Certificates" (the "Certificates") to various financial institutions, *i.e.*, the Investor Institutions. Each Certificate represented an undivided interest in an individual pool. The Certificate holder was entitled to receive interest at a fixed "pass-through" rate, regardless of the rates paid by individual mortgagors. NMEC solicited buyers of Certificates, *i.e.*, Investor Institutions, through various means, including, as alleged by B of A, through Private Placement Memoranda ("PPM"). The PPM were prepared by defendant law firm Lord, Bissell and Brook ("Lord Bissell"). Defendant Leslie W. Michael ("Michael"), is a partner in Lord Bissell and was also a part owner and officer of NMEC.

NMEC was responsible for the initial selection of loans to be included in the pools. B of A was to act as escrow agent for each pool. Advance was to act as servicer on the mortgages for at least some of the pools, and did so act until March, 1983, when it resigned and was replaced by NMEC. NMEC apparently at all times acted as servicer for all the loans in the pools that form the basis of B of A's complaint. A trustee was appointed for each pool. B of A was trustee for most of the pools, but with respect to four pools, Wells Fargo acted as trustee. In their respective roles as trustees, Wells Fargo and B of A were to review the documentation NMEC provided regarding each mortgage in order to determine whether it complied with all the applicable standards set out in the pooling and service agreements.

NMEC, Feldman, Lord Bissell and Michael made numerous representations to the Investor Institutions regarding the nature of the mortgages selected for the pools. Defendants represented that the underlying loans were made in arms-length transactions, the borrowers were capable of servicing their debts on the loans, the values of the residential properties involved were determined by independent appraisals, each loan was fully protected by mortgage insurance and that Glacier General Assurance Company ("Glacier") and Pacific American Insurance Company ("Pacific American"), the primary insurers, had the financial resources to cover any likely defaults and had also secured reinsurance.

The essence of the fraud allegations is that despite defendants' representations respecting the high standards used to select mortgages for the pools, defendants actually were engaged in a widespread series of sham mortgage transactions between various related entities that diverted the Investor Institutions' funds for defendants' personal benefit. Entities and individuals related to or controlled by NMEC, including Michael, Glacier, Energy Resources Financial Inc. ("Energy Resources"), Marvin Weiss ("Weiss"), West Pac Corporation ("West Pac"), and Kent B. Rogers ("Rogers") would obtain funds from NMEC. These entities or individuals would then use these funds to purchase properties through still other related entities. After obtaining a fraudulently inflated appraisal of the property, the related entities would arrange a "loan" between themselves, secured by a note and deed of trust on the overvalued property. The "loan" would then be transferred to NMEC's mortgage pools in exchange for cash the Investor Institutions had entrusted to NMEC.

B of A alleges that Glacier and Pacific American were an integral part of this scheme. It is alleged that these insurance companies were selected to insure the mortgages not because of their ability to provide adequate coverage but because they were related, through common principals, to one or more of the other participants in the scheme. It also is alleged that the insurance companies actively participated in the scheme by recycling properties on which borrowers had defaulted back into the NMEC pools.

This scheme began to unravel in late 1984 and early 1985. In October, 1984, the Seaman's Bank for Savings, one of the Investor Institutions for which B of A acted as trustee, advised the Bank of "certain irregularities in the processing and documentation" of the mortgages comprising Seaman's pool. B of A responded by conducting an investigation into NMEC pools. Through this investigation, the Bank learned not only of the NMEC-managed fraud, but also that its own employees had not, in the Bank's words, "adequately discharged the Bank's responsibilities" as escrow agent and trustee. As a result of its investigation, B of A filed an action in California state court against several of its own employees for their roles in the handling of the NMEC pools.

B of A's investigation also led it to conclude that as a result of the fraud, the Investor Institutions for which it had acted as trustee stood to lose all or most of their investments in the NMEC pools. The Bank, therefore, decided to "resolve its liability" to those Investor Institutions by repurchasing their Certificates or by replacing the mortgages in the pools represented by the Certificates. The Bank paid in cash and replacement collateral to the Investor Institutions a total of $133 million (which apparently was 100 percent of the funds invested in Certificates by them). It expects to realize $38 million on liquidation of the collateral and from the mortgage guarantee insurance claims assigned to it, leaving a net loss of $95 million from its resolving its liability to the Investor Institutions. In return, the Investor Institutions assigned to B of A any claims they might have against any of the defendants. B of A then filed this action, both for damages sustained in its own right and as assignee of the Investor Institutions' claims.

Unlike B of A, Wells Fargo chose not to pay off its beneficiaries. Therefore, Wells Fargo, which had performed essentially the same trustee functions as B of A with respect to Riverhead's, Missouri's and First Federal's mortgage pools, was named by its beneficiaries as a defendant in this litigation. * * *

In their motion to dismiss B of A's complaint, Lord Bissell and Michael (hereinafter, collectively "Lord Bissell") assert that each of the claims the Bank brings against them n11 as assignee should be dismissed under the "one-satisfaction rule," which is set forth in the Restatement (Second) of Torts § 885(3) (1979). The one-satisfaction rule recognizes the principle that an injured party may recover only once for a single injury;

its corollary is that any payment made by any person in compensation for a harm diminishes proportionally the injured party's claim against any tortfeasors. Lord Bissell contends that B of A's payments to its Investor Institutions constitute full satisfaction of those Investor Institutions' claims and, thus, operate to discharge fully all other tortfeasors from any liability to those Investor Institutions. *See* Restatement § 900(1)(b) & comment *b*. n13 Lord Bissell argues further that B of A should not be permitted to avoid the effect of the one-satisfaction rule by purporting to obtain assignments of the Investor Institutions' claims. Instead, they contend, the Bank must pursue the traditional remedies available to joint tortfeasors, *i.e.*, actions for contribution and/or indemnity.

The Court agrees with Lord Bissell's contentions with respect to the applicability of the one-satisfaction rule here and the assignability of the federal and state securities claims and the common law fraud claim. Consequently, those counts must be dismissed; however, B of A will be granted leave to file an amended complaint for contribution and/or indemnity, if it so elects.I further conclude that the RICO claims are assignable and that B of A should be permitted to pursue the Investor Institutions' RICO claims, as their assignee. * * *

However, the Bank's single RICO claim (which does not distinguish between its own claim and the assigned claims) is deficient in failing adequately to allege a RICO "enterprise" and a RICO conspiracy. Leave to amend will be granted to allow B of A the opportunity to amend its complaint in accordance herewith.

BANCA CREMI, S.A. v. ALEX. BROWN & SONS, INC.

132 F.3d 1017 (4th Cir.1997).

MAGILL, SENIOR CIRCUIT JUDGE.

Banca Cremi, S.A., Institucion de Banca Multiple, Grupo Financiero Cremi and Banca Cremi Grand Cayman (together, the Bank) purchased a number of collateralized mortgage obligations (CMOs) through John Isaac Epley, a broker with the brokerage firm of Alex. Brown & Sons, Incorporated (Alex. Brown). Although most of its CMO purchases were profitable, the Bank lost money on six CMO purchases after the market in CMOs collapsed in 1994. The Bank brought suit in the district court against Epley and Alex. Brown, alleging that Epley and Alex. Brown had committed securities fraud in violation of § 10(b) of the Securities and Exchange Act of 1934, 15 U.S.C. § 78j(b), and Rule 10b–5, 17 C.F.R. § 240.10b–5, by making material misrepresentations and omissions regarding the CMOs, by selling securities that were unsuitable, and by charging excessive markups. The Bank also alleged Texas state common-law tort claims for fraud, negligence, negligent misrepresentation, and breach of fiduciary duty, and a claim based on the Maryland Securities Act. The district court granted Epley and Alex. Brown's motion for summary judgment on all of the Bank's claims, and the Bank now appeals. We affirm.

CMOs, first introduced in 1983, are securities derived from pools of private home mortgages backed by U.S. government-sponsored enterprises.[28] From 1987 to 1993, U.S. government-sponsored CMO issuances grew dramatically, from $900 million to $311 billion per year. The market in CMOs largely collapsed in 1994, and in 1995 new issuances fell to $25.4 billion.

Historically, investments in fixed-rate home mortgages have not been attractive to institutional investors. Investors in most fixed-rate securities benefit when interest rates fall. The fixed-rate security then earns interest at a rate higher than decreased prevailing rates. However, unlike other fixed-rate investments such as U.S. treasuries, fixed-rate home mortgages do not benefit from declines in interest rates. Because home mortgages may be freely prepaid, home owners frequently refinance their homes to take advantage of a drop in interest rates. When the mortgage is prepaid, the investor's funds are returned. If the investor seeks to reinvest those funds, as would be the case with most institutional investors, they must be reinvested at the low prevailing rate, rather than earning interest at the higher rate of the original mortgage. This is called the "prepayment risk." If interest rates rise, home mortgages are generally not refinanced, and they lose value just like any other fixed-rate security. Thus, investments in home mortgages perform poorly both when interest rates rise and when they fall.

CMOs concentrate the prepayment risk in some securities in order to reduce that risk in other securities. In so doing, CMOs were designed to make home mortgage investments more attractive to institutional investors, increase the liquidity in the secondary home mortgage market, and reduce the interest costs to consumers buying homes.

A CMO issuer begins with a large pool of home mortgages, often worth billions of dollars. Each pool of home mortgages generates two streams of income. The first income stream is the aggregate of all interest payments made on the underlying mortgages. The second income stream is the aggregate of all principal payments made on the underlying mortgages. These income streams are divided into numerous CMO "tranches," which are the securities sold to investors. To determine what portion of the two income streams are received by an investor in a CMO tranche, each tranche has two unique formulae: one that determines the tranche's interest rate, and the other that determines the tranche's principal repayment priority.

The interest rate on a CMO tranche can be a fixed rate, a floating rate, or a rate that floats inversely to an index rate. Floating interest rates can also be leveraged, meaning that the interest rate shifts more dramatically than the index rate. For example, where a floating rate CMO is

---

28. These entities include the Federal National Mortgage Association, the Federal Home Loan Mortgage Corporation, and the Government National Mortgage Association.

leveraged by a multiplier of two, the CMO's interest rate will increase by two percent when the index rate increases by one percent.

The tranche's principal repayment priority determines when the tranche will receive principal payments made on the underlying mortgages. Each principal payment is divided among all of the tranches in a CMO issuance. High priority tranches receive principal payments first. Support tranches receive principal payments last. Because of this, support tranches are the most sensitive to "extension risk." Extension risk is the opposite of prepayment risk: when interest rates rise, the expected maturity of the support tranche CMO increases, often dramatically.

CMO tranches are categorized into classes which have similar properties and risks. The least risky is the planned amortization class (PAC). PACs have little prepayment risk, and appeal to institutional investors for this reason. Two of the riskiest classes of CMOs, inverse floaters and inverse interest-only strips, are at issue in this litigation.

Inverse floaters have a set principal amount and earn interest at a rate that moves inversely to a specified floating index rate. Inverse floaters will often be leveraged, so a small increase in interest rates causes a dramatic decrease in the inverse floating rate. Usually, inverse floaters are also support tranches, so an increase in interest rates causes their maturity date to extend. Inverse floaters earn high returns if interest rates decline or remain constant, but lose substantial value if interest rates increase.

Inverse interest-only strips (inverse IOs) do not receive principal payments. The interest rate for an inverse IO floats inversely to a specified index rate, like an inverse floater. Interest is calculated by reference to the outstanding principal amount of another reference tranche. As the reference tranche is paid off, the principal on which the inverse IO earns interest decreases accordingly. Like an inverse floater, a rate increase reduces the inverse IO's floating rate. According to some investors, a rate increase also reduces prepayment of the reference tranche, extending the maturity of the inverse IO and, ultimately, increasing the total interest payments made on the inverse IO.

Inverse floaters were first introduced in 1986. Inverse IOs were introduced in 1987. Markets for both of these securities remained strong in the environment of decreasing or stable interest rates that predominated between 1986 and the beginning of 1994. On February 4, 1994, the Federal Reserve Board increased short-term interest rates for the first time in five years. Over the next nine months, short-term rates increased by a total of 2.5 percent, from 3 percent to 5.5 percent. In response to the rate increases, a wave of selling hit bond markets and investors in all types of bonds suffered significant losses.[29]

---

29. Most fixed-rate investments dropped significantly in value. Five-year bonds had their worst year since 1926. The price on zero-coupon treasuries dropped 18.7 percent, while long-term treasury bonds lost 7.5 percent in value.

CMOs were particularly hard hit, for a variety of reasons. The jump in rates halted mortgage prepayments. This in turn extended the average maturity of all CMOs, including, most dramatically, support tranche CMOs such as inverse floaters. Because of their degree of leverage, certain CMOs were extremely sensitive to the interest rate jumps, and their holders flooded the market after the first interest rate increase. CMO liquidity, which had never been a problem in the stable or declining interest rate environment that had existed since their introduction, dried up as all CMO holders tried to sell. The fear of liquidity problems built on itself, reducing the number of willing purchasers during the critical period after the Federal Reserve Board increased interest rates. In April 1994 an investment fund which primarily invested in CMOs filed for bankruptcy, reporting near total losses of its $600 million CMO investment. As a result of these incidents, the market in CMOs virtually collapsed in 1994.

Alex. Brown is a securities brokerage firm, incorporated under the laws of Maryland, with its principal place of business in Baltimore, Maryland. Alex. Brown is registered as a broker-dealer under § 15 of the Securities and Exchange Act of 1934, 15 U.S.C. § 78o. Beginning in April 1993, John Isaac Epley was employed by Alex. Brown in its Houston, Texas office as a vice president. Prior to his employment by Alex. Brown, Epley had worked in Houston as a securities broker for MMAR Group.

Banca Cremi, S.A., is a credit institution incorporated under the laws of Mexico. Banca Cremi Grand Cayman is its wholly owned subsidiary, incorporated under the laws of the Cayman Islands. Both institutions have their principal place of business in Mexico City, Mexico. On June 30, 1993, the Bank had assets of nearly $5 billion and an annual operating income in excess of $36 million.

The Bank's Nuevos Negocios Internacionales (NNI) unit specialized in international investment transactions. The unit engaged in Eurobond issuances, interest rate swaps, investments in Brady Bonds, and various other esoteric investments. According to the NNI monthly reports, the NNI unit held investments with a face value of up to $115 million during 1993 and accumulated income of over $6 million that year. * * *

The Bank filed a complaint for securities fraud against Epley and Alex. Brown in the United States District Court for the District of Maryland. The Bank claimed that Epley and Alex. Brown violated § 10(b) and Rule 10b–5 by: (1) making material misstatements and omissions regarding the CMOs sold to the Bank; (2) selling the Bank the CMOs which it knew to be unsuitable investments for the Bank; and (3) failing to disclose fraudulently excessive markups totaling $2 million on the CMO sales. The Bank also claimed violations of the Maryland Securities Act, common law breach of fiduciary duty, negligence, negligent misrepresentation, and fraud.

In support of their claim that Epley and Alex. Brown made numerous material omissions and misstatements, the Bank alleged that Epley and Alex. Brown failed to provide the Bank with material information about the functioning of each of the CMOs, including: (1) the impact of interest rates on CMO price; (2) the precise principal repayment priority; and (3) the impact of interest rates on CMO liquidity. The Bank also alleged that the defendants failed in their duty to provide: (1) information normally included in a CMO prospectus; (2) sophisticated computer software to reverse engineer new issue CMOs to reveal their performance in various market conditions; (3) information regarding the CMOs' qualification under Mexico's Circular 292; and (4) information regarding the CMOs' qualification under U.S. banking regulations. The Bank also alleged that Epley and Alex. Brown made material misstatements when they: (1) downplayed the impact of a change in interest rates on CMO prices by comparing it to that of other fixed income securities; (2) stated that demand for CMOs currently far exceeds supply; (3) claimed that CMOs had relatively low risk levels; (4) claimed that the inverse IOs sold to the Bank had a self-hedging feature; and (5) told the Bank that the criticisms in the Barron's *Pinocchio Security* article should be less of a concern for institutional investors than for individual investors.* * *

To establish liability under § 10(b), the Bank must prove that "(1) the defendant[s] made a false statement or omission of material fact (2) with scienter (3) upon which the plaintiff justifiably relied (4) that proximately caused the plaintiff's damages." *Cooke v. Manufactured Homes, Inc.,* 998 F.2d 1256, 1260–61 (4th Cir.1993) (quotations and citation omitted). In this case, the Bank has failed to present evidence that would permit a reasonable jury to find that the Bank justifiably relied on any omissions or misstatements made by Epley and Alex. Brown.

A dissatisfied investor cannot recover for a poor investment on the basis of a broker's alleged omission or misstatement where, "through minimal diligence, the investor should have discovered the truth." *Brown v. E.F. Hutton Group, Inc.,* 991 F.2d 1020, 1032 (2d Cir.1993). Because the justifiable reliance requirement "requir[es] plaintiffs to invest carefully," it "promotes the anti-fraud policies" of the securities acts by making fraud more readily discoverable. *Dupuy v. Dupuy,* 551 F.2d 1005, 1014 (5th Cir.1977). A plaintiff's failure to prove that it justifiably relied on a broker's alleged omission or misstatement is necessarily fatal to a securities fraud claim. *See Myers,* 950 F.2d at 167.

An investor's reliance on a broker's omission or misstatement is never justified when the "investor's conduct rises to the level of recklessness." *Brown,* 991 F.2d at 1032. A plaintiff is reckless if he "intentionally refuse[s] to investigate in disregard of a risk known to him or so obvious that he must be taken to have been aware of it, and so great as to make it highly probable that harm would follow." *Dupuy,* 551 F.2d at 1020 (quotations and citation omitted). Stated differently, a plaintiff is reckless if he "possesses information sufficient to call [a mis-]representation into question," but nevertheless "close[s] his eyes to a known risk." *Teamsters Local 282 Pension Trust Fund v. Angelos,* 762 F.2d 522, 530 (7th Cir.1985) (citation omitted). Thus, "[i]f the investor knows enough so that the lie or

omission still leaves him cognizant of the risk, then there is no liability."
Id. * * *

Despite its extensive investment experience and extraordinary resources, the Bank nevertheless contends that, while it may be sophisticated in certain types of investments, it was not sophisticated in CMO investments. *See, e.g., McAnally v. Gildersleeve,* 16 F.3d 1493, 1500 (8th Cir.1994) (recognizing that an individual's sophistication in "stocks and bonds" did not necessarily suggest sophistication in commodities futures options); *Order Approving NASD Suitability Interpretation,* 61 Fed.Reg. 44,100, 44,112 (1996) (NASD Fair Practice Rules) (in approving NASD fair practice rules, SEC recognized that even a sophisticated institutional investor may not be capable of understanding a "particular investment risk"). The Bank argues that deposition testimony of its employees and an expert witness that the Bank was unsophisticated in CMO investments created a genuine issue of fact.

We reject this argument. The Bank's NNI unit, whose function was to invest Bank funds in dollar-denominated investments, employed three well-educated investment professionals to select a sound, but profitable, investment strategy. Mendez, Aguirre, and Buentello conducted a thorough, independent investigation of the benefits and risks of CMO investments by attending seminars, purchasing treatises on the subject, and developing a multi-step review process for each CMO investment. Rather than blindly relying on Epley and Alex. Brown, the record shows that the Bank rejected Epley's suggested investments far more often than it accepted them. Indeed, the Bank consulted with five other brokerage houses regarding CMO investments, and each of these brokerage houses gave the Bank detailed information describing the benefits and the risks of CMO investments. After a year of trading in CMOs, the Bank displayed a knowledge and an aggressiveness that belie its current claim that it did not understand CMO investments. NASD Fair Practice Rules, 61 Fed.Reg. at 44,105 n. 20 ("[An institution] who initially needed help understanding a potential investment may ultimately develop an understanding and make an independent investment decision."). Accordingly, we agree with the district court that the Bank was a "sophisticated investor" for the purposes of this case. *See Banca Cremi v. Alex. Brown,* 955 F.Supp. 499, 515 (D.Md.1997). * * *

In this case, there is no allegation that Epley or Alex. Brown concealed specific risks of individual investments, but rather that they misrepresented the risks associated with an entire field of investment. Clearly, the Bank—through its independent research, contacts with other brokerage houses, and discussions with Epley and Alex. Brown—not only had access to, but actually possessed more than sufficient information to make it aware of the substantial risks of investing in CMOs. The Bank knew that, although it could enjoy substantial earnings from CMO investments if interest rates decreased or remained the same, any increase in interest rates could wreak havoc on its CMO investment strategy. The Bank also knew that more sophisticated analyses of its CMO portfolio was available, such as the price analysis performed by Alex. Brown on the Bank's portfolio in July 1993. The July 1993 price analysis indicated that both inverse floaters and inverse IOs were more sensitive to interest rate increases than other types of CMOs, not to mention other more conservative fixed-rate investments such as U.S. Treasury Bonds. Despite possessing this information, the Bank purchased the six CMOs and never requested any analysis either before or after purchase.

The fourth *Myers* factor, whether the defendants owed a fiduciary duty to the plaintiff, is also not implicated in this case. As will be discussed below, *see infra,* § V, Epley and Alex. Brown were not the agents of the Bank, but rather interacted with the Bank at arm's length in principal-to-principal dealings, and no common law fiduciary duty was ever created. * * *

In sum, in this case the Bank had access to an extraordinary wealth of information regarding CMOs. With few exceptions, the depth and breadth of this information illustrated one overriding point: investments in CMOs, while potentially very profitable, were undoubtedly highly risky. As a sophisticated business entity handling five billion dollars of other people's money, the Bank had the advice of its own employees and a horde of the defendants' competitors. Nevertheless, the Bank invested in CMOs through arm's length dealings with the defendants. While the vast majority of these investments were profitable for the Bank, a half-dozen proved disastrously timed, and the Bank now alleges that its misfortune resulted from its justifiable naivete in listening to the defendants' purported lies.

As in any "action[ ] for fraud, reliance on false statements must be accompanied by a right to rely." *Foremost Guar. Corp. v. Meritor Sav. Bank,* 910 F.2d 118, 125 (4th Cir.1990). Here, the Bank lost its right to rely by its own recklessness. The Bank continued to purchase CMOs after it had sufficient information, given its sophistication, to be well apprised of the risks it would face were interest rates to rise. Given that the Bank was aware of the risks involved in investing in CMOs, the Bank was not justified in relying on Epley and Alex. Brown's alleged omissions and misstatements. Accordingly, we affirm the district court's grant of summary judgment against the Bank on this claim. * * *

NOTES

1. As is clear from this case, the CMO presents a host of risks to investors. One brokerage firm lost $377 million in 1988 as the result of its trading in these instruments, and an investment fund lost $600 million when interest rates spiked in 1994. The time to maturity will vary in a CMO tranche even with separate IO and PO classes, especially if there are significant interest rate changes. Prepayment assumptions used to model the separate tranches have been wrong. The price of these securities are, therefore, quite volatile when interest rates change.

2. CMOs pose a complexity risk, i.e., these securities are so complex it is difficult to measure the full extent of the investor's risks. Indeed, these securities were "blindly com[plex]. Analysts at Goldman Sachs had to rent time on two Cray supercomputers to run simulations of mortgage securities cash flows under different interest rate scenarios." I Barrie A. Wigmore, Securities Markets in the 1980s: The New Regime, 1979–1984, 144 (1997). See also Mortgage–Backed Securities: Not For Widows, Orphans-or Hedge Funds, the Economist, July 9, 1994, at 81 (brokerage firms were having difficulties with the unpredictability of mortgage backed securities).

3. An SEC administrative law judge found that a mutual fund had failed to disclose the risks to investors of switching its trading from pass-through certificates to CMOs. In doing so it addresses the risks of the latter:

> * * * "duration" reflects the immediate percentage change in value a security or portfolio would experience in reaction to an interest rate change. Duration therefore is a risk indicator—an attempt to quantify the price sensitivity or "volatility" of a particular security or portfolio. * * * The record is conclusive that duration and convexity are intricately interrelated. Convexity is the rate at which duration (i.e. price volatility) changes. If duration is analogized to the speed of price changes, convexity would represent acceleration. Negative convexity indicates that a security or portfolio will increase in duration/volatility (i.e. lose value) at a faster rate as interest rates rise than the security or portfolio will decrease in duration/volatility (i.e. gain value) as interest rates fall. All things being equal, a negatively convex security or portfolio exhibits more potential to lose value than it does to gain value in an uncertain interest rate environment. Because CMO derivative securities have embedded prepayment options, they exhibit negative convexity.

In the Matter of Piper Capital Management, Inc., 2000 WL 1759455 (S.E.C. 2000).

4. The reinvestment and prepayment risks of mortgage-backed securities were encountered once again in early 2003 when mortgage rates dropped to levels unseen in decades. This resulted in a massive refinancing boom for home mortgages. As a result, investors in mortgage-backed instruments found "themselves with an estimated $800 billion in cash–perhaps the largest wave of money to flow back to investors in such securities in any quarter." Agnes T. Crane, Investors in Mortgage Bonds are Awash in Cash, Wall St. J., April, 7, 2003, at C13.

Disguised Loans

JPMORGAN CHASE BANK v. LIBERTY MUTUAL INSURANCE CO.

189 F.Supp.2d 24 (S.D.N.Y. 2002).

RAKOFF, DISTRICT JUDGE.

By this lawsuit, plaintiff JPMorgan Chase Bank, for and on behalf of Mahonia Limited and Mahonia Natural Gas Limited (collectively "Mahonia"), seeks to compel the eleven defendant insurance companies (collectively the "Sureties") to pay Mahonia over $1 billion, pursuant to six surety bonds (the "Bonds") that guaranteed the obligations of Enron Natural Gas Marketing Corporation and Enron North America Corporation (collectively "Enron") on six corresponding natural gas and crude oil forward sales contracts (the "Contracts") entered into between June, 1998 and December, 2000.

According to plaintiff, the facts are simple and straightforward. Under each of the Contracts, Mahonia paid Enron a set sum in return for subsequent deliveries of natural gas or crude oil extending over many months. To insure against the risk that Enron might default in part or whole on its promise to deliver the gas and oil, Mahonia not only obtained contractual guarantees from Enron to make monetary payments in the event of such failures but also simultaneously obtained from the Sureties the Bonds here in issue, which guaranteed payment to Mahonia upon any default by Enron.

In due course, Enron did indeed default, following which, on December 7, 2001, plaintiff, on behalf of Mahonia, sent written notices to the Sureties demanding payment in accordance with the terms of the Bonds. When the sureties demurred, plaintiff brought this lawsuit and promptly moved for summary judgment in Mahonia's favor, contending that, by the express terms of the Bonds, the Sureties' obligation to pay was immediate and unconditional.

In response to the motion, defendants allege quite different facts. They allege that, unbeknownst to the Sureties at the time they issued the Bonds, the Contracts between Mahonia and Enron were part of a fraudulent arrangement by which simple loans to Enron by plaintiff's predecessor, the Chase Manhattan Bank ("Chase"), were disguised as sales of assets. Specifically, they allege that Chase lent Mahonia the money used to pay Enron on the Contracts, and that, at the very time Enron was contracting to sell to Mahonia future deliveries of gas and oil, Enron was secretly contracting to repurchase the very same gas and oil from one or more entities commonly controlled with Mahonia, at a price equal to what was owed by Mahonia to Chase on the loan. The net effect was simply a series of loans from Chase to Enron; but by disguising them as sales of assets, Enron could book them as revenue while Chase and Mahonia could, among other things, induce the Sureties to issue Bonds that would effectively guarantee repayment of the loans—something the Sureties were otherwise forbidden to do under applicable New York law (which here governs). See N.Y. Ins. Law §§ 1102, 1113(16)(E); 6901(a)(1)(A) (McKinney 2000). In short, defendants allege that the Bonds were the product of fraudulent inducement and fraudulent concealment by the plaintiff.

Fraudulent inducement and fraudulent concealment are familiar defenses to contractual performance. Yet, New York law does not permit a contracting party to lightly evade its contractual obligations by simply crying "fraud." Thus, for example, under New York law, a claim for breach of contract cannot be converted into a fraud claim by simply alleging that the promisor intended not to perform its promise. *See Papa's–June Music v. McLean,* 921 F.Supp. 1154, 1160–1161 (S.D.N.Y. 1996) (collecting cases). Also, of particular relevance here, New York law will not permit a sophisticated party that, in negotiating a contract, has expressly disclaimed reliance on specific oral representations extrinsic to the contract to thereafter claim that the fraudulence of these representations is a defense to contractual performance. *See Danann Realty Corp. v. Harris,* 5 N.Y.2d 317, 320–21, 184 N.Y.S.2d 599, 157 N.E.2d 597 (1959).

Here, defendants, in seeking to defeat plaintiff's motion for summary judgment on the grounds of fraudulent inducement and/or fraudulent concealment, face three principal hurdles.

First, paragraph 7 of each of the Bonds states, in pertinent part:

> The obligations of each Surety hereunder are absolute and unconditional, irrespective of the value, validity or enforceability of the obligations of [Mahonia] under the [corresponding Contract] or Enron under [its separate guarantees] or any other agreement or instrument referred to therein and, to the fullest extent permitted by applicable law, irrespective of any other circumstance whatsoever that might otherwise constitute a legal or equitable discharge or defense of a surety in its capacity as such.

Disclaimer language similar to this was given effect in the decision of the New York Court of Appeals in *Citibank, N.A. v. Plapinger,* 66 N.Y.2d 90, 495 N.Y.S.2d 309, 485 N.E.2d 974 (1985), in which, extrapolating on *Danann,* the Court held that corporate officers who had signed guarantees of corporate debt containing such language could not escape payment by arguing that they had been fraudulently induced to sign the guarantees in reliance on the lenders' unfulfilled oral promises to extend a further line of credit to the corporation.

But neither *Plapinger* nor its progeny, *see, e.g., Banco Do Estado De Sao Paulo, S.A. v. Mendes Jr. International Co.,* 249 A.D.2d 137, 672 N.Y.S.2d 28, 29 (1st Dep't 1998); *Preferred Equities Corp. v. Ziegelman,* 190 A.D.2d 784, 593 N.Y.S.2d 548, 549 (2d Dep't 1993), avails plaintiff here, for several reasons. To begin with, a full and fair reading of *Plapinger* makes plain that it does *not* stand for the extraordinary proposition—the logical extension of plaintiff's interpretation—that a general sweeping disclaimer can serve to disclaim any and all extrinsic fraud between sophisticated parties. As the Second Circuit stated in *Manufacturers Hanover Trust Company v. Yanakas,* 7 F.3d 310, 316 (2d Cir.1993), "the mere general recitation that a guarantee is 'absolute and unconditional' is insufficient under *Plapinger* to bar a defense of fraudulent inducement ...". Rather, the Court continued, "the touchstone is specificity," that is, a clear indication that the disclaiming party has knowingly disclaimed reliance on the specific representations that form the basis of the fraud claim. *Id.* Thus, in *Plapinger,* even though the disclaimer language may have been broad and general, it was negotiated as part of the same negotiations in which, the defendants later claimed, they were orally promised an additional line of credit, so that, in agreeing to the disclaimers, the corporate officers had to know that, at a minimum, the disclaimers precluded reliance on any specific oral promises made during the defendants' negotiations with the lenders.

Here, by contrast, even if one assumes *arguendo* that the disclaimers in paragraph 7 of the Bonds preclude reliance on the representations in the underlying Contracts of which the Sureties knew or were on notice, there is no suggestion that the Sureties knew or were on notice of the allegedly circular arrangements between Mahonia, Enron, and other entities that transformed what purported to be insurable sales contracts into disguised loans that the Sureties were prohibited by law from insuring. *See generally Turkish v. Kasenetz,* 27 F.3d 23, 27–28 (2d Cir.1994) ("It is well settled that parties cannot use contractual limitation of liability clauses to shield themselves from liability for their own fraudulent conduct.").

Furthermore, nothing in the doctrine of *Plapinger* precludes a defense of fraudulent inducement or concealment premised on fraudulent misrepresentations in the Bonds themselves. Here each of the Bonds is expressly premised on Mahonia's having entered with Enron into a gas or oil "Inventory Forward Sale Contract" and expressly recites that once all the contracted-for gas or oil "is fully delivered" the Sureties' obligations will cease. Plainly implicit in these representations is the assertion that the Sureties are being asked to insure the sale and future delivery of a commodity, rather than being asked to insure, unlawfully, a disguised loan transaction.

In short, nothing in the broad disclaimer language of the Bonds excludes the defense—whether characterized as a defense of fraudulent inducement or fraudulent concealment—that the insured arrangements were a total sham whose reality was totally concealed from the Sureties.

Second, plaintiff points out that under New York Insurance Law, a surety that illegally guarantees repayment of a loan is still obligated to make good on that surety. *See* N.Y. Ins. Law § 1303. But as the few cases applying this provision indicate, *see, e.g., Posner v. United States Fidelity & Guaranty Company,* 33 Misc.2d 653, 226 N.Y.S.2d 1011, 1014–1016 (N.Y.Sup.Ct.1962) (describing the rationale behind the almost verbatim predecessor statute, N.Y. Ins. Law § 143), this is a statutory embodiment of the familiar equitable principle that a wrongdoer, whether willful or negligent, should not benefit from his own wrongdoing. By contrast, there is no reason to believe that the statute applies to an innocent, unknowing insurer who is fraudulently induced to illegally insure loans that the insurer has no reason to believe were loans at all. To put it another way, there is nothing to suggest that the statute was intended to change prior law and preclude an insurer from raising a fraud-in-the-inducement defense—a radical change that, absent legislative history, the legislature can not be supposed to have intended. *See Dornberger v. Metropolitan Life*

Ins. Co., 961 F.Supp. 506, 538 (S.D.N.Y.1997) ("cases holding that an insurer who engages in illegality is not permitted to avoid liability on a policy are inapposite—they do not affect the general rule that an innocent party is entitled to rescind a contract based on illegality.").

Third, plaintiff argues that defendants' allegations of fraud are too speculative and unsupported by admissible evidence to rebut the solid showing plaintiff has made in support of plaintiff's motion for summary judgment. Even if this were true, however, it would not preclude the Court from refusing to enter summary judgment on plaintiff's behalf at this time, *see* Fed.R.Civ.P. 56(f), for defendants have provided a reasonable justification for further discovery. In particular, defendants have offered substantial evidence that, even while plaintiff was moving with alacrity to obtain summary judgment, defendants were repeatedly rebuffed in their informal attempts to obtain the information regarding the underlying transactions needed to confirm (or refute) defendants' theory.

In any event, despite such obstacles, defendants have managed to obtain some important evidence that, taken most favorably to them (as it must be for purposes of this motion), inferentially but materially supports their theory. For example, with respect to the last of the six underlying Contracts here in question, which was entered into between Enron and Mahonia on December 28, 2000, defendants have obtained evidence that, on that very same day, Enron entered into an agreement with an entity called Stoneville Aegean Limited ("Stoneville") to purchase from Stoneville the identical quantities of gas that Enron was that same day agreeing to sell to Mahonia, to be delivered to Enron on the very same future dates as Enron was supposed to deliver the same quantities of gas to Mahonia.

The fact that Enron would be simultaneously buying from Stoneville the very gas it was selling to Mahonia becomes even more suspicious when considered in light of the further evidence adduced by defendants to the effect that both Mahonia and Stoneville—offshore corporations set up by the same company, Mourant & Company—have the same director, Ian James, and the same shareholders.

What, finally, turns suspicion to reasonable inference is defendants' further evidence that, whereas Mahonia agreed in its Contract with Enron to pay Enron $330 million for the gas at the moment of contracting (December 28, 2000), Enron, in its agreement with Stoneville, agreed to pay Stoneville $394 million to buy back the same quantities of gas on the same delivery schedule—but with the $394 million to be paid at specified future dates.

Taken together, then, these arrangements now appear to be nothing but a disguised loan—or at least have sufficient indicia thereof that the Court could not possibly grant judgment to plaintiff.

The Court has also considered plaintiff's other arguments but finds them to be without merit. Accordingly, plaintiff's motion for summary judgment is hereby denied. * * *

NOTE

J. P. Morgan Chase & Co. settled the $1 billion lawsuit it brought against the surety companies at the conclusion of the trial ordered by the judge in the above decision. Christopher Oster & Randall Smith, Enron Deals Cost J.P. Morgan; Bank Takes $1.3 Billion Charge, Wall St. J., Jan. 3, 2003, at A1. That bank and Citigroup were also fined by regulators for their role in aiding Enron disguise its true financial condition. Ben White and Peter Behr, Citigroup, J.P. Morgan Settle Over Enron Deals, Wash. Post, Wash. Post, July 29, 2003, at AO1 (settlement totaled over $300 million).

Before employing the surety companies, J.P. Morgan Chase had used stand-by letters of credit from other banks to guard against default by Enron on the prepay contracts. Under those letters of credit, the banks were required to pay if Enron defaulted on its delivery obligations. One of the syndicates issuing such letters of credit refused to pay $165 million after Enron defaulted. J.P. Morgan Chase then sued the syndicate in England. An English judge, in a lengthy opinion, ruled that the prepay transactions had been properly accounted for by Enron and that U.S. securities laws were not violated by that accounting treatment. Mahonia v. West LB AG, [2004] EWHC 1938 (Comm), Royal Court of Justice London (August 3, 2004).

The collapse of the Enron Corp. raised concerns with other structured financing arrangements that kept debt off the balance sheet and distorted the accounting treatment for revenues and expenses. Enron's stock traded as high as $90 before dropping below $1 just before it declared bankruptcy. Enron's demise was triggered by accounting issues over special purpose entities ("SPEs") called such things as "Raptors," "Chewco" and "JEDI." They were special purpose entities that operated as limited partnerships and were used to take losses off of its books and to increase earnings. *See generally* Report of Investigation by the Special Investigative Committee of the Board of Directors of Enron Corp. (Feb. 1, 2002) (describing accounting short cuts taken by Enron).

The following decision describes the allegations in more detail, as well as claims made against Enron's accountants lawyers who were involved in resolving legal issues, as well as documenting and even structuring these financial transactions.

IN RE ENRON CORP. SECURITIES, DERIVATIVE & ERISA LITIGATION

235 F.Supp.2d 549 (S.D.Tex.2002).

MELINDA HARMON, UNITED STATES DISTRICT JUDGE.

* * * Lead Plaintiff asserts that Defendants participated in "an enormous Ponzi scheme, the largest in history," involving illusory profits "generated by phony, non-arm's-length transactions with Enron-controlled entities and improper accounting tricks" in order to inflate Enron's

reported revenues and profits, conceal its growing debts, maintain its artificially high stock prices and investment grade credit rating, as well as allow individual defendants to personally enrich themselves by looting the corporation, while continuing to raise money from public offerings of Enron or related entities' securities to sustain the scheme and to postpone the collapse of the corporation, a scenario characterized by Lead Plaintiff as "a hall of mirrors inside a house of cards." The consolidated complaint sets out an elaborate scheme of off-the-books, illicit partnerships, secretly controlled by Enron and established at times critical for requisite financial disclosures by Enron in order to conceal its actual financial status. These Enron-controlled entities typically would buy troubled assets from Enron, which Enron would have had difficulty selling in an arm's length transaction to an independent entity and which otherwise would have to be reported on Enron's balance sheet, by means of sham swaps, hedges, and transfers, to record phony profits and conceal debt on Enron's balance sheet. Lead Plaintiff further paints a picture of participation in the scheme by Enron's accountants, outside law firms, and banks, which all were the beneficiaries of such enormous fees and increasing business, as well as investment opportunities for personal enrichment, with the result that their opinions were rubber stamps that deceived investors and the public.

According to the consolidated complaint, in 1997 Enron suffered a substantial financial setback because of a British natural gas transaction, resulting in a loss of one-third of its stock's value and analysts' downgrading its stock and lowering their forecasts of its future earnings' growth. Moreover, Enron had been involved in transactions with a special purpose entity ("SPE")[30] known as Joint Energy Development Incorporated ("JEDI"), which Enron, as a partner, had established in 1993 with an outside investor that held a 50% interest in JEDI. Because initially JEDI was independent, Enron was able to report JEDI's profits, but not carry JEDI's debt on Enron's books. According to the complaint, JEDI generated 40% of the profits that Enron reported in 1997 alone. In December 1997, ten months before the Class Period, a crisis arose when the independent investor sought to withdraw, forcing Enron either to restructure with a new, independent investor or to consolidate JEDI with Enron, and thereby wipe out 40% of the profits that Enron had reported earlier in 1997, and to report JEDI's $700 million debt on Enron's balance sheet, as well as lose the ability to generate future profits by utilizing JEDI as an SPE.

30. As one means of effectuating the alleged Ponzi scheme to defraud investors, a series of partnerships and SPEs clandestinely controlled by Enron were allegedly created, structured, financed and utilized by Defendants to inflate Enron's profits and conceal its debt. The complaint explains, "A public company that conducts business with an SPE may treat the SPE as if it were an independent entity only if it does not control the SPE. At a bare minimum, two conditions must be met: (i) an owner independent of the company must make an equity investment of *at least 3% of the SPE's assets, and that 3% must remain at risk throughout the transaction*; and (ii) *the independent owner must exercise control of the SPE.*"

Unable to find a legitimate, independent outside investor to replace the one withdrawing, Enron, along with Vinson & Elkins and Kirkland & Ellis, resorted to forming another entity, Chewco, totally controlled by Enron, to buy the outsider's investment in JEDI. Enron then arranged with Barclays Bank to lend $240 million to Chewco to allow Chewco to invest in JEDI and obtain the necessary 3% equity interest to maintain the appearance that JEDI was independent. According to the consolidated complaint, pursuant to advice from Vinson & Elkins, Michael Kopper (an Enron employee who worked for Andrew Fastow) was made manager of Chewco because he was not a senior officer of Enron and therefore his role in Chewco would not have to be disclosed. Vinson & Elkins prepared the legal documentation for JEDI and Chewco. On December 12, 1997 Kopper transferred his ownership interest in Chewco to his domestic partner, William Dodson, in a sham transaction effected solely to make it appear that Kopper, and through him, Enron, had no formal interest in Chewco.

Because in actuality there was no outside, independent equity investor with a 3% stake in Chewco, Enron arranged for Barclays Bank to lend $11.4 million to two "straw" parties, Little River and Big River, to permit them to make the requisite 3% "equity" investment in Chewco.

According to the complaint, Kirkland & Ellis helped structure these deals and represented the straw parties, Little River and Big River, as part of the scheme to conceal Enron's debt and losses, and therefore the law firm had knowledge of the manipulation. Barclays and the Enron Defendants prepared the documentation characterizing the advances as loans, while Enron and Chewco characterized them as equity contributions to serve as the 3% equity investment needed for nonconsolidation of JEDI. The loans were noted in documents that resembled promissory notes and loan agreements, but which were titled "certificates" and "funding agreements" that required the borrowers to pay "yield" at a particular percentage rate, i.e., interest. Nevertheless, reflecting Barclays' knowledge about Chewco's lack of an independent third-party investor and the resulting creation of strawmen Little River and Big River, Barclays insisted that the borrowers/Enron secretly establish cash "reserve accounts" in the amount of $6.6 million to secure repayment of Barclay's $11.4 million. The complaint further states that a clandestine agreement for Enron to provide the $6.6 million to fund Chewco's reserve accounts for Big River and Little River was drawn up by Vinson & Elkins, which therefore had to have knowledge of the manipulation and of the absence of outside equity. To fund the reserve accounts, JEDI wired $6.58 million to Barclay's on 12/30/97, thus cutting in half Chewco's illusory 3% equity interest in JEDI, essential for JEDI to be independent of Enron. Because Chewco did not have the requisite equity at risk and did not qualify as an adequately capitalized SPE, it, like JEDI, should have been consolidated into Enron's consolidated financial statements from the outset, but was not.

The complaint further alleges that Enron guaranteed the $240 million unsecured loan from Barclays to Chewco in December 1997, and that in exchange, Chewco agreed to pay Enron a guaranteed fee of $10 million up front (cash at closing) plus 315 basis points annually on the average outstanding balance of the loan. The fee calculation was not based on the risk involved, but on benefitting Enron's financial statement. Furthermore, during the year the loan was outstanding, JEDI, through Chewco, paid Enron $17.4 million under the fee arrangement. Enron characterized these payments as "structuring fees" and recognized income from the $10 million up-front fee in December 1997, when in actuality, the payments were improper transfers from one Enron pocket to another.

Thus Chewco was allegedly financed with debt, not equity, and neither JEDI nor Chewco was a valid SPE because neither met the requirements for nonconsolidation. The establishment of Chewco not only allowed Enron to report JEDI profits of $45 million illicitly, inflating Enron's 1997 reported profits, and to keep $700 million of debt off Enron's books, but it also provided Enron with the opportunity in the future to do non-arm's-length-transactions with an Enron-controlled entity that no independent entity would have done nor agreed to do and which provided a stream of sham profits onto Enron's books.

Chewco became a template for subsequent entities that Enron continued to establish in increasing numbers and size, all secretly controlled by Enron, which Enron and its banks would use to generate enormous phony profits and conceal massive debt. Moreover, contrary to representations made to investors, many of these entities were capitalized with Enron common stock, and Enron guaranteed that if the stock price declined below a certain "trigger" price level and Enron lost its investment grade credit rating, Enron would become liable for the debt of those entities. To pay such a debt, Enron would have to issue substantial amounts of new stock, which in turn would dilute the holdings of current stockholders to their detriment. In sum, Chewco was less than 3% owned by parties independent of Enron, was improperly excluded from Enron's financial statements despite being controlled by Enron, and was never disclosed in Enron's SEC filings during the Class Period. Furthermore, Enron continued to use Chewco/JEDI in non-arm's-length transactions to generate false profits and conceal Enron's actual indebtedness from 1997 through 2001 in transactions that Vinson & Elkins participated in structuring and provided false "true sale" opinions to effectuate.

Two other SPEs, LJM Cayman L.P. ("LJM1") and LJM2 Co–Investment, L.P. ("LJM2"), were structured, reviewed, and approved by Arthur Andersen LLP, Vinson & Elkins, Kirkland & Ellis, individual Enron Defendants, and certain Enron bankers, and controlled by Enron's Chief Financial Officer Andrew Fastow to inflate Enron's financial results by more than a billion dollars, as well as to enrich Fastow and selected others by tens of millions of dollars. LJM1 provided Enron employees an opportunity to enrich themselves personally and quickly. For instance, in March 2000, Enron employees Andrew Fastow, Michael Kopper, Ben Glisan, Kristina Mordaunt, Kathy Lynn and Anne Yaeger Patel obtained financial interests in LJM1 for initial contributions of $25,000 by Fastow, $5,800 each for Glisan and Mordaunt, and lesser amounts for the others, totaling

$70,000. They quickly received extraordinary returns on their invest-ments: on May 1, 2000, Fastow received $4.5 million, while Glisan and Mordaunt within a couple of months received approximately $1 million. * * *

Lead Plaintiff claims that LJM2 was used to create a number of SPEs known as the Raptors, which Defendants utilized in turn to artificially inflate profits and conceal debt that should have been included on Enron's balance sheet. Enron or Enron-related entities entered into twenty-four business relationships from June 1999 through September 2001, crucially timed just before financial reporting deadlines. These transactions includ-ed asset sales by Enron to LJM2 or vice versa; purchases of debt or equity interests by LJM1 or LJM2 in Enron affiliates or Enron SPEs or other entities in which Enron was an investor; purchases of equity investments by LJM1 or LJM2 in SPEs designed to mitigate market risk in Enron's investments; sale of a call option and a put option by LJM2 on physical assets; and a subordinated loan to LJM2 from an Enron affiliate. Further-more these transactions were recorded as generating $229 million in "earnings" for Enron in the second half of 1999, out of total reported earnings of $549 million during that period. * * *

Enron was Vinson & Elkins' largest client, accounting for more than 7% of the firm's revenues. Over the years more than twenty Vinson & Elkins lawyers have left the firm and joined Enron's in-house legal department. The complaint recites a long history of alleged improprieties by Vinson & Elkins as part of the elaborate Ponzi scheme.

The complaint asserts that Vinson & Elkins participated in the negotiations for, prepared the transactions for, participated in the struc-turing of, and approved the illicit partnerships (Chewco/JEDI and the LJMs) and the SPEs (Raptors/Condor, etc.) with knowledge that they were manipulative devices, not independent third parties and not valid SPEs, designed to move debt off Enron's books, inflate its earnings, and falsify Enron's reported financial results and financial condition at crucial times. Vinson & Elkins repeatedly provided "true sale" and other opinions that were false and were indispensable for the sham deals to close and the fraudulent scheme to continue. Vinson & Elkins also allegedly drafted and/or approved the adequacy of Enron's press releases, shareholder reports, and SEC filings, including Form 10Ks and Registration State-ments that Vinson & Elkins knew were false and misleading. Vinson & Elkins also drafted the disclosures about the related party transactions, which it also knew were false and misleading because they concealed material facts. It also was involved in structuring and providing advice about the bogus commodity trades utilized by JP Morgan and Enron with the involvement of Mahonia. Moreover, the firm continually issued false opinions about the illegitimate business transactions, such as that they were "true sales." When the scheme began to collapse in August 2001 and Skilling resigned, whistle-blower Sherron Watkins sent her August 9, 2001 memorandum warning Kenneth Lay not to use Vinson & Elkins to handle an investigation of her voiced concerns about Enron's accounting practices because Vinson & Elkins had a conflict in that "they provided some 'true sale' opinions on some of the [Condor and Raptor] deals." Despite Watkins's warning, Vinson & Elkins was called and allegedly conducted a whitewash investigation of what it knew were accurate allegations of fraudulent misconduct that also involved Vinson & Elkins. Vinson & Elkins received over $100 million in legal fees from Enron. * * *

Contrary to Vinson & Elkins' contention, the situation alleged in the consolidated complaint is not one in which Vinson & Elkins merely represented and kept confidential the interests of its client, which has "the final authority to control the contents of the registration statement, other filing, or prospectus." Instead, the complaint alleges that the two were in league, with others, participating in a plan, with each participant making material misrepresentations or omissions or employing a device, scheme or artifice to defraud, or engaging in an act, practice or course of business that operated as a fraud, in order to establish and perpetuate a Ponzi scheme that was making them all very rich.

Vinson & Elkins was necessarily privy to its client's confidences and intimately involved in and familiar with the creation and structure of its numerous businesses, and thus, as a law firm highly sophisticated in commercial matters, had to know of the alleged ongoing illicit and fraudulent conduct. Among the complaint's specific allegations of acts in furtherance of the scheme are that the firm's involvement in negotiation and structuring of the illicit partnerships and off-the-books SPEs, whose formation documentation it drafted, as well as that of the subsequent transactions of these entities. It advised making Kopper manager of Chewco so that Enron's involvement in and control of the SPE would not have to be disclosed, drafted "true sales" opinions that Lead Plaintiff asserts were essential to effect many of the allegedly fraudulent transactions. Vinson & Elkins was materially involved in the New Power IPO, and it structured and provided advice on the Mahonia trades, all actions constituting primary violations of § 10(b). In other words, it "effected the very" deceptive devices and contrivances that were the heart of the alleged Ponzi scheme. *SEC v. U.S. Environmental*, 155 F.3d at 112. According to the allegations in the complaint, Vinson & Elkins chose to engage in illegal activity for and with its client in return for lucrative fees. Contrary to the Rules of Professional Conduct, it did not resign and thereby violated its professional principles and ethics. Nevertheless, had Vinson & Elkins remained silent publicly, the attorney/client relationship and the traditional rule of privity for suit against lawyers might protect Vinson & Elkins from liability to nonclients for such alleged actions on its client's (and its own) behalf.

But the complaint goes into great detail to demonstrate that Vinson & Elkins did not remain silent, but chose not once, but frequently, to make statements to the public about Enron's business and financial situation. Moreover in light of its alleged voluntary, essential, material, and deep involvement as a primary violator in the ongoing Ponzi scheme, Vinson &

Elkins was not merely a drafter, but essentially a co-author of the documents it created for public consumption concealing its own and other participants' actions. Vinson & Elkins made the alleged fraudulent misrepresentations to potential investors, credit agencies, and banks, whose support was essential to the Ponzi scheme, and Vinson & Elkins deliberately or with severe recklessness directed those public statements toward them in order to influence those investors to purchase more securities, credit agencies to keep Enron's credit high, and banks to continue providing loans to keep the Ponzi scheme afloat. Therefore Vinson & Elkins had a duty to be accurate and truthful. Lead Plaintiff has alleged numerous inadequate disclosures by Vinson & Elkins that breached that duty.

Vinson & Elkins protests that its purported "whitewash" investigation and report in the wake of Sherron Watkins' August 1999 memorandum were not disclosed to the public until after Enron waived the attorney/client privilege and produced the report for Congressional hearings in 2002, after the Class Period ended, and thus cannot be the basis of a § 10(b) misrepresentation claim by the investors. Nevertheless the investigation and report can serve as the basis of a § 10(b) [of the Securities Exchange Act of 1934] and Rule 10b–5(a) or (c) claim alleging use of a device, scheme or artifice to defraud or engagement in an act, practice or course of business that operated as a fraud in the perpetuation of the Ponzi scheme.

Furthermore, the complaint references, summarizes, and quotes from the Powers' investigative committee report the negatively critical findings about Vinson & Elkins' substantial and dubious role in the events of the Class Period, as delineated in the complaint, which support Lead Plaintiff's allegations.

For these reasons the Court finds that Lead Plaintiff has stated claims under § 10(b) against Vinson & Elkins. * * *

NOTE

Michael Kopper, a financial executive at Enron, pleaded guilty to two felony counts of fraud in connection with special purpose entities used by Enron including Chewco. The Enron and Tyco Cleanups, Wall St. J., Aug. 22, 2002, at A12. The FASB later increased the independence requirement for SPE ownership, adding some additional control tests. Jack Spinner, Rule Means Uncertainty for Enron–Style SPEs, Wash. Post, Jan. 24, 2003, at E01.

Project Finance

CARL S. BJERRE
INTERNATIONAL PROJECT FINANCE TRANSACTIONS:
SELECTED ISSUES UNDER REVISED ARTICLE 9
73 Am. Bankr. L.J. 261 (1999).

[There are] two intractable realities that do much to explain the demand for project finance transactions: the enormous amounts of money that many infrastructure and other large projects require, and the difficulty that governments may face in mustering that money via general public revenues. Both of these realities tend to be particularly compelling in less-developed nations, which may have a pressing need for even the most basic infrastructure projects, and in which an infant or ailing economy may severely limit governmental resources. Project finance transactions respond to both of these realities: they are a means by which infrastructure and other large projects can be funded through private capital rather than through government programs.

The term "project finance" is misleadingly broad: it might seem to include all transactions in which investors advance funds for the purpose of supporting a particular project, as opposed to supporting the borrower's operations in general. In fact, however, the term is used to denote only a subset of project-oriented transactions—those in which the lenders expect repayment primarily from the cash flows of the project itself (and, if necessary, from the project's other assets). Accordingly, project finance transactions invariably involve the development of revenue-generating facilities. Typical examples include power plants, oil or gas pipelines, desalinization plants, wastewater treatment facilities, toll roads, telephone infrastructure networks, and mining facilities. As is evident from this list of examples, project finance transactions can have a startlingly deep reach into an economy (and particularly into an economy that is relatively unindustrialized), and can have profound effects on the fabric of the populace's daily life.

The most salient characteristic of project finance transactions is their large scale. To take one example, the cost of construction of a power plant will often reach several hundred million dollars, and these large dollar amounts entail correspondingly large scales in other facets of the transactions. In order to make available the necessary funds, the number of financing parties is large (e.g., bondholders, subordinated bondholders, syndicates of bank lenders, trustees and collateral agents). In order to allow time for the project's expected flow of revenue to reimburse the lenders, the duration of the transactions is large (easily a decade or more). And as a result of all of the foregoing, the volume of documentation and number of legal issues presented by the transactions is also quite large.
* * *

Despite this complexity, one can usefully conceive of project finance transactions as taking a simple, schematic shape: that of a bow tie or butterfly. The butterfly image in particular is appropriate because of the way in which the transactions array dual sets of delicate, elaborately interrelated elements on each side of a central structure. As discussed below, the elements in the two "wings" of a project finance transaction are not exactly mirror images of each other, but they do nonetheless in the aggregate closely reflect each other, and both wings must be sound in order for the transaction to get off the ground, just as the butterfly needs both sets of wings to fly.

A project finance transaction's first wing consists of the agreements and other assets that enable the project's operations to be carried out. A list of examples would begin with agreements with engineers to design the facility, with contractors to build it, and with professionals to operate and maintain it once the facility becomes operational. Other vital examples would include agreements with suppliers to provide coal, crude oil for refinement, waste-water or other raw inputs needed for the facility's operations, and agreements with utilities, ore distributors, or others to purchase the facility's outputs. A third, crucial element in this operational wing would be any licenses and permits granted by governmental authorities of the host country, allowing the project to operate (and often, as a financial incentive, granting it the exclusive right to do so within a certain period). Guarantees of the project's operational agreements also belong in this wing; for example, a guarantee by the host government of a utility's agreement to purchase the facility's power output. Political risk insurance, often present in these transactions in order to protect against various elements of the host country's legal environment, also belongs here.

The transaction's other wing consists of the financing agreements necessary to fund the first wing and provide the lenders with repayment. Important elements of this second wing include credit agreements with bank syndicates; bonds or notes payable to other investors; note purchase agreements; intercreditor agreements; security agreements, in which the project company grants security interests in its assets (including most or all of the assets discussed above in connection with the operational wing) to the lenders; pledge agreements, in which direct owners of the project company grant a security interest in their ownership interests to the lenders; and a collateral agency agreement, providing for one lending institution to act in specified respects as agent for all of the various secured lenders. In this financing wing there are also agreements governing the deposit and securities accounts associated with the project. These accounts play a vital role in regulating the project's cash flow, both as it moves in from the lenders at the transaction's closing and as it moves back out to them during the life of the deal.

Between these two wings, and joining them to each other, the project finance transaction has a set of owners. These can be divided into three: the project company, its intermediate owners, and the ultimate project sponsors. The project company is a special-purpose entity (that is, one with power only to enter into and carry out the agreements and own the assets that constitute the project) that is structured so as to be bankruptcy remote. It is the nerve center of the project, in that it is a party to the preponderance of the agreements described above. For reasons related to local law or political pressure, it is usually organized under the local law of the host country. Principally for reasons related to taxation and liability, the project company is directly owned by one or more intermediate tiers of entities. Owning these intermediate tiers and situated at the metaphorical top of the structure is the project sponsor itself, which is typically a large, well-established concern (or a joint venture among multiple entities of this sort) operating in the general industry sector represented by the project.

CHAPTER ELEVEN

EXCHANGE TRADED FUTURES AND OPTIONS

■ ■ ■

Chapter objectives

- To understand the building blocks of derivative transactions and to see how futures contracts create, shift, and manage price risk on particular commodities.

- To appreciate the regulatory competition between the Commodities Futures Trading Commission and the Securities and Exchange Commission over financial futures contracts.

- To identify price manipulation and other trading abuses that can occur in the futures markets.

- To analyze how single stock futures products are structured and how they trade.

- To learn about how option contracts are structured and how they trade both in listed markets and over-the-counter.

SECTION 1. INTRODUCTION

The derivatives markets indirectly supply liquidity pricing information and risk protection to the securities markets. Derivatives have also become a significant force in other areas of corporate finance, providing such benefits as hedges against commercial and financial risks.

Cash Transactions

The key to understanding derivatives is to understand their building blocks. We first begin with the "cash" or "actual" or "spot" transaction as they are variously called. These are simply cash and carry transactions in which one party buys a commodity for immediate delivery. Say you go to the grocery store and buy bread on the spot and take it home from the store. You have just engaged in a "cash" or "actual transaction" in the "spot" market. The payment terms may vary, you could pay at the time of purchase or buy on credit for later payment, but delivery is immediate.

Forward Transactions

The next building block is the "forward" contract (or "to arrive" contract as it was initially called). This is a transaction for deferred delivery. For example, you visit your nursery and select and buy some shrubs for delivery 60 days later, which is when your house will be completed and ready for landscaping. You have just engaged in a contract for forward delivery. Once again, payment terms could vary. Payment could be immediate or deferred. In some more complex forward contracts pricing may be based on some reference index, say in the case of a forward contract for soybeans, the price of soybeans on the deferred delivery day on a futures exchange.

Options

An elemental derivative is the options contract. This contract gives the buyer the right but not the obligation to do something. The buyer pays the seller a "premium" for that right. For example, Farmer A sells you the right to buy his land for $1 million (the "strike" price) at any time over the next 90 days (the "expiration" date) for which right you pay the farmer $10,000 (the premium). Say you resell the land for $1,100,000 before the expiration date. You then "exercise" the option by purchasing the land from the farmer for the agreed $1million and resell it for $1,100,000. This gives you a profit of $90,000 after the premium is deducted. Say you cannot sell the land. You are out of pocket $10,000 for the option premium but are not stuck with buying a $1 million property.

The option just described is a "call" option that gives you the right to buy something at a specific price, while a "put" option gives you the right to sell something at a specific price. An "American" option allows you to exercise the option at any time before its expiration date. A "Bermuda" option is one that allows exercise only on or after particular dates. You may want to look up other option forms like the "European" and "Asian" options.

Futures Contracts

These contracts are more fully described in the following materials, but briefly they are contracts traded on an exchange that have standardized terms. The buyer and seller of a futures contract are contractually bound to make and take delivery on a specific date at a specified price. However, parties may offset those obligations before delivery and pay or receive the profit or losses from any price change that occurs between the time of entry into the contract and the offset.

Swap Contracts

A swap contract is simply an exchange of payments from some revenue stream or asset. For example, a "plain vanilla" swap could involve an exchange of fixed for floating interest rates. Say you took out a loan for $1 million on which you are paying a fixed rate of 6 percent per year for 30 years, but you later become concerned that interest rates will drop below six percent. That would mean that you would be paying an above market rate. Another party has a $1 million floating rate mortgage at LIBOR who is concerned that interest rates will rise instead of fall. So the two parties agree in essence to swap each other's mortgage payments. You will exchange your fixed rate payment for the other party's floating payment and that party in turn will, effectively, make you fixed payments.

The following is a description of the traditional derivatives markets.

JERRY W. MARKHAM
UNITED STATES SECURITIES AND INVESTMENTS REGULATION HANDBOOK

(Eds. Peter Farmery and Keith Walmsley)
Chapter 8 (1992).

Commodity futures contracts began trading on organized exchanges in the United States in the middle of the nineteenth century. These contracts evolved from so called "to arrive" contracts in which grain was sold pursuant to an agreement that the delivery of the grain would be at a specified future date rather than the immediate delivery. The terms of these to-arrive contracts were standardized on the Chicago Board of Trade and, as such, they became known as futures contracts. This standardization of contract terms allowed futures contracts to be offset so that delivery was not required. This offset feature quickly became the subject of widespread interest to speculators and commercial traders because they could buy and sell these contracts without actually making or taking delivery. Commodity option contracts were also developed for trading on the futures exchanges, but speculative abuses led to their suppression for varying periods. In fact, after 1936, federal law banned commodity option contracts on agricultural commodities.

Traditionally, futures trading was conducted on agricultural commodities. However, inflation and wide scale speculative interest in the 1970s led to the development of a number of new futures contracts, including stock index futures contracts that allowed traders to benefit from changes in the overall value of the stock market. The 1970s also saw the creation of a new exchange that traded stock option contracts: the Chicago Board Options Exchange Inc.

These developments led to explosive growth in the futures and options industry. In 1970, the volume of futures contracts was some 13.6 million. By 1980 that figure had increased to 92 million contracts and by 1990 volume had risen to some 275 million contracts. Trading volume in the new financial futures alone reached 42 million contracts in 1982. By 1989 the number of financial futures contracts that were traded was approaching 200 million, far exceeding the number of agricultural commodity futures contracts that was the traditional basis for futures trading. In 2002, the number of exchange traded futures contracts in the United States soared to 491.5 million contracts and an additional 157 million options contracts were traded on exchanges. About 85 percent of that volume were futures and options on financial instruments. * * *

A commodity futures contract is a bilateral obligation in which the seller (also known as the "short") agrees to deliver a specified amount of an identified grade of commodity at a specified date in the future. The purchaser (also known as the "long") agrees to buy the specified amount of the identified commodity at the agreed date in the future at the price negotiated with the seller. The terms of commodity futures contracts are standardized, but futures contracts typically have a wide range of standardized delivery dates. The only term that is negotiated is the price. That negotiation occurs in an auction-style process on the floors of the commodity exchanges.

Until 2000, commodity futures contracts originating in the United States could be traded only on exchanges in the United States that are licensed by the CFTC as "contract markets". An exchange must be designated as a contract market for each futures contract traded on its floor. * * * The ... largest commodity futures exchange in the United States ... Chicago Mercantile Exchange. [which handles virtually all of U.S. futures trading]* * *

Each futures exchange has a "clearing house" that guarantees performance on the futures contracts traded on the exchange. To effectuate that guarantee, the clearing house is interceded between each buyer and seller of a futures contract. The clearing house, therefore, becomes the buyer and the seller in every futures transaction. Because the terms of futures contracts are standardized, and due to the intercession of the clearing house, futures contracts also become fungible. Consequently, traders can close out their positions without taking delivery, and most do. Some futures contracts provide for cash settlement rather than actual delivery of the underlying commodity. In other futures contracts, particularly agricultural contracts, delivery remains available.

Futures contracts are traded on margin. There are two types of margin. The first is initial margin. This is simply a good faith deposit of money to assure that the parties will perform on their contract. Both the buyer and seller must post this initial margin. Generally, the amount of the margin is only a small percentage of the actual purchase price.

The second form of margin is called variation margin. Futures contracts are marked-to-market each day. That is, if there has been a fluctuation in price, the theoretical gain or loss to each party is computed. Those funds are then credited to the account of the purchaser, through the clearing house and then to the purchaser's broker. This marking-to-market process occurs every day and each party must pay or receive to reflect their gains or losses.

The small amount of initial margin required for futures contracts means that the transaction is highly leveraged. Because of that high leverage, margin requirements are strictly enforced to assure that the parties perform. There is no Securities Investors Protection Corporation

("SIPC") or other federal insurance such as that for stock brokerage firms, banks, or savings and loan association failures in the United States. Because commodity futures brokers remain liable in the event that customers default, they are very aggressive in assuring that margin requirements are met. This margin system has worked well in the past. There have been relatively few failures of commodity futures firms.

The following illustration explains how a futures contract may operate in practice. Assume that in January a trader in Miami wishes to purchase a 5,000 ounce silver futures contract ... in New York for delivery in the following May. The trader would call his broker in Miami to place the order. The broker there would in turn transmit the order to the floor of the exchange for execution in the pit. Assuming that the trader wishes to buy the silver at the existing market price, which we will assume is $5.00, the order would be offered to the ring and executed. At that point, a seller would agree to the contract, i.e., the seller would agree to deliver the silver at that market price. The trade is then reported to the clearing house, and the clearing house is interceded as the buyer and seller. At that point, the purchaser is obligated to take delivery of the silver in New York in May at the price of $5.00 per ounce [silver was trading at nearly $30 per ounce in 2010 but the $5 per ounce is a simpler illustration] or a total of $25,000. The seller has a reciprocal obligation of delivering the silver at that time for that price. Assuming an initial margin requirement of 5%, each party will post margin of $1,250 on the opening of the contract. Assume further that the price of silver jumps $1.00 on the next trading day. This would mean that the purchaser has a gain of $5,000. But the seller has a reciprocal loss of $5,000. The seller would, therefore, be required to post an additional $5,000 to reflect that loss, and the reciprocal gain would be credited to the purchaser. This process continues throughout the period the parties hold their contracts.

NOTES

1. The commodity exchange clearing house serves several important functions. As the buyer and seller of every contract, it allows positions to be closed out without the actual traders having to negotiate with each other. Rather, they simply enter a liquidating order on the floor that when executed will offset and close out the open position of the trader.

2. The clearing house also acts as a guarantor on each contract. That guarantee is backed by margin requirements and the capital of the executing member. If that is not enough, liability may be imposed on all clearing members which include some of the largest financial institutions in the world. Further protection is offered by a clearing fund generated by transaction fees on each contract. This system has proved to be a hardy one, and clearing house risk of default is generally considered to be remote.

MERRILL LYNCH, PIERCE, FENNER & SMITH INC. v. CURRAN

456 U.S. 353, 102 S.Ct. 1825, 72 L.Ed.2d 182 (1982).

JUSTICE STEVENS delivered the opinion of the Court.

The Commodity Exchange Act (CEA), 7 U.S.C. § 1 *et seq.* (1976 ed. and Supp.IV), has been aptly characterized as "a comprehensive regulatory structure to oversee the volatile and esoteric futures trading complex." The central question presented by these cases is whether a private party may maintain an action for damages caused by a violation of the CEA. The United States Court of Appeals for the Sixth Circuit answered that question affirmatively, holding that an investor may maintain an action against his broker for violation of an antifraud provision of the CEA. The Court of Appeals for the Second Circuit gave the same answer to the question in actions brought by investors claiming damages resulting from unlawful price manipulation that allegedly could have been prevented by the New York Mercantile Exchange's enforcement of its own rules. * * *

Prior to the advent of futures trading, agricultural products generally were sold at central markets. When an entire crop was harvested and marketed within a short time-span, dramatic price fluctuations sometimes created severe hardship for farmers or for processors. Some of these risks were alleviated by the adoption of quality standards, improvements in storage and transportation facilities, and the practice of "forward contracting"—the use of executory contracts fixing the terms of sale in advance of the time of delivery.

When buyers and sellers entered into contracts for the future delivery of an agricultural product, they arrived at an agreed price on the basis of their judgment about expected market conditions at the time of delivery. Because the weather and other imponderables affected supply and demand, normally the market price would fluctuate before the contract was performed. A declining market meant that the executory agreement was more valuable to the seller than the commodity covered by the contract; conversely, in a rising market the executory contract had a special value for the buyer, who not only was assured of delivery of the commodity but also could derive a profit from the price increase.

The opportunity to make a profit as a result of fluctuations in the market price of commodities covered by contracts for future delivery motivated speculators to engage in the practice of buying and selling "futures contracts." A speculator who owned no present interest in a commodity but anticipated a price decline might agree to a future sale at the current market price, intending to purchase the commodity at a reduced price on or before the delivery date. A "short" sale of that kind would result in a loss if the price went up instead of down. On the other hand, a price increase would produce a gain for a "long" speculator who had acquired a contract to purchase the same commodity with no intent to take delivery but merely for the purpose of reselling the futures contract at an enhanced price.

In the 19th century the practice of trading in futures contracts led to the development of recognized exchanges or boards of trade. At such exchanges standardized agreements covering specific quantities of graded agricultural commodities to be delivered during specified months in the future were bought and sold pursuant to rules developed by the traders themselves. Necessarily the commodities subject to such contracts were fungible. For an active market in the contracts to develop, it also was essential that the contracts themselves be fungible. The exchanges therefore developed standard terms describing the quantity and quality of the commodity, the time and place of delivery, and the method of payment; the only variable was price. The purchase or sale of a futures contract on an exchange is therefore motivated by a single factor—the opportunity to make a profit (or to minimize the risk of loss) from a change in the market price.

The advent of speculation in futures markets produced well-recognized benefits for producers and processors of agricultural commodities. A farmer who takes a "short" position in the futures market is protected against a price decline; a processor who takes a "long" position is protected against a price increase. Such "hedging" is facilitated by the availability of speculators willing to assume the market risk that the hedging farmer or processor wants to avoid. The speculators' participation in the market substantially enlarges the number of potential buyers and sellers of executory contracts and therefore makes it easier for farmers and processors to make firm commitments for future delivery at a fixed price. The liquidity of a futures contract, upon which hedging depends, is directly related to the amount of speculation that takes place.

Persons who actually produce or use the commodities that are covered by futures contracts are not the only beneficiaries of futures trading. The speculators, of course, have opportunities to profit from this trading. Moreover, futures trading must be regulated by an organized exchange. In addition to its regulatory responsibilities, the exchange must maintain detailed records and perform a clearing function to discharge the offsetting contracts that the short or long speculators have no desire to perform.[1] The operation of the exchange creates employment opportunities for futures commission merchants, who solicit orders from individual traders, and for floor brokers, who make the actual trades on the floor of the exchange on behalf of futures commission merchants and their customers. The earnings of the persons who operate the futures market—the exchange itself, the clearinghouse, the floor brokers, and the futures commission merchants—are financed by commissions on the purchase and sale of futures contracts made over the exchange.

---

1. ... only about "3% of all futures contracts traded are normally settled by an actual delivery."

Thus, in a broad sense, futures trading has a direct financial impact on three classes of persons. Those who actually are interested in selling or buying the commodity are described as "hedgers"; their primary financial interest is in the profit to be earned from the production or processing of the commodity. Those who seek financial gain by taking positions in the futures market generally are called "speculators" or "investors"; without their participation, futures markets "simply would not exist."[2] Finally, there are the futures commission merchants, the floor brokers, and the persons who manage the market; they also are essential participants, and they have an interest in maximizing the activity on the exchange. The petitioners in these cases are members of this third class whereas their adversaries, the respondents, are speculators or investors.

Because Congress has recognized the potential hazards as well as the benefits of futures trading, it has authorized the regulation of commodity futures exchanges for over 60 years. In 1921 it enacted the Future Trading Act, 42 Stat. 187, which imposed a prohibitive tax on grain futures transactions that were not consummated on an exchange designated as a "contract market" by the Secretary of Agriculture. The 1921 statute was held unconstitutional as an improper exercise of the taxing power in *Hill v. Wallace*, 259 U.S. 44, 42 S.Ct. 453, 66 L.Ed. 822 (1922), but its regulatory provisions were promptly re-enacted in the Grain Futures Act, 42 Stat. 998, and upheld under the commerce power in *Chicago Board of Trade v. Olsen*, 262 U.S. 1, 43 S.Ct. 470, 67 L.Ed. 839 (1923). Under the original legislation, the principal function of the Secretary was to require the governors of a privately organized exchange to supervise the operation of the market. Two of the conditions for designation were that the governing board of the contract market prevent its members from disseminating misleading market information and prevent the "manipulation of prices or the cornering of any grain by the dealers or operators upon such board." The requirement that designated contract markets police themselves and the prohibitions against disseminating misleading information and manipulating prices have been part of our law ever since. * * *

---

2. "Broadly speaking, futures traders fall into two general classifications, i.e. 'trade' hedging customers, and speculators. All orders which reach the trading floor originate with one or the other group of traders. The 'trade' customer is the hedger who seeks, at low cost, to protect himself or his company against possible loss due to adverse price fluctuations in the market place. Speculators, on the other hand, embrace all representatives of the general public, including some institutions, plus floor scalpers and position traders, who seek financial gain by taking positions in volatile markets. The principal role of the speculator in the markets is to take the risks that the hedger is unwilling to accept. The opportunity for profit makes the speculator willing to take those risks. The activity of speculators is essential to the operation of a futures market in that the composite bids and offers of large numbers of individuals tend to broaden a market, thus making possible the execution with minimum price disturbance of the larger trade hedging orders. By increasing the number of bids and offers available at any given price level, the speculator usually helps to minimize price fluctuations rather than to intensify them. Without the trading activity of the speculative fraternity, the liquidity, so badly needed in futures markets, simply would not exist. Trading volume would be restricted materially since, without a host of speculative orders in the trading ring, many larger trade orders at limit prices would simply go unfilled due to the floor broker's inability to find an equally large but opposing hedge order at the same price to complete the match."

In 1968 the CEA again was amended to enlarge its coverage and to give the Secretary additional enforcement authority. Act of Feb. 19, 1968, 82 Stat. 26. The Secretary was authorized to disapprove exchange rules that were inconsistent with the statute, and the contract markets were required to enforce their rules; the Secretary was authorized to suspend a contract market or to issue a cease-and-desist order upon a showing that the contract market's rules were not being enforced. In addition, the criminal sanctions for price manipulation were increased significantly, and any person engaged in price manipulation was subjected to the Secretary's authority to issue cease-and-desist orders for violations of the CEA and implementing regulations.

In 1974, after extensive hearings and deliberation, Congress enacted the Commodity Futures Trading Commission Act of 1974. 88 Stat. 1389. Like the 1936 and the 1968 legislation, the 1974 enactment was an amendment to the existing statute that broadened its coverage and increased the penalties for violation of its provisions. The Commission was authorized to seek injunctive relief, to alter or supplement a contract market's rules, and to direct a contract market to take whatever action deemed necessary by the Commission in an emergency. The 1974 legislation retained the basic statutory prohibitions against fraudulent practices and price manipulation, as well as the authority to prescribe trading limits. The 1974 amendments, however, did make substantial changes in the statutory scheme; Congress authorized a newly created Commodities Futures Trading Commission to assume the powers previously exercised by the Secretary of Agriculture, as well as certain additional powers. The enactment also added two new remedial provisions for the protection of individual traders. The newly enacted § 5a(11) required every contract market to provide an arbitration procedure for the settlement of traders' claims of no more than $15,000. And the newly enacted § 14 authorized the Commission to grant reparations to any person complaining of any violation of the CEA, or its implementing regulations, committed by any futures commission merchant or any associate thereof, floor broker, commodity trading adviser, or commodity pool operator. This section authorized the Commission to investigate complaints and, "if in its opinion the facts warrant such action," to afford a hearing before an administrative law judge. Reparations orders entered by the Commission are subject to judicial review.

The latest amendments to the CEA, the Futures Trading Act of 1978, 92 Stat. 865, again increased the penalties for violations of the statute. The enactment also authorized the States to bring *parens patriae* actions, seeking injunctive or monetary relief for certain violations of the CEA, implementing regulations, or Commission orders.

Like the previous enactments, as well as the 1978 amendments, the Commodity Futures Trading Commission Act of 1974 is silent on the subject of private judicial remedies for persons injured by a violation of the CEA.

In the four cases before us, the allegations in the complaints filed by respondents are assumed to be true. The first involves a complaint by customers against their broker. The other three arise out of a malfunction of the contract market for futures contracts covering the delivery of Maine potatoes in May 1976, " 'when the sellers of almost 1,000 contracts failed to deliver approximately 50,000,000 pounds of potatoes, resulting in the largest default in the history of commodities futures trading in this country.' "[3]* * *

One of the futures contracts traded on the New York Mercantile Exchange provided for the delivery of a railroad car lot of 50,000 pounds of Maine potatoes at a designated place on the Bangor and Aroostook Railroad during the period between May 7, 1976, and May 25, 1976. Trading in this contract commenced early in 1975 and terminated on May 7, 1976. On two occasions during this trading period the Department of Agriculture issued reports containing estimates that total potato stocks, and particularly Maine potato stocks, were substantially down from the previous year. This information had the understandable consequences of inducing investors to purchase May Maine potato futures contracts (on the expectation that they would profit from a shortage of potatoes in May) and farmers to demand a higher price for their potatoes on the cash market.

To counteract the anticipated price increases, a group of entrepreneurs described in the complaints as the "short sellers" formed a conspiracy to depress the price of the May Maine potato futures contract. The principal participants in this "short conspiracy" were large processors of potatoes who then were negotiating with a large potato growers association on the cash market. The conspirators agreed to accumulate an abnormally large short position in the May contract, to make no offsetting purchases of long contracts at a price in excess of a fixed maximum, and to default, if necessary, on their short commitments. They also agreed to flood the Maine cash markets with unsold potatoes. This multifaceted strategy was designed to give the growers association the impression that the supply of Maine potatoes would be plentiful. On the final trading day the short sellers had accumulated a net short position of almost 1,900 contracts, notwithstanding a Commission regulation limiting their lawful net position to 150 contracts. They did, in fact, default.

The trading limit also was violated by a separate group described as the "long conspirators." Aware of the short conspiracy, they determined that they not only could counteract its effects but also could enhance the price the short conspirators would have to pay to liquidate their short positions by accumulating an abnormally large long position—at the close of trading they controlled 911 long contracts—and by creating an artificial shortage of railroad cars during the contract delivery period. Because the long conspirators were successful in tying up railroad cars, they prevented

---

3. "The default was virtually unprecedented and, in the words of CFTC officials and members of the industry, shocked the commodity markets and the participants more than any other single event in recent years." H.R. Rep. No. 95–1181, p. 99 (1978), U.S.Code Cong. & Admin.News 1978, p. 2087.

the owners of warehoused potatoes from making deliveries to persons desiring to perform short contracts.[4]

Respondents are speculators who invested long in Maine futures contracts. Allegedly, if there had been no price manipulation, they would have earned a significant profit by reason of the price increase that free market forces would have produced. * * *

We granted certiorari. For the purpose of considering the question whether respondents may assert an implied cause of action for damages, it is assumed that each of the petitioners has violated the statute and thereby caused respondents' alleged injuries. * * *

In determining whether a private cause of action is implicit in a federal statutory scheme when the statute by its terms is silent on that issue, the initial focus must be on the state of the law at the time the legislation was enacted. More precisely, we must examine Congress' perception of the law that it was shaping or reshaping. When Congress enacts new legislation, the question is whether Congress intended to create a private remedy as a supplement to the express enforcement provisions of the statute. When Congress acts in a statutory context in which an implied private remedy has already been recognized by the courts, however, the inquiry logically is different. Congress need not have intended to create a new remedy, since one already existed; the question is whether Congress intended to preserve the pre-existing remedy. * * *

The inference that Congress intended to preserve the preexisting remedy is compelling. As the Solicitor General argues on behalf of the Commission as *amicus curiae*, the private cause of action enhances the enforcement mechanism fostered by Congress over the course of 60 years. In an enactment purporting to strengthen the regulation of commodity futures trading, Congress evidenced an affirmative intent to preserve this enforcement tool. It removed an impediment to exchange rulemaking caused in part by the implied private remedy not by disapproving that remedy but rather by giving the Commission the extraordinary power to supplement exchange rules. And when several Members of Congress expressed a concern that the exclusive-jurisdiction provision, which was intended only to consolidate federal regulation of commodity futures trading in the Commission, might be construed to affect the implied cause of action as well as other court actions, Congress acted swiftly to dispel any such notion. Congress could have made its intent clearer only by expressly providing for a private cause of action in the statute. In the legal context in which Congress acted, this was unnecessary. * * *

The judgments of the Courts of Appeals are affirmed.

It is so ordered.

---

4. ''Because the long conspirators had successfully tied up all the freight cars of the Bangor & Aroostook, Incomco was unable to deliver its warehoused potatoes to persons seeking delivery to fulfill short contracts. As the warm weather set in, the 1,500,000 pounds of potatoes became rotten, and Incomco's total investment was lost.'' 638 F.2d, at 291.

JUSTICE POWELL, with whom THE CHIEF JUSTICE, JUSTICE REHNQUIST, and JUSTICE O'CONNOR join, dissenting. * * *

NOTES

1.   Congress subsequently amended the Commodity Exchange Act to restrict the availability of private rights of action under the Commodity Exchange Act to those directly damaged by a violation. 7 U.S.C. § 25.

2.   The traditional system of trading on regulated contract markets was somewhat unique. Orders from customers were transmitted from "futures commission merchants" (the futures industry analog to the broker-dealer in the securities business) to a "floor broker" in the pit on the floor of the contract market. There the order was executed by "open outcry" in auction style trading. The order could be bid on by other floor brokers representing their own customers or by "floor traders" (sometimes called "locals") bidding for their own account. This trading was colorful and was often shown on news reports. Take a moment to watch the trading on YouTube and note the hand signals being used by the buyers and sellers, which was often the only way to communicate in the chaotic conditions in some pits. There was no market-maker or specialist in these pits. The location on the floor gave the traders there a time an place advantage over other traders who had to enter orders indirectly through a futures commission merchant. No one had an obligation to trade for their own account at any time or to maintain a fair and orderly market. In recent years, those colorful scenes have been largely replaced by electronic trading systems that remove the time and place advantage of the floor trader and provides equal access to the market by everyone. See Jerry W. Markham & Daniel J. Harty, For Whom the Bell Tolls: The Demise of Exchange Trading Floors and the Growth of ECNs, 33 J. Corp. L. 865 (2008).

3.   Futures trading rewards speculators for bringing information to the market. Traders are even rewarded for trading on nonpublic information, provided that the information has not been misappropriated. The information brought to the market by traders assures better pricing of the underlying commodity.

4.   The Pentagon was considering the creation of an online futures market in 2003 that would predict terrorist and political events in the Middle East. The Pentagon sought to capture such an information flow to assist in its intelligence activities. When made public, however, that proposal was met with derision in Congress and was quickly dropped. Was it such a bad idea? The University of Iowa has operated the Iowa Elections Market for several years. That market has consistently been a better predictor of elections than pollsters. Rana Foroohar; With Michael Hastings, Reading the Tea Leaves, Newsweek, Aug. 11, 2003, at 39. The Iowa Elections Market in 2010 was also offering a contract with a payoff based on Federal Reserve Board monetary policy decisions. The Iowa Elections Market may be accessed at: http://tippie.uiowa.edu/iem/ index.cfm. Would not the same principles apply to other political events? Do you see any concerns with insider trading if the terror

exchange was operational. Would a burst of trading suggest inside knowledge of an event? Would this tip off American intelligence of an impending event? Could such trading be used to divert attention away from an area where an actual attack was planned?

5.   In Fadem v. Ford Motor Co., 2003 WL 22227961 (S.D.N.Y. 2003), the court dismissed a complaint that charged the Ford Motor Co. violated the federal securities laws in failing to disclose that it was speculating instead of hedging. The court found no factual basis for the charge, but described the claim as follows:

> Ford is the world's second-largest automobile producer. Pursuant to the Clean Air Act, 42 U.S.C. § 7401, *et seq.*, the company makes use of autocatalysts to limit emissions from the internal combustion engines in its automobiles. In order for these autocatalysts to function properly, they are coated with a solution of chemicals and non-ferrous metals, typically including platinum group metals. It is the purchase of one of these metals, palladium, that is at issue in this case.

> Between July 31, 2000 and February 9, 2001, Ford entered into a series of forward contracts to purchase palladium at fixed prices. The market for this commodity was highly volatile at the time—due in part to factors such as periodic interruptions in supplies from Russia, as well as increased demand stemming from tighter controls on engine emissions. As a result, Ford's contracts were purchased at historically high prices.

> By the fourth quarter of 2001, Ford engineers validated an improved catalyst design technology that sharply reduced the company's need for palladium. As a result, Ford no longer needed the large supply of palladium it had either purchased or promised to purchase. After several unsuccessful attempts to dispose of this excess supply, Ford eventually entered into cash settling contracts in lieu of taking physical delivery of the metals. As required by Financial Accounting Standards ("FAS") 133, it marked to market its forward purchase contracts as of December 31, 2001, resulting in a non-cash charge to earnings in the amount of $953 million.

> Ostensibly, the metals covered by the forward purchase contracts were intended for normal use in production. The plaintiffs allege, however, that Ford's actual purpose was to engage in a speculative bet that the price of palladium would continue to rise, so that Ford and its officials could resell the commodity for a profit. Moreover, the plaintiffs allege that Ford and its officers knew or should have known that it was purchasing a far greater supply of palladium than it needed, as demonstrated by the allegation that Ford and its officers knew the company was in the midst of implementing the new palladium-reducing technology at the time it entered into the contracts.

A similar problem was encountered by California during an energy crisis in that state. Brownouts and rolling blackouts were being experienced by California during the summer of 2000 and were reaching a crisis stage in the winter and spring of 2001. The governor, Gray Davis, entered into long term supply contracts to prevent future shortages. Those contracts were signed at a period of price peaks, assuring high electricity prices in California for years to come. Even worse, the electricity purchases were made from state funds. This raid on the treasury and a declining economy transformed a projected California state budgetary surplus of $8 billion for 2001 to a deficit of almost $6 billion. That deficit resulted in a recall of the state Democratic governor, Gray Davis, and the election of Republican movie star Arnold Schwarzenegger in 2003. For a description of the California energy crisis see James L. Sweeny, The California Electricity Crisis (2002).

SECTION 2.   FINANCIAL FUTURES

Commodity futures contracts were traditionally traded on agricultural commodities. That was changed by the creation of futures contracts on financial instruments in the 1970s. The following is a description of stock index futures that quickly became a popular product:

> In a stock index futures contract, the purchaser of the contract is buying a theoretical portfolio of stocks contained in an index such as Value Line or the Dow Jones Industrial Average. The purchaser of such a contract will profit if the index increases in value. Conversely, the seller will profit, and the purchaser will lose, if the value of the index declines. Unlike other futures contracts, delivery of the actual commodity (i.e., the stocks in the index) is not permitted. Rather, a cash settlement of price differences is made between the parties.

> Stock index futures may be used by speculators who wish to profit from their predictions on the course of the stock market, by allowing such speculation without requiring a major commitment of resources. Thus, stock index futures allow speculators to purchase a diversified portfolio that would reflect such an overall movement in the market, while obtaining a large amount of leverage in their trading, since margin requirements represent a small percentage of the value of the stocks in the index. These futures also provide an opportunity for institutions to hedge their portfolios against market declines. For example, an institution holding a diversified portfolio may believe that the market is going to decline on an overall basis for a period of three months. Rather than liquidate the portfolio, the institution could sell a stock index futures contract. If the market declines as predicted, the profits from the stock index future are then used to offset the loss in the portfolio value of the securities held by the institution.

Jerry W. Markham & David J. Gilberg, "Washington Watch," 6 Corp. L. Rev. 59, 61 (1983).

The use of stock index products coincided with the development of modern portfolio theory, which posits that a trader, no matter how astute, will not be able to pick individual stocks whose gains will out perform the market. This meant that a portfolio containing stocks from all sectors of the economy would out perform a portfolio selected by traders on the basis of their analysis of how those individual stocks would perform. *See generally* Bevis Longstreth, "Fiduciaries, Capital Markets and Regulation: The Current Challenge," 7 Ann. Rev. Banking L. 237 (1988) (discussion of application of modern portfolio theory).

The creation of index and other securities related derivative products led to clashes between the CFTC and the SEC over their respective jurisdiction. The decision of the CFTC to approve commodity futures trading on GNMA certificates set off one such battle. The SEC contended that such contracts were the equivalent of "when issued" GNMA's that were already regulated by the SEC. This resulted in an exchange of acrimonious correspondence between the two agencies. At the end of the day, the SEC lost that battle, and GNMA futures continued to trade. Undaunted by this challenge, the CFTC approved a futures contract on Treasury Bills on the Chicago Mercantile Exchange in 1976. The SEC retaliated by approving the trading of options on GNMA certificates on the CBOE. The commodity exchanges challenged that action in court and won before the Seventh Circuit.

BOARD OF TRADE OF THE CITY OF CHICAGO v. SECURITIES AND EXCHANGE COMMISSION

677 F.2d 1137 (7th Cir.1982), vacated as moot, 459 U.S. 1026, 103 S.Ct. 434, 74 L.Ed.2d 594 (1983).

CUMMINGS, CHIEF JUDGE.

The issue in this case is whether the Securities and Exchange Commission (SEC) has authority to regulate trading in options on Government National Mortgage Association mortgage-backed pass-through certificates (GNMA's), given that GNMA's are both "commodities" and "securities." We hold that pending further action by the Commodity Futures Trading Commission (CFTC), all trading of options on GNMA's is prohibited and that the SEC has no jurisdiction of its own to permit trading in GNMA options.

Last April the Board of Trade of the City of Chicago (Board of Trade) petitioned us to set aside an order of the SEC approving rule changes of the Chicago Board Options Exchange, Incorporated (CBOE). The CBOE rule changes would have allowed trading on the CBOE of exchange-formed off-set options on GNMA's. The underlying instruments, GNMA's or Ginnie Maes, are the product of a program administered by the Government National Mortgage Association, a Government corporation within the Department of Housing and Urban Development. See 12 U.S.C. §§ 1716 et seq.; 24 C.F.R. ch. III. The program is designed to increase liquidity in the secondary mortgage market and attract new private sources of funds into residential loans. Under this program, GNMA certificates are issued by private institutions (primarily mortgage bankers) to represent interests in pools of Government-underwritten residential mortgages. The owner of a GNMA certificate receives a proportion of the income generated as mortgagors in the pool repay their loans, and the timely payment of principal and interest to the GNMA owner is guaranteed by the Government National Mortgage Association. GNMA's, like most securities or commodities, are fully transferable from one investor to another. As the CBOE has advised us, "Institutional investors of all types have been attracted to GNMA's because such investments have favorable yields, good liquidity and a high degree of safety" (Br. 5). Although the regular payments of principal and interest are guaranteed, they are fixed for the life of the pooled mortgages, and consequently GNMA owners bear the risk that mortgage interest rates may fluctuate, making the GNMA certificates more or less valuable. The two derivative instruments at issue here, GNMA options and GNMA futures, allow GNMA traders to transfer the risks associated with value fluctuations to speculators.

The CBOE's proposed market in GNMA options differs from the market in the underlying GNMA's in that when an option contract is traded no GNMA's change hands. The purchaser or "holder" of a GNMA option acquires only the right to buy or sell a specified quantity and quality of GNMA's at a specified price prior to a specified date. Conversely, in return for a premium, the seller or "writer" of the option (here, the CBOE's clearing house) undertakes the obligation of either selling or buying the GNMA's in the event that the holder "exercises" the purchased option. Under the CBOE's proposed rule changes, however, neither party need ever own or deliver any GNMA's in order to profit from the option transaction. The writer of the option may liquidate his position prior to the holder's exercise by purchasing an identical option, in effect transferring the obligation to a new option writer. Likewise, the option holder may recover the value of his option without actually exercising it simply by purchasing an equal but opposite option (an option to buy to match an option to sell, or vice versa). The original option and its opposite, "offsetting" option are then cancelled through the CBOE clearing house. Thus the CBOE's proposed options market could exist and prosper without any of the traders ever exercising the options and buying or selling the GNMA's.

The Board of Trade, a separate market from the CBOE, has since 1975 traded a different GNMA derivative-futures on GNMA's-pursuant to the designation of the other regulatory agency involved in this case, the CFTC. GNMA futures are obligations to make or take delivery of a specified quantity and quality of GNMA's at a particular time in the future and at an agreed price. Both parties to a futures contract are obligated to perform; there is no choice by either party to exercise a right to performance as there is with options. Nevertheless, investors may deal in GNMA futures without ever intending to deliver or take delivery of GNMA's because, like the proposed options, futures contracts may be offset by purchase or sale of an equal and opposite contract. Indeed, futures markets generally are not used to obtain actual delivery of a commodity. Most contracts are fulfilled by entering into an offsetting contract, and fewer than 3% of all futures contracts are fulfilled by taking (or making) actual delivery of the underlying commodity. The differences between options and futures may be quite technical, see, e.g., Moriarty, Phillips & Tosini, A Comparison of Options and Futures in the Management of Portfolio Risk, Financial Analysts J. 61 (Jan./Feb. 1981), but a complete understanding of the differences has not been necessary to decide this case.[5]

Important for understanding the motivation behind this and related lawsuits, however, is the great similarity of functions served by the two GNMA derivatives and the tremendous revenue they may generate for the exchanges on which they are traded. Both options and futures allow GNMA traders to shift to speculators the risk of changing mortgage interest rates, and the volume of risk-shifting and speculation has been tremendous. In 1981, for example, there were approximately 2,293,000 sales of GNMA futures contracts on the Board of Trade, each contract representing $100,000 in unpaid mortgage principal. Thus when the CBOE proposed rule changes with the SEC to accommodate the creation of a market in exchange-formed off-set options on GNMA's, the Board of Trade filed comments criticizing the CBOE proposal.[6] The Board of Trade argued to the SEC that the proposed options are prohibited under Section 4c(c) of the Commodity Exchange Act, 7 U.S.C. § 6c(c), and that they fall within the CFTC's exclusive jurisdiction over commodity options under Sections 2(a)(1) and 4c(b) of the Act.

The SEC nevertheless approved the proposed rule changes on February 28, 1981, and the Board of Trade filed this petition for review as a person "aggrieved" by the SEC order. Securities Exchange Act of 1934, § 25(a)(1). * * *

---

5. Yet another GNMA derivative, options on GNMA futures, may soon be traded under new rules of the CFTC. See 46 Fed.Reg. 54500 (Nov. 3, 1981). The holder of an option on GNMA futures has the right, until a specified date, to buy from or sell to the option writer a futures contract in GNMA's. When the holder exercises such an option, he purchases (or sells) a futures "position" rather than the actual GNMA's.

6. Much of the division between futures and options trading has been fortuitous. In the beginning, both futures and options were regulated together under the Future Trading Act of 1921. The two were then cast asunder in 1922 by the Supreme Court decision of Hill v. Wallace, 259 U.S. 44, 42 S.Ct. 453, 66 L.Ed. 822, which by happenstance invalidated only the futures portion of the 1921 Act. Following reenactment of the futures regulation in the Grain Futures Act of 1922 and invalidation in 1926 of the 1921 options remnant by Trusler v. Crooks, 269 U.S. 475, 46 S.Ct. 165, 70 L.Ed. 365, futures and options regulations were rejoined within the Commodity Exchange Act of 1936. For some 30 years, futures and options led a happy life together; futures being perceived as the legitimate hedging and price-discovery vehicle and options as the farmer-feared device of reckless speculators. Then the Board of Trade, long known as the premier commodity market, Chicago Board of Trade v. Olsen, 262 U.S. 1, 33, 43 S.Ct. 470, 476, 67 L.Ed. 839, decided to begin trading in securities derivatives. In its submissions to the SEC, the Board of Trade explained: The CBOE itself, the nation's first central market for securities options, evolved from an effort by the Chicago Board of Trade in the late 1960's to develop futures contracts in securities. At that time, however, such activity did not fall within the Commodity Exchange Act, the statute governing other Chicago Board of Trade activity. As a result, the plan was modified to qualify it as an options program under the Federal securities laws. Had the plan emerged after the 1974 amendments to the Commodity Exchange Act, when the term "commodity" was broadened to encompass securities and the CFTC was awarded exclusive regulatory jurisdiction, the Chicago Board of Trade could have retained its original objective of trading securities futures contracts on its own floor under the same statute-the Commodity Exchange Act-governing its other activities. The divergence of securities options trading from futures trading was fortuitous, therefore, due to a state of the law at the time that no longer applies.

Before 1974, the Commodity Exchange Act of 1936 applied mostly to agricultural commodities. Essentially all commodity options transactions were prohibited. CEA of 1936, § 4c (current version at § 4c(a), 7 U.S.C. § 6c(a)). In 1974, Congress enacted the Commodity Futures Trading Commission Act, which amended the CEA's definition of "commodity" to include "all other goods and articles, except onions * * *, and all services, rights, and interests in which contracts for future delivery are presently or in the future dealt in * * *." CEA §§ 2(a)(1), 7 U.S.C. § 2. By this amendment, literally anything other than onions[7] could become a "commodity" and thereby subject to CFTC regulation simply by its futures being traded on some exchange. The legislative history shows that the purpose of the enlarged definition was to allow regulation of futures contracts and other transactions in a growing number of commodities such as coffee, sugar, and foreign currencies that were then being traded on and off commodity exchanges and that had been unregulated under the prior version of the CEA. This language was also meant to encompass futures markets that were expected to be expanded to cover non-traditional goods and services such as GNMA's. See S.Rep.No.1131, 93d Cong., 2d Sess. 19, reprinted in (1974) U.S.Code Cong. & Ad.News 5843, 5859; H.R.Rep.No.975, 93d Cong., 2d Sess. 41–42, 62 (1974); Philip F. Johnson, The Commodity Futures Trading Commission Act: Preemption as Public Policy, 29 Vand.L.Rev. 1, 25 (1976) ("Congress was well aware, for example, that a futures contract based upon mortgage interest rates was under development in 1973 and 1974."). Under the expanded definition, the SEC concedes that GNMA's became a commodity when the Board of Trade began trading GNMA futures in 1975. * * *

Recent experience also supports the wisdom of Congress' decision in 1974 to expand the scope of commodities that could become the subject of regulated futures trading. Futures contracts based on these new commodities have enjoyed a rapid expansion. In fact, futures contracts on financial instruments-short term commercial paper, mortgaged-backed certificates guaranteed by the Government National Mortgage Association, Treasury bonds and Treasury bills-are among the most active new contracts currently traded. Many hedgers, including banks, businessmen, and home builders are attracted to these futures contracts as a method for planning their enterprises by ensuring against sudden and expensive decreases in value of the instruments used to finance their commercial operations. This experience establishes that the substantive economic value of futures trading is the same for a farmer, a manufacturer, or a financial institution. Participants in the futures markets utilize the hedging or risk-shifting element of futures contracts, whether the contracts involve soybeans or GNMA's.

---

7. Onions were excepted from the amended definition pursuant to Pub.L. 85–839, s 1, 72 Stat. 1013 (1958) (codified at 7 U.S.C. § 13–1), which prohibited all trading in onion futures. Congress had passed the prohibition following complaints by onion producers that price fluctuations in the futures market adversely affected the cash price of onions. See S.Rep.No.1631, 85th Cong., 2d Sess. (1958); H.R.Rep.No.1036, 85th Cong., 1st Sess. (1957), reprinted in (1958) U.S.Code Cong. & Ad.News 4210–4215. But see Precious Metals Associates v. CFTC, 620 F.2d 900, 905 n.8 (1st Cir.1980) (suggesting a physiological basis for the onion producers' crying).

[The court holds that these contracts fell within the exclusive jurisdiction of the CFTC. The Supreme Court, however, vacated the decision after, as explained in the following note, a jurisdictional agreement between the CFTC and the SEC was enacted into law.]

NOTES

1. In the midst of this court battle, a demarche was reached between the Chairmen of the SEC and CFTC (the "Shad–Johnson Accords"). This agreement allocated jurisdiction between their two agencies. *Joint Explanatory Statement of the SEC and CFTC*, Comm. Fut. L. Rep. (CCH) ¶ 21,332 (Feb. 2, 1982). Congress, thereafter, enacted that agreement into law. Futures Trading Act of 1982, Pub. L. No. 97–444, 96 Stat. 2294. In brief, the CFTC was given exclusive jurisdiction over all commodity futures trading on any instrument, except that single stock futures were prohibited, joining onions as the only commodity on which futures trading was banned. The ban on single stock futures, however, was lifted in 2000 to allow such trading. The regulation of those instruments was to be shared by both the SEC and CFTC. Commodity Futures Modernization Act of 2000, Public L. No. 106–554, 114 Stat. 2763 (Dec. 21, 2000). The SEC was given what amounted to a veto over commodity futures contracts on indexes under the legislation that adopted the Shad Johnson Accords. The SEC retained jurisdiction over options trading on the stock exchanges, including options on indexes. This veto authority led to another dispute with the CFTC that was ironed out temporarily by another inter-agency agreement. Several years later, however, the SEC approved options trading on two Dow Jones indexes and then used its veto power to deny trading of commodity futures on those same indexes. The Seventh Circuit set that arbitrary action aside. Board of Trade v. SEC, 187 F.3d 713 (7th Cir.1999).

2. The Shad–Johnson Accords allowed options on foreign currency to be regulated by the SEC when traded on a national securities exchange and by the CFTC when traded on a commodity exchange or over-the-counter. 1 Phillip McBride Johnson & Thomas Lee Hazen, Derivatives Regulation § 2.02 (2004).

3. The Shad–Johnson Accords did not resolve all jurisdictional issues arising from the statutory schemes administered by the CFTC and the SEC, as seen from the following cases.

ABRAMS v. OPPENHEIMER GOVERNMENT SECURITIES, INC.

737 F.2d 582 (7th Cir.1984).

CUMMINGS, CHIEF JUDGE.

This interlocutory appeal presents the issue of whether a Government National Mortgage Association ("GNMA") forward contract constitutes the purchase and sale of the underlying GNMA security and therefore is regulated by the antifraud provisions of the securities laws, even though the GNMA forward contract itself is not a security as defined by the securities laws. We affirm the district court's holding that the antifraud provisions apply.

On February 6, 1981, plaintiff Richard Abrams entered into an agreement with defendant Oppenheimer Government Securities, Inc. ("OGS"), for the purchase and delivery of approximately $200,000 of GNMA 30–year, 13% interest, mortgage-backed pass-through certificates (also known as Ginnie Maes). Briefly, the program involves, *inter alia*, the GNMA itself, which is a Government corporation within the Department of Housing and Urban Development, see 12 U.S.C. §§ 1716 *et seq.*, 24 C.F.R. ch. III, private issuers (primarily mortgage bankers), broker-dealers such as defendant OGS, and investors such as plaintiff. The private institutions issue GNMA certificates which evidence an interest in a pool of Government-underwritten residential mortgages. The holder of a GNMA receives a proportion of the income generated as mortgagors in the pool repay their loans, and the timely payment of principal and interest to the GNMA holder is guaranteed by the Government. GNMA's are considered securities (as well as commodities), and like most securities or commodities are freely transferrable from one investor to another. The main objectives of the program are to increase liquidity in the secondary mortgage market and attract new private sources of funds into residential loans. *See Board of Trade of City of Chicago v. S.E.C.*, 677 F.2d 1137, 1139 (7th Cir.1982), vacated as moot, 459 U.S. 1026, 103 S. Ct. 434, 74 L. Ed. 2d 594–595; Dep't of Housing and Urban Development, *Analysis And Report On Alternative Approaches To Regulating The Trading Of GNMA Securities*, vol. I, at 1–15 (1978) (HUD Report).

The agreement entered into by the parties is known as a forward contract. The trade date is the date the contract here was purchased, February 6, 1981, but the settlement date, *i.e.*, the date upon which plaintiff was to remit the balance of the purchase price in exchange for delivery of the GNMA certificates, is May 20, 1981. Delayed delivery is in part a result of the lead time required by the issuer to effectuate the mortgage loans once the issuer receives assurance of a ready market for the GNMA's. To hedge against the possibility of falling interest rates between the date the issuer makes a firm commitment to a home buyer or builder and the date the securities are actually issued, issuers generally sell GNMA forward contracts to broker-dealers such as defendant OGS, who in turn enter into contracts for forward delivery with investors such as Abrams. Because GNMA's (GNMA "actuals") and GNMA forward contracts are fully transferrable from one investor to another, markets for these instruments have evolved, and their value may vary. Purchasers of GNMA forwards such as plaintiff typically speculate that the value of the GNMA certificates will increase. A myriad of factors can influence the market value of GNMA's. Most notably, as a long-term fixed interest security, outstanding GNMA's will become more attractive comparatively and their value will generally (though not necessarily) rise in the event that the prevailing long-term interest rates fall. In such a situation the purchaser of the forward would take delivery of the GNMA securities with a market value exceeding the purchase price. Another avenue is available: though the purchaser is obligated by the forward contract to take delivery of the GNMA's, he may assign his rights and obligations by selling the contract before the settlement date. The same alternatives are of course available in the event the market value falls, the deflated value being reflected in the price if the purchaser sells before the settlement date.

From this somewhat simplified background of GNMA's and GNMA forwards we now turn to the transaction at issue. In the agreement negotiated by the parties, plaintiff orally agreed with defendant James Zurek, an employee of OGS, to provide a "good faith" deposit of 10% of the purchase price. Abrams remitted the deposit of $19,200 on March 10, 1981. Plaintiff then received a demand from OGS on or about April 10 for an additional deposit of $9,647 by April 13. According to the demand letter the additional deposit was necessary "due to a decrease in the market value of the GNMA securities." Plaintiff refused to remit the requested funds on the ground that he had not been informed such demands could be made. The very purpose of the original deposit is also in dispute. According to plaintiff, the good faith deposit was to be applied to the balance of the total GNMA purchase price, with the balance due on the settlement date of May 20, 1981. Defendants assert that "the deposit would be returned after the GNMA forward transaction was completed." Defendants' Reply Br. at 1. Defendants also allege in effect the original agreement contemplated that the amount of the deposit returnable to plaintiff could be reduced to compensate OGS for any loss OGS sustained in the transaction.

Plaintiff also alleges that Zurek made material misrepresentations in regard to the expected value of the GNMA certificates and their relationship with the prime lending rate. Zurek allegedly represented that the value of a GNMA certificate would increase by six points (*i.e.*, six-hundredths of one percent) for each one point decrease in the prime rate. The origin of this litigation is that while the prime rate declined during the pre-settlement period, so did the market value of the plaintiff's soon-to-be-issued GNMA's, to the extent of approximately seven points since, possibly along with other contributing factors, prevailing long-term interest rates did not fall contemporaneously with the prime rate at this given time. In addition, Zurek, according to plaintiff, told him that "he [Zurek] had never seen the bonds so low and recommended immediate purchase." Plaintiff's Complaint, Count I, par. 9. Finally, plaintiff claims that Zurek told him he would receive 18–1/2% interest on his deposit. Plaintiff claims the deposit accrued interest at a rate of approximately 14–1/2% to 15%.

When plaintiff did not accede to the request for additional funds, OGS sold plaintiff's contract and returned only $1,700 of the deposit, retaining $17,500 on the grounds that plaintiff breached the contract and that the

$17,500 fairly compensates OGS for the decrease in the market value of the GNMA securities. * * *

Section 10(b) of the 1934 Act prohibits, *inter alia*, any manipulative or deceptive device "in connection with the purchase or sale of any security * * *." 15 U.S.C. § 78j(b). Similarly, Rule 10b–5 prohibits material misrepresentations and omissions "in connection with the purchase or sale of any security." 17 C.F.R. 240.10b–5 (1980). Section 3(a) of the 1934 Act, 15 U.S.C. § 78c(a), states that "the terms 'buy' and 'sell' each include any contract to buy, purchase, or otherwise acquire" and that "the terms 'sale' and 'sell' each include any contract to sell or otherwise dispose of". Section 17(a) of the 1933 Act prohibits the making of any untrue statement or omission of material fact "in the * * * sale of any securities * * *." 15 U.S.C. § 77q(a). The term "sale" is defined in Section 2(3) of the 1933 Act to "include every contract of sale or disposition of a security or interest in a security, for value." 15 U.S.C. § 77b(3).

From this language, it is apparent that the antifraud provisions apply to the transaction at issue. GNMA certificates are considered securities (exempted from registration) n5 pursuant to Section 2(1) of the 1933 Act n6 and Section 3(a)(10) of the 1934 Act, being a "note * * * bond, [or] debenture" with a maturity exceeding nine months. * * *

Defendants assert that if the contract at issue is deemed to constitute a contract for the purchase and sale of securities for purposes of the antifraud provisions, such a holding would encroach upon the jurisdiction of the Commodity Futures Trading Commission (CFTC). We find no merit in this assertion. The CFTC does not possess any statutory authority to regulate the trading of GNMA forward contracts. The "Treasury Amendment" of 1974 to the CEA provides in pertinent part:

> Nothing in this chapter shall be deemed to govern or in any way be applicable to transactions in foreign currency, security warrants, security rights, resales of installment loan contracts, repurchase options, government securities, or mortgages and mortgage purchase commitments, unless such transactions involve the sale thereof for future delivery conducted on a board of trade.

7 U.S.C. § 2. Forward contracts by definition are traded through party-to-party negotiation (over the counter), unlike futures which are traded on an organized exchange. The legislative history behind the 1974 amendment indicates the Treasury Department was concerned that the CFTC might exceed its jurisdiction in regulating financial instruments such as GNMA forwards which are not traded on an organized exchange. n9 See S. Rep. No. 93–1131, 93d Cong., 2d Sess., reprinted in [1974] U.S. Code Cong. & Ad. News 5843, 5863, 5889. Our holding therefore does not in any way intrude upon CFTC jurisdiction.

Defendants also assert that in effect GNMA futures are essentially indistinguishable from GNMA forwards, and therefore applying the antifraud provisions to GNMA forwards but not to GNMA futures is an untenable distinction. We agree with defendants that both forwards and futures are "derivative" contracts created for the purposes of shifting risk, and that both at least in theory obligate the purchaser to take delivery of a commodity such as GNMA's at some date in the future. Yet the fundamental distinction remains that GNMA futures are traded on an organized exchange and are subject to CFTC jurisdiction, whereas GNMA forwards are not. As a result, GNMA futures are highly standardized, whereas the critical terms of GNMA forwards are the result of negotiation between purchaser and broker-dealer. See HUD Report, *supra*, at 111, 131. Forward contracts allow purchasers to negotiate, *inter alia*, the quantity of the commodity (and, in the case of tangible good commodities, the grade or purity), the time and place of delivery, the manner of payment, and deposit or margin requirements, the latter being a primary subject of dispute between the parties in the underlying litigation herein. See Note, *The GNMA Securities Market: An Analysis Of Proposals For A Regulatory Scheme*, 9 Fordham Urb. L.J. 457, 463 n.29 (1980) ("GNMA forward contracts must be distinguished from GNMA futures contracts, which are standardized commodities contracts traded on a Board of Trade."). In addition, many investors are deterred from directly participating in GNMA futures trading on organized exchanges due to the complexity of internal exchange rules or simply due to the limited nature of their investment activities.

Moreover, futures and forwards differ in the purpose of the investment and expectations of the investors. The vast majority of GNMA futures contracts are traded without the commodity ever being ultimately delivered. Indeed, futures markets generally are not used to obtain actual delivery of a commodity. Most contracts are discharged by entering into an offsetting contract, *e.g.*, the seller of a futures contract will later purchase a future of the same commodity, hoping in the interim that the price at which he sold is greater than the price at which he will buy. Such speculation generates profit for those who speculate accurately. Empirical data suggest that fewer than 3% of all futures contracts are fulfilled by taking (or making) actual delivery of the underlying commodity. In contrast, the purchasers of forwards generally adopt a more long-term position, often actually taking delivery of the underlying commodity. * * *

The transactions in question must be distinguished from sales of GNMA futures contracts which are presently being traded on the Chicago Board of Trade. The Board of Trade transactions are highly standardized; the futures contracts are sold at an auction, with the only term in the transaction being the price. Delivery is very rarely taken in such transactions. In the forward contracts under consideration, the parties negotiate all the terms of the sale, including the interest rate, date of delivery, and price, and the purchaser most often takes actual delivery of the underlying certificate. Transactions involving futures contracts require the participation of a clearing house which buys from the seller and sells to the buyer; forward contracts, or contract for delayed delivery, are negotiated directly between the buyer and seller, and no third party is ever involved. Futures contract trading may be carried on through a discretionary account managed by a broker-dealer; the forward contracts involved here require party-to-party negotiation. The current dispute between the SEC and the Commodities Futures Trading Commission (CFTC) concerns jurisdiction over futures contracts trading and possible registration and does not bear on the issue presently before the Court. * * *

In sum, we affirm the district court's holding that the purchase of GNMA forwards is in connection with the purchase and sale of the underlying GNMA securities, and therefore the antifraud provisions of the securities laws apply to the purchase and sale of GNMA forwards.

CHICAGO MERCANTILE EXCHANGE v. SECURITIES AND EXCHANGE COMMISSION

883 F.2d 537 (7th Cir.1989), cert. denied sub nom. Investment Company
Institute v. Securities and Exchange Commission, 496 U.S. 936, 110
S.Ct. 3214, 110 L.Ed.2d 662 (1990).

EASTERBROOK, CIRCUIT JUDGE.

The Commodity Futures Trading Commission has authority to regulate trading of futures contracts (including futures on securities) and options on futures contracts. The Securities and Exchange Commission has authority to regulate trading of securities and options on securities. If an instrument is both a security and a futures contract, the CFTC is the sole regulator because "the Commission shall have exclusive jurisdiction with respect to ... transactions involving ... contracts of sale (and options on such contracts) for future delivery of a group or index of securities (or any interest therein or based upon the value thereof)", 7 U.S.C. § 2a(ii). See also 7 U.S.C. § 2 ("the Commission shall have exclusive jurisdiction, except to the extent otherwise provided in section 2a of this title"); *Chicago Board of Trade v. SEC,* 677 F.2d 1137 (7th Cir.), vacated as moot, 459 U.S. 1026, 103 S.Ct. 434, 74 L.Ed.2d 594 (1982) (*GNMA Options*). If, however, the instrument is both a futures contract and an option on a security, then the SEC is the sole regulator because "the [CFTC] shall have no jurisdiction to designate a board of trade as a contract market for any transaction whereby any party to such transaction acquires any put, call, or other option on one or more securities ... including any group or index of such securities, or any interest therein or based on the value thereof." 7 U.S.C. § 2a(i).

The CFTC regulates futures and options on futures; the SEC regulates securities and options on securities; jurisdiction never overlaps. Problem: The statute does not define either "contracts ... for future delivery" or "option"—although it says that " 'future delivery' ... shall not include any sale of any cash commodity for deferred shipment or delivery". See Lester G. Telser, *Futures and Actual Markets: How They Are Related,* 59 J. Business S5 (1986). Each of these terms has a paradigm, but newfangled instruments may have aspects of each of the prototypes.

Our case is about such an instrument, the index participation (IP). We must decide whether tetrahedrons belong in square or round holes.

Index participations are contracts of indefinite duration based on the value of a basket (index) of securities. The seller of an IP (called the "short" because the writer need not own the securities) promises to pay the buyer the value of the index as measured on a "cash-out day". Any index, such as the Standard & Poor's 500, can be used. The buyer pays for the IP in cash on the date of sale and may borrow part of the price (use margin) on the same terms the Federal Reserve sets for stock—currently 50%. The exchange designates a conversion ratio between the index and the IP, so that (say) each IP unit entitles the holder on cash-out day to the value of the index times 100. Until cash-out the IP may trade on the exchange just like any other instrument. At the end of each quarter the short must pay the buyer (the "long") a sum approximating the value of dividends the stocks in the index have paid during the quarter. From the perspective of the long, then, an IP has properties similar to those of a closed-end mutual fund holding a value-weighted portfolio of the securities in the index: the IPs last indefinitely, pay dividends, and may be traded freely; on cash-out day the IP briefly becomes open-end, and the investor can withdraw cash without making a trade in the market.

Things differ from the short's perspective. Unlike the proprietor of a mutual fund, the short need not own the securities in the index; it will own them (equivalently, a long futures contract based on the same index) only to reduce risk. The short receives the long's cash but must post margin equal to 150% of the value of the IP, similar to the margin required for a short sale of stock. The short sees the IP as a speculative or hedging instrument scarcely distinguishable from a futures contract that terminates on the cash-out day, plus an option held by the long to roll over the contract to the next cash-out date. Cash-out days for an IP generally are the third Friday of March, June, September, and December, the expiration dates of the principal stock-index futures contracts, making the link even more apparent.

Longs and shorts do not deal directly with each other. After the parties agree on the price, the Options Clearing Corporation (OCC) issues the IP to the long, receiving the cash; at the same time the OCC pays the short and "acquires" the short's obligation to pay at cash-out time. OCC guarantees the short's obligations to the long, to secure which it holds the short's 150% margin. As the quarter progresses the short must pony up cash to cover dividend-equivalent obligations. When a long exercises the cash-out privilege, the OCC chooses a short at random to make the payment. Any link between the original buyer and seller of an IP thus does not extend beyond the formation of the instrument; after that instant, each person's rights and obligations run to the OCC exclusively. This arrangement also permits either party to close its position by making an offsetting transaction. If the seller of an IP buys an identical contract in the market, the OCC cancels the two on its books.

The Philadelphia Stock Exchange asked the SEC in February 1988 for permission to trade IPs. The American Stock Exchange and the Chicago Board Options Exchange later filed proposals of their own. Each exchange's IP differs slightly from the others. Philadelphia's IP, called a "Cash Index Participation", allows the long to exercise the cash-out privilege on any business day, at a discount of 0.5% from the value of the index. (The long may cash out on a quarterly date without penalty.) The AMEX's IP, called the "Equity Index Participation", permits the long to cash out quarterly for money or shares of stock in a ratio matching the index. Holders of 500 or more EIP trading units based on the S & P 500 index (each the equivalent of 100 multiples of that index) may exercise the right to receive securities, and they must pay a "delivery charge" to be established by the AMEX. Writers of EIPs may volunteer to deliver stock; if not enough do, a "physical delivery facilitator" at the AMEX will buy stock in the market, using money provided by the shorts whose positions have been liquidated. The CBOE's product, the "Value of Index Participation", has a semi-annual rather than quarterly cash-out date. CBOE's wrinkle is that the short as well as the long may cash out, by tendering the value of the index on the cash-out date. If shorts seeking to close their positions exceed the number of longs who want cash, the OCC will choose additional long positions at random to pay off.

The three stock exchanges and the OCC asked the SEC to allow them to trade these varieties of IP. Each contended that the SEC has exclusive jurisdiction because IPs are securities and not futures contracts. The AMEX added that in its view an IP is an option on securities, activating the savings clause of § 2a(i). The Chicago Board of Trade and the Chicago Mercantile Exchange, supported by the CFTC, asked the SEC to deny the requests. Each futures market, and the CFTC, argued that IPs are futures and not securities, so that the CFTC's jurisdiction is exclusive under 7 U.S.C. §§ 2 and 2a(ii). Complicating the picture, the Investment Company Institute argued that if IPs are securities and not futures, the OCC is an "investment company", offering a product combining features of closed-end and open-end mutual funds, and must register under the Investment Company Act of 1940, 15 U.S.C. §§ 80a–1 to 80a–64.

On April 11, 1989, the SEC granted the exchanges' requests. Release No. 34–26709, 54 Fed.Reg. 15280 (1989). At the same time, its Division of Market Regulation, acting with delegated authority, allowed the OCC to change its rules so that it could issue, settle, and clear IPs. Release No. 34–26713, 54 Fed.Reg. 15575 (1989). The SEC concluded that IPs are "stock" within the meaning of § 3(a)(10) of the Securities Exchange Act of 1934, 15 U.S.C. § 78c(a)(10). IPs are negotiable, pay dividends, may appreciate in value, and may be hypothecated; the only attribute of stock missing from IPs is voting rights, which the SEC thought unimportant. 54 Fed.Reg. at 15285–86. If not stock, the SEC concluded, IPs are "certificates of interest or participation in" stock, another of the instruments defined as "securities" in § 3(a)(10). See 54 Fed.Reg. at 15286. Next the SEC found that IPs are not "futures", *id.* at 15286–89, because they lack two features the SEC thought essential: "futurity" and "bilateral obligation". "Futurity" means that value is set in the future, while as the SEC observed the buyer of an IP pays a price fixed at the time of sale; "bilateral obligation" means that the contract is executory on both sides until expiration or settlement, while the long on an IP performs at the time of purchase, leaving only the short with executory obligations. The SEC went on to say, *id.* at 15289–90, that the OCC need not register under the Investment Company Act because there is no "issuer" within the meaning of § 3(a)(1) of that statute, 15 U.S.C. § 80a–3(a)(1). Concluding that IPs may serve as substitutes for "program trading", provide "an additional layer of liquidity to the market", and afford "an alternative vehicle for retail customers to invest in 'the market' ", 54 Fed.Reg. at 15290, the SEC allowed the exchanges to proceed with their plans. We denied the futures markets' request for a stay but accelerated the hearing of the case on the merits. IPs have been trading on the three exchanges since May. * * *

[T]he futures markets are not plagued by regulation of their own activities. They complain, instead, that the SEC has passed up an opportunity to throttle three competitors. * * *

A futures contract, roughly speaking, is a fungible promise to buy or sell a particular commodity at a fixed date in the future. Futures contracts are fungible because they have standard terms and each side's obligations are guaranteed by a clearing house. Contracts are entered into without prepayment, although the markets and clearing house will set margin to protect their own interests. Trading occurs in "the contract", not in the commodity. Most futures contracts may be performed by delivery of the commodity (wheat, silver, oil, etc.). Some (those based on financial instruments such as T-bills or on the value of an index of stocks) do not allow delivery. Unless the parties cancel their obligations by buying or selling offsetting positions, the long must pay the price stated in the contract (e.g., $1.00 per gallon for 1,000 gallons of orange juice) and the short must deliver; usually, however, they settle in cash, with the payment based on changes in the market. If the market price, say, rose to $1.50 per gallon, the short would pay $500 (50¢ per gallon); if the price fell, the long would pay. The extent to which the settlement price of a commodity futures contract tracks changes in the price of the cash commodity depends on the size and balance of the open positions in "the contract" near the settlement date. When the contract involves financial instruments, though, the price is fixed by mechanical computation from the instruments on which the contracts are based. See *Leist v. Simplot,* 638 F.2d 283, 286–87 (2d Cir.1980) (Friendly, J.), affirmed on other grounds under the name *Merrill Lynch, Pierce, Fenner & Smith, Inc. v. Curran,* 456 U.S. 353, 102 S.Ct. 1825, 72 L.Ed.2d 182 (1982); Philip McBride Johnson & Thomas Lee Hazen, 1 *Commodities Regulation* §§ 1.03–.04, 1.10 (2d ed. 1989); Bryan Byrne, Jr., *The Stock Index Futures Market* (1987).

A security, roughly speaking, is an undivided interest in a common venture the value of which is subject to uncertainty. Usually this means a claim to the assets and profits of an "issuer". Shares of stock entitle their holders to receive dividends and payments on liquidation (or a change in corporate form), see *Landreth Timber Co. v. Landreth,* 471 U.S. 681, 105 S.Ct. 2297, 85 L.Ed.2d 692 (1985); bonds and other debt instruments promise interest plus a balloon payment of principal at the end. Unusual interests such as rights in orange groves still may be "securities" if they represent a pro rata share of a variable pool of earnings. *SEC v. W.J. Howey Co.,* 328 U.S. 293, 66 S.Ct. 1100, 90 L.Ed. 1244 (1946). See generally Louis Loss & Joel Seligman, 2 *Securities Regulation* 926–89 (3d ed. 1988).

Securities usually arise out of capital formation and aggregation (entrusting funds to an entrepreneur), while futures are means of hedging, speculation, and price revelation without transfer of capital. So one could think of the distinction between the jurisdiction of the SEC and that of the CFTC as the difference between regulating capital formation and regulating hedging. Congress conceived the role of the CFTC in that way when it created the agency in 1974 to assume functions that had been performed by the Department of Agriculture but which were no longer thought appropriate for that Department as futures markets expanded beyond commodities into financial instruments. See *GNMA Options* for a recap of the history. Unfortunately, the distinction between capital formation and hedging falls apart when it comes time to allocate the regulation of options.

A call option is a promise by the writer to deliver the underlying instrument at a price fixed in advance (the "strike price") if the option is exercised within a set time. The buyer pays a price (the "premium") in advance for the opportunity; the writer may or may not own the instrument he promises to deliver. Call options are written "out of the money"—that is, the exercise price exceeds the market price at the outset. The writer will make money if by the time the option expires the market price is less than the strike price plus the premium (plus the interest earned on the premium in the interim); the buyer of the option hopes that the market price will rise above the strike price by enough to cover the premium, the time value of money, and the transactions costs of executing the option. Options play valuable roles in price-discovery, and they also allow the parties to adjust the net riskiness of their portfolios. Writers of call options reduce the risk they bear if the market falls while limiting gains if the market rises; buyers hope for large proportional gains if the market rises while accepting the likelihood that the options will turn out to be worthless. Options are side deals among investors, which do not augment an entrepreneur's coffers (except to the extent greater liquidity and opportunities to adjust risk increase social marginal propensity to invest). Dwight M. Jaffee, *The Impact of Financial Futures and Options on Capital Formation,* 4 J. Futures Markets 417 (1984). Unlike financial and index futures, options call for delivery of the underlying instrument—be it a share of stock or a futures contract.

The SEC consistently has taken the position that options on securities should be regulated as securities. For some years the CFTC maintained that options on securities should be regulated as futures because options are extrinsic to capital formation and because it is almost always possible to devise an option with the same economic attributes as a futures contract (and the reverse). Matters came to a head in 1980, when both agencies asserted jurisdiction over options on securities based on pools of notes. The Government National Mortgage Association (GNMA) sold pass-through certificates representing proceeds of mortgage notes, and persons started writing options on them to allow hedging against movements in interest rates. The SEC observed that options written on securities are securities under § 3(a)(10) of the '34 Act; indeed the SEC contended that because options are securities it should regulate all options. The CFTC countered that options on financial instruments are futures under § 4c(b) of the CEA, 7 U.S.C. § 6c(b), and added that because its jurisdiction is exclusive, it is the sole lawful regulator. When the SEC allowed stock exchanges to start trading GNMA options, the futures markets sought review in this court and the CFTC howled bloody murder.

While the case was pending, the agencies reached a pact, which the SEC calls the Shad–Johnson Agreement and the CFTC calls the Johnson–Shad Agreement. (John Shad was the SEC's Chairman at the time, and Phillip Johnson the CFTC's.) This Accord (as we shall call it to avoid offending either agency) provided that jurisdiction over options follows jurisdiction over the things on which the options are written. So the SEC received jurisdiction of options on securities, while the CFTC got jurisdiction of options on futures contracts. Things were not quite done, though, because we held in *GNMA Options* that the agencies could not alter their jurisdiction by mutual agreement. 677 F.2d at 1142 n. 8. Starting from the proposition that options on GNMAs are both securities and futures, we held that the CFTC's jurisdiction is exclusive in light of 7 U.S.C. §§ 2 and 2a.

Congress then enacted the Accord almost verbatim, producing the explicit reference to options in § 3(a)(10) of the '34 Act, the SEC savings clause in § 2a(i) of the CEA, and a small change in 7 U.S.C. § 6n to implement an understanding about pools. The legislature thought that this Accord would resolve things and restore a regime in which the SEC supervises capital formation and the CFTC hedging. See S.Rep. No. 97–384, 97th Cong., 2d Sess. 21–24 (1982); H.R.Rep. No. 97–565, 97th Cong., 2d Sess., Part I at 38–40 (1982), U.S.Code Cong. & Admin.News 1982, p. 3871; H.R.Rep. No. 97–626, 97th Cong., 2d Sess., Part II at 3 (1982), U.S.Code Cong. & Admin.News 1982, p. 2780; 128 Cong.Rec. 24910 (1982) (Rep. De La Garza); Loss & Seligman, 2 *Securities Regulation* at 1064–80; Jerry W. Markham & David J. Gilberg, *Stock and Commodity Options— Two Regulatory Approaches and Their Conflicts,* 47 Albany L.Rev. 741 (1983).

The legislation implementing the Accord left in place the premise on which *GNMA Options* was founded: if an instrument is *both* a security and a futures contract, then the CFTC's jurisdiction is exclusive. Section 2a(ii) has no other possible meaning. Like many an agreement resolving a spat, the Accord addressed a symptom rather than the problem. Options are only one among many instruments that can have attributes of futures contracts as well as securities. Financial markets work best when they offer every possible combination of risk and return—a condition financial economists call "spanning"—so that investors can construct a portfolio to each need and taste. Exchanges and professional investors therefore continually devise financial products to fill unoccupied niches. See Dennis W. Carlton, *Futures Markets: Their Purpose, Their History, Their Growth, Their Successes and Failures,* 4 J. Futures Markets 237 (1984); William L. Silber, Innovation, Competition and New Contract Design in Futures Markets, 1 J. Futures Markets 123 (1981). These products are valuable to the extent that they do *not* match the attributes of instruments already available. New products, offering a new risk-return mixture, are designed to depart from today's models.

Which means that the dispute of 1980–82 about options will be played out—is being played out—about each new instrument. Today's case repeats the conflict. Other novel instruments are being handled by regulation. For example, on July 17, 1989, the CFTC adopted rules exempting from its regulation certain hybrid instruments combining equity or debt with payments based on the price of commodities. 17 C.F.R. Part 34, 54 Fed.Reg. 30684 (1989). Only merger of the agencies or functional separation in the statute can avoid continual conflict. Functional separation is hard to achieve (new instruments will appear at any border). The SEC favors merger; it has asked Congress repeatedly for jurisdiction over all products (including stock-index and financial futures) based on securities, which would relegate the CFTC to its original role as superintendent of commodities futures. The CFTC has so far defended its position, in part with the argument that multiple regulatory bodies allow greater competition and experimentation—a new product can reach market if either agency approves the variant within its domain. See Daniel R. Fischel, *Regulatory Conflict and Entry Regulation of New Futures Contracts,* 59 J. Business S85 (1986); Ronald W. Anderson, *The Regulation of Futures Contracts Innovations in the United States,* 4 J. Futures Markets 297 (1984).

Unless Congress changes the allocation of jurisdiction between the agencies, the question a court must resolve is the same as in *GNMA Options:* is the instrument a futures contract? If yes, then the CFTC's jurisdiction is exclusive, unless it is also an option on a security, in which case the SEC's jurisdiction is exclusive. So long as an instrument is a futures contract (and not an option), whether it is also a "security" is neither here nor there. Still, if IPs really are "stock" they almost certainly are not "futures contracts", so the inquiries aren't so distinct as the statutes imply.

From the perspective of the long, IPs look like an interest in a portfolio of stock. IPs last indefinitely (except for the chance that a long may be cashed out involuntarily on the CBOE), may be sold like stock or used to secure margin and other loans, change in value with the market, and pay dividends. IPs lack other common attributes of stock: they do not confer voting rights and are not "certificated"; owners of IPs receive dividend-equivalent payments quarterly, not when the firms pay dividends. We need not debate whether these differences come to anything, for they pale beside the larger difficulties in calling IPs "stock". The greatest is that IPs are not stock *in* anything. There isn't an issuer— which the SEC emphasized when concluding that the Investment Company Act is inapplicable, 54 Fed.Reg. at 15289–90. Stock is an equity interest in an issuer, the residual claim to the profits of a venture. *United Housing Foundation, Inc. v. Forman,* 421 U.S. 837, 95 S.Ct. 2051, 44 L.Ed.2d 621 (1975). *Landreth* rejected the "sale-of-business doctrine" because the owner of 100% of the equity interest in a firm still owns "stock". Purchasers of IPs don't own equity, directly or indirectly; they don't have a claim to the proceeds and liquidating distribution of a business; there isn't an underlying pool of assets; there is only a "short" on the other side. The absence of an issuer—IPs don't carry votes because they don't have anything to do with equity—tells all. There is no common venture, not even the commonality represented by a mutual fund (which reinvests in real stock and creates the risk that the stakeholder will join Robert Vesco with the kitty). * * *

Although the SEC found IPs to be securities by looking at the promises made *to* the longs, the CFTC found them to be futures by virtue of the promises made *by* the shorts, a perspective implied by the CEA's references to "contracts . . . for future delivery"—emphasizing the shorts' obligation. Shorts on IPs make the same pledge as shorts on stock-index futures contracts: to pay the value of an index on a prescribed day (the expiration date for the futures contract, the cash-out date for the IP). The short owes this obligation to the clearing house rather than to the long. IPs may be settled by buying or selling an offsetting obligation, after which the clearing house cancels the two on the books, just as with futures contracts. Shorts on IPs must put up more margin than shorts on futures contracts and must make dividend-equivalent payments, but the CFTC did not find these differences any more dispositive than the SEC found the IPs' lack of voting rights. Shorts also face an obligation of indefinite duration on the Philadelphia and AMEX IPs, but the CFTC and the futures markets treat this as no more than a prepaid rollover privilege.

Despite the congruence of futures and IPs on the short side, the SEC and the stock exchanges say that both "futurity" and "bilateralism" are missing. According to the SEC, IPs lack "futurity" because an IP is the "present obligation to pay current value". And IPs are not bilateral because the long performs in full by paying up front, although in a futures contract both sides must perform on settlement or expiration.

With respect to bilateralism, the SEC's point is inescapable. With respect to futurity, the SEC is wrong. IPs are no more a "present obligation to pay current value" than are futures contracts. The holder of either an IP or a stock-index futures contract may go to market and trade it; the price necessarily tracks current value. Neither the long on an IP nor the long on a futures contract can compel the short to *pay* current value, however. Both the futures contract and the IP are settled quarterly (the same dates for both kinds of instrument, except for the CBOE's omission of two of the four dates). The short's obligation is to pay the value of the index *on that date*—which lies in the future to the same extent as the settlement date of any futures contract. Even from the long's point of view, IP and futures contract ultimately look the same. The long pays up front for the IP, but the long on a futures contract *promises* up front to make a defined payment on the settlement date; the difference in the timing of the payment does not affect the fact that valuation comes at the defined future date.

So the IP has futurity but not bilateralism. It looks like a futures contract to the short—except that it is of indefinite duration, carries a dividend-equivalent obligation, and requires higher margin. It looks like a mutual fund to the long—except that it has no voting rights, does not represent any interest in an underlying pool of stock, and may be settled by executing an offsetting transaction. Fact is, it is no less a future than it is a security, and no more. It just doesn't fit. Which is the whole point. It isn't supposed to be just like something else; the IP was designed as a novel instrument so that it could offer attributes previously missing in the market.

The only thing of which we are sure is that an IP is not an option on a security. The AMEX contends that it is a prepaid option, with a premium equal to the full value and an exercise price of zero. The SEC did not accept this contention, writing:

> [W]hile IPs contain some characteristics of stock index options (*e.g.,* the issuance and clearance and settlement features of IPs are analogous to those of stock index options), the Commission believes that IPs predominantly have the attributes of a portfolio of common stock.

54 Fed.Reg at 15286 n. 57. The only "characteristics of stock index options" that either the AMEX or the SEC identified are those introduced by the presence of a clearing house—characteristics that the IP shares with stock-index futures to the last detail. Unless we were to say that all futures are also options (they aren't), these features do not make IPs options. The very features that the SEC emphasizes to show that IPs are securities—indefinite duration, payment up front in cash, dividend equivalency, and so on—show that IPs cannot be options. Options are written out of the money, limited in time, and establish a careful balance among premium, strike price, and duration; the writer retains dividends. IPs possess none of these distinguishing features. As the AMEX defines an "option", someone who buys an automobile for cash and drives it away really has obtained an option with a high premium, zero strike price, perpetual duration, and 100% probability of exercise. Words are useful

only to the extent they distinguish some things from others; symbols that comprise everything mean nothing. IPs are not options.

Having concluded that neither the '34 Act nor the CEA addresses the status of IPs in a straightforward way, the logical thing to do is to defer to the agency's resolution of the problem. *Chevron U.S.A. Inc. v. Natural Resources Defense Council, Inc.*, 467 U.S. 837, 104 S.Ct. 2778, 81 L.Ed.2d 694 (1984). But which agency? Each claims to be exercising its discretion; each claims entitlement to deference on a subject within its domain. * * *

If each agency's interpretation of its own statute is entitled to some deference, then the IP is both a security and a futures contract. It has some attributes of both, and all attributes of neither, as we have laid out in excessive detail. Neither characterization can be called wrong.

The only element of financial futures contracts that is missing is "bilateralism". Yet bilateralism is not essential to a futures contract. *CFTC v. Co Petro Marketing Group, Inc.*, 680 F.2d 573 (9th Cir.1982), held that a contract that imposes performance obligations only on the short may be a futures contract. Co Petro sold interests in gasoline that were designed to look like forward contracts, which under the CEA are not futures contracts. Buyers put down deposits to obtain Co Petro's promise to deliver gasoline on future dates. These contracts could not be traded on any market, but Co Petro promised to pay the investor in cash if the market price should rise (that is, the investor could sell the contract back to Co Petro). The investor risked no more than 95% of his deposit; if the price of gasoline fell, the investor's position would be closed. Thus buyers of Co Petro's contracts performed fully on the date they posted the deposit; thereafter only Co Petro had obligations. Despite that, and despite the fact that the contracts were illiquid, the court of appeals concluded that they were futures contracts because their value depended entirely on the price of the commodity at their expiration date, and they were not formed in contemplation of physical delivery.

The SEC brushes off *Co Petro* and similar cases in district courts as based on the principle that once it smells sulfur (Co Petro may have been a bucket shop), either agency may protect the investor. No such principle may be found in the '34 Act or the CEA, however. An instrument either is or is not a futures contract. If it is, the CFTC has jurisdiction; if it is not, the CFTC lacks jurisdiction; if the CFTC has jurisdiction, its power is exclusive. The SEC's position entails the proposition that if Co Petro Marketing Group, Inc., had approached the CFTC after losing in the Ninth Circuit and applied for permission to trade its gasoline contracts as futures, the CFTC would have had to say no, *on the ground that the contracts are not "contracts . . . for future delivery"* under the CEA. That can't be right. * * *

From time to time, the Supreme Court has looked to the purposes of the '34 Act to define "securities", usually with a view to enlarging the definition. (The exception is *Marine Bank v. Weaver*, 455 U.S. 551, 102 S.Ct. 1220, 71 L.Ed.2d 409 (1982).) With the SEC urging it on, the Court has drawn in orange groves covered by joint harvesting contracts, *W.J. Howey,* leaseholds in land near oil wells, *SEC v. C.M. Joiner Leasing Corp.,* 320 U.S. 344, 64 S.Ct. 120, 88 L.Ed. 88 (1943), and other unusual instruments that have some (but far from all) attributes of conventional securities. Obviously the SEC does not ask us to abandon this approach— for itself. It demands, however, that we apply *strictissimi juris* to the CEA, to hold that only an instrument with *every* attribute of a conventional futures contract may be one. Why? If the interpretive approach is proper for the securities acts, it is no less proper for the futures acts. It has been employed under both statutes—not only in *Co Petro* but also in redefining futures contracts to omit the delivery obligation. Recall the statutory scope of the CEA: contracts "for future delivery". Commodity futures contracts may be settled by delivery; financial futures contracts are settled exclusively in cash. One might have thought the prospect of "future delivery" the *sine qua non* of a "futures" contract. Yet no one, not even the SEC, doubts that a contract may be a futures contract even though it provides for cash settlement. If delivery is not essential, then the "traditional" elements of futures contracts are not invariable ingredients of the CFTC's jurisdiction.

Perhaps the SEC wants us to put a thumb on the scales, enlarging the category "securities" while shrinking the category "futures" because of the exclusivity clauses in the CEA: if both categories expand, then the SEC's jurisdiction shrinks. We do not conceive it our function, however, to invent counterweights to statutes; judges should be interpreters rather than sappers and miners. As we said in *GNMA Options,* 677 F.2d at 1161, "[o]ur task should not reflect a value judgment as to which of the competing agencies is best equipped to regulate these [products]."

To the extent instrumental arguments influence the coverage of the laws, they do not necessarily cut for the SEC. The futures markets' reply brief invites us to imagine a "Wheat Index Participation" (WIP) having the same characteristics as the IP except that it is based on an index of wheat prices rather than of stock prices. The buyer would pay cash for the WIP and be able to trade it freely; on a date identical to the expiry of the wheat futures contracts, the writer could be required to pay cash measured by the value of the wheat index. According to the SEC, such an instrument would not be a futures contract because it would lack both futurity and bilateralism (and we would agree on the latter point). So the CFTC could not allow it to be traded, no matter how valuable participants in the market might find it. On the other hand, the WIP certainly would not be "stock" and probably would not meet the criteria for being a "security" of any kind. So the SEC could not allow it to be traded on stock exchanges (anyway, the WIP would be a duck out of water on the AMEX!). We could escape from such silliness by reaching the logical conclusion that a WIP would be a futures contract. Yet if the WIP is a futures contract, it is hard to avoid the conclusion that the IP is one, too.

The petition for review in No. 89–1538 is dismissed for want of jurisdiction. The Investment Company Institute's petition, No. 89–2012, presents questions that we need not reach in light of our disposition of the futures markets' claims. On petition Nos. 89–1763 and 89–1786, the SEC's orders approving the applications of the stock exchanges and the OCC are set aside. * * *

Notes

1. Futures contracts were efficient and presented low costs to traders. It was not necessary to buy and sell the stock underlying the index in order to profit from, or hedge against, price fluctuations. This avoided the transaction costs associated with buying and selling the underlying securities. Low margins and liquidity made stock futures extremely popular with institutional investors. Interest rate futures were of equal or greater interest to portfolio managers with investments in fixed income securities. Futures trading on indexes and interest rate instruments soon outstripped volume on the more traditional agriculture futures contracts.

2. Financial futures contracts could be used for many purposes. For example, assume that the manager of a portfolio that tracks the S & P 500 stock index believes that the market will be falling over the next three months. The manager could sell out the portfolio and buy it back in when he anticipates recovery. Alternatively, the manager could passively invest and do nothing, a popular strategy but one that assumes a market recovery before the portfolio funds are needed. Alternatively, the manager could hedge by selling the S & P 500 futures contract. This locks in the value of the portfolio in the event of a market decline. Of course, the portfolio value is also locked in if the portfolio manager was wrong. For those interested, and many were, stock baskets matching the S & P 500 and other indexes could be purchased through the stock markets. This of course required payment for at least the margin value (50 percent) of the stocks in the basket, as compared to the five percent or less that had to be placed only as margin for index futures trading.

3. The stock markets and futures markets were soon intermingled and interdependent from this trading. The danger of that interdependence was brought dramatically home in the stock market crash of 1987.

JERRY W. MARKHAM & RITA McCLOY STEPHANZ
THE STOCK MARKET CRASH OF 1987—THE UNITED STATES LOOKS AT NEW RECOMMENDATIONS

76 Georgetown Law Journal 1993 (1988).

Between October 13 and October 19, 1987, the stock market suffered its worst decline since the Great Depression. New York Stock Exchange (NYSE) stocks lost $1 trillion in value and the Dow Jones Industrial Average plunged 508 points in a day that came to be known as Black Monday. * * * Various segments of the financial industry blamed each other for the 1987 market break. The New York Stock Exchange, for example, blamed the futures exchanges for helping precipitate the crash. Its report charged that activities associated with commodity exchanges, such as 'program trading' and 'portfolio insurance,' accelerated the decline. The NYSE reported that on Black Monday three portfolio insurers, pursuant to such trading programs, bought and sold $2 billion of stocks and $2.8 billion in futures. On the other hand, the commodity exchanges claimed that their products prevented even greater losses. The media, for its part, alleged that New York Stock Exchange specialists had abandoned their duty to maintain orderly markets and that a stock-index futures contract had been manipulated. Federal agencies prepared their own reports, which, not surprisingly, defended their respective turfs. Congress, meanwhile, held hearings.

To obtain a less partisan analysis, President Reagan created the Presidential Task Force on Market Mechanisms to investigate the collapse and propose regulatory reforms. The resulting report (the Brady Report) concluded, among other things, that the stock and commodity markets are inextricably linked and require coordinated regulation. * * *

'Hedging.' a critical justification for futures trading, allows consumers and producers to shield themselves from the risks of adverse price changes. For example, by selling a contract to deliver wheat at some future date at the current price, a wheat farmer protects himself from the risk of a subsequent decline in the price of wheat. 'Portfolio insurance' is a sophisticated type of hedging used primarily by institutional traders; it was the focus of many explanations of the October 1987 crash. For instance, a portfolio manager expecting the stock market to drop would sell an S & P 500 futures contract, which obligates him to deliver in the future a basket of stock at today's prices. If the market declines, he profits because he then can buy the basket for less than the price at which he has agreed to sell it. If the stock market rises, he profits on his stock portfolio although he loses money on the stock-index futures contract. When the market declines, the profit on the index offsets, in whole or in part, the loss on the stocks. The degree of offset increases as the manager's portfolio more closely resembles the S & P index. By giving up a portion of his potential profit in such a manner, a manager is able to insure his portfolio against sudden drops in the market, yet avoids the transaction costs and the depressing effect that the outright selling of stocks has on the stock price.

'Program trading,' often cited as a cause of the 1987 crash, refers to trading systems, including portfolio insurance, that are directed by computer programs. Changes in market prices prompt these programs to issue orders to buy or sell futures contracts and baskets of stock. For example, in response to a two-point drop in a stock index, programs may order the sale of futures based on a prediction that the market will continue to drop. These programs, although proprietary, confidential, and tailored to specific portfolio strategies, share many characteristics, including a tendency to issue sell orders in response to large drops in prices. Many experts believed that this common characteristic accentuated the October crash. A large market drop prompted virtually all programs to issue sell orders, causing additional massive selling. This additional selling prompted the programs to issue even more sell orders, contributing to an accelerating downward spiral.

The 'triple witching hour' refers to the once shared expiration date of certain equity options, stock-index and other commodity futures, and stock index options. Before federal regulators stepped in, the triple witching hour was infamous for the volatile price fluctuations in the stock market and the unusually heavy trading it produced—a reflection of the close link between the market securities and the futures market. The CFTC and the SEC jointly solved this problem by improving order handling and by separating expiration times to avoid the compounding effect of simultaneous expirations.

In 'index arbitrage,' traders seek to make a profit off minor differences in the prices of certain stock-index futures and the underlying stocks. If the underlying stocks sell for more than the stock-index futures, the arbitrageur buys futures and sells the underlying stocks. Arbitrageurs, during the triple witching hour, used to take advantage of the chaotic trading conditions and the disparate prices created by common expiration times. This increased buying and selling by arbitrageurs escalated market confusion.

Portfolio insurance and index arbitrage, in combination, have the potential to create a self-perpetuating downward spiral known as the 'cascade scenario.' Portfolio managers forecasting a drop in stock prices sell index futures to offset expected losses. The price of the futures then declines and sells at a discount to the underlying stocks. In an effort to profit from the difference, arbitrageurs buy futures and sell stocks. This may depress stock prices and prompt portfolio managers to begin the cycle anew. * * *

In 1982, all major stock markets began a long period of growth spurred by rising corporate earnings, reduced inflation, and falling interest rates. The Dow Jones Industrial Average rose from 777 in August 1982 to 1,896 in December 1986. In 1987, stock prices continued to climb despite rapidly rising interest rates. In August of that year, the Dow hit 2,722 due, in part, to increased foreign investment in United States equities. The growing popularity of portfolio insurance strategies also contributed to the market's rise. On October 14, 1987, however, the 'U.S. equity market began the most severe one-week decline in its history.' From the morning of Wednesday, October 14, to the following Tuesday, the Dow plummeted from over 2,500 to barely 1,700, a drop of nearly one third.

Two events contributed to the October 14 'revaluation of stock prices': (1) the announcement that the August merchandise trade deficit was $15.7 billion, $1.5 billion more than anticipated by financial markets; and (2) the House Ways and Means Committee's proposal to eliminate tax benefits associated with the financing of corporate takeovers. In response, arbitrageurs and other investors sold their positions in takeover candidates and the prices of those stocks collapsed. On October 14 alone, the Dow dropped 95 points on a trading volume of 207 million shares. Index-arbitrage sales accounted for seventeen percent of the volume. The twenty largest New York Stock Exchange members sold $689 million of stock while futures investors sold $500 million of futures.

The next day, October 15, traders in the United States awoke to news of continued selling in Tokyo and London. The Dow opened twenty points down from its close on the previous day; during the first half hour of trading, some 2,500 futures contracts and 48 million shares were traded. Although the Dow recovered slightly during the course of the day, it fell fifty-three points in the final half hour of trading, closing fifty-seven points down for the day. Index arbitrageurs sold almost $175 million on the NYSE that day, and sales of 'stock baskets' totaled another $100 million. These two strategies accounted for a quarter of the volume during the last half hour of trading.

On Friday, October 16, the Dow dropped another 108 points, its largest single-day drop to that point. In the securities markets, four trading institutions sold over $600 million of stock, indicating heavy, concentrated institutional trading. In the futures markets, portfolio insurers and index arbitrageurs sold the equivalent of $2.1 billion of stock. Index arbitrageurs also accounted for $1.7 billion of sell orders. The following Monday—Black Monday—was 'perhaps the worst day in the history of U.S. equity markets.'

On Black Monday the Dow plummeted 508 points on a trading volume of 604 million shares. This 23–percent drop is almost twice the percentage drop of 1929's 'Black Thursday.' S & P 500 futures fell 29 percent on a total volume of 162,000 contracts. This sudden decline had been foreshadowed by precipitous drops in stock markets abroad, which open earlier than U.S. markets. In Tokyo, the Nikkei Index, the Dow equivalent, fell 2.5 percent; by midday, the London market had dropped ten percent. The U.S. markets, including the Major Market Index (MMI) futures and the S & P 500 futures, opened down. Large order imbalances forced many specialists to halt trading in their stocks during the first hour. Nevertheless, two billion shares had traded hands thirty minutes after the opening bell. One mutual fund group accounted for a quarter of that volume.

Index arbitrageurs and portfolio insurers also engaged in heavy trading during the first hour of Black Monday. The discounted openings of stock-index futures resulted in an apparent record discount for futures in relation to stocks. New York Stock Exchange specialists, however, opened trading in their stocks at sharply lower levels. Index arbitrageurs, who had sold stock in anticipation of large futures discounts, rushed to cover their positions by purchasing futures. By 11:00 A.M., rising index-futures prices made stocks more attractive and the stock market rallied.

Between 11:40 A.M. and 2:00 P.M., portfolio insurance sales and rumors that the NYSE might close squelched the rally; the Dow and the futures index fell nine percent and fourteen percent, respectively. During this period, portfolio insurers had sold approximately 10,000 futures contracts, the equivalent of $1.3 billion or forty-one percent of total futures volume, and unloaded $900 million worth of stock on the NYSE. Portfolio insurers in the stock and futures markets provided over $3.7 billion of selling pressure by early afternoon. Selling pressure paused, however, because delays in transmitting orders slowed index-arbitrage activities and because one institution that had already sold $1.3 billion of stock discontinued a sell program. As a result, the Dow rallied to the 2,000 level by 2:45 P.M.

The remainder of the afternoon 'was disastrous.' In the last hour and a half of trading, one portfolio insurer sold over 6,000 futures contracts, the equivalent of $660 million of stock. Some index arbitragers refused to sell stock through DOT and withdrew from the futures market, causing the futures market to fall to a discount of twenty index points. The Dow closed at 1738, with a near 300–point loss in the last seventy-five minutes of trading.

A small number of institutions, portfolio insurers, and mutual funds were central to Monday's crash. In the stock market, the four largest sellers accounted for $2.85 billion or fourteen percent of the total sales. A few mutual fund groups sold $900 million; one such group accounted for 90 percent of these sales. Three portfolio insurers sold approximately $2 billion or about ten percent of total NYSE sales. Futures-market portfolio insurers, in all, sold the equivalent of $4 billion of stocks. Yet, portfolio insurance sales, although large, comprised a small portion of the total sales dictated by computer model formulas.

After the U.S. markets closed on October 19, the Tokyo and London stock markets fell almost fifteen percent. Nevertheless, U.S. stock and futures markets opened with dramatic increases the next day, partly due to the Federal Reserve's statement that it would provide badly needed liquidity for the financial system. By midmorning, the rally ended and a number of exchanges temporarily halted trading. The Chicago Board Options Exchange suspended trading because New York Stock Exchange trading was not open in at least eighty percent of the stocks constituting the option index. Shortly after noon, the Chicago Mercantile Exchange, reacting to closings on the New York Stock Exchange, suspended trading of the S & P 500. The closing of the markets created a virtual freefall. Typically, the futures market discount would have attracted buyers, but many were afraid of the perceived credit risk. And the buying of stocks was stifled because the huge discount made stocks seem so expensive. Thus, both markets were imbalanced by sell orders. In the afternoon, however, the stock market received reassurance when several major corporations announced stock purchase programs. But the financial markets had 'approached breakdown' on Tuesday because of a complete disconnection between the futures and stock markets. * * *

The SEC's Division of Market Regulation conducted a detailed study of the crash to provide the agency with an independent basis for determining the proper regulatory response. The SEC reported the following: Institutional investors are increasingly using derivative index products, i.e., products based on stock indexes, to trade indirectly in certain stocks. This creates an alternative or "synthetic" stock market. In fact, this method of investing has become so prevalent that it has replaced hedging—once the sole justification behind market indexes—as investors' primary reason for trading index futures. The increasing participation of institutional investors also has changed the character of this active futures market. While stock prices once led futures prices, the situation has recently reversed itself. Although there is 'nothing inherently wrong' with futures prices leading stock markets, this phenomenon has two implications: (1) exchange specialists' become less willing to aggressively provide orderly markets by offsetting imbalances when futures markets are trading at a discount or premium; and (2) the less restrictive futures markets encourage additional trading in both markets. These two effects increase the volatility in the stock market.

Five factors contributed to the initial price decline: (1) rising interest rates, (2) persistent trade and budget deficits, (3) concerns about overvalued stock, (4) the decline in the dollar, and (5) a proposed tax change that would make corporate takeovers more costly. Furthermore, the market break strained the New York Stock Exchange specialist system. Although specialists as a group met their obligations, there were instances of questionable actions by individual specialists. The over-the-counter market also performed unsatisfactorily during the crash, despite having executed a record number of transactions. * * *

NOTES

1. The SEC and the CFTC became involved in another regulatory clash after the Stock Market Crash of 1987. The SEC wanted to impose higher margins on futures contracts in order to discourage speculation and price volatility. Congress responded by granting the power to regulate margin on stock index futures to the Federal Reserve Board. The Fed, however, delegated that authority to the CFTC, which delegated it back to the commodity exchanges, leaving the situation unchanged. III Jerry W. Markham, A Financial History of the United States, From the Age of Derivatives into the New Millennium (1970–2001) 159 (2002).

2. A Presidential Working Group on Financial Markets was created to pursue the Brady Commission recommendations. It urged the use of trading halts on the securities exchanges when prices moved substantially. Such market time-outs or "circuit breakers" had long been used in the commodity futures markets to allow traders to obtain margin funds and to assess market conditions with calmer reflection. The circuit breakers were adopted but

proved unpopular and their use was later curbed by expanding the size of the market movement required for their invocation.

Jurisdictional clashes continued between the SEC and CFTC.

———————

BOARD OF TRADE v. SEC
187 F.3d 713 (7th Cir.1999).

Before CUDAHY, COFFEY, and EASTERBROOK, CIRCUIT JUDGES.

EASTERBROOK, CIRCUIT JUDGE.

Although the Dow Jones Industrial Average may be the world's most famous stock market index, the Dow Jones Transportation Average is its most venerable, having been established in 1884. The Dow Jones Utilities Average, which dates from 1929, is another well known indicator. An index uses a few stocks to approximate the performance of a market segment. For example, the 20 stocks in the transportation index are designed to track a portfolio of approximately 145 transportation stocks with a capitalization exceeding $200 billion. The 15 stocks in the utilities index stand in for a utilities segment of 145 firms with a capitalization near $300 billion. When Charles Dow designed these indexes, long before instantaneous worldwide networks, a "computer" was a person who calculated tables of artillery trajectories in longhand on foolscap. In that era a reference to a few stocks as an approximation of many was a valuable time-saving device. Today it is easy to follow the average value-weighted price of a whole market, which an electronic computer can produce at the touch of a button. Each investor can specify and follow the portfolio that seems most interesting or important. Still, indexes have retained their fascination with the media and the public, and they have developed a new use—as the base of futures contracts. Our case presents the question whether futures exchanges may trade contracts based on the Dow Jones Utilities Average and the Dow Jones Transportation Average. For many years Dow Jones was unwilling to license its indexes (rather, the trademarks used to denote them) for use in futures contracts. In 1997 it changed its mind and set in train these proceedings.

"A futures contract, roughly speaking, is a fungible promise to buy or sell a particular commodity at a fixed date in the future. Futures contracts are fungible because they have standard terms and each side's obligations are guaranteed by a clearing house. Contracts are entered into without prepayment, although the markets and clearing house will set margin to protect their own interests. Trading occurs in 'the contract,' not in the commodity." *Chicago Mercantile Exchange v. SEC*, 883 F.2d 537, 542 (7th Cir.1989). *See also Dunn v. CFTC*, 519 U.S. 465, 117 S.Ct. 913, 137 L.Ed.2d 93 (1997). The classic futures contract involves a commodity such as wheat, but in principle any measure of value can be used. Financial futures usually take the form of a contract that depends on the value of an index at some future date. Thus, for example, the buyer (the "long") of a futures contract based on the Standard & Poor's 500 Index future might promise to pay 100 times the value of that index on a defined future date, and the seller (the "short") will receive that price. Either side may close the position by buying or selling an offsetting obligation before the expiration date of the contract.

Financial futures contracts are useful for hedging or portfolio adjustment. They facilitate risk management—that is, assignment of the inevitable risks of markets to those best able to bear them. See generally Merton H. Miller, *Merton Miller on Derivatives* 79–100 (1997); Robert C. Merton, Applications of Option–Pricing Theory: Twenty–Five Years Later, 88 Am. Econ. Rev. 323 (1998); Myron S. Scholes, *Global Financial Markets, Derivative Securities, and Systemic Risks*, 12 J. Risk & Uncertainty 271 (1996). Someone who owns a mutual fund containing all of the Standard & Poor's 500 stocks can cut risk in half by selling a futures contract based on the S & P 500 index, or double the market return (and the risk of loss) for the same financial outlay by buying a S & P 500 futures contract. A futures contract based on a market segment (such as utilities) also may be used for portfolio adjustment. Suppose the investor wants to hold a diversified portfolio of stocks that does not include utilities. This investor might own a broadly representative mutual fund and then sell a futures contract based on a utilities index. Similarly, a person who wants to obtain the returns (and take the risks) of particular market segments that do not have their own mutual fund—for example, a combination of utilities and transportation stocks, but no industrials—could purchase an appropriate combination of futures contracts. Using these contracts for portfolio adjustment is attractive because the transactions costs of trading futures are much smaller (by an order of magnitude) than the costs of trading the underlying stocks in equivalent volumes. A pension fund that wants to move from stocks to the equivalent of a mixed stock-and-bond portfolio, without incurring the costs of trading the stocks, can do so by selling a futures contract on an index.

For many years the traditional futures markets, such as the Chicago Board of Trade, have been at odds with the traditional stock markets, such as the New York Stock Exchange, about where financial futures would be traded—and whether they would be traded at all. The stock exchanges prefer less competition; but, if competition breaks out, they prefer to trade the instruments themselves. The disagreement has spilled over to the regulatory bodies. The Securities and Exchange Commission, which regulates stock markets, has sided with its clients; the Commodities Futures Trading Commission, which regulates boards of trade, has done the same. In 1982 this court held that institutions within the CFTC's domain are authorized to trade financial futures (including options on these futures), and, because of an exclusivity clause in the Commodity Exchange Act, that the stock markets are not. Because the stock exchanges long had traded options, a financial derivative related to futures, a political donnybrook accompanied the regulatory dispute among the markets and agencies. Shortly after our opinion issued, Congress amended the Commodity Exchange Act to reflect a compromise among the CFTC, the SEC, and the exchanges.

Congress allocated securities and options on securities to exchanges regulated by the SEC, futures and options on futures to boards of trade regulated by the CFTC. If an instrument is both a security and a futures contract, then it falls within the CFTC's domain. (This is the basis of *Chicago Mercantile Exchange*, which held that a novel "index participation" is a futures contract that belongs to boards of trade.) Options on single securities are allowed, but futures contracts on single securities are not. This allocation appears to be a political compromise; no one has suggested an economic rationale for the distinction. Having drawn this line, however, Congress had to make it stick. Futures contracts thus must reflect "all publicly traded equity or debt securities or a substantial segment thereof". 7 U.S.C. § 2a(ii)(III). Finally, both agencies participate in the process of reviewing applications to trade new financial futures contracts. Before a new contract may start trading, both the SEC and the CFTC must certify that it meets the statutory criteria. Regulation of the trading process belongs exclusively to the CFTC.

A year after this statute was enacted, the SEC and the CFTC issued a Joint Policy Statement spelling out the kinds of financial futures that the agencies believed suitable for trading. The Joint Policy Statement is not a regulation and lacks legal force, but for many years the markets observed its limits when proposing new contracts. One element of the Joint Policy Statement is that any index used as the basis of a futures contract contain at least 25 domestic equity issuers. The Dow Jones Transportation Average is based on 20 stocks, the Utilities Average on 15. The second element is that, in a price-weighted index, no single security may have a weight exceeding 10% of the entire index, if its price weighting exceeds its capitalization weighting by a factor of three. In April 1997 Dow Jones replaced one firm in its Utilities Average with Columbia Gas, which accounts for 2.93% of the Utilities Average by capitalization weight, but 12.56% by price weight. The Transportation Average does not contain a stock with a similar disparity. * * *

[A] few words about manipulation. Although the SEC did not find that a futures contract based on either of the Dow Jones averages would be "readily susceptible to manipulation" of the index itself or the market segment it reflects, the SEC's order contains an undercurrent of misgiving. To the extent the SEC disagrees with the legislative judgment—that is, to the extent the SEC believes that trading in a futures contract should be forbidden when manipulation is a possibility, rather than a high probability (which we take the word "readily" to signify)—it should present that view openly to Congress, rather than engage in self-help measures that cannot be reconciled with the statute. What is more, we cannot see either in the record or in the nature of the proposed futures contracts any reason for concern.

Squeezes, corners, and other forms of manipulation in futures markets for physical commodities depend on hogging the deliverable supply. See Stephen Craig Pirrong, *The Economics, Law, and Public Policy of Market Power Manipulation* 18–90 (1996). A person who owns a substantial portion of the long interest near the contract's expiration date also obtains control over the supply that the shorts need to meet their obligations. Then the long demands delivery, and the price of the commodity skyrockets. It takes time and money to bring additional supplies to the delivery point, and the long can exploit these costs to force the shorts to pay through the nose. Futures markets deal with the prospect of squeezes and corners by expanding the deliverable supply (allowing, for example, delivery in Kansas City as well as Chicago), by imposing position limits (so that no one long can hold contracts for more than the deliverable supply), and by monitoring positions so that irregularly large positions may be subject to orderly liquidation before the expiration date. But the need for these precautions, like the possibility of manipulation itself, comes from the potential imbalance between the deliverable supply and investors' contract rights near the expiration date. Financial futures contracts, which are settled in cash, have no "deliverable supply"; there can never be a mismatch between demand and supply near the expiration, or at any other time.

Although it is impossible to rule out the use of financial futures contracts to affect the price in the underlying securities, it is hard to see how the effort could be profitable to the would-be manipulator. Financial markets such as all utilities, or all transportation stocks, are so large (many hundreds of billions), liquid, and competitive that their manipulation is almost unimaginable. If someone were determined to drive the price of transportation stocks up or down, buying and selling thousands of futures contracts on the Chicago Board of Trade would be like pouring a Dixie cup of water into Lake Michigan: there would be an effect, but it would not be detectable. One test of the manipulation hypothesis is whether financial futures contracts increase aggregate price volatility, either over the long term or near the expiration date. Economists who have explored this subject agree that on balance stock-index futures contracts have reduced volatility in stock prices, and that the effect on volatility near expiration is trivial. See, e.g., Hendrik Bessembinder & Paul J. Seguin, *Futures–Trading Activity and Stock Price Volatility*, 47 J. Finance 2015 (1992); Richard Roll, *Price Volatility, International Market Links and their Implications for Regulatory Policies*, 3 J. Fin. Services Res. 211 (1989); George Sofianos, *Expirations and Stock Price Volatility*, 13 Rev. Futures Markets 39 (1994).

If the design were to manipulate the price of a single stock rather than the index or its market segment, then smaller investments of capital would suffice—but for the reasons covered in discussing surrogate trading, transactions in an index futures contract are lousy ways of approximating transactions in individual stocks. People who want to manipulate the price of Acme Widget Corp. will deal in that stock, or options in it. Data show that options reduce volatility in the security they represent. Aswath Damodaran & Marti Subrahmanyan, *The Effects of Derivative Securities on the Market for the Underlying Assets in the United States: A Survey*, Fin. Markets Institutions & Instruments 1 (Dec.1992). And if one-stock derivatives do not conduce to manipulation, any futures contract where the index is based on two or more stocks must be *less* readily manipulable. Whether even single-stock options and futures on physical commodities are subject to (reliably profitable) manipulation is an interesting question, see Daniel R. Fischel & David J. Ross, *Should the Law Prohibit "Manipulation" in Financial Markets?*, 105 Harv. L. Rev. 503, 542–52 (1991), but not one we need consider. It is enough to say that manipulation of stock prices through transactions in index futures contracts is hard to do, and a finding that these markets are "readily susceptible to manipulation of the price" would require a great deal more support than the ominous foreboding manifested in the SEC's order—an order that did not begin to discuss the vast empirical literature about the effects of options, futures contracts, and other derivatives on market efficiency.

* * *

The order of the Securities and Exchange Commission is vacated.

SECTION 3.   REGULATORY DISPARITIES—CFTC AND SEC

JERRY W. MARKHAM
SUPER–REGULATOR: A COMPARATIVE ANALYSIS OF SECURITIES AND DERIVATIVES REGULATION IN THE UNITED STATES, GREAT BRITAIN AND JAPAN

28 Brooklyn Journal of International Law (2003).

During the first forty years of its existence, the SEC found little reason to compete with the Commodity Exchange Authority ("CEA") because commodity futures and securities operated pretty much independently. To be sure, in considering the adoption of the Commodity Exchange Act of 1936, Congress found that some large speculators had transferred their manipulative activities from the stock markets to the grain exchanges in order to escape regulation under the Securities Exchange Act of 1934. SEC Chairman William O. Douglas, therefore, sought further regulation of grain speculators, especially those dealing in puts and calls. President Roosevelt responded to that concern by asking his Secretary of Agriculture, Henry Wallace, to take action against the commodity exchanges. Wallace refused to do so, viewing the SEC's concern as cloaking a power grab by the very ambitious Douglas.

The regulatory structures over securities and commodity futures were, therefore, allowed to develop separately. They were distinctive. The cornerstone of SEC regulation is full disclosure to the public in securities offerings. There is no comparable concept in the Commodity Exchange Act of 1936. The SEC was also given authority to enforce margin requirements for securities set by the Federal Reserve Board, a device Congress concluded would curb speculation and avoid the diversion of scarce credit into such activities. The CEA had no such authority. The agency informed Congress during the hearings on the Commodity Exchange Act of 1936 that such authority was not needed. Rather, the CEA wanted to impose limits on the amount of trading that could be conducted by the large speculators. Those speculators were then the principal perpetrators of market manipulations. That authority was granted by Congress in the Commodity Exchange Act of 1936. The SEC had no comparable power. Although the CEA not long afterward changed its position and sought authority to control margins as well after its position limits proved ineffective in curbing price rises in commodity markets, Congress refused to grant the CEA such power. Margins on futures were viewed to be a device to protect the exchanges and futures commission merchants from customer defaults, rather than a credit allocation issue or a means to control speculation. Congress thought that the commodity exchanges were in a better position than the government to assure that margin levels were adequate for their protection.

Although both agencies had anti-fraud provisions to administer, the Commodity Exchange Act provision is more narrowly focused and was never given the expansive interpretation applied to Section 10(b) of the Securities Exchange Act of 1934, the most broadly applied of the antifraud provisions administered by the SEC. The SEC adopted Rule 10b–5 under that provision. It applies to all security transactions. The SEC has used that authority to create whole regulatory programs, the most famous of which has been its insider trading prosecutions. Demonstrating the flexibility of that rule, the SEC's insider trading program was not begun until over a quarter of a century after the SEC was created and almost twenty years after the adoption of Rule 10b–5. Although sometimes likened to Section 10(b) of the Securities Exchange Act of 1934, Section 4b of the Commodity Exchange Act of 1936 was limited to specific fraudulent practices made in connection with futures traded on contract markets. There was no interest by commodity regulators in creating an insider trading program in the futures industry.

Additional regulatory disparities existed in the two regulatory schemes. A cornerstone of SEC regulation of broker-dealers became the suitability requirement, *i.e.*, a broker-dealer may not recommend securities to a customer that are unsuitable in light of the customer's own particular financial circumstances and objectives. The SEC made that doctrine up out of whole cloth. The CEA invented no comparable regulatory concept. The Commodity Exchange Act prohibited over-the-counter dealings in commodity futures—the contract markets were given a monopoly on such transactions, at least for the "regulated" commodities. The SEC, in contrast, regulated a broad-based over-the-counter market. The

SEC imposed affirmative obligations on market makers and exchange specialists to make a "fair and orderly" market, *i.e.*, a market that was not volatile. There was no comparable requirement imposed on the floor traders on the commodity exchanges. Instead, trading was conducted in an auction style open outcry system in which traders could participate, or not, as they themselves chose.

SEC regulation was paternalistic in other ways. It imposed a duty of supervision on broker-dealers that required them to affirmatively supervise their employees with a view toward preventing violations. The CEA imposed no such obligation on futures commission merchants. The CEA did have a large trader reporting system, a power that the SEC did not receive until 1990. The CEA required large traders to file a report disclosing the identity of the trader and any affiliates or entities under common control. The size of the trader's position was then monitored by the CEA to assure that the trader posed no danger to the market.

The securities and commodity futures regulatory schemes were different, but no one really noticed before the 1970s. The product mix of the two industries was such that, aside from some mobile speculators, there was little overlap between commodity and futures trading. That situation began to change dramatically as inflation heated the economy during the Viet Nam war. The resulting price hikes turned investors' attention toward inflation hedges such as gold and silver. Restrictions on their trading allowed those metals to be the subject of commodity futures trading. Similarly, President Nixon's action in taking the United States off the gold standard and out of the International Monetary Fund's fixed rate currency regime led to fluctuating exchange rates that provided a basis for currency trading, as well as trading in precious metals.

Volatility in interest rates and stock prices also led the commodity exchanges to consider commodity futures trading on those items. A committee of the Chicago Board of Trade began to explore whether commodity futures trading principles could be applied to stocks. The result was the CBOE. Prior to the creation of the CBOE, stock options were sold only on a limited basis in the over-the-counter market. The CBOE introduced a commodity futures concept of trading standardized options contracts on an exchange floor. That standardization and the introduction of a clearing house, the Options Clearing Corporation ("OCC"), created a secondary market in options. The CBOE trading floor borrowed from both the securities and commodity exchanges. There was no specialist. Instead, competing market makers were used to create liquidity in an open outcry system like that on the commodity exchanges.

The SEC asserted regulatory control over the CBOE under the provisions of the Securities Exchange Act of 1934. The SEC also became involved in the regulation of over-the-counter commodity options. A loophole in the Commodity Exchange Act of 1936 allowed options trading on "unregulated" commodities such as sugar, coffee and silver. Harold Goldstein, a twenty-six year old commodity trader discovered that loophole and built one of the largest brokerage firms almost over night through the sale of "naked" options that were not backed by anything other than the dubious credit of Goldstein's firm, Goldstein, Samuelson. Increasing prices resulted in customer gains that Goldstein could not cover. The SEC shut down his and similar options firms by claiming that these contracts were securities. State securities administrators aided the SEC in these efforts. Goldstein was jailed.

The Goldstein, Samuelson debacle caused concern in Congress, as did the large jump in commodity prices during this period. Congressional hearings found fault with the CEA's deference to the commodity exchanges. Congress concluded that new legislation was needed to close the regulatory gap in the Commodity Exchange Act that allowed Goldstein, Samuelson to operate. Congress thought that all commodity option and futures trading should be subject to regulation. The Commodity Futures Trading Commission Act of 1974 ("CFTC Act") created the CFTC and brought all commodity futures and options trading under a "single regulatory umbrella." The CFTC was "patterned" after the SEC and was granted strengthened enforcement powers. Among other things, the CFTC was given authority to seek injunctive relief, a favorite weapon employed by the SEC. Self-regulation by the commodity exchanges was strengthened. The National Futures Association was later created to act as an analogue to the NASD. The CFTC Act gave the CFTC some authority that the SEC did not have. The CFTC could impose civil penalties of up to $100,000 per violation (a power that the SEC did not receive until 1984), to bar violators from trading on contract markets (a power that the SEC was not given) and to grant reparations to investors injured by violations committed by registered persons (again this was not a power given to the SEC).

There were other differences in the agencies regulation. Congress passed the Securities Investor Protection Corporation Act ("SIPC") in 1970, after the securities industry nearly broke down during the "paperwork" crisis at the end of the 1970s. That statute provided insurance to securities customers (now $500,000, of which up to $100,000 may be in cash) in the event of a broker-dealer insolvency. The CFTC Act directed the CFTC to consider whether such legislation was needed in the futures industry. The CFTC study compared loss ratios of firms under government insurance programs with the loss ratios of commodity futures customers. The loss ratios for futures commission merchant customers were substantially lower than insured firms, leading the CFTC to conclude that insurance was unnecessary. This was a marked difference in competing regulatory approaches. Insurance creates a moral hazard that the firm being insured will attract funds at low cost from investors on the strength of the government's credit and then use those funds for high return, high risk ventures. The savings and loan debacle of the 1980s is a good example of a glutinous feast on insured funds. The futures industry uses market discipline to protect customers, which seems an unlikely undertaking when the nature of futures trading is considered. Commodity futures contracts are highly leveraged. The low margin requirements set by the exchanges are only a very small percent of the notional amount at risk. Small moves mean large debits to at least half of the market participants. Futures contracts are also selected on the basis of a high degree of price volatility, and speculation is encouraged. Yet, despite that leverage (and attending risk) and the large element of speculation present, there are fewer customer losses due to the bankruptcy of a financial intermediary than in the insured industries that have less risk, volatility and speculation.

The answer lies in the way in margin trading is regulated in the futures industry. The exchanges set margin for the protection of their clearing houses and positions are marked-to-market each day. Losses must be recognized through variation margin payments that must be made before the firm can trade the next day. Futures commission merchants are forced, therefore, to recognize customer losses each day. Losses cannot be put off in the hope of a market recovery. Losses cannot accumulate. The securities industry in contrast had no comparable market discipline. Securities transactions were settled on a $T + 5$ basis, *i.e.*, settlement was not made until five days after the execution of the trade. This left plenty of time for losses to mount or for customers to engage in reckless conduct to make up for losses. The SEC has since imposed a $T + 3$ requirement on settlement but that is still three days more than required in the futures industry.

The SEC was in the midst of defending an expansive interpretation of its insider trading program carried out under Rule 10b–5 at the time the CFTC was created. The CFTC later conducted a study to determine whether such a rule was needed in the futures industry. The CFTC concluded it was not appropriate to impose such a rule on futures traders. Many participants in the futures markets had superior access to information and that traders on exchange floors had time and place advantages for the use of information. The CFTC did not believe that it was practical or desirable to require traders to have equal access to information as required by the SEC.

The CFTC did seek to adopt some regulatory requirements that would have more closely conformed its regulatory structure to that of the SEC. That effort was due largely to the fact that several newly arrived staff members at the CFTC had formerly served on the SEC staff. One SEC style proposal that was enacted was a net capital rule. The SEC had adopted a Uniform Net Capital Rule in the aftermath of the paperwork crisis. As a result of the failure of the stock exchanges failed to enforce their capital rules during that event, the SEC concluded that a more stringent federal rule was needed to protect the customers and the SIPC insurance fund. The futures industry had no paperwork crisis. Its overnight settlement requirement and paperless trading assured that result. Nevertheless, the newly arrived SEC staff members were fresh from their exposure to the SEC Uniform Net Capital Rule, and they thought a net capital rule was needed. The CFTC net capital rule does not appear to have had much effect in preventing insolvencies by futures commission merchants. If anything the low rate of failures increased. The CFTC net capital rule is also flawed and out of date in its risk measurement criteria. The rule, nevertheless, remains on the books.

The CFTC staff also tried to borrow wholesale from the SEC's rulebook through the proposal of a set of customer protection rules. Among other things, those proposals included a rule imposing a supervision requirement such as that employed by the SEC. That rule was adopted, albeit in a more simplified form. A proposal to adopt a suitability requirement did not fare as well. That effort set off a firestorm of controversy and was not adopted. Instead, the CFTC adopted a risk disclosure statement that advised customers in a one page statement of the risks of trading commodity futures, and that customers should themselves consider whether commodity futures trading was suitable in light of the customers particular circumstances and financial resources. Customers were required to sign that statement and confirm that they read and understood its risks. This was a very visible difference from the paternalistic approach of the SEC. The CFTC was requiring individuals to take responsibility for their own investment decisions. Regulatory competition was indeed having an effect on the manner in which the two industries would be regulated. That competition also led to much strife.

In March 2008, the Treasury Department proposed a merger of the CFTC and SEC. However, the cultures and political backing of each agency in congress derailed that effort. See Jerry W. Markham, Merging the SEC and CFTC—A Clash of Cultures, 78 U. Cin. L. Rev. 537 (2009).

SECTION 4. MANIPULATION AND OTHER ABUSES

Commodity markets have long suffered under speculative traders that engage in various practices designed to create a better price for their goods. One type of such activity was referred to in ancient times as "forestalling," i.e., securing control of a commodity on the way to market and holding them off the market in order to obtain a higher price. This practice was condemned in the Bible: Proverbs 11:26 "He that withholdeth grain the people shall curse him; but blessing shall be upon the head of him that selleth it." Other condemned practices were "regrating" (buying commodities and then reselling at a higher price) and "engrossing" (cornering or monopolizing the market) were made medieval crimes and were later enforced by the Star Chamber in England. The statute making such actions a crime was later repealed, except that market monopolization was not permitted. See IV William Blackstone, Commentaries on the Laws of England 158 (1769) and Black's Law Dictionary (4th ed. 1968) (describing these activities). Some of this law was brought to

America. The Carolinas passed a statute in colonial times that sought to stop buying and selling commodities at a higher price by middlemen, but that measure had to be dropped because the middlemen stopped selling, cutting off the flow of goods. Pennsylvania had adopted a statute in 1774 that prohibited such practices. George Washington was also complaining of merchants holding goods off the market in order to obtain higher prices during the Revolution. He wanted them "hung in gibbets." Particularly troubling were the merchants refusing to sell to the Continental Army in Philadelphia in anticipation of being paid in Sterling when the British seized the city. Jerry W. Markham, A Financial History of the United States, From Christopher Columbus to the Robber Barons (1492–1900) 63–65 (2002).

JERRY W. MARKHAM
MANIPULATION OF COMMODITY FUTURES PRICES— THE UNPROSECUTABLE CRIME

8 Yale J. on Reg. 281 (1991).

Commodity futures trading has a long history, but its development in the United States can be traced to the end of the Civil War when, at the Chicago Board of Trade, contracts for the delivery of grain were converted into transferable contracts that often were used to offset each other. Speculators soon learned that these contracts offered opportunities to engage in manipulative activities as well as speculation. Corners and squeezes became widespread and manipulators became veritable legends as witnessed by the story of Joe Leiter, a Harvard graduate who attempted unsuccessfully to corner the wheat market. His corner was broken when a fleet of boats hired by P.D. Armour broke through the ice on Lake Michigan and flooded the Chicago markets with grain. Another even more famous corner of the gold market by Fisk and Gould became a legend in American history.

By 1868 there was a corner a month, and these manipulations continued into the twentieth century. In 1902, for example, James A. Patten made a two million dollar profit in a wheat squeeze in which he pushed prices from $1.00 a bushel to a $1.34. Another famous manipulator was Jesse Livermore, whose corners included the purchase of 120,000 bales of cotton in 1908. In order to inflate the value of his purchases, he planted a front page article in a New York newspaper that stated that Livermore had cornered July cotton, causing speculators to rush in and buy cotton in order to jump on his bandwagon. The result was even larger profits for Livermore. The market later turned on Livermore, however, and he lost his fortune. But "King Jack" Sturges, Benjamin Hutchinson, "Crazy Harper" and others still vied to place themselves in the headlines as "wheat kings," and Chicago became a veritable Valhalla of these anti-heroes.

These "play boys of speculation" aroused much populist animosity and much congressional ire. Nevertheless, repeated efforts to impose federal controls over futures trading in the late 1800's and the turn of the century all failed. One such effort, the "Hatch Act," passed both houses but failed in the Conference Committee. Similarly doomed to failure was an effort to include provisions in the Sherman Anti–Trust Act that would have applied to commodity futures trading. Theodore Roosevelt also sought to curb large short sales that were disrupting the markets. He stated that there "should be measures taken to prevent at least the grosser forms of gambling in securities and commodities, such as making large sales of what men do not possess and 'cornering' the market." Over thirty bills were introduced in response to this Presidential message, but none were adopted.

At the outbreak of World War I, a short wheat crop resulted in new levels of frenzied speculation and caused widespread concern. The Chicago Board of Trade was forced to adopt emergency measures that stopped all wheat trading in its May wheat contract. Legislation was also adopted to control food prices during the war, and President Wilson was authorized to regulate or prohibit transactions on exchanges. President Wilson and his Commerce Secretary, Herbert Hoover, used that authority to form the Food Administration Grain Corporation. Thereafter, the corporation began buying grain and essentially eliminated the exchanges from this process until the end of the war. Nevertheless, the speculation at the outset of the war resulted in a massive study by the Federal Trade Commission (FTC) of the grain trade. As part of that study, the FTC conducted extensive hearings on the issue of manipulation in the commodity futures markets.

The FTC Study focused principally on the critical period in futures trading when contracts are expiring and futures prices merge into cash market prices. It is at this stage that the greatest danger of price distortion appears because only specified grades of a commodity held in approved exchange warehouses can be used for delivery. In instances where there is a shortage of grain that meets those specifications, and where supplies cannot be brought into the market quickly, traders may stand for delivery and attempt to "squeeze" or "corner" the market. The FTC Study found that, if a cornering condition becomes known early in the delivery month, it may be possible to rush large quantities of grain to Chicago to prevent its success. But corners often happen too late in the delivery month for such efforts to work.

A "squeeze" is similar to an intentional corner that falls short of being complete. The FTC Study found that a squeeze is generally more successful from a profit standpoint because someone who is cornering the entire market must "bury the corpse." That is, the person must ultimately dispose of the actual grain used in the corner without greatly depressing prices; otherwise, the value of the corner will be lost. Because the cash grain accumulated to offset the corner must generally be disposed of at a sacrifice price much of the profit on the futures side of the corner is dissipated. The FTC Study noted that traders had found effective methods of burying the corpse. One way is to hold the grain by storing it. However, this tends to increase the difficulty in getting rid of the grain after the effects of the manipulation have dissipated, i.e., grain prices may remain depressed. A more artful method is to render the commodity undeliverable on the futures exchange, as was done in a notorious case of a corner in pork ribs where, prior to being sold, the pieces were cut in such a way as to make them irregular, and therefore unacceptable, for delivery. In other instances, as occurred in several grain corners, the cornering party sold the grain that was taken on delivery in Chicago outside that market, for example, in Buffalo. The trader then provided in its contracts of sale in Buffalo that the grain could not be returned to Chicago.

The FTC Study found statistical evidence showing that, where corners occur, the price of the grain is "artificially enhanced because it is temporarily in extraordinary demand for the sole and only purpose of using it to meet futures contracts." This causes a general loss to the public because the direction, rate, and flow of grain is distorted in a terminal market. The terminal market eventually becomes clogged with grain that is actually needed elsewhere, as traders rush grain to the market to counter the corner or to take advantage of rising prices. * * *

In determining what legislation was needed to prevent manipulation, Congress * * * decided that manipulation would be prevented by requiring a record to be kept of transactions by large traders. As stated in congressional testimony, it was thought that such records would prevent manipulation because, if a man "is undertaking to 'bear' the market and the whole world's knowing he is doing it, he is the only loser. Secrecy is absolutely necessary to such efforts and that is the reason why the Chicago Board of Trade keeps no records."

The legislation also sought to prevent manipulation by requiring all futures contracts to be traded on exchanges and then requiring the exchanges to prevent manipulation. If the exchanges failed to do so, they would lose their privilege to conduct futures trading. It was thought that this legislation would be a mandate to the exchanges that would require them to "drive from their midst the man who is prostituting the machinery of grain market for his own selfish purpose by manipulating the price to his own advantage." Although one Congressman suggested that the manipulators should be hit with a sledge hammer, it was thought that punitive legislation would not be wise and that exchanges should be permitted to clean their own houses.

The legislation that was enacted, the Future Trading Act of 1921, was based on the taxation powers of Congress. It was founded on a Congressional conclusion that futures contracts are susceptible to manipulation and to sudden and unreasonable price fluctuations. It sought to tax out of existence futures transactions that were not conducted on licensed exchanges. The Supreme Court, however, did not believe that Congress could use its taxation powers in such a method and declared the Futures Trading Act of 1921 unconstitutional shortly after its adoption.

After the Court's decision, Henry C. Wallace, the Secretary of Agriculture, pointed out to Congress that dramatic and recent fluctuations in the price of wheat had "strengthened the farmer in his belief that prices had been manipulated to his great disadvantage." A House Report noted that the day after the Supreme Court's decision the price of wheat advanced four cents a bushel. Thereafter, wheat prices declined at a time when there was no reason for them to do so, leading to the conclusion that this was "evidently a straight-out manipulation of the market."

Congress quickly responded by passing new legislation, the Grain Futures Act of 1922, which substantially resembled the Future Trading Act, except that it was based on the commerce power of Congress. The Grain Futures Act was "designed to prevent speculative manipulation of the price of wheat." As the Supreme Court later noted, its purpose "was to control the evils of manipulation of prices in grain. Such manipulation, Congress found, was effected through dealings in grain futures...."

Although "[m]any persons had advocated, as a remedy, that all futures trading be abolished," the Grain Futures Act established a licensing system pursuant to which commodity exchanges were required to be designated as "contract markets." All futures trading was required to be conducted on exchanges so designated. * * * The Grain Futures Act was administered by a small agency in the Department of Agriculture, the Grain Futures Administration (GFA). The GFA carried out the day-to-day regulatory activities under the statute and was subject to supervision by the Secretary of Agriculture, who was one of three members on a commission that was responsible for overall regulation under the Act. The other two members of this commission were the Secretary of Commerce and the Attorney General of the United States. In carrying out its functions, the GFA generally deferred to the exchanges.

[Additional legislation was found to be needed after the stock market crash of 1929 and the ensuing great depression pushed down commodity prices]. In the hearings on that legislation, it was stated that speculative trading had resulted in a substantial burden on the wheat and other grain markets because "commissions and gambling profits" were taken out before the farmer was given any payment. It was charged that "farmers of this country have lost hundreds of millions of dollars through the manipulation of the market on these exchanges. Those manipulators toil not neither do they spin, but they invariably take all of the profit of the farmer's crop and leave him with the bills to pay." Concern was expressed that manipulation had been occurring in the cotton exchange "so as to drive the price down when the farmer is selling and to raise it after his crop is all gone."

One Congressman was incensed that "[w]hile the farmer [was] harvesting his wheat or grain, prices [were] hammered down to the extreme low point, but the moment the farmer parts with his grain the speculators start to raise the price and the result is that both the consumers and the farmers are mulcted by a bunch of professional dishonest speculators, . . . [who] sell millions of bushels of wheat, corn, or rye, just for the purpose of artificially lowering the price so that they can buy the grains back at a much lower price." He stated that such "dastardly tactics have been followed from day to day and year to year to the detriment of the growers, legitimate dealers, and the public." Another Congressman wanted to stop "manipulative short selling; that is the use of the market by the speculator who wishes to depress it, or advance it, as his interest may dictate." * * *

Congress was also concerned with the "sensational price collapse" in the Chicago wheat and corn futures markets on July 19 and 20, 1933, when the exchange was closed. A subsequent investigation by the GFA disclosed that this situation principally was the result of the activities of some traders who controlled fifteen large speculative accounts and who had accumulated an inordinately large holding of wheat and corn. Prices collapsed when a large portion of those positions were suddenly dumped upon the market. * * *

Congress additionally examined a drop of nearly 200 points in cotton futures prices in March of 1935. It was charged: "That is not supply and demand. That is caused by manipulation." Congress was also aware that the futures markets were extremely sensitive and that "false or misleading statements or fictitious trading might in a few minutes turn thousands of dollars into the pocket of some unscrupulous trader." In determining what legislation was needed to prevent these abuses, members of Congress sought ways to stop "racketeering" by a few large professional traders, and to give the government enough "teeth" to properly regulate the exchanges. One Congressman claimed that the Grain Futures Act had been almost a complete failure, lamenting, "It has no teeth." * * *

[Congress responded by enacting the Commodity Exchange Act of 1936]. In considering how to prevent this conduct, it was asked in the hearings whether a statute could be framed in order to allow the government to proceed against an individual who had acquired a large amount of wheat for the purpose of either depressing or boosting the market. The response was that this would be a difficult statute to draft. Instead, drafters thought that limitations should be placed on the amount of trading by large traders. Such position limits would prevent transactions that resulted in a cornering of the market or which resulted in an excess of large scale trading. This policy would "prevent upsetting or disturbing the market; in other words . . . prevent manipulation".

The Commodity Exchange Act, as adopted, thus not only prohibited manipulation, but it also allowed the government to set position limits, [but]. . . . Congress did not define the term manipulation. * * * Because the Commodity Exchange Act did not define manipulation, the task of interpretation was left to the courts and to another small agency within the Department of Agriculture—the Commodity Exchange Authority

("CEA")—which administered the statute under the direction of the Secretary of Agriculture and a Commodity Exchange Commission composed of the Secretaries of Agriculture and Commerce and the Attorney General. During its nearly 40 year existence, the CEA continually faced concerns of congestion and manipulation, which it often sought to resolve by deferring to the exchanges. * * *

Several ... critical events focused attention on the inadequacy of the CEA. Perhaps the most important was the so-called great "Grain Robbery" of 1972 in which the Soviet Union made huge purchases of grain in the United States and drove grain prices to new levels. These purchases were not announced publicly for some months, during which time hedgers and others traded on the markets with knowledge of the sales. Apparently, the Soviets were secretly buying large futures positions as well as large amounts of cash grain. The rising futures prices caused by their purchases of cash grain were said to give the Soviets substantial profits, while consumers paid higher prices. It was further claimed that the closing price on the Kansas City Board of Trade had been raised in order to affect the U.S.D.A. subsidized program in connection with those sales. The CEA initially deferred to an exchange investigation to determine if there had been such a manipulation. The Exchange found no misconduct. However, the CEA later conducted its own investigation and found that the market had been manipulated on the close for several days, resulting in payments of millions of dollars in additional foreign export subsidies. This matter was referred to the Justice Department. * * *

Congress determined that the problems in the commodity futures industry had brought about a crisis of public confidence, and it was determined that CEA resources were "totally inadequate to police the industry." Congress found that self-regulation by the exchanges had not been effective in stopping abusive trading. Further, many futures contracts were completely unregulated because the Commodity Exchange Act had not kept pace with developments in the industry. These contracts included silver, gold, coffee, sugar, cocoa and plywood and foreign currencies. There were also plans to expand futures trading to such things as home mortgages, all of which would be unregulated under the existing regulatory scheme.

To remedy this concern, Congress passed the Commodity Futures Trading Commission Act of 1974. It substantially amended the Commodity Exchange Act by creating a new federal regulatory commission to regulate the CEA. This agency, the Commodity Futures Trading Commission (CFTC), was designed to be comparable to the Securities and Exchange Commission. The CFTC was given expanded powers under the Commodity Exchange Act, including injunctive authority, and was given exclusive jurisdiction over all futures trading. A significant provision that was enacted as a means of preventing violations gave authority to the CFTC to declare a market emergency. Whenever it had reason to believe that an emergency existed, the amendment allowed the CFTC to direct a contract market to take such action as the CFTC believed necessary to maintain or restore orderly trading in, or liquidation, of any futures contract. Such emergencies would include "threatened or actual market manipulation and corners," any act of the United States or a foreign government that would affect a commodity, or any "major market disturbance which prevents the market from accurately reflecting the forces of supply and demand for such commodity."

CFTC v. HUNT

591 F.2d 1211 (7th Cir.), cert. denied, 442 U.S.
921, 99 S.Ct. 2848, 61 L.Ed.2d 290 (1979).

SWYGERT, CIRCUIT JUDGE.

This case presents several issues arising out of a complaint brought by the Commodity Futures Trading Commission, pursuant to the Commodity Exchange Act, against seven members of the Hunt family and an affiliated company. The complaint was instituted by the Commission on April 28, 1977 to compel the defendants to comply with limits established by the Commission on the speculative position that any individual or group may have in soybean futures contracts. See Commodity Exchange Act, § 4a(1), 7 U.S.C. § 6a(1) (Supp.1978); Rule 150.4, 17 C.F.R. § 150.4 (1977).

The Commission's complaint alleges that from at least January 17, 1977 and continuing to the commencement of the court action, two brothers, Nelson Bunker Hunt and William Herbert Hunt, five of their children, and a corporation they control, had been exceeding collectively the limit of three million bushels that had been set for soybean futures contracts. The complaint sought preliminary and permanent injunctions against future violations of these limits, the disgorgement of any profits the Hunts had obtained as a result of their unlawful conduct, and an order requiring the Hunts to liquidate all existing positions in soybean futures in excess of the speculative limits. Contemporaneous with the filing of the complaint, the Commission, pursuant to section 8a(6) of the Commodity Exchange Act, 7 U.S.C. § 12a(6) (1978), publicly disclosed the soybean trading activity and positions of the Hunts. * * *

Section 4a(1) of the Commodity Exchange Act, 7 U.S.C. § 6a(1), authorizes the Commodity Futures Trading Commission to set commodity trading limits. Congress concluded that excessive speculation in commodity contracts for future delivery can cause adverse fluctuations in the price of a commodity, and authorized the Commission to restrict the positions held or trading done by any individual person or by certain groups of people acting in concert. Pursuant to this statutory authority, the Commodity Exchange Authority, the predecessor of the Commodity Futures Trading Commission, established trading limits on a variety of commodities, including soybeans. * * *

Section 4a(1) provides for the aggregation of commodity positions for purposes of determining whether the speculative limit has been exceeded, when one person "directly or indirectly" controls the trading of another, or when two persons are acting "pursuant to an express or implied agreement or understanding...." 7 U.S.C. § 6a(1). Thus, even though two persons acting in concert might each individually have a commodity position below the limit, if their combined position exceeds the limit they have violated the statute. Further, contrary to the arguments advanced by the Hunts, there is nothing in either the statutory language or legislative history which suggests that intent either to affect market prices or specific intent to exceed the speculative limits is a necessary element of a violation of section 4a(1). In fact, the Senate Report to the 1968 amendments to the statute states that a speculative futures position exceeding the limit can constitute a statutory violation "regardless of how or when or for what purpose such position was created." 1968 U.S.Code Cong. & Admin.News 1673, 1678. A violation occurs simply when an individual or several individuals acting in concert exceed the commodity position limits set pursuant to the statute.

The Hunts contend that the evidence compiled in the district court is insufficient to prove a violation of the statute. In assessing the district court's findings, we must defer to the reasonable inferences of the trial court. Fed.R.Civ.P. 52(a). See SEC v. Parklane Hosiery Co., 558 F.2d 1083, 1086 (2d Cir.1977); Markiewicz v. Greyhound Corp., 358 F.2d 26 (7th Cir.), Cert. denied, 385 U.S. 828, 87 S.Ct. 64, 17 L.Ed.2d 65 (1966). Under this rule, the trial court's conclusion that the Hunts violated section 4a(1) by collectively exceeding the speculative limits of Rule 150.4 must be upheld.

A brief survey of the Hunt family's complicated soybean trading substantiates this conclusion. Nelson Bunker Hunt and William Herbert Hunt were the principal family figures in these transactions. They are brothers, and the chief officers of the Hunt Energy Corporation. In mid–1976 N. B. and W. H. Hunt entered the soybean market. By August 1 each brother consistently held a long position at the three million bushel limit, usually for the closest delivery month. Through a series of purchases the date, timing, and size of which were virtually identical each brother, by January 1977, held a three million bushel position in March 1977 soybeans. Over the next six weeks each of the Hunt brothers entered into eight transactions on the same days, using the same broker, involving virtually identical quantities and prices. Throughout this time an employee of the Hunt Energy Corporation, Charles Mercer, prepared commodity position statements for the brothers reflecting their combined holdings and unrealized profits and losses.

On February 25, with both N. B. and W. H. Hunt at the personal position limit, N. B. Hunt ordered a purchase, through one of his brokers, of 750,000 bushels of May soybeans in the name of his son, Houston Hunt. On March 3 he ordered the purchase of 750,000 May bushels to be allocated equally among accounts he had opened on behalf of his three daughters. And, although the bank accounts of the various children lacked the funds to cover these purchases, the transactions were made possible by a short-term transfer of interest-free funds from their father's account. N. B. Hunt's children did not participate in these initial soybean transactions made in their names: they had nothing to do with opening the accounts, placing the first order, or arranging financing for their purchases. And once these family members had entered the soybean market, their transactions were added to the composite report sent to N. B. Hunt.

A similar relationship existed between W. H. Hunt and his son, Douglas. On March 1 W. H. Hunt and his wife transferred their interests in Hunt Holdings, Inc. to their three sons. Less than a week later Douglas Hunt personally and through Hunt Holdings, whose trading he controlled, began purchasing July soybeans. These purchases were financed in part by money advanced by his father.

The overall involvement of the Hunt family in the soybean market also was increased by the spread trading purchasing old crop contracts and selling contracts in new crop markets of N. B. and W. H. Hunt. Some of N. B. Hunt's purchases in this period were financed by temporary advances from his brother. As of April 14, 1977 the Hunt family's collective position involved over twenty-three million bushels of old crop soybeans: over 10.8 million in May futures, 7.7 million in July futures, and 5.2 million in August futures. These collective figures, of course, put the Hunt family well over the speculative limits in soybeans set by Rule 150.4. And the evidence presented in the district court clearly indicates that the individual positions of the family members should be aggregated. Thus, the Hunt family soybean transactions constituted a violation of section 4a(1) of the Commodity Exchange Act, 7 U.S.C. § 6a(1).

Pursuant to section 6c of the Commodity Exchange Act, 7 U.S.C. § 13a–1, the Commodity Futures Trading Commission is authorized to institute an action seeking injunctive relief whenever it appears that any person "has engaged, is engaging, or is about to engage in any act or practice constituting a violation of any provision of this Act or any rule, regulation, or order thereunder." Section 6c further provides that upon a proper showing, a permanent or temporary injunction or restraining order shall be granted by the district court without bond. The discretion afforded the district court in deciding whether to issue such relief, while broad, See United States v. W. T. Grant, 345 U.S. 629, 633–34, 73 S.Ct. 894, 97 L.Ed. 1303 (1953), is not completely unfettered. This court has noted that when Congress has integrated traditional modes of equitable relief into a statutory enforcement scheme, the court's equitable power should be exercised in harmony with the overall objectives of the legislation. SEC v. Advance Growth Capital Corp., 470 F.2d 40, 53 (7th Cir. 1972). In that case we cautioned that

> ... while trial courts should properly be accorded wide latitude in fashioning equitable remedies in cases of this type, it is the inescapable function of the appellate court to make sure that the fashioned remedy meets that criterion in accordance with the regulatory scheme and adequately serves the particularized needs of the case before the

court. Although injunctive relief is never automatic upon the showing of a violation of the Act or regulations (See Hecht Co. v. Bowles (321 U.S. 321, 64 S.Ct. 587, 88 L.Ed. 754), Supra), we should not hesitate to reverse an order denying such relief when it is evident that the trial court's discretion has not been exercised to effectuate the manifest objectives of the specific legislation involved.

Id.

Actions for statutory injunctions need not meet the requirements for an injunction imposed by traditional equity jurisprudence. Once a violation is demonstrated, the moving party need show only that there is some reasonable likelihood of future violations. * * *

In light of these standards, we conclude that the district court was incorrect in denying the injunctive relief sought by the Commission. It would be anomalous to conclude, as did the district court, that the carefully organized, large scale, and long term soybean trading activities of the Hunts constituted a violation of Section 4a(1) of the Commodity Exchange Act, but that relief under section 6c of the Act was inappropriate. Their misconduct was systematic and carefully preconceived. Their soybean positions which were challenged by the Commission were maintained throughout the enforcement proceedings until the futures contracts came to their natural conclusion. Further, the Hunts consistently maintained that their conduct was blameless. And finally, the prominent place of the Hunt family in the commodity markets generally, suggests that it is not unlikely that they will be regular participants in the soybean markets in the future. Thus, they will be in a position in which they are capable of committing future violations. Given the presence of all these factors, injunctive relief should have been granted. * * *

MARKEY, CHIEF JUDGE, concurring and dissenting. * * *

MINPECO, S.A. v. CONTICOMMODITY SERVICES, INC.

673 F.Supp. 684 (S.D.N.Y.1987).

LASKER, DISTRICT JUDGE.

In this action arising out of the crisis in the silver market in 1979–1980, Minpeco alleges that, under the leadership of Bunker and Herbert Hunt, a number of silver futures traders and the brokerage houses who handled their silver futures accounts participated in a conspiracy to manipulate upward the price of silver and silver futures. Five defendants have moved for summary judgment on the ground that the evidence of record is insufficient to establish their participation in this conspiracy. Moving defendants are ACLI International Commodity Services, Inc. ("ACS"), Prudential–Bache Securities, Inc. ("Bache"), and Merrill Lynch, Pierce, Fenner & Smith, Inc. ("Merrill Lynch"), brokerage houses who provided services to the alleged trading conspirators, and Mahmoud Fustok and Lamar Hunt, who were individual silver traders. Although these well-briefed and argued motions present difficult and close questions, I conclude that the record contains sufficient evidence from which a reasonable jury could find that these five defendants participated in a conspiracy to manipulate silver prices. The jury, aided by the live testimony of witnesses subject to cross-examination, must decide whether the moving defendants participated in the conspiracy alleged. Accordingly, the motions for summary judgment are denied.

The gravamen of Minpeco's claims is that a conspiracy led by Bunker and Herbert Hunt, supported by two groups of wealthy investors, including Lamar Hunt and Fustok, and knowingly assisted by the defendant brokerage firms, caused the dramatic rise in silver prices from August 1979 to January 1980. The goal of the alleged conspiracy was to manipulate upward the price of silver and silver futures contracts. Minpeco alleges that defendants' conspiratorial activity violated 1) §§ 1 and 2 of the Sherman Act, 15 U.S.C. §§ 1–2; 2) § 9(b) of the Commodity Exchange Act, 7 U.S.C. § 13(b); 3) the Racketeer Influenced and Corrupt Organizations Act, 18 U.S.C. §§ 1961–65; and 4) N.Y.Gen.Bus.Law § 340 and New York common law.

According to Minpeco, there were two so-called "groups" of trading conspirators: the Hunt Group and the Conti Group. The key members of the Hunt group were the three Hunt brothers and the International Metals Investment Company ("IMIC"), a Bermudian corporation established in July 1979 and controlled by Herbert and Bunker Hunt and several Arab investors. The Conti Group consisted of a coalition of Swiss and Arab bankers and traders, including Naji Nahas, moving defendant Fustok, and Advicorp Advisory Financial Services S.A. ("Advicorp"), who traded in large part through ACS and through Norton Waltuch, a trader with ContiCommodity Services, Inc. ("Conti"). The trading defendants' role in the alleged conspiracy was to create the appearance of new investor demand in silver and to buy as much of the certificated silver bullion in the Commodity Exchange, Inc. ("Comex") and Chicago Board of Trade ("CBT") warehouses as possible by taking delivery on silver futures contracts.

The broker defendants are alleged to have known about the conspiracy both through objective market conditions indicating that the silver market was being manipulated, and through the direct knowledge of their employees from working with and observing the Hunt and Conti groups. Minpeco claims that, motivated by the opportunity to profit from increased trading and higher prices in silver and by the desire to curry favor with the Hunts, the broker defendants joined the conspiracy by assisting the Hunt and Conti groups in three major ways: 1) allowing manipulative trading; 2) financing the conspiracy; and 3) deceiving the exchanges and the Commodity Futures Trading Commission ("CFTC"). * * *

The brokers' motions for summary judgment present substantial questions, particularly whether Minpeco has produced sufficient evidence of the brokers' knowing participation in the conspiracy. * * *

It is not disputed that during the 1979–1980 period, at least twelve entities and individuals with some connection to Advicorp, the largest of which were BPS and Litardex, traded silver futures contracts through commodity trading accounts at ACLI Commodity Services, S.A. ("ACS Geneva"), ACS' Geneva branch, as did Herbert and Bunker Hunt. In addition, ACLI International, Inc., ACS' parent company, loaned Herbert and Bunker Hunt as much as $135 million in the period from October 1979 to March 1980, collateralized by silver. * * *

Minpeco has presented sufficient evidence from which a jury could reasonably conclude that ACS knew that the Conti group and the Hunt group were collectively engaged in manipulative trading. First, it could be reasonably concluded, based on the testimony on letters rogatory of Jean–Francois St. Severin, an account executive at ACS Geneva in 1979, combined with statements in the affidavits submitted by higher-level ACS officials, that for at least a significant period of the conspiracy ACS knew that Advicorp was related to and had some control over the twelve accounts opened at ACS' Geneva branch in 1979–1980, and that Nahas was also related to these Geneva accounts. It could also be inferred that ACS knew that the Conti group was acting together with the Hunt group, based on evidence of Bunker Hunt's presence at a meeting between Nahas, Selim Nassif, and ACS officials to discuss problems with the Advicorp accounts, coupled with evidence of knowledge that Advicorp was placing trades for the Hunts.

Second, a jury could reasonably conclude that ACS knew that at least some of the holders of the Advicorp-related accounts at ACS Geneva were engaged in manipulative trading. In addition to the alleged changes in BPS' silver trading pattern—such as increased deliveries and trading in congested months—which Minpeco argues displayed the classic indicia of manipulative trading and which ACS argues were consistent with normal, legal behavior, there is also evidence that ACS knew that BPS was resisting Comex's efforts to regulate the silver futures market by encouraging traders to reduce their long silver positions in congested months.

Minpeco alleges that ACS engaged in three types of actions in furtherance of the conspiracy: 1) ACS permitted its Advicorp-related accounts to engage in manipulative trading; 2) ACS knowingly loaned money to the Hunts to finance the conspiracy's manipulative activities; and 3) ACS deceived the CFTC and Comex to shield the conspirators from adverse regulation. The cumulative weight of this evidence is sufficient to permit a juror reasonably to infer that ACS knowingly engaged in acts which furthered the alleged conspiracy.

First, the evidence of record permits a reasonable inference that ACS allowed the Advicorp-related accounts to engage in manipulative trading activity and that ACS knowingly financed the conspiracy through loans to the Hunts. The types of trading and financial services which ACS provided to the Advicorp-related accounts were routine and legal and can not, without more, give rise to an inference of participation in a conspiracy.

Evidence of record, however, suggests that by allowing its Advicorp-related accounts to take large positions in silver, in combination with the extension of loans collateralized by silver, ACS exposed itself to potential liability far exceeding its net worth. This over-extension could permit an inference that ACS was acting against its economic interest, one of the "plus" factors which tends to exclude the possibility of independent legitimate behavior. Furthermore, there are genuine issues as to whether BPS' and Litardex' large-scale trading in December 1979 silver violated an ACS internal policy of limiting its customers to no more than 10% of the open interest in a particular month, further excluding the possibility of independent behavior.

ACS also argues that its termination of BPS' account at the end of November 1979 contradicts Minpeco's conspiracy claim. Clearly this termination could be viewed as inconsistent with the charge that ACS was assisting the conspiracy. But the evidence as to the circumstances of this termination, which apparently was sparked by a dispute over the terms for a delivery of December silver, including evidence that ACS attempted to obtain for BPS the financing necessary for the account to remain at ACS, is also subject to the conflicting reasonable interpretation that in fact ACS did everything possible to try to keep BPS' account.

ACS' trading and financial assistance to the Advicorp-related accounts and the Hunts might, in isolation, be viewed as equally consistent with legitimate, independent business activity as with participation in the conspiracy, and hence insufficient under *Matsushita* and *Apex* to allow a reasonable inference in support of Minpeco's claims. However, Minpeco has also produced evidence which could be interpreted as establishing that ACS, despite ample notice of its obligation to assist Comex in regulating the silver futures market, intentionally withheld from Comex pertinent information about the Advicorp-related accounts. This evidence, again, is subject to conflicting interpretations. But, drawing justifiable inferences in favor of the non-moving party, it does tend to exclude the possibility of legitimate business activity. * * *

The most significant motive for ACS' alleged participation in the conspiracy is the stake of its parent, ACLI, Inc., in the price of silver. ACLI, Inc. traded silver futures contracts and physical silver. The record shows that ACLI, Inc.'s silver positions were largely hedged, rendering the bulk of its silver holdings impervious to shifts in price, but it is also undisputed that ACLI, Inc. was "net at risk," holding net unhedged long silver positions. Although these net unhedged positions were not large, they demonstrate that to an extent ACLI, Inc. was enriched by the rise in silver prices. Of course, as a broker, ACS also had a motive to preserve an orderly and healthy silver futures market, and the jury will have to weigh the significance of these competing motivations. However, Minpeco has established that this is not a case in which Minpeco's claim as to ACS "simply makes no economic sense."

In the early 1970s, Bunker and Herbert Hunt opened substantial silver futures trading accounts at Bache, and by October 1979, the Hunt accounts had the largest credit line at Bache. From October 1979 through March 1980, Bache approved loans to the Hunts collateralized by silver which eventually totaled approximately $233 million. Bache argues that provision of these normally legitimate trading and financial acts to Bunker and Herbert Hunt cannot support an inference that Bache knew about, let alone assisted, the multi-member conspiracy charged. However, as described below, Minpeco has presented evidence which raises genuine issues for trial, particularly as to Bache's knowledge of the conspiracy through its employee Scott McFarland and as to Bache's motive to participate in the alleged conspiracy.

Although only Bunker and Herbert Hunt had trading accounts at Bache, there is sufficient evidence to permit the conclusion that Bache knew not only of manipulative trading on the part of the Hunts but also knew that other traders were acting together with the Hunts.

In addition to the general evidence as to objective market indicators discussed above, Minpeco has presented specific evidence from which it could be inferred that Bache knew of the Hunts' manipulative intent. Minpeco's evidence permits the inference that by October 1979 Bache knew that the Hunts' position at Bache of 6,900 silver futures contracts was one-third of the Hunts' over-all long silver futures positions. This meant that the Hunts controlled 100,000,000 ounces of silver, close to 100% of the Comex and CBT warehouse stocks at that time. Hence, Bache had information strongly suggesting that the Hunts were in the process of establishing a dominant position in the silver futures market, an important indicator of manipulative intent. *See Cargill, Inc. v. Hardin,* 452 F.2d 1154, 1164 (8th Cir.1971), *cert. denied,* 406 U.S. 932, 92 S.Ct. 1770, 32 L.Ed.2d 135 (1972). Evidence of Bache's knowledge of this trading behavior, coupled with evidence of other indicia of manipulative trading at Bache, and with Bache's knowledge of Bunker and Herbert Hunt's prior unusual, if not suspicious, silver trading behavior while at Bache, permits a reasonable inference that Bache knew of the Hunts' manipulation. * * *

There is sufficient evidence of record to permit an inference that Bache knowingly participated in the conspiracy by allowing manipulative trading, providing the Hunts with financial assistance and by shielding them from the regulators. Two genuine issues for trial will be mentioned briefly.

From October 1979 to March 1980, Bache made three loans to the Hunts, totalling $233,000,000, collateralized by silver, and authorized a fourth loan which was never made. The timing of these loans, two of which were authorized just after Comex raised its margin requirements for silver futures accounts, permits the inference that Bache knew that the purpose of these loans was to help the Hunts maintain and build their silver positions in the face of Comex's efforts to force them to reduce their positions.

There is also evidence permitting the inference that Bache protected the Hunts from Comex regulation by refusing to aggregate and reduce the Hunt accounts after Comex imposed position limits and aggregation rules on January 7, 1980, despite two instructions from Comex to do so.

Minpeco has produced evidence which supports two motives for Bache's participation in the alleged conspiracy. First, in 1979 commissions from the Hunt loans constituted almost 90% of the annual income of Charles Mattey, the Hunts' senior account executive at Bache. Bache treasurer Langdon Stevenson testified on deposition that he thought that at least "to some degree" these commissions affected Mattey's objectivity in casting votes on the Bache commodity credit committee in favor of extending credit to the Hunts. Second, beginning in October 1979, Bache received significant assistance from Bunker and Herbert Hunt in fending off a hostile take-over. In April 1980, William Marlin, vice-chairman of the Bache Board, told the Bache audit committee investigating Bache's involvement in the silver crisis that the fact that the Hunts owned Bache stock had an impact on the Bache board's dealings with the Hunts—although his testimony also indicates that he did not think that Bache gave the Hunts extra time to meet their obligations when the price of silver plummeted. This evidence permits an inference that the financial well-being of Mattey, Bache, and the Hunts were highly inter-connected and demonstrates, at the least, that this is not a case where there was no rational economic motive to conspire.

The record reflects that beginning in 1974, Merrill Lynch maintained a close financial relationship with Herbert and Bunker Hunt. IMIC from its inception also traded through Merrill Lynch, and in 1979–1980 Merrill Lynch lent both the Hunts and IMIC substantial sums. As with ACS and Bache, Minpeco has presented evidence which raises genuine issues for trial as to Merrill Lynch's knowledge of and participation in the conspiracy.

In addition to the evidence of economic indicators demonstrating market manipulation discussed above, Minpeco has presented evidence permitting an inference that Merrill Lynch had specific knowledge of the scope of the conspiracy. First, there is evidence supporting the claim that Merrill Lynch knew, as early as August 1979, that IMIC was a partnership between the Hunts and several Arab investors. There is also evidence to support an inference that Merrill Lynch knew of the connection between BPS and Fustok by December 1979. Finally, it is undisputed that Merrill Lynch knew that in 1977, after Merrill Lynch had financed the Hunts' trading in soybean futures, the Hunts were found guilty by the CFTC of violating commodities laws in connection with the soybean futures market. This knowledge of the Hunts' past commodities violations, in combination with the objective economic factors indicating market manipulation in 1979–1980, supports a reasonable inference that Merrill Lynch knew of the alleged conspiracy.

As with Bache and ACS, Minpeco alleges that Merrill Lynch assisted the conspiracy by permitting manipulative trading, loaning money to the conspirators, and deceiving the regulators. Two genuine issues for trial deserve mention. First, there is evidence which could permit the inference that the purpose of the large loans made to the Hunts and IMIC in 1979–1980 was to finance the Hunts' deliveries of silver in furtherance of the alleged conspiracy. Although Merrill Lynch characterizes the loans as normal business transactions equally consistent with permissible behavior as with participation in a conspiracy, there is support in the record for the conclusion that the decision to finance the Hunts' deliveries was a controversial departure from the norm. Second, there is evidence that when the CFTC contacted Merrill Lynch in early September 1979 to inquire who owned and controlled IMIC, Merrill Lynch representatives denied having such information, even though it is clear that Merrill Lynch knew from the time of IMIC's incorporation that the Hunts substantially controlled IMIC. While Merrill Lynch has presented evidence indicating that later in September Merrill Lynch pressured IMIC to disclose the Hunts' interest to the CFTC, it is the jury which must decide the weight to be assigned to conflicting evidence.

Minpeco alleges that Merrill Lynch's motivation to participate in the conspiracy arose from the significant commission and interest income produced by the Hunt accounts and from Merrill Lynch's desire to keep the Hunts' goodwill. Merrill Lynch, in response, argues that any interest it had in keeping the Hunts' accounts was far outweighed by its interest in preserving its reputation and maintaining a healthy commodities market for all of its customers. Merrill Lynch also contends that Minpeco's claims against it are internally inconsistent: in its conspiracy claims, Minpeco charges that Merrill Lynch schemed to assist traders with long silver futures positions to raise silver prices, but in its breach of fiduciary duty claims, Minpeco charges that Merrill Lynch encouraged Minpeco to sell silver short on a massive scale, which would tend to lower silver prices. These arguments, however, must be made to the jury. It cannot be concluded on the present record that Merrill Lynch's alleged participation in the conspiracy is wholly implausible. * * *

Fustok, a Lebanese citizen, business associate of Nahas, and active investor and trader in race horses: * * *

During September, October, and November 1979, Fustok met Nahas every two days at the racetrack, on which occasions, according to Fustok's deposition, they discussed silver and Nahas informed Fustok that Bunker Hunt had invested $150 to $200 million in silver. Fustok's deposition also indicates that he and Nahas, in a phone call during those months, discussed the facts that Advicorp's planes were shipping Fustok's silver from the United States to Switzerland and that Nahas and Bunker Hunt were also shipping silver out of the United States. * * *

Fustok participated in meetings and agreements to share losses with other alleged conspirators once the price of silver fell. At one meeting in

March 1980, Nahas and Bunker Hunt sought Fustok's participation in their plan to pool their silver and use it to back bonds so silver would return to its old price, since the three owned "more than half of the world." Fustok, upon learning that Hunt was going to Saudi Arabia, gave him names of people who might help him with his finances. There is a factual dispute whether Fustok proposed an agreement, which was never finalized and which would have provided that Fustok, Nahas, and Bunker Hunt would cover, jointly and severally, 50% of the losses sustained by Advicorp because of its trading in BPS' omnibus account. * * *

Lamar Hunt, youngest brother of Bunker and Herbert Hunt * * * While evidence of Lamar Hunt's allegedly conspiratorial conduct is limited primarily to his development of large silver positions during 1979–80, often in more distant months than other conspirators, Minpeco has produced sufficient evidence from which a reasonable juror could conclude that he participated in the conspiracy. * * *

First, the evidence of record indicates Lamar Hunt's high level of communication with other conspirators. Hunt and his brothers shared information about the silver market. It is undisputed that Lamar began trading in silver on the advice of his brothers, who discussed with him many articles about the silver market over a period of years, including articles about the Comex investigations and Comex rule changes.

The brothers did more than communicate; they also facilitated one another's actions. Herbert Hunt placed the order for Lamar Hunt's 1000 contract straddle, although, according to Lamar, he (Lamar) decided the size and position of the straddle and his brother placed the call primarily because Lamar had never previously ordered a straddle. The brothers also loaned money to each other to finance their silver margin calls.

Finally, Minpeco's evidence that Lamar Hunt engaged in transactions contrary to his self-interest tends to exclude the possibility that he was acting independently.

First, Lamar Hunt sustained large losses in silver transactions. For example, on November 15, 1979, Lamar Hunt lost $1.6 million while liquidating December 1979 and March 1980 contracts and rolling them into September 1980. Minpeco maintains that Hunt was willing to incur this loss in order to increase congestion in the September 1980 position, as other alleged conspirators later began to do. Hunt's explanation that he executed this transaction so that the September contracts would be subject to long-term capital gains treatment when they expired is plausible, but not compelling. A reasonable juror could find the explanation insufficient. Hunt has not produced documents relating to the tax treatment of his silver transactions and the affidavit of Sidney Meyer, Hunt's tax expert, does not purport to determine the specific tax consequences of Hunt's transactions although it does support the plausibility of the general purposes of Lamar's explanations.

Second, in December 1979 Lamar Hunt, contrary to his previous investment pattern, rolled his positions forward into distant months, purportedly to secure long-term gain tax treatment on the transactions. However, one week later he acquired positions in congested months that would be subject to short-term capital gain taxes. Although Hunt's explanation that he made the latter purchases because his straddle could cover additional short-term gains is plausible, it is subject to a conflicting, reasonable interpretation that his participation in the conspiracy explains this seemingly inconsistent conduct. * * *

NOTES

1. The "silver crisis" brought on by the Hunts' trading shook the markets and raised concerns with the CFTC's regulatory role:

In one of its more severe market crises, the CFTC neither took emergency action nor sought injunctive relief. This was the so-called "Silver Crisis" that occurred after the price of silver increased from less than $9 an ounce in 1979 to a peak of approximately $50 dollars an ounce in January of 1980. On March 18, 1980, silver prices dropped thirty-three percent in twenty-four hours. Silver was then trading at $10.80 an ounce—off from $39.50 the day before. The Hunt family then failed to meet hundreds of millions of dollars in margin calls, which threatened the financial stability of Wall Street.

The SEC suspended trading in the stock of various major Wall Street firms in response to reports that these firms were suffering heavy losses because of the Hunts' failure to meet margin calls. The CFTC Chairman was of the view that the entire "financial fabric of the United States was endangered" as a result of the Hunts' activities. Although this proved to be overblown, it was truly an emergency situation that required the combined force of numerous senior government officials to deal with and monitor. The Silver Crisis had a serious impact on other financial markets regulated by those entities, it adversely affected commercial productivity and individual users of silver, and the tremendous amounts of credit extended for the Hunt silver purchases affected monetary policy, causing the Federal Reserve to ask the banks not to extend loans for speculative trading. Nevertheless, "faced with dramatic and disorderly market conditions, the CFTC took none of the specific preventive or emergency actions allowed under the Commodity Exchange Act, although it had both the statutory duty to act and the requisite information." A Congressional Committee asserted that the CFTC could have alleviated the situation by declaring a market emergency but did not do so.

A subsequent CFTC investigation found that the Hunts had at least three billion dollars in silver futures contracts at the exchanges. The Hunts were trading in large amounts through a company they owned jointly with two Arab Sheiks. The CFTC also determined that the Hunts were acting with a group of foreign traders who also held huge silver positions. Several years later the CFTC charged the Hunts and those foreign traders with manipulation. Several of these respondents consented to sanctions, and in 1989 Nelson Bunker Hunt and his brother, Herbert Hunt, agreed to a permanent bar from trading on all commodity exchanges. They also each agreed to pay a ten million dollar civil penalty. But those sanctions were all but meaningless. The Hunt brothers were insolvent and only $1.5 million was allowable as a claim in their bankruptcies, along with hundreds of millions of dollars of claims by other creditors.

The Hunts and others were the subject of several private actions in which it was claimed that their trading activities had caused damages. The most significant of these was the case Minpeco, S.A. v. ContiCommodity Serv. There it was claimed that a government agency in Peru had suffered sharp losses from its speculations in the silver futures markets during the time the Hunts were trading. After years of discovery, the case was tried for several months in the Southern District of New York. On September 1, 1988, a judgment in the amount of $132 million was entered against the Hunts and others. The jury found that they had violated the Commodity Exchange Act, federal antitrust statues, New York common law fraud and the Racketeer Influenced and Corrupt Organizations Act. However, the Hunts subsequently filed bankruptcy which made collection doubtful. Minpeco did obtain substantial settlements from various brokerage firms which had handled the Hunt and other accounts.

Jerry W. Markham, Manipulation of Commodity Futures Prices—The Unprosecutable Crime, 8 Yale J. on Reg. 281 (1991).

2. The California energy crisis in 2001 and 2002 caused further concerns with price manipulation. The Enron Corp. was found to have engaged in a number of "gaming" transactions to take advantage of regulatory disparities. These transactions were imaginatively called such things as "Fat Boy," "Death Star,"and "Get Shorty." Three Enron traders pleaded guilty to criminal charges for engaging in certain of those transactions. Jeff Manning, Helpful Enron Trader Won't See Prison, The Oregonian, Feb. 16, 2007, at DO1. The scandal in the energy markets spread with the discovery that several energy trading firms were using "round trip" trades, or "bragawatts" as they were sometimes called. This trading involved the buying and selling by the same traders to themselves in offsetting transactions in order to boost their trading volumes or to set prices for actual contracts. This became an industry wide practice in natural gas. The CFTC brought actions against several of those firms, which agreed to pay in total over $300 million to settle those charges. Jerry W. Markham, *A Financial History of Modern U.S. Corporate Scandals: From Enron to Reform* 129–140 (2006). The Commodity Futures Modernization Act of 2000 deregulated much derivative trading, particularly where institutions were involved. Nevertheless, the CFTC charged that these round trip trades constituted an attempted manipulation of the commodity markets, even though a regulated commodity exchange was not involved. The CFTC further charged the involved firms with making false reports of these and other trades to various industry publications such as the *Inside FERC Gas Market Report. See* Jerry W. Markham, Lawrence H. Hunt, Jr. & Michael S. Sackheim, Market Manipulation—From Star Chamber to Lone Star, 23 Futures and Derivatives Law Report 7 (2003). Criminal charges were brought against Michelle Valencia, a trader at Dynegy, for engaging in

round trip trades in violation of the Commodity Exchange Act. A federal court initially dismissed those charges as unconstitutionally overbroad, but that decision was reversed on appeal. United States v. Valencia, 394 F.3d 352 (5th Cir. 2004). Valencia was subsequently convicted on mail and wire fraud charges brought against her, but the jury acquitted or were hung on the Commodity Exchange Act claims of false reporting. The Energy Policy Act of 2005 gave the Federal Energy Regulatory Commission ("FERC") authority to sanction manipulation of natural gas prices. That action has raised the issue of whether the FERC or to CFTC (or both) have regulatory authority over the manipulation of prices of natural gas futures contracts that are normally regulated by the CFTC.

The grant of additional power to FERC still did not alleviate congressional concerns that more regulation was needed. Congress subsequently granted the Federal Trade Commission authority to prosecute false reporting and market manipulation in the wholesale petroleum market. Energy Policy Act of 2007, Pub. L. No. 110–140, § 811, 121 Stat. 1492 (2007). The terms of this prohibition are modeled after those of section 10(b) of the Securities Exchange Act of 1934, 15 U.S.C. § 78j(b) (2000).

3. This means that there are now three agencies directly charged with regulating trading in the energy markets, i.e., the CFTC, FERC, and the FTC. In addition, Section 753 of Dodd–Frank Wall Street Reform and Consumer Protection Act of 2010 expanded the manipulation provisions in the Commodity Exchange Act of 1936 to prohibit any "manipulative or deceptive device or contrivance" in violation of CFTC rules adopted within one year of the enactment of Dodd–Frank. The "manipulative or deceptive device or contrivance" language in Section 753 was taken from Section 10(b) of the Securities Exchange Act ("34 Act") where the FTC language was also drawn. Section 753 of Dodd–Frank further contains a special provision for manipulation for "false reporting" of trades or prices.

Both the CFTC and FERC charged Energy Transfer Partners, L.P. with manipulating physical natural gas prices. CFTC v. Energy Transfer Partners, L.P., CIV. NO. 07 CV1301–K (N.D. Tex. 2007); In the Matter of Energy Transfer Partners, L.P., Doc. No. IN06–3–002 (F.E.R.C. 2007). Another such dual prosecution was brought against a hedge fund, Amaranth Advisors, after it lost over $6 billion in a single week during 2006 from its trades in energy products. A district court refused to enjoin the joint proceedings even though both actions were directed at the same conduct. Commodity Futures Trading Comm'n v. Amaranth Advisors, LLC, 523 F. Supp. 2d 328, 331–32 (S.D.N.Y. 2007). The CFTC argued in an appeal of the FERC case against the Amaranth trader that the FERC had no jurisdiction because the trading involved futures contracts over which the CFTC has exclusive jurisdiction. Do you think this is an efficient use of government resources?

SECTION 5. TRADING PRACTICES

Other regulatory concerns in the commodity markets were raised by trading practices on the exchange floors. One such practice involved something called "tax straddles."

JERRY W. MARKHAM
PROHIBITED FLOOR TRADING ACTIVITIES UNDER THE COMMODITIES EXCHANGE ACT

58 Fordham L. Rev. (1989).

A trader wishing to defer gains or to convert short-term gains into long-term capital gains would purchase the right to buy a commodity under a futures contract in a particular delivery month. At the same time, the trader could sell the same futures contract with a different delivery month. If commodity prices thereafter dropped uniformly in both contracts, the futures customer would have a gain in one leg of the transaction and a loss in the other. To illustrate, assume that a trader entered into a futures contract to sell 5,000 ounces of silver at $10 with delivery to be in March; such a tactic is called going short. At the same time, the trader agreed to buy 5,000 ounces of silver at $10.10 with delivery to be in November. The trader, in the second transaction, was going long. Assume silver prices subsequently rose $1.00 in both contracts. The trader would then have a gain of $5,000 in the long transaction and an offsetting $5,000 loss in the short leg. In the short transaction, he was agreeing to sell something that was worth more than what he had agreed to sell it for and, in the long transaction, he had agreed to buy something that was worth more than what he had agreed to pay for it.

If the taxpayer then liquidated the short leg in which there was a loss, he would realize a loss for tax purposes. If he offset the gain from the profitable leg of the transaction in the following tax year, the overall result would be a loss in the first year that could be used to offset other income or to convert income into long-term capital gain, while the overall transaction had no real economic effect.

If done legitimately, the tax straddle was an acceptable means of deferring taxes. Not all traders, however, wanted to engage in legitimate tax straddles because they presented a risk that actual trading losses could be incurred that would not offset the tax benefits of a transaction. For example, if silver prices reversed themselves after liquidating the loss transaction, the trader could have an actual economic loss that would not be offset by the liquidated leg of the transaction. To legitimately foreclose this possibility, traders would, after liquidating the loss leg, reestablish a similar leg, which would continue to offset any further changes in futures prices. In the following year, the trader could then liquidate both legs and thereby avoid the possibility of large losses.

Nevertheless, there remains a small risk of loss between the liquidation of the first leg and its reestablishment. In addition, variations in silver prices between different delivery months could actually result in a loss or, if a trader was lucky, an outright gain. Possible price fluctuations motivated so-called spread or straddle traders to profit from changes between delivery months. These changes were caused by events that might not affect all prices the same way because of differing perceptions of the long-term effects of the events. To negate such risks in tax straddles, traders sometimes engaged in illegal wash transactions by entering into buy and sell transactions in the same commodity for the same delivery month. These wash sales effectively eliminated the risk of price variations in the liquidation and reestablishment of the loss legs.

Tax straddle traders also engaged in transactions that were fictitious and prearranged to ensure that no outright losses occurred. These transactions sometimes took the form of round-robin or rollover tax spreads. In these prearranged transactions, three exchange members engaged in multiple round-robin transactions in particular futures contracts. The buy and sell orders for these transactions, entered simultaneously on the floor, were generally for large blocks of futures in illiquid delivery months. Because of their simultaneous entry, large size and the illiquidity of the contracts, the participants usually were assured that their prearranged buy and sell orders would be matched. The first round of those transactions resulted in large tax losses to participants in the current tax year. In the next tax year, however, the round-robin transactions were reversed so that the prior year's loss was, for the most part, recovered as a taxable gain. Predictably, a similar but greater series of such transactions would be conducted in subsequent tax years to create tax losses to apply against the gains from the prior rollover tax spreads and from other trading activities.

Tax straddle traders also sometimes manipulated prices in illiquid commodity markets to acquire the necessary gains and losses and to protect against actual outright losses. These and other fraudulent trading practices became the subject of several CFTC enforcement actions. The CFTC was also responsible for the institution of grand jury proceedings in New York and Chicago. Numerous criminal indictments were returned in both cities. Investigators also discovered that the Commodity Exchange Inc. ("Comex") in New York had special trading rules that allowed straddles to be established in after-hours trading at any price that occurred during the trading range of the day, ensuring price fluctuations for tax purposes. The CFTC later prohibited this practice.

In Chicago, grand juries indicted several soybean traders and in New York over forty traders were the subject of enforcement actions, all arising out of passing money, fraudulent trading and tax straddles. * * * The CFTC's concern about tax straddles resulted in the passage of the Economic Recovery Tax Act of 1981, which changed the ways in which commodities futures transactions are taxed. Under the Act, tax straddles are now taxed at year-end by being marked to their market price even if the transaction has not been liquidated. If there is an open gain in one leg of a straddle and a realized loss of the closing of the other leg, the gain is taxed as if it had been closed. This eliminates the usefulness of tax straddles as well as the need for wash sales and other trading techniques which sought to reduce trading risks.

UNITED STATES v. WINOGRAD

656 F.2d 279 (7th Cir.1981), cert. denied, sub nom., 455
U.S. 989, 102 S.Ct. 1612, 71 L.Ed.2d 848 (1982).

PELL, CIRCUIT JUDGE.

At the conclusion of a jury trial, the defendants were found guilty of conspiracy to defraud the United States by impairing the United States Treasury Department's collection of income taxes in violation of 18 U.S.C. § 371, aiding the preparation of fraudulent United States income tax returns in violation of 26 U.S.C. § 7206(2), and entering into fixed and uncompetitive commodity futures transactions and wash sales in violation of 7 U.S.C. § 6c(a)(A). This appeal followed the entry of judgment on the jury verdict.

In the fall of 1974, Harold Brady, repeatedly characterized by the parties as "one of the world's largest copper traders," and apparently being desirous of providing himself with a tegurium protecting himself to some extent from the inevitable result of an overabundance of otherwise taxable income, employed the Siegel Trading Company to execute various commodity futures transactions in order to defer certain tax payments otherwise due that year. Appellant Siegel was the president of the company, appellant Winograd was vice-president, and both appellants were active floor-traders in commodities futures. After negotiations between the appellants and agents for Brady, it was decided that one of the procedures that would be utilized to achieve this objective was the placement of "tax straddles" in Mexican peso futures contracts on the International Monetary Market in Chicago. "Tax straddles" or "tax spreads" were, at the time at least, legitimate means to accomplish the deferring of tax payments from one year to the next and sometimes the conversion of short-term gains into long-term gains. The basis of the procedure is that normally price changes in two different future month contracts of the same commodity move in the same direction and in the same amount. The deferral or conversion is accomplished by going "long" or being a net buyer in one future month of the commodity, and going "short" or being a net seller in another month of the same commodity. When the prices of the future contracts change (generally increasing in peso futures), one account will show a loss while the other shows the corresponding, and hopefully equal, gain. The key to the transaction is to liquidate the loss-bearing account or "leg" during the first tax year or in the short-term, and to liquidate the gain-bearing account or "leg," if possible, in the following tax year or in the long-term. The legs are usually immediately reestablished for future months, thus "rolling over" the transaction. If all goes as expected, the losses should nearly or exactly equal the gains and thus there would be no real economic impact on the investor. Beneficial tax treatment results, however, when, as here, the short term "losses" shelter other unrelated short-term gains in the first year, in effect converting the amount which would have been short-term gain in the first year into gain in the second year.

As stated previously, "tax straddles" were legitimate and legal means of deferring or converting tax consequences when properly executed on an established commodities futures exchange or market and through bona fide competitive trades. The Government's position in this case, however, is that the appellants executed Brady's peso trades not through bona fide trades and open-outcry on an established market, but through prearranged and uncompetitive trades done between various employees of the Siegel Trading Company. The Government concludes, therefore, that Brady improperly deducted his short-term losses and that the appellants are guilty of the charged violations. * * *

One of the more fundamental issues appellants present is that the Government's evidence was insufficient to convict them. In this argument, appellants contend that it was the Government's burden under the income tax counts to establish that the peso transactions were "risk-free" so that the short-term "losses" were improperly deducted, and that the Government failed to establish this fact by the requisite proof.

Appellants' characterization of the Government's case is in a sense warranted. We disagree, however, with their conclusion. The Government contends, basically, that the transactions were "risk-free" because they were prearranged and thus Brady had a guaranteed seller or buyer for his position when he had accomplished his tax objectives and liquidated one leg of his position. It is true that Brady had little or no risk of market entry or exit. However, the transactions appellants executed for Brady nevertheless incorporated substantial "risks" relevant to the income tax counts because appellants did not have control over the market price of pesos and therefore Brady stood to lose substantial amounts of money if the price moved contrary to their expectations, or if the spreads between the two months' prices changed relative to each other or, in the words of Winograd on one occasion, "the spread (price) differential" had gotten "out of whack."

Notwithstanding this "risk," however, we find that the district court correctly held that the Brady "losses" were not properly deducted. Our conclusion is not based upon weighing the risks involved in the peso transactions, but is based upon the fact that the appellants did not accomplish their tax objectives through bona fide transactions in the competitive open market. The Government presented substantial evidence that Brady's trades were not done in the usual manner of open-outcry in the peso area or "pit" of the IMM, but were prearranged "crosses" done in-house between traders in the Siegel Trading Company. The trades often were not done within the relevant day's price range, and in some cases

Winograd would engage in the irregular practice of "bidding" for a contract at a price lower than he was "offering." In essence, therefore, appellants appeared to be utilizing the organized market, but were in fact creating a market for their transactions at the prices they established for ulterior purposes. Such prearranged trades are not bona fide transactions supporting loss deductions. * * *

For the reasons given herein the judgments of conviction are Affirmed.

NOTES

1. A number of wealthy individuals had used tax straddles to evade taxes and were forced to pay those taxes and penalties when these practices were attacked by the Internal Revenue Service. Among those affected was singer Willie Nelson. He was nearly bankrupted by the tax straddle transactions conducted for him in the commodity markets. Todd Mason, *Momma, Don't Let Your Babies Grow Up to Work for the Tax Boys*, Wall St. J., Jan. 29, 1991, at C1.

2. For other tax straddle cases see United States v. Turkish, 623 F.2d 769 (2d Cir.1980), *cert. denied*, 449 U.S. 1077, 101 S.Ct. 856, 66 L.Ed.2d 800 (1981) (conviction upheld for conspiracy to defraud United States and tax evasion through rigged trades and wash sales in the crude oil futures market); DeMartino v. Commissioner of Internal Revenue, 862 F.2d 400 (2d Cir.1988) (crude oil futures in New York market). The IRS also prosecuted numerous cases in which tax losses were disallowed for trading in the London forward market, which did not expressly prohibit such activities. *See e.g.*, Gardner v. Commissioner of Internal Revenue, 954 F.2d 836 (2d Cir.1992), *cert. denied, sub nom.*, Falk v. Commissioner, 504 U.S. 910, 112 S.Ct. 1940, 118 L.Ed.2d 546 (1992) (listing cases and denying deductions for transactions on London commodity markets that had no economic substance).

3. Spread transactions involve the purchase and sale of offsetting futures contracts for the same commodity but with different delivery dates. This illustrates a couple of important aspects of futures trading. First, generally, the price of a futures contract with a more distant delivery date will trade at a higher price than one with a shorter delivery date. This reflects theoretical interest rates and storage charges for the commodity for the longer period and is referred to as the "contango" in the industry. These price relations between futures contracts may vary and even invert as market events have differing effects on particular delivery periods. This gives rise to spread or straddle trading that seeks to take advantage of those "basis" differences.

4. Another basis concern is that commodity futures are delivered at a specific delivery point (except for certain financial futures including stock index futures that settle in cash) such as Chicago for grain traded there. A trader in say Georgia hedging grain prices on the Chicago Board of Trade may experience a difference in actual grain prices in Georgia because of transpor-

tation and other disparities, creating a basis risk and leaving the farmer not fully hedged.

JERRY W. MARKHAM
THE COMMODITY EXCHANGE MONOPOLY—REFORM IS NEEDED

48 Washington & Lee Law Review 977 (1991).

Perhaps the most significant regulatory event in the futures industry in recent years was the announcement in early 1989 that the office of the United States Attorney in Chicago had conducted massive undercover operations on the Chicago Mercantile Exchange and the Chicago Board of Trade. Disguised FBI agents acted as traders on the exchange floors and tape recorded their conversations with traders. The result was the indictment of forty-six traders, charging hundreds of violations of federal laws. The trials in those actions have not been a complete success for the government. They have, however, shown that illegal after hours trading and petty theft is prevalent on the floors of the commodity exchanges.

The Chicago sting operation also revealed that a widespread, pernicious and symbiotic relationship exists between "floor brokers" who execute customer orders and so-called "locals" who trade for their own accounts. This situation has developed as a result of the fact that the locals and floor brokers enjoy a statutory monopoly over the handling and execution of orders on the exchange floor. As will be described below, the Commodity Exchange Act requires all customer orders to be transmitted to the floor for execution by a floor broker. The customer order flow handled by floor brokers is a prime source of profitability for the locals, who trade for their own accounts. The locals feed off that order flow and they profit even more to the extent they can obtain executions from floor brokers at non-competitive prices.

Floor brokers are willing to provide non-competitive prices because they are susceptible to errors that can cost them thousands of dollars. As shown by the Chicago sting operation, the locals, in exchange for non-competitive executions, often cover up these errors. The locals are then repaid or prepaid by kickbacks from profits obtained by cheating other customers of the floor broker. Indeed, the Chicago sting operation revealed that floor brokers established elaborate banks or pools with locals that were built up by cheating customers so that floor broker errors could be covered and floor traders allowed to profit without competition.

Government witnesses testified that these trading practices included what were identified as "edges," "leads," "matches," and "trading off" an order. An "edge" seems to be simply a competitive advantage that particular traders are given over other traders because of their willingness to trade in large volume with floor brokers that are executing customer orders. This assists the trader given the edge to buy at the bid and sell at the offering price, or vice versa, thereby profiting on the spread between the bid and ask prices in the pit. The giving of an edge by a floor broker is designed to reward large floor traders who are willing to participate in large volume at or near current market levels and who will cover errors of the broker, as for example, by taking trades that were missed by the floor broker because of chaotic market conditions. Although giving an edge to a large floor trader does not guarantee him a profit and is not viewed to be a payback to cover errors, the floor trader is better assured of a profit because of the competitive advantage he is given. The giving of an edge, therefore, may deliberately exclude competition from the order execution process.

An ever more malignant form of trading is the so-called "lead." Simply stated, a lead is an order given by a floor broker to a floor trader at a price that is slightly different from that existing at other points in the trading pit. This allows the floor trader to accept the customer order and immediately execute an opposite trade with another trader in the pit to obtain a profit. A lead does not guarantee a profit because market conditions can change before the order is executed. Nevertheless, it does provide a clear competitive advantage, even greater than an edge, for a floor trader and is intentionally designed to allow the execution of a customer order at a price that is not competitive in the market place. The giving of a lead is often done to repay a trader for prior errors suffered by the floor broker, which were taken into the account of the floor trader and then later paid back by leads.

A third form of fraudulent trading practice exposed by the Chicago sting operation involves so-called "matches." A match occurs when a floor broker gives a buy order and a sale order to a floor trader at disparate prices that provide a profit or a "scratch"—i.e., no profit—to the floor trader. This is done without any exposure to the marketplace. These traders often involve a third party who acts as an intermediary in order to conceal the non-competitive nature of the trades. Matches often occur because floor brokers are too busy to execute all the trades they hold in their "deck." Observing that trades can be matched off before or at the close of trading, the floor broker may simply leave the orders in the deck until market chaos diminishes and they can be matched off with each other in a noncompetitive manner. This assures the floor broker of an execution and allows him to build up his bank or pool with other traders so that he can pay off errors that can not be concealed. A related form of fraud involves trading against an order. This occurs when a floor broker takes the opposite side of his customer's order by using an intermediary broker or brokers.

Another problem dramatized by the FBI sting operation are so-called "curb" trades which are trades conducted after the close of trading. Since such trading is outside trading hours, it constitutes off-exchange trading in violation of the Commodity Exchange Act. Often such trading simply involves floor brokers attempting to fill orders that were missed by mistake or inadvertence during closing sessions, which are often chaotic.

In other instances, curb trading is conducted, often long after the close, in order to cheat customers. * * *

The fraud revealed by the Chicago sting operation initially raised widespread consternation in the press. That concern diminished, however, after an examination of the indictments revealed that, even though hundreds of trades were involved, many of the dollar amounts for each trade were small—often less than a few hundred dollars. Consequently, the total amount of money involved was not great, at least as compared to some of the financial scandals that have been observed in recent years in the securities markets. The government also met an initial lack of success in its first trial involving traders in the Swiss franc pit on the Chicago Mercantile Exchange—i.e., convictions were obtained only on a limited number of charges. In addition, in a subsequent trial, the district court severed one trader after the trial began because that trader's defense conflicted with those of his fellow codefendants, raising concern that other traders there would have a basis for appeal in the event of an adverse verdict. Interestingly, the trader was severed because his defense was that the practices at issue were so widespread that they could not be considered to be anything other than normal practice. Those setbacks seemed to have been overcome when the government obtained a number of convictions in its trial involving the soybean pit. More recently, however, the Japanese yen pit trial resulted in a severe setback for the government. The jury announced that it was hung on many of the charges, and it acquitted some of the defendants. Nevertheless, over thirty of the forty-eight traders indicted as a result of the Chicago sting operation have been convicted. Retrials are also scheduled for other defendants and more indictments are expected.

The press initially suggested that the problems exposed by the Chicago sting operation could be corrected by prohibiting so-called "dual" trading that now exists on the floors of the exchanges. Dual trading allows floor brokers who are executing customer orders also to trade for their own accounts. Another suggestion was that an improved audit trail would permit detection of these practices and would provide deterrence to traders. In fact, the CFTC has considered both of these issues for over fifteen years. It has made some progress in improving audit trails, and the CFTC and Congress are now proposing restrictions on dual trading. It is doubtful, however, whether those efforts will effectively prevent the type of conduct at issue in the Chicago sting operation because many of the practices at issue in the operation did not involve dual trading. Further, the transactions at issue were often accomplished shortly before or after the close of trading, when timing is most difficult.

NOTES

1. Section 4c of the Commodity Exchange Act of 1936 (7 U.S.C. § 6c) prohibits certain improper trading practices such as "wash" sales, "accommodation" trades and "fictitious" trades. Section 747 of the Dodd–Frank Wall Street Reform and Consumer Protection Act of 2010 expanded those prohibited trading activities to include other "disruptive" trading such as "spoofing" (bidding or offering with the intent to cancel the bid or offer before execution), violating bids and offers and any other trading action that "demonstrates intentional or reckless disregard for the orderly execution of transactions during the closing period." Section 747 also authorizes the CFTC to promulgate rules that would prohibit "any other trading practice that is disruptive of fair and equitable trading."

2. The CFTC continues to prosecute improper trading practices by floor traders, even though they are a dying breed as the result of electronic trading. See e.g., In the Matter of ConAgra Trade Group Inc. (firm agrees to pay $12 million to settle charges that one of its floor traders disrupted the crude oil futures market by engaging in a stunt to push that market over $100 per barrel for the first time in history); In the Matter of Moore Capital Management, LP, CFTC Doc. No. 10–09 (C.F.T.C. 2010) (respondent was "banging the close"). In *In the Matter of DiPlacido*, Comm. Fut. L. Rep. (CCH) ¶ 30,970 (C.F.T.C. 2008), *aff'd sub nom., DiPlacido v. CFTC*, 364 Fed. Appx. 657, *cert. denied*, ___ U.S. ___, 130 S.Ct. 1883, 176 L.Ed.2d 399 (2010), the Second Circuit found manipulative activity where a floor trader was seeking an "ugly" close, and traded through the orders of other market participants by violating bids and offers.

3. The growth of electronic trading is gradually reducing the role of floor traders and many trading floors have been shuttered in favor of electronic trading. See Jerry W. Markham and Daniel J. Harty, For Whom the Bell Tolls: The Demise of Exchange Trading Floors and the Growth of ECNs, 33 J. Corp. L. 865 (2008). This migration has reduced floor trader fraud, but there are still some trading abuses even on electronic exchanges. See *In re Lui*, Comm. Fut. L. Rep. (CCH) ¶ 30,491 (C.F.T.C. 2007), where the CFTC, by consent, imposed sanctions against a respondent for knowingly and illegally prearranging trades on the Globex electronic trading platform at the Chicago Mercantile Exchange. The respondent was trading several of his customer accounts against each other, resulting in profits for the favored customers on one side of the trades and losses to customers on the other side. Electronic trading poses other dangers such as the "fat finger" syndrome in which a larger than sought order is entered by mistake. Computer systems may also malfunction. The London Stock Exchange's computers malfunctioned on September 8, 2008, and traders were frozen out of that market, which was rallying, for more than seven hours. The Toronto Stock Exchange was closed on December 17, 2008, because of computer problems, and the Globex electronic market was shut down for over three hours on December 24, 2008. On September 14, 2010, the Chicago Mercantile Exchange entered some 30,000 test trades by mistake into the live energy and metals markets, causing a drop in prices.

SECTION 6. DEREGULATION AND SINGLE STOCK FUTURES[8]

The Commodity Futures Modernization Act of 2000 (the "CFMA"), Pub. Law 106–554, 114 Stat 2763 (December 21, 2000), introduced dramatic changes in futures market regulation. For the first time in the history of federal futures law, trading away from the regulated markets is now permissible. The previous ban on securities based futures contracts has been lifted. That massive overhaul of commodities markets regulation resulted in a three-tiered layer of regulation for those markets. The highest degree of regulation remains with the designated contract markets where retail futures trading takes place in the more traditional commodities products including agricultural commodities. There is virtually no regulation for off-exchange principal-to-principal transactions among institutions or sophisticated and wealthy investors that fall within the statutory concept of eligible contract participants ("ECPs"), consisting of institutional and highly accredited customers. ECPs include financial institutions, insurance companies, registered investment companies; corporations, partnerships, trusts, and other entities having total assets exceeding $10,000,000, employee benefit plans subject to ERISA that have total assets exceeding $5,000,000; governmental entities, as well as some other categories of investors. Commodity Exchange Act § 1a(12), 7 U.S.C. § 1a(12), CFMA § 101.

The CFMA abolished the former contract market monopoly for commodities futures and options contracts that prohibited the trading of those contracts other than on an organized exchange. The Act thus permits, for the first time, over-the-counter markets for commodities futures and options. The Act also introduced a new category of futures markets for certain commodities-based products. This new category of commodities market is open not to retail investors generally (unless participating through a registered futures commission merchant) but rather is open only to specified qualified investors or other investors who trade through a futures commission merchant. This new market was created by the Modernization Act's new category known as a derivatives transaction execution facility ("DTEF").

The CFMA permits the trading of futures contracts on single stocks and narrow-based security indices. These transactions are referred to as stock futures and had been previously prohibited by a jurisdictional agreement between the CFTC and the SEC. These products may be traded on either securities or futures exchanges, and the SEC and CFTC are directed by the CFMA to coordinate their regulatory oversight over such products. A stock future is defined as a security, which makes the Securities Exchange Act of 1934 generally applicable to their operations.

---

8. The material in this section is drawn from 23 Jerry W. Markham & Thomas Lee Hazen, Broker–Dealer Operations Under Securities and Commodities Law § 3:11, § 8:24 & 10:16.1 (2d ed.2003).

Securities futures can be traded only on common stock registered under Section 12 of the Securities Exchange Act of 1934, which subjects them to periodic reporting requirements of the SEC.

Securities futures may be traded either on a national securities exchange or a contract market, but in either case the exchange must be cross-registered with the other regulator. The CFTC and the SEC adopted joint regulations concerning listing standards for securities exchanges and associations trading securities futures products. Securities broker-dealers were allowed to register by notice with the CFTC as futures commission merchants or introducing brokers, but their involvement was limited to trading securities futures products. This "passport" concept is also applied to investment advisers and commodity trading advisers. An investment adviser is given an exemption under the Investment Advisers Act, where they are solely providing advice as to securities futures. Normally investment advisers are exempted from the Commodity Exchange Act. Cross-registration is also applied to investment companies and commodity pools, but it appears that it primarily has to be an investment company that would be cross-registered as a commodity pool. "Dual" trading (in which floor brokers also act as floor traders) is prohibited in trading single stock futures, but floor brokers and floor traders trading stock futures on a futures exchange are exempted from the registration requirements and other provisions of the Securities Exchange Act of 1934.

The National Futures Association ("NFA") was allowed to adopt streamlined securities requirements and be designated as a national securities association. The NFA was required by the CFMA to conform its customer protection rules to those in the securities industry in order for stock futures to be traded by futures industry markets and registrants. Among other things, the NFA adopted provisions to make its rules closely conform to securities industry suitability requirements, including a prohibition against making unsuitable recommendations.

The CFMA amended Section 7(c) of the Securities Exchange Act of 1934 to provide the Federal Reserve Board with authority to set margin requirements for futures on individual securities and narrow based indexes. The Federal Reserve Board delegated this rule making authority jointly to the CFTC and the SEC. The SEC and CFTC, thereafter proposed margin rules for these products. The statutory amendments required such margin to be not lower than the lowest level of margin required for comparable options contract traded on national securities exchanges. Rules adopted by the CFTC and SEC established a minimal initial and maintenance margin level of twenty percent of the current market value of the position. 17 C.F.R. § 242.403. The rule would allow lower margin for positions that are offset by positions in derivatives. This twenty percent level is far in excess of the normal margin requirements for futures contracts in the commodity futures industry, where margins are often less than five percent of the value of the contract. In proposing these rules, the SEC and CFTC noted that listed options have margin requirements of twenty percent for short sellers. The purchaser of an option on stock is generally required to pay the full amount of the premium. The CFTC and SEC required both the purchasers and sellers of stock futures to be subject to a twenty percent margin requirement.

The CFTC and the SEC adopted rules that permit customers of futures commission merchants and broker-dealers to choose whether securities futures products (single stock futures and futures on narrow based indices) will be held in a futures account subject to Commodity Exchange Act segregation requirements or in a securities account subject to Rule 15c3–3 and the Securities Investor Protection Association insurance provisions. Customers electing segregation treatment under the Commodity Exchange Act will not have any account insurance protection. Conversely, customers holding such positions in a broker-dealer would have such protection. Firms are required to furnish a disclosure document to customers that provide a general description of the protection afforded futures accounts under the Commodity Exchange Act and securities accounts under the federal securities laws. The firm would have to advise the customer whether the security futures products would be held in a futures account or in a securities account.

Single stock futures trading has not enjoyed much success in the United States. Most futures contracts have initial margins of less than five percent of the notional amount of the contract. However, the SEC mandated a margin of twenty percent for single stock futures. The result was to discourage trading in single stock futures in the United States. Rather, South Africa now hosts the largest single stock futures exchange. Jerry W. Markham, Merging the SEC and CFTC—A Clash of Cultures, 78 U. Cinn. L. Rev. 537, 597 (2009).

The CFTC had mandated a single page risk disclosure document for futures contracts it regulates as a substitute for the "suitability" doctrine imposed by the SEC. However, the SEC concluded that traders in single stock futures needed both the protection of a suitability requirement and additional disclosures. As one author noted:

> The CFTC had mandated a single page risk disclosure document for futures contracts it regulates as a substitute for the "suitability" doctrine imposed by the SEC. However, the SEC concluded that traders in single stock futures needed both the protection of a suitability requirements and additional disclosures. Perhaps, the SEC thought that traders of such products are particularly stupid people. The result was a twenty-six page disclosure statement, rather than the single page disclosure form used for all other futures contracts.

Lawrence Hunt Jr., The Paulson Report is a Non–Starter, 67 Financier World Wide 53 (July 2008).

Single stock futures did prove useful during the subprime crisis in 2008 when the SEC suspended shot sales in the stocks of financial services firms. Those traders were still able effectively to short those stocks on OneChicago, the largest single stock futures exchange in the United

States. See Jerry W. Markham, A Financial History of the United States, From the Subprime Crisis to the Great Recession (2006–2009) 531 (2011).

NOTES

The CFMA also symbolized a growing concern that United States exchanges were becoming less competitive and that the exchange trading requirement in the Commodity Exchange Act was causing derivatives business to migrate abroad. The open outcry system of trading also was under challenge with the growth of the Internet and electronic trading facilities. European exchanges began trading futures electronically and their volume rose rapidly. The Chicago commodity exchanges created something called Globex that allowed limited electronic order execution outside normal trading hours. The members of American commodity exchanges, however, resisted broader electronic trading because they did not want to forfeit their time and place advantage on the trading floor. As a result, the American commodity exchanges lost their leadership role in futures trading.

The Eurex, an electronic futures exchange in Germany, became the world's largest futures exchange, displacing the Chicago exchanges from that position at the end of the twentieth century. The Chicago Board of Trade and Chicago Mercantile Exchange agreed to merge in October 2006 in order to meet this competitive threat. However, before that merger could be completed, the IntercontinentalExchange ("ICE") made an unsolicited offer to buy the Chicago Board of Trade. ICE is an Atlanta based electronic trading platform for energy products. Tom Walker, IntercontinentalExchange to Buy Commodity-trading Platform; Transactions Estimated at $150 Billion a Year, Atlanta Journal–Constitution, June 5, 2007, at 1D. ICE lost that fight. The Chicago Mercantile Exchange also subsequently merged with the New York Mercantile Exchange, giving it control of all but a very small share of futures trading in the United States. Efforts to establish competing exchanges in recent years have failed. See Jerry W. Markham, A Financial History of the United States, From Enron Era Scandals to the Subprime Crisis (2004–2006) 190, 215–217 (2011).

JERRY W. MARKHAM & DANIEL J. HARTY
FOR WHOM THE BELL TOLLS: THE DEMISE OF EXCHANGE TRADING FLOORS AND THE GROWTH OF ECNS

33 J. Corp. L. 865 (2008).

The colorful "open outcry" trading in the "pits" of the Chicago futures exchanges and the bell-ringing opening of trading on the floor of the New York Stock Exchange (NYSE) has long dominated the public perception of how those markets operate. However, exchange trading floors are fast fading into history because the trading of stocks and derivative instruments are moving to electronic communications networks

(ECNs) that simply match trades by computers through algorithms at incredibly high speeds and volumes. Competition from ECNs has already forced the NYSE and the Chicago futures and options exchanges to demutualize, consolidate, and reduce the role of their trading floors, while expanding their own electronic execution facilities.[9] * * *

The ECNs arrived in force in the financial markets beginning in the early 1990s in the form of automated trading systems for institutional traders in the third [off-exchange] market. In some ways they were actually a creation of the exchanges' efforts to automate. "Electronic trading" encompasses a wide range of systems that facilitate the entry and execution of orders electronically by algorithms. * * * Some commentators view the development of trade-matching algorithms as the democratization of the financial markets. They suggest that the adoption of algorithms replaces the "privileged market access," conferred by open outcry trading and permits exchanges to differentiate between each order, let alone between members and non-members. * * * Participants in these new ventures soon learned the benefits of electronic trading systems and order matching algorithms. These benefits include the reduction in costs and trading errors, enhancement of operational efficiencies, and benefits associated with risk management. All of the major algorithms share some common characteristics. In particular, they provide for the anonymity of market users, something more difficult to disguise when traders stand face-to-face. Algorithms that survive the exchange development and consolidation phase will strike the right balance of fundamental qualities important to users: anonymity, speed, capacity, and stability. * * *

The open outcry trading systems on the futures exchanges' floors were clearly being overwhelmed as the new century began. Responding to those competitive threats, the CME and CBOT merged their clearing operations in 2003, and both the CME (in 2002) and the CBOT (in 2005) demutualized and became public companies. Still, the percentage of open outcry trades declined between 2000 and 2007 from 90% to 22%. Recognizing that the end was near, the CBOT and CME merged all of their operations in 2007. * * * After their merger, the CME and CBOT announced that they were consolidating their trading floors and would be

---

9. As one author has noted:

With increased competition caused by deregulation, technological advances, and globalization, the organization of stock exchanges is at a crossroads. Traditionally, stock exchanges were organized as not-for-profit organizations, founded and owned by brokers and dealers who managed "their" stock exchange like an exclusive club, with high barriers for new entrants and a regional or even national monopoly, comparable to a medieval gild [sic]. Today, domestic and international competition increasingly compel stock exchanges to give up their exclusivity, undergo restructuring, and become publicly traded for-profit companies, a process referred to as demutualization.

Andreas M. Fleckner, Stock Exchanges at the Crossroads, 74 Fordham L. Rev. 2541, 2541–42 (2006). See generally Roberta S. Karmel, Turning Seats Into Shares: Causes and Implications of Demutualization of Stock and Futures Exchanges, 53 Hastings L.J. 367 (2002) (discussing the implications of exchange demutualizations). Another demutalization occurred on the Chicago Board Options Exchange Inc. in the summer of 2010. Lynn Cowan, New Offerings Take a Holiday, Wall St. J., June 21, 2010 at C6.

shifting several contracts to their electronic trading platform (Globex), including agricultural products.[10] * * *

SECTION 7. STOCK OPTIONS TRADING

CHICAGO BOARD OPTIONS EXCHANGE, INC. LEARNING CENTER

www.cboe.com (visited March 9, 2003).

The Basics

You buy or trade stocks, bonds and mutual funds. Perhaps you invest in a 401(k) plan. You've come to www.cboe.com for information and education about options and how they can be used as part of your short or long term investment objectives. Did you know you may be using a form of options as part of your everyday life? Do you pay a premium every quarter for house, auto, and medical insurance? You have purchased insurance as a safeguard against a fire in your home, a crash in your car, or large medical bills. Some investors use options on stocks or cash indexes to protect and insure the value of their portfolios.

A major advantage of options is their versatility. They can be as conservative or as speculative as your investing strategy dictates. Options enable you to tailor your position to your own set of circumstances. Consider the following benefits of options:

! You can protect stock holdings from a decline in market price

! You can increase income against current stock holding

! You can prepare to buy a stock at a lower price

! You can position yourself for a big market move even when you don't know which way prices will move

! You can benefit from a stock price rise without incurring the cost of buying the stock outright * * *

How Options Work

Much like stocks, options can be used to take a position on the market in an effort to capitalize on an upward or downward market move. Unlike stocks, however, options can provide an investor the benefits of leverage

---

10. Pit Trading to End for Pork Bellies And Selected Products in Chicago, N.Y. Times, Aug. 29, 2007, at C7. The CME website now notes that:

> The CME open outcry platform and trading floor systems are linked to the CME® Globex® electronic trading platform, which allows market participants to buy and sell whether they're sitting at trading booths on our Chicago trading floors, working at offices or homes thousands of miles away, or making trades during and after regular trading hours. At CME, some traders prefer face-to-face interaction on the CME trading floors while an increasing number prefer to trade electronically.

CME, Open Outcry to eTrading, http://www.cme.com/about/ins/caag/index.html (last visited Oct. 21, 2007).

over a position in an individual stock or basket of stocks reflecting the broad market. At the same time, options buyers also can take advantage of predetermined, limited risk. Conversely, options writers assume significant risk if they do not hedge their positions.

An option is the right, but not the obligation, to buy or sell a stock (or other security) for a specified price on or before a specific date. A call is the right to buy the stock, while a put is the right to sell the stock. The person who purchases an option, whether it is a put or a call, is the option "buyer." Conversely, the person who originally sells the put or call is the option "seller."

Options are contracts in which the terms of the contract are standardized and give the buyer the right, but not the obligation, to buy or sell a particular asset (e.g., the underlying stock) at a fixed price (the strike price) for a specific period of time (until expiration). To the buyer, an equity call option normally represents the right to buy 100 shares of underlying stock, whereas an equity put option normally represents the right to sell 100 shares of underlying stock. The seller of an option is obligated to perform according to the terms of the options contract— selling the stock at the contracted price (the strike price) for a call seller, or purchasing it for a put seller—if the option is exercised by the buyer. All option contracts trade on U.S. securities exchanges are issued, guaranteed and cleared by the Options Clearing Corporation (OCC). OCC is a registered clearing corporation with the SEC and has received "AAA" credit rating form Standard & Poor's Corporation. The "AAA" credit rating corresponds to OCC's ability to fulfill its obligations as counterparty for options trades.

The price of an option is called its "premium." The potential loss to the buyer of an option can be no greater than the initial premium paid for the contract, regardless of the performance of the underlying stock. This allows an investor to control the amount of risk assumed. On the contrary, the seller of the option, in return for the premium received from the buyer, assumes the risk of being assigned if the contract is exercised. In accordance with the standardized terms of their contracts, all options expire on a certain date, called the "expiration date." For conventional listed options, this can be up to nine months from the date the options are first listed for trading. There are longer-term option contracts, called LEAPS, which can have expiration dates up to three years from the date of the listing. Harrison Roth, LEAPS, What they Are and How to Use Them For Profit vii (1994).

American-style options (the most commonly traded) and European-style options possess different regulations relating to expiration and the exercising of an option. An American-style option is an option contract that may be exercised at any time between the date of purchase and the expiration date. Conversely, a European-style option (used primarily with cash settled options) can only be exercised during a specified period of time just prior to expiration.

Call Options

The buyer of an equity call option has purchased the right to buy 100 shares of the underlying stock at the stated exercise price. Thus, the buyer of one XYZ June 110 call option has the right to purchase 100 shares of XYZ at $110 up until June expiration. The buyer may do so by filing an exercise notice through his broker or trading firm to the Options Clearing Corporation prior to the expiration date of the option. All calls covering XYZ are referred to as an "option class." Each individual option with a distinctive trading month and strike price is an "option series." The XYZ June 110 calls would be an individual series.

Put Options

The buyer of a put option has purchased the right to sell the number of shares of the underlying stock at the contracted exercise price. Thus, the buyer of one ZYX June 50 put has the right to sell 100 shares of ZYX at $50 any time prior to the expiration date. In order to exercise the option and sell the underlying at the agreed upon exercise price, the buyer must file a proper exercise notice with the OCC through a broker before the date of expiration. All puts covering ZYX stock are referred to as an "option class." Each individual option with a distinctive trading month and strike price is an "option series." The ZYX June 50 puts would be an individual series.

How You Can Use Options

If you anticipate a certain directional movement in the price of a stock, the right to buy or sell that stock at a predetermined price, for a specific duration of time can offer an attractive investment opportunity. The decision as to what type of option to buy is dependent on whether your outlook for the respective security is positive (bullish) or negative (bearish). If your outlook is positive, buying a call option creates the opportunity to share in the upside potential of a stock without having to risk more than a fraction of its market value. Conversely, if you anticipate downward movement, buying a put option will enable you to protect against downside risk without limiting profit potential. Purchasing options offer you the ability to position yourself accordingly with your market expectations in a manner such that you can both profit and protect with limited risk.

NOTES

1. A "capped" option has a limited profit potential. "FLEX" options allow large traders to negotiate the terms of the option, which is not possible for other exchange traded options that have standardized terms for everything but the premium, which is negotiated.

2. Exchange traded stock options are listed in series with varying expiration dates, providing flexibility in pricing and trading strategies, of

which there are many. Some common strategies include "spreads" or "straddles" in which the trader may, for example, buy a put and call on the same security. The nature of such trading is quite complex and includes the following types of spreads: "box," "delta," "butterfly," "diagonal horizontal," and "ratio calendar." For definitions of these trading practices see www.cboe.com (glossary).

3.   The pricing of the option premium is quite a complicated process. Its value will depend on a number of factors including the time until expiration, and the volatility of the stock: "beta," *i.e.*, how the stock's price correlates to the entire market. One popular options pricing model, "Black–Scholes," was innovative enough to win its creators a Nobel price in economics.

4.   The secondary market on the CBOE allows option traders to close out their positions without having to actually exercise their option. Instead an offsetting transaction is entered into by the trader. The purchaser of call option will thus have a gain or loss equal to the difference between the exercise price and the market price of the underlying security less the premium and any transaction costs. This allows the trader to avoid the larger transaction and other costs that would be incurred if the option were exercised by buying and then reselling the underlying security.

JERRY W. MARKHAM & DAVID J. GILBERG
STOCK AND COMMODITY OPTIONS—TWO REGULATORY APPROACHES AND THEIR CONFLICTS

47 Albany Law Review 741–791 (1983).

Until 1973, stock option trading was generally limited to executive compensation plans and individualized transactions conducted over the counter and to members of the New York Stock Exchange and its Association of Member Firm Option Departments. The latter were not large markets, principally because of the difficulty of bringing buyers and sellers together and having all parties agree on the terms of the options. Moreover, there was no "secondary" market for stock options, which often precluded a party to the option agreement from liquidating the right or obligation before its expiration. These problems were eliminated, however, in 1973 with the advent of "listed" stock options on the CBOE, a concept created by a special committee of the Board of Trade of the City of Chicago (Chicago Board of Trade), a commodity futures exchange. That committee had been appointed to study the feasibility of applying commodity futures trading principles to options on securities, "to develop *futures contracts* in securities."

Exchange listed options standardized the terms of option contracts and created an auction market, as well as a secondary market, where option buyers and sellers could competitively bid for and offset their positions by opposite transactions, thereby granting flexibility and liquidity to option traders. Standardization was further effected by using a single buyer and seller for each transaction, the CBOE Clearing Corporation, later renamed the Options Clearing Corporation (OCC). The OCC is the ultimate writer and holder of each option, a concept that was also borrowed from commodity futures trading. * * *

[Each] trade is confirmed with the OCC which becomes the seller of the contract to the customer. The opposite side of the transaction is also formally undertaken by the OCC in that it intercedes between the customer and the opposite party, the market maker or other customer who was the writer of the contract. Consequently, the obligation of the seller of a call option to deliver stock upon payment of the exercise price runs to the OCC, and the OCC is obligated to pay him the exercise price if the option is exercised. The buyer of a call option is obligated to pay the OCC the exercise price if he chooses to exercise, and the OCC is then obligated to [obtain the stock from the writer and to deliver it to the purchaser].

This system offers several advantages to investors. For example, for a low premium, a call option holder may obtain a great deal of leverage and can profit from that leverage by price changes in stock, with liability limited to the premium cost. A writer owning the stock, on the other hand, can obtain additional income from stockholdings during periods when the writer does not expect the stock to increase in value.

Following the CBOE's market creating, other security exchanges sought entry into this new field. The American Stock Exchange (Amex) was the first, later to be followed by others. The exchanges initially traded call options, but later added put options as well.

Stock options, albeit non-exchange listed options, were at the center of the Congressional investigations that followed the stock market crash of 1929. It was found that "[t]he granting of options to pool syndicates has been ... at the bottom of most manipulative [stock] operations, because the granting of these options permits large-scale manipulations t be conducted with a minimum of financial risk to the manipulators."

In order to eliminate such abuses, the initial drafts of the legislation that ultimately led to the enactment of the Securities Exchange Act of 1934 proposed to ban all forms of stock options contracts. The Committee of Put and Call Brokers and Dealers in the City of New York argued, however, that stock options had been traded successfully for over two hundred years, and that they should not be banned because they served important functions in the securities markets. Stock options offered "assurance against loss"; they had a "stabilizing quality"; and they "afforded the operator of moderate means [an opportunity] to protect a position in the market at a minimum risk," thereby serving as "insurance" in a manner similar to "hedging" operations which guard against price changes in commodity futures trading.

As a result of this testimony, the Securities Exchange Act of 1934, as adopted, did not ban options, but rather subjected them to the rulemaking authority of the SEC under Section 9 of the Securities Exchange Act of 1934. No rules were adopted by the SEC under that authority, however, until the creation of the CBOE, when Rule 9b–1 was adopted. That rule prohibited options trading on any exchange except in accordance with a plan regulating options trading approved by the SEC. The rule also permitted the SEC to require changes in approved options plans and to disapprove amendments to such plans. In adopting this rule, the SEC stressed that option trading on exchanges was on a "pilot basis" only and that the flexible regulatory control permitted by Rule 9b–1 was necessary because of the novelty of exchange option trading, and because such trading might involve complex problems and pose special risks to investors and to the integrity of the marketplace. In granting the CBOE application to trade options, the SEC emphasized that it was recognizing the CBOE as an "experimental project," a "test market," and the SEC cautioned that it would maintain close surveillance over its progress.

Several trading innovations and regulatory safeguards were adopted by the CBOE as a part of this pilot program. For example, the CBOE clearing corporation (which was the issuer of the options) agreed to comply with the registration provisions of the Securities Act of 1933. This resulted in the dissemination of prospectuses to each customer effecting transactions in options through the options exchanges—at an annual cost of some 1.2 million dollars.

The CBOE agreed with the SEC to limit the number of the stocks it would initially trade options on and agreed to expand trading gradually. The CBOE also provided in its rules that the securities underlying its options must be registered and listed on another national securities exchange and have broad distribution and volume characteristics. These rules were designed to preclude an adverse effect on the market in the underlying security. CBOE rules additionally imposed limits on the number of options reporting requirements for large traders. These limit requirements, alien to the securities markets generally, parallel provisions utilized by commodity futures exchanges and the CFTC under the Commodity Exchange Act.

Before allowing the Amex to trade, however, the SEC decided to restrict the expansion of the CBOE and the entry of Amex into the market until they sufficiently "addressed," among other SEC concerns, the following areas: "development of programs [for] common clearing; dissemination of last-sale price data; standardized options terms; availability of options quotations; and appropriate regulatory controls relating to trading in "away-from-the-money options."

In addressing these issues, the exchanges proposed to use clearing principles and contracted standardization methods substantially identical to those already in use by the CBOE. The Amex, however, proposed to use its unitary specialist system, which does not segregate the functions of broker and dealer. The CBOE and Amex also agreed to a proposal whereby the CBOE Clearing Corporation was renamed the OCC and became owned jointly by Amex and the CBOE and other exchanges which later traded options.

The CBOE and Amex also proposed a plan for a common options tape and public reporting of last-sale information. This plan established the Option Price Reporting Authority (OPRA), which was directed to establish "a separate common option tape on the floor of both exchanges" and to disseminate "option last-sale date from these exchanges to vendors of automated interrogation devices." The SEC approved these proposals in principle and approved the options program of the Amex on an "experimental basis."

With the rapid growth and widespread interest in stock options, however, abuses were discovered which precipitated enforcement actions by both the exchanges and the SEC. In one such case, the SEC instituted an administrative proceeding and injunctive actions as the result of its discovery of the reporting of fictitious options transactions on the Amex in the spring of 1976. These proceedings involved a total of nineteen registered Amex specialists.

These and other abuses were of serious concern to the SEC. Indeed, from the inception of exchange listed stock option trading, the SEC closely monitored its progress and watched for abuses and adverse economic effects. Thus, in a study conducted in 1973, the SEC first sought to determine whether options should be traded on more than one exchange and, if so, whether uniform procedures should be required. The study also examined the economic functions of options trading; the nature of the participation (small, institutional and others); the effects of options trading on the underlying securities markets; and whether there should be limits on the outstanding number of option contracts and the terms of option contracts. The SEC's study also sought to determine whether the traditional exchange specialist system should be permitted in connection with option trading or whether the innovation adopted by the CBOE for the separation of the broker-dealer function by a competitive market marker system should be employed.

The SEC did not reach any immediate conclusions from this study, but it did continue its stringent regulation of the options exchanges.

NOTES

1. The CBOE started options trading on just 16 stocks. Twenty years later, options were being traded on over 1,000 stocks through over thirty exchanges worldwide. Harrison Roth, LEAPS, What they Are and How to Use Them For Profit vii (1994).

2. Competition from an electronic stock exchange, the Internet stock exchange, also affected the options markets. The Boston Options Exchange became all-electronic, and the AMEX began electronic trading in its options in 2004. The CBOE was forced to develop a new electronic exchange called "C2."

3. A holder of a call option faces what kinds of risks? What are the risks to a short seller of a call option? How do those risks differ with a put option?

BELENKE v. SECURITIES AND EXCHANGE COMMISSION

606 F.2d 193 (7th Cir.1979).

SWYGERT, CIRCUIT JUDGE.

This is a proceeding on a petition for review of an order of the Securities and Exchange Commission ("SEC") entered January 11, 1979 approving an amendment to the rules of the Chicago Board Options Exchange, Inc. ("CBOE") pursuant to section 19(b) of the Securities Exchange Act of 1934, as amended. 15 U.S.C. § 78s(b). Petitioners are eighteen members of the CBOE appointed to serve as board brokers who have joined together as the Board Brokers Association ("BBA") to pursue this claim. They contend that the order must be set side because the SEC failed to follow the appropriate procedures when it approved the amendments to the CBOE's rules and because these amendments are inconsistent with the requirements of the Act.

The CBOE was organized in 1973 as a Delaware nonstock corporation to provide an exchange on which options contracts in various common stocks could be traded. As a securities exchange, it is subject to the self-regulatory responsibilities imposed by the Securities Exchange Act of 1934, primarily under section 6(b). 15 U.S.C. § 78f(b).

Prior to the approval of the proposal question, the members of the CBOE could act in one of three capacities: as a market maker, a floor broker, or a board broker. A market maker buys and sells options strictly for his own account, whereas a floor broker acts solely as an agent, earning commissions by executing orders for others. A member can be registered both as a market maker and as a floor broker but cannot act as both with respect to the same underlying security on the same business day. A board broker also performs functions as an agent, but deals only in specified classes of options for which he has been given an exclusive appointment to maintain the public limit order book. A "limit order" is an order to buy or sell an option at a specified price in contrast to a "market order" to buy or sell at the prevailing price. If the prevailing price and the specified price differ, a limit order cannot be executed immediately. Rather than hold a limit order indefinitely, the floor brokers may, for a fee, place such orders in the board broker's book to be executed when the specified price is reached. Orders placed in these books have priority over other orders at the same price.

With the goal of achieving maximum efficiency in the maintenance of its public limit order books, the CBOE submitted a proposal to the SEC on July 28, 1978. The proposal involved replacing the board brokers with

CBOE employees, Order Book Officials ("OBOs"), compensated at a fixed rate. The CBOE believed that such direct control over this service would better meet the needs of its member firms and their customers. More specifically, under the plan the CBOE would be able to take action against those OBOs with insufficient staff and to transfer option classes from one OBO to another to accommodate flow stress or floor congestion. The board broker system provided the CBOE with little flexibility to take such action.

Upon the filing of the CBOE rule changes, the SEC, pursuant to section 19(b) (1) of the Act, provided notice and the opportunity for written comment on the proposals. The BBA filed extensive written comments in opposition to the proposals, in which they raised many of the objections they raise in this petition. The BBA contended that the Securities Exchange Act prohibited the CBOE from maintaining an OBO-type plan; that the plan would reduce the efficiency of floor transactions and compromise the self-regulatory responsibilities of the CBOE; and that the proposals would frustrate competition and unfairly discriminate against CBOE members acting as board brokers. The BBA also asserted that the proposal constituted the fixing of commission rates thereby requiring hearings pursuant to section 6(e) of the Act prior to their approval.

After consideration of the proposal and the written comments submitted regarding it, the SEC concluded that the amendments to the CBOE's rules were consistent with the requirements of the Securities Exchange Act. Accordingly, on January 11, 1979, the SEC issued an approval order pursuant to section 19(b) (2). This order determined, with supporting reasoning, that nothing in the Act prohibited the plan; that the proposal did not trigger the procedural requirements of section 6(e); that it would not reduce the CBOE's self-regulatory capacity; that it would not unfairly discriminate against board brokers; and that the plan would not impose inappropriate burdens upon competition. * * *

Petitioners contend that the SEC violated the procedures required by the Securities Exchange Act by failing to make an independent determination that the OBO rules were consistent with the requirements of the Act. The SEC approval order, to which petitioners give such short shrift, See supra 195–196 n.1, belies this argument. The Order responds to the written objections submitted by petitioners and explains its finding that the proposed rule changes were consistent with the terms of the Act, with particular reference to sections 6(b)(1), 6(b)(5), 11A(a)(1)(C)(i), 11A(a)(1)(C)(ii) and 19(g)(1) of the Act.

Petitioners also argue that the "record" before the SEC did not contain "substantial evidence" to support its decision that the factual premises were inadequate for the SEC's conclusion. This argument ignores the character of the procedures Congress established for SEC review of rule changes proposed by self-regulatory organizations. A detailed factual record is not required in this context. * * *

[P]etitioners' contention that the SEC's order was arbitrary and capricious with respect to the competition issue is [also] untenable. The order fulfilled its statutory responsibility by analyzing the OBO proposal and demonstrating that specific statutory purposes would be served by it. See, supra, 198. For example, the SEC order stated:

> The Commission finds that the CBOE's proposal to assume responsibility for maintenance of the limit order book as an Exchange-offered service should enable the Exchange to standardize further the operation of all limit order books, to deploy its employees efficiently from stations of light volume to stations of heavy volume in response to shifting market conditions and to hire additional staff to meet additional market demands.

SEC Approval Order, p. 14. And the SEC balanced the goal of competition with other goals that would be served by the proposal which is all that is required by section 6(b)(8), the most specific statutory requirement regarding competition:

> The Commission believes that the CBOE proposal does not impose any burden upon competition not necessary or appropriate in furtherance of the purposes of the Act, but rather furthers the public policy goals of enhancing the potential for competition among markets as set forth under the Act. To the extent that centralization of limit order book services in the CBOE may impose any specific burden on competition, the Commission finds that any potential anti-competitive effect is outweighed by the CBOE proposal's furtherance of the purposes of the Act in fostering economically efficient executions of securities transactions, and by enhancing the regulatory capabilities of the CBOE to monitor and enforce compliance by its members with the Act, rules thereunder, and rules of the Exchange.

Id. at 22 * * *

Accordingly, the order of the Commission is affirmed.

NOTES

1. The trading system on the CBOE is a hybrid of the auction style of trading in the commodity markets and the specialist system used on the stock exchanges. The specialist's functions were split between the market makers and the Order Book Officials ("OBO"). The OBO assumed the specialist's duty of maintaining the book of limit orders, while the market makers assumed the duty of maintaining a continuous and orderly market. Unlike the specialist system, there are competing market makers on the floor of the CBOE. Nevertheless, the CBOE may designate one market maker as "primary":

> The CBOE and OCC have disseminated a good deal of information to the public in order to solicit business. These defendants maintain a website,

http://www.cboe.com, with information about the options, the trading systems, market information, tips on strategy, and free software. This website material represents that CBOE order handling, routing, and execution systems "guarantee our customers the fastest and most equitable transactions." Two documents, one dated April 30, 1997, that the OCC identifies as a "prospectus," and another headed with the CBOE logo and available on the Internet, titled *Characteristics and Risks of Standardized Options*, which is furnished to investors as required by law, state that the CBOE ordinarily becomes obligated to accept an option transaction on the next business day if reported in a timely way, and that premiums for multiply traded options may differ across markets. An investor may therefore buy a multiply-listed option on the CBOE and offset his position on another exchange.

The CBOE also published an information booklet called *Welcome to the Chicago Board Options Exchange* (the "*Welcome* booklet") representing that all equity options are traded under the "Designated Primary Market Maker" ("DPM") system to ensure a fair and orderly, continuous, two-sided market. DPMs are individuals designated to "make" the markets by trading in certain specific ways. The *Welcome* booklet states that DPMs determine the formula for generating automatically generated market quotations, that the system that disseminates the quotations is accurate, and that DPMs must participate at all times in any automated execution system that may be open, and, moreover, are present at the trading post through the business day, and, with respect to their trades as market makers, effect trades that correlate well with the overall trading pattern for each series in the options classes involved. The *Welcome* booklet states that if a DPM quotes a price that matches the order of a floor broker's customer, "a trade occurs." CBOE Rule 8.51 states that a "firm quote requirement generally applies at all times" and "obligates the trading crowd to sell (buy) at least the established number of contracts at the offer (bid) which is displayed when an ... order reaches the trading station."

The CBOE has also developed an electronic order execution system called the Retail Automatic Execution System ("RAES"). Literature available on the CBOE website says that orders "that fall within designated premium levels, contract size, and series parameters are guaranteed a fill at the current market bid and offer." The DPMs are authorized to deactivate RAES, thus preventing a trade from being executed automatically, in only two circumstances. The first is if floor conditions become too heavy. In that case, the floor brokers can use a "Public Automated Routing System" ("PAR") to execute trades. This is a PC-based touch-screen, order routing and execution system that allows brokers to present a customer order to DPMs and other market makers. It also allows DPMs to determine the identity of a retail customer or his clearing house before executing the trade. When RAES is deactivated because of heavy trading, the floor brokers can send all their orders from their PAR workstations to an automated customer order book known as the "Electronic Book" ("EBOOK") that automatically sorts and files trades in price and time sequence. The other circumstance in which

CBOE represents that RAES may be deactivated is when a competing exchange offers a better price on a multiply-listed option, in which case the order is printed in the public order book and announced to the trading crowd for execution. CBOE rule 6.8 requires market markers to sell/buy a customer's RAES order.

Cathedral Trading, LLC v. Chicago Board Options Exchange, 199 F.Supp.2d 851 (N.D.Ill.2002).

2. The American and Philadelphia exchanges also trade stock options, but they use their specialist systems for that trading. An experiment to trade options on the New York Stock Exchange did not succeed but a subsequent venture, NYSE Arca, and the acquisition of the options trading of the Amex, a long time CBOE competitor, gained some traction. The NYSE was the third largest options exchange for U.S. equities in 2010. http://www.nyse.com/futuresoptions/ nyseamex/1218155409117.html.

SHULTZ v. SECURITIES AND EXCHANGE COMMISSION

614 F.2d 561 (7th Cir.1980).

SWYGERT, CIRCUIT JUDGE.

This appeal arises from a final order of the Securities and Exchange Commission ("the Commission") affirming the disciplinary action taken by the Chicago Board Options Exchange, Inc. ("Exchange") against petitioner, Howard J. Shultz. * * *

On July 19, 1976, the Business Conduct Committee of the Exchange initiated disciplinary proceedings against Howard Shultz, a registered market maker, and three other Exchange market makers. A market maker is a member of the Exchange who buys and sells options for his own account, in contrast to a broker member of the Exchange who acts as an agent for public investors by executing option trades on their behalf. The function of the market maker is to aid in maintaining a stable market by engaging in options transactions during temporary gaps in public supply and demand for options.

Shultz and the three other market makers were charged with violating Exchange Rule 4.1, requiring market makers to refrain from conduct inconsistent with just and equitable principles of trade; Exchange Rule 8.7(a), requiring market makers to engage in dealings reasonably calculated to contribute to the maintenance of a fair and orderly market and forbidding transactions that are inconsistent with that purpose; and Exchange Rule 4.2, prohibiting conduct in violation of another rule.

These charges were based on a series of circular transactions engaged in by petitioner and the other market makers on three separate days, transactions which left each in exactly the same position he had been in prior to the trades. Each market maker purchased from and sold to another of the market makers a single Eastman Kodak "July 90" call option contract at the same price within an interval of one to two minutes. On each of the three occasions, the price at which the transactions were consummated was lower by $7/8 or $1 than the previous sale price for the option series. On each occasion the price of the security underlying the option varied by $1/2 or less on the New York Stock Exchange, its primary market. In each instance the circular trade was followed by an offer to sell which further lowered the price of the option. Because no one purchased at the lower price, that offer to sell became the "final" offer at which the options market closed.

Petitioner Shultz and at least one of the other market makers who participated in the circular trades were "short" with respect to the option series.[12]

Having found probable cause that a violation of the Exchange's rules had occurred, the Business Conduct Committee of the Exchange ordered disciplinary proceedings against the four market makers engaged in the circular trades. Shultz requested an evidentiary hearing. The remaining three market makers submitted offers of settlement which were accepted by the Business Conduct Committee, in which the allegations were neither admitted nor denied. * * *

The Exchange's Director of Investigations presented documentary evidence establishing Shultz' participation in the circular trades. Shultz testified that he had been a professional in various phases of the securities industry for eleven years and that as a market maker, he considered himself a scalper.[13] He admitted engaging in the transactions at issue, but he stated that the pattern of circular transactions purchase and sale of an option contract within the space of one or two minutes was consistent with his trading patterns which frequently included "scratched trades."[14] Because of his daily volume of trades, petitioner stated he had no independent recall of the trades in question. He testified that none of the other market makers engaged in these transactions were his personal friends and that he had no acquaintance with them off the floor of the Exchange. He denied either soliciting or being solicited concerning these transactions. Petitioner also stated that because of the profitable nature of his business, he had no pressing need for money at the time of these transactions. When asked by various members of the Business Conduct Committee for an explanation of his reasons for entering into both a transaction to sell and a transaction to buy at the same price ($7/8 to $1 lower than the previous sale price for the option series) and then choosing

---

12. To be "short" in the context of options means to have sold options not yet purchased. One way to eliminate a short position is to purchase an option contract.

13. A scalper seeks to profit by taking advantage of changing market conditions which will affect prices of options before those conditions become manifest in the market.

14. "Scratched trades," sometimes called reverse trades, were defined by the Business Conduct Committee as "a purchase and sale of the same quantity of an option series at the same price during the same day."

not to buy again at the subsequent lower offer made immediately after these transactions, Shultz offered no explanation.

Bernard Carey, a board broker assigned to Polaroid options, Chairman of the Floor Officials Committee, and a member of the Board of Directors of the Exchange, testified as a witness for Shultz. He said that he had never seen the "triple reverse" pattern presented by the trades in question nor had he seen a scratch trade between market makers during closing rotation. Carey indicated that, if he had seen a triple reverse in Polaroid followed by a lower offer that was allowed to stand, he would have reported the transaction. Gerald Wood, a floor broker in Eastman Kodak options and a member of several committees including the Floor Officials Committee, was also a witness for Shultz and stated that a series of transactions such as the ones in question would be an abnormal occurrence which he had never seen. Wood testified that, had he been aware of the pattern of the transactions when they occurred, he would have tried to stop them. Scott Schwab, a market maker in Polaroid options, testified that he frequently scratched trades, but had never seen a series of transactions like those in question.

In its decision the Business Conduct Committee found that Shultz had entered into the transactions alleged, and that the trades were not legitimate scratch trades or trades where prevailing market conditions could justify reversal of one's position. According to the Committee, trades involving only one lot, at or near the close of trading where a second trade was made with the same individual within a short time period, would have the appearance of impropriety. In this case, the Committee stated, there was in addition a pattern of transactions over a number of days in an illiquid series involving the same individuals with no change in their relative option position and no other apparent purpose but to influence the price of the last sale in that option series; the Committee found such activity to be "clearly improper."[15] The Committee held that because the transactions at issue were the last transactions of the day and because they preceded the final offer and moved the option down the maximum amount the option could be moved under Rule 8.7(b)(ii), and yet there was not a corresponding change in price of the underlying security, and an offer lower than the last sale did not result in a transaction; the conclusion was inescapable that the trades were in violation of the Exchange rules. Petitioner was found to have entered into transactions which were inconsistent with just and equitable principles of trade and which did not constitute a course of dealings reasonably calculated to contribute to the maintenance of a fair and orderly market, in violation of Exchange Rules 4.1, 8.7, and 4.2. The Committee determined that Shultz did not have the intent to create a false and misleading appearance of activity, so the charge under Rules 4.7 and 4.2 was dismissed. The penalty assessed was a three week suspension and a $2,500 fine.

---

15. A "series" of options is all options of the same type covering the same underlying security and having the same exercise price and expiration date.

Shultz petitioned the Board of Directors of the Exchange for review of the Business Conduct Committee's decision pursuant to Exchange Rule 17.9. The Board upheld the Committee's decision in all respects.

Shultz sought the Commission's review of the Exchange's disciplinary action, pursuant to Section 19(d) of the Securities Exchange Act, 15 U.S.C. § 78s(d). The Commission, after considering briefs filed by Shultz and the Exchange and hearing oral argument, issued an opinion and order affirming the Exchange's disciplinary action. In its opinion, the Commission found the evidence of Shultz' violations "clear and convincing."

In reviewing a decision of the Exchange, the Commission makes a de novo determination of the facts and the law. The Commission must find that the member charged

> has engaged in such acts or practices, or has omitted such acts, as the (Exchange) has found him to have engaged in or omitted (and) that such acts or practices, or omissions to act, are in violation of such provisions of (the Securities Exchange Act), the rules or regulations thereunder, (or) the rules of the self-regulatory organization.

Section 19(e)(1)(A) of the Securities Exchange Act, 15 U.S.C. § 78s(e)(1)(A). After giving notice and the opportunity for a hearing, which may include the presentation of additional evidence, the Commission makes an "independent decision on the violation and penalty." Todd & Co. v. Securities and Exchange Commission, 557 F.2d 1008, 1012 (3d Cir. 1977); R. H. Johnson & Co. v. Securities and Exchange Commission, 198 F.2d 690, 695 (2d Cir.), cert. denied, 344 U.S. 855, 73 S.Ct. 94, 97 L.Ed. 664 (1952) (emphasis added).

This court does not review actions of the Exchange Committee because Exchange disciplinary actions

> are subject to full review by the Securities and Exchange Commission, a wholly public organ, with a hearing before it if requested, the taking of further evidence it may deem relevant, and a decision based on its own findings.

Nassau Securities Service v. Securities and Exchange Commission, 348 F.2d 133 (2d Cir. 1965). Our role is to review the order of the Commission. We will consider errors in the Exchange proceedings "only if and to the extent that they infected the Commission's action by leading to error on its part." R. H. Johnson & Co. v. Securities and Exchange Commission, 198 F.2d 690, 695 (2d Cir.), cert. denied, 344 U.S. 855, 73 S.Ct. 94, 97 L.Ed. 664 (1952). We are persuaded that no such errors occurred here.
* * *

The Commission found that the evidence supporting the findings of violations was clear and convincing. We have determined that there was substantial evidence to support the findings of the Commission under the standard used by the Commission.

On each of the three days in question, petitioner and two other market makers engaged in identical transactions. None of the trades was in response to an order by a public customer, and the transactions were in a series that was infrequently traded. The result of the trades in terms of the option was a lowering of the price; but in terms of the positions of petitioner and the other market makers, the result was a nullity each wound up in precisely the same position he was in prior to the trades. We agree with the Commission that "(c)ircular trades with virtually the same individuals on three occasions do not occur by chance." There was therefore substantial evidence to support the Commission's inference that the transactions were contrived.

Further, the Commission's inference that the transactions served no legitimate economic purpose is also supported by substantial evidence. No such purpose has been suggested by petitioner. There is no dispute that the transactions were in an illiquid option series and at a price lower than the preceding sale price. Each of the three transactions occurred during or near closing rotation and each was followed by a lower offer which was not accepted by any of the market makers. Three experienced options traders testifying for petitioner conceded that these trades were unusual and two stated that, had they witnessed such transactions, they would have attempted to stop them. Under Exchange Rule 8.7(a), petitioner must engage only in transactions reasonably necessary to maintain a fair and orderly market, and under Rule 4.1, must avoid conduct inconsistent with just and equitable principles of trade. The Commission has long made clear that these obligations are affirmative and cannot be met by a showing of no undesirable effect or even no discernable effect. Securities Exchange Act Release No. 1117 (March 30, 1937). Given these affirmative obligations embodied in the Exchange rules, the Commission correctly concluded that three contrived transactions serving no legitimate economic purpose constituted violations of Rules 8.7(a), 4.1, and 4.2.[16] * * *

The order of the Commission is affirmed.

SPICER v. CHICAGO BOARD OF OPTIONS EXCHANGE, INC.

977 F.2d 255 (7th Cir.1992).

FLAUM, CIRCUIT JUDGE.

Section 6 of the Securities Exchange Act of 1934 (Exchange Act), 15 U.S.C. § 78f (1988), governs, among other things, the registration of national securities exchanges with the Securities and Exchange Commis-

---

16. The Commission concluded that the purpose of petitioner's transactions was to lower the price of the option series. The Commission reached this conclusion because petitioner and one other market maker were "short" with respect to that option series and because petitioner could give no alternative explanation. We have determined that the trades were in violation of Exchange Rules 4.1, 8.7(a), and 4.2 because they were not reasonably calculated to contribute to the maintenance of a fair and orderly market, and because they were inconsistent with the just and equitable principles of trade required of market makers; therefore, we need not reach the issue of petitioner's specific purpose in making the trades.

sion (the Commission). Subsection 6(b), *id.* § 78f(b), provides that the Commission may register an exchange only if the exchange has established rules to govern trading, internal operations, and the discipline of wayward exchange members, and has demonstrated the capacity to comply with those rules and enforce compliance by its members. The plaintiffs, who purchased securities on a national securities exchange, maintain that § 6(b) furnishes them an implied private right of action against members of the exchange who allegedly violated certain exchange trading rules, and against the exchange itself for failing to enforce compliance with those rules, and for violating, on its own accord, other exchange rules. We decline to announce a categorical rule regarding all potential private actions under this provision. We hold only that § 6(b) may never support a private suit against an exchange for violating or failing to enforce its own rules, and that it does not support an action against exchange members for violating the exchange rules at issue in this case.

This lawsuit, like many before it, arises from the ashes of Black Monday, the stock market crash of October 19, 1987. *See, e.g., Ruffolo v. Oppenheimer & Co.,* 949 F.2d 33 (2d Cir.1991); *DeBruyne v. Equitable Life Assurance Soc'y,* 920 F.2d 457 (7th Cir.1990); *Thomas McKinnon Sec., Inc. v. Clark,* 901 F.2d 1568 (11th Cir.1990), *cert. denied,* 498 U.S. 1027, 111 S.Ct. 678, 112 L.Ed.2d 670 (1991). The plaintiff class consists of all investors, other than the individual defendants, who purchased certain Standard & Poors 100 (S & P 100) index options during trading rotations at the Chicago Board of Options Exchange (CBOE) on October 20. The defendants are the CBOE, a national securities exchange registered to conduct options trading, and 35 individual "market-makers" in the S & P 100 pit, all of whom are CBOE members. Market-makers are individual traders appointed by the CBOE to maintain a fair, orderly and liquid market in one or more classes of option contracts. Their function is similar, although not identical, to that of "specialists" on national stock exchanges. The market-makers trade for their own account on the floor of the exchange, buying options from brokers representing investors who wish to sell, and selling options to brokers representing investors who wish to buy. Of the individual defendants here, 24 traded on the day in question and 11 did not; we shall refer to the two groups as the "participants" and the "nonparticipants," respectively.

On October 20, the plaintiffs issued "market orders"—meaning orders to buy (or, as the case may be but is not here, sell) S & P 100 options at the prevailing market price—to their brokers. The gravamen of their lawsuit is that when their brokers executed those orders, the participants, who sold the options, charged grossly inflated prices to recoup losses they had suffered the previous day. The CBOE, the investors allege, facilitated the participants' wrongdoing by violating the securities laws and certain CBOE rules, and by failing to enforce compliance by the market-makers with other exchange rules. The nonparticipants are also alleged to have facilitated the wrongdoing by failing to appear for trading on October 20, in violation of yet another CBOE rule.

The basis of the plaintiffs' lawsuit might appear odd from the perspective of commonly accepted finance principles. The price of an option is determined by a number of factors, one being the price volatility of the underlying security, *see generally* Julian Walmsky, *The New Financial Instruments* 156–61 (1988), which in this case is the S & P 100 stock index. October 19 and 20 were arguably the most volatile days in the history of the stock market. *See* Report of the Presidential Task Force on Market Mechanisms (The Brady Report), [1987–88 Transfer Binder] Fed. Sec.L.Rep. (CCH) ¶ 84,213. The S & P 100 stock index lost about 21% of its value on October 19; in the first two and one-half hours of trading on October 20, the Dow Jones Industrial Average experienced more than a 23% swing in value. In light of this unprecedented volatility, it should have come as no surprise that the price of S & P 100 index options was much higher than usual. But these observations are relevant primarily to liability and damages; at issue here is whether the plaintiffs' complaint states a valid cause of action under federal law. * * *

The plaintiffs maintain that the participants, in violation of CBOE Rules 4.1 and 8.7, fraudulently charged exorbitant prices for S & P 100 index options during trading on October 20, 1987. They also allege that the non-participants willfully breached CBOE Rule 8.7 by failing to appear and trade for their accounts on that day. These violations, the investors contend, are actionable in federal court under § 6(b)(5).

Such a contention surely cannot rest upon the plain language of that statute. Section 6(b)(5) provides that the Commission may not register an exchange unless it has promulgated rules designed to prevent fraudulent practices, promote just and equitable principles of trading, perfect the mechanism of a free and open market, and the like. 15 U.S.C. § 78f(b)(5). True, § 6(b)(5) is tangentially related to the actions of exchange members, a group which includes market-makers; it requires that an exchange, as a prerequisite to registration, establish rules prohibiting fraudulent practices by its members. But that is a far cry from providing a private remedy for an exchange member's violation of those rules. As we discussed earlier, the provision pertains solely to the registration of national securities exchanges, and does not confer any rights upon private parties. More important, it does not make unlawful any act or omission by an exchange member. *Touche Ross,* 442 U.S. at 569–71, 99 S.Ct. at 2485–86. By its terms, then, § 6(b)(5) provides no basis upon which we can discern Congress' intent to imply a private remedy of the sort sought by the plaintiffs.

The legislative history of § 6(b) is silent on this issue, which compels the plaintiffs once again to turn to *Curran.* They contend that when Congress enacted the 1975 Amendments to the Exchange Act, federal courts had routinely and consistently held that § 6 granted an implied remedy against exchange members who violated internal rules designed to protect investors. The market-makers respond that *Curran* may be distinguished, and rely upon many of the same points raised by the CBOE. We earlier sidestepped some difficult issues raised by the CBOE and the investors regarding the meaning of "routine and consistent" under *Curran* because § 19(g)(1) made their resolution unnecessary. Here, we are afforded no such luxury, for Congress has not enacted a provision, analogous to § 19(g)(1), explicitly requiring exchange members to comply with exchange rules. * * *

The plaintiffs, as noted, charge that the participants violated CBOE Rules 4.1 and 8.7(a) by fraudulently charging exorbitant and unreasonable prices for certain index options. We assume at this stage of the litigation that their charge is accurate. Rule 4.1 provides that exchange members shall not "engage in acts or practices inconsistent with just and equitable principles of trade." Rule 8.7(a) provides that market makers should engage in transactions that "constitute a course of dealings reasonably calculated to contribute to the maintenance of a fair and orderly market." The investors do not cite, nor did our research discover, any case recognizing an implied remedy under § 6(b)(5) for the violation of an exchange rule similar to either Rule 4.1 or 8.7(a). * * *

The investors also charge that the non-participants violated CBOE Rule 8.7(b) by failing to appear and trade for their accounts on the day following Black Monday. The non-participants concede that they did not show up for trading, and we assume without deciding that this constitutes a violation of Rule 8.7(b). Nonetheless, the investors again do not cite, nor could we find, any pre–1975 case recognizing an implied remedy against an exchange member for anything remotely resembling this conduct. * * *

We hold, in conclusion, that § 6(b) does not grant an implied private right of action to investors who charge that market-makers, or any exchange member, violated CBOE Rules 4.1, 8.7(a) or 8.7(b). * * *

AFFIRMED.

ABRAMS v. PRUDENTIAL SECURITIES, INC.

2000 WL 390494 (N.D.Ill.2000).

GEORGE W. LINDBERG, UNITED STATES DISTRICT JUDGE.

Plaintiffs, a number of market makers on the Chicago Board of Options Exchange (CBOE), bring this action against defendant, Prudential Securities, Inc., alleging violations of federal securities law and Illinois common law. Prudential filed a motion to dismiss the original complaint, which was based only on Illinois securities law. In response, plaintiffs filed the instant complaint. Prudential has again moved to dismiss the complaint pursuant to Fed.R.Civ.P. 12(b)(6).

According to the allegations in the complaint, Prudential is a full service brokerage firm servicing the investment needs of individuals and institutions, including clients trading on the CBOE. The CBOE is a national securities exchange subject to regulation by the Securities and Exchange Commission (SEC). CBOE market makers trade stock options, which are contracts that convey the right to buy or sell a specified amount or value of a particular underlying security, or stock, at a fixed price, called the "strike price." An option giving the right to buy an underlying security is a "call" option and an option giving the right to sell the underlying security is a "put" option. The market maker is obligated to perform according to the terms of the option and have no discretion over whether or not to fulfill the terms of the option once they sell the option. The unit of trading or contract size of a physical delivery option is the amount of the underlying stock that the holder can buy or sell pursuant to the option contract. The unit of trading is generally 100 shares. In sum, for example, a "physical delivery 50 call" gives the holder the right to purchase 100 shares at $50 per share.

In mid April 1998, Prudential began purchasing call options of Chrysler Corporation, the third-largest U.S. automaker, at strike prices that were well above the current market price for Chrysler stock. It purchased more than 15,000 such contracts for Chrysler stock. This was far in excess of the other options traded for Chrysler during the same period.

On May 7, 1998, Chrysler announced a $40 billion merger with Daimler–Benz AG, a German automaker, resulting in a new company called DaimlerChrysler. After this announcement, the price of shares for Chrysler went up 30 percent in three days. Plaintiffs filled Prudential's orders, which were far out of the money at that point, although they believed the trades were based on insider information. They estimate that Prudential profited more than $10 million as a result of the trades.

According to plaintiffs' theory, Prudential's purchase of Chrysler options was economically irrational and therefore had to be based on knowledge of the impending merger. They allege that unknown insiders at Daimler–Benz, Chrysler or both, provided insider information about the impending merger to Prudential and its customers, whom it refers to as "undisclosed principals." Plaintiffs further claim that Prudential traded and substantially assisted its undisclosed principals in trading with knowledge that, or in reckless disregard of whether, the trading was on the basis of material, non-public, insider information. The insiders of Daimler and Chrysler and their tippees owed a fiduciary duty to their respective corporations not to trade on the basis of inside information or to tip that information to others. The insiders and their tippees were also subject to a duty to the investing public to either abstain from trading or disclose the information at issue, which they breached when they or their tippees purchased options of Chrysler stock. Prudential knew or should have known that the trades they executed were illegal, fraudulent and based upon insider information. At all relevant times, Prudential had a duty to exercise ordinary care in its conduct as a brokerage firm conducting business at the CBOE and it breached this duty by trading on insider information.

Based on these allegations, plaintiffs brings claims of: 1) a violation of the Insider Trading and Securities Fraud Enforcement Act, section 20(A) of the Securities Exchange Act, 15 U.S.C. § 78t–1; 2) a violation of section 10(b) of the Securities Exchange Act, and 3) common law negligence. Prudential claims that plaintiffs have failed to adequately plead that Prudential is a corporate insider or assumed any fiduciary duty, that Daimler–Benz or Chrysler derived any benefit from any alleged tip, that Prudential acted with the required state of mind, or that plaintiffs experienced transaction or loss causation or damages. In addition, Prudential claims that plaintiffs have failed to plead fraud with particularity, that their claim is untimely, and that their state law negligence claim is precluded under Illinois law. Because plaintiffs' § 20(A) claim is reliant upon its § 10(b) claim, defendant claims it is subject to dismissal as well.
* * *

Plaintiffs admit that they have not alleged that Prudential was a corporate insider or quasi-insider of Chrysler or Daimler–Benz that had a direct fiduciary dutyto shareholders. They maintain, however, that they have met the standard established in *Dirks* by pleading that Prudential was a "tippee," someone that has received insider information from a corporate fiduciary. A tippee may be found liable for insider trading under § 10(b), if: (1) tipper possessed material, nonpublic information regarding corporation; (2) tipper disclosed this information to tippee; (3) tippee traded in corporation's securities while in possession of that nonpublic information provided by tipper; (4) tippee knew or should have known that tipper violated relationship of trust by relaying the information; and (5) tipper benefitted by the disclosure to tippee. *SEC v. Warde*, 151 F.3d 42, 46 (2nd Cir.1998).

The complaint states that prior to the public announcement of the merger, unknown insiders at Daimler–Benz or Chrysler tipped insider information concerning the pending merger to Prudential; that these insiders as well as their tippees owed a fiduciary duty to their respective corporations not to trade on the basis of inside information or to tip that information to others; that Prudential traded with knowledge that, or in reckless disregard for, whether the trading was based on material, non-public, insider information; that Prudential knew or should have known that the trades they executed were illegal, fraudulent, and based on insider information. * * *

Pleading fraud requires disclosing the "who, what, when, where, and how: the first paragraph of any newspaper story." *In re HealthCare Compare Corp. Sec. Litig.*, 75 F.3d 276, 281 (7th Cir.1996) (quoting *DiLeo v. Ernst & Young*, 901 F.2d 624, 627 (7th Cir.1990)). Prudential maintains that plaintiffs have not identified who at Prudential engaged in insider trading; who at Chrysler or Daimler–Benz tipped the insider information, in breach of their fiduciary duty, to the unidentified person at Prudential; or what relationship existed between these two (or more) parties. In addition, according to Prudential, plaintiffs have inadquately alleged when or how Prudential received the insider information and therefore whether

Prudential was actually tipped or whether they merely "should have known that the trades they executed were illegal, fraudulent and based upon insider information." Prudential claims that the entire amended complaint is based on speculation and information and belief, and accuses plaintiffs of using it as a vehicle to discover information for use against others, something Rule 9(b) is designed to prevent. *Vicom, Inc. v. Harbridge Merchant Servs., Inc.*, 20 F.3d 771, 777 (7th Cir.1994).

Although the court acknowledges that Rule 9(b) does not transform federal notice pleading under Fed.R.Civ.P. 8 to fact pleading, plaintiffs simply have no response to defendant's pointing out specific deficiencies in the complaint. They state only that they have satisfied Rule 9(b), without citing any factual allegations from the complaint that support this assertion. It appears that defendant's belief that plaintiffs are on a "fishing expedition" may be correct. The court finds that plaintiffs have not met the pleading requirements of Fed.R.Civ.P. 9(b).

For these reasons, plaintiffs' § 10(b) claim fails. Prudential points out that a § 20(A) claim is predicated upon a successful § 10(b) claim. *Jackson Nat. Life Ins. Co. v. Merrill Lynch & Co.*, 32 F.3d 697, 703 (2nd Cir.1994). Because plaintiffs' 10(b) claim fails, the court must also dismiss their § 20(A) claim. * * *

NOTES

1. The leverage afforded by options makes them a favorite tool for insider trading abuses. See, e.g., United States v. O'Hagan, 521 U.S. 642, 117 S.Ct. 2199, 138 L.Ed.2d 724 (1997) (lawyer used misappropriated information to trade 2,500 options contracts covering 25,000 shares of Pillsbury stock).

2. The Prudential case demonstrates that the use of inside information may be difficult to prove. Compare Securities and Exchange Commission v. Unifund SAL, 910 F.2d 1028 (2d Cir.1990) where the court affirmed the entry of a preliminary injunction against foreign traders in options and stock even though no tipper of merger information could be identified.

MILLER v. AMERICAN STOCK EXCHANGE

317 F.3d 134 (2d Cir. 2003).

KEARSE, CIRCUIT JUDGE.

* * * The present litigation involves the trading of equity options on various stock exchanges. The facts material to the district court rulings that are the subject of this appeal are not in dispute.

Plaintiffs are persons who purchased equity options after December 31, 1994. Defendants are AMEX, the Chicago Board Options Exchange,

Inc. ("CBOE"), the New York Stock Exchange, Inc. ("NYSE"), the Pacific Stock Exchange, Inc. ("Pacific Exchange"), the Philadelphia Stock Exchange, Inc. ("Philadelphia Exchange") (collectively "the Exchanges"), and members of the Exchanges that acted as market makers and specialists in options trading (the "market maker defendants"). In early 1999, various plaintiffs commenced more than 20 class actions alleging that defendants had conspired to restrict the listing and trading of particular options to one stock exchange at a time, thereby restraining trade in such options in violation of § 1 of the Sherman Act. * * *

The trading of options on national exchanges began in 1973 when CBOE became registered as a national exchange; such trading was regulated in Rule 9b–1, promulgated by the Commission under the Exchange Act, *see* SEC Rule 9b–1, 17 C.F.R. § 240.9b–1. When other exchanges proposed to list options for trading, the SEC commenced a study of the practice, including the question of whether the trading of options on a given class of securities should be allowed to proceed on multiple exchanges. *See* SEC Release No. 10490 (Nov. 14, 1973). After a public hearing, the Commission concluded in 1974 that additional study was required before allowing, inter alia, "multiple exchange option trading." SEC Release No. 11144, 1974 (Dec. 19, 1974). At that time, the SEC authorized AMEX to allow options trading, and it noted that AMEX did not intend to allow dual trading.

In 1976, the SEC allowed CBOE to list options that were already traded on another exchange. *See generally* 49 S.E.C. 1158, SEC Release No. 26809, 1989 (May 11, 1989). It also allowed the Pacific Exchange to commence options trading and noted that that Exchange planned to list options that were being traded on other exchanges. *See* SEC Release No. 12283, (Mar. 30, 1976). In early 1977, the Commission invited public comment on multiple listing, *see* SEC Release No. 13325 (Mar. 3, 1977), and expressed concern that, in the course of trading options listed on more than one exchange, floor members of certain exchanges might be violating the Exchange Act, *see* SEC Release No. 13433 (Apr. 5, 1977). Later in 1977, the Commission requested that the exchanges voluntarily cease the listing of new options classes pending a comprehensive SEC review of options trading. *See* SEC Release No. 13760 (July 18, 1977). It proposed to issue a rule temporarily barring such new listings if the exchanges would not suspend them voluntarily; the rule became unnecessary because the exchanges complied voluntarily, *see* SEC Release No. 15026 (Aug. 3, 1978), and continued to comply until the SEC lifted the moratorium in 1980, *see* SEC Release No. 16701 (Mar. 26, 1980) ("SEC Mar. 26, 1980 Release").

In 1980, the Commission permitted the resumption of new listings and trading generally, but it stated that it needed to consider further

> whether to continue its current policy of restricting multiple trading in exchange-traded options or whether to permit a more unfettered competitive environment in which an options exchange would be free

to trade any eligible options class, subject to the adequacy of its surveillance and other self-regulatory capabilities.

Id. at *22–*23. As the district court noted,

> [t]he SEC identified a number of possible adverse effects from multiple trading, including (i) market fragmentation; (ii) the likelihood that meaningful competition among market centers may be, at best, transitory because of member firms' automatic order routing practices; and (iii) the potential negative impact on the financial position of the regional exchanges. [SEC Mar. 26, 1980 Release]. The Commission believed that some of its concerns might be alleviated by the development of market integration facilities, and expressed an inclination toward multiple trading. However, the SEC deferred further action, requesting that the exchanges consider "whether, and to what extent, the development of market integration facilities would minimize concerns regarding market fragmentation and maximize competitive opportunities in the options markets."

On May 30, 1980, the SEC approved a plan, formulated by the exchanges jointly, for the single, or exclusive, listing of any new equity option. *See* SEC Release No. 16863 (May 30, 1980). The new listings were to be allocated among the several exchanges on a rotating basis. *See id.* While permitting multiple listings of other types of options and of over-the-counter securities, the Commission remained concerned that "unlimited multiple trading of equity options at this time might result in significant deleterious structural changes in the markets, with a resultant decrease in competition in other areas such as services relating to execution and clearing functions." SEC Release No. 17577 (Feb. 26, 1981) (footnote omitted).

In 1987, the Commission proposed the adoption of a multiple-trading rule and announced the commencement of a proceeding to consider, inter alia, whether to permit such multiple-market trading. *See* SEC Release No. 34–24613 (June 18, 1987). In 1989, the Commission announced the adoption of Rule 19c–5, which it described as allowing "an exchange unilaterally [to] decide, as a business matter, not to multiply trade any particular option," but prohibiting an exchange from "reaching an agreement with one or more other exchanges to refrain from multiple trading." SEC Release No. 34–26870 (May 26, 1989). Multiple listing was to be implemented gradually. Rule 19c–5 provided that, as of January 22, 1990, an exchange was to be prohibited from adopting any rule, policy, or practice that limited its ability to list any equity options that had first been listed on an exchange on or after that date, *see* SEC Rule 19c–5(a)(1), 17 C.F.R. § 240.19c–5(a)(1) (2002); from January 22, 1990, to January 21, 1991, an exchange was to be prohibited from adopting such a rule, policy, or practice with respect to 10 classes of options that had been listed on another exchange prior to January 22, 1990, see SEC Rule 19c–5(a)(2), 17 C.F.R. § 240.19c–5(a)(2) (2002); and effective January 21, 1991, an exchange was to be prohibited from adopting such a rule, policy, or practice with respect to any equity options, *see* SEC Rule 19c–5(a)(3), 17 C.F.R. § 240.19c–5(a)(3) (2002) ("No rule, stated policy, practice, or interpretation of this exchange shall prohibit or condition, or be construed to prohibit or condition or otherwise limit, directly or indirectly, the ability of this exchange to list any stock options class because that options class is listed on another options exchange.").

Notwithstanding the terms of Rule 19c–5, the SEC, shortly before the Rule was to become effective, asked exchanges to refrain from the multiple listing of such options as had previously been listed only singly.

The SEC's moratorium on multiple listing was lifted beginning in November 1992. By the end of 1994, all equity options were eligible for multiple listing. The Commission had noted, however, that it retained ultimate authority over such listings. In 1997, the SEC exercised this authority to approve the sale by NYSE of its options business to CBOE. The SEC rejected assertions that the sale tended to create a monopoly, stating that it "would regard any anticompetitive arrangements in the trading of options to be of very serious concern, but [that] after reviewing the proposed transfer closely, the Commission disagrees with these assertions." SEC Release No. 34–38542, 1997 SEC LEXIS 900 (Apr. 23, 1997). * * *

In September 2000, the SEC found that certain exchanges had improperly followed a course of conduct that limited multiple listing. *See, e.g.,* SEC Release No. 43268 (Sept. 11, 2000) ("Member firms of certain of the respondent exchanges made proposals to multiply list options. In order to avoid or defeat multiple listing, the respondent exchanges rebuffed or denied these proposals without an adequate basis in their rules and, in some instances, threatened or harassed member firms who made the proposals."). The exchanges in question were censured, and they agreed, inter alia, to change certain procedures that had facilitated exclusivity of listing. * * *

In the present case, we agree with the district court's conclusion that the Exchange Act impliedly repeals § 1 of the Sherman Act with respect to the listing and trading of equity options, because the implied repeal is necessary to preserve the authority of the SEC to regulate that conduct. The Exchange Act itself does not prohibit agreements for exclusivity in options listing, and, as described, the Commission has taken varied positions with respect to the appropriateness of multiplicity, in part because under the Exchange Act it is concerned with more than just the protection of competition, which is "the sole aim of antitrust legislation," "The SEC must consider, in addition, the economic health of the investors, the exchanges, and the securities industry." *Id.* Thus, in evaluating the wisdom under the Exchange Act of requiring or prohibiting multiple listings, the Commission has perforce balanced the interest of promoting competition, on the one hand, against undesirable potential effects, on the other hand, such as market fragmentation and "deleterious structural changes in the markets," in order to carry out its statutory duty to enhance "the 'economically efficient execution of securities transactions.' " * * *

NOTES

1. Initially, by agreement, there was no competition in options trading on the stocks of the companies listed on the equity options exchanges. The SEC ordered the exchanges to stop that practice and to permit multiple listings, but the option exchanges simply ignored that order until that order was enforced in the Miller case. The International Stock Exchange ("ISE"), a new all-electronic exchange, was then able to compete head-to-head with the floor trading operations of the stock options exchanges. ISE soon became the world's largest equity options exchange, supplanting the CBOE in that role. Jerry W. Markham, A Financial History of the United States, From Enron Era Scandals to the Subprime Crisis (2004–2006) 158 (2010). The SEC found that this competition was beneficial, in addition to narrowing spreads, the expansion of multiple trading led to "market structure innovations that were designed to attract more order flow by enhancing the efficiency, transparency and liquidity of their markets." 69 Fed. Reg. 6124, 6126 (Feb. 9, 1004).

SECTION 8. COMMODITY OPTIONS

JERRY W. MARKHAM & DAVID J. GILBERG STOCK AND COMMODITY OPTIONS—TWO REGULATORY APPROACHES AND THEIR CONFLICTS

47 Albany Law Review 741–791 (1983).

In many respects, stock options are similar to commodity futures contracts. Both constitute agreements to buy or sell a given quantity of a particular security or commodity and both are intended for use principally as hedging and speculative investments, not as contracts for actual delivery. Like stock options, commodity options and commodity futures in various forms have been traded for hundreds of years, serving a wide range of economic and speculative functions.

Under a commodity futures contract, the trader is responsible for the total change in value of the contract during the period of his ownership; if the price of the commodity moves adversely, the trader is obligated to make additional payments equal to the amount of the adverse price change. Because options carry no such obligations for the option *holder*, they are often more popular among small investors. Thus, because the option can be permitted to lapse, the holder can limit losses to the initial price of the option, the premium paid. The writer of the option, however, would not be so limited and would be liable for delivery of the commodity regardless of any adverse price changes. This can cause serious loss to the writer where the writer is uncovered or "naked"; that is, where the writer does not own the commodity or an offsetting futures contract.

Another type of commodity option is issued by the producer of a particular commodity. It gives the holder of the option the right to buy or sell a given quantity of the goods produced by that company at a fixed price. These became known as "dealer" options because they were backed by the actual physical inventory of the issuing company. This type of investment, also known as "Mocatta" options after the Mocatta Metals Corporation, which initiated the plan, is based on more secure backing but, as is true of naked options, the investor undertakes the risk that the issuing company will be unable to fulfill its obligations when the option is exercised.

Still another type of option is the so-called "London" option, so named because of the relationship it bears to options traded on London exchanges. These exchanges have, for many years, conducted a reputable and respected trading in options and have developed a sound system by which in turn has established margin requirements and imposed other safeguards successfully used by futures exchanges to assure performance. American firms marketing such options in the United States, however, often failed to effect the transaction on the London exchanges, thus "bucketing" the order and creating a "naked" option. Moreover, even if the order was effected, it was done in the name of the London broker through an omnibus account of the American dealer, who generally was not a member of the London exchange. As a consequence, the customer had no contractual relationship whatsoever with any individual on that exchange, and thus was dependent solely on the financial integrity of the American dealer, integrity which was often sorely lacking. Only the American dealer, or some other entity, such as the record owner of the option, was known to the London broker. As a result, none of the protections afforded to option traders by the ICCH were extended to the American customer.

Commodity options have been traded on exchanges in the United States for over one hundred years, but they too have encountered serious abuses. Indeed, after speculation on commodities and options in particular had been blamed in large part for the collapse of the wheat market in the Great Depression, Congress enacted the Commodity Exchange Act (CEA), which imposed a flat prohibition on the trading on any options in the agricultural commodities then regulated under the CEA. For more than thirty years, this legislative proscription operated to ban options both on and off exchanges and, as will be discussed, was only recently removed by Congress.

In the early 1970s, a loophole in the law was discovered, which ultimately allowed a resurgence of off-exchange options trading far beyond anything previously experienced. The mastermind of this loophole was a twenty-six-year-old trader named Harold Goldstein, who put his scheme into operation in 1971. Starting with an initial capitalization of $800, by the end of 1972, Goldstein's firm, Goldstein–Samuelson, Inc., had offices worldwide and a gross income of $45 million. Goldstein relied on high pressure, mass-marketing techniques, and the naivete and greed on unsophisticated investors. The loophole used by Goldstein was simple. The CEA prohibited only the trading of options on those agricultural commodities within its scope. Several commodities, including the so-called "world" commodities, such as silver, platinum and coffee, were not then subject to the option ban contained in the CEA, and it was on these commodities that Goldstein conducted his trading.

Goldstein's adventure quickly turned to disaster because he was selling naked options. As large price increases in certain commodities began to occur, Goldstein became unable to pay, and by 1973 he was out of business, leaving behind some $85 million in unpaid "options." These were not the only losses, however, because several other firms had followed Goldstein's lead and losses of many millions more ensued.

As a result of these and other abuses, Congress sought to create a stronger and more coherent federal regulatory structure in the commodities field. The Commodity Futures Trading Commission Act (CFTC Act) was enacted in 1974 to meet this concern. The CFTC Act, which constituted amendments and extensions of the CEA, established the CFTC as an independent federal agency and vested it with "exclusive" jurisdiction over futures contracts trading and other activities, including the trading of commodity options. In particular, the CFTC Act attempted to fill the legislative gaps and "loopholes."

The CFTC Act extended the coverage of the CEA to all previously unregulated commodities, and it maintained the ban on options trading in the previously regulated commodities. It did not, however, prohibit options trading in the previously unregulated commodities. Rather, it gave the CFTC plenary authority to regulate such transactions.

As a result of the enactment of the CFTC Act and its grant of exclusive jurisdiction to the CFTC, the authority of the SEC and the states was preempted. Although initially ineffective, by the 1974 the states and the SEC had taken action to prevent abuses in the sale of commodity options. With the preemption of that authority, however, the widespread sale of commodity options began once again. The result was a debacle vividly illustrated by a number of cases against brokers dealing in the so-called London options. * * *

Through these types of operations, which often resulted in insolvency proceedings, London and other options traded in the United States developed a reputation as shady investments pushed on unsophisticated investors by unscrupulous brokers. In the process, commodity options came increasingly to be viewed by the public as imprudent and disreputable investment vehicles.

One of the CFTC's first actions was its adoption in June 1975 of a rule broadly prohibiting the use of any deceptive acts or practices in connection with transactions in commodity options. This "antifraud" rule, however, proved ineffective against the proliferating option firms, and in October 1975, the CFTC sought public comment on additional rules for options trading. At the time, the CFTC noted that many commodity option offerings appeared questionable since in most cases investors were not given adequate assurance that the issuers of the options would be able "to perform their obligation under the option contracts when and if required to do so." In order to remedy this situation, the CFTC suggested several approaches. Those proposals were also considered by a CFTC Advisory Committee which, in July 1976, recommended that options be permitted to be traded only on designated contract markets subject to the type of regulations governing the trading of futures contracts.

That plan was not immediately adopted. Rather, effective January 1977, the CFTC required persons engaged in options trading to register with the CFTC as futures commission merchants (brokers); additionally, such persons were required to comply with the minimum net capital requirements of the CFTC. A "segregation" provision was included as well, along with specific risk disclosure and recordkeeping requirements.

By the time of the 1978 Congressional hearings on the reauthorization of the CFTC, however, it had become clear that effective control of commodity options would not be possible even under this new regulatory approach. The CFTC openly acknowledged this situation, noting that the lack of a sufficient enforcement staff and the absence of developed case law in the field had rendered its regulation of options completely unmanageable. As a result, the CFTC proposed, and on June 1, 1978 enacted, a total moratorium on trading of commodity options, which was to be continued indefinitely until such time as the CFTC again authorized options trading. The only exemptions to this trading suspension were for commercial or trade options, which are traded between members of the same industry and do not involve the public, and for dealer options, previously described.

In the Congressional hearings that followed, there was considerable discussion concerning whether commodity options should be completely banned. The House Committee on Agriculture proposed legislation that would have prohibited "all commodity option transactions involving those commodities not set forth in section 2(a)(1) of the Act" but allowing the CFTC the authority to permit such transactions by its subsequent enactment of rules and regulations. The bill approved by the Senate Committee on Agriculture, Nutrition and Forestry went somewhat further, granting the CFTC no authority to create exemptions, except through a program of trading on domestic exchanges. As finally enacted, the Futures Trading Act of 1978 included the CFTC's ban on options trading and the exemption for trade and dealer options but permitted the CFTC to develop a new program for regulating options, the acceptance of which by Congress would result in a lifting of the ban.

On November 3, 1981, the CFTC announced a three year "pilot program" for the trading of options on futures contracts through designated contract markets [which was later made permanent]. During that time the CFTC will collect data and study the ability of the contract markets, and the CFTC itself, to control abusive options trading effectively. Under the pilot program, domestic exchanges designed by the CFTC as contract markets for the trading of futures contracts may apply for designation as markets for options trading. Each board of trade may offer options on futures contracts in one underlying commodity only, on which it is already trading futures contracts. To assure effective regulatory control over such trading, the CFTC also adopted a number of regulatory controls, including requirements that futures contracts subject to options trading be highly liquid (they must average trading at least 1000 contracts per week); that contract markets demonstrate a legitimate economic purpose for the options traded; that contract markets and their members establish supervisory procedures for sales personnel; that a simplified disclosure document be presented to and signed by customers and that the document explain the nature of and risks associated with options trading, as well as define those persons suitable for such trading, all in a manner prescribed by the CFTC.

The trading of commodity options on exchanges is conducted in a manner similar to that of stock options and commodity futures contracts. Thus, orders to buy and sell options are transmitted to a futures commission merchant who communicates such orders to a "floor broker" on the floor of an exchange. Orders are then executed through a process of open bidding between competing floor brokers representing buyers and sellers. A confirmation of the transaction is thereafter forwarded to the trader's local brokerage office. In addition, every transaction is cleared by a clearinghouse, such as the CBOT's Board of Trade Clearing Corporation, which acts as the actual buyer and seller for every trade and operates like the OCC.

Unlike stock option trading, however, commodity options traded on exchanges do not involve market-makers or a specialist system. Instead, floor brokers may serve the functions of executing the orders of others as well as making a market, and no specific obligation to maintain an orderly market is imposed.

Subject to certain restrictions, the trading of exchange-listed options on futures contracts is now permitted by statute and regulation. Because the enactment of the pilot program did not purport to affect options governed by existing CFTC regulations, however, the provisions for trade and dealer options involving off-exchange sales remain in effect. Moreover, on November 9, 1982, the CFTC extended the pilot program to options on physical commodities as well as futures contracts, and Congress has recently passed legislation allowing the CFTC to approve trading of options on agriculture commodities....

These measures, thus, reestablish the trading of commodity options, subject to exchange and federal regulation. The availability of such instruments will permit commodity traders as well as producers to employ a broader variety of trading strategies, thereby enhancing market liquidity and flexibility. The approval of agricultural options trading is particularly significant for farmers, grain elevator operators and other agricultural businesses because it provides an additional means by which they can hedge against price fluctuations. Indeed, this use of the commodity markets represents, in part, a return to their origins and traditional functions.

KELLEY v. CARR

442 F.Supp. 346 (W.D.Mich. 1977).

Fox, Chief District Judge,

This case was initiated by the Attorney General of Michigan in the Circuit Court for Ingham County. It was alleged that defendants were in violation of various sections of both the Michigan Uniform Securities Act, MCLA §§ 451.501 *et seq.* (1977), and the Michigan Consumer Protection Act, MCLA §§ 445.901 *et seq.* (1977) by transacting business as unregistered commodities broker-dealers and agents, transacting business fraudulently, and offering and selling unregistered securities. Plaintiff subsequently amended his complaint to allege violations of the anti-fraud provisions of the federal Commodity Exchange Act, 7 U.S.C. §§ 1 *et seq.* (1977). Defendant Lloyd, Carr & Co. petitioned this court for removal of the action from the state court. The Commodity Futures Trading Commission (C.F.T.C.) then moved to intervene as a party plaintiff.

On November 7, 1977, I issued a temporary restraining order basically enjoining defendants from engaging in any sort of fraudulent or deceitful business activities. I also granted the C.F.T.C.'s motion to intervene. The matter is now here on motions by plaintiffs for preliminary injunctive relief.

Lloyd, Carr & Co. and Lloyd Carr Financial Co. were both founded in mid–1976, and are now partnerships between James A. Carr and Charles P. LeMieux, III. Lloyd, Carr & Co. engages in the business of soliciting and selling so-called London commodity options on futures contracts. Lloyd Carr Financial is a commodity trading advisor; that is, it "engages in the business of advising others either directly or through publications or writings, as to the value of commodities or as to the advisability of trading in any commodity...." On August 1, 1977, the C.F.T.C. issued an opinion in an administrative proceeding instituted against Lloyd, Carr in early 1977. The Commission ruled that Lloyd, Carr was engaged in the business of selling and offering to sell commodity futures options without proper registration under federal regulations. It revoked the existing registration of Lloyd Carr Financial as a commodity trading advisor, denied the application for registration of Lloyd, Carr & Co. as a futures commission merchant, and entered a cease and desist order barring further violations of the Commodity Exchange Act. Lloyd, Carr appealed that ruling to the Second Circuit Court of Appeals, which stayed enforcement pending its determination.

Lloyd, Carr has its principal place of business in Boston, and has offices in several cities across the country, including one in Detroit. Activities in the Detroit office led to the initiation of this action by the Attorney General of Michigan, although plaintiff C.F.T.C. alleges unlawful activities in all Lloyd, Carr operations.

A futures contract is an agreement to purchase or sell a fixed amount of a commodity of a certain grade at a certain future date for a fixed price. Futures contracts may be settled by delivery of the goods, but in the vast majority of cases an offsetting transaction occurs in which the holder of a contract to sell liquidates his position by purchasing a contract to buy the same commodity or the holder of a contract to buy cancels his position by acquiring a contract to sell. An option on a futures contract is a right to buy or sell the contract for a particular commodity at a specified price, known as the "strike price," within a specified period of time. The purchaser pays a premium for the option in addition to broker's fees at the time of purchase and, if the option is exercised, at the time of sale. Options may be supported by an underlying futures contract at the time of their creation. Increasingly, however, so-called "naked options" are being sold. This type of option is one created without backing by either futures contracts or actual ownership of the commodities involved, and may be written by anyone willing to risk that he will be able to cover his obligation should the option be exercised.

It is evident that options are attractive to sellers in that capital requirements are minimal, and to buyers because costs are usually somewhat lower than purchasing a futures contract outright since the premium and initial broker's fees should run less than the margin requirements of the underlying contract, and investors can limit their potential losses. Owing to the ease of market entry, however, fly-by-night organizations are often attracted.

The potential for abuse in the field of option trading created a great deal of pressure for legislation outlawing fraudulent dealings in commodity options. The Commodity Exchange Act, passed in 1936, banned option trading in all domestic commodities within its scope. International commodities, such as those traded on the London exchanges, were not covered, however. In 1974 Congress responded by passing the Commodity Futures Trading Commission Act, which created the C.F.T.C. as an independent regulatory body paralleling the Securities and Exchange Commission and broadened the coverage of the 1936 Act. In section 6c(b) of the 1974 amendments it was provided that the C.F.T.C. should have broad authority to regulate, through its rule-making powers, commodity options transactions. Pursuant thereto, the C.F.T.C. adopted Rule 32.9. * * *

Plaintiffs allege that this provision has been violated by defendants. I conclude that the affidavits, exhibits, and testimony produced by plaintiffs clearly show that "the defendants purposefully engaged in the sort of continuous, concerted fraudulent practices that lie at the core of the prohibitions contained in Rule 32.9." *Commodity Futures Trading Comm'n v. Crown Colony Commodity Options, Ltd.*, 434 F.Supp. 911, 914–15 (S.D.N.Y.1977).

It is charged by plaintiffs that Lloyd, Carr has engaged in a high-pressure "boiler room" sales campaign in its efforts to sell commodity options.[17] The supporting evidence creates a picture of an operation that has no place in an industry where "it is essential ... that the highest ethical standards prevail...." Defendants have responded by asserting that no "boiler room" exists since Lloyd, Carr rents space in fashionable buildings and conducts its business in well-appointed offices. They have not denied that they offer options "in large volume by means of an intensive selling campaign through numerous salesmen by telephone" without regard to the suitability to the needs of the customer. All that really appears to have happened is that the boiler room has been moved to the executive suite.

The first step in Lloyd, Carr's marketing program is the recruitment of sales personnel. In order to attract salespersons, advertisements soliciting applicants are placed in the daily newspapers in the cities where Lloyd, Carr has, or intends to open, offices. These advertisements state that "almost all [of our sales people] came to us from other industries with neither experience in nor knowledge of commodities as investment vehicle.... Income in the upper half of this group, ..., ranges from $24,000 to $138,000 on an annual basis." The ads also indicate that salespersons receive intensive training. It is clear that Lloyd, Carr sales personnel have no background in the commodity options industry; the ads themselves provide sufficient support for that proposition. It is equally evident from the record before me, however, that despite its representation to the contrary, Lloyd, Carr fails to give salespersons adequate training concerning London commodity options before permitting them to solicit funds from prospective investors for option purchases and to advise investors as to the suitability of such investments.

The "intensive training" that Lloyd, Carr provides does not fully educate the newly-hired individual in the intricacies of the commodity industry. Rather, the training received is primarily in telephone sales techniques. The emphasis is on pressuring potential investors into purchasing. Scripts of "canned" sales pitches are often distributed to sales personnel and they are instructed to maintain control of the conversation at all times.

---

17. Boiler room activity has been described as consisting essentially of "offering to customers securities of certain issuers in large volume by means of an intensive selling campaign through numerous salesmen by telephone or direct mail, without regard to the suitability to the needs of the customer, in such a manner as to induce a hasty decision to buy the security being offered without disclosure of the material facts about the [security]." *SEC v. R. J. Allen & Assocs., Inc.*, 386 F.Supp. 866, 874 (S.D.Fla. 1974).

This type of sales technique is known as a "cold calling" or "cold canvassing" approach. Salespersons make their calls to potential investors with whom neither they nor the company has had prior contacts. Names are collected from lists purchased from commercial customer list firms. After the initial, or "set-up" call, sales personnel begin a series of follow-up calls to pressure their potential client into buying an option. The evidence indicates that some people received daily calls for a month or more. The total number of calls made by Lloyd, Carr's salespersons is staggering. In the Detroit office alone over 50,000 long distance calls have been made in a 30–day period. Intense pressure is imposed on salespersons by supervisors who constantly monitor the sales force and often interject pep talks, exhorting the callers to make more sales. The managers of some branches have resorted to bizarre actions to stimulate sales; one often wears a gorilla suit and mask while roaming the sales floor, while another masquerades in a Superman costume. When a sale is made, bells are often rung throughout the office, and personnel stand to cheer. In effect, a circus atmosphere is created. Prizes are often awarded to provide incentives for higher sales. For each sale made by a salesperson, he receives a commission of ten percent. A quota system is employed whereby quota sheets requiring that certain targets be met are distributed each day. If the quota for the number of daily phone calls or monthly sales is not met, salespersons often are fired.

The pressure brought to bear on those receiving calls from Lloyd, Carr is enormous. In the set-up call, the primary objective is to "qualify" the prospect by determining the extent of his resources and interest. This initial contact is intended to stimulate interest by emphasizing the get-rich-quick potential of commodity options. Toward that end, callers have made a number of false, deceptive, or misleading representations, such as statements that investors would double or triple their money if they invested now, that the most conservative estimates call for the price of a particular commodity to rise by 100 to 200 percent within one year, and that every time the market price of a commodity rises, the investor makes large profits. The record contains a number of references to statements made by Lloyd, Carr salespersons that the investor is in a can't-lose position by purchasing commodity options.

Following the initial contact, the prospect sometimes receives a number of pamphlets and other sales literature. Like the set-up calls, this literature contains several misleading representations. It is stated, for example, that: (1) The London options offered by Lloyd, Carr are guaranteed by the International Commodities Clearing House (ICCH). In fact, only member firms of London exchanges are protected against default by the ICCH, and Lloyd, Carr is not a member. (2) The investor realizes a profit for every increase in the price of the commodity future underlying the option. In point of fact, no profit is realized until the price moves above a break-even point which is substantially above the market price due to Lloyd, Carr's excessive premiums. (3) Lloyd, Carr offers discounts off going option prices. In truth, the prices Lloyd, Carr charges are substantially higher than those charged by other dealers. In Michigan, for example, Lloyd, Carr charges approximately $8,000 for a single option while other firms charge approximately $2,500 for the same item. (4) Investment in commodity options offers limited risk. Such investments are, however, actually highly speculative. The only limitation of risk involves a limited *loss* potential since an investor could refuse to exercise his option if the market price fell below the strike price, thus limiting his loss to the premium and commission paid. Since Lloyd, Carr charges a premium of as much as $10,000, however, the loss can clearly be destructive to some investors. Moreover, by trading in options the investor sacrifices the opportunity to profit on small increases in market price. (5) Lloyd, Carr is "long known for the quality, depth and reliability of its research; the training, motivation, knowledge and integrity of its brokers; the magnitude and liquidity of its capital assets; and the efficiency of its coast to coast offices and incomparable worldwide communication network...." In fact, Lloyd, Carr was founded only in June or July of 1976. At the time the statement regarding Lloyd, Carr's "long known" qualities was first published, the company had been in existence for approximately six months.

Shortly after receiving the sales literature, prospects are usually deluged with phone calls in an attempt to consummate a sale. It is apparent from the record that salespersons wilfully make any misrepresentations necessary to effect a sale.

It is frequently stated that last year 82 percent of Lloyd, Carr's customers made money. In point of fact, one of Lloyd, Carr's operations' leaders testified that the reference to 82 percent represented only that percentage of about 200 customers in 1976, and that the figure was intended to suggest that that percentage did not *lose* money. Several customers have indicated that they were continuously given the impression that their investment was guaranteed, when in fact, of course, no such protection exists. Moreover, prospective customers are assured prior to purchasing an option that Lloyd, Carr will keep in constant touch with them regarding their investment. Once the money has changed hands, however, investors often find it next to impossible to contact the salesperson with whom they dealt. Rather, a different salesperson takes any inquiries. Should the investor ask to speak with his original salesperson, he is often told that that individual no longer works for Lloyd, Carr, or some other excuse, such as "he was recently involved in an automobile accident and will be hospitalized indefinitely." If at that point the investor questions the new contact about the wisdom of his original investment, it is not unusual for that salesperson to begin another sales pitch, confirming that the original investment will probably result in a total loss and that the investor should buy a second option to cover his losses. This process is often repeated with still other salespersons.

Salespersons do not disclose the mark-up on the options. Indeed, it appears that salespersons are not told themselves what the mark-up is. If asked, it is divulged that commissions range between 10 and 30 percent. Actually, the total mark-up ranges between 300 and 400 percent.

Salespersons are not subtle in attempting to induce potential customers to act quickly. If a customer ultimately agrees to purchase an option, Lloyd, Carr sends out a messenger to his home or business within a few hours of the telephone call to pick up payment. Often, however, orders are not filled for several days.

The overriding flavor of the solicitations, and that which makes them patently deceitful, is the unrestrained and unambiguous prediction of certain or enormous profits. Potential investors are inundated with assurances of large, low-risk gains. There is no attempt on the part of Lloyd, Carr salespersons to counsel their clients or to consider financial positions so that it can be determined whether they can realistically afford to enter the commodities market. The one and only concern is sell, sell, sell. Unsubstantiated predictions of increases in the market prices of whatever commodity is being pushed are made to sound like calculated fact to potential investors. In many cases, explanatory literature—some of which may in fact be helpful, as indicated below—is never sent despite promises to the contrary. In almost no cases is there an adequate explanation of how the commodity options market operates so that prospects can become aware of how much the market price of the commodity must increase before a break-even point is reached. Instead, sellers give the impression that profits are reaped with every price rise, however incremental it might be.

It does appear that Lloyd, Carr has attempted to provide sufficient disclosure in two items sometimes mailed to potential customers. It is expressly stated in one leaflet that the purpose of the publication is to conform with Rule 32.5 adopted under the 1974 amendments to the Commodity Exchange Act. Lloyd, Carr therein informs investors that:

RISK

No individual or firm, even with the experience and extensive research and world-wide communication facilities Lloyd Carr possesses, can with certainty predict specific market movements of the futures contract or the commodity underlying the option offered.

ACCORDINGLY, AND BECAUSE OF THE VOLATILE NATURE OF THE COMMODITIES MARKET, THE PURCHASE OF COMMODITY OPTIONS IS NOT SUITABLE FOR MANY MEMBERS OF THE PUBLIC. AN INVESTOR SHOULD NOT PURCHASE A COMMODITY OPTION UNLESS HE IS AWARE OF THE POTENTIAL FOR LOSS, IS PREPARED TO SUSTAIN A TOTAL LOSS OF THE PURCHASE PRICE OF THE OPTION WHICH WILL OCCUR SHOULD THE PRICE OF THE UNDERLYING FUTURES CONTRACT NOT MOVE BEYOND THE STRIKE PRICE IN THE ANTICIPATED DIRECTION AND UNDERSTANDS THE NATURE AND EXTENT OF HIS RIGHTS AND OBLIGATIONS.

Yet the volatility of these markets is one of the compelling reasons we do recommend to those who meet the requirements, the purchase of commodity options, which couple high leverage and unlimited profit potential with assurance of known and limited loss possibility and elimination of margin calls. This assurance is totally absent from entry into straight commodity futures contracts and makes speculation in the latter infinitely more unsuitable, even foolhardy, for a far greater number of investors.

THESE COMMODITY OPTIONS HAVE NOT BEEN APPROVED OR DISAPPROVED BY THE COMMODITY FUTURES TRADING COMMISSION NOR HAS THE COMMISSION PASSED UPON THE ACCURACY OR ADEQUACY OF THIS STATEMENT. ANY REPRESENTATION TO THE CONTRARY IS A VIOLATION OF THE COMMODITY EXCHANGE ACT AND THE REGULATIONS THEREUNDER.

LLOYD CARR BELIEVES, HOWEVER, AND HAS BEEN ADVISED BY LEGAL COUNSEL, THAT THE STATEMENTS AND INFORMATION CONTAINED HEREIN ARE IN FULL CONFORMITY WITH DISCLOSURE SEC. 325 OF THE RULES AND REGULATIONS ISSUED UNDER THE COMMODITY FUTURES TRADING ACT OF 1974.

This language does in fact conform with Rule 32.5(5).

This disclosure does not suffice to save Lloyd, Carr's operations, however. First, there is no disclosure of the actual cost to the customer broken down into the various components including fees, commissions, or any other charges. Second, it is apparent from the description of the overall sales activities presented above that disclosure of risk was not emphasized, indeed it was generally omitted entirely. Salespersons were neither interested in performing nor qualified to undertake the necessary fiduciary responsibilities that inhere in the investment advisor field. Moreover, Lloyd, Carr management actively encouraged the types of pressure sales tactics used exclusively. Lloyd, Carr represents in one of its publications that "our high standards of moral responsibility and zealous desire to protect the confidence and reputation for integrity we have earned from our clients and the investing public, dictate that we not only emphasize the unusual profit potentials [options] transactions may offer, but carefully and candidly indicate the inherent risk and cost factors." There can be no doubt that this policy was not adhered to, and that the "high standards of moral responsibility" are in dramatic need of reappraisal.

In light of this factual background, it is not difficult to pass on plaintiffs' motions for preliminary injunctive relief. All factors point to the conclusion that the motions should be granted. Indeed, in a brief filed with the court defendants Lloyd, Carr & Co. and James A. Carr admitted that Lloyd, Carr "has thus far been unable to conform its business practices to the dictates of this Act [the Commodity Exchange Act]." * * *

The case before me falls within that category in which the fact of violation and the likelihood of future infractions are clear. The C.F.T.C. has succeeded in showing a number of egregious, inexcusable violations of

federal law. It is hard to imagine a more straightforward prohibition against fraud than § 32.9 of the rules promulgated under the Commodity Exchange Act. I deem it inherently fraudulent for an organization like Lloyd, Carr to make bold predictions of astronomical returns on investment in a field as speculative and uncertain as commodity options. *See United States v. Wolfson*, 405 F.2d 779 (2d Cir.), *cert. denied*, 394 U.S. 946, 22 L. Ed. 2d 479, 89 S.Ct. 1275 (1969); *United States v. Herr*, 338 F.2d 607 (7th Cir.1964), *cert. denied*, 382 U.S. 999, 15 L.Ed.2d 487, 86 S.Ct. 563 (1966). In addition, of course, the plethora of specific misrepresentations and omissions discussed above clearly falls within the purview of Rule 32.9. Moreover, there are indications that defendants continued their operations unaltered even in the face of a temporary restraining order. I have no hesitation in stating that a preliminary injunction should be granted on the basis of the "likelihood of future violations" standard.
* * *

NOTES

1. The Lloyd, Carr & Co., scandal widened after the owner was arrested for criminal contempt of Judge Fox's injunction. He was released on bail and then became a fugitive. A fingerprint check disclosed that he was actually Alan Abrahams, an escaped felon from a New Jersey prison. He was later captured and jailed.

2. The CFTC's suspension of over-the-counter options trading did not stop these fraudulent sales operations. They began calling their contracts "deferred delivery contracts," which were not subject to CFTC jurisdiction. The CFTC brought enforcement actions against some sixty firms to stop such sales. Numerous boiler rooms selling these contracts and their predecessor options were located in an area of Miami, Florida that regulators were soon calling "Maggot Mile." An old regulatory nemesis returned to engage in this business. Harold Goldstein, the principal of Goldstein Samuelson, the firm whose abuses resulted in CFTC regulation of options trading, tried to sell commodity options contracts by calling them unregulated deferred derivative contracts. As will be seen in the next chapter, that effort failed.

CHAPTER TWELVE

OVER-THE-COUNTER DERIVATIVES

■ ■ ■

Chapter objectives

- To learn about how financial derivative contracts are designed, traded, and settled in over-the-counter markets.

- To evaluate the ongoing legislative and judicial attempts to regulate or exempt over-the-counter derivatives.

- To understand the investment risks to end-users from using financial derivatives, including swap agreements.

- To appreciate the range of financial engineering products that involve derivative contracts.

SECTION 1. INTRODUCTION[1]

Historians have traced transactions in derivative instruments to 2000 B.C. In the United States, futures style contracts were slow to develop. The State of Massachusetts Bay, however, did issue some derivative instruments that appear to contain a crude form of cost of living index. One such instrument was a two year note for three hundred seventy pounds at six percent to be paid in currency "in a greater or less Sum, according as Five Bushels of CORN for, Sixty-eight Pounds and four-seventh Parts of a Pound of BEEF, Ten Pounds of SHEEPS WOOL, and Sixteen Pounds of SOLE LEATHER shall then cost, more or less than One Hundred and Thirty Pounds current Money, at the then current Prices of said Articles." Commodity markets also existed in Colonial America. They were auction style markets, a form of trading that is still in use in today's commodity futures markets.

The Civil War saw the development of a derivative instrument whose complexity and financial elegance matches anything that exists today on Wall Street. This was the so-called Erlanger bond that was issued in

---

1. The following discussion is drawn from Jerry W. Markham, "Confederate Bonds," "General Custer," and the Regulation of Derivative Financial Instruments, 25 Seton Hall Law Review 1 (1994) and Regulation of Hybrid Instruments Under the Commodity Exchange Act—Alternatives Are Needed, 1990 Columbia Business Law Review 1 (1990).

Europe by Emile Erlanger & Co. and J. Henry Schroder & Co. for the Confederate States of America. See chapter 10. The Erlanger bond was a tri-valued derivative instrument. One such bond provided for payment at maturity in the buyer's choice of 100 pounds sterling, 2500 French francs, or 4000 pounds of cotton Still another Confederate bond provided for the Treasury of the Confederate States to pay principal and interest in either cash or cotton. Interest coupons were attached to these bonds for payment in Confederate dollars or New Orleans Middling Grade Cotton. Here, however, the derivative function worked against the purchaser because the Confederate States could choose to pay the lesser of the two valued items. Perhaps evidencing the dangers of derivative instruments, the default risk on these cotton bonds proved to be quite high.

Difference trading on price changes also became commonplace in the over-the-counter market. The states attempted to stop this trading through legislation that prohibited such contracts or made them unenforceable as gambling contracts. Difference trading also occurred in the securities markets. A speculator could "place a wager on a stock, in much the same way as he might bet on a prize fight or a horse race." In one famous case, Justh v. Holliday, 13 D.C. (2 Mackay) 346 (1883), a broker was denied enforcement of a note against a decedent's estate because the note had been given to cover losses from betting on price differences in stocks. The surreptitious nature of the trading, and the fact that the decedent did not have the wherewithal to actually buy the stocks purportedly being traded, convinced the court that these were illegal gambling contracts. The decedent won that skirmish but lost a much bigger battle, and his life, only a few months after issuing this note. He was General George Armstrong Custer.

SECTION 2. CFTC PROBLEMS AND OTC DERIVATIVES

COMMODITY FUTURES TRADING COMMISSION v. CO PETRO MARKETING GROUP, INC.

680 F.2d 573 (9th Cir.1982).

CANBY, CIRCUIT JUDGE.

Co Petro Marketing Group, Inc., and individual appellants, Harold Goldstein and Michael Krivacek, (Co Petro) appeal from an order of the district court, 502 F.Supp. 806, permanently enjoining them from offering, selling, or otherwise engaging in futures contracts in petroleum products, in violation of §§ 4 and 4h of the Commodity Exchange Act, as amended, (the Act), 7 U.S.C. §§ 6, 6h (1976). Co Petro contends that the contracts it sold were not subject to the Act. Co Petro also appeals from the district court's award of relief ancillary to the permanent injunction. The district court appointed a receiver, ordered Co Petro to permit the receiver access to the firm's books and records, ordered an accounting, and generally ordered the disgorgement of unlawfully obtained funds. Co Petro further assigns as error the district court's taking judicial notice of three prior proceedings against defendant Goldstein. We affirm the district court's judgment that Co Petro was offering and selling "contracts of sale of a commodity for future delivery" (futures contracts) within the meaning of section 2(a)(1) of the Act, 7 U.S.C.§ 2 (1976). We also agree with the district court that Co Petro violated sections 4 and 4h of the Act, 7 U.S.C. §§ 6, 6h (1976), by trading these contracts otherwise than by or through a member of a board of trade which has been designated by the Commodity Futures Trading Commission as a contract market. Finally we affirm the award of ancillary relief and find no error in the district court's taking judicial notice of the three prior proceedings against defendant Goldstein.

Co Petro is licensed by the State of California as a gasoline broker. It operated a chain of retail gasoline outlets and also acted as a broker of petroleum products, buying and reselling in the spot market several hundred thousand gallons of gasoline and diesel fuel monthly. While part of its business operations involved the direct sale of gasoline to industrial, commercial, and retail users of gasoline, Co Petro also offered and sold contracts for the future purchase of petroleum products pursuant to an "Agency Agreement for Purchase and Sale of Motor Vehicle Fuel" (Agency Agreement).

Under the Agency Agreement, the customer (1) appointed Co Petro as his agent to purchase a specified quantity and type of fuel at a fixed price for delivery at an agreed future date, and (2) paid a deposit based upon a fixed percentage of the purchase price. Co Petro, however, did not require its customer to take delivery of the fuel. Instead, at a later specified date the customer could appoint Co Petro to sell the fuel on his behalf. If the cash price had risen in the interim Co Petro was to (1) remit the difference between the original purchase price and the subsequent sale price, and (2) refund any remaining deposit. If the cash price had decreased, Co Petro was to (1) deduct from the deposit the difference between the purchase price and the subsequent sale price, and (2) remit the balance of the deposit to the customer. A liquidated damages clause provided that in no event would the customer lose more than 95% of his initial deposit.

Co Petro marketed these contracts extensively to the general public through newspaper advertisements, private seminars, commissioned telephone solicitors, and various other commissioned sales agents. The Commodity Futures Trading Commission brought this statutory injunctive action under section 6c of the Act, 7 U.S.C.§ 13a–1 (1976), seeking to enjoin Co Petro's sales of petroleum products pursuant to its Agency Agreements. The Commission's complaint generally charged and the district court held that Co Petro was in violation of the Act by offering and selling contracts of sale of commodities for future delivery outside of a licensed contract market.

Co Petro contends that the Commission lacks jurisdiction over transactions pursuant to its Agency Agreements because these agreements are "cash forward" contracts expressly excluded from regulation by section 2(a)(1) of the Act, 7 U.S.C.§ 2 (1976). While section 2(a)(1) provides the Commission with regulatory jurisdiction over "contracts of sale of a commodity for future delivery," it further provides that the term future delivery "shall not include any sale of any cash commodity for deferred shipment or delivery." Cash commodity contracts for deferred shipment or delivery are commonly known as "cash forward" contracts, while contracts of sale of a commodity for future delivery are called "futures contracts". See H.R.Rep.No.93–975, 93d Cong., 2d Sess. 129–30 (1974). The Act, however, sets forth no further definitions of the term "future delivery" or of the phrase "cash commodity for deferred shipment or delivery." The statutory language, therefore, provides little guidance as to the distinctions between regulated futures contracts and excluded cash forward contracts and, to our knowledge, no other court has dealt with this question. Where the statute is, as here, ambiguous on its face, it is necessary to look to legislative history to ascertain the intent of Congress. See United States v. Turkette, 452 U.S. 576, 580, 101 S.Ct. 2524, 2527, 69 L.Ed.2d 246 (1981). Our examination of the relevant legislative history leads us to conclude that the Co Petro's Agency Agreements are not cash forward contracts within the meaning of the Act.

The exclusion for cash forward contracts originated in the Future Trading Act, Pub.L.No.67–66,§ 2, 42 Stat. 187 (1921). Congress passed the Future Trading Act as a result of excessive speculation and price manipulations occurring on the grain futures markets. S.Rep.No.212, 67th Cong., 1st Sess. 4–5 (1921). See S.Rep.No.93–1131, 93d Cong., 2d Sess. 13 (1974), reprinted in (1974) U.S.Code & Ad.News 5843, 5854–55. To curb these abuses, the Future Trading Act imposed a prohibitive tax on all futures contracts with two exceptions. Section 4(a) of the Act exempted from the tax future delivery contracts made by owners and growers of grain, owners and renters of land on which grain was grown, and associations of such persons. 42 Stat. 187. Section 4(b) of the Act exempted from the tax future delivery contracts made by or through members of boards of trade which had been designated by the Secretary of Agriculture as contract markets. Id. During hearings on the bill that became the Future Trading Act, various witnesses expressed concern that the exemption for owners and growers of grain, owners and renters of land on which grain was grown, and associations of such persons, was too narrow. By its terms, this section might not exempt from the tax a variety of legitimate commercial transactions, such as cash grain contracts between farmers and grain elevator operators for the future delivery of grain. Hearings on H.R. 5676 Before the Senate Committee on Agriculture and Forestry, 67th Cong., 1st Sess. 8–9, 213–214, 431, 462 (1921). As a result, the Senate added language to section 2 of the bill, excluding "any sale of cash grain for deferred shipment" from the term "future delivery". S.Rep.No.212, 67th Cong., 1st Sess. 1 (1921). There is no indication that Congress drew this exclusion otherwise than to meet a particular need such as that of a farmer to sell part of next season's harvest at a set price to a grain elevator or miller. These cash forward contracts guarantee the farmer a buyer for his crop and provide the buyer with an assured price. Most important, both parties to the contracts deal in and contemplate future delivery of the actual grain.

The exclusion was carried forward without change into the Grain Futures Act, Pub.L.No.67–331, § 2, 42 Stat. 998 (1922). In 1936, Congress enacted the Commodity Exchange Act, Pub.L.No.74–675, 49 Stat. 1491 (1936). This Act expanded the scope of federal regulation to include certain specified commodities in addition to grain, id.,§ 3, and reworded the exclusion to except "any cash commodity for deferred shipment or delivery." Id.,§ 2. The Commodity Exchange Act also deleted the express exemption for owners and growers of grain, owners and renters of land, and associations of such persons. Congress considered the exemption redundant since section 2 of the Act, which excluded cash commodity contracts for deferred shipment or delivery, served to protect the same interests that had been protected by the exemption for owners and growers. H.R.Rep.No.421, 74th Cong., 1st Sess. 4–5 (1935). Although the Act has been amended numerous times since 1936, the language excluding cash commodities for deferred shipment or delivery has remained the same.

A more recent House Report on the 1974 Amendments to the Act reconfirms the narrowness of the exclusion. H.R.Rep.No.93–975, 93d Cong., 2d Sess. 129–30 (1974). The House Report describes a typical cash transaction as involving, for example, a farmer who wants to convert 5,000 bushels of wheat into cash. He seeks a buyer such as a grain elevator for whom the wheat has "inherent value." The wheat has "inherent value" for the grain elevator because the elevator "is in contact with potential buyers such as the flour miller, and has the facilities to store, condition, and load out the grain and earn additional income from these services." Id. at 129. The wheat also has "inherent value" to the flour miller, who can increase its utility and value by grinding it into flour. Id. A cash forward contract is common in these kinds of transactions because it guarantees the miller, for example, a price but allows delivery to be deferred "until such time as he could process the wheat." Id. This House Report therefore supports prior history indicating that a cash forward contract is one in which the parties contemplate physical transfer of the actual commodity.

The situation for which the exclusion for cash forward contracts was designed is not present here. Co Petro's Agency Agreement customers were, for the most part, speculators from the general public. The underlying petroleum products had no inherent value to these speculators. They had neither the intention of taking delivery nor the capacity to do so. Yet it was to the general public that Co Petro made its strongest sales pitches. For example, in an advertisement in the Los Angeles Times under the headline "Invest in Gasoline," Co Petro stated: "The Sophisticated Small

Investor Can Make Money Buying Gasoline. It's a high risk-high potential yield opportunity." In addition to advertising extensively in newspapers of general circulation, Co Petro ran seminars to explain its investment vehicle to the general public. It also hired sales agents experienced in marketing commodities to investors. In an apparent attempt to protect itself, Co Petro required the investor in one version of its Agency Agreement to initial the following statement: "I realize that a motor vehicle fuel purchase is a high risk speculative venture and I fully understand that I could lose most or all of my entire deposit and by virtue of my own business experience or independent advice, I am capable of evaluating the hazards and merits of this motor vehicle fuel purchase."

There is nothing in the legislative history surrounding cash forward contracts to suggest that Congress intended the exclusion to encompass agreements for the future delivery of commodities sold merely for purposes of such speculation. Congress has recognized the vital role speculators play in the proper functioning of futures markets, H.R.Rep.No.93–975, supra, at 138, and has expressed its desire to protect speculators through expansive federal regulation. See Merrill Lynch, Pierce, Fenner & Smith, Inc. v. Curran, 456 U.S. 353, 102 S.Ct. 1825, 1845, 72 L.Ed.2d 182 (1982). Prior to the 1974 Amendments to the Act, only certain specified commodities were regulated. In 1974, Congress not only expanded the list of commodities subject to regulation, but also extended regulation to "all other goods and articles, ... and all services, rights, and interests in which contracts for future delivery are presently or in the future dealt with." 7 U.S.C.§ 2 (1976). The House Report on these amendments stated: "There is no reason why a person trading in one of the currently unregulated futures markets should not receive the same protection afforded to those trading in the currently regulated markets." H.R.Rep. No.93–975, supra, at 76. See S.Rep.No.93–1131, supra, at 19. This recent expression of legislative intent to protect persons like Co Petro's customers, who deal in previously unregulated commodity futures, is consonant with a narrow reading of the exclusion for sales of cash commodities for deferred shipment or delivery. We hold, therefore, that this exclusion is unavailable to contracts of sale for commodities which are sold merely for speculative purposes and which are not predicated upon the expectation that delivery of the actual commodity by the seller to the original contracting buyer will occur in the future. See In re Stovall, (Current) Commodity Futures Law Reports (CCH) § 20,941 at 23, 778 (Dec. 6, 1979).

This does not end our inquiry, however. Even though Co Petro's Agency Agreements do not fall within the exclusion for cash forward contracts, there remains the question whether they are "contracts of sale of a commodity for future delivery" (futures contracts) within the meaning of section 2(a)(1) of the Act, 7 U.S.C.§ 2 (1976). Co Petro contends that its Agency Agreements cannot be futures contracts because they lack most of the common distinguishing features of futures contracts as they are known in the industry. Futures contracts traded on the designated markets have certain basic characteristics. Except for price, all the futures contracts for a specified commodity are identical in quantity and other terms. The fungible nature of these contracts facilitates offsetting transactions by which purchasers or sellers can liquidate their positions by forming opposite contracts. The price differential between the opposite contracts then determines the investor's profit or loss. See Cargill, Inc. v. Hardin, 452 F.2d 1154, 1157 (8th Cir.1971), cert. denied, 406 U.S. 932, 92 S.Ct. 1770, 32 L.Ed.2d 135 (1972); H.R.Rep.No.93–975, supra, at 130.

While contracts pursuant to Co Petro's Agency Agreements were not as rigidly standardized as futures contracts traded on licensed contract markets, neither were they individualized. Tables furnished by Co Petro to its sales agents demonstrate uniformity in the basic units of volume, multiples of which were offered for sale. Similarly, relevant dates in Co Petro's Agency Agreements were uniform. The date on which an investor had to notify Co Petro of his intent to take delivery or appoint Co Petro as his agent to resell the contract was set at approximately eight months from the purchase date. An investor could not give notice prior to the specified notice date. The delivery date was always ten months from the purchase date.

More important, however, than the degree to which Co Petro's Agency Agreements conform to the precise features of standardized futures contracts is the rationale for standardization in futures trading. Standardized form contracts facilitate the formation of offsetting or liquidating transactions. The ability to form offsetting contracts is essential, since investors rarely take delivery against the contracts. Pursuant to provisions in Co Petro's Agency Agreements, Co Petro was obliged to perform an offsetting service for its customers by reselling contracts for their accounts. Customers also could liquidate their positions in the face of adverse price movements by canceling their contracts with Co Petro and paying only the liquidated damages provided for in the Agency Agreements. Therefore, Co Petro's customers, like customers who trade on organized futures exchanges, could deal in commodity futures without the forced burden of delivery. Disregarding form for substance, Tcherepnin v. Knight, 389 U.S. 332, 336, 88 S.Ct. 548, 553, 19 L.Ed.2d 564 (1967), we find without merit Co Petro's argument that its Agency Agreement represents a radical departure from the classic elements of a standardized futures contract. We also reject Co Petro's final contention that, contrary to the practice in organized futures markets where price is established by public auction, it negotiated prices directly with its Agency Agreement customers. The evidence indicates that, for the most part, Co Petro unilaterally set prices for its products according to the then-prevailing market rates, with the spot market determining resale prices to subsequent purchasers. Moreover, the fact that public auction did not determine Co Petro's prices is merely a result of Co Petro's failure to seek Commission licensing for organized exchange trading in petroleum futures.

In determining whether a particular contract is a contract of sale of a commodity for future delivery over which the Commission has regulatory jurisdiction by virtue of 7 U.S.C.§ 2 (1976), no bright-line definition or list of characterizing elements is determinative. The transaction must be viewed as a whole with a critical eye toward its underlying purpose. The contracts here represent speculative ventures in commodity futures which were marketed to those for whom delivery was not an expectation. Addressing these circumstances in the light of the legislative history of the Act, we conclude that Co Petro's contracts are "contracts of sale of a commodity for future delivery." 7 U.S.C.§ 2 (1976). * * *

We hold that Co Petro was a board of trade as defined by section 2(a)(1) of the Act, 7 U.S.C.§ 2 (1976), and that its failure to trade futures contracts through a designated contract market was in violation of section 4, 7 U.S.C. § 6 (1976). * * *

RUSSELL E. SMITH, DISTRICT JUDGE, dissenting. * * *

NOTES

Harold Goldstein continued his life of crime. He created an offshore bank and used it to defraud individuals through loan schemes. He was indicted but fled, only to be captured by authorities aboard a stolen yacht carrying illegal firearms.

SECTION 3.   TREASURY AMENDMENT

The next round in this saga of fraudulent over-the-counter derivatives involved options on currency. Dealers in those instruments claimed they were exempt from CFTC regulation by the so-called Treasury Amendment in the Commodity Exchange Act.

DUNN v. COMMODITY FUTURES TRADING COMMISSION

519 U.S. 465, 117 S.Ct. 913, 137 L.Ed.2d 93 (1997).

JUSTICE STEVENS delivered the opinion of the Court.

The question presented is whether Congress has authorized the Commodity Futures Trading Commission (CFTC or Commission) to regulate "off-exchange" trading in options to buy or sell foreign currency.

The CFTC brought this action in 1994, alleging that, beginning in 1992, petitioners solicited investments in and operated a fraudulent scheme in violation of the Commodity Exchange Act (CEA), 7 U.S.C. § 1 *et seq.*, and CFTC regulations. See 7 U.S.C. § 6c(b); 17 CFR § 32.9 (1996). The CFTC's complaint, affidavits, and declarations submitted to the District Court indicate that customers were told their funds would be invested using complex strategies involving options to purchase or sell various foreign currencies. Petitioners apparently did in fact engage in many such transactions. *Ibid.;* 58 F.3d 50, 51 (C.A.2 1995). To do so, they contracted directly with international banks and others without making use of any regulated exchange or board of trade. In the parlance of the business, petitioners traded in the "off-exchange" or "over-the-counter" (OTC) market. No options were ever sold directly to petitioners' customers. However, their positions were tracked through internal accounts, and investors were provided weekly reports showing the putative status of their holdings. Petitioners and their customers suffered heavy losses. *Id.,* at 51–52. Subsequently, the CFTC commenced these proceedings. * * *

The outcome of this case is dictated by the so-called "Treasury Amendment" to the CEA. 88 Stat. 1395, 7 U.S.C. § 2(ii). We have previously reviewed the history of the CEA and generally described how it authorizes the CFTC to regulate the "volatile and esoteric" market in futures contracts in fungible commodities. See *Merrill Lynch, Pierce, Fenner & Smith, Inc. v. Curran,* 456 U.S. 353, 356, 357–367, 102 S.Ct. 1825, 1828–1834, 72 L.Ed.2d 182 (1982). As a part of the 1974 amendments that created the CFTC and dramatically expanded the coverage of the statute to include nonagricultural commodities "in which contracts for future delivery are presently or in the future dealt in," see 88 Stat. 1395, 7 U.S.C. § 2 (1970 ed., Supp. IV), Congress enacted the following exemption, which has come to be known as the "Treasury Amendment":

> "Nothing in this chapter shall be deemed to govern or in any way be applicable to *transactions in foreign currency,* security warrants, security rights, resales of installment loan contracts, repurchase options, government securities, or mortgages and mortgage purchase commitments, unless such transactions involve the sale thereof for future delivery conducted on a board of trade." 7 U.S.C. § 2(ii) (emphasis added).

The narrow issue that we must decide is whether the italicized phrase ("transactions in foreign currency") includes transactions in options to buy or sell foreign currency. An option, as the term is understood in the trade, is a transaction in which the buyer purchases from the seller for consideration the right, but not the obligation, to buy or sell an agreed amount of a commodity at a set rate at any time prior to the option's expiration. We think it plain that foreign currency options are "transactions in foreign currency" within the meaning of the statute. We are not persuaded by any of the arguments advanced by the CFTC in support of a narrower reading that would exempt futures contracts (agreements to buy or sell a specified quantity of a commodity at a particular price for delivery at a set future date) without exempting options. * * *

Indeed, adopting the Commission's reading would deprive the exemption of the principal effect Congress intended. The CFTC acknowledges that futures contracts fall squarely within the Treasury Amendment's exemption, and there is no question that the exemption of off-exchange foreign currency futures from CFTC regulation was one of Congress' primary goals.[2] Yet on the CFTC's reasoning the exemption's application to futures contracts could not be sustained.

A futures contract is no more a transaction "in" foreign currency as the Commission understands the term than an option. The Commission argues that because a futures contract creates a legal obligation to purchase or sell currency on a particular date, it is somehow more clearly a transaction "in" the underlying currencies than an option, which generates only the right to engage in a transaction. This reasoning is wholly unpersuasive. No currency changes hands at the time a futures contract is made. And, the existence of a futures contract does not guarantee that currency will actually be exchanged. Indeed, the Commission concedes that, in most cases, futures contracts are "extinguished before delivery by entry into an offsetting futures contract." Adopting the CFTC's reading would therefore place both futures and options outside the exemption, in clear contravention of Congress' intent.

Furthermore, this interpretation would leave the Treasury Amendment's exemption for "transactions in foreign currency" without any significant effect at all, because it would limit the scope of the exemption to "forward contracts" (agreements that anticipate the actual delivery of a commodity on a specified future date) and "spot transactions" (agreements for purchase and sale of commodities that anticipate near-term delivery). Both are transactions "in" a commodity as the CFTC would have us understand the term. But neither type of transaction for *any* commodity was subject to intensive regulation under the CEA at the time of the Treasury Amendment's passage. See 7 U.S.C. § 2 (1970 ed., Supp. IV) ("term 'future delivery,' as used in this chapter, shall not include any sale of any cash commodity for deferred shipment or delivery"); Snider § 9.01; J. Markham, The History of Commodity Futures Trading and Its Regulation 201–203 (1987). Our reading of the exemption is therefore also consonant with the doctrine that legislative enactments should not be construed to render their provisions mere surplusage. * * *

JUSTICE SCALIA, concurring in part and concurring in the judgment. * * *

---

2. The amendment was enacted on the suggestion of the Treasury Department at the time of a dramatic expansion in the scope of federal commodities regulation. The Department expressed concerns in a letter to the relevant congressional committee that this development might lead, inter alia, to the unintended regulation of the off-exchange market in foreign currency futures. See S.Rep. No. 93–1131, pp. 49–50 (1974) ("The Department feels strongly that foreign currency futures trading, other than on organized exchanges, should not be regulated by the new agency") (letter of Donald Ritger, Acting General Counsel). The Treasury Amendment, which tracks almost verbatim the language proposed by the Department, cf. id., at 51, was included in the legislation to respond to these concerns. Id., at 23. The CFTC is therefore plainly correct to reject the suggestion of its amici that the Treasury Amendment's exemption be construed not to include futures contracts within its coverage.

NOTES

1. The CFTC continued to pursue the currency option dealers after the *Dunn* case, claiming that those dealers were boards of trade that were outside the scope of the Treasury Amendment. Congress then made things easier for the CFTC by including a provision in the Commodity Futures Modernization Act of 2000 ("CFMA") that allowed the CFTC to regulate these operations. Pub. L. No. 106–554, 114 Stat. 2763 (2000). Under the CFMA, the CFTC has the authority to regulate options on currencies, if such transactions are traded on an "organized exchange." An organized exchange is defined as one that permits trading by non-institutional participants or on other than a principal-to-principal basis. 7 U.S.C. § 1a(27). This change allowed the CFTC to attack retail firms that previously had sought to avoid CFTC jurisdiction under the Treasury Amendment. The CFTC was dealt a setback in that effort, however, after the Seventh Circuit ruled that a currency dealer's contracts were forward rather than futures contracts, which meant they were outside the CFTC's jurisdiction. CFTC v. Zelener, 373 F.3d 861 (7th Cir. 2004). The CFTC Reauthorization Act of 2008 sought to overturn the *Zelener* decision by granting the CFTC regulatory authority over all-exchange retail transactions in foreign currency that are offered on a leveraged or margin basis or financed by the offeror or its affiliates. Persons engaged in such activity must register with the CFTC as "retail foreign exchange dealers." Those registrants, and futures commission merchants engaged in such activity, are required to have minimum adjusted net capital of $20 million. The CFTC was also given broader regulatory authority over other foreign currency market participants, including commodity pool operators and commodity trading advisors. Jerry W. Markham, 13A Commodities Regulation: Fraud, Manipulation & Other Claims, § 27:14.50 (2010). Under the CFMA, foreign currency transactions that are futures or options contracts are allowed for "eligible" contract participants[3] with counterparties that are not regulated financial institutions. The CFMA allows retail sales of foreign currency futures or options contracts only if the counterparty, or the person offering to be the counterparty, of the retail customer is a futures commission merchant or certain other financial institutions. CFTC v. Valko, 2006 WL 2582970 (S.D. Fla. 2006).

2. The foreign currency ("Forex") market is two tiered. At the top, are the banks that provide and trade foreign currency with large institutions. That market trades trillions of dollars every day. A second tier is the retail market where you obtain foreign currency when you travel abroad. The spreads in that market are much larger and less competitive than those in the institutional market, as you may have discovered when you changed money on the street and compared that with the rate on your credit card.

3. Salomon Brothers (now a part of Citigroup, Inc.) developed something called Range Forward Contracts for institutional clients. That provided for a range of rates at which currencies could be exchanged on a forward contract basis.

---

3. Section 1a(12) of the Commodity Exchange Act now defines an eligible contract participant to include an individual who has total assets in an amount in excess of $10,000,000 and investment advisers subject to regulation under the Investment Advisers Act of 1940. 7 U.S.C. § 1a(12).

SECTION 4.   FINANCIAL OTC INSTRUMENTS

Financial engineering in the last part of the twentieth century sparked a near revolution in finance. These instruments took many forms and come in literally hundreds of varieties.[4] One of the first of these instruments was a silver bond offered by the Sunshine Mining Company in 1980. These bonds were indexed to the price of silver and were redeemable at the indexed price if it were greater than $1000, the face value of the bond. The bond offered investors an opportunity to receive a fixed minimum return at a reduced interest rate and also to receive the opportunity to profit should the price of silver rise. The investor paid a premium for that opportunity in the form of reduced interest rates on the bond.

The CFTC was either unaware of, or did not concern itself with, the offering of this bond. That attitude was to change as the growth of similar derivatives and more exotic investments began to multiply in the 1980s. During this period, the CFTC began to consider these instruments on an ad hoc basis. Some passed muster, while others did not. For example, the CFTC staff authorized an offering of subordinated debentures that were to be paid an annual rate of ten-and-a-half percent with additional payments based on increases in the price of natural gas. The CFTC, however, questioned another proposal involving oil under which the Standard Oil Company sought to issue notes attached to a debenture that would be separately tradeable. The holder of this instrument was to be given a principal sum plus a premium for increases in crude oil prices over a specified amount. The CFTC eventually allowed this offer to go forward but asserted that it would not allow similar offerings in the future.

The CFTC staff also concluded that certain gold warrants were options that were subject to the exchange trading restrictions of the Commodity Exchange Act. The gold warrants in question were associated with a proposed equity offering in a particular company. The company was organized for the purpose of acquiring, exploring and developing precious metals mining properties. The company filed with the SEC a registration statement covering 1.3 million units consisting of one share of common stock, one common stock purchase warrant and one warrant to purchase a specified amount of gold. The stock warrants and gold warrants were detachable and transferable commencing no later than 100 days from the date of registration with the SEC. Each gold warrant gave the holder the right to purchase 0.01 Troy ounces of gold from the company at an initial price of $6, subject to production by the company of sufficient gold to permit exercise. The gold warrant price was tied to a base production cost that initially would be $300 per ounce and would be adjusted quarterly in proportion to increases or decreases in the consumer price index. The

---

4. This note is excerpted from Jerry W. Markham, Regulation of Hybrid Instruments Under the Commodity Exchange Act—Alternatives Are Needed, 1990 Columbia Business Law Review 1 (1990).

CFTC staff was of the view that these warrants were commodity options because they gave the holder the conditional right, but not the obligation, to purchase physical gold. Moreover, part of the purchase price of the offer was directly attributable to the value of the gold warrant and would serve the economic purpose of an option premium.

In *CFTC v. Wells Fargo Bank, N.A.*, Civ. No. 87–07992 Wdk. (BX) (Nov. 18, 1987) the CFTC charged that Wells Fargo was illegally offering and selling options contracts to the general public in the form of "Wells Fargo Gold Market Certificates.'" Purchasers of these certificates deposited a sum of money (ranging from $2500 to $1 million) with the bank and paid a non-refundable premium or fee for the right to earn a return based on the increase, if any, in gold prices at the conclusion of a 26 week deposit period. The investor in this program could select a "Full Option'" or a "Half Option.'" Under the former, the investor's earnings were calculated by multiplying the deposit amount by 100% of any increase in the price of gold at the conclusion of the 26–week period. Half Options were multiplied by 50% of the increase in gold prices and could be purchased for a lower premium than a Full Option. In addition to paying a premium, investors had to forego interest on the deposit of their funds. Wells Fargo consented to a permanent injunction that enjoined it from selling these instruments, and it agreed to refund the customer funds and premiums and to pay interest on the use of the customer funds.

In the 1980s, a major brokerage house developed agreements that effectively allowed the holder of variable rate interest obligations to hedge the risk of adverse changes in those rates. These agreements simply set floors or caps on the amount of fluctuation in a variable rate commitment. In the event that interest rates fluctuated beyond that range, the brokerage firm would pay the customer an amount equivalent to such increase over the ceiling or decrease under the floor. The differences were periodically computed and payments made to the customer, if any were due. These interest rate obligation agreements effectively assured that the variable rate was converted into a fixed rate mortgage, although a limited amount of variation could be permitted between the floor or cap.

In exchange for this commitment, the brokerage firm was paid a fee. The brokerage firm would hedge its risk in this transaction on a futures exchange that offered interest rate futures contracts. Floor and cap contracts were generally offered only to large commercial customers and only for substantial amounts, which effectively excluded the public from participating. The terms of the agreements were to some extent standardized but the essential terms of the contracts such as price, duration and interest rate were individually negotiated. In addition, there were no margin requirements. Nevertheless, the contracts effectively allowed the shifting of the risk of change in value of the interest rates, just as does a commodity futures contract traded on a contract market. There was, however, no provision for an offsetting contract under the floor and cap agreements. Rather, the contract was for a specific duration. The CFTC did not conclude that these contracts were futures or commodity options.

Another over-the-counter derivative is the swap contract. These agreements have become widespread and are engaged in by many major financial institutions. Under an interest rate swap arrangement, one company effectively swaps its fixed interest rate obligations for the varia- ble rate obligations of another. These transactions may also involve currencies, stocks and other instruments. The following example of a swap transaction may best help explain how they work. Assume that a construc- tion company has a floating interest rate that is reset periodically on the basis of some interest rate index such as LIBOR (London Interbank Offered Rate). The construction company is concerned that interest rates will increase, causing a large jump in its interest costs. Separately, a finance company has loaned a large amount of its funds at a fixed rate. The finance company fears that interest rates will decrease, which will reduce the return on its loan note. The finance company, therefore would like to have a floating rate note, rather than a fixed rate. The concerns of both the finance company and the construction company can be solved through a swap in which they simply agree to exchange payment streams. That is, the two companies will periodically pay each other the difference in the event of an interest rate fluctuation. So, assume that interest rates increase, the finance company will have to pay the construction company the amount of the difference between the fixed rate and the new rate. If interest rates go down the construction company will pay the finance company an amount equal to the decrease. This is a simple example of a derivative, but many derivative transactions are infinitely more complex and exotic. *See Frank Partnoy, F.I.A.S.C.O.: Blood in the Water on Wall Street* 94 (1997) (describing a "quanto constant maturity swap yield curve flattening trade").

The swap market has become a sophisticated market for major financial institutions. Generally, it does not involve individual customers and does not permit speculation. In addition, the transactions are individ- ually negotiated for terms, amounts and other items, although many terms are standardized. These transactions do not generally involve mar- gin and, while they allow the shifting of the risk that interest rates will change, just as does a futures contract, there is no provision to allow speculation. The CFTC rendered an interpretation that allows these transactions to occur without being treated as commodity option or commodity futures contracts.

By the 1990s, more than 1200 financial derivative products were being offered over-the-counter. They include such things as swaptions, embedded options, synthetic indexing, synthetic stocks, barrier options, best-of-two-options, down-and-out options, deferred stop or deferred start options, lateral options, look back options, performance options, and exploding options. The CFTC had previously adopted rules to deal with the increased rate of new derivative financial instruments. 17 C.F.R. Part 34 (1989). In adopting those rules, the CFTC concluded that instruments containing more futures or options elements than typical interest rate or similar instruments would be treated as regulated futures or options. The rules exempted hybrid debt instruments, certain preferred equity or depository instruments with commodity option components and demand deposits, bond deposits, or transactions accounts offered by federally insured financial institutions. For other instruments, the value of implied option premiums could not outweigh the commodity independent components. The CFTC established a complex formula for making that determination. A CFTC Task Force on Off–Exchange Instruments also finally focused on swap transactions. It concluded that they should not be regulated as futures or commodity options.

NOTES

1. Important to the development of the swaps market was the creation of standardized documentation. This was carried out through the International Swaps and Derivatives Association (ISDA):

> The International Swaps and Derivatives Association is the global trade association representing leading participants in the privately negotiated derivatives industry, a business which includes interest rate, currency, commodity, credit and equity swaps, as well as related products such as caps, collars, floors and swaptions. ISDA was chartered in 1985, and today numbers over 575 member institutions from 44 countries on six continents. These members include most of the world's major institutions who deal in and leading end-users of privately negotiated derivatives, as well as associated service providers and consultants.

> Since its inception, the Association has pioneered efforts to identify and reduce the sources of risk in the derivatives and risk management business. Among its most notable accomplishments are: developing the ISDA Master Agreement; publishing a wide range of related documentation materials and instruments covering a variety of transaction types; producing legal opinions on the enforceability of netting (available only to ISDA members); securing recognition of the risk-reducing effects of netting in determining capital requirements; promoting sound risk management practices, and advancing the understanding and treatment of derivatives and risk management from public policy and regulatory capital perspectives.

www.isda.org

2. The CFTC's rulemaking efforts for hybrid instruments did not bring any degree of certainty into the regulation of these new derivative financial instruments. To the contrary, confusion seemed to grow, as seen from the following case.

TRANSNOR (BERMUDA) LTD. v. B.P. NORTH AMERICAN PETROLEUM

738 F.Supp. 1472 (S.D.N.Y. 1990).

WILLIAM C. CONNER, DISTRICT JUDGE.

* * * Plaintiff Transnor (Bermuda) Ltd. ("Transnor") is a corporation established under the laws of Bermuda and with its principal place of business there. Transnor's suit arises out of its purchase of two cargoes of North Sea Crude Oil in December 1985 at an average price of $24.50 per barrel for delivery in Scotland in March 1986. Transnor refused to take delivery of these cargoes because their market value had declined after Transnor entered into the contracts.

Transnor claims that remaining defendants Conoco Inc., Conoco (U.K.) Ltd. (collectively "Conoco") and Exxon Corporation ("Exxon"), conspired with the settling defendants to cause a decline in crude oil prices by jointly selling cargoes of Brent blend crude oil ("Brent Oil") at below-market prices. Brent Oil is a blend of oils produced in various fields in the North Sea and delivered through pipelines for loading onto cargo ships at Sullem Voe in the Shetland Islands. By the end of March 1986, the price of a barrel of Brent Oil had dropped substantially to $13.80 per barrel, from $29.05 per barrel in November 1985. Transnor asserts claims against defendants for violations of the Sherman Act, 15 U.S.C. § 1 (1982), and sections 4(c), 6(b), and 6(a) of the Commodity Exchange Act ("CEA"), 7 U.S.C. §§ 6(c), 9 and 13(b) (1980 & 1989 Supp.). * * *

Transnor claims that defendants carried out their conspiracy through "tax spinning"—the arm's-length sale by an integrated oil producer to a third party and a substantially simultaneous purchase of a similar quantity of oil at substantially the same price for use in that producer's refineries—which, depending on the relation between the average market price and the price at which the trades were made, created the possibility of substantial tax savings under U.K. tax law. The crux of Transnor's claim is that from approximately November 1985 through mid-March 1986, defendants conspired to tax spin Brent Oil at below-market prices in order to reduce the U.K. taxes paid by defendants. Transnor also claims that the artificially reduced price of the spin sales drove down the market price of Brent Oil, a benchmark crude oil, as well as that of other crude oils such as West Texas Intermediate ("WTI"), an oil traded on the New York Mercantile Exchange, with which Brent Oil is virtually interchangeable.

Under the U.K. Oil Taxation Act of 1975 ("Taxation Act"), the applicable petroleum revenue tax rate between April 2, 1985 and March 31, 1986 was 87%. Under the then-applicable provisions of the Taxation Act, the taxed price on sales of oil differed depending on whether the sale was at arm's length on the open market or the oil was transferred directly to an integrated producer's affiliated entity. Transfers to affiliated companies were taxed at an assessed market value, known as the tax reference price ("TRP"), which, beginning in 1984, was determined by the Inland Revenue's Oil Taxation Office ("OTO") based on an average of prices established retrospectively for a period of time prior to the interaffiliate transfer. Defendants argue that because of declining oil prices from other causes, primarily the excess supply in the world oil market caused by OPEC, the TRP was higher than the current market price and thus led to payment of taxes on sales to affiliated entities based on an artificially high rate. Rather than pay taxes based on such an inflated price, defendants entered into matched buy/sell transactions in the open market instead of transferring oil directly to their refineries. Defendants claim that tax spinning thus resulted in payment of taxes based on a more accurate market rate, not, as Transnor claims, at below-market rates. This would furnish a logical explanation of tax spinning if it was done only in a declining market, in which the tax-spin transactions were at an actual market price lower than the TRP—i.e. lower than the average market prices over the past month. Whether the tax spinning was done only in such circumstances is unclear from the present record.

Both parties spend considerable energy debating whether these transfers violate U.K. tax law. In brief, Transnor contends that while it was legal for an integrated oil company to sell its oil in the open market and to buy oil for its own needs, it was not legal to enter into a large number of matched buy/sell contracts at the same price in order to establish a "portfolio" of contracts for delivery months in the future. Defendants held these contracts open until the delivery month and then selected from their "portfolio" the lowest-priced sale and assigned to it oil they produced that month, known as "equity production." Producers were also able to choose among their affiliated businesses in assigning the sale, which was then reported to the tax authorities as the arms-length price at which they sold their equity production. In order to balance its portfolio for the month, other buy/sells for that month would be disposed of by "booking out"[5] or by entering into an offsetting transaction. * * *

[D]efendants challenge the Court's subject matter jurisdiction over the commodities claims, contending that the Brent transactions were "cash forward contracts" specifically exempted from the scope of the CEA. While section 2(a)(1) of the CEA provides the Commission with regulatory jurisdiction over "contracts of sale of a commodity for future delivery," it further provides that the term future delivery "shall not include any sale of a cash commodity for deferred shipment or delivery." This case presents the Court with a novel type of transaction, which appears to be a hybrid of a futures contract and a forward contract. Examination of the distinctions between the two, their purposes and the caselaw construing them, leads the Court to conclude that Transnor's 15–day Brent transac-

---

5. "Bookout" contracts are separate contracts entered into by the parties to the original contracts whereby they settle their respective obligations under the original contracts by paying each other the difference between the contract price and an agreed reference price.

tions are futures contracts within the meaning of the Act, and are therefore subject to the Commission's regulatory powers.

Sales of cash commodities for deferred shipment or delivery generally have been recognized to be transactions in physical commodities in which delivery in fact occurs but is delayed or deferred for purposes of convenience or necessity. See *Commodity Futures Trading Comm. v. Co Petro Marketing Group, Inc.*, 680 F.2d 573 (9th Cir.1982); *In re Stovall*, [1977–1980 Transfer Binder] Comm.Fut.L.Rep. (CCH) & 20,941, 23,777 (CFTC 1979); 52 Fed.Reg. 47022 ("Regulation of Hybrid and Related Instruments: Advance Notice of Proposed Rulemaking") (CFTC, December 11, 1987). Forward contracts have thus been defined as transactions in which the commercial parties intend and can accommodate physical transfer of the actual commodity. *See Co Petro*, 680 F.2d at 578–79; *NRT Metals, Inc. v. Manhattan Metals (Non–Ferrous), Ltd.*, 576 F.Supp. 1046, 1050–51 (S.D.N.Y.1983). By contrast, futures contracts are undertaken primarily to assume or shift price risk without transferring the underlying commodity. As a result, futures contracts providing for delivery may be satisfied either by delivery or offset. *See* 54 Fed.Reg. 30694, 30695 ("Policy Statement Concerning Swap Transactions") (CFTC, July 21, 1989). Once distinguished by unique features, futures and forward contracts have begun to share certain characteristics due to increasingly complex and dynamic commercial realities. The predominant distinction between the two remains the intention of the parties and the overall effect of the transaction.

The Commodity Futures Trading Commission ("CFTC") has recognized that commodity transactions between commercial participants in certain markets have evolved from privately negotiated contracts for deferred delivery of a physical commodity under which delivery generally occurs to transactions that have highly standardized terms and are frequently satisfied by payments based upon intervening market price changes. *See* Regulation of Hybrid and Related Instruments: Advance Notice of Proposed Rulemaking, *supra* at 47027. 15–day Brent is such a market. The 15–day Brent market involves sales or purchases of a cargo for delivery on an unspecified day of a given month. The actual delivery dates are determined at the seller's option, the buyer being entitled to clear notice of a three-day loading range. 15–day Brent sales are therefore highly specialized forward sales which start out "dry"[6] but ultimately become "wet,"[7] subject to liquidation of the contract. *See* The Legal Aspects of the 15–Day Brent Market, at 110. Because the contracts do not provide for offset without the consent of the parties and because the sellers cannot predict in advance whether a particular buyer will insist on physical delivery, the market remains one based on physical trading. *Id.* at 116. Yet, because 15–day Brent oil can be sold without physical cover initially, participants can take long or short positions in the market for

---

6. A "dry" or "paper" deal refers to the purchase or sale of a claim on a cargo of Brent in some future month.

7. A "wet" deal refers to a physical transaction in which a specific cargo actually changes hands.

purposes of hedging and speculation, explaining the high ratio between barrels traded and barrels delivered. The three major motivations in Brent market activity, hedging, speculation and tax spinning, *id.*; R. Bacon, The Brent Market: An Analysis of Recent Developments, Oxford Institute for Energy Studies (1986), have led at least one commentator to describe the market as an "unregulated and unguaranteed form of futures trading." The Legal Aspects of the 15–Day Brent Market, *supra,* at 117 (quoting International Petroleum Exchange of London: "Brent Crude Oil, Trading of Brent Crude. Notes for Discussion," February 26, 1986). The 15–day Brent Market has thus assumed aspects of the futures market while retaining elements of the forward contract.

The legislative history of the forward contract exclusion, fully set forth by the Ninth Circuit Court in *Commodity Futures Trading Comm. v. Co Petro Marketing Group, Inc.,* 680 F.2d 573 (9th Cir.1982), reveals its narrow purpose: to facilitate commodities transactions within the commercial supply chain. Policy Statement Concerning Swap Transactions, *supra,* at 30695. The exemption originated in the 1921 Act to meet the particular need of a farmer to sell part of next season's harvest at a set price to a grain elevator or miller. *See* S.Rep. No. 212, 67th Cong. 1st Sess. 1 (1921), H.R.Rep. No. 345, 67th Cong. 1st Sess. 7 (1921). The exemption was predicated upon the contemplation of actual, albeit future, delivery of the underlying commodity. *Co Petro,* 680 F.2d at 578; *NRT Metals, Inc. v. Manhattan Metals (Non–Ferrous), Ltd.,* 576 F.Supp. 1046, 1050 (S.D.N.Y. 1983). The more recent 1974 version of the Act has left unchanged the exemption's limited scope, confirming the view that a forward contract is one in which the parties contemplate the future transfer of the commodity. *See Co Petro,* 680 F.2d at 578 (citing H.R.Rep. No. 975, 93rd Cong.2d Sess. 129–30 (1974)); *NRT Metals,* 576 F.Supp. at 1050. "[N]othing in the legislative history surrounding ... [the exemption] suggest[s] that Congress intended to encompass agreements for the future delivery of commodities sold ... for ... speculative purposes." *Co Petro,* 680 F.2d at 579. The *Co Petro* Court summed up that,

> this exclusion is unavailable to contracts for sale for commodities which are sold merely for speculative purposes and which are not predicated upon the expectation that delivery of the actual commodity by the seller to the original contracting buyer will occur in the future. *Id.; see NRT Metals,* 576 F.Supp. at 1051.

In determining whether a particular transaction is exempt from the Act's jurisdiction as a forward contract, the Courts and the CFTC have required that the contract's terms and the parties' practice under the contract make certain that both parties to the contract deal in and contemplate future delivery of the commodity. *See Co Petro,* 680 F.2d at 578; 50 Fed.Reg. 39656, 39657–58 ("Characteristics Distinguishing Cash and Forward Contracts and 'Trade' Options") (CFTC, September 30, 1985).

In *Co Petro,* the relevant agency agreements in gasoline obligated Co Petro to perform an offsetting service for its customers which would satisfy their contractual duties without delivery. Co Petro customers could also liquidate their positions in the face of adverse price fluctuations through a cash settlement by cancelling their contracts and paying only the liquidated damages provided for in the agreements. The Ninth Circuit Court likened Co Petro's customers to those customers who trade on organized futures markets because they could deal in commodities futures without the forced burden of actual delivery, *Co Petro,* 680 F.2d at 570, 580, and accordingly held that "the contracts here represent speculative ventures in commodities which were marketed to those for whom delivery was not an expectation." *Id.* at 581.

In *Commodity Futures Trading Comm. v. Comercial Petrolera International S.A.,* [1980–82 Transfer Binder] Comm.Fut.L.Rep. (CCH) & 21,222 at 25,088 (S.D.N.Y.1981), Judge Knapp similarly held that the relevant oil contracts were intended as "investment vehicles" in which the parties had never anticipated delivery. *Id.* at 25,098. The court's reasoning emphasized the language in the contracts that obligated the buyers to "purchase a specified amount of oil at a fixed price *or* to notify the dealer to sell the oil at the going price on or before a specified future date." *Id.* at 25,092–93. * * *

The Court acknowledges that 15–day Brent contracts may represent binding commitments to buy or sell physical oil. The real question, however, is whether the transactions are more like bargains for the purchase and sale of crude oil than speculative transactions tacitly expected to end by means other than delivery. The Ninth Circuit Court's "forced burden of delivery" language in *Co Petro* does not mandate forward contract classification of those contracts imposing a forced burden which is not expected to be enforced. The Ninth Circuit Court held only that the *absence* of a forced burden of delivery is indicative of the speculative nature of futures contracts. That court did not have before it contracts imposing a forced burden of delivery, and thus did not rule on the effect of the *presence* of such a burden. Accordingly, this Court need not disagree with or deviate from *Co Petro,* but merely considers as relevant whether the contracts provide for an opportunity to avoid delivery. * * *

The customary use of offsetting and booking out strongly suggests that physical delivery was not contemplated by the parties.

Moreover, the high degree of standardization of terms such as quantity, grade, delivery terms, currency of payment and unit of measure, which facilitate offset, bookout and other clearing techniques available on the Brent market, further evidence the investment purpose of Brent trading. The 15–day Brent market does not remotely resemble the commercial trading originally excepted from the Act. While this Court recognizes that commercial transactions have increased in complexity since the predecessor to the CEA was enacted, the interests of Brent participants, which include investment and brokerage houses, do not parallel those of the farmer who sold grain or the elevator operator who bought it for deferred delivery, so that each could benefit from a guaranteed price.[8]

While there is no contractual entitlement to satisfy Brent obligations by means other than delivery, the likelihood of avoiding delivery has enabled participants to develop what is essentially a "paper" market for speculative or hedging purposes rather than one for physical transfer. The Court therefore concludes that the 15–day Brent transactions do not constitute forward contracts excepted from the CEA.

After deciding that the relevant contracts were not forward contracts, the *Co Petro* court considered whether the contracts constituted futures contracts. In making that determination, the court found that,

> no bright line definition or list of characterizing elements is determinative. The transaction must be viewed as a whole with a critical eye toward its underlying purpose.

Co Petro, 680 F.2d at 581. The Ninth Circuit Court then held that, due to their speculative nature, the contracts at issue were "contracts for sale of a commodity for future delivery." In a recent policy statement, the Commodity Futures Trading Commission affirmed and amplified *Co Petro's* holding by declaring,

> In determining whether a transaction constitutes a futures contract, the Commission and the courts have assessed the transaction "as a whole with a critical eye toward its underlying purpose" [citing *Co Petro*]. Such an assessment entails a review of the "overall effect" of the transaction as well as a determination as to "what the parties intended." Although there is no definitive list of the elements of futures contracts, the CFTC and the courts recognize certain elements as common to such contracts. Futures contracts are contracts for the purchase or sale of a commodity for delivery in the future at a price that is established when the contract is initiated, with both parties to the transaction obligated to fulfill the contract at the specified price. In addition, futures contracts are undertaken principally to assume or shift price risk without transferring the underlying commodity. As a result, futures contracts providing for delivery may be satisfied either by delivery or offset. The Commission has explained that this does not mean that all commodity futures contracts must have these elements [citation omitted]. * * *

Transnor's contracts for 15–day Brent, a commodity within the CEA's meaning, were dated December 1985 and called for March 1986 delivery, indicating that sales of 15–day Brent could occur several months ahead of the specified loading month. Transnor's Brent contracts established a price for a standardized volume when the contract was initiated in December 1985, despite the +–5% volume tolerance, and both parties to

---

8. Nor will finding the 15–day Brent transactions to constitute futures contracts effectively eliminate the CEA's forward contract exception. The intentions of the parties still govern and the opportunity to satisfy a contract through means other than delivery is alone insufficient to categorize the nature of the transaction.

the contracts were obligated to fulfill the contract at the specified price. Most importantly, the Brent contracts were undertaken mainly to assume or shift price risk without transferring the underlying commodity. Defendants acknowledge that the volume of Brent contract trading greatly exceeded the amount of physical oil available to satisfy such contracts. The volume of contracts traded and the high standardization of the contracts demonstrate the essential investment character of the 15–day Brent market. "With an eye toward [their] underlying purpose," the Court concludes that Transnor's 15–day Brent transactions constitute futures contracts. * * *

For the reasons outlined above, defendants' motion for summary judgment is denied.

SECTION 5.   LEGISLATIVE RESPONSE

The decision of the court in the Transnor meant that the international Brent Oil Market would have to register with the CFTC as a contract market and that the contracts that had theretofore traded on that market were illegal because the market had not been so licensed. Recognizing the uncertainty that lay in the area of these developing derivative financial instruments, particularly swaps which had grown to monumental proportions, Congress enacted the Futures Trading Practices Act of 1992. That legislation amended the Commodity Exchange Act to provide the CFTC with some exemptive power for institutional traders. This was needed, not only to remove the legal uncertainties of swaps and other over-the-counter derivatives, but also because the derivative products traded by institutions were individually negotiated and would not fit within the standardized format required for exchange trading. In addition, the institutions did not need the protections for small a customer that is a central part of the CFTC's regulatory efforts.

The Futures Trading Practices Act of 1992 allowed the CFTC to exempt any transaction by "appropriate persons" from the exchange—trading requirement. Appropriate persons include institutional participants such as banks, insurance companies, investment companies, commodity pools, broker-dealers, corporations of a specific size, and the "other persons." The CFTC has adopted regulations to implement that legislation by, among other things, exempting swaps transactions by institutions. The Brent Oil Market was also exempted.

Hybrid instruments or OTC (over-the-counter) derivatives as they came to be called became an enormous market within a short period of time. The growth of the market was fostered by dealers that were heavily capitalized subsidiaries of major banks and brokerage firms. The triple AAA rating given to these firms by the ratings agencies removed most concerns with counterparty risk by end users. The dealers served as a substitute trading floor and clearing house found in the futures markets.

The determination in 1992 by Congress to exempt institutional investors from the reach of the Commodity Exchange Act was a wise one. Certainly, such institutions did not require the public customer protections that are imposed by the Commodity Exchange Act. On the other hand, some of those institutions discovered that derivative financial transactions posed risks that they neither understood nor appreciated. Indeed, the size and complexity of the market was such that there was a serious danger that these instruments could jeopardize the health of even the most powerful financial institution and even pose a threat to our financial system.

Experience thus proved all too soon that concerns with the dangers presented by derivative instruments were not entirely unwarranted. To cite some examples, the English House of Lords ruled that municipal governments in England that had engaged in swap transactions were not authorized to do so and that, therefore, the transactions were invalid. Macy's defaulted on a swap contract that involved $83 million in interest payments; a unit of Metallgesellschaft A.G. lost $1.37 billion from mismatched derivative transactions; Kashima Oil in Japan lost $1.5 billion in currency transactions; Gibson Greetings Inc. lost $19 million from derivative trading; Kidder Peabody lost $350 million in "phantom" derivative trades; a New York municipal bond fund failed to disclose that 40 percent of its assets were invested in derivatives; Procter & Gamble lost over $150 million from derivative trading; Orange County in California lost $140 million; David Askin's Granite Hedge Fund had losses of an estimated $600 million from "market neutral" derivatives; City College of Chicago sued claiming that it was misled in the purchase of $100 million in derivative obligations; Cargill's hedge funds lost $100 million from mortgage backed securities; Piper Capital Management was having difficulty valuing its derivatives and lost $700 million from derivative transactions; HYM Financial Inc. in New Jersey lost all of its capital from derivatives; Dell Computer lost $26 million from derivative based transactions; Air Products took a loss of $69 million on derivative contracts; an employee investment fund of Atlantic Richfield Company lost $22 million in derivative trades; several mutual funds were compensated by their advisors or brokers for millions of dollars in losses suffered from derivatives transactions; and Mead Corporation lost over $12 million from derivatives trading.

If all those losses were not enough, a twenty-eight year old commodity futures trader at the Barings bank bankrupted that 300 year-old firm. It had helped America finance the Louisiana Purchase. See Jerry W. Markham, Protecting the Institutional Investor—Jungle Predator or Shorn Lamb? 12 Yale J. on Reg. 345 (1995) (describing losses from derivatives trading). In January 2008, Jérôme W. Kerviel, a rouge trader at Société Générale (Soc Gen), lost $7.2 billion from a futures contrast position on stocks. This caused a worldwide stock market selloff and the U.S. Federal Reserve Board cut its interest rates in order to rally the market. Jerry W.

Markham, A Financial History of the United States: From the Subprime Crisis to the Great Recession, 475 (2011).

PROCTER & GAMBLE CO. v. BANKERS TRUST CO.

925 F.Supp. 1270 (S.D.Ohio 1996).

FEIKENS, DISTRICT JUDGE, sitting by Designation.

Plaintiff, The Procter & Gamble Company ("P & G"), is a publicly traded Ohio corporation. Defendant, Bankers Trust Company ("BT"), is a wholly-owned subsidiary of Bankers Trust New York Corporation ("BTNY"). BTNY is a state-chartered banking company. BT trades currencies, securities, commodities and derivatives. Defendant BT Securities, also a wholly-owned subsidiary of BTNY, is a registered broker-dealer. The defendants are referred to collectively as "BT" in this opinion.

P & G filed its Complaint for Declaratory Relief and Damages on October 27, 1994, alleging fraud, misrepresentation, breach of fiduciary duty, negligent misrepresentation, and negligence in connection with an interest rate swap transaction it had entered with BT on November 4, 1993. This swap, explained more fully below, was a leveraged derivatives transaction whose value was based on the yield of five-year Treasury notes and the price of thirty-year Treasury bonds ("the 5s/30s swap"). * * *

Financial engineering, in the last decade, began to take on new forms. A current dominant form is a structure known as a derivatives transaction. It is "a bilateral contract or payments exchange agreement whose value derives ... from the value of an underlying asset or underlying reference rate or index." Global Derivatives Study Group of the Group of Thirty, *Derivatives: Practices and Principles* 28 (1993). Derivatives transactions may be based on the value of foreign currency, U.S. Treasury bonds, stock indexes, or interest rates. The values of these underlying financial instruments are determined by market forces, such as movements in interest rates. Within the broad panoply of derivatives transactions are numerous innovative financial instruments whose objectives may include a hedge against market risks, management of assets and liabilities, or lowering of funding costs; derivatives may also be used as speculation for profit. Singher, *Regulating Derivatives: Does Transnational Regulatory Cooperation Offer a Viable Alternative to Congressional Action?* 18 Fordham Int'l. Law J. 1405–06 (1995).

This case involves two interest rate swap agreements. A swap is an agreement between two parties ("counterparties") to exchange cash flows over a period of time. Generally, the purpose of an interest rate swap is to protect a party from interest rate fluctuations. The simplest form of swap, a "plain vanilla" interest-rate swap, involves one counterparty paying a fixed rate of interest, while the other counterparty assumes a floating interest rate based on the amount of the principal of the underlying debt.

This is called the "notional" amount of the swap, and this amount does not change hands; only the interest payments are exchanged.

In more complex interest rate swaps, such as those involved in this case, the floating rate may derive its value from any number of different securities, rates or indexes. In each instance, however, the counterparty with the floating rate obligation enters into a transaction whose precise value is unknown and is based upon activities in the market over which the counterparty has no control. How the swap plays out depends on how market factors change.

One leading commentator describes two "visions" of the "explosive growth of the derivatives market." Hu, *Hedging Expectations: "Derivative Reality" and the Law and Finance of the Corporate Objective,* Vol. 73 Texas L.Rev. 985 (1995). One vision, that relied upon by derivatives dealers, is that of perfect hedges found in formal gardens. This vision portrays

> the order—the respite from an otherwise chaotic universe—made possible by financial science. Corporations are subject to volatile financial and commodities markets. Derivatives, by offering hedges against almost any kind of price risk, allow corporations to operate in a more ordered world.

Id. at 994.

The other vision is that of "science run amok, a financial Jurassic Park." *Id.* at 989. Using this metaphor, Hu states:

> In the face of relentless competition and capital market disintermediation, banks in search of profits have hired financial scientists to develop new financial products. Often operating in an international wholesale market open only to major corporate and sovereign entities—a loosely regulated paradise hidden from public view—these scientists push the frontier, relying on powerful computers and an array of esoteric models laden with incomprehensible Greek letters. But danger lurks. As financial creatures are invented, introduced, and then evolve and mutate, exotic risks and uncertainties arise. In its most fevered imagining, not only do the trillions of mutant creatures destroy their creators in the wholesale market, but they escape and wreak havoc in the retail market and in economies worldwide.

Id. at 989–90.

Given the potential for a "financial Jurassic Park," the size of the derivatives market[9] and the complexity of these financial instruments, it is not surprising that there is a demand for regulation and legislation. Several bills have been introduced in Congress to regulate derivatives. BT Securities has been investigated by the Securities and Exchange Commission ("SEC") and by the Commodities Futures Trading Commission

---

9. Estimates of the amount of usage of derivatives range from $14 trillion to $35 trillion in face or notional amounts. Cohen, The Challenge of Derivatives, Vol. 63 Fordham L.Rev. 1993 (1995).

("CFTC") regarding a swap transaction with a party other than P & G. *In re BT Securities Corp.,* Release Nos. 33–7124, 34–35136 and CFTC Docket No. 95–3 (Dec. 22, 1994). Bankers Trust has agreed with the Federal Reserve Bank to a Consent Decree on its leveraged derivatives transactions.

At present, most derivatives transactions fall in "the common-law no-man's land beyond regulations—... interest-rate and equity swaps, swaps with embedded options ('swaptions')," and other equally creative financial instruments. Cohen, *The Challenge of Derivatives,* Vol. 63 Fordham L.Rev. at 2013. This is where the two highly specialized swap transactions involved in this case fall.

Those swaps transactions are governed by written documents executed by BT and P & G. BT and P & G entered into an Interest Rate and Currency Exchange Agreement on January 20, 1993. This standardized form, drafted by the International Swap Dealers Association, Inc. ("ISDA"), together with a customized Schedule and written Confirmations for each swap, create the rights and duties of parties to derivative transactions. By their terms, the ISDA Master Agreement, the Schedule, and all Confirmations form a single agreement between the parties.

During the fall of 1993, the parties began discussing the terms of an interest rate swap which was to be customized for P & G. After negotiations, the parties agreed to a swap transaction on November 2, 1993, which is referred to as the 5s/30s swap; the written Confirmation is dated November 4, 1993.

In the 5s/30s swap transaction, BT agreed to pay P & G a fixed rate of interest of 5.30% for five years on a notional amount of $200 million. P & G agreed to pay BT a floating interest rate. For the first six months, that floating rate was the prevailing commercial paper ("CP") interest rate minus 75 basis points (0.75%). For the remaining four-and-a-half years, P & G was to make floating interest rate payments of CP minus 75 basis points plus a spread. The spread was to be calculated at the end of the first six months (on May 4, 1994) using the following formula:

$$\text{Spread} = \frac{(98.5 * [5 \text{ year CMT}] - 30 \text{ T Price})}{100} \quad 5.78\%$$

In this formula, the "5 year CMT" (Constant Maturity Treasury) represents the yield on the five-year Treasury Note, and the "30 T Price" represents the price of the thirty-year Treasury Bond. The leverage factor in this formula meant that even a small movement up or down in prevailing interest rates results in an incrementally larger change in P & G's position in the swap.

The parties amended this swap transaction in January 1994; they postponed the date the spread was to be set to May 19, 1994, and P & G was to receive CP minus 88 basis points, rather than 75 basis points, up to the spread date.

In late January 1994, P & G and BT negotiated a second swap, known as the "DM swap", based on the value of the German Deutschemark. The Confirmation for this swap is dated February 14, 1994. For the first year, BT was to pay P & G a floating interest rate plus 233 basis points. P & G was to pay the same floating rate plus 133 basis points; P & G thus received a 1% premium for the first year, the effective dates being January 16, 1994 through January 16, 1995. On January 16, 1995, P & G was to add a spread to its payments to BT if the four-year DM swap rate ever traded below 4.05% or above 6.01% at any time between January 16, 1994, and January 16, 1995. If the DM swap rate stayed within that band of interest rates, the spread was zero. If the DM swap rate broke that band, the spread would be set on January 16, 1995, using the following formula: Spread = 10 * [4–year DM swap rate − 4.50%].

The leverage factor in this swap was shown in the formula as ten.

P & G unwound both of these swaps before their spread set dates, as interest rates in both the United States and Germany took a significant turn upward, thus putting P & G in a negative position vis-a-vis its counterparty BT. BT now claims that it is owed over $200 million on the two swaps, while P & G claims the swaps were fraudulently induced and fraudulently executed, and seeks a declaratory verdict that it owes nothing.

In the 1933 Securities Act, Congress defined the term "security" as

> any note, stock, treasury stock, bond, debenture, evidence of indebtedness, certificate of interest or participation in any profit-sharing agreement, collateral-trust certificate, preorganization certificate or subscription, transferrable share, investment contract, voting-trust certificate, certificate of deposit for a security, fractional undivided interest in oil, gas, or other mineral rights, any put, call, straddle, option, or privilege on any security, certificate of deposit, or group or index of securities (including any interest therein or based on the value thereof), or any put, call, straddle, option, or privilege entered into on a national securities exchange relating to foreign currency, or, in general, any interest or instrument commonly known as a "security", or a certificate of interest or participation in, temporary or interim certificate for, receipt for, guarantee of, or warrant or right to subscribe to or purchase, any of the foregoing.

15 U.S.C. § 77b(1). The definition section of the 1934 Act, 15 U.S.C. § 78c(a)(10), is virtually identical and encompasses the same instruments as the 1933 Act. *Reves v. Ernst & Young,* 494 U.S. 56, 61 n. 1, 110 S.Ct. 945, 949 n. 1, 108 L.Ed.2d 47 (1990).

P & G asserts that the 5s/30s and DM swaps fall within any of the following portions of that definition: 1) investment contracts; 2) notes; 3) evidence of indebtedness; 4) options on securities; and 5) instruments commonly known as securities.

Congress intended a broad interpretation of the securities laws and flexibility to effectuate their remedial purpose of avoiding fraud. *SEC v. Howey,* 328 U.S. 293, 66 S.Ct. 1100, 90 L.Ed. 1244 (1946). The United States Supreme Court has held, however, that Congress did not "intend" the Securities Acts "to provide a broad federal remedy for all fraud." *Marine Bank v. Weaver,* 455 U.S. 551, 556, 102 S.Ct. 1220, 1223, 71 L.Ed.2d 409 (1982). The threshold issue presented by P & G's securities fraud claims is whether a security exists, *i.e.,* whether or not these swaps are among "the myriad financial transactions in our society that come within the coverage of these statutes." *Forman,* 421 U.S. at 849, 95 S.Ct. at 2059.

Economic reality is the guide for determining whether these swaps transactions that do not squarely fit within the statutory definition are, nevertheless, securities. *Reves,* 494 U.S. at 62, 110 S.Ct. at 949–50. In order to determine if these swaps are securities, commodities, or neither, I must examine each aspect of these transactions and subject them to the guidelines set forth in Supreme Court cases.

For purposes of the federal securities laws, an "investment contract" is defined as "a contract, transaction or scheme whereby a person invests his money in a common enterprise." *Howey,* 328 U.S. at 298–99, 66 S.Ct. at 1102–03. Stated differently, the test whether an instrument is an investment contract is whether it entails "an investment in a common venture premised on a reasonable expectation of profits to be derived from the entrepreneurial or managerial efforts of others." *Forman,* 421 U.S. at 852, 95 S.Ct. at 2060. * * *

While the swaps may meet certain elements of the *Howey* test whether an instrument is an investment contract, what is missing is the element of a "common enterprise." P & G did not pool its money with that of any other company or person in a single business venture. How BT hedged its swaps is not what is at issue—the issue is whether a number of investors joined together in a common venture. Certainly, any counterparties with whom BT contracted cannot be lumped together as a "common enterprise." Furthermore, BT was not managing P & G's money; BT was a counterparty to the swaps, and the value of the swaps depended on market forces, not BT's entrepreneurial efforts. The swaps are not investment contracts.

BT asserts that the swaps are not notes because they did not involve the payment or repayment of principal. P & G responds that the counterparties incurred payment obligations that were bilateral notes or the functional equivalent of notes.

As with the test whether an instrument is an investment contract, these swap agreements bear some, but not all, of the earmarks of notes. At the outset, and perhaps most basic, the payments required in the swap agreements did not involve the payment or repayment of principal. *See*

Sanderson v. Roethenmund, 682 F.Supp. 205, 206 (S.D.N.Y.1988) (promises to pay a specified sum of principal and interest to the payee at a specified time are to be analyzed as "notes" for the purposes of the Securities Acts).

In *Reves,* 494 U.S. at 64–67, 110 S.Ct. at 950–52, the Supreme Court set out a four-part "family resemblance" test for identifying notes that should be deemed securities. Those factors are: 1) the motivations of the buyer and seller in entering into the transaction (investment for profit or to raise capital versus commercial); 2) a sufficiently broad plan of distribution of the instrument (common trading for speculation or investment); 3) the reasonable expectations of the investing public; and 4) whether some factor, such as the existence of another regulatory scheme, significantly reduces the risk of the instrument, thereby rendering application of the securities laws unnecessary.

In explaining the first prong of the "family resemblance" test, the Court in *Reves* distinguished between the motivations of the parties in entering into the transaction, drawing a line between investment notes as securities and commercial notes as non-securities. The Court said:

> If the seller's purpose is to raise money for the general use of a business enterprise or to finance substantial investments and the buyer is interested primarily in the profit the note is expected to generate, the instrument is likely to be a "security." If the note is exchanged to facilitate the purchase and sale of a minor asset or consumer good, to correct for the seller's cash-flow difficulties, or to advance some other commercial or consumer purpose, on the other hand, the note is less sensibly described as a "security."

Reves, 494 U.S. at 66, 110 S.Ct. at 951–52.

There is no "neat and tidy" way to apply this prong of the test, in part because P & G and BT were counterparties, not the typical buyer and seller of an instrument. BT's motive was to generate a fee and commission, while P & G's expressed motive was, in substantial part, to reduce its funding costs. These motives are tipped more toward a commercial than investment purpose. As to P & G, there was also an element of speculation driving its willingness to enter a transaction that was based on its expectations regarding the path that interest rates would take. Thus, this prong of the *Reves* test, standing alone, is not a sufficient guide to enable one to make the determination whether the 5s/30s and DM swaps were notes within the meaning of the Securities Acts.

The second prong of the *Reves* test examines the plan of distribution of the instrument "to determine whether it is an instrument in which there is 'common trading for speculation or investment.'" *Id.,* quoting *SEC v. C.M. Joiner Leasing Corp.,* 320 U.S. 344, 351, 64 S.Ct. 120, 123–24, 88 L.Ed. 88 (1943). While derivatives transactions in general are an important part of BT's business, and BT advertises its expertise in putting together a variety of derivatives packages, the test is whether the 5s/30s and DM swaps in particular were widely distributed. These swaps are analogous to the notes that were held not to be securities on the basis that the plan of distribution was "a limited solicitation to sophisticated financial or commercial institutions and not to the general public." *Banco Español de Credito v. Security Pacific Nat'l Bank,* 763 F.Supp. 36, 43 (S.D.N.Y.1991), *aff'd* 973 F.2d 51 (2d Cir.1992). The 5s/30s and DM swaps were customized for Procter & Gamble; they could not be sold or traded to another counterparty without the agreement of BT. They were not part of any kind of general offering.

Thus, I conclude that the 5s/30s and DM swaps were not widely distributed and do not meet the second prong of the *Reves* test.

Application of the third *Reves* factor—the public's reasonable perceptions—does not support a finding that these swap agreements are securities. They were not traded on a national exchange, "the paradigm of a security." *Reves,* 494 U.S. at 69, 110 S.Ct. at 953. I recognize that some media refer to derivatives generally as securities and that some commentators assume that all derivatives are securities. Other commentators understand that many swap transactions are customized, bilateral contracts not subject to regulation. Cohen, 63 Fordham L.Rev. at 2013. However, what is relevant is the perception of those few who enter into swap agreements, not the public in general. P & G knew full well that its over-the-counter swap agreements with BT were not registered with any regulatory agency. P & G's "perception" that these swap agreements were securities did not surface until after it had filed its original Complaint in this case.

Thus, I conclude that the 5s/30s and DM swaps do not meet the third prong of the *Reves* test.

The fourth *Reves* factor is whether another regulatory scheme exists that would control and thus reduce the risk of the instrument, making application of the securities laws unnecessary. At about the time these swaps were entered into, the guidelines of the Office of the Comptroller of Currency ("OCC") and the Federal Reserve Board went into effect. OCC Banking Circular 277, *Risk Management of Financial Derivatives,* Fed.Banking L.Rep. (CCH) & 62,154, at 71,703 (Oct. 27, 1993); Federal Reserve Board Supervisory Letter SR 93–69, *Examining Risk Management and Internal Controls for Trading Activities of Banking Organizations,* Fed.Banking L.Rep. & 62–152, at 71,712 (Dec. 20, 1993); OCC Bulletin 94–31, *Questions and Answers for BC–277: Risk Management of Financial Derivatives,* Fed.Banking L.Rep. & 62–152, at 71,719 (May 10, 1994).

While these guidelines are useful in regulating the banking industry, their focus is the protection of banks and their shareholders from default or other credit risks. They do not provide any direct protection to counterparties with whom banks enter into derivatives transactions. While the 5s/30s and DM swaps may meet this prong of the *Reves* "family resemblance" test, this is not enough to bring these transactions within the statutory definition of a "note" for purposes of the securities laws.

Balancing all the *Reves* factors, I conclude that the 5s/30s and DM swaps are not notes for purposes of the Securities Acts.

P & G argues that if the swaps are not notes, they are evidence of indebtedness because they contain bilateral promises to pay money and they evidence debts between the parties. It argues that the counterparties promised to pay a debt, which consists of future obligations to pay interest on the notional amounts. Indeed, BT now claims that it is owed millions of dollars on the swaps. P & G points out that the phrase "evidence of indebtedness" in the statute must have a meaning other than that given to a "note" so that the words "evidence of indebtedness" are not redundant. Thus, it argues, without citation to authority, that if the swaps are not notes, then they should be construed as an evidence of indebtedness "either because they may contain terms and conditions well beyond the typical terms of a note and beyond an ordinary investor's ability to understand, or because the debt obligation simply does not possess the physical characteristics of a note."

The test whether an instrument is within the category of "evidence of indebtedness" is essentially the same as whether an instrument is a note. *Holloway v. Peat, Marwick, Mitchell & Co.,* 879 F.2d 772, 777 (10th Cir.1989), *judgment vacated on other grounds sub nom. Peat Marwick Main Co. v. Holloway,* 494 U.S. 1014, 110 S.Ct. 1314, 108 L.Ed.2d 490 (1990), *reaff'd on remand,* 900 F.2d 1485 (10th Cir.), *cert. den.* 498 U.S. 958, 111 S.Ct. 386, 112 L.Ed.2d 396 (1990) (passbook savings certificates and thrift certificates were analyzed under the "note" or "evidence of indebtedness" categories, as they represented a promise to repay the principal amount, plus accrued interest); *In re Tucker Freight Lines, Inc.,* 789 F.Supp. 884, 885 (W.D.Mich.1991) (The Court's "method [in *Reves*] seems applicable to all debt instruments, including evidences of indebtedness.").

I do not accept P & G's definition of "evidence of indebtedness" in large part because that definition omits an essential element of debt instruments—the payment or repayment of principal. Swap agreements do not involve the payment of principal; the notional amount never changes hands. * * *

Five-year notes and thirty-year Treasury bonds are securities; therefore, P & G contends that the 5s/30s swap is an option on securities. It argues that because the 5s/30s swap spread was based on the value of these securities, it falls within the statutory definition: "any put, call, straddle, option or privilege on any security, group or index of securities (including any interest therein or based on the value thereof)." It describes the 5s/30s swap as "a single security which can be decomposed into a plain vanilla swap with an embedded put option. The option is a put on the 30–year bond price with an uncertain strike price that depends on the level of the 5–year yield at the end of six months."

BT contends that the 5s/30s swap is not an option because no one had the right to take possession of the underlying securities. BT argues that although both swaps contained terms that functioned as options, they were not options because they did not give either party the right to sell or buy anything. According to BT, the only "option-like" feature was the spread calculation that each swap contained; that any resemblance the spread calculations had to options on securities does not extend to the underlying swaps themselves, which had no option-like characteristics. I agree that the 5s/30s swap was not an option on a security; there was no right to take possession of any security.

The definition of a "security" in the 1933 and 1934 Acts includes the parenthetical phrase "(including any interest therein or based on the value thereof)," which could lead to a reading of the statute to mean that an option based on the value of a security is a security. Legislative history, however, makes it clear that that reading was not intended. The U.S. House of Representatives Report ("House Report") on the 1982 amendments that added this parenthetical phrase provides that the definition of "security" includes an option on "(i) any security, (ii) any certificate of deposit, (iii) any group or index of securities (including any interest therein or based on the value thereof), and (iv) when traded on a national securities exchange, foreign currency." H.R.Rep. No. 626, 97th Cong., 2d Sess., pt. 2, at 4 (1982), *reprinted in* 1982 U.S.C.C.A.N. 2780, 2795. Thus, even though the statute jumbles these definitions together, it is clear from the House Report that the parenthetical phrase "(. . . based on the value thereof)" was intended only to modify the immediately preceding clause— "group or index of securities"—and not the words "any option" or "any security."

Two Orders by the Security and Exchange Commission must be considered. These rulings involve transactions between BT and Gibson Greetings, Inc. in swaps that have some similarities to the 5s/30s swap. *In re BT Securities Corp.*, Release Nos. 33–7124, 34–35136 (Dec. 22, 1994), and *In the Matter of Mitchell A. Vazquez*, Release Nos. 33–7269, 34–36909 (Feb. 29, 1996). In these cases, the SEC ruled that a "Treasury–Linked Swap" between BT and Gibson Greetings, Inc. was a security within the meaning of the federal securities laws. The SEC stated: "While called a swap, the Treasury–Linked Swap was in actuality a cash-settled put option that was written by Gibson and based initially on the 'spread' between the price of the 7.625% 30–year U.S. Treasury maturity maturing on November 15, 2022 and the arithmetic average of the bid and offered yields of the most recently auctioned obligation of a two-year Treasury note."

These SEC Orders were made pursuant to Offers of Settlement made by BT Securities and Vazquez. In both Orders, the SEC acknowledged that its findings were solely for the purpose of effectuating the respondents' Offers of Settlement and that its findings are not binding on any other person or entity named as a defendant or respondent in any other proceeding. They are not binding in this case, in part because of the differences between the transactions; nor do they have collateral estoppel effect. *See also SEC v. Sloan*, 436 U.S. 103, 118, 98 S.Ct. 1702, 1711–12,

56 L.Ed.2d 148 (1978) (citations omitted) (The "courts are the final authorities on the issues of statutory construction and are not obliged to stand aside and rubber-stamp their affirmance of administrative decisions that they deem inconsistent with a statutory mandate or that frustrate the congressional policy underlying a statute.").

Even though both the Gibson Greetings, Inc. swap and the P & G 5s/30s swap derived their values from securities (Treasury notes), they were not options. While these swaps included option-like features, there is a missing essential element of an option. These swaps were exchanges of interest payments; they did not give either counterparty the right to exercise an option or to take possession of any security. Neither party could choose whether or not to exercise an option; the stream of interest payments under the swap was mandatory. Consequently, I conclude that the 5s/30s swap is not an option on a security or an option based on the value of a security.

Finally, P & G contends that both the 5s/30s and the DM swaps are securities simply because that is how these instruments were offered and how they have become known through a course of dealing. In support of this position, P & G points to the SEC Orders in the Gibson Greetings matter and asserts that BT labels leveraged derivatives as investments, speculative, and options; and that the financial markets and the media characterize derivatives as securities.

The Supreme Court uses the *Howey* test for both "investment contracts" and the more general category of an "instrument" commonly known as a "security." *Landreth Timber Co. v. Landreth*, 471 U.S. 681, 691 n. 5, 105 S.Ct. 2297, 2304 n. 5, 85 L.Ed.2d 692 (1985); *Forman*, 421 U.S. at 852, 95 S.Ct. at 2060 ("We perceive no distinction, for present purposes, between an 'investment contract' and an 'instrument' commonly known as a 'security.' " In either case, "the basic test for distinguishing the transaction from other commercial dealings is 'whether the scheme involves an investment of money in a common enterprise with profits to come solely from the efforts of others.' " *Howey,* 328 U.S. at 301, 66 S.Ct. at 1104).

Even before the *Howey* decision, the Supreme Court established a contextual connection between an "investment contract" and "instrument commonly known as a 'security' " in *Joiner Leasing,* 320 U.S. at 351, 64 S.Ct. at 123–24, where the Supreme Court stated:

> In the Securities Act the term "security" was defined to include by name or description many documents in which there is common trading for speculation or investment. Some, such as notes, bonds, and stocks, are pretty much standardized and the name alone carries well-settled meaning. Others are of more variable character and were necessarily designated by more descriptive terms, such as "transferable share," "investment contract," and "in general any interest or instrument commonly known as a security." We cannot read out of the statute these general descriptive designations merely because

more specific ones have been used to reach some kinds of documents. Instruments may be included within any of these definitions, as matter of law, if on their face they answer to the name or description. However, the reach of the Act does not stop with the obvious and commonplace. Novel, uncommon, or irregular devices, whatever they appear to be, are also reached if it be proved as a matter of fact that they are widely offered or dealt in under terms or courses of dealing which established their character in commerce as "investment contracts," or as "any interest or instrument commonly known as a 'security.'"

While neither *Joiner Leasing,* nor *Landreth,* nor *Forman* dealt with instruments comparable to the leveraged derivatives involved in this case, the reasoning of the Supreme Court is applicable. In each of these cases, the Court emphasized that when a party seeks to fit financial instruments into the non-specific categories of securities, those instruments must nevertheless comport with the *Howey* test, which "embodies the essential attributes that run through all of the Court's decisions defining a security. The touchstone is the presence of an investment in a common venture premised on a reasonable expectation of profits to be derived from the entrepreneurial or managerial efforts of others." *Forman,* 421 U.S. at 852, 95 S.Ct. at 2060.

In determining whether the 5s/30s and DM swaps are instruments commonly known as securities, P & G's own pleadings are telling in defining how P & G viewed these transactions. In recent motions, P & G asserts that it knew of the alleged fraud in the 5s/30s swap in mid-April 1994. Yet, P & G did not bring securities claims when it filed its original Complaint in October 1994. P & G did not assert a claim for securities violations until January 1995, after the SEC and CFTC issued their rulings in the Gibson Greetings matter. If P & G itself had really thought it was dealing with securities, it is fair to assume that P & G would have included securities counts in its original Complaint.

In any event, the contracts between P & G and BT do not meet the *Howey* criteria, particularly because there is no way that they can be construed to be a pooling of funds in a common enterprise. These swaps do not qualify as securities.

It is important to point out that the holdings in this case are narrow; I do not determine that all leveraged derivatives transactions are not securities, or that all swaps are not securities. Some of these derivative instruments, because of their structure, may be securities. I confine my ruling to the 5s/30s and the DM swaps between P & G and BT. * * *

The Commodity Exchange Act ("CEA") includes in its definition of a commodity "all services, rights, and interests in which contracts for future delivery are presently or in the future dealt in." 7 U.S.C. § 1a(3). BT asserts that the swaps are not futures contracts; P & G claims that they are.

Under the CEA, The Commodity Futures Trading Commission has exclusive jurisdiction over "accounts, agreements ... and transactions involving contracts of sale of a commodity for future delivery traded or executed on a contract market ... or any other board of trade, exchange, or market, and transactions [in standardized contracts for certain commodities]." As of January 19, 1996, the CFTC had "not taken a position on whether swap agreements are futures contracts." Letter from Mary L. Schapiro, Chair of U.S. Commodity Futures Trading Commission to Congressmen Roberts and Bliley, p. 4 (Jan. 19, 1996). This opinion does not decide that issue because the 5s/30s and DM swaps are within the Swaps Exemption to the CEA and because P & G has not stated a claim under § 4b, § 4o, or 17 C.F.R. § 32.9, as discussed below.

Even if the 5s/30s and DM swaps are defined as commodities, swap agreements are exempt from all but the antifraud provisions of the CEA under the CFTC Swap Exemption. Title V of the Futures Trading Practices Act of 1992 granted the CFTC the authority to exempt certain swaps transactions from CEA coverage. 7 U.S.C. § 6(c)(5). In response to this directive, on January 22, 1993, the CFTC clarified its July 1989 safe-harbor policy regarding swap transactions[10] in order to "promote domestic and international market stability, reduce market and liquidity risks in financial markets, including those markets (such as futures exchanges) linked to the swap market, and eliminate a potential source of systemic risk. To the extent that swap agreements are regarded as subject to the provisions of the Act, the rules provide that swap agreements which meet the terms and conditions [of the rules] are exempt from all provisions of the Act, except section 2(a)(1)(B)." *Exemption for Certain Swap Agreements,* 58 Fed. Reg. 5587, 5588 (Jan. 22, 1993).

To qualify for exemption, a transaction must fit within the CFTC's definition and meet four criteria. The CFTC defines a "swap agreement" as

(i) An agreement (including terms and conditions incorporated by reference therein) which is a rate swap agreement, basis swap, forward rate agreement, commodity swap, interest rate option, forward foreign exchange agreement, rate cap agreement, rate floor agreement, rate collar agreement, currency swap agreement, cross-currency rate swap agreement, currency option, any other similar agreement (including any option to enter into any of the foregoing);

(ii) Any combination of the foregoing; or

(iii) A master agreement for any of the foregoing together with all supplements thereto.

---

10. The CFTC identified those swap transactions that would not be regulated as futures or commodity options transactions under the CEA to include those that had 1) individually-tailored terms; 2) an absence of exchange-style offset; 3) an absence of a clearing organization or margin system; 4) limited distribution with the transaction undertaken in conjunction with the parties' lines of business, thus precluding public participation; and 5) a prohibition against marketing to the public. Policy Statement Concerning Swap Transactions, 54 Fed.Reg. 30,694 (July 21, 1989).

17 C.F.R. § 35.1(b) (1993). The 5s/30s and DM swaps fit within this definition.

The four criteria for exemption are: 1) The swap must be entered into solely between "eligible swap participants;" 2) the swap may not be part of a fungible class of agreements standardized as their material economic terms; 3) counterparty creditworthiness is a material consideration of the parties in entering into the swap agreement; and 4) the swap is not entered into and is not traded on or through an exchange market. 17 C.F.R. § 35.2 (1993).

The 5s/30s and DM swaps meet these criteria. First, the definition of "eligible swap participants" in 17 C.F.R. § 35.1(b)(2) includes a "bank or trust company (acting on its own behalf or on behalf of another eligible swap participant)" and corporations with total assets exceeding $10,000,000. BT and P & G are within this definition. Second, these swaps are customized and not fungible as they could not be sold to another counterparty without permission. Third, creditworthiness is a consideration of the parties. Fourth, the swaps are private agreements not traded on any exchange. * * *

NOTES

1. As will be seen in section 7, a different court did not completely agree with the analysis in this case. Additional litigation was brought against Bankers Trust by other customers:

> One such dispute involved Bankers Trust and an Indonesian financial services company named PT Dharmala Sakti Sejahtera ("Dharmala"). The dispute between Dharmala and Bankers Trust centered on a series of U.S. dollar interest rate swap agreements with a total notional value of US$50 million that the two companies had entered into in 1994.
>
> Like Procter & Gamble and Gibson Greetings, Dharmala had speculated that United States interest rates would not rise shortly before the first of the Federal Reserve's six increases of the federal funds rate during 1994. Dharmala initially refused to pay Bankers Trust any of the amount that was owed under the swap agreements. Similar to the allegations made by Procter & Gamble and Gibson Greetings, Dharmala claimed, among other things, that Bankers Trust had misrepresented the risk of the swap agreements. Bankers Trust and Dharmala eventually settled their dispute after a court in the United Kingdom ruled that Dharmala was capable of understanding the risks involved in the transaction and therefore was liable for the losses. (Bankers Trust International PLC v. PT Dharmala Sakti Sejahtera, Queen's Bench Division (Commercial Court) (Dec. 1, 1995)).

Michael S. Bennett & Michael J. Marin, The Casablanca Paradigm: Regulatory Risk in the Asian Financial Derivatives Markets, 5 Stan. J. L. Bus. & Fin. 1, 7 (1999).

2. Calls for regulation of over-the-counter derivative instruments followed the losses suffered by Procter & Gamble Co. and several other large companies. One effort involved imposing a "suitability" requirement on dealers in derivative instruments, a regulatory safeguard that had traditionally prohibited broker-dealers in the securities industry from recommending transactions to unsophisticated investors that were unsuitable for such investors in light of their particular financial circumstances and needs. Although large institutions were previously thought capable of fending for themselves, regulators did impose such a modified form of suitability requirements on derivative dealers in the wake of the losses suffered by institutions in the early 1990s. For a debate over whether such a requirement is necessary see Norman S. Poser, Liability of Broker–Dealers for Unsuitable Recommendations to Institutional Investors, 2001 B.Y.U. L. Rev. 1493 (arguing that it is needed) and Jerry W. Markham, Protecting the Institutional Investor—Jungle Predator or Shorn Lamb? 12 Yale J. on Reg. 345 (1995) (arguing that institutional investors can protect themselves).

The flip side of this argument is what actions should institutional investors take to protect themselves from the risk of loss from derivative transactions, particularly losses from rogue traders who incur and conceal large trading losses from their institutional employer. See Jerry W. Markham, Guarding the Kraal—On the Trail of the Rogue Trader, 21 Iowa J. Corp. L 131 (1995). One result of the losses experienced from OTC derivatives was the development of more sophisticated internal controls that were designed to assure that firms using those instruments were properly managing their risks. Complex value-at-risk ("VAR") models were developed to assess the effects of probable market movements on particular derivative products so that firms would have an idea as to their risk exposure. These VAR models will assume a time line of say three weeks and assess historical price movements during that period of time in relation to the sensitivity of the instrument being assessed to such movements. Using mathematical formulas, the potential risk from that instrument can be given a value. Of course, prices may not always follow historical trends and particular instruments may be affected by extraneous events that the VAR formula does not capture—that flaw in VAR models became apparent during the financial crisis in 2007–2009, but had been foreseen even before that event. See Nassim N. Taleb, The Black Swan (2007).

Derivative dealers and other firms exposed to derivative risks from counterparties may take their monitoring even further by stressing positions and exposures under "worst case" scenarios of possible market movements and protect themselves accordingly. Firms with such exposures may also employ an "Enterprise Risk Management" model that will have a risk management process that assesses all risks from all trading centers in order to measure firm wide exposures and to limit losses from any particular counterparty or instrument deemed a danger. Risk is assessed across the enterprise: " 'Enterprise wide' means the removal of traditional functional, divisional, departmental, or cultural barriers. A truly holistic, integrated, future focused, and process-oriented approach helps an organization manage all key business risks and opportunities with the intent of maximizing shareholder value for the enterprise as a whole." Scott A. Reed, The Audit

Committee and Enterprise Risk Management, 1496 PLI/Corp. 127 (June 2005). These firms also use multiple monitoring points, rather than a straight-line reporting relationship, for traders and trading desks in order to have as many eyes as possible on their trading, making it harder to engage in rogue activities. See generally Standard & Poor's Enterprise Risk Management For Financial Institutions, Rating Criteria and Best Practices (Nov. 2005).

3. Another concern was that the risks of derivatives were not being properly disclosed to shareholders of the companies investing in such instruments. To remedy that situation more disclosure was required in the footnotes to the balance sheet, but concerns continued. Finally, Financial Accounting Standard Board ("FASB") Statement of Financial Accounting Standards No. 133, effective 15 June 2000, required corporations to recognize derivatives as either assets or liabilities at their fair value. The corporation must disclose its purpose in entering into the derivative transactions and its management policies for managing the risks associated with derivatives.

4. Each quarter, the Comptroller of the Currency prepares a public report of bank derivatives activity reporting trade volume by product type and participant (available at http://www.occ.treas.gov/deriv/deriv.htm). The main types of derivatives that banks engage in are based on foreign exchange, credit, interest rate, equity, and commodities (including gold and silver). The financial return on derivatives varies by type of derivative. For example, in the first quarter of 2009, national banks lost $3.2 billion from credit derivatives while earning over $9 billion from interest rate derivatives.

SECTION 6. HEDGE–TO–ARRIVE AND MARKETING CONTRACTS

The restrictions in the Commodity Exchange Act on off-exchange futures and options continued to cause concern. One product in particular, the "hedge-to-arrive" contract, generated a great deal of litigation.

LACHMUND v. ADM INVESTOR SERVICES, INC.

191 F.3d 777 (7th Cir.1999).

RIPPLE, CIRCUIT JUDGE.

* * * A hedge-to-arrive contract ("HTA") is an agreement between a farmer and a grain elevator for the sale of a fixed quantity of grain for delivery at a specific time in the future. The parties agree to a price per bushel set by reference to the Chicago Board of Trade ("CBOT") futures price for a particular month, plus or minus a basis (an adjustment that reflects local variables, such as the cost of transportation, storage, labor, and utilities). The futures reference price is fixed at the time of contracting, but the basis floats until the farmer decides to fix it, sometime before an agreed upon pricing deadline. If the farmer does not fix the basis within the specified time, it will be set automatically by the terms of the

HTA. *See Eby v. Producers Co-op, Inc.,* 959 F.Supp. 428, 430 n. 1 (W.D.Mich.1997); *Farmers Co-op. Co. v. Lambert,* No. LACV305569, 1999 WL 177473, at *3 (Iowa Dist.Ct.1999); Matthew J. Cole, Note, *Hedge–To–Arrive Contracts: The Second Chapter of the Farm Crisis,* 1 Drake J. Agric. L. 243, 246 (1996).

HTA contracts benefit farmers by permitting them to lock in a particular price and to guarantee themselves a buyer for their grain prior to delivery. They face a risk, however, that grain prices will rise and that they will be committed to selling their grain at an agreed price below the current market value. By the same token, the elevator faces a risk that the futures reference price will fall, leaving the elevator locked into a price above the current market price. Each party can hedge against these risks by establishing a position in the futures market that is opposite to its contract position. For example, the elevator would hedge its risk when it contracts with a farmer by simultaneously establishing a "short" position (an obligation to sell) in the futures market for the month of delivery to offset its obligation to buy from the farmer. *See Eby,* 959 F.Supp. at 430 n. 1; *Lambert,* 1999 WL 177473, at *4; Cole, *supra,* at 246.

Some HTA contracts (or the parties' practice under such contracts) allow the farmer to "roll" the delivery obligation to some future date, either to accommodate shortfalls in the crop yield or to allow the farmer to sell the grain on the "spot" (cash) market for a better price. When a farmer opts to roll an HTA to a later month, the elevator cancels or offsets its futures hedge in the original delivery month (by entering an obligation to buy the same quantity that it is obligated to sell) and then rehedges by establishing a new short position in the new delivery month. The price difference, as of the date of the roll, between the new and old futures months—the "spread"—is then added to the price per bushel of the original HTA. The farmer thus absorbs this spread, whether it is positive or negative. *See Eby,* 959 F.Supp. at 430 n. 1; *Lambert,* 1999 WL 177473, at *4–5; Cole, *supra,* at 250.

ADM Investor Services, Inc. ("ADMIS") is a corporation registered with the Commodity Futures Trading Commission ("CFTC") as a Futures Commission Merchant. A/C Trading Co. ("A/C") is an Indiana general partnership registered with the CFTC as an Introducing Broker ("IB").[11] A/C Trading 2000 ("A/C 2000") is an Indiana general partnership run by James Gerlach and engaged in the business of agricultural consulting. Demeter, Inc. ("Demeter") is a corporation operating a grain elevator. Plaintiff Tom Lachmund is an Indiana farmer.

In January 1995, Mr. Lachmund entered into a consulting agreement with A/C 2000. Pursuant to A/C 2000's (Gerlach's) advice and consultation, Mr. Lachmund opened a commodity futures and options trading

---

11. An IB may solicit commodity customer accounts and introduce those accounts to a Futures Commission Merchant such as ADMIS. ADMIS executed a Guarantee Agreement on behalf of A/C. By this agreement, ADMIS guaranteed the performance of, and agreed to be jointly and severally liable for, all obligations of A/C under the Commodity Exchange Act and its rules and regulations.

account with ADMIS and entered into a series of HTA grain contracts with Demeter for the sale of Mr. Lachmund's estimated annual yield in 1995 and 1996. He also purchased some off-exchange options directly from Demeter in 1995 and conducted some options transactions in his ADMIS account in 1996 to hedge against loss on the HTA contracts.

When Mr. Lachmund's crop yield fell short of the contract amounts, he was able to roll the undelivered amounts forward to later crop futures months, even to the next crop year. After a series of rolls, however, Demeter informed Mr. Lachmund in 1996 that it would no longer allow HTA contracts to be rolled beyond the end of a crop year so that each HTA contract had to be settled at the end of the crop year, either by delivery of grain or by cash transaction. Demeter then charged Mr. Lachmund's account with a debit of $304,597.26. Meanwhile, the options Mr. Lachmund had purchased failed to buffer his losses on the HTA contracts.

Mr. Lachmund brought this action under the CEA, RICO, and state law, alleging a conspiracy of fraudulent misrepresentation with respect to his contracts with Demeter. In his complaint, Mr. Lachmund claims that ADMIS, A/C, and other entities conspired to evade the CFTC's futures market regulations by engaging in off-exchange futures market activities through HTA contracts with farmers. The purpose of this alleged conspiracy, according to Mr. Lachmund, was to attract business to ADMIS and its IBs by misrepresenting the HTA contracts as a risk-free method of selling future crops. The HTA contracts were in fact, Mr. Lachmund claims, illegal off-exchange futures contracts because the grain purportedly sold by the contracts did not have to be delivered within the crop year. That the purpose of the contracts was not to transfer actual grain, he alleges, is evidenced by the fact that farmers were encouraged to enter into HTAs for grain quantities greater than they could produce in a crop year, that many HTAs did not specify a delivery date, that the farmers could engage in unlimited rolling of their delivery obligations, and that the contracts could be settled by a cash buy-out at any time. Mr. Lachmund claims that Gerlach failed to inform him of various material facts concerning the risks involved in the contracts and options program. He claims that Gerlach falsely led him to believe that the only risk would be the price of the options purchased to hedge against the risk of price movement between the time of contracting and the time of delivery. Gerlach failed to inform him of the risk of unlimited liability for inverse crop year spreads in a program in which shortfalls are rolled into the next year. Had the defendants informed him of the actual risks associated with the HTA contracts, Mr. Lachmund asserts, he would not have entered into the contracts, and he would not have opened a trading account with ADMIS.
* * *

The [Commodity Exchange Act of 1936] ("CEA"), 7 U.S.C. § 1 et seq. prohibits transactions involving contracts for the purchase or sale of a commodity for "future delivery" unless such transactions are conducted on or subject to the rules of a board of trade designated by the CFTC as a "contract market" for that commodity. 7 U.S.C. § 6(a) (Supp.1999). However, the CEA excludes from the definition of "future delivery" any "sale of any cash commodity for deferred shipment or delivery." *Id.* § 1a(11). Thus, contracts for the sale of a cash commodity for deferred shipment or delivery—commonly known as "cash forward contracts"—are exempt from regulation under the CEA. *See Andersons, Inc. v. Horton Farms, Inc.,* 166 F.3d 308, 318 (6th Cir.1998); *CFTC v. Co Petro Marketing Group, Inc.,* 680 F.2d 573, 576–77 (9th Cir.1982).

Cash forward contracts permit parties who contemplate the physical transfer of a commodity to guarantee themselves, prior to the time of delivery, a buyer (or a seller) at a particular price, even though convenience or necessity requires delayed delivery or shipment. *See Andersons,* 166 F.3d at 318; *Co Petro,* 680 F.2d at 577–78. The CEA's prohibition of off-exchange contracts for "future delivery" seeks to regulate not this type of contract for the actual physical transfer of a commodity, but instead transactions driven by price speculation. *See Andersons,* 166 F.3d at 318; *Co Petro,* 680 F.2d at 577–78 (tracing the cash forward exclusion back to Congress' enactment of the Future Trading Act of 1921, which exempted from regulation future delivery contracts made by owners and growers of grain). In *Salomon Forex, Inc. v. Tauber,* 8 F.3d 966 (4th Cir.1993), *cert. denied,* 511 U.S. 1031, 114 S.Ct. 1540, 128 L.Ed.2d 192 (1994), the Fourth Circuit explained:

> Because the [CEA] was aimed at manipulation, speculation, and other abuses that could arise from the trading in futures contracts and options, as distinguished from the commodity itself, Congress never purported to regulate "spot" transactions (transactions for the immediate sale and delivery of a commodity) or "cash forward" transactions (in which the commodity is presently sold but its delivery is, by agreement, delayed or deferred).... Transactions in the commodity itself which anticipate actual delivery did not present the same opportunities for speculation, manipulation, and outright wagering that trading in futures and options presented. From the beginning, the CEA thus regulated transactions involving the purchase or sale of a commodity "for future delivery" but excluded transactions involving "any sale of any cash commodity for deferred shipment or delivery." 7 U.S.C. § 2. The distinction, though semantically subtle, is what the trade refers to as the difference between "futures," which generally are regulated, and "cash forwards" or "forwards," which are not.

Id. at 970–71.

In contrast to cash forward contracts, futures contracts are mechanisms used to shift price risk and generally do not contemplate or result in the physical transfer of the underlying commodity:

> [A futures contract] is generally understood to be an executory, mutually binding agreement providing for the future delivery of a commodity on a date certain where the grade, quantity, and price at the time of delivery are fixed. To facilitate the development of a liquid

market in these transactions, these contracts are standardized and transferrable. Trading in futures seldom results in physical delivery of the subject commodity, since the obligations are often extinguished by offsetting transactions that produce a net profit or loss. The main purpose realized by entering into futures transactions is to transfer price risks from suppliers, processors and distributors (hedgers) to those more willing to take the risk (speculators). Since the prices of futures are contingent on the vagaries of both the production of the commodity and the economics of the marketplace, they are particularly susceptible to manipulation and excessive speculation.

Id. at 971 (footnote omitted).

Mr. Lachmund's claim for violations of the CEA is premised on the conclusion that the HTA contracts between him and Demeter are off-exchange futures contracts and not cash forward contracts exempt from the CEA. Although cash forward contracts and futures contracts are easily distinguishable in theory, it is frequently difficult in practice to tell whether a particular arrangement between two parties is a bona fide cash forward contract for the delivery of grain or whether it is a mechanism for price speculation on the futures market. Our task, therefore, is to establish a methodology for determining whether a particular contract is a cash forward contract exempt from regulation under the CEA or a futures contract subject to the requirements of the CEA. We then must apply that test to the facts of the case before us to determine whether Count IV of Mr. Lachmund's complaint states a claim for violation of the CEA.

In determining whether a contract is a cash forward contract or a futures contract, our starting point must always be the words of the contract itself. The contract's terms will provide several indications of the nature of the transaction it memorializes. The document itself will reveal whether the agreement contemplates actual delivery, by indicating the following: whether the parties to the contract are in the business of producing or obtaining grain; whether the parties are capable of delivering or receiving actual grain in the quantities provided for in the contract; whether there is a definite date of delivery; whether the agreement explicitly requires actual delivery, as opposed to allowing delivery obligations to be rolled indefinitely into the future; whether payment takes place only upon delivery; and whether the contract's terms are individualized, as opposed to standardized. *See* CFTC Interpretive Statement, Characteristics Distinguishing Cash and Forward Contracts and "Trade" Options, 50 Fed.Reg. 39,656, 39,658 (1985); *see also Andersons,* 166 F.3d at 320 (citing *In re Grain Land Coop.,* 978 F.Supp. 1267, 1273–74 (D.Minn. 1997)); *Co Petro,* 680 F.2d at 578.

This list of factors characterizing cash forward contracts, however, is neither exhaustive nor definitive. Indeed, because the CEA regulates transactions, it is often necessary to look beyond the written contract. *See Andersons,* 166 F.3d at 319–20 (cautioning that "self-serving labels" that parties place on their contracts are not dispositive on the issue whether a contract is a cash forward contract or a futures contract); *Co Petro,* 680 F.2d at 581 (noting that "no bright-line definition or list of characterizing elements is determinative"). In order to gain the fullest understanding possible of the parties' agreement and their purpose, we often must consider the course of dealings between the parties and the totality of the business relationship. *See id.* ("The transaction must be viewed as a whole with a critical eye toward its underlying purpose.").

We note that the CFTC—the agency charged with administering the CEA—advocates such an approach that considers the totality of the circumstances. *See* Amicus Br. at 4 ("[A] court must look beyond the four corners of a written agreement and take into account all relevant circumstances in deciding the issue of the underlying nature of the transaction."); *see also* CFTC Interpretive Statement, Characteristics Distinguishing Cash and Forward Contracts and "Trade" Options, 50 Fed.Reg. 39,656, 39,657 (1985) (noting that both courts and the Commission "have required that the contract's terms *and the parties' practice* under the contract" indicate that both the buyer and seller deal in and contemplate future delivery of the actual commodity (emphasis added)); *see also id.* at 39,658 (noting that "the courts and the Commission have examined whether the parties to the contracts are commercial entities that have the capacity to make or take delivery and *whether delivery, in fact, routinely occurs under such contracts*" (emphasis added)). Other courts have adopted a similar approach, looking not only at the characteristics of the contracts themselves but also at the history of dealings between the parties. *See, e.g., Andersons,* 166 F.3d at 320 (including as a consideration whether "delivery and payment routinely occurred between the parties in past dealings"); *Co Petro,* 680 F.2d at 581; *Farmers Co-op. v. Lambert,* No. LACV 305569, 1999 WL 177473, at *12 (Iowa Dist.Ct.1999) ("Past actual delivery patterns and course of dealing between the parties are relevant....").

With these principles in mind, we turn now to the facts in the case before us. We begin by examining the terms of the HTA contracts between Mr. Lachmund and Demeter. First, the contracts, on their faces, clearly contemplate the actual delivery of grain. Several terms, which appear in each HTA contract, indicate that the purpose of each agreement is the physical transfer of actual grain (or soybeans): Term 4 governs the circumstance in which the grain delivered is of an improper grade or is out of condition or unmerchantable; term 5 governs the time of shipment; term 6 allows the buyer to route the grain to an alternate destination if it is unable to receive the grain at the time of delivery; term 7 allows the seller to fulfill the contract requirements with not only grain from his own production but also grain from a different source; term 9 requires that the grain delivered conform to Pure Food and Drug regulations; term 10 requires the seller to warrant that the grain is free and clear of all liens; and the payment term provides that payment will be made "upon delivery and pricing." These terms clearly contemplate actual delivery, rather than mere speculation on price movements in the market for grain.

Second, it is undisputed that the parties to the contract are in the business of producing or obtaining grain. The seller, Mr. Lachmund, is a farmer who produces corn and soybeans; the buyer, Demeter, operates a grain elevator. Moreover, the parties are reasonably capable of delivering or receiving actual grain in the quantities provided for in the contract. Mr. Lachmund's complaint avers that the grain quantities in the contracts were based on his estimated annual crop yield. Therefore, it cannot be said that, although the parties are in the business of producing and buying grain, the contract quantities are so much greater than the parties' capacities that the contract, on its face, must not contemplate actual delivery. *See Lambert,* 1999 WL 177473, at *10.

Third, the contracts provide a definite time of delivery. For example, the May 1995 corn contract provided for delivery in October 1995; the February 1996 corn contract provided for delivery in October 1996. The soybean contracts similarly provided for specific times of delivery. The terms of the contracts also require actual delivery and do not allow delivery obligations to be rolled to a future date, let alone rolled indefinitely into the future. Term 5 provides:

> It is expressly understood that the grain herein mentioned is to be shipped as specified and be bought in or canceled only at the option of the buyer. The time of shipment can be extended by the buyer only. When grain is not shipped within specified time, this contract remains in force until the grain is shipped, or the contract canceled by the buyer.

Although a section labeled "remarks" in each contract states that "if buyer and seller mutually agree, they may continue to amend this contract until" a specific date subsequent to the delivery date, no term explicitly allows rolling of any kind.

Finally, the contracts are individualized with respect to such terms as the quantity of grain, the grade and type of grain, the time of delivery, the point of delivery, and which weights and grades will govern.

The HTA contracts, on their faces, contain all of the features characteristic of a cash forward contract for the physical transfer of actual grain. The contracts' terms contemplate actual delivery of the grain and reflect the parties' intention and purpose to buy and sell grain rather than to engage in price speculation on the futures market.

The contract terms, however, do not end our inquiry. Mr. Lachmund alleges that the parties engaged in a course of dealing not reflected in the written contracts that indicates a purpose other than the purchase and sale of actual grain. Mr. Lachmund's complaint alleges that the contracts' speculative nature is apparent from the parties' course of dealings outside of the contracts' written terms: The farmers could engage in unlimited rolling of their delivery obligations, and the contracts could be settled by a cash buy-out at any time.

As to whether parties engaged in a course of dealing that allowed unlimited and indefinite rolling of delivery obligations, Mr. Lachmund's own pleadings contradict this allegation. Although he avers that he and Demeter agreed to several rolls outside of the original terms of the contract, he also alleges that Demeter refused, in May or June of 1996, to allow continued rolling across crop years and demanded settlement of the contracts. It is thus clear that the parties did not engage in a course of dealing consisting of unlimited and indefinite rolling of delivery obligations to the point where it can be said that no actual delivery obligation existed.

Mr. Lachmund also alleges that Demeter, in practice, did not require delivery but would instead accept a cash buy-out in lieu of delivery. In reviewing a dismissal under Rule 12(b)(6), we must assume that this allegation is true. However, even if true, Demeter's willingness to settle the contracts by cash buy-out is not sufficient, in light of all the other facts discussed above, to establish that no delivery obligation existed or that the fundamental, underlying purpose and intention of the parties was anything other than the physical delivery of actual grain. Under the contract, Demeter retained the right to cancel the contract if the grain was not shipped in time. It stands to reason that Demeter would agree to cancel a contract that the seller could not perform only on the condition that the seller pay Demeter, through a cash buy-out, the damages Demeter would suffer in finding an alternate source of grain to replace the undelivered amounts.

In sum, Mr. Lachmund's pleadings concerning the parties' course of dealing are insufficient to overcome the written contracts' unambiguous character as cash forward contracts for the transfer of grain. We hold, therefore, that the HTA contracts at issue in this case are cash forward contracts exempt from the purview of the CEA and that, accordingly, Count IV of Mr. Lachmund's complaint does not state a claim for violations of the CEA.

For the foregoing reasons, the judgment of the district court is affirmed. AFFIRMED

NOTES

1. For other decisions addressing the nature of hedge-to-arrive contracts *see e.g.*, The Andersons, Inc. v. Horton Farms, Inc., 166 F.3d 308 (6th Cir.1998); Haren v. Conrad Cooperative, 198 F.3d 683 (8th Cir.1999).

2. The Commodity Futures Trading Commission concluded that at least some hedge-to-arrive contracts were futures and options contracts when they were regularly offset without delivery of the grain. See e.g., In re the Andersons, Comm. Fut. L. Rep. (CCH) ¶ 27,526 (C.F.T.C. 1999).

MG REFINING & MARKETING, INC.
v. KNIGHT ENTERPRISES, INC.

25 F.Supp.2d 175 (S.D.N.Y.1998).

SONIA SOTOMAYOR, U.S.D.J. by designation.

These cross-motions for summary judgment arise from a dispute between MG Marketing & Refining, Inc. ("MG") and eighteen of its customers, including Knight Enterprises, Inc. (collectively the "Customers"), in which the Customers allege breaches of certain 45–day contracts. In its pleadings, MG has admitted non-performance but asserts the affirmative defenses of illegality and impossibility. MG now moves for summary judgment on the ground that the contracts at issue were illegal and therefore void. The Customers move for summary judgment dismissing MG's illegality and impossibility defenses.

For the reasons discussed below, this Court denies both parties' motions with respect to the defense of illegality, and grants the Customers' motion with respect to the defense of impossibility.

The following facts are not disputed in any material way. The Customers are commercial entities that either use or engage in business activity relating to the wholesale, retail, supply, storage or distribution of diesel fuel and other petroleum products. MG was at one time the primary operating subsidiary of MG Corporation, and was at all relevant times herein a trader, distributor and marketer of oil and other oil related products.

Beginning as early as December 1991 and continuing through December 1993, MG marketed and sold to the Customers certain long-term contracts for the delivery of unleaded gasoline or heating oil at a fixed price and over a term of five or ten years. Without the use of a regulated exchange market, the parties entered into agreements with an aggregate stated volume of 160 million barrels by the end of 1993. The contracts themselves came in two forms. Under the first kind (the "ratables"), the Customers were required to take monthly deliveries on a ratable basis, and MG was required to meet the stated requirements. Except in a few cases where ratables were repudiated early in 1994, physical delivery occurred regularly under these contracts, and all of the Customers had the physical capacity to take these deliveries.

The second kind of contract (the "flexie" or "45–day contract") was nearly identical to the first, but the delivery requirements were modified to read as follows:

> Delivery under this Agreement shall be made no earlier than the Term Commencement Date and no later than the Term End Date. Purchaser shall notify Seller in writing of each Lifting date, which shall be no earlier than forty-five (45) days after such written notification has been received by Seller. Such written notice shall also include the quantity of the Product to be transferred from Seller to Purchaser

on such Lifting Date. If as of the day that is forty-five (45) days prior to the Term End Date (the "Last Notice Date"), Purchaser has not provided Seller with written notice of the Lifting Date with respect to any quantity of Product remaining to be delivered as of such Last Notice Date, the Lifting Date for such quantity of undelivered Product shall be the Term End Date.

Although MG sold flexies to the Customers with an aggregate stated volume of approximately 60 million barrels, none of the Customers has ever requested physical deliveries under a flexie, and few, if any, had the capacity to take the full stated volumes all at once.

Both the ratables and the flexies also contained a provision (the "blow out" provision), which allowed the Customers to cash out their contracts and terminate any remaining delivery requirements in the event of a "price spike"—i.e., if the price of petroleum futures on the New York Mercantile Exchange ("NYMEX") rose higher than a level stated in the contracts. This provision reads as follows:

> At any time during the Term of this Agreement that the Fixed Cash Price is less than the bid price for the applicable NYMEX Futures Contract . . ., Purchaser may, in lieu of accepting all or part (in lots of 42,000 gallons) of the remaining deliveries of Product, accept cash payments from Seller based on the average of bid prices obtained by Seller in totally or partially liquidating its long hedge positions for this Agreement (the "Average Bid Price") in the applicable NYMEX Futures Contract. . . . Upon Purchaser's receipt of cash payments from Seller representing all of the remaining deliveries of Product, Seller shall have no obligation to deliver any further Product under this Agreement and this Agreement shall terminate.

The contracts specified that "the cash payment to be received by Purchaser shall be an amount equal to [either 100% or 50%, depending on whether this is a flexie or a ratable, respectively, of] the product of the number of gallons represented by the long hedge positions to be liquidated multiplied by the difference between the Average Bid Price for the applicable NYMEX Futures Contract and the Fixed Cash Price."

Relations between the parties continued normally and without interruption until 1994, when the CFTC's Division of Enforcement began investigating the flexies and announced in November that they might be illegal off-exchange futures contracts. The Commodity Exchange Act ("CEA"), 7 U.S.C. § 1 et seq., requires that futures contracts be marketed and entered into only through certain designated "contract markets," which meet very specific CEA requirements. To call the flexies "illegal off-exchange futures contracts" is thus to suggest that they are illegal because they are futures contracts, subject to CEA regulation, but were entered into without the aid of a contract market.

These investigations continued for some time, until MG submitted an offer of settlement that the CFTC accepted, and which was formally entered into on July 27, 1995. The resulting order stopped the initiation of any full-scale enforcement proceedings against MG, assessed MG a $2.25 million penalty, established a series of oversight requirements for the corporation, declared the contracts to be "illegal off-exchange futures contracts", and required MG to certify within five days that it had notified "all Purchasers of existing 45 Day Agreements that the Commission has entered this Order finding that the 45 Day Agreements are illegal and therefore void ... and directing [MG] to cease and desist from violating" the relevant sections of the CEA. On July 27, 1995, MG's President issued letters to the Customers explaining the CFTC's Order and claiming that MG was "barred ... from performance" under the flexies. In 1996, when the NYMEX reference price exceeded the fixed contract price, every Customer wrote in to MG and asked to exercise their contractual rights to cash out all of their flexies. MG refused to perform.

Although disputes between the present parties began as early as April 8, 1994, when MG filed its original complaint against Knight Enterprises on a related matter, the Court consolidated all of the Customers' action for pre-trial purposes on March 11, 1996. By then, the Customers had alleged breach of the 45–day contracts, and MG subsequently responded to these claims by moving to dismiss. In its motion, MG argued that the Customers were collaterally estopped from denying an affirmative defense of illegality because the CFTC had already declared the flexies illegal and therefore void, that the present action amounted to an illicit collateral attack on the CFTC Order, and that MG could not be held liable for damages because the Order made performance under the flexies impossible. The Customers countered that MG was judicially estopped from asserting the illegality of the flexies because MG had advanced an inconsistent position in a prior arbitration proceeding. The Customers also argued that MG waived its right to deny the legality of the flexies under the express terms of the contracts. * * *

The issue of illegality arises in this case because § 4a of the CEA makes it "unlawful for any person to offer to enter into, to enter into, to execute, [or] to confirm the execution of ... a contract for the purchase or sale of a commodity for future delivery ... unless ... such transaction is conducted on or subject to the rules of a board of trade which has been designated by the Commodity Futures Trading Commission as a 'contract market' for such commodity...." 7 U.S.C. § 6(a)–(a)(1). MG's illegality defense rests on the fact that the flexies, which appear to be "contracts for the purchase or sale of a commodity for future delivery," were never entered into in accordance with the rules that this section specifies. Absent some exception to § 4a, the flexies would therefore qualify as illegal off-exchange futures contracts.

The Customers argue that MG's illegality defense must fail as a matter of law because the flexies fit into one or more of the following three exceptions to § 4a: the "trade option" exception, see 17 C.F.R. § 32.4(a) (exempting commodity options when the offeror has a "reasonable basis to believe" that it is offering the option to "a producer, or commercial user of, or merchant handling, the commodity which is the subject of the commodity option transaction . . . and that such producer, processor, or commercial user or handler is offered or enters into the commodity option transaction solely for purposes related to its business as such"), the "swaps" exception, see 17 C.F.R. § 35.2 (exempting certain swap agreements, as specified therein), or the "forward contract" exception, see 7 U.S.C. § 2 (1988)[12] (exempting transactions for "any sale of any cash commodity for deferred delivery or shipment").

The first two of these contentions can be dismissed with little difficulty. As MG points out in its papers, the trade option exception was meant to be a "narrowly defined" and "very limited exception" to the general rule set forth in § 4a of the CEA, which prohibits the trading of commodity options through unregulated markets. See Policy Statement Concerning Swap Transactions, 54 Fed. Reg. 30694, 30694 (CFTC July 21, 1989) (referring to trade option exemption as "narrowly defined" exception to CEA); CFTC Interpretive Letter No. 84–7, [1982–1984] Transfer Binder Comm. Fut. L. Rep. (CCH) P 22,025, at 28,595 (Feb. 22, 1984) (referring to trade option exemption as "very limited exception" to CEA's general ban on unregulated options trading). To qualify as a "commodity option" at all, however, an instrument must give the offeree a right, but no obligation, to make or take delivery of a physical commodity at a fixed price and within a specified time. See United States v. Bein, 728 F.2d 107, 111–12 (2d Cir.1984); CFTC v. U.S. Metals Depository Co., 468 F.Supp. 1149, 1154–55 (S.D.N.Y.1979); Characteristics Distinguishing Cash and Forward Contracts and Trade Options, 50 Fed. Reg. 39656, 39658 (CFTC Sept. 30, 1985). Although the Customers suggest that the flexie language makes them "offerees" of a "trade option", § 2 of these contracts unambiguously places an obligation on each Customer to take delivery sometime within the five or ten year terms set by the individual instruments. The blow-out provisions of these contracts are, moreover, only triggered in the event of a price spike. Because the flexies contain an obligation in all other circumstances, they cannot be considered options at all under the law, and so cannot meet an important threshold requirement for application of the CEA's trade option exception.

The flexies similarly fail to meet the very basic definition of a "swap" under the law, and so fail to meet the threshold requirement for application of the CEA's swap exception. As MG correctly points out, the CFTC has defined a "swap" as "an agreement between parties to exchange a series of cash flows measured by different interest rates, exchange rates, or prices with payments calculated by reference to a principal base." Policy Statement Concerning Swap Transactions, 54 Fed. Reg. at 30695; see also 17 C.F.R. § 35; Exemption for Certain Swap Agreements, [1992–94 Transfer Binder] Comm. Fut. L. Rep. § 25,539, at 39,592; Exemption for Certain Swap Agreement, 58 Fed. Reg. 5587, 5589 (CFTC January 22,

---

12. The CEA has been amended so that the language concerning exceptions for forward contracts now appears in § 1a(11), see 7 U.S.C. § 1a(11). This language is, however, identical to that of former CEA § 2(a)(1)(A), 7 U.S.C. § 2 (1988). Because the present action arose under the older statute, this opinion will continue to refer to the forward contract exception using its older numbering system.

1993); Procter & Gamble Co. v. Bankers Trust Co., 925 F. Supp. 1270, 1275 (S.D. Ohio1996) ("[A] swap is an agreement between two parties ('counterparties') to exchange cash flows over a period of time."). By contrast, the flexies do either one of two things. Either they oblige the Customers to take delivery of petroleum at a set price in the future, in which case they function as agreements for the simple sale and delivery of commodities. Or, during a price spike, they give the Customers the right to cash out the contracts, in which case the Customers are entitled to receive a cash settlement based on a principal amount but are obliged to give MG no similar cash flow in return. In either case, although the CFTC has tended to take a rather liberal view of swaps in order to recognize "the diversity and evolving nature of swap transactions", see Exemption for Certain Swap Agreements, 58 Fed. Reg. at 5589, 5593, it would stretch the definition of a "swap" beyond recognition to include these transactions within its purview. The flexies therefore fail to meet the basic requirement for exemption under the swaps exception as well.

Whether the flexies qualify for the "forward contract" exception thus presents the critical, and ultimately much more difficult, question. As both parties acknowledge, until at least 1990, the forward contracts exception was meant to exempt from CFTC jurisdiction any transaction in which "the desire to acquire or dispose of a physical commodity [was] the underlying motivation for entering [the] contract, [but in which] delivery may be deferred for purposes of convenience or necessity." In re Stovall, [1977–1980 Transfer Binder] 1979 CFTC LEXIS 10, Comm. Fut. L. Rep. (CCH) P 20,941, at 23,778; see also Statutory Interpretation Concerning Forward Transactions, 55 Fed. Reg. 39188, 39190 (CFTC Sept. 25, 1990). By contrast, the "exclusion [was] unavailable to contracts of sale for commodities which [were] sold merely for speculative purposes and which [were] not predicated upon the expectation that delivery of the actual commodity by the seller to the original contracting buyer [would] occur in the future." CFTC v. Co Petro Mktg. Group, Inc., 680 F.2d 573, 579 (9th Cir.1982). To determine whether a given contract was entered for one or the other reason, each transaction was "viewed as a whole, with a critical eye towards its underlying purpose." Id. at 581.

Given the nature of this test, the CFTC made it quite clear that there was no exhaustive list of elements that would serve to establish the existence of a forward contract. See Policy Statement Concerning Swap Transactions, 54 Fed. Reg. at 30694–95. Rather, the "overall effect" of a transaction as well as "what the parties intended" had to be examined in most cases. See id. Certain factors did, however, commonly contribute to a favorable finding, such as: non-standardized, individually negotiated terms, capacities on the part of the buyer to take and the seller to make delivery, routine physical delivery of the underlying commodities, absence of exchange-style offset provisions granting the counterparties a right to cash out the contracts, absence of any other settlement systems or rights of assignment under the contracts themselves, and marketing or sales only to commercial entities, who regularly dealt in the commodities at issue, rather than to the general public. See, e.g., Co Petro, 680 F.2d at 578, 580. Each of these factors were deemed to lend support to the notion that the underlying purpose of a given transaction was to effect physical delivery.

The Customers argue, however, that in its 1990 Statutory Interpretation Concerning Forward Transactions, 55 Fed. Reg. 39188, the CFTC radically revised this underlying purpose test and replaced it with a more "objective" one, under which MG's illegality defense must fail as a matter of law. Under this objective test, contracts should be considered legal forward contracts whenever they are entered into between commercial parties in connection with their businesses, and when the contracts set forth specific delivery obligations imposing on the parties substantial economic risks of a commercial nature. The first question to address is thus whether the underlying purpose test has been replaced.

The Customers cite the 1990 Statutory Interpretation because it effectively reversed the holding of Judge Conner in Transnor (Bermuda) Ltd. v. BP North America Petroleum, 738 F.Supp. 1472 (S.D.N.Y.1990), a case which involved the legality of the so-called "15–day Brent market", and upon which MG has partly relied in arguing for the relevance of the underlying purpose test. This case involved an unregulated and highly complex set of transactions, which were something of "a hybrid of a future contract[s] and forward contract[s]." Id. at 1489. Employing the traditional criteria and principles identified above, but emphasizing the routine physical delivery requirement, Judge Conner noted that there was an extremely low ratio of actual to negotiated deliveries in this market. See id. at 1490–91 (noting that contracts were "routinely settled by means other than delivery"). This ratio suggested to him that the underlying purposes of the transaction must have been "hedging, speculating and tax spinning." Id. at 1490. Judge Conner therefore held that the unregulated Brent activity was illegal under the CEA.

The CFTC ultimately disagreed with this holding. In its 1990 Statutory Interpretation, the CFTC explained that Congress had not yet provided enough guidance on the scope of the forward contracts exclusion:

> in the content [sic] of today's commercial environment, including with regard to the concept of what constitutes delivery for the purposes of the exclusion ... From 1974 and with increasing frequency, there have evolved in the commercial segments of the economy a diverse variety of transactions involving commodities.... These transactions, which are entered into between commercial counterparties in the normal commercial channels, serve the same commercial functions as did those forward contracts which were originally the subject of the section 2(a)(1) exclusion notwithstanding the fact that, in specific cases and as separately agreed to between the parties, the transactions may ultimately result in performance through the payment of cash as an alternative to actual physical transfer or delivery of the commodity.

Statutory Interpretation Concerning Forward Transactions, 55 Fed. Reg. at 39191. The CFTC then held that the forward contract exclusion applied to transactions in the 15–day Brent market, as well as any other markets with analogous delivery mechanisms.

Although the Customers are correct to note that the 1990 Statutory Interpretation clarified that routine physical delivery under a contract is not an absolute precondition for application of the forward contract exception, the Customers overstate the CFTC's holding when they contend that this opinion marks an abandonment of the underlying purpose test altogether. The transactions examined in the 1990 Statutory Interpretation involved commercial buyers and sellers of crude oil, who entered into sometimes lengthy "chains" of transactions rather than simple bilateral agreements. Because of the chain-like structure of this activity, counterparties in a given series would sometimes find themselves in multiple, offsetting positions with respect to one another, thus making it more convenient and less risky simply to cash out these positions and allow delivery to pass through one less layer of exchange. Still, "the market [itself] remained one based on physical trading", and each chain normally effectuated the delivery of crude oil. Transnor, 738 F.Supp. at 1489. The CFTC noted that title and bills of lading passed between the various members of a chain, as did "substantial risk[s] of a commercial nature", including those of "demurrage, damage, theft or deterioration of the commodity as well as other risks associated with owning the commodity delivered." Statutory Interpretation Concerning Forward Transactions, 55 Fed. Reg. at 39191. It was only in this specific context that the CFTC concluded that cashed-out 15–day Brent contracts ought to be considered agreements appurtenant to the more primary goal of obtaining deferred delivery of underlying commodities.

In fact, far from undermining the traditional forward contract analysis, the CFTC explicitly reiterated the proposition that to identify a forward contract, the "transaction[s] must be viewed as a whole, with a critical eye towards [their] underlying purpose." Id. at 39190 (quoting Co Petro, 680 F.2d at 581). The CFTC also reconfirmed that there is no definitive list of elements for determining this purpose, and that "such an assessment entail[s] ... a review of the 'overall effect' of the transaction as well as a determination of 'what the parties intended'" Id. Although the CFTC decided to de-emphasize the importance of routine physical delivery in discerning the purposes of the 15–day Brent contracts, the CFTC found it particularly salient, in reaching this decision, that the 15–day Brent contracts contained "no right of offset, [did] not rely on a variation margining and settlement system, and [did] not permit assignment of contractual obligations without counterparty consent." Id. at 39189 (emphasis added); see also id. at 39192 (noting that offsets resulted from "separate, individually negotiated, new agreements, [that] there [was] no obligation or arrangement to enter into such agreements, [and that they were] not provided for by the terms of the contracts as initially entered into"). The CFTC's decision thus indicated its expert opinion that contracts containing no rights to offset, but that are nevertheless cashed out pursuant to separately negotiated agreements, should not be deemed to serve a speculative purpose just because they do not end in physical delivery. * * *

MG argues that when applied to the facts produced thus far in discovery, the underlying purpose test entitles MG, rather than the Customers, to summary judgment on the defense of illegality. If the flexies were viewed in isolation, this Court might be inclined to grant MG's motion against most of the Customers in this case. This is because the record contains overwhelming and nearly uncontradicted evidence that the flexies were never thought of as ways independently to effectuate physical deliveries. Although the right to cash out the flexies was triggered only during price spikes, the record contains ample evidence, for example, that the chance of a price spike occurring within the terms of the flexies was objectively very high, and price spikes sufficient to trigger the blowout provisions did in fact occur in every case. Moreover, when these spikes occurred in 1996, every single Customer asked to cash out the flexies, and no delivery has ever occurred under a flexie. * * *

The record also contains direct deposition testimony, from some or all of the Customer representatives who negotiated the flexies with MG, that the Customers expected a price spike to occur, that they never intended to take delivery under the contracts, and that they hoped to cash out the contracts and make money on future price fluctuations. * * *

"Summary judgment is [however] rarely appropriate when subjective matters such as intent are material", see Abrams v. United States, 797 F.2d 100, 105 (2d Cir.1986), and the record does contain some evidence that may be more helpful to the Customers' underlying position. Namely, the record contains evidence that the flexies may have been negotiated as part of larger transactions, which included the sale not only of flexies but of certain ratable contracts. * * * The notion of "hedging," however, unlike that of "speculating," means "to limit the financial risk of (e.g., a bet) by a counterbalancing transaction," see American Heritage Dictionary 389 (3d ed. 1994), and it is undisputed that physical delivery occurred under the ratable contracts on a regular basis. When viewed as part of these larger, ongoing transactions, some of the descriptions of the transactions between MG and the Customers might thus be read to suggest that the flexies were viewed by both as instruments for insuring against certain price fluctuations that might arise as petroleum was delivered under the terms of the ratable or other contracts. This sort of conclusion would, in turn, be strengthened by the facts that both parties are commercial dealers, and that none appeared to deal regularly on any orthodox futures markets.

In light of the underlying purpose test, and heeding the CFTC's acknowledgment that commodities markets have been evolving to meet increasing complex needs through increasingly complex markets, a critical set of questions therefore remains. Were the flexies entered into by commercial dealers, who were primarily in the business of buying and selling petroleum, but who were also willing to seize on the opportunity to speculate on an unregulated futures market price, thereby obtaining a second source of income? Or were the flexies entered into primarily as ways of "shifting future price risks incidental to commercial operations and other forward commitments," which involved the transfer of unleaded gasoline and heating oil? See Statutory Interpretation Concerning Forward Transactions, 55 Fed. Reg. at 39191. To answer these questions, a decision-maker will have to look not only at the contract language itself but at what was happening in and around the negotiations of all the contracts, and in particular of the flexies. Because this inquiry will require the relevant decision maker to weigh the evidence, assess the credibility of its various sources, and reconcile any inconsistencies that may arise, the inquiry is one that lies squarely within the province of the jury, and MG's motion for summary judgment is denied. * * *

For the reasons discussed, the Court denies the Customers' motion for summary judgment dismissing MG's illegality defense because the test for whether these contracts are illegal will require a fact-finder to look at the purposes underlying the instruments. The Court also denies MG's motion for summary judgment on the basis of its illegality defense because there is still a genuine issue of material fact concerning the underlying purposes of the flexie contracts. The Court grants the Customers' motion for summary judgment dismissing MG's impossibility defense because, under the only set of assumptions in which impossibility is relevant to this case, MG's defense is premised on an order that was caused by MG's consent.

NOTES

An MG affiliate, MG Trade Finance Corp., a subsidiary of Metallgesellschaft AG, had other problems. A trader at that company entered into "hedged" futures positions that were showing losses of over $2 billion when spot oil prices fell below the company's futures positions. MG Trade Finance closed out the positions, taking the loss, and was rescued by a loan of over $2 billion that was arranged by the Deutsche Bank. The trader was fired, but sued MG for $1 billion for defamation and other claims. A Nobel Prize winning economist, Merton Miller, added to the controversy by claiming in the *Wall Street Journal* that MG management had panicked because they did not understand the futures markets and should have let the hedge continue and avoid losses. Management claimed that the company would have incurred losses of $50 billion if they had not liquidated the position.

SECTION 7. COMMODITY FUTURES MODERNIZATION ACT OF 2000

The SEC and CFTC continued their rivalry as the last century closed. The SEC created a safe harbor from its otherwise onerous regulation for dealers in derivative instruments through something called "Broker–Dealer Lite" registration. 17 C.F.R. § 240.3b–13. Those dealers often engaged in securites transactions in connection with their derivatives business, subjecting them to regulation as broker-dealers. The Broker–Dealer Lite registration eased the application of broker-dealer regulations on those derivative dealers. The CFTC viewed this as a threat to its jurisdiction and announced a plan to conduct an investigation of over-the-counter derivatives to determine whether they should be subject to CFTC regulation. The industry viewed this simply as a cover to lay the groundwork for such regulation. The SEC, the Treasury Department and the Federal Reserve Board all weighed in against this jurisdictional grab. Congress responded with legislation that stopped the CFTC. All of this commotion was for nothing because the CFTC did a volte face in its regulatory approach and adopted rules deregulating most over-the-counter derivative trading when conducted between institutions. That approach was then adopted into law by Congress through the Commodity Futures Modernization Act of 2000 ("CFMA"), Pub L. No. 106–554, 114 Stat. 2763 (2000).[13]

The CFMA created two tiers of regulated markets that included designated contract markets and registered derivative transaction execution facilities ("DTFs"). The amendments further provided for two categories of markets to be exempted from regulation. They are exempt boards of trade and exempt commercial markets. Designated contract markets are the traditional commodity exchanges where futures contracts are traded by any type of market participant, including unsophisticated customers. These contract markets are still regulated. The CFMA requires those designated contract markets to have sixteen core principles that include such things as monitoring trading to prevent manipulation, publishing market information, preventing abuses, arbitration procedures and antitrust restrictions. The CFTC's regulatory role over contract markets is to be more one of oversight than direct involvement.

The CFMA additionally removed from the reach of the Commodity Exchange Act certain "excluded commodities." These include most financial instruments including interest rate, exchange rate, security index, debt or equity instruments, and other indexes including inflation indexes or other rate differential index or measures of economic or commercial risk. This exemption applies where the excluded commodity is traded by "eligible contract participants" and provided that the contract is not

---

13. The following discussion of the CFMA is adopted from Jerry W. Markham & Thomas Lee Hazen, Broker–Dealer Operations Under Securities and Commodity Laws § 2:43 (2002).

executed on a "trading facility." Eligible contract participants are large institutions as defined in the Act. A trading facility is one that allows multiple participants to trade contracts by accepting bids and offers. It does not apply to systems that enable participants to negotiate and enter into bilateral transactions or trading by a government securities broker-dealer in government securities and facilities where bids and offers and their acceptance are not binding. The CFMA additionally excluded from the reach of most of the provisions of the Commodity Exchange Act over-the-counter transactions in excluded commodities where they are conducted on a principal-to-principal basis by eligible contract participants on an electronic trading facility. The legislation further confirms the exclusion of swap transactions from the Commodity Exchange Act where they are between eligible contract participants, subject to individual negotiations, and are not executed on a trading facility. See generally United States v. Radley, ___ F.3d ___, 2011 WL 241984 (5th Cir. 2011) (discussing exclusions).

CAIOLA v. CITIBANK, N.A.

295 F.3d 312 (2d Cir.2002).

B.D. PARKER JR., CIRCUIT JUDGE.

Plaintiff-appellant Louis S. Caiola brought federal securities fraud and state law claims against defendant-appellee Citibank, N.A., New York arising from extensive physical and synthetic investments. * * *

The allegations in the Complaint are as follows. Caiola, an entrepreneur and sophisticated investor, was a major client of Citibank Private Bank, a division of Citibank, from the mid–1980s to September 1999. During this relationship, Citibank assisted Caiola with a wide range of business and personal financial services. As a result of these transactions, which involved hundreds of millions of dollars, Caiola became one of Citibank's largest customers.

Beginning in the mid–1980s, Caiola undertook high volume equity trading, entrusting funds to Citibank who in turn engaged various outside brokerage firms. Caiola specialized in the stock of Philip Morris Companies, Inc. ("Philip Morris") and regularly traded hundreds of thousands of shares valued at many millions of dollars. To hedge the risks associated with these trades, Caiola established option positions corresponding to his stock positions.

As Caiola's trades increased in size, he and Citibank grew increasingly concerned about the efficacy of his trading and hedging strategies. Caiola's positions required margin postings of tens of millions of dollars and were sufficiently large that the risks to him were unacceptable unless hedged. But the volume of options necessary to hedge effectively could impact prices and disclose his positions—effects known as "footprints" on the market. In early 1994, Citibank proposed synthetic trading. A synthetic transaction is typically a contractual agreement between two counterparties, usually an investor and a bank, that seeks to economically replicate the ownership and physical trading of shares and options. The counterparties establish synthetic positions in shares or options, the values of which are pegged to the market prices of the related physical shares or options. The aggregate market values of the shares or options that underlie the synthetic trades are referred to as "notional" values and are treated as interest-bearing loans to the investor. As Citibank explained to Caiola, synthetic trading offers significant advantages to investors who heavily concentrate on large positions of a single stock by reducing the risks associated with large-volume trading. Synthetic trading alleviates the necessity of posting large amounts of margin capital and ensures that positions can be established and unwound quickly. Synthetic trading also offers a solution to the "footprint" problem by permitting the purchase of large volumes of options in stocks without affecting their price.

Taking Citibank's advice, Caiola began to engage in two types of synthetic transactions focusing on Philip Morris stock and options: equity swaps and cash-settled over-the-counter options. In a typical equity swap, one party (Caiola) makes periodic interest payments on the notional value of a stock position and also payments equal to any decrease in value of the shares upon which the notional value is based. *See* Note, *Tax–Exempt Entities, Notional Principle Contracts, and the Unrelated Business Income Tax,* 105 Harv.L.Rev. 1265, 1269 (1992). The other party (Citibank) pays any increase in the value of the shares and any dividends, also based on the same notional value. *See id.*

For example, if Caiola synthetically purchased 1000 shares of Philip Morris at $50 per share, the notional value of that transaction would be $50,000. Because this notional value would resemble a loan from Citibank, Caiola would pay interest at a predetermined rate on the $50,000. If Philip Morris's stock price fell $10, Caiola would pay Citibank $10,000. If the stock price rose $10, Citibank would pay Caiola $10,000. Citibank also would pay Caiola the value of any dividends that Caiola would have received had he actually owned 1000 physical shares.

Caiola also acquired synthetic options, which were cash-settled over-the-counter options. Because these options were not listed and traded on physical exchanges, their existence and size did not impact market prices. Caiola and Citibank agreed to terms regarding the various attributes of the option in a particular transaction (such as the strike price, expiration date, option type, and premium). They agreed to settle these option transactions in cash when the option was exercised or expired, based on the then-current market price of the underlying security.

Caiola and Citibank documented their equity swaps and synthetic options through an International Swap Dealers Association Master Agreement ("ISDA Agreement")[14] dated March 25, 1994. The ISDA Agreement established specific terms for the synthetic trading. After entering into the ISDA Agreement, Caiola, on Citibank's advice, began to enter into "cou-

---

14. The International Swap Dealers Association, now known as the International Swap and Derivatives Association, is a global trade association that developed a master agreement for interest rate and currency exchange swaps. See First Nat'l Bank of Chicago v. Ackerley Communications, Inc., 2001 WL 15693, at *4 n. 3 (S.D.N.Y.2001).

pled" synthetic transactions with Citibank. Specifically, Caiola's over-the-counter option positions were established in connection with a paired equity swap, ensuring that his synthetic options would always hedge his equity swaps. This strategy limited the amount he could lose and ensured that his risks would be both controllable and quantifiable.

Citibank promised Caiola that as his counterparty it would control its own risks through a strategy known as "delta hedging." Delta hedging makes a derivative position, such as an option position, immune to small changes in the price of an underlying asset, such as a stock, over a short period of time. *See* John C. Hull, *Options Futures, and Other Derivatives* 311–12 (4th ed.2000). The "delta" measures the sensitivity of the price of the derivative to the change in the price of the underlying asset. *Id.* at 310. Specifically, "delta" is the ratio of the change in the price of the derivative to that of the underlying asset. *Id.* Thus, if an option has a delta of .5, a $1 change in the stock price would result in a $.50 change in the option price. Caiola's synthetic positions contained a number of components, such as a stock position plus one or more option positions. For each of these coupled or integrated transactions a "net delta" was calculated which helped Citibank determine the amount of securities necessary to establish its "delta core" position. By maintaining a "delta core" position in the physical market, Citibank could achieve "delta neutrality," a hedge position that would offset Citibank's obligations to Caiola.

Effective delta hedging is a sophisticated trading activity that involves the continuous realignment of the hedge's portfolio. Because the delta changes with movements in the price of the underlying asset, the size of the delta core position also constantly changes. Although a certain delta core position might sufficiently hedge Citibank's obligations at one point, a different delta core position may become necessary a short time later. *See* Hull, *supra,* at 310–11. Thus, as markets fluctuate, the net delta must be readjusted continuously to ensure an optimal exposure to risk. *Id.;* Adam R. Waldman, Comment, *OTC Derivatives & Systemic Risk: Innovative Finance or the Dance into the Abyss?,* 43 Am.U.L.Rev. 1023, 1044 (1994). Citibank told Caiola that as his counterparty it would continuously adjust its delta core positions to maintain delta neutrality. Also, Caiola routinely altered his transactions to account for their effect on Citibank's delta core positions. This arrangement was satisfactory so long as Citibank adhered to its delta hedging strategy, which involved comparably small purchases in the physical market. However, if Citibank fully replicated Caiola's stock and option positions in the physical market instead of delta hedging, the benefits of synthetic trading would disappear and he would be exposed to risks that this strategy was designed to avoid.

Each synthetic transaction was governed by an individualized confirmation containing a number of disclaimers. A confirmation for Caiola's purchase of 360,000 cash-settled over-the-counter options dated December 9, 1998 ("Confirmation"), for instance, provides that each party represents to the other that "it is not relying on any advice, statements or recommendations (whether written or oral) of the other party," that each is entering the transaction "as principal and not as an agent for [the] other party," and that "[Caiola] acknowledges and agrees that [Citibank] is not acting as a fiduciary or advisor to [him] in connection with this Transaction." Further, the ISDA Agreement and accompanying Schedule, which governed the overall synthetic relationship, provides:

> This Agreement constitutes the entire agreement and understanding of the parties with respect to its subject matter and supersedes all oral communication and prior writings with respect thereto. (ISDA Agreement & 9(a).) [Caiola] has such knowledge and experience in financial, business and tax matters that render him capable of evaluating the merits and risks of this Agreement and the Transactions contemplated hereunder; [Caiola] is able to bear the economic risks of this Agreement and the Transaction contemplated hereunder; and, after appropriate independent investigations, [Caiola] has determined that this Agreement and the Transactions contemplated hereunder are suitable for him. . . . (ISDA Agreement, Schedule to the Master Agreement, Part 5, & 2(a)(ii).)

In October 1998, Citicorp, Citibank's parent company, merged with Travelers Group, Inc. ("Travelers"). Caiola feared that Salomon Smith Barney ("SSB"), a Travelers affiliate, might become involved in his account. At a November 18, 1998 meeting, Citibank informed Caiola that SSB would become involved in Caiola's synthetic equities trading. At this meeting, Caiola stated that he did not wish to become a client of SSB and that, unless his relationship with Citibank were to continue as it had previously existed, he would terminate it. Citibank assured Caiola then and subsequently that their relationship would continue unchanged and, specifically, that his synthetic trading relationship with Citibank would remain unaltered by SSB's involvement.

Relying on these assurances, Caiola maintained his account at Citibank and continued to establish sizeable positions with the understanding that they would be managed synthetically, with Citibank continuing to serve as the delta hedging counterparty. From January 1999 through March 1999, Caiola bought and sold more than twenty-two million options, established a swap position involving two million shares of Philip Morris stock with a notional value of eighty million dollars, and paid Citibank millions of dollars in commissions and interest.

However, after November 1998, and contrary to its representations and unknown to Caiola, Citibank had secretly stopped delta hedging and transformed Caiola's synthetic portfolio into a physical one by executing massive trades in the physical markets that mirrored Caiola's synthetic transactions. In other words, when Caiola sought to open an integrated synthetic position in shares of synthetic stock and synthetic options, Citibank, instead of delta hedging, simply executed physical trades on stock and options. These transactions, Caiola alleges, exposed him to the risks—"footprints" and a lack of liquidity—that synthetic trading was intended to avoid.

On March 12, 1999, Citibank told Caiola that it intended to early exercise certain options in his portfolio for physical settlement, a demand inconsistent with a synthetic relationship. One week later Citibank for the first time refused to establish a synthetic option position Caiola requested. Growing concerned, on March 26, 1999, Caiola inquired and was told that SSB was unwilling to assume the risks associated with synthetic trading. During this time period, although Caiola had taken a large position in Philip Morris stock that was declining in value, he wrote options expecting to recoup his losses and to profit from an anticipated rise in the value of the shares. The strategy, Caiola claims, failed because Citibank had secretly and unilaterally terminated synthetic trading. This termination cost Caiola tens of millions of dollars because the price of Philip Morris rebounded as he had expected.

At this point, Caiola investigated and discovered that Citibank had ceased treating his investments synthetically as early as November 1998. Two Citibank officers informed Caiola that "many" of his trades had been executed on the physical market, although they had been submitted and accepted by Citibank as synthetic transactions. The only explanation Caiola received was that "[t]his is how SSB wanted it done."

Caiola unearthed additional evidence that Citibank had transformed his portfolio when he attempted to unwind his account in September 1999. When Caiola placed unwind transactions, Citibank refused to execute the trades without a commission—a further indication to Caiola that what he thought were synthetic positions were being handled by Citibank as physical transactions. In addition, as Citibank executed certain option transactions during this unwind period, Citibank sent Caiola confirmations reflecting that the transactions were for physical, instead of cash, settlement. Caiola also was told by a Citibank official that it was holding hundreds of thousands of physical shares of Philip Morris stock in his account and that Citibank had executed certain unwind transactions by going to the physical market to sell millions of options and shares. Finally, when Citibank failed to completely unwind a certain swap position, it told Caiola that hundreds of thousands of physical shares—for which he had no hedge protection and was financially responsible—were being sold on his behalf.

In July 2000, Caiola sued Citibank alleging violations of section 10(b) and Rule 10b–5. He also asserted state law claims for fraud, breach of fiduciary duty, and breach of contract. Generally, the Complaint alleged that Citibank violated section 10(b) and Rule 10b–5 when it misrepresented that it would continue its pre-existing synthetic trading relationship but secretly abandoned its role as delta hedging counterparty and, instead, bought and sold exchange-traded stock and options on Caiola's behalf Caiola further claims that Citibank's misrepresentations were material, he relied on them, and, as a result, he experienced massive losses.

Citibank moved to dismiss under Rule 12(b)(6) on the grounds that Caiola was neither a purchaser nor a seller of securities, that the synthetic transactions were not "securities," and that the confirmations established that neither party was entitled to rely on the representations of the other. *See* Fed.R.Civ.P. 12(b)(6). The District Court granted Citibank's motion. *Caiola v. Citibank, N.A.,* 137 F.Supp.2d 362, 367–73 (S.D.N.Y.2001). * * *

The District Court ... concluded—without distinguishing between options and swaps—that Caiola failed to allege the purchase or sale of a security because his synthetic transactions were not "securities." The District Court analyzed Caiola's options in light of the conventional understanding that "[a]n option contract 'entitles a purchaser to buy or sell a commodity by some specific date at a fixed price known as the "strike price"....'" *Caiola,* 137 F.Supp.2d at 370 (quoting *United States v. Bein,* 728 F.2d 107, 111 (2d Cir.1984)). The District Court believed that no court previously had considered "whether the types of transactions at issue in this case constitute securities, although in [*Procter & Gamble*], the court held that certain interest rate swap contracts were not 'securities.'" *Id.* at 369. The court concluded that "for many of the same reasons offered in *Procter and Gamble,* the transactions at issue were not 'securities.'" *Id.* In particular, the District Court held that Caiola's synthetic transactions did not fit the definition of "securities" in section 3(a)(10) of the 1934 Act because they were not investment contracts, notes, or evidence of indebtedness. *Id.* at 369–70. The court also held that the synthetic transactions were not "options on securities" as defined by that section because, drawing on *Procter & Gamble,* " 'they did not give either counterparty the right to exercise an option or to take possession of any security.'" *Id.* at 370 (quoting *Procter & Gamble,* 925 F.Supp. at 1282).

Caiola's synthetic transactions, however, involved two distinct instruments: cash-settled over-the-counter options and equity swaps. The two must be analyzed separately. We conclude that Caiola's synthetic options are "securities" subject to section 10(b). Caiola does not argue on appeal that his equity swaps met the definition of a security under section 3(a)(10) at the time of his trades, but instead urges us to apply retroactively the Commodities Futures Modernization Act of 2000 ("CFMA"), Pub.L. No. 106–554, 114 Stat. 2763 (2000). Because Caiola did not adequately raise this issue before the District Court, we decline to consider it on appeal.

The anti-fraud provisions of the federal securities laws cover options on securities. Section 3(a)(10) of the 1934 Act defines "security" to include "any put, call, straddle, option, or privilege on any security, certificate of deposit, or group or index of securities (including any interest therein or based on the value thereof)...." 15 U.S.C. § 78c(a)(10) (2000). Citibank contends that this definition of "security" does not include all options without limitation. Citibank argues that only an option on a security would be covered, not an option based on the value of a security. In other words, according to Citibank, an option that involves the right to take possession of a security fits the statutory definition but a synthetic option that merely obligates the counterparty to make cash payments based on the value of a security does not. The District Court agreed with this analysis. *Caiola*, 137 F.Supp.2d at 370–72. Caiola, on the other hand, alleges that his synthetic options were simply cash-settled over-the-counter options on Philip Morris stock and therefore are securities. We agree that these instruments are securities under section 3(a)(10) for a number of reasons.

The Confirmation, on which Citibank relies for its argument that Caiola's options are not securities, indicates that the transactions are commonly used cash-settled over-the-counter options. The Confirmation expressly states that the "particular Transaction to which this Confirmation relates is an Option" and the "Type of Transaction" is an "Equity Option" on the "common stock of Philip Morris Cos." Options have been covered under section 10(b) since the 1934 Act was amended in 1982. Securities Exchange Act of 1934 Amendments of 1982, Pub.L. No. 97–303, 96 Stat. 1409 (1982). The parties dispute whether cash-settled over-the-counter options on the value of a security are covered by section 10(b). We hold that they are.

The Supreme Court has cautioned that "[i]n searching for the meaning and scope of the word 'security' ... the emphasis should be on economic reality." *United Hous. Found. v. Forman*, 421 U.S. 837, 848, 95 S.Ct. 2051, 44 L.Ed.2d 621 (1975) (quoting *Tcherepnin v. Knight*, 389 U.S. 332, 336, 88 S.Ct. 548, 19 L.Ed.2d 564 (1967)). The definition of security is construed in a "flexible" manner, so as to "meet the countless and variable schemes devised by those who seek the use of the money of others on the promise of profits." *SEC v. W.J. Howey Co.*, 328 U.S. 293, 299, 66 S.Ct. 1100, 90 L.Ed. 1244 (1946). In this way, the economic reality approach "permit[s] the SEC and the courts sufficient flexibility to ensure that those who market investments are not able to escape the coverage of the Securities Acts by creating new instruments that would not be covered by a more determinate definition." *Reves v. Ernst & Young*, 494 U.S. 56, 63 n. 2, 110 S.Ct. 945, 108 L.Ed.2d 47 (1990).

Under section 3(a)(10) "security" includes (i) an option on any "security," (ii) an option on any "certificate of deposit," and (iii) an option on any "group or index of securities." Therefore, "option" under section 3(a)(10) is not limited to "conventional" exchange-traded options. It applies to both exchange-traded as well as over-the-counter options and does not distinguish between physically-settled and cash-settled options. Nor does the definition distinguish between options documented as swaps as opposed to options documented in some other fashion.

We find further support for our conclusion in section 3(a)(10)'s definition of "security" to include an option on any "group or index of securities." An option on a security can be physically settled by delivery of physical stock. An index of securities, however, is simply a benchmark against which financial performance is measured. An option on an index of securities is settled by cash since physical delivery is not possible. *See* 5

Louis Loss & Joel Seligman, *Securities Regulation* 2650 (3d ed.1999). Consequently, the right to take possession does not define an "option" under section 3(a)(10), which covers options that can be physically delivered as well as those that cannot.

Both the District Court and Citibank rely heavily on *Procter & Gamble* for their conclusion that cash-settled over-the-counter options are not securities. *Procter & Gamble,* however, held that a very different type of transaction—swaps linked to the price of Treasury notes—were not securities. The plaintiff in *Procter & Gamble* argued that even though the instrument in question was technically an interest rate swap, it had option-like features and thus could be characterized as an "option on a security" under section 3(a)(10). *Procter & Gamble,* 925 F.Supp. at 1280–81. The court, however, rejected this argument because the swap "did not give either counterparty the right to exercise an option or to take possession of any security." *Id.* at 1282. The District Court imported this language from *Procter & Gamble,* finding it dispositive. *Caiola,* 137 F.Supp.2d at 370 (quoting *Procter & Gamble,* 925 F.Supp. at 1282). Unlike the plaintiff's argument in *Procter & Gamble* that an interest rate swap with option-like features could be characterized as an option on a security, *Caiola's* transactions involve the much more straightforward question of whether a cash-settled over-the-counter option on Philip Morris stock—similar to options commonly traded on the market—is an option on a security. *Procter & Gamble* does not address this issue.

Further, *Procter & Gamble* concluded that a critical feature of an option was the right to exercise and to take possession of the security because the parenthetical "based on the value thereof" in section 3(a)(10) applied only to the immediately preceding phrase, "group or index of securities" and not to "any security." *Procter & Gamble,* 925 F.Supp. at 1281–82. We believe this conclusion is incorrect, and we decline to follow its lead. We hold that the parenthetical applies to "any security." The text of the statute itself includes cash-settled options by defining "option" to include an option on a "group or index of securities." This provision is sufficiently clear that a resort to legislative history is not necessary.[15] *See Lee v. Bankers Trust Co.,* 166 F.3d 540, 544 (2d Cir.1999). A contrary reading would mean that the statute illogically both includes and excludes cash-settled options in the same sentence. In other words, there is no basis for reading into the term "option" as used in the phrase "option ... on any security" a limitation requiring a particular method of settlement—a

---

15. The District Court examined the CFMA and its legislative history for insight into the status of Caiola's transactions, which were entered into prior to the enactment of the CFMA. Because section 3(a)(10) is clear, that inquiry was unnecessary. In any event, we disagree with the District Court's conclusion that Caiola's options were "security based swap agreements" exempted from the CFMA's definition of security. *Caiola,* 137 F.Supp.2d at 371–72. The CFMA provides that a "swap agreement" is not a security under section 3(a)(10) of the 1934 Act. CFMA § 303, 114 Stat. at 2763A–452–57. However, section 301 of the CFMA excludes from the definition of "swap agreement" "any ... option ... on any security ... or group or index of securities, including any interest therein and based on the value thereof." Id. § 301, 114 Stat. at 2763A–450. Thus, options based on the value of a security are not "swap agreements;" they are securities. The District Court's analysis failed to account for this exclusion.

limitation that clearly does not apply to "option" as used in the phrase "option . . . on any . . . index of securities." The *Procter & Gamble* court's application of the parenthetical also produced the odd consequence that Rule 10b–5 would cover options based on the value of two securities but not options based on the value of single security. We do not agree with this interpretation and, accordingly, we hold that there is no textual basis for reading section 3(a)(10) to define "option" as including only transactions that give the holder the right to receive the underlying securities.

Thus, section 3(a)(10)'s broad definition of "security" to include an option on any "security" as well as an option on any "group or index of securities" permits no distinction between cash-settled options and those that are settled by physical delivery. Accordingly, Caiola's cash-settled over-the-counter options are securities under section 3(a)(10).

Caiola does not argue that, at the time of his trades, his equity swaps were covered by section 10(b), but urges us to apply retroactively the CFMA's amendments to section 10(b). In December 2000, Congress enacted the CFMA to, among other things, clarify the status of swap agreements under the securities laws. CFMA § 2, 114 Stat. at 2763A–366. Sections 302 and 303 of the CMFA define "swap agreements" and then expressly exclude them from the definition of "securities," but amend section 10(b) to reach swap agreements. *Id.* §§ 302, 303, 114 Stat. at 2763A–452. Had Caiola entered into his synthetic stock transactions after the enactment of the CFMA, they clearly would now be covered under Rule 10b–5. To prevail on a retroactivity argument, Caiola faces a substantial burden. "Elementary considerations of fairness dictate that individuals should have an opportunity to know what the law is and to conform their conduct accordingly; settled expectations should not be lightly disrupted." *Landgraf v. USI Film Prods.,* 511 U.S. 244, 265, 114 S.Ct. 1483, 128 L.Ed.2d 229 (1994); *see Hughes Aircraft Co. v. United States,* 520 U.S. 939, 946, 117 S.Ct. 1871, 138 L.Ed.2d 135 (1997) ("[W]e apply this time-honored presumption [against retroactive legislation] unless Congress has clearly manifested its intent to the contrary.").

We find it unnecessary to resolve whether Caiola has overcome this hurdle because he failed to raise the issue properly in the District Court and we generally do not consider arguments not raised below. *First City, Texas Houston, N.A. v. Rafidain Bank,* 281 F.3d 48, 52–53 (2d Cir.2002); *Pulvers v. First UNUM Life Ins. Co.,* 210 F.3d 89, 95 (2d Cir.2000); *cf. Readco, Inc. v. Marine Midland Bank,* 81 F.3d 295, 302 (2d Cir.1996) (stating that the "general rule" of not considering matters not raised before the district court "may be disregarded in two circumstances: (1) where consideration of the issue is necessary to avoid manifest injustice or (2) where the issue is purely legal and there is no need for additional fact-finding").

The District Court ordered the parties to brief "the impact of the [CFMA] on whether the transactions at issue in this case constitute 'securities' under federal law." The order provided Caiola with the opportunity to argue retroactivity, but his response was insufficient to preserve the issue for appellate review. Although, in a footnote, Caiola mentions "settled expectations" and cites cases applying statutes to pre-enactment conduct, he never discusses retroactivity. Consequently, we conclude that the issue was not properly raised below and, because there is no manifest injustice in our declining to hear this argument in the first instance here, we choose not to consider it. *Cf. United States v. Restrepo*, 986 F.2d 1462, 1463 (2d Cir.1993) (refusing to consider argument raised only in an appellate brief footnote because "[w]e do not consider an argument mentioned only in a footnote to be adequately raised or preserved for appellate review"). * * *

SECTION 8. ENRON LOOPHOLE CLOSED

Dodd–Frank

Concerns over swaps trading arose during the subprime crisis that occurred between 2007 and 2009. The administration of President Barack Obama sought legislation that would repeal the "Enron loophole" in the CFMA for OTC derivatives being traded on the "Exempt Commercial Markets," such as the IntercontinentalExchange ("ICE"), that had been exempted from regulation under the Commodity Futures Modernization Act of 2000. That legislation was contained in the Dodd–Frank Wall Street Reform and Consumer Protection Act that was passed on July 15, 2010.[16] That legislation gave the SEC jurisdiction over security based swaps and the CFTC jurisdiction over other swaps, except that joint regulatory authority is given to both agencies for "mixed" swaps that have elements of both securities and commodities.[17]

Most swaps will now be traded on a regulated exchange and will be cleared through a regulated central counterparty. In addition, many swap market participants will now be regulated, including swap dealers and "major swap participants."[18] Firms acting as swap dealers and major swap participants must register with the CFTC or the SEC before they can engage in swap transactions. Firms engaged in securities based swaps must register with the SEC.[19] The CFTC may also require the registration of foreign boards of trade that allow U.S. traders to access their electronic trading systems.[20]

Dodd–Frank requires parties to swap contracts to be eligible contract participants (institutions or wealthy individuals) if the swap is not traded on a regulated contract market.[21] Dodd–Frank also requires swaps to be cleared by a registered derivatives clearing organization (DCO) unless the

---

16. Pub. L. 111–203.

17. Dodd–Frank § 722.

18. Id. at § 723.

19. Id. at § 764.

20. Id. at § 738a.

21. Id. at § 723.

CFTC rules otherwise.[22] Swaps cleared by a DCO must be maintained at a registered futures commission merchant that is subject CFTC segregation requirements for customer funds. Segregation may also be demanded for non-cleared swaps.[23] The CFTC was allowed to regulate margin requirements when necessary to protect the integrity of derivative clearing organizations.[24] Dodd–Frank requires the CFTC to make public disclosures concerning the volume and nature of cleared swaps, but disclosure of trader identity is restricted.[25] The act requires the reporting of non-cleared swaps to registered "swap data repositories" or (if the former doesn't accept them) to the CFTC.[26] Dodd–Frank directs the CFTC to establish position limit requirements on swaps.[27]

The SEC and CFTC are directed to coordinate their regulations and to consult with each other and with prudential regulators. Most swaps will now be traded on a regulated exchange and cleared through a regulated central counterparty. The Dodd–Frank Act allows regulators to impose capital and margin requirements on swap dealers and major swap participants, but not end-users.

The Treasury Secretary is authorized to exempt foreign exchange swaps from the federal regulation imposed on other swap market participants. In order to prevent any future bailouts like the one at AIG, federal assistance to any swap related transaction or entity is prohibited.

SECTION 9. FINANCIAL ENGINEERING

Financial engineers developed a broad range of complex derivative instruments. One such instrument, "Prides" ("Provisionally Redeemable Income Debt Exchangeable for Stock"), was described by a court as follows:

> Cendant was formed on December 17, 1997, through the merger of CUC International, Inc. ("CUC") and HFS, Inc. ("HFS"). In February, 1998, Cendant and its wholly owned subsidiary, Cendant Capital I, issued a derivative-type convertible security known as Cendant FELINE PRIDES ("Prides") in an initial public offering ("Prides Offering") pursuant to a registration statement, a prospectus, and a prospectus supplement filed with the Securities Exchange Commission ("SEC"). The registration statement and the prospectus contained Cendant's audited and consolidated statements of income for the three years ended December 31, 1996 and the Company's unaudit-

---

22. Id. at § 725.

23. Id. at § 724.

24. Id. at § 736.

25. Id. at § 727.

26. Id. at § 736.

27. Id. at § 733.

ed financial results for 1997. The Prides Offering, which involved the sale of approximately 29,900,000 Prides valued at $1.5 billion, closed on March 2, 1998. Defendants Merrill Lynch & Co., Merrill Lynch, Pierce, Fenner & Smith Inc. (collectively "Merrill Lynch"), and Chase Securities Inc. ("Chase") were the underwriters.

The registration statement and the prospectus offered two types of Prides: Income Prides and Growth Prides. Each of the Income Prides consists of a unit comprised of a Purchase Contract under which the holder will purchase from Cendant on February 16, 2001 a specified number of newly issued shares of Cendant common stock for $50 (the "Stated Amount") in cash. Cendant will pay the holders of Income Prides "Contract Adjustment Payments" at the rate of 5% of the Stated Amount per year, an interest in Trust Preferred Securities paying 6.45% of the Stated Amount per year, and $50 at maturity. Each of the Growth Prides consists of a unit comprised of a Purchase Contract under which the holder will purchase from Cendant on February 16, 2001 a specified number of newly issued shares of Cendant common stock for the Stated Amount in cash. Cendant will pay the holders of Growth Prides "Contract Adjustment Payments" at the rate of 5% of the Stated Amount per year and a 1/20th undivided beneficial interest in a treasury security having a principal amount of $1000 and maturing in 2001.

In re Cendant Corp. Prides Litigation, 51 F.Supp.2d 537 (D.N.J.1999), vacated in part, 243 F.3d 722 (3d Cir.), cert. denied, 534 U.S. 889, 122 S.Ct. 202, 151 L.Ed.2d 143 (2001). This financial engineering did not save the company from scandal. Cendant Corp., a marketer and hotel franchiser that owned the Days Inn chain of motels and Century 21, the large real estate broker, was found to have inflated its revenues by more than $500 million over the course of several years. The company's stock dropped from $35 to $19 after that revelation, reducing the capitalization of the company by $19 billion, $14 billion of that amount was lost in a single day. That was the largest accounting fraud up to that date, but that title was lost to Enron and others. Cendant agreed to pay investors $3.5 billion to settle claims involving its accounting manipulations. Three company officers pled guilty to criminal fraud charges. Two juries jury could not reach a verdict in the trial of Walter Forbes, former head of Cendant Corp., but the government obtained a conviction in his third trial.

NOTE

What is the corporate purpose in issuing Prides? What advantages do they offer to investors? What are the disadvantages?

An effort to deconstruct the elements of common stock were attempted through the use of "unbundled stock units," which are described as following:

American Express Company, a New York corporation (the "Company"), hereby offers, upon the terms and conditions set forth in this Prospectus and in the accompanying Letter of Transmittal (which together constitute the "Exchange Offer"), to exchange up to 60,000,-000 of its Common Shares, par value $.60 per share (the "Shares"), for its Unbundled Stock Units ("USUs"), on the basis of ___ USUs for each Share tendered. Each USU consists of three securities: $75 principal amount of Base Yield Bonds, Due 2019 (the "Bonds"), one Incremental Dividend Depositary Preferred Share (the "IDP"), representing an interest in 1/10 of one Incremental Dividend Preferred Share (the "Incremental Dividend Preferred Shares"), and one Equity Appreciation Certificate (the "EAC"). If more than 60,000,000 Shares are validly tendered and net withdrawn on or prior to the expiration date of the Exchange Offer, the Company will accept such Shares for exchange on a pro rata basis as described herein. The Exchange Offer is subject to certain conditions as set forth under "The Exchange Offer B Certain Conditions to the Exchange Offer," including a minimum of 40,000,000 Shares being validly tendered and not withdrawn on or prior to the expiration date of the Exchange Offer. * * *

In July 1987, the Company's Board of Directors authorized a repurchase of 40,000,000 of the Company's outstanding Common Shares over the next two to three years, extending a repurchase program pursuant to which the Company had repurchased an additional 40,000,000 shares. The Exchange Offer will permit the Company to complete and increase this program.

The Board of Directors of the Company believes that, given the Company's business, assets and prospects, and the current market price of the Shares, the purchase of Shares by the Company is an attractive investment. The Board of Directors believes that the Exchange Offer is a more cost-effective method of repurchasing a significant number of Shares than other repurchase methods. The Company will also realize increased cash flow by replacing a portion of its common equity capitalization with USUs. In addition, the Company may realize an increased earnings per share depending on the level of income in any period. Based on 417,083,333 Shares outstanding at October 31, 1988, if 60,000,000 Shares are exchanged for USUs, the number of outstanding Shares will be reduced by approximately 14.4% to 357,083,333 Shares.

The Company believes that it should provide investors with the opportunity to separately evaluate the prospects that (i) the Company will maintain its current common dividend, (ii) such dividend may be increased and (iii) the Company's Common Shares will appreciate in value.

Shareholders who exchange their Shares for USUs will be able to choose between the various investment attributes of Share ownership represented by the securities included in a USU. Holders may thereby focus their investment in the Company on those aspects of ownership most consistent with their investment objectives. For example, investors who seek level annual income may wish to own Bonds. Investors desiring to share on an annual basis in the future dividend growth, if any, of the Company may wish to own the IDPs. Investors who do not require annual income and seek a leveraged investment in the Company may wish to own the EACs. Investors with multiple objectives may wish to own some combination of the securities included in a USU, such as the ESU, or the entire USU. Alternatively, holders of Shares may wish to retain all of the existing investment and voting rights represented by their Shares.

Prospectus, American Express Company, Offer to Exchange Up to 60,000,-000 of its Common Shares on the Basis of, Per Share, Unbundled Stock Units, Each Unit Consisting of $75 Principal Amount of Base Yield Bonds, Due 2019, One Incremental Dividend Depositary Preferred Share, Representing 1/10 of One Incremental Dividend Preferred Share, and One Equity Appreciation Certificate.

These units were kept off the market as a result of objections by the staff of the Securities and Exchange Commission. III Jerry W. Markham, A Financial History of the United States, From the Age of Derivatives to the New Millennium (1970–2001) 194 (2002).

Another way of selling elements of a corporation was more successful. It was called "tracking stock." This stock grants the holder rights to only a portion of the business of a corporation. Say large corporation has a profitable division and several not-so-profitable ones. You would like to invest in the profitable line of business but not the others. Tracking stock permits such an arrangement. In Sedighim v. Donaldson, Lufkin & Jenrette, Inc., 167 F.Supp.2d 639 (S.D.N.Y.2001), the district in dismissing a lawsuit described one tracking stock arrangement:

> Plaintiffs assert claims that raise questions of first impression with respect to the rights of holders of "tracking stock." This is a purported class action on behalf of all holders of DLJdirect stock, a type of common stock designed to "track" the performance of the online brokerage business of Donaldson, Lufkin & Jenrette, Inc. ("DLJ"). * * * In late May, 1999, DLJ issued 16 million shares of DLJdirect stock for $20 per share in an initial public offering ["IPO"]. It retained 84.3 million DLJdirect shares. The DLJdirect stock was intended to "track" the DLJdirect online brokerage business. In other words, the value of DLJdirect shares would vary with the performance of the online brokerage business. The DLJdirect business was separated from the rest of DLJ's business for accounting purposes. A wholly-owned subsidiary of DLJ, DLJdirect Holdings ("Holdings"),

held title to a majority of DLJdirect assets, but DLJdirect, itself, was a division of DLJ and not a separate corporate entity.

In connection with the IPO, DLJ filed a Registration Statement and Prospectus (the "Prospectus") with the SEC. The Prospectus stated the following:

> Holders of DLJdirect common stock will not have any claims on the assets of DLJdirect. Even though from a financial reporting standpoint we have allocated our consolidated assets, liabilities, revenue, expenses and cash flow between DLJdirect and DLJ, that allocation will not change the legal title to any assets or responsibility for any liabilities ... Further, in any liquidation, holders of DLJdirect common stock will receive a share of the net assets of [DLJ] based on the relative trading prices of DLJdirect common stock and DLJ common stock rather than on any assessment of the actual value of DLJdirect or DLJ.

It also said that holders of DLJdirect stock will have no voting rights, except in limited circumstances where a separate class vote is required by Delaware law.

In the section on risk factors, the Prospectus stated that DLJ could not guarantee that the price of the stock would track the performance of the DLJdirect business as intended, and that DLJdirect shareholders would be common shareholders of DLJ, subject to all of the risks of investment in DLJ and all its businesses. It also said that material financial events which occur at DLJ may affect DLJ direct's financial position.

Contrary to plaintiffs' allegations, the Prospectus did not represent that DLJdirect shareholders would be entitled to all the benefits of ownership of DLJ common stock. The Prospectus said that DLJdirect shareholders would be "common shareholders of Donaldson, Lufkin and Jenrette, Inc.," but it made clear that DLJdirect common stock was not the same as DLJ common stock. For example, the Prospectus Summary stated that "[w]e are offering you shares of DLJdirect common stock, but we are not offering you any shares of DLJ common stock."

The Prospectus further disclosed that there would be conflicts of interest between DLJ shareholders and DLJdirect shareholders, and that the DLJ board might make decisions favoring DLJ shareholders. As an example of the type of decisions in which a conflict might arise, the Prospectus mentioned "decisions on how to allocate consideration received from a merger involving [DLJ] between holders of DLJ common stock and DLJdirect common stock."

The Prospectus also stated that in the event of a sale of more than 80% of the assets of DLJdirect, DLJdirect shareholders would be entitled to one of the following: (1) a dividend in an amount equal to the proportionate interest in the net proceeds of the sale, (2) redemption of DLJdirect shares for an amount equal to the proportionate interest in the net proceeds of the sale, or (3) issuance of DLJ stock at a 10% premium over the value of DLJdirect shares.

Finally, in a paragraph captioned "Relationship with DLJ," in which the Prospectus discussed potential conflicts between DLJdirect and DLJ with respect to cash management and allocation policies, the Prospectus stated that

> DLJ intends to reconstitute the board of [Holdings].... Shortly after the consummation of the offering, DLJ intends to add two outside directors to the board of directors of [Holdings]. DLJ's current intent is to submit all significant transactions including significant "intercompany" transactions between DLJ and DLJdirect, for approval by the board of directors of [Holdings]. The decisions of the board of DLJ and Holdings would be subject to the board of directors general fiduciary duty. However, there can be no assurance that transactions between DLJdirect and DLJ could not be effected on more favorable terms with unaffiliated, third parties. * * *

See also The Loews Corp. also created a tracking stock for its profitable, but threatened, tobacco subsidiary, Lorillard, Inc. These tracking stock shares, called the "Carolina Group," were created as class of common stock of Loews, rather than Lorillard. The Carolina Group shareholders were given one tenth of a vote for each share of tracking stock they hold. Dean Foust, "This Stock May Harm Your Portfolio's Health," Business Week, Feb. 4, 2002, at 80. *See also* In re General Motors Class H Shareholders Litigation, 734 A.2d 611 (Del.Ch.1999) (rejecting breach of fiduciary duty claims in connection with tracking stock).

Tracking stock has raised concerns with the fiduciary duties of directors. Where do their loyalties lie when their decisions will benefit one tracked area of the firm over another in say budgeting? If directors have options on tracked stock, will they be conflicted by their decisions? See Jeffrey J. Schick, Toward Transaction Specific Standards of Directorial Fiduciary Duty in the Tracking Stock Context, 75 Wash. L. Rev. 1365 (2001) (discussing possible conflicts of interest); Jesse Drucker, Sprint Shows Pitfalls of Investing in Tracking Stock, Wall St. J., March 7, 2003, at C1 (discussing concerns with tracking stock).

Another popular device is the weather derivative that is used to provide protection against price risks caused by weather events and to allow speculation on such risks. Andrea S. Kramer & Willlliam R. Pomierski, What You Need to Know About Weather Derivatives, 19 Fut. & Derv. L. Rep. 11 (1999). Those price risks include everything from higher heating costs in a cold winter to reduced profits from snow plow sales because of a warm winter, or the cancellation of a concert because of a rain storm. The Enron Corp. before its demise, sold weather hedge contracts that provided payments in the event of higher than expected utility charges as the result of adverse weather.

The Chicago Climate Exchange allows trading on cap and trade allowances for green house gases.

So called CAT Bonds (Catastrophe Bonds) are securitized offerings that pay investors a return on their funds, but those investors may lose principal if there is a "trigger event" such as a hurricane. U.S. General Accounting Office, Catastrophe Insurance Risks, Status of Efforts to Securitize Natural Catastrophe and Terrorism Risk 10–11 (Sept. 2003). One company announced that it was offering earnings protection insurance that would cover lower than expected earnings by insurance companies. The Florida Hurricane Catastrophe Finance Corp. was created by the state legislature to act as a co-insurer of hurricane losses with private companies. It is authorized to issue tax-free bonds when total hurricane losses exceed $6.3 billion. Those bonds will be paid off with special assessments on every person in Florida insured under any casualty policy. Christopher McEntee, Florida Agency Gets IRSOK to Sell Hurricane Relief bonds, Bond Buyer, April 16, 1998, at 1.

Although hedging is often likened to insurance in the sense that it protects against a risk of loss, there has historically been a fundamental distinction drawn between products regulated as insurance and those that are viewed to be derivatives. Thomas Lee Hazen, Disparate Regulatory Schemes for Parallel Activities: Securities Regulation, Derivatives Regulation, Gambling, and Insurance, 24 Ann. Rev. Bank. & Fin. L. 375 (2005). In that regard, the General Counsel for the New York State Insurance Department concluded that weather derivatives are not insurance, because insurance covers a specific casualty event for the insured,[32] while derivatives pay with or without such an event, allowing them to be used for speculation or hedging of weather related price risks. Specifically, the General Counsel stated that:

> Weather derivatives do not constitute insurance contracts under ... the New York Insurance Law because the terms of the instrument do not provide that, in addition to or as part of the triggering event, payment to the purchaser is dependent upon that party suffering a loss. Under such instruments, the issuer is obligated to pay the purchaser whether or not that purchaser suffers a loss. Neither the amount of the payment nor the trigger itself in the weather derivative bears a relationship to the purchaser's loss. Absent such obligations, the instrument is not an insurance contract.

State of New York Insurance Dep't, Office of General Counsel, "Weather Financial Instruments (derivatives, hedges, etc.)" (Feb. 15, 2000). *See also* State of New York Insurance Dep't, Office of General Counsel, "Catastrophe Options" (June 25, 1998).

---

32. As noted in Chapter 15, the insured must have an "insurable interest" in the casualty event, a requirement that was adopted to prevent gambling on the lives of others.

The distinction between casualty insurance that is regulated as insurance on the one hand and hedging with a derivative contract on the other is exemplified by crop insurance. Crop insurance insures against crop failures under the Federal Crop Insurance Act. 7 U.S.C. § 1503. Crop loss is regulated as insurance under that act because it insures against a casualty event, *i.e.*, a crop failure from, say, a drought. Futures or other derivative contracts may be used to hedge the very same crop that is protected by crop insurance. However, the hedge provided by the derivative contract guards only against the risk of a price decline in the market for the crop, not the destruction or failure of the crop itself, which is covered by crop insurance. The futures contract, protects against a price risk, not a casualty loss and, therefore, is not regulated as insurance. Similarly, weather derivatives, such as weather swaps, act as hedges against price risks from weather changes or weather events such as a hurricane. They do not insure against the casualty losses caused by the hurricane itself.

The National Association of Insurance Commissioners ("NAIC") also decided that it would not treat weather derivatives as insurance because no specific property was tied to a specific casualty event in which there was an insurable interest. That same reasoning was applied to credit default swaps ("CDS") (which are discussed below in Section 10) by the New York Department of Insurance in 2000. However, the New York State Superintendent of Insurance announced during the financial crisis in 2008 that a CDS with an actual risk of loss from the underlying security created an insurable interest that was subject to insurance regulation, but not "synthetic" CDS that did not involve the ownership of the actual underlying security. NAIC also announced that it was considering whether it should regulate credit default swaps. See Jerry W. Markham, "Regulating Credit Default Swaps in the Wake of the Subprime Crisis." Working Paper for the International Monetary Fund Seminar on Current Developments in Monetary and Financial Law. Wash. D.C. (Dec. 2, 2009). However, Section 722 of Dodd–Frank Wall Street Reform and Consumer Protection Act of 2010 rejected that position and exempted swaps from state insurance regulation.

In another context, the New York Department of Insurance General Counsel ruled that a home equity protection program was not insurance because it was not tied to a specific casualty event. Under that program, homeowners could hedge against declines in property values in their neighborhood by paying a fee to the issuer. Such payments were to be based on overall declines in the neighborhood and not that of any specific property. New York Insurance Department General Counsel Opinion No. 5–1–2002 (#2) (May 1, 2002).

The following is a description of some of the instruments issued by Nomura Derivative Products, Inc., a derivatives dealer:

1. Dual Currency swap ("Dual")

A fixed/floating cross-currency swap with, say, floating Libor payments in JPY (Japanese Yen) and fixed payments in USD (U.S. dollars). There may also be exchange of notionals in USD and JPY at the start and/or end of the contract.

2. Reverse Dual Currency swap ("Reverse Dual")

A Dual Currency swap, except that the currency roles are reversed, with floating payments in USD and fixed payments in JPY. Analytically, these products are exactly the same, and the difference in names arises purely from marketing considerations.

3. Power Reverse Dual

A Reverse Dual Currency swap except that instead of a fixed coupon there is an "indexed" coupon that is linked to an FX rate (usually USD/JPY). The contract behaves exactly as a swap floating leg (in USD) and a strip of FX options (cash settled in JPY). Precisely: the indexed coupon is equal to max (a.C–b,k), where C is the FX rate and a, b and k are strike constants set in the contract.

4. Callable Power Reverse Dual

A swap, like Power Reverse Dual, with the additional feature that the party making the indexed payments has the (Bermudan-style) right to terminate the contract on a coupon payment date. In this respect the product strongly resembles a Bermudan swaption/callable swap. The option-holder will exercise the option and terminate the product when the FX rate is judged by them to be "too" high.

5. Trigger Power Reverse Dual

A swap, like Power Reverse Dual, with the feature of automatic termination if an FX observation is higher (alternatively, lower) than a pre-set threshold. Trigger observation is made periodically on or around the coupon payment dates. The product is similar to Callable Power Reverse Dual except that termination is automatic on high FX rates, rather than at the discretion of the option-holder. The same Fingal function (CallablePRD) is used to price both trade types.

6. Callable Reverse Floater

A swap with, say, floating Libor payments in USD and indexed JPY payments inked to (but not equal to) JPY–Libor as per Cap Floor. One of the parties has the Bermudan-style right to cancel the trade at any coupon payment date. This product is very similar to a cross-currency Bermudan swaption/callable swap, with the one difference being the indexed JPY coupons which are not fixed but equal to one of the formulas: max (b–a.L,k) or min (a.L–b,k), where L is JPY–Libor and a, b and k are strike constants set in the contract. NOTE. The word "Reverse" is not used here in the same sense as the other trades, but arises instead because the size of the indexed coupon goes down when the JPY–Libor rate goes up.

7. Dual Barrier Option

This contract can be broken down into a collection of trades, most of which are vanilla components such as Fixed Leg and Swap Floating Leg. The exotic part of the trade is a final exchange of notionals which depends on a barrier-style observation of an FX rate. For instance, we observe the USD/JPY FX rate every day for a period of time during the contract. If the rate was ever on any day less than, say, 103, the barrier would have "knocked out". The final payment might be a fixed amount of JPY if the barrier did not knock, and a fixed amount of USD if the barrier did knock. This product is exactly equivalent to a standard FX barrier contract paying off an FX forward. It is priced with the same valuation function, called FxBarrier2.

8. Bermudan Zero Swaption

This trade is swap-based (and single currency). On the floating side, Libor payments are made as usual. On the indexed ("fixed") side, no payments are made until maturity, when one large payment is made (this can be thought of as one fixed interest payment whose accrual period is the entire length of the swap). Without any additional features, this is called a zero-coupon swap; it can be priced with the functions Swap Floating Leg and Fixed Cash Flows. The exotic trade gives the Bermudan-style option to enter into a zero-coupon swap on one of a number of regularly spaced exercise dates. There may be a cash-flow on entry to compensate for the periods passed before entry into the swap.

9. Periodic Cap

This product resembles a Cap, in that it consists of a regular strip of payments based on the corresponding Libor observations and some strikes. Unlike a cap, the current strike is not set in the contract but is equal to the value of the previous coupon (plus a spread). For example, a contract may be based on USD 3m-Libor, with payments every 3m. The payment on any payment date is a rate equal to the minimum of the current Libor setting and the sum of the last coupon rate and 40bp. This "caps" the coupon each period at no more than 40bp higher than the coupon at the previous period. In symbols:

$$\text{Coupon(i)} = \min (\text{Libor(i)}, \text{Coupon(I–1)} + 40bp).$$

NORMAN MENACHEM FEDER
DECONSTRUCTING OVER–THE–COUNTER DERIVATIVES

2002 Columbia Business Law Review 677.

Credit derivatives are relatively recent OTC products that are intended to transfer credit exposure vis-a-vis specific obligors. Essentially, credit derivatives, like other derivatives, isolate specific risk—either credit risk only or credit risk together with market risk—and transfer that risk to a willing party. Transfer of the isolated credit risk protects the risk transferor from, and exposes the risk transferee to, the risk that an obligor—whom often is called a reference credit or reference entity—may experience a credit event, such as a default under a specified debt instrument or a certain decline in creditworthiness. Notably, the transfer need not disturb the original credit relationship between reference credit and creditor. The reference asset can be anything whose value reflects the credit of a certain entity, but tradable bonds are the most logical because their price is most easily discovered. Bank loans too may one day become important reference assets.

Credit risk protection provided by third parties is hardly new. For ages, guarantees and letters of credit have protected creditors from obligor defaults. What sets credit derivatives apart from predecessor techniques is separation of the protection from the reference asset. This allows the market to trade credit risk separately from the instrument that creates the risk. This also allows the market to price that risk and for various investors to mitigate or amplify for themselves the credit risk of specific entities with relative ease.

Credit derivatives usually comprise one of three forms: credit default swap, total return swap and credit spread option. Additionally, there is a fourth form, credit-linked debt, which is not a pure credit derivative, but a hybrid of a debt instrument and credit derivative. As a general matter, the maturities of credit derivatives do not exceed, and usually do not even match, the maturities of the underlying obligations of the reference credit. The exact form of credit derivative will determine how much credit risk is being transferred, but every form involves the sale of credit protection from a protection seller to a protection buyer (although other correlative phrasing is used with certain types of credit derivatives).

A credit default swap transfers potential credit loss, usually, but not necessarily, in connection with a specific reference asset. Under a typical credit default swap, the protection buyer makes a single payment or periodic payments to the protection seller as premium, and the protection seller is obligated to pay a credit event payment to the protection buyer if a credit event occurs. Because the reference asset may retain residual value after default by the reference credit, the benefit to the protection buyer from receipt of the credit event payment is usually structured to equal something less than the gross value of the reference asset.

Credit event payments can take on various forms. In a cash-settled arrangement, the protection seller will pay cash, and usually only the difference between the principal amount and recovery value of the reference asset. Specifically, the credit event payment will equal the difference between the market value of the reference asset after default, as determined by dealer quotes or market price, and its par value. Alternatively, the cash-settlement arrangement can be binary. In that case, the protection seller will pay a stipulated amount. This amount would likely equal the par value of the reference asset minus some amount that represents the parties' expectation of the reference asset's residual value following default, based on market experience. Or, the amount will equal a pre-determined percentage of the par value of the reference asset; this amount is meant to reflect the parties' expectation when entering into the swap of prospective credit loss.

In a physically-settled arrangement, the credit event payment amount will equal the par value of the reference asset and, in exchange for payment by the protection seller of that amount, the protection buyer will physically deliver the reference asset to the protection seller. The protection seller will then have a right to claim on the reference asset from the obligor. The advantage of physical settlement, particularly to the protection buyer, is that it results in a precise credit risk transfer and lets the parties avoid valuing prospectively the post-default reference asset to pre-determine the amount of the credit event payment.

The credit event commonly portends the insolvency of the issuer of the reference asset. The event can be instrument-specific, such as failure of the obligor to make a payment when due under the reference asset. Alternatively, it can be defined more generally to include a credit rating downgrade or a failure of the obligor to make any payment under any obligation. In any event, the credit-dependant trigger is the basis for the transfer of credit risk from the protection buyer to the protection seller.

For example: Party A holds a bond issued by Company C and would like to manage the risk that Company C will fail. Party A can enter into a credit-default swap with Bank B, under which Party A will periodically pay Bank B a floating rate (e.g., LIBOR plus fifty basis points) on a notional amount and Bank B will be obligated to pay Party A the principal amount minus any residual value of the bond if B fails. In this example, Party A is the protection buyer and Bank B is the protection seller. Company C is unaffected by the transaction, at least until it defaults, whereupon its creditor may be Party A or Bank B, depending on whether the swap requires Party A to transfer the bond to Bank B after Bank B makes the credit-default payment to party A.

The reference asset in a credit default swap can be a single item or a basket of items. In the case of a basket, the contract will often include a first-to-default feature, whereby the protection seller's payment obligations are triggered upon the first default of any of the assets in the basket (and the derivatives contract thereafter may or may not automatically terminate). Sometimes, a contract referencing a basket of assets will include instead a green bottle feature, which allocates protection to all the assets in the basket according to proportions described in the contract. Additionally, some credit-default swaps will incorporate a materiality threshold, meaning that the protection seller's payment obligations will be triggered only if the protection buyer first experiences a pre-determined amount of loss.

Perhaps because the protection buyer's payment obligations can be periodic, or perhaps because credit default swaps sometimes refer to notional amounts for purpose of calculating the protection buyer's payment obligations or the protection seller's credit default payment amount, the transactions are considered swaps. Nevertheless, the protection seller's payment obligations are contingent; thus it may be more accurate to think of credit default swaps as options. Certainly, a credit default swap in which the protection buyer must deliver the reference asset to the protection seller to obtain the credit default payment resembles a physically-settled put option.

With a total return swap, also known as a total rate-of-return swap, the protection buyer, or total return seller, artificially sells a reference asset to the protection seller, or total return buyer. Technically, the total return seller agrees to pay the total return associated with a reference asset to the total return buyer. Total return equals interest plus fees and appreciation in market value at maturity. In exchange, the total return buyer agrees to make payments to the total return seller. These payments are formulated from either fixed or floating rates on a notional amount and cover depreciation in value at maturity. To compensate the total return buyer for the risk it undertakes, the notional amount is usually less than the principal amount of the reference asset. The transaction may or may not provide for termination and a cash settlement between the parties if a credit event occurs.

For example: Party A holds a bond issued by Company C, and Bank B would like to obtain both the credit risk and the market risk under the bond. Party A can swap with Bank B all the returns on the bond, including any increase in value of the bond, measured at maturity, in exchange for (i) periodic payments by Bank B to Party A at a floating rate (e.g., LIBOR plus fifty basis points) on a notional amount, and (ii) a payment equal to any decrease in value of the bond measured at maturity (or early termination of the bond, if applicable). In this example, Party A is the total return seller and the protection buyer, and Bank B is the total return buyer and the protection seller.

The nature of the risks protected distinguishes a total return swap from a credit-default swap. A credit default swap transfers only credit risk. A total return swap, however, transfers both credit risk and market risk. Indeed, because a total return swap synthetically transfers ownership in an asset, some market professionals do not see the transaction as a true credit derivative, even though credit risk is shifted. This may also explain why total return swap terminology prefers the terms total return buyer and total return seller to the terms protection seller and protection buyer, respectively. Interestingly, a total return swap can engender a basis swap. This would occur if both the reference asset and the total return buyer's payment obligations were set at a floating rate. Because both sides of the swap relate to floating rates, the market risk that the total return swap transfers is basis risk.

Credit spread options are designed to capture changes in yield between (i) a reference asset and a relatively risk-free baseline, such as a U.S. Treasury Bill or market rate swap, of similar maturity; (ii) similar securities of two different issuers; or (iii) two obligations of the same issuer but with differing maturities. The spread between the two items is the quantification by the market of the credit risk in holding a certain asset. What makes credit spread options unique among credit derivatives is the disregard of credit events and sole focus on the differences between two references. The protection offered by a credit spread option usually can be invoked long before a true credit event occurs because yield differences express the market's anticipation of credit or credit-like events. In this sense, it might not be appropriate to call a credit spread option a credit derivative; ultimately, however, the moniker is fair because the product does address credit risk, just not credit-default alone.

In a credit spread option, the party buying protection, as it were, pays a premium and obtains a right to buy from or sell to the other party the reference asset at a pre-determined price, should the spread reach a certain trigger point. When the option is a put, the option holder will sell the asset once the spread indicates unpalatable risk. When the option is a call, the option holder will buy the asset once the spread, hence return, appears sufficiently large to justify tolerating the risk. The protection provided by a credit spread option is wider than that provided by a credit swap or a total-return swap because a credit spread option protection trigger can occur long before a credit event arises and payment is due regardless of what causes the credit spread movement.

For example: Party A holding a rated bond issued by Company C with one-year maturity can buy a credit spread put option from Bank B for an upfront premium. The option gives Party A the right to sell the bond to Bank B at a pre-determined strike value. The strike value is expressed in terms of credit spread over a one year U.S. Treasury bond. On the option's strike date, if the actual spread of the bond is less than the strike value, the option is worthless and simply will expire. If the spread is higher than the strike value on the strike date, Party A will deliver the underlying bond to Bank B and Bank B will pay an agreed-upon compensation. In this example, Party A is the spread buyer and Bank B is the spread seller.

Credit-linked debt is only a credit derivative in part. Most commonly, it takes the form of a credit-linked note, which is a combination of a structured note and a funded credit-default swap. In a credit-linked note, the protection seller pays the protection buyer a principal amount, in exchange for a note issued by the protection buyer. Under the note, the protection buyer obligates itself to pay periodic interest. The principal is redeemed upon maturity or a credit event, whichever comes first. In the case of a first-occurring credit event, however, the note holder will suffer. If the arrangement is cash-settled, the note issuer will deduct a stipulated credit-default amount from the principal. If the arrangement is physically-settled, the note issuer will deliver the reference asset to the note holder, instead of redeeming with cash.

For example: Bank B issues a note to Party A, under which Party A lends a principal amount to Bank B at a pre-determined interest rate.

Bank B will pay periodic interest payments to Party A. However, if a certain Company C defaults on a certain bond that it has issued before the note's maturity, Party A will forfeit its rights to return of some or all of the principal and any remaining interest payments. In this example, Party A is the protection seller and Bank B is the protection buyer.

A credit-linked deposit is similar to a credit-linked note. In a credit-linked deposit, the protection seller deposits a principal amount into an account with the protection buyer. Additionally, the protection seller agrees to forfeit some or all of the contents of the account in the event of a credit-default of the reference obligor.

In contrast to the protection seller in a credit-default swap, the protection seller in credit-linked debt ensures its contingent payment obligation in advance by way of a forfeitable loan. In this manner, the protection seller funds or collateralizes the original credit risk with a principal amount. The protection buyer is thus also protected from the credit risk of the protection seller. It is this funding that most distinguishes credit-linked debt from a credit default swap. This funding is particularly attractive to regulated entities, as the credit risks of both the obligor and of the credit derivative counterparty are neutralized, reducing the need for regulatory capital. As in the case of a credit default swap, credit-linked debt transfers only credit risk.

ETERNITY GLOBAL MASTER FUND LIMITED v. MORGAN GUARANTY TRUST COMPANY

375 F.3d 168 (2d Cir. 2004).

JACOBS, CIRCUIT JUDGE:

Plaintiff–Appellant Eternity Global Master Fund Limited ("Eternity" or "the Fund") purchased credit default swaps ("CDSs" or "the CDS contracts") from Defendants–Appellees Morgan Guaranty Trust Company of New York and JPMorgan Chase Bank (collectively, "Morgan") in October 2001. Eternity appeals from a final judgment entered in the United States District Court for the Southern District of New York (McKenna, J.), dismissing with prejudice its complaint alleging breach of contract, fraud, and negligent misrepresentation by Morgan in connection with the CDSs. The CDS contracts were written on the sovereign bonds of Argentina and would be "triggered" upon the occurrence of a "credit event,' such that if Argentina restructured or defaulted on that debt, Eternity would have the right to put to Morgan a stipulated amount of the bonds for purchase at par value.

In late November 2001, the government of the Republic of Argentina, in the grip of economic crisis, initiated a "voluntary debt exchange" in which bondholders had the option of turning in their bonds for secured loans on terms less favorable except that the loans were secured by certain

Argentine federal tax revenues. Eternity informed Morgan that the voluntary debt exchange was a credit event that triggered Morgan's obligations under the CDS contracts. Morgan disagreed. * * *

On appeal, Eternity challenges the dismissal of its claims. For the reasons set forth below, we affirm the dismissal of the fraudulent and negligent misrepresentation claims but reverse the dismissal of the contract claim and remand for further proceedings.

On behalf of its investors, Eternity trades in global bonds, equities and currencies, including emerging-market debt. During the relevant period, Eternity's investment portfolio included short-term Argentine sovereign and corporate bonds. In emerging markets such as Argentina, a significant credit risk is "country risk," i.e., "the risk that economic, social, and political conditions and events in a foreign country will adversely affect an institution's financial interests," including "the possibility of nationalization or expropriation of assets, government repudiation of external indebtedness, . . . and currency depreciation or devaluation." Credit risk can be managed, however. Banks, investment funds and other institutions increasingly use financial contracts known as "credit derivatives" to mitigate credit risk. In October 2001, in light of Argentina's rapidly deteriorating political and economic prospects, Eternity purchased CDSs to hedge the credit risk on its in-country investments.

By way of introduction, we briefly review the terminology, documentation, and structure of Eternity's credit default swaps. A credit default swap is the most common form of credit derivative, i.e., "[a] contract which transfers credit risk from a protection buyer to a credit protection seller." Protection buyers (here, Eternity) can use credit derivatives to manage particular market exposures and return-on-investment; and protection sellers (here, Morgan) generally use credit derivatives to earn income and diversify their own investment portfolios. Simply put, a credit default swap is a bilateral financial contract in which "[a] protection buyer makes[] periodic payments to . . . the protection seller, in return for a contingent payment if a predefined credit event occurs in the reference credit," i.e., the obligation on which the contract is written.

Often, the reference asset that the protection buyer delivers to the protection seller following a credit event is the instrument that is being hedged. But in emerging markets, an investor may calculate that a particular credit risk "is reasonably correlated with the performance of [the sovereign] itself," so that (as here) the investor may seek to isolate and hedge country risk with credit default swaps written on some portion of the sovereign's outstanding debt. In many contexts a "default" is a simple failure to pay; in a credit default swap, it references a stipulated bundle of "credit events" (such as bankruptcy, debt moratoria, and debt restructurings) that will trigger the protection seller's obligation to "settle" the contract via the swap mechanism agreed to between the parties. The entire bundle is typically made subject to a materiality threshold. The occurrence of a credit event triggers the "swap," i.e., the protection seller's obligation to pay on the contract according to the settlement mechanism. "The contingent payment can be based on cash settlement ... or physical delivery of the reference asset, in exchange for a cash payment equal to the initial notional [i.e., face] amount [of the CDS contract]." A CDS buyer holding a sufficient amount of the reference credit can simply tender it to the CDS seller for payment; but ownership of the reference credit prior to default is unnecessary. If a credit event occurs with respect to the obligation(s) named in a CDS, and notice thereof has been given (and the CDS buyer has otherwise performed), the CDS seller must settle. Liquidity in a secondary market increases the usefulness of a CDS as a hedging tool, though the limited depth of that market "can make it difficult to offset.... positions prior to contract maturity."

The principal issue dividing the parties is whether the CDS contracts at issue are ambiguous in any material respect. In this case, we assess ambiguity in the disputed CDS contracts by looking to (i) the terms of the three credit default swaps; (ii) the terms of the International Swaps and Derivatives Association's ("ISDA" or "the Association") "Master Swap Agreement," on which those swaps are predicated, (iii) ISDA's 1999 Credit Derivatives Definitions—which are incorporated into the disputed contracts; and (iv) the background "customs, practices, [and] usages" of the credit derivatives trade, Because customs and usages matter, and because documentation promulgated by the ISDA was used by the parties to this dispute, we briefly review some relevant background.

The term "derivatives" references "a vast array of privately negotiated over-the counter ... and exchange traded transactions," including interest-rate swaps, currency swaps, commodity price swaps and credit derivatives—which include credit default swaps. A derivative is a bilateral contract that is typically negotiated by phone and followed by an exchange of confirmatory faxes that constitute the contract but do not specify such terms as events of default, representations and warranties, covenants, liquidated damages, and choice of law. These (and other) terms are typically found in a "Master Swap Agreement," which, prior to standardization efforts that began in the mid–1980s, "took the form of separate 15–to 25–page agreements for each transaction."

Documentation of derivatives transactions has become streamlined, chiefly through industry adherence to "Master Agreements" promulgated by the ISDA. In 1999, Eternity and Morgan entered the ISDA Multicurrency–Cross Border Master Agreement, which governs, inter alia, the CDS transactions disputed on appeal. Each disputed CDS also incorporates the 1999 ISDA Credit Derivatives Definitions, the Association's first attempt at a comprehensive lexicon governing credit derivatives transactions. Last year, due to the rapid evolution of "ISDA documentation for credit default swaps," the Association began market implementation of the 2003 Credit Derivatives Definitions, which evidently constitutes a work in progress.

Eternity's Global Master Fund is managed by HFW Capital, L.P., including its Chief Investment Officer, Alberto Franco. In 2001, Franco engaged Morgan to facilitate Eternity's participation in the Argentine corporate debt market. Fearing that a government debt crisis would impair the value of Eternity's Argentine investments, Franco sought to hedge using credit default swaps written on Argentine sovereign bonds. In October 2001, the Fund entered into three such contracts. Each CDS incorporated (i) the ISDA Master Swap Agreement, and (ii) the 1999 ISDA Definitions. The total value of the contracts was $14 million * * * Except as to value and duration, the terms were virtually identical, as follows:

(i) Eternity would pay Morgan a fixed periodic fee tied to the notional value of each respective credit default swap.

(ii) The swaps would be triggered upon occurrence of any one of four credit events—as defined by the 1999 ISDA Credit Derivative Definitions—with respect to the Argentine sovereign bonds: Failure to pay, Obligation Acceleration, Repudiation/Moratorium, and Restructuring.

(iii) Each CDS called for physical settlement following a credit event, specifically:

(a) Upon notification (by either party to the other) of a credit event, and confirmation via two publicly available sources of information (e.g., the Wall Street Journal), and

(b) delivery to Morgan of the requisite amount of Argentine sovereign bonds,

(c) Morgan would pay Eternity par value for the obligations tendered.

It is alleged (and we therefore assume) that Eternity entered the swaps in reliance on Morgan's representations that it would provide access to a liquid secondary market that would enable the Fund to divest the contracts prior to termination.

The parties dispute whether any of certain actions taken by Argentina with respect to its debt obligations in November and December 2001 constituted a credit event. The district court thought not, and dismissed Eternity's contract claim at the pleading stage. With the background and structure of the disputed CDS contracts in mind, we turn to Eternity's principal allegations. * * *

The contracts at issue were signed in October 2001. By then, international financial markets had been speculating for months that Argentina might default on its $132 billion in government and other public debt. At an August 2001 meeting of bondholders in New York, Morgan acknowledged the possibility of a sovereign-debt default and advised that it was working with the Argentine government on restructuring scenarios. On October 31, 2001—after the effective date of the swap contracts at issue on this appeal—Morgan sent Eternity a research report noting that there was a "high implied probability of [a] restructuring" in which bondholders would likely receive replacement securities with a less-favorable rate of return. One day later, Argentine President Fernando de la Rua asked sovereign-bond holders to accept lower interest rates and longer maturities on approximately $95 billion of government debt.

On November 19, 2001, the Argentine government announced that a "voluntary debt exchange" would be offered to sovereign-bond holders. According to various public decrees, willing bondholders could exchange their obligations for secured loans that would pay a lower rate of return over a longer term, but that would be secured by certain federal tax revenues. So long as the government made timely payments on the loans, the original obligations would be held in trust for the benefit of Argentina; if the government defaulted, however, bondholders would have recourse to the original obligations, which were to "remain effective" for the duration of their life-in-trust. From late November through early December 2001, billions of dollars in sovereign bonds were exchanged for the lower-interest loans.

The complaint alleges that the debt exchange amounted to a default because local creditors had no choice but to participate, and that the financial press adopted that characterization. On November 8, 2001 Eternity served the first of three notices on Morgan asserting that the planned debt exchange was a restructuring credit event as to all three CDS contracts; but Morgan demurred.

On December 24, newly-installed interim President Adolfo Rodriguez Saa-appointed by the Argentine Congress on December 23 to replace President de la Rua-announced a public-debt moratorium. On December 27, Morgan notified Eternity that the moratorium constituted a credit event and subsequently settled the outstanding $2 million and $9 million credit default swaps (otherwise set to terminate on October 22, 2006 and March 31, 2002, respectively). According to Morgan, the third swap (valued at $3 million) had expired without being triggered, on December 17, 2001.

It is undisputed that the December 24 public-debt moratorium was a trigger of Eternity's outstanding swaps; in Eternity's view, however, the voluntary debt exchange had triggered Morgan's settlement obligations as early as November 8, 2001, as the Fund had been insisting throughout November and December of that year. In that same period, Eternity asked Morgan to liquidate the swaps on a secondary market. Notwithstanding Morgan's representations in February 2001 regarding the existence of a secondary market for the CDSs, it refused to quote Eternity any secondary-market pricing, though it did offer to "unwind" the contracts by returning the premiums Eternity had paid from October through November 2001. * * *

The question is whether at this stage it can be decided as a matter of law that the voluntary debt exchange was not a "restructuring credit event" covered by the Fund's CDS contracts with Morgan. * * * [The court concludes that it could not be decided as a matter of law that was the case.] * * *

The district court ruled, and we agree, that Morgan's representations as to (i) Eternity's ability to liquidate the credit default swaps at some future time, and (ii) Morgan's ability to assist Eternity in such a liquidation, cannot support a claim for negligent misrepresentation because they are promissory representations about future events. * * *

For the foregoing reasons, we affirm the judgment insofar as it dismissed Eternity's claims premised on fraud and negligent misrepresentation. We reverse the judgment insofar as it dismissed Eternity's claim for breach of contract, and remand for further proceedings consistent with this opinion, on the ground that certain material terms of the contracts cannot be found unambiguous on the basis of the pleadings alone.

NOTES

1. Banks and insurance companies are the principal issuers of credit derivatives. In 2003, the credit derivatives market was valued at some $2 trillion in notional amount. Henny Sender & Marcus Walker, Selling Default Protection, Wall St. J., April 2, 2003, at C13. The size of that market exploded over the next few years, reaching $26 trillion in 2007.

2. Standardized credit default swaps have been developed that are comprised of baskets of credit default swaps on individual companies. These indexes allow hedging against default on fixed income securities issued by corporations in the same way as stock index derivatives are used for portfolio protection. Michael Mackenzie, New Credit Products to be Launched, Wall St. J., April 2, 2003, at C15.

Derivatives have been made available for retail customers. The Chase Manhattan Bank (now JP Morgan Chase) created a time deposit account called the "Market Index Investment Account." This account paid interest computed on the basis of increases, if any, in the Standard & Poor's 500 Composite Stock Price Index.

Merrill Lynch & Co. sold something called Market Index Target Term Securities ("MITTS") in 1997. These instruments were essentially notes that repaid the principal amount in five years. Instead of interest, the holder received a payment based on the percentage increase, if any, in the Dow Jones Industrial Average ("Dow") above a benchmark value set at 6 to 10 percent above the value of that index on the pricing date for the instrument. The Dow would have to increase by that 6 to 10 percent amount before the holder received any return on the loan of principal. These instruments were registered with the SEC under the Securities Act of 1933. The stock market was rising at the time they were issued. Indeed, it was in the midst of a bubble. The MITTS assured the customer of a return of principal (assuming no default) and the possibility of profiting from that historic advance in security prices. As things turned out, the investors purchasing MITTS received only a return of their principal because the stock market collapsed after their issuance. Nevertheless, those investors were spared principal losses, unlike investors holding the common stocks that make up the Dow, which was down some thirty percent from its high.

Salomon Brothers created something called "SPINS." The principal repayment under this instrument was based on the value of the S & P 500 Index. The interest rate was set at two percent. The dividend rate on the stocks in the index, however, were greater than that amount, allowing Salomon Brothers to keep the difference. It could avoid market exposure from increases in the S & P 500 Index by hedging that risk. III Jerry W. Markham, A Financial History of the United States, From the Age of Derivatives to the New Millennium (1970–2001) 194 (2002).

The Magma Copper Company was issuing Copper Interest Indexed Senior Subordinated Notes in 1988. As suggested by their name, the return on these instruments was based on copper prices. Marriott Corp. and other companies were offering "Real Yield Securities" ("REALS"), a product developed by Morgan Stanley. Reals were 10 year notes that paid an interest rate that was the greater of a less than market rate or a rate based on inflation as determined from the Consumer Price Index published by the Department of Labor. As things turned out, there was only a low rate of inflation during that period. These securities were also registered with the SEC. Fannie Mae was also issuing inflation indexed notes and as seen in Chapter 9 the federal government began issuing such debt.

In 1994, Morgan Stanley created a new derivative, called PLUS notes ("Peso–Linked U.S. Dollar Secured Note"), to permit certain Mexican banks (particularly Banco Nacional de Mexico) to remove what [one author] ... describes as "undervalued and illiquid" inflation-linked bonds from their balance sheets without having to record any losses for accounting purposes. Banco Nacional was unwilling to simply sell the bonds, which are known as Bonos Ajustables del Gobierno Federal (adjustable bonds of the Mexican government), because a straightforward sale would have forced the bank to record an accounting loss.

Investment banks trying to help Banco Nacional and other Mexican banks sell Mexican sovereign debt to institutional investors in the United States and Europe faced the problem that these investors wanted highly rated (that is, investment grade) securities, and they wanted them denominated in U.S. dollars rather than in Mexican pesos. These twin preferences were problematic because only Mexican debt denominated in pesos was investment grade. This was due to the fact that rating agencies are very comfortable in assuring investors that the Mexican government will pay back its obligations that are denominated in pesos, because the government can always simply print more pesos to cover its debt. But if the peso falls in value against the dollar, the Mexican government might not be able to meet its obligations to repay in dollars. It might, for example, suspend the convertibility of its currency, as it had done in the past. Thus, the Bonos Ajustables that Banco Nacional wished to sell were given a high, investment grade AA-rating by Standard & Poor's, but they were payable in Mexican pesos rather than in U.S. dollars.

In order to rid Banco Nacional of its Bonos Ajustables, Morgan Stanley created a Bermuda corporation, which in turn created and sold its own bonds backed by the Mexican securities. These were the bonds known as PLUS notes. Unlike the Bonos Ajustables, the PLUS notes were denominated in U.S. dollars. Morgan Stanley convinced Standard & Poor's to give the new bonds issued by the Bermuda company the same AA-rating given to Mexico's peso-denominated sovereign debt, instead of the much lower rating given to Mexico's U.S. dollar-denominated debt.

Jonathan R. Macey, Wall Street Versus Main Street: How Ignorance, Hyperbole, and Fear Lead to Regulation, 65 U. Chi. L. Rev. 1487, 1497–1498 (1998).

Salomon Brothers developed something called "Zones" that were issued by Comcast Corp but were exchangeable into Sprint PCS shares. Comcast also sold Participating hybrid option note exchangeable Securities ("PHONES") that was a debt instrument that paid interest plus dividends on the stock of another company owned by Comcast. The holder could exchange the PHONE at maturity for the cash value of the associated stock. This allowed Comcast to defer capital gains by avoiding a sale and providing it what amounted to a loan secured by the stock. These instruments were a creation of Merrill Lynch which was also underwriting Pharmaceutical HOLDRs which were depository receipts for an undivided beneficial ownership interest in the common stocks of twenty pharmaceutical companies.

Another offering involved Premium Income Exchangeable Securities ("PIES") for the MediaOne Group. These were notes that paid seven percent and were exchangeable into American Depository Receipts for the ordinary shares of a foreign registrant, Vodafone AirTouch.

Morgan Stanley Dean Witter & Co. was selling "BOXES," which are senior debt securities issued by Morgan Stanley exchangeable for a cash amount determined by the market prices of the seventeen component stocks contained in the AMEX Biotechnology Index. The price of the BOXES would in turn depend on the changes in the values of those Stocks. Biotech Boxes, 2002, SEC No–Act LEXIS 309 (March 27, 2002). Microsoft was selling put warrants on its stock in 1998, thereby generating large revenues, but exposing it to risk. III Jerry W. Markham, A Financial History of the United States, From the Age of Derivatives to the New Millennium (1970–2001) 258, 275–76 (2002).

The use of derivatives for consumers is expected to expand in the future. One proposal would allow students to hedge against a drop in the number of jobs in their proposed career. Robert J. Shiller, The New Financial Order, Risk in the 21st Century 110–15 (2003). A college tuition plan that was tied to future income failed at Yale. Students there (from 1971 to 1978) could pay 0.4 percent of their income after graduation in lieu of a student loan at a conventional interest rate. President Clinton was among those taking advantage of that program, but income levels proved insufficient to provide an adequate return to the school. Id. at 143. NYSEG, the New York electric company, was offering an "electricity supply pricing option" that allowed consumers to choose various pricing options for their electricity. They could elect either a fixed or floating amount payment for electricity. The floating amount selection allowed the consumer to bet that electricity prices would be decreasing.

SECTION 10. CREDIT DEFAULT SWAPS

JERRY W. MARKHAM
REGULATING CREDIT DEFAULT SWAPS IN THE WAKE OF THE SUBPRIME CRISIS

A Working Paper Prepared for the International Monetary Fund Seminar
on Current Developments in Monetary and Financial Law (2009).

The subprime crisis focused much attention on credit default swaps (CDS) and the role they played in the failure of the American International Group Inc. (AIG). The bailout of AIG by the U.S. government was unprecedented in size and scope, and the amount of the bill to the taxpayers for that and other failures is yet to be tallied. The U.S Government, and those in Europe, are seeking to regulate the previously unregulated CDS market. To date, that effort has focused on the creation of central clearinghouses for CDS, which, it is hoped, will lead to greater transparency. The development of such clearinghouses is supported by the derivatives industry, and several clearinghouses have already been formed to carry out this activity. "Legacy" swaps are being registered with those clearinghouses and plans are underway for listing new originations. More troubling to the industry is the Obama administration's request for broader, more intrusive, indeed pervasive, regulation of CDS by the Securities and Exchange Commission (SEC) and other over-the-counter (OTC) derivatives by the Commodity Futures Trading Commission (CFTC). * * *

This paper will review the role played by CDS in the subprime crisis and the Great Panic of 2008. It will describe how the subprime crisis caused a sharp, probably unjustified, devaluation in the so-called "Super Senior" component of collateralized debt obligations (CDOs), which were at the heart of the crisis, and which in many instances were covered by CDS.* * *

Securitization provided the banks with a way to move subprime loans off their balance sheets, and it allowed "lenders to shift mortgage credit risk and interest rate risk to investors who have greater risk tolerance."[33]

---

33. Division of Insurance and Research of the Federal Deposit Insurance Corporation, *Breaking New Ground in U.S. Mortgage Lending*, FDIC Outlook (Fed. Deposit Ins. Corp.), Summer 2006, at 21.

The amount of securitized subprime mortgages grew from about $11 billion in 1994 to over $100 billion in 2002. Bear Stearns made its first subprime securitization offering in 1997 for mortgages totaling $385 million, and it underwrote an additional $1.9 billion in securitizations over the next ten months. "By 2005, almost 68 percent of home mortgage originations were securitized."[34] The FDIC noted, in 2006, that:

> A significant development in the mortgage securities market is the recent and dramatic expansion of 'private-label, [mortgage-backed securities] MBS ... Total outstanding private-label MBS represented 29 percent of total outstanding MBS in 2005, more than double the share in 2003. Of total private-label MBS issuance, *two thirds comprised non-prime loans in 2005*, up from 46 percent in 2003.[35]

The securitization process was carried out through CDOs that were distributed through "warehouse" operations, in which mortgages were purchased from non-bank originators by investment banks and then resold through securitizations. These warehousing operations became a part of an unregulated "shadow banking" system.[36] A shareholder report by UBS AG described its CDO facility as follows:

> In the initial stage of a CDO securitization, the [CDO] desk would typically enter into an agreement with a collateral manager. UBS sourced residential mortgage backed securities ('RMBS') and other securities on behalf of the manager. These positions were held in a CDO Warehouse in anticipation of securitization into CDOs. Generally, while in the Warehouse, these positions would be on UBS's books with exposure to market risk. Upon completion of the Warehouse, the securities were transferred to a CDO special-purpose vehicle, and structured into tranches. The CDO desk received structuring fees on the notional value of the deal, and focused on Mezzanine ('Mezz') CDOs, which generated fees of approximately 125 to 150 bp [basis points](compared with high-grade CDOs, which generated fees of approximately 30 to 50 bp). . . .

> Under normal market conditions, there would be a rise and fall in positions held in the CDO Warehouse line as assets were accumulated ('ramped up') and then sold as CDOs. There was typically a lag of between 1 and 4 months between initial agreement with a collateral manager to buy assets, and the full ramping of a CDO Warehouse.[37]

Subprime CDOs were broken up into separate tranches. The less secure tranches were required to absorb any larger than expected losses from mortgage defaults, providing a cushion from loss for the most secure tranche, called the "Super–Senior." As a result of this credit enhancement

---

34. FDIC, *Breaking New Ground in U.S. Mortgage Lending* FDIC Outlook 21 (Summer 2006) (emphasis supplied).

35. *Id.*

36. These warehousing operations often involved the purchase on non-bank subprime mortgage originations by investment banks like Bear Stearns and Merrill Lynch. *See* PAUL MUOLO & MATHEW PADILLA, CHAIN OF BLAME (2008) (describing these warehousing operations).

37. UBS AG, SHAREHOLDER REPORT ON UBS'S WRITE-DOWNS § 4.22 (2008).

feature, the Super–Seniors were considered to be more credit-worthy than the underlying subprime mortgages themselves. * * *

A CDS is an agreement by one party to make a series of payments to a counter party, in exchange for a payoff, if a specified credit instrument goes into default. As one court defined these instruments:

> a common type of credit derivative in which the protection buyer makes a fixed payment to the protection seller in return for a payment that is contingent upon a 'credit event'—such as a bankrupt-cy—occurring to the company that issued the security (the 'reference entity') or the security itself (the 'reference obligation'). The contingent payment is often made against delivery of a 'deliverable obligation'—usually the reference obligation or other security issued by the reference entity—by the protection buyer to the protection seller. This delivery is known as the 'physical settlement.'[38]

Although CDS were widely used as a form of insurance against a default from that credit instrument, they were also used for speculation on whether a default will occur.[39] It was estimated that eighty percent or more of the giant CDS market was speculative. The CDS, in all events, proved to be a popular instrument. Outstanding notional value of the CDS was over $42 trillion in debt at year-end 2007.

CDS were used to enhance the creditworthiness of subprime securitizations. As an April 2008 UBS shareholder report noted, "[k]ey to the growth of the CDO structuring business was the development of the credit default swap ('CDS')...."[40] With the credit enhancement of a CDS, the credit rating agencies often gave the Super Seniors their highest triple-A rating. This was the same credit rating enjoyed by the federal government, which signaled to the world that a default on those Super Senior tranches was highly unlikely. Unfortunately, the rating agencies' risk models for awarding the triple-A rating on CDOs did not take into account the

---

38. Deutsche Bank AG v. Ambac Credit Products LLC, 2006 U.S. Dist. LEXIS 45322 (S.D.N.Y. 2006). * * *

39. An ABX Index was created to track the value of mortgaged-backed securities based on credit default swaps.

The ABX Index is a series of credit-default swaps based on 20 bonds that consist of subprime mortgages. ABX contracts are commonly used by investors to speculate on or to hedge against the risk that the underling mortgage securities are not repaid as expected. The ABX swaps offer protection if the securities are not repaid as expected, in return for regular insurance-like premiums. A decline in the ABX Index signifies investor sentiment that subprime mortgage holders will suffer increased financial losses from those investments. Likewise, an increase in the ABX Index signifies investor sentiment looking for subprime mortgage holdings to perform better as investments.

Housing Derivatives: ABX Index, *available at* http://www.housingderivatives.typepad.com/housing _ Derivatives/abx _ index/. The CBOE also began trading credit default options in 2007 that were automatically exercised upon the occurrence of specified credit events. Press Release, Chicago Board Options Exchange, CBEO to Launch Exchange–Traded Credit Default Options in Second Quarter (Mar. 14, 2007), http://www.cboe.com/AboutCBOE/ShowDocument.aspx?DIR=ACNews& FILE=cboe _ 20070314a.doc. The Chicago Board of Trade (CBOT) also developed CDS Index Futures contracts. CBOT CREDIT DEFAULT SWAP INDEX FUTURES REFERENCE GUIDE (2008), *available at* http://www.cmegroup.com/trading/interest-rates/files/Swap _ Futures _ Reference _ Guide _ 2008 _ Oct _ doc.pdf.

40. *See* UBS AG, SHAREHOLDER REPORT ON UBS'S WRITE-DOWNS § 4.22 (2008).

possibility of a major downturn in the real estate market. That flaw was not spotted until the subprime crisis arose. * * *

A credit down grade at the American International Group, Inc. (AIG) in September 2008 raised concerns that large losses would be experienced in the financial community if AIG defaulted on its $500 billion CDS portfolio. This spurred the federal government to mount a $183 billion rescue of that firm. AIG entered the CDS market in a big way in 2005 through its division called AIGFP, which had been founded by a group of traders from Drexel Burnham Lambert, the failed junk bond broker of Michael Milken fame. AIGFP's risk model predicted that, based on historic default rates, the economy would have to fall into depression before AIG would experience losses from its CDS exposures. AIGFP assured investors in August 2007 that "it is hard for us, without being flippant, to even see a scenario within any kind of realm of reason that would see us losing $1 in any of those transactions."[42]

AIG's share price dropped sharply after it reported a large 2007 fourth quarter loss that was accompanied by a $5.29 billion write-down of its mortgage related business, including a write-down of its credit CDS business by $4.88 billion. AIG reported a loss of $7.81 billion in the first quarter of 2008, largely due to a write down of $11 billion related to losses from Super Senior CDS written by the AIG Financial Products Corp. (AIGFP). Another $3.6 billion was written off by AIG for those instruments in the second quarter of 2008, adding to the $5.36 billion loss by AIG in that quarter. AIG reported a loss in the third quarter of $24.47 billion, including losses of $7.05 billion in AIGFP.

Fed chairman Ben Bernanke turned AIG and the CDS market into a pariah when he declared in congressional testimony that nothing had made him more angry than the AIG failure, which he attributed to AIG's exploitation of "a huge gap in the regulatory system."[43] He asserted that AIGFP was nothing more than a hedge fund attached to large and stable insurance company that "made huge numbers of irresponsible bets, [and] took huge losses. There was no regulatory oversight because there was a gap in the system."[44] Bernanke stated that the government was forced to expend billions of dollars to save AIG because its failure would have been "disastrous for the economy."[45]

Actually, it appears that AIG's failure was the result of credit downgrades, prompted by AIG's write-downs of its CDS positions. Those writedowns were caused by a lack of a market that could accurately price the

---

42. Robert O'Harrow, Jr. & Brady Dennis, *Credit Rating Downgrade, Real Estate Collapse Crippled AIG—Third of Three Parts*, L.A. TIMES, Jan. 2, 2009, *available at* http://articles.latimes.com/2009/jan/02/ business/fi-aig2.

43. DAVID WESSEL, IN FED WE TRUST, 194 (2009).

44. *Id.*

45. *Id.* A report by TARP Inspector General (the TARP Cop) Neil Barofsky issued in November 2009 charged that the Fed's takeover of AIG had been badly flawed in paying Goldman Sachs and other large investment banks in full for their AIG CDS. *AIG and Systemic Risk*, WALL ST. J., Nov. 20, at A26.

underlying Super Seniors. The subsequent credit downgrades caused large collateral calls that AIG did not have the liquidity to meet.

AIG's CEO, Martin Sullivan blamed mark-to-market accounting requirements for the losses sustained by AIGFP. Sullivan complained that AIG was required to markdown its inventories even though it had no intention of selling them. He may have had a point, as this was a common complaint in the industry. Fair value pricing was resulting in a procyclical progression of write-downs that bore no relation to actual value.

Critics of fair value accounting charged that, because liquidity in subprime investments had dried up as the subprime crisis blossomed, the only prices available for "fair value" accounting were fire sale prices from desperate sellers. Those prices in no way reflected the actual value of the Super Seniors as measured by their cash flows or defaults. One accountant complained to the FASB that: "May the souls of those who developed FASB 157 burn in the seventh circle of Dante's Hell."[46] Warren Buffett likened mark-to-market requirements for measuring bank regulatory capital to throwing "gasoline on the fire in terms of financial institutions."[47]

Dodd–Frank

The Obama administration submitted a lengthy legislative proposal to Congress, which sought to repeal the regulatory exemption for swaps that was added to the Commodity Exchange Act in 1992 and expanded in 2000. As described in section 8, the Dodd–Frank Wall Street Reform and Consumer Protection Act of 2010 enacted that proposal into law. The Securities and Exchange Commission ("SEC") was given jurisdiction over security based swaps and the Commodity Futures Trading Commission ("CFTC") was given jurisdiction over non-security swaps, swaps on broad-based indexes and swaps on federal government obligations and certain other securities that are exempt from SEC regulation. Joint regulatory authority is given to both agencies for "mixed" swaps that have elements of both securities and commodities. The SEC has described this allocation of jurisdiction as follows:

> The Dodd–Frank Act divides regulatory authority over swap agreements between the CFTC and SEC (though the prudential regulators, such as the Federal Reserve Board, also have an important role in setting capital and margin for swap entities that are banks). The SEC has regulatory authority over "security-based swaps," which are defined as swaps based on a single security or loan or a narrow-based group or index of securities (including any interest therein or the

---

46. *Accounting Principles*, 40 SEC. REG. & L. REP. (BNA) 1767 (2008).

47. Holman W. Jenkins, Jr., *Buffett's Unmentionable Bank Solution*, WALL ST. J., Mar. 11, 2009, at A13. As one author noted:

The argument against fair value is a compelling one: volatile markets make securities valuation difficult and undermine investors' confidence, forcing companies to mark down values, leading to greater illiquidity and further markdowns. The more the markdowns impair capital, the greater the loss of investor confidence, and the faster the churn of the self-reinforcing cycle.

Todd Davenport. *Fair Value: Few Fans, But Fewer Alternatives; Despite Widespread Frustration, Changes Don't Seem Likely*, 173 AM. BANKER 1 (Mar. 24, 2008).

value thereof), or events relating to a single issuer or issuers of securities in a narrow-based security index. Security-based swaps are included within the definition of "security" under the Securities Exchange Act of 1934 and the Securities Act of 1933.

The CFTC has primary regulatory authority over all other swaps, such as energy and agricultural swaps. The CFTC and SEC share authority over "mixed swaps," which are security-based swaps that also have a commodity component.

In addition, the SEC has anti-fraud enforcement authority over swaps that are related to securities but that do not come within the definition of "security-based swap." These are called "security-based swap agreements." The Dodd–Frank Act provides the SEC with access to information relating to security-based swap agreement in the possession of the CFTC and certain CFTC-regulated entities, such as derivatives clearing organizations, designated contract markets, and swap data repositories.

http://www.sec.gov/spotlight/dodd-frank/derivatives.shtml.

CHAPTER THIRTEEN

INVESTMENT COMPANIES AND OTHER FINANCIAL INTERMEDIARIES

■ ■ ■

Chapter objectives

- To recognize the different liquidity and investment features of closed-end mutual funds, open-ended mutual funds, unit investment trusts, and real estate investment trusts.

- To identify an investment company as defined in the federal Investment Company Act of 1940.

- To see how private equity and hedge, also serve as financial intermediaries.

SECTION 1. INTRODUCTION

One important institutional investor that plays a significant role in corporate finance is the mutual fund. These "buy side" securities market entities are responsible for investing an estimated $6 trillion into corporate and other securities. In September 2002, mutual funds held 18 percent of all publicly traded equity securities in the United States. Securities and Exchange Commission Release No. 33–8188, January 31, 2003. They also provide an investment medium for corporations in the form of money market funds and play a significant role in the savings and retirement plans provided by corporations to employees. This chapter will examine the operations of mutual funds and other investment companies and their regulation.

"The investment company concept dates to Europe in the late 1700s, according to K. Geert Rouwenhorst in The Origins of Mutual Funds, when 'a Dutch merchant and broker ... invited subscriptions from investors to form a trust ... to provide an opportunity to diversify for small investors with limited means.' "[1] Investment companies also trace their history back to the Societe de Belgique, a trust originally created in 1822 by King William of the Netherlands that allowed the trust beneficiaries to hold

---

1. Investment Company Institute, 2005 Mutual Fund Fact Book, A Guide to Trends and Statistics in the Mutual Fund Industry Appendix B (2005), available at ICI.org.

interests in government loans.[2] Another trust in the 1830s was used to sell the stocks held by a bank that were acquired from defaulting borrowers. In France, in 1852, the Societe Generale de Credit Mobilier, (no relation to the American Credit Mobiler railroad construction company that caused much scandal in America) used shareholder funds to invest in the operations of other companies, including the dynamite business of Alfred Nobel.

Investment companies were also formed in London in the 1860s. These entities used investor funds to finance the purchase of shares of other companies. The Foreign and Colonial Government Trust was one such entity. It purchased the securities of several foreign firms. Another trust, formed in the 1870s, was the Submarine Cables Trust that invested in the securities of telegraph companies. The stock of that trust itself traded on the London Stock Exchange. The Scottish American Investment Trust was established in 1873 by Robert Fleming. He was the grandfather of Ian Fleming, the creator of James Bond. Fleming's trust company used a professional board of advisors to select investments. Some 500 investors participated in that trust.

Investment companies were slow to arrive in the United States. The Massachusetts Hospital Life Insurance Company, a company originally formed in 1818 as a insurance company, did operate a trust that had some characteristics of an investment company. It invested the commingled funds of beneficiaries, including the sum of $37,000 donated by friends of Daniel Webster while he was Secretary of State. This fund provided Webster with an income of about $1,000 annually. However, "someone remarked that the proposition was 'indelicate' and he wondered how Mr. Webster would take it? 'How will he take it?' snorted [Harrison Gray] Otis. 'Why, quarterly, to be sure!' " Samuel Eliot Morison, John Paul Jones, A Sailor's Biography 359 (1959).

Some other investment operations appeared at the end of the nineteenth century, but the real growth in investment companies in America would await the stock market boom of the 1920s. That speculative era witnessed a "veritable epidemic of investment trusts [that] inflicted the Nation." S. Rep. No. 1455, 73d Cong., 2d Sess. 339 (1934). By 1929, an investment company was being formed every day in America. Their allure was the result of claims of diversification and expert management. Investors were told that the investment company allowed them to make a small investment that would be pooled with other investor funds and used to purchase a diversified range of securities issued by other companies. Expert managers were to select those stocks based on a professional analysis.

Many of the investment companies operating in the 1920s were "closed end." This meant that they were corporations that invested in

---

2. Even earlier, in 1664, the East India Company agreed to repurchase its own shares from shareholders at book value, providing some of the elements of a mutual fund See Jonathan B. Baskin & Paul J. Miranti, Jr., A History of Corporate Finance 77 (1997) (describing this arrangement).

stocks, instead of say making automobiles. Closed end companies obtained funds by issuing its own common and preferred stock to investors and by borrowing through bond issues, providing the common shareholders with leverage. The stock of closed end companies traded in secondary markets and was even listed on the stock exchanges.

Another form of investment company were the "fixed trusts," which are now referred to as "unit investment trusts" or "defined asset" funds. These were a pool of stocks usually held by a bank in trust. Ownership interests in that pool were sold to the public. These entities did not have managers and did not trade the stocks in the pool. The portfolio remained fixed, unlike the closed end companies that could buy and sell stocks according to market conditions and the judgment of its managers.

"Face amount" certificates were still another way to entice small investors into the market. These were actually periodic investment plans in which the investor paid a fixed amount each month and was entitled to receive the face amount of the certificate on maturity. The investors' funds were invested by the issuer to provide that return.

The "open end" or "mutual" fund appeared in the 1924 but did not have time to develop before the stock market crashed in 1929. The mutual fund was the invention of Edward G. Leffler in Boston. Such companies continually sell and redeem their shares at their net asset value. This means that an investor wishing to liquidate his or her investment simply notifies the company of that desire, and the company will return the investor's aliquot portion of the total fund based on its net asset value on the day of redemption. Similarly, new investors would invest by purchasing an interest in the company based on current net asset value.

Mutual funds provide many advantages. They include the use of expert managers and diversification that could not be possible for investors with only small amounts of funds to invest. The mutual fund also provides liquidity to investors because they are normally able to have their investment redeemed at any time at its net asset value. In contrast, liquidation of an ownership interest in a closed end fund will require the location of a willing buyer. Closed end companies often trade at less than their net asset value.

During the 1920s, one out of every ten investors was a holder of investment company shares or certificates. The stock market crash of 1929 was a disaster for those investors. The Goldman Sachs Trading Corporation, a closed end investment company, raised over $100 million for its operations. Its shares traded at one point before the crash at $326. They were selling for $1.75 in 1932. Another investment company saw its share prices drop from $100 to 63 cents. Subsequent investigations revealed a number of abuses by the investment companies. They included speculative investments, failure to diversify as promised, undue leverage obtained from bond sales and the purchase of stock on margin and self dealing on the part of the organizers of the investment companies.

After its creation in 1934, the Securities and Exchange Commission ("SEC") conducted an inquiry into the operations of investment companies. That study discovered a number of abuses that resulted in the passage of the Investment Company Act of 1940. 15 U.S.C. § 80a–1 *et seq.* This legislation has been said to be "the most intrusive financial legislation known to man or beast." Clifford E. Kirsch ed., The Financial Services Revolution: Understanding the Changing Role of Banks, Mutual Funds, and Insurance Companies 382 (1997). Among other things, this act required that forty percent of an investment company's board of directors be independent, and transactions with affiliated persons were restricted. Investment companies were prohibited from issuing debt securities or preferred stock that would allow them to leverage their market positions. See Matthew Fink, The Rise of Mutual Funds (2008) (describing growth of mutual funds).

The investment companies began a recovery in the 1950s, but the mutual fund replaced the closed end company as the investment vehicle of choice for many investors. Scandal soon returned with the collapse of Investors Overseas Services ("IOS"), a giant off-shore mutual fund that had been structured to avoid regulation by the SEC. IOS was managed by a very colorful character, Bernie Cornfeld, who traveled on his own jet with a bevy of beautiful women. IOS managed a "fund-of-funds" that invested in the shares of other investment companies. It had two classes of share. The class sold to the public was non-voting. The voting class was held by Cornfeld and his cronies, giving them complete control over investor funds. Cornfeld's loose administration led to sales to United States investors, as well as fraud and dubious investments. That activity gave rise to regulatory action by the SEC. IOS was, thereafter, sold to Robert Vesco, a financier with a troubled background. He then looted the company of hundreds of millions of dollars. Vesco fled to the Caribbean. Although he was subsequently jailed in Cuba for other misdeeds, Vesco remains a fugitive from justice in the United States.

Despite that set back, mutual funds continued to gain favor with investors. Their popularity soared with the invention of the money market fund in 1971. This was simply a mutual fund that invested in short term debt instruments. Investors could continually add and remove funds from the money market fund. The net asset value of each share in these funds was maintained at one dollar. Increases in the value of the fund were paid out as "dividends" in the form of additional shares, thus maintaining a dollar based account for additions and withdrawals. In the rare event of losses, however, the money market fund could "break the buck."

The money market fund was used as the functional equivalent of a bank account, but one that paid a market rate of interest. The money market fund paid higher rates of return than time deposits at a bank because then existing government regulations capped interest rates paid on time deposits and precluded interest on demand deposits. With the creation of the Cash Management account, which is described in Chapter 3, investors could effectively treat their money market fund accounts as bank accounts and earn money market interest rates on all their idle cash.

With these advantages, the money market fund became the most popular investment in America.

Money market funds administered by non-banks such as broker-dealers compete with bank accounts but have some substantial differences. Losses may be sustained in a money market fund because it is investing in securities that pose investment risks. Because these funds only invest in high-grade, short-term securities, however, the risk of breaking the buck, *i.e.*, returning to the investor less than a full dollar for each dollar invested, is remote. Nevertheless, federal Securities Investor Protection Corporation ("SIPC") account insurance does not protect investors in the event of a loss because SIPC insures only the solvency of broker-dealers, not investment performance.

The stock market bubble of the 1990s furthered the growth of mutual funds. The number of mutual funds increased from 360 in 1970 to over 8000 at the beginning of the century. Many mutual funds were organized into complexes that provided a broad array of investment choices to investors and allowed switching among individual mutual funds in the complex as investors' investment objectives changed.

Investors do, indeed, have a broad range of investment choices in mutual funds. For example, an investor seeking to invest in fixed income instruments may choose among mutual funds that invest in money market instruments (with sub choices of municipal, federal or private securities) longer term municipal securities (with sub choices of states and instruments), United States government securities (with sub choices of bills, notes and bonds with varying maturities and mortgage backed instruments) and corporate bonds (with sub choices on convertible bonds, global bonds and differing maturities, and ratings grades down to and including junk bonds).

Equity investors may choose from index funds on a broad range of indexes, sector funds that invest in a particular business sector such as automobiles, option funds, growth funds, aggressive growth funds, contrarian funds that trade against popular investment views, global funds, emerging market funds for stocks of companies in lesser developed countries, balanced funds (with varying balances) that invest in both fixed income and equity securities, "quant" funds that use computer programs to make stock picks and vulture funds that invest in failing companies. A "stable value" mutual fund is one that provides a guaranteed rate of return. The guarantee is backed by a bank or insurance company. Bridget O'Brian, SEC Looks Into Stable–Value Funds, Wall St. J., March 27, 2003, at D9.

Remember that a mutual fund is simply a pool of investment funds. It is not itself an investment. It is surprising how many people, when asked what they are investing in, will just say "mutual funds." That response is pretty much meaningless, except to tell you that someone else is managing a portfolio with objectives that the investor found desirable. A more complete answer would be, for example, "a long term, high quality (AA+

rated) corporate bond mutual fund. This identifies the nature of the investment and alerts the participants to the risks being incurred. For example, with respect to the aforementioned bond fund, safety of principal appears to be its objective, and the high credit rating of the bonds being purchased offers some analytical assurance that the default rate should be low. A concern for mutual funds investing in fixed income instruments, however, is that the mutual fund is perpetual in existence. When bond prices decrease from an increase in interest rates, a bondholder can hold the bond to maturity and receive back the complete principal invested, assuming no default. In a mutual fund, the decrease in the value of the bonds in the fund will decrease the net asset value of the fund immediately, reducing the principal investment of the investor. The mutual fund may make an investment decision not to hold the bonds to maturity, giving the investor no choice except to accept the loss. Even a mutual fund buying highly rated bonds could incur large losses if it has an aggressive trading strategy that seeks to profit from anticipated changes in interest rates by buying and selling bonds to achieve that goal."

Mutual funds are independent entities but are organized by varying groups. Some mutual fund distributors are principally engaged in the mutual fund business. Other distributors are broker-dealers that have significant other business lines. The banks have also become large distributors of mutual funds.

A key aspect of the mutual fund's operation is its contract with an investment advisor that will trade the funds contributed by the individual investors. That adviser's investment objectives and choices will measure the success of the investors in the mutual fund. Investors must also consider fees and expenses charged or incurred by the mutual fund since those items will reduce their investment return. Those concerns are more specifically addressed in Section 5 of this chapter.

A REPORT TO CONGRESS IN ACCORDANCE WITH § 356(C) OF THE UNITING AND STRENGTHENING AMERICA BY PROVIDING APPROPRIATE TOOLS REQUIRED TO INTERCEPT AND OBSTRUCT TERRORISM ACT OF 2001 (USA PATRIOT ACT)

Secretary of the Treasury, Federal Reserve Board, Securities and Exchange Commission and Commodity Futures Trading Commission (December 31, 2002).

The 1940 [Investment Company] Act classifies almost all registered investment companies as either "management companies" or "unit investment trusts."[3] Management companies, which often adjust (or "man-

---

3. A "management company" is any investment company other than a unit investment trust or a face-amount certificate company. 15 U.S.C. 80a–4(3). A "unit investment trust" is an "investment company which (A) is organized under a trust indenture, contract of custodianship or agency, or similar instrument, (B) does not have a board of directors, and (C) issues only redeemable securities, each of which represents an undivided interest in a unit of specified

age") their portfolios in an active manner, are subclassified as "open-end" and "closed-end" companies. An open-end investment company is a management company that is offering or has outstanding any redeemable securities that it issued. Open-end investment companies, which are more commonly called "mutual funds," are by far the most prevalent type of registered investment company. * * *

Mutual funds are today one of the most popular ways individual investors participate in the securities markets. In 2001, more than 8,300 active mutual funds, with approximately $7 trillion in assets, were registered with the SEC. Mutual funds are held by more than half of U.S. households. A mutual fund, like any other investment company, is a trust, partnership, or corporation whose assets consist of a portfolio of securities, interests in which are represented by the shares that the fund issues. A mutual fund raises money from shareholders and invests it in accordance with the fund's stated objectives. Mutual funds are generally grouped into stock funds, bond funds, and money market funds. In addition, like most investment companies, mutual funds usually do not have their own employees. One or more third-party service providers (which may or may not be affiliated with the mutual fund) conduct all of a mutual fund's operations.

Unlike other investment companies, a mutual fund typically offers its shares continuously to the public, and redeems its shares on demand by investors, at a price based on the fund's net asset value. A mutual fund usually offers its shares to the public through a principal underwriter, which is a registered broker-dealer. Shares also may be purchased directly from some funds (called "direct-sold funds"). In addition, they may be purchased through a variety of alternative distribution channels, such as fund "supermarkets" (through which investors may purchase shares of several different mutual funds), insurance agents, financial planners, and banks. Mutual funds employ transfer agents to conduct record keeping and related functions. * * *

A closed-end investment company (or "closed-end fund") is a management company other than an open-end investment company. Like a mutual fund, a closed-end fund is a trust, partnership, or corporation whose assets consist of a portfolio of securities, interests in which are represented by the shares that the fund issues. Closed-end funds differ from mutual funds in that they do not offer their shares continuously, nor do they redeem their shares on demand. Instead, a closed-end fund issues a fixed number of shares, which typically trade on a stock exchange or in

---

securities, but does not include a voting trust." 15 U.S.C. 80a–4(2). A "face-amount certificate company" is "an investment company which is engaged or proposes to engage in the business of issuing face-amount certificates of the installment type, or which has been engaged in such business and has any such certificate outstanding." 15 U.S.C. 80a–4(1). A "face amount certificate" is "any certificate, investment contract, or other security which represents an obligation on the part of its issuer to pay a stated or determinable sum or sums at a fixed or determinable date or dates more than twenty-four months after the date or issuance, in consideration of the payment of periodic installments or a stated or determinable amount" or "any security which represents a similar obligation on the part of a face-amount certificate company, the consideration for which is the payment of a single lump sum." 15 U.S.C. 80a–2(a)(15).

the over-the-counter market. Investors seeking to buy or sell these shares must buy or sell them through a broker-dealer on the exchange. Like other publicly traded securities (and unlike the shares of a typical mutual fund), shares of a closed-end fund trade at a market price that fluctuates and is determined by supply and demand in the marketplace.

Closed-end funds typically do not have an account relationship with their investors. * * * Although most closed-end funds do not redeem their shares, a category of closed-end funds—"interval funds"—do have limited redemption features. Interval funds rely on rule 23c–3 under the 1940 Act to periodically offer to repurchase from shareholders a limited number of fund shares at net asset value. Rule 23c–3 describes the intervals at which such repurchase offers may be made (three, six or twelve months) and the amount of stock that may be the subject of a repurchase offer (not less than five percent nor more than twenty-five percent of the fund's outstanding stock). There are currently an estimated 30 interval funds.

NOTES

Consider the following description of the distinctions between open-end mutual funds closed-end investment companies:

> Unlike a traditional mutual fund in which investors purchase and redeem shares directly from and with the mutual fund, a closed-end fund has a fixed number of shares and (after the initial public offering) investors may only purchase shares from an existing shareholder through a stock exchange on which such shares are listed. Thus, shares in a closed-end fund are traded exactly like the shares of any other publicly-owned corporation. By contrast with an "open-end" mutual fund, in which the number of shares is not fixed and investors can purchase or redeem shares at current net asset value ("NAV") (calculated by dividing the fund's total assets by the number of shares outstanding), a closed-end fund has a fixed number of shares that originally were sold in a public offering. Per-share trading prices may be at either a premium or a discount to NAV, but more often are at a discount.

> Because closed-end funds operate with a fixed number of shares, they have limited options for obtaining capital to make new investments. Once a fund's initial capital has been fully invested, new investments generally can be made only if the fund sells existing portfolio holdings. Other options for raising capital include secondary public offerings at net asset value, or rights offerings to current investors at or below NAV.

Strougo on Behalf of Brazil Fund, Inc. v. Scudder, Stevens & Clark, Inc., 964 F.Supp. 783, 788 (S.D.N.Y.1997).

Money Market Funds

A popular form of the mutual fund is the "money market fund" that invests in short term money market instruments that are highly liquid. The money market fund was designed to allow retail and institutional investors to earn interest on their idle funds while at the same time having maintaining their liquidity and safety of principle. The money market fund concept was invented by Bruce Bent and Henry B.R. Brown in 1971. Within five years, money market funds were holding assets valued at $3 billion, a number that increased to $230 billion by 1982. See Jerry W. Markham, III A Financial History of the United States, From the Age of Derivatives into the New Millennium (1970–2001) 6–7 (2002). The total amount of assets held in institutional and retail money market funds exceeded $2.8 trillion in September 2008, about $1 trillion of that amount was held in retail funds.

The Reserve Primary Fund that was created Bent and Brown encountered a spectacular loss during the subprime crisis in 2008. That failure was due to the fact that this fund held commercial paper issued by Lehman Brothers, which became worthless after Lehman declared bankruptcy on September 15, 2008. The Reserve Primary Fund then "broke-the-buck," which meant that investors would receive less than one dollar for each dollar they invested in the fund. The failure of the Reserve Primary Fund set off a panic among investors in other money market funds. Money market funds had a net outflow of $200 billion in the two-week period following the Reserve Primary Fund's failure, reversing a net inflow of $28.4 billion in August. This panic was quelled after the Treasury Department announced on September 19 that it would provide $50 billion to act as a temporary guarantee to protect money market funds from investment losses. That stabilized the situation, and the guarantee ended one year later. Jerry W. Markham, A Financial History of the United States, From the Subprime Crisis to the Great Recession (2006–2009) 531–534 (2010).

SECTION 2. THE INADVERTENT INVESTMENT COMPANY?

SECURITIES AND EXCHANGE COMMISSION v. FIFTH AVENUE COACH LINES, INC.

435 F.2d 510 (2d Cir.1970).

ADAMS, CIRCUIT JUDGE.

This appeal raises important questions regarding the application of the Investment Company Act of 1940 ('the 1940 Act'), 15 U.S.C. § 80a–1 et seq. As we view the case, the central issue is whether Fifth Avenue Coach Lines, Inc. ('Fifth') had become an investment company within the meaning of § 3(a)(1)[4] of the 1940 Act (15 U.S.C.§ 80a–3 (a)(1)) by June

---

4. § 3(a): 'When used in this subchapter, 'investment company' means any issuer which (1) is or holds itself out as being engaged primarily, * * * in the business of investing, reinvesting, or trading in securities'.

30, 1967. Also presented is the question whether an injunction prohibiting further violations of § 10(b) of the Securities Exchange Act of 1934 ('the 1934 Act'), 15 U.S.C. § 78j(b), is justified against the defendants, Victor Muscat and Roy M. Cohn.

The Securities and Exchange Commission ('SEC') sought an injunction in the District Court for the Southern District of New York against the individual defendants to prevent further violations of the 1934 Act and the 1940 Act, and requested the appointment of a receiver for Fifth. The Honorable Edward C. McLean, United States District Judge, in a decision at 289 F.Supp. 3 (1968), found Fifth to be, as of June 30, 1967, an investment company which, because it had not registered under the 1940 Act, was acting in violation of § 7(a) of the Act (15 U.S.C. § 80a–7(a)). * * *

Until March, 1962, Fifth operated in New York City one of the nation's largest privately owned municipal transit systems. Fifth's transformation from a company primarily engaged in the transportation business began in March, 1962, when the City of New York acquired by condemnation all the bus lines of Fifth within the City. Since that time, Fifth and the City have been litigating Fifth's claims for compensation for such taking. The City satisfied Fifth's claim with respect to physical assets in October, 1966, and only recently settled Fifth's claims with respect to going concern assets and other intangibles. From 1962 to 1966, however, Fifth had little to do except to litigate these claims and to resolve old tort claims remaining from its period as an operating company. The receipt in 1966 of an initial condemnation award of more than $11,500,000, free of all liabilities, consequently breathed new life into Fifth.

After the City had taken Fifth's operating assets, a group composed of Krock, Muscat and Robert L. Huffines, Jr., acquired control of Fifth through a pyramid of interlocking shareholdings at the peak of which rested Defiance Industries, Inc. (Defiance). In 1966, Defiance had only one class of stock outstanding, consisting of 892,894 shares of common stock. Of this total, Muscat owned about 27% And Huffines about 9%. Huffines sold his Defiance stock to William P. Ruffa, an attorney in the firm of Saxe, Bacon & Bolan, to which Cohn is 'of counsel.' Ruffa, however, acted merely as nominee for the stock which was owned by Muscat and Cohn. As of December 12, 1966, Cohn owned 7% Of Defiance, Bolan and Krock each owned 1%, and Muscat 27%, totaling for this control group 36% Of Defiance's stock.

Defiance, in turn, owned about 32% Of BSF Company, a registered investment company. BSF owned 20% Of Gray Line, an inactive corporation. BSF also owned 9% Of Fifth, and Gray Line owned 23% Of Fifth, the only substantial asset of Gray Line. Surface Transit, Inc., a wholly-owned subsidiary of Fifth, owned 33% Of Gray Line and Fifth itself owned 45% Of Gray Line. Thus, in this circle, BSF, Fifth and Surface together owned 98% Of Gray Line, while BSF and Gray Line owned 32% Of Fifth. The remainder of Fifth's stock, however, was owned by about 2,000 public shareholders. Further control over BSF was obtained by Cohn and Bolan through the purchase of 18,735 shares of BSF stock on July 6, 1966, Cohn taking 16,735 shares and Bolan 2,000 shares. Moreover, when Fifth received its condemnation award from the City, it purchased about 3.4% Of Defiance's stock. There were several other companies which eventually touched Fifth in the pyramid topped by Defiance, but the above describes the basic skeleton.

In addition to being officers and directors of many of the other companies in the group, Muscat, Bolan, and Krock formed the executive committee of Fifth's Board of Directors. Muscat was president of the company, Bolan was secretary, and Krock the treasurer. Others on the ten-man board of directors included Krock's personal physician, Krock's son-in-law, who was a director of BSF and American Steel and Pump Corp. (57% Owned by BSF), and a vice president and controller of American Steel. Saxe, Bacon & Bolan were general counsel for most of the companies in the group including Fifth. Cohn was neither an officer nor director of any of the companies, but the District Court found him to be an active participant in controlling the affairs of Fifth and Defiance.

In a letter dated July 28, 1966, accompanying Fifth's annual report to its shareholders for 1965, Muscat (as president of the company) stated that as soon as the condemnation award was paid by the City, 'the Company intends to make proper and advantageous investments for the benefit of the Company.' The annual meeting was held on August 10, 1966, and Cohn there read another letter from Muscat to the shareholders stating in part:

> 'There are bargains available today in the form of investments in transportation, in related fields, and in brand new fields—bargains which others cannot take advantage of because they do not have the cash available.

> 'We have been actively exploring several of these opportunities and we will be ready to move forward boldly when the funds are paid over to us.

> 'We have waited more than four years. But we will be in a position to put the money to work profitably for you as soon as it is received.'

Cohn then rejected a proposal made by Lewis Gilbert, an active shareholder in many companies, that the proceeds of the condemnation award be immediately distributed to Fifth's shareholders.

When the $11.5 million condemnation funds were received from the City in October, 1966, Fifth immediately began its investing program, purchasing within a month stock in Wilson Brothers, Standard Packaging, Horn & Hardart, Defiance Industries, American Steel and Pump, Republic Corporation and others. In December, Fifth made the first of several tender offers for the stock of Austin, Nichols & Company. By December 31, 1966, Fifth had placed more than $8 million of its $11.5 million either in stocks or time deposits, some of the above investments having been sold and others purchased. Further investments and trading reduced available cash to $843,000 by June 30, 1967.

The District Court found that as of June 30, 1967, Fifth had become an investment company within the meaning of § 3(a)(1) of the 1940 Act. Fifth contends it was not engaged in the business of investing or trading in securities, but was seeking ventures in which to purchase control for the purpose of operating companies. Judge McLean found that while Fifth's intention may have been as stated, Fifth was 'markedly unsuccessful in carrying out that policy' (having gained control only of Mercantile National Bank of Chicago), and that by June 30 'the only business that it can fairly be found to be primarily engaged in was the business of investing in securities.' The District Court did not find Fifth to be an investment company at an earlier date because Judge McLean thought 'a company which has suddenly come into possession of a substantial amount of cash is entitled to a reasonable time to decide what to do with it without violating the Investment Company Act.'

Professor Louis Loss has noted that 'the problems of the (investment company) industry flow from the very nature of the assets of investment companies. Because those assets are usually liquid and readily negotiable, control of the companies' large funds of cash and securities (offer) many opportunities for exploitation by unscrupulous management.'

Pursuant to § 30 of the Public Utility Holding Company Act of 1935, 15 U.S.C. § 79z–4, the SEC made a four-year study, completed in 1941, of investment companies. In Part One of its Report, the SEC undertook to classify investment companies-to distinguish between companies owning securities in other corporations and those in the business of investing in other corporations. SEC, Report on the Study of Investment Trusts and Investment Companies, Part One, H.R.Doc. No. 707, 75th Cong., 3rd Sess. (1938). See especially pp. 15–20, 22–29. The first group of companies includes those with holdings primarily in wholly-owned or non-wholly-owned subsidiaries (defined as companies owned 50% or more). The business of such companies may be considered to be the same as that of their subsidiaries, and the SEC excluded such companies from the scope of its study. On the other hand, companies with investments primarily in diversified securities or corporations in which they have working control (defined as ownership of 10% To 50% Of the outstanding voting power) were found to be part of the industry needing regulation. Where this line between the management of subsidiaries (the characteristic mode of operation of 'conglomerate' corporations), and the control of other companies becomes hazy, the Report suggested an analysis of other factors, including the degree of integration or non-integration of the company and its affiliates, the volume of trading by the company in its portfolio securities, the frequency of shifts in portfolio securities, and the representations made to the public or its shareholders regarding the nature of its business. The Report examined in detail the activities and abuses of such 'quasi-holding' companies, and revealed the same type of abuses which were found to have occurred in the management of Fifth.

Fifth argues that from the time it received the proceeds of the condemnation award from the City, it was endeavoring to gain operating control of companies—to become a conglomerate—and that it therefore should not be denominated an investment company. However, when Fifth's statements to its shareholders are viewed against the backdrop of Fifth's actual securities trading and Judge McLean's findings that 'Fifth never came close to achieving that objective' (gaining control of Austin, Nichols), and that 'Fifth has been markedly unsuccessful in carrying out * * * (its) policy' of obtaining control of other companies, Fifth's activities come within the ambit of § 3(a)(1) of the Act.

From an historical viewpoint, there is nothing surprising about considering Fifth to be an investment company. The transformation of an industrial company into an investment company, which occurred with Fifth, was anticipated by events preceding the enactment of the 1940 Act. For example the Adams Express Company controlled large portions of the nation's express forwarding business before World War I. The United States Government, however, after entering the War, took over all express business in the country and placed it in the American Railway Express Company, an entity formed by the Government. As a result of this transaction—somewhat analogous to the taking of Fifth's business by New York City—Adams Express became an investment-holding company, rather than an operating company. * * *

Accordingly, the order of the District Court will be affirmed.

NOTES

1. The Investment Company Act creates a presumption that a company holding investment securities in excess of forty percent of its total non-cash and government securities asset value is an investment company. SEC v. S & P National Corp., 360 F.2d 741, 746 (2d Cir.1966).

2. There are a number of exemptions from the registration and other requirements of the Investment Company Act including broker-dealers, banks and insurance companies. 5 Thomas Lee Hazen, The Law of Securities Regulation § 20.4 (5th ed. 2005). Berkshire Hathaway, the investment fund headed by Warren Buffett, perhaps America's most famous investor, engages in a broad range of investment activities. Had it been required to register as an investment company, its decidedly non-independent board composed of Buffett family members and his lawyer and co-investors,[5] would have to be restructured and its operations modified or terminated. "Berkshire Hathaway escapes the 1940 Act only by folding its strategic investment activities into an

5. Arthur Levitt, Take On the Street, What Wall Street and Corporate America Don't Want You to Know, What You Can Do to Fight Back 210 (2002). Buffett has himself been critical of the sometimes too cozy relationships on other boards of directors. Andrew Hill, Buffett Urges Tighter Boardroom Supervision, Financial Times, March 10, 2003, at 1. The Berkshire Hathaway board was restructured to add a majority of independent directors after the Enron and other scandals resulted in such a mandate from securities self-regulatory bodies.

insurance subsidiary, and exploiting Nebraska's permissive insurance statute in a fashion that no other company can be expected to duplicate." Ronald J. Gilson & Reinier Kraakman, Investment Companies as Guardian Shareholders: The Place of the MISC in the Corporate Governance Debate, 45 Stan. L. Rev. 985, 1003 (1993). The Investment Company Act thus exempts insurance companies from its provisions even though they engage in a broad range of investment activities for their reserves. 15 U.S.C. § 80a–2(a)(17). Do you think that Berkshire Hathaway should be exempted from that statute? Does its exemption suggest that the market rather than statutes govern investment success?

SECTION 3. HEDGE FUNDS

A REPORT TO CONGRESS IN ACCORDANCE WITH § 356(C) OF THE UNITING AND STRENGTHENING AMERICA BY PROVIDING APPROPRIATE TOOLS REQUIRED TO INTERCEPT AND OBSTRUCT TERRORISM ACT OF 2001 (USA PATRIOT ACT)

Secretary of the Treasury, Federal Reserve Board, Securities and Exchange Commission and Commodity Futures Trading Commission (December 31, 2002).

The term "hedge fund" refers generally to a privately offered investment vehicle that pools the contributions of its investors in order to invest in a variety of asset classes, such as securities, futures contracts, options, bonds, and currencies. A precise figure for the size of the hedge fund industry, in terms of the number of funds and the total value of assets managed, is unavailable because no official reporting organization exists for hedge funds. As of the last quarter of 2001, however, it was estimated that there were between 4,000 and 5,000 hedge funds worldwide that managed between $400 and $500 billion in capital. Although the hedge fund industry remains small in relation to the mutual fund industry, investment in hedge funds is growing (peaking in 2008 with some $2.5 trillion under management).

Hedge funds domiciled in the United States are usually organized as limited partnerships or limited liability companies. The sponsor/general partner/manager usually holds an interest in the fund along with investors/limited partners/members, who are, in most circumstances, either wealthy individuals or institutions such as savings associations, broker-dealers, investment companies, and employee benefit plans. Further, hedge funds do not engage in "public offerings" of the interests in the funds. The sponsor often handles marketing and investor services, and often serves as the fund manager with responsibility for making decisions regarding operations and investment strategy. A hedge fund also may retain an investment adviser or multiple advisers. It is not uncommon, however, for the sponsor, manager, and investment adviser(s) to be either the same legal entity or separate legal entities that might be owned by the sponsor. A typical hedge fund is similar to a mutual fund in that it maintains several contractual relationships that are integral to the operation of the hedge fund, including relationships with prime brokers, executing brokers, custodians, administrators, placement agents, registrars and transfer agents.

For various reasons arising from tax, administrative, and regulatory concerns, hedge funds often are established under U.S. law as partnerships ("U.S. domestic hedge funds") or as corporations in a foreign jurisdiction ("U.S. hedge funds with an offshore related fund"). Hedge funds that are offered to U.S. investors tend to be structured in ways to address the needs of either tax-exempt investors or taxable investors. U.S. domestic hedge funds are usually in the form of limited partnerships to accommodate taxable U.S. investors. Partnerships provide favorable tax treatment for individual investors because the partnership's income is taxed only at the level of the individual investors in the partnership, as opposed to a corporation's income that is taxed at both the entity and individual investors' levels. In contrast, some U.S. hedge funds with an offshore related fund accommodate tax-exempt U.S. investors, such as pension funds and university endowments, and non-U.S. investors.

Generally, all hedge funds require investors to complete subscription agreements that detail the investors' identity, domicile, and net worth, among other information. The investor then returns the subscription agreement to the hedge fund manager or administrator and forwards his initial investment to the hedge fund's account with its custodian or its prime broker. For the redemption of investment assets, U.S. domestic hedge funds usually rely on their custodian or prime broker to forward assets from the hedge fund's account to the investor's account. A U.S. hedge fund with an offshore related fund generally processes a redemption through its fund administrator, which sends the redeemed investment to the investor's bank account identified in the subscription documents. A typical hedge fund often has a one-year "lock-up" period from the date of investment, during which the investor cannot redeem his investment. Once the initial lock-up period is over, the right of an investor to redeem is governed by the partnership agreement. Most investors may demand a redemption during a set period that occurs on a quarterly, semi-annual, or annual basis. There is no formal domestic secondary market for hedge fund shares, but a few hedge funds have made public offerings.

Alfred Winslow Jones is credited with the creation of the modern hedge fund concept through his company A.W. Jones & Co. that was founded in 1949. That hedge fund made gains of over 1000 percent in a ten-year period. As manager, he received twenty percent of profits, the rest going to the investors. These gains and the featuring of his hedge fund in a *Fortune* magazine article in 1966 spurred others to mimic his success. Within three years, some 150 hedge funds were managing $1 billion in customer funds. Their number would increase to 800 by 1994, and funds under management rose to $75 billion. Included among the investors in these hedge funds were several university endowment funds. Minimum investments ranged from $250,000 to $5 million.

Hedge funds were initially excluded from registration under the Investment Company Act of 1940 under a provision in that statute that exempted from regulation investment companies with less than 100 investors. 15 U.S.C. § 80–a3(c)(1). An additional exemption was added in 1996 that allowed inclusion of an unlimited number of "qualified purchasers," *i.e.*, wealthy, sophisticated individuals (e.g., an individual with more than $5 million in investments) and institutions. 15 U.S.C. § 80–a3(c)(7).

Hedge funds are high-risk, highly-leveraged investment pools. Gains made by hedge funds and their managers became legendary. One such manager, Paul Tudor Jones, made nearly $100 million in 1987. George Soros was among those espying the advantages of hedge funds. His hedge funds would grow large enough to move entire markets. In one famous event that occurred in 1992, Soros sold the British pound short to the tune of $10 billion. His hedge fund made profits of $2 billion and drove Great Britain out of a stabilization agreement with other European nations that was then seeking to create a common currency—the euro. Michael T. Kaufman, Soros, The Life and Times of a Messianic Billionaire (2002).

Tales of success turned to legendary losses in 1998 as markets turned volatile. George Soros lost large amounts in his hedge funds after the Russian government defaulted on obligations in which he had invested. Soros had to shut down one of the hedge funds he managed. He was also later indicted and found guilty of insider trading in France for hedge fund activities in that country. Another hedge Fund, Tiger Management, lost $2 billion in a single day from currency trading. Although it managed to make money for the year, this hedge fund complex suffered losses in later years and was liquidated in 2000.

A more spectacular failure involved a hedge fund complex named Long Term Capital Management ("LTCM"). This hedge fund's market analysts included twenty-five economists with Ph.Ds, two Nobel prize winners in economics and the former vice chairman of the Federal Reserve Board. LTCM was headed by John Meriwether. He had been forced previously to leave Salomon Brothers after a scandal involving the rigging of the Treasury market by a trader at that firm. See chapter 9. Meriwether was a gambler extraordinaire, having once proposed a bet with John Gutfreund at Salomon Brothers in a game of Liar's Poker for $10 million: "One Hand," "No tears." Michael Lewis, Liar's Poker: Rising Through the Wreckage on Wall Street (1989). LTCM was an even bigger bet, using large amounts of borrowed funds to gain leverage and engaging in complex and high risk trading strategies such as "convergence" trading.

In one strategy, LTCM borrowed Brady bonds (described in chapter 9) sold them short and then bought the non-Brady bond debt of the same country. LTCM was anticipating a change of the price spread between those two different forms of bonds. LTCM also engaged in "total return" swaps in which it agreed to pay an institutional investor a fixed interest rate on the amount required to buy a block of stock. In return, the institution agreed to pay LTCM the amount of any dividends paid on the designated block of stock. LTCM and the investor further agreed that LTCM would pay the investor for the amount of any decreases in market value of the block, and the investor paid LTCM the amount of any increases.

LAKONIA MANAGEMENT LTD. v. MERIWETHER

106 F.Supp.2d 540 (S.D.N.Y.2000).

SCHEINDLIN, DISTRICT JUDGE.

This action arises out of the near-collapse in September 1998 of the initially heralded, and now infamous, Long Term Capital Hedge Funds (the "LTC Funds" or "Funds"). Plaintiff Lakonia Management Limited ("Lakonia") is a former investor in the Funds. Plaintiff alleges that defendants—individuals, partnerships and corporations associated with the Funds—violated sections 1962(b) and 1962(d) of the Racketeer Influenced and Corrupt Organizations Act ("RICO"), 18 U.S.C. § 1962(b), (d), by engaging in a fraudulent scheme to gain control of the Funds and to "squeeze out" plaintiff and other investors for insufficient consideration. In addition to its federal RICO claims, plaintiff asserts related state law claims for breach of fiduciary duty. * * *

Defendant Meriwether is a recognized expert in sophisticated investment strategies. In 1993, Meriwether, joined by a group of nine similarly renowned financiers, started the LTC Funds.[6]

The Funds were composed of various domestic and foreign corporate entities. These entities operated through a bi-level master fund/feeder fund structure as follows. Investors purchased shares in one of several feeder funds. The feeder funds in turn invested substantially all of their assets in a single master fund—defendant LTC Portfolio—which utilized the capital to make sophisticated and highly-leveraged investments.[7]

Defendant LTC Management, a Delaware limited partnership, served as investment manager of LTC Portfolio. As investment manager, LTC Management had complete investment authority over the assets of LTC Portfolio. Meriwether and his nine colleagues were limited partners and

---

6. The group of nine comprised Victor J. Haghani, Gregory Hawkins, Lawrence Hilibrand, William Krasker, Richard F. Leahy, James J. McEntee, Robert C. Merton, Eric Rosenfeld and Myron S. Scholes.

7. The stated investment objective of LTC Portfolio was:

"to maximize the expected total return on its portfolio on a risk-adjusted basis.... by employing sophisticated analytical models and by undertaking complex proprietary trading strategies on a leveraged basis, primarily in fixed-income securities denominated in any currencies and associated derivative instruments such as warrants, options, forward contracts, futures contracts and customized contractual agreements."

principals of LTC Management. Thus, Meriwether and his colleagues (collectively, the "Principals") effectively controlled the investment of LTC Portfolio's assets.

Defendant LTC V, a Cayman Islands limited liability company, was one of the several feeder funds that invested in LTC Portfolio. Only those investors with a net worth of $10 million or greater were eligible to purchase shares in LTC V. Meriwether was a director of LTC V.

Prior to the events of September 1998 which are described in detail below, the Bank Defendants were primarily creditors of the LTC Funds. The Funds' investment strategy was based upon extensive use of borrowed funds and other forms of leverage. The Bank Defendants provided the financing necessary to pursue such a strategy on terms highly favorable to the Funds.

For example, according to the Complaint, creditors typically require debtors to post collateral worth slightly more than the amount loaned. This extra collateral is known as a "haircut." Plaintiff alleges that, on many occasions, the Bank Defendants loaned money to the Funds without requiring the Funds to provide "haircuts".

In addition to their role as creditors, the Bank Defendants sometimes acted as counterparties for the Funds in derivative contracts such as futures, swaps and options. And, one of the Bank Defendants—Merrill Lynch—invested $22 million in the Funds through a deferred compensation plan. Finally, the Complaint alleges that the Bank Defendants "competed" with the Funds because those defendants "were, and are, heavily involved in financial markets as brokers for customers, as traders for their own proprietary accounts and/or as market makers for various securities also traded by [the Funds]."

In 1994, plaintiff Lakonia invested $50,039,887 in LTC V through a private offering of LTC V securities. The Offering Memorandum for those securities made clear that investment in LTC V was a high-risk financial venture and warned potential purchasers that returns would be both volatile and uncertain. Specifically, the Offering Memorandum stated:

Investment in [LTC V] entails a high degree of risk and is suitable only for sophisticated investors for whom an investment in [LTC V] does not represent a complete investment program and who fully understand and are capable of bearing the risks of an investment in [LTC V].... There can be no assurance that [LTC Portfolio] will be able to achieve its investment objective or that investors will receive a return of their capital, and investment results may vary substantially on a quarterly or annual basis.

The Offering Memorandum informed prospective purchasers that shares of LTC V were not registered under domestic or foreign securities laws, and that there was no public market for shares of LTC V. In addition, the Offering Memorandum stated that LTC V had authority to mandatorily redeem "all or any part of a Shareholder's Shares at any time and for any reason, in its sole and absolute discretion." Any mandatory redemption would be at the then-current net asset value per share. Finally, the Offering Memorandum disclosed that the Principals would initially invest an aggregate of at least $100 million in LTC Portfolio—as distinct from LTC V.

Pursuant to its investment strategy, LTC Management leveraged the assets of LTC Portfolio, taking on "huge" amounts of debt. For example, in 1996, LTC Portfolio's leverage ratio was approximately 30 to 1. That is, LTC Portfolio carried $30 of debt for every $1 of available capital.

From late winter 1994 through spring 1998, LTC Management's strategy worked well. Investors earned profits of 20% in 1994; 43% in 1995; 41% in 1996 and 17% in 1997. By fall 1997, the reported capital of LTC Portfolio was approximately $7 billion. Similarly, by November 30, 1997, the value of Lakonia's investment in LTC V had increased from $50,039,887 to $137,931,042—a profit of $87,891,155.

In December 1997, after determining that $7 billion was too much capital for the available investment opportunities, the Funds redeemed $2.5 billion worth of shares to investors. Pursuant to this mandatory redemption, Lakonia received $55,571,546—the full amount of its original investment plus approximately $5.5 million. Following the mandatory redemption, Lakonia retained a substantial investment in LTC V. On July 31, 1998, the value of Lakonia's remaining investment was $72,768,929.

On August 17, 1998, Russia devalued the ruble and declared a debt moratorium. Russia's actions precipitated an international financial crisis. Among other things, the Russian debt moratorium sparked a "flight to quality" by investors; that is, investors sought safe, high-quality investments and avoided risk. The Complaint alleges that this flight to quality caused:

> credit risk spreads and liquidity premiums [to rise] sharply in markets around the world. The size, persistence, and pervasiveness of the widening of risk spreads represented an extreme deviation from the risk management models employed by the [LTC Funds], which were based on assumptions that did not take into account such dramatic circumstances but rather were historical in nature. As a result, the [LTC Funds] (and other market participants) suffered losses in individual markets that greatly exceeded what conventional (so called value at risk) models, estimated during more stable periods, suggested were probable.

The flight to quality "also resulted in a substantial reduction in the liquidity of many markets, which made it difficult for the [LTC Funds] to reduce exposure quickly without incurring further ('fire sale') losses—particularly given the large positions it held in certain markets." At the same time, the Funds were finding it difficult to raise capital or to obtain additional financing. By the end of August 1998, LTC Portfolio's available capital was $2.3 billion compared to $4.7 billion in December 1997—a loss of equity totaling more than fifty percent.

In early September 1998, the Bank Defendants modified their previously favorable credit arrangements with the Funds. For example, the Complaint charges that "certain Bank Defendants required [LTC Portfolio] to collateralize not only current but future risk." Other Bank Defendants, in their role as counterparties to LTC Portfolio in derivative contracts, sought "as much collateral as possible from the [F]unds through the daily margining process, refusing previously extended intra day credits and in many cases seeking to apply possible liquidation values to market-to-market valuations." In plain language, the Bank Defendants effectively raised the margin percentage requirements imposed on the Funds, further straining the Funds' available cash flow.

Faced with the possibility that they would be unable to meet margin and collateral payments due at the end of September, the Funds employed defendant Goldman Sachs to find investors willing to infuse the failing venture with additional capital. On September 18, 1998, after trying unsuccessfully to raise additional capital for the Funds, Goldman Sachs telephoned William J. McDonough, President of the Federal Reserve Bank of New York (the "Federal Reserve"). Goldman Sachs informed McDonough that the Funds were "in dire straits, such that they might not be able to continue operations the following week." Two days later, representatives from the Federal Reserve and the Treasury traveled to the Connecticut offices of LTC Management to review the Funds' books and records. According to the Complaint, the government representatives were "shocked by the volume in off-balance sheet trading activity" which "far exceeded the on-balance sheet assets of the [F]unds and massively exceeded the [F]unds remaining capital."

By September 21, the Funds' liquidity situation had deteriorated further. That evening, defendants Goldman Sachs, J.P. Morgan and Merrill Lynch met with Peter Fisher of the Federal Reserve to discuss various options for salvaging the Funds. The meeting continued the following day with the added participation of President McDonough and defendant UBS AG.

The group of commercial banks and government representatives focused primarily on a salvage option called the "consortium approach." Under the consortium approach, a group of the Funds' major creditors—namely, the thirteen Bank Defendants—would recapitalize LTC Portfolio by investing $3.6 billion in a newly created feeder fund and a newly created limited liability company (collectively, the "New Funds"). The New Funds would then invest their combined $3.6 billion in LTC Portfolio in exchange for (i) a 90% interest in the assets of LTC Portfolio; and (ii) operational control of LTC Management. The original investors in LTC Portfolio would retain an aggregate 10% interest in the master fund.

On September 23, Warren Buffet, American International Group and Goldman Sachs contacted McDonough and made a joint offer to purchase 100% of the Funds for $250 million in cash (the "Buffet Offer"). Pursuant to the Buffet Offer, the original investors in LTC Portfolio would no longer have any equity interest in the master fund. Instead, the original investors, and in turn their shareholders, would receive an aggregate cash-out payment of $250 million. Meanwhile, the Funds' new owners—Buffet, American International Group and Goldman Sachs—would infuse LTC Portfolio with $4 billion and then "gradually liquidate at what Buffet thought could be a decent profit." Buffet requested that the Funds respond to his Offer within 1.5 hours.

McDonough contacted Meriwether via telephone and informed him of the Buffet Offer. Meriwether told McDonough that the Buffet Offer was not feasible because Meriwether did not have authority to sell 100% of the Funds. However, Meriwether did not obtain an independent legal opinion regarding his ability to sell 100% of the Funds. Nor did Meriwether (i) attempt to negotiate the terms of the Buffet Offer; (ii) contact the other Principals to discuss the Buffet Offer; or (iii) conduct due diligence for purposes of comparing the Buffet Offer with the consortium approach.

One day later, on September 24, the Bank Defendants formalized their consortium offer and collectively invested $3.6 billion in the New Funds as described above. The New Funds in turn invested $3.6 billion in LTC Portfolio in exchange for a 90% equity stake in LTC Portfolio and operational control of LTC Management. The remaining 10% equity stake was held by the original investors in LTC Portfolio, including LTC V.

Following the Bank Defendants' recapitalization, the financial health of the Funds greatly improved. By February 26, 1999, LTC Portfolio had earned returns of more than 20%. By March 30, 1999, the Funds' risk dropped by more than 50%, and the value of LTC Portfolio's assets increased to $5 billion. The Bank Defendants announced that, as a result of the reduction in risk and an increase in the value of LTC Portfolio's net assets, they anticipated returning some capital to investors during the second half of 1999.

In a letter dated June 17, 1999, Meriwether notified plaintiff and "the original 1994 investors" that their shares would be mandatorily redeemed "in the near future." On July 6, 1999, the "Funds eliminated the interests of all of its outside investors, including the plaintiff, by redeeming their interests with a $300 million redemption payment." Pursuant to the redemption, Lakonia received $8,157,379.[8] Thus, Lakonia ultimately recouped $63,728,925—a 27% return on its original investment of $50,039,887. Also on July 6, the Funds made a $1 billion payment to the Bank Defendants. The payment represented a return of 27.5% of the Bank Defendants' $3.6 billion investment in the Funds.

On July 13, exactly one week after the redemption, plaintiff filed its initial complaint. Plaintiff filed its Amended Complaint on November 3, 1999.

---

8. By way of comparison, Lakonia's investment had a value of $72,768,929 on July 31, 1998. By October 31, 1998—one month after the Bank Defendants' recapitalization—the value of Lakonia's investment had dropped to $6,693,747. Presumably, the value of Lakonia's investment was even lower in August and September 1998. However, plaintiff does not provide that figure.

The gravamen of the Complaint is that, under the guise of salvaging the distressed Funds, the Bank Defendants conspired with each other and with Meriwether to gain control of the Funds and to eliminate plaintiff and other shareholders for a fraction of the value they would have otherwise received. * * *

Despite the complexity of the events and financial transactions underlying this litigation, resolution of the pending motions is relatively straightforward. * * * [Plaintiff claims] that defendants "usurped 90% of plaintiff's equity interest in [the Funds] at a grossly deficient price, and subsequently took the rest." No matter how inflammatory the language plaintiff chooses to use, it cannot transform what is, in essence, a challenge to the substantive fairness of the Bank Defendants' recapitalization. The Bank Defendants did not "usurp", steal or swindle 90% of LTC Portfolio's equity interests. Rather, it paid for those interests with $3.6 billion of much-needed capital. Absent even the hint of any other dishonest or deceitful conduct, the mere fact that plaintiff believes the Bank Defendants should have paid more cannot and does not constitute fraud. * * *

THE PENSION COMMITTEE OF THE UNIVERSITY OF MONTREAL PENSION PLAN v. BANC OF AMERICA SECURITIES, LLC

568 F.3d 374 (2d Cir. 2009).

LEVAL, CIRCUIT JUDGE.

Plaintiffs appeal from the judgment of the United States District Court for the Southern District of New York dismissing their claims against Banc of America Securities LLC ("BAS"), without leave to replead, for failure to state a claim upon which relief may be granted. Plaintiffs were investors in two hedge funds based in the British Virgin Islands, Lancer Offshore, Inc. and OmniFund Ltd. ("the Funds"). They brought this action to recover losses they suffered on the liquidation of the Funds. Plaintiffs alleged that their losses resulted from frauds committed by Michael Lauer, who managed the Funds through Lancer Management Group, LLC ("Lancer Management").

Plaintiffs' claims against BAS allege that, in its role as the prime broker for the Funds, BAS aided and abetted the frauds and breaches of fiduciary duty committed by Lauer and Lancer Management. The district court dismissed the claims, ruling that Plaintiffs failed to satisfy their burden of pleading proximate causation for their losses. We disagree. The complaint includes allegations that BAS knowingly and substantially assisted Lauer and Lancer Management in deceiving Plaintiffs as to the net asset values of the Funds by falsifying the values of the Funds' holdings on Position Reports, which BAS knew would be relied upon by the Funds' auditor and administrators in calculating and verifying the

Funds' net asset values ("NAVs"). It alleges further that the Plaintiffs "reasonably relied upon the [false] representations regarding the Funds' NAVs [net asset values] ... in deciding to invest in and/or remain invested in the Funds," and that the falsely inflated net asset values were used to justify the payment of fees to Lauer, Lancer Management, and others, which drained the assets of the Funds. In our view, the complaint sufficiently pleaded that BAS's actions proximately caused the Plaintiffs' losses. * * *

Lauer was the founder, manager and sole shareholder of Lancer Management, which was the Funds' investment manager. Lauer and Lancer Management were responsible for all investment decisions for the Funds. Lancer Management managed the Funds in exchange for fees, which were based on the Funds' NAVs. Lauer and Lancer Management solicited investors in the Funds through personal contacts, third-party marketers or finders, and letters and other mailings, marketing materials, newsletters and private placement memoranda ("PPMs").

The PPMs represented that the majority of the Funds' assets would be invested in common stocks traded on the New York Stock Exchange, the American Stock Exchange or in the U.S. over-the-counter market. However, Lauer and Lancer Management caused the Funds to pursue an increasingly risky strategy, investing the Funds' assets in restricted (and thus not freely marketable) shares, warrants, and non-equity investments of a small number of "micro-cap and small-cap companies ... many of [which] were not publicly traded at all." The majority of the securities in which the Funds invested were not listed on any exchange and were quoted, if at all, on the Over-the-Counter Bulletin Board and/or pink sheets.

The PPMs provided that the NAVs of the Funds would be determined based on the market values of the securities held by the Funds. Specifically, the PPMs provided that listed or quoted securities were to "be valued at their last sales price on the date of determination." The PPMs also provided that listed or quoted securities not sold on the date of determination as well as unlisted securities were to "be valued at the mean between the 'bid' and 'asked' prices" of the most recent date on which such prices were quoted, and if no quotes had been [made] in the past 15 business days, then at a valuation assigned by the Board of Directors. The PPMs also contained a caveat that, in the event the directors determined that the listed valuation method did not represent its market value, the directors would value the securities.

As early as March 2000, the Funds began losing money on a massive scale. To hide the Funds' losses and show increasing NAVs, Lauer and Lancer Management embarked on a scheme to manipulate and inflate their valuation of the securities held by the Funds to the extent of hundreds of millions of dollars: Lauer and Lancer Management purchased for the Funds substantial and sometimes controlling stakes in companies whose shares were thinly-traded on the open market. The Funds' purchases were made in private transactions; they did not involve free-trading common stock, but rather securities not traded on the open market. Prior to the end of the Funds' reporting periods, Lauer and Lancer Management would purchase small amounts of the unrestricted, free-trading stock of these companies in such a manner as to drive up the "market price" of those shares. They would then improperly assign these artificially inflated values to the Funds' restricted holdings, thereby generating the appearance of large paper profits, and triggering payment of larger fees to Lauer and Lancer Management.

These false inflated valuations were used in calculating the Funds' NAVs, and the false NAVs were disseminated to investors each month and used to prepare the Funds' audited financial statements. Lancer Offshore's annual reports for 2000, 2002, and 2003 also included fraudulent NAV figures. The fraudulent NAV statements and audit reports were intended to and did induce Plaintiffs to invest, and remain invested, in the Funds and to artificially and improperly inflate the Fund management, incentive, and administrative fees, thereby draining the Funds' remaining assets. * * *

As the Funds' prime broker, BAS cleared and settled trades, provided portfolio management services, and served as the central custodian for some of the securities held by the Funds. BAS received a commission on each of the trades it cleared and settled. Because Lancer Management executed a high volume of trades through BAS and therefore generated substantial commissions for the bank, BAS provided Lauer with substantial goods and services, such as funding construction of, paying rent on, and providing the infrastructure for Lancer Management's Park Avenue office space.

Each month, BAS prepared monthly account statements ("Account Statements"), which purported to reflect the value of the securities held in its custody on behalf of the Funds. In order to collect the valuation information needed to generate account information, BAS received an electronic data feed from one or more third-party data providers who, in turn, obtained market prices from various securities exchanges and market makers.

BAS also permitted Lauer and Lancer Management to access reports from its computer system through a website called www.primebroker.com. Upon request from Lauer and Lancer Management, BAS periodically posted reports generated by BAS's computer system on its website. Using logins and passwords provided by BAS, Lauer and Lancer Management were able to access the BAS website on a "read-only" basis and view, download and print various reports posted by BAS, including Position Reports, which purported to show the Funds' holdings and the values of those holdings. The Position Reports were the only documents in existence that listed and depicted the values of both the Fund positions in BAS's custody and those held "away" from BAS.

The Position Reports contained BAS's name at the top of each page. When downloaded and printed, the Position Reports contained no disclaimer or other marking to suggest that they were anything other than official documents prepared by BAS and bearing its imprimatur. BAS also gave the Funds' service providers access to the BAS website so that they could view, download, and print Position Reports for the Funds.

Lauer and Lancer Management used Letters of Authorization ("LOAs") both to instruct BAS to transfer money for the purchase of securities and to instruct BAS how to input valuations and other information about the securities in the Funds' portfolios. * * *

BAS, according to the allegations of the complaint, participated and directly assisted in Lauer and Lancer Management's fraud by presenting false values of the Funds' holdings on the Position Reports at the request of Lauer and Lancer Management with actual knowledge that the information being supplied by Lauer and Lancer Management was false and was being used to mislead investors about the Funds' condition and performance. The Position Reports misrepresented the values of the Funds' holdings in at least five ways: (1) they overvalued unregistered warrants; (2) they valued securities at values higher than the last quoted public price for the shares; (3) they reported unrealistic and misleading increases in the values of unregistered shares and unregistered warrants; (4) they depicted unregistered shares and warrants which could not be publicly traded as registered, free-trading shares; and (5) they valued unregistered shares at the last quoted public price for the registered shares (although their unmarketable status necessarily gave them a lower value than otherwise identical marketable shares). * * *

According to the allegations of the complaint, BAS had actual knowledge that the Position Reports would be relied upon by the Funds' auditor and administrators in calculating and verifying the Funds' NAVs because: (a) BAS knew that the Position Reports were the only reports reflecting the entirety of the Funds' holdings by depicting the values of the positions held both in the custody of BAS and away from BAS; (b) BAS knew that Lauer and Lancer Management were downloading and printing the Position Reports and providing them to third parties, including the Funds' auditor and administrators; and (c) BAS itself provided these parties with direct access to the BAS computer system for the purpose of allowing them to review, download, and print the Position Reports generated and posted there by BAS. BAS also had actual knowledge that investors and potential investors would receive the NAV statements and audits based on the falsified valuations and rely on them in making investment decisions.

Moreover, Lauer and Lancer Management managed the funds in exchange for receiving certain fees, which were based on the Funds' NAVs. The fraudulent inflation of the Funds' NAVs, which BAS assisted, was intended to, and did, artificially and improperly inflate the management, incentive, and administrative fees claimed by Lauer, Lancer Management, and others. As an experienced prime broker for hedge funds,

BAS knew the importance of portfolio valuations and NAV statements, and the ways that Lauer, Lancer Management, the Funds' auditors and administrators, investors, and potential investors would use them. * * *

Plaintiffs contend that the complaint sufficiently alleged proximate causation by setting forth that the investors' losses were the direct or reasonably foreseeable result of BAS's role in falsifying and disseminating the BAS reports that were used to prepare the NAV statements and audited financial statements on which the investors relied for financial decisions. We agree. The complaint did not contain merely "conclusory assertions." * * *

Specifically, the complaint pleads that, at the request of Lauer and Lancer Management, BAS placed false values of the Funds' holdings on the Position Reports, which contained BAS's name at the top of each page, without any disclaimer or other marking to suggest that they were anything other than official documents prepared by and bearing the imprimatur of BAS. The complaint provided specific examples of BAS's role in the fraud, involving BAS's participation in falsifying values for XtraCard warrants, Nu–D–Zine restricted shares, and a publicly traded stock (FFIRD). * * *

Whether the Plaintiffs will be able to prove the allegations set forth in the complaint is quite another matter. Since we are at the pleading stage, we need not resolve this question. Accepting all factual allegations in the complaint as true, and drawing all reasonable inferences from them in the Plaintiffs' favor, we must conclude that Plaintiffs have adequately pled that BAS aided and abetted frauds and breaches of fiduciary duty in a manner which proximately caused losses to the Plaintiffs.

For the reasons set forth above, the judgment of the district court is vacated and the case is remanded for further proceedings consistent with this opinion.

NOTES

1. In Gredd v. Bear, Stearns Securities Corp. (In re Manhattan Investment Fund Ltd.), 359 B.R. 510, 47 Bankr. Ct. Dec. 185 (Bkrtcy. S.D.N.Y. 2007), a bankruptcy judge ruled that funds received by a prime broker could be treated as voidable transfers where the prime broker was on inquiry notice that a hedge fund manager was reporting large gains when it was actually experiencing large losses in its accounts at the prime broker. A prime broker:

> clears and finances the trades of customers executed by other brokers at the customer's direction. The prime broker clears and executes the trades of the executing brokers for the customer. The customer maintains its funds and securities in an account with the prime broker. The executing brokers execute the trades in the name of the prime broker but for the benefit of the customer. The prime broker is responsible for margin

requirements for the customer. The prime broker provides financing and clearing for the customer's securities transactions wherever they are executed. This means that the customer does not need to maintain funds at numerous broker-dealers. Prime broker arrangements are particularly popular with hedge funds.

23A Jerry W. Markham & Thomas Lee Hazen, Broker–Dealer Operations Under Securities and Commodities Law: Financial Responsibilities, Credit Regulation, and Customer Protection, § 13:15 (2d ed. 2007).

2. The hedge fund is a prime example of the immutable rule of risk versus reward. The higher the risk, the higher the expected return and the greater the risk of loss. There is no way to change that equation, no matter how smart the investor.

3. Hedge funds were intended only for institutions and sophisticated wealthy investors that could understand and absorb the risks incurred by their managers. The large gains from these funds, however, attracted the interest of small investors, viewing their spectacular gains as offsetting the risk of loss. Small investors do not qualify for the exemption in the Investment Company Act ($5 million in investment assets) for participation in a hedge fund. Wall Street, however, found a way around that limitation. Registered investment companies did qualify for the exemption, allowing them to invest in the hedge funds and sell their own securities to retail investors. The NASD cautioned its members that sales of such investments must be carefully conducted. A determination should be made that each investor is suitable for such risks and the strategies and risks of the underlying hedge fund must be fully explained. NASD Notice to Members No. 0307 (Feb. 2003).

SEC and Hedge Funds

The SEC staff conducted a study of hedge funds and expressed concern with their unregulated status. The staff asserted that the lack of regulation prevented the SEC from monitoring the activities of these funds, resulting in a lack of uniform or prescribed disclosures to investors. Smaller investors were also being involved in these funds indirectly and problems were occurring. The staff recommended that hedge fund advisers be required to register with the SEC as investment advisors under the Investment Advisers Act of 1940. SEC Staff Report, The Implications of the Growth of Hedge Funds. (Sept. 29, 2003). The SEC then adopted an investment adviser registration requirement for hedge funds. That proposal aroused intense opposition, even though about half of the larger hedge funds were already registered as advisors. That registration requirement was adopted by a 3–2 vote of the Commission. 17 C.F.R. § 275.205–3. Excepted from the registration requirement were hedge funds that required clients to keep their funds invested in the hedge fund for at least two years, absent extraordinary circumstances. 17 C.F.R. § 275.203(b)(3)–1(d)(2).

The rule was challenged and the District of Columbia Court of Appeals set it aside, concluding that the SEC had acted in an arbitrary fashion in adopting it. Goldstein v. SEC, 451 F.3d 873 (D.C. Cir.2006). Several hundred hedge funds then deregistered as investment advisers, but some 2,000 hedge funds remained registered. Following that decision, the President's Working Group on Financial Markets concluded that the regulation of hedge funds should be left to market discipline. "Financial Regulation and the Invisible Hand," Remarks by Ben S. Bernanke, Chairman Federal Reserve Board, at the New York University Law School, New York, N.Y. (April 11, 2007). For a discussion of the regulation of hedge funds see Jerry W. Markham, Mutual Fund Scandals—A Comparative Analysis of the Role of Corporate Governance in the Regulation of Collective Investments, 3 Hastings Bus. L. J. 67, 99–121 (2006). The SEC, nevertheless, adopted an anti-fraud rule for hedge funds under the Investment Advisers Act of 1940. 17 C.F.R. § 275.206(4)–8.

The hedge funds came under renewed regulatory scrutiny and renewed demands for their regulation as investment advisers after the exposure of the largest ever financial fraud by Bernie Madoff whose hedge fund was actually a Ponzi scheme. Ironically, Madoff had registered as an investment adviser under the SEC hedge fund rule that was stricken by the D.C. Circuit. Unlike many hedge funds, Madoff did not withdraw that registration after the D.C. Circuit's decision. It also appeared that the SEC had blundered several times in failing to uncover the fraud during its audits of Madoff as an investment adviser. See Jerry W. Markham, A Financial History of the United States, From the Subprime Crisis to the Great Recession (2006–2009) 609–613 (2010). Nevertheless, the Dodd–Frank Dodd–Frank Wall Street Reform and Consumer Protection Act of 2010 required hedge fund managers to register with the SEC as investment advisers, if the assets they manage in the United States exceed $150 million. Registered hedge fund managers must keep books and records that disclose the amount of assets under management, the degree of leverage in the funds they manage, any side pocket arrangements giving some investors greater rights than others, and trading practices. The SEC was also authorized to make periodic and surprise examinations of registered hedge funds.

Private Equity

In 2007, hedge funds were estimated to have some 1.5 trillion under management in some 8,000 or more funds. This figure on funds under management may actually understate the buying power of hedge funds since they often trade with borrowed funds and highly leveraged instruments. The buying power of the hedge funds has been estimated to exceed that of mutual funds and private equity. The latter (private equity) is another growing phenomenon in finance.

Private equity does not have to worry about Sarbanes–Oxley and SEC regulations that have sapped executive time, resulted in enormous expense, driven foreign listings offshore and discouraged initial public offerings ("IPOs"). Many talented individuals were avoiding service on public company boards because of fears of liability. In light of Sarbanes–Oxley and ill thought out regulations, "who in their right mind would want to sit on a corporate board these days." Michael S. Malone, "The Pump-and-Dump Economy," Wall St. J., Dec. 21, 2006, at A16. Private equity firms are also raiding public companies and taking them private. "Going-private transactions have risen dramatically in recent years, topping 25 percent of public takeovers in the last three years." Interim Report of the Committee on Capital Markets Regulation X (Nov. 30, 2006). Over 2100 private equity buyouts were consummated in the first ten months of 2006 at $583 billion, up $138 billion from the prior 12 months. The total buyouts in 2006 reached $709.8 billion by year end. The NYSE experienced delistings valued at 38.8 billion in 2006 and Nasdaq had withdrawals valued at $11 billion. The value of companies going private trebled between 2004 and 2006. The value of initial public offerings in the United States in 2006 was less than one half that of the public companies that went private. That trend was expected to grow in 2007.

More capital was going into private equity funds than net flows into mutual funds in 2006. Private equity was accounting for more than 20 percent of acquisitions in the United States and Europe. Hedge funds and other private equity also supplied $27.7 billion in financing to public companies in 2006 through "PIPES" (private investments in public equity). Private equity groups now control vast enterprises. They include the Blackstone Group with $71 billion under management; the Carlyle Group with $47 billion; Bain Capital—$40 billion; Kohlberg Kravis Roberts—$30 billion—Texas Pacific Group—$30 billion and Cerberus Capital Management—$24 billion. Charles Duhigg, "Can Private Equity Build a Public Face?" N.Y. Times, Dec. 24, 2006, § 3, at 1, 4.

These private equity groups are intensely private and seek to prevent any public or regulatory scrutiny of their activities. That benefit makes them more nimble and exposes them to less regulatory costs, including the shareholder class action lawsuits that every public company must now endure. However, in a surprising turn around large private equity funds and hedge funds were themselves making public offerings of their own shares in 2007 in order reap the rewards of their investments. See Dennis K. Berman & Henny Sender, "KKR's IPO May Set Firm on Rugged Path," Wall St. J., July 5, 2007, at C1; James Politi et al., "Blackstone Founders to Collect $2.6 Billion," Fin. Times (London), June 12, 2007 at 1; and Michael J. de la Merced & Jenny Anderson, "Hedge Funds Continue Public Path", N.Y. Times, July 3, 2007, at C1. Lawmakers then began considering legislation that would tax away much of the private equity profits from such offerings. Francesco Guerrera et al., "Blackstone

Faces IPO Challenge in the Senate," Fin. Times (London), June 15, 2007, at 1.

The private equity buyout binge peaked in July 2007 as the credit crunch tightened and the subprime crisis began. Leveraged loans to private equity groups were an early victim of that credit crunch. Banks closed down their syndicated loan underwritings. Private equity deals virtually stopped in August 2007 as the credit crunch further tightened. Another effect of the credit crunch was to disrupt closings of acquisitions agreed to before the credit crunch. For example, Cerberus Capital Management walked away from a $6.6 billion takeover of United Rentals, an equipment leasing company. KKR and Goldman Sachs backed out of an agreement to purchase Harman International for $8 billion. Thomas H. Lee Partners and Bain Capital withdrew from a $19 billion purchase agreement for Clear Channel Communications. A consortium of six banks, which included Citigroup, Deutsche Bank and Wachovia backed out of a deal to provide nearly $20 billion in financing to those two private equity firms. See Jerry W. Markham, VI A Financial History of the United States: The Subprime Crisis (2006–2009) 249–276 (2011).

The difficulties experienced in the private equity market and concerns over hedge funds resulted in a provision in the Dodd–Frank Wall Street Reform and Consumer Protection Act of 2010 that generally bans banks from investing in or sponsoring private equity and hedge funds. There are, however, some exceptions, including one that permits banking entities to invest in aggregate up to three percent of their Tier 1 capital in such enterprises.

There is no technical distinction between hedge funds and private equity. Typically, however, hedge funds are usually short-term traders of financial instruments in one form or another, while private equity takes control and manage the companies they buy, often for extended periods of time.

SECTION 4. ROLE OF INVESTMENT ADVISORS

The Investment Company Act of 1940 seeks to assure that the investment advisers managing the portfolio of a mutual fund do not take advantage of investors. The Supreme Court explained why:

> The Court of Appeals correctly noted that Congress was concerned about the potential for abuse inherent in the structure of investment companies. A mutual fund is a pool of assets, consisting primarily of portfolio securities, and belonging to the individual investors holding shares in the fund. Congress was concerned because

> > "[m]utual funds, with rare exception, are not operated by their own employees. Most funds are formed, sold, and managed by

external organizations, [called 'investment advisers,'] that are separately owned and operated. . . .

The advisers select the funds' investments and operate their businesses. . . . Since a typical fund is organized by its investment adviser which provides it with almost all management services . . ., a mutual fund cannot, as a practical matter sever its relationship with the adviser. Therefore, the forces of arm's-length bargaining do not work in the mutual fund industry in the same manner as they do in other sectors of the American economy." S.Rep.No. 91–184, p. 5 (1969); U.S.Code Cong. & Admin.News 1910, pp. 4897, 4901.

As a consequence, "[t]he relationship between investment advisers and mutual funds is fraught with potential conflicts of interest," * * *

The cornerstone of the Investment Company Act's (ICA) effort to control conflicts of interest within mutual funds is the requirement that at least 40% of a fund's board be composed of independent outside directors. 15 U.S.C. § 80a–10(a). As originally enacted § 10 of the Act required that these 40% not be officers or employees of the company or "affiliated persons" of its adviser. In 1970, Congress amended the Act to strengthen further the independence of these directors adding the stricter requirement that the outside directors not be "interested persons." See 15 U.S.C. §§ 80a–10(a), 80a–2(a)(19). To these statutorily disinterested directors, the Act assigns a host of special responsibilities involving supervision of management and financial auditing. They have the duty to review and approve the contracts of the investment adviser and the principal underwriter, 15 U.S.C. § 80a–15(c); the responsibility to appoint other disinterested directors to fill vacancies resulting from the assignment of the advisory contracts, 15 U.S.C. § 80a–16(b); and are required to select the accountants who prepare the company's Securities and Exchange Commission financial filings, 15 U.S.C. § 80a–31(a).

Burks v. Lasker, 441 U.S. 471, 480–483, 99 S.Ct. 1831, 60 L.Ed.2d 404 (1979).

JONES v. HARRIS ASSOCIATES, L.P.

—— U.S. ——, 130 S.Ct. 1418, 176 L.Ed.2d 265 (2010)

JUSTICE ALITO delivered the opinion of the Court.

We consider in this case what a mutual fund shareholder must prove in order to show that a mutual fund investment adviser breached the "fiduciary duty with respect to the receipt of compensation for services" that is imposed by § 36(b) of the Investment Company Act of 1940, 15 U.S.C. § 80a–35(b) (hereinafter § 36(b)).

The Investment Company Act of 1940 (Act), 54 Stat. 789, 15 U.S.C. § 80a–1 *et seq.*, regulates investment companies, including mutual funds.

"A mutual fund is a pool of assets, consisting primarily of [a] portfolio [of] securities, and belonging to the individual investors holding shares in the fund." *Burks v. Lasker,* 441 U.S. 471, 480, 99 S.Ct. 1831, 60 L.Ed.2d 404 (1979). The following arrangements are typical. A separate entity called an investment adviser creates the mutual fund, which may have no employees of its own. The adviser selects the fund's directors, manages the fund's investments, and provides other services. See *id.,* at 481. Because of the relationship between a mutual fund and its investment adviser, the fund often " 'cannot, as a practical matter sever its relationship with the adviser. Therefore, the forces of arm's-length bargaining do not work in the mutual fund industry in the same manner as they do in other sectors of the American economy.' "*Ibid.* (quoting S.Rep. No. 91–184, p. 5 (1969) (hereinafter S. Rep.)).

"Congress adopted the [Investment Company Act of 1940] because of its concern with the potential for abuse inherent in the structure of investment companies." *Daily Income Fund,* 464 U.S., at 536, 104 S.Ct. 831 (internal quotation marks omitted). Recognizing that the relationship between a fund and its investment adviser was "fraught with potential conflicts of interest," the Act created protections for mutual fund shareholders. *Id.,* at 536–538, 104 S.Ct. 831 (internal quotation marks omitted); *Burks, supra,* at 482–483, 99 S.Ct. 1831. Among other things, the Act required that no more than 60 percent of a fund's directors could be affiliated with the adviser and that fees for investment advisers be approved by the directors and the shareholders of the fund. See §§ 10, 15(c), 54 Stat. 806, 813.

The growth of mutual funds in the 1950's and 1960's prompted studies of the 1940 Act's effectiveness in protecting investors. See *Daily Income Fund,* 464 U.S., at 537–538, 104 S.Ct. 831. Studies commissioned or authored by the Securities and Exchange Commission (SEC or Commission) identified problems relating to the independence of investment company boards and the compensation received by investment advisers. See *ibid.* In response to such concerns, Congress amended the Act in 1970 and bolstered shareholder protection in two primary ways.

First, the amendments strengthened the "cornerstone" of the Act's efforts to check conflicts of interest, the independence of mutual fund boards of directors, which negotiate and scrutinize adviser compensation. The amendments required that no more than 60 percent of a fund's directors be "persons who are interested persons," *e.g.,* that they have no interest in or affiliation with the investment adviser. 15 U.S.C. § 80a–10(a); § 80a–2(a)(19). These board members are given "a host of special responsibilities." *Burks,* 441 U.S., at 482–483, 99 S.Ct. 1831. In particular, they must "review and approve the contracts of the investment adviser" annually, *id.,* at 483, 99 S.Ct. 1831, and a majority of these directors must approve an adviser's compensation, 15 U.S.C. § 80a–15(c). Second, § 36(b), 84 Stat. 1429, of the Act imposed upon investment advisers a "fiduciary duty" with respect to compensation received from a mutual fund, 15 U.S.C. § 80a–35(b), and granted individual investors a private right of action for breach of that duty, *ibid.*

The "fiduciary duty" standard contained in § 36(b) represented a delicate compromise. Prior to the adoption of the 1970 amendments, shareholders challenging investment adviser fees under state law were required to meet "common-law standards of corporate waste, under which an unreasonable or unfair fee might be approved unless the court deemed it 'unconscionable' or 'shocking,' "and "security holders challenging adviser fees under the [Investment Company Act] itself had been required to prove gross abuse of trust." *Daily Income Fund,* 464 U.S., at 540, n. 12, 104 S.Ct. 831. Aiming to give shareholders a stronger remedy, the SEC proposed a provision that would have empowered the Commission to bring actions to challenge a fee that was not "reasonable" and to intervene in any similar action brought by or on behalf of an investment company. *Id.,* at 538, 104 S.Ct. 831. This approach was included in a bill that passed the House. H.R. 9510, 90th Cong., 1st Sess., § 8(d) (1967); see also S. 1659, 90th Cong., 1st Sess., § 8(d) (1967). Industry representatives, however, objected to this proposal, fearing that it "might in essence provide the Commission with ratemaking authority." *Daily Income Fund,* 464 U.S., at 538, 104 S.Ct. 831.

The provision that was ultimately enacted adopted "a different method of testing management compensation," *id.,* at 539, 104 S.Ct. 831 (quoting S.Rep., at 5 (internal quotation marks omitted)), that was more favorable to shareholders than the previously available remedies but that did not permit a compensation agreement to be reviewed in court for "reasonableness." This is the fiduciary duty standard in § 36(b).

Petitioners are shareholders in three different mutual funds managed by respondent Harris Associates L.P., an investment adviser. Petitioners filed this action in the Northern District of Illinois pursuant to § 36(b) seeking damages, an injunction, and rescission of advisory agreements between Harris Associates and the mutual funds. The complaint alleged that Harris Associates had violated § 36(b) by charging fees that were "disproportionate to the services rendered" and "not within the range of what would have been negotiated at arm's length in light of all the surrounding circumstances." App. 52.

The District Court granted summary judgment for Harris Associates. Applying the standard adopted in *Gartenberg v. Merrill Lynch Asset Management, Inc.,* 694 F.2d 923 (C.A.2 1982), the court concluded that petitioners had failed to raise a triable issue of fact as to "whether the fees charged . . . were so disproportionately large that they could not have been the result of arm's-length bargaining." App. to Pet. for Cert. 29a. The District Court assumed that it was relevant to compare the challenged fees with those that Harris Associates charged its other clients. *Id.,* at 30a. But in light of those comparisons as well as comparisons with fees charged by other investment advisers to similar mutual funds, the Court held that it could not reasonably be found that the challenged fees were outside the range that could have been the product of arm's-length bargaining. *Id.*, at 29a–32a.

A panel of the Seventh Circuit affirmed based on different reasoning, explicitly "disapprov[ing] the *Gartenberg* approach." 527 F.3d 627, 632 (2008). Looking to trust law, the panel noted that, while a trustee "owes an obligation of candor in negotiation," a trustee, at the time of the creation of a trust, "may negotiate in his own interest and accept what the settlor or governance institution agrees to pay." *Ibid.* (citing Restatement (Second) of Trusts § 242, and Comment *f*). The panel thus reasoned that "[a] fiduciary duty differs from rate regulation. A fiduciary must make full disclosure and play no tricks but is not subject to a cap on compensation." 527 F.3d, at 632. In the panel's view, the amount of an adviser's compensation would be relevant only if the compensation were "so unusual" as to give rise to an inference "that deceit must have occurred, or that the persons responsible for decision have abdicated." *Ibid.*

The panel argued that this understanding of § 36(b) is consistent with the forces operating in the contemporary mutual fund market. Noting that "[t]oday thousands of mutual funds compete," the panel concluded that "sophisticated investors" shop for the funds that produce the best overall results, "mov[e] their money elsewhere" when fees are "excessive in relation to the results," and thus "create a competitive pressure" that generally keeps fees low. *Id.*, at 633–634. The panel faulted *Gartenberg* on the ground that it "relies too little on markets." 527 F.3d, at 632. And the panel firmly rejected a comparison between the fees that Harris Associates charged to the funds and the fees that Harris Associates charged other types of clients, observing that "[d]ifferent clients call for different commitments of time" and that costs, such as research, that may benefit several categories of clients "make it hard to draw inferences from fee levels." *Id.*, at 634.

The Seventh Circuit denied rehearing en banc by an equally divided vote. 537 F.3d 728 (2008). The dissent from the denial of rehearing argued that the panel's rejection of *Gartenberg* was based "mainly on an economic analysis that is ripe for reexamination." 537 F.3d, at 730 (opinion of Posner, J.). Among other things, the dissent expressed concern that Harris Associates charged "its captive funds more than twice what it charges independent funds," and the dissent questioned whether high adviser fees actually drive investors away. *Id.*, at 731.

Since Congress amended the Investment Company Act in 1970, the mutual fund industry has experienced exponential growth. Assets under management increased from $38.2 billion in 1966 to over $9.6 trillion in 2008. The number of mutual fund investors grew from 3.5 million in 1965 to 92 million in 2008, and there are now more than 9,000 open-and closed-end funds.

During this time, the standard for an investment adviser's fiduciary duty has remained an open question in our Court, but, until the Seventh Circuit's decision below, something of a consensus had developed regarding the standard set forth over 25 years ago in *Gartenberg, supra.* The *Gartenberg* standard has been adopted by other federal courts, and "[t]he SEC's regulations have recognized, and formalized, *Gartenberg*-like factors." Brief for United States as *Amicus Curiae* 23. See 17 CFR § 240.14a–101, Sched. 14A, Item 22, para. (c)(11)(i) (2009); 69 Fed.Reg. 39801, n.31, 39807–39809 (2004). In the present case, both petitioners and respondent generally endorse the *Gartenberg* approach, although they disagree in some respects about its meaning.

In *Gartenberg,* the Second Circuit noted that Congress had not defined what it meant by a "fiduciary duty" with respect to compensation but concluded that "the test is essentially whether the fee schedule represents a charge within the range of what would have been negotiated at arm's-length in the light of all of the surrounding circumstances." 694 F.2d, at 928. The Second Circuit elaborated that, "[t]o be guilty of a violation of § 36(b), ... the adviser-manager must charge a fee that is so disproportionately large that it bears no reasonable relationship to the services rendered and could not have been the product of arm's-length bargaining." *Ibid.* "To make this determination," the Court stated, "all pertinent facts must be weighed," *id.,* at 929, and the Court specifically mentioned "the adviser-manager's cost in providing the service, ... the extent to which the adviser-manager realizes economies of scale as the fund grows larger, and the volume of orders which must be processed by the manager." *Id.,* at 930.[5] Observing that competition among advisers for the business of managing a fund may be "virtually non-existent," the Court rejected the suggestion that "the principal factor to be considered in evaluating a fee's fairness is the price charged by other similar advisers to funds managed by them," although the Court did not suggest that this factor could not be "taken into account." *Id.,* at 929. The Court likewise rejected the "argument that the lower fees charged by investment advisers to large pension funds should be used as a criterion for determining fair advisory fees for money market funds," since a "pension fund does not face the myriad of daily purchases and redemptions throughout the nation which must be handled by [a money market fund]." *Id.,* at 930, n. 3.[6]

The meaning of § 36(b)'s reference to "a fiduciary duty with respect to the receipt of compensation for services" is hardly pellucid, but based on the terms of that provision and the role that a shareholder action for breach of that duty plays in the overall structure of the Act, we conclude

---

5. Other factors cited by the *Gartenberg* court include (1) the nature and quality of the services provided to the fund and shareholders; (2) the profitability of the fund to the adviser; (3) any "fall-out financial benefits," those collateral benefits that accrue to the adviser because of its relationship with the mutual fund; (4) comparative fee structure (meaning a comparison of the fees with those paid by similar funds); and (5) the independence, expertise, care, and conscientiousness of the board in evaluating adviser compensation. 694 F.2d, at 929–932 (internal quotation marks omitted).

6. A money market fund differs from a mutual fund in both the types of investments and the frequency of redemptions. A money market fund often invests in short-term money market securities, such as short-term securities of the United States Government or its agencies, bank certificates of deposit, and commercial paper. Investors can invest in such a fund for as little as a day, so, from the investor's perspective, the fund resembles an investment "more like a bank account than [a] traditional investment in securities." *Id.,* at 925.

that *Gartenberg* was correct in its basic formulation of what § 36(b) requires: to face liability under § 36(b), an investment adviser must charge a fee that is so disproportionately large that it bears no reasonable relationship to the services rendered and could not have been the product of arm's length bargaining.

We begin with the language of § 36(b). As noted, the Seventh Circuit panel thought that the phrase "fiduciary duty" incorporates a standard taken from the law of trusts. Petitioners agree but maintain that the panel identified the wrong trust-law standard. Instead of the standard that applies when a trustee and a settlor negotiate the trustee's fee at the time of the creation of a trust, petitioners invoke the standard that applies when a trustee seeks compensation after the trust is created A compensation agreement reached at that time, they point out, " 'will not bind the beneficiary' if either 'the trustee failed to make a full disclosure of all circumstances affecting the agreement' ''which he knew or should have known or if the agreement is unfair to the beneficiary. (quoting Restatement (Second) of Trusts § 242, Comment *i*). Respondent, on the other hand, contends that the term "fiduciary" is not exclusive to the law of trusts, that the phrase means different things in different contexts, and that there is no reason to believe that § 36(b) incorporates the specific meaning of the term in the law of trusts.

We find it unnecessary to take sides in this dispute. In *Pepper v. Litton,* 308 U.S. 295, 60 S.Ct. 238 (1939), we discussed the meaning of the concept of fiduciary duty in a context that is analogous to that presented here, and we also looked to trust law. At issue in *Pepper* was whether a bankruptcy court could disallow a dominant or controlling shareholder's claim for compensation against a bankrupt corporation. Dominant or controlling shareholders, we held, are "fiduciar[ies]" whose "powers are powers [held] in trust." *Id.,* at 306, 60 S.Ct. 238. We then explained:

> "Their dealings with the corporation are subjected to rigorous scrutiny and where any of their contracts or engagements with the corporation is challenged the burden is on the director or stockholder not only to prove the good faith of the transaction but also to show its inherent fairness from the viewpoint of the corporation and those interested therein.... *The essence of the test is whether or not under all the circumstances the transaction carries the earmarks of an arm's length bargain. If it does not, equity will set it aside.*" *Id.,* at 306–307[, 60 S.Ct. 238] (emphasis added; footnote omitted); see also *Geddes v. Anaconda Copper Mining Co.,* 254 U.S. 590, 599, 41 S.Ct. 209, 65 L.Ed. 425 (1921) (standard of fiduciary duty for interested directors).

We believe that this formulation expresses the meaning of the phrase "fiduciary duty" in § 36(b), 84 Stat. 1429. The Investment Company Act modifies this duty in a significant way: it shifts the burden of proof from the fiduciary to the party claiming breach, 15 U.S.C.

§ 80a–35(b)(1), to show that the fee is outside the range that arm's-length bargaining would produce.

The *Gartenberg* approach fully incorporates this understanding of the fiduciary duty as set out in *Pepper* and reflects § 36(b)(1)'s imposition of the burden on the plaintiff. As noted, *Gartenberg* insists that all relevant circumstances be taken into account, see 694 F.2d, at 929, as does § 36(b)(2), 84 Stat. 1429 ("[A]pproval by the board of directors ... shall be given such consideration by the court as is deemed appropriate under *all the circumstances*" (emphasis added)). And *Gartenberg* uses the range of fees that might result from arm's-length bargaining as the benchmark for reviewing challenged fees.

Gartenberg's approach also reflects § 36(b)'s place in the statutory scheme and, in particular, its relationship to the other protections that the Act affords investors.

Under the Act, scrutiny of investment adviser compensation by a fully informed mutual fund board is the "cornerstone of the ... effort to control conflicts of interest within mutual funds." *Burks*, 441 U.S., at 482, 99 S.Ct. 1831. The Act interposes disinterested directors as "independent watchdogs" of the relationship between a mutual fund and its adviser. *Id.*, at 484, 99 S.Ct. 1831 (internal quotation marks omitted). To provide these directors with the information needed to judge whether an adviser's compensation is excessive, the Act requires advisers to furnish all information "reasonably ... necessary to evaluate the terms" of the adviser's contract, 15 U.S.C. § 80a–15(c), and gives the SEC the authority to enforce that requirement. See § 80a–41. Board scrutiny of adviser compensation and shareholder suits under § 36(b), 84 Stat. 1429, are mutually reinforcing but independent mechanisms for controlling conflicts. See *Daily Income Fund*, 464 U.S., at 541, 104 S.Ct. 831 (Congress intended for § 36(b) suits and directorial approval of adviser contracts to act as "independent checks on excessive fees"); *Kamen*, 500 U.S., at 108, 111 S.Ct. 1711 ("Congress added § 36(b) to the [Act] in 1970 because it concluded that the shareholders should not have to rely solely on the fund's directors to assure reasonable adviser fees, notwithstanding the increased disinterestedness of the board" (internal quotation marks omitted)).

In recognition of the role of the disinterested directors, the Act instructs courts to give board approval of an adviser's compensation "such consideration ... as is deemed appropriate under all the circumstances." § 80a–35(b)(2). Cf. *Burks*, 441 U.S., at 485, 99 S.Ct. 1831 ("[I]t would have been paradoxical for Congress to have been willing to rely largely upon [boards of directors as] 'watchdogs' to protect shareholder interests and yet, where the 'watchdogs' have done precisely that, require that they be totally muzzled").

From this formulation, two inferences may be drawn. First, a measure of deference to a board's judgment may be appropriate in some instances.

Second, the appropriate measure of deference varies depending on the circumstances.

Gartenberg heeds these precepts. *Gartenberg* advises that "the expertise of the independent trustees of a fund, whether they are fully informed about all facts bearing on the [investment adviser's] service and fee, and the extent of care and conscientiousness with which they perform their duties are important factors to be considered in deciding whether they and the [investment adviser] are guilty of a breach of fiduciary duty in violation of § 36(b)." 694 F.2d, at 930.

While both parties in this case endorse the basic *Gartenberg* approach, they disagree on several important questions that warrant discussion.

The first concerns comparisons between the fees that an adviser charges a captive mutual fund and the fees that it charges its independent clients. As noted, the *Gartenberg* court rejected a comparison between the fees that the adviser in that case charged a money market fund and the fees that it charged a pension fund. 694 F.2d, at 930, n. 3 (noting the "[t]he nature and extent of the services required by each type of fund differ sharply"). Petitioners contend that such a comparison is appropriate, Brief for Petitioners 30–31, but respondent disagrees. Brief for Respondent 38–44. Since the Act requires consideration of all relevant factors, 15 U.S.C. § 80a–35(b)(2); see also § 80a–15(c), we do not think that there can be any categorical rule regarding the comparisons of the fees charged different types of clients. See *Daily Income Fund, supra,* at 537, 104 S.Ct. 831 (discussing concern with investment advisers' practice of charging higher fees to mutual funds than to their other clients). Instead, courts may give such comparisons the weight that they merit in light of the similarities and differences between the services that the clients in question require, but courts must be wary of inapt comparisons. As the panel below noted, there may be significant differences between the services provided by an investment adviser to a mutual fund and those it provides to a pension fund which are attributable to the greater frequency of shareholder redemptions in a mutual fund, the higher turnover of mutual fund assets, the more burdensome regulatory and legal obligations, and higher marketing costs. 527 F.3d, at 634 ("Different clients call for different commitments of time"). If the services rendered are sufficiently different that a comparison is not probative, then courts must reject such a comparison. Even if the services provided and fees charged to an independent fund are relevant, courts should be mindful that the Act does not necessarily ensure fee parity between mutual funds and institutional clients contrary to petitioners' contentions. See *id.,* at 631. ("Plaintiffs maintain that a fiduciary may charge its controlled clients no more than its independent clients").

By the same token, courts should not rely too heavily on comparisons with fees charged to mutual funds by other advisers. These comparisons are problematic because these fees, like those challenged, may not be the product of negotiations conducted at arm's length. See 537 F.3d, at 731–

732 (opinion dissenting from denial of rehearing en banc); *Gartenberg, supra,* at 929 ("Competition between money market funds for shareholder business does not support an inference that competition must therefore also exist between [investment advisers] for fund business. The former may be vigorous even though the latter is virtually non-existent").

Finally, a court's evaluation of an investment adviser's fiduciary duty must take into account both procedure and substance. See 15 U.S.C. § 80a–35(b)(2) (requiring deference to board's consideration "as is deemed appropriate under all the circumstances"); cf. *Daily Income Fund,* 464 U.S., at 541, 104 S.Ct. 831 ("Congress intended security holder and SEC actions under § 36(b), on the one hand, and directorial approval of adviser contracts, on the other, to act as independent checks on excessive fees"). Where a board's process for negotiating and reviewing investment-adviser compensation is robust, a reviewing court should afford commensurate deference to the outcome of the bargaining process. See *Burks,* 441 U.S., at 484, 99 S.Ct. 1831 (unaffiliated directors serve as "independent watchdogs"). Thus, if the disinterested directors considered the relevant factors, their decision to approve a particular fee agreement is entitled to considerable weight, even if a court might weigh the factors differently. Cf. *id.,* at 485, 99 S.Ct. 1831. This is not to deny that a fee may be excessive even if it was negotiated by a board in possession of all relevant information, but such a determination must be based on evidence that the fee "is so disproportionately large that it bears no reasonable relationship to the services rendered and could not have been the product of arm's-length bargaining." *Gartenberg, supra,* at 928.

In contrast, where the board's process was deficient or the adviser withheld important information, the court must take a more rigorous look at the outcome. When an investment adviser fails to disclose material information to the board, greater scrutiny is justified because the withheld information might have hampered the board's ability to function as "an independent check upon the management." *Burks, supra,* at 484, 99 S.Ct. 1831 (internal quotation marks omitted). "Section 36(b) is sharply focused on the question of whether the fees themselves were excessive." *Migdal v. Rowe Price–Fleming Int'l, Inc.,* 248 F.3d 321, 328 (C.A.4 2001); see also 15 U.S.C. § 80a–35(b) (imposing a "fiduciary duty with respect to the *receipt of compensation* for services, or of payments of a material nature "(emphasis added)). But an adviser's compliance or noncompliance with its disclosure obligations is a factor that must be considered in calibrating the degree of deference that is due a board's decision to approve an adviser's fees.

It is also important to note that the standard for fiduciary breach under § 36(b) does not call for judicial second-guessing of informed board decisions. See *Daily Income Fund, supra,* at 538, 104 S.Ct. 831; see also

Burks, 441 U.S., at 483, 99 S.Ct. 1831 ("Congress consciously chose to address the conflict-of-interest problem through the Act's independent-directors section, rather than through more drastic remedies"). "[P]otential conflicts [of interests] may justify some restraints upon the unfettered discretion of even disinterested mutual fund directors, particularly in their transactions with the investment adviser," but they do not suggest that a court may supplant the judgment of disinterested directors apprised of all relevant information, without additional evidence that the fee exceeds the arm's-length range. *Id.*, at 481, 99 S.Ct. 1831. In reviewing compensation under § 36(b), the Act does not require courts to engage in a precise calculation of fees representative of arm's-length bargaining. See 527 F.3d, at 633 ("Judicial price-setting does not accompany fiduciary duties"). As recounted above, Congress rejected a "reasonableness" requirement that was criticized as charging the courts with rate-setting responsibilities. Congress' approach recognizes that courts are not well suited to make such precise calculations. Cf. *General Motors Corp. v. Tracy,* 519 U.S. 278, 308, 117 S.Ct. 811, 136 L.Ed.2d 761 (1997) ("[T]he Court is institutionally unsuited to gather the facts upon which economic predictions can be made, and professionally untrained to make them"); *Verizon Communications Inc. v. FCC,* 535 U.S. 467, 539, 122 S.Ct. 1646, 152 L.Ed.2d 701 (2002); see also *Concord v. Boston Edison Co.,* 915 F.2d 17, 25 (CA1 1990) (opinion for the court by Breyer, C.J.) ("[H]ow is a judge or jury to determine a 'fair price'?"). *Gartenberg*'s "so disproportionately large" standard, 694 F.2d, at 928, reflects this congressional choice to "rely largely upon [independent director] 'watchdogs' to protect shareholders interests." *Burks, supra,* at 485, 99 S.Ct. 1831.

By focusing almost entirely on the element of disclosure, the Seventh Circuit panel erred. See 527 F.3d, at 632 (An investment adviser "must make full disclosure and play no tricks but is not subject to a cap on compensation"). The *Gartenberg* standard, which the panel rejected, may lack sharp analytical clarity, but we believe that it accurately reflects the compromise that is embodied in § 36(b), and it has provided a workable standard for nearly three decades. The debate between the Seventh Circuit panel and the dissent from the denial of rehearing regarding today's mutual fund market is a matter for Congress, not the courts.

For the foregoing reasons, the judgment of the Court of Appeals is vacated, and the case remanded for further proceedings consistent with this opinion.

It is so ordered.

[Justice Thomas' concurring opinion is omitted]

NOTES

Section 913 of the Dodd–Frank Wall Street Reform and Consumer Protection Act of 2010 directed the SEC to conduct a study on the effectiveness of existing standards of care for broker-dealers, investment advisers and their associated persons in providing personalized investment advice to retail customers. Among other things, the SEC staff report concluded that there should be a uniform fiduciary for broker-dealers and investment advisers when they supply personalized advice to customers. SEC Staff, Study on Investment Advisers and Broker–Dealers: As Required by Section 913 of the Dodd–Frank Wall Street Reform and Consumer Protection Act 9 (Jan. 2011).

SECTION 5.   SALES LOADS AND OTHER REGULATORY ISSUES

KRULL v. SECURITIES AND EXCHANGE COMMISSION

248 F.3d 907 (9th Cir.2001).

McKEOWN, CIRCUIT JUDGE.

  * * * Kenneth C. Krull became a registered securities representative in 1981. At the time of the transactions at issue, Krull was a general securities principal, branch manager, and sole registered representative in the Marysville, Washington office of Investment Management and Research, Inc. Investment Management is a member firm of the National Association of Securities Dealers, Inc. ("NASD").

From November 1990 through July 1993, Krull repeatedly switched eight customers, holding ten accounts, in and out of a series of common stock mutual funds. With one exception, these funds were front-end "loaded"; that is, they charged a transaction fee at the time of purchase. The remaining fund was subject to a contingent deferred sales charge if sold within a six-year holding period. Krull recommended all of the more than one hundred transactions in question to customers who invariably heeded his advice. Customers held the mutual funds on average for just over ten months. Although the customers consented to each transaction by signing a "switch form," Krull failed to follow company policy to keep such activity to a minimum, to execute short-term mutual fund trades only at the shareholder's request, and to submit switch forms to the home office for review.

Krull's recommendations in the Franklin Rising Dividends Fund ("Franklin Fund"), a common stock fund with an income and growth objective, are illustrative of what the Securities and Exchange Commission ("Commission" or "SEC") labeled a "clear pattern[]" of excessive trading. Between June and October 1992, all eight customers purchased Franklin Fund shares on Krull's recommendation. Krull recommended the fund because of its Morningstar five-star rating,[11] one-year superior performance, management's disciplined approach, and the protection offered in the shaky economy. Krull's enthusiasm for the fund was short-lived and somewhat inconsistent. Soon after recommending purchase of this fund, Krull began switching customers out of the fund and, between December 1992 and June 1993, seven of the eight customers sold their Franklin Fund shares. In December, when other customers were selling their shares on Krull's advice, Krull recommended to one customer that he purchase this very same mutual fund and then in February and April 1993 switched this same customer out of the Franklin Fund and into funds outside the Franklin family of funds. As it turns out, intra-family switches

---

11.   Morningstar, established by Morningstar, Inc. of Chicago, is a mutual fund rating system ranging from one to five stars. Five stars is the highest rating.

within the Franklin family incurred no sales charge, and yet Krull offered no explanation why other Franklin family funds were not suitable investments. Nor did he explain the rationale for the quick switches in light of his strong buy recommendation. And when queried about the customer who was buying Franklin when Krull was recommending a sell to other clients, he conceded that, "looking back on it, it doesn't [make any sense]."

Krull followed this same pattern of switching in other funds-Phoenix Growth Fund, Franklin Growth Fund, Idex Fund, Templeton World Fund, Sogen International Fund, and others. Although all of his customers ultimately profited from these transactions in absolute terms, six of the eight collectively earned $81,705 less by following Krull's recommendations than they would have by holding their initial fund investments. Krull, however, earned more than $171,000 in commissions on the switches.

The disciplinary review process for a securities representative involves multiple levels of alphabet-soup entities. Here the process began with the District Business Conduct Committee ("DBCC") of the NASD and culminated in the SEC order that is on direct appeal to this court.

Established pursuant to the 1938 Maloney Act Amendments to the Securities Exchange Act of 1934, the NASD is a nonprofit corporation registered with the Commission as a national securities association.

The NASD is required to promulgate rules "to protect investors and the public interest," 15 U.S.C. § 78o–3(b)(6), and to enforce these rules through disciplinary proceedings and sanctions, 15 U.S.C. §§ 78o–3(b)(7)–(8), 78o–3(h), 78s(g). The Commission approves proposed NASD rules, such as the Rules of Fair Practice (now known as Conduct Rules). 15 U.S.C. § 78s(b)(1), (b)(2).

At the time of this proceeding, the DBCC and the National Business Conduct Committee ("NBCC") were a part of the NASD's regulatory arm, or NASD Regulation, Inc. NASD Manual–Administrative 151, 153–54 (1996/1997). The regulatory and disciplinary process was restructured after Krull's case was filed. *See* Order, Exchange Act Release 34–38908, 1997 WL 441929, at *32–35, 38 (Aug. 7, 1997) (approving proposed rule changes whereby DBCC and NBCC were restructured). The members of these committees were brokers and dealers within the securities community, thus assuring the collective business experience of securities professionals in each disciplinary decision.

Under this disciplinary regime, the DBCC makes the first determination as to a member's alleged misconduct. The DBCC's decisions are reviewable by the NBCC on its own motion or upon application of an aggrieved party. The final stop in the administrative process is review of the NBCC decision, essentially the final NASD ruling, by the Commission. 15 U.S.C. § 78s(d), (e). Although the Commission reviews the record de novo, its review of the sanction is narrower-the sanction may be modified or canceled only if it is "excessive or oppressive." 15 U.S.C. § 78s(e);

Hateley v. SEC, 8 F.3d 653, 655 n. 6 (9th Cir.1993); *Sartain,* 601 F.2d at 1371 n. 2.

After a four-day hearing, the DBCC found that Krull had violated the Rules of Fair Practice by recommending purchases and sales of mutual fund shares without reasonable grounds to believe such transactions were suitable for his customers. A total of 147 transactions, or switches, were deemed unreasonable, in part because of NASD's presumption that short-term trading in mutual funds is improper. * * *

Krull appealed ... to the Commission, which, after an independent review of the record, confirmed the unsuitability of Krull's mutual fund recommendations and sustained the finding of violation of the Rules of Fair Practice. The Commission did, however, modify the sanction by reducing the restitution. The parties stipulated that two of the eight customers made more through the switching than they would have through a "buy and hold" strategy. The Commission then ordered restitution of $81,705 to the remaining six customers representing the amount they would have earned had they held their initial investments without switches. The one-year suspension and $20,000 fine were affirmed. This petition for review of the SEC's order followed. * * *

Mutual funds have long been categorized as suitable only as long-term investments and not a vehicle for short-term trading. Article III, Section 2 of the NASD's Rules of Fair Practice (now Conduct Rule 2310), sets out principles for fair dealing with customers and the broad parameters for suitability of securities transactions:

> In recommending to a customer the purchase, sale or exchange of any security, a member shall have reasonable grounds for believing that the recommendation is suitable for such customer upon the basis of the facts, if any, disclosed by such customer as to his other security holdings and as to his financial situation and needs.

The Policy Statement of the Board of Governors issued under this rule admonishes that trading in mutual funds on a short-term basis violates a responsibility for fair dealing and explicitly states that "normally [fund shares] are not proper trading vehicles and such activity on its face may raise the question of Rule violation."

The Commission has consistently considered short-term trading in mutual funds as inappropriate and violative of the rules on fair dealing because of the costs associated with front-loaded funds. The Commission pointedly noted in *In re Winston H. Kinderdick* that

> [m]utual fund shares generally are suitable only as long-term investments and cannot be regarded as a proper vehicle for short-term trading, especially where such trading involves new sales loads. A pattern of switches from one fund to another by several customers of a registered representative, where there is no indication of a change in the investment objectives of the customers and where new sales

loads are incurred, is not reconcilable with the concept of suitability.
* * *

Krull failed to meet his burden to justify more than one hundred of the challenged switches. For example, in the case of the Franklin Fund, Krull justified his sale recommendations based on his belief that newly-elected President Clinton seemed favorable to business and would institute policies favorable to domestic growth. The explanation for his sell recommendations was hardly convincing, however, when he was simultaneously making a buy recommendation to another customer. The pattern that emerges is one of Krull maximizing his commissions at the expense of the customer.

Krull's argument that his customers did not face excessive commissions when compared to churning (excessive trading) claims[12] or wrap fee accounts[13] does little to bolster his defense. This attempt to justify his recommendations on the premise that his customers profited, albeit not as much as they could have without excessive costs, ignores the fact that the focus of this suitability claim is not whether customers made money, but whether switches served a reasonable investment objective when made. The NASD, in a careful decision of more than fifty pages, analyzed each transaction and Krull's purported trading strategy, and found that the pattern of switching between funds was inconsistent with Krull's claimed rationale. In reviewing the record of Krull's trades, the Commission agreed with the NASD's assessment that Krull's explanations were "implausible and lacking any reasonable basis." The Commission also noted that it had previously rejected comparisons between churning and suitability claims, *see Kinderdick,* Exchange Act Release No. 34–12818, 46 S.E.C. at 640, 1976 WL 18843, at *3, and found comparisons to wrap accounts to be inapposite because switching here reduces the assets on which the representative's fee is based. * * *

NOTES

1. Consider the following explanation of the fees charged on mutual fund shares:

"Unquestionably, the unique characteristic of mutual funds is that they are permitted, under the [Investment Company] Act, to market their

---

12. Churning claims arise when a broker, exercising control over an account, abuses a customer's confidence for personal gain by initiating transactions that are excessive in view of the character of the account. *See Mihara v. Dean Witter & Co., Inc.,* 619 F.2d 814, 821 (9th Cir.1980). Suitability claims are distinct from churning claims but may overlap when a broker recommends unsuitable trades for the purpose of churning. The distinction between the claims, however, is that unsuitability requires showing the quality of the investment is inappropriate whereas churning requires showing the quantity of trades is improper. *See Tiernan v. Blyth, Eastman, Dillon & Co.,* 719 F.2d 1, 5 (1st Cir.1983).

13. A wrap fee account is an investment program that "bundles or 'wraps' a number of services (brokerage, advisory, research, consulting, management, etc.) together and covers them with a single fee based on the value of the assets under management."

shares continuously to the public, but are required to be prepared to redeem outstanding shares at any time. § 80a–22(e). The redemption 'bid' price that a shareholder may receive is set by the Act at approximately the fractional value per share of the fund's net assets at the time of redemption. § 80a–2(a)(32). In contrast, the 'asked' price, or the price at which the fund initially offers its shares to the public, includes not only the net asset value per share at the time of sale, but also a fixed sales charge or 'sales load' assessed by the fund's principal underwriter who acts as an agent in marketing the fund's shares. § 80a–2(a) (35). Sales loads vary within fixed limits from mutual fund to mutual fund, but all are paid to the funds' underwriters; the charges do not become part of the assets of the fund. The sales loads of the funds held by the decedent ranged from seven and eight percent to one percent of the fractional net asset value of the funds' shares.

"Private trading in mutual fund shares is virtually nonexistent. Thus, at any given time, under the statutory scheme created by the Investment Company Act, shares of any open-end mutual fund with a sales load are being sold at two distinct prices. Initial purchases by the public are made from the fund, at the 'asked' price, which includes the load. But shareholders 'sell' their shares back to the fund at the statutorily defined redemption or bid price."

United States v. Cartwright, 411 U.S. 546, 547–549, 93 S.Ct. 1713, 36 L.Ed.2d 528 (1973). The Court further stated that:

"Mutual fund shares are not traded on exchanges or generally in the over-the-counter market, as are other securities, but are sold by the fund through a principal underwriter, and redeemed by the fund, at prices which are related to 'net asset value.' The net asset value per share is normally computed twice daily by taking the market value at the time of all portfolio securities, adding the value of other assets and subtracting liabilities, and dividing the result by the number of shares outstanding. Shares of most funds are sold for a price equal to their asset value plus a sales charge or commission, commonly referred to as the 'sales load' * * *. A few funds, however, known as 'no-load' funds, offer their shares for sale at net asset value without a sales charge. Shares of most funds are redeemed or repurchased by the funds at their net asset value, although a few funds charge a small redemption fee. The result of this pricing system, it is apparent, is that the entire cost of selling fund shares is generally borne exclusively by the purchaser of new shares and not by the fund itself. In this respect the offering of mutual fund shares differs from, say, the offering of new shares by a closed-end investment company or an additional offering 'at the market' of shares of an exchange-listed security, where at least a portion of the selling cost is borne by the company selling the shares."

411 U.S. at 548, n.3 (citation omitted)

2. FINRA rules limit the amount the sales load that may be charged on mutual fund sales. In most instances, that maximum sales load is 7.25 percent. Mutual funds may have multiple classes of shares charging differing loads. These options may include classes with front-end commissions, back

end commissions, periodic commissions, and contingent deferred commissions that are reduced if the shares are held for some specific period. Particularly popular are no load funds that do not charge a commission. These shares are purchased by the investor directly from the mutual fund, rather than through a broker. See generally Tom Lauricella, Mutual–Fund Investors Take Quiz: A, B or C? Wall St. J., March 7, 2003, at C1 (describing differing classes and no loads). Even no-load shares may be charged something called "12b–1 fees." The SEC thus allows mutual funds to adopt a "12b–1 plan" that permits the mutual fund to charge shareholders a fee that will cover their distribution costs. 17 C.F.R. § 270.12b–1. No load fund investors will also pay advisory fees and other operational costs from their invested funds. Arthur Levitt, Take On the Street, What Wall Street and Corporate America Don't Want You to Know, What You Can Do to Fight Back 48 (2002).

3. Mutual funds may have breakpoints that allow a discount for larger purchases, which may be accumulated over time. Accumulation is allowed for more than one fund in a complex in order to meet the breakpoint. 17 C.F.R. § 270.22d–1. Customers must be advised off the availability of these breakpoints (through a "breakpoint letter"), and it is an improper practice for sales personnel to structure trades in order to stay under the breakpoint. See generally Tom Lauricella, Morgan Stanley Is Sued on Break Points, Wall St. J., March 5, 2003, at C1 (describing breakpoint abuses).

4. Investment companies must file periodic reports with the SEC and must file their sales literature with that agency. In the wake of the Enron and other corporate governance scandals, the SEC required mutual funds to disclose whether they have a code of ethics. Do you think such codes will prevent fraud?

5. The share holdings of mutual funds are considerable and would allow them to strongly influence management if voted actively. Most mutual funds, however, are passive investors that vote with their feet rather than to try to actively manage a company. In 2001, however, the SEC adopted rules requiring investment companies to disclose their practices in voting the shares of companies they hold. 17 C.F.R. § 270.13b1–4. See generally Alan R. Palmiter, Mutual Fund Voting of Portfolio Shares: Why Not Disclose? 23 Cardozo L. Rev. 1419 (2002) (advocating such a requirement). Do you think mutual fund advisors are in a position to actively manage the companies in which they invest assets of a mutual fund?

6. The SEC issued a concept release seeking comment on whether a self-regulatory organization (SRO), such as the FINRA, is needed in the mutual fund industry. Securities and Exchange Commission Release No. IC–25925 (Feb. 5, 2003). The Dodd–Frank Act of 2010 (§ 416) also directed a study on whether a SRO is needed for private funds. The SEC is still considering an SRO for investment adviser.

UNITED STATES v. NATIONAL ASSOCIATION OF SECURITIES DEALERS, INC.

422 U.S. 694, 95 S.Ct. 2427, 45 L.Ed.2d 486 (1975).

Opinion of the Court by MR. JUSTICE POWELL, announced by MR. JUSTICE BLACKMUN.

* * * An 'investment company' invests in the securities of other corporations and issues securities of its own. Shares in an investment company thus represent proportionate interests in its investment portfolio, and their value fluctuates in relation to the changes in the value of the securities it owns. The most common form of investment company, the 'open end' company or mutual fund, is required by law to redeem its securities on demand at a price approximating their proportionate share of the fund's net asset value at the time of redemption. In order to avoid liquidation through redemption, mutual funds continuously issue and sell new shares. These features—continuous and unlimited distribution and compulsory redemption—are, as the Court recently recognized, 'unique characteristic(s)) of this form of investment.' United States v. Cartwright, 411 U.S. 546, 547, 93 S.Ct. 1713, 1714, 36 L.Ed.2d 528 (1973).

The initial distribution of mutual-fund shares is conducted by a principal underwriter, often an affiliate of the fund, and by broker-dealers who contract with that underwriter to sell the securities to the public. The sales price commonly consists of two components, a sum calculated from the net asset value of the fund at the time of purchase, and a 'load,' a sales charge representing a fixed percentage of the net asset value. The load is divided between the principal underwriter and the broker-dealers, compensating them for their sales efforts.[14]

The distribution-redemption system constitutes the primary market in mutual-fund shares, the operation of which is not questioned in this litigation. The parties agree that § 22(d) of the Investment Company Act requires broker-dealers to maintain a uniform price in sales in this primary market to all purchasers except the fund, its underwriters, and other dealers. And in view of this express requirement no question exists that antitrust immunity must be afforded these sales. This case focuses, rather, on the potential secondary market in mutual-fund shares.

Although a significant secondary market existed prior to enactment of the Investment Company Act, little presently remains. The United States agrees that the Act was designed to restrict most of secondary market trading, but nonetheless contends that certain industry practices have

---

14. The Act defines 'sales load' to be the difference between the public offering price and the portion of the sales proceeds that is invested or held for investment purposes by the issuer. § 80a–2(a)(35). Most mutual funds charge this sales load in order to encourage vigorous sales efforts on the part of underwriters and broker-dealers. There are some funds that do not charge this additional sales fee. These 'no load' funds generally sell directly to the investor without relying on the promotional and sales efforts of underwriters and broker-dealers. See SEC Report of the Division of Investment Management Regulation, Mutual Fund Distribution and Section 22(d) of the Investment Company Act of 1940, p. 112 (Aug. 1974) (hereinafter 1974 Staff Report).

extended the statutory limitation beyond its proper boundaries. The complaint in this action alleges that the defendants, appellees herein, combined and agreed to restrict the sale and fix the resale prices of mutual-fund shares in secondary market transactions between dealers, from an investor to a dealer, and between investors through brokered transactions. Named as defendants are the National Association of Securities Dealers (NASD), and certain mutual funds, mutual-fund underwriters, and securities broker-dealers. * * *

The Investment Company Act of 1940 originated in congressional concern that the Securities Act of 1933, 48 Stat. 74, 15 U.S.C. § 77a et seq., and the Securities Exchange Act of 1934, 48 Stat. 881, 15 U.S.C. § 78a et seq., were inadequate to protect the purchasers of investment company securities. Thus, in § 30 of the Public Utility Holding Company Act, 49 Stat. 837, 15 U.S.C. § 79z–4, Congress directed the SEC of study the structures, practices, and problems of investment companies with a view toward proposing further legislation. Four years of intensive scrutiny of the industry culminated in the publication of the Investment Trust Study and the recommendation of legislation to rectify the problems and abuses it identified. After extensive congressional consideration, the Investment Company Act of 1940 was adopted.

The Act vests in the SEC broad regulatory authority over the business practices of investment companies.[15] We are concerned on this appeal with § 22 of the Act, 15 U.S.C. § 80a–22, which controls the sales and distribution of mutual-fund shares. The questions presented require us to determine whether § 22(d) obligates appellees to engage in the practices challenged in Counts II–VIII and thus necessarily confers antitrust immunity on them. If not, we must determine whether such practices are authorized by § 22(f) and, if so, whether they are immune from antitrust sanction. Resolution of these issues will be facilitated by examining the nature of the problems and abuses to which § 22 is addressed, a matter to which we now turn.

The most thorough description of the sales and distribution practices of mutual funds prior to passage of the Investment Company Act may be bound in Part III of the Investment Trust Study. H.R.Doc.No.279, 76th Cong., 1st Sess. (1940) (hereinafter Investment Trust Study pt. III). That

---

15. For example, the Act requires companies to register with the SEC, 15 U.S.C. § 80a–8. See also § 80a–7. Companies also must register all securities they issue, see Securities Act of 1933, 15 U.S.C. § 77f; Investment Company Act, 15 U.S.C. § 80a–24(a), and must submit for SEC inspection copies of the sales literature they send to prospective investors. § 80a–24(b). The Investment Company Act requires the submission and periodic updating of detailed financial reports and documentation and the semiannual transmission of reports containing similar information to the shareholders. § 80a–29. It also imposes controls and restrictions on the internal management of investment companies: establishing minimum capital requirements, § 80a–14; limiting permissible methods for selecting directors, § 80a–16; and establishing certain qualifications for persons seeking to affiliate with the companies, § 80a–9. Finally, the Act imposes a number of controls on the internal practices of investment companies. For example, it requires a majority shareholder vote for certain fundamental business decisions, § 80a–13, and limits certain dividend distributions, § 80a–19. See generally The Mutual Fund Industry: A Legal Survey, 44 Notre Dame Law. 732 (1969).

Study, as Congress has recognized, see 15 U.S.C. § 80a–1, forms the initial basis for any evaluation of the Act.

Prior to 1940 the basic framework for the primary distribution of mutual-fund shares was similar to that existing today. The fund normally retained a principal underwriter to serve as a wholesaler of its shares. The principal underwriter in turn contracted with a number of broker-dealers to sell the fund's shares to the investing public. The price of the shares was based on the fund's net asset value at the approximate time of sale, and a sales commission or load was added to that price.

Although prior to 1940 the primary distribution system for mutual-fund shares was similar to the present one, a number of conditions then existed that largely disappeared following passage of the Act. The most prominently discussed characteristic was the 'two-price system,' which encouraged and active secondary market under conditions that tolerated disruptive and discriminatory trading practices. The two-price system reflected the relationship between the commonly used method of computing the daily net asset value of mutual-fund shares and the manner in which the price for the following day was established. The net asset value of mutual funds, which depends on the market quotations of the stocks in their investment portfolios, fluctuates constantly. Most funds computed their net asset values daily on the basis of the fund's portfolio value at the close of exchange trading, and that figure established the sales price that would go into effect at a specified hour on the following day. During this interim period two prices were known: the present day's trading price based on the portfolio value established the previous day; and the following day's price, which was based on the net asset value computed at the close of exchange trading on the present day. One aware of both prices could engage in 'riskless trading' during this interim period. See Investment Trust Study pt. III, pp. 851–852.

The two-price system did not benefit the investing public generally. Some of the mutual funds did not explain the system thoroughly, and unsophisticated investors probably were unaware of its existence. See id., at 867. Even investors who knew of the two-price system and understood its operation were rarely in a position to exploit it fully. It was possible, however, for a knowledgeable investor to purchase shares in a rising market at the current price with the advance information that the next day's price would be higher. He thus could be guaranteed an immediate appreciation in the market value of his investment, although this advantage was obtained at the expense of the existing shareholders, whose equity interests were diluted by a corresponding amount. The load fee that was charged in the sale of mutual funds to the investing public made it difficult for these investors to realize the 'paper gain' obtained in such trading. Because the daily fluctuation in net asset value rarely exceeded the load, public investors generally were unable to realize immediate profits from the two-price system by engaging in rapid in-and-out trading. But insiders, who often were able to purchase shares without paying the load, did not operate under this constraint. Thus insiders could, and sometimes did, purchase shares for immediate redemption at the appreciated value.

The two-price system often afforded other advantages to underwriters and broker-dealers. In a falling market they could enhance profits by waiting to fill orders with shares purchased from the fund at the next day's anticipated lower price. In a similar fashion, in a rising market they could take a 'long position' in mutual-fund shares by establishing an inventory in order to satisfy anticipated purchases with securities previously obtained at a lower price. In each case the investment company would receive the lower of the two prevailing prices for its shares, and the equity interests of shareholders would suffer a corresponding dilution.

As a result, an active secondary market in mutual-fund shares existed. Principal underwriters and contract broker-dealers often maintained inventory positions established by purchasing shares through the primary distribution system and by buying from other dealers and retiring shareholders. Additionally, a 'bootleg market' sprang up, consisting of broker-dealers having no contractual relationship with the fund or its principal underwriter. These bootleg dealers purchased shares at a discount from contract dealers or bought them from retiring shareholders at a price slightly higher than the redemption price. Bootleg dealers would then offer the shares at a price slightly lower than that required in the primary distribution system, thus 'initiating a small scale price war between retailers and tend(ing) generally to disrupt the established offering price.'

Section 22 of the Investment Company Act of 1940 was enacted with these abuses in mind. Sections 22(a) and (c) were designed to 'eliminat(e) or reduc(e) so far as reasonably practicable any dilution of the value of other outstanding securities ... or any other result of (the) purchase, redemption, or sale (of mutual fund securities) which is unfair to holders of such other outstanding securities,' 15 U.S.C. § 80a–22(a). They authorize the NASD and the SEC to regulate certain pricing and trading practices in order to effectuate that goal. Section 22(b) authorizes registered securities associations and the SEC to prescribe the maximum sales commissions or loads that can be charged in connection with a primary distribution; and § 22(e) protects the right of redemption by restricting mutual funds' power to suspend redemption or postpone the date of payment. * * *

Section 22(d) prohibits mutual funds from selling shares at other than the current public offering price to any person except either to or through a principal underwriter for distribution. It further commands that 'no dealer shall sell (mutual-fund shares) to any person except a dealer, a principal underwriter, or the issuer, except at a current public offering price described in the prospectus.' 15 U.S.C § 80a–22(d). By its terms, § 22(d) excepts interdealer sales from its price maintenance requirement. Accordingly, this section cannot be relied upon by appellees as justification for the restrictions imposed upon interdealer transactions. At issue, rather, is the narrower question whether the § 22(d) price maintenance mandate for sales by 'dealers' applies to transactions in which a broker-dealer acts as a statutory 'broker' rather than a statutory 'dealer.' The District Court concluded that it does, and thus that § 22(d) governs transactions in which the broker-dealer acts as an agent for an investor as well as those in which he acts as a principal selling shares for his own account. * *

In view of the scope of the SEC's regulatory authority over the activities of the NASD, the Government's decision to withdraw from direct attack on the association's rules was prudent. The SEC's supervisory authority over the NASD is extensive. Not only does the Maloney Act require the SEC to determine whether an association satisfies the strict statutory requirements of that Act and thus qualifies to engage in supervised regulation of the trading activities of its membership, 15 U.S.C. § 78o–3(b), it requires registered associations thereafter to submit for Commission approval any proposed rule changes, § 78o–3(j). The Maloney Act additionally authorizes the SEC to request changes in or supplementation of association rules, a power that recently has been exercised with respect to some of the precise conduct questioned in this litigation, see n. 31, supra. If such a request is not complied with, the SEC may order such changes itself. § 78o–3(k)(2).

The SEC, in its exercise of authority over association rules and practices, is charged with protection of the public interest as well as the interests of shareholders, see, e.g., § 78o–3(a)(1), (b)(3), and (c), and it repeatedly has indicated that it weighs competitive concerns in the exercise of its continued supervisory responsibility. * * *

Here implied repeal of the antitrust laws is 'necessary to make the (regulatory scheme) work.' Silver v. New York Stock Exchange, 373 U.S., at 357, 83 S.Ct., at 1257. In generally similar situations, we have implied immunity in particular and discrete instances to assure that the federal agency entrusted with regulation in the public interest could carry out that responsibility free from the disruption of conflicting judgments that might be voiced by courts exercising jurisdiction under the antitrust laws. See Hughes Tool Co. v. Trans World Airlines, 409 U.S. 363, 93 S.Ct. 647, 34 L.Ed.2d 577 (1973); Pan American World Airways, Inc. v. United States, 371 U.S. 296, 83 S.Ct. 476, 9 L.Ed.2d 325 (1963). In this instance, maintenance of an antitrust action for activities so directly related to the SEC's responsibilities poses a substantial danger that appellees would be subjected to duplicative and inconsistent standards. This is hardly a result that Congress would have mandated. We therefore hold that with respect to the activities challenged in Count I of the complaint, the Sherman Act has been displaced by the pervasive regulatory scheme established by the Maloney and Investment Company Acts.

Affirmed.

Mr. Justice White, with whom Mr. Justice Douglas, Mr. Justice Brennan, and Mr. Justice Marshall join, dissenting.

Late Trading and Market Timing Scandals

The bursting of the stock market bubble in 2000 and increased competition resulted in a decline in assets held by mutual funds and a decrease in advisory fees. Mutual funds were also encountering competition from exchange traded funds (ETFs) that were becoming increasingly popular. ETFs are essentially investments that are traded on an exchange and track the value of a particular index. The first of these contracts appeared in 1993 and were called SPDRs (Standard & Poor's Depository Receipts) or "spiders." They were the equivalent of a diversified mutual fund but allowed intra-day trading. In order to meet this competition, and declining fees as net asset values dropped, mutual fund advisors began allowing hedge funds and other professional traders to engage in "market timing" and "late trading" transactions. These practices allowed traders to profit from market events occurring after 4:00 p.m., which is when the net asset value is computed for mutual funds. Late trading assured the trader a virtually risk free profit when he obtains information with market effect after the 4:00 p.m. pricing. For a further description of these scandals see Jerry W. Markham, Mutual Fund Scandals—A Comparative Analysis of the Role of Corporate Governance in the Regulation of Collective Investments, 3 Hastings Bus. L. J. 67, 99–121 (2006).

Eliot Spitzer, the New York Attorney General, began a broad scale attack on market timing and late trading in mutual funds in 2003. He charged Edward J. Stern and a hedge fund he managed, Canary Capital Partners, with improperly late trading mutual fund shares. The SEC was severely embarrassed by Spitzer's suit and his claim that late trading and market timing abuses were widespread in the mutual funds industry. In an effort to reclaim some of its lost regulatory ground, the SEC started filing its own suits, claiming that late trading arrangements were not properly disclosed under its full disclosure regimen. Spitzer and the SEC collected over $3.5 billion in fines and restitution from mutual funds that had allowed late trading and market timing. The SEC also adopted more regulations for mutual funds. Among other things, mutual funds were required to create compliance programs and hire compliance officers. The SEC required investment advisers to have a code of ethics and to disclose the effects of market timing transactions and the policies of the mutual fund concerning such trading.

One particularly controversial rule adopted by the SEC required the chairman of mutual fund boards be independent from that of the chief executive officer and that outside directors comprise at least seventy-five percent of mutual fund boards. Those outside directors would have to meet in separate sessions at least quarterly. The SEC rule was approved despite a study showing that mutual funds with non-independent chairman charged expenses that were on average lower than those with an independent chairman. Boards with management chairman also performed better on average. In response to the SEC rule proposal, legislation was introduced requiring the SEC to conduct a study of whether companies with independent chairman actually perform better. Consolidated

Appropriations Act, 2005, Pub. L. No. 108–447, 118 Stat. 2809 (2004). This was an effort to shame the SEC into reversing its rule but had no effect. The U.S. Chamber of Commerce sued the SEC to block implementation of that rule, which was approved by a split 3–2 vote of the Commission. The District of Columbia Court of Appeals concluded that the SEC had the authority to adopt such a proposal, but held that the SEC had not adequately considered its costs or available alternatives. Chamber of Commerce of the United States v. Securities and Exchange Commission, 412 F.3d 133 (D.C. Cir. 2005). That ruling was brushed aside by the SEC. The agency readopted the same rule only one week after it was stricken, without even awaiting the mandate of the court of appeals. The passage of the rule was also once again highly politicized, being passed over the dissenting votes of the two Republican commissioners, one of whom apologized to the Court of Appeals for the majority's high-handed approach. 70 Fed. Reg. 39,390 (July 7, 2005). That rule was again challenged and set aside by the court of appeals. Chamber of Commerce of the United States v. Securities and Exchange Commission, 443 F.3d 890 (D.C. Cir. 2006). Incredibly, the SEC was again considering adopting such a requirement in 2007 despite those setbacks in the court of appeals. Peter J. Wallison, Mutual Madness, Wall St. J., July 6, 2007.

SECTION 6. UNIT INVESTMENT TRUSTS

The unit investment trust is another form of investment company that has proved popular with investors. Like any investment vehicle, it provides advantages and disadvantages.

THOMAS S. HARMAN
EMERGING ALTERNATIVES TO MUTUAL FUNDS: UNIT INVESTMENT TRUSTS AND OTHER FIXED PORTFOLIO INVESTMENT VEHICLES

1987 Duke L. J. 1045.

The unit investment trust (UIT) has experienced many changes since its inception some sixty years ago as a "fixed trust." Some of the early fixed trusts were created as a result of the distrust of the excesses of the managed investment companies revealed in the aftermath of the Depression. Others were created because of the diversification they provided and because they allowed small investors to obtain an interest in a portfolio of securities that had become unaffordably expensive. Today such trusts compete with mutual funds for many consumers' investment dollars. * * *

A UIT is an unmanaged investment vehicle that invests in securities and sells interests ("units") in itself. As such, it meets the definition of "investment company" in section 3 of the Investment Company Act of 1940 (the 1940 Act). The 1940 Act specifically defines a UIT as an investment company, organized under a trust indenture, that has no board of directors and that "issues only redeemable securities, each of which represents an undivided interest in a unit of specified securities." While the UIT, like a mutual fund, issues redeemable securities, it nonetheless is different from a mutual fund in that the entity sponsoring the UIT nearly always creates a secondary market in the units sold by the trust. Both the sponsor and the trust benefit from the creation of the secondary market. The sponsor receives a sales charge on each unit resold in the secondary market, often at a higher rate than that received on units sold in the primary market. Unitholders enjoy a trust that does not have to deplete itself of its assets—possibly under disadvantageous circumstances—to meet redemptions. Redemptions of portfolio securities could cause premature termination of the trust if substantial enough or, more likely, create distributions of principal to remaining unitholders that could be reinvested only less advantageously or upon payment of a sales load or commission.

UITs are attractive investments because they offer liquidity and diversity at an affordable price. They allow investors of even moderate means to own an interest in a pool of diversified securities and, because they issue redeemable securities, they allow investors to liquidate their investments quickly and avoid many of the market's vagaries. While a mutual fund also offers diversification and liquidity, the UIT can provide those attributes at a lower cost because it has no investment adviser to whom it must pay an annual management fee. Moreover, because the UIT has a relatively fixed portfolio, the brokerage commissions it incurs are small in comparison to those of a mutual fund, the portfolio of which often changes. Finally, because of its relatively fixed portfolio, the UIT offers a "known" return. Conversely, a mutual fund's investment return may rise or fall as it trades its portfolio or invests additional proceeds from new shareholders.

UITs now invest in a variety of securities. Many invest in municipal bonds, but others invest in mortgage-backed securities. A third type of UIT invests in corporate securities, particularly preferred stock and corporate bonds. Although the vast majority of UITs invest in either municipal or corporate bonds, some UITs even invest in equity securities. In contrast, the early UITs essentially served as vehicles through which one could invest in common stocks, particularly securities listed on the New York Stock Exchange. The common stocks tended to represent a cross section of various issuers, although a number of early UITs specialized in the equity securities of banks, railroads, insurance, public utility or oil companies.

Because UITs, unlike mutual funds, have no investment adviser or board of directors, certain provisions of the 1940 Act clearly are irrelevant to them. Section 15, which governs the investment company's contract with the adviser, and sections 10 and 16, which govern an investment company's board of directors, are just a few examples. Section 18's extensive regulation of an investment company's capital structure is also irrelevant to UITs, because that provision applies only to management investment companies. Because a UIT is an essentially static entity, the provision of the 1940 Act that governs an investment company's transactions with its affiliates is also mostly irrelevant. This static nature has even been recognized in the context of periodic reporting to the Securities and Exchange Commission (the Commission); while mutual funds must file reports semi-annually with the Commission, UITs need only file annually. Moreover, because the 1940 Act requires only management investment companies to issue voting stock, the proxy provision of the 1940 Act is also largely irrelevant. UITs are, however, subject to certain important provisions under the 1940 Act.

The trust indenture, under which a UIT must be organized, governs the administration of the trust and the activities of those associated with it: the trustee, the depositor and the evaluator. The trust indenture also provides for the termination of the trust and the distribution of its assets. Many indentures stipulate that the trust will terminate after twenty years, although some trusts have a shorter duration and others exist for as many as fifty years. The 1940 Act, section 26 in particular, governs certain aspects of the indenture and, in so doing, controls the identity and activities of a UIT's trustee.

The trust indenture typically does not govern the underwriting of the trust. Instead, a separate agreement governs the distribution of the trust. UIT underwritings generally are not conducted like the "best efforts" underwriting of a mutual fund. Rather, each underwriter of a UIT becomes the owner of a specific number of trust units on a certain date. For so risking their capital and performing other activities, the underwriters receive a concession out of the public offering price of the units. The concession is often 3.5 to 3.7% of the public offering price, depending upon how many units the underwriter has agreed to purchase. The public offering price includes the sales charge, which often ranges from 4 to 6% of the public offering price. The underwriters may earn more than just a concession. If a profit is made on the deposit of securities into the UIT, all underwriters typically share in that profit. Any aggregate loss on the acquisition of securities deposited in the UIT, however, is usually borne solely by the sponsor. * * *

In addition to the underwriters, the sponsor, the trustee and the evaluator perform integral functions with respect to the UIT. The sponsor, of course, figures prominently in the life of the UIT. It organizes the trust and generally bears all of the accompanying organizational expenses. The sponsor is usually one of the underwriters of the trust. In fact, sometimes all of the underwriters of a trust serve as sponsor or co-sponsor. The sponsor earns money from the sales charge that constitutes a portion of the sale price of the units, and from the spread between the price at which it sells portfolio securities to the trust and the price it pays for the portfolio securities—the difference between the "offering side" and the "bid side." The sponsor may also receive compensation for providing portfolio supervisory services, because nothing requires only the evaluator to provide those services. The sponsor may even profit from the use of

cash paid to it before the date of settlement for the purchase of units.
* * *

NOTES

1.   The unit investment trust ("UIT") allows an investor seeking current income to make a more diversified investment. UIT shares are usually priced at $1,000 or less to attract smaller investors seeking diversification and who could not otherwise afford to diversify by buying several individual securities.

2.   The UIT portfolio is selected by expert analysts (the sponsor), but the investor is spared from active portfolio management by a third party that incurs costs and may cause losses. Of course, that limitation may be a disadvantage if the portfolio needs rebalancing. The most popular portfolio securities for a UIT are municipal bonds, which also bring tax advantages to the investor. See Chapter 9.

3.   The organizer of the UIT, the sponsor, is typically a broker-dealer. After the sponsor selects the securities for a particular UIT, it is closed. This means that, typically, no new securities will be sold or added to the UIT. The securities are deposited with a trustee under a trust indenture agreement that governs their handling.

U.S. TRUST CO. OF NEW YORK v. JENNER

168 F.3d 630 (2d Cir.1999).

VAN GRAAFEILAND, CIRCUIT JUDGE.

* * * The Trusts herein are unit investment trusts ("UITs"), entities that invest in fixed portfolios of securities and issue interests ("units") in their investments to third parties. *See* 15 U.S.C. § 80a–4(2). From 1977 to early 1982, these UITs bought Washington Public Power Supply System ("WPPSS") bonds that were issued to finance construction of two nuclear power plants. On January 22, 1982, WPPSS announced that the plants would not be built because of cost overruns and other problems. On June 15, 1983, the Washington Supreme Court held that State guarantees of the bonds were *ultra vires* and therefore unenforceable. Following the resultant default, bondholders brought numerous securities law class actions against WPPSS and other defendants connected to the bond issue or the underlying construction project. These actions were consolidated into a multi-district case ("MDL 551") in the United States District Court for the District of Arizona (Browning, *J.*). * * *

It suffices to say that a settlement ultimately was reached, as part of which the Trustees herein have received or will receive substantially in excess of $150 million. The instant interpleader actions were brought to determine how this money should be disbursed.

On December 29, 1992, U.S. Trust Company of New York, the Bank of New York, and Chase Manhattan Bank, as Trustees for 335 UITs, brought the first action (the "US Trust" action). On June 10, 1993, Investors Fiduciary Trust Company, as trustees for 11 UITs, filed the second action (the "Investors Fiduciary" action). The district court certified three classes of defendants for both actions: Class A—the Current Holders—those investors who acquired UIT units after June 15, 1983, the date of the State's disclaimer, and who held them either until the date that the UITs received and recorded the MDL 551 settlement funds or until the UIT's termination; Class B—the Former Holders—those investors who acquired UIT units before June 15, 1983 and who disposed of them before the UIT received the Settlement Funds or if the UIT was terminated prior to receipt of the Settlement Funds, before the UIT was terminated; Class C—the Continuous Holders—those investors who acquired UIT units before June 15, 1983 and who held them until the UIT received the Settlement Funds or until the UIT was terminated.

Essentially, the interpleader actions pit the Current and Continuous Holders against the Former Holders. The Former Holders, who owned the UIT units at the time of the WPPSS bond default, argue that even though they disposed of their UIT units before any MDL 551 settlement funds came into the UITs, they should get a share of the proceeds because, they say, they were the ones who were injured by the default. The Current and Continuous Holders argue that the UIT trust indentures expressly provide that only those investors who owned the UIT units when the settlement funds came into the UITs should get the money.

In order to resolve the issue thus created, the district court correctly looked to the language of the trust indentures. *See Elliott Assoc. v. J. Henry Schroder Bank & Trust Co.*, 838 F.2d 66, 71 (2d Cir.1988); *Meckel v. Continental Resources Co.*, 758 F.2d 811, 816 (2d Cir.1985). The Certificates of Ownership, which represented ownership of the trust units in the instant case, provide in almost identical language that the Certificate holder is bound by the terms of the indentures. New York and Missouri, whose laws are expressly made pertinent herein, enforce this mandate.

The indentures herein provide, again in almost identical language:

1. that all moneys received by the Trustee shall be held without interest in trust as part of the Trust Fund until required to be disbursed in accordance with the provisions of the indenture;

2. that the Trustee shall establish an Interest Account, a Principal Account and a Reserve Account;

3. that all interest received by the Trustee with respect to the Bonds held by the Trust shall be credited to the Interest Account; and

4. that all moneys received by the Trustee in respect of the Bonds, other than amounts credited to the Interest Account shall be credited to the Principal Account; and

5. that payments on "Principal Distribution Days" shall be made from the Principal Account and computed as of the close of business on the preceding "Record Day."

These provisions are clear and unambiguous, and ambiguity is not created simply because the parties urge different interpretations. *Metropolitan Life Ins. Co. v. RJR Nabisco, Inc.,* 906 F.2d 884, 889 (2d Cir.1990). Moreover, where, as here, a contract is unambiguous, "courts are required to give effect to the contract as written and may not consider extrinsic evidence to alter or interpret its meaning." *Consarc Corp. v. Marine Midland Bank, N.A.,* 996 F.2d 568, 573 (2d Cir.1993); *Cruden v. Bank of New York,* 957 F.2d 961, 976 (2d Cir.1992). The affidavit of the proposed witness Harmon was of this nature and appellants' reliance upon it is misplaced.

Equally misplaced is appellants' attempt to give *res judicata* or collateral estoppel effect to Judge Browning's comments in the MDL 551 litigation that only those bondholders who purchased WPPSS bonds prior to June 15, 1983 have a viable cause of action for securities fraud. In the first place, the record in the MDL 551 litigation contains no judicial finding or participant stipulation that such fraud exists. Indeed, the existence of securities fraud was negated consistently throughout the MDL 551 settlement proceedings. More importantly, the terms "bondholder" and "unitholder" are not synonymous, and the legal ramifications of the two statuses differ substantially. As the district court correctly put it, "the MDL 551 Litigation involved neither the same parties nor the same issues involved herein."

We obviously have not discussed all of the arguments made by competent counsel for the Former Holders, and we see no need to do so. These are not securities fraud actions. They are contract interpretation cases, i.e., were the terms of the trust indentures complied with? The district court correctly held that they were. Accordingly its judgment of April 6, 1986 encompassing all the summary judgments is affirmed.

NOTES

1. The trustee for a UIT has only a limited role: "The trustee, usually a major bank, is unlike a trustee in most other contexts in that it typically performs only "ministerial duties," collecting and distributing the interest and dividends due on the portfolio securities and providing the unit holders with periodic reports concerning the interest received, amounts distributed and securities in the portfolio." U.S. Trust Co. of New York v. Alpert, 10 F.Supp.2d 290 (S.D.N.Y.1998), aff'd, 168 F.3d 630 (2d Cir.1999). This role is similar to that of trustee under a trust indenture for bonds. See Ch. 4. The trustee of a UIT may be authorized by the trust indenture to dispose of portfolio securities upon the occurrence of certain specified events, such as threat of default of a portfolio security.

2.   A concern in investing in UITs is liquidity. That concern is met by the fact that there is often a secondary market in UIT shares. A sponsor may thus agree to redeem and resell interests in the UIT. To assure the redemption at a fair price, the sponsor will usually have an independent third party price the UIT:

> Some indentures, including those involved herein, are also executed by an "evaluator," who, together with the trustee, values the trust's assets for purposes of fixing the net asset value at which units are redeemed and based on which they will trade in the secondary market.

U.S. Trust Co. of New York v. Alpert, 10 F.Supp.2d 290 (S.D.N.Y.1998), aff'd, 168 F.3d 630 (2d Cir.1999). There is, of course, no free lunch on Wall Street, so the sponsor may profit by buying these units back at their lower bid price and reselling them at a higher asked price.

3.   UITs have their limitations. Sales commissions, underwriting charges and assembling the portfolio all add to the cost and reduce the amount of their return. The UIT is usually less diversified than the diversified mutual funds. The absence of an advisor, will leave the UIT owner to their own devices in determining whether the investment should be sold.

4.   The UIT will usually be rated by a ratings agency such as Standard & Poors. The rating will reflect the views of those agencies on the creditworthiness of the portfolio securities. Those ratings are only as good as the raters and may change over time. See Ch. 3.

5.   Some UITs have offered insurance, letters of credit or other devices to guarantee against a default on the securities held in the portfolio. Of course, such features will add to the cost of the UIT and are themselves only as good as the credit of the issuer of the guarantee.

6.   The UIT is usually used for fixed income instruments or dividend paying securities, but may also be used for a portfolio of indexed securities. The American Stock Exchange has created such a product:

> DIAMONDS represent ownership in the DIAMONDS, Trust Series 1, a unit investment trust established to accumulate and hold a portfolio of the equity securities that comprise the Dow Jones Industrial Average. DIAMONDS seek investment results that, before expenses, generally correspond to the price and yield performance of the DJIA. There is no assurance that the price and yield performance of the DJIA can be fully matched.

www.amex.com (visited March 17, 2003).

7.   As a result of the late trading and market timing scandals at the mutual funds consideration is being given to whether alternative investment forms such as UITs might be more cost effective and subject to less abuse. After extensive study, two authors have recommended the use of a "managed investment trust" ("MIT") as an alternative governance structure. The MIT would use the UIT as a model. Peter J. Wallison & Robert E. Litan, Competitive Equity, A Better Way to Organize Mutual Funds 100 (2007).

Another alternative is the unitary investment fund ("UIF") that is widely employed outside the United States. This "is a contract type entity which is not independent of its sponsor or manager," as is the case for the open end mutual fund. Stephen K. West, The Investment Company Industry in the 1990s, A Rethinking of the Regulatory Structure Appropriate for Investment Companies in the 1990s. 64 (March 1990). The UIF may allow redemption of investments, but it operation and success is vested in the manager. The UIFs have an "all in" annual management fees plus transaction costs. "They existed in 1940 and in fact were the preferred form in Boston" and were grandfathered by the Investment Company Act "with limited corporate democracy imposed by permitting the unit holders to remove the trustee by a two-thirds vote." *Id.* at 65 "The benefits of a unitary form are realism and the elimination of large amounts of administrative work at the state and federal level involved with the corporate governance structure, to say nothing of the internal administration and legal work involved." *Id.*

In 1978, the SEC staff examined whether the UIF concept was appropriate for America. As a part of that study, the use of such entities in England was examined. The SEC staff and the Investment Company Institute then sought to draft model legislation for UIFs. The SEC also sought public comment on the concept in 1982, but "[m]ost commentators opposed the UIF, based largely on concerns about the adequacy of investor protections for UIF investors and unresolved questions about how the concept would work in practice." SEC Division of Investment Management, "Protecting Investors: A Half Century of Investment Company Regulation" 282, n. 107 (May 1992). That response cooled interest in the UIF for a time but a study conducted for the Investment Company Institute by Stephen K. West in 1990 advocated the adoption of a UIF structure. The SEC staff rejected that recommendation in 1992, concluding that, while the UIF approach to fees "generally is sound," cost savings appeared to be "minimal." The SEC staff further contended that "there is no practical substitute for the oversight of boards of directors regarding investment company operations." *Id.* at 283. The issue was revisited in 2005 by the American Enterprise Institute as a part of a series of conferences that considered the issue of whether there is a better way to regulate mutual funds. Stephen West appeared at one of those conferences with a revised proposal that would create a UIF with a board of directors.

SECTION 7.   FACE AMOUNT CERTIFICATES

SECURITIES AND EXCHANGE COMMISSION v. MOUNT VERNON MEMORIAL PARK

664 F.2d 1358 (9th Cir.1982), cert. denied, 456 U.S.
961, 102 S.Ct. 2037, 72 L.Ed.2d 485 (1982).

POOLE, CIRCUIT JUDGE.

In this appeal, we must decide whether the Mount Vernon Memorial Park (Mount Vernon), a Sacramento cemetery and mortuary which issued debentures in connection with the sale of its services, is an "investment company" within the meaning of the Investment Company Act of 1940

(Act), 15 U.S.C. § 80a–1 et seq. In a two-count complaint filed in the district court, the Securities and Exchange Commission (Commission) alleged that Mount Vernon had failed to comply with the regulatory provisions of the Act and violated provisions of the Securities Act of 1933, § 77t(b), and the Securities and Exchange Act of 1934, §§ 78u(d), 78u(e), in connection with its funeral debenture program.* * *

Mount Vernon is a California corporation operating a licensed mortuary and cemetery in Sacramento, California. Appellee Foy E. Bryant was the president and principal shareholder since Mount Vernon's incorporation and throughout the critical period at issue in this case.

In addition to the sale of its services for cash, Mount Vernon began in the mid-sixties to sell cemetery plots and funeral services on an anticipatory or "pre-need" basis. A pre-need customer would contract for purchase of a plot and a funeral service in the event of death. Under an installment sales arrangement, Mount Vernon agreed to provide a specified funeral service at a fixed price; customer was obligated to make payments spread over several years. Mount Vernon was free to use the monies received to cover its general operating expenses. If the "need" for service arose before all installments had been met, the payments made would be credited toward the price.

In October 1969, the California Attorney General issued an opinion interpreting California's Short Act, Cal.Bus. & Prof.Code § 7735 et seq., as applied to the sales of pre-need cemetery and mortuary services. He concluded that the Act required all consideration paid pursuant to installment sale funeral contracts to be held in trust until the services were actually performed. Furthermore, the opinion indicated that a refund of 90% of installment payments had to be available to any pre-need purchaser at any time under the contract arrangement. Under such an interpretation of California law, companies such as Mount Vernon could no longer use installment payment revenue to meet current operating expenses.

Mount Vernon altered its pre-need sales contract in an effort to avoid the trust fund requirements of the Short Act promulgated in the Attorney General's decision. Exempted from the Short Act were sellers of pre-need funeral contracts who issued securities as a part of the program. Thus, once securities were registered with the California Department of Corporations, they could be offered for sale as part of a pre-need funeral program and the seller was free to use 85% of the proceeds from the sale of the debentures for any purpose, retaining only 15% in a sinking fund.

Beginning in September 1970, Mount Vernon offered "Pre–Need Funeral Service Debentures." Under the restructured program, a purchaser executed two documents: a funeral service contract and a subscription agreement. The contract obligated Mount Vernon to provide future services at a fixed price so long as the purchaser continued to make installment payments toward purchase of the debentures. Under the subscription agreement, purchaser agreed to buy a certain number (equivalent to the approximate contract price for funeral services) of "Pre–Need

Funeral Service Debentures," in amounts of $100 each. The debentures were interest bearing; the term of the subscription could run up to eight years. Monthly payments, which could be as low as $7.50, were accumulated by Mount Vernon until they reached the subscription price, at which time a debenture was issued. Upon default on the installment payment obligation under the subscription agreement, Mount Vernon was released from its commitment to provide funeral services at a fixed price under the contract.

Once purchased, the debentures were redeemable for funeral and cemetery services or for cash at maturity, twenty years after purchase. If, upon the arrival of the contingency, the debentures were insufficient to cover the contract price of the services, they could be redeemed up to the amount of their value so long as the contract balance for the services was paid at the time services were rendered. The subscription agreement was cancellable at will upon notice by the purchaser. If cancelled, Mount Vernon immediately refunded only the installment payments made since the issuance of the last debenture; the balance was redeemable at maturity.

Between September 1970 and January 1975, Mount Vernon made four offerings of the debentures, each totaling one million dollars. The interest rate of the first offering was 4 1/2% while the remaining offerings provided for interest of 3%, in each case payable either directly to the purchaser or creditable toward the next installment payment. Mount Vernon retained 15% of installment payments in a sinking fund; the remaining 85% was available to meet the company's operating expenses.

Mount Vernon discontinued its debenture contract offerings in 1975 after approximately 4,900 such contracts had been sold. In 1976, the Commission indicated in an administrative decision that it viewed debentures similar to those issued by Mount Vernon to be "face-amount certificates of the installment type," rendering issuers of such certificates investment companies by virtue of § 80a–3(a)(2). See In re International Funeral Service of California, Inc., (1975–1976 Transfer Binder) Fed.Sec. L.Rep. (CCH) P 80,363, at 85,960 (1976). Shortly thereafter, the Commission advised Mount Vernon that it considered the firm an investment company because of the outstanding funeral debentures.

In February 1976, Mount Vernon began to deposit revenue from the existing debenture contracts into a separate bank account. Thus, after paying 15% of the revenue into the sinking fund, as required by the subscription agreement, the balance has been held in this bank account, monies from which are used for investment with the profits on such investments paid to Mount Vernon.

On February 17, 1977, this suit was commenced by the Commission in the Eastern District of California. Count one alleged that Mount Vernon and Bryant violated the Act by issuing face-amount certificates of the installment type without complying with the Act's registration requirements. Count two charged fraudulent and materially misleading activities in connection with the sale of these debentures, in violation of the Securities Acts of 1933 and 1934.

The Commission moved for a preliminary injunction against the appellees on both counts and appellees sought dismissal of count one for failure to state a claim, theorizing that Mount Vernon was not a regulable investment company. * * *

An investment company within the meaning of the Act is defined in § 80a–3. For our purposes, it is undisputed that Mount Vernon is an investment company if it

> is engaged or proposes to engage in the business of issuing face-amount certificates of the installment type, or has been engaged in such business and has any such certificates outstanding(.)

§ 80a–3(a)(2). A face-amount certificate is defined in § 80a–2(a)(15):

> (a) When used in this subchapter, unless the context otherwise requires:

> > (15) "Face amount certificate" means any certificate, investment contract, or other security which represents an obligation on the part of its issuer to pay a stated or determinable sum or sums at a fixed or determinable date or dates more than twenty-four months after the date of issuance, in consideration of periodic installments of a stated or determinable amount (which security shall be known as a face-amount certificate of the installment type)(.)

A threshold requirement for applicability of the above quoted section is that the instrument in question be a "certificate, investment, or other security." The parties do not appear to contest that the funeral service debentures are investment contracts or securities, and we do not find it necessary to examine the point. Appellees admit that Mount Vernon has outstanding certificates which literally fit the definition in subsection 15. They theorize, however, and the district court agreed, that the Act was intended to regulate only issuers of certificates defined in subsection 15 who use the proceeds from the sale of such certificates for reinvestment in other companies' securities and not in the issuers' own business (hereinafter "reinvestment requirement"). * * *

In the Public Utility Holding Company Act of 1935, § 79z–4, Congress instructed the Commission to investigate the activities and problems of investment companies and to propose regulatory legislation. A detailed investigation lead to proposed legislation, which was subsequently modified in light of suggestions and criticism from the investment industry. It was only in this modified version of the bill that (a)(2) appeared as part of the investment company definition. The inclusion was made "in order to eliminate any doubt that the face-amount-certificate companies are within the category of investment companies contemplated by this legislation...." House Hearings, supra, at 101.

The ultimate objective of the Act was to regulate "liquid pools of public savings entrusted to the (investment) company management for investment in productive enterprise." Note, The Investment Company Act of 1940, 50 Yale L.J. 440, 440 (1941). Viewing the Act in light of its broadest objectives, we acknowledge that Congress focused primary attention on companies "invest(ing) in securities of other corporations and issu(ing) securities of (their) own." United States v. National Association of Securities Dealers, 422 U.S. 694, 697–98, 95 S.Ct. 2427, 2432–2433, 45 L.Ed.2d 486 (1975). But this is hardly a surprising revelation in light of (a)(1) and (a)(3), which define investment companies as those significantly engaged in the business of investing in the securities of others. * * *

Since we have rejected Mount Vernon's theory that an (a)(2) investment company must be primarily engaged in reinvestment in other companies' securities, Mount Vernon cannot seriously contest that it falls within the terms of the Act. We therefore reverse the judgment of the district court dismissing count one of the Commission's complaint and remand this case to that court for further proceedings consistent with this opinion.

SECTION 8. DERIVATIVES

Like other areas of finance, financial engineers have been at work on creating investment company-like products. One disadvantage of the mutual fund was that a customer buying or selling received the net asset value only as calculated at particular times at day's end and not continuously. A new product was invented that sought to provide the advantages and diversification of a mutual fund but also allow liquidation and purchase continuously throughout the day at then current prices. They were called exchange traded funds, a particularly popular such instrument was the "Spider."

> New York, January 29, 2003–With assets topping more than $35 billion and average daily trading of 34 million shares, the American Stock Exchange (Amex) today celebrates the 10–year anniversary of the start of trading in its flagship exchange traded fund (ETF), SPDR—Standard & Poor's Depositary Receipts ("Spider"). * * * "As ETFs have surged in popularity and as investors have poured $100 billion into our 122 ETFs over the last ten years, investors see the inherent benefits that ETFs offer: tax efficiency, diversification and transparency."

> ETFs are akin to index funds that trade like a single stock. They are liquid and easy to use, and offer diversification, market tracking, low expenses and tax efficiency. ETFs offer a flexible mechanism to get needed exposure, while at the same time are more transparent and provide greater control than traditional mutual funds.

The Amex pioneered the concept of ETFs in the U.S. in 1993 with the introduction of trading in SPDRs—Standard & Poor's Depositary Receipts (AMEX: SPY), an exchange-traded unit investment trust based on the Standard & Poor's 500 Index.

www.amex.com (visited March 17, 2003). These instruments are further described as follows:

> Exchange traded funds (ETFs) are index funds or trusts that are listed on an exchange and can be traded intraday. Investors can buy or sell shares in the collective performance of an entire stock or bond portfolio as a single security. Exchange traded funds add the flexibility, ease and liquidity of stock trading to the benefits of traditional index fund investing.

Id.

Mutual funds are not supposed to be used for "market timing" trading, *i.e.*, buying and selling rapidly in order to take advantage of short-term market movements. Rather, mutual funds are used for long-term "buy and hold" strategies. This is because of the high fees associated with mutual fund transactions and because of their pricing at the close of trading only, which restricts the ability to take advantage of market movements. How does this concern square with the trading of ETFs? Some large traders were allowed to avoid the restriction of trading only at day's end in mutual funds by being allowed to trade at night at the preceding closing price. This allowed those traders to take advantage of over-night price movements at the preset price. Civil and criminal enforcement actions were brought to stop such activities. Riva D. Atlas, Ex-Hedge Fund Trader Pleads Guilty in Inquiry, New York Times, Oct. 3, 2003, at C1.

Commodity Pools[16]

A "commodity pool" is another investment creature with hybrid characteristics. Introduced to federal regulation at the same time as commodity trading advisors (in 1974), the "commodity pool operator" ("CPO") represents a relatively new entrant into the commodity industry. A commodity pool is typically an organization that raises capital through the sale of interests in it, such as shares or limited partnerships, and uses that capital to invest in commodity contracts. In its features, the typical commodity pool bears a strong resemblance to mutual funds and similar investment companies that have operated for decades in the securities industry. See Rosenthal & Co. v. Commodity Futures Trading Commission, 802 F.2d 963 (7th Cir.1986) ("A commodity pool is the commodity-futures equivalent of a mutual fund; the investor buys shares in the pool and the operator of the pool invests the proceeds in commodity futures.").

---

16. The following note is drawn principally from Phillip Johnson & Thomas Hazen, Derivatives Regulation (4th ed. 2004).

A commodity pool must register with the Commodity Futures Trading Commission ("CFTC"). 7 U.S.C. § 6m.

As a rule, the interests purchased by investors carry a right to participate in the results of the investment program but limit their personal liability to the amount of their investment in the venture. Principal attractions of the commodity pool are its ability to assume diversified positions in the futures market due to its substantial resources; the elimination of margin calls directly to investors; the avoidance by investors of any personal duty to make or take delivery on futures contracts; and, as noted above, limited liability for investors. In addition to the typical commodity pool, created and marketed as such, "inadvertent" commodity pools can arise—for example, when securities trading partnerships enter the futures or commodity options market. Similarly, problems relating to inadvertent commodity pools can arise when insurance companies and other financial institutions aggregate client accounts (for example, pension funds) to take positions in futures.

In Lopez v. Dean Witter Reynolds, Inc., 805 F.2d 880, 883–884 (9th Cir.1986) the court stated that:

> While numerous courts have dealt with the concept of commodity pools in the abstract, few have specifically attempted to define what constitutes a pool. The Commodity Exchange Act fails to provide any assistance in this regard. * * * Those courts which have raised the issue require the following factors to be present in a commodity pool: (1) an investment organization in which the funds of various investors are solicited and combined into a single account for the purpose of investing in commodity futures contracts; (2) common funds used to execute transactions on behalf of the *entire* account; (3) participants share pro rata in accrued profits or losses from the commodity futures trading; and (4) the transactions are traded by a commodity pool operator in the name of the pool rather than in the name of any individual investor.

In 1982, Congress made it clear that the federal securities laws of 1933 and 1934 apply to the sale and purchase of interests in a commodity pool that qualify as "securities." Thus when an investment company invests in derivative instruments several complexities are raised. Even if the derivative investments are limited exclusively to those regulated by the CFTC, dual regulatory requirements may be imposed. The provisions of the federal securities laws and the rules of the Securities and Exchange Commission ("SEC") will apply to the offering of the units in the pool to the public, but the pool will not be regulated as an investment company under the provisions of the Investment Company Act of 1940. Instead, the Commodity Exchange Act of 1936 will govern the pool's operations. As noted, this will require registration with the CFTC as a CPO, unless exempted, as in the case of a small pool. The adviser to the pool will also have to register with the CFTC as a "commodity trading adviser", unless exempted. 7 U.S.C. § 6o.

In addition to registration requirements, all nonexempt commodity pool operators must comply with strict operational standards set forth in CFTC Regulations 4.20 through 4.26 of the Commission. Except in the case of offerings made to a person satisfying the standards of an "accredited investor" under the securities laws, CFTC Regulation 4.21 provides that "on or before" the date when the commodity pool operator solicits, accepts, or receives any funds (including securities or property) from a prospective participant in a pool, and Commission Regulation section 4.24 requires that it must deliver to that person a disclosure document containing the following:

1. The name and main address of the commodity pool operator and each of its principals as well as their business background for the preceding five years;

2. The business background, for the same period, of any commodity trading advisor to the pool (and its principals);

3. "Any actual or potential conflict of interest" in regard to the pool by the operator or manager, commodity trading advisor (or their principals), or carrying futures commission merchant (or their principals or introducing brokers);

4. Under standards set in Commission Regulation section 4.25, the "actual performance" of the pool (and its principals), of the commodity trading advisor (and its principals), and of any other pool of the operator or a commodity trading advisor (and their principals), for the preceding five years or lesser term of their existence, to be calculated and presented in strict conformity with specifications contained in that Regulation;

5. Whether the operator, commodity trading advisor, or any principal has a beneficial interest in the pool and, if so, the extent of that interest;

6. An identification of all types of expenses and fees that were incurred by the pool in the preceding fiscal year and are expected to be incurred in the current year;

7. Information regarding any minimum or maximum contribution requirements and, if applicable, what will be done with the funds until trading begins;

8. How the pool will fulfill its margin requirements on transactions, and how it will use funds in excess of margin requirements;

9. Any restrictions upon transfer or redemption of interests in the pool;

10. The extent to which pool participants may be liable in excess of their capital contributions;

11. The pool's distribution policy with respect to profits or capital, and its federal income tax effects for the participants;

12. Any "material" administrative, civil, or criminal action against the operator, commodity trading advisor, or a principal in the preceding five years;

13. Any fee payable by the operator, commodity trading advisor, or a principal to any person for soliciting capital contributions to the pool;

14. Whether the operator, commodity trading advisor, or a principal trades (or intends to) and, if so, whether participants will be permitted to inspect those trading records;

15. A statement that all participants will receive monthly or quarterly account statements and either a certified or uncertified annual financial report; and

16. On the cover page of the disclosure document, a disclaimer that the Commission has neither reviewed nor passed on the accuracy or completeness of that document.

In addition, the first page of the disclosure document must set forth a specific "risk disclosure statement" as set forth verbatim in Regulation section 4.24, which, in addition to stating certain risks of joining a pool, repeats again the disclaimer of Commission review of the disclosure document. Moreover, in the event that the operator "knows or has reason to know" that the disclosure document is materially inaccurate or incomplete, a corrected disclosure document must be furnished to all existing and prospective participants in the pool within five business days thereafter. To the extent that commodity pools invest in foreign futures and commodity options, they are subject to the disclosure requirements set out in Commission Regulation section 4.24. Similarly, commodity pool operators are subject to the antifraud provisions in the Commodity Exchange Act.

Mutual funds regulated by the SEC may also trade derivative instruments without having to register with the CFTC as a commodity pool operator where those transactions are used to hedge the securities portfolio.

Many hedge funds trade regulated commodity futures and option contracts. That trading activity initially led those funds to register with the CFTC as CPOs and CTAs. However, "[i]n 1992, the CFTC adopted a key liberalizing measure, Rule 4.7, which preserved CPO registration requirements but provided an exemption from most regulatory requirements for pools offered only to highly accredited investors," which composed most of those persons investing in hedge funds. Susan C. Ervin, "Letting Go: The CFTC Rethinks Managed Futures Regulation," 24 Futures & Derivatives L. Rep. 1, 8, n. 5 (May 2004). Similar relief was not given for CTA registration. However, the CFTC began rethinking its regulatory role after the enactment of the Commodities Futures Modernization Act of 2000. Pub. L. Rep. No. 106–554, 114 Stat. 2763 (2000). That statute was a statutory reflection of the CFTC's decision to deregulate the commodity markets for transactions in which only wealthy and sophisticated investors are involved. The CFTC was, therefore, receptive to a petition from the "Managed Funds Association . . . a trade association for hedge fund managers and CPOs" that sought "a 'sophisticated investor' exemption" from registration as a CTA for advisors advising only wealthy and sophisticated clients. Ervin, supra, at p. 3. That exemption was adopted by the CFTC on August 8, 2003. 68 Fed. Reg. 47221 (Aug. 8, 2003). This was exactly the opposite of the approach of the SEC, as described above.

ROBERT A. ROBERTSON & BRADLEY W. PAULSON REGULATION OF FINANCIAL DERIVATIVES: A METHODOLOGY FOR MUTUAL FUND DERIVATIVE INSTRUMENTS

1 Stanford Journal of Law, Business & Finance 237 (1995).

The term "derivatives" covers a broad array of financial instruments. They are perhaps best defined as instruments whose value is based upon (or "derives" from) the value of an underlying asset, index, or reference rate. The term includes financial products traded on an exchange, such as futures and options, as well as products traded over-the-counter ("OTC") or negotiated privately, such as forwards, swaps, OTC options, structured notes, and certain mortgage backed securities. * * *

The fact that an instrument is a "derivative" by no means implies that it is an improper investment for mutual funds. Funds invest in derivatives for many legitimate reasons, which include reducing ("hedging") their risks and investing funds in anticipation of future market movements. For example, foreign equity funds might use derivatives to hedge against currency risks. If a Latin American stock fund has equity investments in Mexico, and the fund's investment adviser believes the Mexican peso might fall relative to the U.S. dollar, the adviser might enter into a currency forward contract. The forward would enable the fund to trade its pesos for dollars at a predetermined rate of exchange and guard against the risk that the dollar value of the peso might fall.

Similarly, a fund manager may need funds in a foreign currency at a specified time in the future. The manager might want to purchase from a creditworthy domestic issuer a structured note that will pay principal and interest in the foreign currency. By doing so, the manager could be assured of having the right amount of foreign funds available when needed. The transaction might entail less risk than buying a similar note issued by a less creditworthy foreign issuer or bank.

The dangers associated with mutual fund derivative investments typically arise when a fund manager uses fund assets to gamble on market movements, and investors do not expect the fund manager to take these risks. Despite large losses by some mutual funds during 1994 that were attributable to investments in derivatives, we believe that many, if not the overwhelming majority, of mutual fund derivative investments are entirely appropriate—provided that these investments are consistent with investor expectations. * * *

Two types of laws govern a mutual fund's derivative investment activities: substantive laws and disclosure laws. Substantive laws govern how a mutual fund may engage in derivative investments, regardless of any disclosures made to the fund's investors. Disclosure laws, on the other hand, describe how permissible derivative investments must be disclosed to a fund's investors and require that those investments be consistent with what has been disclosed.

The Investment Company Act ("Act") governs the pricing practices of mutual fund shares. Section 22(c) provides the Commission with the authority to make rules governing these practices, and Rule 22c–1 generally requires a fund to calculate the current net asset value of its shares every business day.

In addition, the Act requires a fund (other than certain money market funds) to value its portfolio securities at market value. Market quotations must be used for those securities where available. For all other securities, a fund's board of directors is required to determine the assets' fair value. The consequences of a mistake can be serious.

The SEC's Division of Investment Management (the "Division") requires that funds correct any pricing errors and that fund sponsors reimburse shareholders who suffer a material economic loss due to the errors. Accordingly, funds must ensure that they can appropriately price any derivative instrument they acquire.

The Investment Company Act also indirectly governs a mutual fund's liquidity requirements. Section 22(e) requires that a fund make payment for redeemed shares within seven days after the tender of the shares. Thus, funds must maintain liquid investment portfolios that will enable them to meet this obligation. In this regard, the Commission requires funds to limit their investments in illiquid portfolio securities to fifteen percent of net assets. The limit is ten percent, however, in the case of money market funds. An asset is considered "illiquid" if a fund cannot sell the asset in the ordinary course of business within seven days at the approximate price at which the fund has valued the asset.

Mutual funds generally must determine if a particular security, including a derivative instrument, is illiquid. The Division, however, has taken the position that particular derivative instruments may be illiquid under all or most conditions. Derivatives may be illiquid if the derivative is designed to meet the needs of a particular fund. Such a derivative might not have the market depth required to support a finding that the instrument is liquid. Some instruments may be liquid in one market environment and not in another. A fund must continually make liquidity determinations, especially with derivatives, to ensure that it meets the liquidity requirements.

Although the leverage restrictions of the Investment Company Act were not originally designed to govern most of the derivative transactions that mutual funds engage in today, those provisions have been used to a limited extent. Section 18(f) restricts leveraged capital structures by prohibiting a fund from issuing any class of "senior security," which is any bond, note, or similar security evidencing indebtedness. The Division has stated that a mutual fund's derivative investments may involve two types of leverage: "indebtedness leverage" and "economic leverage." Certain derivatives entail "indebtedness leverage" because they consist of, in part at least, an obligation or indebtedness to someone other than the fund's shareholders and enable the fund to participate in gains or losses in excess of its initial investment. For example, the writer of a stock put option makes no initial investment but is obligated to purchase the underlying stock at a fixed price, thereby participating in any losses to the extent of the full stock price. Other derivatives involve "economic leverage" because they display heightened price sensitivity to market fluctuations, such as stock prices or interest rates. For instance, leveraged inverse floaters, which have an interest rate that moves inversely to a designated rate, experience market fluctuations equivalent to those that would be experienced with a conventional bond of a larger principal amount or with investments that the fund purchased on margin.

Section 18 has been applied to derivatives that create indebtedness leverage. The Commission and the Division have required funds to "cover" the obligations that indebtedness leverage creates by establishing segregated accounts consisting of cash or high grade debt securities. These accounts must be in an amount at least equal to the value of the fund's obligations. The Division has expressed concern about derivatives that create economic leverage because of their increased volatility. At this time, the Division believes that one of the most effective means for addressing these concerns is improved risk disclosure. If this approach does not sufficiently protect fund shareholders, the Division may reconsider whether to recommend that the Investment Company Act be amended to place substantive limits on derivative use.

Thus, mutual funds must pay close attention to pricing, liquidity, and leverage restrictions when they make investments in derivative instruments. The substantive laws that govern these areas have helped to shape present mutual fund structures and, as a consequence, investor expectations of these investments. Of course, disclosure laws play a more direct role developing these expectations. These laws, in conjunction with the methodology, will now be considered. * * *

In essence, Rule 2a–7 under the Investment Company Act requires all mutual funds holding themselves out to the public as money market funds to invest in securities that allow the fund to maintain a stable net asset value. Rule 2a–7 was adopted by the Commission in 1983. The intent of the rule was to limit money market fund investments "to those instruments that have a low level of volatility" and to "provide greater assurance that the money market fund will continue to be able to maintain a stable price per share that fairly reflects the current net asset value per share of the funds."

Since the Commission adopted amendments to Rule 2a–7 in 1991, most money market funds have been required to maintain a dollar-weighted average portfolio maturity of not more than 90 days. Additionally, all instruments held by these funds must have a remaining maturity of 13 months (397 days) or less. An instrument maturing in more than 13 months is deemed to mature within that time if its interest rate adjusts within 13 months. Shortly after the Commission adopted the 1991 amendments, interpretive problems arose. Many fund managers believed they were permitted under the rule to hold any medium-or long-term security if its interest rate adjusted within 13 months—*despite the fact that its value may not return to par upon readjustment.* Consequently, the SEC began a protracted campaign to reign in fund managers who were reaching too high in their quest for returns.

Marianne K. Smythe, Director of the Division, sent a letter to the ICI [Investment Company Institute] in late 1991 stating that inverse floaters are not appropriate instruments for money market funds. Ms. Smythe stated,

> ... An investment in an inverse floater will ordinarily expose the money market fund to a degree of interest rate risk and volatility more characteristic of a long-term instrument. Investment in an inverse floaters [sic] would circumvent the provisions of Rule 2a–7 governing the maximum maturity of individual securities and the average weighted portfolio maturity where a sufficient amount of a fund's assets is invested in these instruments.

The letter closed with a warning that the Division would recommend enforcement action against funds holding these instruments. Later, in July 1992, the Division stated in a letter to Morgan Keegan & Company that, with respect to government securities with maturities of more than 13 months, the interest rate readjustment provisions must reset at a rate such that the instrument "can reasonably be expected to have a market value that approximates their par value." In June 1993, the Division sent another letter to the ICI stating that capped floaters that mature in more than 13 months are impermissible under Rule 2a–7. * * *

In mid-June 1994, the Chairman of the Commission, Arthur Levitt, sent letters to the ICI and the chief executives of eighty fund complexes in which he stated, "I strongly encourage the management of every fund that holds derivative instruments to take steps that will ensure the proper understanding and effective management of derivatives risk." Later that same month, Barry P. Barbash, Director of the Division of Investment Management, sent a letter to the ICI explaining that the

> ... maturity limiting provisions of the rule are designed to ensure that money market funds invest in securities characterized by a low level of volatility and whose market-based values do not differ significantly from [the values ascribed to the securities on the funds'

books].... In analyzing whether a particular adjustable rate security is appropriate for a money market fund, an adviser must determine not only that holding the security is not specifically prohibited by the rule, but also that the security meets the general rule applicable to all investments by a money market fund: that investment in the security is consistent with maintaining a stable net asset value.

In addition to the derivatives identified as inappropriate in the December release, the letter stated that range floaters and dual index floaters are also among the types of instruments that are unsuitable for money market funds. This letter, following closely on the heels of Chairman Levitt's letter, should have prompted fund managers to reexamine closely their derivative investments. * * *

NOTES

1. The Investment Company Act of 1940 sought to curb the leveraging of investment companies through borrowed funds. Nevertheless, closed end investment companies investing in hybrid preferred stock that had elements of debt and equity were becoming popular in 2003. Tom Lauricella, Wall St. J., May 2, 2003, at C1. Why do you think such securities are attractive to closed-end funds and not mutual funds?

2. The creation of single stock futures raises further complexities in the regulation of pooled investments. Under the Commodity Futures Trading Modernization Act of 2000 the CFTC and SEC are to share jurisdiction over those instruments. See Chs. 11, 12. How does that shared jurisdiction affect mutual funds or commodity pools trading single stock futures?

SECTION 9.   REAL ESTATE INVESTMENT TRUSTS

Another pooled investment mechanism is the Real Estate Investment Trust ("REIT"). This vehicle is a creature created by Congress that offers pass-through tax treatment to participants as long as certain restrictions are met.

AMERICAN REALTY TRUST v. UNITED STATES OF AMERICA

498 F.2d 1194 (4th Cir. 1974).

ADAMS, CIRCUIT JUDGE.

After the sale and lease-back of a particular piece of commercial real estate, who, as between the seller-lessee and the buyer-lessor, is entitled to claim, for federal tax purposes, a depreciation deduction for the property? That is the key issue in this case, and it arises from the attempt by a real estate investment trust to take a depreciation deduction on an apartment house that it purchased and then leased back to the seller.

The taxpayer, American Realty Trust ("ART"), is a real estate investment trust, that since its inception in 1961 has sought the favorable tax treatment afforded such trusts by the Internal Revenue Code. 26 U.S.C. §§ 856–858. To qualify for such treatment under the Code, each trust must pay out at least 90 per cent of its taxable income each taxable year in dividends to its shareholders. If the trust qualifies, such income is taxed only to the shareholders. Failure to qualify results in the dividend income being subjected to taxation twice—once to the real estate investment trust, and once to its shareholders as dividends.

On January 29, 1965, ART entered into an agreement with one Harry Helmsley, a real estate entrepreneur. By the terms of the agreement, Helmsley conveyed to ART for seven million dollars a resort property in Palm Beach, Florida, called the Palm Beach Towers.

The sale price, seven million dollars, was composed of $2,500,000. in cash, and the balance by ART's taking the property subject to a mortgage of $4,500,000. The agreement provided that if the mortgage were reduced to less than $4,500,000. by the date of closing, ART, the buyer, would still make cash payments totaling $2,500,000.

ART agreed to lease the property on a "net lease" basis to Palm Beach Towers, Inc., Helmsley's wholly-owned corporation, with certain provisions under the lease to be undertaken or guaranteed by Helmsley personally. At the closing, ART was to provide Helmsley with a written option to repurchase the property.

On February 8, 1965, ART and Palm Beach Towers, Inc. entered into a lease of the Palm Beach property with ART as lessor and Towers as lessee. The lengthy and complex lease contained the following pertinent provisions:

(1) The rental term was to run until January 31, 1986, or 21 years, with two successive twenty-five year renewal options.

(2) A net rental averaging $645,000. per year was stipulated. Related provisions insured that every cost would be borne by the tenant. These costs included, *inter alia*, all operating expenses, taxes, levies, insurance, and repairs. In addition, Helmsley was to bear the cost of some capital improvements made to the property.

(3) The rental rate was to be reduced by 50 per cent of any reduction in the amount paid annually on the mortgage.

(4) In the event the mortgage was increased, the tenant, Palm Beach Towers, Inc., would be entitled to 50 per cent of the addition.

(5) Any condemnation award for the property was to be applied in the following manner: (a) to the mortgagee to the extent of the outstanding principal balance; (b) to the landlord up to $2,525,000; (c) to the tenant up to the value of its leasehold estate; and (d) the remainder to be shared by the landlord (60 per cent) and the tenant (40 per cent).

(6) If less than all the property were taken by condemnation, the net rent was to be reduced by an amount equal to 10–1/2 per cent of any sum received by the landlord and not applied to the reduction of the mortgage principal.

(7) The landlord, ART, was to consent to any assignment of the lease, except that it could withhold its consent if any transfer prior to February 1, 1971, were to a corporation or partnership in which Helmsley had less than a 25 per cent interest.

(8) The lease incorporated Helmsley's personal guarantee to meet the lease obligations through January 31, 1971, and bound Helmsley to own at least 25 per cent of the tenant organization, and personally to oversee the operation of the property.

Executed contemporaneously with the lease was a document styled "Option Agreement," between Helmsley and ART, under which Helmsley was granted an option to repurchase the Palm Beach property. The option was to be exercisable only at one of the following times, and at the indicated price:

August, 1969—$6,560,000.

August, 1970—6,440,000.

August, 1971—6,320,000.

August, 1972—6,190,000.

The option price was to be paid by Helmsley's assuming the mortgage as it existed at the time of exercise of the option, and by his paying the balance of the purchase price in cash.

On September 17, 1971, Helmsley assigned the option contract to his "Subchapter S" corporation, which proceeded to exercise the option. Helmsley testified that he was motivated to exercise the option by the sudden availability of "wrap around" financing,[17] which enabled him, through his corporation, to acquire title with little cash outlay of his own.

ART elected to be taxed as a real estate investment trust for fiscal year 1968 under sections 856 through 858 of the Code. In its computation of its taxable income for that year, ART included in its gross income the rental payments from Palm Beach Towers, and took a large depreciation deduction for the Palm Beach property as well as a deduction for the interest payments it had made on the mortgage. ART computed its "overall" 1968 income on the same basis, and distributed to its shareholders 90 per cent of its computed "real estate investment trust taxable income," so as to qualify for favorable tax treatment under the Code.

Upon audit of ART's 1968 federal income tax return, the Commissioner determined that the "sale and lease-back" arrangement between ART and Helmsley did not result in a transfer of "true" ownership of Palm Beach Towers to ART, but rather constituted a "secured-lending arrange-

---

17. This sort of financing arrangement allows a borrower to give what is essentially a second mortgage on a property, but have it treated as a first mortgage.

ment" by which Helmsley retained ownership of the property, while ART acquired, in effect, only a security interest in it. The whole transaction, maintained the Commissioner, was thus in the nature of a "loan" by ART to Helmsley, secured by the Palm Beach property.

Accordingly, the Commissioner denied ART any deduction for depreciation on the Palm Beach property, and characterized Helmsley's rental payments as "interest" on the ART loan. The disallowance of the depreciation deduction resulted in a substantial increase in ART's taxable income and, consequently, caused the amount distributed to its shareholders to be less than the requisite 90 per cent of ART's taxable income.[18] The Commissioner therefore denied ART its status as a qualifying real estate investment trust under the Code, and levied an increased tax.

ART paid the tax, with interest, and filed a claim for a refund. Upon administrative denial of its claim, ART brought suit in the district court for the refund. The jury, by "special verdict," found the ART–Helmsley transaction to constitute a "good faith" purchase and lease-back by ART, and not merely a "financial arrangement." Based on that verdict, the trial court entered a judgment directing the government to pay ART a refund. The government has appealed. * * *

... [I]t would seem that our primary function on this appeal is to determine whether there was sufficient evidence to support the jury's verdict. We emphasize that appellate review of a jury verdict presents no occasion for the reviewing court to sift and weigh competing factual assertions, to draw its own inferences from contradictory evidence, or to choose between the more persuasive of two plausible but contradictory inferences. * * *

Applying these standards, we are disinclined to disturb the jury's verdict. There was extensive testimony to the effect that the Helmsley–ART deal was *not* merely a tax avoidance device, that commercial considerations underlay it, and that the parties intended that the ownership of the Palm Beach property would pass to ART. In short, there was evidence that the transaction "was a good faith purchase and lease-back" and not a mere "financial arrangement." Given the presence in the record of such evidence, we cannot say the jury's verdict was clearly erroneous. Neither can we say that the record so overwhelmingly supported the government's position that a directed verdict or a judgment n.o.v. should have issued. * * *

---

18. Disallowance of the depreciation deduction caused ART's taxable income to increase. ART had distributed 90 per cent of taxable income calculated with the deduction. The amount thus distributed was, of course, less than 90 per cent of taxable income calculated *without* the depreciation deduction. The difference between the dividend distribution and the amount ART would have had to distribute under the Commissioner's computation of its taxable income was about $19,000. ART's failure to pay out this amount resulted in a claimed increased tax liability of $279,642.66, exclusive of interest.

NOTE

Harry Helmsley, a billionaire hotel magnate in New York City, was married to Leona Helmsley. Leona managed the Helmsley hotel chain and was portrayed in the chain's advertisements as an elitist who assures the highest quality in her luxury hotels. Mrs. Helmsley was famous for the demands she placed on employees, earning her the title of "Queen of Mean." She and her husband were indicted for tax evasion. He was found incompetent to stand trial, but Leona was convicted of 333 counts of tax evasion. Her defense was not helped by her remark that "only the little people pay taxes." After being released from prison, Leona was hit with a $10 million judgment for firing the manager of one of her hotels because he was gay. The court reduced that figure down to $500,000 because the jury had been unduly affected by her abrasive personality. Apparently, Harry Helmsley was a much nicer person. A large memorial was erected near Wall Street in honor of his development activities in New York. Jerry W. Markham, *A Financial History of Modern U.S. Corporate Scandals: From Enron to Reform* 392 (2006).

CHARLES E. WREN III
"SPARING CAIN: EXECUTIVE CLEMENCY IN CAPITAL CASES": THE STAPLED REIT ON ICE: CONGRESS' 1988 FREEZE OF THE GRANDFATHER EXCEPTION FOR STAPLED REITS

28 Capital University Law Review 717 (2000).

The REIT is a creature of the Internal Revenue Code (Code) which permits many investors to pool capital and real estate assets while providing beneficial tax consequences. These tax savings are accomplished in a fashion similar to the manner in which the mutual fund benefits the securities investor; that is, REIT investors obtain a return from their pooled resources without paying a corporate or entity-level tax on any gain.

However, in exchange for these tax benefits, the Code prescribes that the REIT's involvement in income-producing real estate must be limited to a passive role. Generally, this means REITs cannot actively manage or operate the properties they own.

The REIT investor benefits most by the REIT's embodiment of the advantages of both the corporation and the partnership (or limited liability company). Like corporate shareholders, REIT investors enjoy limited liability and transferability of shares (i.e., liquidity). At the same time, the REIT is afforded conduit or pass-through tax treatment similar to a partnership. This conduit status permits the REIT to avoid taxation at both the entity and investor level (i.e., double taxation) by passing its tax attributes through to its shareholders.

However, there are significant distinctions between the REIT and the corporate and partnership forms. Primarily, the REIT's pass-through status is accomplished by what is essentially a "dividends-paid deduction." The REIT is required to distribute to its shareholders nearly all of its taxable income, whereupon, unlike a corporation, the REIT is permitted to deduct these distributions. As a result, the REIT pays no federal income tax on this distributed income. Also, the REIT can only pass through gains from its activities, losses are not permitted. For this reason, REITs are generally not viewed as tax shelter vehicles.

Three basic varieties of REITs exist: the equity, mortgage, and hybrid REIT. Equity REITs pool investor capital and own real estate, such as apartment complexes, shopping centers, industrial parks, and office buildings. They derive income primarily from rentals on these properties. Mortgage REITs invest in real estate mortgage lending and derive income from the fees and interest on these loans. The hybrid REIT holds both mortgage and real estate assets. Thus, it provides the investor with a hedge position against both markets.

The REIT was created under the Real Estate Investment Trust Act of 1960. Congress passed this legislation with two interrelated considerations in mind. First, using the mutual fund as an analogy, Congress wished to provide the small investor with a less-risky access to the real estate investment market. Second, in order to hedge against the business risks associated with real estate investment, the REIT was intended to be a passive real estate investment vehicle.

For Congress, the REIT could provide the small investor this access because, like the mutual fund, the REIT's method of investment would consist of pooling arrangements whereby investors could secure advantages traditionally only available to those with larger resources, (i.e., institutional and wealthy investors). These advantages would include the spreading of risk through diversification, professional management, and direct ownership.

Particularly, Congress stated that, "[t]hese advantages include the spreading of the risk of loss by the greater diversification of investment which can be secured through the pooling arrangements; the opportunity to secure the benefits of expert investment counsel; and the means of collectively financing projects which the investors could not undertake singly." These considerations, which lay behind the creation of the REIT, ought to similarly apply to the various REITs that exist today.

The second rationale underlying the creation of the REIT was the requirement that the REIT be a passive investment vehicle. Congress emphasized that "[t]his bill restricts this 'pass through' of the income for tax purposes to what is clearly passive income from real estate investments, as contrasted to income from the active operation of businesses involving real estate." Further, "any real estate trust engaging in active business operations should continue to be subject to the corporate tax in the same manner as is true in the case of similar operations carried on by other comparable enterprises."

The justification for requiring that REIT income be passive in nature is grounded in the fact that the REIT is a hybrid entity. That is, it is afforded pass-through treatment like a partnership, and yet, it also enjoys the corporate advantages of limited liability and liquidity. Consequently, Congress subjected REITs to strict organizational and operational rules to ensure that REITs would be passive entities. These rules demand that a REIT is not actively managed by shareholders who organized the REIT simply to escape double taxation. Additionally, the rules prevent active real estate operating companies from taking advantage of these special tax incentives, thereby protecting small investors from risks associated with active businesses.

Subsequent tax developments, most importantly the 1984 Act and the Tax Reform Act of 1986 (1986 Act), significantly changed the market landscape for the REIT. Generally, the 1986 Act impacted the REIT industry in two important ways.

First, by curtailing tax shelter abuses, especially with regard to real estate investments, the 1986 Act demanded that in the future such investments "needed to be on a more economic and income-oriented footing." Second, the 1986 Act allowed REITs, for the first time, to directly provide certain "customary" services to their tenants. This enabled REITs to "operate and manage—in addition to owning—most types of income-producing commercial properties." As a result, it was no longer necessary for REITs to use independent contractors to furnish their tenants these services. Furthermore, REITs could now provide a greater variety of services to their tenants without violating the tax rules.

Even though Congress created the REIT in 1960, according to the National Association of Real Estate Investment Trusts (NAREIT), REITs enjoyed little growth until the early 1990s, when "new publicly traded REITs infused much needed equity capital into the over-leveraged real estate industry."

In 1992, the market capitalization of the United States REIT industry was around $13 billion. In 1998, there were more than 200 publicly traded REITs with an equity market capitalization exceeding $150 billion. Since the 1960 legislation, however, tax developments and creative business innovations have enabled some REITs to expand beyond their original conception to active investment vehicles operating under a single tax regime.

To qualify under the Code as a REIT and receive pass-through treatment, an entity must satisfy four tests on a year-by-year basis which relate to the REIT's organizational structure, source of income, nature of assets, and distribution of income. "The ... purpose of these tests is to ensure that the REIT operates ... as a passive real estate investment vehicle."

Organizational Structure Test: Under this test, an entity must meet six organizational requirements. First, it must be managed by one or more trustees or directors for the entire taxable year. Second, the beneficial ownership of the entity must be evidenced by transferable shares. Third, the entity must be one that would be taxed as a domestic corporation but for the REIT provisions. Fourth, the entity cannot be either a section 582(c)(5) financial institution or a life insurance company. Fifth, the beneficial ownership of the entity must be held by 100 or more persons. And sixth, the entity must not have five or fewer persons owning more than fifty percent of the entity.

These requirements reflect the original policy justification to create a real estate investment vehicle that is accessible to the small investor. The five person fifty percent (or "5–50") requirement and the 100 person beneficial ownership requirement are most important to ensuring that REIT ownership will not be concentrated in the hands of a few wealthy individuals.

Source of Income Test: After meeting the six organizational tests, an entity must meet several complex and mechanical income tests. Generally, an entity must satisfy a seventy-five percent gross income test and a ninety-five percent gross income test.

Under the former, at least seventy-five percent of REIT gross income for the taxable year must be derived from: (1) rent on real property, (2) interest on obligations secured by real property, (3) gain from the sale of interests in real property, other than property held for sale in the ordinary course of a trade or business, (4) dividends and gains from a REIT, and (5) other limited sources. Under the latter test, at least ninty-five percent of REIT gross income must be derived from sources described in the seventy-five percent test, plus dividends, interest, and gain from the disposition of stock or securities.

These tests are intended to limit the REIT's investments to those closely connected to real estate activities and certain other types of passive investments.

Nature of Assets Test: An entity wishing to qualify for REIT status must also satisfy several requirements based on the nature of the assets to be held by the REIT. First, at least seventy-five percent of the value of the REIT's assets must be comprised of real estate assets, cash, and cash items (including receivables), and government securities. Second, not more than twenty-five percent of the REITs assets can be invested in securities. Finally, securities of a single issuer included under the twenty-five percent test cannot comprise more than five percent of the REIT's total assets, or more than ten percent of the outstanding voting stock of the issuer.

These requirements ensure that the assets held by a REIT are comprised primarily of real property or assets connected to real property ownership.

Distribution Test: Section 857 of the Code prescribes a number of requirements concerning the distribution of REIT income to its shareholders. These rules ensure that the REIT operates as a pass-through entity.

The most important of these rules is that at least ninety-five percent of the REIT's annual taxable income must be distributed to its shareholders as dividends. If the REIT meets the distribution requirements, it is permitted to deduct the amount so distributed as a dividends-paid deduction.

Upon meeting the organizational requirements under the Code, a REIT will not be subject to federal income taxes on that portion of income distributed to its shareholders, as required by the ninety-five percent distribution requirement of section 857. While the REIT will still be subject to a corporate level tax on the undistributed portion of its income, the REIT will effectively avoid the double taxation of income to which corporations are exposed. However, if the REIT fails to qualify under the Code, it will be taxed as a regular corporation on all of its income, whether or not such income was distributed to its shareholders. * * *

JACK H. McCALL
A PRIMER ON REAL ESTATE TRUSTS: THE LEGAL BASICS OF REITS

2 Transactions 1 (2001).

REITs—particularly the publicly-traded REITs—generally provide investors with liquidity, diversification, security, and performance in at least five ways.

First, REIT investors can freely trade shares of the over 200 publicly-traded REIT stocks daily on the New York and American Stock Exchanges, the Nasdaq Stock Market, and in over-the-counter trading. Second, REIT investors are able to maintain highly diverse real estate investment portfolios by investing in any or all of the categories of REITs discussed below and by selecting from REITs that specialize in a variety of property types, including retail shopping centers and malls, apartments, warehouses, office buildings, industrial parks, health care facilities and hotels. (Even real estate assets as highly specialized as self-storage units, golf courses, movie theaters, auto dealership lots and prisons have now been added to the host of investment options available to REIT investors.)

Next, publicly-traded REITs offer investors the protection of investing (1) in a public company that owns long-life, income-producing physical assets or, in the case of mortgage REITs, the "bundle" of rights adhering to real estate mortgages and secured financings underlying those physical assets, and (2) in the securities of a company subject to SEC and stock exchange regulation. REITs are professionally managed by officers generally skilled in real estate acquisition, management, financing, development and operations, and the performance of public REITs is overseen by independent directors, independent public auditors and financial analysts, whose collective scrutiny helps provide investors with an added degree of protection and accountability. Fourth, the low levels of debt currently maintained by most REITs—frequently coupled with board-mandated policies and governing documents' requirements (*i.e.*, charter, articles of incorporation or declaration of trust, and related organizational documents like bylaws) that are intended to maintain conservative debt levels and modest fiscal practices—provide a degree of greater security for the financial system at large. Finally, total returns on REITs have routinely matched the performance levels attained by several leading market indices and have regularly exceeded returns on fixed debt instruments and direct investments in real estate. Because REITs must pay out a large amount of their taxable income on an annual basis.

There are two main, overarching types of REITs: *equity REITs* and *mortgage REITs*. An equity REIT specializes in *property ownership*. By directly owning, investing in or acquiring, managing, or developing real property, an equity REIT derives its revenue primarily from income generated by rental and lease payments. An equity REIT can benefit from appreciation in its underlying real properties; its income can grow through increases in rents from such properties; and cash in excess of taxable income can be produced through property depreciation, which the equity REIT can use to reinvest in its own operations.

On the other hand, a mortgage REIT concentrates on *financing activities*. A mortgage REIT invests in the mortgages, mortgage-backed securitizations and whole or subprime loans, or portions thereof, on real property assets. In essence, mortgage REITs loan money to real estate owners, and such REITs generate their revenue from the interest earned on such loans. Unlike equity REITs, however, "pure" mortgage REITs do not own real property. Rapid, successive increases in interest rates can raise borrowing costs without corresponding increases in income. While all REITs depend on the maintenance of favorable interest rates, mortgage REITs are particularly susceptible to the adverse effects of interest rate and credit fluctuations and loan defaults. * * *

Several REIT subtypes have developed from the two main types of REITs (*i.e.*, equity and mortgage REITs), and these have established niches in the REIT market at large. These species of REITs include the following:

A hybrid REIT, as the name suggests, owns a combination of equity and mortgage interests in properties. A finite life REIT, or "FREIT", sets forth in the offering documents for its securities a termination date (usually, seven to fifteen years from the REIT's date of inception) and an investment strategy.

A special purpose or dedicated REIT invests in a single type of property and may be tied to a particular developer or user of real estate. Certain REITs invest in a variety of property types (*e.g.*, apartments, hotels, self-storage facilities, restaurants, golf courses, office buildings, shopping centers, etc.), while many more tend to specialize in one exclusive property type or in certain segments within a particular real estate property market (*e.g.*, not merely hotels, but in full-service, limited service or extended stay hotels). Additionally, some REITs focus their investments in specific geographical regions (e.g., ownership of properties located only in the southeastern United States).

A single property REIT invests in one, usually very large, property (*e.g.*, Rockefeller Center is currently owned by a single property REIT).

An umbrella partnership REIT ("UPREIT") is a REIT in which the REIT itself does not own a direct interest in properties. Rather, the REIT owns a direct interest, as the general partner (either itself or through a wholly-owned subsidiary), in an "umbrella" limited partnership. The UPREIT umbrella partnership (also frequently called the REIT's operating partnership) owns a direct interest in properties.

An IPO surge in 1992–93 because of the cheaper costs of capital then available in the public markets meant better returns on investment and led to the rejuvenation of REITs. In this period, the UPREIT concept was first adopted by tax and securities lawyers. At roughly the same time, the UPREIT model was discovered by investment bankers to be an ideal vehicle by which a newly formed REIT could reach an appropriate size to readily access the public capital markets. This major structural innovation helped foster the move from private to public ownership, led to the creation of the "baby" REITs, *i.e.*, those formed from 1992 today, and revitalized the REIT industry at large. When adapted by older REITs to become the basis for the DOWNREIT structure (see below), additionally, the UPREIT model helped provide a new lease on life for several older REITs whose opportunities for growth had hitherto been thwarted.

DOWNREITs: By comparison to UPREITs, "DOWNREITs" (also called "Down–REITs") are now encountered more frequently with many REITs formed before 1992. In such older REITs, properties may have been initially held at the REIT level, but, in order to obtain many of the benefits of the UPREIT model—particularly the ability to defer taxable gains through issuance of limited partnership interests to sellers of real property-one or more new subsidiary partnerships may be formed, and many or all newly acquired properties will be held and owned at the level of these subsidiary partnerships.

Another prime example of the trend towards specialization in the REIT industry is the healthcare REIT, which is treated by some industry experts as a different category from equity, mortgage and hybrid REITs and which operates either through purchase/sale lease-backs of healthcare facilities or through mortgages that are secured by healthcare facilities.

The primary advantage of the *paired-share REIT* and *stapled REIT* models is the ability of these two types of REITs both to own *and* operate virtually any real estate asset class in a more tax-efficient structure than can either conventional REITs or "C" corporations. While most REITs cannot directly operate properties in which their earnings are not derived from rents or leases but result from other types of sales (*e.g.*, gaming casinos, hotel operations and stores), paired-share and stapled REITs can effectively both own *and* manage such properties, deriving their revenues not only from rental income but from property operations as well. Hence, paired-share and stapled REITs have at least three advantages: (1) they receive the tax benefits offered by the REIT provisions of the Code; (2) unlike conventional equity REITs, they can invest in operationally intensive businesses, yet maintaining operational control over their real estate assets; and (3) also unlike conventional equity REITs, their investors derive the full economic benefits of both ownership *and* management of those real estate assets.

Paired-share and stapled REITs are considered (and are often called) "grandfathered" REITs, inasmuch as these REITs were formed in the 1970s and 1980s before the implementation of 1984 federal legislation that eliminated the ability to create new paired-share or stapled REITs but that granted the few then-existing REITs of that type the right to continue to operate in such form. These included Hotel Investors Trust (later acquired by Starwood Capital, which then formed Starwood Lodging); Santa Anita Realty (later acquired by Meditrust); California Jockey Club (later acquired by Patriot American Hospitality); First Union Real Estate; Hollywood Park; and Corporate Property Investors (a private REIT).

The primary difference between paired-share and stapled REITs is structural. In essence, however, both paired-share and stapled REITs contain two companies whose stock is "paired" or "stapled," so that their shares trade as a single unit. As a result, the two companies—the REIT and the operating company—are owned by the same stockholders.

The leading competitive advantages—or, rather, the perceived advantages—of the "grandfathered" REITs include the following: (a) the elimination of conflicts of interest that arise from leasing properties to a management-owned lessee and operational conflicts created by the potentially divergent interests between an asset's owner and manager; (b) the elimination of *leakage (i.e.,* the excess profits created at a lessee level after payment of all operating expenses and lease payments back to the REIT under a percentage lease operating structure) because any economic advantage lost to the REIT under the participating lease structure and retention of leakage by the lessee is still ultimately retained by the REIT's shareholders, who also own shares in the "C" corporation operating company/lessee; (c) the benefit to shareholders of management teams' operational expertise in driving property-level performance; (d) the benefit of the operating company's unrestricted ability to operate businesses otherwise precluded to a REIT, so that it can operate certain real estate-related businesses (*e.g.,* casinos, hotels or golf courses) that typically demand high levels of customer service; and (e) the ability to pay marginally higher prices for assets and charge marginally lower rents for the same assets than their similarly valued but fully taxed counterparts structured as "C" corporations or as non-paired REITs with some leakage.

Recent criticisms (some of which are erroneous, including the charge that they are totally exempt from federal taxation) may potentially threaten many of the tax advantages offered by the paired-share and stapled REITs. The Clinton administration's budget proposals for the 1999 federal fiscal year recommended tax legislation with significant potential effects on various REITs. Among other things, the practical effect of these proposals would, if enacted, "freeze" the ability of the "grandfathered" REITs to acquire substantially new assets or to engage in a new line of business after the date of first committee action by the Ways and Means Committee of the House of Representatives. These concerns have partially helped encourage the development of yet another type of REIT structure—the "paperclip" REIT. * * * In this case, the REIT forms an operating company (usually, a "C" corporation) that will (1) lease properties from the REIT; (2) pursue certain opportunities that cannot be undertaken by the REIT; and (3) acquire certain assets that cannot be held by the REIT due to the tax concerns arising from the two asset tests' requirements. Moreover, the same leading advantage offered by the "grandfathered" REIT structure—the elimination of leakage and the operation of the REIT's assets within a relatively self-contained, autarchic universe, while avoiding the obvious conflicts of interest inherent in a system in which the lessee/operating company is largely owned by the REIT's own management—are offered to the REIT's shareholders by the paperclip REIT structure. Unlike the paired-share REIT, though, where both companies' stocks trade as a single linked unit, the REIT and the "C" corporation are separate public companies, whose stocks trade separately. The two organizations are "paperclipped" together through an inter-company agreement. This agreement (a) gives the operating company a right of first refusal to lease and manage all future properties acquired by the REIT, and (b) provides the REIT with a similar right of first refusal to acquire properties presented to it by the operating company. In addition, the two companies share certain senior members of management and board members, which arrangements are intended to fully align the two companies' interests for the benefit of both companies' shareholders.

Once formed, the newly formed operating company is "spun off" to create a new publicly traded corporation, complete with its own majority of independent directors on its board who are, moreover, largely separate from the REIT's board, so as to reduce (if not eliminate outright) the potential conflicts of interest within the system. Each shareholder of the REIT receives one or more shares of the operating company's separately traded common stock, thus giving the REIT's shareholders the benefits of (a) the REIT's ownership of real estate and (b) the "paperclipped" operator's management and operational capabilities. In theory, if the REIT's and operating company's separate teams of independent board members do their jobs correctly, the potential and actual conflicts of interest facing the paperclip REIT system would be minimized.

As compared to a conventional REIT, the paperclip REIT structure provides investors with greater flexibility. They may invest separately (a) at the REIT level for steady real estate growth and income, (b) at the operating company level for growth through operating leverage, or (c) in both entities jointly. Compared to a paired-share REIT, a paperclip REIT also costs much less to structure and implement; offers significantly easier tax-free acquisitions of corporate targets; and enables investors to invest independently in two different entities, depending on their investment objectives. Like the UPREIT and DOWNREIT, moreover, a paperclip REIT may also use units of limited partnership interest (as will be explored in the next part) as an alternative "acquisition currency" for tax-sensitive real property sellers.

NOTES

1. Modern portfolio theory seeks diversification. How does a REIT fit into that picture? Is a portfolio that does not have real estate investments diversified?

2. The stock market downturn that began in 2000 was not accompanied by a similar downturn in the residential real estate market. Near record low interest rates spurred residential real estate investments in 2003. At the same time, bond returns were being reduced and commercial real estate was lagging, while gold prices were soaring as the War in Iraq approached. Does this underscore the importance of diversification or do you think an investor would be better off by trying to anticipate these developments? Is there an instrument available that will allow you to capture the overall upswing in the residential real estate market? Remember that what goes up may come down as demonstrated by the slump in the residential real estate market during 2006–2010.

3. In April 2003, REITS were estimated to hold only "about $378 billion in assets, 34 percent less than General Electric." Bloomberg News, REITs Said at Risk of Irrelevancy, Raleigh News & Observer, April 7, 2003, at 10B. Does this mean that the REIT is not a significant force in the commercial real estate market or that investors were anticipating the downturn in commercial real estate and were trying to avoid that risk? What effect did the subprime crisis in 2007–2009 have on REITS?

INDEX

References are to Pages

†